202

ENGLISH–ARABIC
AND
ARABIC–ENGLISH
DICTIONARY

JOHN WORTABET, M. D.
AND
HARVEY PORTER, Ph.D.

With a Supplement of Modern Words
and New Meanings by

JOHN L. MISH, Ph.D.
Chief, Oriental Division, New York Public Library

FREDERICK UNGAR PUBLISHING CO.
NEW YORK

PREFACE

No up-to-date Arabic dictionary for English-speaking students has been available for almost half a century. Those dictionaries that could be bought either did not contain the new words coined since 1900, or else they neglected to show grammatical forms which are indispensable to the non-Arab, such as broken plurals or the vowels of the imperfect. There can thus be no question about the urgent need for such a dictionary; but until such a work appears, and that will take time, the publishers believed that the gap might be filled temporarily by reprinting a basic Arabic-English, English-Arabic dictionary—in this case Wortabet's, which has been out of print for many years—and adding a good selection of modern words and expressions. This should enable the student to read the average Arabic newspaper or book without missing the sense of many words.

It is hoped that within this modest framework, this dictionary will be of real help to all English-speaking students of Arabic.

John L. Mish

New York, 1954

ABBREVIATIONS. إِخْتِصَارَاتْ

a. = adjective.	صفة	ppr. = present participle.	اسم فاعل
ad. = adverb.	حال او ظرف	p. pron. = personal pronoun.	ضمير
con. = conjunction.	حرف عطف	int. = interrogation.	اسم استفهام
n. = noun.	اسم	rel. = relative.	اسم موصول
pl. = plural.	جمع	dem. = demonstrative.	اسم إشارة
pp. = past participle.	اسم مفعول	pp. = preposition.	حرف جر

ENGLISH-ARABIC DICTIONARY

قاموس انكليزي وعربي

A

A *or* an.	حَرْفُ نَكِرَةٍ	Abdomen *n.*	بَطْنٌ
Abaft *ad.*	عِنْدَ مُؤَخَّرِ ٱلْمَرْكَبِ	Abdominal *a.*	بَطْنِيٌّ
Abandon *v. t.*	تَرَكَ . هَجَرَ	Abduct *v. t.*	خَطَفَ ـ إِخْتَلَسَ
Abase *v. t.*	أَذَلَّ . وَضَعَ ـ حَطَّ	Abduction *n.*	خَطْفٌ . إِخْتِلَاسٌ
Abasement *n.*	ذُلٌّ . ضَعَةٌ	Abet *v. t.*	حَرَّضَ . عَاوَنَ . عَاضَدَ
Abash *v. t.*	خَجَّلَ . أَخْجَلَ	Abhor *v. t.*	مَقَتَ . كَرِهَ
Abate *v. t.* or *i.*	نَقَصَ . نَقَّصَ	Abhorrence *n.*	مَقْتٌ . كَرَاهَةٌ
Abatement *n.*	تَقْلِيلٌ . تَخْفِيضٌ	Abide *v. i.* or *t.*	أَقَامَ بِ . إِنْتَظَرَ
Abbess *n.*	رَئِيسَةُ دَيْرٍ	Abiding *a.*	ثَابِتٌ . مُسْتَمِرٌّ
Abbey *n.*	دَيْرٌ	Ability *n.*	قُدْرَةٌ . طَاقَةٌ . إِسْتِطَاعَةٌ
Abbot *n.*	رَئِيسُ دَيْرٍ	Abject *a.*	ذَلِيلٌ . دَنِيٌّ . حَقِيرٌ
Abbreviate *v. t.*	قَصَّرَ . إِخْتَصَرَ	Abjure *v. t.*	رَفَضَ . إِرْتَدَّ عَنْ
Abbreviation *n.*	تَقْصِيرٌ . إِخْتِصَارٌ	Able *a.*	قَادِرٌ . مُسْتَطِيعٌ
Abdicate *v. t.* or *i.*	خَلَعَ نَفْسَهُ مِنْ	Able-bodied *a.*	صَحِيحُ ٱلْجِسْمِ
Abdication *n.*	تَنَازُلٌ عَنْ	Ablution *n.*	غَسْلٌ . وُضُوءٌ

Ably *ad.*	بِقُدْرَة بِمَهَارَة
Abnegation *n.*	إِنْكَارُ ٱلنَّفْس
Abnormal *a.*	غَيْرُ قِيَاسِيّ . شَاذٌّ
Aboard *ad.*	فِي السَّفِينَة
Abode *n.*	مَقَامٌ . مَنْزِلٌ . مَسْكِنٌ
Abolish *v. t.*	نَسَخَ . — ٱلْغَى . أَبْطَلَ
Abolition *n.*	نَسْخٌ . إِلْغَاء
Abominable *a.*	كَرِيهُ . قَبِيحٌ
Abominate *v. t.*	كَرِهَ — إِسْتَقْبَحَ
Abomination *n.*	قَبِيحَةٌ . رِجْسٌ
Aborigines *n. pl.*	(سُكَّانٌ) أَصْلِيُّونَ
Abortion *n.*	سِقْطٌ . إِسْقَاطُ ٱلْجَنِين
Abortive *a.*	مُخِيبٌ . غَيْرُ مُنْتِج
Abound *v. i.*	كَثُرَ . — وَفَرَ يَفُرُ
About *pr.*	حَوْلَ نَحْوَ
Above *pr.*	فَوْقَ . اكْثَرُ مِنْ
Abrasion *n.*	كَشْطٌ . إِحْتِكَاك
Abridge *v. t.*	قَصَّرَ . أَوْجَزَ . إِخْتَصَر

Abridgement *n.*	إِيجَازٌ . إِخْتِصَارٌ
Abroad *ad.*	خَارِجًا . فِي ٱلْخَارِج
Abrogate *v. t.*	ٱلْغَى . ابْطَلَ . نَسَخَ
Abrupt *a.*	فُجَائِيٌّ . مَقْطُوعٌ
Abruptness *n.*	مُفَاجَأَةٌ . إِنْقِطَاعٌ
Abcess *n.*	خُرَّاجٌ . خَرَّاجَةٌ
Abscond *v. i.*	تَوَارَى . إِخْتَفَى . إِنْسَلَّ
Absence *n.*	غَيْبَةٌ . غِيَابٌ
Absent *a.* Absentee *n.*	غَائِبٌ
Absolute *a.*	غَيْرُ مُقَيَّد . مُطْلَقٌ
Absolutely *ad.*	مُطْلَقًا . قَطْعًا
Absolution *n.*	حَلٌّ . غُفْرَانٌ
Absolve *v. t.*	حَلَّ — . غَفَرَ —
Absorb *v. t.*	إِمْتَصَّ . إِسْتَغْرَقَ
Absorption *n.*	إِمْتِصَاصٌ
Abstain *v. i.*	إِمْتَنَعَ عَنْ
Abstenious *a.*	قَلِيلُ ٱلْأَكْلِ . عَفِيفٌ
Abstinence *n.*	إِمْتِنَاعٌ . عِفَّةٌ

Abstinent a.	زَاهِدٌ عَفِيفٌ	Accent n.	شِدَّةٌ في اللَّفظِ . نَبْرَةٌ
Abstract v. t.	جَرَّدَ . إِختْلَسَ	Accentuate v. t.	شَدَّدَ. أَظْهَرَ أَهمِّيتَهُ
Abstract a.	مُجَرَّدٌ . تَجْريدِيٌّ	Accept v. t.	قَبِلَ ـ رَضِيَ
Abstraction n.	تَجْريدٌ . (غَيْبَة)	Acceptable a.	مَقْبولٌ. مَرْضِيٌّ
Abstractly ad.	مُجَرَّدًا	Acceptance n.	قَبُولٌ
Abstruse a.	عَويصٌ مُشْكِلٌ	Acceptation n.	قَبُولٌ . مَعْنًى
Absurd a.	باطِلٌ . مُخَالِفٌ العَقْلَ	Accepted a.	مَقْبولٌ
Absurdity n.	بُطْلٌ . بُطْلَانٌ	Access n.	دُخُولٌ . وُصُولٌ
Abundance n.	كَثْرَةٌ . وَفْرٌ	Accessible a.	سَهْلُ الوُصُولِ. اليِفٌ
Abundant a.	كَثِيرٌ . وافِرٌ	Accession n.	زِيَادَةٌ . وُصُولٌ جُلُوسٌ (ملك)
Abuse v. t.	شَتَمَ ـ أَسَاءَ آسْتِعْمَالَهُ		
Abuse n.	شَتيمَةٌ . سُوءُ الاستِعْمَالِ	Accident n.	عَرَضٌ . آفَةٌ
Abusive a.	شَاتِمٌ مُهينٌ	Accidental a.	عَرَضِيٌّ . إِتِّفَاقِيٌّ
Abyss n.	هاوِيَةٌ . وَهْدَةٌ	Acclamation n.	تَصْفيقٌ . إِسْتِحْسَانٌ
Acacia n.	شَجَرُ السَّنْطِ	Acclimate Acclimatize v. t.	عَوَّدَ عَلَى المَنَاخِ
Academy n.	مَدْرَسَةُ العُلُومِ أَوْ مَجْمَعُهَا	Acclimation n.	تَعَوُّدُ المَنَاخِ
Accede v. t.	قَبِلَ . رَضِيَ بِهِ ـ	Acclivity n.	مَطْلَعٌ . مَصْعَدٌ
Accelerate v. t.	اسْرعَ . عَجَّلَ	Accommodate v. t.	أَمَدَّ . وَفَّقَ

Accommodating a.	مُوَفِّقٌ. مُلَاطِفٌ
Accommodation n.	مُوَافَقَةٌ
Accompaniment n.	مُرَافَقَةٌ
Accompany v. t.	رَافَقَ
Accomplice n.	شَرِيكٌ فِي ذَنْبٍ
Accomplish v. t.	أَكْمَلَ. أَنْجَزَ
Accomplishment n.	إِنْجَازٌ. إِتْمَامٌ
Accord n.	إِتِّفَاقٌ. إِتِّحَادٌ
Accordance n.	إِتِّفَاقٌ
According to.	عَلَى مُوجِبٍ. بِحَسَبِ
Accordingly ad.	لِذَلِكَ
Accost v. t.	خَاطَبَ كَلَّمَهُ أَوَّلاً
Account v. t.	حَسَبَ ـُ. عَدَّ
Account n.	حِسَابٌ. قِصَّةٌ. خَبَرٌ
Accountability n.	مَسْؤُولِيَّةٌ
Accountable a.	مَسْؤُولٌ
Accountant n.	كَاتِبُ الْحِسَابَاتِ
Accrue v. i.	زَادَ. نَشَأَ ـَ أُضِيفَ
Accumulate v. t. or i.	جَمَعَ ـ. إِزْدَادَ
Accumulation n.	إِزْدِيَادٌ. تَجَمُّعٌ
Accumulative a.	جَامِعٌ. مُزْدَادٌ
Accuracy n.	ضَبْطٌ. إِتْقَانٌ
Accurate a.	مَضْبُوطٌ. مُتْقَنٌ
Accurately ad.	بِضَبْطٍ. بِإِتْقَانٍ
Accursed a.	مَلْعُونٌ
Accusation n.	إِشْتِكَاءٌ. شِكَايَةٌ
Accuse v. t.	شَكَا. إِتَّهَمَ. سَعَى بِهِ
Accuser n.	شَاكٍ. مُتَّهِمٌ
Accustom v. t.	عَوَّدَ
Acerbity n.	حَرَافَةٌ. فَظَاظَةٌ
Ache n.	وَجَعٌ. أَلَمٌ
Ache v. i.	تَوَجَّعَ. تَأَلَّمَ
Achieve v. t.	عَمِلَ. تَمَّمَ. فَازَ
Achievement n.	عَمَلٌ. إِنْجَازُ أَمْرٍ
Acid n.	حَامِضٌ
Acidity n.	حُمُوضَةٌ

Acknowledge v. t.	إِعْتَرَفَ . أَقَرَّ
Acme n.	رَأْسٌ . قِمَّةٌ
Acknowledgement n.	إِعْتِرافٌ
Acorn n.	بَلُّوطٌ
Acoustics n.	عِلْمُ ٱلسَّمْعِيَّاتِ
Acquaint v. t.	أَعْلَمَ . عَرَّفَ
Acquaint-ance n.	مَعْرِفَةٌ . أَحَدُٱلْمَعَارِفِ
Acquiesce v. t.	قَبِلَ . رَضِيَ بِ
Acquire v. t.	حَصَّلَ . إِقْتَنَى
Acquisition n.	تَحْصِيلٌ . قِنْيَةٌ
Acquit v. t.	بَرَّأَ . أَطْلَقَ
Acquittal n.	تَبْرِئَةٌ . إِطْلَاقٌ
Acre n.	فَدَّانٌ (إِنْكِلِيزِيٌّ)
Acreage n.	عَدَدُ ٱلْفَدَادِينِ فِي أَرْضٍ
Acrid a.	قَارِصٌ . حِرِّيفٌ
Acrimony n.	حَرَافَةٌ . حِدَّةٌ
Across pr.	عَرْضًا . عَبْرَ
Act n.	فِعْلٌ . عَمَلٌ

Act v. t. or i.	فَعَلَ . عَمِلَ . تَصَرَّفَ
Action n.	فِعْلٌ . مَعْرَكَةٌ . دَعْوَى
Active a.	فَعَّالٌ . نَشِيطٌ
Actively ad.	بِنَشَاطٍ . بِهِمَّةٍ
Activity n.	نَشَاطٌ . هِمَّةٌ
Actor n.	فَاعِلٌ . مُشَخِّصٌ فِي مَلْعَبٍ
Actual a.	فِعْلِيٌّ . حَقِيقِيٌّ
Actually ad.	فِعْلًا . حَقًّا
Actuate v. t.	حَمَلَهُ عَلَى . سَاقَ إِلَى
Acumen n.	ذَكَاءٌ . حِذَاقَةٌ
Acuminate a.	مُحَدَّدُ ٱلرَّأْسِ . مُسَنَّنٌ
Acute a.	حَادٌّ . ذَكِيٌّ . حَاذِقٌ
Acuteness n.	حِدَّةٌ . حِذَاقَةٌ
Adage n.	مَثَلٌ
Adamant n.	حَجَرٌ صَلْبٌ . مَاسٌ
Adapt v. t.	نَاسَبَ . وَافَقَ
Adapted a.	جَدِيرٌ بِهِ . مُنَاسِبٌ
Adaptable a.	قَابِلُ ٱلْمُنَاسَبَةِ

Adaptation *n.*	مُنَاسَبَةٌ . مُوَافَقَةٌ
Add *v. t.*	جَمَعَ ـَ أَضَافَ إِلَى
Adder *n.*	أَفْعَى ج أَفَاعٍ
Addict *v. t.*	اولَعَ بِ . عَكَفَ عَلَى
Addicted *pp,*	مُوْلَعٌ . مُنْعَكِفٌ
Addition *n.*	جَمْعٌ . إِضَافَةٌ
Additional *a.*	مُضَافٌ . زَائِدٌ
Addle *v. t. & a.*	أَفْسَدَ . قَذَرَ
Address *v. t.*	خَاطَبَ . عنْوَنَ
Address *n.*	خِطَابٌ .عنْوَانٌ . حِذَاقَةٌ
Adduce *v. t.*	أَوْرَدَ . جَآءَ بِ
Adept *n.*	مَاهِرٌ . لَبِيبٌ
Adequate *a.*	كَافٍ . مُسَاوٍ
Adhere *v. t.*	لَصَقَ . لَزِقَ ـَ
Adherence *n.*	لَصْقٌ . لُزُوقٌ
Adherent *a. n.*	حَلِيفٌ . مُلْتَصِقٌ بِ
Adhesion *n.*	لَصْقٌ . إِلْتِصَاقٌ
Adhesive *a.*	لَزِجٌ . دَابِقٌ
Adieu *ad.*	أَسْتَوْدِعُكُم اَللّه
Adjacent *a.*	مُجَاوِرٌ . مُتَاخِمٌ
Adjective *n.*	نَعْتٌ . صِفَةٌ
Adjoin *v. t. or i.*	إِتَّصَلَ بِ .جَاوَرَ
Adjoining *a.*	مُتَصِلٌ بِ
Adjourn *v. t.*	أَجَّلَ . اخَّرَ
Adjournment *n.*	تَأْجِيلٌ . تَأْخِيرٌ
Adjudicate *v. t.*	قَضَى ـَ حَكَمَ
Adjunct *n. or a.*	مُضَافٌ . مُلْحَقٌ
Adjure *v. t.*	إِسْتَحْلَفَ
Adjust *v. t.*	نَاسَبَ . ضَبَطَ
Adjustment *n.*	ضَبْطٌ . تَعْدِيلٌ
Adjutant *n.*	مُعَاوِنٌ عَسْكَرِيٌّ
Administer *v. t.*	أَدَارَ . أَجْرَى
Administration *n.*	إِدَارَةٌ . إِجْرَآءٌ
Administrator *n.*	مُدِيرٌ . وَكِيلٌ
Admirable *a.*	عَجِيبٌ .بَاهِرٌ
Admiral *n.*	أَمِيرُ اَلْبَحْرِ

Admiralty n.	إِمَارَةُ آلْبَحْرِيَّةِ
Admiration n.	تَعَجُّبٌ . إِسْتِحْسَانٌ
Admire v. t.	تَعَجَّبَ مِنْ . إِسْتَحْسَنَ
Admissible a.	مُسَلَّمٌ بِهِ . جَائِزٌ
Admission n.	تَسْلِيمٌ بِ . دُخُولٌ
Admit v. t.	سَلَّمَ بِهِ . أَدْخَلَ
Admittance n.	دُخُولٌ . تَسْلِيمٌ
Admix v. t.	مَزَجَ . خَلَطَ
Admixture n.	مَزِيجٌ
Admonish v. t.	نَبَّهَ . اَنْذَرَ
Admonition n.	إِنْذَارٌ . نَصِيحَةٌ
Admonitive a. } Admonitory a. }	مُنْذِرٌ
Ado n.	تَعَبٌ . ضَجِيجٌ
Adolescence n.	شُبُوبِيَّةٌ . مُرَاهَقَةٌ
Adopt v. t.	تَبَنَّى . إِتَّخَذَ
Adoption n.	تَبَنٍّ . إِتِّخَاذٌ
Adorable a.	مُسْتَحِقٌّ آلْعِبَادَةِ
Adoration n.	عِبَادَةٌ . مَحَبَّةٌ فَائِقَةٌ
Adore v. t.	عَبَدَ . أَحَبَّ
Adorn v. t.	زَيَّنَ . زَخْرَفَ
Adornment n.	تَزْيِينٌ . زِينَةٌ
Adrift a. or ad.	عَائِمٌ . سَائِبٌ
Adroit a.	مَاهِرٌ . أَرِيبٌ . حَاذِقٌ
Adroitness n.	مَهَارَةٌ . حَذَاقَةٌ
Adulation n.	تَمَلُّقٌ . إِطْرَاءٌ
Adulatory a.	مُتَمَلِّقٌ . مُطْرٍ
Adult n.	بَالِغُ آلسِّنِّ
Adulterate v. t.	أَفْسَدَ . غَشَّ
Adulterer n. } Adulterous a. }	زَانٍ
Adultery n.	زِنًى
Advance v. i. or t.	تَقَدَّمَ . قَدَّمَ . رَقَّى
Advance n.	تَقَدُّمٌ . تَرَقٍّ
Advance guard n.	طَلِيعَةُ آلْجَيْشِ
Advanced a.	مُقَدَّمٌ . مُرَقًّى . مُتَقَدِّمٌ
Advancement n.	تَقْدِيمٌ . تَرْقِيَةٌ
Advantage n.	فَائِدَةٌ . مَصْلَحَةٌ
Advantageous a.	مُفِيدٌ . نَافِعٌ

Advent n.	مَجِيءٌ . ظُهُورٌ
Adventitious a.	عَرَضِيٌّ
Adventure n.	حَادِثَةٌ غَرِيبَةٌ . مَشْرُوعٌ
Adventurous ⎰ Adventuresome ⎱ a.	مُخَاطِرٌ بِنَفْسِهِ
Adverb n.	ظَرْفٌ أَوْحَالٌ
Adverbial a.	ظَرْفِيٌّ أَوْحَالِيٌّ
Adversary n.	خَصْمٌ . مُقَاوِمٌ
Adverse a.	مُضَادٌّ . مُعَاكِسٌ
Adversity n.	مُصِيبَةٌ . بَلِيَّةٌ
Advert v. i.	اِلْتَفَتَ إِلَى . أَشَارَ
Advertise v. t.	أَعْلَنَ . اخْبَرَ
Advertisement n.	إِعْلَانٌ . إِخْبَارٌ
Advice n.	نَصِيحَةٌ . مَشُورَةٌ
Advisable a.	مُوَافِقٌ . مُسْتَحْسَنٌ
Advise v. t.	نَصَحَ . أَخْبَرَ
Advisory n.	شُورِيٌّ
Advocacy a.	مُحَامَاةٌ . شَفَاعَةٌ
Advocate n.	مُحَامٍ (أَفُوكَاتُو)
Advocated v. t.	حَمَى عَنْ . عَضَدَ
Advocation n.	مُحَامَاةٌ . إِحْتِجَاجٌ
Adz or Adge n.	قَدُومٌ
Aerial a.	هَوَائِيٌّ . عَالٍ
Aerolite n.	حَجَرٌ جَوِّيٌّ . نَيْزَكُ
Aeronaut n.	مُسَافِرٌ فِي الْهَوَاءِ
Aesthetics n. pl.	عِلْمُ الْجَمَالِ
Afar ad.	عَلَى بُعْدٍ
Affability n.	أُنْسٌ وَبَشَاشَةٌ
Affable a.	أَنِيسٌ . لَيِّنُ الْجَانِبِ
Affably ad.	بِبَشَاشَةٍ . بِلُطْفٍ
Affair n.	أَمْرٌ . شَأْنٌ . قَضِيَّةٌ
Affect v. t.	أَثَّرَ فِي . هَيَّجَ . تَصَنَّعَ
Affectation n.	تَصَنُّعٌ
Affected a.	مُتَأَثِّرٌ . مُصَابٌ . مُتَصَنِّعٌ
Affecting a.	مُؤَثِّرٌ
Affection n.	مَحَبَّةٌ . مَوَدَّةٌ

Affectionate a.	مُحِبٌّ . وَدُودٌ
Affective a.	مُهَيِّجُ العَواطِفِ
Affiance v. t.	خَطَبَ ـُ (المَرْأَةَ)
Affidavit n.	إِقْرَارٌ بِاليَمِينِ
Affiliate v. t.	تَبَنَّى . أَشْرَكَ
Affiliation n.	تَبَنٍّ . إِشْرَاكٌ
Affinity n.	قَرَابَةٌ . مُجَانَسَةٌ
Affirm v. t.	حَقَّقَ . أَكَّدَ
Affirmable a.	مُمْكِنٌ تَأْكِيدُهُ
Affirmation n.	تَأْكِيدٌ . إِيجَابٌ
Affirmative a. or n.	إِيجَابِيٌّ . مُوجَبٌ
Affirmatory a.	مُثْبِتٌ
Affix v	ألصَقَ بِ وَصَلَ
Affix n	مُضَافٌ
Afflict v.	كَدَّرَ . ضَايَقَ
Afflicting Afflictive	مُكَدِّرٌ . مُغِمٌّ
Affliction n.	ضِيقَةٌ . بَلِيَّةٌ
Affluence n.	غِنًى . وَفْرَةٌ
Affluent a.	غِنِيٌّ . وَافِرٌ
Afford v. t.	أَنْتَجَ . قَدَّمَ . قَدَرَ عَلَى
Affray n.	مُشَاجَرَةٌ . شَغَبٌ
Affright v. t.	أَفْزَعَ . خَوَّفَ
Affront v. t.	أَهَانَ . عَيَّرَ
Affront n.	إِهَانَةٌ . تَعْيِيرٌ
Affusion n.	سَكْبٌ . رَشٌّ
Afloat ad.	عَائِمٌ
Afoot ad.	مَاشٍ . جَارٍ
Aforesaid a.	المَارُّ ذِكْرُهُ
Afraid a.	خَائِفٌ . مُرْتَعِبٌ
Afresh ad.	حَدِيثًا . أَيْضًا
Aft a. or ad.	عِنْدَ المُؤَخِّرِ
After ad. or pr.	بَعْدُ . خَلْفُ . بِحَسَبِ
Afternoon n.	بَعْدَ الظُّهْرِ
After-thought n.	تَأَمُّلٌ . مُعَادٌ
Afterwards ad.	بَعْدَ ذَلِكَ
Again ad.	أَيْضًا . مَرَّةً أُخْرَى

Against *pr.*	ضِدٌّ . تُجَاهَ
Age *n.*	عُمْرٌ . عَصْرٌ
Aged *a.*	طَاعِنٌ فِي السِّنِّ
Agency *n.*	فَاعِلِيَّةٌ . وَكَالَةٌ
Agent *n.*	فَاعِلٌ . وَكِيلٌ
Agglomerate *v. t.*	كَتَّلَ
Agglomeration *n.*	تَكْتِيلٌ . تَرَاكُمٌ
Agglutinate *v. t.*	غَرَّى . أَلْصَقَ
Agglutination *n.*	تَغْرِيَةٌ . إِلْزَاقٌ
Aggrandize *v. t.*	عَظَّمَ . كَبَّرَ
Aggrandizement *n.*	تَعْظِيمٌ
Aggravate *v. t.*	زَادَ . بَالَغَ فِي
Aggravation *n.*	زِيَادَةٌ . تَثْقِيلٌ
Aggregate *v. t.*	جَمَّعَ ـَـ . بَلَغَ ـُـ
Aggregate *n.* or *a.*	اَلْكُلُّ . مَجْمُوعٌ
Aggregation *n.*	جَمْعٌ
Aggress *v. t.*	تَعَدَّى عَلَى
Aggression *n.*	تَعَدٍّ

Aggressive *a.* Aggressor *n.*	مُتَعَدٍّ
Aggrieve *v. t.*	أَحْزَنَ . كَدَّرَ
Aghast *ad.*	مُنْذَهِلٌ . مَرْعُوبٌ
Agile *a.*	حَرِكٌ . خَفِيفٌ
Agility *n.*	خِفَّةٌ . سُرْعَةٌ
Agitate *v. t.*	حَرَّكَ . هَيَّجَ . أَقْلَقَ
Agitation *n.*	تَحْرِيكٌ . إِنْزِعَاجٌ
Agitator *n.*	مُهَيِّجٌ . مُحَرِّكٌ
Ago *ad.*	سَابِقًا . مِنْ مُدَّةٍ
Agonize *v. i.*	تَعَذَّبَ
Agony *n.*	أَلَمٌ شَدِيدٌ . نَزْعٌ
Agrarian *a.*	مُخْتَصٌّ بِالْحُقُولِ
Agrarian *n.*	مَنْ يَطْلُبُ قِسْمَةَ } الْأَرَاضِي بِالتَّسَاوِي }
Agree *v. i.*	إِتَّفَقَ عَلَى . سَلَّمَ بِ
Agreable *a.*	مُرْضٍ . سَارٌّ
Agreement *n.*	إِتِّفَاقٌ . عَهْدٌ
Agricultural *a.*	زِرَاعِيٌّ . فَلَاحِيٌّ

Agriculture n.	اَلْفِلَاحَةُ . اَلزِّرَاعَةُ
Agriculturist n.	فَلَّاحٌ . زَارِعٌ
Aground ad.	عَلَى الْأَرْضِ (مَرْكَبٌ)
Ague n.	بُرَدَآءُ . بَرْدِيَّةٌ
Ah ! Aha ! ex.	آهِ . آهَاً
Ahead ad.	امَامَ . إِلَى قُدَّامٍ
Aid v. t.	سَاعَدَ . أَعَانَ
Aid n.	مُسَاعَدَةٌ . عَوْنٌ . مَدَدٌ
Ail v. i.	إِعْتَلَّ . تَشَكَّى مِنْ مَرَضٍ
Ail n. Ailment n.	عِلَّةٌ . مَرَضٌ
Aim v. t. or i.	قَصَدَ . إِعْتَرَضَ . صَوَّبَ
Aim n.	قَصْدٌ . غَرَضٌ
Aimless a.	بِلَا قَصْدٍ أَوْ غَرَضٍ
Air n.	هَوَاءٌ . نَغْمَةٌ . هَيْئَةٌ
Air v. t.	عَرَّضَ لِلْهَوَاءِ . هَوَّى
Airing n.	تَنَزُّهٌ
Airless a.	بِلَا هَوَاءٍ
Airy a.	مَكْشُوفٌ لِلْهَوَاءِ . مَرِحٌ
Akin a.	ذُو قَرَابَةٍ . نَسِيبٌ
Alacrity n.	إِسْتِعْدَادٌ لِلْعَمَلِ . نَشَاطٌ
Alarm v. t.	خَوَّفَ . أَرْعَبَ
Alarm n.	إِنْذَارٌ بِالْخَطَرِ . خَوْفٌ
Alarm-clock n.	سَاعَةٌ مُنَبِّهَةٌ
Alarming a.	مُخِيفٌ . مُفْزِعٌ
Alas ! ex.	وَاأَسْفَاهُ
Albeit ad.	مَعَ أَنَّ وَلَوْ أَنَّ
Albumen n.	زُلَالٌ
Alchemy n.	الْكِيمْيَاءُ الْقَدِيمَةُ
Alcohol n.	(اَلْكُحُولُ)
Alcoholic a.	(كُحُولِيٌّ)
Alderman n.	شَيْخُ بَلَدٍ
Ale n.	جِعَةٌ
Alert a.	مُنَبِّهَةٌ . مُتَيَقِّظٌ . خَفِيفٌ
Alertness n.	خِفَّةٌ . يَقْظَةٌ . نَشَاطٌ
Algebra n.	عِلْمُ الْجَبْرِ
Algebraist n.	مَاهِرٌ فِي عِلْمِ الْجَبْرِ

Algerine a.	جَزَائِرِيٌّ	Allegory n.	مَجَازٌ . رَمْزٌ
Alien a. or ad.	أَجْنَبِيٌّ	Alleviate v. t.	خَفَّفَ . لَطَّفَ
Alienate v. t.	نَقَلَ . أَبْعَدَ	Alleviation n.	تَسْكِينٌ . تَلْطِيفٌ
Alienation n.	بَعْجٌ . نَقْلٌ . هِجْرَانٌ	Alley n.	زُقَاقٌ ج أَزِقَّةٌ
Alight v. i.	تَرَجَّلَ . وَقَعَ عَلَى	Alliance n.	مُعَاهَدَةٌ . مُحَالَفَةٌ . مُصَاهَرَةٌ
Alignment n.	تَرْتِيبٌ عَلَى خَطٍّ	Allied pp.	مُتَعَاهِدٌ . مُنْتَسِبٌ . مُصَاهِرٌ
Alike a.	شَبِيهٌ . نَظِيرٌ	Alligator n.	ضَرْبٌ مِنَ التِّمْسَاح
Aliment n.	غِذَاءٌ ج أَغْذِيَةٌ	Allot v. t.	خَصَّصَ . اعْطَى نَصِيبًا
Alimental, alimentary a.	مُغْذٍ	Allotment n.	نَصِيبٌ . تَقْسِيمٌ
Alive a.	حَيٌّ	Allow v. t.	سَمَحَ . أَذِنَ . أَجَازَ
Alkali n.	الْقِلْيُ . الْقِلَى	Allowable a.	جَائِزٌ . مُبَاحٌ
Alkaline n.	قَلَوِيٌّ	Allowance n.	إِذْنٌ . رَاتِبٌ
Alkoran n.	الْقُرْآنُ	Alloy v. t. or n.	مَزِيجُ الْجَيِّدِ مَعَ الرَّدِي
All a. or n.	كُلٌّ . الْكُلُّ	Allude v. t.	اشَارَ أَوْ لَمَّحَ إِلَى
Allay v. t.	اخْمَدَ . خَفَّفَ . خَفَضَ	Allure v. t.	إِسْتَمَالَ . إِجْتَذَبَ . اغْوَى
Allegation n.	تَأْكِيدٌ . حُجَّةٌ . إِدِّعَاءٌ	Allurement n.	جَذْبٌ . إِسْتِمَالَةٌ . إِغْوَاءٌ
Allege v. t.	صَرَّحَ . إِدَّعَى	Alluring a.	مُسْتَمِيلٌ . مُغْوٍ
Allegiance n.	طَاعَةٌ . امَانَةٌ		

Allusion n.	إِشَارَة . تَلْمِيحْ
Alluvium n.	غَرْبَل . رُسُوبُ ٱلْمَاء
Ally n. or v. t.	مُحالِفْ . مُعَاهِدٌ . حَالَف
Almanac n.	رُزْنَامَةٌ . تَقْوِيمُ ٱلسنة
Almighty a. or n.	قَادِر على كلِّ شَيْء
Almond n.	اوزْ
Almoner n.	وَكِيلُ ٱوْمُوَزِّعُ صَدَقات
Almost ad.	تَقْرِيباً
Alms n.	صَدَقَةٌ . إِحْسان
Aloft ad.	فِي ٱلْعَالِي . فَوْق
Alone a.	على ٱنْفِرَاد . وَحْدَه
Along ad. or pr.	إِلى قُدَّامٍ . بِجَانِب
Aloof ad.	بِمَعْزِل عَنْ . على بَعْد
Aloud ad.	بِصَوْت وَاضِحٍ اوْ عال
Alphabet n.	حُرُوف ٱلهِجَاء
Alphabetic a.	نِسْبة لِحُرُوف ٱلهِجَاء
Alpine a.	مُخْتَصٌّ بِجَبَلٍ عال
Already ad.	

Also ad.	ايْضا . كَذلِك
Altar n.	مَذْبَحْ
Alter v. t.	غَيَّرَ . بَدَّلَ . حَوَّل
Alterable a.	قَابِلُ ٱلتَّغْيِير
Alteration n.	تَغْيِير . تَحْوِيل
Altercation n.	مُخَاصَمَة . مُشَاجَرَةٌ
Alternate a.	مُتَبَادِلٌ . مُتَعَاقِبْ
Alternate v. i.	بَادَلَ . نَاوَب
Alternation n.	تَبَادُلٌ . تَنَاوُب
Alternative n.	احَدُ امْرَيْنِ
Although con.	مَع انَّ . وَلَوْ ان
Altitude n.	عُلُوٌّ . إِرْتِفَاعْ
Altogether ad.	جُمْلَةً . ٱلْكل مَعاً
Alum n.	شَبٌّ ابْيَضْ
Always ad.	دائِماً . عَلَى ٱلدَّوَام
Amalgamate v. t.	خَلَط مَعْدَناً بِالزِّئْبَق مَزَج
Amalgamation n.	مَزْجُ ٱلْمَعَادِنِ بِالزِّئْبَق

Amanuensis *n.* كَاتِبٌ ما يُمْلَى عَلَيْهِ	Ambler *n.* خَابٌّ . رَهوَانٌ
Amass *v. t.* جَمَعَ . كَوَّمَ	Ambrosia *n.* عنبَرِيَّةٌ . طَعَامُ الآلِهَةِ
Amateur *n.* مُغْرَمٌ بالفنونِ هاوٍ	Ambulance *n.* مَحْمَلُ المَرْضَى
Amatory *a.* حُبِّيٌّ . عِشْقِيٌّ	Ambuscade *n.* مَكْمَنٌ
Amaze *v.t.* أَدْهَشَ . أَذْهَلَ	Ambush *n.* كَمِينٌ
Amazement *n.* دَهْشَةٌ . إِنْذِهَالٌ	Ameliorate *v. t.* حَسَّنَ . أَصْلَحَ
Amazing *a.* مُدْهِشٌ . عَجِيبٌ	Amelioration *n.* تَحْسِينٌ
Amazon *n.* إِمْرَأَةٌ حَرْبِيَّةٌ . سَلِيطَةٌ	Amenable *a.* مَسْؤُولٌ . مُطَالَبٌ
Ambassador *n.* سَفِيرٌ ج سُفَرَاءُ	Amend *v. t.* اصْلَحَ . عَدَّلَ . حَسَّنَ
Amber *n.* كَهْرَبَاءُ	Amendment *n.* إِصْلَاحٌ . تَحْسِينٌ
Ambergris *n.* عَنْبَرٌ	Amends *n.* تَعْوِيضٌ
Ambiguity *n.* إِلْتِبَاسٌ . إِبْهَامٌ	Amenity *n.* لُطْفٌ . أُنْسٌ
Ambiguous *a.* مُلْتَبِسٌ . مُبْهَمٌ	Amerce *v. t.* غَرَّمَ
Ambition *n.* طَلَبُ الرِّفْعَةِ . حُبُّ الرِّآسَةِ	Amethyst *n.* جَمَشْتٌ . بَنَفْشٌ
Ambitious *a.* طَالِبُ الرِّفْعَةِ . مُحِبُّ الرِّآسَةِ	Amiable *a.* أَنِيسٌ . مَحْبُوبٌ
	Amiably *ad.* بِلُطْفٍ . بِرِقَّةٍ . بِوُدٍّ
	Amiable *a.* سَلَمِيٌّ . وِدَادِيٌّ
Amble *v. i.* خَبَّ . رَهَا	Amid *pr.* بَيْنَ . فِيمَا بَيْنَ

Amiss *a.* or *ad.*	غَيْرُ مُوَافِقٍ . بِخَطَأٍ	Amuse *v. t.*	سَلَّى . أَلْهَى
Amity *n.*	مَحَبَّةٌ . صُحْبَةٌ	Amusement *n.*	تَسْلِيَةٌ
Ammonia *n.*	نُشَادِرٌ	Amusing *a.*	مُسَلٍّ . مُضْحِك
Ammunition *n.*	مُؤْنَةُ الْحَرْبِ	Anachronism *n.*	خَطَأٌ تَارِيخِيٌّ
Amnesty *n.*	أَمَانٌ . عَفْوٌ	Anæsthetic *n.*	مُخَدِّرٌ
Among Amongst } *pr.*	بَيْنَ . فِيمَا بَيْنَ	Analogous *a.*	مُقَابَنٌ . تَمْثِيلِيٌّ
Amorous *a.*	عَاشِقٌ . غَرَامِيٌّ	Analogy *n.*	تَمْثِيلٌ . مُمَاثَلَةٌ
Amount *v. i.* or *n.*	بَلَغَ . مَبْلَغٌ	Analysis *n.*	تَحْلِيلٌ . تَفْصِيلٌ
Amphibious *a.*	(حَيَوَانٌ) مَائِيٌّ بَرِّيٌّ	Analytic *a.*	تَحْلِيلِيٌّ . مُفَصَّلٌ
Amphitheatre *n.*	مَلْعَبٌ مُدَوَّرُ الْبِنَاءِ	Analyze *v. t.*	حَلَّلَ . فَصَّلَ
Ample *a.*	فَسِيحٌ . وَاسِعٌ . كَافٍ	Anarchic *a.*	بِلَا حُكُومَةٍ أَوْ تَرْتِيبٍ
Amplification *n.*	تَوْسِيعٌ . إِسْهَابٌ	Anarchy *n.*	عَدَمُ الْحُكْمِ . فَوْضَى
Amplify *v. t.*	وَسَّعَ . أَسْهَبَ	Anathema *n.*	حَرْمٌ
Amplitude *n.*	إِتِّسَاعٌ . كِبَرٌ	Anathematize *v. t.*	حَرَمَ
Amply *ad.*	كِفَايَةً . بِسِعَةٍ	Anatomical *a.*	تَشْرِيحِيٌّ
Amputate *v. t.*	بَتَرَ . قَطَعَ	Anatomist *n.*	عَالِمٌ فِي التَّشْرِيحِ
Amputation *n.*	بَتْرٌ . قَطْعٌ	Anatomy *n.*	عِلْمُ التَّشْرِيحِ
Amulet *n.*	عُوذَةٌ . تَمِيمَةٌ	Ancestor *n.*	سَلَفٌ . جَدٌّ

Ancestral *a.*	مُخْتَصٌّ بِالْأَجْدَادِ
Ancestry *n.*	سِلْسِلَةُ الْأَجْدَادِ نَسَبٌ
Anchor *n.*	مِرْسَاةٌ ج مَرَاسٍ
Anchorage *n.*	مَرْسًى. مَرْفَأٌ
Anchorite *n.*	نَاسِكٌ . زَاهِدٌ
Ancient *a.*	قَدِيمٌ
Ancients *n. pl.*	الْقُدَمَاءُ
And *con.*	وَاوُ الْعَطْفِ
Anecdote *n.*	حِكَايَةٌ . قِصَّةٌ
Anemone *n.*	شَقِيقَةٌ . (نَبَاتٌ)
Anew *ad.*	جَدِيدًا . أَيْضًا
Angel *n.*	مَلَاكٌ
Angelic *a.*	مَلَكِيٌّ
Anger *n.*	غَضَبٌ . غَيْظٌ
Angle *n.*	زَاوِيَةٌ ج زَوَايَا
Angle *v.i.*	صَادَ (السَّمَكَ) بِالصِّنَّارَةِ
Angler *n.*	صَيَّادٌ بِالصِّنَّارَةِ
Anglican *a.*	تَابِعُ الْكَنِيسَةِ الْإِنْكِلِيزِيَّةِ
Anglicism *n.*	لَهْجَةٌ إِنْكِلِيزِيَّةٌ
Anglicize *v. t.*	حَوَّلَ إِلَى الْإِنْكِلِيزِيِّ
Angling *n.*	صَيْدٌ بِالصِّنَّارَةِ
Angrily *ad.*	بِغَيْظٍ . بِغَضَبٍ
Angry *a.*	غَضْبَانُ . مُغْتَاظٌ
Anguish *v.*	عَذَابٌ . أَلَمٌ شَدِيدٌ
Angular *a.*	ذُو زَوَايَا
Animadversion *v.*	مَلَامَةٌ . تَنْكِيتٌ
Animadvert *v. i.*	اِلْتَفَتَ إِلَى . نَكَّتَ
Animal *n.*	حَيَوَانٌ
Animalcule *n.*	حُوَيْوِينَةٌ
Animate *v. t.*	أَحْيَا . أَنْعَشَ . نَشَّطَ
Animating *a.*	مُحْيٍ . مُنَشِّطٌ
Animation *n.*	نَشَاطٌ . حَيَاةٌ . رُوحٌ
Animosity *n.*	بُغْضٌ . حِقْدٌ
Ankle *n.*	رُسْغُ الْقَدَمِ
Anklet *n.*	خَلْخَالٌ
Annalist *n.*	مُؤَرِّخٌ

Annals *n.*	أَخْبَارٌ سَنَوِيَّةٌ مُتَتَابِعَةٌ	Annulment *n.*	إِلْغَاءٌ. إِبْطَالٌ
Annex *v. t.*	أَوْصَلَ. اضَافَ	Annulet *v. t.*	زَرَدَةٌ. حَلْقَةٌ
Annexation *n.*	إِيصَالٌ. إِضَافَةٌ	Annunciate *v. t.*	أَعْلَنَ. أَتَى بِأَخْبَارٍ
Annihilate *v. t.*	أَعْدَمَ. اَبَادَ	Annunciation *n.*	إِعْلَانٌ. خَبَرٌ. بِشَارَةٌ
Annihilation *n.*	إِعْدَامٌ. إِبَادَةٌ	Anoint *v. t.*	مَسَحَ
Anniversary *n. or a.*	عِيدٌ سَنَوِيٌّ	Anointing *n.*	مَسْحٌ
Annotate *v. t.*	شَرَحَ. حَشَى	Anomalous *a.*	غَيْرُ قِيَاسِيٍّ. شَاذٌّ
Annotation *n.*	شَرْحٌ. حَاشِيَةٌ	Anomaly *n.*	شُذُوذٌ. عَدَمُ نِظَامٍ
Annotator *n.*	شَارِحٌ. مُحَشٍّ	Anon *ad.*	عَنْ قَرِيبٍ. حَالاً
Announce *v. t.*	أَعْلَنَ. أَخْبَرَ. أَنْبَأَ	Anonymous *a.*	بِلَا اسْمٍ
Announcement *n.*	إِعْلَانٌ إِنْبَاءٌ	Another *a.*	آخَرُ غَيْرٌ
Annoy *v. t.*	كَدَّرَ. أَزْعَجَ	Answer *n. or v. t.*	جَوَابٌ. اجَابَ
Annoyance *n.*	إِزْعَاجٌ. أَمْرٌ مُكَدِّرٌ	Answerable *a.*	مَسْئُولٌ. مُوَافِقٍ
Annual *a. or n.*	سَنَوِيٌّ. نَبَاتٌ سَنَوِيٌّ	Ant *n.*	نَمْلَةٌ
Annually *ad.*	سَنَوِيًّا	Antagonism *n.*	مُضَادَّةٌ. مُقَاوَمَةٌ
Annuity *n.*	مَعَاشٌ سَنَوِيٌّ	Antagonist *n.*	مُقَاوِمٌ. خَصْمٌ
Annul *v. t.*	أَلْغَى. أَبْطَلَ	Antagonistic *a.*	مُضَادٌّ. مُقَاوِمٌ
Annular *a.*	حَلْقِيٌّ. مُسْتَدِيرٌ	Antagonize *v. t.*	ضَادَّ. قَاوَمَ

Antractic a.	مُخْتَصٌّ بِٱلْقُطْبِ ٱلْجَنُوبِيِّ
Antecedence n.	أَسْبَقِيَّةٌ . سَبْقٌ
Antecedent a.	سَابِقٌ
Antechamber n.	غُرْفَةٌ مُقَدَّمَةٌ
Antedata v. t.	أَرَّخَ قَبْلَ (ٱلتَّارِيخ ٱلْحَقِيقِيِّ)
Antediluvian a. or n.	قَبْلَ ٱلطُّوفَانِ
Antelope n.	رِئْمٌ ج آرَامٌ
Antepenult a.	مَقْطَعُ ٱلْكَلِمَةِ قَبْلَ ٱلْأَخِيرِ
Anterior a.	سَالِفٌ . مُتَقَدِّمٌ
Anthem n.	نَشِيدٌ
Anteroom n.	غُرْفَةٌ . قُدَّامَ غُرْفَةٍ
Anther n.	طَرَفُ سِدَاةِ ٱلنَّبَاتِ
Anthracite n.	فَحْمٌ حَجَرِيٌّ صَلْبٌ
Anthropology n.	عِلْمٌ يَبْحَثُ عَنْ ٱلْإِنْسَانِ
Antichrist n.	ضِدّ ٱلْمَسِيحِ
Anticipate v. t.	سَبَقَ ـ رَأَى مِنْ قَبْلُ
Anticipation n.	سَبْقٌ . حِسٌّ . سَابِقٌ
Antidote n.	تِرْيَاقٌ
Antimony n.	إِثْمِدٌ . اِنْتِيمُنُ
Antipathy n.	نُفُورٌ . كَرَاهَةٌ
Antipodes n.	السَّاكِنُونَ أَقْطَارَ ٱلْأَرْضِ ٱلْمُتَقَابِلَةِ
Antiquarian a.	مُخْتَصٌّ بِٱلزَّمَانِ ٱلْقَدِيمِ
Antiquarian n. } Antiquary n. }	عَالِمٌ بِٱلْآثَارِ ٱلْقَدِيمَةِ
Antiquated a. or pp.	قَدِيمٌ . عَتِيقٌ
Antique a. or n.	أَثَرٌ قَدِيمٌ . قَدِيمٌ
Antiquity n.	ٱلزَّمَانُ ٱلْقَدِيمُ . أَثَرٌ قَدِيمٌ
Antiseptic a. or n.	مُضَادُّ ٱلْفَسَادِ وَٱلْعُفُونَةِ
Antithesis n.	تَبَايُنٌ فِي ٱلْكَلَامِ
Antitype n.	ٱلْمَرْمُوزُ إِلَيْهِ

Antler *n.*	قَرْنُ الْوَعْلِ	Apish *a.*	قِرْدِيٌّ . نَظِيرُ الْقِرْدِ
Anus *n.*	إِسْتٌ	Apocalypse *n.*	الرُّؤْيَا . سِفْرُ الرُّؤْيَا
Anvil *n.*	سِنْدَانٌ . زُبْرَةٌ	Apocrypha *n.*	الْكُتُبُ غَيْرُ الْقَانُونِيةِ
Anxiety *n.*	هَمٌّ . قَلَقٌ	Apocryphal *a.*	غَيْرُ ثَابِت . بَاطِلٌ
Anxious *a.*	مُهْتَمٌّ . مَشْغُولُ الْبَال	Apologetic *a.*	إِعْتِذَارِيٌّ . إِحْتِجَاجِيٌّ
Any *a.*	احَدٌ . ايَّا كَان	Apologist *n.*	مُحْتَجٌّ . مُحَامٍ
Apace *ad.*	سَرِيعاً	Apologize *v. i.*	إِعْتَذَرَ . دَافَعَ عَنْ
Apart *ad.*	عَلَى جَانِبٍ . على حِدَة	Apology *n.*	اِعْتِذَارٌ . مُحَامَاةٌ
Apartment *n.*	غُرْفَةٌ . مُخْدَعٌ	Apoplexy *n.*	دَآءُ السَّكْتَةِ
Apathetic *a.*	غَيْرُ حَاسٍّ أَوْ مُبَالٍ	Apostasy *n.*	إِرْتِدَادٌ . جُحُودُ الدِّينِ
Apathy *n.*	عَدَمُ الآكْتِرَاثِ أَوِ الْمُبَالَاةِ	Apostate *n.*	مُرْتَدٌّ . جَاحِدٌ
Ape *n.* or *v. t.*	قِرْدٌ . قَلَّدَ	Apostatize *v. t.*	إِرْتَدَّ . جَحَدَ الآيمَان
Aperient *a.*	مُسْهِلٌ . خَفِيفٌ . مُلَيِّنٌ	Apostle *n.*	رَسُولٌ ج رُسُل
Aperture *n.*	نَافِذَةٌ . ثَقْبٌ	Apostleship *n.*	رَسُولِيَّة . رِسَالَة
Apex *n.*	قُمَّةٌ . رَأْسٌ	Apostolic *a.*	رَسُولِيٌّ
Apiary *n.*	مَنْحِلة	Apostrophe *n.*	حَذْفُ حَرْفٍ وعلامتهُ
Apiece *ad.*	نَصِيبُ كُلٍّ . لِكُلٍّ وَاحِدٍ	Apothecary *n.*	اجْزَائِيٌّ (صَيْدَلانِيّ)
		Appall *v. t.*	أَرْعَبَ . رَاعَ

Appalling a.	مُرْعِبٌ . رَائِعٌ
Apparatus n.	ادَوَاتٌ
Apparel n.	لِبَاسٌ . كِسَاءٌ
Apparent a.	ظَاهِرٌ . وَاضِحٌ
Apparently ad.	بِحَسَبِ الظَّاهِرِ
Apparition n.	ظُهُورٌ . طَيْفٌ
Appeal v. t.	رَفَعَ الدَّعْوَى
Appeal n.	إِسْتِئْنَافٌ . رَفْعُ الدَّعْوَى
Appear v. t.	ظَهَرَ ـَ . بَانَ ـَ
Appearance n.	ظُهُورٌ
Appease v. t.	سَكَّنَ (غَيْظَهُ) . هَدَّأَ
Appellant n.	رَافِعُ الدَّعْوَى
Appellation n.	لَقَبٌ . تَسْمِيَةٌ
Appellative a. or n.	عَامٌّ . إِسْمٌ عَامٌّ
Append v. t.	عَلَّقَ او الْحَقَ بِ
Appendage n.	مُلْحَقٌ . ذَيْلٌ
Appendix n.	مُلْحَقٌ . ذَيْلُ كِتَابٍ
Appertain v. i.	إِخْتَصَّ بِ
Appetite n.	(قَابِلِيَّةٌ) شَهْوَةُ آلأَكْلِ
Appetizing a.	مُهَيِّجٌ لِشَهْوَةِ آلأَكْلِ
Applaud v. t.	مَدَحَ . صَفَقَ مَدْحًا
Applause n.	مَدْحٌ . تَصْفِيقٌ إِسْتِحْسَانٍ
Apple n.	تُفَّاحَةٌ
Appliance n.	وَضْعٌ . تَخْصِيصٌ . وَاسِطَةٌ
Applicable a.	مُطَابِقٌ . مُوَافِقٌ
Applicant n.	طَالِبٌ ج طَلَبَةٌ
Application n.	مُوَاظَبَةٌ . طَلَبٌ . وَضْعٌ
Apply v. t. or i.	أَطْلَقَ عَلَى . إِسْتَعْمَلَ لِ
Apply to-for v. t.	طَلَبَ مِنْ
Appoint v. t.	عَيَّنَ . أَقَامَ عَلَى
Appointee n.	مُعَيَّنٌ لِوَظِيفَةٍ
Appointment n.	تَعْيِينٌ . رَاتِبٌ
Apportion v. t.	قَسَّمَ . أَحْصَّ
Apportionment n.	تَقْسِيمٌ . إِحْصَاصٌ
Apposite a.	مُوَافِقٌ . لَائِقٌ
Apposition n.	بَدَلٌ (فِي النَّحْوِ)

Appraisal Appraisment } n.	تَثْمِين . (تَقْدِيرٌ)
Appraise v. t.	ثَمَّن (قَدَّرَ)
Appreciable a.	قَابِلُ التَّثْمِينِ وَالتَّقْدِيرِ
Appreciate v. t.	ثَمَّنَ . إِعْتَبَرَ
Appreciation n.	تَثْمِينٌ . إِعْتِبَارٌ
Apprehend v. t.	فَهِمَ . أَدْرَكَ . قَبَضَ
Apprehension n.	إِدْرَاكٌ . خَوْفٌ
Apprehensive a.	مُدْرِكٌ . خَائِفٌ
Apprentice n.	تِلْمِيذُ صِنَاعَةٍ
Apprise v. t.	أَخْبَرَ . اعْلَمَ
Approach v. t.	دَنَا . قَرُبَ . مِنْ
Approachable a.	سَهْلُ الْإِقْتِرَابِ إِلَيْهِ
Approbation n.	إِسْتِحْسَانٌ . رِضًى
Appropriate v. t.	خَصَّصَ . أَفْرَزَ
Appropriate n.	مُنَاسِبٌ . لَائِقٌ
Appropriate a.	تَخْصِيصٌ
Approval n.	إِسْتِحْسَانٌ . قُبُولٌ
Approve v. t.	إِسْتَحْسَنَ . رَضِيَ بِهِ
Approximate v. t. or a. }	إِقْتَرَبَ إِلَى . تَقْرِيبِيٌّ
Approximately ad.	تَقْرِيباً
Approximation n.	تَقْرِيبٌ . إِقْتِرَابٌ
Appurtenance n.	مُلْحَقٌ . مُخْتَصٌّ
Apricot n.	مِشْمِشَةٌ
April n.	نِيسَانٌ
Apron n.	(مِرْيُولٌ) وَزْرَةٌ
Apt a.	مُسْتَعِدٌّ . خَلِيقٌ ب
Aptitudes Aptness } n.	مَيْلٌ طَبِيعِيٌّ . اهْلِيَّةٌ
Aptly ad.	كَمَا يَجِبُ . بِلِيَاقَةٍ
Aquarium n.	حَوْضُ السَّمَكِ وَالنَّبَاتِ
Aquatic a.	عَائِشٌ فِي الْمَاءِ
Aqueduct n.	قَنَاةُ مَاءٍ
Aqueous a.	مَائِيٌّ
Arabian a.	عَرَبِيٌّ
Arabic n.	الْعَرَبِيَّةُ
Arable a.	صَالِحٌ لِلْحَرْثِ او الزَّرْعِ
Arbiter Arbitrator } n.	فَيْصَلٌ . حَكَمٌ

Arbitrary n.	غَيْرُ مُقَيَّدٍ . مُسْتَبِدٌّ
Arbitrate v. t. or i.	تَوَسَّطَ بِحُكْمٍ بَيْنَ
Arbitration n.	حُكْمُ ٱلْفَيَاصِلِ
Arbour n.	عَرِيشٌ ج عَرَائِشُ
Arboreous a.	شَجَرِيٌّ
Arc d.	قَوْسٌ ج قُسِيٌّ
Arcade n.	رُوَاقٌ ج أَرْوِقَةٌ
Arch n. or v. t.	قَنْطَرَةٌ . قَنْطَرَ
Archæology n.	عِلْمُ ٱلْآثَارِ ٱلْقَدِيمَةِ
Archaic a.	قَدِيمٌ
Archangel n.	رَئِيسُ مَلَائِكَةٍ
Archbishop n.	رَئِيسُ أَسَاقِفَةٍ
Archbishop-ric n.	مَقَامُ رَئِيسِ ٱلْأَسَاقِفَةِ
Archduchess n.	أَمِيرَةٌ فِي دَوْلَةِ ٱلنَّمْسَا
Archduke n.	أَمِيرٌ فِي دَوْلَةِ ٱلنَّمْسَا
Arched a.	مُقَوَّسٌ . مَقْبُوٌّ
Archer n.	رَامِي ٱلسِّهَامِ . رَامٍ
Archery n.	صِنَاعَةُ ٱلرَّمْيِ بِٱلْقَوْسِ

Archetype n.	أَنْمُوذَجٌ أَصْلِيٌّ
Archipelago n.	مَجْمُوعُ جُزَائِرَ . أَرْخِبِيلٌ
Architect n.	مُهَنْدِسُ بِنَاءٍ
Architectural a.	مُتَعَلِّقٌ بِعِلْمِ ٱلْبِنَاءِ
Architecture n.	عِلْمُ ٱلْبِنَاءِ وَهَنْدَسَتُهُ
Archives n. pl.	سِجِلَّاتٌ وَخَزَائِنُهَا
Archway n.	مَمْشًى تَحْتَ قَنَاطِرَ
Arctic a.	مُخْتَصٌّ بِٱلْقُطْبِ ٱلشَّمَالِيِّ
Ardent a.	حَارٌّ . غَيُورٌ
Ardour n.	حَرَارَةٌ . حَمِيَّةٌ . حَمَاسَةٌ
Arquous a.	صَعْبٌ . شَاقٌّ
Area n.	سَاحَةُ أَرْضٍ . إِتِّسَاعُهَا
Arena n.	مَيْدَانٌ ج مَيَادِينُ
Arenaceous a.	رَمْلِيٌّ
Argillaceous a.	صَلْصَالِيٌّ
Argue v. i. or t.	نَاظَرَ . إِحْتَجَّ . جَادَلَ
Argument n.	دَلِيلٌ . حُجَّةٌ
Argumentation n.	إِقَامَةُ ٱلدَّلِيلِ

Argumentation *n.*	إِحْتِجَاجِيّ
Arid *a.*	قَاحِلٌ . جَافٌّ
Aridity *n.*	قُحُولَةٌ . يُبُوسَةٌ
Aries *n.*	بُرْجُ ٱلْحَمَلِ
Aright *ad.*	مُسْتَقِيمًا
Arise *v. i.*	قَامَ . طَلَعَ . ظَهَرَ
Aristocracy *n.*	الأَشْرَافُ . حُكُومَتُهُم
Aristocrat *n.*	أَحَدُ ٱلْأَشْرَافِ
Aristocratic *a.*	مُخْتَصٌّ بِٱلْأَشْرَافِ
Arithmetic *n.*	عِلْمُ الْحِسَابِ
Arithmetical *a.*	حِسَابِيّ
Arithmetician *n.*	عَالِمٌ بِٱلْحِسَابِ
Ark *n.*	فُلْكٌ . تَابُوتٌ
Arm *n.*	ذِرَاعٌ . سَاعِدٌ . فَرْعٌ مِنَ الْعَسْكَرِ
Arm *v. t.*	سَلَّحَ
Armada *n.*	مَجْمُوعُ بَوَارِجَ . اسْطُولٌ
Armament *n.*	جِهَازٌ لِلْحَرْبِ
Arm-chair *n.*	كُرْسِيّ ذُو يَدَيْنِ
Armful *n.*	مِلْ قَبْضَةِ الذِّرَاعِ
Armhole *n.*	ثَقْبُ ثَوْبٍ لِلذِّرَاعِ
Armistice *n.*	هُدْنَةٌ
Armlet *n.*	سِوَارٌ
Armour *n.*	عُدَّةُ حَرْبٍ . سِلَاحٌ
Armoured *a.*	مُصَفَّحٌ بِٱلْحَدِيدِ . مُلَبَّسٌ بِصَفَائِحِ حَدِيدٍ
Armourer *n.*	صَانِعُ أَسْلِحَةٍ أَوْ بَائِعُهَا
Armoury *n.*	مَخْزَنُ اسْلِحَةٍ
Armpit *n.*	إِبْطٌ ج آبَاطٌ
Arms *n. pl.*	عُدَّةُ حَرْبٍ . اسْلِحَةٌ
Army *n.*	جَيْشٌ ج جُيُوشٌ
Aroma *n.*	رَائِحَةٌ عِطْرِيَّةٌ
Aromatic *a.*	عَطِرٌ . طِيبِيّ
Around *pr.* or *ad.*	حَوْلَ
Arouse *v. t.*	أَيْقَظَ . نَبَّهَ . حَرَّضَ
Arraign *v. t.*	دَعِيَ لِلْمُحَاكَمَةِ
Arraignment *n.*	مُحَاكَمَةٌ

Arrrange v. t.	رَتَّبَ . دَبَّرَ
Arrangement n.	تَرْتِيبٌ . تَدْبِيرٌ
Arrant a.	شَهِيرٌ بِالشَّرِّ
Array n.	مُصَافٌ . لِبَاسٌ
Array v. t.	صَفَّ . لَبِسَ . زَيَّنَ
Arrears n. pl.	بَقَايَا دَيْنٍ مُسْتَحِقٍّ
Arrest v. t.	اَلْقَى اَلْقَبْضَ عَلَى . وَقَفَ
Arrest n.	اِلْقَاءُ الْقَبْضِ . تَوْقِيفٌ
Arrival n.	مَجِيءٌ . وُصُولٌ
Arrive v. i.	أَتَى . وَصَلَ . بَلَغَ
Arrogance n.	غَطْرَسَةٌ . تَكَبُّرٌ
Arrogant a.	مُتَجَبِّرٌ . مُتَكَبِّرٌ
Arrogate v. t.	اِدَّعَى . نَسَبَ لِنَفْسِهِ
Arrow n.	سَهْمٌ ج سِهَامٌ
Arsenal n.	مَخْزَنُ مُؤْنَةٍ حَرْبِيَّةٍ
Arsenic n.	زِرْنِيخٌ . سَمُّ الْفَارِ
Arson n.	حَرْقُ بَيْتٍ عَنْ ضَغِينَةٍ
Art n.	فَنٌّ . صِنَاعَةٌ . مَكْرٌ

Arterial a.	شِرْيَانِيٌّ
Artery n.	شِرْيَانٌ ج شَرَايِينُ
Artful a.	مَكَّارٌ . مَاهِرٌ
Artichoke n.	(أَرْضِي شَوْكِي) خُرْشُوفٌ
Article n.	بَنْدٌ . مَادَّةٌ . آلُ التَّعْرِيفِ
Articulate a.	ذُو مَفَاصِلَ أَوْ مَقَاطِعَ
Articulate v. t.	لَفَظَ وَاضِحًا
Articulation n.	لَفْظٌ . مَفْصِلٌ . اِتِّصَالٌ
Artifice n.	حِيلَةٌ تَدْبِيرٌ
Artificer n.	صَاحِبُ حِرْفَةٍ . مُخْتَرِعٌ
Artificial a.	مُصْنَعٌ . غَيْرُ حَقِيقِيٍّ
Artillery n.	مَدَافِعُ (طُوبْجِيَّةٌ)
Artisan n.	صَاحِبُ صِنَاعَةٍ
Artist n.	إِسْتَاذُ صِنَاعَةٍ . مُصَوِّرٌ
Artistic a.	مُطَابِقٌ لِلصِّنَاعَةِ . نَفِيسٌ
Artless a.	سَاذِجٌ سَلِيمُ النِّيَّةِ

As _ad._	كَمَا . مِثْلُ . لَمَّا . بَيْنَمَا
Ascend _v. t._ or _i._	صَعِدَ . طَلَعَ ـِ
Ascendant _a._ or _n._	فَائِقٌ . سَطْوَةٌ
Ascendency _n._	سَطْوَةٌ . سلْطَة
Ascension _n._	صُعُودٌ
Ascent _n._	طُلُوعٌ . مَرْقًى . إِرْتِقَاءٌ
Ascertain _v. t._	كَشَفَ ـِ حَقَّقَ
Ascetic _n._	نَاسِكٌ . زَاهِدٌ
Asceticism _n._	تَنَسُّكٌ . زُهْدٌ
Ascribe _v. t._	نَسَبَ ـِ إِلَى
Ascription _n._	نِسْبَةٌ . تَخْصِيصٌ
Ash _n._	دَرْدَارٌ (شَجَرَة)
Ashamed _a._	خَجْلَانُ . مُسْتَحٍ
Ashen _a._	دَرْدَارِيٌّ . رَمَادِيٌّ
Ashes _n. pl._	رَمَادٌ
Ashore _ad._	عَلَى الْبَرّ او إِلَيْهِ
Ashy _a._	رَمَادِيٌّ . مُصْفَرٌّ
Asiatic _a._	نِسْبَةٌ لآسِيَّا

Aside _ad._	عَلَى جَانِبٍ . عَلَى إِنْفِرَادٍ
Asinine _a._	حِمَارِيٌّ . بَلِيدٌ
Ask _v. t._	طَلَبَ ـِ سَأَل
Asleep _a._	نَائِمٌ . رَاقِدٌ
Asp _n._	صِلٌّ . أفْعَى
Asparagus _n._	هَلْيُونٌ
Aspect _n._	مَنْظَرٌ . هَيْئَةٌ
Asperity _n._	خُشُونَة . غِلاَظَة
Asperse _v. t._	قذفَ ـِ طَعَنَ في
Aspersion _n._	قذفٌ . طَعْنٌ . رَشٌّ
Asphyxia _n._	إِخْتِنَاقٌ
Aspirant _n._	طَالِبٌ . تَوَّاقٌ
Aspirate _n._	صَوْتٌ كَالْهَاء
Aspiration _n._	شَوْقٌ . مَطْأَبٌ . تَلَهُّفٌ
Aspire _v. i._	طَلَبَ بِشَوْقٍ . تَاقَ إِلَى
Ass _n._	حِمَارٌ ج حَمِيرٌ
Assail _v. t._	هَجَمَ عَلَى . إِقْتَحَم
Assailant _n._	مُهَاجِمٌ . مقْتَحِمٌ

Assassin n.	قاتِلٌ سِرًّا
Assassinate v. t.	قَتَلَ سِرًّا
Assassination n.	قَتْلٌ سِرًّا
Assault v. t. or n.	هَاجَمَ مُهَاجَمَةٌ
Assay v. t. or i. or n.	جَرَّبَ إِمْتِحَان
Assayer n.	مُمْتَحِنُ الْمَعَادِن
Assemblage n.	إِجْتِمَاعٌ . مَحْفَلٌ
Assemble v. i. or t.	جَمَعَ . إِجْتَمَعَ
Assembly n.	مَجْمَعٌ . مَجْلِسٌ
Assent v. i. or n.	سَلَّمَ . تَسْلِيمٌ
Assert v. t	زَعَمَ . إِدَّعَى . تَأَكَّدَ
Assertion n.	زَعْمٌ . إِدِّعَاءٌ . تَأْكِيدٌ
Assess v. t.	قَدَّرَ . ثَمَّنَ
Assessment n.	تَثْمِينٌ
Assessor n.	مُثَمِّنٌ . مَنْ يَضَعُ الرَّسْمَ
Assets n. pl.	مَوْجُودَاتٌ
Asseverate v. t.	اَكَّدَ صَرَّحَ
Assiduity n.	مُوَاظَبَةٌ . مُثَابَرَةٌ

Assiduous a.	مُوَاظِبٌ . مُثَابِرٌ
Assign v. t.	خَصَّصَ . أَفْرَزَ
Assignation n.	تَعْيِينٌ . مِيعَادُ لِقَاءٍ
Assignee n.	مَنْ يُسَلَّمُ لَهُ شَيْءٌ
Assignment n.	تَعْيِينٌ . تَحْوِيلٌ . إِحَالَةُ امُورِ مُفْلِسٍ إِلَى وُكَلَاءٍ
Assimilate v. t.	مَثَّلَ . شَبَّهَ . أَدْغَمَ
Assist v. t.	أَعَانَ . سَاعَدَ . اغَاثَ
Assistance n.	مُسَاعَدَةٌ . عَوْنٌ
Assistant n.	مُسَاعِدٌ . مُعِينٌ
Assizes n.	مَحْكَمَةٌ . مَجْلِسُ الْحُقُوقِ
Associate v. t. or i.	اشْرَكَ . إِشْتَرَكَ
Associate n. or a.	شَرِيكٌ . رَفِيقٌ
Association n.	مُشَارَكَةٌ . جَمْعِيَّةٌ
Assort v. t.	رَتَّبَ . جَنَّسَ
Assorted a.	مُتَنَوِّعٌ . مُشَكَّلٌ
Assortment	تَرْتِيبٌ . بَضَائِعُ مُتَنَوِّعَةٌ
Assuage v. t.	خَفَّفَ . اخْمَدَ

Assume *v. t.*	اِدَّعَى . اِتَّخَذَ
Assuming *a.*	مُدَّعٍ . مُتَكَبِّرٌ . مُعْجَبٌ
Assumption *n.*	اِدِّعَاءٌ . اِتِّخَاذٌ
Assurance *n.*	تَأْكِيدٌ . يَقِينٌ
Assure *v. t.*	أَكَّدَ . حَقَّقَ
Asteroid *n.*	سَيَّارٌ صَغِيرٌ
Astern *ad.*	عَلَى مُؤَخَّرِ السَّفِينَةِ أَوْ خَلْفَهَا
Asthma *n.*	دَاءُ الرَّبْوِ
Asmatic *a.*	مُصَابٌ بِدَاءِ الرَّبْوِ
Astonish *v. t.*	أَدْهَشَ . حَيَّرَ
Astonishing *a.*	مُدْهِشٌ . مُحَيِّرٌ
Astonishment *n.*	دَهْشَةٌ . تَعَجُّبٌ
Astound *v. t.*	أَدْهَشَ حَيَّرَ
Astray *ad.*	تَائِهاً . شَارِداً
Astrine *ad.*	مُفَرْشِحاً
Astringent *a. or n.*	قَابِضٌ ج قَوَابِضُ
Astrologer *n,*	مُنَجِّمٌ
Astrology *n.*	عِلْمُ التَّنْجِيمِ

Astronomer *n.*	عَالِمٌ بِعِلْمِ الْهَيْئَةِ
Astronomy *n.*	عِلْمُ الْهَيْئَةِ
Astute *a.*	ذَكِيٌّ . حَاذِقٌ
Astuteness *n.*	دَهَاءٌ فَرَاسَةٌ
Asunder *ad.*	مَفْصُولاً عَنْ
Asylum *n.*	مَلْجَأٌ . بِيمَارِسْتَانٌ
At *pr.*	عِنْدَ . فِي
Atheism *n.*	اَلإِنْكَارُ وُجُودِ اللهِ
Atheist *n.*	مُنْكِرُ وُجُودِ اللهِ . مُلْحِدٌ
Athirst *a.*	عَطْشَانُ . ظَمْآنُ
Athlete *n.*	مُصَارِعٌ . مُتْقِنُ الرِّيَاضَةِ
Athletic *a.*	قَوِيُّ الْجِسْمِ . ضَلِيعٌ
Athwart *ad.*	عَرْضاً
Atlas *n.*	(أَطْلَسُ . مَجْمُوعُ خَارِطَاتٍ)
Atmosphere *n.*	هَوَاءٌ . جَوٌّ
Atmospheric *a.*	هَوَائِيٌّ . جَوِّيٌّ
Atom *n.*	ذَرَّةٌ . جَوْهَرُ الْفَرْدِ
Atomic *a.*	مُخْتَصٌّ بِجَوْهَرِ الْفَرْدِ

Atone *v. t.* or *i.*	كَفَّرَ عَنْ
Atonement *n.*	كَفَّارَة
Atrocious *a.*	فَظِيعٌ . فَاحِشٌ
Atrocity *n.*	كَبِيرَة . فَظَاعَة
Attach *v. t.*	وَصَلَ ـ عَلَّقَ
Attachment *n.*	ضَبْطَ . حَجْزٌ (آلأمْوَال) . وُدٌّ
Attack *v. t.* or *n.*	هَاجَمَ . مُهَاجَمَة
Attain *v. t.*	حَصَّلَ . بَلَغَ ـ
Attainment *n.*	تَحْصِيلٌ . بُلُوغٌ
Attaint *v. t.*	أَفْسَدَ . أَثْبَتَ خِيَانَتَهُ
Attempt *v. t.* or *n.*	جَرَّبَ . حَاوَلَ تَجْرِبَة
Attend *v. t.* or *i.*	رَافَقَ . إِعْتَنَى . حَضَرَ
Attendance *n.*	حُضُورٌ . مُلَازَمَة
Attendant *n.*	تَابِعٌ . خَادِمٌ . إِصْغَاء
Attention *n.*	إِنْتِبَاه . مَعْرُوف
Attentive *a.*	مُصْغٍ . مُلَازِمٌ
Attenuate *v. t.*	رَقَّقَ . خَفَّفَ
Attenuation *n.*	تَرْقِيقٌ . تَخْفِيفٌ
Attest *v. t.*	شَهِدَ . اثْبَتَ . أَكَّدَ
Attestation *n.*	شَهَادَةٌ . إِثْبَاتٌ
Attire *v. t.* or *n.*	أَلْبَسَ . لِبَاسٌ
Attitude *n.*	حَالَة . هَيْئَة
Attorney *n.*	وَكِيلُ دَعَاوٍ
Attract *a. t.*	جَذَبَ ـ إِسْتَمَالَ
Attraction *n.*	جَذْبٌ . جَاذِبِيَة
Attracting Attractive *a.*	جَاذِبٌ . مُسْتَمِيلٌ . سَارٌّ
Attractiveness *n.*	صِفَةُ الْجَذْبِ جَاذِبِية . حُسْن
Attribute *v. t.* or *n.*	نَسَبَ إِلَى . صِفَة
Attribution *n.*	نِسْبَة . وَصْف
Attrition *n.*	فَرْكُ . سَحْق
Attuned *pp.*	مُوَفَّق . مُدَوْزَن
Auction *n.*	مَزَاد . حَرَاج
Auctioneer *n.*	دَلَّال

Audacious *a.*	جَسُورٌ . وَقِحٌ
Audacity *n.*	جَسَارَةٌ . وَقَاحَةٌ
Audible *a.*	مَسْمُوعٌ
Audience *n.*	اَلسَّامِعُونَ اَلْحَاضِرُونَ
Audit *v. t.*	فَحَصَ حِسَابًا وَضَبَطَهُ
Auditor *n.*	فَاحِصُ حِساب . سَامِعٌ
Auditory *a.*	سَمْعِيٌّ
Auger *n.*	مِثْقَبٌ
Aught *n.*	شَيْءٌ ما
Augment *v. t. or i.*	زَادَ . إِزْدَادَ
Augment Augmentation } *n.*	زِيَادَة
Augury *n.*	فَأْلٌ . تَطَيُّرٌ
August *a.*	عَظِيمٌ . سَامِي الشَّأْن
August *n.*	شَهْرُ آب
Aunt *n.*	عَمَّةٌ أَوْ خَالَة
Auricle *n.*	صِيوَانَةُ الاذُنِ أُذَيْنَةُ الْقَلْب
Auriferous *a.*	ذُو ذَهَب
Aurora *n.*	شَفَقٌ
Auspicious *a.*	ذُو حَظٍّ . سَعِيدٌ
Austere *a.*	عَابِسٌ . صَارِمٌ
Austerity *n.*	صَرَامَةٌ . عُبُوسٌ
Authentic *a.*	حَقِيقِيٌّ
Authenticate *v. t.*	حَقَّقَ . أَثْبَتَ
Authenticity *n.*	حَقِيقَةٌ . حَقَّانِيَّة
Author *n.*	مُؤَلِّفٌ . مُصَنِّفٌ . مُسَبِّبٌ
Authoritative *a.*	جَازِمٌ . ذُو سُلْطَةٍ
Authority *n.*	سُلْطَةٌ . حَقُّ التَّسَلُّطِ
Authorization *n.*	تَفْوِيضٌ . إِجَازَةٌ
Authorize *v. t.*	فَوَّضَ . أَجَازَ . رَخَّصَ
Authorship *n.*	صِنَاعَةُ التَّأْلِيف
Autobiography *n.*	تَرْجَمَةُ الإِنْسَانِ لِحَيَاتِه
Autocracy *n.*	سُلْطَةٌ مُطْلَقَة
Autocrat *n.*	حَاكِمٌ مُطْلَقٌ
Autograph *n.*	خَطُّ الْمُؤَلِّفِ . إِمْضَاءٌ

Automatic a.	مُتَحَرِّكٌ مِنْ ذَاتِهِ
Autonomy n.	حُكْمٌ ذَاتِيٌّ إِسْتِقْلَالِيٌّ
Autopsy n.	تَشْرِيحُ جُثَّةٍ
Autumn n.	أَلْخَرِيفُ
Autumnal a.	خَرِيفِيٌّ
Auxiliary a. or n.	مُسَاعِدٌ
Avail v. i. or t. or n.	نَفَعَ. أَفَادَ. نَفْعٌ
Available a.	مَوْجُودٌ. مُفِيدٌ
Avails n. pl.	الْحَاصِلُ مِنْ بَيْعٍ
Avalanche n.	هَيَارُ الثَّلْجِ مِنْ جَبَلٍ
Avarice n.	بُخْلٌ. شُحٌّ
Avaricious a.	بَخِيلٌ. شَحِيحٌ
Avenge v. t.	إِنْتَقَمَ مِنْ. عَاقَبَ
Avenger n.	مُنْتَقِمٌ
Avenue n.	شَارِعٌ عَرِيضٌ. مَدْخَلٌ
Aver v. t.	اكَّدَ. جَزَمَ
Average n. or v. t.	مُعَدَّلٌ. عَدَّلَ

Averse a.	غَيْرُ رَاضٍ. مُنَافٍ. كَارِهٌ
Aversion n.	نُفُورٌ. كَرَاهَةٌ
Avert v. t.	حَوَّلَ عَنْ. مَنَعَ
Aviary n.	قَفَصٌ. بَيْتُ الطُّيُورِ
Avidity n.	شَرَهٌ. حِرْصٌ
Avocation n.	حِرْفَةٌ. مَشْغَلَةٌ
Avoid v. t.	جَانَبَ. تَحَوَّلَ عَنْ
Avoirdupois n.	عِيَارٌ فِيهِ اللِّبْرَا ١٦ أُوقِيَّةً إِنْكْلِيزِيَّةً
Avouch v. t.	اكَّدَ. صَرَّحَ بِ
Avow v. t.	صَرَّحَ. أَقَرَّ بِ
Avowal n.	إِقْرَارٌ. إِشْهَارٌ
Await v. t.	إِنْتَظَرَ. تَوَقَّعَ
Awake Awaken } v. t. or i.	ايْقَظَ اِسْتَيْقَظَ
Awake a.	يَقْظَانُ
Award v. t. or n.	حَكَمَ قَضَى. حُكْمٌ
Aware a.	عَارِفٌ. مُنْتَبِهٌ

Away ad.	عَلَى بُعْدٍ . غَائِباً	Ax or Axe n.	فَأْسٌ ج فُؤُوسٌ
Awe n. or v. t.	رَوْعَةٌ . خَشْيَةٌ . اِرْعَبْ	Axillary a.	اِبْطِيٌّ
Awe-struck a.	مُرْتَعِدٌ . رَاهِبٌ	Axiom n.	مَبْدَأ . اوَّلِيَّةٌ
Awful a.	مُخِيفٌ . هَائِلٌ	Axiomatic a.	مَبْدَئِيٌّ . اوَّلِيٌّ
Awhile ad.	إِلَى حِينٍ . مُدَّةً	Axail a.	مِحْوَرِيٌّ
Awkward a.	أَخْرَقُ . مُتَلَبِّكٌ	Axis n.	مِحْوَرٌ
Awkwardness n.	خُرْقٌ . تَلَبُّكٌ	Axle n.	مِحْوَرُ دُولَابٍ . قُطْبٌ
Awl n.	مَخْرَزٌ ج مَخَارِزٌ	Ay or Aye adv.	بَلَى . نَعَمْ . دَائِماً
Awning n.	مَظَلَّةٌ ج مَظَالُّ	Azure a. or n.	اِسْمَانْجُونِيٌّ
Awry a. or ad.	مُنْحَرِفٌ مُعَوَّجٌ بِانْحِرَافٍ		

B

Babble v. i. or n.	بَقَّ هَذَرَ هَذْرٌ	Baboon n.	نَوْعٌ مِنَ القُرُودِ
Babbler n.	بَقَّاقٌ . مِهْذَارٌ	Babyish a.	سَرِيعُ التَّكَدُّرِ كَالطِّفْلِ
Babe or Baby n.	طِفْلٌ ج اطْفَالٌ	Bachelor n.	عَزَبٌ ج عُزَّابٌ

Bachelorship n.	عُزُوبَةٌ	Baggage n.	أَمْتِعَةُ السَّفَرِ
Back n. or ad.	ظَهْرٌ ج ظُهُورٌ	Bagging n.	خَيْشٌ لِلْأَكْيَاسِ
	إِلَى الْوَرَاءِ	Bail n. or v. t.	كَفِيلٌ كَفَالَةٌ
Back and forth ad.	إِقْبَالًا وَإِدْبَارًا		أَطْلَقَ بِكَفَالَةٍ
To go back	رَجَعَ –	Bait n. or v. t.	طُعْمٌ لِلسَّمَكِ . طَعَّمَ
Backbite v. t.	غَابَ . إِغْتَابَ	Bake v. t.	طَبَخَ بِفُرْنٍ . خَبَزَ
Backbiting n.	غِيبَةٌ. إِغْتِيَابٌ	Baker n.	فُرَّانٌ . خَبَّازٌ
Backbone n.	ٱلسِّلْسِلَةُ الْفَقَرِيَّةُ	Bakery n.	مَخْبَزٌ . دُكَّانُ الْخُبْزِ
Backing n.	عَوْنٌ . سَنَدٌ . بِطَانَةٌ	Balance n. or v. t.	مِيزَانٌ . وَازَنَ
Backside n.	ظَهْرٌ . قَفَاءٌ	Balcony n.	شُرْفَةٌ . كُشْك
Backslide v. i.	مَالَ عَنْ . إِرْتَدَّ	Bald a.	أَقْرَعُ
Backward ad. or a. }	إِلَى الْخَلْفِ . مُتَأَخِّرٌ	Baldness n.	قَرَعٌ
Bacon n.	لَحْمُ خِنْزِيرٍ مُجَفَّفٌ	Bale n.	(طَرْدٌ) حُزْمَةٌ ج حُزَمٌ
Bad a.	شِرِّيرٌ . رَدِيٌّ . مُضِرٌّ	Baleful a.	مُضِرٌّ . مُحْزِنٌ . مُكَدِّرٌ
Bade v. t.	أَمَرَ (مَاضِي bid)	Balk v. t.	خَيَّبَ أَعَاقَ
Badge n.	عَلَامَةٌ (نِيشَانٌ)	Ball n.	كُرَةٌ . رَصَاصَةٌ (طَابَةٌ)
Baffle v. t.	خَيَّبَ .غَلَبَ بِحِيلَةٍ	Ballad n.	أُغْنِيَةٌ.اغَانٍ
Bag n.	كِيسٌ ج ا كْيَاسٌ	Ballast n. or v. t.	صَابُورَةٌ . صَبَّرَ
Bag v. t.	وَضَعَ فِي كِيسٍ		

Balloon *n.*	مَرْكَبَةٌ هَوَائِيَّةٌ (بالُون)
Ballot *n.* or *v. t.*	وَرَقَةُ انْتِخابٍ.إِنْتَخَبَ بِهَا
Balm *n.*	رِيحَان .مَرْهَمٌ عَطِرٌ
Balmy *a. n.*	عَطِرٌ . لَطِيفٌ . لَذِيذٌ
Balsam *n.*	بَلْسَمٌ
Balustrade *n.*	دَرَابِزُون
Bamboo *n.*	خَيْزَرَانٌ
Ban *n.*	نَهْيٌ عَامٌ . لَعْنٌ (حِرْمٌ)
Banana *n.*	مَوْزٌ
Band *n.* or *v. t.*	رِبَاطٌ.فِرْقَةٌ. إِرْتَبَطَ
Bandage *n.* or *v. t.*	عِصَابَةٌ . ضِمَادَةٌ لَفَّ ُ. ضَمَدَ
Bandbox *n.*	عُلْبَةٌ لِلْبَرَاتِيطِ
Bandit *n.*	قَاطِعُ ٱلطَّرِيقِ
Bane *n.*	سَمٌّ . أَذِيَّةٌ . شَرٌّ
Baneful *a.*	سَامٌّ . مُضِرٌّ . مُهْلِكٌ
Bang *v. t. or n.*	ضَرَبَ ـِ. صَوْتٌ بِشِدَّةٍ.ضَرْبَةٌ
Banish *v. t.*	نَفَى ـ طَرَدَ ـُ
Banishment *n.*	نَفْيٌ
Bank *n.*	شَطٌّ . سَدٌّ . مَقْعَدٌ . بَنْكٌ
Bank-bill Bank-note *n.*	كَمْبِيَالَةُ بَنْكٍ.بنكـنوت
Banker *n.*	صَاحِبُ بَنْكٍ صَرَّافٌ ج صَيَارِفَةٌ
Banking *n.*	(صَرَافَةٌ)
Bankrupt *a. or n.*	مُفْلِسٌ
Bankruptcy *n.*	إِفْلَاسٌ
Bank-stock *n.*	أَسْهُمُ بَنْكٍ
Banner *n.*	رَايَةٌ . بَيْرَقٌ
Banquet *n.*	وَلِيمَةٌ . مَأْدَبَةٌ
Banter *v. i. or n.*	مَزَحَ ـَ. سَخِرَ ـَ مَزْحٌ
Baptism *n.*	مَعْمُودِيَّةٌ
Baptist *n.*	مُعْتَقِدٌ بِالتَّغْطِيسِ فِي ٱلْمَعْمُودِيَّةِ
Baptize *v. t.*	عَمَّدَ
Bar *n. or v. t.*	(دِقٌّ) قَضِيبٌ . سَدَّ

Barb n.	سِنَان . شَوْكَة
Barbarian n.	بَرْبَرِيّ . مُتَوَحِّشٌ
Barbaric a. Barbarous a.	بربريّ . فظيع
Barbarism n.	بَرْبَرِيَّة . تَوَحُّشٌ
Barbarity n.	فَظَاظَة . قَسَاوَة
Barbed n.	ذُو سِنَانٍ أوْ شوْكٍ
Barber n.	حَلَّاقٌ
Bard n.	شَاعِرٌ . مُغَنٍّ . مُنْشِدٌ
Bare a. or v. t.	عَارٍ . مُجَرَّدٌ . عَرَّى
Barefaced a.	وَقِحٌ بِدُونِ حَيَاءٍ
Barefoot a.	حَافٍ
Bareheaded a.	مَكْشُوفُ الرَّأْسِ
Barely ad.	بِالجَهْدِ . فَقَطْ
Bareness n.	عُرْيَة
Bargain n. or v. i.	مُسَاوَمَة . سَاوَمَ
Barge n.	جَرْمٌ . سَفِينَةٌ لِلشَّحْنِ
Bark n or v. t. or i.	قِشْرٌ . قَشَّرَ . قَلَفَ . نَبَحَ
Bark Barque n.	سَفِينَةٌ بِثَلَاثَةٍ صَوَارٍ
Barking n.	نَبِيحٌ . عُوَاءٌ
Barley n.	شَعِيرٌ
Barn n.	هُرْيٌ . بِنَاءٌ لِلْمَوَاشِي
Barometer n.	مِيزَانٌ لِلْهَوَاءِ
Baron n.	(بَارُونٌ)
Baronage n.	رُتْبَة مِنَ الأَشْرَافِ
Baronet n.	رُتْبَة دُونَ البَارُونِ
Barrack n.	قَشْلَاقٌ . ثُكْنَة
Barrel n.	بِرْمِيلٌ
Barren a.	عَاقِرٌ . عَقِيمٌ . مَحْلٌ
Barrenness n.	عُقْرٌ . مَحْلٌ
Barricade n. or v. t.	سَدٌّ . حَاجِزٌ . سَدَّ
Barrier n.	سَدٌّ . حَاجِزٌ . حَدٌّ . مَانِعٌ
Barrister n.	وَكِيلُ دَعَاوٍ
Barter n. or v.t.	مُبَادَلَة . بَادَلَ البَضَائِعَ
Basalt n.	حَجَرٌ نَارِيٌّ أَسْوَدُ
Base n. or a.	قَاعِدَة . دَنِيءٌ . خَسِيسٌ
Baseless a.	بِلَا أَسَاسٍ . بَاطِلٌ

Basement n.	طَبَقَةُ ٱلْبَيْتِ ٱلسُّفْلَى	Bathe v.t. or i.	حَمَّمَ . غَسَلَ . إِسْتَحَمَّ
Baseness n.	دَنَاءَةٌ . لُؤْمٌ	Bathing n.	إِسْتِحْمَامٌ . إِغْتِسَالٌ
Bashful a.	مُسْتَحٍ . خَجِلٌ	Battalion n.	تَابُورٌ ج تَوَابِيرُ . اورْطَة
Bashfulness n.	حِشْمَةٌ . حَيَاءٌ	Batter v. t.	هَدَمَ ـ . هَدَّ
Basin n.	طَسْت . حَوْضٌ	Battering-ram n.	مَنْجَنِيقٌ
Basilisk n.	حَيَّةٌ خُرَافِيَّةٌ أَوْ تِنِّين	Battery n.	مَجْمُوعُ مَدَافِعَ . بَطَّارِيَّةٌ
Basis n.	أَسَاسٌ . أَصْلٌ	Battle n.	قِتَالٌ . مَعْرَكَةٌ . حَرْبٌ
Bask v. i.	تَشَمَّسَ	Battle-axe n.	بَلْطَة
Basket n.	سَلَّة ج سِلَالٌ . قُفَّة ج قُفَفٌ	Battlement n.	شُرْفَة ج شُرَفٌ
Bastard n.	نَغْلٌ إِبْنُ زِنَا	Bauble n.	لُعْبَةٌ . شَيْءٌ زَهِيدٌ
Baste v. t.	شَلَّ ـُ شَرَّجَ	Bawl v. i.	صَرَخَ ـُ . صَيَّحَ
Bastinade) Bastinado) v. t. or n.	ضَرَبَ بِعَصًا خَاصَّةً عَلَى أَسْفَلِ ٱلْقَدَمَيْن . ضَرْبٌ بِهِ	Bay a.	أَحْمَرُ ٱللَّوْنِ
Bastion n.	بُرْجٌ اوِ ٱلْبَارِزُ مِنْهُ	Bay n.	خَلِيجٌ . شَجَرُ ٱلْغَارِ
Bat n.	وَطْوَاطٌ . خُفَّاشٌ	Bayonet n.	حَرْبَة
Batch n.	كَمِّيَّةٌ مِقْدَارٌ	Bazaar n.	سُوقٌ ج أَسْوَاقٌ
Bated a.	خَفِيٌّ (صَوْت)	Be v. i. (was, been)	كَانَ يَكُونُ
Bath n.	حَمَّامٌ	Beach n.	شَطٌّ (رَمْلِيٌّ) شَاطِئٌ

Beacon n.	مَنَارَةٌ ج مَنَائِرُ	Beau n.	لَبِقٌ. بَشُوشٌ لِلنِّسَاء
Bead n.	خَرَزَةٌ ج خَرَزٌ	Beau-ideal n.	خَيَالٌ. غَايَةُ ٱلْجَمَالِ
Beak n.	مِنْقَادٌ. مِنْقَارٌ	Beauteous a.	حَسَنٌ. جَمِيلٌ
Beaker n.	كَأْسٌ قَدَحٌ	Beautiful a.	حَسَنٌ. جَمِيلٌ
Beam v. t.	اشْرَقَ لَاحَ	Beautify v. t	حَسَّنَ. زَخْرَفَ
Beam n.	جِسْرُ خَشَبٍ. شُعَاعٌ	Beauty n.	حُسْنٌ. جَمَالٌ
Bean n.	حَبَّةٌ مِنَ ٱللُّوبِيَا اوِ ٱلْفُولِ	Beaver n.	كَلْبُ ٱلْمَاءِ
Bear n.	دُبٌّ ج ادْبَابٌ. شَرِسٌ	Becalm v. t.	هَدَّأَ. سَكَّنَ
Bear v. t. or i.	حَمَلَ ــ وَٱحْتَمَلَ. اثْمَرَ	Because con.	لِأَنَّ. بِسَبَبِ ان
Bearable a.	مَا يُحْتَمَلُ اوْ يُطَاقُ	Beckon v. t.	أَوْمَأَ. أَشَارَ
Beard n.	لِحْيَةٌ ج لِحًى	Become v. i. or t.	صَارَ ــ. لَاقَ
Bearded a.	ذُو لِحْيَةٍ أَوْ شَوْكٍ	Becoming a.	لَائِقٌ. مُوَافِقٌ
Beardless a.	بِلَا لِحْيَةٍ. امْرَدُ	Bed n.	فِرَاشٌ. مَجْرَى (نَهْرٍ)
Bearer n.	حَامِلٌ. نَاقِلٌ	Bedaub v. t.	طَلَى. دَهَنَ ــ
Beast n.	بَهِيمَةٌ ج بَهَائِمُ. وَحْشٌ	Bedding n.	فِرَاشٌ وَمَفْرُوشَاتُهُ
Beat v. t.	ضَرَبَ ــ غَلَبَ ــ	Bedeck v. t.	زَيَّنَ. زَخْرَفَ
Beating n.	ضَرْبٌ بَالِغٌ	Bedew v. t.	نَدَّى
Beatitude n.	غِبْطَةٌ. طُوبَى	Bedim v. t.	اظْلَمَ

Bedlam n.	بِيمَارِسْتَانٌ	Beforehand ad.	قَبْلاً . مِنْ قَبْلُ
Bed-quilt n.	لِحَافٌ ج لَحُفٌ	Befoul v. t.	وَسَّخَ . دَنَّسَ . لَوَّثَ
Bedridden n.	مُلَازِمُ ٱلْفِرَاشِ	Befriend v. t.	وَالَى . اعَان
Bedroom n.	غُرْفَةُ ٱلنَّوْمِ	Beg v. t. or i.	إِلْتَمَسَ . تَسَوَّلَ
Bedstead n.	تَخْتٌ . سَرِيرٌ	Beget v. t.	وَلَدَ يَلِدُ . أَنْتَجَ
Bee n.	نَحْلَةٌ	Beggar n. or v. t.	شَحَّاذٌ . افْقَرَ
Beef n.	لَحْمُ بَقَرٍ	Beggarly a.	حَقِيرٌ . دَنِيٌّ
Beefsteak n.	شَرِيحَةُ بَقَرٍ لِلشَّيِّ	Beggary n.	فَقْرٌ . مَسْكَنَة
Bee-hive n.	خَلِيَّةٌ . كَوَّارَة	Begging n.	تَسَوَّلَ . شِحَاذَةٌ
Beer n.	جِعَةٌ (بِيرَا)	Begin v. t.	بَدَأَ ـَ . إِبْتَدَأَ ب
Beeswax n.	شَمْعٌ عَسَلِيٌّ	Beginning n.	بَدْءٌ . بِدَاءَة
Beet n.	(شَمَنْدُورٌ) . (بَنْجَرٌ)	Begird v. t.	زَنَّرَ . نَطَّقَ . طَوَّقَ
Beetle n.	خُنْفَسَاءٌ	Begrudge v. t.	حَسَدَ ـُ عَلَى
Beeves (pl. of beef.)	بَقَرٌ	Beguile v. t.	غَرَّ ـُ . خَدَعَ
Befall v. t.	اصَابَ . إِعْتَرَى	Begun(pp. of Begin)	مَبْدُوءٌ
Befit v. t.	نَاسَبَ . لَاقَ ـ	Behalf n.	مَنْفَعَة . لِأَجْلِ . بِالنِّيَابَةِ عَنْ
Befool v. t.	إِفْتَتَنَ . خَدَعَ	Behave v. i.	تَصَرَّفَ . أَحْسَنَ سُلُوكَهُ
Before ad. or pr.	قَبْلُ . قُدَّامُ . امَامُ	Behaviour n.	تَصَرُّفٌ . سِيرَة

Behead v. t.	قَطَعَ رَأْسَهُ	Bell n.	جَرَسٌ ج أَجْرَاسٌ
Beheld v. t. (Behold.)	رَأَى (مَاضِي)	Belle n.	إِمْرَأَةٌ حَسَنَةٌ . حَسْنَاهُ
Behind pr. or ad.	وَرَآءَ . خَلْفُ	Belles-lettres n.	آدَابُ اللُّغَةِ
Behindhand ad.	مُتَأَخِّرًا	Belligerent a.	مُحَارِبٌ
Behold v.t. or ad.	رَاى ـ هُوَ ذَا	Bellow v. i. or n.	جَأَرَ . صَرَخَ . جَأْرٌ
Beholden a. (to)	شَاكِرٌ لِ	Bellows n.	مِنْفَخٌ . مِنْفَاخٌ
Beholder n.	مُشَاهِدٌ . مُعَايِنٌ	Belly n.	بَطْنٌ . جَوْفٌ
Behoove v. t.	لَزِمَ ـ . وَجَبَ ـ	Belly-band n.	حِزَامُ الفَرَسِ
Being n.	كَوْنٌ . وُجُودٌ . كَائِنٌ	Belong v. i.	إِخْتَصَّ بِ
Belabour v. t.	ضَرَبَ ـ كَثِيرًا	Belonging a.	مُخْتَصٌّ . ذَيْلٌ
Belate v. t.	أَخَّرَ . أَبْطَأَ	Beloved a.	مَحْبُوبٌ . حَبِيبٌ
Belch v. t.	قَذَفَ ـ تَجَشَّا	Below pr. or ad.	تَحْتَ . دُونَ
Beleaguer v. t.	حَاصَرَ . أَحَاطَ بِ	Belt n.	زِنَّارٌ . حِزَامٌ . مِنْطَقَة
Belfry n.	قُبَّةُ الجَرَسِ	Bemoan v. t.	نَدَبَ ـ . نَاحَ ـ
Belie v. t.	كَذَّبَ	Bench n.	مَقْعَدٌ . دَكَّةُ القُضَاةِ
Belief n.	تَصْدِيقٌ . إِعْتِقَادٌ	Bend v. t. or i.	حَنَا . ثَنَى . تَلَوَّى
Believe v. t.	صَدَّقَ . إِعْتَقَدَ . آمَنَ	Bend n.	حَنْوٌ . ثَنْيٌ . عَطْفٌ
Believer n.	مُصَدِّقٌ . مُؤْمِنٌ	Beneath pr. or ad.	تَحْتَ . أَسْفَلَ

Benediction n.	بَرَكَةٌ إِنْعَامٌ
Benefaction n.	إِحْسَانٌ . خَيْرٌ
Benefactor n.	مُحْسِنٌ . عَامِلُ خَيْرٍ
Beneficence n.	إِحْسَانٌ عَمَلُ ٱلْخَيْرِ
Beneficent a.	مُحْسِنٌ . جَوَّادٌ
Beneficial a.	مُفِيدٌ . نَافِعٌ
Beneficiary n.	أَلْمُحْسَنُ إِلَيْهِ
Benefit n.	نَفْعٌ فَائِدَةٌ
Benevolence n.	إِحْسَانٌ جُودٌ
Benevolent n.	مُحْسِنٌ . مُحِبُّ ٱلْخَيْرِ
Benighted a.	ذَاهِبٌ فِي الظَّلَامِ
Benign a.	حَلِيمٌ . لَطِيفٌ
Benignity n.	حِلْمٌ . لُطْفٌ
Bent a. or n.	مَعْطُوفٌ . مَيْلٌ
Benumb v. t.	خَدَّرَ
Bequeath v. t.	وَصَّى بِ
Bequest n.	وَصِيَّةٌ . ٱلْمُوَصَّى بِهِ
Berate v. t.	عَنَّفَ . وَبَّخَ

Bereave v. t.	اثْكَلَ . أَفْقَدَ
Bereavement n.	فُقْدَانُ الْحَبِيبِ
Bereft (pp. of Bereave).	فَاقِدٌ
Berry n.	تُوتَةٌ . حَبَّةُ تُوت
Berth n.	سَرِيرٌ فِي سَفِينَةٍ . مَنْصِبٌ
Beseech v. t.	تَوَسَّلَ تَضَرَّعَ إِلَى
Beseem v. t.	لَاقَ . وَافَقَ
Beseemly a.	لَائِقٌ . مُوَافِقٌ
Beset v. t.	أَحَاطَ. لَازَمَ
Besetting a.	مُحِيطٌ . مُلَازِمٌ
Beside pr.	بِجَانِبِ عِنْدَ
Besides ad.	فَضْلًا عَنْ . عَدَا . غَيْرَ
Besiege v. t.	حَاصَرَ
Besmear v. t.	طَلَى ـ . لَوَّثَ
Besotted a.	سَكِّيرٌ . أَبْلَهُ
Besought (pret of Beseech).	تَوَسَّلَ
Bespangle v. t.	زَيَّنَ . رَصَّعَ
Bespatter v. t.	لَطَخَ

Besprinkle v. t.	رَشَّ
Best a.	أَلْأَحْسَنُ . ٱلْأَفْضَلُ
Bestial a.	بَهِيمِيٌّ . قَذِرٌ
Bestir v. t.	حَرَّكَ
Bestow v. t.	اعطَى وَهَبَ يَهِب
Bestowal Bestowment } n.	إِعْطَاءٌ . مَنْحٌ
Bestride v. t.	فَرْشَحَ رَكِب
Bet n. or v. t. or i.	مُرَاهَنَةٌ . رَاهَنَ
Betake v. t.	لَجَأَ إِلَى . عَكَف
Bethink v. t.	فَطِنَ ـُ . تَأَمَّلَ
Betide v. t. or i.	حَدَثَ ـُ . صَارَ ـ
Betimes ad.	فِي وَقْتٍ مُنَاسِب . بَاكِرًا
Betoken v. t.	أَشَارَ . دَلَّ ـ
Betray v. t.	سَلَّمَ . خَانَ
Betrayal n.	تَسْلِيم . خِيَانَة
Betroth v. t.	خَطَبَ ـ (إِمْرَأَة)
Betrothal n.	خِطْبَة
Better a.	إِحْسَنُ . افضلُ . خَيْرٌ
Bettor n.	مُرَاهِنٌ
Between Betwixt } pr.	بَيْنَ . مَابَيْن
Beverage n.	شَرَابٌ . مَشْرُوبٌ
Bevy n.	سِرْبٌ . جَمَاعَة
Bewail v. t.	نَاحَ . نَدَبَ ـُ
Beware v. t.	حَذِرَ ـ . تَحَرَّزَ مِن
Bewilder v. t.	حَيَّرَ
Bewitch v. t.	إِفْتَنَ . سَحَرَ
Beyond ad. or pr.	عَبَرَ . بَعَدَ
Bias n. or v. t.	مَيْلُ . إِنْحِرَافُ . امَالَ
Bib n.	صَدْرِيَّةُ ٱلطِّفْل
Bibber n.	شِرِّيبٌ
Bible n.	ٱلْكِتَابُ ٱلْمُقَدَّسُ
Bibli- cal a.	مُخْتَصٌّ بِٱلْكِتَابِٱلْمُقَدَّسِ
Bibliography n.	تَارِيخُ ٱلْكُتُب أَوْ وَصْفُهَا
Bicephaleus a.	ذو رَأْسَيْن
Bid v. i. or n.	امَرَ ـُ . زَايَدَ . دَفْعٌ

Bidden (*pp. Bid*)	مَأْمُورٌ
Bidding *n.*	اَمْرٌ . دَعْوَةٌ
Bid *v. t. or i.*	إِنْتَظَرَ . أَقَامَ . سَكَنَ
Biennial *a.*	حَادِثٌ مَرَّةً كُلَّ سَنَتَيْنِ
Bier *n.*	نَعْشٌ ج نُعُوشٌ
Bifold *a.*	مُزْدَوِجٌ . ذُو ثِنْيَتَيْنِ
Big *a.*	كَبِيرٌ . ضَخْمٌ
Bigamy *n.*	اَلتَّزَوُّجُ بِامْرَأَتَيْنِ مَعًا
Bight *n.*	خَلِيجٌ صَغِيرٌ
Bigness *n.*	كِبَرٌ . ضَخَامَة
Bigot *n.* Bigoted *a.* }	مُتَعَصِّبٌ بِالدِّينِ
Bigotry *n.*	تَعَصُّبٌ بِالدِّينِ
Bile *n.*	صَفْرَاءُ . مِرَّةٌ
Bilingual *n.*	ذُو لُغَتَيْنِ
Bilious *a.*	صَفْرَاوِيٌّ
Bill *n.*	مِنْقَارٌ . قَائِمَةُ حِسَابٍ
Bill of exchange *n.*	سَفْتَجَة
Billet *n.*	رُقْعَة . كَتِيبَة

Bil- lion *n.*	اَلْفُ مَلْيُونٍ أَوْ اَلْفُ اَلْفِ اَلْفٍ
Billow *n.*	مَوْجَةٌ ج مَوْجَاتٌ
Billowy *a.*	مُتَمَوِّجٌ
Bimonthly *a.*	مَا يَظْهَرُ كُلَّ شَهْرَيْنِ
Bin *n.*	صَنْدُوقٌ لِلْمُؤْنَةِ
Binary *a.*	مُزْدَوِجٌ . ثُنَائِيٌّ
Bind *v. t.*	رَبَطَ ـُ . أَوْثَقَ . جَلَدَ
Binder *n.*	مُجَلِّدُ كُتُبٍ
Bindery *n.*	مَحَلُّ اَلتَّجْلِيدِ
Binding *n.*	رَبْطٌ . تَجْلِيد
Biographer *n.*	كَاتِبُ تَرْجَمَةِ إِنْسَانٍ
Biography *n.*	تَرْجَمَةُ إِنْسَانٍ
Biology *n.*	عِلْمُ اَلْحَيَاةِ
Biped *n.*	ذُو رِجْلَيْنِ اوْ سَاقَيْنِ
Birch *n.*	بَتُولَا (شَجَرٌ) قَضِيبٌ
Bird *n.*	طَائِرٌ . عُصْفُورٌ
Bird-lime *n.*	دَابُوقٌ (دَبَقٌ)
Birth *n.*	وِلَادَة . مَوْلِدٌ

Birthday n.	مِيلَادٌ . مَوْلِدٌ
Birthplace n.	مَسْقَطُ آلرَّأْسِ . مَوْلِدٌ
Birthright n.	بُكُورِيَّة
Biscuit n.	(بَقْسِمَاط)
Bisect v. t.	نَصَفَ ـُ . شَطَرَ ـُ
Bisection n.	شَطْرٌ . تَنْصِيفٌ
Bishop n.	أُسْقُفٌ ج أَسَاقِفَة
Bishopric n.	أَبْرَشِيَّة أُسْقُفٍ
Bisextile n.	سَنَة كَبِيسَة
Bison n.	جَامُوسٌ أَمْرِيكَانِيٌّ
Bit n.	شَكِيمَة . قِطْعَة صَغِيرَة
Bitch n.	كَلْبَة
Bite v. t. or n.	عَضَّ ـُ . عَضَّة
Bitter a.	مُرٌّ . شَدِيدٌ . مُحْزِن
Bitterness n.	مَرَارَةٌ . بُغْضَة . حُزْن
Bitumeen n.	حُمَّرٌ وَحُمَرٌ
Bituminous a.	حُمَرِيٌّ
Bivalve n. or a.	صَدَفٌ . صَدَفِيٌّ
Bivouac n. or v. t.	اَلْمَبِيتُ فِي آلْعَرَاءِ بَاتَ بِدُونِ خِيَمٍ
Blab v. t. or i.	أَفْشَى آلسِّرَّ . هَذِرَ
Blackguard n.	ثَالِبٌ . وَبَشٌ
Block a. or n.	أَسْوَدُ . زِنْجِيٌّ
Blackberry n.	تُوتٌ اسْوَدٌ
Blackboard n.	لَوْحٌ أَسْوَدٌ
Blacken v. t.	سَوَّدَ
Blacksmith n.	حَدَّادٌ
Bladder n.	مَثَانَة
Blade n.	نَصْلٌ . وَرَقَةُ عِشْبٍ
Blamable Blameworthy n.	مُسْتَحِقُّ آللَّوْمِ
Blame n. or v.t.	لَوْمٌ . لَامَ ـُ . عَاتَبَ
Blameless a.	بِلَا لَوْمٍ . بَرِيءٌ
Blanch v. t.	بَيَّضَ . قَصَّرَ
Bland a.	لَطِيفٌ . أَنِيسٌ
Blandish v. t.	لَاطَفَ . مَلِقَ ـُ
Blandishment n.	مُلَاطَفَة . مَلِقٌ
Blandness n.	لُطْفٌ . مُؤَانَسة

Blank a. or n.	خَالٍ .وَرَقَةٌ بَيْضَاءُ
Blanket n.	حِرَامٌ. دِثَارٌ
Blaspheme v. t.	جَدَّفَ
Blasphemous a.	تَجْدِيفِيٌّ . مُجَدِّفٌ
Blasphemy n.	تَجْدِيفٌ
Blast v. t.	لَفَحَ _ . فجَّرَ (بِلُغْم)
Blast n.	هَبَّةُ رِيحٍ . لَفْوحٌ (لُغْمٌ)
Blaze v. i. or n.	إِنْتَهَبَ . أَذاعَ . لَهِيبٌ
Bleach v. t.	بَيَّضَ . قَصَرَ _
Bleaching n.	تَبْيِيضٌ . قِصَارَةٌ
Bleak a.	بَارِدٌ. مُعَرَّضٌ لِلرِّيحِ ٱلْبَارِدَةِ
Blear v t.	سَبَّبَ ٱلْعَمَشَ
Blear-eyed a.	اعْمَشُ
Bleat v. i. or n.	ثَغَا يَثْغُو . ثُغَاءٌ
Bleed v. i. or i.	فَصَدَ _ . نَزَفَ
Bleeding n.	فَصَادٌ . نَزْفٌ
Blemish v. t. or n.	أَعَابَ . عَيْبٌ
Blend v. t. or i.	مَزَجَ _ إِمْتَزَجَ
Bless v. t.	بَارَكَ . حَمَّدَ _
Blessed a.	مُبَارَكٌ . مَغْبُوطٌ . سَعِيدٌ
Blessedness n.	غِبْطَةٌ . سَعَادَةٌ
Blessing n.	بَرَكَةٌ . نِعْمَةٌ
Blight v. t. or n.	لَفَحَ_لَفُوحٌ . آفَةٌ
Blind a. or n.	أَعْمَى . ضَرِيرٌ . غَبِيٌّ
Blind v. t.	أَعْمَى . عَمَّى
Blindfold v. t.	غَطَّى ٱلْعَيْنَيْنِ
Blindness n.	عَمًى . غَبَاوَةٌ
Blindly ad.	بِدُونِ فِكْرٍ . بِغَبَاوَةٍ
Blink v. i.	غَمَزَ _ . جَهَرَ _
Bliss / Blissfulness } n.	سَعَادَةٌ . غِبْطَةٌ
Blissful a.	سَعِيدٌ . مَغْبُوطٌ
Blister n. or v. t.	نَفْطَةٌ . حَرَّافَةٌ . نَقَطَ
Blithe / Blithesome } a.	فَرِحٌ . مُبْتَهِجٌ . مَسْرُورٌ
Bloat v. t. or i.	وَرَّمَ . نَفَخَ . إِنْتَفَخَ
Block n. or v. t.	قِطْعَةُ خَشَبٍ . سَدَّ
Blockade v. t. or n.	حَاصَرَ . احَاطَ . حِصَارٌ

Blockhead *n.*	بَكِيدٌ . أَبْلَهُ
Block-house *n.*	بُرْجٌ مِنْ أَخْشَابٍ ضَخْمَةٍ
Blood *n.*	دَمٌ
Blood-hound *n*	كَلْبُ صَيْدٍ كَبِيرٌ
Bloodless *a.*	بِلَا دَم
Bloodshed *n.*	سَفْكُ الدَّمِ . قَتْلٌ
Blood-thirsty *a.*	سَفَّاكُ الدَّمِ
Blood-vessel *n.*	وِعَاءٌ دَمَوِيٌّ . عِرْقٌ
Bloody *n.*	دَمَوِيٌّ . مُلَطَّخٌ بِالدَّمِ
Bloom *n.* or *v. i.*	زَهْرَةٌ . جَمَالٌ . أَزْهَرَ
Blooming *a.*	مُزْهِرٌ . نَضِيرٌ . جَمِيلٌ
Blossom *n.* or *v. i.*	زَهْرَةٌ . اَزْهَرَ
Blot *n.* or *v. t.*	لَطْخَةٌ . عَارٌ . لَطَخَ . مَحَا
Blotch *n.*	لَمْعَةٌ . بَثْرَةٌ
Blotting-paper *n.*	وَرَقٌ نَشَّاشٌ
Blow *n.* or *v. t.* or *i.*	ضَرْبَةٌ . هَبَّ
Blower *n.*	نَافِخٌ . مِنْفَخٌ
Blubber *n.*	شَحْمُ الحُوتِ
Blue *a.*	ازْرَقُ
Blueness *n.*	زُرْقَةٌ
Bluff *n.* or *a.*	جَرْفٌ شَاهِقٌ . فَظٌّ
Bluish *a.*	ضَارِبٌ إِلَى الزُّرْقَةِ
Blunder *n.* or *v. i.*	خَطَأً . غَلِطَ
Blundering *a.*	كَثِيرُ الخَطَأِ
Blunt *a.* or *v. t.*	كَلِيلٌ . شَرِسٌ فَلَّ حَدَّ السِّكِّينِ
Bluntness *n.*	كَلَالٌ . خُشُونَةٌ
Blur *n.* or *v. t.*	لَطْخَةٌ . لَاثَ
Blurred *pp.*	غَيْرُ وَاضِحٍ
Blush *v.i.* or *n.*	خَجِلَ . احْمِرَارٌ
Bluster *v. t.* or *n.*	هَاجَ . تَصَلَّفَ . تَصَلُّفٌ
Boa *n.*	ضَرْبٌ مِنَ الحَيَّاتِ الضَّخْمَةِ
Boar *n.*	خِنْزِيرٌ
Board *n.*	لَوْحُ خَشَبٍ . قُوتٌ . مَجْلِسٌ
Board *v. t.* or *i.*	غَطَّى بِالوَاحِ . صَعَدَ إِلَى مَرْكَبٍ . أَكَلَ قَاتَ
Boarder *n.*	نَزِيلٌ بِالأُجْرَةِ

Boarding *n.* تَسْمِيرُ الْوَاح . طعامٌ	Boisterous *a.* هائِجٌ . صيَّاح
Boast *v. i.* or *n.* إفتخرَ . إفْتِخَارٌ	Bold *a.* جَسُورٌ . شُجَاعٌ
Boastful *a.* مُفتخرٌ . مُتَعَظِمٌ	Boldness *n.* جَسارَةٌ شَجَاعَة
Boasting *n.* إفْتِخَارٌ . تعظمٌ	Bolster *n.* or *v. t.* وسَادَةٌ . سندَ
Boat *n.* قاربٌ . زَوْرَقٌ . سفينةٌ	Bolt *n.* or *v. t.* مِزْلَاجٌ (دُقرَة . دَقَرَ)
Boating *n.* ألتنزُهُ بالقَارب	Bomb *n.* (قَنبرَة) قُنبلَة
Boatman *n.* بَحْرِيٌّ	Bombard *v. t.* رَمَى بالقنَابل
Boatswain *n.* مُدِيرُ قَارب	Bombardment *n.* إطْلَاقُ القَنابل
Bob *v. i.* إهتَزَ . إرْتَجَّ	Bombast *n.* التفخر في الكَلَام
Bode *v. t.* or *i.* انبَأ بهِ . شَوَّمَ	Bond *n.* قيد . رباط . عَهد
Bodiless *a.* بلاجِسْم او جسدٍ	Bondage *n.* عبُودية
Bodily *a.* or *ad.* جَسَدِيٌّ . كُلِّيًّا	Bondman Bondservant } *n.* عبدٌ . رَقِيقٌ
Body *n.* جسمٌ . جَسَدٌ . بَدَنٌ	Bondsman *n.* كَافلٌ . ضَامِنٌ
Bog *n.* مُسْتَنْقَعٌ	Bone *n.* عظمٌ ج عظَام
Boggy *a.* مُسْتَنْقَعِيٌّ	Bone-setter *n.* مُجَبِّرُ العِظَام
Bogus *a.* مُزَوَّرٌ . كاذِبٌ	Bonfire *n.* نارٌ تُشعَلُ للفرح
Boil *n.* or *v. i.* or *v. t.* دُمَّلٌ . غَلَى ـ .سَلَقَ ـ	Bonnet *n.* قُبَّعة . بُرْنَيْطَة
Boiler *n.* مِرْجَلٌ (دَسْتٌ)	Bonny *a.* جميلٌ . بَدِيعٌ . فرحٌ

Bonus n.	نافِلَة . جزاءُ فَوقَ المَفرُوضِ
Bony a.	كَثِيرُ العِظامِ . ضَلِيعٌ
Boody n.	أَبلَهُ . غَبِيٌّ
Book n.	كِتابٌ . سِفرٌ
Book-binder n.	مُجَلِّدُ كُتُبٍ
Book-case n.	خِزانَةُ كُتُبٍ
Book-keeping n.	مَسكُ الدَّفاتِرِ
Book-store n.	مَخزَنُ كُتُبٍ
Book-worm n.	مُغرَمٌ بِالكُتُبِ
Boom v. i. or n.	عَجَّ . هَدَرَ . زَئِيرٌ
Booming n.	مُنقَضٌّ بِشِدَّةٍ . عاجٌّ
Boon n. or a.	هِبَةٌ . بَشُوشٌ
Boor n. Boorish a.	غَلِيظٌ . جافٍ . غَيرُ مُهَذَّبٍ
Boot n. or r. t.	حِذاءٌ (جِزمَةٌ) . نَفَعَ ـَ
Booth n.	خَيمَةٌ . مَظَلَّةٌ
Bootless n.	غَيرُ نافِعٍ . عَبَثٌ
Booty n.	غَنِيمَةٌ
Borax n.	بُورَقٌ

Border n.	حافَّةٌ . حَدٌّ . تَخَّمٌ
Bore v. t.	قَدَحَ ـَ . أَتعَبَ . اضجَرَ
Bore n.	(قَدحٌ) ثَقبٌ . مُضَنجِرٌ
Boreal n.	شِمالِيٌّ
Born p.p. of bear.	مَولُودٌ
Borne p.p. of bear.	مَحمُولٌ
Borrow v. t.	إِستَعارَ . إِستَقرَضَ
Bosom n.	حِضنٌ . صَدرٌ
Botanist a.	عالِمٌ بِالنَّباتِ
Botanize v. t.	جَمعُ النَّباتِ
Botany n.	عِلمُ النَّباتِ
Botch n. or v. t.	رَقعٌ رَدِيٌّ . رَقَعَ رَدِيئاً
Both a.	كِلاَ وَكِلتا
Bother n. or v. t.	إِنزِعاجٌ . ازعَجَ
Bottle n.	زُجاجَةٌ . قارُورَةٌ
Bots n. pl.	دُودُ إِمعاءِ الخَيلِ
Bottom n.	قَعرٌ . قاعٌ . اسفَلٌ
Bottomless a.	بِلاَ قَعرٍ

Bough n.	غُصْنٌ
Bought p.p. of buy.	مُبْتَاعٌ
Bounce v. i. or n.	وَثَبَ . وَثْبَةٌ
Bound p.p. of bind.	مُقَيَّدٌ . مُلْتَزِمٌ
Bound v. t. or i.	حَدَّدَ . قَفَزَ
Bound Boundary } n.	حَدٌّ . تُخْمٌ
Bounteous Bountiful } a.	كَرِيمٌ . جَوَّادٌ
Bounty n.	كَرَمٌ . سَخَاءٌ
Bouquet n.	بَاقَةُ زُهُورٍ
Bout n.	دَوْرٌ
Bovine a.	بَقَرِيٌّ
Bow v. t. or i.	حَنَا ـ إِنْحَنَى
Bow n.	إِنْحِنَاءٌ . قَوْسٌ
Bowlder n.	صَخْرَةٌ كَبِيرَةٌ كَرَوِيَّة
Bowman n.	رَامٍ بِالقَوْسِ
Bowels n. pl.	أَمْعَاءٌ . أَحْشَاءٌ
Bower n.	مَظَلَّةٌ . عَرِيشٌ
Bowl n.	كَأْسٌ . طَاسٌ

Bowsprit n.	خَشَبَةُ مُقَدَّمِ السَّفِينَةِ
Bowstring n.	وَتَرُ القَوْسِ
Box n. or v. t.	صُنْدُوقٌ . لَكَمَ
Boxer n.	مُقَاتِلٌ بِقَبْضَةِ اليَدِ
Boy n.	صَبِيٌّ . غُلَامٌ
Boyhood n.	صَبْوَةٌ
Boyish a.	وَلَدِيٌّ . طَفِيفٌ
Brace n. or v. t.	مِشَدٌّ . شَدَّ ـ
Bracelet n.	سِوَارٌ ج اَسَاوِرُ
Bracket n.	رَفٌّ صَغِيرٌ بَارِزٌ مِنَ الحَائِطِ
Brackets n. pl.	هِلَالَانِ كَذَا ( )
Brackish a.	مَالِحٌ . مَائِلٌ لِلْمُلُوحَةِ
Brad n.	مِسْمَارٌ صَغِيرٌ بِلَا رَأْسٍ
Brag v. i.	تَصَلَّفَ . فَاخَرَ
Braggadocio Braggart } n.	مُتَصَلِّفٌ . نَفَّاخٌ
Braid v. t. or n.	ضَفَرَ ـ . ضَفِيرَةٌ
Brain n.	دِمَاغٌ ج اَدْمِغَةٌ
Brake n.	آلَةٌ لِتَوْقِيفِ دُولَابٍ . (فَرْمَلَةٌ)

Bramble n.	عَوْسَج . عُلَّيْق
Bran n.	نُخَالة
Branch n. or v. i.	غُصْنٌ . تَفَرَّعَ
Brand v. t.	وَسَمَ ـ . عاب ـ
Brand n.	وَسْمٌ أَوْسِمَةٌ . عَيْبٌ
Brandish v. t.	هَزَّ . حَرَّكَ
Brandy n.	كُونْياك
Brasier n.	كانُونٌ . نَحَّاسٌ
Brass n.	نُحَاسٌ أَصْفَرُ
Brassy n.	نُحَاسِيٌّ
Bravado n.	تَصَلُّفٌ . تَعَظُّمٌ
Brave a. or n.	شُجَاعٌ . بَاسِلٌ
Brave v. t.	إِقْتَحَمَ . بَارَزَ
Bravery n.	شَجَاعَةٌ . بَسَالَةٌ
Bravo n. or int.	جَسُورٌ . أَحْسَنْتَ
Brawl n. or v. i.	مُشَاجَرَةٌ . تَشَاجَرَ
Brawny a.	قَوِيٌّ . ضَلِيعٌ
Bray v. t. or i.	سَحَقَ ـ . شَهَقَ ـ

Bray }n. Braying	شَهِيقٌ . نَهِيقٌ
Brazen a.	نُحَاسِيٌّ
Brazen }a. Brazen-faced	جَسُورٌ . وَقِحٌ
Breach n.	خَرْقٌ . نَكْثٌ
Bread n.	خُبْزٌ . عَيْشٌ
Breadstuff n.	دَقِيقٌ . حُبُوبٌ
Breadth n.	عَرْضٌ
Break v. t. or i.	كَسَرَ ـ . إِنْكَسَرَ
Break n.	كَسْرٌ . فَتْحَةٌ
Breakage n.	كَسْرٌ
Breaker n.	كَاسِرٌ . صَخْرَةٌ بَحْرِيَّةٌ
Breakfast n. or v. i.	فُطُورٌ . فَطَرَ ـ (تَرَوَّقَ)
Breakwater n.	سَدٌّ لِمَنْعِ الأَمْوَاج
Breast n. or v. t.	صَدْرٌ . صَادَرَ
Breastplate n.	دُرْعٌ ج دُرُوعٌ
Breastwork n.	مِتْرَاسٌ
Breath n.	نَفَسٌ . نَسْمَةٌ
Breathe v. i.	تَنَفَّسَ

Breathing n.	تَنَفُّسٌ
Breathless n.	مَقطوعُ النَّفَسِ
Breeches n. pl.	سَراويلُ (سِروالٌ)
Breed v. t. or i.	وَلَّدَ . رَبَّى . وَلَدَ
Breed n.	ذُرِّيَّةٌ . نَسْلٌ . جِنْسٌ
Breeding n.	تَوليدٌ . تَربِيةٌ . سَجايا
Breeze n.	نَسيمٌ
Brethren n. pl. of brother.	إِخوَةٌ
Brevity n.	اِختِصارٌ . إيجازٌ
Brew v. t.	خَمَّرَ (جِعَةً (بيرا)
Brewery n.	مَصنَعُ الجِعَةِ
Bribe n. or v. t.	بَرطيلٌ . بَرطَلَ
Bribery n.	بَرطَلةٌ . رَشوَةٌ
Brick n.	آجُرٌّ . قِرميدٌ
Brick-bat n.	قِطعةُ قِرميدٍ
Brick-kiln n.	أَتونُ الآجُرِّ
Bridal a. or n.	عُرسِيٌّ . عُرسٌ
Bride n.	عَروسٌ
Bridegroom n.	عَريسٌ

Bridemaid Bride's maid } n.	شَبينةُ العَروسِ
Bridge n. or v. t.	جِسرٌ . قَنطَرةٌ . نَصَبَ جِسراً
Bridle n. or v. t.	لِجامٌ . أَلجَمَ
Brief a. or n.	قَصيرٌ . عَرضُ حالٍ مُختَصَرٌ
Brier n.	عُلَّيقٌ . عَوسَجٌ
Brig n.	سَفينةٌ ذاتُ صارِيَينِ
Brigade n.	لِواءٌ مِن الجُندِ
Brigadier n.	قائِدٌ فَوقَ اميرِ الآي . لِواءٌ
Brigand n.	لِصٌّ . قاطِعُ طُرُقٍ
Brigandage n.	قَطعُ الطُّرُقِ
Bright a.	لامِعٌ . بَرَّاقٌ . ذَكِيٌّ
Brighten v. t. or i.	أَنارَ . لَمَعَ
Brightness n.	أَلمَعانٌ . رَونَقٌ
Bright's disease n.	مَرَضٌ في الكُليَتَينِ
Brilliancy n.	رَونَقٌ . بَهاءٌ
Brilliant a.	بَهِيٌّ . لامِعٌ
Brim n.	شَفةٌ . حَرفٌ . حافةٌ
Brimful Brimming } a.	مَملوءٌ إلى شَفتِهِ

Brimstone n.	كِبْرِيت
Brine n.	مَاءٌ كَثِيرُ ٱلْمُلُوحة
Bring v. t.	أَتَى بِهِ . احْضَرَ
Brink n.	حَافَة
Brisk a.	نَشِيطٌ . سَرِيعٌ . خَفِيفٌ
Briskness n.	نَشَاطٌ . خِفَّةٌ
Bristle n. or v. i.	هَلَبَة . تَنَفَّشَ
Bristly a.	اهْلَبُ اوْ هُلْبِيٌّ
Brittle a.	قَصِمٌ . قَصِفٌ
Brittleness n.	سِرْعَةُ ٱلِٱنْكِسَار
Broad a.	عَرِيضٌ . مُتَّسِعٌ
Broadcloth n.	جُوخٌ
Broaden v. t. or i.	أَوْسَعَ . عَرَّضَ . إِتَّسَعَ
Broad-side n.	إِطْلَاقَ مَدَافِعِ جَانِبِ ٱلْبَارِجَةِ
Brocade n.	دِيبَاجٌ . سُنْدُسٌ
Brochure n.	كُرَّاسَة
Brouge n.	لَفْظٌ فَاسِدٌ
Broil v.t. or n.	شَوَى . إِنْشَوَى . خِصَامٌ

Broken pp. (break	مَكْسُورٌ (مِنْ
Broker n.	سِمْسَارٌ ج سَمَاسِرَة
Brokerage n.	سَمْسَرَة
Bronchitis n.	إِنْتِهَابُ شُعَبِ ٱلرِّئَة
Bronze n.	خَلِيطٌ مِنْ نِحَاسٍ وَقَصْدِيرٍ
Brooch n.	دَبُّوسٌ لِلصَّدْرِ
Brood n.	فَرْخٌ ج فِرَاخ . نَسْلٌ
Brood v. t.	حَضَنَ ٱلْفِرَاخَ
Brood v. i.	ثَابَرَ عَلَى ٱلْهَمِّ
Brook n. or v. t.	سَاقِيَة . إِحْتَمَلَ
Brooklet n.	سَاقِيَة صَغِيرَة
Broom n.	مِكْنَسَة ج مَكَانِسُ
Broomstick n.	قَضِيبُ مِكْنَسَةِ
Broth n.	مَرَقٌ
Brothel n.	بَيْتُ ٱلْعَوَاهِرِ
Brother n.	أَخٌ . إِخْوَة
Brotherhood n.	اخْوِيَّة ج إِخَاءٌ
Brought pp. of bring.	مُحْضَرٌ . مُؤْتًى بِهِ
Brow n.	جَبْهَة . جَبِينٌ . حَافَة

Brown a. or v. t. أَسْمَرُ . جَعَلَهُ اسْمَرَ	Bud n. or v. i. بُرْعُمٌ . أَخْرَجَ البَرَاعِمَ
Brownish a. مَائِلٌ إِلَى السُّمْرَةِ	Budge v. i. تَحَرَّكَ . إِنْطَلَقَ
Browse v. t. or i. رَعَى . إِرْتَعَى	Budget n. قَائِمَةٌ مَالِيَّةٌ . مِيزَانِيَّةٌ
Bruin n. لَقَبٌ لِلدُّبِّ	Buffalo n. جَامُوسٌ ج جَوَامِيسُ
Bruise v. t. رَضَّ ـ رَضْرَضَ	Buffet v. t. لَكَمَ ـ لَطَمَ ـ قَاوَمَ
Brunt n. شِدَّةٌ . صَدْمَةٌ	Buffoon n. مَازِحٌ . مَاجِنٌ
Brush n. فُرْشَةٌ . اغصانٌ مَقطوعة	Bug n. بَقَّةٌ . فِسْفِسٌ ج فَسَافِسُ
Brush v. i. or t. مَسَحَ (بِالفُرْشَةِ)	Bugbear n. هَائِلٌ . وَهْمِيٌّ
Brusque a. خَشِنُ المُعَامَلَةِ . عنيفٌ	Bugle n. نَفِيرٌ
Brutal } Brutish } a. وَحْشِيٌّ . فَظٌّ	Build v. t. بَنَى ـ عَمَّرَ
Brutality n. وحشِيَّةٌ . فَظَاظَةٌ	Building n. بِنَاءٌ . عَمَارٌ
Brutalize v. t. وَحَّشَ	Built pp. of build. مَبْنِيٌّ
Brute n. وَحْشٌ . جَافٍ . قَاسٍ	Bulb n. بَصَلَةُ نَبَاتٍ
Bubble n. فُقَّاعَةٌ . مَشْرُوعٌ بَاطِلٌ	Bulbous a. ذو بَصَلٍ
Buck n. ذَكَرُ الغَنَمِ وَالوَعْلِ	Bulge v. i. تَقَبَّبَ . بَرَزَ
Bucket n. دَلْوٌ . سَطْل	Bulk n. حجمٌ . مِقْدَارٌ
Buckle n. or v.t. إِبْزِيمٌ . شَدَّ (بِهِ)	Bulky n. جَسِيمٌ . ضَخْمٌ . كَبِيرٌ
Buckler n. تُرْسٌ ج اتْرَاسٌ	Bull n. ثَوْرٌ ج ثِيرَان

Bull-dog n.	كَلْبٌ كَبِيرٌ ضَارٍ
Bullet n.	كُلَّةٌ بُنْدُقِيَّةٌ . رَصَاصَةٌ
Bulletin n.	تَقْرِيرٌ رَسْمِيٌّ
Bull-frog n.	ضِفْدَعٌ كَبِيرٌ
Bullion n.	سَبَائِكُ ذَهَبٍ أَوْ فِضَّةٍ
Bullock n.	ثَوْرٌ صَغِيرٌ اوْ خَصِيٌّ
Bully n.	مُتَوَعِّدٌ . مُتَصَلِّفٌ
Bullrush n.	حَلْفَاةٌ . بَرْدِيٌّ
Bulwark n.	حِصْنٌ . مِتْرَاس
Bumble-bee n.	نَحْلَةٌ كَبِيرَةٌ
Bump n.	صَدْمَةٌ . لَطْمَةٌ . وَرَمٌ
Bump v. t. or i.	صَدَمَ بِصَوْتٍ قَوِيٍّ
Bumper n.	كَأْسٌ مَمْلُوءَةٌ
Bun n.	نَوْعٌ مِنَ ٱلْكَعْكِ
Bunch n. or v. t.	عُنْقُودٌ . عِذْقٌ . جَمَّعَ
Bundle n.	رَبْطَةٌ . رِزْمَةٌ . حُزْمَةٌ
Bung n.	سَدَادُ بَرْمِيلٍ
Bungle v. i.	خَبَّصَ
Bunion n.	ثُؤْلُولٌ فِي ٱلرِّجْلِ
Bunting n.	نَسِيجُ صُوفٍ لِلرَّايَاتِ
Buoy n.	عَوَّامَةٌ لِدَلَالَةِ ٱلْمَرَاكِبِ
Buoyant n.	عَائِمٌ . خَفِيفٌ . مَسْرُورٌ
Bur or burr n.	غِلَافُ نَبَاتٍ ذُوْ شَوْكٍ
Burden n. or v. t.	حِمْلٌ . ضَايَقَ
Burdensome a.	ثَقِيلٌ . مُتْعِبٌ
Bureau n.	خِزَانَةٌ . مَكْتَبٌ
Burglar n.	سَارِقُ بَيْتٍ بِٱللَّيْلِ
Burglary n.	سِرْقَةُ بَيْتٍ بِٱللَّيْلِ
Burial n.	دَفْنٌ . جَنَازَةٌ
Burlesque a or n.	مُضْحِكٌ . أُضْحُوكَةٌ
Burly a.	جَسِيمٌ . ضَخْمٌ
Burn v. t. or n.	حَرَقَ . إِحْتَرَقَ . كَيٌّ
Burnish v. t.	صَقَلَ
Burrow n. or v. i.	وِجَارٌ . إِحْتَقَرَ
Burst v. t. or i.	فَجَرَ . إِنْفَجَرَ . إِنْفَلَقَ
Bury v. t.	دَفَنَ . قَبَرَ

Bush _n._	شُجَيْرَةٌ . دَغَلٌ
Bushel _n._	مِكْيَالٌ انْكِلِيزِيٌّ
Bushy _a._	كَثٌّ
Busily _ad._	بِجِدٍّ أَوْ بِاجْتِهَادٍ
Business _n._	شُغْلٌ . مَصْلَحَةٌ . حِرْفَةٌ
Bust _n._	تِمْثَالُ الرَّاسِ إِلَى الصَّدْرِ
Bustle _n._ or _v. i._	جَلَبَةٌ . عَجَلَةٌ . — ضَجَّ
Busy _a._	مَشْغُولٌ . مُهْتَمٌّ
Busybody _n._	فُضُولِيٌّ
But _conj._ or _pr._	لَكِنَّ . غَيْرَ انْ . إِلَّا
Butcher _n._	لَحَّامٌ . قَصَّابٌ . جَزَّارٌ
Butchery _n._	ذَبْحٌ . قَتْلٌ عَظِيمٌ
Butler _n._	سَاقِي الخَمْرِ
Butt _n._	هَدَفٌ . بَرْمِيلٌ كَبِيرٌ
Butter _n._	زُبْدَةٌ . سَمْنٌ

Buttery _n._	بَيْتُ المُؤُونَةِ
Butterfly _n._	فَرَاشَةٌ ج فَرَاشٌ
Buttock _n._	عَجُزٌ ج أَعْجَازٌ
Button _n._	زِرٌّ ج ازْرَارٌ
Buttonhole _n._	عُرْوَةٌ لِلزِّرِّ
Buttress _n._	دِعَامَةٌ
Buxom _a._	جَسِيمٌ . طَرِبٌ
Buy _v. t._	إِبْتَاعَ . إِشْتَرَى
Buzz _v. i._ or _n._	دَوَى . دَوِيٌّ
Buzzard _n._	ضَرْبٌ مِنَ البَازِ
By _pr._	عِنْدَ . قُرْبَ . بِ
By-and-by _ad._	بَعْدَ حِينٍ
By-path By-way } _n._	مَسْلَكٌ صَغِيرٌ
By-word _n._	عِبْرَةٌ . مَثَلٌ

C

Cab n.	نَوْعٌ مِنَ ٱلْمَرْكَبَاتِ
Cabal n.	عُصْبَةٌ سِرِّيَّةٌ
Cabbage n.	كُرْنُبٌ . مَلْفُوفٌ
Cabin n.	كُوخٌ . حُجْرَةٌ فِي سَفِينَةٍ
Cabinet n.	خِزَانَةٌ . وِزَارَةٌ
Cabinet-maker n.	نَجَّارٌ
Cable n.	جُمَّلٌ (حَبْلُ ٱلْمِرْسَاةِ أَوْ سَلْسِلَتُهَا) . حَبْلٌ غَلِيظٌ
Cackle v. i. or n.	قَاقَ ـُ . قَوْقَ
Cadaverous a.	شَبِيهٌ بِٱلْجُثَّةِ . مُصْفَرٌّ
Cadence n.	هُبُوطُ ٱلصَّوْتِ . لَحْنٌ
Cadet n.	تِلْمِيذُ مَدْرَسَةٍ حَرْبِيَّةٍ
Café n.	قَهْوَةٌ
Cage n.	قَفَصٌ
Cajole v. t.	دَاهَنَ . تَمَلَّقَ
Cake n.	قُرْصٌ . كَعْكَةٌ
Calamitous a.	مُسِيءٌ . نَكِبٌ
Calamity n.	مُصِيبَةٌ . بَلِيَّةٌ
Calcareous a.	كِلْسِيٌّ
Calcedony n.	عَقِيقٌ أَبْيَضُ
Calcine v. t.	كَلَّسَ بِٱلنَّارِ
Calculate v. t.	حَسَبَ ـُ . أَحْصَى
Caldron n.	قِدْرٌ . خَلْقِينٌ
Calendar n.	تَقْوِيمُ ٱلسَّنَةِ (رُزْنَامَةٌ)
Calf (pl. calves) n.	عِجْلٌ ج عُجُولٌ
Calf of the leg n.	بَطْنُ ٱلسَّاقِ
Calibre n.	قَطْرٌ . إِتِّسَاعٌ . عِيَارٌ
Calico n.	شِيتٌ . خَامٌ
Call v. t. or i.	دَعَا . سَمَّى . نَادَى

Call *n.*	دَعْوَةٌ . طَلَبٌ . مُنَادَاةٌ
Calling *n.*	حِرْفَةٌ . مَصْلَحَةٌ . مُنَادَاةٌ
Callous *a.*	مُتَصَلِّبٌ . مُكَنِّبٌ
Calm *a.* or *v. t.*	هَادِئٌ . هَدَّأَ . اسْكَنَ
Calm } Calmness } *n.*	هُدُوءٌ . سُكُونٌ
Caloric *n.*	أَلْحَرَارَةُ
Calorific *n.*	مُوَلِّدٌ لِلْحَرَارَة
Calumniate *v. t.*	وَشَى بِ . نَمَّ ـِ
Calumny *n.*	نَمِيمَةٌ . إِفْتِرَاءٌ
Calve *v. t.*	وَلَدَتْ (أَلْبَقَرَةُ)
Calyx *n.*	كَأْسُ ٱلزَّهْرَةِ
Came (Come *v. i.* ماضي)	جَاءَ . أَتَى
Camel *n.*	جَمَلٌ . بَعِيرٌ . نَاقَةٌ
Camelopard *n.*	زَرَافَةٌ
Cameo *n.*	حَجَرٌ كَرِيمٌ نَافِرُ ٱلنَّقْشِ
Camera *n.*	آلَةٌ لِلتَّصْوِيرِ ٱلشَّمْسِيِّ
Camomile } Chamomile } *n.*	بَابُونَجٌ
Camp *n.*	مَحَلَّةٌ . مُعَسْكَرٌ
Campaign *n.*	غَزْوَةٌ . حَرْبٌ
Camphor *n.*	كَافُورٌ
Can *v. i.* or *n.*	قَدَرَ ـِ . كُوزٌ
Canal *n.*	قَنَاةٌ . تُرْعَةٌ
Canary *n.*	عُصْفُورٌ مُغَرِّدٌ
Cancel *v. t.*	مَحَا . أَلْغَى . أَبْطَلَ
Cancellation *n.*	مَحْوٌ
Cancer *n.*	سَرَطَانٌ
Cancerous *a.*	سَرَطَانِيٌّ
Candid *a.*	مُخْلِصٌ . سَلِيمُ ٱلنِّيَّة
Candidate *n.*	طَالِبُ ٱلِانْتِخَاب
Candidly *ad.*	بِإِخْلَاصٍ . مُخْلِصًا
Candy *n.*	فَنْدٌ . نَوْعٌ مِنَ ٱلْحَلْوَى
Candle *n.*	شَمْعَةٌ . قِنْدِيلٌ
Candlestick *n.*	شَمْعَدَانٌ . مَغَارَةٌ
Candour *n.*	إِخْلَاصٌ . سَلَامَةُ ٱلنِّيَّة
Cane *n.*	قَصَبَةٌ . عَصًا
Canine *a.*	كَلْبِينٌ
Canine-tooth *n.*	نَابٌ

Canker n. or v i.	قُرْحُ ٱڪَّالُ . فَسَدَ —
Canker-worm n.	دُودُ النَّبَاتَاتِ
Cannibal n.	آكلُ لُحُومِ ٱلْبَشَر
Cannibalism n.	أَكْلُ لُحُومِ ٱلْبَشَر
Cannon n.	مَدْفَعٌ ج مَدَافِعُ
Cannonade n.	ضَرْبٌ بِالْمَدَافِعِ
Cannoneer } Cannonier } n.	ٱلرَّامِي بِالْمَدَافِعِ
Canoe n.	قَارِبٌ هِنْدِيٌّ
Canon n.	قَانُونٌ
Canonical a.	قَانُونِيٌّ
Canonize v. t.	صَرَّحَ بِقَدَاسَةِ مَيْتٍ
Canopy n.	مِظَلَّةٌ
Cant n. or v. i.	تَظَاهُرٌ بِكَلَامِ ٱلتَّقْوَى . تَظَاهَرَ
Canter v. i. or n.	خَبَّ . خَبَبٌ
Canto n.	قَصِيدَةٌ
Canton n.	مُقَاطَعَةٌ . إِقْلِيمٌ
Cantonment n.	مَحَلَّةٌ
Canvas n.	جِنْفِيصٌ . خَيْشٌ

Canvass v. t.	بَحَثَ عَنْ — طَلَبَ
Cap n. or v. t.	(طَرْبُوشٌ) . غَطَّى
Capability n.	مَقْدُرَةٌ . طَاقَةٌ
Capable a.	قَادِرٌ . اهْلٌ
Capacious a.	مُتَّسِعٌ فَسِيحٌ
Capacity n.	سَعَةٌ . قُدْرَةٌ
Cap-a-pie ad.	مِنَ ٱلرَّأْسِ إِلَى ٱلْقَدَمِ
Cape n.	رَأْسُ (أَرْضٍ) بُرْنُسٌ
Capillary a. or n.	شَعْرِيٌّ
Capital n. or a.	رَأْسُ مَالٍ . قَصَبَةٌ مَمْلَكَةٍ . رَئِيسِيٌّ . نَفِيسٌ
Capitalist n.	ذُو مَالٍ مُثْمِرٍ
Capitol n.	سَرَايَ ٱلْحُكُومَة ٱلْأَمِيرِكِيَّة
Capitulate v. i.	سَلَّمَ تَحْتَ شُرُوطٍ
Caprice n.	تَقَلُّبُ ٱلْخَاطِرِ
Capricious a.	مُتَقَلِّبٌ
Capsize v. t. or i.	قَلَبَ . إِنْقَلَبَ
Captain n.	قِبْطَانٌ . يُوزْبَاشِي

Capricorn n.	بُرْجُ الْجَدْي	Card v. t.	مَشَط . حَلَج
Captious a.	كَثِيرُ آلِانْتِقَاد	Cardiac a.	مُخْتَصٌّ بِالْقَلْب
Captivate v. t.	أَسَرَ — إِفْتَنَ	Cardinal n. or a.	كَرْدِنَالٌ . أَوَّلِيٌّ
Captive n. or a.	أَسِيرٌ . مَسْبِيٌّ	Care n. or v. i.	إِعْتِنَاءٌ . هَمٌّ . إِعْتَنَى
Captivity n.	أَسْرٌ . سَبْيٌ	Careen v.i.or t.	مَالَتِ آلسَّفِينَةُ . أَمَالَهَا
Captor n.	آسِرٌ . سَالِبٌ	Career n.	مَجْرًى . مَسِيرٌ
Capture n. or v. t.	قَبْضٌ . قَبَضَ عَلَى	Careful a.	حَذِرٌ . كَثِيرُ آلِاعْتِنَاء
Car n.	عَجَلَة . مَرْكَبَة	Carefulness n.	إِعْتِنَاءٌ . مُبَالَاة
Carat n.	قِيرَاط (فِي وَزْنِ آلذَّهَبِ)	Careless a.	غَيْرُ مُبَالٍ . غَافِلٌ
Caravan n.	قَافِلَة ج قَوَافِلُ	Carelessness n.	إِهْمَالٌ . غَفْلَة
Caraway n.	كَرْوِيَآء (كَرَاوِيَا)	Caress v. t or n.	لَاطَف . دَلَّلَ . مُلَاطَفَة
Carbine n.	(قَرَابِينَة) بُنْدُقِيَّة قَصِيرَة	Cargo n.	شَحْنٌ . وَسْقُ سَفِينَةٍ
Carbon n.	فَحْمٌ (كَرْبُونٌ)	Caricature n.	صُورَة هَزْلِيَّة
Carbonaceous a.	فَحْمِيٌّ	Carious a.	نَخِر
Carbonize v. t.	صَيَّرَهُ فَحْمًا	Carmine n.	لَوْن دُودِيٌّ
Carbuncle n.	دُمَّلٌ كَبِيرٌ	Carnage n.	مَلْحَمَة . مَقْتَلَة عَظِيمَة
Carcass n.	جُثَّة جِيفَة	Carnal a.	جَسَدَانِيٌّ . شَهْوَانِيٌّ
Card n.	وَرَقَة زِيَارَةٍ . مُشْطٌ لِلصُّوف	Carnally ad.	بِشَهْوَةٍ جَسَدِيَّة

Carnival *n.*	مَرْفَعٌ ج مَرَافِعُ
Carnivorous *a.*	آكِلُ لُحُومٍ . ضَارٍ
Carob *n.*	خَرُّوبٌ
Carol *n.* or *v. i.*	اغْنِيَّةٌ . غَنَّى
Carousal *n.*	وَلِيمَةٌ لِلشُّرْبِ وَالفَرَحِ
Carouse *v. i.*	شَرِبَ وَفَرِحَ . قَصَفَ
Carp *v. i.*	لامَ ـُ . عَذَلَ ـُ
Carpenter *n.*	نَجَّارٌ
Carpet *n.*	سُجَّادَةٌ . بِسَاطٌ
Carriage *n.*	مَرْكَبَةٌ . (عَرَبِيَّةٌ)
Carrion *n.*	جِيفَةٌ لَحْمٌ نَتِنٌ
Carrot *n.*	جَزَرَةٌ ج جَزَرٌ
Carry *v. t.*	حَمَلَ ـِ . نَقَلَ ـُ
Cart *n.*	عَجَلَةُ النَّقْلِ
Cartage *n.*	نَقْلٌ . اجْرَةُ آلنَّقْلِ
Carter *n.*	سَائِقُ عَجَلَةِ النَّقْلِ
Cartilage *n.*	غُضْرُوفٌ ج غَضَارِيفُ
Cartilaginous *a.*	غُضْرُوفِيٌّ
Cartridge *n.*	(فَشَكَةٌ ج فَشَكٌ)
Carve *v. t.*	قَشَّ ـُ قَطَعَ (لَحْمًا)
Cascade *n.*	شَلَّالٌ
Case *n.*	صَنْدُوقٌ . حَالٌ . قَضِيَّةٌ
Casement *n.*	صَنْدُوقُ شُبَّاكٍ
Cash *n.* or *v. t.*	نُقُودٌ . قَبَضَ ـِ نَقْدًا
Cash-book *n.*	دَفْتَرُ النُّقُودِ
Cashier *n.* or *v. t.*	أَمِينُ الصَّنْدُوقِ . عَزَلَ
Cashmere *n.*	كَشْمِيرٌ
Casing *n.*	غِطَاءٌ . بِرْوَازٌ
Cask *n.*	بَرْمِيلٌ
Casket *n.*	عِلْبَةٌ لِلْحُلِيِّ أَوْ اِكِلٌّ شَيْءٌ ثَمِينٍ
Casque *n.*	خُوذَةٌ ج خُوَذٌ
Cast *v. t.*	رَمَى . صَبَّ . سَبَكَ
Cast *n.*	رَمْيَةٌ . هَيْئَةٌ . سَبِيكَةٌ
Castaway *n.*	مَرْفُوضٌ . مَرْذُولٌ
Caste *n.*	طَائِفَةٌ . فِئَةٌ
Castigate *v. t.*	أَدَّبَ . ضَرَبَ بِآلسَّوْطِ

Casting n.	رَمْيٌ . سَبِيكة
Cast-iron n.	جَدِيدٌ صَبٌّ
Castor-oil n.	زَيْتُ خَرْوَع
Castle n.	حِصْنٌ . قَلعَة . صَرْحٌ
Castrate v. t.	خَصَى —
Casual a.	عَرَضِيٌّ . إِتِّفَاقِيٌّ
Casually ad.	عَرَضًا . إِتِّفَاقًا
Casualty n.	حَادِثَةٌ عَرَضِيَّة
Cat n.	قِطٌّ . هِرٌّ
Catacomb n.	مَغَارَةٌ لِلدَّفْنِ تَحْتَ الأَرْض
Catalogue n.	قَائِمَة . جَدْوَلٌ
Cataract n.	شَلَّالٌ . مَاءٌ أَزْرَقُ في العَيْنَيْن
Catarrh n.	زُكَامٌ
Catastrophe n.	مُصِيبَةٌ . نَكْبَة
Catch v. t.	أَدْرَكَ . قَبَضَ . تَنَاوَلَ
Catching a.	مُعْدٍ
Catechetical a.	بِالسُّؤَالِ وَالجَوَاب
Catechise v. t.	عَلَّمَ بِالسُّؤَالِ
Catechism n.	اصُولُ الإِيمَان
Categorical a.	صَرِيحٌ . قَاطِعٌ
Category n.	صَفٌّ . طَبَقَة
Cater v. t.	رَوَّدَ . قَدَّمَ طَعَامًا
Caterpillar n.	دُودَة . فَرَاشَة
Catgut n.	وَتَرٌ مِنْ مِعًى
Cathartic n. or a.	مُسْهِلٌ
Cathedral n.	كَنِيسَةُ اسْقُف
Catholic a.	جَامِعٌ . كَاثُولِيكِيٌّ
Catholocism n.	النِّظَامُ الكَاثُولِيكِيُّ
Cattle n. pl.	مَاشِيَةٌ ج مَوَاش
Caudal a.	ذَنَبِيٌّ
Caught pp. of catch.	مَقْبُوضٌ
Caul n.	نَزْبٌ
Cauliflower n.	قَرْنَبِيط أَوْ قُنْبِيط
Causal a.	سَبَبِيٌّ
Causalty n.	سَبَبِيَّة
Causation n.	تَسْبِيبٌ

Causative a.	مُسَبِّبٌ
Cause n.	سَبَبٌ . عِلَّةٌ
Caustic a. or n.	حَارِقٌ . كَاوٍ
Cauterize v. t.	كَوَى ـِ . وَسَمَ ـِ
Cautery n.	كَيٌّ
Caution n. or v. t.	حَذَرٌ . حَذَّرَ
Cautious a.	حَذِرٌ . مُحْتَرِسٌ
Cavalcade n.	مَوْكِبُ فُرْسَانٍ
Cavalier n.	فَارِسٌ . خَيَّالٌ
Cavalry n.	فُرْسَانٌ . خَيَّالَةٌ
Cave Cavern } n.	مَغَارَةٌ ج مَغَائِرُ
Cavil v. i. or n.	مَاحَكَ . مُمَاحَكَةٌ
Cavity n.	وَقْبَةٌ . تَجْوِيفٌ
Cease v. i.	كَفَّ عَنْ . إِنْقَطَعَ
Cedar n.	أَرْزٌ
Cede v. t.	تَرَكَ ـُ . تَخَلَّى عَنْ
Ceil v. t.	سَقَفَ ـُ . طَيَّنَ . بَطَّنَ
Ceiling n.	سَقْفٌ (طَوَانٌ)
Celebrate v. t.	عَظَّمَ . إِحْتَفَلَ
Celebrated a.	مَشْهُورٌ
Celebrity n.	شُهْرَةٌ . صِيتٌ
Celerity n.	سُرْعَةٌ . عَجَلَةٌ
Celery n.	كَرْفْسٌ
Celestial a.	سَمَاوِيٌّ
Celibacy n.	عُزُوبَةٌ . عُزْبَةٌ
Cell n.	صَوْمَعَةٌ . خَلِيَّةٌ . حُوَيْصَلَةٌ
Cellar n.	قَبْوٌ . بَيْتٌ تَحْتَانِيٌّ
Cellular n.	حُوَيْصَلِيٌّ . ذُو تَجَاوِيفٍ
Cement n. or v. t.	مِلَاطٌ . مَلَطَ
Cemetry n.	مَقْبَرَةٌ
Censer n.	مِبْخَرَةٌ . مِجْمَرَةٌ
Censor n.	مُرَاقِبٌ . مُؤَدِّبٌ . مُنْتَقِدٌ
Censorious a.	قَاسٍ . كَثِيرُ ٱلْمَلَامَةِ
Censurable a.	قَابِلُ ٱلْمَلَامَةِ
Censure v. t. or n.	لَامَ . مَلَامَةٌ
Census n.	تَعْدَادُ ٱلنُّفُوسِ
Cent n.	جُزْءٌ مِنَ ٱلْمِئَةِ مِنَ ٱلرِّيَالِ
Centaur n.	فَرَسٌ خُرَافِيٌّ لَهُ رَأْسُ إِنْسَانٍ

Centennial a.	مَرَّةً كُلِّ مِئَةِ سَنَةٍ	Certainly n.	مُحَقَّقًا
Centenarian n.	ذو مِئَةِ سَنَةٍ	Certainty n.	يَقِين . قَطْع
Centigrade a.	قِيَاسُ مِئَةِ دَرَجَةٍ	Certificate n.	شَهَادَة . وَثِيقَة
Centipede n.	ذو مِئَةِ رِجْلٍ . أَمْ أَرْبَع وَأَرْبَعِين	Certify v. t.	حَقَّقَ . شَهِدَ بِ
		Certitude n.	يَقِين . عَدَمُ الشَكِّ
Central a.	مَرْكَزِيٌّ	Cerulean a.	سَمَاوِيُّ اللَّوْنِ
Centrality n.	مَرْكَزِيَّة	Cessation n.	إِنْقِطَاع . تَوَقُّف
Centre n.	مَرْكَز . وَسْط	Cession n.	تَسْلِيم . تَخْلِيَة
Centrifugal a.	مَائِل عَنِ المَرْكَز	Cess-pool n.	مَحَلُّ الأَقْذَارِ . بَالُوعَة
Centripetal n.	مَائِل إِلَى المَرْكَز	Chafe v.i.or t.	دَعَكَ ـَ . ضَجِرَ ـَ
Centurion n.	قَائِدُ مِئَةٍ	Chaff n. or e. i.	عُصَافَة . مَازَح
Century n.	مِئَة سَنَةٍ . قَرْن	Chaffer v. i.	سَاوَمَ
Cereals n. pl.	حُبُوب تُؤْكَل	Chagrin n. or v.t.	خَجَل . ضَجَر . أَزْعَجَ
Cerebrum n	الدِّمَاغ	Chain n. or v. i.	سِلْسِلَة . رَبَطَ بِهَا
Cerebral a.	دِمَاغِيّ	Chair n.	كُرْسِيّ ج كَرَاسِيّ
Ceremonial a.	إِحْتِفَالِيّ . طَقْسِي	Chairman n.	صَاحِبُ الكُرْسِيِّ
Ceremonial Ceremony } n.	إِبْتِذَال . طَقْس	Chaise n.	مَرْكَبَة بِعَجَلَتَيْنِ
Certain a.	أَكِيدٌ . مُحَقَّق	Chalcedony n.	عَقِيق ابْيَضُ

Chalice n.	كَأْسُ ٱلْعَشَاءِ ٱلرَّبَّانِي
Chalk n.	طَبَاشِيرُ
Challenge v. t. or n.	إِسْتَدْعَى لِلْمُبَارَزَةِ . تَحَدَّ
Chamber n.	غُرْفَةٌ . حُجْرَةٌ
Chamberlain n.	حَاجِب
Chameleon n.	حِرْبَاءٌ
Champ v.t. or i.	صَكَمَ عَلَى . عَضَّ
Champagne n.	شَمْبَانِيَا
Champion n.	مُبَارِزٌ . مُحَامٍ . بَطَلٌ
Chance n.	صُدْفَةٌ . عَرَضٌ . إِتِّفَاقٌ
Chance v. i.	إِتَّفَقَ . حَدَثَ
Chancellor n.	وَزِيرٌ . رَئِيسُ قُضَاةٍ
Chandler n.	بَائِعُ شَمْعٍ
Change n. or v. t.	تَغْيِيرٌ . غَيَّرَ
Changeable a.	قَابِلُ ٱلتَّغْيِيرِ . مُتَقَلِّبٌ
Channel n.	مَجْرًى . مَضِيقٌ . تَلَم
Channelled a.	مُتَلَّم
Chant v. t. or i. or n.	أَنْشَدَ . غَنَّى . نَشِيد
Chaos n.	هِيُولِيٌّ . عَدَمُ ٱنْتِظَام
Chaotic a.	غَيْرُ مُنْتَظِمٍ . مُشَوَّشٌ
Chapel n.	مَعْبَدٌ . كِنِيسَةٌ
Chaplain n.	قِسِّيسٌ فِي ٱلْجَيْشِ
Chaplet n.	إِكْلِيلُ زَهْرٍ او أَوْرَاقٍ
Chapter n.	بَابٌ . فَصْلٌ
Char v. t.	صَبَّرَ فَحْمًا . حَرَقَ
Character n.	سَجِيَّةٌ . خُلْقٌ . صِفَةٌ
Characteristic a. or n	خَاصٌّ . مَزِيَّةٌ
Characterize v. t.	وَصَفَ . مَيَّزَ
Charcoal n.	فَحْمٌ (مِنْ خَطَب)
Charge v. t. or n.	هَاجَمَ . شَكَا . أَوْصَى دَكَّ . مُهَاجَمَةٌ . شَكْوَى
Charge n.	قَيْدٌ فِي حِسَاب
Charger n.	صَحْفَةٌ . جَوَادٌ
Chariot n.	مَرْكَبَةٌ
Charitable a.	مُحْسِنٌ . مُتَصَدِّق
Charity n.	صَدَاقَةٌ . إِحْسَان

Charlatan *n.*	ذجّالٌ	Cheap *a.*	رخيص
Charm *n.*	طَلْسَمٌ . حُسْنٌ . لُطْفٌ	Cheapen *v. t.*	رخّصَ
Charm *v.t.*	سَحَرَ ـُ . فَتَنَ ـِ . ابْهَجَ	Cheapness	رُخْصٌ
Charming *a.*	سَارٌّ جدًّا . مُبْهِجٌ	Cheat *v. t.*	غشَّ ـُ . غَبَنَ ـِ
Chart *n.*	خَرِيطةٌ	Cheat *n.*	مُحْتَالٌ . خِدَاعٌ
Charter *n.* or *v. t.*	صكٌّ . إمْتِيازٌ . إسْتَأْجَرَ	Check *v. t.*	ردَعَ . اوقَفَ . عَاقَ
Chary *a.*	حذِرٌ . مُتَيَقِّظٌ	Check *n.*	رَدْعٌ . تَوْقِيفٌ . تَحْوِيلٌ
Chase *v. t.*	طَارَدَ . إصْطَادَ	Checker *v. t.*	نوَّعَ
Chase *n.*	مُطَارَدَةٌ . صَيْدٌ	Checkers *n. pl.*	لعِبُ الدَّامَا
Chasm *n.*	شقٌّ عَميقٌ في الأرضِ	Cheek *n.*	خدٌّ . خُدُودٌ . وَجْنَةٌ
Chaste *a.*	عفِيفٌ	Cheer *v. t.* or *n.*	فرّحَ . شَرَحَ . إنْشِرَاحٌ
Chasten *v. t.*	أدَّبَ	Cheerful Cheery *n.*	مَسْرُورٌ . بشّاشٌ
Chastise *v. t.*	قاصَّ . ادّبَ	Cheese *n.*	جبن
Chastisement *n.*	قصاصٌ . تأْديبٌ	Chemical *a.*	كيميّ او كِيمَاوِيٌّ
Chastity *n.*	عفّةٌ	Chemicals *n. pl.*	مَوَادٌّ كِيميّةٌ
Chat *v. i.*	حَادَثَ . كَالَمَ	Chemise *n.*	قَميصُ امْرَأةٍ
Chatter *v. i.*	هذرَ . بقَّ ـُ	Chemist *n.*	عالِمٌ بالْكِيميا
Chatterer *n.*	بقّاق	Chemistry *n.*	ألكِيميا

Cheque n.	تَحْوِيْلٌ (مَالِيٌّ)
Cherish v. t.	رَبَّى . أَعَزَّ . لَاطَفَ
Cherry n. or a.	كَرَزٌ . كَرَزِيُّ اللَّوْنِ
Cherub n.	كَرُوْبٌ أَوْ كَرُوْبِيْمٌ
Chess n.	شَطَرَنْجٌ
Chest n.	صُنْدُوْقٌ . صَدْرٌ
Chestnut n.	كَسْتَنَا . أَبُو فَرْوَة
Chevalier n.	فَارِسٌ (شَفَلِيرٌ)
Chew v. t.	مَضَغَ ـُ
Chick Chicken } n.	فَرْخٌ ج فُرُوْخ وَفِرَاخ
Chicken-pox n.	جَدْرِيُّ المَاءِ
Chick-peas n. pl.	حِمَّصٌ
Chide v. t.	عَاتَبَ زَجَرَ ـُ
Chief a.	رَئِيْسِيٌّ . أَوَّلِيٌّ . اَهَمُّ
Chief Chieftain } n.	رَئِيْسٌ . قَائِدٌ
Chiefly ad.	خُصُوْصاً . بِالأَخَصِّ
Child pl. Children n.	وَلَدٌ ج اوْلَادٌ
Childhood n.	زَمَانُ الصِّبَا . صَبْوَةٌ

Childish a.	وَلَدِيٌّ . بَاطِلٌ
Chill a. or n.	بَارِدٌ . قَشْعَرِيْرَةٌ
Chilly v. t.	بَرَّدَ
Chilly a.	بَارِدٌ
Chime n.	الْحَانُ اجْرَاسٍ مُوَقَّعَةٍ
Chimera n.	تَصَوُّرٌ وَهْمِيٌّ
Chimerical a.	وَهْمِيٌّ . بَاطِلٌ
Chimney n.	مَدْخَنَةٌ . دَاخِنَةٌ
Chin n.	ذَقْنٌ ج ذُقُوْن
China n.	خَزَفٌ صِيْنِيٌّ . بِلَادُ الصِّيْنِ
Chinese a.	صِيْنِي
Chine n.	فَقَارَةٌ
Chink n.	شَقٌّ ضَيِّقٌ
Chink v. i. or t.	إِنْشَقَّ . طَنَّ . أَطَنَّ
Chintz n.	شِيْتٌ مُخْتَلِفُ الأَلْوَانِ
Chip n.	قِطْعَةُ خَشَبٍ صَغِيْرَةٌ
Chirography n.	خَطٌّ . صِنَاعَةُ الْكِتَابَةِ
Chirp v. i.	غَرَّدَ . صَوَّتَ

Chisel n. or v. t.   إِزْمِيلٌ ج اَزَامِيلُ. نَحَتَ بِهِ

Chivalrous a.   شَرِيفٌ. ذُو شَهَامَةٍ

Chivalry n.   فُرُوسِيَّةٌ. بَسَالَةٌ

Chloroform n.   بَنْجٌ (كْلُورُفُورم)

Chocolate n.   (شُوكَلاتَا)

Choice n. or a.   إِخْتِيَارٌ. نَفِيسٌ. فَاخِرٌ

Choir n.   زُمْرَةُ مُرَنِّمِين

Choke v. t. or i.   خَنَقَ. سَدَّ. إِخْتَنَقَ

Choler n.   صَفْرَاءُ. غَضَبٌ

Cholera n.   اَلْهَوَاءُ اَلْأَصْفَرُ

Choleric a.   سَرِيعُ اَلْغَضَبِ. غَضُوبٌ

Choose v. i.   إِخْتَارَ. إِنْتَخَبَ

Chop v. t. or n.   قَطَعَ. قِطْعَةُ لَحْمٍ

Chord n.   وَتَرٌ وَوَتَرٌ ج أَوْتَارٌ

Chorister n.   مُغَنٍّ. مُرَنِّمٌ

Chorus n.   قَرَارٌ فِي اَلتَّرْنِيمِ   زُمْرَةُ مُرَنِّمِينَ

Christ n.   اَلْمَسِيحُ

Christen v. t.   عَمَّدَ. سَمَّى

Christendom n.   اَلْعَالَمُ اَلْمَسِيحِي

Christening n.   مَعْمُودِيَّةٌ مَعَ تَسْمِيَةٍ

Christian a. or n.   مَسِيحِيٌّ

Christianity n.   اَلدِّيَانَةُ اَلْمَسِيحِيَّةُ

Christianize v. t.   نَصَّرَ

Christmas n.   عِيدُ اَلْمِيلاد

Chromatic a.   مُخْتَصٌّ بِالْأَلْوَانِ

Chronic n.   مُزْمِنٌ

Chronicle n.   سِفْرُ اَلْأَخْبَارِ. تَأْرِيخٌ

Chronological a.   تَارِيخِيٌّ

Chronologer Chronologist n.   عَالِمٌ بِالتَّارِيخِ

Chronology n.   حِسَابُ اَلتَّوَارِيخِ

Chronometer n.   سَاعَةٌ تَضْبُطُ نَفْسَهَا

Chrysalis n.   شَرْنَقَةٌ ج شَرَانِق

Chubby a.   ضَخْمُ اَلْجِسْمِ وَقَصِيرُهُ

Chuckle v. i.   ضَحِكَ سِرًّا

Chum n.   زَمِيلٌ. رَفِيق

Church *n.*	كَنِيسَةٌ	Circulate *v. i.* or *t.*	دَازَ . نَشَرَ ــُ
Churchyard *n.*	مَقْبَرَةٌ	Circulation *n.*	دَوَرَانٌ . نَشْرٌ
Churl *n.*	خَشِنٌ . فَظٌّ	Circulatory *a.*	دَائِرٌ
Churn *v. t.* or *n.*	مَخَضَ ــُ مِمْخَضٌ	Circumambulate *v. t.*	طَافَ ــُ حَوْلَ
Cicatrice Cicatrix } *n.*	نَدْبَةٌ	Circumcise *v. t.*	خَتَنَ ــِ . طَهَّرَ
Cider *n.*	عَصِيرُ التُّفَّاحِ	Circumcision *n.*	خِتَان
Cigar *n.*	سِيكَارَةٌ	Circumference *n.*	مُحِيط
Ciliary *a.*	هُدْبِيٌّ . شَعْرِيٌّ	Circumflex *n.* (ٛ)	عَلَامَةُ مَدّ حَرْفٍ
Cimeter Cimerer } *n.*	سَيْفٌ مُقَوَّسٌ	Circumjacent *a.*	مُحِيطٌ (بِهِ)
Cincture *n.*	زُنَّارٌ . مِنْطَقَةٌ	Circumlocution *n.*	إِسْهَابٌ
Cinders *n. pl.*	بَقَايَا الْوَقِيدِ الْمَحْرُوقِ	Circumnavigate *v. t.*	طَافَ بَحْرًا
Cinnamon *n.*	قِرْفَةٌ	Circumnavigation *n.*	أَلطَّوَافُ بَحْرًا
Cipher *n.*	صِفْرٌ	Circumscribe *v. t.*	أَحَاطَ بِهِ . حَصَرَ ــُ
Ciphering *v.*	حِسَابُ الْأَرْقَامِ	Circumscription *n.*	إِحَاطَةٌ . حَصْرٌ
Circle *n.* or *v. i.*	دَائِرَةٌ . دَارَ ــُ	Circumspect *a.*	حَذِرٌ . مُحْتَرِسٌ
Circuit *n.*	دَوَرَانٌ . إِقْلِيمٌ	Circumspection *n.*	حَذَرٌ . إِحْتِرَاسٌ
Circuitous *a.*	دَوْرِيٌّ . غَيْرُ مُسْتَقِيمٍ	Circumspectly *ad.*	بِحَذَرٍ . إِحْتِرَاسًا
Circular *a.*	مُدَوَّرٌ . نَشْرَةٌ	Circumstance *n.*	حَالَةٌ . ظَرْفٌ

Circumstantial *a.* مَفْصَلٌ. عَرَضِيٌّ	Clack *v. i.* or *n.* طَقْطَقَ. قَعْقَعَ. طَقْطَقَة
Circumvent *v. t.* غَلَبَهُ بِالْحِيلَة	Clad *pp.* of clothe لَابِسٌ. مَكْسُوٌّ
Circus *n.* مَلْعَبٌ مُسْتَدِيرٌ لِلْخَيْل	Claim *v. t.* or *n.* اِدَّعَى بِهِ. اِدِّعَاءٌ
Cistern *n.* صِهْرِيجٌ. حَوْضٌ	Claimant *n.* طَالِبٌ. مُدَّعٍ
Citadel *n.* بُرْجٌ. قَلْعَة	Clam *n.* بَطْلِينُوس
Citation *n.* اِقْتِبَاس. اِسْتِدْعَاءٌ	Clamber *v. i.* تَسَلَّقَ
Cite *v. t.* اِقْتَبَسَ. اِسْتَشْهَدَ. اِسْتَدْعَى	Clammy *a.* دَبِقٌ. لَزِجٌ
Citizen *n.* مَدَنِيٌّ تَابِعٌ لِدَوْلَةٍ	Clamour *n.* صِيَاحٌ. ضَجَّة
Citizenship *n.* حُقُوقُ الْمَدَنِيَّة	Clamorous *a.* صِيَاح. صَخَّاب
Citron *n.* لَيْمُونٌ حَامِضٌ. اتْرُجّ	Clamp *v. t.* or *n.* شَدَّ بِكَلَّاب. كَلَّاب
Citric *n.* لَيْمُونِيٌّ. اتْرُجِّيّ	Clan *n.* عَشِيرَة. قَبِيلَة
City *n.* مَدِينَةٌ. بَلْدَة	Clandestine *a.* خَفِيٌّ. مَسْتُورٌ
Civil *a.* مَدَنِيٌّ. سِيَاسِيٌّ. انِيسٌ	Clang *v. t.* or *n.* طَنَّ. رَنَّ
Civilian *n.* { مَدَنِيٌّ. عَالِمٌ بِالشَّرِيعَة الْمَدَنِية	Clangour *n.* طَنِينٌ
	Clank *n.* or *v. t.* قَعْقَعَة. قَعْقَعَ
Civilry *n.* انِسٌ. لَطُفَ	Clap *v. t.* or *n.* صَفَّقَ. تَصْفِيق
Civilization *n.* تَمَدُّنٌ. تَهْذِيب	Claper *n.* مِدَقُّ الْجَرَس او الْبَاب
Civilize *v. t.* مدَّنَ. هَذَّبَ	Claret *n.* نَوْعُ خَمْر فَرَنْسَاوِية

Clarify v. t.	صَفَّى . رَوَّقَ
Clarion n.	بُوقٌ ج أَبْوَاقٌ
Clash v. i. or t.	إِصْطَدَمَ . ضَادَّ
Clashing n. or a.	تَصَادُمٌ . تَعَارُضٌ
Clasp n. or v. t.	إِبْزِيمٌ . عَانَقَ . قَبَضَ
Class n.	صَفٌّ . فَصِيلَةٌ . رُتْبَةٌ
Classic a. or n.	مُؤَلَّفٌ شَهِيرٌ
Classification n.	صَفٌّ . تَرْتِيبٌ
Classify v. t.	صَفَّ . رَتَّبَ
Clatter n. or v. i.	طَقْطَقَ . طَقْطَقَةٌ
Clause n.	جُزْءُ جُمْلَةٍ . عِبَارَةٌ
Clavicle n.	تَرْقُوَةٌ ج تَرَاقٍ
Claw n. or v. t.	مِخْلَبٌ . خَلَبَ ـِ
Clay n.	طِينٌ . صَلْصَالٌ
Clayey a.	طِينِيٌّ . صَلْصَالِيٌّ
Clean a. or ad.	نَظِيفٌ . نَقِيٌّ . تَمَامًا
Clean v. t.	نَظَّفَ . نَقَّى
Cleanliness n.	نَظَافَةٌ . نَقَاوَةٌ

Cleanse v. t.	طَهَّرَ . نَقَّى
Clear a.	صَافٍ . رَائِقٌ
Clear v. t. or i.	صَفَّى . بَرَّأَ . إِنْجَلَى
Clearance n.	تَصْفِيَةٌ . إِجَازَةٌ
Clearly ad.	وَاضِحًا . جَلِيًّا
Clearness n.	وُضُوحٌ . بَيَانٌ . بَهَاءٌ
Cleavage n.	شَقٌّ . شَقٌّ إِلَى طَبَقَاتٍ
Cleave v. t. or i.	شَقَّ ـُ . إِلْتَصَقَ
Cleft n. or pp.	شَقٌّ . مَشْقُوقٌ
Clemency n.	رَأْفَةٌ . حِلْمٌ
Clement a.	رَؤُوفٌ . حَلِيمٌ
Clergy n.	إِكْلِيرُوسٌ
Clergyman n.	قَسٌّ أَوْ قِسِّيسٌ
Clerical a.	إِكْلِيرِيٌّ
Clerk n.	كَاتِبٌ ج كُتَّابٌ
Clerkship n.	مَقَامُ الْكَاتِبِ
Clever a.	ذَكِيٌّ . حَاذِقٌ . أَرِيبٌ
Cleverness n.	ذَكَاءٌ . حَذَاقَةٌ

Clew *n.*	دَلِيلٌ . إِشَارَةٌ
Click *v. i.* or *a.*	تَكْنَكَ . تَكْتَكَةٌ
Client *n.*	زَبُونُ ٱلْمُحَامِي . تَابِعٌ
Cliff *n.*	صَخْرَةٌ شَاهِقَةٌ
Climate Clime } *n.*	مَنَاخٌ . إِقْلِيمٌ
Climatic *a.*	إِقْلِيمِيٌّ
Climax *n.*	نِهَايَةٌ . تَدَرُّجٌ
Climb *v. t.* or *i.*	تَسَلَّقَ . صَعِدَ ـَ
Clinch *v. t.*	ضَبَطَ ـِ شَدَّ ـُ . أَثْبَتَ
Clincher *n.*	كُلَّابٌ . بُرْهَانٌ قَاطِعٌ
Cling *v. i.*	إِلْتَصَقَ بِ . تَعَلَّقَ عَلَى
Clinic Clinical } *n.*	(كَلِينِيك) . سَرِيرِيٌّ
Clink *v. i.* or *t.*	طَنَّ ـِ رَنَّ ـِ
Clip *v. t.*	قَرَمَ ـُ قَصَّرَ . قَلَّمَ
Clipper *n.*	سَفِينَةٌ سَرِيعَةُ السَّيْرِ
Clique *n.*	عُصْبَةٌ
Cloak *n.* or *v. t.*	رِدَاءٌ . سَتَرَ ـِ
Clock *n.*	سَاعَةٌ كَبِيرَةٌ
Clock-maker *n.*	سَاعَاتِيٌّ
Clockwork *n.*	آلَاتُ سَاعَةٍ
Clod *n.* or *v. i.*	مَدَرٌ . تَكَتَّلَ
Clog *v. t.* or *n.*	عَاقَ . ثَقَّلَ . عَائِقٌ
Cloister *n.*	دَيْرٌ
Close *v. t.* or *n.*	غَلَفَ ـِ . أَنْجَزَ . خِتَامٌ
Close *a.*	ضَيِّقٌ . مَحْصُورٌ . قَرِيبٌ
Closely *ad.*	مُلَاصِقًا . عَنْ قُرْبٍ
Closet *n.*	مُخْدَعٌ . حُجْرَةٌ صَغِيرَةٌ
Closing *n.* or *a.*	نِهَايَةٌ . خِتَامٌ . آخِرٌ
Closure *n.*	إِنْجَازٌ . خَتْمٌ . حَوْشٌ
Clot *n.* or *v. i.*	خِثْرَةٌ . خَنَرَ ـَ
Cloth *n.*	نَسِيجٌ . قُمَاشٌ . جُوخٌ
Clothe *v. t.*	كَسَا ـُ أَلْبَسَ
Clothes Clothing } *n.*	لِبَاسٌ . ثِيَابٌ . كِسْوَةٌ
Clothes-line *n.*	حَبْلُ الْغَسِيلِ
Clothier *n.*	صَانِعُ ثِيَابٍ وَبَائِعُهَا
Cloud *n.*	غَيْمٌ . سَحَابٌ

Cloud v. t. or i.	اظلمَ . سوَّدَ . تغيَّم	Coachman n.	سائقُ مرْكبة
Cloudiness n.	تغيّم	Coadjutor n.	معاونٌ . مساعدٌ
Cloudy a.	مغيّم . مظلم	Coagulate v. t. or i.	خثَّرَ . خثَرَ
Cloves n. pl.	كبشُ القرَنْفل	Coagulation n.	روبٌ . تجمُّدٌ . خثَرٌ
Cloven pp. of cleave.	مشقوق	Coal n.	فحمٌ . فحمٌ حجريٌّ
Cloven-footed a.	مشقوق الظلْف	Coal v.	إتحدَ . إتصلَ
Clover n.	نفْلة . برْسيم	Coaling n.	تقديمُ فحم
Clown n	فظٌّ . مهرّج	Coalition n.	إعتصابٌ . إتحاد
Clay v. t.	ملا ــ . أشبعَ	Coal-mine n.	معدنُ فحم حجري
Club n.	عصاً . نبّوتٌ . منتدًى	Coarse a.	خشِنٌ . ثخين . غليظ
Club-footed	أخنفُ	Coar en ss n.	خشونة . فظاظة
Clue see clew	دليلٌ . إشارة	Coast n.	شاطئُ البحْر
Clump n.	دغْلٌ (من شجر)	Coaster n.	مسافرٌ قرْب الشّاطئ
Clumsy a.	أخرقُ	Coat n.	ردآءٌ . جبّة
Clung pp. of cling.	تعلّق على وب	Coating n	تغطية . غطآءٌ
Cluster n. or v. i.	عنقودٌ . تجمّعَ	Coax v. t.	تملّقَ
Clutch v. t. or n.	قبضَ ــ . قبضٌ	Cobble v. t	رقعَ (أحذيةً)
Coach n.	عجلة . عربة . مركبة	Cobble-stone n.	حصاة مستديرة

Cobbler n.	مُرَقِّعُ احْذِيَةٍ
Cobweb n.	نَسِيجُ الْعَنْكَبُوت
Cock n.	دِيك . حَنَفِيَّة
Cockade n.	عُقْدَةُ شَرِيطٍ لِلرَّأْسِ
Cockatrice n.	افْعُوَان
Cockle n.	نَوْعٌ مِنَ الصَّدَف
Cockroach n.	صُرْصُورٌ
Cockscomb n.	عُرْفُ الدِّيكِ
Cockswain n.	رَئِيسُ قَارِبٍ
Cocoanut n.	جَوْزُ هِنْدٍ . نَارِجِيلٌ
Cocoon n.	شَرْنَقَة
Cod · Codfish } n.	نَوْعٌ مِنَ السَّمَك
Coddle v. t.	دَلَّلَ
Code n.	دُسْتُورُ شَرَائِعَ . مَجَلَّة
Codicil n.	ذَيْلُ وَصِيَّةٍ
Codify v. t.	جَمَعَ . لَخَّصَ الشَّرَائِعَ
Co-efficient n. or a.	مُعَيِّن . مُسَاعِد
Co-equal a.	كُفُوٌ . مَثِيلٌ . عَدِيلٌ

Coerce v. t.	غَصَبَ . أَجْبَرَ
Coercion n.	غَصْبٌ . إِجْبَارٌ
Coercive a.	غَاصِبٌ . مُجْبِرٌ
Coeval a. or n.	مُعَاصِرٌ . مُتَسَاوٍ
Co-existent a.	مَوْجُودٌ فِي زَمَانٍ وَاحِدٍ
Co-existence n.	التَّعَادُلُ فِي الْوُجُودِ
Co-extensive a.	مُعَادِلٌ فِي الْامْتِدَاد
Coffee n.	بُنّ . قَهْوَة
Coffer n.	صَنْدُوقٌ لِلْمَال
Coffin n.	تَابُوتٌ . نَعْشٌ
Cog n.	سِنُّ دُولَاب
Cogency n.	قُوَّة . شِدَّة
Cogent a.	قَوِيٌّ . مُقْنِع
Cogitate v. i.	تَأَمَّلَ . فَكَّرَ
Cogitation n.	تَأَمُّلٌ . تَفْكِيرٌ
Cognate n.	نَسِيبٌ . مُجَانِسٌ
Cognition n.	عِلْم . إِدْرَاك
Cognizable a.	قَابِلُ الْمَعْرِفَةِ

Cognomen n.	إِسْمُ ٱلْعَائِلَةِ	Coldness n.	بُرُودَةٌ . بَرْدٌ
Cogwheel n.	دُوْلَابٌ ذُو أسنَانٍ	Colic n.	مَغْصٌ . (قُولَنْجٌ)
Cohabit v. i.	سَاكَنَ	Collaborator n.	شَرِيكٌ فِي عَمَلٍ
Co-heir n.	قَسِيمُ ٱلْمِيرَاثِ	Collapse v. i. or n.	هَبَطَ ـُ . تَهَوُّرٌ
Cohere v. i.	إِلْتَصَقَ . إِتَّحَدَ	Collar n. or v. t.	طَوْقٌ . قَبَّةٌ . طَوَّقَ
Coherence Cohesion n.	إِلْتِصَاقٌ . إِلْتِحَامٌ	Collate v. i.	قَابَلَ . جَمَعَ . رَتَّبَ
Coherent a.	مُلْتَصِقٌ . مُنْتَظِمٌ	Collateral a.	مُجَانِبٌ مُرَافِقٌ
Cohesive a.	لَزِجٌ مُلْتَصِقٌ	Collation n.	مُقَابَلَةٌ . لُمْجَةٌ
Cohort n.	كَتِيبَةٌ	Colleague n.	شَرِيكٌ . رَصِيفٌ
Coil v. t. or n.	لَفَّ . طَوَى ـ لَفَّةٌ	Collect v. t. or i.	جَمَعَ . إِجْتَمَعَ
Coin n. or v. t.	قِطْعَةُ نُقُودٍ . سَكَّ ـُ	Collected pp. or a.	مَجْمُوعٌ . رَزِينٌ
Coinage n.	سَكُّ ٱلنُّقُودِ . ٱلْمَسْكُوكَاتُ	Collection n.	جَمْعٌ . مَجْمُوعٌ
Coincide v. i.	إِتَّفَقَ	Collectively ad.	جُمْلَةً . بِالْإِجْمَالِ
Coincidence n.	إِتِّفَاقٌ . مُطَابَقَةٌ	Collector n.	جَامِعٌ . جَابٍ
Coincident n.	مُتَّفِقٌ . مُطَابِقٌ	College n.	مَدْرَسَةٌ عَالِيَةٌ أَوْ كُلِّيَّةٌ
Coke n.	نَوْعُ فَحْمٍ حَجَرِيٍّ	Collegiate a.	مُخْتَصٌّ بِمَدْرَسَةٍ كُلِّيَّةٍ
Cold a. or n.	بَارِدٌ . بَرْدٌ . زُكَامٌ	Collide v. i.	تَصَادَمَ
Coldly ad.	بَارِداً. بِعَدَمِ اكْتِرَاثٍ	Collier n.	فَحَّامٌ . سَفِينَةٌ لِحَمْلِ ٱلْفَحْمِ

Colliery *n.*	مَعْدِنُ الْفَحْمِ
Collision *n.*	تَصَادُمٌ
Collocate *v. t.*	رَتَّبَ . نَظَّمَ
Colloquial *n.*	عَامِيٌّ . تَحَاوُرِيٌّ
Colloquy *n.*	مُحَاوَرَةٌ
Collude *v. i.*	تَآمَرَ
Collusion *n.*	مُؤَامَرَةٌ لِلْخِدَاعِ
Collusive *a.*	خِدَاعِيٌّ
Colon *n.*	عَلَامَةُ وَقْفٍ (:)
Colonel *n.*	أَمِيرُ آلَاي
Colonial *a.*	مُخْتَصٌّ بِمُسْتَعْمَرَةٍ
Colonist *n.*	مُسْتَعْمِرٌ . مُهَاجِرٌ
Colonization *n.*	إِنْشَاءُ مُسْتَعْمَرَاتٍ
Colonize *v. t.*	أَنْشَا مُسْتَعْمَرَةً
Colonade *n.*	صَفُّ أَعْمِدَةٍ
Colony *n.*	مُسْتَعْمَرَةٌ . مُهَاجِرُونَ
Colossal *a.*	جَسِيمُ الْقَدِّ
Colossus *n.*	تِمْثَالٌ عَظِيمُ الْقَدِّ

Colour *n.* or *v. t.* or *i.*	لَوْنٌ . لَوَّنَ . إِحْمَرَّ
Colouring *n.*	تَلْوِينٌ . تَلَوُّنٌ . صِبْغٌ
Colours *n. pl.*	رَايَةٌ . عَلَمٌ
Colporteur *n.*	بَيَّاعٌ يَدُورُ بِكُتُبٍ
Colt *n.*	فِلْوٌ . مُهْرٌ
Column *n.*	عَمُودٌ ج أَعْمِدَةٌ
Columnar *a.*	عَمُودِيٌّ
Comb *n.*	مُشْطٌ ج أَمْشَاطٌ
Combat *n.* or *v. t*	قِتَالٌ . قَاتَلَ
Combatant *n.*	مُقَاتِلٌ
Combative *a.*	مَائِلٌ إِلَى الْقِتَالِ . خَصُومٌ
Combination *n.*	إِتِّحَادٌ . إِتِّفَاقٌ
Combine *v. i.* or *t.*	إِجْتَمَعَ . جَمَعَ
Combustible *a.*	قَابِلُ الْإِشْتِعَالِ
Combustion *n.*	إِشْتِعَالٌ . إِحْتِرَاقٌ
Come *v. i.* (came, come)	جَاءَ اتَى
Comedian *n.*	كَاتِبُ رِوَايَاتٍ هَزْلِيَّةٍ . مُشَخِّصُهَا
Comedy *n.*	رِوَايَةٌ هَزْلِيَّةٌ

Comely a.	حَسَنُ ٱلصُّورَة
Comet n.	نَجْمٌ ذُو ذَنَبٍ
Comfort n. or v. t.	تَعْزِيَة . عَزَّى
Comfortable a.	مُرِيحٌ . مُسْتَرِيحٌ
Comforter n.	مُعَزٍّ . ٱلرُّوحُ ٱلْقُدُسُ
Comic / Comical } a.	مُضْحِكٌ . هَزْلِيٌّ
Coming a. or n.	آتٍ إِتْيَانٌ . مَجِيءٌ
Comma n. (,)	عَلَامَةُ وَقْفٍ قَصِيرٍ
Command v. t. or n.	اَمَرَ . أَمْرٌ
Commandant / Commander } n.	أَمِيرٌ . قَائِدٌ
Commanding ppr.	آمِرٌ . مُشْرِفٌ عَلَى
Commandment n.	أَمْرٌ . وَصِيَّةٌ
Commemorable a.	مُسْتَحِقُّ ٱلذِّكْرِ
Commemorate v. t.	إِحْتَفَلَ . عَيَّدَ
Commemorative a.	تَذْكَارِيٌّ
Commence v. t. or i.	بَدَا . إِبْتَدَأَ
Commencement n.	بَدْءٌ
Commend v. t.	مَدَحَ ـ إِسْتَوْدَعَ
Commendable a.	مُسْتَحِقُّ ٱلْمَدْحِ
Commendation n.	مَدْحٌ . تَوْصِيَةٌ
Commensurable / Commensurate } a.	مُتَسَاوٍ
Comment v. i. or n.	شَرَحَ . تَفْسِيرٌ
Commentary n.	تَفْسِيرٌ . شَرْحٌ
Commentator n.	مُفَسِّرٌ . شَارِحٌ
Commerce n.	تِجَارَةٌ . مَتْجَرٌ
Commercial a.	تِجَارِيٌّ . مَتْجَرِيٌّ
Commingle v. t. or i.	مَزَجَ . إِمْتَزَجَ
Commiserate v. t.	أَشْفَقَ عَلَى
Commiseration n.	شَفَقَةٌ
Commissary n }	مُفَوَّضٌ . مَأْمُورٌ . ٱلْمَأْكُولَاتِ فِي جَيْشٍ
Commission n.	وَكَالَةٌ . لَجْنَةٌ
Commission v. t.	فَوَّضَ إِلَى
Commissioner n.	وَكِيلٌ مُفَوَّضٌ
Commit v. t.	سَلَّمَ . إِرْتَكَبَ
Commitment n.	إِبْدَاعٌ . سِجْنٌ

Committal n.	تَسْلِيمٌ . إِرْتِكابٌ
Committee n.	لَجْنَةٌ . وُكَلاءُ
Commodious a.	مُرِيحٌ . رَحْبٌ
Commodity n.	سِلْعَةٌ . بِضاعَةٌ
Commodor n.	رَئِيسُ أَسْطُولٍ
Common a.	عامٌّ . إِعْتِيادِيٌّ
Commoner n.	احَدُ الْعامَّةِ
Commonly a.	غالِبًا . إِعْتِيادِيًّا
Common-wealth n.	حُكُومَةٌ جُمْهُورِيَّةٌ
Commotion n.	ضَجَّةٌ . إِضْطِرابٌ
Commune v. i.	إِشْتَرَكَ . كالَمَ
Communicant n.	مُشْتَرِكٌ
Communicate v. t.	ابْلَغَ . أَخْبَرَ
Communication n.	تَبْلِيغٌ . مُراسَلَةٌ
Communicative a.	مُبْلِغٌ
Communion n.	مُخالَطَةٌ . إِشْتِراكٌ
Community n.	جَماعَةٌ . إِشْتِراكٌ
Commutable a.	قابِلُ الاسْتِبْدالِ
Commutation n.	تَبادُلٌ . إِسْتِبْدالٌ
Commute v. t.	إِسْتَبْدَلَ . غَيَّرَ
Compact a. or n.	مُتَلَبِّدٌ . مُعاهَدَةٌ
Compactness n.	تَلَبُّدٌ . مَتانَةٌ
Companion n.	رَفِيقٌ . عَشِيرٌ
Companionable a.	أَنِيسٌ
Companionship n.	مُعاشَرَةٌ . صُحْبَةٌ
Company n.	جَماعَةٌ . شِرْكَةٌ
Comparable a.	قابِلُ الْمُقابَلَةِ
Comparative a. or n.	نَسْبِيٌّ . أَفْعَلُ التَّفْضِيلِ
Compare v. t. or i.	قابَلَ . شابَهَ
Comparison n.	مُقابَلَةٌ . مُشابَهَةٌ
Compartment n.	قِسْمٌ . بَيْتٌ
Compass v.t.	أَحاطَ بِ . أَنْجَزَ . نالَ
Campass n.	مُحِيطٌ . حُكُّ
Compasses n. pl.	بِرْكارٌ أَوْ بِيكارٌ
Compassion	شَفَقَةٌ . رَأْفَةٌ

Compassionate a.	شَفُوقٌ . رَؤُوفٌ
Compatibility n.	مُوَافَقَةٌ . مُلَاءَمَةٌ
Compatible a.	مُوَافِقٌ . مُلَائِمٌ
Compeer n.	قَرِينٌ . شَرِيكٌ
Compel v.	أَجْبَرَ الزَمَ . غَصَبَ
Compend } Compendium } n.	مُخْتَصَرٌ
Compensate v. t.	عَوَّضَ . كَافَأَ
Compensation n.	مُكَافَأَةٌ . تَعْوِيضٌ
Compete v. i.	سَابَقَ . بَارَى . نَاظَرَ
Competence } Competency } n.	كِفَايَةٌ . جَدَارَةٌ
Competent a.	جَدِيرٌ . قَادِرٌ عَلَى
Competition n.	مُسَابَقَةٌ . مُبَارَاةٌ
Competitor n.	مُسَابِقٌ . مُبَارٍ
Competitive a.	سِبَاقِيٌّ
Compilation n.	مَجْمُوعَةٌ . تَأْلِيفٌ
Compile v. t.	جَمَّعَ . أَلَّفَ
Complacence n.	سُرُورٌ بِ . رِضًى بِ
Complacent a.	رَاضٍ بِ . مَسْرُورٌ بِ

Complain v. i.	شَكَا . تَظَلَّمَ مِنْ
Complainant } Complainer } n.	مُشْتَكٍ
Complaint n.	شِكَايَةٌ . عِلَّةٌ
Complaisance n.	مُلَاطَفَةٌ . مُرَاعَاةٌ
Complaisant a. }	مُلَاطِفٌ . مُرَاعِي الخَاطِرِ
Complement n.	تَتِمَّةٌ . تَكْمِلَةٌ
Complemental a.	مُتَمِّمٌ . تَكْمِيلِيٌّ
Complete v. t. or a.	تَمَّمَ . ا كْمَلَ . كَامِلٌ
Completely ad.	تَمَامًا
Completement } Completion } n.	إِتْمَامٌ . تَكْمِيلٌ
Complex a.	مُرَكَّبٌ . مُشْتَبِكٌ
Complexion n.	لَوْنُ الوَجْهِ
Complexity n.	إِشْتِبَاكٌ . تَعَقُّدٌ
Compliance n.	إِذْعَانٌ . إِجَابَةٌ
Compliant a.	مُذْعِنٌ . مُنْقَادٌ
Complicate v. t. or a.	عَوْقَلَ . مُعَقَّدٌ
Complicated a.	مُعَرْقَلٌ . مُعَقَّدٌ

Complication n.	عَرْقَلَةٌ . تَشْوِيشٌ
Complicity n.	إِشْتِرَاكٌ فِي ذَنْبٍ
Compliment n.	قَوْلُ مَدْحٍ . تَحِيَّةٌ
Complimentary a.	مَادِحٌ
Comply v. i.	أَذْعَنَ . اجَابَ . إِنْقَادَ
Component a. or n.	تَرْكِيبِيٌّ . جُزْءٌ
Comport v. i.	وَافَقَ . لَاءَمَ
Compose v. t.	رَكَّبَ . اَلَّفَ . هَدَّأَ
Composed a.	مُرَكَّبٌ . مُؤَلَّفٌ رَزِينٌ
Composer n.	مُؤَلِّفٌ . جَامِعٌ
Composite a.	مُرَكَّبٌ مِنْ أَجْزَاءَ
Composition n.	تَرْكِيبٌ . تَأْلِيفٌ
Compositor n.	صَفَّافُ اُحْرُفٍ لِلطَّبْعِ
Compost n.	سَمَادٌ
Composure n.	رَزَانَةٌ . هُدُوءٌ
Compound a. or n.	مُرَكَّبٌ . مَزِيجٌ
Compound v. t.	رَكَّبَ . مَزَجَ
Component a. or n.	مُرَكَّبٌ . جُزْءٌ جَوْهَرِيٌّ

Comprehend v. t.	اَدْرَكَ . فَهِمَ
Comprehensible a.	مُمْكِنٌ إِدْرَاكُهُ
Comprehension n.	إِدْرَاكٌ . شُمُولٌ
Comprehensive a.	شَامِلٌ . جَامِعٌ
Compress v. t.	كَبَسَ . ضَغَطَ
Compression n.	كَبْسٌ
Comprise v. t.	تَضَمَّنَ . إِشْتَمَلَ عَلَى
Compromise v. t. or n.	اِتَّفَقَ . إِتِّفَاقٌ
Compulsion n.	غَصْبٌ . إِكْرَاهٌ
Compulsive } a. Compulsory }	غَاصِبٌ . مُجْبِرٌ
Compunction n.	تَوْبِيخُ الضَّمِيرِ
Computable a.	قَابِلُ الإِحْصَاءِ
Compute v. t.	اَحْصَى . حَسَبَ
Comrade n.	رَفِيقٌ . صَاحِبٌ
Con v. t.	تَأَمَّلَ . دَرَسَ
Concatenation n.	تَسَلْسُلٌ . سِلْسِلَةٌ
Concave a.	مُقَعَّرٌ . مُجَوَّفٌ
Concavity n.	تَجْوِيفٌ . قَعْرَةٌ

Conceal *v. t.*	اخفى . سَتَرَ ـِ . كَتَمَ ـُ
Concealment *n.*	إخفاء . كِتْمَان
Concede *v. t.*	مَنَحَ — سَلَّمَ بهِ
Conceit *n.*	تَخَيُّل . رَأْي . عُجْب
Conceited *a.*	مُعْجَب بنفسِهِ
Conceivable *a.*	مُمْكِن تَصَوُّرُهُ
Conceive *v. t.*	تَصَوَّرَ في الذِّهْنِ
Concentrate *v. t.*	جَمَعَ في مَرْكَزٍ
Concentration *n.*	جَمْع . تَجَمُّع
Concentric *a.*	ذو مَرْكَزٍ وَاحِدٍ
Conception *n.*	تَصَوُّر . فِكْر . حَبَل
Concern *v. t. or n.*	هَمَّ ـُ . هَمّ . قَضِيَّة
Concerning *pr.*	بخُصُوص . مِنْ جِهَةِ
Concert *v. t. or i.*	دَبَّرَ . إتَّفَقَ
Concert *n.*	إتِّفَاق . مَحْفَل مُوسِيقِيّ
Concession *n.*	تَسْلِيم بِ . هِبَة . رُخْصَة
Conciliate *v. t.*	سَالَمَ . وَفَّقَ بَيْنَ
Conciliation *n.*	مُسَالَمَة
Conciliatory *a.*	مُسْتَعْطِف . مُسَالِم
Concise *a.*	مُخْتَصَر . وَجِيز
Conciseness *n.*	إخْتِصَار . إيجَاز
Conclave *n.*	مَجْمَع سِرِّي
Conclude *v. t. or i.*	أنهى . إسْتَنْتَجَ
Concluding *a.*	خَاتِم . أخِير
Conclusion *n.*	خَاتِمَة . نَتِيجَة
Conclusive *a.*	قَاطِع . جَازِم
Concoct *v.*	دَبَّرَ . رَكَّبَ طَبِيخًا
Concoction *n.*	هَضْم . تَدْبِير
Concomitant *a.*	مُرَافِق . مُلَازِم
Concord *n.*	إتِّفَاق . وِفَاق
Concordance *n.*	فِهْرِس
Concordat *n.*	صَكّ . إتِّفَاق
Concourse *n.*	إجْتِمَاع
Concrete *a. or n.*	مُتَجَمِّد . مُرَكَّب
Concretion *n.*	كُتْلَة مُتَجَمِّدَة
Concubine *n.*	سُرِّيَّة ج سَرَارِيّ

Concupiscence n.	شَهْوَة . هَوًى
Concur v. i.	إِتَّفَقَ
Concurrence n.	إِتِّفَاق
Concurrent a.	مُرَافِق . مُجَارٍ
Concussion n.	هَزّ . صَدْمَة
Condemn v. t.	حَكَمَ عَلَى . دَانَ ـ
Condemnation n.	حُكْم . دَيْنُونَة
Condemnatory a.	دَائِن . حَاكِم بِدَيْنُونَة
Condensation n.	تَكْثِيف
Condense v. t.	كَثَّفَ . اوْجَزَ . قَطَّرَ
Condescend v. i.	تَنَازَلَ . تَسَاهَلَ
Condescension n.	تَنَازُل
Condign a.	مُسْتَحِقّ . مُوَافِق
Condiment n.	تَابِل ج تَوَابِل
Condition n. or v. t.	حَالَة . شَرْط . إِشْتَرَطَ
Conditional a.	شَرْطِيّ
Conditioned a.	مَشْرُوط او مُشْتَرَط
Condole v. i. or t.	حَزِنَ مَعَ غَيْرِه
Condolence n.	الأَسَف مَعَ الْغَيْر
Condone v. t.	غَفَرَ ـ . سَامَحَ
Condor n.	حَدَأَة أَمِيرِكِيَّة كَبِيرَة
Conduce v. i.	أَفْضَى أَوْ آلَ إِلَى
Couducible Conducive a.	مُفْضٍ أَوْ آيِل إِلَى
Conduct v. t.	قَادَ . أَدَارَ
Conduct n.	تَصَرُّف . قِيَادَة
Conductor n.	قَائِد . مُوصِل كَهْرَبَائِيّ
Conduit n.	قَنَاة ج قُنِيّ وَقَنَوَات
Cone n.	مَخْرُوط
Confection Confectionery n.	حَلْوَى أَوْ حَلْوَاء
Confectioner n.	حَلْوَانِيّ
Confederacy n.	عُصْبَة . مُعَاهَدَة
Confederate v. i. or a.	إِعْتَصَبَ . مُتَعَاهِد
Confederation n.	تَعَاهُد . تَحَالُف
Confer v.i. or t.	تَشَاوَرَ . مَنَحَ ـ
Conference n.	مُشَاوَرَة . مُؤْتَمَر

Confess v. t.	أَقَرَّ . إِعْتَرَفَ	Conflagration n.	إِحْتِرَاقٌ . حَرِيقٌ
Confessedly ad.	بِإِقْرَارِ ٱلْعُمُومِ	Conflict n.or v.t.	قَتَالٌ. خِصَامٌ. نَازَعَ
Confession n.	إِعْتِرَافٌ . إِقْرَارٌ	Conflicting a.	مُتَنَاقِضٌ . مُتَخَالِفٌ
Confessional n.	كُرْسِيُّ ٱلِاعْتِرَافِ	Confluent a.	جَارٍ مَعَ غَيْرِه
Confessor n.	مُعَرِّفٌ . مُعْتَرِفٌ	Conform v. t. or i.	شَاكَلَ . إِمْتَثَلَ
Confidant n.	صَفِيٌّ . خِلٌّ اَمِينٌ	Conformable a.	مُطَابِقٌ . مُوَافِقٌ
Confide v. i. or t.	اَمَنَ - أَرْكَنَ إِلَى	Conformation n.	تَرْكِيبٌ . جَبْلَةٌ
Confidence n.	ثِقَةٌ . إِرْكَانٌ	Conformity n.	مُوَافَقَةٌ . مُطَابَقَةٌ
Confident a.	مُتَأَكِّدٌ . وَاثِقٌ	Confound v. t.	خَلَطَ . حَيَّرَ
Confidential a.	سِرِّيٌّ . اَمِينٌ	Confounded a.	مُخْتَلِطٌ . مُتَحَيِّرٌ
Configuration n.	صُورَةٌ . هَيْئَةٌ	Confront v. t.	وَاجَهَ . قَابَلَ
Confine v. t.	حَجَزَ - حَصَرَ -	Confuse v. t.	خَلَطَ - بَلْبَلَ . أَخْجَلَ
Confinement n.	حَصْرٌ . حَبْسٌ	Confusion n.	بَلْبَالٌ . تَشْوِيشٌ
Confirm v. t.	اَثْبَتَ . شَدَّدَ	Confutation n.	دَحْضٌ . إِبْطَالٌ
Confirmation n.	إِثْبَاتٌ . تَأْيِيد	Confute v. t.	اِدْحَضْ . أَبْطَلَ
Confirmative } a. Confirmatory }	مُثْبِتٌ . مُؤَيِّد	Congeal v. t. or t.	جَمَّدَ . جَمُدَ -
Confiscate v. t. }	ضَبَطَ مُلْكاً (ٱلْحَكُومَةَ)	Congelation n.	جَمْدٌ أَوْجُمُودٌ
Confiscation n.	ضَبْطُ ٱلْمِلْكِ	Congenial n.	مِنْ خُلْقٍ وَاحِدٍ .مُوَافِقٌ

Congeniality n.	مُوَافَقَةُ ٱلْخُلُقِ
Congenital a.	خِلْقِيٌّ . مِنَ ٱلْخِلْقَةِ
Congested a.	مُحْتَقِنٌ
Congestion n.	إِحْتِقَانٌ
Conglomerate v. t. or a.	كَتَلَ . مُكَتَّلٌ
Conglomeration n.	تَكَتُّلٌ
Congratulate v. t.	هَنَّأَ
Congratulation n.	تَهْنِئَةٌ
Congratulatory a.	مُهَنِّي
Congregate v. t. or i.	حَشَدَ ـُ . إِحْتَشَدَ
Congregation n.	جَمَاعَةٌ . مَحْفَلٌ
Congregational a.	جُمْهُورِيٌّ (فِي ٱلدِّينِ)
Congress n.	مُؤْتَمَرٌ . مَجْمَعٌ
Congruity n.	مُنَاسَبَةٌ . مُطَابَقَةٌ
Congruous a.	مُنَاسِبٌ . مُوَافِقٌ
Conical a.	مَخْرُوطِيُّ ٱلشَّكْلِ
Conicsections n.	عِلْمُ قَطْعِ ٱلْمَخْرُوطِ
Coniferous a.	ذُو ثَمَرٍ كَٱلصَّنَوْبَرِ

Conjectural a.	حَدْسِيٌّ . تَخْمِينِيٌّ
Conjecture n.	حَدْسٌ . تَخْمِينٌ
Conjoin v. t.	وَصَلَ ـِ . قَرَنَ ـِ
Conjointly ad.	مَعًا
Conjugal a.	زَوَاجِيٌّ . بَعْلِيٌّ
Conjugate v. t.	صَرَّفَ (ٱلْفِعْلَ)
Conjugation n.	تَصْرِيفُ ٱلْفِعْلِ
Conjunction n.	وَصْلٌ . حَرْفُ عَطْفٍ
Conjunctive a.	عَاطِفٌ . مُوصِلٌ
Conjuncture n.	إِتِّحَادٌ . وَقْتٌ مُهِمٌّ
Conjure v. t. or i.	رَقَّى ـِ . إِسْتَحْلَفَ
Conjurer n.	رَاقٍ . مَشْعُوذٌ
Connect v. t.	وَصَلَ ـِ . قَرَنَ ـِ
Connection Connexion n.	وَصْلٌ . إِتِّصَالٌ
Connective n. or a.	مُوصِلٌ . رَابِطٌ
Connivance n.	إِغْضَاءٌ عَنْ زَلَّةٍ
Connive v. t.	تَغَاضَى عَنْ
Connubial a.	زِيجِيٌّ أَوْ زَوْجِيٌّ

Conoid ⎰	شَبِيهَةٌ بِالْمَخْرُوطِ
Conoidal ⎱ a.	
Conquer v. t.	غَلَبَ ـِ . ظَفَرَ بِـ
Conqueror n.	غَالِبٌ . ظَافِرٌ . فَاتِحٌ
Conquest n.	غَلَبَةٌ . ظَفَرٌ . فَتْحٌ . فُتُوحٌ
Consanguinity n.	قَرَابَةٌ . نَسَبٌ
Conscience n.	الضَّمِيرُ . ذِمَّةٌ
Conscientious a.	صَاحِبُ ذِمَّةٍ . أَمِينٌ
Conscientiousness n.	ذِمَّةٌ . امَانَةٌ
Conscious a.	عَارِفٌ . يَقْظَانُ
Consciously ad.	عَنْ عِلْمٍ . عَمْدًا
Consciousness n.	إِدْرَاكٌ . يَقْظَةٌ
Conscript a.	جُنْدِيٌّ مَأْخُوذٌ بِالْقُرْعَةِ
Conscription n. ⎰	قُرْعَةُ الْعَسْكَرِ
⎱	إِكْتِتَابٌ
Consecrate v. t.	قَدَّسَ . كَرَّسَ
Consecration n.	تَقْدِيسٌ . تَكْرِيسٌ
Consecutive a.	مُتَتَابِعٌ . مُتَوَالٍ
Consent n. or v. i.	رِضًى . رَضِيَ بِـ
Consentient a.	مُتَّفِقُ الرَّأْيِ
Consequence n.	نَتِيجَةٌ . اهَمِّيَّةٌ
Consequent a. or n.	تَابِعٌ . تَالٍ
Consequential a.	نَاتِجٌ . مُهِمٌّ . مُعْجَبٌ
Consequently ad.	مِنْ ثَمَّ . إِذًا
Conservation n.	حِفْظٌ . وِقَايَةٌ
Conservatism n. ⎰	الْمُحَافَظَةُ عَلَى
⎱	النِّظَامِ الْحَالِيِّ
Conservative a. or n.	مُحَافِظٌ
Conservatory ⎰	حَافِظٌ . كِنٌّ لِلنَّبَاتِ
a. or n. ⎱	
Conserve v. t.	حَفِظَ ـَ . صَانَ ـُ
Consider v. t. or i.	إِعْتَبَرَ . تَبَصَّرَ
Consider- ⎰	مُسْتَحِقُّ الِاعْتِبَارِ . وَافِرٌ
able a. ⎱	
Considerate a.	مُتَبَصِّرٌ . حَازِمٌ
Consideration n.	تَفَكُّرٌ . إِعْتِبَارٌ
Considering ppr.	نَظَرًا إِلَى . مُتَأَمِّلٌ
Consign v. t.	سَلَّمَ إِلَى . اوْدَعَ
Consignee n.	الْمُتَسَلِّمُ . الْمُرْسَلُ إِلَيْهِ

Consignment n.	تَسْلِيمٌ . إِرْسَالِيَّةٌ
Consist v. i.	تَكَوَّنَ (مِنْ)
Consistence Consistency } n.	قِوَامٌ . مُوَافَقَةٌ
Consistent a.	جَامِدٌ . مُوَافِقٌ
Consistently ad.	مُطَابَقَةً ل
Consolable a.	قَابِلُ التَّعْزِيَةِ
Consolation n.	تَعْزِيَةٌ . سَلْوَى
Consolatory a.	مُعَزٍّ . مُسَلٍّ
Console v. t.	عَزَّى . سَلَّى
Consolidate v. t. or i. }	ثَبَّتَ . مَكَّنَ . تَجَمَّدَ
Consolidation n.	تَثْبِيتٌ . تَجَمُّدٌ
Consonant a. or n.	مُوَافِقٌ . الأَحْرُفُ الصَّحِيحُ
Consort n.	زَوْجٌ او زَوْجَةٌ . قَرِينٌ
Consort v. i.	تَشَارَكَ . تَرَافَقَ
Conspicuous a.	بَيِّنٌ . جَلِيٌّ . ظَاهِرٌ
Conspiracy n.	فِتْنَةٌ . مُؤَامَرَةٌ
Conspirator n.	مُتَآمِرٌ
Conspire v. i.	قَنَ تَ . تَآمَرَ
Constable n.	مَأْمُورٌ لِحِفْظِ السَّلَامِ
Constant a.	ثَابِتٌ . دَائِمٌ . امِينٌ
Constancy n.	ثَبَاتٌ . عَزْمٌ . امَانَةٌ
Constantly ad.	عَلَى الدَّوَامِ
Constellation n.	جَمَاعَةُ نُجُومٍ . بُرْجٌ
Consternation n.	دَهْشَةٌ . رُعْبٌ
Constipate v. t.	قَبَضَ الأَمْعَاءَ
Constipation n.	قَبْضُ الأَمْعَاءِ
Constituency n.	جَمَاعَةُ المُنْتَخِبِينَ
Constituent a. or n. }	مُكَوِّنٌ . مُوَكِّلٌ . جَوْهَرِيٌّ
Constitute v. t.	قَامَ . نَصَبَ . رَكَّبَ
Constitution n.	بُنْيَةٌ . نِظَامٌ
Constitutional a.	نِظَامِيٌّ . مِزَاجِيٌّ
Constitutive a.	مُقِيمٌ . مُكَوِّنٌ
Constrain v. t.	اجْبَرَ . الزَمَ
Constraint n.	إِلْزَامٌ . حَصْرٌ
Constrict v. t.	شَدَّ . ضَغَطَ

Constriction n. شدٌّ.ضغطٌ. إِقباضٌ	Consumption n. إِتلافٌ. دَآءُ ٱلسُّلِّ
Constringent a. قابِضٌ. مُقَلِّصٌ	Consumptive a. مُصَابٌ بِالسُّلِّ
Construct v. t. بَنَى ـ اِنشَأَ . دَبَّرَ	Contact n. مُمَاسَّةٌ . مُلَامَسَة
Construction n. بِنَاءٌ . تَرْكِيبٌ	Contagion n. عَدْوَى مِنَ ٱلْمُمَاسَةِ
Constructor n. بَانٍ . بَنَّاءٌ	Contagious a. مُعْدٍ بِمُمَاسَةٍ
Constructive a. بَانٍ . إِسْتِدْلَالِيٌّ	Contain v. t. وَسِعَ ـ . إِحْتَوَى
Construe v. i. فَسَّرَ مَعْنَى . أَعْرَبَ	Contaminate v. t. أَفْسَدَ . دَنَّسَ
Consul n. قُنْصُلٌ ج قَنَاصِلُ	Contamination n. إِفْسَادٌ . تَنْجِيسٌ
Consular a. قُنْصُلِيٌّ	Contemn v. t. أَهَانَ . كَرِهَ ـَ
Consulship n. مَقَامُ ٱلْقُنْصُل	Contemplate v. t. or i. } تَأَمَّلَ . قَصَدَ ـ
Consulate n. مَكْتَبُ ٱلْقُنْصُل	Contemplation n. تَأَمُّلٌ
Consult v. t. or i. شَاوَرَ . تَشَاوَرَ	Contemplative a. مُتَفَكِّرٌ
Consultation n. مُشَاوَرَةٌ . مُفَاوَضَةٌ	Contemporaneous a. مُعَاصِرٌ
Consume v. t. or i. } أَتْلَفَ . ابَادَ . فَنِيَ ـَ	Contempt n. إِهَانَةٌ . إِحْتِقَارٌ
Consumer n. آكِلٌ .مُسْتَعْمِلٌ.نَافِذٌ	Contemptible a. مُحْتَقَرٌ . دَنِيءٌ
Consummate a. تَامٌّ . مُكَمَّلٌ	Contemptuous a. مُحْتَقِرٌ . مُهِينٌ
Consummate v. t. كَمَّلَ . تَمَّمَ	Contend v. t. نَازَعَ . حَاجَّ . قَاوَمَ
Consummation n. إِتْمَامٌ . إِنْجَازٌ	Content v. t. أَرْضَى . أَقْنَعَ

Content n.	المَضْمُونُ . فَحْوَى
Content Contented } n.	رَاضٍ . مُكتَفٍ . قَانِعٌ
Contention n.	مُنَازَعَةٌ . مُشَاجَرَةٌ
Contentious a.	مُشَاجِرٌ . خُصُومٌ
Contentment n.	قَنَاعَةٌ . رِضًى
Contest n.	مُجَاهَدَةٌ . مُقَاوَمَةٌ
Contest v. t.	نَازَعَ . قَاوَمَ . نَاظَرَ
Contstant n.	مُقَاوِمٌ . مُنَاظِرٌ
Conterminous a.	مُتَاخِمٌ . مُجَاوِرٌ
Context n.	قَرِينَةٌ . سِيَاقُ الْكَلَامِ
Contiguity n.	مُمَاسَّةٌ . قُرْبٌ
Contiguous a.	مُمَاسٌّ . مُتَّصِلٌ بِ
Continence Continency } n.	عِفَّةٌ . إِمْسَاكٌ
Continent a. or n.	عَفِيفٌ . قَارَّةٌ
Continental a.	مُخْتَصٌّ بِقَارَّةٍ
Contingence Contingency } n.	حَادِثَةٌ عَرَضِيَّةٌ
Contingent a. or n.	عَرَضِيٌّ . مَشْرُوطٌ . عَارِضٌ
Contingently ad.	عَرَضًا . إِتِّفَاقًا
Continual a.	دَائِمٌ . مُسْتَمِرٌّ
Continuance n.	دَوَامٌ . بَقَاءٌ
Continuation n.	تَتَابُعٌ . تَوَالٍ
Continue v. i. or t.	دَامَ . دَاوَمَ
Continuity a.	مُوَاصَلَةٌ . إِتِّصَالٌ
Continuous a.	مُتَّصِلٌ . دَائِمٌ
Contortion n.	إِعْوِجَاجٌ . تَفَتُّلٌ
Contort v. t.	فَتَلَ . لَوَى
Contour a.	صُورَةُ حُدُودِ الشَّيْءِ
Contraband a.	مَمْنُوعٌ شَرْعًا
Contract n.	عَقْدٌ . شَرْطٌ . إِتِّفَاقٌ
Contract v. t. or i. }	قَلَّصَ . شَارَطَ . تَقَبَّضَ
Contracted a.	مُتَقَلِّصٌ مُنْقَبِضٌ مُضَيَّقٌ
Contractible a.	قَابِلُ التَّقَلُّصِ
Contraction n.	تَقَلُّصٌ . إِنْقِبَاضٌ
Contractor n.	مُشَارِطٌ . مُعَاقِدٌ . مُقَاوِلٌ
Contradict v. t.	نَاقَضَ . ضَادَّ . نَافَى
Contradiction n.	مُنَاقَضَةٌ . تَنَاقُضٌ

Contradictory a.	مُتَناقِضٌ
Contrariety n.	مُعَاكَسَة . مُغَايَرَةٌ
Contraries n. pl.	اضْدَادٌ
Contrary n.	مُضَادٌّ . ضِدٌّ . مُخَالِفٌ
Contrast n. or v. t. or i.	تَبَايُنٌ. قَابَلَ. مَيَّزَ بَيْن
Contravene v. t.	خَالَفَ . عَارَضَ
Contravention n.	مُخَالَفَةٌ . مُعَارَضَة
Contribute v. t.	وَهَب ـ . أَعْطَى
Contribution n.	هِبَة . إِعْطَاءٌ
Contributive a.	آئِلٌ إِلَى . مُفِيْدٌ
Contributor n.	مُعْطٍ
Contrite a.	مُنْكَسِرُ الْقَلْبِ. مُتَخَشِّعٌ
Contrition n.	إِنْكِسَارُ الْقَلْبِ . تَخَشُّعٌ
Contrivance n.	حِيْلَة . تَدْبِيْرٌ
Contrive v. t.	دَبَّرَ . إِبْتَدَعَ
Control n. or v. t.	سُلْطَةٌ . ادَارَ . سَادَ
Controllable a.	مُمْكِنٌ إِدَارَتُهُ
Controller n.	مُدِيْرٌ . مُرَاقِبٌ

Controversial a.	جَدَلِيٌّ
Controversy n.	جِدَالٌ . مُنَاظَرَة
Controvert v. t.	خَاصَمَ . جَادَلَ
Controvertible n.	مُمْكِنٌ مُقَاوَمَتُهُ
Contumacious a.	عَنِيْدٌ . مَارِدٌ
Contumacy n.	عِنَادٌ
Contumelious a.	مُهِيْن . عَاتٍ . شَاتِمٌ
Contumely n.	شَتِيْمَةٌ . إِهَانَة
Contusion n.	رَضٌّ. رَضَّة
Conundrum n.	ضَرْبٌ مِنَ اللُّغْزِ
Convalescense n.	نَقَهٌ . تَعَافٍ
Convalescent a.	نَاقِةٌ . مُتَعَافٍ
Convene v. t. or i.	جَمَعَ . ـ . إِلْتَأَمَ
Convenience n.	مُوَافَقَة . رَاحة
Convenient a.	مُوَافِق . مُلَائِم . مُرِيح
Conveniently ad.	بِسُهُوْلَةٍ . بِرَاحةٍ
Convent n.	دَيْرٌ ج أَدْيِرَة
Conventicle n.	إِجْتِمَاعٌ دِيْنِيٌّ

Convention n. مَجْمَعٌ. مُؤْتَمَرٌ. مُعَاهَدَةٌ	Convey v. t. نَقَلَ. حَمَلَ ـ
Conventional a. إِصْطِلاَحِيٌّ. إِعْتِيَادِيٌّ	Conveyance n. نَقْلٌ. مَرْكَبَةٌ
Converge v. i. إِتَّجَهَ إِلَى مَرْكَزٍ	Convict v. t. or n. أَثْبَتَ ذَنْبَهُ. مُذْنِبٌ
Convergence n. إِتِّجَاهٌ إِلَى مَرْكَزٍ	Conviction n. إِثْبَاتُ الذَّنبِ. يَقِين
Convergent Converging a. مُتَقَارِبٌ. مُتَّجِهٌ إِلَى مَرْكَزٍ	Convince v. t. اقْنَعَ
Conversant a. عَارِفٌ. خَبِيرٌ	Convivial a. مُبْهِجٌ. قَصُوفِيٌّ
Conversation n. مُفَاوَضَةٌ. حَدِيثٌ	Conviviality n. إِنْشِرَاحٌ. قَصُوفٌ
Conversational a. مُخْتَصٌّ بِالْحَدِيثِ	Convocation n. جَمْعٌ. مَجْمَعٌ
Converse v. i. تَفَاوَضَ. تَحَادَثَ	Convoke v. t. إِسْتَدْعَى. جَمَعَ ـ
Converse n. or a. عَكْسٌ. مَعْكُوسٌ	Convolute Convoluted a. مُلْتَفٌّ
Conversly ad. بِالْعَكْسِ	Convolution n. لَفٌّ. إِلْتِفَافٌ
Conversion n. تَحْوِيلٌ. تَوْبَةٌ	Convoy v. t. or n. خَفَرَ ـ. خَفَرٌ
Convert v. t. حَوَّلَ. بَدَّلَ. هَدَى	Convulse v. t. شَنَّجَ. رَجَّ ـ
Convert n. مُهْتَدٍ إِلَى دِينٍ	Convulsive a. مُشَنِّجٌ
Convertible a. قَابِلُ التَّبْدِيلِ	Cony n. وَبْرٌ ج وُبُورٌ
Convex a. مُحَدَّبٌ	Coo v. i. هَدَرَ. سَجَعَ ـ
Convexity n. تَحَدُّبٌ	Cook v. t. or n. طَبَخَ ـ. طَبَّاخٌ (عَشِّيٌّ)
	Cookery n. صِنَاعَةُ الطَّبْخِ

Cool *a.*	بَارِدٌ . مُعْتَدِلُ ٱلبُرُودَةِ	Copt *n.* Coptic *a.* }	قِبْطِي
Cool *v. t.* or *i.*	بَرَّدَ . هَدَّأ . بَرَدَ ـُ	Copula *n.*	رَابِط . صِلة
Cooler *n.*	بَرَّادَةٌ . مُبَرِّدٌ	Copulate *v. t.* or *i.*	جَامَعَ
Coolly *ad.*	بِهُدُوءٍ . بِضَبْطِ ٱلنَفْسِ	Coping *n.*	إِفْرِيز . سَقِيفَةُ حَائِطٍ
Coolness *n.*	بُرُودَةٌ . رِبَاطَةُ جَأْشٍ	Copy *n.* or *v. t.*	نُسْخَةٌ . نَسَخَ ـَ
Coop *n.* or *v. t.* }	قَفَصٌ . حَبَسَ فِي قَفَصٍ	Copyer Copyist } *n.*	نَاسِخ
Cooper *n.*	صَانِعُ بَرَامِيلَ	Copyright *n.*	حَقُّ طَبْعِ كِتَابٍ
Co-operate *v. i.*	تَعَاوَنَ . تَشَارَكَ	Coquet *v. i.*	غَنِجَ ـَ
Co-operative *a.*	مُشْتَرِكٌ فِي عَمَلٍ	Coquetry *n.*	غُنْجٌ ـ غُنَاجٌ
Co-ordinate *a.*	مُتَسَاوِي ٱلرُّتْبَةِ	Coquette *n.*	غَنِجَةٌ . (غَنُوجَة)
Co-partner *n.*	شَرِيك ج شُرَكَآءُ	Coquettish *a.*	غَانِج . غَنِجٌ
Co-partnership *n.*	شِرْكَة	Coral *n.* or *a.*	مَرْجَان . مَرْجَانِيٌّ
Cope *v.i.*	بَارَى . سَابَقَ . نَاظَرَ	Cord *n.* or *v. t.*	مَرَسٌ . شَدَّ بِمَرَسٍ
Copious *a.*	وَافِرٌ . غَزِيرٌ	Cordage *n.*	حِبَالُ ٱلسَّفِينَةِ
Copper *n.*	نُحَاسٌ احْمَرُ	Cordate *a.*	قَلْبِيُّ ٱلشَّكْلِ
Copperas *n.*	زَاجٌ	Cordial *v.* or *n.* }	قَلْبِيٌّ . مُخْلِصٌ . شَرَابٌ مُنْعِشٌ
Copper-smith *n.*	نَحَّاسٌ		
Copse *n.*	غَابَةُ اشْجَارٍ صَغِيرَةٍ . دَغْلٌ	Cordiality *n.*	وُدٌّ . إِخْلَاصٌ

Cordon *n.*	نِطَاقٌ مِنَ الجُنْد
Core *n.*	قَلْبٌ . لُبٌّ
Coriander *n.*	كُزْبَرَةٌ
Cork *n.* or *v. t.*	سَدَّادَةٌ . (فَلِّينٌ) سَدَّ بِهَا
Corky *a.*	(فَلِّينِيٌّ)
Cork-screw *n.*	بِرِيمٌ . (بَرِّيمَةٌ)
Corn *n.*	حَبٌّ . ذُرَةٌ . مِسْمَارٌ
Cornea *n.*	قَرْنِيَةُ العَيْن
Cornelian *n.*	عَقِيقٌ
Corner *n.*	زَاوِيَةٌ . قَرْنَةٌ
Corner-stone *n.*	حَجَرُ الزَّاوِيَة
Cornet *n.*	صُورٌ . نَفِيرٌ
Cornice *n.*	إِفْرِيزٌ . طَنَفٌ
Corolla *n.*	تُوَيْجُ زَهْرَة
Corollary *n.*	تَابِعَةٌ . نَتِيجَةٌ
Coronation *n.*	تَتْوِيجٌ
Coroner *n.*	مَأْمُورٌ يَفْحَصُ سَبَبَ مَوْتٍ فُجَائِيٍّ

Coronet *n.*	تَاجُ آلاشْرَاف . إِكْلِيل
Corporal *a.* or *n.*	جَسَدِيٌّ . (أُونْبَاشِي)
Corporation *n.*	شِرْكَةٌ
Corporeal *a.*	ذُو جَسَدٍ . جَسَدَانِيٌّ
Corps *n.*	فَيْلَقُ عَسْكَرٍ . جَمَاعَةٌ
Corpse *n.*	جُثَّةُ المَيْت
Corpulence Corpulency *n.*	سَمَانَةٌ . جَسَامَةٌ
Corpulent *a.*	سَمِينٌ . جَسِيمٌ
Corpuscle *n.*	ذَرَّةٌ . جُسَيْمٌ
Correct *v. t.*	اصْلَحَ . نَقَّحَ . اَدَّبَ
Correct *a.*	صَحِيحٌ . مَضْبُوط
Correction *n.*	إِصْلَاحٌ . تَنْقِيحٌ . تَأْدِيبٌ
Corrective *a.*	مُصْلِحٌ . تَأْدِيبِيٌّ
Correctly *ad.*	بِضَبْطٍ . تَمَامًا
Correctness *n.*	ضَبْط . مُطَابَقَةٌ لِلْحَقِّ
Correlate *v.t.* or *i.*	نَاسَبَ . تَنَاسَبَ
Correlation *n.*	نِسْبَةٌ . مُنَاسَبَة
Correlation *n.*	نِسْبَةٌ مُتَبَادَلَة

Correlative *a.* or *n.*	نِسْبِيٌّ مُتَبَادَلٌ . ذُو نِسْبَةٍ مُتَبَادَلَةٍ
Correspond *v. i.*	طَابَقَ . رَاسَلَ
Correspondence *n.*	مُرَاسَلَةٌ . مُنَاسَبَةٌ
Correspondent *n.* or *a.*	مُرَاسِلٌ . مُنَاسِبٌ
Corridor *n.*	رِوَاقٌ . أَرْوِقَة
Corroborate *v. t.*	شَدَّدَ . اثْبَتَ . أَيَّدَ
Corroboration *n.*	إِثْبَاتٌ . تَأْيِيدٌ
Corrode *v. i.* or *t.*	صَدِئَ . قَرَضَ
Corrodent Corrosive } *a.*	آكِلٌ . قَارِضٌ
Corrosion *n.*	صَدَأٌ . قَرْضٌ
Corrugation *n.*	تَجَعُّدٌ
Corrupt *v. t.* or *a.*	افْسَدَ . نَجَّسَ . فَاسِدٌ
Corruptible *a.*	فَاسِدٌ . فَانٍ
Corruption *n.*	فَسَادٌ . نَجَاسَةٌ
Corruptive *a.*	مُفْسِدٌ . مُنَجِّسٌ
Corruptness *n.*	فَسَادٌ
Corsair *n.*	قُرْصَانُ البَحْر

Corselet *n.*	زُرْدِيَّةٌ . دِرْعٌ
Corset *n.*	مِشَدٌّ لِلنِّسَاء
Cortege *n.*	مَوْكِبٌ
Coruscate *v. i.*	بَرَقَ . لَمَعَ
Corvée *n.*	سُخْرَة
Corvette *n.*	بَارِجَةٌ صَغِيرَةٌ
Cosmetic *a.* or *n.* }	مُحَسِّنٌ لِلَوْنِ الوَجْهِ
Cosmogony *n.*	عِلْمُ تَكْوِينِ الكَوْنِ
Cosmography *n.*	عِلْمُ وَصْفِ الكَوْنِ
Cosmology *n.*	عِلْمٌ يَبْحَثُ عَنِ الكَوْنِ
Cosmopolitan *n.*	رَجُلٌ وَطَنُهُ العَالَم
Cost *n.* or *v. t.* or *i.*	قِيمَةٌ . سِعْرٌ . كَلَّفَ
Costal *a.*	ضِلْعِيٌّ
Costive *a.*	قَابِضُ الأَمْعَاء
Costiveness *n.*	قَبْضُ الأَمْعَاء
Costliness *n.*	غَلَاءٌ
Costly *a.*	غَالٍ
Costume *n.*	زِيٌّ ج أَزْيَاء

Cot *n.*	كُوخ . فِرَاشٌ صَغِيرٌ
Cote *n.*	حَظِيرَةٌ . صِيرَةٌ
Coterie *n.*	جَمَاعَةُ اصْحَابٍ
Cotemporaneous *a.* Cotemporary *n.*	مُعَاصِرٌ
Cottage *n.*	كُوخ . بَيْتٌ صَغِيرٌ
Cottager *n.*	سَاكِنُ كُوخٍ
Cotton *n.* or *a.*	قُطْنٌ . قُطْنِيٌّ
Cotton-gin *n.*	مَحْلَجُ القُطْنِ
Cotyledon *n.*	فِلْقَةُ بِزْرَةٍ
Couch *v. i.* or *t.*	إضْطَجَعَ . كَمَنَ أضْجَعَ
Couch *n.*	فِرَاشٌ
Cough *v. i.* or *n.*	سَعَلَ ـ سُعَالٌ
Council *n.*	مَجْلِسُ الشُّورَى
Councillor *n.*	عَضْوُ مَجْلِسٍ . مُشِيرٌ
Counsel *n.* or *v. t.*	نَصِيحَةٌ . نَصَحَ
Counsellor *n.*	نَاصِحٌ . مُشِيرٌ . فَقِيهٌ
Count *v. t.* or *n.*	عَدَّ . احْصَى . امِيرٌ

Countenance *n.*	مُحَيَّا . طَلْعَةٌ
Countenance *v. t.*	عَضَدَ ـ
Counter *n.* or *ad.*	مَائِدَةُ مَخْزَنٍ . ضِدَّ
Counteract *v. t.*	ضَادَّ . خَيَّبَ
Counteraction *n.*	مُضَادَّةٌ . إِبْطَالٌ
Counterbalance *n.* or *v. t.*	مُوَازَنَةٌ . وَازَنَ . عَادَلَ
Counterfeit *a.* or *n.* or *v. t.*	مُزَوَّرٌ . زَوَّرَ
Countermand *n.* or *v. t.*	أَمْرٌ يُبْطِلُ امْراً . أَلْغَى
Countermarch *v. i.* or *n.*	قَهْقَرَ . قَهْقَرَى
Counterpane *n.*	لِحَافُ فِرَاشٍ
Counterpart *n.*	قِسْمٌ مُقَابِلَ قِسْمٍ
Counterplot *n.*	حِيلَةٌ ضِدَّ حِيلَةٍ
Counterpoise *n.* or *v. t.*	ثِقَلٌ . مُوَازِنٌ . وَازَنَ
Countersign *n.*	كَلِمَةُ سِرِّ اللَّيْلِ
Countersign *v. t.*	امْضَى إِثْبَاتاً لإِمْضَاءٍ
Countess *n.*	امِيرَةٌ
Counting-house *n.*	مَكْتَبُ التَّاجِرِ

Countless *a*.	مَا لَا يُحْصَى
Country *n*.	بِلَاد . بَرِّيَّة
Countryman *n*.	اِبْنُ بِلَادٍ . فَلَّاحٌ
County *n*.	لِوَاءٌ مِنْ بِلَادٍ
Couple *n*. or *v. t*.	زَوْجٌ . اِثْنَانِ . وَصَلَ
Couplet *n*.	بَيْتَا شِعْرٍ
Coupling *n*.	رَابِطٌ . مُوصِلٌ . وَصْلٌ
Courage *n*.	شَجَاعَة . بَسَالَةٌ
Courageous *a*.	شُجَاعٌ . بَاسِلٌ
Courier *n*.	رَسُولٌ . بَرِيدٌ
Course *n*.	سَيْرٌ . طَرِيقٌ . نَاحِيَةٌ
Courser *n*.	فَرَسٌ سَرِيعٌ
Court *n*. or *v. t*.	دَارٌ . مَحْكَمَةٌ . تَمَلَّقَ
Courteous *a*.	اَنِيسٌ . اَدِيبٌ
Courtesan *n*.	زَانِيَة . فَاجِرَةٌ
Courtesy *n*.	اُنْسٌ . اَدَبٌ . اِنْسَانِيَّةٌ
Courtier *n*.	مُلَازِمُ بِلَاطِ آلْمَلِكِ
Courtliness *n*.	اَدَبٌ . لُطْفٌ مَعَ شَرَفٍ

Courtly *a*.	اَدِيبٌ . شَرِيفٌ
Court-martial *n*.	مَحْكَمَة عَسْكَرِيَّة
Court-plaster *n*.	لَزُوقٌ مِنْ حَرِيرٍ
Courtship *n*.	تَمَلُّقٌ
Courtyard *n*.	حَوْشٌ . دَارٌ
Cousin *n*.	اِبْنُ عَمٍّ اوْ عَمَّةٍ اوْ خَالٍ اوْ خَالَةٍ اوِ اِبْنَتُهُمْ
Cove *n*.	خَلِيجٌ صَغِيرٌ . خَوْرٌ
Covenant *n*. or *v. t*.	عَهْدٌ . عَاهَدَ
Cover *v. t*. or *n*.	سَتَرَ . غَطَّى . غِطَاءٌ
Covering *n*.	غِطَاءٌ . سِتْرٌ
Coverlet *n*.	لَحَافٌ . دِثَارٌ
Covert *n*. or *a*.	مَأْوًى . مَسْتُورٌ . سِرِّيٌّ
Covertly *ad*.	سِرًّا . خُفْيَةً
Covet *v. t*.	اِشْتَهَى . طَمِعَ فِي
Covetous *a*.	مُشْتَهٍ . طَمَّاعٌ
Covetousness *n*.	شَهْوَةٌ . طَمَعٌ
Covey *n*.	سِرْبٌ مِنْ (طُيُورٍ)
Cow *n*.	بَقَرَةٌ

Coward *n.*	جَبَانٌ ج جُبَنَاء
Cowardice *n.*	جَبَانَة . جُبْن
Cowardly *a.* or *ad.*	جَبَانٌ . بِجِبَانَةٍ
Cower *v. i.*	خَرَّ أَوْ تَرَدَّدَ مِنَ ٱلْخَوْفِ
Cowherd *n.*	رَاعِي بَقَرٍ
Cowhide *n.*	جِلْدُ بَقَرٍ أَوْ سَوْطٌ مِنْهُ
Cowl *n.*	قَلَنْسُوَةٌ ج قَلَانِس
Coxcomb *n.*	مُعْجَبٌ . مُتَحَذْلِقٌ . بَلْتَعَانِيٌّ
Cowpox *n.*	جَدَرِيُّ ٱلْبَقَرِ
Coy *a.*	مُتَصَاوِنٌ . مُعْتَزِلٌ عَنِ ٱلْمُعَاشَرَةِ
Cozen *v. t.*	خَدَعَ . غَشَّ
Cozy *a.*	مُسْتَرِيحٌ
Crab *n.*	سَرَطَانٌ
Crabbed *a.*	خَشِنُ ٱلْجَانِبِ . فَظٌّ
Crack *n.* or *v. t.* or *i.*	شَقٌّ . شَقَّ . تَشَقَّقَ (طَقَّ)
Cracker *n.*	كَعْكٌ يَابِسٌ . بَقْسُمَاط
Crackle *v. i.*	(قَرْقَعَ . طَقْطَقَ)
Cradle *n.* or *v. t.*	سَرِيرٌ . وَضَعَ فِي سَرِيرٍ

Craft *n.*	حِرْفَة سَفِينَةٌ صَغِيرَة
Craft Craftiness *n.*	دَهَاءٌ . مَكْرٌ
Craftsman *n.*	صَانِعٌ . مُحْتَرِفٌ
Crafty *a.*	دَاهٍ . مُحْتَالٌ
Crag *n.*	صَخْرٌ شَاهِقٌ . غَلِيظ
Cragged Craggy *a.*	صَخْرِيٌّ . غَلِيظ
Cram *v. t.* or *i.*	حَشَا . أَفْعَمَ
Cramp *n.* or *v. t.*	كُزَازٌ . كُلَّابٌ ضَيَّقَ عَلَى . اعَاقَ
Crane *n.*	كُرْكِيٌّ آلَةٌ لِرَفْعِ ٱلْأَثْقَالِ
Cranial *a.*	قِحْفِيٌّ
Cranium *n.*	جُمْجُمَة . قِحْفٌ
Crank *n.*	يَدُ دُولَابٍ أَوْ آلَةُ ٱلتَّدْوِيرِ
Crape *n.*	(كُرِيشَة) . نَسِيجٌ
Crash *v. i.* or *n.*	صَوَّتَ صَوْتُ كَسْرٍ
Crass *a.*	خَشِنٌ . غَلِيظ
Crate *n.*	قَفَصٌ لِنَقْلِ صُحُونٍ فَخَّارِيةٍ
Crater *n.*	فُوهَةُ بُرْكَان

Craunch v.t. مَضَغَ. سَحَقَ بِالْأَسْنَانِ	Credence n. ثِقَة . تَصْدِيق
Cravat n. رِبَاطُ رَقَبَةٍ	Credentials pl. شَهَادَاتٌ رَسْمِيَّة
Crave v. t. إِشْتَهَى إِشْتَاق . طَلَب	Credibility n. إِسْتِحْقَاقُ التَّصْدِيقِ
Craven a. or n. جَبَانٌ . نَذْلٌ	Credible a. مُسْتَحَقُّ التَّصْدِيقِ
Craving n. تَلَهُّفٌ . إِشْتِهَاءٌ	Credit n. or v. t. ثِقَة . امَّن
Crawl v. i. دَبَّ ـ . زَحَفَ ـ	Creditable a. مَوْثُوق بِهِ . مُعْتَبَر
Crayon n. or v. t. قَلَمُ رَصَاصٍ . رَسَمَ بِهِ	Creditor n. دَائِنٌ . صَاحِبُ دَيْنٍ
Craze v. t. جَنَّنَ	Credulity n. سُهُولَةُ التَّصْدِيقِ
Craziness n. جُنُونٌ. إِخْتِلَالُ الْعَقْلِ	Credulous a. سَهْلُ التَّصْدِيقِ
Crazy a. مَجْنُونٌ.مُخْتَلُّ الْعَقْلِ	Creed n. مَذْهَبٌ . قَانُونُ الْإِيمَانِ
Creak v. i. صَرَفَ ـ ضَرِيفًا	Creek n. جُونٌ . نَهْرٌ صَغِيرٌ
Cream n. زُبْدَةُ اللَّبَنِ . قِشْدَة	Creep v. i. دَبَّ ـ . زَحَفَ ـ
Crease v. t. or n. غَضَّنَ . غَضْن	Creeper n. نَبْتٌ مُتَعَرِّشٌ اوْ مُتَسَلِّق
Create v.t. خَلَقَ ـ . بَرَأَ ـ ابدَعَ	Cremation n. حَرْق . حَرْقُ الْجُثَّةِ
Creation n. خَلْقٌ خَلِيقَة . بَرِيَّة	Crescent n. هِلَالٌ
Creative a. خَالِقٌ . مُبْدِع	Cress n. رَشَادٌ . قُرَّةُ الْعَيْنِ
Creator n. خَالِق . الْبَارِئُ	Crest n. قُنْبُرَة . قِمَّة
Creature n. خَلِيقَة . مَخْلُوق . بَرِية	Crest-fallen a. مُنْحَطّ . ذَلِيل

Cretacious a.	طَبَاشِيرِيّ	Crisp a.	قَصِم . مُجَعَّد
Crevice n.	شَقّ ج شُقُوق	Criterion n.	دَلِيلٌ . مِقْيَاسٌ
Crew n.	مَلَّاحُو السَّفِينَة . جَمَاعَة	Critic n.	مُنْتَقِدٌ . مُنَكِّتٌ
Crib n.	مِذْوَد . مَهْد	Critical a.	إِنْتِقَادِيّ . مُدَقِّقٌ . مُخْطِرٌ
Cricket n.	صُرْصُر	Criticise v. t.	إِنْتَقَدَ . نَكَّتَ
Crier n.	مُنَادٍ . مُؤَذِّن	Criticism } Critique } n.	إِنْتِقَادٌ . تَنْكِيتٌ
Crime n.	جَرِيمَة . جِنَايَة . جُنَاح	Croak v. i. or n.	نَعَقَ ـَ . نَعِيقٌ
Criminal n. or a.	مُذْنِبٌ . جِنَائِيّ	Croaker n.	نَاعِقٌ . مُتَذَمِّرٌ
Criminality n.	جِنَائِيَّة . ذَنْبِيَّة	Crockery n.	خَزَفٌ . فَخَّارٌ
Criminate v. t.	إِسْتَذْنَبَ . جَنَّحَ	Crocodile n.	تِمْسَاح
Crimination n.	إِسْتِذْنَابٌ . تَجْنِيحٌ	Crocus n.	زَعْفَرَان
Crimp v. t. or a.	جَعَّدَ . قَصَّمَ	Crony n.	خِلٌّ . نَدِيمٌ
Crimson n. or a.	قِرْمِزٌ . قِرْمِزِيّ	Crook v. t. or n.	عَقَفَ ـَ . عَصَا الرَّاعِي
Cringe v. i.	تَذَلَّلَ لـ	Crooked a.	أَعْقَفُ . مُلْتَوٍ
Cringer } Cringeling } n.	مُتَذَلِّلٌ	Crookedness n.	إِعْوِجَاجٌ . إِنْعِقَافٌ
Cripple n. or v. t.	كَسِيحٌ . صَيَّرَ كَسِيحًا	Crop n.	غَلَّة . حَوْصَلَة
Crisis n.	بُحْرَان . نُقْطَة الخَطَرِ وَالتَّغَيُّر . أَزْمَة	Crosier n.	عُكَّاز الأَسْقُف
		Cross n. or a.	صَلِيبٌ . نَكِدٌ

Cross *v. t. or i.*	عَبَرَ ـُ عَارَضَ	Crown-prince *n.*	وَلِيُّ ٱلْعَهْدِ
Cross-bow *n.*	قَوْسُ ٱلسِّهَامِ	Crucial *a.*	صَلِيبِيٌّ . شَدِيدٌ . حَتْمِيٌّ
Cross-eyed *a.*	أَحْوَلُ	Crucible *n.*	بُوتَقَة
Crossing *n.*	مَعْبَرٌ . عُبُورٌ	Crucifix *n.*	صَلِيبٌ عَلَيْهِ صُورَةُ ٱلْمَسِيحِ
Crossgrained *a.*	شَابَك . نَكِدٌ	Crucifixion *n.*	صَلْبٌ
Crosslegged *a.*	مُتَرَبِّعٌ	Cruciform *a.*	صَلِيبِيُّ ٱلشَّكْلِ
Cross-purpose *n.*	قَصْدٌ مُتَضَادٌّ	Crucify *v. t.*	صَلَبَ ـ
Cross-question *v. t.*	إِسْتَنْطَقَ . حَقَّقَ	Crude *a.*	نِيَّ . غَيْرُ مُتْقَن
Cross-road *n.*	مُصْلَبُ ٱلطُّرُقِ	Crudity *n.* Crudeness	عَدَمُ إِتْقَانٍ . فَجَاجَة
Crosswise *ad.*	عَرْضاً	Cruel *a.*	قَاسٍ . صَارِمٌ
Crotch *n.*	مَفْرَقُ أَغْصَانٍ	Cruelty *n.*	قَسَاوَة . صَرَامَة
Crotchet *n.*	وَهْمٌ . تَصَوُّرٌ بَاطِلٌ	Cruet *n.*	قَارُورَة
Crouch *v. i.*	رَبَضَ . جَثَا ـُ	Cruise *n.* or *v. i.*	طَافَ ـ . طَوَافٌ بَحْراً
Croup *n.*	دَاءُ ٱلذِّبْحَة	Cruiser *n.*	بَارِجَة طَوَّافَةٌ أَوْ سَرِيعَة
Crow *n.* or *v. i.*	غُرَابٌ . صَاحَ (ٱلدِّيكُ)	Crum Crumb *n.*	كِسْرَة صَغِيرَة
Crow-bar *n.*	مُخْلٌ ج أَمْخَالٌ	Crumble *v. t. or i.*	فَتَّ . تَفَتَّتَ
Crowd *n. or v. t.*	زَحْمَة . زَاحَمَ	Crumple *v. t. or i.*	غَضَّنَ تَغَضَّنَ
Crown *n. or v. t.*	تَاجٌ . تَوَّجَ	Crupper *n.*	(قُوشٌ) . (اصَالُ)

Crusade n. حَرْبُ ٱلصَّلِيبِيَّةِ . جِهَادٌ	Cud n. · جَرَّةٌ
Crusader n. مُحَارِبٌ صَلِيبِيٌّ	Cuddle v. i. or t. إِسْتَكَنَّ عِنْدَ. حَضَنَ
Crush v. t. سَحَقَ . حَطَّمَ . اذَلَّ	Cudgel n. نَبُّوتٌ . هِرَاوَةٌ
Crust n. or v. t. قِشْرٌ . لَبَّسَ بِقِشْرٍ	Cue n. ذَيْلٌ . إِشَارَةٌ . تَلْمِيحٌ
Crustacious a. ذُو قِشْرٍ أَوْصَدَفَةٍ	Cuff n. or v. t. كُمُّ ٱلْقَمِيصِ. لَطَمَ ـ
Crusty a. فَظٌّ . شَرِسٌ . قِشْرِيٌّ	Cuirass n. دِرْعٌ ج ادْرَاعٌ وَدُرُوْعٌ
Crutch n. عُكَّازٌ	Cuirassier n. لَابِسُ دِرْعٍ . مُدَرَّعٌ
Cry v. i. صَرَخَ ـُ . بَكَى ـِ . صُرَاخٌ or n.	Culinary a. طَبْخِيٌّ
Crying a. صَارِخٌ . مَشْهُورٌ . عَظِيمٌ	Cull v. t. نَخَبَ . ـُ إِنْتَخَبَ
Crypt n. مُخْدَعٌ تَحْتَ ٱلْأَرْضِ	Cullender n. مِصْفَاةٌ
Crystal n. بَلُّوْرٌ وَبِلُّوْرٌ	Culminate v. i. بَلَغَ اعْلَاهُ
Crystalline a. بَلُّوْرِيٌّ . شَفَّافٌ	Culmination n. غَايَةُ ٱلْبُلُوْغِ
Crystallize v. i. or t. تَبَلْوَرَ . بَلْوَرَ	Culpable a. مَلُومٌ . مُخْطِئٌ
Cub n. جَرْوٌ . شِبْلٌ	Culpability n. ذَنْبٌ. إِسْتِحْقَاقُ ٱللَّوْمِ
Cube n. or v. t. كَعَّبَ . مُكَعَّبٌ . كَعْبٌ	Culprit n. مُذْنِبٌ
Cubic Cubiform } a. مُكَعَّبُ ٱلشَّكْلِ	Cultivable a. قَابِلُ ٱلْحِرَاثَةِ
Cubit n. ذِرَاعٌ ج أَذْرُعٌ	Cultivate v. t. حَرَثَ ـُ . هَذَّبَ
Cucumber n. خِيَارٌ . قُثَّاءٌ	Cultivation Culture } n. حِرَاثَةٌ . تَهْذِيبٌ

Cumber v. t.	ثَقَّلَ . أَعَاقَ . لَبَّكَ
Cumbersome } a. Cumbrous }	ثَقِيلٌ . مُلَبِّكٌ
Cumulate v. t.	رَكَمَ ـ كَوَّمَ
Cumulative a.	مُتَجَمِّعٌ . مُتَزَايِدٌ
Cuneiform } a. Cuniform }	إِسْفِينِيُّ الشَّكْلِ
Cunning a. or n.	دَاهٍ . دَاهِيَة . دَهَاءٌ
Cup n. or v. t.	كَاسٌ . فِنْجَان. حَجَمَ ـ
Cupbearer n.	سَاقٍ . سَاقِي مَلِكٍ
Cupboard n.	(خِزَانَةٌ) (دُوْلَابٌ)
Cupidity n.	طَمَعٌ . جَشَعٌ
Cupola n.	قُبَّة
Cur n.	كَلْبٌ . شَاكِسٌ . فَظٌّ
Curable a.	قَابِلُ الشِّفَاءِ
Curacy n.	مَقَامُ قَسِّيسٍ أَوْ خُورِيٍّ
Curate n.	قَسِّيسٌ . خُورِيٌّ
Curative a.	شَافٍ
Curator n.	وَكِيْلٌ . حَافِظ
Curb n. or v. t.	شَكِيمَة . صَدَّ . كَبَحَ ـ

Curd n.	رَوْبٌ . خَثْرَة . لَبَنٌ رَائِبٌ
Curdle v. i. or t.	خَثَرَ . خَثَّرَ
Cure v. t. or n.	شَفَى . شِفَآءٌ
Curiosity n.	إِسْتِطْلَاعٌ . نَادِرَة
Curious a.	مُسْتَطْلِع . نَادِرٌ
Curl n. or v. t. or i.	جُعْدَة . جَعَّدَ . تَجَعَّدَ
Curly a.	مُتَجَعِّدٌ . جُعْدِيٌّ
Currants n. pl.	عِنَبُ الثَّعْلَبِ. كِشْمِشٌ
Currency n.	مُعَامَلَة . نُقُوْدٌ . جَرَيَانٌ
Current a. or n.	جَارٍ . مَجْرًى
Currier n.	مُصْلِحُ جُلُوْدٍ مَدْبُوغَةٍ
Curry v. t.	اصْلَحَ (جُلُوداً) حَسَّ (فَرَساً)
Curse v. t. or n.	لَعَنَ . لَعْنَة
Cursed a.	مَلْعُونٌ . مَكْرُوْهٌ
Cursorily ad.	بِسُرْعةٍ . بِلَا دِقَّةٍ
Cursory a.	سَرِيْعٌ . غَيْرُ مُدَقَّق
Curt a.	قَصِيرٌ . فَظٌّ
Curtail v. t.	قَصَّرَ . اوْجَزَ

Curtain n. or v. t.	ستارْ نصبَ ستاراً
Curvature) Curve } n.	إنْحِنَاءْ . قَوْسْ
Curve v. t. or i.	قَوَّسَ . إنْحَنَى
Cushion n.	وِسَادَة . مخدَّة
Custodian n.	وَكِيلْ . مُحَافِظ
Custody n.	وَكَالَة . مُحَافظة . حبْسْ
Custom n.	عَادَة . دَأْبْ
Customary a.	إعْتِيَادِيّ . مَأْلُوفْ
Cutomer n.	زَبُون ج زُبنَاءْ
Custom-house n.	(جُمْرُكْ) دِيوَان الرُّسُومَات
Customs n.	رُسُومَات . (جمَارِكْ)
Cut v. t. or n.	قَطعَ _ . قَطْعْ
Cutaneous a.	جِلْدِيّ
Cuticle n.	بَشَرَة الجِلْد
Cutlass n.	سَيْفْ عَرِيضْ قَصِيرْ
Cutlery n.	ادَوَاتُ القَطْعِ كالسَّكَاكِين
Cutlet n.	قِطعة لحم لِلشَّيّ (كستلاتا)
Cutter n.	سَفِينَة صَغِيرة
Cutting a. or n.	قَاطِعْ . مُؤْلِمْ . قطعَة
Cwt n.	عَلامَةُ مِئَةِ لِيرَا انكليزيَّة
Cyclamen n.	بَخُورُ مَرْيَمْ (نبات)
Cycle n.	دَائِرَة . دَوْرْ
Cyclone n.	زَوْبَعَة عظيمة
Cyclopean a.	كبِير جدًّا
Cyclopedia n.	دَائِرَةُ المَعَارِفِ
Cylinder n.	اسْطُوَانَةْ ج اسَاطِين
Cylindrical a.	اسْطُوَانِيّ
Cymbal n.	صنْجْ ج صنوجْ
Cynic n. Cynical a. }	شَرِسْ . فَظّ
Cypress n.	سَرْوْ . سَرْوَة
Cyprian Cypriote } a. or n.	قبْرُسِيّ
Cyst n.	كِيسْ غِشَائِيّ
Czar n.	قَيْصَرُ رُوسِيًّا
Czarina n.	إمْرَاةُ القَيصرِ
Czarowitz n.	وليّ عهْد رُوسِيًّا

D

Dab v. t.	ملَثَ ـُ . لطَخَ ـَ
Dabble v. i.	لعِب في وبِ . لَطَخَ
Dad Daddy } n.	أبْ (بلُغَةِ ٱلاوْلادِ)
Daft a.	بليدٌ . مَجْنونٌ
Dagger n.	خنْجرٌ ج خَنَاجرُ
Dahlia n.	دَاليَا (نَبَاتٌ)
Daily a. or ad.	يوْميٌّ . يوْميًّا
Daintly ad.	بتأنُّقٍ
Daisy n.	أقحُوَانٌ
Dainty a.	نفيسٌ . أنيقٌ
Dairy n.	مَلْبَنٌ . مَجْبنةٌ
Dale n.	وَادٍ ج اوديةٌ
Dalliance n.	مُدَاعَبةٌ . مُلاَعَبةٌ
Dally v. i.	دَاعَبَ . غَازَلَ . لاَعَبَ

Dam v. t.	سدَّ ـُ . حَجَرَ
Dam n.	سدٌّ . امُّ بَهيمَةٍ
Damage n. or v. t.	ضَرَرٌ . أضرَّ
Damask n.	نَسيجٌ نَفيسٌ منقشٌ
Dame n.	سيِّدَة
Damn v. t.	دَانَ ـِ . لعَنَ ـَ
Damnable a.	ملْعُونٌ . مَكْرُوهٌ
Damnation n.	دَينُونةٌ . هَلاَكٌ
Damp a. or n.	رَطبٌ . رُطوبةٌ
Dampen v. t.	رَطَّبَ . بَلَّ ـُ
Damper n.	صِمَامُ مَدْخنَةٍ
Dampness n.	رُطوبةٌ
Damsel n.	فَتَاةٌ . بنْتٌ
Dance v. i. or n.	رَقصَ ـُ . رَقصٌ

Dandelion n.	نَابُ الأسدِ (نَبَاتٌ)
Daddle v. t.	رَقَّصَ (طِفْلاً) . دَلَّلَ
Dandruff n.	هِبْرِيَّةُ الرَّأْسِ. أَقْشَرَةٌ
Dandy n.	أَنِيقٌ . مُتَأَنِّقٌ
Danger n.	خَطَرٌ
Dangerous a.	خَطِرٌ . مُخْطِرٌ
Dangle v. i.	تَدَلَّى
Dank a.	مُبْتَلٌّ . رَطْبٌ
Dapple Dappled } a.	أَرْقَطُ
Dard v. i. or t.	تَجَاسَرَ . إِقْتَحَمَ
Daring a.	مُتَجَاسِرٌ . جَسُورٌ
Dark a. or n.	مُظْلِمٌ . أَغْبَشُ. ظَلامٌ
Darken v. t. or i.	أَظْلَمَ . عَتَّمَ
Darkly ad.	مُظْلِماً
Darkness n.	ظَلامٌ . قَتَامٌ
Darling a. or n.	عَزِيزٌ . حَبِيبٌ
Darn v. t.	رَتَقَ ـِ . رَفَأَ ـَ
Darnel n.	زِوَانٌ
Dart n. or v. t. or i. }	سَهْمٌ . رَمَى . إِنْقَضَّ
Dash v. t.	صَدَمَ ـِ . إِقْتَحَمَ . كَسَّرَ
Dash n.	عَلامَةُ فَصْلٍ كَذَا (—)
Dastard n.	خَسِيسٌ . لَئِيمٌ
Dastardly a.	جَبَانٌ . لَئِيمٌ
Data n. pl.	مَوَادٌّ . مَوْضُوعٌ
Date n. or v. t.	تَارِيخٌ . تَمْرَةٌ. أَرَّخَ
Daub v. t.	طَيَّنَ . دَهَنَ
Daughter n.	بِنْتٌ أَوْ ابْنَةٌ
Daughter-in-law n.	كَنَّةٌ
Daunt v. t.	أَفْزَعَ . أَرْهَبَ
Dauntless a.	جَسُورٌ . جَرِيْءٌ
Dauphin n.	وَلِيُّ عَهْدِ فَرَنْسَا
Dawn n. or v. i.	فَجْرٌ . أَفْجَرَ
Day n.	يَوْمٌ . نَهَارٌ
Day-break Day-spring } n.	فَجْرٌ . فَلَقٌ
Daylight n.	ضَوْءُ النَّهَارِ
Daze Dazzel } v. t.	جَهَرَ ـَ . أَسْدَرَ

Deacon n.	شَمَّاسْ ج شَمَامِسَة
Dead a. or n.	مَيْتٌ ج أَمْوَاتٌ
Deaden v. t.	أَضْعَفَ . أَخْمَدَ
Dead-letter n.	مُهْمَلٌ
Deadlock n.	وَرْطَةٌ . مُعْضِلَة
Deadly a.	مُهْلِكٌ . مُمِيتٌ
Deaf a.	أَصَمُّ . اطْرَشُ
Deafen v. t.	أَصَمَّ
Deaf-mute n.	أَطْرَشُ . اخْرَسُ
Deafness n.	صَمَمٌ . طَرَشٌ
Deal v. t. or i.	وَزَّعَ . تَاجَرَ . عَامَلَ
Dealer n.	تَاجِرٌ . بَيَّاعٌ
Dean n.	ثَانِي الأُسْقُفِ . رَئِيسُ عُمْدَة مَدْرَسَةٍ أَوْ كَاتِبُهَا
Dear a.	عَزِيزٌ . غَالٍ
Dearth n.	مَجَاعَةٌ . قَحْطٌ
Death n.	مَوْتٌ
Deathless a.	خَالِدٌ

Debar v. t.	مَنَعَ ـ . صَدَّ عَنْ
Debase v. t.	أَذَلَّ . افْسَدَ
Debasement n.	إِذْلَالٌ . دَنَاءَة
Debasing a.	مُفْسِدٌ . مُذِلٌّ
Debate v. t. or n.	نَاظَرَ بَاحَثَ . مُنَاقَشَةٌ
Debauch n. or v. t.	خَلَاعَة . أَفْسَدَ
Debauchery n.	خَلَاعَةٌ . فِسْقٌ
Debilitate v. t.	أَضْعَفَ . اوْهَنَ
Debility n.	ضَعْفٌ . وَهْنٌ . وَنَاءٌ
Debt n.	دَيْنٌ ج دُيُونٌ
Debtor n.	مَدْيُونٌ
Decade n.	مُدَّةُ عَشْرِ سِنِينَ
Decadence n.	إِنْحِطَاطٌ
Decalogue n.	الْوَصَايَا الْعَشْرُ
Decamp v. i.	بَرَحَ الْمَحَلَّةَ . إِنْسَلَّ
Decanter n.	قَنِّينَة
Decapitate v. t.	قَطَعَ الرَّأْسَ
Decay v. i. or n.	إِنْحَطَّ . فَنِيَ ـ فَنَاءٌ

Decease v. i. or n.	مَاتَ . مَوْتٌ . وَفَاةٌ
Deceased a.	مَيْتٌ . مَرْحُومٌ
Deceit n.	غِشٌّ . مَكْرٌ . خَدِيعَة
Deceitful a.	غَاشٌّ . خَدَّاعٌ
Deceive v. t.	غَشَّ ُ . خَدَعَ . خَادَع
December n.	شَهْرُ كَانُونَ الْأَوَّلِ
Decency n.	لِيَاقَة . حِشْمَة
Decennial a.	حَادِثٌ كُلَّ عَشْرِ سِنِينَ مَرَّةً
Decent a.	لَائِقٌ . مُوَافِقٌ
Deception n.	خَدِيعَة . غُرُورٌ . غِش
Deceptive a.	غَرَّارٌ . غَاشٌّ
Decide v. t.	عَزَمَ ِ . حَتَمَ ـ . أَنْهَى
Decided a.	مَحْتُومٌ . عَزُومٌ . وَاضِحٌ
Decimal a.	عَشْرِيٌّ
Decimate v. t.	قَتَلَ عُشْرًا
Decipher v. t.	فَسَّرَ . حَلَّ
Decision n.	حَتْمٌ . حُكْمٌ . فَتْوى
Decisive a.	فَاطِع . جَازِمٌ . حَتْمِيٌّ
Deck v.t. or n.	زَيَّنَ . ظَهْرُ السَّفِينَة
Declaim v. i.	خَطَبَ ُ . أَكْثَرَ الْكَلَام
Declamation n.	خِطَابٌ . خُطْبَة
Declamatory a.	خِطَابِيٌّ كَثِيرُ الْكَلَامِ
Declaration n.	قَرَارٌ . تَصْرِيحٌ
Declare v. t.	أقَرَّ . صَرَّحَ بِ . شَهَرَ
Declension n.	تَصْرِيفُ الْأَسْمَاءِ
Declination n.	إِنْحِرَافٌ
Decline v. t. or i.	إِنْحِرَافٌ . رَفْضٌ
	صَرَفَ . إِنْحَرَفَ . إِنْحَطَ
Declivity n.	اِحْدُورٌ . مُتَحَدِّرٌ
Decoct v. t.	غَلَى ِ
Decoction n.	مَغْلِيٌّ
Decompose v.t. or i.	حَلَّ . فَسَدَ ُ
Decomposition n.	إِنْحِلَالٌ . فَسَادٌ
Decorate v. t.	زَيَّنَ . زَخْرَفَ
Decoration n.	زِينَة . نِيشَانٌ

Decorative *a.*	مُزَيَّنٌ.مُزَخْرَفٌ	Deer *n.*	اَبلٌ إِبَلٌ ج اَيَائِلٌ
Decorous *a.*	اَدِيبٌ . لَائِقٌ	Deface *v. t.*	شَوَّهَ . مَحَا ـُ
Decorum *n.*	اَدَبٌ. لِيَاقَةُ التَّصَرُّفِ	Defacement *n.*	تَشْوِيهٌ
Decoy *v. t* or *n.*	اَغْوَى . حِيلَةٌ	Defalcation *n.*	إِخْتِلَاسٌ
Decrease *v. t.* or *i.* or *n.*	قَلَّلَ . نَقَصَ ـُ نَقْصٌ	Defamation *n.*	هَتْكَةٌ . وِشَايَةٌ
Decree *v. t.* or *n.*	اَصْدَرَ اَمْرًا.اَمْرٌ	Defame *v. t.*	وَشَى يَشِي بِهِ . هَتَكَ
Decreed *a.* or *pp.*	مَحْتُومٌ . مُقَدَّرٌ	Default *v. t.* or *n.*	إِخْتَلَسَ مَالاً قَصَّرَ عَنْ
Decrepitude *n.*	هَرَمٌ . عَجْزٌ	Default *n.*	إِخْتِلَاسٌ.ذَنْبٌ. تَقْصِيرٌ
Dedicate *v. t.*	قَدَّسَ . كَرَّسَ (دَشَّنَ)	Defeat *v. t.* or *n.*	غَلَبَ ـِ هَزَمَ ـ هَزِيمَةٌ
Dedication *n.*	تَقْدِيسٌ. تَكْرِيسٌ	Defect *n.*	نَقْصٌ . خَلَلٌ . عَيْبٌ
Deduce *v. t.*	إِسْتَدَلَّ . إِسْتَنْتَجَ	Defection *n.*	تَرْكٌ . خِيَانَةٌ
Deducible *a.*	مُمْكِنٌ إِسْتِنْتَاجُهُ	Defective *a.*	نَاقِصٌ . كَثِيرُ الْخَلَلِ
Deduct *v. t.*	طَرَحَ ـَ اَسْقَطَ	Defence Defense *n.*	حِمَايَةٌ . مُدَافَعَةٌ
Deduction *n.*	إِسْقَاطٌ . إِسْتِنْتَاجٌ	Defenceless *a.*	خَالٍ مِنَ الْحِمَايَةِ
Deed *n.*	عَمَلٌ . فِعْلٌ	Defend *v. t.*	حَمَى . دَفَعَ عَنْ
Deem *v. t.* or *i.*	ظَنَّ ـُ إِرْتَأَى	Defendant *n.*	مُدَافِعٌ مُدَّعًى عَلَيْهِ
Deep *a.* or *n.*	عَمِيقٌ . الْبَحْرُ	Defender *n.*	مُحَامٍ . مُدَافِعٌ
Deepen *v. t.* or *i.*	عَمَّقَ . زَادَ عُمْقًا	Defensive *a.*	دِفَاعِيٌّ

Defer v. t.	أَمْهَلَ . أَخَّرَ . أَجَّلَ
Deference n.	إِحْتِرَامٌ . إِعْتِبَارٌ
Deferential a.	إِحْتِرَامِيٌّ
Defiance n.	تَحَدٍّ . تَعْيِيرٌ
Deficiency n.	نَقْصٌ . قُصُورٌ
Deficient a.	نَاقِصٌ . قَاصِرٌ
Deficit n.	نَقْصٌ فِي ٱلْمَالِ
Defile v. t. or i.	دَنَّسَ . مَشَى صَفًّا
Defile n.	مَضِيقٌ
Defilement n.	نَجَاسَةٌ . تَدْنِيسٌ
Definable a.	قَابِلُ ٱلتَّحْدِيدِ
Define v. t.	حَدَّدَ . عَرَّفَ . بَيَّنَ
Definite a.	مَحْدُودٌ . وَاضِحٌ
Definition n.	حَدٌّ . تَعْرِيفٌ
Definitive a.	مُحَدِّدٌ . قَاطِعٌ . جَازِمٌ
Deflect v. t. or i.	حَرَّفَ . إِنْحَرَفَ
Deflection n.	تَحْرِيفٌ . إِنْحِرَافٌ
Deform v. t.	شَوَّهَ . بَشَّعَ

Deformed a.	مُشَوَّهٌ . مَعْيُوبُ ٱلْخِلْقَةِ
Deformity n.	عَيْبُ ٱلْخِلْقَةِ
Defraud v. t.	غَبَنَ ـ . خَدَعَ ـ
Defry v. t.	قَامَ بِٱلنَّفَقَةِ
Defunct a.	مُتَوَفًّى . مَيِّتٌ
Defy v. t.	تَحَدَّى . بَارَزَ . عَيَّرَ
Degenerate a. or v. i	مُنْحَطٌّ . إِنْحَطَّ . فَسَدَ
Degeneracy Degeneration } n.	فَسَادٌ . إِنْحِطَاطٌ
Degradation n.	ذُلٌّ . هَوَانٌ
Degrade v. t.	اذَلَّ . حَطَّ ٱلشَّانَ ـ
Degraded a.	مُذَلٌّ . مُحْتَقَرٌ
Degrading a.	مُذِلٌّ . شَائِنٌ
Degree n.	رُتْبَةٌ . دَرَجَةٌ
Deify v. t.	أَلَّهَ
Deign v. i.	تَنَازَلَ . تَكَرَّمَ
Deism n.	إِعْتِقَادٌ بِٱللهِ دُونَ ٱلْوَحْيِ
Deist n.	مُعْتَقِدٌ بِٱللهِ دُونَ ٱلْوَحْيِ
Deity n.	الوهِيَّةٌ . إِلهٌ

Deject v. t.	اغم . بَرَّدَ هِمَّته
Dejected a.	كَثِيبٌ . مَغْمُومٌ
Dejection n.	غَمٌّ . كَآبَةٌ
Delay v.t. or n.	أَخَّرَ . أَعَاقَ . تَأَخُّرٌ
Delectable a.	مُبْهِجٌ . سَارٌّ جِدًّا
Delegate v. t. or n.	فَوَّضَ . نَائِبٌ . رَسُولٌ
Delegation n.	تَفْوِيضٌ . جَمَاعَةُ نُوَّابٍ
Deleterious a.	ضَارٌّ . مُؤْذٍ . مُهْلِكٌ
Deliberate v. i. or t.	تَأَمَّلَ . تَبَصَّرَ
Deliberate a.	مُتَمَهِّلٌ . مَقْصُودٌ . مُتَأَمِّلٌ
Deliberately ad.	مُتَمَهِّلاً . عَمْداً
Deliberation n.	تَأَمُّلٌ . تَبَصُّرٌ . تَمَهُّلٌ
Delicacy n.	رِقَّةٌ . حِشْمَةٌ . لَذَّةٌ
Delicate a.	غَضٌّ . لَطِيفٌ . لَذِيذٌ
Delicious a.	شَهِيٌّ . لَذِيذٌ
Delight n. or v.i.	بَهْجَةٌ . إِبْتَهَجَ
Delighted a.	مُبْتَهِجٌ . مَسْرُورٌ جِدًّا
Delightful a.	مُبْهِجٌ . سَارٌّ
Delineate v. t.	رَسَمَ ـ صَوَّرَ . وَصَفَ ـ
Delineation n.	رَسْمٌ . وَصْفٌ
Delinquency n.	قُصُورٌ . خَطَآءٌ
Delinquent a.	مُقَصِّرٌ . مُذْنِبٌ
Delirious a.	هَاذٍ
Delirium n.	هَذَيَانٌ (بُحْرَانٌ)
Deliver v. t.	نَجَّى . اطْلَقَ . سَلَّمَ
Deliverance n.	نَجَاةٌ . إِطْلاقٌ . تَخْلِيصٌ
Delivery n.	نَجَاةٌ . تَسْلِيمٌ . وِلَادَةٌ
Dell n.	وَادٍ صَغِيرٌ
Delta n.	قِطْعَةُ أَرْضٍ مُثَلَّثَةٌ
Delude v. t.	خَدَعَ ـ أَغْوَى . اضَلَّ ـ
Deluge n. or v. t.	طُوفَانٌ . غَمَرَ ـ
Delusion n.	وَهْمٌ . ضَلَالٌ . غُرُورٌ
Delusive a.	خَادِعٌ . مُضِلٌّ
Demagogue n.	زَعِيمُ ٱلْعَوَامِّ . مُهَيِّجُهُمْ
Demand v.t. or n.	طَلَبَ ـ طَلَبٌ
Demarcation Demarkation n.	تَخْطِيطُ ٱلْحُدُود

Demean v. t.	سَلَكَ ـُ . تَصَرَّفَ . دَنَّا
Demeanor n.	سُلُوك . تَصَرُّف
Demented a.	مُخْتَلُّ ٱلْعَقْلِ
Demerit n.	نَقْصٌ ادبِيٌّ . قُصُور
Demigod n.	نِصْفُ إِلهٍ . بَطَل
Demise n.	وَفَاة . مَوْت
Democracy n.	حُكْمٌ جُمْهُورِيٌّ
Democrat n.	أَحَدُ حِزْبِ ٱلْجُمْهُورِيِّين
Democratic Democratical } a.	جُمْهُورِيٌّ
Demolish v. t.	هَدَمَ ـِ . هَدَّ ـُ
Demolition n.	هَدْم . هَدّ
Demon n.	جِنِّيٌّ . رُوحٌ نَجِس
Demoniac n.	مَنْ بِهِ رُوحٌ نَجِس مَجْنُون
Demonstrate v. t.	بَرْهَنَ . أَثْبَتَ
Demonstration n.	إِثْبَات . دَلَالَة
Demonstrative a.	دَالٌّ مُظْهِرٌ عَوَاطِفَهُ
Demoralization n.	فَسَادُ ٱلآدَاب

Demoralize v. t.	افْسَدَ ٱلآدَابَ او النخْوَة
Demur v. i.	تَرَدَّدَ فِي . تَأَخَّرَ
Den n.	عَرِينٌ . عَرِّيس
Denial n.	إِنْكَار . رَفْض
Denizen n.	سَاكِن
Denominate v. t.	لَقَّبَ . سَمَّى
Denomination n.	تَسْمِية . طَائِفَة
Denominator n.	مَخْرَجُ ٱلْكُسُور
Denote v. t.	أَشَارَ إِلَى . دَلَّ عَلَى
Denounce v. t.	شَهَّرَ . إِشْتَكَى على
Dense a.	كَثِيف . مُلْتَفّ . مُتَلَبِّد
Density n.	كَثَافَة
Dent n. or v. t.	نَقِيرَة . نَقَرَ قَلِيلاً
Dental a.	سِنِّيٌّ او ضِرْسِيٌّ
Dentate n.	ذُو اسْنَان
Dentiform a.	شَبِيهٌ بالسِّنِّ
Dentist n.	طَبِيبُ ٱلأَسْنَان
Dentistry n.	طِبُّ ٱلاسْنَان

Dentition *n.*	زَمَنُ ٱلتَّسْنِينِ . بُرُوزُ ٱلْأَسْنَانِ
Denude *v. t.*	عَرَّى . جَرَّدَ
Denunciation *n.*	تَعْدِيلٌ . تَهْدِيدٌ
Deny *v. t.*	أَنْكَرَ . رَفَضَ طَلَبًا
Deodorize *v. t.*	أَزَالَ ٱلرَّائِحَة
Depart *v. i.*	ذَهَبَ ـَ رَحَلَ
Department *n.*	دَائِرَةُ أَعْمَالٍ . قِسْمٌ
Departure *n.*	ذَهَابٌ . رَحِيلٌ
Depend *v. i.*	إِسْتَنَدَ إِلَى . وَثِقَ بِ . تَدَلَّى
Dependence *n.*	إِتِّكَالٌ . إِسْتِنَادٌ . تَعَلُّقٌ
Dependent *a.*	مُسْتَنِدٌ . تَابِعٌ وَخَاضِعٌ لِ
Depict *v. t.*	صَوَّرَ . وَصَفَ ـِ
Deplorable *a.*	مُحْزِنٌ . مَا يُرْثَى لَهُ
Deplore *v. t.*	اسِفَ ـَ عَلَى . حَزِنَ عَلَى
Depopulate *v. t.*	قَرَضَ ٱلسُّكَّانَ
Depopulation *n.*	إِنْقِرَاضُ ٱلسُّكَّانِ

Deport *v. t.*	تَصَرَّفَ . نَقَلَ . نَفَى
Deportation *n.*	إِجْلَاءُ ٱلسُّكَّانِ
Deportment *n.*	تَصَرُّفٌ . سُلُوكٌ
Depose *v. t. or i.*	عَزَلَ ـِ شَهِدَ ـَ
Deposit *v. t. or n.*	أَوْدَعَ . وَضَعَ ـَ وَدِيعَةٌ
Deposition *n.*	عَزْلٌ . شَهَادَةٌ
Depository *n.*	مَخْزَنٌ . مُسْتَوْدَعٌ
Depot *n.*	مَخْزَنٌ . مَحَطَّةٌ
Deprave *v. t.*	أَفْسَدَ
Depraved *a.*	فَاسِدٌ . شِرِّيرٌ
Depravity *n.*	فَسَادٌ . شَرٌّ
Deprecate *v. t.*	تَوَسَّلَ . أَسِفَ عَلَى
Depreciate *v. t. or i.*	وَكَّسَ . وَكَسَ
Depreciation *n.*	إِسْتِخْفَافٌ . هُبُوطُ ٱلْقِيمَةِ
Depredation *n.*	سَلْبٌ . نَهْبٌ
Depress *v. t.*	خَفَضَ . أَذَلَّ . أَغَمَّ
Depressing *a.*	مُكَدِّرٌ . مُغِمٌّ

Depression n. تَخَفُّضٌ . كَآبَةٌ . كَسَادٌ	Dervish n. دَرْوِيشٌ
Depriva-tion n. نَزْعٌ . فُقْدَانٌ . حِرْمَانٌ	Descend v. i. نَزَلَ ـِ . إِنْحَدَرَ
Deprive v. t. أَخَذَ مِنْ . نَزَعَ ـِ	Descendant n. سَلِيلٌ . أَحَدُ الذُّرِّيَّةِ
Depth n. عُمْقٌ	Descent n. نُزُولٌ . أُحْدُورٌ
Deputation n. تَوْكِيلٌ . وَفْدٌ	Describe v. t. وَصَفَ ـِ . أَوْضَحَ
Depute v. t. وَكَّلَ . أَوْفَدَ	Description n. وَصْفٌ
Deputy n. نَائِبٌ . وَكِيلٌ . وَافِدٌ	Descriptive a. وَصْفِيٌّ . وَاصِفٌ
Derange v. t. قَلَبَ ـِ . شَوَّشَ	Descry v. t. رَأَى . او مِنْ بَعِيدٍ
Deranged a. مَقْلُوبٌ . مُشَوَّشٌ . مُخْتَلٌّ	Desecrate v. t. نَجَّسَ . دَنَّسَ
Derangement n. تَشْوِيشٌ . إِخْتِلَالٌ	Desert v. t. or i. تَرَكَ ـُ . هَجَرَ ـُ
Deride v. t. إِزْدَرَى بِ . هَزَأَ بِ ـَ	Desert n. قَفْرٌ . صَحْرَآءُ . إِسْتِحْقَاقٌ
Derisive / Derisory a. إِسْتِهْزَائِيٌّ . إِزْدِرَائِيٌّ	Deserter n. هَارِبٌ . آبِقٌ
Derision n. إِزْدِرَآءٌ . هُزْءٌ	Deserve v. t. إِسْتَحَقَّ . إِسْتَوْجَبَ
Derivation n. إِشْتِقَاقٌ	Desiccate v. t. نَشَّفَ . جَفَّفَ
Derivative a. or n. مُشْتَقٌّ	Desideratum n. مَطْلُوبٌ . بُغْيَةٌ
Derive v. t. إِشْتَقَّ . إِسْتَخْرَجَ مِنْ	قَصَدَ ـُ . نَوَى ـِ . قَصْدٌ
Derogate v. t. or i. نَقَصَ . إِسْتَخَفَّ بِ	Design v. t. or n. رَسَمَ ـُ . رَسْمٌ
Derogative / Derogatory a. مُسْتَخِفٌّ . مُسْتَحْقِرٌ	Designate v. t. أَشَارَ إِلَى . عَيَّنَ . دَلَّ

Designation _n._	تَعْيِينٌ . دَلَالَةٌ
Designedly _ad._	قَصْدًا . عَمْدًا
Designer _n._	مُسْتَنْبِطٌ . رَاسِمٌ . مُصَوِّرٌ
Designing _a._	رَاسِمٌ . مُحْتَالٌ . دَاهٍ
Desirable _a._	مَرْغُوبٌ . مُبْتَغًى
Desire _n._ or _v. t._	رَغْبَةٌ . بُغْيَةٌ . إِبْتَغَى
Desirous _a._	رَاغِبٌ . مُبْتَغٍ
Desist _v. i._	كَفَّ عَنْ ُ . عَدَلَ عَنْ
Desistance _n._	تَرْكٌ . كَفٌّ عَنْ
Desk _n._	مَائِدَةٌ لِلْكِتَابَةِ
Desolate _v. t._ or _a._	دَمَّرَ . خَرَّبَ . مُقْفِرٌ
Desolation _n._	دَمَارٌ . وَحْشَةٌ . خَرَابٌ
Despair _v. i._ or _n._	يَئِسَ ـ . يَأْسٌ . قُنُوطٌ
Despairing _a._	يَآئِسٌ . بِلَا رَجَاءٍ
Despatch _see_ Dispatch.	
Desperado _n._ Desperate _a._	يَآئِسٌ . فَاتِكٌ . هَائِجٌ
Desperation _n._	يَأْسٌ . قُنُوطٌ
Despicable _a._	خَسِيسٌ . مُحْتَقَرٌ . مُهَانٌ
Despise _v. t._	إِحْتَقَرَ . اهَانَ

Despite _n._	ضَغِينَةٌ . حِقْدٌ
Despite of.	رَغْمًا عَنْ
Despoil _v. t._	نَهَبَ . سَلَبَ
Despond _v. i._	يَئِسَ ـ قَنِطَ
Despondency _n._	يَأْسٌ . قُنُوطٌ
Despondent Desponding _a._	خَائِبُ الْأَمَلِ . قَانِطٌ
Despot _n._ Despotic _a._	حَاكِمٌ مُطْلَقٌ . ظَالِمٌ
Despotism _n._	سُلْطَةٌ مُطْلَقَةٌ . ظُلْمٌ
Dessert _n._	فَاكِهَةٌ أَوْ حَلْوَى بَعْدُ الطَّعَامِ
Destination _a._	مَكَانٌ مَقْصُودٌ
Destinate Destine _v. t._	قَدَّرَ . عَيَّنَ . خَصَّصَ
Destiny _n._	قَدَرٌ . قِسْمَةٌ . نَصِيبٌ
Destitute _a._	مُحْتَاجٌ . خَالٍ مِنْ . فَقِيرٌ
Destitution _n._	فَاقَةٌ . عَوَزٌ
Destroy _v. t._	اهْلَكَ . أَبَادَ . ازَالَ
Destruction _n._	إِبَادَةٌ . هَلَاكٌ
Destructive _a._	مُهْلِكٌ . مُمِيتٌ
Desultory _a._	غَيْرُ مُنْتَظِمٍ . مُنْقَطِعٌ

Detach v. t.	فَصَلَ ـ فَكَّ ـ	Detestable a.	مَكْرُوهَة . مَمْقُوتْ
Detachment n.	سَرِيَّةٌ مِنَ ٱلْجُنْدِ	Detestation n.	كُرْهٌ . مَقْتٌ
Detail n. or v. t.	تَفْصِيلٌ . اسْهَابٌ . اسْهَبَ	Dethrone v. t.	خَلَعَ عَنِ ٱلْمُلْكِ
Detain v. t.	حَجَزَ ـ . صَدَّ ـ . مَنَعَ ـ	Dethronement n.	خَلْعٌ
Detect v. t.	كَشَفَ ـ . وَجَدَ ـ	Detonation n.	صَوْتُ ٱنْفِجَارٍ
Detection n.	كَشْفٌ . إِظْهَارٌ	Detour n.	دَوْرَةٌ
Detention n.	حَجْزٌ . تَوْقِيفٌ . تَأْخِيرٌ	Detract v. t.	قَلَّلَ . ذَمَّ ـ
Deter v. t.	أَعَاقَ . صَدَّ . مَنَعَ ـ	Detraction n.	ذَمٌّ . نَمِيمَةٌ
Deteriorate v. i.	إِنْحَطَّ . فَسَدَ ـ	Detriment n.	ضَرَرٌ . خَسَارَةٌ
Deterioration n.	إِنْحِطَاطٌ . فَسَادٌ	Detrimental a.	مُضِرٌّ
Determinable a.	قَابِلُ التَّحْدِيدِ أَوِ التَّعْرِيفِ	Deuteronomy n.	سِفْرُ التَّثْنِيَةِ
Determinate a.	مَحْدُودٌ . جَازِمٌ	Devastate v. t.	خَرَّبَ . دَمَّرَ
Determination n.	تَحْدِيدٌ . عَزْمٌ . حُكْمٌ	Devastation n.	تَخْرِيبٌ . دَمَارٌ
Determine v. t.	حَكَمَ فِي . عَزَمَ عَلَى حَقَّقَ	Develop v. i. or t.	نَشَأَ ـ . إِنْتَشَرَ ـ نَشَرَ
		Development n.	نُشُوءٌ . نَشْرٌ
Determined a.	عَزُومٌ . مَحْكُومٌ بِهِ	Deviate v. i.	حَادَ ـ . مَالَ ـ
		Deviation n.	إِنْحِرَافٌ . حَيَدَانٌ
Detest v. t.	كَرِهَ ـ . مَقَتَ ـ	Device n.	حِيلَةٌ . تَدْبِيرٌ . عَلَامَةٌ

Devil *n.*	شَيْطَان
Devilish *a.*	شَيْطَانِيٌّ . خَبِيثٌ
Deviltry *n.*	شَيْطَنَة . تَصَرُّفٌ شَيْطَانِيٌّ
Devious *a.*	زَائِغٌ . مُنْحَرِفٌ مُعْوَجٌّ
Devise *v. t.*	دَبَّرَ . إِخْتَرَعَ . وَصَّى بَعْدَ المَوْتِ
Devoid *a.*	خَالٍ . مُجَرَّدٌ . فَارِغٌ
Devolve *v. t.* or *i.*	كَلَّفَ . سَلَّمَ . إِنْتَقَلَ
Devote *v. t.*	أَفْرَزَ . خَصَّصَ
Devoted *a.*	مُفْرَزٌ
Devotedness *n.*	غَيْرَةٌ . وُلُوعٌ
Devotee *n.*	زَاهِدٌ . مُتَعَبِّدٌ
Devotion *n.*	غَيْرَةٌ . عِبَادَة
Devour *v. t.*	إِبْتَلَعَ . إِفْتَرَسَ
Devout *a.*	دَيِّنٌ . تَقِيٌّ
Dew *n.*	نَدًى . طَلٌّ
Dexterity *n.*	خِفَّةٌ . مَهَارَة
Dexterous *a.*	خَفِيفٌ . مَاهِرٌ

Diabolic Diabolical } *a.*	شَيْطَانِيٌّ خَبِيثٌ
Diadem *n.*	تَاجٌ . عِصَابَة
Diagnosis *n.*	تَشْخِيصٌ
Diagonal *n.*	خَطٌّ بَيْنَ زَاوِيَتَيْنِ مُتَقَابِلَتَيْنِ
Diagram *n.*	رَسْمٌ . شَكْلٌ هَنْدَسِيٌّ
Dial *n.*	مِينَا سَاعَةٍ . شَمْسِيَّة
Dialect *n.*	لُغَة . لَهْجَة
Dialectic Dialectical } *a.*	نُطْقِيٌّ . لَهْجِيٌّ
Dialogue *n.*	مُحَاوَرَةٌ . مُكَالَمَة
Diameter *n.*	قُطْرُ دَائِرَةٍ
Diametrical *a.*	قُطْرِيًّا أَبْعَدُ مَا يُمْكِنُ
Diamond *n.*	مَاسٌ
Diaphragm *n.*	حِجَابٌ . الْحِجَابُ الْحَاجِزُ (فِي الطِّبِّ)
Diarrhœa *n.*	إِسْهَالٌ
Diary *n.*	يَوْمِيَّة
Dice *n. pl. of* Die	زَهْرُ النَّرْدِ
Dicephalous *a.*	ذُو رَأْسَيْنِ

Dictate *v.* or *n.*	أَمْلَى عَلَى . أَمَرَ ـُ . أَمْر
Dictation *n.*	إِمْلَاء . أَمْر
Dictator *n.*	مُطْلَقُ ٱلسُّلْطَةِ
Dictatorial *a.*	مُسْتَبِدّ
Diction *n.*	أُسْلُوبُ ٱلْكَلَامِ
Dictionary *n.*	قَامُوس ج قَوَامِيس
Dictum *n.*	قَوْلٌ جَازِمٌ
Didactic Didactical } *a.*	تَعْلِيمِيّ . مُوَافِق لِلتَّعْلِيمِ
Die *v. i.*	مَاتَ ـُ . تُوُفِّيَ
Diet *n.* or *v. i.*	طَعَام . إِحْتَمَى بِالطَّعَامِ
Differ *v. i.*	إِخْتَلَفَ . تَبَايَنَ
Difference *n.*	إِخْتِلَاف . فَرْق
Different *a.*	مُخْتَلَف
Difficult *a.*	صَعْب . عَسِر . شَاقّ
Difficulty *n.*	صُعُوبَة . عَائِقَة . إِرْتِبَاك
Diffident *a.*	غَيْر وَاثِق بِنَفْسِهِ
Diffuse *v. t.* or *a.*	نَشَرَ ـُ مُنْتَشِر . مُسْهِب
Diffusion *n.*	نَشْر . إِمْتِدَاد
Diffusive *a.*	مُمْتَدّ . مُنْتَشِر . مُسْهِب
Dig *v. t.* or *i.* (dug)	حَفَرَ ـِ . نَقَبَ ـُ
Digest *v. t.* or *n.*	هَضَمَ ـِ . مَجْمُوعُ شَرَائِع
Digestible *a.*	سَهْلُ ٱلْهَضْمِ
Digestion *n.*	هَضْم
Digestive *a.*	هَاضِم
Dignified *a.*	ذُو وَقَار
Dignify *v.t.*	كَرَّمَ . شَرَّفَ . وَقَّرَ
Dignitary *n.*	صَاحِبُ رُتْبَةٍ عَالِيَةٍ
Dignity *n.*	وَقَار . كَرَامَة . جَاه
Digress *v. i.*	حَادَ ـِ . إِسْتَطْرَدَ
Digression *n.*	حَيَدَان . إِسْتِطْرَاد
Digressive *a.*	مُسْتَطْرِد . مُعْتَسِف
Dike *n.*	سَدّ . خَنْدَق
Dilapidated *a.*	خَرِب . مُتَسَاقِط
Dilate *v. t.* or *i.*	وَسَّعَ . مَدَّ ـُ . إِتَّسَعَ
Dilatory *a.*	بَطِيّ . مُتَكَاسِل . مُتَرَاخٍ
Dilemma *n.*	مُشْكِل . وَرْطَة

Diligence n.	جَدٌّ . مُثَابَرَةٌ . مُوَاظَبَةٌ
Diligent a.	مُجْتَهِدٌ . مُثَابِرٌ
Dilute v. t.	خَفَّفَ سَائِلاً . أَضَافَ مَاءً
Dilution n.	تَخْفِيفٌ
Dim a. or v. t.	مُظْلِمٌ . مُكَدَّرٌ . كَدَّرَ
Dimension n.	قِيَاسٌ . إِمْتِدَادٌ . قَدْرٌ
Diminish v. t. or i.	قَلَّلَ . نَقَصَ . قَلَّ . نَقَصَ
Diminution n.	تَقْلِيلٌ . نَقْصٌ
Diminutive n. or a.	إِسْمُ التَّصْغِيرِ . صَغِيرٌ جِدًّا
Dimly ad.	مُكَدَّرًا
Dimple n.	نُونَةٌ . (غَمَّازَةٌ)
Dimpled a.	ذُو نُونَاتٍ
Din n. or v. t.	صَخَبٌ . قَعْقَعَةٌ . قَعْقَعَ
Dine v. i.	تَغَدَّى . تَعَشَّى
Dinginess n.	غُبْسَةٌ
Dingy a.	مُكَمَّدُ اللَّوْنِ
Dinner n.	غَدَاءٌ . فَطُورٌ
Diocese n.	أَبْرَشِيَّةٌ
Dip v. t. or n.	غَمَسَ _ . حُدُورٌ
Diphthong n.	إِجْتِمَاعُ حَرْفَيْ عِلَّةٍ بِصَوْتٍ وَاحِدٍ
Diploma n.	شَهَادَةٌ مَدْرَسِيَّةٌ
Diplomacy n.	سِيَاسَةُ الدُّوَلِ
Diplomatic a.	مُخْتَصٌّ بِالسِّيَاسَةِ
Diplomatist n.	خَبِيرٌ بِالسِّيَاسَةِ الدَّوْلِيَّةِ
Dipper n.	غَاطِسٌ . مِغْرَفَةٌ
Dire a.	هَائِلٌ . مُرْعِبٌ
Direct v. t. or a.	أَرْشَدَ . أَدَارَ . أَمَرَ _ . مُسْتَقِيمٌ
Direction n.	جِهَةٌ . إِرْشَادٌ . أَمْرٌ
Directly ad.	رَأْساً . بِإِسْتِقَامَةٍ . حَالاً
Directness n.	إِسْتِقَامَةٌ . خُلُوصٌ
Director n.	مُدِيرٌ . مُدَبِّرٌ . نَاظِرٌ
Directory n.	جَمَاعَةُ مُدِيرِينَ كِتَابٌ مُرْشِدٌ . دَلِيلٌ
Direful a.	هَائِلٌ . رَائِعٌ

Dirge n.	تَرْنِيمَةُ جَنَازَةٍ
Dirk n.	خِنْجَرٌ ج خَنَاجِرُ
Dirt n.	وَسَخٌ . قَذَرٌ
Dirtly a.	وَسِخٌ . قَذِرٌ
Disability n.	عَجْزٌ . عَدَمُ ٱقْتِدَارٍ
Disable v. t.	اعْجَزَ . أَوْهَنَ
Disabuse v. t.	بَيَّنَ غَلَطَهُ . أَصْلَحَ فِكْرَهُ
Disadvantage n.	خِسَارَةٌ . عَاقَةٌ
Disadvantageous a.	غَيْرُ نَافِعٍ
Disaffected a.	فَاتِرُ ٱلْمَحَبَّةِ . سَاخِطٌ
Disagree v. i.	تَخَالَفَ
Disagreeable a.	غَيْرُ مُرْضٍ . غَيْرُ مَقْبُولٍ
Disagreement n.	إِخْتِلَافٌ . إِنْشِقَاقٌ
Disallow v. t.	أَنْكَرَ عَلَى . رَفَضَ
Disappear v. i.	غَابَ . تَوَارَى
Disappearance n.	مُوَارَاةٌ . إِخْتِفَاءٌ
Disappoint v. t.	خَيَّبَ . خَذَلَ
Disappointment n.	خَيْبَةٌ . خِذْلَانٌ
Disapprobation } n. Disapproval }	إِنْكَارٌ عَلَى عَدَمُ رِضًى
Disapprove v. t.	أَنْكَرَ عَلَى . عَابَ
Disarm v. t.	جَرَّدَ مِنَ ٱلسِّلَاحِ نَزَعَ ٱلْقُوَّةَ
Disarrange v. t.	أَخَلَّ بِالتَّرْتِيبِ . قَلَبَ
Disaster n.	مُصِيبَةٌ . نَازِلَةٌ . نَكْبَةٌ
Disastrous a.	مَشْؤُومٌ . جَالِبُ مُصِيبَةٍ
Disavow v. t.	أَنْكَرَ . رَفَضَ
Disavowal n.	إِنْكَارٌ . رَفْضٌ
Disband v. t.	فَضَّ . فَرَّقَ
Disbelief n.	عَدَمُ تَصْدِيقٍ
Disbelieve v. t.	أَنْكَرَ . كَفَرَ
Disburden v. t.	نَزَعَ حِمْلَهُ
Disburse v. t.	أَنْفَقَ . صَرَفَ
Disbursement n.	إِنْفَاقٌ . صَرْفٌ
Disc n. see Disk.	
Discard v. t.	رَفَضَ . أَبْعَدَ . طَرَحَ
Discern v. t.	رَأَى . مَيَّزَ

Discernible a.	مُمْكِنٌ مُشَاهَدَتُه
Discerning a.	مُمَيِّزٌ . بَصِيرٌ
Discernment n.	تَمْيِيز . إِدْرَاكٌ. فِطْنَة
Discharge v. t. or n.	أَطْلَقَ.طَرَدَ.صَرَفَ أَجْرَى . تَخْلِيَة
Disciple n.	تِلْمِيذ ج تَلَامِيذ وَتَلَامِذَة
Disciplinary a.	تَأْدِيبِيٌّ
Disicpline. v. t. or n.	أَدَّبَ ,هَذَّبَ . تَأْدِيب
Disclaim v. t.	أَنْكَرَ . رَفَضَ ـُ
Disclose v. t.	أَظْهَرَ . بَيَّنَ . أَعْلَنَ
Disclosure n.	إِظْهَارٌ. إِعْلَانٌ.إِبَاحَة
Discolour v. t.	غَيَّرَ لَوْنَهُ . لَطَّخَ
Discomfit v. t.	هَزَمَ ـِ . كَسَرَ ـِ
Discomfiture n.	هَزِيمَة .خَيْبَة
Discomfort n.	كَدَرٌ. عَدَمُ رَاحَةٍ
Discommode v. t.	أَقْلَقَ . ثَقَلَ عَلَى
Discompose v. t.	شَوَّشَ . بَلْبَلَ
Disconcert v. t.	أَقْلَقَ . حَيَّرَ
Disconnect v. t.	فَصَلَ ـِ . قَطَعَ ـَ
Disconsolate a.	كَئِيبٌ . حَزِينٌ
Discontented a.	غَيْرُ رَاضٍ. ضَجِرٌ
Discontent Discontentment } n.	عَدَمُ رِضًى ضَجَرٌ
Discontinue v. t. or i.	أَبْطَلَ . إِنْقَطَعَ
Discontinuous a.	مُنْقَطِعٌ
Discord n.	خِصَامٌ . عَدَمُ إِتِّفَاقٍ
Discordant a.	غَيْرُ مُتَّفِق . مُغَايِرٌ
Discount v. t. or n.	خَفْضُ الثَّمَنَ. إِسْقَاطٌ (خَصْمٌ)
Discountenance v. t.	عَارَضَ.قَاوَمَ
Discourage v. t.	بَرَّدَ هِمَّتَه
Discouragement n.	فَشَّلَ . ضَعْفُ الْعَزْم
Discouraging a.	مُضْعِفُ الْعَزْم وَالرَّجَاءِ
Discourse n. or v.i.	خِطَابٌ. خَاطَبَ
Discourtesy n.	سُوءُ الآدَب . فَظَاظَةٌ

Discover v. t.	كَشَفَ ـ وَجَدَ ـ إِكْتَشَفَ
Discovery n.	إِكْتِشَافٌ . إِخْتِرَاعٌ
Discredit v. t. or n.	لَمْ يُصَدِّقْ . شَيْنٌ
Discreditable a.	شَائِنٌ . مُخِلٌّ بِالشَّرَفِ
Discreet a.	عَاقِلٌ . حَازِمٌ
Discreetness Discretion } n.	تَعَقُّلٌ . بَصِيرَةٌ . تَمْيِيزٌ
Discretionary a.	مَتْرُوكٌ لِحُكْمِهِ
Discrepance Discrepancy } n.	إِخْتِلَافٌ . مُغَايَرَةٌ
Discriminate v. t.	مَيَّزَ بَيْنَ
Discuss v. t.	بَحَثَ ـ فِي او بَاحَثَ
Discussion n.	مُبَاحَثَة
Disdain v. t. or n.	إِزْدَرَى بِ . إِحْتِقَارٌ
Disdainful a.	مُسْتَحْقِرٌ . مُتَعَجْرِفٌ
Disease n.	مَرَضٌ . دَاءٌ . عِلَّة
Diseased a.	مَرِيضٌ . سَقِيم
Disembark v. t. or i.	نَزَّلَ أَوْ نَزَلَ مِنْ سَفِينَةٍ
Disembarrass v. t.	أَزَالَ ارْتِبَاكًا

Disenchant v.t.	حَرَّرَ مِنْ سِحْرٍ او رُقْيَةٍ
Disencumber v. t.	حَرَّرَ مِنْ أَثْقَال
Disengage v. t.	فَكَّ مِنْ عَهْدٍ . أَطْلَقَ
Disentangle v. t.	فَكَّ ـُ . حَلَّ ـُ
Disfavour n.	عَدَمُ قُبُولٍ . نُفُورٌ
Disfiguration n.	تَشْوِية
Disfigure v. t.	شَوَّهَ . أَخَلَّ بِالهَيْئَةِ
Disfranchise v. t.	نَزَعَ الحُقُوقَ السِّيَاسِيَّة
Disgorge v. t.	أَخْرَجَ . قَذَفَ . إِسْتَفْرَغَ
Disgrace v. t. or n.	فَضَحَ ـَ . شَانَ . عَيَّبَ . عَارٌ
Disgraceful a.	شَائِنٌ . مُعِيبٌ
Disguise v.t. or n.	سَتَّرَ . اخْفَى . تَسَتَّرَ . تَنَكَّرَ
Disgust n. or v. t.	كُرْهٌ . قَزَّزَ
Disgusting a.	مُقَزِّزٌ . كَرِيهة
Dish n.	صَحْنٌ . قَصْعَةٌ . طَبَقٌ
Dishearten v. t.	أَضْعَفَ العَزْمَ او الهِمَّةَ
Dishonest a.	غَيْرُ أَمِين . غَابِنٌ

Dishonesty n.	غَبْنٌ . عَدَمُ أَمَانَةٍ
Dishonour n. or v. t.	هَوَانٌ . عَارٌ . أَهَانَ
Dishonorable a.	شَائِنٌ . مُعِيبٌ
Disinclination n.	مَيْلٌ عَنْ . نُفُورٌ
Disincline v. t.	أَمَالَ عَنْ . نَفَرَ
Disinfect v. t.	طَهَّرَ مِنْ أَسْبَابِ ٱلْعَدْوَى
Disingenuous a.	غَيْرُ مُخْلِصٍ
Disinherit v. t.	حَرَمَ مِنَ ٱلْإِرْثِ
Disintegrate v. t.	حَلَّ . فَرَّقَ أَجْزَاءَهُ
Disinterested a.	صَافِي النِّيَّةِ
Disjoin v. t.	فَصَلَ ـ
Disjoint v. t.	خَلَعَ ـ
Disk or Disc n.	قُرْصٌ ج اقْرَاصٌ
Dislike v. t. or n.	كَرِهَ ـ . سَئِمَ ـ
Dislocate v. t.	خَلَعَ ـ ازَاحَ
Dislocation n.	خَلْعٌ . إِزَاحَةٌ
Dislodge v. t.	أَخْرَجَ مِنْ مَكَانِهِ
Disloyal a.	خَائِنٌ . غَيْرُ امِينٍ
Disloyalty n.	خِيَانَةٌ عَدَمُ امَانَةٍ
Dismal a.	مُظْلِمٌ . مُغِمٌّ
Dismantle v. t.	عَرَّى . نَزَعَ أَدَوَاتِ التَّحْصِينِ
Dismast v. t.	نَزَعَ سَوَارِيَ سَفِينَةٍ
Dismay n. or v. t.	رَوْعٌ . رَوَّعَ
Dismember v. t.	فَصَلَ ـ ٱلْأَجْزَآءَ
Dismiss v. t.	صَرَفَ ـ . طَرَدَ ـ
Dismissal Dismission } n.	فَصْلٌ . عَزْلٌ
Dismount v. i. or t.	نَزَلَ عَنْ دَابَّةٍ . نَزَّلَ
Disobedience n.	عَدَمُ طَاعَةٍ . عِصْيَانٌ
Disobey v. t.	عَصَى ـ . خَالَفَ أَمْراً
Disoblige v. t.	خَالَفَ خَاطِرَهُ اوْ كَدَّرَهُ
Disorder n. or v. t.	تَشْوِيشٌ . شَوَّشَ
Disorderly a.	مُشَوَّشٌ . غَيْرُ مُنْتَظِمٍ
Disorganize v. t.	أَخَلَّ بِنِظَامٍ او تَرْتِيبٍ
Disown v. t.	رَفَضَ ـ . أَنْكَرَ
Disparage v. t.	عَبَّ . إِحْتَقَرَ

Dispassionate .	رَزِينٌ. هَادِئُ ٱلطَّبْعِ
Dispatch *v.t.*	اَرْسَلَ . أَنْجَزَ
Dispatch *n.*	سِرْعَةٌ . رِسَالَةٌ
Dispel *v. t.*	بَدَّدَ . ازَالَ
Dispensary *n.*	صَيْدَلِيَّةٌ. مَجَّانِيَّةٌ
Dispensation *n.*	نِظَامٌ . تَحْلِيلٌ إِجَازَةٌ
Dispense *v.t.*	اعْفَى مِنْ. وَزَّعَ. اجْرَى
Disperse *v. t.*	بَدَّدَ . شَتَّتَ
Dispersion *n.*	تَشْتِيتٌ . تَشَتُّتٌ
Dispirited *a.*	فَشِلٌ. مُنْكَسِرُ ٱلْعَزْمِ
Displace *v. t.*	أَزَاحَ مِنْ مَكَانِهِ
Displacement *n.*	إِزَاحَةٌ مِنْ مَكَانِهِ
Display *v.t.* or *n.*	اظْهَرَ. مَنْظَرٌ بَاطِلٌ
Displease *v. t.*	كَدَّرَ. غَمَّ. احْزَنَ
Displeasure *n.*	كَدَرٌ. غَمٌّ. (زَعَلٌ)
Disposal *n.*	تَصَرُّفٌ. تَرْتِيبٌ. تَدْبِيرٌ
Dispose *v. t.*	رَتَّبَ. تَصَرَّفَ فِي. امَالَ
Disposition *n.*	تَرْتِيبٌ. خُلْقٌ . مَيْلٌ
Dispossess *v. t.*	حَرَمَهُ مُلْكَهُ . سَلَبَ
Disproportion *n.*	عَدَمُ تَنَاسُبٍ او تَعَادُلٍ
Disproof *n.*	إِدْحَاضٌ. رَدٌّ
Disprove *v. t.*	أَدْحَضَ . رَدَّ
Disputable *a.*	قَابِلُ ٱلرَّدِّ. فِيهِ خِلَافٌ
Disputant *n.*	مُنَاظِرٌ . مُجَادِلٌ
Disputation *n.*	مُجَادَلَةٌ . مُنَاظَرَةٌ
Dispute *v. t.* or *i.*	جَادَلَ . نَازَعَ
Disqualify *v.t.*	ازَالَ اهْلِيَّتَهُ. اعْجَزَ
Disquiet *v. t.*	أَزْعَجَ . أَخَلَّ بِٱلرَّاحَةِ
Disregard *v. t.* or *n.*	إِسْتَخَفَّ بِهِ. إِهْمَالٌ
Disrelish *n.* or *v. t.*	كُرْهٌ . تَقَزَّزَ
Disreputable *a.*	شَائِنٌ. مُضِرٌّ بِٱلصِّيتِ
Disrepute *n.*	صِيتٌ رَدِيٌّ او مَعِيبٌ
Disrespect *n.*	جَفَاءٌ . عَدَمُ ٱحْتِرَامٍ
Disrespectful *a.*	جَافٍ . مُهِينٌ
Disrobe *v. t.*	خَلَعَ ٱلثِّيَابَ

Dissatisfaction n.	عَدَمُ الرِّضى
Dissatisfactory a.	غَيْرُ رَاضٍ
Dissatisfied a.	غَيْرُ رَاضٍ أَوْ مُكْتَفٍ
Dissatisfy v. t.	أَضْجَرَ . لَمْ يُرْضِ
Dissect v. t.	شَرَّحَ
Dissemble v. t. or i.	تَظَاهَرَ . تَسَتَّرَ . رَاءَى
Disseminate v. t.	بَثَّ ـُ . نَثَرَ ـُ
Dissension n.	إِنْشِقَاقٌ . نِزَاعٌ
Dissent v. i. or n.	خَالَفَ الرَّأْيَ . خِلَافٌ
Dissenter n.	مُخَالِفٌ خَاصَّةً فِي الدِّينِ
Dissertation n.	خِطَابٌ . مَقَالَةٌ
Dissever v. t.	فَصَلَ ـِ . قَطَعَ ـَ
Dissimilar a.	مُخْتَلِفٌ . غَيْرُ مُشَابِهٍ
Dissimilarity Dissimiltude } n.	إِخْتِلَافٌ
Dissimulation n.	تَظَاهُرٌ . رِيَاءٌ
Dissipate v. t.	بَذَّرَ . أَسْرَفَ . شَتَّتَ
Dissipated a.	مُتَشَتِّتٌ . خَلِيعٌ
Dissipation n.	خَلَاعَةٌ . لَهْوٌ . إِسْرَافٌ
Dissoluble a.	قَابِلُ الذَّوَبَانِ
Dissolute a.	خَلِيعٌ . فَاجِرٌ
Dissolution n.	إِنْحِلَالٌ . فَنَاءٌ . مَوْتٌ
Dissolve v. t. or i.	ذَوَّبَ . حَلَّ ـُ . ذَابَ ـُ
Dissolvent n.	مُحَلِّلٌ . مُذِيبٌ
Dissuade v. t.	ثَنَى عَنْ
Dissuasion n.	إِقْنَاعٌ بِالْعُدُولِ عَنْ
Dissuasive a.	مُمِيلٌ عَنْ . ثَانٍ عَنْ
Dissyllable n.	لَفْظَةٌ ذَاتُ مَقْطَعَيْنِ
Distaff n.	عِرْنَاسٌ ج عَرَانِيسُ
Distance n. or v. t.	بُعْدٌ . مَسَافَةٌ . سَبَقَ ـِ
Distant a.	بَعِيدٌ
Distaste n.	عَيْفٌ . كَرَاهَةٌ
Distasteful a.	كَرِيهَةٌ . غَيْرُ لَذِيذٍ
Distemper n.	مَرَضٌ . سُوءُ الْخُلُقِ
Distend v. t. or i.	وَسَّعَ . مَدَّدَ . إِنْتَفَخَ
Distill v. t. or i.	قَطَّرَ . تَقَطَّرَ
Distillery n.	مَعْمَلُ المُسْكِرَاتِ

Distinct a.	وَاضِحٌ . بَيِّنٌ . مُمْتَازٌ
Distinction n.	تَمْيِيزٌ . سُمُوٌّ . رِفْعَةٌ
Distinctive a.	مُمَيِّزٌ . فَاصِلٌ
Distinctly ad.	وَاضِحاً . بَيِّناً
Distinctness n.	وُضُوحٌ . صَرَاحَةٌ
Distinguish v. t.	مَيَّزَ . فَصَلَ بَيْنَ
Distinguished a.	مُمْتَازٌ . شَهِيرٌ
Distort v. t.	لَوَى . عَوَّجَ . حَرَّفَ
Distract v. t.	شَوَّشَ . حَيَّرَ . أَلْهَى
Distraction n.	تَشْوِيشٌ . لَهْوٌ
Distress n. or v.t.	ضِيقٌ . أَلَمٌ شَدِيدٌ . ضَايَقَ
Distressing / Distressful } a.	مُؤْلِمٌ . شَاقٌّ . مُكَدِّرٌ
Distribute v. t.	وَزَّعَ . قَسَّمَ
Distribution n.	تَوْزِيعٌ . تَقْسِيمٌ
District n.	اقْلِيمٌ . كُورَةٌ . مَرْكَزٌ
Distrust n. or v. t.	عَدَمُ ثِقَةٍ . إِرْتَابَ
Distrustful a.	غَيْرُ وَاثِقٍ . مُرْتَابٌ
Disturb v. t.	أَقْلَقَ . شَوَّشَ . ازْعَجَ
Disturbance n.	تَشْوِيشٌ . إِضْطِرَابٌ
Disunion n.	إِنْشِقَاقٌ . إِنْفِصَالٌ
Disunite v. t.	فَصَلَ . فَرَّقَ
Disuse v. t. or n.	أَهْمَلَ . إِهْمَالٌ
Ditch n.	خَنْدَقٌ . حُفْرَةٌ
Ditto n.	مِثْلُهُ . ذَاتُ الشَّيءِ
Diurnal a.	يَوْمِيٌّ . نَهَارِيٌّ
Divan n.	دِيوَانٌ . مَقْعَدٌ
Dive v. i. or n.	غَطَسَ . غَاصَ . غَطْسَةٌ
Diverge v. i.	إِفْتَرَقَ . إِنْحَرَفَ
Divergence n.	تَشَعُّبٌ . إِقْتِرَاقٌ
Divergent / Diverging } a.	مُفْتَرِقٌ . مُنْفَصِلٌ
Divers / Diverse } a.	مُخْتَلِفٌ . مُتَنَوِّعٌ
Diversify v. t.	نَوَّعَ . جَعَلَهُ أَشْكَالاً
Diversion n.	تَحْوِيلٌ . لَهْوٌ . تَسْلِيَةٌ
Diversity n.	تَنَوُّعٌ . تَعَدُّدُ الاشْكَال
Divert v. t.	أَلْهَى عَنْ . سَلَّى
Diverting a.	مُلْهٍ . مُسَلٍّ . مُحَوِّلٌ

Divest v. t.	عَرَّى . نَزَعَ ــَ
Divide v. t. ـ	قَسَمَ ــ . جَزَّأَ . فَصَلَ ــ
Dividend n.	حِصَّةٌ . اَلْعَدَدُ اَلْمَقْسُومُ
Divider n.	قَاسِمٌ . قَسَّامٌ
Divine a. or v. t.	إِلَهِيٌّ . تَكَهَّنَ
Divinity n.	أُلُوهِيَةٌ . لَاهُوتٌ
Divisible a.	قَابِلُ اَلْقِسْمَةِ
Division n.	قِسْمَةٌ . تَقْسِيمٌ . فِرْقَةٌ
Divisor n.	مَقْسُومٌ عَلَيْهِ
Divorce v. t. or n.	طَلَّقَ . طَلَاقٌ
Divulge v. t.	اذَاعَ . بَاحَ ب
Dizziness n.	دُوَارٌ . رَنَحٌ
Dizzy a.	مُصَابٌ بِالدَّوَارِ . مُتَرَنِّحٌ
Do v. t. (did, done).	عَمِلَ ــَ . فَعَلَ ــَ
Docile a.	سَهْلُ اَلتَّعْلِيمِ . مُطِيعٌ
Docility n.	إِنْقِيَادٌ
Dock n. or v.t.	مَرْبَطُ اَلسُّفُنِ . قَصَّرَ
Dockyard n.	تَرْسَخَانَةٌ

Doctor n.	طَبِيبٌ (دَكْتُورٌ)
Doctorate n.	رُتْبَةُ اَلدَّكْتُورِ
Doctrine n.	تَعْلِيمٌ دِينِيٌّ . عَقِيدَةٌ
Document n.	رَقِيمٌ . صَكٌّ
Doged v. t. or i.	جَانَبَ . تَنَحَّى عَنْ
Doe n.	ظَبْيَةٌ . اُنْثَى اَلْإِيِّلِ اوِ اَلْوَعْلِ
Doff v. t.	نَزَعَ ــَ كُسْوَةً
Dog n.	كَلْبٌ ج كِلَابٌ
Dog-days n. pl.	ايامُ اَلشِّعْرَى
Dogged a.	عَنِيدٌ . عَازِمٌ . فَظٌّ
Dogma n.	عَقِيدَةٌ . مَذْهَبٌ
Dogmatic } a. Dogmatical }	جَازِمُ اَلرَّأْيِ . تَجَبُّرٌ
Dogmatism n.	جَزْمُ اَلرَّأْيِ . تَجَبُّرٌ
Dogmatize v. t.	جَزَمَ فِي اَلرَّأْيِ
Dog-star n.	اَلشِّعْرَى (نَجَمَةٌ)
Dole n. or v.t.	نَصِيبٌ . هِبَةٌ حَقِيرَةٌ اعْطَى صَدَقَةً زَهِيدَةً
Doleful a.	مُغِمٌّ . مُحْزِنٌ

Doll n.	اَلعُوْبَة . لُعْبَة
Dollar n.	رِيَالٌ ج رِيَالَاتٌ
Dolorous a.	مُؤْلِمٌ . مُحْزِنٌ
Dolphin n.	دُلْفِيْنٌ ج دَلَافِيْنُ
Dolt n.	بَلِيْدٌ . أَبْلَهُ
Domain n.	مُلْكٌ . رِزْقٌ . مَمْلَكَةٌ
Dome n.	قُبَّةٌ
Domestic a.	بَيْتِيٌّ . عَائِلِيٌّ . دَاجِنٌ
Domesticate v. t.	دَجَّنَ . أَنَسَ
Domicile n. or v. t.	مَسْكَنٌ . مَقَامٌ . اسْكَنَ
Dominant a.	مُتَسَلِّطٌ . سَائِدٌ . شَائِعٌ
Domination n.	تَسَلُّطٌ . سِيَادَةٌ
Domineer v. i.	تَسَلُّطٌ . بِغَطْرَسَةٍ وَتَعَجْرُفٍ
Dominion n.	مَمْلَكَةٌ . تَسَلُّطٌ
Don v. t.	لَبِسَ ـ
Donate v. t.	مَنَحَ ـَ وَهَبَ . يَهَبُ
Donation n.	هِبَةٌ . هَدِيَّةٌ
Donkey n.	حِمَارٌ ج حَمِيْرٌ
Donor n.	وَاهِبٌ . مُعْطٍ
Doom n.	قَضَاءً . نَصِيْبٌ . هَلَاكٌ
Doomsday n.	يَوْمُ الدَّيْنُوْنَةِ
Door n.	بَابٌ . مَدْخَلٌ
Dormant n.	نَائِمٌ . غَيْرُ عَامِلٍ
Dormitory n.	غُرْفَةُ النَّوْمِ . مَنَامٌ
Dorsal a.	ظَهْرِيٌّ
Dose n. or v. t.	جَرْعَةٌ . سَقَى جُرْعَةً
Dot n. or v. t.	نُقْطَةٌ . نَقَطَ
Dotage n.	خَرَفٌ . ضَعْفُ العَقْلِ كِبَرًا
Dotard n.	خَرِفٌ
Dote v. i.	خَرِفَ ـَ وَلِعَ
Double a. or v. t.	مُزْدَوِجٌ . ضَاعَفَ
Double-dealing n.	خِدَاعٌ . مُخَاتَلَةٌ
Doubt n. or v. t.	شَكٌّ . رَيْبٌ . شَكَّ ـُ
Doubtful a.	مَشْكُوْكٌ فِيْهِ . مُرْتَابٌ
Doubtless ad.	بِلَا شَكٍّ أَوْ رَيْبٍ
Dough n.	عَجِيْنٌ

Dove n.	حَمَامَةٌ ج حَمَامٌ
Dove-cote n.	بُرْجُ حَمَامٍ
Dower / Dowry } n.	صَدَاقٌ . مَهْرٌ
Down pr. or n.	إِلَى تَحْتُ . زَغَبٌ
Downfall n.	هُبُوطٌ . خَرَابٌ
Downcast / Downhearted } a.	مَكْسُورُ الْخَاطِرِ مَغْمُومٌ
Downright a.	وَاضِحٌ . صَافٍ . مُسْتَقِيمٌ
Downward / Downwards } ad.	إِلَى تَحْتُ او اسفَلَ
Doxology n.	تَسْبِحَةٌ
Doze v. i.	نَعَسَ ــَ نَامَ خَفِيفًا
Dozy a.	نَاعِسٌ . نَعْسَانٌ
Dozen n.	إِثْنَا عَشَرَ (دَرْزِينَة)
Drachm n.	دِرْهَمٌ
Draft n.	سَحْبٌ . سَفْتَجَةٌ . حَوَالَة
Drag v. t. or i.	سَحَبَ ــ جَرَّ ــ تَأَخَّرَ
Dragoman n.	تُرْجُمَانٌ
Dragon n.	تِنِّينٌ

Dragoon n.	جُنْدِيٌّ مِنَ ٱلْفُرْسَانِ
Drain n. or v. t.	قَنَاةٌ . فَرَّغَ بِقَنَاةٍ
Drainage n.	صَرْفٌ . قَنَوَاتُ مَاءٍ
Drake n.	ذَكَرُ ٱلْبَطِّ
Dram n.	دِرْهَمٌ . جُرْعَةٌ مُسْكِرَةٌ
Drama n.	رِوَايَةٌ تَشْخِيصِيَّةٌ
Dramatic a.	مُخْتَصٌّ بِرِوَايَةٍ تَشْخِيصِيَّةٍ
Dramatist n.	مُؤَلِّفُ رِوَايَاتٍ
Dramatize v. t.	كَتَبَ رِوَايَاتٍ تَشْخِيصِيَّةً
Drape v. t.	غَطَّى بِسُتُرٍ او سُجُوفٍ
Draper n.	تَاجِرٌ بِالنَّسِجِ ٱلصُّوفِيَّةِ
Drapery n.	أَصْوَافٌ سُجُوفٌ
Draught n.	مَجْرَى هَوَاءٍ . جُرْعَةٌ
Draughts n.	لَعْبُ ٱلدَّامَا
Draughtsman n.	رَسَّامٌ
Draw v. t.	سَحَبَ ــ جَرَّ ــ جَذَبَ
Drawback n.	عَائِقَةٌ . مَانِعٌ
Drawer n.	سَاحِبٌ . (جَرَّارٌ) . (دَرْجٌ)

Drawers n. pl.	سِرْوَالٌ تَحْتِيٌّ
Drawing n.	رَسْمٌ . تَخْطِيطٌ . سَحْبٌ
Drawing-room n.	غُرْفَةُ إِسْتِقْبَال
Drawl v. i. or n.	اطَالَ الصَّوْتَ فِي النُّطْقِ
Dray n.	مَرْكَبَةٌ لِنَقْلِ البَضَائِعِ
Dread n. or v. t.	خَوْفٌ . هَوْلٌ . خَافَ
Dreaded Dreadful } a.	هَائِلٌ . مُخِيفٌ
Dream n. or v. i.	حُلْمٌ . حَلَمَ
Dreamless a.	خَالٍ مِنَ الأَحْلَام
Dreamy a.	كَثِيرُ الأَحْلَامِ
Dreariness n.	وَحْشَةٌ . كَآبَة
Dreary a.	مُغِمٌّ . مُسْتَوْحِشٌ
Dredge v. t. or n.	جَرَفَ . مِجْرَفَةٌ بَحْرِيَّة
Dregs n. pl.	ثُفْلٌ . دُرْدِيٌّ
Drench v. t.	بَلَّلَ
Dress n. or v. t.	لِبَاسٌ . لَبَسَ . كَسا
Dressmaker n.	خَيَّاطَة
Dribble v. i.	قَطَرَ

Driblet n.	كَمِّيَّة قَلِيلَة . جُزْءٌ صَغِيرٌ
Drift v. i. or n.	تَكَوُّمُ إِنْسَاق . كَوْمَةُ ثَلْجٍ
Drill n.	تَمْرِينُ الجُنُودِ . مِثْقَبٌ
Drill v. t.	ثَقَبَ . مَرَّنَ الجُنُودَ
Drink (drank, drunk) v. t.	شَرِبَ
Drip v. i.	قَطَرَ
Drive v. t. or i.	سَاقَ . حَرَّضَ . أَلْزَمَ
Drizzle v. i. or n.	أَرَذَّ . نَضَّ . رَذَاذٌ
Droll a.	مُضْحِك
Drollery n.	مَزْحٌ . دُعَابَةٌ
Dromedary n.	بَعِيرٌ مُسْرِعٌ . هِجِينٌ
Drone n.	ذَكَرُ النَّحْلِ . كَسْلَانٌ
Droop v. i.	ذَبَلَ . ضَنِيَ
Drop n. or v. t.	قَطْرَةٌ . قَطَرَ . أَسْقَطَ
Dropsy n.	إِسْتِسْقَاءٌ
Dropsical a.	مُسْتَسْقٍ
Dross n.	رَغْوَةُ مَعْدَن (زَغَلٌ)
Drought n.	قَيْظٌ . قَحْطٌ

Drove n.	قَطِيعُ ج قُطْعَانٌ
Drown v. t. or i.	غَرَّقَ . غَرِقَ ـَ
Drowsiness n.	نُعَاسٌ
Drowsy a.	نَعْسَانُ
Drudge n. or v. i.	كَثِيرُ ٱلْكَدِّ . كَدَّ . جَدَّ
Drudgery n.	عَنَاءٌ . شُغْلٌ مُمِلٌّ
Drug n. or v. t.	عَقَّارٌ . عَالَجَ بِٱلْعَقَاقِيرِ
Drugget n.	لِبْدٌ ج لُبُودٌ
Druggist n.	صَيْدَلَانِيٌّ . اِجْزَائِيٌّ
Drum n. or v. i.	طَبْلٌ . طَبَّلَ
Drummer n.	طَبَّالٌ
Drunk Drunken } a.	سَكْرَانُ ج سَكَارَى
Drunkard n.	سِكِّيرٌ
Drunkenness n.	سُكْرٌ
Dry a. or v. t.	يَابِسٌ . يَبَّسَ
Dry-goods n. pl.	مَنْسُوجَاتٌ
Dryly ad.	بِتَحَكُّمٍ
Dryness n.	يُبُوسَةٌ

Dual a.	مُثَنَّى
Dub v. t.	سَمَّى . لَقَّبَ
Dubious a.	مَشْكُوكٌ فِيهِ . مُشْتَبَهٌ
Ducal a.	أَمِيرِيٌّ . دُوقِيٌّ
Ducat n.	دِينَارٌ أُورُبِّيٌّ
Duchess n.	أَمِيرَةٌ إِمْرَأَةُ دُوقٍ
Duchy Dukedom } n.	إِيَالَةُ دُوقٍ
Duck n. or v. t.	بَطٌّ . غَطَّسَ
Duckling n.	فَرْخُ ٱلْبَطِّ
Duct n.	اِنْبُوبَةٌ . قَنَاةٌ
Ductile a.	مُتَمَعِّطٌ . مَرِنٌ
Ductility n.	لِينَةٌ . إِمْتِغَاطِيَّةٌ
Due n. or a.	حَقٌّ . مُسْتَحَقٌّ . مَطْلُوبٌ
Duel n.	مُبَارَزَةُ ٱثْنَيْنِ
Duelist Dueller } n.	مُبَارِزٌ
Dug pp. or n.	مَحْفُورٌ . ضَرْعٌ ج ضُرُوعٌ
Duke n.	امِيرُ (دُوقٌ)

Dull *a.* or *v. t.*	كَالٌ . بَلِيدٌ . اكَلَ
Dullness *n.*	كَلَالَةٌ . بَلَادَةٌ . بَلَاهَةٌ
Duly *ad.*	كَمَا يَجِبُ . فِي حِينِهِ
Dumb *a.*	أَخْرَسُ . أَبْكَمُ
Dumbness *n.*	خَرَسٌ . بَكَمٌ
Dumpish *a.*	كَئِيبٌ . مَغْمُومٌ . بَلِيدٌ
Dun *a.* or *v. t.*	كُمَيْتُ اللَّوْنِ . طَلَبَ بِلَجَاجَةٍ
Dunce *n.*	غَبِيٌّ . أَبْلَهُ
Dung *n.* or *v. t.*	زِبْلٌ . سَمَادٌ . دِمَالٌ . سَمَّدَ
Dungeon *n.*	حَبْسٌ . غَائِرٌ
Duodecimal *a.* or *n.*	إِثْنَاعَشَرِيٌّ . جُزْءٌ مِنْ ١٢
Duodenum *n.*	الْمِعَى الْاِثْنَا عَشَرِيُّ
Dupe *n.* or *v. t.*	غَرِيرٌ . غَرَّ
Duplicate *n.* or *v. t.*	نُسْخَةٌ ثَانِيَةٌ . ثَنَّى
Duplicity *n.*	مُخَادَعَةٌ . مُخَاتَلَةٌ
Durability *n.* Durableness	صِفَةُ الْبَقَاءِ
Durable *a.*	مُسْتَمِرٌّ . بَاقٍ
Duration *n.*	بَقَاءٌ . دَوَامٌ . مُدَّةٌ
During *pr.*	اثْنَاءَ . مُدَّةَ . خِلَالَ
Dusk *n.*	غَسَقٌ . غَبَشٌ
Dusky *a.*	غَاسِقٌ . مَائِلٌ إِلَى السَّوَادِ
Dust *n.* or *v. t.*	غُبَارٌ . مَسَحَ مِنَ الْغُبَارِ
Duster *n.*	مَاسِحُ الْغُبَارِ . مِمْسَحَةٌ
Dustpan *n.*	مَجْرُودُ الْغُبَارِ
Dusty *a.*	مُغَبَّرٌ . مُنَغِّرٌ
Duteous Dutiful *a.*	مُتَمِّمٌ وَاجِبَاتِهِ . مُطِيعٌ
Duty *n.*	فَرْضٌ . وَاجِبٌ . رَسْمُ جُمْرُكٍ
Dwarf *n.* or *a.* Dwarfish *a.*	قَزْمٌ . قَصِيرُ الْقَدِّ
Dwarf *v. t.*	صَيَّرَهُ قَزْمًا . مَنَعَ نُمُوَّهُ
Dwell *v. i.*	سَكَنَ . قَطَنَ
Dwelling *n.*	مَسْكَنٌ . بَيْتٌ
Dwindle *v. i.*	صَغُرَ . إِنْحَطَّ . قَلَّ
Dye *v. t.* or *n.*	صَبَغَ . صِبْغَةٌ . صِبَاغٌ
Dyeing *n.*	صَبْغٌ . صِبَاغَةٌ
Dyer *n.*	صَبَّاغٌ
Dying *pp.* of *die.*	مَائِتٌ . فَانٍ

Dynasty n.	دَوْلَةُ مُلُوكٍ
Dysentery n.	سَحْجٌ . دُوسَنْطَارِيَا

Dyspepsia n.	تُخْمَةٌ . سُوءُ ٱلْهَضْمِ
Dyspeptic a. or n.	مُتَعَلِّقٌ بِٱلتُّخْمَةِ . مُصَابٌ بِهَا

E

Each a.	كُلٌّ . كُلُّ وَاحِدٍ
Eager a.	رَاغِبٌ . تَائِقٌ . مُلْهِفٌ لِ
Eagerness n.	رَغْبَةٌ . شَوْقٌ
Eagle n.	نَسْرٌ ج نُسُورٌ
Eaglet n.	فَرْخُ نَسْرٍ
Ear n.	أُذُنٌ ج آذَانٌ
Ear of corn n.	سُنْبُلَةٌ
Earl n.	رُتْبَةٌ بَيْنَ ٱمَرَاءِ ٱلْاِنْكَلِيزِ
Early a. or ad.	مُبَكِّرٌ . بَاكِرًا
Earn v. t.	إِسْتَحَقَّ اجْرَةً . كَسَبَ _
Earnest a. or n.	جَادٌّ . عَرْبُونٌ

Earnestness n.	غَيْرَةٌ . جِدٌّ . إِهْتِمَامٌ
Earnings n.	أَجْرٌ . كَسْبٌ
Ear-ring n.	قُرْطٌ ج أَقْرَاطٌ
Earth n.	ٱلْأَرْضُ . تُرَابٌ
Earthen a.	تُرَابِيٌّ . مِنْ طِينٍ
Earthen-ware n.	أَوَانٍ خَزَفِيَّةٌ
Earthquake n.	زَلْزَلَةٌ ج زَلَازِلُ
Ease n. or v. t.	رَاحَةٌ سُهُولَةٌ . اراحَ
Easiness n.	سُهُولَةٌ . رَاحَةٌ
East n.	ٱلشَّرْقُ . ٱلْمَشْرِقُ
Easter n.	عِيدُ ٱلْفِصْحِ

Easterly } a. شَرْقِيٌّ
Eastern }

Eastward ad. نَحْوَ ٱلشَّرْقِ . شَرْقاً

Easy a. سَهْلٌ . هَيِّنٌ

Eat v.t. or i. أَكَلَ

Eatable n.or a. مَأْكُولٌ . مَا يُؤْكَلُ

Eaves n. pl. أَطْنَافُ ٱلسَّقْفِ

Ebb v. i. or n. جَزْرٌ . جَزَرَ

Ebony n. أَبْنُوسٌ

Ebullition n. غَلَيَانٌ . فَوَرَانٌ

Eccentric n. or a. مُنْحَرِفٌ . غَرِيبٌ

Ecclesiastic n. } أَكْلِيرِكِيٌّ كَنَائِسِيٌّ
Ecclesiastical a. }

Eaves n. or v. i. or t. صَدَى . أَصْدَى

Eclipse n. كُسُوفٌ . خُسُوفٌ

Ecliptic n. مَدَارُ ٱلشَّمْسِ

Economic } a. إِقْتِصَادِيٌّ
Economical }

Economize v. t. or i. إِقْتَصَدَ

Economy n. إِقْتِصَادٌ

Ecstasy n. شَغَفٌ . ذُهُولٌ

Ecstatic n. شَغَفِيٌّ . مُفْتَنٌ

Eddy n. دَرْدُورٌ

Eden n. عَدْنٌ

Edge n. حَدٌّ . حَافَةٌ

Edgewise ad. جَانِبِيًّا

Edible see eatable.

Edict n. أَمْرٌ سُلْطَانِيٌّ . فَرْمَانٌ

Edifice n. بِنَاءٌ . عِمَارَةٌ

Edify v. t. بَنَى . أَفَادَ . هَذَّبَ

Edit v.t. هَذَّبَ لِلطَّبْعِ . نَقَّحَ

Edition n. طَبْعٌ . طَبْعَةٌ

Editor n. مُهَذِّبٌ . رَئِيسُ تَحْرِيرِ جَرِيدَةٍ

Educate v. t. عَلَّمَ . رَبَّى . دَرَّبَ

Education n. تَعْلِيمٌ . تَرْبِيَةٌ . تَهْذِيبٌ

Educe v. t. إِسْتَخْرَجَ . اِنْتَجَ

Eel n. سَمَكٌ كَأَكْلِيَّةِ . حَنْكَلِيسٌ

Efface v. t. مَحَا . طَلَسَ

Effect n. or v. t. نَتِيجَةٌ . تَأْثِيرٌ . سَبَّبَ

Effective } a. فَعَّالٌ . مُنْتِجٌ . عَامِلٌ
Effectual }

Effects n. pl.	أَمْتِعَة . أَثَاثٌ
Effeminacy n.	خُنَاثَة . تَخَنُّثٌ
Effeminate a. or v. t.	خَنِثَ . خَنَّثَ
Effervesce v. t.	فَارَ . ازْبَدَ
Effervescence n.	فَوَرَانٌ
Effervescent a.	فَوَّارٌ . مُزْبِدٌ
Effete a.	غَيْرُ مُنْتِجٍ . مَنْهُوكٌ
Efficacious a.	فَعَّالٌ . عَامِلٌ
Efficacy Efficiency } n.	قُوَّةٌ فَعَّالَة . فَاعِلِيَّة
Efficient a.	فَعَّالٌ . مُنْتِجٌ
Effigy n.	تِمْثَالٌ . صُورَة
Efflorescence n.	إِزْهَارٌ
Effort n.	إِجْتِهَادٌ . سَعْيٌ
Effrontery n.	وَقَاحَةٌ . عَجْرَفَةٌ
Effulgence n.	بَهَآءٌ . رَوْنَقٌ
Effulgent a.	بَهِيٌّ . لَامِعٌ
Effusion n.	سَفْكٌ . إِهْرَاقٌ
Egg n.	بَيْضَة ج بُيُوضٌ وَبَيْضَات

Egg-plant n.	بَاذِنْجَانٌ
Egoism Egotism } n.	عُجْبٌ . تَعْظِيمُ الذَّات
Egotist n. Egotistic a. }	مُعْجَبٌ بِنَفْسِهِ
Egregious a.	فَائِقٌ (فِي السُّوءِ)
Egress n.	خُرُوجٌ . مَخْرَجٌ
Egyptian a.	مِصْرِيٌّ
Eight n.	ثَمَانِيَة . ثَمَانٍ
Eighth a.	الثَّامِنُ
Eighteen n.	ثَمَانِيَةَ عَشَرَ وَثَمَانِي عَشْرَةَ
Eighty n.	ثَمَانُونَ
Either a. or pron.	إِمَّا . كُلٌّ مِنَ اثْنَيْنِ
Ejaculate v. t.	نَطَقَ بِصُرَاخٍ اوْ دُعَاءٍ
Eject v. t.	قَذَفَ . أَخْرَجَ . طَرَدَ
Ejection n.	قَذْفٌ . إِخْرَاجٌ
Elaborate v. t. or a.	تَمَّمَ . أَتْقَنَ . مُتْقِنٌ
Elapse v. i.	مَضَى . إِنْقَضَى
Elastic a.	مَرِنٌ . لَدِنٌ
Elasticity n.	مُرُونَة . لُدُونَة

Elated *pp.*	مُفْتَخِرٌ . مُبْتَهِجٌ
Elation *n.*	تَشَامُخٌ . إِبْتِهَاجٌ
Elbow *n.* or *v. t.*	مِرْفَقٌ دَفَعَ بِهِ
Elder *a.* or *n.*	اَكْبَرُ عُمْراً . شَيْخٌ
Elder *n.* (plant).	بَلَسَانٌ
Elderly *a.*	مُتَقَدِّمٌ فِي السِّنِّ
Eldest *a.*	الأَكْبَرُ فِي الْعُمْرِ
Elect *v. t.* or *a.* or *n.*	إِنْتَخَبَ . مُخْتَارٌ
Election *n.*	إِنْتِخَابٌ
Electric Electrical } *a.*	كَهْرَبَائِيٌّ
Electricity *n.*	كَهْرَبَائِيَّةٌ
Electrify *v. t.*	كَهْرَبَ
Elegance *n.*	ظَرَافَةٌ . لَبَاقَةٌ
Elegant *a.*	ظَرِيفٌ . كَيِّسٌ . مَلِيحٌ
Elegy *n.*	مَرْثَاةٌ ج مَرَاثٍ
Element *n.*	عُنْصُرٌ . مَبْدَأٌ
Elemental Elementary } *a.*	عُنْصُرِيٌّ . اوَّلِيٌّ
Elephant *n.*	فِيلٌ ج افْيَالٌ
Elevate *v. t.*	رَفَعَ . رَقَّى . عَلَّى
Elevation *n.*	رَفْعٌ . إِرْتِفَاعٌ
Elevator *n.*	رَافِعٌ . مُعَلٍّ
Eleven *n.*	احَدَ عَشَرَ
Eleventh *a.*	الْحَادِي عَشَرَ
Elicit *v. t.*	إِسْتَخْرَجَ . إِسْتَبَانَ
Elide *v. t.*	حَذَفَ
Eligible *a.*	جَدِيرٌ بِالإِنْتِخَابِ
Eliminate *v. t.*	اخْرَجَ . حَذَفَ ـ
Elimination *n.*	إِخْرَاجٌ
Elision *n.*	حَذْفٌ
Elk *n.*	نَوْعٌ مِنَ الإِيَّلِ
Ellipse *n.*	إِهْلِيلَجٌ
Elliptical *a.*	إِهْلِيلَجِيُّ الشَّكْلِ
Elm *n.*	دَرْدَارٌ (نَوْعٌ مِنَ الشَّجَرِ)
Elocution *n.*	نُطْقٌ . فَصَاحَةٌ
Elocutionist *n.*	إِسْتَاذُ الْخِطَابَةِ
Elongate *v. t.*	أَطَالَ طَوَّلَ

Elope _v. i._	هَرَبَ سِرًّا
Eloquence _n._	فَصَاحَةٌ . بَلَاغَةٌ
Eloquent _a._	فَصِيحٌ . بَلِيغٌ
Else _pron._ or _a._	غَيْرُ . وَإِلَّا
Elsewhere _ad._	بِغَيْرِ مَكَانٍ
Elucidate _v. t._	اوْضَحَ. شَرَحَ ـَ
Elude _v. t._	تَمَلَّصَ مِنْ . تَجَنَّبَ
Emaciate _v. i._ or _t._	هُزِلَ ـُ
Emaciation _n._	هُزَالٌ
Emancipate _v. t._	حَرَّرَ . اعْتَقَ
Emancipation _n._	تَحْرِيرٌ
Emanate _v. i._	نَشَأَ ـَ . صَدَرَ ـُ
Emasculate _v. t._	اضْعَفَ . خَصَى
Embalm _v. t._	حَنَّطَ
Embankment _n._	سَدٌّ . حَاجِزٌ
Embargo _n._	حَجْزُ ٱلسُّفُنِ عَنِ ٱلسَّفَرِ
Embark _v. t._	رَكِبَ سَفِينَةً . بَاشَرَ
Embarkation _n._	نُزُولٌ فِي سَفِينَةٍ

Embarrass _v. t._	لَبَّكَ . رَبَكَ ـُ
Embarrassment _n._	إِرْتِبَاكٌ . لَبَكَةٌ
Embassy _n._	سِفَارَةٌ
Embellish _v. t._	زَيَّنَ . زَخْرَفَ
Embellishment _n._	زِينَةٌ . زَخْرَفَةٌ
Embezzle _v._	إِخْتَلَسَ
Embezzlement _n._	إِخْتِلَاسٌ
Emblem _n._	رَمْزٌ . كِنَايَةٌ
Emblematic Emblematical } _a._	رَمْزِيٌّ
Embody _v. t._	جَسَّمَ . ضَمَّنَ
Embolden _v. t._	شَجَّعَ . جَرَّأَ
Embrace _v. t._ or _n._	عَانَقَ . تَضَمَّنَ . مُعَانَقَةٌ
Embroider _v. t._	طَرَّزَ
Embroidery _n._	تَطْرِيزٌ
Embroil _v. t._	شَوَّشَ . هَيَّجَ . افْتَنَ
Embryo _n._	جَنِينٌ ج اجِنَّةٌ . جُرْثُومَةٌ
Embryology _n._	عِلْمٌ يَبْحَثُ عَنِ ٱلاجِنَّةِ
Emerald _n._	زُمُرُّدٌ

Emerge v. i.	خَرَجَ ـِ . ظَهَرَ ـَ
Emergency n.	حَادِثَةٌ غَيْرُ مُنْتَظَرَةٍ ضَرُورَةٌ
Emetic a. or n.	مُقَيِّئٌ
Emigrant n.	مُهَاجِرٌ
Emigrate v. i.	هَاجَرَ الْوَطَنَ
Emigration n.	مُهَاجَرَةٌ
Eminence n.	إِرْتِفَاعٌ . سُمُوٌّ
Eminent a.	سَامٍ . شَهِيرٌ
Emissary n.	رَسُولٌ . جَاسُوسٌ
Emission n.	إِصْدَارٌ . نَشْرٌ
Emit v. t.	أَصْدَرَ . نَشَرَ ـُ
Emollient a.	مُلَيِّنٌ
Emotion n.	اِنْفِعَالٌ نَفْسَانِيٌّ
Emotional a.	اِنْفِعَالِيٌّ . سَرِيعُ الْاِنْفِعَالِ
Empale v. t.	خَوْزَقَ
Emperor v. t.	سُلْطَانٌ (اِمْبَرَاطُورٌ)
Emphasis n.	تَأْكِيدٌ . تَشْدِيدُ الصَّوْتِ
Emphasize v. t.	أَكَّدَ . شَدَّدَ . اللَّفْظَ
Emphatic a.	مُؤَكَّدٌ . مُشَدَّدٌ
Empire n.	مَمْلَكَةٌ . سَلْطَنَةٌ
Employ v. t.	إِسْتَخْدَمَ . شَغَّلَ
Employé n.	مُسْتَخْدَمٌ . اجِيرٌ
Employer n.	مُسْتَخْدِمٌ . مُشَغِّلٌ
Employment n.	شُغْلٌ . مَصْلَحَةٌ
Empower v. t.	قَدَّرَ . مَكَّنَ . فَوَّضَ
Empress n.	سُلْطَانَةٌ (أَمْبَرَاطُورَةٌ)
Emptiness n.	فَرَاغٌ . خُلُوٌّ
Empty a.	خَالٍ . فَارِغٌ . بَاطِلٌ
Empty v. t.	افْرَغَ
Emulate v. t.	نَافَسَ . بَارَى
Enable v. t.	قَدَّرَ . مَكَّنَ
Enact v. t.	سَنَّ . رَسَمَ ـُ
Enactment n.	سُنَّةٌ . شَرِيعَةٌ
Enamel n. or v. t.	مِينَاءٌ . غَشَّى بِالْمِينَاءِ
Enamour v. t.	عَشِقَ . افْتَتَنَ

Encamp v. t. or i.	نَزَلَ ـِ . عَسْكَرَ
Encampment n.	مَحَلَّة . مُعَسْكَرٌ
Enchain v. t.	غَلَّ . سَلْسَلَ . أَوْثَقَ
Enchant v. t.	سَحَرَ ـَ . فَتَنَ ـِ . رَقَى
Enchantment n.	سِحْرٌ . رُقْيَةٌ
Encircle v. t.	أَحَاطَ . أَحْدَقَ ب
Enclosure n.	حَوْشٌ . سِيَاجٌ
Encompass v. t.	احَاطَ . أَحْدَقَ ب
Encounter n. or v. t.	مُصَادَفَةٌ . مَعْرَكَةٌ . صَادَفَ . بَارَزَ
Encourage v. t.	شَجَّعَ ، حَرَّضَ عَلَى
Encouragement n.	تَشْجِيعٌ
Encouraging a.	مُشَجِّعٌ.مُقَوِّي ٱلْأَمَلِ
Encroach v. t.	تَعَدَّى عَلَى
Encroachment n.	تَعَدٍّ عَلَى
Encumber v. t.	ثَقَّلَ . أَعَاقَ . عَرْقَلَ
Encumbrance n.	ثِقْلٌ . إِعَاقَةٌ
Encyclopedia n.	دَائِرَةُ ٱلْمَعَارِفِ

End n. or v. t.	نِهَايَة . غَايَة . أَنْهَى
Endanger v. t.	أَوْقَعَ فِي ٱلْخَطَرِ
Endear v. t.	حَبَّبَ . صَيَّرَ عَزِيزاً
Endeavour v. t. or n.	إِجْتَهَدَ . سَعَى ـ
Ending n.	إِنْتِهَاءٌ . خِتَامٌ
Endless a.	غَيْرُ مُتَنَاهٍ . بِلَا نِهَايَةٍ
Endow v. t.	وَقَفَ لَهُ رِزْقاً . امْهَرَ
Endowment n.	وَقْفٌ . مَهْرٌ
Endurable a.	مُمْكِنٌ إِحْتِمَالُهُ.مُحْتَمَل
Endurance n.	إِحْتِمَالٌ . بَقَاءٌ
Endure v. t. or i.	بَقِيَ ـَ . إِحْتَمَلَ
Enemy n.	عَدُوٌّ ج أَعْدَاءٌ
Energetic Energetical } a.	نَشِيطٌ . هُمَامٌ
Energize v. t.	قَوَّى . شَدَّدَ
Energy n.	هِمَّة . جِدٌّ . نَشَاطٌ
Enervate Enfeeble } v. t.	اضْعَفَ . أَوْهَنَ
Enforce v. t.	أَجْرَى . أَنْفَذَ
Enforcement n.	إِجْرَاءٌ . إِنْفَاذٌ

Enfranchise v. t.	مَنَحَ حُقُوقَ ٱلْأُمَّةِ
Engage v. t.	عَاهَدَ . إِسْتَخْدَمَ . بَارَزَ
Engaged a.	مَشْغُولٌ . مُقَيَّدٌ . مَخْطُوبٌ
Engagement n.	وَعْدٌ . خِطْبَةٌ قِتَالٌ
Engaging a.	فَاتِنٌ . مُسْتَمِيلُ ٱلْعَوَاطِفِ
Engender v. t.	وَلَّدَ . أَوْجَدَ . سَبَّبَ
Engine n.	آلَةٌ بُخَارِيَّةٌ
Engineer n.	مُهَنْدِسٌ
English a. or n.	إِنْكِلِيزِيٌّ . ٱلْإِنْكِلِيزُ
Engrave v. t.	حَفَرَ ـِ . نَقَشَ ـُ
Engraver n.	حَفَّارٌ . نَقَّاشٌ
Engraving n.	نَقْشٌ . صُورَةٌ مَحْفُورَةٌ
Engross v. t.	شَغَلَ . نَسَخَ بِخَطٍّ وَاضِحٍ
Engulf v. t.	إِبْتَلَعَ
Enhance v. t.	رَقَّى . عَظَّمَ
Enigma n.	لُغْزٌ . اُحْجِيَّةٌ
Enigmatic Enigmatical } a.	لُغْزِيٌّ . غَامِضٌ
Enjoin v. t.	أَمَرَ ـُ

Enjoy v. t.	إِلْتَذَّ . تَمَتَّعَ بِ
Enjoyable a.	لَذِيذٌ . مُفْرِحٌ
Enjoyment n.	لَذَّةٌ . حَظٌّ . تَمَتُّعٌ
Enlarge v. t. or i.	وَسَّعَ . إِتَّسَعَ
Enlargement n.	تَوْسِيعٌ . تَوَسُّعٌ
Enlighten v. t.	عَلَّمَ . أَنَارَ
Enlist v. t. or i.	ضَمَّ . دَوَّنَ اسْمًا
Enlistment n.	تَقْيِيدٌ . تَدْوِينٌ
Enliven v. i.	أَنْعَشَ . أَبْهَجَ
Enmity n.	عَدَاوَةٌ
Ennoble v. t.	شَرَّفَ . رَقَّى
Enormity n.	جَسَامَةٌ . فَظَاعَةٌ
Enormous a.	عَظِيمٌ جِدًّا . مُفْرِطٌ
Enough n. or ad.	كَافٍ
Enrage v. t.	أَغَاظَ . أَغْضَبَ
Enrich v. t.	أَغْنَى . أَخْصَبَ
Enrol v. t.	سَجَّلَ . دَوَّنَ
Ensign n.	عَلَمٌ . ضَابِطٌ

Enslave v. t.	إِسْتَعْبَدَ . إِسْتَرَقَّ	Entomb v. t.	قَبَرَ ـُ . دَفَنَ ـِ
Ensnare v. t.	أَخَذَ بِحِيلَةٍ . شَبَكَ	Entrails n. pl.	أَحْشَاءٌ . أَمْعَاءٌ
Ensue v. i.	تَلَا ـُ . تَبِعَ ـَ	Entrance n.	مَدْخَلٌ . دُخُولٌ
Entail v. t.	أَوْقَفَ . جَرَّ	Entrance v. t.	سَحَرَ ـَ . أَبْهَجَ
Entangle v. t.	عَرْقَلَ . شَبَكَ ـِ	Entrap v. t.	شَبَكَ ـِ . أَخَذَ بِحِيلَةٍ
Enter v. t. or i.	أَدْخَلَ أَوْ دَخَلَ ـُ	Entreat v. t.	تَوَسَّلَ . تَضَرَّعَ
Enterprise n.	مَسْعًى . مَشْرُوعٌ	Entreaty n.	تَوَسُّلٌ . إِلْتِمَاسٌ
Eeterprising a.	ذُو إِقْدَامٍ . هُمَامٌ	Entry n.	دُخُولٌ . مَدْخَلٌ . تَقْيِيدٌ
Entertain v. t.	ضَافَ . سَلَّى	Entwine v. t.	فَتَلَ ـِ . حَبَكَ ـِ
Entertaining a.	مُسَلٍّ . سَارٌّ	Enumerate v. t.	عَدَّ ـُ . أَحْصَى
Entertainment a.	تَسْلِيَةٌ . ضِيَافَةٌ	Enunciate v. t.	أَعْلَنَ . نَطَقَ ـِ
Enthrone v. t.	أَجْلَسَ عَلَى الْعَرْشِ	Envelop v. t.	غَلَفَ . لَفَّ ـُ
Enthusiasm n.	حَمَاسَةٌ . نَشَاطٌ	Envelope n.	غِلَافٌ . ظَرْفٌ
Enhusiast n. } Enthusiastic a.}	حَمِسٌ . نَشِيطٌ	Envenom v. t.	سَمَّ ـُ . أَحْقَدَ
Entice v. t.	أَغْوَى . رَاوَدَ . تَمَلَّقَ	Enviable a.	مُهَيِّجُ الْحَسَدِ . مُشْتَهًى
Entire a.	كَامِلٌ بِكُلِّ . صَحِيحٌ	Envious a.	حَاسِدٌ . حَسُودٌ
Entirely ad.	تَمَامًا . بِكُلِّيَتِهِ	Environ v. t.	أَحَاطَ . أَحْدَقَ بِهِ
Entitle v. t.	لَقَّبَ . أَعْطَى حَقًّا فِي	Environment n.	إِحَاطَةٌ

Environs *n. pl.*	سَوَادٌ . ضَوَاحٍ
Envoy *n.*	رَسُولٌ . مُعتَمَدٌ . سَفِيرٌ
Envy *n.* or *v. t.*	حَسَدٌ . حَسَدَ ــِ
Ephemeral *a.*	فَانٍ . قَلِيلُ البَقَاءِ
Epic *a.* or *n.*	قِصَّةٌ شِعرِيَّةٌ
Epicure *n.* } Epicurean *a.* }	مُتَنَعِّمٌ . شَهوَانِيٌّ
Epidemic *n.* or *a.*	وَبَأٌ . وَبَائِيٌّ
Epidermis *n.*	بَشَرَةٌ
Epiglottis *n.*	لِسَانُ المِزمَارِ
Epigram *n.*	شِعرٌ . قَصِيرٌ . فَكِه
Epilepsy *n.*	دَاءُ الصَّرعِ
Epileptic *a.*	صَرِيعٌ . مُصَابٌ بِالصَّرعِ
Episcopal *a.* } Episcopalian *n.* }	أُسقُفِيٌّ
Episode *n.*	حَادِثَةٌ . إِستِطرَادِيَّةٌ
Epistle *n.*	رِسَالَةٌ
Epitaph *n.*	كِتَابَةٌ عَلَى قَبرٍ
Epithet *n.*	صِفَةٌ . لَقَبٌ
Epitome *n.*	مُختَصَرٌ . خُلَاصَةٌ
Epitomize *v. t.*	لَخَّصَ . أَوجَزَ . إِختَصَرَ
Epoch *n.*	عَصرٌ . زَمَنٌ
Equable *a.*	مُتَسَاوٍ
Equal *a.* or *n.* or *v. t.*	مُسَاوٍ . قَرِينٌ . سَاوَى
Equality *n.*	مُسَاوَاةٌ . مُعَادَلَةٌ
Equalize *v. t.*	سَاوَى . عَدَّلَ
Equanimity *n.*	هُدُوءُ العَقلِ
Equation *n.*	تَسوِيَةٌ . مُعَادَلَةٌ جَبرِيَّةٌ
Equator *n.*	خَطُّ الإِستِوَاءِ
Equatorial *a.*	مَنسُوبٌ لِخَطِّ الإِستِوَاءِ
Equestrian *a.* or *n.*	مُتَعَلِّقٌ بِرُكُوبِ الخَيلِ . خَيَّالٌ . فَارِسٌ
Equiangular *a.*	مُتَسَاوِي الزَّوَايَا
Equidistant *a.*	مُتَسَاوِي البُعدِ
Equilateral *a.*	مُتَسَاوِي الأَضلَاعِ
Equilibrium *n.*	تَوَازُنٌ
Equinoctial *a.*	إِعتِدَالِيٌّ
Equinox *n.*	إِعتِدَالُ اللَّيلِ وَالنَّهَارِ

Equip v. t.	جَوَّزَ . أَهَبَ
Epuipage n.	مُهِمَّاتٌ . اتْبَاعٌ
Equipment n.	تَجْهِيزٌ . جِهَازٌ
Equitable a.	عَادِلٌ . مُنْصِفٌ
Equity n.	عَدْلٌ . إِنْصَافٌ
Equivalent n.	مُسَاوٍ . مُعَادِلٌ
Equivocal a.	ذُو مَعْنَيَيْنِ . مُشْتَبِه
Equivocate v. t.	لَبَّسَ فِي الكَلَامِ
Era n.	عَصْرٌ . مُدَّةٌ
Eradicate v. t.	إِسْتَأْصَلَ
Erase v. t.	مَحَا ـُ . سَحَقَ ـ
Erasure n.	مَحْوٌ
Ere ad.	قَبْلَ أَنْ . قَبْلُ
Erect a. or v. t.	مُنْتَصِبٌ . نَصَبَ ـُ . أَقَامَ
Erection n.	إِقَامَةٌ . نَصْبٌ
Erelong ad.	بَعْدَ قَلِيلٍ
Erosion n.	قَضْمٌ . قَرْضٌ
Erosive a.	آكِلٌ . قَاضِمٌ
Err v. i.	غَلِطَ ـَ . ضَلَّ ـِ . خَطِئَ
Errand n.	عَرَضٌ
Erratic a.	ضَالٌّ . زَائِغٌ . غَيْرُ مَضْبُوطٍ
Erratum Errata pl. n. } n.	غَلَطٌ . خَطَأٌ
Erroneous a.	مَغْلُوطٌ
Error n.	غَلَطٌ . خَطَأٌ
Erudition n.	عِلْمٌ غَزِيرٌ
Eruption n.	إِنْفِجَارٌ . بَثَرٌ
Erysipelas n.	مَرَضُ الحُمْرَة
Escape n. or v. i.	نَجَاةٌ . نَجَا ـُ
Eschew v. t.	رَفَضَ ـِ . تَنَحَّى عَنْ
Escort v. t. or n.	خَفَرَ ـِ . خَفَرٌ
Esophagus n.	المَرِيءُ
Especial a.	خَاصٌّ . خُصُوصِيٌّ
Especially ad.	خَاصَّةً
Espouse v. t.	خَطَبَ ـُ (إِمْرَأَةً)
Espy v. t.	إِسْتَطْلَعَ . إِسْتَكْشَفَ
Esquire n.	سَيِّدٌ

Essay v. t.	جَرَّبَ	Ethical a.	ادَبِيٌّ
Essay n.	تَجْرِبَةٌ . مَقَالَةٌ	Ethics n. pl.	عِلْمُ الآدَابِ
Essence n.	مَاهِيَّةٌ . عِطْرٌ	Ethnology n.	البَحْثُ عَنْ أَجْنَاسِ البَشَرِ
Essential a.	جَوْهَرِيٌّ . ضَرُورِيٌّ	Etiquette n.	آدَابُ الإِكْرَامِ
Essentially ad.	حَقِيقَةً	Etymology n.	إِشْتِقَاقُ الكَلَامِ
Establish v. t.	أَقَامَ . ثَبَّتَ	Eulogy n.	تَقْرِيظٌ . تَابِينٌ
Establishment n.	إِقَامَةٌ . بِنَاءٌ	Eunuch n.	خَصِيٌّ
Estate n.	حَالٌ . مُلْكٌ	European n.	اورُبِّيٌّ
Real-estate n.	الأَمْلَاكُ غَيْرُ المَنْقُولَةِ	Evacuate v. t.	أَخْلَى . تَرَكَ
Esteem n. or v. t.	إِعْتِبَارٌ. إِعْتَبَرَ	Evacuation n.	إِخْلَاءٌ . تَرْكٌ
Estimable a.	مُسْتَحِقُّ المَدْحِ	Evade v. t.	إِجْتَنَبَ. مَلَصَ مِنْ
Estimate v. t.	حَسَبَ . ثَمَّنَ	Evanescent a.	فَانٍ . زَائِلٌ
Estimation n.	تَثْمِينٌ . إِعْتِبَارٌ	Evangelical a.	إِنْجِيلِيٌّ
Estrange v. t.	نَفَّرَ	Evangelist n.	مُبَشِّرٌ إِنْجِيلِيٌّ
Estuary n.	مَصَبُّ نَهْرٍ	Evaporate v. i.	تَحَوَّلَ بُخَارًا
Eternal a.	سَرْمَدِيٌّ . أَبَدِيٌّ	Evasion n.	إِجْتِنَابٌ . مُوَارَبَةٌ
Eternity n.	الأَبَدُ . الأَزَلُ	Evasive a.	مُجْتَنِبٌ. مُحَاوِلٌ .مُوَارِبٌ
Ether n.	إِثِيرٌ	Eve Evening } n.	مَسَاءٌ . عَشِيَّةٌ

Even a.	سَهْل . مُسْتَوٍ	Evolve v. t.	نَشَرَ ـُ . اخْرَجَ
Even ad.	حَتَّى . كَذَلِكَ . اَيْضاً	Ewe n.	شَاةٌ . نَعْجَةٌ
Event n.	حَادِثَةٌ . نَتِيجَةٌ	Exact a. or v. t.	مَضْبُوطٌ . اَلْزَمَ
Eventful a.	كَثِيرُ الْحَوَادِثِ	Exaction n.	بَلَصَ . ظُلْمٌ فِي الْأَخْذِ
Eventually a.	فِي النِّهَايَةِ . اَخِيراً	Exactly ad.	تَمَاماً . بِضَبْطٍ
Ever ad.	دَائِماً . كُلَّ حِينٍ	Exactness n.	ضَبْطٌ . إِتْقَانٌ
Evergreen n.	نَبَات دَائِمُ الْإِخْضِرَارِ	Exaggerate v. t.	بَالَغَ . غَالَى فِي
Everlasting a.	اَبَدِيٌّ . بَاقٍ	Exaggeration n.	مُبَالَغَةٌ . مُغَالَاةٌ
Evermore ad.	دَائِماً . اَبَداً	Exalt v. t.	رَقَّى . عَظَّمَ . فَخَّمَ
Every a.	كُلٌّ	Exaltation n.	تَرْقِيَةٌ . سُمُوٌّ . رِفْعَةٌ
Everywhere ad.	فِي كُلِّ مَكَانٍ	Exalted a.	مُرْتَفِعٌ . سَامٍ
Evict v. t.	اَخْرَجَ . طَرَدَ ـُ	Examination n.	فَحْصٌ . إِمْتِحَانٌ
Evidence n.	بُرْهَانٌ . دَلِيلٌ . شَهَادَةٌ	Examine v. t.	فَحَصَ . إِمْتَحَنَ
Evident a.	وَاضِحٌ . ظَاهِرٌ . جَلِيٌّ	Example n.	مِثَالٌ . نَمُوذَجٌ . قُدْوَةٌ
Evil n. or a.	شَرٌّ . شِرِّيرٌ	Exasperate v. i.	اَغَاظَ . اَسْخَطَ
Evince v. t.	اَظْهَرَ . بَيَّنَ	Exasperation n.	إِغَاظَةٌ . حَنَقٌ
Evoke v. t.	إِسْتَدْعَى	Excavate v. t.	حَفَرَ ـُ . نَبَشَ ـُ
Evolution n.	نَشْرٌ . نُشُوءٌ	Excavation n.	حَفْرٌ . حَفْرَةٌ

Exceed *v.t.* or *i.*	زَادَ ـ . فَاقَ ـ . جَاوَزَ
Exceeding *a.*	فَائِقٌ . عَظِيمٌ جِدًّا
Exceedingly *ad.*	جِدًّا . لِلْغَايَةِ
Excel *v. t.* or *i.*	فَاقَ ـ . سَبَقَ ـ
Excellence Excellency	*n.* فَضْلٌ . جُوْدَةٌ . سُمُوٌّ
Excellent *a.*	فَاضِلٌ . فَاخِرٌ . نَفِيسٌ
Except *v. t.*	إِسْتَثْنَى مِنْ
Except Excepting	*pr.* إِلاَّ . غَيْرُ . مَا عَدَا
Exception *n.*	إِسْتِثْنَاءٌ . شُذُوذٌ
Exceptional *a.*	شَاذٌّ . إِسْتِثْنَائِيٌّ
Excess *n.*	زِيَادَةٌ . مُجَاوَزَةُ الْحَدِّ
Excessive *a.*	زَائِدٌ جِدًّا . مُفْرِطٌ
Exchange *v. t.* or *n.*	بَادَلَ . مُبَادَلَةٌ
Excision *n.*	قَطْعٌ . بَتْرٌ
Excitable *a.*	سَرِيعُ الْهَيَجَانِ
Excite *v. t.*	هَيَّجَ . أَثَارَ . حَرَّكَ
Excited *a.*	مُتَهَيِّج . ثَائِرٌ
Exciting *a.*	مُهَيِّجٌ . مُحَرِّكٌ
Excitement *n.*	هَيَجَانٌ . ثَوَرَانٌ
Exclaim *v. i.*	صَاحَ ـ . صَرَخَ ـ
Exclamation *n.*	صُرَاخٌ . صَيْحَةٌ
Exclude *v. t.*	اخْرَجَ . إِسْتَثْنَى
Exclusion *n.*	إِخْرَاجٌ . نَفْيٌ . مَنْعٌ
Exclusive *a.*	نَافٍ . مَانِعٌ . خَاصٌّ
Excommunicate *v. t.*	حَرَّمَ ـ
Excommunication *n.*	حِرْمٌ
Excrement *n.*	بَرَازٌ . رَوْثٌ
Excrescence *n.*	نُتُوٌّ غَيْرُ طَبِيعِيّ
Excretion *n.*	إِفْرَازُ الْفُضُولِ
Excruciating *a.*	أَلِيمٌ جِدًّا . مُعَذِّبٌ
Exculpate *v. t.*	بَرَّأَ . زَكَّى
Excursion *n.*	سَفْرَةٌ قَصِيرَةٌ
Excusable *a.*	مَعْذُورٌ
Excuse *v. t.*	عَذَرَ ـ . سَامَحَ
Excuse *n.*	عُذْرٌ
Execrate *v. t.*	لَعَنَ ـ . كَرِهَ ـ

Execute v. t. أَنْجَزَ . أَعْدَمَ (اَلْحَيَاةَ)	Exhort v. وَعَظَ . اَنْذَرَ . حَثَّ ـُ
Executioner n. مُعْدِمُ اَلْحَيَاةِ . جَلَّادٌ	Exhortation n. وَعْظٌ . إِنْذَارٌ
Executive a. or n. مُجْرٍ . مُنْفِذ . رَئِيسٌ	Exhume v. t. نَبَشَ ـَ اَلْمَدْفُونَ
Executor a. وَكِيلُ تَرِكَةٍ . وَصِيٌّ	Exigence Exigency n. إِحْتِيَاجٌ . إِضْطِرَارٌ
Exemplary a. مُسْتَحِقُّ اَلْإِقْدَاءِ بِهِ	Exile n. or v. t. مَنْفًى . نَفَى ـِ
Exemplify v. t. مَثَّلَ . نَسَخَ ـَ	Exist v. i. كَانَ ـُ . وُجِدَ
Exempt v. t. أَعْفَى مِنْ	Existence n. وُجُودٌ
Exemption n. إِعْفَاءٌ . تَحْرِيرٌ مِنْ	Existent a. Existing ppr. or a. مَوْجُودٌ . كَائِنٌ
Exercise n. مُمَارَسَةٌ . رِيَاضَةٌ	Exodus n. خُرُوجٌ . سِفْرُ اَلْخُرُوجِ
Exert v. t. بَذَلَ اَلْجُهْدَ ـُ . سَعَى ـَ	Exonerate v. t. بَرَّا
Exertion n. إِجْتِهَادٌ . سَعْيٌ . جِدٌّ	Exorbitant a. مُفْرِطٌ . بَاهِظٌ
Exhale v. i. or t. زَفَرَ ـِ	Exotic a. or n. اَجْنَبِيٌّ . (نَبَاتٌ)
Exhaust v. t. فَرَّغَ . أَفْنَى	Expand v. t. or i. مَدَّ ـُ . إِمْتَدَّ
Exhaustion n. نَفَادٌ . كَلَالٌ	Expanse n. إِنْبِسَاطٌ . فُسْحَةٌ
Exhaustive a. مُدَقِّقُ اَلْبَحْثِ . كَامِلٌ	Expantiate v. i. اَطْنَبَ . تَوَسَّعَ فِي
Exhibit v. t. أَظْهَرَ . عَرَضَ ـِ	Expatriate v. t. أَجْلَى عَنِ اَلْوَطَنِ
Exhibiton n. إِظْهَارٌ . مَعْرَضٌ	Expect v. t. إِنْتَظَرَ . تَوَقَّعَ
Exhilarate v. t. ابْهَجَ . أَنْعَشَ	Expectancy Expectation n. إِنْتِظَارٌ . تَوَقُّعٌ

Expectorate v. t.	بَصَقَ ـُ . نَفَثَ ـُ
Expectoration n.	بَصْق . نَفْث
Expedience ⎱ n. Expediency ⎰	مُوَافَقَة . مُنَاسَبَة
Expedient a.	مُوَافِق . نَافِع
Expedient n.	وَسِيلَة . وَاسِطَة
Expedite v. t.	عَجَّلَ . بَعَثَ ـَ
Expedition n.	سُرْعَة . إِرْسَالِيَّة
Expel v. t.	طَرَدَ ـُ . أَخْرَجَ
Expend v. t.	صَرَفَ ـِ . أَنْفَقَ
Expenditure n.	صَرْف . نَفَقَة
Expense n.	نَفَقَة . مَصْرُوف
Expensive a.	غَالٍ . (مُكَلِّف)
Experience n. or v. t.	إِخْتِبَار . إِخْتَبَرَ
Experienced a.	خَبِير . مُخْتَبِر
Experiment n.	إِمْتِحَان . تَجْرِبَة
Expert n.	مَاهِر . بَارِع . خَبِير
Expiate v. t.	كَفَّرَ عَنْ ●
Expiration n.	إِنْقِضَاءٌ . نِهَايَة

Expire v. i.	مَاتَ . إِنْقَضَى . زَفَرَ ـِ
Explain v. t.	فَسَّرَ . أَوْضَحَ
Explanation n.	تَفْسِير . إِيضَاح
Explanatory a.	مُفَسِّر . تَفْسِيرِيّ
Explicit a.	صَرِيح . وَاضِح
Explode v. i.	إِنْفَجَرَ
Exploration n.	إِكْتِشَاف . رَوْد
Explore v. t.	زَادَ ـُ . إِكْتَشَفَ
Explosion n.	إِنْفِجَار
Explosive a. or n.	مُسَبِّبُ ٱلْإِنْفِجَار
Export v. t.	أَصْدَرَ بَضَائِع
Exports n. pl.	بَضَائِع صَادِرَة
Expose v. t.	كَشَفَ ـِ . عَرَضَ ـِ
Exposition n.	عَرْض . تَفْسِير
Expostulate v. i.	نَصَحَ ـَ عَاقَبَ
Exposure n.	كَشْف . عَرْض
Expound v. t.	فَسَّرَ . شَرَحَ ـَ
Express a. or n.	صَرِيح . خَاصّ

Express *n.*	رَسُولٌ خَاصٌّ . مَرْكَبَةٌ خَاصَّةٌ
Express *v. t.*	عَصَرَ ـ أَظْهَرَ
Expressed *a.*	مَقُولٌ . مَنْطُوقٌ بِهِ
Expression *n.*	عِبَارَةٌ . أُسْلُوبُ النُّطْقِ
Expressive *a.*	بَلِيغٌ . مُفِيدُ الْمَعْنَى
Expressly *ad.*	خَاصَّةً . صَرِيحاً
Expulsion *n.*	طَرْدٌ . إِخْرَاجٌ
Expunge *v. t.*	مَحَا ـ أَزَالَ
Expurgate *v. t.*	طَهَّرَ . نَقَّحَ
Exquisite *a.*	نَفِيسٌ . فَاخِرٌ
Extant *a.*	بَاقٍ فِي الْوُجُودِ
Extemporaneous Extemporary } *a.*	مُرْتَجِلٌ
Extempore *ad.*	إِرْتِجَالاً
Extemporize *v. t.*	إِبْتَدَهَ . أَرْتَجَلَ
Extend *v. t.* or *i.*	مَدَّ . إِمْتَدَّ
Extension *n.*	مَدٌّ . إِمْتِدَادٌ . إِتِّسَاعٌ
Extensive *a.*	مُمْتَدٌّ . مُتَّسِعٌ
Extent *n.*	إِمْتِدَادٌ . سِعَةٌ
Extenuate *v. t.*	خَفَّفَ . خَفَّضَ
Exterior *a.* or *n.*	خَارِجِيٌّ . الْخَارِجُ
Exterminate *v. t.*	إِسْتَأْصَلَ . أَبَادَ
External *a.*	خَارِجِيٌّ . عَرَضِيٌّ
Extinct *a.*	مُنْقَرِضٌ . مَعْدُومٌ
Extinction *n.*	إِنْقِرَاضٌ
Extinguish *v. t.*	أَطْفَأَ . أَزَالَ
Extirpate *v. t.*	إِسْتَأْصَلَ . أَبَادَ
Extol *v. t.*	مَجَّدَ . فَخَّمَ
Extort *v. t.*	بَلَصَ
Extortion *n.*	بَلْصٌ
Extortionate *a.* Extortioner *n.* }	بَلَّاصٌ
Extra *n.* or *a.*	زِيَادَةٌ . زَائِدٌ
Extract *n.*	جُمْلَةٌ مُقْتَبَسَةٌ . خُلَاصَةٌ
Extract *v. t.*	إِسْتَخْرَجَ . إِقْتَبَسَ
Extraction *n.*	إِسْتِخْرَاجٌ . نَسَبٌ
Extraordinary *a.*	فَوْقَ الْعَادَةِ . غَرِيبٌ

Extravagance n.	إِسْرَافٌ . إِفْرَاطٌ	Eye n. or v. t.	عَيْنٌ ج أَعْيُن . رَاقَبَ
Extravagant a.	مُسْرِفٌ . مُفْرِطٌ . مُبَالِغٌ	Eyeball n.	مُقْلَةٌ . مَقَلٌ
Extreme a.	اقْصَى . اشَدُّ	Eye-brow n.	حَاجِبٌ ج حَوَاجِبُ
Extremely ad.	لِلْغَايَةِ . جِدًّا	Eye-glass n.	مَنْظَرٌ
Extreme Extremity } n.	طَرَفٌ . حَاجَةٌ شَدِيدَةٌ	Eye-lashes n. pl.	هُدْبٌ ج أَهْدَابٌ
Extricate v. t.	نَشَلَ ـَ . أَنْقَذَ . فَكَّ	Eyelid n.	جَفْنٌ ج أَجْفَانٌ
Exuberance n.	وَفْرَةٌ . غَزَارَةٌ . خِصْبٌ	Eye-sight n.	بَصَرٌ . عِيَانٌ
Exude v. t. or i.	رَشَحَ . أَفْرَزَ	Eye-tooth n. Tusk.	نَابٌ ج أَنْيَابٌ
Exult v. i.	إِبْتَهَجَ . تَهَلَّلَ		

F

Fable n.	خُرَافَةٌ . خُزَعْبَلَةٌ	Face n. or v. t.	وَجْهٌ . سَطْحٌ . وَاجَهَ
Fabric n.	بِنْيَةٌ . نَسِيجٌ	Facetious a.	مَازِحٌ . هَازِلٌ
Fabricate v. t.	صَنَعَ . إِخْتَلَقَ	Facilitate v. t.	سَهَّلَ . يَسَّرَ
Fabulous a.	خُرَافِيٌّ . خُزَعْبَلِيٌّ	Facility n.	سُهُولَةٌ . يُسْرٌ

Fac-simile n.	نُسْخَة طِبْق ٱلْأَصْلِ
Fact n.	حَقِيقَة . أَمْرٌ . وَاقِعٌ
Faction n.	عَصَبَة . حِزْبٌ
Factious a.	حِزْبِي . مُتَحَزِّبٌ
Factitious a.	مَصْنَع
Factor n.	عَامِل . أَصْلُ ٱلْحَاصِلِ . ضِلْع
Factory n.	مَعْمَل
Faculty n.	قُوَّة . طَاقَة . (عُمْدَة)
Fade v. i.	ذَبَلَ . جَرِدَ . بَاخَ
Fagot n.	حُزْمَة قُضْبَان
Fail v. t. or i.	خَابَ . اَفْلَسَ
Failure n.	خَيْبَة . إِفْلَاسٌ
Fain a. or ad.	مَسْرُورٌ . بِرِضًى
Faint a. or v. i.	مَعِي . أَعْيِي . غُشِيَ عَلَيْهِ
Faint-hearted a.	جَبَان . خَائِفَ
Faintly ad.	بِضُعْف . قَلِيلاً
Faintness n.	إِعْيَاءٌ . إِغْمَاءٌ
Fair a. or n.	حَسَنٌ . صَافٍ . سُوقٌ

Fairly ad.	بِإِسْتِقَامَة . بِعَدْل
Fairness n.	عَدَالَة . حُسْنٌ . بَيَاضٌ
Fairy n. or a.	جِنِّيَة . جِنِّيّ
Faith n.	إِيمَان . إِعْتِقَاد . مَذْهَبٌ
Faithful a.	أَمِين . صَادِقٌ
Faithfulness n.	أَمَانَة
Faithless a.	غَيْرُ مُؤْمِنٍ . خَائِنٌ
Falcon n.	بَاز . صَقْر
Falconer n.	مُرَبِّي اوْ مُطَبِّعُ ٱلْبُزَاةِ
Fall v. i. or n.	سَقَطَ . وُقَعَ . سُقُوط
Fallacious a.	خَادِعٌ . سَفْسَطِيّ
Fallacy n.	خَطَأً . إِسْتِدْلَالٌ . فَاسِدٌ
Fallible a.	قَابِلُ ٱلْخَطَأِ اوْ ٱلزَّلَلِ
Fallow a. or n.	أَرْضٌ غَيْرُ مَزْرُوعَةٍ
False a.	كَاذِبٌ . مُزَوَّرٌ . بَاطِل
Falsehood n.	كِذْبٌ . زُوْرٌ
Falsify v. t. or i.	زَوَّرَ . كَذَّبَ
Falter v. i.	تَرَدَّدَ . قَصَّرَ . أَعْتَم

Fame *n.*	صِيتٌ عَظِيمٌ . شُهْرَةٌ
Famed *a.*	مَشْهُورٌ . شَهِيرٌ
Familiar *a.* or *n.*	مَأْلُوفٌ . مَعْرُوفٌ
Familiarity *n.*	أُلْفَةٌ . صَدَاقَةٌ . مَعْرِفَةٌ
Familiarize *v. t.*	أَلَّفَ . عَوَّدَ . سَهَّلَ
Family *n.*	عَائِلَةٌ . آلٌ . نَسَبٌ
Famine *n.*	مَجَاعَةٌ . قَحْطٌ . غَلَاءٌ
Famish *v. i.* or *t.*	مَاتَ جُوعاً . جَوَّعَ
Famous *a.*	شَهِيرٌ . كَثِيرُ الذِّكْرِ
Fan *n.* or *v. t.*	مَرْوَحَةٌ . هَوَّى . رَوَّحَ
Fanatic *n.* Fanatical *a.*	مُتَعَصِّبٌ فِي الدِّينِ
Fancied *a.*	مَوْهُومٌ . مُتَصَوَّرٌ
Fanciful *a.*	وَهْمِيٌّ . تَصَوُّرِيٌّ
Fancy *n.* or *v. t.* or *i.*	وَهْمٌ . تَصَوَّرَ
Fang *n.*	نَابٌ . مَخْلَبٌ
Fantasm *n.*	وَهْمٌ . خَيَالٌ
Fantastic Fantastical *a.*	وَهْمِيٌّ . خَيَالِيٌّ
Fantasy *n.*	وَهْمٌ . تَصَوُّرٌ . بَاطِلٌ
Far *a.* or *ad.*	بَعِيذٌ . بَعِيداً
Farce *n.*	رِوَايَةٌ سُخْرِيَّةٌ . بُطْلٌ
Farewell *n.*	اَلْوِدَاعُ
Farm *n.* or *v. t.*	مَزْرَعَةٌ . فَلَجَ . اِقْطَعَ
Farmer *n.*	فَلَّاحٌ . مُلْتَزِمٌ
Farming *n.*	فِلَاحَةٌ
Farrier *n.*	بَيْطَارٌ ج بَيَاطِرَة
Farther *a.*	أَبْعَدُ . أَيْضاً
Farthing *n.*	فَلْسٌ ج فُلُوسٌ
Fascinate *v. t.*	فَتَنَ . خَلَبَ ـ
Fascination *n.*	اِفْتِتَانٌ
Fashion *n.* or *v. t.*	زِيٌّ . عَادَةٌ . جَبَلَ ـِ
Fashionable *a.*	بِحَسَبِ الزِّيِّ اوِ الْعَادَةِ
Fast *a.*	سَرِيعٌ . ثَابِتٌ . مَاكِنٌ
Fast *n.* or *v. i.*	صَوْمٌ . صَامَ ـُ
Fasten *v. t.*	مَكَّنَ . ثَبَّتَ . شَدَّ ـُ
Fastidious *a.*	صَعْبُ الإِرْضَاءِ
Fat *n.* or *a.*	دُهْنٌ . سَمِينٌ

Fatal a.	مُمِيتٌ . مُهْلِكٌ	Fatty a.	دَسِمٌ . دَهِنٌ
Fatalism n.	اَلْإِعْتِقَادُ بِالْقَدَرِ	Faucet n.	اُنْبُوبَةٌ . حَنَفِيَّةٌ
Fatalist n.	مُعْتَقِدٌ بِالْقَدَرِ	Fault n.	عَيْبٌ . ذَنْبٌ . غَلَطٌ
Fatally ad.	مُمِيتًا	Faultless a.	بِلَا عَيْبٍ . كَامِلٌ
Fatality Fate } n.	قَدَرٌ . قَضَاءٌ	Faulty a.	عَائِبٌ . مَغْلُوطٌ . نَاقِصٌ
Fated a.	مُقَدَّرٌ . مَقْضِيٌّ بِهِ	Favour v. t.	أَحْسَنَ إِلَى . اَعَانَ
Fates n. pl.	تَقَادِيرُ	Favour n.	مَعْرُوفٌ . نِعْمَةٌ . رِضًى
Father n.	أَبٌ ج آبَاءٌ . وَالِدٌ	Favourable a.	مُوَافِقٌ . لَطِيفٌ
Father-in-law n.	حَمٌ أَوْ حَمُو	Favourite n. or a.	خَلِيلٌ . عَزِيزٌ . حَبِيبٌ
Fatherland n.	وَطَنٌ ج أَوْطَانٌ	Favouritism n.	مُحَابَاةٌ
Fatherless a.	بِلَا أَبٍ . يَتِيمٌ	Fawn v. t.	تَذَلَّلَ لَهُ . دَاهَنَ
Fatherly a.	أَبَوِيٌّ	Fawn n. or a.	وَلَدُ الْأَيِّلِ . مِنْ لَوْنِهِ
Fathom n. or v. t.	قَامَةٌ . سَبَرَ	Fealty n.	أَمَانَةٌ . طَاعَةٌ
Fathomless a.	عَمِيقٌ لَا يُسْبَرُ غَوْرُهُ	Fear n. or v. t.	خَوْفٌ . خَافَ
Fatigue n. or v. t.	وَنًى . تَعَبٌ . اتْعَبَ	Fearful a.	خَائِفٌ . مُخِيفٌ . رَائِعٌ
Fatling n.	مُسَمَّنٌ . مَعْلُوفٌ	Fearfulness n.	خَوْفٌ . حَالَتُهُ
Fatness n.	سَمَانَةٌ . دَسَمٌ	Fearless a.	بِلَا خَوْفٍ . جَسُورٌ
Fatten v. t.	سَمَّنَ . دَسَّمَ	Feasible n.	مُمْكِنٌ فِعْلُهُ

Feast *n.* or *v. t.* or *i.*	عِيدٌ . وَلِيمَةٌ . أَوْلَمَ
Feat *n.*	عَمَلٌ . عَجِيبٌ
Feather *n.*	رِيشَةٌ ج رِيشٌ
Feature *n.*	هَيْئَةٌ . طَلْعَةٌ . صِفَةٌ
February *n.*	شَهْرُ شُبَاطٍ (فبراير)
Fecund *a.*	مُخْصِبٌ. مُثْمِرٌ (لِلْحَيَوَانِ)
Fee *n.* or *v. t.*	أُجْرَةٌ . هِبَةٌ . آجَرَ
Feeble *a.*	ضَعِيفٌ . عَاجِزٌ
Feebleness *n.*	ضُعْفٌ . وَهْنٌ
Feed *a.* or *v. t.*	عَلَفٌ . أَطْعَمَ
Feel *v. t.* or *i.*	لَمَسَ . حَسَّ
Feeling *n.*	حِسٌّ . شُعُورٌ . إِنْفِعَالٌ
Feign *v. t.*	تَظَاهَرَ . تَرَاءَى
Feint *n.*	حِيلَةٌ . تَظَاهُرٌ
Felicitate *v. t.*	هَنَّا
Felicity *n.*	سَعَادَةٌ . غِبْطَةٌ
Fell *v. t.*	رَمَى . أَلْقَى
Fellow *n.*	رَفِيقٌ . قَرِينٌ
Fellowship *n.*	أُلْفَةٌ. صُحْبَةٌ. شِرْكَةٌ
Felon Felonious *a.*	مُجْرِمٌ بِذَنْبٍ عَظِيمٍ
Felony *n.*	جَرِيمَةٌ عَظِيمَةٌ . جِنَايَةٌ
Felt *n.*	اِبْدَجْ لِبُودٌ . وَالْبَادْ
Female *n.* or *a.*	أُنْثَى ج اِنَاثٌ
Feminine *a.*	مُؤَنَّثٌ . اِنْثَوِيٌّ
Fen *n.*	مُسْتَنْقَعٌ
Fence *n.* or *v. t.*	سِيَاجٌ . سَيَّجَ
Ferment Fermentation *a.*	إِخْتِمَارٌ . هَيَجَانٌ
Ferment *v. i.* or *t.*	خَمَّرَ . إِخْتَمَرَ
Fern *n.*	خَنْشَارٌ (نَبَاتٌ)
Ferocious *a.*	ضَارٍ . مُفْتَرِسٌ
Ferocity *n.*	تَوَحُّشٌ . قَسَاوَةٌ
Ferry *n.* or *v. t.*	مَعْبَرٌ . عَبَّرَ
Fertile *a.*	مُخْصِبٌ . مُثْمِرٌ
Fertility *n.*	خِصْبٌ
Fertilize *v. t.*	خَصَّبَ . لَقَّحَ
Fervency *n.*	حَرَارَةٌ . حَمَاسَةٌ

Fervent / Fervid *a.*	حَارٌّ . غَيُورٌ . حَادٌّ
Fervour *n.*	حَرَارَةٌ . حَمَاسَةٌ . حَمِيَّةٌ
Festal *a.*	مُفَرِّحٌ . عِيدِيٌّ
Fester *v. i.* or *n.*	تَقَيَّحَ . قَيْحٌ
Festival *n.*	عِيدٌ . فَرَحٌ
Festivity *n.*	فَرَحٌ . بَسْطٌ . عِيدٌ
Fetch *v. t.*	جَاءَ بِهِ . أَحْضَرَ
Fetid *a.*	مُنْتِنٌ . مُحَمّمٌ
Fetter *n.* or *v. t.*	قَيْدٌ . قَيَّدَ
Fetus *n.*	جَنِينٌ ج أَجِنَّةٌ
Feud *n.*	نِزَاعٌ . شِقَاقٌ
Fever *n.*	حُمَّى
Feverish *a.*	مَحْمُومٌ
Few *a.*	قَلِيلٌ . يَسِيرٌ
Fib *n.* or *v. i.*	كِذْبَةٌ . كَذَبَ
Fibre / Fibril *n.*	لِيفَةٌ . لِيفٌ . لُوَيْفَةٌ
Fickle *a.*	مُتَقَلِّبٌ . مُتَرَدِّدٌ
Fickleness *n.*	تَقَلُّبٌ . طَيْشٌ
Fiction *n.*	خُرَافَةٌ . كَذِبٌ
Fictitious *a.*	كَاذِبٌ . وَهْمِيٌّ
Fiddle *n.*	كَمَنْجَة
Fidelity *n.*	أَمَانَةٌ . صِدْقٌ
Fidget *v. t.*	قَلِقَ . ضَجِرَ
Fidgety *a.*	قَلِقٌ . مُضْطَرِبٌ . ضَجِرٌ
Field *n.*	حَقْلٌ . سَاحَةٌ
Field-piece *n.*	مَدْفَعٌ . صَغِيرٌ
Fiend *n.*	عَدُوٌّ . خَبِيثٌ . شَيْطَان
Fierce *a.*	عَنِيفٌ . حَادٌّ . شَرِسٌ
Fiery *a.*	نَارِيٌّ . حَادُّ الطَّبْعِ
Fife *n.*	مِزْمَارٌ
Fifteen *a.*	خَمْسَةَ عَشَرَ . خَمْسَ عَشْرَةَ
Fifteenth *a.*	الْخَامِسَ عَشَرَ
Fifth *a.* or *n.*	خَامِسٌ . خُمْسٌ
Fiftieth / Fifty *a.*	الْخَمْسُونَ . خَمْسُونَ
Fig *n.*	تِينَة
Fight *n.* or *v. t.*	قِتَالٌ . قَاتَلَ

Figurative a.	مَجَازِيٌّ . إِسْتِعَارِيٌّ
Figure n. or v.t. or i.	صُورَة . صَوَّرَ . حَسَبَ . ظَهَرَ
Filbert n.	بُنْدُقَة
Filch v. t.	سَرَقَ ـِ . أَسَلَ
File n. or v. t.	مِبْرَدٌ . صَفٌّ . بَرَدَ ـُ
Filial a.	بَنَوِيٌّ . وَلَدِيٌّ
Fill v. t.	مَلَأَ . أَفْعَمَ
Filly n.	فِلْوٌ . مُهْرَة
Film n.	غِشَاوَة
Filter n. or v. t.	مِصْفَاة . صَفَّى
Filth Filthness } n.	وَسَخٌ . قَذَرٌ
Filthy a.	وَسِخٌ . قَذِرٌ
Filtrate v. t.	صَفَّى
Fin n.	زِعْنِفَة (اَلسَّمَك)
Final a.	نِهَائِيٌّ . أَخِيرٌ
Finally ad.	أَخِيرًا
Finance n.	مَالِيَّة
Financial a.	مَالِيٌّ
Financier n.	مَاهِرٌ بِالأُمُورِ اَلْمَالِيَّة
Find v. t. (pp. Found)	وَجَدَ ـِ
Fine a.	دَقِيقٌ . نَاعِمٌ
Fine n. or v. t.	غَرَامَة . غَرَّمَ
Fineness n.	دِقَّة . رِقَّة
Finery n.	زِينَة . حِلْيَة
Finesse n.	دَهَاءٌ . حِيلَة
Finger n. or v.t.	إِصْبَع . مَسَّ . جَسَّ ـُ
Finish v. t.	أَنْهَى . أَنْجَزَ . أَكْمَلَ
Finite a.	مَحْدُودٌ . مُتَنَاهٍ
Fir n.	شَرْبَين . (شَجَر)
Fire n.	نَارٌ . حَرَارَةُ اَلْخُلُق
Fire v. t.	اوْقَدَ . أَطْلَقَ (اَلأَسْلِحَة)
Fire-arms n. pl.	أَسْلِحَة . نَارِيَّة
Fire-engine n.	آلَة لِإِطْفَاءِ اَلنَّار
Firefly n.	حَبَاحِبُ
Fire-place n.	مَوْقِدٌ
Fireside n.	مَوْقِدُ اَلْعَائِلَة . أَلْبَيْت

Fireworks *n. pl.*	أَلْعَابٌ . نَارِيَةٌ	Fit *a.* or *v. t.*	مُنَاسِبٌ . نَاسَبَ
Firm *a.* or *n.*	ثَابِتٌ . رَاسِخٌ شِرْكَةٌ (تُجَّار)	Fitful *a.*	مُتَغَيِّرٌ . غَيْرُ مَضْبُوطٍ
Firmament *n.*	جَلَدٌ . جَوٌّ	Fitness *n.*	لِيَاقَةٌ . مُنَاسَبَةٌ
Firman *n.*	فَرَمَانٌ	Five *n.* or *a.*	خَمْسَةٌ
Firmly *ad.*	بِثَبَاتٍ . بِعَزْمٍ	Fivefold *a.* or *ad.*	خَمْسَةُ أَضْعَافٍ
Firmness *n.*	ثَبَاتٌ . عَزْمٌ . مَتَانَةٌ	Fix *v. t.* or *i.*	ثَبَّتَ . مَكَّنَ . أَرْسَخَ
First *a.* or *ad.*	اَلْأَوَّلُ . أَوَّلاً . اِبْتِدَاءً	Fizz *v. i.* / Fizzle *v. i.*	صَفَرَ ﹻ (نَارٌ)
First-born *n.*	بِكْرٌ ج أَبْكَارٌ	Flabby / Flaccid *a.*	رَخْوٌ . مُرْتَخٍ
First-rate *a.*	عَالٍ . فَائِقٌ	Flag *n.*	حَلْفَاءُ . رَايَةٌ . بَلَاطَةٌ
Fiscal *a.*	مُخْتَصٌّ بِالْمَالِيَّةِ	Flag *v. t.*	ضَعُفَ ﹷ . اِسْتَرْخَى
Fish *n.* or *v. t.* or *i.*	سَمَكٌ . صَادَ ﹻ	Flagitious *a.*	خَبِيثٌ . فَاجِرٌ
Fisherman *n.*	صَيَّادُ سَمَكٍ	Flagon *n.*	إِبْرِيقٌ لِلْمُسْكِرَاتِ
Fishery *a.*	صَيْدُ السَّمَكِ أَو مَحَلُّهُ	Flagrant *a.*	مُفْرِطٌ . قَبِيحٌ
Fish-hook *n.*	صِنَّارَةُ الصَّيْدِ	Flag-ship *n.*	بَارِجَةُ أَمِيرِ الْبَحْرِ
Fishing *n.*	صَيْدُ السَّمَكِ	Flag-staff *n.*	سَارِيَةُ الرَّايَةِ
Fissure *n.*	شِقٌّ . فَلْقٌ	Flag-stone *n.*	بَلَاطَةٌ
Fist *n.*	قَبْضَةُ الْيَدِ	Flake *n.*	صَفِيحَةٌ رَقِيقَةٌ
Fit *n,*	نَوْبَةٌ . صَرْعٌ . دَوْرٌ	Flame *n.* or *v. i.*	لَهِيبٌ . اِلْتَهَبَ

Flaming a. ملْتهِب . برّاق . مُحْتدٌّ	Fleece n. or v. t. جَزَّة . جَزَّ. سَلَبَ
Flank n. or v. خاصِرَة أتَى آلجانبَ	Fleet a. or n. سَرِيعٌ. اسطُولٌ
Flannel n. نَسِيجٌ صُوفيٌّ (فَلازنلاً)	Fleeting a. وقْتيٌّ. فَان
Flap n. or v. t. or i. ذَيْلَ (ثَوْب) خَفَقَ ـِ	Flesh n. لَحْمٌ . جَسَدٌ . أَلبَشَرُ
Flare v. i. خَفَقَ (آللهيبُ)تألّقَ	Fleshly a. حيوانيٌّ . شَهوانيٌّ
Flash n. or v. i. وَميضٌ. أُومضَ . برقَ ـ	Fleshy a. سَمِينٌ. لَحِميٌّ
Flask n. قنِّينَةٌ . قَارُورَةٌ	Flew pret. of fly طَارَ
Flat a. or n. مُسَطّح. طبقة . سَهلٌ	Flexibility n. لِينٌ .مُرُونَةٌ
Flatten v. t. or i. سَطّحَ. تَسطّحَ	Flexible a. لَيّنٌ . مَرِنٌ . مُنقَادٌ
Flatter v. t. مَلقَ ـَ . داهَنَ	Flicker v. i. خَفَقَ ـِ لَالأَ
Flatterer Flattering } مُتملِّق.مُداهِنٌ	Flight n. طيرانٌ.هرَبٌ . فَرَارٌ
Flattery n. مَلقٌ . مُداهنةٌ	Flighty a. طائشٌ.مُتخيِّلٌ
Flavour n. or v. t. طَعمٌ. رَائِحَة. تبّلَ	Flimsy a. سَخيفٌ . ضَعيفٌ.باطلٌ
Flaw n. عيبٌ . خلَلٌ . شَقٌّ	Fling v. t. or n.رمَى ـِ.طرَحَ ـَ.رَمْيٌ
Flax n. كَتّانٌ (نبَاتٌ) قنّبٌ	Flint n. صوّانٌ
Flay v. t. سلَخَ ـَ . كَشطَ ـِ	Flippant a. خَفيفُ آلـكلَامِ .ثقباقٌ
Flea n. بُرغُوثٌ ج. برَاغيثُ	Flirt v. t., i. or n.غازَلَ. غنِجَ.غنجةٌ
Flee(Fled) v. i. هرَبَ ـُ . فرَّ ـِ	Flirtation n. غنجٌ. مُغَازَلَةٌ

Flit v. i. Flitter v. i.	هَفَتَ ـِ . حَامَ ـُ
Float v. t. or i.	عَامَ ـُ . سَبَّحَ
Flock n. or v.i.	قَطِيعٌ . سِرْبٌ تَجَمَّعَ
Flog v. t.	جَلَدَ ـِ . سَاطَ ـُ
Flogging n.	جَلْدٌ . سَوْطٌ
Flop v. t.	صَفَقَ . تَقَلَّبَ
Flood n. or v. t.	طُوفَانٌ . غَمَرَ ـُ
Floor n. or v. t.	أَرْضُ ٱلْبَيْتِ . طَبَقَةٌ . بَلَّطَ
Flora n.	نَبَاتُ إِقْلِيمٍ . شَرْحُهُ
Floral a.	زَهْرِيٌّ
Florid a.	أَحْمَرُ . زَاهِرٌ . مُزَوَّقٌ
Florist n.	مُرَبِّي ٱلزُّهُورِ
Flotilla n.	أُسْطُولٌ صَغِيرٌ
Flounce Flounder } v. i.	تَمَرَّغَ . تَقَلَّبَ
Flour n.	طَحِينٌ . دَقِيقٌ
Flourish v.t. or i.	هَنَّى . أَزْهَرَ . أَفْلَحَ
Flow v. i.	جَرَى ـِ . سَالَ ـِ . نَبَعَ ـُ
Flower n.	زَهْرَةٌ . زُبْدَةٌ

Flowery a.	زَهْرِيٌّ . أَزْهَرَ . زَاهِرٌ
Flown see Fly.	طَارَ . طَيَّرَ
Fluctuatte v.i.	تَقَلَّبَ . تَرَدَّدَ
Fluency n.	طَلَاقَةُ ٱللِّسَانِ
Fluent a.	ذَلِقٌ . طَلِقُ ٱللِّسَانِ
Fluid n.	سَائِلٌ . مَائِعٌ
Fluidity n.	سَيَلَانٌ . مَيْعٌ
Flush n. or v. i.	إِحْمِرَارٌ . إِحْمَرَّ
Flute n.	نَايٌ
Flutter v. i. or n.	خَفَقَ ـِ . خَفَقَانٌ
Fly v. i. or t.	طَارَ . طَيَّرَ
Fly n.	ذُبَابَةٌ ج ذِبَّانٌ وَذُبَابٌ
Fly-leaf n.	وَرَقَةٌ بَيْضَاءُ فِي كِتَابٍ
Foal n. or v. i.	فَلْوٌ . وَلَدَتْ (فَرَسٌ
Foam n. or v. i.	رَغْوَةٌ . زَبَدٌ ازْبَدَ
Foamy Foaming } a.	مُزْبِدٌ
Focus n.	نُقْطَةُ ٱلْإِحْتِرَاقِ
Fodder n. or v.t.	عَلَفٌ . عَلَفَ ـِ

Foe n.	عَدُوٌّ . خَصْمٌ	Foolishness n.	جَهْلٌ . حَمَاقَةٌ
Fog n.	ضَبَابٌ	Foolhardy a	مُتَهَوِّرٌ . مُخَاطِرٌ بِنَفْسِهِ جَهْلًا
Foil v. t. or n.	خَيَّبَ . صَفِيحَةٌ . رَقِيقَةٌ	Foot n.	قَدَمُ رِجْلٍ . وَزْنُ شِعْرٍ
Fold n.	ضِعْفٌ . ثِنْيٌ . حَظِيرَةٌ	Footman n.	خَادِمٌ . تَابِعٌ
Fold v. t.	ثَنَى ﻴﻪ . زَرَبَ ﻴﻪ	Foot-path n.	مَمْشًى . مَسْلَكٌ (لِلرَّاجِلِ)
Foliage n.	أَوْرَاقُ ٱلنَّبَاتِ	Footstep n.	خُطْوَةٌ . أَثَرُ ٱلْقَدَمِ
Folk n.	أَهْلٌ . قَوْمٌ . اناَسٌ	Footstool n.	كُرْسِيٌّ لِلرِّجْلَيْنِ
Follow v. t. or i.	تَبِعَ ﻴﻪ . نَتَجَ مِنْ	For pr. or conj.	لِأَجْلِ . لِ . لِأَنَّ
Follower n.	تَابِعٌ . تِلْمِذٌ	Forage n.	عَلَفٌ . عُلُوفَةٌ
Following n.	قَوْمٌ . اتْبَاعٌ	Forasmuch conj.	حَيْثُ . بِمَا أَنَّ
Folly n.	جَهَالَةٌ . حَمَاقَةٌ . سَفَهٌ	Foray n.	غَزْوَةٌ . غَارَةٌ
Foment v. t.	اثَارَ . هَيَّجَ	Forbear v. t. or i.	إِمْتَنَعَ . كَفَّ ﻴﻪ
Fond a.	مُولَعٌ . مُحِبٌّ	Forbearance n.	إِحْتِمَالٌ . إِمْتِنَاعٌ
Fondle v. t.	دَلَّلَ . لَاطَفَ	Forbid v. t.	نَهَى ﻴﻪ . مَنَعَ ﻴﻪ
Fondness n.	غَرَامٌ . وَدَادٌ	Force n. or v. t.	قُوَّةٌ . فَاعِلِيَّةٌ . أَلْزَمَ
Font n.	طَقْمُ احْرُفٍ . نَبْعٌ	Forceps n. pl.	مِلْقَطٌ . جِرَاحِيٌّ
Food n.	طَعَامٌ . قُوتٌ	Forcible a.	قَوِيٌّ . فَعَّالٌ
Fool n. / Foolish a.	جَاهِلٌ . غَبِيٌّ . سَفِيهٌ	Ford n. or v. t.	مَخَاضَةٌ . خَاضَ ﻴﻪ

Fore-arm n.	سَاعِد	Foremost a.	الاوَّلُ . اَلْمَتَقَدِّمُ
Forebode v.t.	تَشَاءَمَ . أَنْبَأَ بِشَرّ	Forenoon n.	مَا قَبْلَ الظُّهْرِ
Forecast n. or v.t.	تَدْبِيرٌ سَابِقٌ . دَبَّرَ	Foreordain v. t.	سَبَقَ فَعَيَّنَ
Forecastle n.	أَعْلَى مُقَدَّمِ السَّفِينَةِ	Foresee v. t.	سَبَقَ فَنَظَرَ أَوْ عَرَفَ
Forefather n.	جَدٌّ . سَلَف	Foresight v.	سَبَقَ النَّظَرِ . عِنَايَة
Forefinger n.	سَبَّابَة	Forest n.	غَابَة . عَرِينٌ
Forefoot n.	قَائِمَة . مُقَدَّمَةٌ لِلْبَهِيمَةِ	Forestall n. n.	سَبَقَ إِلَى
Forego v. t.	تَنَازَلَ عَنْ . تَرَكَ ـُ	Foretell v. t.	سَبَقَ فَاخْبَرَ . أَنْبَأَ
Foregoing a.	مُتَقَدِّمٌ . سَالِفٌ	Forethought n.	فِكْرٌ سَابِقٌ . تَبَصُّرٌ
Foregone a.	مَعْزُومٌ عَلَيْهِ . مَحْتُومٌ	Forever ad.	إِلَى الآبَدِ
Forehead n.	جِبْهَة	Forewarn v.t.	سَبَقَ فَحَذَّرَ . انْذَرَ
Foreign Foreigner } n.	أَجْنَبِيٌّ . غَرِيبٌ	Forfeit v.t. or n.	غَرِمَ فِي جِنَايَةٍ . غَرَامَة
Forejudge v. t.	سَبَقَ فَقَضَى	Forge n. or v. t.	كُورٌ . زَوَّرَ
Foreknow v. t.	سَبَقَ فَعَرَفَ	Forger n.	حَدَّادٌ . مُزَوِّرٌ
Foreknowledge n.	عِلْمٌ سَابِقٌ	Forgery n.	تَزْوِيرٌ . زَيْفٌ
Forelock n.	نَاصِيَةٌ ج نَوَاصٍ	Forget v. t. (Forgot)	أَسِيَ ـَ
Foreman n.	نَاظِرٌ . رَئِيسُ شُغْلٍ	Forgetful a.	نَاسٍ . غَافِلٌ
Foremast n.	سَارِيَةُ الْمُقَدَّمِ	Forgetfulness n.	نِسْيَانٌ . غَفَلٌ

Forgive v. t.	غَفَرَ ـ لَهُ
Forgiveness n.	غُفْرَانٌ . مَغْفِرَةٌ
Fork n. or v. t.	شَوْكَةٌ . تَشَعَّبَ
Forked a.	مُتَشَعِّبٌ . مُتَفَرِّعٌ
Forlorn a.	مُهْمَلٌ . بَائِسٌ
Form n.	رَسْمٌ . شَكْلٌ . هَيْئَةٌ
Form v. t.	كَوَّنَ . صَوَّرَ . عَمِلَ ـ
Formal a.	رَسْمِيٌّ . خَارِجِيٌّ
Formality n.	عَادَةٌ رَسْمِيَّةٌ . تَكْلِيفٌ
Formally ad.	رَسْماً . بِالظَّاهِرِ فَقَط
Formation n.	تَكْوِينٌ . تَرْكِيبٌ
Former a.	سَابِقٌ . اوَّلُ اثْنَيْنِ
Formerly ad.	سَابِقاً . قَبْلاً
Formidable a.	عَظِيمٌ . مُخِيفٌ
Formulate v. t.	صَرَّحَ بِهِ رَسْمِيًّا
Formication n.	زِنًى . عَهَارَةٌ
Forsake v. t.	تَرَكَ ـ هَجَرَ ـ
Forsaken a.	مَتْرُوكٌ
Fort n.	حِصْنٌ . قَلْعَةٌ
Forth ad.	خَارِجاً . فَصَاعِداً
Forthcoming a.	آتٍ . قَرِيبُ الْحُضُورِ
Forthwith ad.	حَالاً . عَلَى الْفَوْرِ
Fortieth a.	الْأَرْبَعُونَ
Fortification n.	حِصْنٌ . تَحْصِينٌ
Fortify v. t.	حَصَّنَ . قَوَّى
Fortitude n.	تَجَلُّدٌ . عَزْمٌ . ثَبَاتٌ
Fortnight n.	اسْبُوعَانِ
Fortress n.	حِصْنٌ . قَلْعَةٌ
Fortuitous a.	عَرَضِيٌّ . اِتِّفَاقِيٌّ
Fortunate a.	سَعِيدٌ . حَظِيظٌ
Fortune n.	حَظٌّ . نَصِيبٌ
Forty a.	أَرْبَعُونَ
Forward a. or ad.	مُقَدَّمٌ . إِلَى قُدَّامٍ
Forward v. t.	أَرْسَلَ . عَجَّلَ
Fossil n. or a.	مُتَحَجِّرٌ
Foster v. t.	رَبَّى . عَالَ . اعَانَ

— 11 —

Foul a.	قَذِرٌ . نَجِسٌ . قَبِيحٌ
Foul v. t.	وَسَّخَ . نَجَّسَ . لَوَّثَ
Found v. t.	اسَّسَ . انشَأَ . سَبَكَ
Foundation n.	اسَاسٌ . اصلٌ
Founder n.	مُؤَسِّسٌ . سَبَّاك
Foundling n.	وَلَدٌ . لَقِيطٌ
Foundry } n. Foundery }	مَعْمَلُ السَّبْكِ
Fount } n. Fountain }	نَبْعٌ . يَنْبُوعٌ
Four a.	ارْبَعَة او ارْبَعُ
Fourfold a.	ارْبَعَةَ اضعَافٍ
Fourfooted a.	ذَوَاتُ الارْبَعِ
Fourscore a.	ثَمَانُونَ
Fourteen a.	ارْبَعَةَ عَشَرَ . ارْبَعَ عَشْرَةَ
Fourteenth a.	الرَّابِعُ عَشَرَ
Fowl n.	طَيْرٌ . دُجَاجَة
Fowler n.	صَيَّادٌ
Fowling-piece n.	بَارُودَة . بُندُقِيَّةٌ
Fox n.	ثَعْلَبٌ . مَكَّار

Fraction n.	كَسْرٌ . جُزْءٌ
Fracture n. or v. t.	كَسْرٌ . كَسَرَ
Fragile a.	قَصِمٌ . سَهْلُ الانكِسَارِ
Fragment n.	قِطْعَةٌ . كِسْرَةٌ
Fragmentary a	مُؤَلَّفٌ مِنْ كِسَرٍ
Fragrance n.	رَائِحَةٌ . ذَكِيَّةٌ
Fragrant a.	عَطِرٌ . ذَكِيُّ الرَّائِحَةِ
Frail a.	نَحِيفٌ . ضَعِيفٌ . وَاهٍ
Frailty n.	ضَعْفٌ . وَهْنٌ . عجْزٌ
Frame n.	بِنْيَةٌ . قَالِبٌ . بِرْوَازٌ
Franchise n.	إمْتِيَازٌ سِيَاسِيٌّ
Frank a. or n.	مُخْلِصٌ . سَلِيمُ النِّيَّةِ . إفْرَنْجِي
Frankincense n.	بَخُورٌ . لُبَانٌ
Frankness n.	إخْلاصٌ . صَفْوُ النِّيَّةِ
Frantic a.	مَجْنُونٌ . هَائِجٌ غَيْظًا
Fraternal a.	أخَوِيٌّ
Fraternity n.	إخَاءٌ وَإِخَاوَة . شِرْكَةٌ
Fraternize v. t.	آخَى . تَآخَى

Fratricide n.	قَاتِلُ ٱلْأَخِ . قَتْلُ ٱلْأَخِ
Fraud n.	خِدَاعٌ . غَبْنٌ . مَكْرٌ
Freak n.	غَرَابَةُ خَلْقٍ أَوْ فِعْلٍ
Freckle n. or v. t.	كَلَفٌ . كَلِفَ ـَ
Freckled Freckly } a.	أَكْلَفُ
Free v. t.	حَرَّرَ . أَعْتَقَ
Free a.	حُرٌّ . بَرِيءٌ . مَجَّانِيٌّ
Freedom n.	حُرِّيَّةٌ . بَرَاءَةٌ . خُلُوصٌ
Freely ad.	مَجَّانًا . طَوْعًا . بِسَخَاءٍ
Freeman n.	حُرٌّ
Freemason n.	فَرْمَاسُون
Freeness n.	حُرِّيَّةٌ . سَخَاءٌ
Free-thinker n.	مُنْكِرُ ٱلْوَحْيِ
Freewill n.	إِرَادَةٌ حُرَّةٌ
Freeze v. t. or i.	قَرَّسَ . قَرَسَ ـ
Freight n.	شَحْنٌ . اجْرَتُهُ
French n. or a.	فَرَنْسَاوِيٌّ
Frenzy n.	جُنُونٌ . غَيْظ
Frequent a.	كَثِيرُ ٱلْوُقُوعِ . مُتَوَاتِرٌ
Frequent v. t.	تَرَدَّدَ إِلَى . لَازَمَ
Frequently ad.	تَكْرَارًا . كَثِيرًا مَا
Fresco n. or v. t.	تَصْوِيرٌ عَلَى جِصٍّ
Fresh a.	جَدِيدٌ . رَطْبٌ
Freshen v.t. or i.	حَلَّى . رَطَّبَ . أَنْعَشَ . إِشْتَدَّ
Freshet n.	سَيْلٌ . طُغْيَانٌ
Freshman n.	مُبْتَدِئٌ (فِي مَدْرَسَةٍ)
Freshness n.	نَضَارَةٌ . عُذُوبَةٌ
Fret v.t. or i.	كَدَّرَ . تَكَدَّرَ . ضَجِرَ
Fretful a.	نَكِد . شَاكٍ
Fretfulness n.	نَكَدٌ . ضَجَرٌ
Friar n.	رَاهِبٌ ج رُهْبَانٌ
Friction n.	فَرْكٌ . حَكٌّ . دَلْكٌ
Friday n.	يَوْمُ ٱلْجُمْعَةِ
Friend n.	صَاحِبٌ . صَدِيقٌ . خِلٌّ
Friendless a.	بِلَا صَدِيقٍ . مُهْمَل
Friendly a.	وَدُودٌ . مُسَالِم

Friendship n.	صَدَاقَةٌ . الْفَةٌ	Froth n.	رَغْوَةٌ . زَبَدٌ
Frigate n.	بَارِجَةٌ حَرْبِيَّةٌ	Froward a.	مُتَمَرِّدٌ . عَاتٍ
Fright n.	خَوْفٌ . فَزَعٌ . رُعْبٌ	Frown n. or v. t.	عَبُوسَةٌ. عَبَسَ َ
Frighten v. t.	خَوَّفَ . افْزَعَ	Froze see Freeze.	فَرَّسَ
Frightful a.	مُرْعِبٌ . مُخِيفٌ . هَائِلٌ	Fructify v. t.	جَعَلَهُ مُثْمِراً . لَقَّحَ
Frigid a.	بَارِدٌ . قَارِس	Frugal a.	مُقْتَصِدٌ
Frill / Fringe } n.	هُدْبٌ . حَاشِيَةٌ	Frugality n.	إِقْتِصَادٌ
Frisk v. t.	قَفَزَ فَرَحاً . مَرِح ــ	Fruit n.	ثَمَرٌ . فَاكِهَةٌ . حَاصِل
Frisk / Erisky } a.	مَرِح . خَفِيف	Fruitful a.	مُثْمِرٌ . مُخْصِبٌ . مُنْتِجٌ
Frivolity n.	طَيْشٌ . بَطْلٌ	Fruitlessly ad.	عَبَثاً . بَاطِلاً
Frivolous a.	عَبَثٌ . بَاطِلٌ	Frustrate v. t.	خَيَّبَ . أَبْطَلَ
Frock n.	قُفْطَانٌ . (فُسْطَانٌ)	Fry v. t. or i.	قَلَى ــ . إِنْقَلَى
Frog n.	ضَفْدَعٌ ج ضَفَادِعُ	Frying-pan n.	مِقْلاة
Frolic n. or v. i.	لِعْبٌ . مَرِحَ ــ	Fuel n.	وَقِيدٌ . وُقُود
From pr.	مِنْ . عَنْ . مِنْ عِنْدَ	Fugitive n. or a.	هَارِبٌ . زَائِلٌ
Front n.	مُقَدَّمٌ . صَدْرٌ	Fulcrum n.	مُسْنَدٌ . دَارِكٌ
Frontier n.	حَدٌّ . تُخْمٌ	Fulfil v. t.	اكْمَلَ . اتَمَّ
Frost n.	صَقِيعٌ . جَلِيدٌ	Fulfilment n.	إِتْمَامٌ . وَفَاءٌ

Full *a. or v.t.*	مَلآنٌ. وَافِرٌ. تَامٌّ. قَصَرَ
Fuller *n.*	قَصَّارٌ
Fully *ad.*	تَمَاماً
Fume *n. or v. i.*	بُخَارٌ. إِغْتَاظَ. دَخَّنَ
Fumigate *v. t.*	بَخَّرَ. دَخَّنَ
Fumigation *n.*	تَبْخِيرٌ. تَدْخِينٌ
Fun *n.*	مُزَاحٌ. هَزْلٌ
Function *n.*	وَظِيفَةٌ. شُغْلٌ
Fund *n.*	مَالٌ. رَأْسُ مَالٍ
Fundamental *a.*	أَسَاسِيٌّ. جَوْهَرِيٌّ
Funeral *n.*	جِنَازَةٌ
Fungus *n.*	فُطْرٌ (نَبَاتٌ)
Funnel *n.*	قِمَعٌ. مِدْخَنَةٌ
Funny *a.*	مُضْحِكٌ
Fur *n.*	فَرْوٌ. بَيَاضُ اللِّسَانِ
Furious *a.*	هَائِجٌ غَضَباً. مُزْبِدٌ
Furl *v. t.*	طَوَى ـِ لَفَّ ـُ
Furlong *n.*	فَرْسَخٌ ج فَرَاسِخُ
Furlough *n.*	رُخْصَةٌ لِلْغِيَابِ (إِجَازَةٌ)
Furnace *n.*	كُورٌ. اتُونٌ
Furnish *v. t.*	جَهَّزَ. أَهَبَ
Furniture *n.*	أَثَاثٌ. أَمْتِعَةٌ
Furrier *n.*	فَرَّاءٌ. تَاجِرُ الْفَرْوِ
Furrow *n. or v. t.*	ثَلْمٌ. خَدَّةٌ. خَدَّ ـُ
Further *a. or ad.*	أَبْعَدُ. ثُمَّ. أَيْضاً
Further *v. t.*	سَاعَدَ. أَيَّدَ
Furthermore *ad.*	ثُمَّ. أَيْضاً
Furthermost} Furthest *a.*	الْأَبْعَدُ. الْأَقْصَى
Furtive *a.*	سِرِّيٌّ. خَفِيٌّ
Fury *n.*	غَيْظٌ مُزْبِدٌ. جُنُونٌ
Fuse *v. t. or i.*	أَذَابَ. ذَابَ ـُ
Fuse *n.*	فَتِيلَةُ اللَّغْمِ
Fuss *n.*	ضَجِيجٌ. شَغَبٌ
Futile *a.*	بَاطِلٌ. عَبَثٌ
Futility *n.*	عَبَثٌ. عَدَمُ الْفَائِدَةِ
Future *n. or a.*	مُسْتَقْبِلٌ. آتٍ
Futurity *n.*	الْزَّمَانُ الْمُقْبِلُ

G

Gabble *v. i.* or *n.*	نَوْثَرَ . نَوْثَرَة
Gable *n.*	(جَمْلُون)
Gag *v. t.* or *n.*	سَدَّ الفَمِ
Gage *n.* or *v. t.*	رَهْنٌ . عِيَار . عَايَرَ
Gaily } Gayly } *ad.*	سُرُوراً . بَهْجَةً
Gain *n.* or *v. t.* or *i.*	كَسْبٌ . رَبِحَ
Gainful *a.*	مُكْسِبٌ . مُرْبِح
Gainings *n. pl.*	ارْبَاح
Gainsay *v. t.*	نَاقَضَ . قَاوَمَ
Gait *n.*	اَلْمَشْيُ أَوْ نَوْعُهُ
Gaiter *n.*	جُرْمُوق
Galaxy *n.*	اَلْمَجَرَّةُ . مَوْكِبٌ
Gale *n.*	رِيحٌ شَدِيدَةٌ . عَاصِفَةٌ
Gall *n.*	صَفْرَآءُ . مَرَارَةٌ . عَفْصٌ

Gallant *a.*	شُجَاعٌ . لَطِيفٌ . عَاشِقٌ
Gallantry *n.*	بَسَالَةٌ . شَهَامَةٌ
Gallery *n.*	رِوَاقٌ . دِهْلِيزٌ
Galley *n.*	نَوْعٌ مِنَ السُّفُنِ
Gallic *a.*	غَالِيٌّ . فَرَنْسَاوِيٌّ
Gallon *n.*	مِكْيَالٌ لِلسَّائِلَاتِ
Gallop *n.* or *v. i.*	رَكْضُ (اَلْفَرَسِ)
Gallows *n. pl.*	مِشْنَقَةٌ
Galvanic *a.*	كَهْرَبَائِيٌّ . كَلْفَانِيٌّ
Galvanize *v. t.*	كَهْرَبَ . لَبَّسَ بِالْمَعْدَنِ
Gamble *v. t.* or *i.*	قَامَرَ
Gambler *n.*	مُقَامِرٌ
Gambling *n.*	مُقَامَرَةٌ
Gambol *n.* or *v. i.*	رَقْصٌ . قَمَصَ

Game n.	لِعْبَة . قَنَص . صَيداً
Gamester n.	لاعبٌ . مُقَامِر
Gander n.	ذَكَرُ ٱلوَزّ
Gang n.	زُمْرَة . جَماعَة
Gangrene n. or v. i.	غَنْغَرِين تَغَنْغَرَ
Gangway n.	مَعْبَرٌ . مَمَرٌّ
Gaol n.	سِجْن . حَبْس
Gap n.	شَقٌّ . فَتْحَة
Gape v. t.	فَغَرَ ــ
Garb n.	لِبَاس . هَيْئَة
Garden n.	بُستَان . جُنَيْنة
Gardener n.	بُستَانيٌّ
Gargle v. t. or n.	غَرْغَرَ . غَرْغَرَة
Garland n.	إِكْلِيلُ زَهرٍ
Garlic n.	ثُوم
Garment n.	ثَوْبٌ . كِسَاءٌ
Garner n. or v. t.	شُونَة ـ خَزَنَ ـ
Garnish v. t.	زَيَنَ . زَخْرَفَ

Garrison a. or v. t.	حَرَسُ حِصْنٍ . جَهَّزَ بِحَرَسٍ
Garrulity n.	نُرْثَرَة . بَقَاق
Garrulous a.	نُرْثَار . بَقْبَاق
Garter n.	رُبَاط ٱلسَّاق . (وِسَامٌ إِنْكِلِيزِيٌّ)
Gas n.	غَاز
Gaseous a.	غَازِيٌّ
Gash n.	جُرْح
Gas-light n.	نُورُ غَاز
Gasometer n.	مِقْيَاسُ غَاز . مَخْزَنه
Gasp v. i. or n.	إِنْتَهَتَ . لَهْثَة
Gastric a.	مِعَدِيٌّ
Gate n.	بَابٌ . مَدْخَلٌ
Gateway n.	مَدْخَل فِي حَائِط
Gather v. t. or i.	جَمَعَ . إِجْتَمَعَ
Gaudy a.	مُزَخْرَف بِلا ذَوقٍ
Gauge v. t. or n.	قَاس . مِقْيَاسٌ
Gaunt a.	هَزِيل . ضَامِر . أعجَفُ
Gauntlet n.	كَفٌّ مِن حَدِيدٍ

Gawky *a.* or *n.*	غَشِيم . غَلِيظ التَّصرُّفِ
Gauze *n.*	نَسِيج رَقِيق
Gay *a.*	مُبتَهِج . مَرِح . فَاخِر
Gayety *n.*	بهجَة . بَسط . سُرُور
Gaze *n.* or *v.t.*	نظرَة ثَابِتَة . تَفَرَّسَ
Gazelle *n.*	غزَال ج غِزلَان
Gazette *n.*	جَرِيدَة ج جَرَائِد
Gazetteer *n.*	كِتَابُ وَصفِ البُلدَان
Gear *n.*	عُدَّة . جِهَاز . أَدَوَات
Gear *v. t.*	لَبَّسَ بعدَّةٍ
Gelatine *n.*	هُلَام
Gelding *n.*	حِصَان مَخصِيّ
Gem *n.*	جَوهَرَة . فَصّ
Gender *n.*	جِنس ج أَجنَاس
Genealogical *a.*	نَسَبِيّ
Genealogy *n.*	سِلسِلَةُ النَسَب
General *a.* or *n.*	عَامّ . شَائِع . قَائِد
Generality *n.*	عُمُومِيَّة . اغلَبِيَّة
Generalize *v. t.*	عَمَّم
Generally *ad.*	غَالِبًا . عُمُومًا
Generate *v. t.*	وَالَدَ . سَبَّبَ . أَحدثَ
Generation *n.*	حَبَّلَ . تَنَاسُل
Generative *a.*	مُوَلِّد . مُنتِج
Generic Generical *a.*	جِنسِيّ . شَامِل
Generosity *n.*	سَخَاء . كَرَم
Generous *a.*	كَرِيم . سَخِيّ
Genesis *n.*	تَوليد . سِفرُ التَكوِين
Genial *a.*	مُبهِج . بَشُوش
Genii *n. pl.*	جَانّ
Genitive *n.*	المُضَافُ إِلَيه
Genius *n.*	حَذق . قَرِيحَة . صَاحِبُهَا
Genteel *a.*	مُهَذَب . لَطِيف
Gentile *n.* or *a.*	امِي . وَثَنِي
Gentility *n.*	رِقَّة . تَهذِيب . ادَب
Gentle *a.*	لَطِيف . دَمِث . انِيس
Gentleman *n.*	مُهَذَب . (خوَاجَا) سَيِّد

Gentleness n.	رقة . دَمَاثَة . لُطْف
Gently ad.	بِلَطَافَة . بِرقة
Gentry n.	أَلْخَاصَّة . النجبَاء الأعيَان
Genuine a.	حَقِيقِيّ . صَحِيح . خَالِص
Genuineness n.	حَقِيقَة . حَقِيقِيَّة
Genus (pl. Genera) n.	جِنْس . نَوْع
Geographic ⎫ a. Geographical ⎭	جِغْرَافِيّ
Geography n.	جِغْرَافِيَا . رَسْمُ الأرض
Geologic ⎫ a. Geological ⎭	جِيُولُوجِيّ
Geologist n.	عَالِم بالجِيُولُوجِيَا
Geology n.	عِلْمُ طَبَقَاتِ الأرض
Geometric ⎫ a. Geometrical ⎭	هَنْدَسِيّ
Geometrician n.	مَاهِر بعِلْم الهَنْدَسَة
Geometry n.	عِلْمُ الهَنْدَسَة
Germ n.	جُرْثُومَة . اصْل
German ⎫ a. Germanic ⎭	ألْمَانِيّ . جَرْمَانِيّ
Germinate v. i.	نَبَتَ ـُ . افْرَخَ
Gestation n.	حَمْل . مُدةُ الحَمَل
Gesticulate v. i.	اوَّمَأ في الخِطَاب
Gesticulation ⎫ n. Gesture ⎭	إيمَاء . حَرَكَة جَسَدِيَّة
Get (Got) v. t.	حَصَّل . إقْتَنَى
Ghastliness n.	إصْفِرَارُ الوَجِه
Ghastly a.	فَظِيعُ المَنْظَر
Ghost n.	رُوح . طَيْف . خَيَال
Ghostly a.	خَيَالِيّ . رُوحَانِيّ
Ghoul n.	غُوْل ج غِيلَان
Giant n. or a.	جَبَّار . عَظِيم جدًّا
Gibberish n.	تَمْتَمَة
Gibbet n. or v. t.	مِشْنَقَة . شَنَقَ
Gibe v. i. or n.	إزْدَرَى . هَزَأ . هزْء
Gibralter n.	جَبَلُ طَارِق
Giddiness n.	دُوَار . طَيْش
Giddy a.	مُصَاب بالدُّوَار . طَائِش
Gift n.	عَطِيَّة . هِبَة
Gifted a.	حَاذِق . ذو مَوَاهِب

Gig n.	مَرْكَبَةٌ ذَاتُ دُولَابَيْن	Gizzard n.	قَانِصَةٌ ج قَوَانِصُ
Gigantic a.	كَبِيرٌ جِدًّا. ضَخْم	Glacier n.	جُرْفُ جَلِيدٍ
Gild v. t.	مَوَّهَ. ذَهَّبَ	Glad a.	مَسْرُورٌ. فَرْحَان. مَبْسُوط
Gilt n.	مِكْيَالٌ صَغِيرٌ لِلسَّوَائِل	Gladden v. t.	فَرَّحَ. أَسَرَّ. أَبْهَجَ
Gilt a.	مُذَهَّب. مُمَوَّه	Glade n.	مَعْبَرٌ او فُسْحَةٌ فِي غَابَةٍ
Gimlet n.	بَرِّيمٌ صَغِير. بَرِّيمَة	Gladiator n.	مُصَارِع
Gin n.	نَوْعٌ مِنَ الْعَرَقِ. فَخّ	Gladness n.	سُرُورٌ. فَرَحٌ. بَسْط
Ginger n.	زَنْجَبِيل	Glance n. or v. i.	لَمْحَةٌ. لَمَحَ ـ. إِنْعَكَسَ
Gipsy Gypsy n.	نُوري. غَجَري	Gland n.	غُدَّة ج غُدَد
Giraffe n.	زَرَافَة	Glandular Glandulous a.	غُدِّي ذُو غُدَدٍ
Gird v. t.	نَطَّقَ. زَنَّرَ ـ. رَبَطَ ـ	Glare n. or v. i.	لَمَعَانٌ. مُبْهِرٌ. تَوَهَّجَ
Girder n.	جِسْرٌ كَبِير	Glaring a.	لَامِع. مُبْهِر. فَاحِش
Girdle n.	مِنْطَقَة. زُنَّار. حِزَام	Glass n.	زُجَاج. مِرْآة. نَظَّارَة
Girl n.	صَبِيَّة. إِبْنَة. فَتَاة	Glassy a.	زُجَاجِيّ
Girth n.	حِزَام	Glaze v. t.	جَهَّزَ بِزُجَاجٍ
Gist n.	خُلَاصَة. زُبْدَة. جُل	Gleam n. or v. i.	وَمِيضٌ. بَرْقٌ. وَمَضَ ـ
Give v. t.	أَعْطَى. وَهَبَ ـ	Glean v. t.	إِلْتَقَطَ. جَمَعَ الْفَضَلَاتِ
Giving n.	إِعْطَاءٌ. إِهْدَاءٌ	Glee n.	سُرُورٌ. إِبْتِهَاج

Gleeful *a.*	مَسْرُورٌ . فَرِحٌ . مُبْتَهِجٌ
Glen *n.*	وَادٍ ضَيِّقٌ مُنْفَرِدٌ
Glibness *n.*	نُعُومَةٌ . طَلَاقَةُ اللِّسَانِ
Glide *v. i.*	تَزَلَّقَ تَزَلُّجٌ
Glimmer *v. i.*	تَلَأْلَأَ . خَفِيفًا
Glimmering *n.*	تَلَأْلُؤٌ
Glimpse *n.*	لَمْحَةٌ . نَظْرُهُ قَصِيرَةٌ
Glisten Glitter } *v. i.* or *n.*	تَلَأْلَأَ .لَمَعَانٌ
Gloat *v. i.*	تَفَرَّسَ بِعَيْنِ الشَّرِّ
Globe *n.*	كُرَةٌ.الأَرْضُ
Globular Globulous } *a.*	كَرَوِيٌّ
Globule *a.*	كُرَيَّةٌ
Glomerate *v. t.*	كَتَّلَ
Gloom *n.*	قَتَامٌ . غَمٌّ
Gloomy *a.*	مُغِمٌّ . مُكَدِّرٌ
Glorify *v. t.*	مَجَّدَ . عَظَّمَ . أَجَلَّ
Glorious *a.*	مَجِيدٌ . جَلِيلٌ
Glory *n.*	مَجْدٌ . جَلَالَةٌ . شُهْرَةٌ

Gloss Glossiness } *n.*	لَمَعَانٌ . تَأْوِيلٌ
Glossary *n.*	فِهْرِسُ كَلِمَاتٍ مَشْرُوحَةٍ
Glossy *a.*	مَصْقُولٌ . لَامِعٌ
Glottis *n.*	مِزْمَارُ الْحَنْجَرَةِ
Glove *n.*	كَفٌّ ج كُفُوفٌ
Glow *n.* or *v.i.*	تَوَهَّجَ . تَوَقَّدَ . إِحْتَدَمَ
Glowing *a.*	مُتَوَهِّجٌ . مُتَأَجِّجٌ . لَامِعٌ
Glow-worm *n.*	بَرَاعَةٌ (حَشَرَةٌ)
Glue *n.* or *v. t.*	غِرَاءٌ . غَرَّى
Glum *a.*	مَغْمُومٌ . عَبُوسٌ
Glut *v. t.*	أَشْبَعَ
Glutinous *a.*	دَبِقٌ . لَزِجٌ
Glutton *n.* Gluttonous *a.* }	أَكُولٌ . نَهِمٌ . شَرِهٌ
Gluttony *n.*	شَرَهٌ . نَهَمٌ
Gnarled Gnarly } *a.*	مُعَقَّدٌ . مُلْتَفٌّ
Gnash *v. t.*	صَرَّ اسْنَانَهُ
Gnat *n.*	بَعُوضَةٌ . نَامُوسَةٌ
Gnaw *v. t.*	قَرَضَ . قَضَمَ

Go (went, gone) v. i.	ذَهَبَ ـَ. مَضَى ـ
Goad n. or v. t.	مِنْخَسٌ. نَخَسَ ـ
Goal n.	أَمَدٌ. غَايَةٌ. غَرَضٌ
Goat n.	مَاعِزٌ. عَنْزٌ. تَيْسٌ
Goat-herd n.	مَعَّازٌ
Gobble v. t. or i.	إِزْدَرَدَ. لَهِمَ
Go-between n.	وَسِيطٌ
Goblet n.	قَدَحٌ. كَأْسٌ
Goblin n.	جِنِّيٌّ. عِفْرِيتٌ
God n.	إِلهٌ ج آلِهَةٌ. اَللهُ
Goddess n.	إِلَاهَةٌ
Godfather n.	عَرَّابٌ
Godless a.	كَافِرٌ. شِرِّيرٌ. فَاجِرٌ
Godliness n.	تَقْوَى
Godly a.	تَقِيٌّ. صَالِحٌ
Godson n.	فِلْيُونٌ
Gold n.	ذَهَبٌ
Golddust n.	دَقِيقُ الذَّهَبِ. تِبْرٌ
Golden a.	ذَهَبِيٌّ
Goldfinch n.	حَسُّونٌ. (طَائِرٌ)
Goldsmith n.	صَائِغٌ ج صَاغَةٌ
Gondola n.	زَوْرَقٌ. قَارِبٌ
Gong n.	نَاقُوسٌ
Good a.	صَالِحٌ. جَيِّدٌ. طَيِّبٌ
Good n.	خَيْرٌ. نَفْعٌ. فَائِدَةٌ
Good-by Good-bye } n. or int.	تَوْدِيعٌ. بَا مَانِ اللهِ
Good-humour n.	بَشَاشَةٌ
Goodly a.	جَمِيلٌ. حَسَنٌ
Good-natured a.	حَسَنُ الْأَخْلَاقِ
Goodness n.	صَلَاحٌ. جُوْدَةٌ. فَضِيلَةٌ
Goods n. pl.	بَضَائِعُ. سِلَعٌ. أَمْلَاكٌ
Good-will n. }	إِحْسَانٌ. مَسَرَّةٌ. مَعْرُوفٌ
Goose n. (pl. geese)	وَزَّةٌ. غَبِيٌّ
Gore v. or v.t.	دَمٌ. نَطَحَ ـَ. طَعَنَ ـ
Gorge v. t.	إِلْتَهَمَ

Gorgeous a.	فَاخِرٌ . زَاهٍ . بَهِيٌّ
Gorilla n.	اكْبَرُ ٱلْقُرُودِ . جُوْرِلاً
Gory a.	دَمَوِيٌّ . مُضَرَّجٌ بِالدَّمِ
Gosling n.	فَرْخُ ٱلْوَزِّ
Gospel n.	إِنْجِيلٌ . بِشَارَةٌ
Gossip n. or v. i.	فُضُولِيٌّ . مِهْذَارٌ . هَذَرَ ــِ
Gouge n. or v. t.	إِزْمِيلٌ . نَقَرَ ــ
Gourd n.	قَرْعٌ . (نَبَاتٌ)
Gout n.	نِقْرِسٌ . دَاءُ ٱلْمُلُوكِ
Gouty a.	مُصَابٌ بِالنِّقْرِسِ
Govern v. t.	مَلَكَ . سَادَ . حَكَمَ
Governess n.	مُعَلِّمَةُ عَائِلَةٍ
Government n.	حُكُومَةٌ . سِيَاسَةٌ
Governor n.	حَاكِمٌ . وَالٍ . مُدِيرٌ
Governorship n.	مَنْصِبُ ٱلْحَاكِمِ . وِلَايَةٌ
Gown n.	قُفْطَانٌ . جُبَّةُ ٱلْعُلَمَاءِ
Grab v. t. or n.	مَسَكَ . خَطَفَ . خَطْفٌ
Grace n.	نِعْمَةٌ . عَفْوٌ . حُسْنٌ
Grace v. t.	زَيَّنَ . ظَرَّفَ . اكْرَمَ
Graceful a.	رَقِيقٌ . لَطِيفٌ . مُهَذَّبٌ
Graceless a.	شِرِّيرٌ . خَبِيثٌ
Gracious a.	مُنْعِمٌ . جَوَّادٌ . رَحِيمٌ
Graciously ad.	بِلَطَافَةٍ . تَكَرُّمًا
Gradation n.	تَدْرِيجٌ . تَدَرُّجٌ
Grade n.	دَرَجَةٌ . رُتْبَةٌ
Gradual a.	تَدْرِيجِيٌّ
Graduate v. i.	نَالَ رُتْبَةً عِلْمِيَّةً
Graduation n.	نَيْلُ رُتْبَةٍ . تَدْرِيجٌ
Graft n. or v. t.	تَطْعِيمُ ٱلْغُصْنِ . طَعَّمَ
Grain n.	حَبَّةٌ . حُبُوبٌ . حِنْطَةٌ
Gram n.	وَزْنُ ٱلْجِرَامِ
Grammar n.	عِلْمُ ٱلصَّرْفِ وَٱلنَّحْوِ
Grammarian n.	نَاحٍ ج نُحَاةٌ
Grammatical a.	حَسَبَ ٱلنَّحْوِ
Granary n.	مَخْزَنُ ٱلْحُبُوبِ . هُرْيٌ
Grand a.	عَظِيمٌ . فَاخِرٌ . جَلِيلٌ

Grand-child n.	حَفِيدٌ . حَفِيدَةٌ
Granted pp.	مُسَلَّمٌ بِهِ . لِنَفْرِضْ
Grandee n.	احَدُالشَّرَفَاءِ او الْاعْيَانِ
Grandeur n.	عَظَمَةٌ . سُمُوٌّ . فَخَامَةٌ
Grandfather Grandsire } n.	جَدٌّ ج جُدُودٌ
Grandma Grandmother } n.	جَدَّةٌ
Grandson n.	حَفِيدٌ
Granite n.	نَوْعٌ مِنَ الْحَجَرِ الصَّلْبِ
Grant n. or v.t.	هِبَةٌ وهَبَ ـِ . أَجَابَ
Granular Granulate } a.	حِبِّيٌّ . مُحَبَّبٌ
Granulate v. t. or i.	حَبَّبَ . تَحَبَّبَ
Granule n.	حُبَيْبَةٌ . دَقِيقَةٌ
Grape n.	حَبَّةُ عِنَبٍ
Grape-shot n.	دَكَّةُ رَصَاصَاتٍ
Grape-vine n.	دَالِيَةٌ . كَرْمَةٌ
Graphic Graphical } a.	خَطِّيٌّ . بَلِيغُ الْوَصْفِ
Grapple v. t. or n.	قَبَضَ . صَارَعَ . قَبْضٌ
Grasp v.t. or n.	قَبَضَ . مَسَكَ . قَبْضٌ
Grasping a.	طَمَّاعٌ
Grass n.	حَشِيشٌ . كَلَأٌ . عُشْبٌ
Grasshopper n.	جُنْدُبٌ
Grassy a.	عُشْبٌ . مُعْشِبٌ
Grate v. t. or i.	حَكَّ . كَدَّرَ . صَرَفَ
Grate n.	كَانُونٌ . وُجَاقٌ
Grateful a.	شَكُورٌ . مُرْضٍ
Gratefulness n.	إِمْتِنَانٌ . شُكْرٌ
Gratification n.	إِرْضَاءٌ . جَبْرُ الْخَاطِرِ
Gratify v. t.	أَرْضَى . طَيَّبَ الْخَاطِرَ
Grating n.	شَعْرِيَّةٌ
Gratis ad.	مَجَّانًا
Gratitude n.	شُكْرٌ
Gratuitous a.	مَجَّانِيٌّ . بِلَا دَاعٍ
Gratuity n.	عَطِيَّةٌ . هَدِيَّةٌ
Grave n. or a.	قَبْرٌ . مُهِمٌّ . رَصِينٌ
Gravel n. or v. t.	حَصًى او دَقِيقُهَا . فَرَشَ بِهِ
Graven a.	مَنْحُوتٌ . مَنْقُوشٌ

Graver n.	نَقَّاش . حَفَّار
Gravestone n.	رُجمَةٌ ج رُجَم
Graveyard n.	مَقبَرَة
Gravitate v. i.	مَالَ إِلَى . إِنجَذَبَ
Gravity n.	رَزَانَةٌ . عَظَمَةُ الْجَاذِبِيَّةُ
Gravy n.	مَرَقٌ
Gray a.	أَشيَبُ . أَشهَبُ
Grayish a.	ضَارِب إِلَى الشَّيبِ
Grayness n.	شَيبٌ . شُهبَةٌ
Graze v. t. or i.	رَعَى ـَ . مَسَّ ـَ
Grazing n.	مَرعًى
Grease n. or v. t.	دُهنٌ . دَهَنَ ـُ
Greasiness n.	دُهنِيَّةٌ
Greasy a.	دَهِنٌ
Great a.	عَظِيمٌ . كَبِيرٌ . سَامٍ
Greatly ad.	كَثِيرٌ جِدًّا
Greatness n.	عَظَمَةٌ . سُمُوٌّ . كُبرٌ
Greaves n. pl.	جُرمُوق . دِرع لِلأَرجُل
Grecian a.	يُونَانِيٌّ . رُومِيٌّ
Greedily ad.	شَرِهًا . نَهِمًا . تَائِقًا
Greediness n.	شَرَهٌ . شَهوَةٌ . طَمَعٌ
Greedy a.	شَرِهٌ . أَكُولٌ . طَامِع
Greek a. or n.	يُونَانِيٌّ
Green a.	أَخضَرُ . فَجٌّ . عَدِيمُ الْخِبرَةِ
Greenhouse n.	كِنَانٌ لِتَربِيَةِالنَّبَات
Greens n. pl.	خُضَرٌ . بُقُولٌ
Greet v. t.	حَيَّا . سَلَّمَ عَلى
Greeting n.	تَحِيَّةٌ . سَلَامٌ
Greyhound n.	كَلب سَلُوقِيٌّ
Griddle Gridion n.	(مَصبع).سَفُّودٌ . مِقلَاةٌ
Grief n.	حُزنٌ . كَآبَة
Gregarious a.	عَائِشٌ سِربًا(حيوان)
Grievance n.	شَكوَى . ضِيق . اذِيَّة
Grieve v. i. or t.	حَزِنَ ـَ . أَحزَنَ ـَ
Grievous a.	مُحزِنٌ . شَاقَ . شَدِيدٌ
Grill v. t.	شَوَى ـ

Grim a.	عَبُوسٌ. هَائِلٌ. شَرِسٌ	Grog n.	شَرَابٌ مُسْكِرٌ
Grimace n.	إعْوِجَاجُ ٱلْوَجْهِ لِقَصْدٍ	Groin n.	ارْبِيَة
Grime v. t. or n.	قَذَرَ. لَوَّثَ. وَسَخٌ	Groom n. or v. t.	سَائِسٌ. سَاسَ - (ٱلْخَيْلَ)
Grin n. or v. t.	كَشْرَةٌ. كَشَرَ -	Groove n.	خَدَّةٌ. خَطٌّ مَحْفُورٌ. ثُلْم
Grind v. t.	سَنَّ. طَحَنَ. جَرَشَ -	Grope v. i.	تَلَمَّسَ. تَجَسَّسَ
Grind v.t. (the teeth)	قَرَعَ اسْنَانَهُ	Gross a.	غَلِيظٌ. ضَخْمٌ. فَظٌّ
Grinder n.	سِنَّانٌ. مِطْحَنَةٌ. ضِرْسٌ	Gross n.	جُمْلَةٌ. ١٢ دَسْتَةً (دَزِّينَةً)
Grindstone n.	جَلَخَ. مِسَنٌّ	Grossness n.	غِلَاظَةٌ. خُشُونَةٌ
Grip n. or Gripe v. t.	قَبْضٌ. قَبَضَ - . مَغْصٌ	Grotto n.	كَهْفٌ ج كُهُوفٌ
Grist n.	طَحْنَةٌ	Grotesque a.	غَرِيبٌ. مُضْحِكٌ
Gristel n.	غُضْرُوفٌ ج غَضَارِيف	Ground n.	ارْض. اسَاسٌ. دَلِيلٌ
Gristmill n.	طَاحُونٌ ج طَوَاحِينُ	Ground v. t. or i.	اسَّسَ. شَطَّطَتْ (سَفِينَةٌ)
Grit n.	رَمْل. جَرِيشُ ٱلطَّحِينِ	Groundless a.	بَاطِلٌ. لَا اصْلَ لَهُ
Grizzled Grizzly a.	اشْيَبُ. أَرْبَدُ	Groundwork n.	اسَاسٌ. أَصْلٌ
Groan v. t. or n.	انّ. تَأَوَّهَ. انِينٌ	Group n. or v. t.	جَمَاعَةٌ. زُمْرَةٌ. جَمَعَ
Groaning n.	انِينٌ. تَأَوُّهٌ	Grove n.	غَابَةٌ. حَرَجَةٌ
Grocer n.	بَدَّالٌ (بَقَّالٌ). عَطَّارٌ	Grovel v. t.	تَذَلَّلَ. دَبَّ -
Grocery n.	دُكَّانُ ٱلْمَأْكُولَاتِ	Grow v. t. or i.	رَبِّى. نَمَا. زَادَ -

Growl v. t. or i.	هَمْهَمَ . تَقَمْقَمَ
Growth n.	نُمُوٌّ . زِيَادَةٌ . تَقَدُّمٌ
Grub n.	شَحْمَةُ الأَرْضِ دُودَةُ الخُنْفُسَاء
Grudge n. or v. t.	ضَغِينَةٌ . حَسَدَ ـُ
Gruel n.	ثَرِيدٌ لِلْمَرِيضِ
Gruff a.	عَبُوسٌ . شَرِسٌ
Grumble v. i.	تَذَمَّرَ . تَقَمْقَمَ
Grunt v. i. or n.	قَبَعَ ـَ . قَبِيعَةٌ
Guarantee v. t. or n.	كَفَلَ ـِ . كَفَالَةٌ . كَفِيلٌ
Guard n. or v. t.	حِرَاسَةٌ . حُرَّاسٌ حَرَسَ ـُ
Guardian n.	حَارِسٌ . وَصِيٌّ . وَلِيٌّ
Guardianship n.	وِصَايَةٌ . حِرَاسَةٌ
Guess v. t. or n.	خَمَّنَ . تَخْمِينٌ
Guest n.	ضَيْفٌ ج ضُيُوفٌ
Guidance n.	إِرْشَادٌ. هِدَايَةٌ . دِلَالَةٌ
Guide v. t.	أَرْشَدَ.دَلَّ ـُ . هَدَى ـِ
Guide n.	مُرْشِدٌ . دَلِيلٌ

Guile n.	مَكْرٌ . خِدَاعٌ . غِشٌّ
Guileless a.	مُخْلِصٌ . بَرِيءٌ
Guillotine n.	آلَةٌ لِلإِعْدَامِ بِقَطْعِ الرَّأْسِ
Guilt Guiltiness } n.	ذَنْبٌ
Guiltless a.	بَرِيءٌ لَا ذَنْبَ فِيهِ
Guilty a.	مُذْنِبٌ . مُسْتَحِقُّ القِصَاصِ
Guinea n.	٢١ شِلِنًا . جُنَيْهٌ
Guise n.	أُسْلُوبٌ . هَيْئَةٌ . زِيٌّ
Guitar n.	قِيثَارٌ . ج قَيَاثِيرُ
Gulf n.	خَلِيجٌ . جُونٌ
Gull v. t. or n.	خَدَعَ . طَائِرٌ بَحْرِيٌّ
Gullet n.	المَرِيءُ . البُلْعُومُ
Gully n.	مَجْرَى عَمِيقٌ ضَيِّقٌ
Gulp v. t. or n.	لَهِمَ . جَرَعَ . جَرْعَةٌ
Gum n.	لِثَةٌ . صَمْغٌ
Gun n.	بَارُودَةٌ . بُنْدُقِيَّةٌ . مَدْفَعٌ
Gunner n.	طُوبْجِيٌّ
Gunpowder n.	بَارُودٌ

Gunsmith *n.*	صَانِعُ ٱلأَسْلِحَةِ	Gutter *n.*	قَنَاةٌ . بَالُوعَةٌ
Gurgle *v. i.*	تَغَرْغَرَ	Guttural *a.* or *n.*	حَلْقِيٌّ . حَرْفُ ٱلْحَلْقِ
Gush *v. i.*	دَفَقَ –	Guy *n.*	حَبْلٌ لِلإِسْنَادِ
Gust *n.*	نَفْخَةُ رِيحٍ قَوِيَّةٍ	Gymnasium *n.*	مَدْرَسَةُ ٱلرِّيَاضَةِ
Gust *n.*	مِعًى ج أَمْعَاءٌ	Gymnastic *a.*	رِيَاضِيٌّ . جَسَدِيٌّ

H

Ha ! *ex.*	عَجَبًا . هَا	Hackneyed *a.*	كَثِيرُ ٱلإِسْتِعْمَالِ
Habiliment *n.*	ثَوْبٌ	Hackney-coach *n.*	مَرْكَبَةٌ لِلْكِرَاءِ
Habit *n.*	عَادَةٌ . دَأْبٌ . ثَوْبٌ	Haddock *n.*	نَوْعٌ مِنَ ٱلسَّمَكِ
Habitable *a.*	قَابِلُ ٱلسُّكْنَى	Haft *n.*	مَقْبِضٌ وَمِقْبَضٌ . نِصَابٌ
Habitation *n.*	مَسْكِنٌ	Hag *n.*	عَجُوزٌ . قَبِيحَةٌ
Habitual *a.*	عَادِيٌّ . إِعْتِيَارِيٌّ	Haggard *a.*	خَاسِفُ ٱلْوَجْهِ
Habituate *v.t.*	عَوَّدَ . أَلَّفَ	Haggle *v. t.* or *i.*	دَقَّقَ فِي ٱلْمُسَاوَمَةِ . قَطَّعَ
Habitude *n.*	عَادَةٌ	Hail *n.* or *v. t.*	بَرَدَ . نَادَى . حَيَّا
Hack *v. t.* or *n.*	قَطَعَ . فَرَضَ . كَدِيشٌ	Hailstones *n. pl.*	بَرَدَ

Hair n.	شَعْرٌ . شَعَرَة	Hammock n.	سَرِيرٌ مُعَلَّق
Hairless a.	أَجْرَدُ	Hamper n. or v. t.	قُفَّةٌ . عَاقَ . قَيَّدَ
Hairy a.	أَشْعَرُ	Hamstring n. or v. t.	عُرْقُوب . عَرْقَبَ
Hale a.	مُتَعَافٍ . صَحِيحُ ٱلْجِسْمِ	Hand n. or v.t.	يَدٌ . كَفٌّ . نَاوَلَ
Half n. (pl. Halves)	نِصْف	Handbook n.	كِتَابٌ مُخْتَصَرٌ لِلدِّلَالَة
Hall n.	دِهْلِيز . قَاعَة . مُنْتَدَى	Handcraft Handicraft } n.	حِرْفَة . صَنْعَةُ ٱلْيَدِ
Halloo n. or v. i.	صَيْحَة . صَاحَ ــ	Handcuff n.	غُلٌّ . قَيْد لِلْيَد
Hallow v. t.	قَدَّس	Handful n.	قَبْضَة . شِرْذِمَة
Hallucination n.	وَهْم . تَوَهُّم	Handily ad.	بِمَهَارَة . بِسُهُولَة
Halo n.	هَالَة . دَائِرَة مُنِيرَة	Handiwork n.	شُغْلُ ٱلْيَد
Halt n. or a.	وُقُوف . أَعْرَج	Handkerchief n.	(مِحْرَمَة) . مِنْدِيل
Halt v. t. or i.	وَقَّفَ . وَقَفَ ــ . عَرِجَ ــ	Handle n. or v. t.	مِقْبِض . مَسَّ ــ
Halter n. or v.t.	رَسَن . شِنَاق . رَسَنَ	Handmaid n.	جَارِيَة . أَمَة
Halve v. t.	نَصَّفَ ــ . شَطَرَ ــ	Hand-mill n.	جَارُوش ج جَوَارِيش
Ham n.	فَخْذُ خِنْزِير مُمَلَّح	Handsome a.	جَمِيل . حَسَن
Hamlet n.	مَزْرَعَة	Handy a.	مَاهِر . قَرِيب
Hammer n.	مِطْرَقَة . شَاكُوش	Hang v. t. or i.	عَلَّق . شَنَقَ . تَعَلَّقَ
Hammer v. t.	طَرَقَ ــ . دَقَّ ــ	Hangings n. pl.	سَتَائِر . مُعَلَّقَات

Hangman n.	جَلَّادٌ	Hardship n.	مَشَقَّةٌ . صُعُوبَةٌ
Hanker v. i.	تَاقَ ـُ إِلَى	Hardware n.	بَضَائِعُ مَعْدَنِيَّةٌ
Hap-hazard n.	عَرَضٌ . صِدْفَةٌ	Hardy a.	شَدِيدٌ . بَاسِلٌ . ضَلِيعٌ
Hapless a.	نَحِسٌ . مَنْكُودُ ٱلْحَظِّ	Hare n.	أَرْنَبٌ
Happen v. i.	حَدَثَ ـُ صَارَ ـِ	Hare-brained a.	طَائِشٌ
Happiness n.	سَعَادَةٌ . غِبْطَةٌ	Harelip n.	شَفَّةٌ شَرْمَاءُ
Happy a.	سَعِيدٌ . مَغْبُوطٌ . فَرِحٌ	Harem n.	حَرِيمٌ
Harangue n. or v. t.	خِطَابٌ . خَاطَبَ	Hark v. i.	أَصْغَى إِلَى
Harass v. t.	أَزْعَجَ . اضْجَرَ . أَتْعَبَ	Harlot n.	زَانِيَةٌ . عَاهِرَةٌ
Harassing a.	مُزْعِجٌ . مُتْعِبٌ	Harm n. or v. t.	أَذِيَّةٌ . ضَرَرٌ . آذَى
Harbinger n.	سَابِقٌ . مُبَشِّرٌ	Harmful a.	مُؤْذٍ . مُضِرٌّ
Harbour n. or v. t.	مِينَاءٌ . مَرْفَأٌ . آوَى	Harmless a.	غَيْرُ مُضِرٍّ . سَلِيمٌ
Hard a.	قَاسٍ . صَلْبٌ . صَعْبٌ	Harmonious a.	مُتَوَافِقٌ . مُتَنَاسِبٌ
Harden v. t. or i.	صَلَّبَ . قَسَّى . تَصَلَّبَ	Harmonize v. t.	وَفَّقَ . سَاوَى
Hard-hearted a.	قَاسِي ٱلْقَلْبِ	Harmony n.	إِتِّفَاقٌ . مُوَازَنَةٌ
Hardihood n.	جَرَاءَةٌ . إِقْدَامٌ	Harness n.	عُدَّةُ ٱلْفَرَسِ وَٱلْعَسْكَرِيِّ
Hardly ad.	بِصُعُوبَةٍ . بِالْجُهْدِ	Harness v. t.	أَلْبَسَ ٱلْعُدَّةَ . كَدَّنَ
Hardness n.	صَلَابَةٌ . قَسَاوَةٌ	Harp n. or v. i.	عُودٌ . ضَرَبَ عَلَيْهِ

Harper *n.*	ضاربٌ بالعُوْدِ
Harpoon *n.*	خَطّافُ ٱلصَّيدِ
Harrow *n.* or *v. t.*	مِسلَفَة . كَدَرَ . سَلَفَ
Harry *v. t.*	نَهَبَ . سَلَبَ . ازعَجَ
Harsh *a.*	صارِمٌ . فَظٌّ . خَشِنٌ
Harshness *n.*	جَفَاءٌ . خُشُونَةٌ
Hart *n.*	إيَّلٌ . وَعِلٌ ج وُعُولٌ
Harvest *n.* or *v. t.*	حِصادٌ . حَصَدَ ـِ
Hash *n.* or *v. t.*	(لَحمٌ مَفرُومٌ) . قَطَّعَ
Haste Hasten} *v. i.* or *t.*	أسرَعَ . عَجَّلَ
Haste *n.*	عَجَلَةٌ . مُبَادَرَةٌ
Hasty *a.*	عَجُولٌ . مُسرِعٌ . حَادٌّ
Hat *n.*	بُرنَيطَةٌ . قَلَنسُوَةٌ
Hatch *v.t.* or *i.*	فَقَسَ ـِ . إنفَقَسَ
Hatchet *n.*	فَأسٌ
Hatchway *n.*	مَدخَلٌ في ٱلسَّفِينَةِ
Hate *n.* or *v. t.*	بُغضٌ . أبغَضَ . مَقَتَ
Hateful *a.*	مَمقُوتٌ . مَكرُوهٌ
Hatred *n.*	بُغضٌ . مَقتٌ

Hatter *n.*	صانِعُ ٱلبَرَانِيطِ اوْ بائِعُها
Haughty *a.*	مُتَكَبِّرٌ . مُتَعَجرِفٌ
Haul *v. t.*	جَذَبَ . سَحَبَ
Haunch *n.*	وَرْكٌ
Haunt *n.* or *v. t.*	مَزَارٌ . تَرَدَّدَ إلَى
Haunted *a.*	مَأوَى ٱلجَانّ أوِ ٱلطَيفِ
Have *v. t.*	مَلَكَ ـِ . لَهُ
Haven *n.*	مِيناءٌ . مَرسَى
Havoc *n.*	خَرَابٌ . مَقتَلَةٌ
Hawk *n.*	بَازِجٍ بُوازٍ . صَقرٌ ج صُقرٌ
Hawser *n.*	حَبلٌ ضَخمٌ
Hawthorn *n.*	زَعرُورٌ (نَبَاتٌ)
Hay *n.*	قَشٌّ . تِبنٌ . كَلَأٌ
Hazard *n.* or *v.t.*	خَطَرٌ . خَاطَرَ بِ
Hazardous *a.*	مُخطِرٌ . خَطِرٌ
Haze *n.*	ضَبَابَةٌ . إغبِرَارٌ
Hazel *n.* or *a.*	شَجَرُ ٱلبُندقِ . بُندقيٌّ
Haziness *n.*	إغبِرَارٌ

Hazy a.	ضَبَابِيٌّ . مُغبَرٌّ
He pron.	هُوَ
Head n. or v. t.	رَأسٌ . قَادَ . تَرَأَّسَ
Headache n.	وَجَعُ آلرَّأسِ . صُدَاعٌ
Head-dress n.	كِسَاءُ آلرَّأس
Heading n.	أوَّلُ آلشَّيْءِ . عُنْوَانٌ
Headland n.	رَاسٌ (فِي آلْبَحْرِ)
Headlong a. or ad.	آلرَّأسُ إِلَى أَسْفَلَ
Head-quarters n.	مَرْكَزُ آلْقَائِدِ أو آلْحُكُومةِ
Headship n.	رِئَاسَة
Headstrong a.	عَنِيدٌ . صُلْبُ آلرَّأسِ
Heal v. t. or i.	شَفَى ـ . تَعَافَى . إِنْدَمَلَ
Health n.	صِحَّةٌ . عَافِيةٌ
Healthful a.	مُتَعَافٍ . مُفِيدٌ لِلصِّحَّةِ
Healthfulness Healthiness } n.	صِحَّةٌ . عَافِيةٌ
Healthy a.	صَحِيحٌ . نَافِعٌ لِلصِّحَةِ
Heap n. or v. t.	كُوْمَةٌ . عُرْمَةٌ . كَوَّمَ

Hear v. t.	سَمِعَ ـ اصغَى . أطَاعَ
Hearing n.	سَمْعٌ . مَسمَع
Hearken v. t.	أصغَى . إِستَمَعَ
Hearsay n.	قَوْل . قَالَ وَقِيل
Hearse n.	مَرْكَبَةٌ لِحَمْلِ آلْمَوتَى
Heart n.	قَلْبٌ . لُبٌّ
Heart-felt a.	قَلْبِيٌّ . مُخْلِصٌ
Hearth n.	مَوْقِدَةٌ
Heartily a.	قَلْبِيًّا . بِنشَاطٍ
Heartiness n.	خُلوصٌ . هِمَّةٌ
Heartless a.	قَاسٍ . بِلاَ رَأْفَةٍ
Hearty a.	قَلْبِيٌّ . مُخْلِصٌ . مُتَعَافٍ
Heat n. or v. t.	حَرَارَةٌ . سَخَّنَ
Heathen n. Heathenish a. }	وَثَنِي
Heathenism n.	آلدِّيَانَةُ آلْوَثْنِيَّةُ
Heave v. t.	دَفَعَ ـ رَمَى ـ
Heaven n.	آلسَّمَاءُ
Heavenly a.	سَمَاوِيٌّ

Heaviness n.	ثِقَل . غَمّ
Heavy a.	ثَقِيلٌ . شَدِيدٌ . بَطِيءٌ
Hebraic a. Hebrew n.	عِبْرَانِيٌّ
Hedge n. or v. t.	سِيَاجٌ . سَيَّجَ
Hedgehog n.	قُنْفُذٌ ج قَنَافِذ
Heed v. t.	بَالَى . أَصْغَى إِلَى
Heed n.	إِكْتِرَاثٌ . إِعْتِنَاءٌ
Heedful a.	مُبَالٍ . مُنْتَبِهٌ
Heedless a.	غَافِلٌ . غَيْرُ مُبَالٍ
Heedlessness n.	عَدَمُ الْمُبَالَاة
Heel n.	عَقِبٌ ج اعقَابٌ
Hegira n.	هِجْرَةٌ
Heifer n.	عِجْلَة
Height n.	عُلُوٌّ
Heighten v. t.	عَلَّى . زَادَ
Heinous a.	فَظِيعٌ
Heir n.	وَارِثٌ ج وَرَثَةٌ
Heir-apparent n.	وَلِيُّ عَهْد

Hell n.	جَهَنَّم . جَحِيم
Hellenic a.	يُونَانِيٌّ
Helm n.	دَفَّة . قِيَادَة
Helmet n.	خُوذَةٌ ج خُوذٌ
Helmsman n.	مُدِيرُ الدَّفَّة
Help v. t. or n.	سَاعَدَ . مُسَاعَدَة
Helpful a.	مُسَاعِدٌ . مُعَاوِن
Helpless a.	عَاجِزٌ . لَا مُعِينَ له
Helpmate n.	مُعِينٌ . رَفِيق
Hem n. or v. t.	كِفَّة . حَاشِيَة . كَفَّ
Hemisphere n.	نِصْفُ كُرَّة
Hemlock n.	شَوْكَرَان
Hemorrhage n.	نَزْفُ الدَّم
Hemp n.	قِنَّب
Hen n.	دُجَاجَة
Henbane n.	بَنْج (نَبَات)
Hence ad.	مِن هُنَا . لِهٰذَا . إِذًا
Henceforth Henceforward ad.	مِنَ الآنَ فَصَاعِدًا

Hencoop n.	قَفَص . قُنّ
Heptagon n.	مُسَبَّع
Her pro.	لَهَا . هَا (ضَمِير)
Herald n. or v. t.	مُنَادٍ . مُخَبِّر . اخبَر
Herb n.	عُشْب . بَقْل . نَبْت
Herbaceous a.	عُشْبِيّ
Herbage n.	كَلَأ . خُضْرَة
Herbarium n.	مَنْبِت
Harbivorous a.	آكِلُ النَّبَاتِ
Herculean a.	عَظِيم جِدًّا . صَعْب
Herd n. or v. i.	قَطِيع . إِجْتَمَع
Herdsman n.	رَاعٍ ج رُعَاة
Here ad.	هُنَا . هَا هُنَا
Hereabouts ad	فِي هٰذِهِ النَّوَاحِي
Hereafter ad.	فِيمَا بَعْد . بَعْدَ هٰذَا
Hereby ad.	بِهٰذَا . مِنْ هٰذَا
Hereditary a.	إِرْثِيّ . مَوْرُوث
Herein ad.	فِي هٰذَا . مِنْ هٰذَا . لِهٰذَا
Heresy n.	(هَرْطَقَة) بِدْعَة

Heretic n. } Heretical a. }	(هَرْطُوقِي) . خَارِجِي
Heretofore ad.	فِيمَا مَضَى . سَابِقًا
Hereupon ad.	عِنْدَ ذٰلِكَ . مِنْ ثَمَّ
Herewith ad.	بِهٰذَا . مِنْ هٰذَا
Heritage n.	مِيرَاث
Hermetically ad.	بِضَبْطٍ (مَسْدُود)
Hermit n.	نَاسِك . زَاهِد
Hermitage n.	مَنْسَك
Hernia n.	فِتْق
Hero n. (pl. Heroes).	صِنْدِيد . بَطَل
Heroic a.	صِنْدِيدِيّ . مَجِيد
Heroine n.	صِنْدِيدَة . بَطَلَة
Heroism n.	بَسَالَة . إِقْدَام
Herring n.	نَوْع مِنَ السَّمَكِ
Herself pro.	نَفْسِهَا . ذَاتِهَا
Hesitancy } Hesitation } n.	تَرَدُّد . إِرْتِيَاب
Hesitate v. i.	تَرَدَّدَ . إِرْتَابَ
Heterogeneous a.	مُخْتَلِفُ الجِنْسِ
Hew v. t.	نَحَتَ — . قَطَعَ

Hexagon n.	مُسَدَّس
Hexangular a.	مُسَدَّس ٱلزَّوَايَا
Hibernal a.	شَتَوِيّ
Hibernate v. i	شَتَّى (لِلْبَهَائِمِ)
Hibernian n.	إِرْلَانْدِيّ
Hiccough n. or v. i.	فُوَاق . فَاقَ ـَ
Hidden a.	مُخْفِيّ . مَسْتُور
Hide v. t. or i.	أَخْفَى . إِخْتَفَى
Hideous a.	قَبِيح . كَرِيهُ ٱلْمَنْظَرِ
Hierarchy n.	رِئَاسَه دِينِيَّة
Hieroglyphics n. pl.	خَطّ بِصُوَر
High a.	عَالٍ . سَامٍ
Highland n.	نَجْد . أَرْض جَبَلِيَّة
Highly ad.	كَثِيرًا . جِدًّا
Highness n.	سُمُوّ . رِفْعَه
High-priest n.	رَئِيسُ ٱلْكَهَنَة
Hight see Height n.	عُلُوّ
High-water n.	أَعْلَى ٱلْمَدّ
Highway n.	سِكَّه سُلْطَانِيَّة

Highwayman n.	قَاطِعُ ٱلطُّرُق
Hilarity n.	طَرَب فَرَح
Hill n.	تَلّ . أَكَمَة
Hillock n.	قَلِيل . كَثِيب
Hilly a.	كَثِيرُ ٱلتِّلَال
Hilt n.	مِقْبَض . نِصَاب
Himself pro.	نَفْسُه . ذَاتُه
Hind a. or n.	مُؤَخَّرُ ٱلشَّيْءِ . إِيَلَة
Hinder v. t.	عَاقَ . صَدَّ ـُ مَنَعَ ـَ
Hinderance / Hindrance } n.	عَائِق . مَانِع
Hindermost / Hindmost } a.	ٱلْأَخِير
Hindoo n.	هِنْدِيّ
Hinge n. or v. i.	مِفْصَلَة . دَار عَلَى
Hint v. t. or i. or n.	أَوْمَأَ . لَمَّحَ . إِيمَاء . تَلْمِيح
Hip n.	وَرْك
Hippodrome n.	مَيْدَانٌ لِلْخَيْلِ
Hippopotamus n.	فَرَسُ ٱلْمَاء
Hire n. or v. t.	أَجْر . كِرَاء . إِسْتَأْجَرَ
Hireling n. or a.	أَجِير

His pro.	لهُ
Hiss v.t. or i. or n.	صَفَرَ ــِ . فَحَّ ــُ فَحِيحٌ
Historian n.	مُؤَرِّخٌ
Historical a.	تَارِيخِيٌّ
History n.	تَأْرِيخٌ
Hit v.t. or n.	اصَابَ . إِصَابَة
Hitch v.t. or n.	عَلَقَ . رَبَطَ . عَرْقَلَة
Hither ad.	إِلَى هُنَا
Hitherto ad.	إِلَى آلآنَ
Hive n.	قَفِيرٌ
Hoar } Hoary } a.	أَشْيَبُ . أَبْيَضُ
Hoard v.t. or n.	ذَخَرَ ــ . ذَخِيرَة
Hoarfrost n.	مَلَّاحٌ . صَقِيع
Hoariness n.	شَيبٌ
Hoarse a.	أَبَحُّ . مَبْحُوحٌ
Hoarseness n.	بُحَّةٌ
Hoax n. or v.t.	غِشٌّ . أُلْعُوبَة . غَشَّ . مَكَرَ
Hobble v.i. or t.	عَرِجَ . شَكَّلَ
Hobby } Hobbyhorse } n.	مَا يُولَعُ بِهِ
Hobgoblin n.	غَوْلٌ
Hock n. or v.t.	عُرْقُوبٌ . عَرْقَبَ
Hod n.	نَقِّيرٌ ج نِقْرَان
Hoe n. or v.t.	مِجْرَفَة . مِعْزَقَة . عَزَقَ ــ
Hog n.	خِنْزِيرٌ ج خَنَازِيرُ
Hogshead n.	بَرْمِيلٌ كَبِيرٌ
Hog-sty n.	زَرِيبَةُ ٱلْخَنَازِيرِ
Hoist v.t.	رَفَعَ ــ
Hold n.	ضَبْطٌ . دَاخِلُ سَفِينَةٍ
Holde v.t.	ضَبَطَ . حَجَزَ ــُ . وَسِعَ ــ
Hole n.	ثَقْب . خَرْق . وَجَار
Holiday n.	يَوْمُ بَطَالةٍ
Holiness n.	قَدَاسَةٌ
Hollow a.	فَارِغٌ . مُجَوَّفٌ . بَاطِلٌ
Hollow v.t.	جَوَّفَ
Hollow n.	إِنْخِفَاضٌ . غَوْطٌ . جَوْف
Hollow-hearted a.	خَائِنٌ . مُرَاءٍ
Hollyhock n.	الخَطْمِيُّ

Holy a.	مُقَدَّس . قُدُّوس	Honorary a.	إِكْرَامِيّ
Homage n.	إِكْرَام . عِبَادَة . إِحْتِرَام	Hood n.	قَلَنْسُوَة . قُبَّعَة
Home n.	بَيْت . وَطَن	Hoodwink v. t.	خَدَعَ . خَتَلَ ـِ
Homely a.	عَدِيم ٱلْحُسْنِ . بَيْتِيّ	Hoof n.	حَافِر . ظِلْف ج ظُلُوف
Homeopathy n.	ٱلْعِلَاجُ بِٱلْمِثْلِ	Hook n.	شِصّ . كَلَّاب . خُطَّاف
Homesick a.	مُشْتَاق لِلْوَطَنِ او لِلْبَيْتِ	Hoop n. or v. t.	إِطَار . طَوْق . شَدَّ بِإِطَارٍ
Homestead n.	دَارُ عَائِلَةٍ	Hooping-cough n.	مَرَضُ ٱلشَّهْقَة
Homeward ad.	نَحْوَ ٱلْبَيْتِ او ٱلْوَطَنِ	Hoot n. v. i.	صِيَحه . نَعْق . نَعَقَ ـ
Homicide n.	قَاتِل . قَتْل	Hop v. i.	قَفَزَ عَلَى رِجْلٍ وَاحِدَةٍ
Homogeneous a.	مُتَجَانِس	Hop n.	قَفْزَة . حَشِيشَةُ ٱلدِّينَار
Hone n. or v. t.	مِسَنّ رَفِيع . سَنَّ ـُ	Hope n. or v. i.	رَجَاء . رَجَا ـُ
Honest a.	مُسْتَقِيم . أَمِين . مُخْلِص	Hopeful a.	كَثِيرُ ٱلرَّجَاءِ . مَرْجُوّ
Honesty n.	أَمَانَه . إِسْتِقَامَة	Hopeless a.	بِلَا رَجَاءٍ . بَائِس
Honey n.	عَسَل	Horde n.	قَوْم . قَبِيلَة
Honeycomb n.	شَهْدُ ٱلْعَسَلِ	Horizon n.	افق
Honeymoon n.	شَهْرُ ٱلزَّوَاجِ	Horizontal a.	افقيّ
Honour n. or v. t.	إِكْرَام . أَكْرَمَ	Horn n.	قَرْن . بُوْن . نَاقُوْر
Honorable a.	مُكْرَم . شَرِيف	Horned a.	ذو قُرُون

Hornet n.	زنبورٌ	Hostler n.	سائسُ الخيلِ
Horrible a.	هائلٌ . فظيعٌ	Hot a.	حارٌّ . سُخنٌ . حامٍ
Horrid a.	فظيعٌ . قبيحٌ	Hotel n.	فندقٌ . لوكندةٌ
Horrify v. t.	أرْغبَ . أفظعَ	Hotly ad.	بحميةٍ . بشدَّةٍ
Horror n.	هولٌ . رُعبٌ	Hound n.	كلبُ الصَّيدِ
Horse n.	فرَسٌ. حصانٌ ج احصنةٌ	Hour n.	ساعةٌ . زمانٌ
Horseback n.	ظهرُ الفرَسِ	Hour-glass n.	ساعةٌ . رمليَّةٌ
Horseman n.	خيَّالٌ . فارسٌ	Hourly a. or ad.	كلَّ ساعةٍ
Horsemanship n.	فنُّ رُكوبِ الخيلِ	House n.	بيتٌ . دوْلةٌ . شرْكةٌ
Horseshoe n.	نعلُ الفرَسِ	House-breaker n.	لصٌّ ج لُصوصٌ
Horsewhip n.	سوْطٌ . كُرْباجٌ	Household n.	أهلُ البيتِ
Hospitable a.	مِضيافٌ . كريمٌ	Housekeeper n.	مُدبِّرُ المنزلِ .
Hospital n.	مستشفى	Houseless a.	بلا مسكنٍ
Hospitality n.	تضييفٌ.ضيافةٌ	Hovel n.	كوخٌ . خصٌّ
Host Hostess } n.	مُضيفٌ مضيفٌ . مُضيفةٌ	Hover v. i.	حامَ . ترَدَّدَ بقرْبٍ
Hostage n.	رهنٌ . رهينٌ	How ad.	كيفَ
Hostile a.	عدائيٌّ . مُضادٌّ	However ad.	كيفما . إلا انَّ
Hostility n.	عداوةٌ . خصامٌ	Howl v. i. or n.	عوَى ـِ . عُوَاءٌ

Hub *n.*	كَطِّيخة آلدُّولاب	Humiliation *n.*	ذُلٌّ . إنحطاطٌ
Hubbub *n.*	ضَوْضاءٌ . ضَجِيجٌ	Humility *n.*	تَواضُعٌ . خُشوعٌ
Huddle *v. t.*	اسرَعَ. خَلَطَ ـ إِزْدَحَمَ	Humour *v. t.*	لاطَفَ . دَارَى
Hue *n.*	لَوْنٌ	Humour *n.*	طَبْعٌ . سَجِيّةٌ . فكَاهةٌ
Hug *v. t. or n.*	عانَقَ . عِناقٌ	Humorist *n.* } Humorous *a.* }	مَازِحٌ . مُضحِكٌ
Huge *a.*	كَبيرٌ جِدًّا . جَسيمٌ	Hump *n.*	حَدَبةٌ . سِنامٌ
Hull *n.*	قِشرُ آلجُوزَةِ . بدَنُ آلسَّفينةِ	Humpback } Hunchback } *n.*	أحدَبُ . حَدْباءُ
Hull *v. t.*	قَشَّرَ	Hundred *n.*	مِئةٌ ومائةٌ
Hum *v. i. or n.*	دَنْدَنَ. دَنْدَنةٌ .دَوِيٌّ	Hundredth *a.*	ألمِئةُ
Human *a.*	بَشَريٌّ . إِنسَاني	Hunger *n. or v. i.*	جُوعٌ .جَاعَ
Humane *a.*	ذو إِنْسَانيّةٍ . لَطيف	Hungry *a.*	جائِعٌ .جُوعَان
Humanity *n.*	إِنْسَانيّةٌ . لُطْفٌ	Hunt *v. t.* or *n.*	إصطادَ . صَيدٌ . قَنَصٌ
Humble *a.*	وديعٌ . مُتَواضِعٌ	Hunter Huntsman *n.* }	قانِصٌ .صَيّادٌ
Humble *v. t.*	ذَلَّ . وَضَعَ ــ حَطَّ	Hurl *v. t. or n.*	ألقَى . رَمَى ـ رَميةٌ
Humbug *n.* or *v. t.*	شَعبَذةٌ . غَشَّ ــ	Hurrah ! *ex.*	هِتَافُ آلفَرَح
Humid *a.*	رَطْبٌ . مُنَدّى	Hurricane *n.*	زَوْبَعةٌ
Humidity *n.*	رُطُوبةٌ . نَدًى	Hurry *v. t. or i.*	عَجِلَ . إِستَعجَلَ
Humiliate *v. t.*	ذَلَّ .حَطَّ شَأنَهُ	Hurt *n. or v. t.*	ضَرَر . أضَرَّ . آذَى

Hurtful *a.*	مُوْذٍ . مُضِر
Husband *n.* or *v. t.*	زَوْجٌ . بَعْلٌ . إِقْتَصَدَ
Husbandman *n.*	فَلاحٌ . كَرَّامٌ
Husbandry *n.*	فَلاحَة
Hush *v. t.* or *i.*	اسْكَتَ . سَكَتَ ـُ
Husk *n.* or *v. t.*	قِشْرَة . قَشَرَ
Husky *a.*	أَبَحّ
Hustle *v. t.*	زَحَمَ . دَفَعَ ـ عَجَّلَ
Hut *n.*	كُوخ
Huzza *n.*	هِتَافُ الإِسْتِحْسَان
Hybrid *n.*	مَوْلُودٌ مِنْ نَوْعَيْن
Hydraulics *n. sing.*	عِلْمُ السَّوَائِل
Hydrogen *n.*	هِدْرُوجِين
Hydrophobia *n.*	دَاءُ الْكَلَب
Hygiene Hygienics } *n.*	عِلْمُ حِفْظِ الصِّحَّة
Hyena *n.*	ضَبْع ج ضِبَاع
Hymn *n.*	تَرْنِيمة
Hymnal *n.*	كِتَابُ تَرْنِيمَاتٍ
Hyperbola *n.*	قَوْسُ قَطْعِ الْمَخْرُوطِ
Hyperbole *n.*	مُبَالَغَة
Hyphen *n.*	عَلَامَةُ وَصْلٍ (ـ)
Hypochondria *n.*	سَوْدَآء
Hypocrisy *n.*	رِيَاء . نِفَاق
Hypocrite *n.*	مُرَآء . مُنَافِق
Hypothenuse *n.*	وَتَرُ زَاوِيَةٍ قَائِمَة
Hypothssis *n.*	حَدَس . فَرْض
Hyssop *n.*	زُوفَا
Hysterical *a.*	(هِسْتِيرِي)
Hysteria Hysterics } *n.*	(هِسْتِيرِيَا)

I

I *pro.*	انا
Ice *n.*	جَليدٌ
Iceberg *n.*	جَبلُ جَليدٍ عائمٌ
Ice-cream *n.*	(بُوز.جلاته . دَنْدُرْمَه)
Icicle *n.*	جَلِيدٌ مَخْرُوطِيُّ آلشَّكْلِ
Icy *a.*	جَليديٌّ . فَارِسٌ
Idea *n.*	صُورَةٌ عقلِيَّة . فِكْرٌ
Ideal *a.*	تصَوُّرِيٌّ . كَامِل
Idealize *v. t.*	تَصَوَّرَ
Identic / Identical *a.*	عَيْنُهُ . ذَاتُهُ
Identify *v. t.*	حقَّقَ أَنَّهُ هو
Idiocy *n.*	بَلاهَةٌ . عتَه
Idiom *n.*	إِصْطِلاحٌ
Idiomatic / Idiomatical *a.*	إِصطِلاحيٌّ
Idio *n.* / Idiotic *a.*	أَبلهُ . مَعتوهٌ
Idle *a.* / Idler *n.*	بطَّال . كَسْلانٌ
Idleness *n.*	كَسَلٌ . بطَالةٌ
Idol *n.*	صَنَمٌ . وَثَنٌ
Idolater *n.*	وَثَنِيٌّ . عَابد اصنامٍ
Idolatrous *a.*	مُختصٌّ بعِبادَة آلاوثانِ
Idolize *v. t.*	أَفْرَطَ في آلحُبِّ . ولِعَ بِ
Idolatry *n.*	عبادَةُ آلاوثان
If *conj.*	لَوْ . إِنْ . إِذَا
Igneous *a.*	ناريٌّ
Ignite *v. t.*	أَوْقَدَ . أَشْعَلَ
Ignoble *a.*	دَنِيءٌ . خسيسٌ
Ignominious *a.*	مُوجِبُ آلعَارِ . مُخزٍ
Ignominy *n.*	عَارٌ . فَضيحَة . إِبَةٌ

Ignoramus *n.* }	جَاهِلٌ . غَبِي
Ignorant *a.*	
Ignorance *n.*	جَهَالَة . غَبَاوَة
Ignore *v. t.*	تَجَاهَلَ . أَهْمَلَ
Ill *a. or a.*	مَرِيضٌ . سُوءٌ
Ill-bred *a.*	غَيْرُ مُهَذَّبٍ . فَظٌّ
Illegal *a.*	غَيْرُ شَرْعِيٍّ
Illegible *a.*	مُمْتَنِعٌ قِرَاءَتُهُ
Illegitimate *a.*	غَيْرُ شَرْعِيٍّ . نَغْل
Ill-fated *a.*	نَحْس . مَشْؤُومٌ
Ill-favoured *a.*	أَشْوَهُ .سَيِّ ءُ الْمَنْظَرِ
Illiberal *a.*	بَخِيلٌ . خَسِيسٌ
Illicit *a.*	مُحَرَّمٌ . مَمْنُوع
Illimitable *a.*	غَيْرُ مَحْدُودٍ
Illiterate *a.*	أُمِّيٌّ
Ill-nature *n.*	سُوءُ الطَّبْع
Illness *n.*	مَرَضٌ . عِلَّة
Illogical *a.*	غَيْرُ مَنْطِقِيٍّ
Ill-omened *a.*	مَشْؤُومٌ

Ill-starred *a.*	مَشْؤُومٌ
Ill-timed *a.*	فِي غَيْرِ وَقْتِهِ
Illumine } *v. t.*	أَنَارَ . اضَاءَ
Illuminate	
Illumination *n.*	إِنَارَةٌ
Illusion *n.*	وَهْمٌ
Illusive } *a.*	غَرَّارٌ . غَيْرُ حَقِيقِيٍّ
Illusory	
Illustrate *v. t.*	بَيَّنَ . شَرَحَ
Illustration *n.*	إِيضَاحٌ . تَصْوِير
Illustrious *a.*	شَهِيرٌ . جَلِيلٌ
Ill-will *n.*	ضَغِينَة . سُوءُ نِيَّةٍ
Image *n.*	تِمْثَالٌ . صُورَة
Imagery *n.*	التَّصَوُّرُ فِي الْكَلَامِ
Imaginable *a.*	قَابِلُ التَّصَوُّرِ
Imaginary *a.*	تَصَوُّرِيٌّ . وَهْمِيٌّ
Imagination *n.*	التَّصَوُّرُ . الْمُخَيِّلَة
Imaginative *a.*	كَثِيرُ التَّصَوُّرِ
Imagine *v. t.*	تَصَوَّرَ . تَخَيَّلَ
Imbecile *a.*	سَخِيف . عَاجِز

Imbecility n.	سَخَافَةٌ . عَجْزٌ
Imbedded pp.	مَغْرُوزٌ . مَدْفُونٌ
Imbibe v. t.	شَرِبَ ــ . تَشَرَّبَ
Imbrue v. t.	بَلَّلَ . نَقَعَ . لَطَّخَ
Imbue v. t.	صَبَغَ ــ . أَثَّرَ
Imitate v. t.	تَمَثَّلَ بِهِ . حَاكَى
Imitation n.	إِقْتِدَاءٌ . تَزْوِيرٌ
Immaculate a.	بِلَا دَنَسٍ . نَقِيٌّ
Immalleable a.	لَا يُمْطَلُ بِالطَّرْقِ
Immaterial a.	غَيْرُ مَادِّيٍّ . غَيْرُ مُهِمٍّ
Immature a.	فِجٌّ . غَيْرُ بَالِغٍ
Immeasurable / Immensurable } a.	لَا يُقَاسُ
Immediate a.	غَيْرُ مُتَأَخِّرٍ . قَرِيبٌ
Immediately ad.	حَالًا . عَلَى الفَوْرِ
Immemorial a.	قَدِيمٌ جِدًّا
Immense a.	عَظِيمٌ جِدًّا
Immensity n.	كُبْرٌ لَا يُقَاسُ
Immerse v. t.	غَطَسَ ــ . غَمَسَ ــ

Immersion n.	غَطْسٌ . غَمْسٌ
Immigrant a.	مُهَاجِرٌ إِلَى
Immigrate v. i.	هَاجَرَ إِلَى
Imminent a.	قَرِيبٌ . مُوْشِكٌ
Immoderate a.	مُفْرِطٌ . مُتَجَاوِزُ الحَدِّ
Immodest a.	عَدِيمُ الحِشْمَةِ اوِ الحَيَاءِ
Immolate v. t.	ذَبَحَ ــ
Immoral a.	فَاسِدٌ . فَاجِرٌ
Immorality n.	فَسَادُ الآدَابِ
Immortal a.	خَالِدٌ
Immortality n.	خُلُودٌ
Immortalize v. t.	خَلَّدَ
Immovable a. in pl. n.	ثَابِتٌ . رَاسِخٌ . عَقَارٌ
Immunity n.	بَرَاءَةٌ . إِمْتِيَازٌ
Immure v. t.	حَبَسَ ــ
Immutability n.	عَدَمُ التَّغَيُّرِ
Immutable a.	عَدِيمُ التَّغَيُّرِ
Imp n.	عِفْرِيتٌ صَغِيرٌ

Impact n.	صَدْمٌ . دَفْعٌ
Impair v. t.	أَفْسَدَ . أَخَلَّ بِهِ . أَضَرَّ
Impale v. t.	خَوْزَقَ
Impalpable a.	مَا لَا يُدْرَكُ بِٱللَّمْسِ
Impart v. t.	مَنَحَ ـــَ . أَخْبَرَ بِهِ
Impartial a.	عَدِيمُ ٱلْمُحَابَاةِ . عَادِلٌ
Impartiality n.	عَدَمُ ٱلْمُحَابَاةِ
Impassable a.	مَا لَا يُعْبَرُ
Impassioned a.	ثَائِرٌ . مُهَيِّجٌ . مُتَهَيِّجٌ
Impatience n.	عَدَمُ ٱلصَّبْرِ
Impatient a.	عَدِيمُ ٱلصَّبْرِ . جَزِعٌ
Impeach v. t.	أَقَامَ دَعْوَى عَلَيْهِ
Impede v. t.	عَاقَ
Impediment n.	عَائِقٌ
Impel v. t.	دَفَعَ ــ حَرَّضَ
Impending a.	مُوْشِكٌ . مُتَوَعِّدٌ
Impenetrable a.	غَيْرُ قَابِلِ ٱلْإِخْتِرَاقِ
Impenitence n.	عَدَمُ ٱلتَّوْبَةِ
Impenitent a.	عَدِيمُ ٱلتَّوْبَةِ
Imperative a. or n.	ضَرُورِيٌّ . أَمْرٌ
Imperceivable } a. Imperceptible }	لَا يُشْعَرُ بِهِ
Imperfect a.	نَاقِصٌ . غَيْرُ كَامِلٍ
Imperfection n.	نَقْصٌ
Imperial a.	سُلْطَانِيٌّ
Imperil v. t.	أَوْقَعَ فِي خَطَرٍ
Imperious a.	مُتَجَبِّرٌ . ضَرُورِيٌّ
Imperishable a.	عَدِيمُ ٱلزَّوَالِ
Impermeable a.	مَا لَا يَتَخَلَّلُهُ سَائِلٌ
Impersonal a.	غَيْرُ شَخْصِيٍّ
Impersonate v. t.	شَخَّصَ
Impertinence n.	وَقَاحَةٌ
Impertinent a.	وَقِحٌ . فُضُولِيٌّ
Imperturbable a.	رَكِينٌ لَا يُقْلَقُ
Impervious a.	مَا لَا يُخْرَقُ أوْ يُتَخَلَّلُ
Impetuosity n.	إِقْتِحَامٌ . حِدَّةٌ
Impetuous a.	مُتَقَحِّمٌ . مُحْتَدٌّ

Impetus *n.*	قُوَّةٌ دَافِعَةٌ	Importance *n.*	أَهَمِّيَّةٌ . عَظَمَةٌ
Impiety *n.*	عَدَمُ ٱلتَّقْوَى	Important *a.*	مُهِمّ . خَطِيرٌ
Impious *a.*	شِرِّيرٌ . أَثِيمٌ	Importation *n.*	جَلْبٌ مِنْ خَارِجٍ
Implacable *a.*	حَنِقٌ لَا يُرْضَى	Importunate *a.*	لَجُوجٌ . مُلِحّ
Implant *v. t.*	غَرَسَ فِي . أَدْخَلَ	Importune *v. t.*	لَجَّ ـِ . أَلَحَّ عَلَى
Implement *n.*	آلَةٌ . أَدَاةٌ	Importunity *n.*	لَجَاجَةٌ . إِلْحَاحٌ
Implicate *v. t.*	أَوْقَعَ فِي . عَرَّضَ	Impose *v. t.*	وَضَعَ ـَ عَلَى . غَشَّ ـُ
Implication *n.*	تَضَمُّنُ مَعْنًى	Imposing *a.*	عَظِيمٌ . مُؤَثِّرٌ
Implicit *a.*	مُتَضَمَّنٌ . مَوْثُوقٌ بِهِ	Imposition *n.*	تَكْلِيفٌ . مَكْرٌ
Implicitly *ad.*	بِثِقَةٍ تَامَّةٍ . مَعْنَوِيًّا	Impossibility *n.*	عَدَمُ ٱلإِمْكَانِ
Implore *v. t.*	تَوَسَّلَ . إِسْتَغَاثَ	Impossible *a.*	غَيْرُ مُمْكِنٍ . مُسْتَحِيلٌ
Imply *v. t.*	تَضَمَّنَ . دَلَّ عَلَى	Impost *n.*	ضَرِيبَةٌ . مَكْسٌ
Impolite *a.*	قَلِيلُ ٱلأَدَبِ . فَظّ	Impostor *n.*	خَدَّاعٌ . دَجَّالٌ
Impoliteness *n.*	قِلَّةُ ٱلآدَبِ	Imposture *n.*	خُدْعَةٌ
Impolitic *a.*	بِغَيْرِ حِكْمَةٍ . غَيْرُ مُنَاسِبٍ	Impotence *n.*	عَجْزٌ . وَهْنٌ
Imponderable *a.*	عَدِيمُ ٱلثِّقَلِ	Impotent *a.*	عَاجِزٌ . وَاهِنٌ
Import *v. t.*	جَلَبَ ـِ . ادْخَلَ إِلَى	Impoverish *v. t.*	أَفْقَرَ . أَعْوَزَ
Import *n.*	وَارِدٌ . مَعْنًى . اهَمِّيَّةٌ	Impracticable *a.*	مُمْتَنِعُ عَمَلُهُ

Imprecate v. t.	دَعَا عَلَى	Imprudence n.	قِلَّةُ ٱلْحَزْمِ أَوِ ٱلْبَصِيرَةِ
Impregnable a.	مَنِيع	Imprudent a.	غَيْرُ بَصِيرٍ أَوْ حَازِمٍ
Impregnate v. t.	لَقَّحَ . أَشْرَبَ	Impudence n.	وَقَاحَة . سَفَه
Impregnation n.	تَلْقِيح . إِشْرَاب	Impudent a.	وَقِح . سَفِيه
Impress v. t.	أَثَّرَ . سَخَّرَ . خَتَمَ	Impugn v. t.	نَاقَضَ . عَارَضَ
Impress n.	رَسْم . أَثَر . صُورَة	Impulse Impulsion } n.	قُوَّة دَافِعَة
Imprsesion n.	ظَنّ . عَلَامَة . طَابِعَة	Impulsive a.	مُنْدَفِع . دَافِع
Impressive a.	مُؤَثِّر	Impunity n.	عَدَمُ عِقَابٍ . أَمْن
Imprint v. t. or n.	طَبَعَ — . وَسَمَ — وَسْم	Impure a.	فَاسِد . نَجِس
Imprison v. t.	حَبَسَ — . سَجَنَ —	Impurity n.	فَسَاد . قَذَر
Imprisonment n.	حَبْس . سِجْن	Imputation n.	إِتِّهَام . ذَمّ
Improbable a.	غَيْرُ مُحْتَمِلٍ	Impute v. t.	نَسَبَ إِلَى . حَسِبَ لَهُ
Improper a.	غَيْرُ لَائِقٍ	In pr.	فِي . بِ . دَاخِل
Impropriety n.	عَدَمُ لِيَاقَةٍ	Inability n.	عَجْز . عَدَمُ قُدْرَةٍ
Improve v. t. or i.	حَسَّنَ . تَقَدَّمَ	Inaccessible a.	مَنِيع
Improvement n.	تَحَسُّن . تَقَدُّم	Inaccuracy n.	عَدَمُ ضَبْطٍ أَوْ صِحَّةٍ
Improvident a.	عَدَمُ ٱلْعِنَايَةِ . مُتَغَفِّل	Inaccurate a.	غَيْرُ مَضْبُوطٍ أَوْ صَحِيح
Improvise v. i.	إِرْتَجَلَ . إِبْتَدَهَ	Inaction Inactivity } n.	عَدَمُ حَرَكَةٍ . بِطَالَة

Inactive a.	سَاكِنٌ . مُتَكَاسِلٌ
Inadequate a.	غَيْرُ كَافٍ . نَاقِصٌ
Inadmissible a.	مُمْتَنِعٌ قَبُولُهُ
Inadvertence } Inadvertency } n.	غَفْلَةٌ . سَهْوٌ
Inalienable a.	لاَ يُبَاعُ وَلاَ يُوهَبُ
Inane a.	فَارِغٌ . غَيْرُ مُفِيدٍ . خَاوٍ
Inanimate a.	عَدِيمُ ٱلْحَيَاةِ
Inapplicable a.	غَيْرُ مُطَابِقٍ
Inappreciable a.	مَالاَ يُحْسَبُ . زَهِيدٌ
Inappropriate a.	غَيْرُ مُنَاسِبٍ
Inapt a.	غَيْرُ جَدِيرٍ . غَيْرُ مُنَاسِبٍ
Inaptitude a.	عَدَمُ جَدَارَةٍ أَوْ مُنَاسَبَةٍ
Inarticulate a.	غَيْرُ مَلْفُوظٍ
Inasmuch ad.	بِمَا انَّ
Inattention n.	عَدَمُ مُبَالاَةٍ . غَفْلَةٌ
Inattentive a.	غَيْرُ مُبَالٍ . مُتَغَافِلٌ
Inaudible a.	غَيْرُ مَسْمُوعٍ
Inaugural a.	إِفْتِتَاحِيٌّ . إِحْتِفَالِيٌّ
Inaugurate v. t.	إِفْتَتَحَ . رَسَمَ . قَلَّدَ
Inauguration n.	إِفْتِتَاحٌ . تَقْلِيدٌ
Inauspicious a.	مَشْؤُومٌ
Inborn } Inbred } a.	غَرِيزِيٌّ . طَبِيعِيٌّ
Incalculable a.	مَالاَ يُحْصَى
Incandescent a.	وَهَّاجٌ
Incantation a.	رُقْيَةٌ
Incapability n.	عَجْزٌ . قُصُورٌ
Incapable a.	عَاجِزٌ . غَيْرُ قَادِرٍ
Incapacitate v. t.	اعْجَزَ
Incapacity n.	عَجْزٌ
Incarcerate v. t.	حَبَسَ
Incarceration n.	حَبْسٌ
Incarnate a.	مُتَجَسِّدٌ
Incarnation n.	تَجَسُّدٌ
Incase v. t.	وَضَعَ فِي صُنْدُوقٍ
Incautious a.	غَافِلٌ . غَيْرُ مُتَحَذِّرٍ
Incendiary a. or n.	حَارِقُ بُيُوتٍ عَمْدًا
Incense n. Incense v. t. }	بَخُورٌ . بَخَّرَ . اغَاظَ

Incentive *n.*	بَاعِثٌ . حَثٌّ	Incline *v. t. or i.*	أَمَالَ . مَالَ ـِ
Inception *n.*	بَدَاءَةٌ . شُرُوعٌ	Inclose *v. t.*	أَحَاطَ . سَيَّجَ . ضَمَّنَ
Incertitude *n.*	عَدَمُ يَقِينٍ . شَكٌّ	Inclosure *n.*	حَائِطٌ . حَظِيرَةٌ . ضِمْنٌ
Incessant *a.*	غَيْرُ مُنْقَطِعٍ	Include *v. t.*	حَوَى ـِ . شَمِلَ ـَ
Incest *n.*	أَلزِّنَا بَيْنَ أَقْرِبَاءَ	Including *pp.* Inclusive *a.*	شَامِلٌ . حَاوٍ
Inch *n.*	عُقْدَةٌ	Incognito *n. or ad.*	تَنَكُّرٌ
Incidence *n.*	وُقُوعٌ . حُدُوثٌ	Incoherence *n.*	عَدَمُ ارْتِبَاطٍ . هَذَيٌ
Incident *n.*	وَاقِعٌ . حَادِثَةٌ	Incoherent *a.*	هَذَآءٌ . بِلَا مُطَابَقَةٍ
Incidental *a.*	عَرَضِيٌّ . إِتِّفَاقِيٌّ	Incombustible *a.*	مَا لَا يُحْرَقُ
Incipient *a.*	إِبْتِدَائِيٌّ	Income *n.*	إِيرَادٌ . دَخْلٌ
Incision *n.*	شَقٌّ . تَشْرِيطٌ	Incommode *v. t.*	ثَقَّلَ عَلَى . اتْعَبَ
Incisive *a.*	قَاطِعٌ . صَارِمٌ . حَادٌّ	Incommodious *a.*	مُتْعِبٌ
Incisor *n.*	قَاطِعٌ . ثَنِيَّةٌ . (سِنٌّ)	Incommunicative *a.*	كَتُومٌ
Incite *v. t.*	حَمَلَ عَلَى . أَغْوَى . هَيَّجَ	Incomparable *a.*	فَرِيدٌ
Incivility *n.*	غَلَاظَةٌ . عَدَمُ أُنْسٍ	Incompatible *a.*	مُغَايِرٌ . مُتَنَافٍ
Inclement *a.*	صَارِمٌ . قَارِسٌ	Incompetence *n.*	قُصُورٌ . عَجْزٌ
Inclinable *a.*	مَائِلٌ إِلَى	Incompetent *a.*	قَاصِرٌ . عَاجِزٌ
Inclination *n.*	مَيْلٌ	Incomplete *a.*	نَاقِصٌ

Incompleteness *n.*	نَقْص
Incomprehensible *a.*	مُمْتَنِع إِدْرَاكُه
Inconceivable *a.*	مَا لاَ يُتَصَوَّرُ
Inconclusive *a.*	غَيْرُ مُقْنِع
Incongruent Incongruous } *a.*	غَيْرُ مُتَنَاسِب
Incongruity *n.*	عَدَمُ تَنَاسُب
Inconsiderable *a.*	زَهِيد
Inconsiderate *a.*	غَيْرُ مُبَالٍ
Inconsistency *n.*	تَنَاقُض
Inconsistent *a.*	مُخَالِف . مُنَاقِض
Inconsolable *a.*	لاَ يَتَعَزَّى
Inconspiciuous *a.*	غَيْرُ بَيِّنٍ أَوْ وَاضِح
Inconstancy *n.*	تَقَلُّب
Inconstant *a.*	مُتَقَلِّب . مُتَغَيِّر
Incontestable *a.*	مَا لاَ يُنْكَرُ
Incontinence Incontinency } *n.*	عَدَمُ العِفَّة وَالضَّبْط
Incontinent *a.*	غَيْرُ عَفِيفٍ . فَاسِق
Incontrovertible *a.*	مَا لاَ يُرَدُّ
Inconvenience *n.*	عَائِق
Inconvenient *a.*	غَيْرُ مُوَافِقٍ
Incorporate *v. t.*	ضَمَّ إِلَى . أَدْخَلَ أَقَامَ شَرْعًا
Incorporeal *a.*	غَيْرُ مَادِّيٍّ . بِلاَ جِسْم
Incorrect *a.*	غَيْرُ مُصِيب . خَطَأ
Incorrectness *n.*	خَطَأ . عَدَمُ ضَبْط
Incorrigible *a.*	مَا لاَ يُصْلَحُ
Incorrupt *a.*	غَيْرُ فَاسِدٍ . طَاهِر
Incorruptible *a.*	عَدِيمُ الفَسَاد
Increase *v. t. or i.*	زَادَ — نَمَا —
Increment Increase } *n.*	زِيَادَة . نُمُوّ
Incredible *a.*	مُمْتَنِع تَصْدِيقُه
Incredulity *n.*	عَدَمُ تَصْدِيق
Incredulous *a.*	غَيْرُ مُصَدِّق
Incriminate *v. t.*	اِسْتَذْنَبَ . اِتَّهَمَ
Incrust *v. t.*	لَبَّسَ بِقِشْرَة
Incubation *n.*	حَضَانَة . رَحْم
Incubus *a.*	كَابُوس ج كَوَابِيس

Inculcate v. t.	اوصى . أَلَحَّ . عَلَّمَ
Incumbent a. or n.	واجبٌ عَلَى . مُتَوَظِّفٌ
Incumbrance n.-	عَائِقٌ . ثِقَلٌ
Incur v.t.	تَعَرَّضَ لَهُ . جَلَبَ عَلَى نَفْسِهِ
Incurable a.	عَدِيمُ آلشِّفَاءِ
Incursion n.	غَزْوَةٌ . غَارَةٌ
Indebted n.	مَدْيُونٌ
Indecency n.	رَذِيلَةٌ . قَبَاحَةٌ
Indecent a.	رَذِيلٌ . قَبِيحٌ
Indecipherable a.	مَا لَا يُقْرَأُ أَوْ يُحَلُّ
Indecision n.	تَرَدُّدٌ . عَدَمُ ثَبَاتٍ
Indecisive a.	غَيْرُ جَازِمٍ
Indeclinable a.	غَيْرُ مُتَصَرِّفٍ . مَبْنِيٌّ
Indecorous a.	مُخَالِفُ آلْأَدَبِ
Indecorum n.	مُخَالَفَةُ آلْأَدَبِ
Indeed ad.	حَقًّا . صَحِيحٌ
Indefatigable a.	جَادٌّ لَا يَكِلُّ
Indefensible a.	مَا لَا يُحَامَى عَنْهُ
Indefinite a.	غَيْرُ مَحْدُودٍ . مُبْهَمٌ
Indefiniteness n.	عَدَمُ تَحْدِيدٍ
Indelible a.	ثَابِتٌ لَا يُمْحَى
Indelicacy n.	قِلَّةُ آلْأَدَبِ
Indelicate a.	قَلِيلُ آلْأَدَبِ
Indemnification Indemnity n.	تَعْوِيضُ غَرَامَةٍ
Indemnify v. t.	عَوَّضَ عَنْ
Indent v. t.	فَرَضَ — . قَيَّدَ لِخِدْمَةٍ
Indentation n.	فَرْضٌ . أَثَرٌ
Independence Independency n.	اِسْتِقْلَالٌ
Independent a.	مُسْتَقِلٌّ
Indescribable a.	مَا لَا يُوصَفُ
Indestructible a.	مَا لَا يَفْنَى
Indeterminable a.	مَا لَا يُحَدَّدُ
Indeterminate a.	غَيْرُ مُحَدَّدٍ
Index n.	دَلِيلٌ . فِهْرِسٌ . سَبَّابَةٌ
Indian n.	هِنْدِيٌّ
Indiaman n.	سَفِينَةٌ تُسَافِرُ إِلَى آلْهِنْدِ

India-rubber n. (مُغَيِّطٌ) . (لَسْتِك)

Indicate v. t. اشَارَ إِلَى . دَلَّ ـ

Indication n. إِشَارَةٌ . دَلَالَةٌ

Indicative a.
Indicator n. } مُشِيرٌ . دَالٌّ

Indict v. t. أَقَامَ دَعْوَى عَلَيْهِ

Indictment n. إِقَامَةُ ٱلدَّعْوَى

Indifference n. عَدَمُ ٱكْتِرَاثٍ

Indifferent a. غَيْرُ مُكْتَرِثٍ . سَوَآءٌ

Indigence n. فَقْرٌ . فَاقَةٌ

Indigenous a. وَطَنِيٌّ . بَلَدِيٌّ

Indigent a. فَقِيرٌ . مُعْوِزٌ

Indigestible a. مَا لَا يُهْضَمُ

Indigestion n. تُخَمَةٌ . سُوءُ هَضْمٍ

Indignant a. مُغْتَاظٌ

Indignation n. غَيْظٌ . غَضَبٌ

Indignity n. إِهَانَةٌ . إِحْتِقَارٌ

Indigo n. نِيلٌ (الصِّباغ المعروف)

Indirect a. غَيْرُ مُسْتَقِيمٍ . مُنْحَرِفٌ

Indirectness n. إِنْحِرَافٌ

Indiscernible a. مَا لَا يُرَى أَوْ يُمَيَّزُ

Indiscoverable a. مَا لَا يُكْشَفُ

Indiscreet a. غَيْرُ حَازِمٍ او بَصِيرٍ

Indiscretion n. حَمَاقَةٌ . رُعُونَةٌ

Indiscriminate a. غَيْرُ مُمَيَّزٍ . بِلَا فَرْقٍ

Indiscrimination n. عَدَمُ تَمْيِيزٍ

Indispensable a. ضَرُورِيٌّ

Indisposed a. مُنْحَرِفُ ٱلصِّحَّةِ نَافِرٌ مِنْ

Indisposition n. إِنْحِرَافُ ٱلصِّحَّةِ

Indisputable a. مَا لَا يُنْكَرُ . مُسَلَّمٌ

Indissoluble
Indissolvable } a. مَا لَا يَنْحَلُّ

Indistinct n. غَيْرُ وَاضِحٍ . مُبْهَمٌ

Indistinctness n. عَدَمُ وُضُوحٍ

Indistinguishable a. مَا لَا يُمَيَّزُ

Indite v. t. أَلَّفَ . كَتَبَ . أَمْلَى بِ

Individual n. شَخْصٌ . فَرْدٌ

Individualism
Individuality } n. ذَاتِيَّةٌ . فَرْدِيَّةٌ

Individualize v. t.	مَيَز عَلى حِدَة
Individually ad.	إِفرَادًا . شَخصِيًا
Indivisible n.	مَالاَ يَنقَسِم
Indocile a.	غَيرُ طَائِعٍ . عَاص
Indolence n.	كَسَلٌ . تَوَانٍ
Indolent a.	كَسلاَنٌ
Indomitable a.	مَالاَيُقهَرُ اوْ يُذَلّ
Indorse v. t.	صَادَقَ عَلى
Indorsement n.	مُصَادَقَةٌ عَلى
Indubitable a.	لاَ رَيبَ فِيهِ
Induce v. t.	اغرَى . امَال . رَغَب
Inducement n.	دَاعٍ . مُوجِبٌ
Induction n.	إِدخَال . إِستِدلاَل
Inductive a.	إِستِدلاَلِيّ
Indue v. t.	مَنَحَ — . البَس . قلّد
Indulge v. t. or i.	ارضى . اولَعَ
Indulgence n.	تَلَذّذ . عَفوٌ
Indulgent a.	مُدَلِّلٌ . مُسَامِحٌ

Industrial a.	صِنَاعِيّ
Industrious a.	جَادٌّ . مُثَابِرٌ
Industry n.	جِدّ . مُثَابَرَة . صِنَاعَة
Inebriate v. t. or n.	أَسكَرَ . سِكّيرٌ
Inebriation Inebriety } n.	سُكرٌ
Inedited a.	غَيرُ مَطبُوعٍ
Indeffable a.	مَالاَ يُعَبّرُ عَنهُ
Ineffaceable a.	مَالاَ يُمحَى
Ineffective Ineffectual Inefficacious } a.	غَيرُ فَعّالٍ . عَبَثٌ
Inefficacy Inefficiency } n.	عَدَمُ فَاعِلِيَّة
Inefficient a.	غَيرُ فَعّالٍ . عَاجِز
Inelegant a.	غَيرُ ظَرِيفٍ
Inelegant a.	لاَ يَجُوزُ إِنتِخَابُهُ
Inequality n.	عَدَمُ مُسَاوَاةٍ
Inert a.	غَيرُ مُتَحَرِّكٍ . بَلِيدٌ
Inestimable a.	فَائِقُ التّثمِين
Inevitable a.	مَالاَ مَفَرَّ مِنهُ

Inexact a.	غَيْرُ مَضْبُوطٍ	Infamy n.	فَضِيحَةٌ . عَارٌ . قَبِيحَةٌ
Inexactness n.	عَدَمُ ضَبْطٍ . غَلَطٌ	Infancy n.	طُفُولِيَّةٌ
Inexcusable a.	بِلَا عُذْرٍ	Infant n.	طِفْلٌ . رَضِيعٌ
Inexhaustible a.	مَالَا يَفْرَغُ	Infanticide n.	قَتْلُ ٱلْأَطْفَالِ
Inexorable a.	غَيْرُ مُتَغَيِّرٍ . ثَابِتُ ٱلْعَزْمِ	Infantile ⎱ a. Infantine ⎰	طِفْلِيٌّ
Inexpedience ⎱ Inexpediency ⎰	عَدَمُ مُنَاسَبَةٍ	Infantry n.	جُنُودٌ مُشَاةٌ
Inexpedient a.	غَيْرُ مُنَاسِبٍ	Infatuate v. t.	فَتَنَ . شَغَفَ حُبًّا
Inexpensive a.	رَخِيصٌ	Infatuation n.	إِفْتِنَانٌ . كَلَفٌ . وُلُوعٌ
Inexperience n.	عَدَمُ ٱلْإِخْتِبَارِ	Infect v. t.	أَعْدَى . أَفْسَدَ
Inexpiable a.	مَالَا يُمْفَى أَوْ يُكَفَّرُ عَنْهُ	Infection n.	عَدْوَى . إِفْسَادٌ
Inexplicable a.	مَالَا تَفْسِيرَ لَهُ	Infectious a.	مُعْدٍ . مُفْسِدٌ
Inexpressible a.	مَالَا يُعَبَّرُ عَنْهُ	Infelicitous a.	نَحْسٌ . فِي غَيْرِ مَحَلِّهِ
Inexpressive a.	غَيْرُ مُعَبِّرٍ عَنْ	Infelicity n.	نَحْسٌ . بَلِيَّةٌ
Inextinguishable a.	مَالَا يَنْطَفِئُ	Infer v. t.	إِسْتَنْتَجَ . إِسْتَدَلَّ
Inextricable a.	مَالَا يُحَلُّ . مُعَقَّدٌ	Inferable ⎱ a. Inferential ⎰	نَاتِجٌ عَنْ . مُسْتَدَلٌّ
Infallibility n.	عِصْمَةٌ	Inference n.	نَتِيجَةٌ . إِسْتِدْلَالٌ
Infallible a.	مَعْصُومٌ	Inferior a.	دَنِيءٌ . دُونَ
Infamous n.	كَرِيهُ ٱلصِّيتِ	Inferiority n.	دُونِيَّةٌ . أَسْفَلِيَّةٌ

Infernal a.	جهنمِيّ . جحيمِيّ
Infertility n.	عَدَمُ خِصبٍ
Infest v. t.	كَدَّرَ . أَكثَرَ في
Infidel n.	كَافِرٌ ج كفّارٌ وَكَفَرَة
Infidelity n.	كُفرٌ . خِيَانَةٌ
Infinite a.	غَيرُ محدودٍ
Infinitely ad.	بلا نِهَايَةٍ . جِدًّا
Infiniteness Infinity } n.	عَدَمُ حَدٍّ أَوْ نِهَايَةٍ
Infinitesimal a.	دَقِيقٌ جِدًّا
Infinitive a.	صِيغَةُ ٱلمَصدَرِ
Infirm a.	عَاجِزٌ . ضَعِيفٌ
Infirmary n.	مُستَشفى
Infirmity n.	ضَعفٌ . عَجزٌ
Inflame v. t.	أضرَمَ . هَيَّجَ
Inflammable a.	قَابِلُ ٱلإِلتِهَابِ
Inflammation n.	إِلتِهَابٌ
Inflammatory a.	مُلهِبٌ . مُهَيِّجٌ
Inflate v. t.	نَفَخَ — . مَلَأَ هَوَاءً

Inflect v. t.	حَنَى — . صَرَّف
Inflection Inflexion } n.	حِنَايَةٌ . تَصرِيفٌ
Inflexibility n.	صَلَابَةٌ . إِصرَارٌ
Inflexible a.	لَا يُحنَى . مُصِرٌّ
Inflict v. t.	أَبلَى بِهِ . حَمَّلَ بِهِ
Infliction n.	بَلِيَّةٌ . عِقَابٌ
Influence n.	تَأثِيرٌ . نُفُوذٌ . قُوَّةٌ
Influence v. t.	أَثَّرَ في . أَمَالَ
Influential a.	ذو سُطوَةٍ او نُفُوذٍ
Influenza n.	زُكَامٌ وَأفِدِي
Influx n.	وُرُودٌ بِوَفرَةٍ
Infold v. t.	لَفَّ — عَانَقَ
Inform v. t.	اخبَرَ . أَعلَمَ
Informal a.	غَيرُ رَسمِيّ
Informality n.	مُخَالَفَةُ ٱلرُّسُومِ
Information n.	خَبَرٌ . إِنبَاءٌ
Infraction Infringement } n.	نَكثٌ . تَعَدٍّ
Infrequent a.	نَادِرٌ

Inhale v. t.	إِسْتَنْشَقَ

Infringe v. t.	خَالَفَ . تَعَدَّى عَلَى
Infuriate v. t.	أَغَاظَ . هَيَّجَ غَضَبًا
Infuse v. t.	أَدْخَلَ . نَقَعَ
Infusion n.	إِدْخَال . تَنْقِيع
Ingathering n.	حَصَّاد . جَمْع
Ingenious a.	حَاذِق . لَبِيب
Ingenuity n.	حَذَاقَة . مَهَارَة
Ingenuous a.	صَفِيّ . مُخْلِص . نَبِيل
Inglorious a.	عَدِيم المَجْد . مُخْزٍ
Ingot n.	سَبِيكَة ج سَبَائِك
Ingratiate v. t.	إِسْتَعْطَفَ
Ingratitude n.	كُنُود . عَدَم الشُّكْر
Ingredient a.	عُنْصُر مَزِيج
Ingress n.	دُخُول . مَدْخَل
Ingulf v. t.	إِبْتَلَعَ
Inhabit v. t. or i.	سَكَنَ ُ . قَطَنَ ُ
Inhabitable a.	قَابِل السَّكَن
Inhabitant n.	سَاكِن . قَاطِن

Inhere v. i.	إِخْتَصَّ بِهِ . طُبِعَ عَلَيْهِ
Inherent a.	مُلَازِم . حَالّ فِي
Inherit v. t.	وَارَثَ ُ
Inheritance n.	مِيرَاث ج مَوَارِيث
Inheritor n.	وَارِث ج وَرَثَة
Inhibit v. t.	نَهَى ــ . مَنَعَ ــ عَارَضَ
Inhospitable a.	غَيْر مِضْيَافٍ
Inhospitality n.	عَدَم إِكْرَام الضَّيْف
Inhuman a.	عَدِيم الإِنْسَانِيَّة
Inhumanity n.	عَدَم الإِنْسَانِيَّة
Inimical a.	عُدْوَانِيّ . مُقَاوِم
Inimitable a.	لَا يُحَاكَى . لَا مَثِيل لَهُ
Iniquitous a.	أَثِيم . شِرِّير جِدًّا
Iniquity n.	إِثْم . شَرّ
Initial a. or n.	إِبْتِدَائِيّ . اوَّل اسْم
Initiate v. t.	أَدْخَلَ فِي . بَدَأَ . عَلَّمَ
Initiative a. Initiatory	إِبْتِدَائِي . إِنْشَائِيّ

Inject v. t.	حَقَنَ ـُ . أَدْخَلَ فِي
Injection n.	حَقْنَة
Injudicious a.	غَيْرُ مُوَافِقٍ أَوْ بَصِيرٍ
Injunction n.	أَمْرٌ . حُكْمٌ
Injure v. t.	أَضَرَّ . آذَى
Injurious a.	مُضِرٌّ . مُؤْذٍ
Injury n.	ضَرَرٌ . أَذِيَّة
Injustice n.	ظَالِم . جَوْر . بَغْي
Ink n.	حِبْر . مِدَاد
Inkhorn } n. Inkstand }	دَوَاة . مِحْبَرَة
Inkling n.	تَلْمِيح . إِشَارَة
Inland n.	دَاخِل الْبَرِّ
Inlay v. t. (pp. inlaid)	رَصَّع
Inlet n.	مَدْخَل . خَلِيج . جُوْن
Inmate n.	سَاكِن مَعَ غَيْرِهِ
Inmost } a. Innermost }	الْأَكْثَرُ دَاخِلِيَّة
Inn n.	فُنْدُق . خَان
Innate a.	غَرِيزِي . بَدِيهِي
Inner a.	دَاخِلِيٌّ
Inkeeper n.	صَاحِبُ الْفُنْدُق . خَانَاتِي
Innocence n.	بَرَاءَة . طَهَارَة
Innocent a.	بَرِيٌ . سَلِيمُ الْقَلْب
Innocuous a.	غَيْرُ مُضِرٍّ . سَلِيم
Innovation n.	بِدْعَة . إِحْدَاث
Innovator n.	مُبْدِع . مُحْدِث
Innoxious a.	غَيْرُ مُضِرٍّ . سَلِيم
Innuendo n.	تَلْمِيح خَفِي . دَسِيسَة
Innumerable a.	فَائِقُ الْإِحْصَاء
Innutricious } a. Innutritive }	غَيْرُ مُغَذٍّ
Inoculate v. t.	طَعَّم . لَقَّح
Inoculation n.	تَطْعِيم . تَلْقِيح
Inodorous a.	عَدِيمُ الرَّائِحَة
Inoffensive a.	غَيْرُ مُسِيءٍ . بَسِيط
Inoperative a.	غَيْرُ عَامِل
Inopportune a.	فِي غَيْرِ أَوَانِهِ

Inordinate *a.*	مُفْرِط . زَائِدٌ
Inorganic *a.*	غَيْرُ آلِيّ . غَيْرُ عُضْوِيّ
Inquest *n.*	فَحْصٌ . تَفْتِيشٌ
Inquire *v. t.*	إِسْتَخْبَرَ . سَأَلَ
Inquirer *n.*	مُسْتَخْبِرٌ . طَالِبٌ
Inquiry *n.*	سُؤَالٌ . فَحْصٌ . بَحْثٌ
Inquisition *n.*	تَفْتِيشٌ . دِيوَانُهُ
Inquisitive *a.*	كَثِيرُ السُّؤَالِ
Inquisitor *n.*	مُفَتِّشٌ . فَاحِصٌ
Inroad *n.*	غَزْوَةٌ . هَجْمَةٌ
Insalubrious *a.*	وَخِيمٌ . وَبِيلٌ
Insalubrity *n.*	وَبَالٌ . وَخَامَةٌ
Insane *a.*	مَجْنُونٌ . مُخْتَلُّ الْعَقْلِ
Insanity *n.*	جُنُونٌ . إِخْتِلَالُ الْعَقْلِ
Insatiable ⎫ *a.* Insatiate ⎭	لَا يَشْبَعُ
Inscribe *v. t.*	كَتَبَ . حَفَرَ
Inscription *n.*	كِتَابَةٌ
Inscrutable *a.*	مَا لَا يُكْشَفُ لَا يُفْهَمُ

Insect *n.*	دُوَيْبَةٌ . حَشَرَةٌ
Insectivorous *a.*	آكِلُ الْحَشَرَاتِ
Insecure *a.*	غَيْرُ مُطْمَئِنٍّ . خَطِرٌ
Insecurity *n.*	عَدَمُ الْأَمْنِ
Insensate *a.*	عَدِيمُ الْحِسِّ . بَلِيدٌ
Insensibility *n.*	عَدَمُ الْحِسِّ
Insensible *a.*	عَدِيمُ الْحِسِّ
Inseparable *a.*	مَا لَا يُفْصَلُ أَوْ يَنْفَكُّ
Insert *v. t.*	أَدْخَلَ . أَدْرَجَ
Insertion *n.*	إِدْخَالٌ . إِدْرَاجٌ
Inside *ad.* or *a.* or *n.*	دَاخِلًا . دَاخِلٌ
Insidious *a.*	غَدَّارٌ . مُخَاتِلٌ
Insight *n.*	بَصِيرَةٌ . فِطْنَةٌ
Insignia *n.*	عَلَامَاتٌ
Insignificant *a.*	زَهِيدٌ . طَفِيفٌ
Insincere *a.*	غَيْرُ مُخْلِصٍ
Insincerity *n.*	عَدَمُ إِخْلَاصٍ
Insinuate *v. t.*	لَمَّحَ . دَسَّ

Insinuation *n.*	تَلْمِيحٌ . دَسِيسَةٌ	Inspiring *a.*	مُشَجِّعٌ . مُفَرِّحٌ . مُنَشِّطٌ
Insipid *a.*	تَفِهٌ . بَارِدٌ . نَاشِفٌ	Instability *n.*	عَدَمُ ثَبَاتٍ . تَقَلُّبٌ
Insipidity *n.*	تَفَاهَةٌ . بَلَادَةٌ	Instable *a.*	غَيْرُ ثَابِتٍ . مُتَغَيِّرٌ
Insist *v. i.*	أَصَرَّ . أَلَحَّ	Install *v. t.*	قَلَّدَ مَنْصِبًا . أَقَامَ
Insistence *n.*	إِصْرَارٌ . الْحَاحٌ	Installment *n.*	قِسْطٌ . تَقْلِيدٌ
Insolence *n.*	وَقَاحَةٌ . عُتُوٌّ	Instance *n.*	مِثَالٌ . حَادِثَةٌ
Insolent *n.*	وَقِحٌ . عَاتٍ	Instant *a.* or *n.*	حَالِي . مُهِمٌّ . لَحْظَةٌ
Insolubility *n.*	عَدَمُ الذَّوَبَانِ	Instantaneous *a.*	حَالِي . فَجَائِي
Insoluble *a.*	مَا لَا يَذُوبُ . لَا يُحَلُّ	Instantly *ad.*	حَالًا عَلَى الْفَوْرِ
Insolvable *a.*	مَا لَا يُحَلُّ . لَا يُفَسَّرُ	Instead *ad.*	عِوَضًا عَنْ
Insolvency *n.*	إِفْلَاسٌ	Instep *n.*	ظَهْرُ الْقَدَمِ
Insolvent *a.*	مُفْلِسٌ	Instigate *v. t.*	حَمَلَ عَلَى . أَغْرَى
Insomuch *ad.*	حَتَّى أَنْ	Instigation *n.*	إِغْرَاءٌ . تَهْيِيجٌ
Inspect *v. t.*	فَحَصَ ــ . فَتَّشَ	Instigator *n.*	مُغْرٍ . مُهَيِّجٌ
Inspection *n.*	فَحْصٌ . تَفْتِيشٌ	Instill *v. t.*	أَدْخَلَ . تَدْرِيجًا . لَقَّنَ
Inspector *n.*	نَاظِرٌ . مُفَتِّشٌ	Instinct *n.*	سَلِيقَةٌ . فِطْرَةٌ . غَرِيزَه
Inspiration *n.*	شَهِيقٌ . وَحْيٌ	Instinctive *a.*	غَرِيزِيٌّ
Inspire *v. t.*	شَهَقَ ــ أَلْهَمَ	Institute *v. t.*	أَقَامَ . أَنْشَا

Institution n.	إِقَامَةٌ . مَنْصِبٌ . دَارٌ لِلتَّعْلِيم . وَمَا أَشْبَهَ
Instruct v. t.	عَلَّمَ . أَوْصَى
Instruction n.	تَعْلِيمٌ . أَمْرٌ
Instructive a.	مُفِيدٌ . مُثَقِّفٌ
Instructor n.	مُعَلِّمٌ . مُدَرِّسٌ
Instrument n.	آلَةٌ . وَاسِطَةٌ
Instrumental a.	آلِيٌّ . مُفْضٍ إِلَى
Instrumentality n.	وَاسِطَةٌ
Insubordination n.	عِصْيَانٌ
Insufferable a.	مَا لَا يُطَاقُ
Insufficiency n.	نَقْصٌ
Insufficient a.	غَيْرُ كَافٍ . نَاقِصٌ
Insular a.	مُخْتَصٌّ بِجَزِيرَةٍ . مُحَاطٌ بِمَاءٍ
Insulate v. t.	أَفْرَدَ . قَطَعَ عَنْ
Insulator n.	قَاطِعُ مَجْرَى الْكَهْرَبَائِيَّةِ
Insult n. or v. t.	إِهَانَةٌ . أَهَانَ
Insulting a.	مُهِينٌ . شَاتِمٌ

Insuperable a.	مَا لَا يُغْلَبُ
Insupportable a.	مَا لَا يُحْتَمَلُ
Insurance n.	تَأْمِينٌ . ضَمَانٌ
Insure v. t.	أَمَّنَ . ضَمِنَ
Insurgent a.	ثَائِرٌ . مَارِدٌ . عَاصٍ
Insurmountable a.	مَا لَا يُقْوَى عَلَيْهِ
Insurrection n.	ثَوْرَةٌ . فِتْنَةٌ
Insusceptible a.	غَيْرُ مُتَأَثِّرٍ
Intangible a.	مَا لَا يُحَسُّ بِهِ
Intact a.	كَامِلٌ . سَالِمٌ . غَيْرُ مَمْسُوسٍ
Integer n.	عَدَدٌ صَحِيحٌ أَوْ تَامٌّ
Integral n. or a.	صَحِيحٌ . كَامِلٌ
Integrate v. t.	تَمَّمَ . شَمَلَ . جَدَّدَ
Integrity n.	إِسْتِقَامَةٌ . كَمَالٌ
Intellect n.	عَقْلٌ . ذِهْنٌ
Intellectual a.	عَقْلِيٌّ . ذَكِيٌّ
Intelligence n.	فَهْمٌ . ذَكَاءٌ
Intelligent a.	ذَكِيٌّ . عَاقِلٌ

Intelligible *a.*	مَفْهُومٌ . مَعْقُولٌ
Intemperance *n.*	اِفْرَاطٌ . سُكْرٌ
Intemperate *a.*	مُفْرِطٌ . سِكِّيرٌ
Intend *v. t. or i.*	قَصَدَ ـِ . نَوَى ـِ
Intense *a.*	شَدِيدٌ جِدًّا
Intensely *ad.*	جِدًّا . بِشِدَّةٍ
Intensify *v. t.*	شَدَّدَ . قَوَّى
Intensive *a.*	مُشَدِّدٌ . مُقَوٍّ
Intent *n. or a.*	قَصْدٌ . مُنْصَبٌّ عَلَى
Intention *n.*	قَصْدٌ . نِيَّةٌ
Intentional *a.*	مَقْصُودٌ . عَمْدِيٌّ
Intentionally *ad.*	عَمْدًا
Inter *v. t.*	دَفَنَ ـِ . قَبَرَ ـِ
Intercede *v. i.*	شَفَعَ . تَوَسَّطَ
Intercept *v. t.*	عَارَضَ . وَقَفَ
Interception *n.*	مُعَارَضَةٌ . تَوْقِيفٌ
Intercession *n.*	شَفَاعَةٌ
Intercessor *n.*	شَفِيعٌ . وَسِيطٌ

Interchange *v.t. or n.*	بَادَلَ . تَبَادُلٌ
Intercourse *n.*	مُبَاشَرَةٌ . مُخَالَطَةٌ
Interdict *v.t. or n.*	مَنَعَ . نَهْيٌ
Interest *n.*	فَائِدَةٌ . رَغْبَةٌ . نَفْعٌ
Interest *v. t.*	اِسْتَعْمَلَ . رَغَّبَ
Interested *a.*	مَائِلٌ . مُهْتَمٌّ
Interesting *a.*	مُلِذٌّ . مُفِيدٌ
Interfere *v. i.*	تَدَاخَلَ فِي . عَارَضَ
Interference *n.*	مُدَاخَلَةٌ . مُعَارَضَةٌ
Interim *n.*	اَثْنَاءٌ . خِلَالٌ
Interior *a. or n.*	دَاخِلِيٌّ . اَلدَّاخِلُ
Interjection *n.*	حَرْفُ نِدَاءٍ
Interlace *v. t.*	شَبَكَ ـِ
Interleave *v. t.*	أَدْخَلَ أَوْرَاقًا بَيْنَ غَيْرِهَا
Interline *v. t.*	خَطَّ بَيْنَ خُطُوطٍ
Interloper *n.*	فُضُولِيٌّ . طُفَيْلِيٌّ
Intermarriage *n.*	تَزَاوُجٌ
Intermeddle *v. i.*	تَدَاخَلَ

Intermediate a.	مُتَوَسِّط
Intermediation n.	وَسَاطَةٌ . تَوَسُّطٌ
Interment n.	دَفْنٌ . جِنَازَةٌ
Interminable a.	لَا نِهَايَةَ لَهُ
Intermingle v.t. or i.	خَالَطَ . تَخَالَطَ
Intermission n.	فَتْرَةٌ . تَوَقُّفٌ
Intermit v. t. or i.	وَقَفَ . تَوَقَّفَ
Intermittent a.	مُتَقَطِّعٌ . مُتَنَاوِبٌ
Intermix v. t. or i.	مَازَجَ . تَخَالَطَ
Internal a.	دَاخِلِيٌّ . بَاطِنِيٌّ
International a.	مُشْتَرَكٌ بَيْنَ الأُمَمِ
Internecine a.	مُتَبَادِلُ الْقَتْلِ . مُهْلِكٌ
Interpalate v. t.	أَفْسَدَ كِتَابًا وَاوَادْخَلَ فِيهِ
Interpose v. i.	ادْخَلَ أَوْ دَخَلَ بَيْنَ
Interposition n.	مُدَاخَلَةٌ . تَوَسُّطٌ
Interpret v. t.	تَرْجَمَ . فَسَّرَ
Interpretation n.	تَرْجَمَةٌ . تَفْسِيرٌ
Interpreter n.	مُتَرْجِمٌ . مُفَسِّرٌ
Interregnum n.	فَتْرَةٌ فِي السَّلْطَنَةِ
Interrogate v.t.	سَأَلَ ـ . (إِسْتَنْطَقَ)
Interrogation n.	سُؤَالٌ . (إِسْتِنْطَاقٌ)
Interrogative a.	إِسْتِفْهَامِي
Interrupt v. t.	قَطَعَ ـ . تَعَرَّضَ لـ
Interruption n.	قَطْعٌ . إِنْقِطَاعٌ . مَانِعٌ
Intersect v. t.	قَاطَعَ . تَقَاطَعَ
Intersection n.	تَقَاطُعٌ
Intersperse v. t.	بَذَرَ بَيْنَ
Interstice n.	فُسْحَةٌ ضَيِّقَةٌ
Intertwine / Intertwist v.t.	شَبَكَ ـ . حَبَكَ ـ
Interval n.	خِلَالٌ . فَتْرَةٌ
Intervene v. i.	تَخَلَّلَ . تَوَسَّطَ
Intervention n.	مُدَاخَلَةٌ . تَوَسُّطٌ
Interview n.	مُقَابَلَةٌ . مُحَادَثَةٌ
Interweave v. t.	حَاكَ . نَسَجَ مَعًا
Intestate a.	بِدُونِ وَصِيَّةٍ
Intestine a.	دَاخِلِي . وَطَنِيٌّ

Intestines n. pl.	أَمْعَاءُ
Inthrall v. t.	إِسْتَعْبَدَ
Intimacy n.	مَوَدَّة . خَاصَّة
Intimate v. t.	اشَارَ . لَمَّحَ
Intimate a. or n.	خَاصٌّ . خَلِيلٌ
Intimation n.	تَلْمِيحٌ . إِعْلَانٌ
Intimidate v. t.	أَخَافَ . هَدَّدَ
Intimidation n.	تَهْدِيد
Into prep.	فِي . إِلَى دَاخِلٍ
Intolerable a.	مَالَا يُطَاقُ
Intolerance n.	تَعَصُّبٌ
Intolerant a.	مُتَعَصِّبٌ
Intone v. t.	نَغَّمَ . لَحَّنَ فِي القِرَاءَةِ
Intoxicate v. t.	أَسْكَرَ
Intoxication n.	سُكْرٌ
Intractable a.	مَالَا يُذَلَّلُ . عَنِيدٌ
Intransitive a.	لَازِمٌ (فِعْلٌ)
Intrench v. t.	خَنْدَقَ . حَصَّنَ
Intrenchment n.	تَحْصِينٌ . مِتْرَاسٌ
Intrepid a.	جَسُورٌ . شُجَاعٌ
Intrepidity n.	جَسَارَة . جَرَاءَة
Intricacy n.	تَعْقِيدٌ
Intricate a.	مُعَقَّدٌ . مُشَكَّلٌ
Intrigue n. or v. i.	دَسِيسَةٌ . إِحْتَالَ
Intriguer n.	مُحْتَالٌ . صَاحِبُ دَسَائِسَ
Intrinsic a.	حَقِيقِيٌّ . جَوْهَرِيٌّ
Introduce v. t.	دَخَلَ . عَرَّفَ . أَنْشَأَ
Introduction n.	إِدْخَالٌ مُقَدِّمَة
Introductory a.	إِفْتِتَاحِي . دِيبَاجِي
Introspection n.	نَظَرٌ إِلَى دَاخِلٍ
Intrude v. i.	تَطَفَّلَ . تَعَدَّى
Intrusion n.	تَطَفُّل
Intrusive a.	مُتَطَفِّلٌ
Intrust v. t.	امَّنَ أَوْدَعَ
Intuition n.	بَدَاهَةٌ . فِطْرَةٌ
Intuitive a.	بَدِيهِيٌّ

Inundate v. t.	غَمَرَ ـَ . اغْرَقَ
Inundation n.	طُفُوحٌ . فَيَضَانٌ
Inure v. t.	عَوَّدَ
Inutility n.	عَدَمُ فَائِدَةٍ
Invade v. t.	هَجَمَ عَلَى . إِفْتَتَحَ
Invader n.	مُهَاجِمٌ . فَاتِحٌ . غَازٍ
Invalid a. or n.	مَرِيضٌ . بَاطِلٌ
Invalidate v. t.	أَبْطَلَ . أَوْهَنَ
Invalidity n.	بُطْلَانٌ . فَسَادٌ
Invaluable a.	فَائِقُ الثَّمَنِ . سَامٍ
Invariable a.	غَيْرُ مُتَغَيِّرٍ . ثَابِتٌ
Invasion n.	مُهَاجَمَةٌ . فُتُوحٌ . غَزْوٌ
Invective n.	شَتِيمَةٌ . سَبٌّ
Inveigh v. t.	طَعَنَ ـَ . سَعَى بِهِ
Inveigle v. t.	اغْوَى . أَضَلَّ . وَرَّطَ
Invent v. t.	إِخْتَرَعَ . إِخْتَلَقَ
Invention n.	إِخْتِرَاعٌ . إِخْتِلَاقٌ
Inventive a. } Inventor n. }	مُخْتَرِعٌ . مُبْدِعٌ
Inventory n.	قَائِمَةٌ . تَقْيِيدٌ
Inversion n.	عَكْسٌ . قَلْبٌ
Invert v. t.	عَكَسَ ـِ . قَلَبَ ـِ
Invertebrate a.	عَدِيمُ الْفَقَرَاتِ
Inverse a.	مُنْعَكِسٌ . مَقْلُوبٌ
Inverted a.	مَقْلُوبٌ . مَعْكُوسٌ
Invest v. t.	قَلَّدَ . وَقَفَ لِلْفَائِدَةِ
Investigate v. t.	فَحَصَ . إِسْتَقْصَى
Investigation n.	فَحْصٌ . إِسْتِقْصَاءٌ
Investiture n.	تَقْلِيدٌ . إِقَامَةٌ
Investment n.	إِلْبَاسٌ . وَضْعُ مَالٍ
Inveterate a.	مُتَأَصِّلٌ . مُتَعَوِّدٌ
Invidious a.	مُهَيِّجُ الْحَسَدِ أَوِ الْبَغْضِ
Invigorate v. t.	قَوَّى . شَدَّدَ . نَشَّطَ
Invincible a.	مَنِيعٌ . لَا يُغْلَبُ
Inviolable a.	مُحَرَّمٌ . مَالَا يَنْقَضُ
Inviolate a.	مَصُونٌ . مَحْفُوظٌ
Invisible a.	غَيْرُ مَنْظُورٍ

Invitation n.	دَعْوَةٌ . إِسْتِدْعَاءٌ	Ironical a.	تَهَكُّمِيٌّ . إِسْتِهْزَائِيٌّ
Invite v. t.	دَعَاُ . إِسْتَدْعَى	Irony n.	تَهَكُّمٌ . إِسْتِهْزَاآءٌ
Invocation n.	دُعَاءٌ . صَلَاةٌ	Irradiate v. t.	أَضَاءَ . أَشَعَّ . اَنَارَ
Invoice n.	قَائِمَةُ بَضَائِعَ	Irrational a.	غَيْرُ مَعْقُولٍ
Invoke v. t.	دَعَا . إِسْتَغَاثَ	Irreclaimable a.	مَالَا يُسْتَرَدُّ
Involuntary a.	غَيْرُ إِخْتِيَارِيٍّ	Irreconcilable a.	مَالَا يُصَالَحُ
Involution n.	تَرْقِيَةُ ٱلْعَدَدِ (في الحساب)	Irrecoverable a.	مَالَا يُرَدُّ . مَالَا يُعَادُ
Involve v. t.	لَفَّ . تَضَمَّنَ . عَرْقَلَ	Irredeemable a.	مَالَا يُفَدَّى اوْ يُفَكُّ
Invulnerable a.	مَصُونٌ . مَالَا يُجْرَحُ	Irrefutable a.	مَالَا يُدْحَضُ
Inward a.	دَاخِلِيٌّ . بَاطِنِيٌّ	Irregular a.	غَيْرُ قِيَاسِيٍّ . شَاذٌّ
Inwrought a.	مُرَصَّعٌ . مُوَشَّى	Irregularity n.	عَدَمُ ٱنْتِظَامٍ . شُذُوذٌ
Iodine n.	يُوْدٌ (دوا)	Irrelevant a.	غَيْرُ مُطَابِقٍ
Irascible a.	نَزِقٌ . سَرِيعُ ٱلْغَضَبِ	Irreligion n.	كُفْرٌ . زَنْدَقَةٌ
Ire n.	غَضَبٌ . غَيْظٌ	Irreligious a.	قَلِيلُ ٱلدِّينِ
Iridiscent a.	مُلَوَّنٌ كَقَوْسِ قُزَحَ	Irremediable a.	ألَا يُشْفَى اوْ يُصْلَحُ
Iris n.	قَوْسُ قُزَحَ . قَزَحِيَّةُ ٱلْعَيْنِ	Irremovable a.	ألَا يُنْقَلُ اوْ يُنْزَعُ
Irksome a.	مُمِلٌ . مُضْجِرٌ . مُتْعِبٌ	Irreparable a.	ألَا يُعَوَّضُ
Iron n. or a.	حَدِيدٌ . حَدِيدِيٌّ	Irrepressible a.	ألَا يُرْدَعُ اوْ يُضْبَطُ

Irreproachable a.	مَا لَا يُلَامُ
Irresistible a.	مَا لَا يُقَاوَمُ او يُدْفَعُ
Irresolute a.	مُتَرَدِّدٌ . مُتَقَلْقِلٌ
Irresoluteness Irresolution } n.	تَرَدُّدٌ . تَقَلُّبٌ
Irrespective a.	بِلَا ٱلْتِفَاتٍ إِلَى
Irresponsible a.	غَيْرُ مَسْؤُولٍ
Irretrievable a.	مَا لَا يُعَوَّضُ
Irreverence n.	عَدَمُ ٱحْتِرَامٍ
Irrevocable a.	مَا لَا يُلْغَى او يُرَدّ
Irrigate v. t.	سَقَى ـ أَرْوَى
Irrigation n.	سَقْيٌ . رَيٌّ
Irritabiliy n.	سُرْعَةُ ٱلتَّهْيِيجِ
Irritable a.	;حَكِدٌ . نَزِقٌ
Irritant a. or n.	مُهَيِّجٌ
Irritate v. t.	هَيَّجَ . أَثَارَ . أَغَاظَ
Irritation n.	تَهْيِيجٌ . إِلْهَابٌ
Irruption n.	هُجُومٌ . غَارَةٌ . إِنْفِجَارٌ
Is (see to be)	كَائِنٌ . يَكُونُ

Islam Islamism } n.	الإِسْلَامُ
Island Isle } n.	جَزِيرَةٌ ج جَزَائِر
Islet n.	جَزِيرَةٌ صَغِيرَةٌ
Isolate v. t.	أَفْرَدَ
Isosceles n.	مُتَسَاوِي ٱلضِّلَعَيْنِ
Israelite n.	إِسْرَائِيلِيٌّ
Issue v. t. or i.	أَصْدَرَ . صَدَرَ ـ
Issue n.	نَتِيجَةٌ . نَسْلٌ . صُدُورٌ
Isthmus n.	بَرْزَخٌ
It pro.	هُوَ . هِيَ
Italian n. or a.	إِيطَالِيٌّ
Italics n. pl.	حَرْفُ ٱلطَّبْعِ ٱلْمَائِلَةُ
Itch n. or v. t.	جَرَبٌ . حِكَّةٌ . حَكَّ
Item n.	أَيْضًا . نَفْذَةٌ
Iterate v. t.	كَرَّرَ
Itinerant a.	دَائِرٌ . جَائِلٌ
Itinerate v. i.	دَارَ . جَالَ ـ

Itinerary n.	سِيَاحَةٌ أَوْ كِتَابُهَا	Ivory n. or a.	عَاجٌ ۰ عَاجِيٌّ
Itself pro.	ذَاتُهُ ۰ نَفْسُهُ	Ivy n. (نَبَاتٌ)	لَبْلَابٌ أَوْ عَاشِقُ ٱلشَّجَرِ

J

Jabber v. i.	بَقَّ ۔ تَمْتَمَ	Jailer n.	سَجَّانٌ
Jack n.	آلَةٌ لِقَلْعِ ٱلْأَحْذِيَةِ اوْ لِرَفْعِ ٱلْأَثْقَالِ	Jam n. or v. t.	مُرَبًّى ۰ زَحْمَةٌ ۰ زَحَمَ ــ
		Janitor n.	حَاجِبٌ ۰ بَوَّابٌ
Jackal n.	إِبْنُ آوَى ج بَنَاتُ آوَى	Janizary n.	إِنْكِشَارِيٌّ ۰ يَسْقَجِيٌّ
Jackass n.	حِمَارٌ ج حَمِيرٌ	January n.	كَانُونُ ٱلثَّانِي ۰ يَنَايِرُ
Jackdaw n.	نَوْعٌ مِنَ ٱلزَّاغِ	Jar v. t. or i.	هَزَّ ــ ۰ إِهْتَزَّ
Jacket n.	جُبَّةٌ قَصِيرَةٌ	Jar n.	جَرَّةٌ ۰ حِزَّةٌ ۰ خِصَامٌ
Jack-knife n.	سِكِّينُ ٱلْجَيْبِ	Jargon n.	رَطَانَةٌ
Jade n.	كَدِيشٌ ۰ جَارِيَةٌ	Jasmine Jessamine } n.	يَاسَمِينٌ ۰ فُلٌّ
Jaded a.	مُعْيٍ ۰ تَعِبٌ	Jasper n.	يَشْبٌ
Jagged a.	مَحْزُوزٌ ۰ مَشْقُوقٌ	Jaundice n.	يَرْقَانٌ
Jail n.	حَبْسٌ ۰ سِجْنٌ	Jaunty n.	مَرِحٌ ۰ خَفِيفٌ

Javelin *n.*	مِزْرَاق ج مَزَارِيق	Jewel *n.*	جَوْهَرَة . دُرَّة
Jaw *n.*	فَكّ ج فُكُوك	Jeweller *n.*	صَائِغ . جَوْهَرِي
Jealous *a.*	غَيُور . مِغْيَار	Jewelry *n.*	مَصَاغ . حُلِي
Jealousy *n.*	غَيْرَة	Jib *n.*	شِرَاع مُقَدَّم ٱلسَّفِينَة
Jeer *v. i.* or *n.*	هَزَأَ ـَ . هَزْء	Jibe *v. i.* or *n.*	هَزَأَ ـ . هَزْء
Jelly *n.*	هُلَام	Jilt *v. t.*	رَفَضَتْ عَاشِقَهَا
Jeopard Jeopardize } *v. t.*	أَلْقَى فِي خَطَرٍ	Jingle *v. t.*	طَنَّ ـِ . رَنَّ ـِ
Jeopardy *n.*	خَطَر	Job *n.*	شُغْلَة . مُقَاوَلَة .(أَيُّوب ٱلنَّبِيّ)
Jerboa *n.*	يَرْبُوع ج يَرَابِيع (حَيَوَان)	Jockey *n.*	تَاجِر بِٱلْخَيْل . مَكَّار
Jerk *v. t.*	رَمَى . شَدَّ بَغْتَة	Jocose Jocular } *a.*	مَازِح . دَاعِب
Jest *v. i.* or *n.*	مَزَحَ ـ مَزْح	Jog Joggle } *v. t.*	هَزَّ ـ . وَكَزَ يَكِزُ
Jester *n.*	مَازِح . مَاجِن	Jog on *v. t.* or *i.*	مَشَى عَلَى مَهْلٍ
Jesting *n.*	مَزْح	Join *v. t.* or *i.*	وَصَلَ ـ . إِتَّصَلَ
Jesuit *n.* Jesuitical *a.* }	يَسُوعِيّ	Joiner *n.*	نَجَّار
Jesuitism *n.*	مَبَادِئ يَسُوعِيَّة	Joint *n.* or *a.*	مَفْصِل . عُقْدَة . مُشْتَرَك
Jet *n.*	غَايَةُ ٱلسَّوَادِ . فَوَّارَة	Jointed *a.*	ذُو مَفَاصِل أَو عُقَد
Jetty *n.*	لِسَانٌ صِنَاعِي فِي ٱلْبَحْرِ	Jointly *ad.*	مَعًا . بِٱشْتِرَاكٍ
Jew *n.* Jewish *a.* }	يَهُودِي	Joist *n.*	جِسْر . خَشَبَة مُعْتَرِضَة

Joke n. or v. t.	مَزَحَ. هَزْل. هَزَلَ ـ
Jolly a.	مَرَح . فَرِح . بَهِيج
Jolt v. t. or i.	رَجَّ ـ . (خَضَّ ـ) إِرْتَجَّ
Jostle v. t.	صَدَمَ . رَجَّ ـ
Jot n. or v. t.	جُزْءٌ دَقِيق . دَوَّنَ
Journal n.	(يَوْمِيَّة . جَرِيدَة)
Journalism n.	كِتَابَةُ جَرِيدَةٍ. تَحْرِيرٌ
Journalist n.	كَاتِبُ جَرِيدَةٍ. مُحَرِّرٌ
Journey n. or v. i.	سَفَرٌ . سَافَرَ
Jovial a.	مَرَح . فَرِح
Jowl n.	خَدٌّ . فَكٌّ
Joy n.	فَرَح . سُرُور . بَهْجَة
Joyful Joyous } a.	فَرِح . مُبْتَهِج مَسْرُور
Joyless a.	عَدِيمُ ٱلْفَرَحِ . كَئِيب
Jubilant a.	كَثِيرُ ٱلِٱبْتِهَاجِ. مُتَهَلِّل
Jubilee n.	يُوبِيل
Judaism n.	دِيَانَة ٱلْيَهُود
Judge n.	قَاضٍ . دَيَّان

Judge v. t.	قَضَى ـ . حَكَمَ ـ
Judgment n.	قَضَاء. حُكْم . تَمْيِيز
Judicatory a.	مُخْتَصٌّ بِمَحْكَمَةٍ . حُكْمِي
Judicial a.	قَضَائِيّ . قِصَاصِي
Judiciary a. or n.	قَضَائِيّ . دَائِرَةُ ٱلْقُضَاة
Judicious a.	حَكِيم . حَازِم
Jug n.	إِبْرِيق . كُوز
Juggle v. i.	شَعْوَذَ . غَبَنَ ـ
Juggler n.	مُشَعْوِذ . مَكَّار
Jugglery Juggling } n.	شَعْوَذَة
Jugular a. or n.	عُنُقِي. حَبْلُ ٱلْوَرِيدِ
Juice n.	عَصِير. عُصَارَة
Juicy n.	غَضّ . ذُو عُصَارَة
July n.	تَمُّوز . يُولِيُو
Jumble v. t. or n.	خَلَطَ . خِلْط
Jump v. i. or n.	قَفَزَ . قَفْزَة
Junction n.	وَصْل . مُلْتَقَى

Juncture *n.*	آنٌ . وَقْتٌ مُهِمٌّ
June *n.*	حَزِيرَانُ . يُونِيُو
Jungle *n.*	غَابَةٌ . اجَمَ
Junior *n.*	اصغَرُ عُمْراً
Juniper *n.*	عَرْعَرٌ (نَبَاتٌ)
Junk *n.*	سَفِينَةٌ صِينِيَّةٌ . مَوَادٌ عَتِيقَةٌ
Juno *n.*	إِلَهَةٌ رُومَانِيَّةٌ .
Jupiter *n.*	إِحْدَى ٱلسَّيَّارَاتِ ٱلصَّغِيرَةِ . ٱلْمُشْتَرِي (سَيَّارٌ)
Jurisdiction *n.*	حُكْمٌ أَوْ دَائِرَتُهُ
Jurisprudence *n.*	عِلْمُ ٱلْفِقْهِ
Juror Juryman *n.*	عُضْوُ مَحْكَمَةِ ٱلتَّحْقِيقِ
Jury *n.*	مَحْكَمَةٌ تَحْقِيقِيَّةٌ
Just *a. or ad.*	عَادِلٌ . بَارٌّ . تَمَامًا
Justice *n.*	عَدْلٌ . إِسْتِقَامَةٌ . قَاضٍ
Justifiable *a.*	يَتَبَرَّرُ . جَائِزٌ
Justification *n.*	تَبْرِيرٌ . تَبْرِئَةٌ
Justify *v. t.*	بَرَّرَ . بَرَّأَ
Justly *ad.*	بِعَدْلٍ . بِٱسْتِحْقَاقٍ
Jut *v. i.*	بَرَزَ ـُ . نَتَأَ ـَ
Juvenile *a. or n.*	وَلَدِيٌّ . وَلَدٌ
Juxtaposition *n.*	مُقَارَبَةٌ

K

Keel *n.*	قَاعِدَةُ ٱلسَّفِينَةِ
Keen *a.*	حَادٌّ . ذَكِيٌّ
Keep *v. t.*	حَفِظَ ـَ . ضَبَطَ ـُ
Keeper *n.*	حَافِظٌ . حَارِسٌ

Keepsake *n.*	شيْءٌ لِلتَّذْكَار	Kin *n.*	اقَارِبُ . أَنْسِبَاءُ
Keg *n.*	بَرْمِيلٌ صَغِيرٌ	Kind *a.* or *n.*	لَطِيفٌ . مُحْسِنٌ . نَوْعٌ
Ken *v. t.* or *n.*	عَلِمَ ـَ . عَلِمَ	Kindle *v. t.*	اضْرَمَ . اشْعَلَ
Kennel *n.*	زَرِيبَةُ ٱلْكِلَاب	Kindliness *n.*	لُطْفٌ . مَعْرُوفٌ
Kerchief *n.*	مِنْدِيلٌ	Kindly *ad.* or *a.*	بِلُطْفٍ . لَطِيفٌ
Kernel *n.*	حَبَّةٌ . نَوَاةٌ . لُبٌّ	Kindness *n.*	لُطْفٌ . مَعْرُوفٌ
Kerosene *n.*	زَيْت مَعْدِنِيّ	Kindred *n.*	اقَارِبُ . أَنْسِبَاءُ
Kettle *n.*	قِدْرٌ . غَلَّايَةٌ	Kine *n. pl.*	بَقَرٌ
Key *n.*	مِفْتَاحٌ . تَفْسِيرٌ	King *n.*	مَلِكٌ ج مُلُوكٌ
Key-stone *n.*	أَعْلَى حَجَرِ ٱلْقَنْطَرَة	Kingdom *n.*	مَمْلَكَةٌ
Kick *v. t.* or *i.* or *n.*	لَبَطَ ـُ . رَفَسَ ـِ	Kink *v. i.* or *n.*	إِلْتَوَى . لِيَةٌ
Kid *n.*	جَدْيٌ ج جِدَاءٌ	Kinsman *n.*	نَسِيبٌ . قَرِيبٌ
Kidnap *v. t.*	إِخْتَلَسَ بَشَرًا	Kiss *n.* or *v. t.*	قُبْلَةٌ . قَبَّلَ
Kidney *n.*	كُلْيَةٌ ج كِلًى	Kitchen *n.*	مَطْبَخٌ
Kill *v. t.*	قَتَلَ ـُ . اخْمَدَ	Kite *n.*	حِدَاةٌ . طَيَّارَةٌ
Kiln *n.*	أَتُونٌ	Kitten *n.*	جِرْوُ ٱلْقِطِّ . قُطَيْطَةٌ
Kilo Kilogramme *n.*	أَلْفُ جِرَامٍ	Knack *n.*	خِفَّةٌ . بَرَاعَةٌ . مَلَكَةٌ
Kilometre *n.*	أَلْفُ مِتْرٍ	Knapsack *n.*	مِزْوَدُ ٱلْجُنْدِيّ

Knarled a.	مُعَقَّد	Knob n.	عُجْرَة
Knave n. Knavish a.	خَبِيثٌ . مَكَّارٌ	Knock v. t. or n.	قَرَعَ ــَ . ضَرْبَة
Knavery Knavishness	خَبَاثَةٌ . مَكْرٌ	Knocker n.	مِقْرَعَة . مِطْرَقَة
Knead v. t.	عَجَنَ ــِ	Knoll n.	تَلَّة . رَابِيَة صَغِيرَة
Knee n.	رُكْبَة ج رُكَبٌ	Knot n. or v. t.	عُقْدَة . عَقَّدَ
Kneel v. i.	رَكَعَ ــَ . جَثَا ــُ	Knotted Knotty a.	مُعَقَّد . كَثِيرُ الْعَقْدِ
Knee-pan n.	رَضْفَةُ الرُّكْبَةِ	Know v. t.	عَلِمَ ــَ . عَرَفَ ــِ
Knell n.	دَقُّ الْجَرَسِ لِمَيِّت	Knowable a.	مَا يُعْلَمُ أَوْ يُعْرَفُ
Knife n.	سِكِّينٌ	Knowingly ad.	عَمْدًا
Knight n.	فَارِسٌ . لَقَبُ شَرَفٍ	Knowledge n.	عِلْمٌ . مَعْرِفَة
Knighthood n.	فُرُوسِيَّةٌ رُتْبَةُ شَرَفٍ	Knuckle n.	مِفْصَلُ الْإِصْبَع
Knit v. t. or i.	حَبَكَ ــِ . إِحْتَبَكَ	Koran n.	الْقُرْآن

L

Label n. or v. t.	وُرَيْقَةٌ لِعِنْوَانٍ . عَنْوَنَ	Laborious a.	شَاقٌّ . كَدُودٌ
Laboratory n.	مَعْمَلُ فَنٍّ	Labour n. or v. i.	كَدَّ . إِشْتَغَلَ

Labourer *n.*	فَاعِلٌ . شَغَّالٌ
Labyrinth *n.*	أَمْرٌ مُعَقَّدٌ . الْغَازُ
Lace *n.* or *v. t.*	(تَخْرِيم) . شَدَّ بِخَيْطٍ
Lacerate *v. t.*	شَرَّطَ . مَزَّقَ
Laceration *a.*	تَشْرِيطٌ . تَمْزِيقٌ
Lachrymal *a.*	دَمْعِي
Lack *n.* or *v. t.* or *i.*	عَوَزٌ . عَازَ . أَعْوَزَ
Laconic Laconical } *a.*	مَا قَلَّ وَدَلَّ (مِن الْكَلَامِ)
Lacteal Lactic } *a.*	لَبَنِي
Lad *n.*	صَبِيٌّ . وَلَدٌ . فَتًى
Ladder *n.*	سُلَّمٌ ج سَلَالِمُ
Lade *v. t.*	حَمَلَ . شَحَنَ ـ
Lading *n.*	حَمْلٌ . شَحْنٌ
Ladle *n.*	مِغْرَفَةٌ
Lady *n.*	سَيِّدَةٌ . خَاتُونٌ
Ladyship *n.*	مَقَامُ السَّيِّدَةِ
Lag *v. i.*	تَأَخَّرَ . أَبْطَأَ
Laggard *n.*	مُتَأَخِّرٌ . مُتَكَاسِلٌ
Lagoon *n.*	بُحَيْرَةٌ قَلِيلَةُ الْمَاءِ
Laid, lain, *see* Lay.	
Lair *n.*	عَرِينٌ . وِجَارٌ ج أَوْجِرَة مَوْضُوع
Laity *n.*	الْعَوَامُّ . غَيْرُ الإِكْلِيرُسِ
Lake *n.*	بُحَيْرَةٌ
Lamb *n.*	خَرُوفٌ . حَمَلٌ
Lambkin *n.*	خَرُوفٌ صَغِيرٌ
Lame *a.* or *v. t.*	أَعْرَجُ . عَرَّجَ
Lameness *n.*	عَرَجٌ
Lament *n.* or *v. t.*	نَاحَ ـ . رَثَى ـ
Lamentable *a.*	مُحْزِنٌ . مَا يُرْثَى لَهُ
Lamentation *n.*	نَوْحٌ . مَرْثَاةٌ
Lamp *n.*	مِصْبَاحٌ . سِرَاجٌ . قِنْدِيلٌ
Lampoon *v. t.* or *n.*	هَجَا . هَجْوٌ
Lance *n.* or *v. t.*	رُمْحٌ . رَمَحَ . طَعَنَ ـ
Lanceolate *a.*	رُمْحِي الشَّكْلِ
Lancet *n.*	مِشْرَطٌ . مِبْضَعٌ
Land *n.*	أَرْضٌ . بَرٌّ . بِلَادٌ

Land v. t. or i.	اِنْزَلَ او نَزَلَ مِنْ سَفِيْنَة
Landlocked a.	مُحَاط بِالْبَرّ
Landlord n.	رَبُّ اَرْضٍ او مَنْزِلٍ
Landmark n.	عَلَامَةُ حَدٍّ . تُخْم
Landscape n.	مَنْظَرٌ مِنَ الاَرْضِ
Lane n.	زُقَاق . مَضِيْق
Language n.	لُغَة . كَلَام . لِسَان
Languid a.	مُتَوَان . مُتَرَاخٍ
Languish v. i.	خَارَ . اِنْضَنَى . اِرْتَخَى
Languor n.	رَخَاوَة . ضَعْف
Lank a.	رَخْو . نَحِيْف
Lantern n.	(فَنَار . فَانُوْس)
Lap n.	ذَيْل . حِضْن . حِجْر
Lap v. t. or i.	وَلَغَ . طَوَى . اِنْثَنَى
Lapse v. i.	مَضَى وَقْتُهُ . سَقَطَ
Larceny n.	سِرْقَة
Lard n.	دُهْنُ الْخِنْزِيْر
Larder n.	بَيْتُ الْمَؤُوْنَة
Large a.	كَبِيْر . فَسِيْح
Largely ad.	بِوَفْرَة . كَثِيْراً
Lark n.	قُبَّرَة او قُنْبَرَة (طَائِر)
Larynx n.	حَنْجَرَة ج حَنَاجِرُ
Lascivious a.	شَهْوَانِيّ . فَاسِق
Lash n. or v.t.	سَوْط . سَاطَ . شَدَّ
Lass n.	فَتَاة . صَبِيَّة
Lassitude n.	اِسْتِرْخَاء . عَيَاء
Last n. or a.	قَالِبُ الْحِذَاء . الاَخِيْر
Last v. i.	بَقِيَ . دَامَ . اِسْتَمَرَّ
Lastly ad.	أَخِيْراً
Latch n. or v. t.	سِقَّاطَة . اوْصَدَ (الْبَاب)
Latchet n.	شِرَاك . سَيْر
Late a.	مُتَأَخِّر
Lately ad.	حَدِيْثاً
Lateness n.	تَأَخُّر . فَوَاتُ الْوَقْت
Latent a.	مُسْتَتِر . كَامِن
Lateral a.	جَنْبِيّ . جَانِبِيّ

Lather n.	مُخَرْطَةٌ	Laurel n.	غَارٌ (شَجَرٌ)
Lather n.	رَغْوَةُ ٱلصَّابُون	Lava n.	مَوَادٌ تُقْذَفُ مِنْ جَبَلِ ٱلنَّار
Latin a. or n.	لَاتِينِيٌّ . ٱللُّغَةُ ٱللَّاتِينِيَّةُ	Lavatory n.	مَرْحَضَةٌ . مَغْسَلَةٌ . حَمَّامٌ
Latitude n.	عَرْضٌ	Lave v. t.	غَسَلَ ـِ
Latter a.	ٱلأَخِيرُ . ٱلثَّانِي	Laver n.	مَرْحَضَةٌ . جُرْنٌ لِلْغَسْلِ
Latterly ad.	حَدِيثًا	Lavish a. or v. t.	مُسْرِفٌ . أَسْرَفَ . بَذَّرَ
Lattice n.	شُبَّاكٌ	Law n.	شَرِيعَةٌ . نَامُوسٌ . سُنَّةٌ
Laud v. t.	مَدَحَ ـَ ـ . حَمَدَ ـَ	Lawful a.	شَرْعِيٌّ . جَائِزٌ . مُبَاحٌ
Laudable a.	مَمْدُوحٌ . جَدِيرٌ بِالْمَدْحِ	Lawfulness n.	جَوَازٌ
Laudanum a.	صِبْغَةُ أَفْيُون	Lawless a.	مُخَالِفٌ ٱلشَّرِيعَةِ . عَاصٍ
Laudatory a.	مَدْحِيٌّ . مَادِحٌ	Lawn n.	سَهْلَةٌ خَضْرَاءُ . (شَاشٌ)
Laugh n. or v. i.	ضَحْكَةٌ . ضَحِكَ ـَ	Lawsuit n.	دَعْوَى ج دَعَاوٍ
Laughable a.	مُضْحِكٌ	Lawyer n.	فَقِيهٌ . مُحَامٍ (أَفُوكَاتُو)
Laughing Laughter } n.	ضَحْكٌ	Lax a.	مُتَرَاخٍ . مُتَسَاهِلٌ
Laughing-stock n.	أُضْحُوكَةٌ	Laxative a.	مُسْهِلٌ
Launch v. t.	أَنْزَلَ فِي ٱلْمَاء	Laxity n.	تَرَاخٍ . فَسَادٌ
Laundress n.	غَسَّالَةٌ	Lay n. or a.	نَشِيدٌ . عَامِّيٌّ
Laundry n.	مَغْسَلٌ	Lay v. t.	وَضَعَ ـَ . نَظَمَ . بَسَطَ ـ

Layer n.	طَبَقَةٌ
Laziness n.	كَسَل . تَوانٍ
Lazy a.	كَسْلانٌ
Lead n.	رصَاصٌ
Lead v. t.	قَادَ ُ . هدى ـ
Leader n.	قَائِدٌ . مرْشِدٌ
Leadership n.	قِيَادَةٌ . رِيَاسَةٌ
Leaf n.	وَرقَةٌ . مِصْراعٌ
Leaflet n.	وُرَيْقَةٌ
Leafy a.	مُورِقٌ . ذو ورَق
League n.	مُحَالَفَةٌ . عصْبَةٌ . فرْسَخٌ
Leak n. or v. i.	فجْرَةٌ . وكَفَ ـ
Leakage n.	وكْفٌ . تَلَفٌ مِنه
Leaky a.	واكِفٌ . غيْرُ مضبوطٍ
Lean a. or v. i.	نَحِيفٌ . هزِيل . مَالَ ـ
Leanness n.	هزَالٌ . نَحَافةٌ
Leap n. or v. t.	قَفْزَةٌ . قَفَزَ ـ . وثَب
Leap-year n.	سنة كبِيسةٌ

Learn v. t.	تَعلَّمَ . عَلِم ـَ
Learned a.	عَالِمٌ . مَاهِرٌ
Learner n.	متَعلِّمٌ . تِلْميذ
Learning n.	عِلْمٌ . معرِفَة
Lease n. or v. t.	إِيجَارٌ . آجر
Least a.	الأَصغَرُ . الأَقَلُ . الأدنَى
Leather n.	جلْدٌ مدْبوغ
Leathern } a. Leathery }	مِن جِلدٍ . جِلدِي
Leave n. or v. t.	إِذْنٌ . تَركَ ـ
Leaven n. or v. t.	خَميرة . خَمَّرَ ـ
Lecture n.	خطَابٌ
Lecturer n.	خطِيبٌ . مُدرِّسٌ
Led pp. of Lead.	مقود
Ledge n.	طَبَقَةٌ . صخورٌ بَارِزَة
Ledger n.	دفْتَرُ مُختَصرِ الحِسَابَات
Leech n.	علَقة
Lee n. or a.	الجَانبُ المَحْفور مِن الرِّيح
Leeward a. or ad.	مع الرِّيح

Leeway n.	حَرَكَةٌ جَنْبِيَّةٌ مَعَ ٱلرِّيحِ
Left a. or n.	يَسَارٌ . شِمَالٌ
Left-handed a.	أَعْسَرُ
Leg n.	رِجْلٌ . سَاقٌ . قَائِمَة
Legacy n.	وَصِيَّةٌ . وَقْفٌ
Legal a.	شَرْعِيٌّ . قَانُونِيٌّ . جَائِزٌ
Legality n.	شَرْعِيَّةٌ . جَوَازٌ
Legalize v. t.	جَعَلَهُ شَرْعِيًّا
Legate n.	نَائِبٌ . قَاصِدٌ
Legatee n.	ٱلْمُوصَى لَهُ . وَارِثٌ
Legation n.	سِفَارَةٌ
Legend n.	خُرَافَةٌ . عِنْوَانٌ
Legendary a.	خُرَافِيٌّ
Legerdemain n.	شَعْوَذَةٌ . شَعْبَذَةٌ
Legging n.	جَوْرَبٌ لِلرِّجْلِ
Legible a.	مَا يُقْرَأُ . وَاضِحٌ
Legion n.	كَتِيبَةٌ . جَوْقٌ
Legislate v. i.	سَنَّ شَرَائِعَ

Legislation n.	سَنُّ ٱلشَّرَائِعِ
Legislative a.	مُخْتَصٌّ بِسَنِّ ٱلشَّرَائِعِ
Legislator n.	مُشْتَرِعٌ
Legislature n.	مَجْلِسُ ٱلْمُشْتَرِعِينَ
Legitimacy n.	شَرْعِيَّةٌ
Legitimate a.	شَرْعِيٌّ . نِظَامِيٌّ
Leisure n.	عُطْلَةٌ . فَرَاغٌ
Leisurely ad.	بَطِيئًا . رُوَيْدًا
Lemon n.	لَيْمُونٌ
Lemonade n.	شَرَابُ ٱللَّيْمُونِ
Lend v. t.	أَقْرَضَ . أَعَارَ
Length n.	طُولٌ
Lengthen v.t. or i.	أَطَالَ . طَالَ _
Lengthwise ad.	طُولاً
Lengthy a.	طَوِيلٌ
Lenient a.	لَطِيفٌ . حَلِيمٌ
Lenity n.	لُطْفٌ . مُسَاهَلَةٌ
Lens n.	بَلُّورَةٌ مُحَدَّبَةٌ أَوْ مُقَعَّرَةٌ

Lent *n.* or *pp.*	ٱلصَّوْمُ ٱلكَبِيرُ . مُقْرَض
Lentil *n.*	عَدَسَة
Leopard *n.*	نِمْرٌ . نَمِرٌ
Leper *n.* Leprous *a.* } *a.*	مَجْذُومٌ
Leprosy *n.*	جُذَام
Less *a.*	اقَلُّ
Lesion *n.*	أَذِيَّة . ضَرَرٌ . هَتْكٌ
Lessen *v. i.* or *t.*	قَلَّ . نَقَصَ . قَلَّلَ
Lesson *n.*	مَآلَة . تَعْلِيم . عِبْرَةٌ
Lest *conj.*	لِئَلَّا
Let *v. t.*	سَمَحَ . رَخَّصَ . آجَرَ
Lethargy *n.*	سُبَاتٌ . تَغَافُل
Letter *n.*	حَرْفٌ . كِتَابٌ . تَحْرِيرٌ
Letters *pl.*	آدَابٌ . تَهْذِيبٌ
Lettuce *n.*	خَسٌّ
Levant *n.*	شَرْقِيُّ بَحْرِ ٱلرُّوم
Level *a.* or *v.t.*	مُسْتَوٍ . سَهْل . سَوَّى
Level *n.*	سَطْحٌ مُسْتَوٍ مِيزَانٌ (مَنْسُوبٌ)
Levelling *n.*	تَسْوِيَة . تَسْطِيح
Lever *n.*	مِحْل . عَتَلَة
Levity *n.*	خِفَّة . طَيْشٌ
Levy *v. t.*	ضَرَبَ عَلَى . جَبَى ــ
Lewd *a.*	شَهْوَانِيٌّ . مُفْسِدٌ . فَاسِقٌ
Lewdness *n.*	فِسْق . فُجُور
Lexicographer *n.*	مُؤَلِّفُ قَامُوسٍ
Lexicon *n.*	قَامُوسٌ
Liable *a.*	مُعَرَّضٌ لِ . مَسْؤُولٌ
Liability *n.*	تَعَرُّضٌ لِ . مَسْؤُولِيَة
Liar *n.*	كَذَّابٌ
Libel *n.*	هَجْرٌ . طَعْنٌ (قَذْفٌ)
Libeler *n.*	هَاجٍ . طَعَّانٌ (قَاذِفٌ)
Libelous *a.*	هِجَائِيٌّ . طَاعِنٌ
Liberal *a.*	سَخِيٌّ . كَرِيم
Liberality *n.*	سَخَاءٌ . كَرَم
Liberalize *v. t.*	حَرَّرَ مِنَ ٱلتَّعَصُّبِ
Liberate *v. t.*	حَرَّرَ . اعْتَقَ . أَطْلَقَ

Liberation n.	نَحْرِيرٌ . إِطْلَاقٌ
Liberator n.	مُحَرِّرٌ . مُعْتِقٌ
Libertine n.	خَلِيعٌ . فَاسِقٌ . فَاجِرٌ
Liberty n.	حُرِّيَّةٌ . إِسْتِقْلَالٌ
Librarian n.	مُدِيرُ مَكْتَبَةٍ
Library n.	مَكْتَبَةٌ
Lice n. pl.	قَمْلٌ
License n.	إِجَازَةٌ . غُلُوٌّ . خَلَاعَةٌ
Licensed a. Licentiate n. }	ذُو ٱمْتِيَازٍ أَوْ رُخْصَةٍ
Licentious a.	شَهَوَانِي . خَلِيعٌ
Licentiousness n.	خَلَاعَةٌ . دَعَارَةٌ
Lick v. t.	لَحَسَ ـَ . لَعَقَ ـَ
Licorice Liquorice } n.	سُوسٌ (نَبَاتٌ)
Lid n.	غِطَاءٌ ج اغْطِيَة
Lie n.	كِذْبٌ
Lie v. i.	كَذَبَ . إِضْطَجَعَ . إِتَّجَهَ . مَكَثَ
Lieutenant n.	نَائِبٌ . (مُلَازِمٌ)
Life n.	حَيَاةٌ . عُمْرٌ . نَشَاطٌ

Life-boat n.	قَارِبٌ لَا يَغْرَقُ
Lifelike a.	مِثْلُهُ . طِبْقُ ٱلْأَصْلِ
Lifelong a.	مَا يَدُومُ مَدَى ٱلْحَيَاةِ
Lift v. t. or n.	رَفَعَ . عَلَّى . رَفْعٌ
Ligament n.	رِبَاطٌ . عَصَبٌ
Ligature n.	عِصَابَةٌ
Light n. or a.	نُورٌ . ضَوْءٌ . خَفِيفٌ
Light Lighten } v. t.	أَنَارَ . أَضَاءَ
Lighten v. i. or t.	بَرَقَ ـُ . خَفَّفَ
Lighter n.	جَرْمٌ . مَاعُونٌ
Light-headed a.	طَائِشٌ . فِرْقَارٌ
Light-house n.	مَنَارَةٌ
Lightly ad.	بِخِفَّةٍ
Lightness n.	خِفَّةٌ . فَرْفَرَةٌ
Lightning n.	بَرْقٌ
Lightsome a.	نَيِّرٌ . فَرِحٌ . مُفْرِحٌ
Like ad.	عَلَى مِثَالٍ
Like a. or n.	مِثْلٌ . شَبِيهٌ . نَظِيرٌ

Like v. t.	احَبَّ . إِسْتَحْسَن
Likely a. or ad.	مُحْتَمَل . مُمْكِن
Liken v. t.	شَبَّهَ . مَثَّل
Likeness n.	شِبْه . صُورَة
Likewise ad.	ايْضًا . كَذَلِكَ
Liking n.	إِسْتِحْسَان . مَيْل إِلَى
Lily n.	زَنْبَق . سُوسَن
Limb n.	غُصْن . عُضْو
Line n.	كِلْس . (جِير)
Lime-kiln n.	أَتُّون كِلْس
Lime-stone n.	حَجَر ٱلْكِلْس
Limit n. or v. t.	حَدّ . تُخْم . حَدَّد
Limitable a.	قَابِل ٱلتَحْدِيد
Limitation n.	تَحْدِيد . حَصْر
Limitless a.	لِا حَدِّ . غَيْر مَحْدُود
Limp v. i. or a.	عَرِجَ . رَخْو
Limpid a.	صَافٍ . رَائِق
Line n.	خَطّ . سَطْر . صَفّ . مَرَس

Line v. t.	بَطَّن . خَطَّطَ . سَطَّر
Lineage n.	نَسَب . ذُرِّيَّة
Lineal a.	نَسَبِيّ
Lineament n.	رَسْم . هَيْئَة
Linear a.	خَطِّي . مُسْتَقِيم
Linen n.	كَتَّان . ثِيَاب مِنْ كَتَّان
Linger v. i.	ابْطَأَ . تَرَدَّد
Lingering a.	إِبْطَاء . تَأَخُّر
Lingual a.	لِسَانِيّ
Linguist n.	عَالِم بِاللُّغَات
Linguistic Linguistical } a.	مُخْتَصّ بِعِلْم ٱللُّغَات
Lining n.	بِطَانَة . تَبْطِين
Liniment n.	مَرْهَم . دِهْن
Link n. or v. t.	حَلْقَة . زَرَدَة . سَلْسَل
Linseed n.	بِزْر كَتَّان
Lint n.	كَتِيت . مُشَاقَة
Lintel n.	عَتَبَة ج . عَتَب
Lion n.	أَسَد ج اسُود

Lioness n.	لَبْوَةٌ	Lithography n.	صِنَاعَةُ ٱلطَّبْعِ ٱلْحَجَرِيِّ
Lip n.	شِفَةٌ	Litigant n.	خَصِيمٌ . مُدَّعٍ
Liquify v. t.	ذَوَّبَ . أَمَاعَ	Litigate v. i.	خَاصَمَ . اَقَامَ دَعْوَى
Liquid n.	مَائِعٌ . سَائِلٌ	Litigation n.	مُخَاصَمَةٌ . إِجْرَاءُ ٱلدَّعَاوِي
Liquidate v. t.	صَفَّى ٱلْحِسَابَ . اَوْفَى	Litter n.	مَحْمَلٌ . نُثَارَةٌ . أَجْرِيَةٌ
Liquidation n.	تَصْفِيَةُ ٱلْحِسَابِ إِيفَاءً	Little a. or ad.	صَغِيرٌ . قَلِيلٌ . قَلِيلاً
Liquor n.	سَائِلٌ . شَرَابٌ . مُسْكِرٌ	Liturgy n.	خِدْمَةُ ٱلْعِبَادَةِ
Liquorice n.	نَبَاتُ ٱلسُّوسِ اورِبُّهُ	Live v. i.	عَاشَ . أَقَامَ بِ . تَصَرَّفَ
Lisp v. i. or n.	لَثِغَ . لُثْغَةٌ	Live a.	حَيٌّ . نَشِيطٌ
List n.	قَائِمَةٌ . جَدْوَلٌ . مَيْلٌ	Livelihood n.	مَعَاشٌ . مَعِيشَةٌ
Listen v. i.	اصْغَى إِلَى . إِسْتَمَعَ	Liveliness n.	خِفَّةٌ . نَشَاطٌ
Listless a.	غَافِلٌ . غَيْرُ مُبَالٍ	Lively a.	خَفِيفٌ . نَشِيطٌ . بَشَّاشٌ
Literal a.	حَرْفِيٌّ	Liver n.	كَبِدٌ ج اكْبَادٌ
Literary a.	آدَابِيٌّ . عِلْمِيٌّ	Livery n.	زِيٌّ رَسْمِيٌّ لِلْخَدَمِ
Literature n.	آدَابُ ٱللُّغَةِ . كُتُبٌ	Live-stock n.	خَيْلٌ . مَوَاشٍ
Lithe Lithesome } a.	مَرِنٌ . لَيِّنٌ	Livid a.	أَزْرَقُ مُسْوَدٌّ
Lithograph v. t. or n.	طَبَعَ عَلَى حَجَرٍ	Living a. or n.	حَيٌّ . مَعِيشَةٌ
Lithographer n.	طَابِعٌ عَلَى حَجَرٍ	Lizard n.	حِرْذَوْنٌ . ضَبٌّ

Lo ! *ex.*	هُوَذَا . إِذَا بِ . هَا
Load *n.* or *v. t.*	حَمْلٌ . حَمَّلَ . شَحَنَ ـ
Loadstone *n.*	حَجَرُ مَغْنَطِيس
Loaf *n.*	رَغِيفٌ . قَالِبُ (سُكر)
Loafer *n.*	بَطَّال . كَسْلَان
Loam *n.*	تُرْبَةٌ مُخْصِبَة
Loan *v.* or *n.*	اقْرَضَ . اعَارَ . قَرْضٌ
Loath *a.*	غَيْرُ رَاضٍ . نَافِرٌ
Loathe *v. t.*	كَرِه ـ . سَئِم
Loathsome *a.*	مَكْرُوه
Loathsomeness *n.*	كَرَاهة
Lobe *n.*	فَصٌ ج فُصُوصٌ
Lobster *n.*	سَرَطَان بَحْرِيّ
Local *a.*	مَحَلِّيّ
Locality *n.*	مَحَلٌّ . مَوْقِعٌ
Locate *v. t.*	وَضَعَ ـ . انْزَلَ
Location *n.*	وَضْعٌ . مَوْضِعٌ
Lock *n.* or *v. t.*	قُفْلٌ . اقْفَلَ
Locket *n.*	حَمِيلَة
Locksmith *n.*	قَفَّالٌ . (قَرَدَحجِي)
Locomotion *n.*	سَيْرٌ . إِنْتِقَالٌ
Locomotive *n.*	آلَةُ البُخَارِ لِلسَّيْرِ
Locust *n.*	جَرَادَةٌ
Lodge *n.* or *v. i.*	مَأْوَى . آوَى . بَاتَ ـ
Lodger *n.*	نَزِيلٌ . بَاتَّتْ
Lodging *n.*	مَبِيتٌ . مَنْزِلٌ
Loftiness *n.*	عُلُوّ . تَشَامُخ
Lofty *a.*	عَالٍ . رَفِيع . مُتَشَامِخ
Log *n.*	خَشَبَةٌ ضَخْمَة
Logarithms *n. pl.*	عِلْمُ الأَنْسَابِ
Log-book *n.*	كِتَابُ سَيْرِ سَفِينةٍ
Logic *n.*	عِلْمُ المَنْطِقِ
Logical *a.*	مَنْطِقِي . قِيَاسِيّ
Logician *n.*	عَالِمٌ بِالمَنْطِقِ
Loin *n.*	صُلْبٌ ج اصْلَابٌ
Loiter *v. t.*	تَأَخَّرَ . أَبْطَأَ

Lone a.	مُنْفَرِدٌ . مُتَوَحِّدٌ	Lord n.	رَبّ . سَيِّدٌ . شَرِيفٌ
Loneliness n.	وَحْدَةٌ	Lordly a.	شَرِيفٌ . مُتَعَظِّمٌ . سَامٍ
Lonely Lonesome } a.	مُسْتَوْحِشٌ	Lordship n.	رُبُوبِيَّةٌ . سِيَادَةٌ
Long a. or v. i.	طَوِيلٌ . تَاقَ . إِشْتَاقَ	Lose v. t.	ضَيَّعَ . خَسِرَ . فَقَدَ
Longevity n.	طُولُ ٱلْعُمْرِ	Loss n.	خَسَارَةٌ . فَقْدٌ . تَلَفٌ
Longing n.	إِشْتِيَاقٌ . شَوْقٌ	Lot n.	نَصِيبٌ . حِصَّةٌ . قُرْعَةٌ
Longitude n.	طُولٌ	Lotion n.	غَسْلٌ . غِسْلَةٌ
Long-suffering n. or a.	طُولُ ٱلْأَنَاةِ . طَوِيلُهَا	Lottery n.	قُرْعَةٌ . قِمَارٌ
Look v. i.	نَظَرَ . فَتَّشَ . ظَهَرَ	Lotus n.	جَنْدَقُوقٌ
Looking-glass n.	مِرْآةٌ	Loud a.	عَالٍ . مُجْهِرٌ . جَهُورٌ
Loom n. or v. i.	نَوْلٌ . ظَهَرَ	Loudness n.	عُلُوُّ(ٱلصَّوْتِ) . جَهَارَةٌ
Loop n.	عُرْوَةٌ	Lounge v. i.	تَقَاعَدَ . تَكَاسَلَ
Loop-hole n.	فَرَاغُ ٱلْعُرْوَةِ . مَهْرَبٌ	Louse n. (pl. Lice).	قَمْلَةٌ ج قَمْلٌ
Loose Loosen } v. t.	حَلَّ . فَكَّ . أَطْلَقَ	Lovable Lovely } a.	مَحْبُوبٌ . جَدِيرٌ بِٱلْمَحَبَّةِ
Loose a.	مَحْلُولٌ . رَخْوٌ . مُسْتَرْسِلٌ	Love n. or v. t.	مَحَبَّةٌ . أَحَبَّ
Looseness n.	رَخَاوَةٌ . إِنْحِلَالٌ	Loveliness n.	حُسْنٌ . جَمَالٌ
Lop v. t.	قَضَبَ . إِسْتَمَالَ	Lover n. Loving a. }	مُحِبٌّ . عَاشِقٌ
Loquacious a.	كَثِيرُ ٱلْكَلَامِ	Low a.	مُنْخَفِضٌ . دَنِيٌّ . رَخِيصٌ

Lower v. t.	خَفَّضَ . أَنْزَلَ	Luggage n.	أَمْتِعة
Lowering a.	مُظْلِمٌ . عَابِسٌ	Lukewarm a.	فَاتِرٌ
Lowland n.	أَرْضٌ مُنْخَفِضَة	Lull v.t. or i. or n.	هَدَّأ . هَدَا . هدوٌّ
Lowliness n.	مَسْكَنَةٌ . ضَعَة	Lumbre n.	سَقَطُ ٱلْمَتَاع . اخْشَاب
Lowly a.	مُتَوَاضِعٌ . وَدِيعٌ	Luminary n.	جِرْمٌ مُضِيٌّ
Low-spirited a.	كَئِيبٌ	Luminous a.	مُضِيٌّ نَيِّر
Loyal a.	أَمِينٌ . مُخْلِصُ ٱلطَّاعة	Lump n.	كُتْلَة . جُمْلة
Loyalty n.	أَمَانَةٌ . طَاعَة	Lunacy n.	جُنُونٌ
Lubricate v. t.	دَهَّنَ . زَيَّتَ . مَلَّس	Lunar } Lunary } a.	قَمَرِيٌّ
Lucid a.	وَاضِحٌ . صَاف	Lunatic n. or a.	مَجْنُونٌ . جُنُونِيٌّ
Lucidness } Lucidity } n.	وُضُوحٌ . صَفَاءٌ	Lunatic-asylum n.	بِيمَارِسْتَانٌ
Luck n.	حَظٌّ . نَصِيبٌ	Lunch n or v. i.	غَدَاءٌ . تَغَدَّى
Luckily ad.	بِحُسْنِ ٱلْحَظِّ . بِسَعْدٍ	Lung n.	رِئَة
Luckless a.	مَنْكُودُ ٱلْحَظِّ	Lurch v. i. or n.	إِنْدَفَعَ جَانِبًا
Lucky a.	حَظِيظٌ . سَعِيدٌ	Lure v. t.	اغْوَى . غَرَّ
Lucrative a.	مُكْسِبٌ . مُفِيد	Lurid a.	مُصْفَرٌّ . مُغِمٌّ . مُكَدَّر
Lucre n.	رِبْحٌ . مَكْسَب	Lurk v. i.	كَمَنَ . إِخْتَبَأَ
Ludicrous a.	مُضْحِك	Luscious a.	حُلْوٌ . لَذِيذ

Lust n. or v. i.	شَهْوَةٌ . إِشْتَهَى
Lustful a.	شَهْوَانِيٌّ
Lustily a.	بِبَأْسٍ بِشِدَّةٍ
Lustre n.	بَهَاءٌ . رَوْنَقٌ . شُهْرَةٌ
Lustrous a.	لَامِعٌ . بَهِيٌّ
Lusty a.	ضَلِيعٌ . نَشِيطٌ
Lute n.	عود
Luxuriance n.	رَتْعٌ . خِصْبٌ . تَرَفٌ
Luxuriant a.	خِصْبٌ . تَارِفٌ

Luxuriate v. i.	رَتَعَ . تَنَعَّمَ
Luxurious a.	مُتَنَعِّمٌ . مُتْرَفِهٌ
Luxury n.	تَرَفٌ . تَنَعُّمٌ . رَفَاهة
Lyceum n.	جَمْعِية عِلْمِية
Lying n. or a.	كِذْبٌ . كَاذِبٌ
Lynch v. t.	قَاصَّ او قَتَلَ بِلاَ حُكْمٍ شَرْعِي
Lynx n.	نَوْع مِنَ الفَهْدِ
Lyre n.	قِيثَارٌ
Lyric / Lyrical a.	غِنَائِيٌّ . قِيثَارِيٌّ

M

Macadamize v. t.	رَصَف بِالْحَصَى
Mace n.	عصاً . صَوْلَجَانٌ
Macerate v. t.	نَقَعَ . اتْحَفَ
Machination n.	مُؤَامَرَةٌ . مَكْرٌ

Machine n.	آلَةٌ
Machinery n.	آلَاتٌ او اجْزَآؤُها
Machinist n.	صَانِعُ آلَاتٍ
Mackerel n.	سمَكٌ بَحري مُنَقَّط

Mackintosh *n.*	مُشَمَّع
Mad *a.*	مَجْنُون . أَحْمَق
Madam *n.*	سَيِّدَة
Madden *v. t.*	أَغْضَب . جَنَّن
Madhouse *n.*	بِيمَارِسْتَان
Madly *ad.*	بِجُنُون . بِحَمَاقَةٍ
Madman *n.*	مَجْنُون
Madness *n.*	جُنُون . حَمَاقَة
Magazine *n.*	مَخْزَن (جَرِيدَة)
Maggot *n.*	دُودَة
Magic *n.*	سِحْر . رُقْيَة
Magic Magical ⎫ *a.*	سِحْرِيّ
Magician *n.*	سَاحِر . رَاقٍ
Magisterial *a.*	سُلْطَانِيّ . مُتَجَبِّر
Magistracy *n.*	مَأْمُورِيَّةُ حَاكِمٍ
Magistrate *n.*	حَاكِم . مَأْمُور
Magnanimity *n.*	شَرَفُ النَّفْسِ
Magnanimous *a.*	شَرِيفُ النَّفْسِ

Magnate *n.*	عَظِيم . كَبِير . وَجِيه
Magnet *n.*	مِغْنَطِيس
Magnetic Magnetical ⎫ *a.*	مِغْنَطِيسِيّ
Magnetism *n.*	مِغْنَطِيسِيَّة
Magnetize *v. t.*	مَغْنَطَ
Magnificence *n.*	جَلَال . بَهَاء
Magnificent *a.*	بَهِيّ . فَاخِر . جَلِيل
Magnify *v. t.*	كَبَّر . عَظَّم . بَجَّل
Magnitude *n.*	كِبَر . قَدَر . أَهَمِّيَّة
Magpie *n.*	نَوْعٌ مِنَ الْعَقْعَقِ (طَائِر)
Maid Maiden ⎫ *n.*	فَتَاة . عَذْرَاء . جَارِيَة
Maiden-hair *n.*	كُزْبَرَةُ الْبِئْرِ (نَبَات)
Mail *n.*	بَرِيد . دِرْع
Mail *v. t.*	أَرْسَل بِالْبَرِيد . دَرَّع
Maim *v. t.*	جَدَّع . بَتَّر
Main *a. or n.*	رَئِيسِيّ . أَهَمّ . قُوَّة
Mainland *n.*	الْيَابَسَة (غَيْرُ جَزِيرَةٍ)
Mainly *ad.*	غَالِباً . فِي الْأَكْثَرِ

Mainmast n.	الصَّارِي ٱلأَكْبَر	Malefactor n.	مُذْنِب . مُجْرِمٌ
Mainsail n.	الشِّرَاعُ الأَكْبَرُ	Malevolent a.	سيِّءُ ٱلنِّيَةِ . ضَاغِنٌ
Maintain v. t.	حَفِظَ . قَامَ بِ . أَكَّدَ	Malformation n.	سُوءُ ٱلخِلْقَةِ . تَشَوُّهٌ
Maintenance n.	إعَالَةٌ . حِفْظٌ . قِيَامٌ	Malice n.	ضَغِينَةٌ . حِقْدٌ
Maize n.	ذُرَةٌ صَفْرَاءُ	Malicious a.	ضَاغِنٌ . حَقُودٌ
Majestic a.	جَلِيلٌ . رَفِيعٌ . عَظِيمٌ	Malign v. t.	هَتَكَ . نَمَّ مِ . إِفْتَرَى
Majesty n.	جَلالَةٌ . عَظَمَةٌ	Malignancy Malignity } n.	ضَغِينَةٌ . خَبَاثَةٌ
Major a. or n.	أَكْبَرُ . كُبْرَى . (بِكْبَاشِي)	Malignant a.	ضَاغِنٌ . حَقُودٌ . خَبِيثٌ
Major-general n.	قَائِدُ لِوَاءٍ	Malleable a.	قَابِلُ ٱلمَطْلِ بِٱلتَطْرِيقِ
Majority n.	ٱلأَكْثَرِيَّةُ . سِنُّ ٱلبُلُوغِ	Mallet n.	مِطْرَقَةٌ
Make v. t.	عَمِلَ ـَ . صَنَعَ ـَ . اوْجَبَ	Malpractice n.	سُوءُ ٱلعَمَلِ
Maker n.	عَامِلٌ . صَانِعٌ . خَالِقٌ	Maltreat v. t.	عَامَلَ بِٱلسُّوءِ
Maladministration n.	سُوءُ إِدَارَةٍ	Maltreatment n.	مُعَامَلَةٌ . سَيِّئَةٌ
Malady n.	مَرَضٌ . عِلَّةٌ . دَاءٌ	Mameluke n.	مَمْلُوكٌ ج مَمَالِيكُ
Malaria n.	فَسَادُ ٱلهَوَاءِ . مَلارِيَا	Mamma n.	أُمٌّ
Malcontent a.	غَيْرُ رَاضٍ	Mammal i n. Mammalia n. pl. }	ذَوَاتُ ٱلثُّدِيِّ
Male n.	ذَكَرٌ ج ذُكُورٌ	Man n. (pl. Men)	ٱلإِنْسَانُ . رَجُلٌ
Malediction n.	لَعْنَةٌ . شَتِيمَةٌ	Manacle v.t. or n.	غَلَّ ـُ . غُلٌّ ج اغْلَالٌ

Manage v. t.	اَدَارَ . سَاسَ ـُ . دَبَّرَ
Manageable a.	سَهْلُ ٱلتَّدْبِيرِ وَٱلضَّبْطِ
Management n.	تَدْبِيرٌ . إِدَارَةٌ
Manager n.	مُدِيرٌ . مُدَبِّرٌ
Mandate n.	أَمْرٌ رَسْمِيٌّ
Mandrake n.	لُفَّاحٌ (نَبَاتٌ)
Mane n.	عُرْفُ ٱلْفَرَسِ
Maneuvre Manœuvre } n.	حَرَكَاتُ ٱلْعَسْكَرِ حِيلَةٌ
Manful a.	رَجُلِيٌّ . شَهْمٌ
Mange n.	جَرَبُ ٱلْحَيَوَانَاتِ
Manger n.	مِذْوَدٌ . مَعْلَفٌ
Mangle v. t.	مَزَّقَ . فَرَّضَ
Mangy a.	أَجْرَبُ
Manhood n.	رُجُولَةٌ . مُرُوءَةٌ
Mania n.	جُنُونٌ . وَلَعٌ . (هَوَسٌ)
Maniac n. Maniacal a. }	مَجْنُونٌ
Manifest a. or v. t.	ظَاهِرٌ . بَيَّنَ . أَظْهَرَ
Manifestation n.	إِظْهَارٌ . بَيَانٌ
Manifesto n.	إِعْلَانٌ . مَنْشُورٌ
Manifold a.	مُتَنَوِّعٌ . شَتَّى
Mankind n.	نَوْعُ ٱلْإِنْسَانِ . ٱلْبَشَرُ
Manfully ad.	بِمُرُوءَةٍ . بِشَهَامَةٍ . بِشَجَاعَةٍ
Manliness n.	رُجُولِيَّةٌ . شَهَامَةٌ
Manly a.	شَهْمٌ . ذُو مُرُوءَةٍ
Manna n.	مَنٌّ
Manner n.	كَيْفِيَّةٌ . اُسْلُوبٌ . دَأْبٌ
Manners n. pl.	آدَابٌ
Man-of-war n.	بَارِجَةٌ حَرْبِيَّةٌ
Manœuvre see Maneuvre.	
Manor n.	عِقَارٌ . إِقْطَاعَةٌ
Mansion n.	دَارٌ . قَصْرٌ
Manslaughter n.	أَقْتَلُ خَطَأً
Mantel n.	رَفٌّ فَوْقَ ٱلْمَوْقِدِ
Mantle n.	رِدَاءٌ . جُبَّةٌ
Manual a. or n.	شُغْلُ ٱلْيَدِ . كِتَابٌ مُخْتَصَرٌ
Manufactory n.	مَعْمَلٌ

Manufacture n. or v. t.	عَمَلٌ . إِصْطِنَاعٌ
Manufacturer n.	صَانِعٌ . صَاحِبُ مَعْمَلٍ
Manure n.	زِبْلٌ . سَمَادٌ . سِرْقِينٌ
Manuscript n.	كِتَابُ خَطٍّ
Many a.	كَثِيرٌ . عَدِيدٌ
Map n.	(خَارِطَةٌ) . رَسْمُ بِلَادٍ
Mar v. t.	أَضَرَّ . أَفْسَدَ . شَوَّهَ
Marauder n. Marauding a.	نَهَّابٌ . مُغِيرٌ لِلسَّلْبِ
Marble n.	رُخَامٌ . مَرْمَرٌ
March n. or v. i.	اذَارُ . مَسِيرٌ . سَارَ –
Mare n.	أُنْثَى ٱلْفَرَسِ
Margin n.	حَاشِيَةٌ . حَرْفٌ . شَفِيرٌ
Marine a. Mariner n.	بَحْرِيٌّ
Marital a.	زَوْجِيٌّ
Maritime a.	بَحْرِيٌّ . مُجَاوِرُ ٱلْبَحْرِ
Mark n.	عَلَامَةٌ . أَثَرٌ . هَدَفٌ
Mark v. t.	عَلَّمَ عَلَى . لَاحَظَ
Market n.	سُوقٌ ج اسْوَاقٌ
Marketable a.	رَائِجٌ
Marksman n.	رَامٍ . مَاهِرٌ بِٱلرَّمْيِ
Marmalade n.	نَوْعٌ مِنَ ٱلْمُرَبَّى
Marriage n.	عُرْسٌ . زَوَاجٌ
Marriageable a.	خَلِيقٌ بِٱلزَّوَاجِ
Marrow n.	مُخٌّ . لُبٌّ
Marry v. t. or i.	زَوَّجَ . تَزَوَّجَ
Mars n.	ٱلْمَرِّيخُ (سَيَّارٌ) . إِلهُ ٱلْحَرْبِ
Marsh n.	مُسْتَنْقَعٌ . سَبْخَةٌ
Marshal n. or v. t.	اكْبَرُ ٱلْقُوَّادِ . صَفَّ
Marshy a.	مُسْتَنْقَعِيٌّ . سَبْخٌ
Martial a.	حَرْبِيٌّ . عَسْكَرِيٌّ
Martyr n.	شَهِيدٌ ج شُهَدَاءٌ
Martyrdom n.	إِسْتِشْهَادٌ
Marvel v. i. or n.	تَعَجَّبَ . عَجِيبَةٌ
Marvelous a.	عَجِيبٌ . غَرِيبٌ
Masculine a.	مُذَكَّرٌ
Mash v. t.	دَقَّ – . خَبَصَ –

Mask n. or v. t.	وَجْهٌ عَارِيَةٌ . نَكَّرَ . سَتَرَ
Mason n.	بَنَّاءٌ . مِعْمَارٌ
Masonic a.	مَاسُونِيٌّ
Masonry n.	صِنَاعَةُ البِنَاءِ . مَاسُونِيَّةٌ
Masquerade v. i. or n.	تَنَكُّرٌ لِلسُّخْرِيَّةِ
Mass n.	كَوْمٌ . مِقْدَارٌ . قُدَّاسٌ
Massacre n. or v. t.	ذَبْحٌ . مَقْتَلَةٌ . قَتَلَ
Massive a.	جَسِيمٌ . غَلِيظٌ
Mast n.	صَارٍ . دَقَلٌ
Master n. or v. t.	سَيِّدٌ . مُعَلِّمٌ . رَئِيسٌ . غَلَبَ
Master-piece n.	شُغْلٌ سَامٍ فِي بَابِهِ
Mastery n.	ظَفَرٌ . تَسَلُّطٌ
Mastic n.	عِلْكٌ . (مَصْطَكَى)
Masticate v. t.	مَضَغَ . عَلَكَ
Mastication n.	مَضْغٌ . عَلْكٌ
Mastiff n.	كَلْبٌ . كَبِيرٌ . قَوِيٌّ
Mat n. or v. i.	حَصِيرَةٌ . تَلَبَّدَ
Match n.	عُودُ كِبْرِيتِيٍّ . قَرِينٌ . سِبَاقٌ
Match v. t.	وَفَّقَ . أَزْوَجَ
Matchless a.	لَا نَظِيرَ لَهُ
Mate n.	رَفِيقٌ . قَرِينٌ . ثَانِي قِبْطَانٍ
Material n. or a.	مَادَّةٌ . مَادِّيٌّ
Materialism n.	مَذْهَبُ الْمَادِّيِّينَ
Materialist n.	دَهْرِيٌّ
Materially ad.	مَادِّيًّا
Maternal a.	أُمِّيٌّ
Maternity n.	أُمِّيَّةٌ . وَظِيفَةُ الْأُمِّ
Mathematical a.	رِيَاضِيٌّ
Mathematician n.	عَالِمٌ بِالرِّيَاضِيَّاتِ
Mathematics n. pl.	الْعُلُومُ الرِّيَاضِيَّةُ
Matricide n.	قَتْلُ الْآمِّ
Matriculate v. t.	تَسَجَّلَ فِي مَدْرَسَةٍ عَالِيَةٍ
Matrimonial a.	مُتَعَلِّقٌ بِالزِّيجَةِ
Matrimony n.	الزِّيجَةُ
Matron n.	شَيْخَةٌ . رَئِيسَةٌ . قَهْرَمَانَةٌ
Matted a.	مُتَلَبِّدٌ

Matter *v. i.*	هَمَّ . أَغَثَ
Matter *n.*	مَادَّةٌ . هُيُولَى . أَمْرٌ
Mattock *n.*	مِعْوَلٌ ج مَعَاوِلُ
Mattress *n.*	فِرَاشٌ
Mature *a.* or *v. i.*	نَاضِجٌ . بَالِغٌ . نَضَجَ
Matureness } *n.* Maturity }	نَضْجٌ . بُلُوغٌ
Maul *v. t.*	ضَرَبَ شَدِيدًا بِعَصًا . جَرَحَ
Mausoleum *n.*	مَقَامٌ . مَزْخْرَفٌ لِمَيِّتٍ
Maxim *n.*	قَاعِدَةٌ . حِكْمَةٌ ج حِكَمٌ
Maximum *n.*	غَايَةٌ . اعْلَى دَرَجَةٍ
May *n.* or *v. i.*	أَيَّارُ (مَايُو) . أَمْكَنَ
Mayor *n.*	حَاكِمُ مَدِينَةٍ . رَئِيسُ بَلَدِيَّةٍ
Maze *n.*	إِرْتِبَاكٌ . وَرْطَةٌ
Mazy *a.*	مُرْتَبِكٌ . مُبْهَمٌ
Me *pron.*	ضَمِيرُ المُتَكَلِّم . بِي . ي
Meadow *n.*	مَرْجٌ . رَوْضَةٌ
Meagre *a.*	هَزِيلٌ . زَهِيدٌ . سَخِيفٌ
Meal *n.*	طَحِينٌ . أَكْلَةٌ وَاحِدَةٌ

Mealy *a.*	نَاعِمٌ كَالطَّحِين
Mean *a.*	حَقِيرٌ . دَنِيٌّ . وَسَطٌ
Mean *v. t.*	عَنَى ـِ . قَصَدَ ـِ . نَوَى ـِ
Meander *v. t.*	إِنْعَرَجَ . جَرَى عِوَجًا
Meaning *n.*	مَعْنًى . مُرَادٌ . مَرَامٌ
Meanly *ad.*	بِدَنَاءَةٍ . خِسَّةً
Meanness *n.*	خَسِيسَةٌ . دَنَاءَةٌ
Means *n. pl.*	وَاسِطَةٌ . ثَرْوَةٌ
Meantime } Meanwhile } *ad.*	فِي اثْنَاءِ ذٰلِكَ
Measles *n. pl.*	حَصْبَةٌ (مَرَضٌ)
Measurable *a.*	قَابِلُ القِيَاسِ أَوِ الكَيْلِ
Measure *v. t.*	قَاسَ . كَالَ ـِ . مَسَحَ ـِ
Measure *n.*	قِيَاسٌ . كَيْلٌ . وَسِيلَةٌ
Measurement *n.*	قِيَاسٌ . مِسَاحَةٌ
Meat *n.*	لَحْمٌ . طَعَامٌ
Mechanic *n.*	فَاعِلٌ يَعْمَلُ بِالآلَاتِ
Mechanical *a.*	آلِيٌّ . صِنَاعِيٌّ
Mechanics *n. pl.*	عِلْمُ الحِيَلِ

Mechanism n.	تَرْكِيبُ آلَاتٍ
Medal n.	نِيشَانٌ . سِكَّةٌ تَذْكَارِيَّةٌ
Medallion n.	سِكَّةٌ كَبِيرَةٌ . وِسَامٌ
Meddle v. i.	تَطَفَّلَ . تَحَرَّشَ
Meddler n. Meddlesome a. }	مُتَحَرِّشٌ . مُتَطَفِّلٌ
Mediaeval a.	مِنَ ٱلْقُرُونِ ٱلْمُتَوَسِّطَةِ
Mediate v. t.	تَوَسَّطَ . تَشَفَّعَ فِي
Mediation n.	شَفَاعَةٌ . تَوَسُّطٌ
Mediator a.	وَسِيطٌ . شَفِيعٌ
Medical a.	طِبِّيٌّ
Medicate v. t.	خَلَطَ بِعَقَاقِيرَ . عَالَجَ
Medicinal a.	عِلَاجِيٌّ . دَوَائِيٌّ
Medicine n.	دَوَاءٌ . عِلَاجٌ
Mediocre a.	وَسَطٌ أَوْ أَقَلُّ مِنْهُ
Mediocrity n.	اِعْتِدَالٌ . قِلَّةٌ
Meditate v. t. or i.	تَأَمَّلَ . تَفَكَّرَ . نَوَى
Meditation n.	تَأَمُّلٌ . تَفَكُّرٌ
Mediterranean n.	ٱلْبَحْرُ ٱلْمُتَوَسِّطُ

Medium n.	وَاسِطَةٌ . وَسَطٌ . وَسِيطٌ
Medley n.	خَلِيطٌ . عَدَمُ نِظَامٍ
Meek a.	وَدِيعٌ . حَلِيمٌ . لَطِيفٌ . طَائِعٌ
Meekness n.	وَدَاعَةٌ . حِلْمٌ
Meet v. t. or i.	لَقِيَ . اِلْتَقَى . اِجْتَمَعَ
Meet a.	لَائِقٌ . مُوَافِقٌ
Meeting n.	اِجْتِمَاعٌ . مَجْمَعٌ . لِقَاءٌ
Melancholy n.	غَمٌّ . سَوْدَآءُ
Meliorate v. t.	حَسَّنَ . أَصْلَحَ
Melioration n.	تَحْسِينٌ
Mellow a.	نَاضِجٌ . لَيِّنٌ . رُخْوٌ
Mellow v. t. or i.	نَضَّجَ . نَضِجَ
Melodious a.	مُطْرِبٌ . رَخِيمٌ
Melody n.	حُسْنُ ٱلْأَلْحَانِ . إِيقَاعُهَا
Melon n.	جَبَسٌ . بَطِّيخٌ
Melt v. t. or i.	أَذَابَ . ذَابَ
Member n.	عُضْوٌ . جُزْءٌ
Membership n.	عُضْوِيَّةٌ

Membrane *n.*	غِشَاءٌ . نَسِيجٌ
Membranaceous Membranous } *a.*	غِشَائِيٌّ
Memento *a.*	تَذْكِرَةٌ
Memoir *n.*	تَرْجَمَةٌ . تَقْرِيرٌ
Memorable *a.*	مُسْتَحِقُّ الذِّكْرِ
Memorialize *v. t.*	قَدَّمَ عَرْضَ حَالٍ إِلَى
Memorandum *n.*	تَذْكِرَةٌ . مُفَكِّرَةٌ
Memorial *n.* or *a.*	تَذْكِرَةٌ . تَقْرِيرٌ لِلتَّذْكَارِ
Memorize *v. t.*	حَفِظَ . غَيَّبَ
Memory *n.*	ذِكْرٌ . الذَّاكِرَةُ . الْحَافِظَةُ
Menace *v. t.* or *n.*	هَدَّدَ . تَوَعَّدَ . وَعِيدٌ
Menagerie *n.*	مَعْرِضُ الْحَيَوَانَاتِ
Mend *v. t.* or *i.*	أَصْلَحَ . رَقَّعَ . تَحَسَّنَ
Mendacious *a.*	كَاذِبٌ
Mendacity *n.*	كِذْبٌ
Mendicancy Mendicity } *n.*	تَسَوُّلٌ . شِحَاذَةٌ
Mendicant *n.*	شَحَّاذٌ . مُتَسَوِّلٌ
Menial *a.* or *n.*	دَنِيءٌ . ذَلِيلٌ . اجِيرٌ
Menses *n. pl.* Menstruation *n.* }	حَيْضٌ . طَمْثٌ
Menstrual *a.*	حَيْضِيٌّ . شَهْرِيٌّ
Menstruate *v. i.*	حَاضَتْ . طَمِثَتْ
Mensuration *n.*	قِيَاسٌ . مِسَاحَةٌ
Mental *a.*	عَقْلِيٌّ . ذِهْنِيٌّ
Mention *n.* or *v. t.*	ذِكْرٌ . ذَكَرَ
Mercantile *a.*	تِجَارِيٌّ
Mercenary *a.* or *n.*	مُسْتَأْجَرٌ . طَمَّاعٌ
Merchandise *n.*	بَضَائِعُ . تِجَارَةٌ
Merchant *a.*	تَاجِرٌ
Merchantman *n.*	سَفِينَةٌ تِجَارِيَّةٌ
Merciful *a.*	رَحِيمٌ . رَؤُوفٌ
Merciless *a.*	عَدِيمُ الرَّحْمَةِ . صَارِمٌ
Mercurial *a.*	زِئْبَقِيٌّ . حَادُّ الطَّبْعِ
Mercury *n.*	زِئْبَقٌ . مُطَارِدٌ (سَيَّارٌ)
Mercy *n.*	رَحْمَةٌ . رَأْفَةٌ
Mere *a.*	مُجَرَّدٌ . خَالِصٌ
Merely *ad.*	فَقَطْ . لَا غَيْرُ

Merge *v. t. or i.*	غَطَسَ. إِخْتَفَى فِي
Meridian *n.*	نِصْفُ ٱلنهَارِ وَخَطُّهُ
Merit *n.* or *v. t.*	فَضْلٌ. إِسْتِحْقَاقٌ. إِسْتَحَقَّ
Merited *a.*	مُسْتَحِقٌّ. مُسْتَوْجَبٌ
Meritorious *a.*	مُسْتَحِقٌّ ٱلثَّنَاءَ أَوِ ٱلثَّوَابِ
Merriment *n.*	فَرَحٌ. طَرَبٌ. إِنْبِسَاطٌ
Merry *a.*	فَرَحٌ. طَرِبٌ
Mesmerism *n.*	تَنْوِيمٌ إِصْطِنَاعِيٌّ
Mess *n.*	طَبْخَةٌ. حِصَّةٌ. خَلْطٌ
Message *n.*	رِسَالَةٌ. بَلَاغٌ
Messenger *n.*	رَسُولٌ. سَاعٍ
Messiah *n.*	ٱلْمَسِيحُ
Metal *a.*	مَعْدِنٌ
Metallic *n.*	مَعْدِنِيٌّ
Metallurgy *n.*	عِلْمُ ٱلْمَعَادِنِ
Metaphor *n.*	إِسْتِعَارَةٌ. مَجَازٌ
Metaphorical Metaphoric *a.*	إِسْتِعَارِيٌّ مَجَازِيٌّ
Metaphysical *a.*	مُخْتَصٌّ بِعِلْمِ ٱلْمَعْقُولَاتِ
Metaphysician *n.*	عَالِمٌ بِٱلْمَعْقُولَاتِ
Metaphysics *n.*	عِلْمُ مَاوَرَاءَ ٱلطَّبِيعَةِ
Mete *v. t.*	قَاسَ. كَالَ ـِ
Meteor *n.*	شِهَابٌ
Meteorite Meteorolite *n.*	حَجَرٌ مِنَ ٱلْجَوِّ نِيزَكٌ
Meteorology *n.*	عِلْمُ ٱلظَّوَاهِرِ ٱلْجَوِّيَّةِ
Meter *n.*	مِقْيَاسُ ٱلْمَاءِ وَٱلْغَازِ
Metre *n.*	مِتْرٌ. وَزْنُ ٱلشِّعْرِ
Method *n.*	طَرِيقَةٌ. اسْلُوبٌ. نِظَامٌ
Methodic Methodical *a.*	بِتَرْتِيبٍ. بِنِظَامٍ
Metrical *a.*	مَوْزُونٌ. نَظْمِيٌّ
Metropolis *n.*	عَاصِمَةُ بِلَادٍ
Metropolitan *n.*	مَطْرَانٌ مُخْتَصٌّ بِقَصَبَةٍ
Mettle *n.*	مُرُوءَةٌ. نَخْوَةٌ. نَشَاطٌ
Mew *v. i.*	مَاءَ كَٱلْقِطِّ. نَوَّى
Miasma *n.*	أَبْخِرَةٌ سَامَّةٌ
Mice *n.* (*pl.* of Mouse).	فِيرَانٌ
Microscope *n.*	مِجْهَرٌ. (مِكْرُسْكُوبٌ)

Midday n.	نِصْفُ ٱلنَّهَارِ . مُنْتَصَفُهُ
Middle a. or n.	مُنْتَصَفٌ أَوْسَطُ . وَسَطٌ
Middling a.	مُتَوَسِّطٌ . بَيْنَ بَيْنَ
Midnight n.	مُنْتَصَفُ ٱللَّيْلِ
Midriff n.	الْحِجَابُ ٱلْحَاجِزُ
Midshipman n.	ضَابِطٌ صَغِيرٌ فِي بَارِجَةٍ
Midst n.	وَسَطٌ
Midway n.	مُنْتَصَفُ ٱلْمَسَافَةِ
Midwife n.	قَابِلَةٌ ج قَوَابِلُ . (دَايَةٌ)
Midwifery n.	قِبَالَةٌ
Mien n.	هَيْئَةٌ . طَلْعَةٌ
Might n.	قُوَّةٌ . بَأْسٌ . شِدَّةٌ
Mightily ad.	بِشِدَّةٍ . جِدًّا
Mighty a.	قَوِيٌّ . قَدِيرٌ . عَزِيزٌ
Migrate v. i.	هَاجَرَ . إِنْتَقَلَ
Migration n.	مُهَاجَرَةٌ . إِنْتِقَالٌ
Migratory a.	رَاحِلٌ . مُتَنَقِّلٌ
Mild a.	لَطِيفٌ . حَلِيمٌ . مُعْتَدِلٌ

Mildew n.	عَفُونَةٌ
Mildness n.	لُطْفٌ . حِلْمٌ . رِقَّةٌ
Mile n.	مِيلٌ ج أَمْيَالٌ
Militant a.	مُحَارِبٌ . مُجَاهِدٌ
Military a.	حَرْبِيٌّ . عَسْكَرِيٌّ
Militia n.	جُنْدَ ٱلرَّدِيفِ
Milk n. or v. t.	حَلِيبٌ . لَبَنٌ . حَلَبَ ــ
Milkyway n.	الْمَجَرَّةُ
Mill n. or v. t.	مَطْحَنَةٌ . مَعْمَلٌ . طَحَنَ ــ
Millennium n.	أَلْفُ سَنَةٍ
Miller n.	طَحَّانٌ
Millet n.	ذُرَةٌ
Milliner n.	خَيَّاطَةُ لِبَاسُ ٱلنِّسَاءِ
Millinery n.	مَلْبُوسَاتُ ٱلنِّسَاءِ
Million n.	أَلْفُ أَلْفٍ . مَلْيُونٌ
Millionaire n.	وَافِرُ ٱلْغِنَى
Millstone n.	حَجَرُ طَاحُونٍ . رَحَى
Milt n.	طِحَالٌ

Mimic *n.* or *v. t.*	مُقَلِّدٌ . قَلَّدَ هُزْلاً
Minaret *n.*	مَأْذَنَةٌ ج مَآذِن
Mince *v. t.* or *i.*	قَرَّطَ . (فَرَمَ) تَخَطَّرَ
Mind *n.*	عَقْلٌ . ذِهْنٌ . نِيَّةٌ
Mind *v. t.*	بَالَى بِهِ . إِكْتَرَثَ . إِعْتَنَى
Minded *a.*	مُتَفَكِّرٌ . مَائِلٌ إِلَى
Mindful *a.*	مُبَالٍ . مُكْتَرِثٌ . مُعْتَنٍ
Mine *pron.* or *n.*	لِي . مَعْدِنٌ . لُغْمٌ
Miner *n.*	صَانِعٌ فِي مَنَاجِمَ
Mineral *n.* or *a.*	جَمَادٌ . جَمَادِيٌّ
Mineralogist *n.*	عَالِمٌ بِالْجَمَادَاتِ
Mineralogy *n.*	عِلْمُ الْجَمَادِ وَالْمَعَادِنِ
Mingle *v. t.* or *i.*	خَلَطَ ـ مَزَجَ ـ . إِمْتَزَجَ
Miniature *n.*	صُورَةٌ . صَغِيرَةٌ
Minimum *n.*	الْأَقَلُّ . أَقَلُّ مِقْدَارٍ
Mining *n.*	مُعَالَجَةُ الْمَعَادِنِ اوِ اللُّغُومِ
Minister *v. t.*	خَدَمَ ـ . امَدَّ . قَدَّمَ لِ
Minister *n.*	خَادِمٌ قِسِّيسٌ . سَفِيرٌ . وَزِيرٌ

Ministerial *a.*	قَسُّوسِيٌّ . وَزِيرِيٌّ
Ministration *n.*	خِدْمَةٌ
Ministry *n.*	خِدْمَةٌ . وَزَارَةٌ
Minor *a.*	اصْغَرُ عُمْراً . قَاصِرٌ . اصْغَرُ
Minority *n.*	الْعَدَدُ الْأَقَلُّ . سِنُّ الْقُصُورِ
Minstrel *n.*	مُغَنٍّ . عَوَّادٌ
Mint *n.*	مَضْرِبُ نُقُودٍ . نَعْنَعٌ
Minuend *n.*	الْمَطْرُوحُ مِنْهُ
Minus *a.*	عَلَامَةُ الطَّرْحِ (—) . إِلاَّ
Minute *n.*	دَقِيقَةٌ . تَذْكِرَةٌ
Minute *a.*	دَقِيقٌ . مُدَقَّقٌ
Minutely *ad.*	بِدِقَّةٍ . بِضَبْطٍ
Minuteness *n.*	دِقَّةٌ . صِغَرٌ
Miracle *n.*	آيَةٌ . مُعْجِزَةٌ . عَجِيبَةٌ
Miraculous *a.*	عَجِيبٌ . خَارِقُ الْعَادَةِ
Mirage *n.*	سَرَابٌ . لَمْعٌ
Mire *n.*	وَحْلٌ . حَمْأَةٌ
Mirror *n.*	مِرْآةٌ ج مَرَايَا

Mirth n.	فَرَحٌ . سُرُورٌ . طَرَبٌ
Mirthful a.	طَرِبٌ . فَرِحٌ
Miry a.	ذُو وَحَلٍ
Misanthrope n. } Misanthropic a. }	مُبْغِضُ ٱلْبَشَرِ
Misanthropy n.	بُغْضُ ٱلْبَشَرِ . وَحْشَةٌ
Misapplication n.	سُوْءُ ٱلْإِسْتِعْمَالِ
Misapply v. t.	أَسَاءَ ٱلْإِسْتِعْمَالَ
Misapprehend v. t.	أَسَاءَ ٱلْفَهْمَ
Misapprehension n.	سُوْءُ ٱلْفَهْمِ
Misbehave v. i.	أَسَاءَ ٱلتَّصَرُّفَ
Misbehaviour n.	سُوْءُ ٱلتَّصَرُّفِ
Misbelief n.	إِعْتِقَادٌ . فَاسِدٌ
Misbelieve v. t.	أَسَاءَ ٱلْإِعْتِقَادَ
Miscalculate v. t.	أَسَاءَ ٱلْحِسَابَ
Miscarriage n.	خَيْبَةٌ . إِسْقَاطُ ٱلْجَنِينِ
Miscarry v. i.	خَابَ ـ . اسْقَطَتْ
Miscellaneous a.	مُتَنَوِّعٌ . شَتَّى
Miscellany n.	مَجْمُوعُ أَشْيَاءَ . شَتَّى

Mischance n.	مُصِيبَةٌ
Mischief n.	ضَرَرٌ . سُوْءٌ . شَرٌّ
Mischievous a.	مُضِرٌّ . مُسِيءٌ مُكَدِّرٌ
Misconceive v. t.	أَسَاءَ ٱلْفَهْمَ . غَلِطَ ـ
Misconception n.	سُوْءُ ٱلْمَفْهُومِيَّةِ . غَلَطٌ
Misconduct n.	سُوْءُ ٱلتَّصَرُّفِ
Misconstrue v. t.	أَسَاءَ ٱلتَّأْوِيلَ . حَرَّفَ
Miscount v. t.	غَلِطَ فِي ٱلْعَدِّ
Miscreant n.	كَافِرٌ . شِرِّيرٌ . فَاجِرٌ
Misdate v. t.	أَرَّخَ غَلَطًا
Misdeed n.	فِعْلٌ شِرِّيرٌ . سَيِّئَةٌ
Misdemeanor n.	سُوْءُ ٱلسِّيرَةِ . ذَنْبٌ
Misdirect v. t.	أَرْشَدَ او عَنْوَنَ خَطَأً
Misdoing n.	إِسَاءَةٌ . خَطِيئَةٌ
Miser n. } Miserly a. }	بَخِيلٌ . شَحِيحٌ
Miserable a.	تَعِيسٌ شَقِيٌّ . مِسْكِينٌ
Misery n.	مَسْكَنَةٌ . شَقَاءٌ . تَعَاسَةٌ
Misfortune n.	مُصِيبَةٌ . بَلِيَّةٌ . نَكْبَةٌ

Misgiving n.	رِيبَةٌ . قَلَقُ ٱلنَّفْسِ
Misgovern v. t.	أَسَاءَ ٱلسِّيَاسَةَ
Misgovernment n.	سُوءُ ٱلْإِدَارَةِ
Misguide v. t.	أَسَاءَ ٱلْإِرْشَادَ. اضَلَّ
Mishap n.	مُصِيبَةٌ . نَازِلَةٌ
Misinform v.t.	اخْبَرَ بِغَيْرِ ٱلْوَاقِعِ
Misinterpret v. t.	أَسَاءَ ٱلتَّفْسِيرَ
Misjudge v. t.	اخْطَأَ فِي ٱلْحُكْمِ
Mislay v. t.	وَضَعَ فِي غَيْرِ مَحَلِّهِ
Mislead v. t.	أَضَلَّ . اغْوَى
Mismanagement n.	سُوءُ ٱلتَّدْبِيرِ
Misname v. t.	اخْطَأَ فِي ٱلتَّسْمِيَةِ
Misnomer n.	إِسْمٌ فِي غَيْرِ مَحَلِّهِ
Misplace v. t.	وَضَعَ فِي غَيْرِ مَحَلِّهِ
Misprint n.	غَلَطٌ فِي ٱلطَّبْعِ
Mispronounce v. t.	غَلِطَ فِي ٱللَّفْظِ
Mispronunciation n.	خَطَأٌ فِي ٱللَّفْظِ
Misquote v. t.	اخْطَأَ فِي ٱلْإِقْتِبَاسِ
Misrepresent v. t.	حَرَّفَ كَلَامَهُ . مَوَّهَ
Misrule n.	سُوءُ ٱلسِّيَاسَةِ وَٱلْحُكْمِ
Miss n.	فَتَاةٌ . إِخْطَاءٌ
Miss v. t.	اخْطَأَ لَمْ يُصِبْ . اعْوَزَهُ
Misshaped / Misshapen a.	مُشَوَّهٌ . قَبِيحُ ٱلْخِلْقَةِ
Missile n.	مِرْمَاةٌ
Missing a.	مَفْقُودٌ . ضَائِعٌ
Mission n.	إِرْسَالِيَّةٌ . جَمَاعَةٌ مُرْسَلَةٌ
Missionary n.	مُرْسَلٌ . مُبَشِّرٌ
Missive n.	رِسَالَةٌ
Misspell v. t.	اخْطَأَ فِي ٱلتَّهْجِئَةِ
Misspend v. t.	صَرَفَ بَاطِلاً
Misstatement n.	تَحْرِيفٌ . تَمْوِيهٌ
Mist n. or v. i.	ضَبَابٌ رَذَاذٌ . ارَذَّ
Mistake n. or v. t.	خَطَأٌ . سَهْوٌ . اخْطَأَ
Mistaken a.	مُخْطِئٌ
Mister n.	سَيِّدٌ . افَنْدِي . خَوَاجَا
Mistranslate v. t.	اخْطَأَ فِي ٱلتَّرْجَمَةِ

Mistress n.	سَيِّدَةٌ. مُعَلِّمَةٌ. سِرِّيَّةٌ
Mistrust n. or v. t.	عَدَمُ ثِقَةٍ. شَكَّ في
Mistrustful a.	عَدِيمُ الثِّقَةِ
Misty a.	ذُو ضَبَابٍ. ضَبَابِيٌّ
Misunderstand v. t.	أَسَاءَ الفَهْمَ
Misunderstanding n.	سُوءُ فَهْمٍ. خِلَافٌ
Misuse v. t. or n.	أَسَاءَ الاسْتِعْمَالَ
Mite n.	شَيْءٌ يَسِيرٌ. فِلْسٌ. سُوَيْسَةٌ
Mitre n.	تَاجُ أُسْقُفٍ أَوْ قَلَنْسُوَتُهُ
Mitigate v. t.	خَفَّضَ. خَفَّفَ. لَيَّنَ
Mitten n.	كَفٌّ بِلَا أَصَابِعَ
Mix v. t. or i.	مَزَجَ. امْتَزَجَ
Mixture n.	مَزِيجٌ
Moan v. i. or n.	أَنَّ. أَنِينٌ
Moat n.	خَنْدَقٌ تَحْصِينٍ
Mob n. or v. t.	الأَوْبَاشُ. قَامَ الأَوْبَاشُ عَلَيْهِ
Mobile a.	سَهْلُ الحَرَكَةِ أَوِ التَّغَيُّرِ
Mobility n.	سُهُولَةُ الحَرَكَةِ. خِفَّةٌ
Mobilize v. t.	عَبَّأَ (جَيْشًا) لِلْحَرْبِ
Mock v. t. or a.	هَزَأَ. سَخِرَ. مَصْنَعٌ
Mockery n.	هَزْءٌ. سُخْرَةٌ
Mode n.	كَيْفِيَّةٌ. أُسْلُوبٌ. عَادَةٌ
Model n. or v. t.	نَمُوذَجٌ مِثَالٌ عَمِلَ عَلَى الرَّسْمِ
Moderate a. or v. t.	مُعْتَدِلٌ. خَفَّفَ. خَفَّضَ
Moderation n.	اعْتِدَالٌ. ضَبْطُ النَّفْسِ
Modern a.	حَدِيثٌ. مُتَأَخِّرٌ
Modest a.	مُحْتَشِمٌ. حَيِيٌّ. مُعْتَدِلٌ
Modesty n.	حِشْمَةٌ. حَيَاءٌ
Modification n.	تَغْيِيرٌ. نَوْعٌ
Modify v. t.	غَيَّرَ صِفَاتِهِ. نَوَّعَ
Modulate v. t.	أَوْقَعَ عَلَى وَزْنٍ
Mohammedan n. or a.	مُسْلِمٌ. إِسْلَامِيٌّ
Moiety n.	نِصْفٌ
Moist a.	رَطْبٌ. مُنَدَّى
Moisten v. t.	رَطَّبَ. نَدَّى. تَرَّى
Moisture n.	رُطُوبَةٌ. نَدًى

Molasses *n. pl.*	دِبْسُ سُكَّرٍ
Mold } *n. or v. i.* Mould} or *t.*	عَفَّنَ . قَالَبَ . تَعَفَّنَ . صَبَّ فِي قَالَبٍ
Moldy } Mouldy} *a.*	مُتَعَفِّنٌ
Molder } Moulder} *v.i.*	إِنْحَلَّ . بَلِيَ —
Mole *n.*	خَالٌ . خُلْدٌ . سَدٌّ فِي ٱلْبَحْرِ
Molecule *a.*	ذَرَّةٌ
Molest *v. t.*	كَدَّرَ . ازْعَجَ
Mollify *v. t.*	لَيَّنَ . طَيَّبَ ٱلْخَاطِرَ
Molten *a.*	ذَائِبٌ . مَسْبُوكٌ
Moment *n.*	دَقِيقَةٌ . أَهَمِّيَّةٌ
Momentary *a.*	لَحْظَةٌ . وَقْتِيٌّ
Momentous *n.*	مُهِمٌّ جِدًّا . خَطِيرٌ
Momentum *n.*	قُوَّةُ ٱلْإِنْدِفَاعِ
Monarch *n.*	مَلِكٌ . سُلْطَانٌ
Monarchical *a.*	مَلَكِيٌّ
Monarchy *n.*	مَمْلَكَةٌ . مَلَكِيَّةٌ
Monastery *n.*	دَيْرٌ ج أَدِيرَةٌ
Monastic *a.*	رَهْبَانِيٌّ . نَسْكِيٌّ
Monday *n.*	يَوْمُ ٱلْإِثْنَيْنِ
Money *n.*	دَرَاهِمُ . نُقُودٌ
Moneyed *a.*	ذُو مَالٍ . غَنِيٌّ
Mongrel *a. or n.*	نَغْلٌ . خِلَاسِيٌّ
Monition *n.*	إِنْذَارٌ . إِنْبَاءٌ . تَنْبِيهٌ
Monitor *n.*	مُنْذِرٌ . عَرِيفٌ
Monk *n.*	رَاهِبٌ . نَاسِكٌ
Monkey *n.*	قِرْدٌ . (سَعْدَانٌ)
Monogamy *n.*	زَوَاجٌ بِٱمْرَأَةٍ وَاحِدَةٍ
Monogram *n.*	طُغْرَاءٌ
Monomaniac *a.*	مَجْنُونٌ فِي أَمْرٍ وَاحِدٍ
Monopolize *v. t.*	إِحْتَكَرَ . خَصَّصَ لِنَفْسِهِ
Monopoly *n.*	إِحْتِكَارٌ . إِمْتِيَازٌ فِي أَمْرٍ
Monosyllable *n.*	لَفْظَةٌ مِنْ مَقْطَعٍ وَاحِدٍ
Monotheism *n.*	التَّوْحِيدُ
Monotonous *a.*	مُمِلٌّ . بَارِدٌ
Monotony *n.*	عَدَمُ تَغَيُّرٍ او تَنَوُّعٍ

Monster *n.*	وحشٌ غَريبُ ٱلْخِلْقَةِ
Month *n.*	شَهْرُ ج اشْهُرٌ وَشُهُورُ
Monthly *a.*	شَهْرِيّ
Monument *a.*	بِنَاءٌ لِلتّذْكَارِ . ضَرِيحُ
Monumental *a.*	تَذْكَارِيّ
Mood *n.*	حَالَةٌ . مِنْوَالٌ . صِيغَةُ فِعْلٍ
Moody *a.*	مَهْمُومٌ . مَغْمُومٌ . نَكِدٌ
Moon *n.*	قَمَرُ ج اقْمَارٌ
Moonshine *n.*	ضَوْءُ ٱلْقَمَرِ . تَظَاهُرٌ
Moor *v.t.* or *n.*	رَبَطَ سَفِينَةً . مَغْرِبِيّ
Moorings *n. pl.*	رُبُطُ ٱلسَّفِينَةِ
Mop *n.* or *v. t.*	مِمْسَحَةٌ . مَسَحَ ـ بِهَا
Mope *v. i.*	مَلَّ ـ . ضَجِرَ ـ
Moral *a.*	أَدَبِيّ . فَاضِلٌ . مُسْتَقِيمٌ
Moral *n.*	مَغْزَى مَثَلٍ او مَقْصِدُهُ
Morality *n.*	إِسْتِقَامَةُ ٱلسِّيرَةِ . فَضِيلَةٌ
Moralize *v. t.*	فَسَّرَ بِمَعْنًى أَدَبِيٍّ
Morally *ad.*	أَدَبِيًّا

Morals *n. pl.*	ٱلْآدَابُ . صِفَاتٌ ادَبِيّة
Morass *n.*	مُسْتَنْقَعٌ . سَبْخَةٌ
Morbid *a.*	سَقِيمٌ . وَبِيلٌ . مُغِمٌّ
More *a.* or *ad.*	اكْثَرُ . ازْيَد
Moreover *ad.*	ايضًا . ثُمَّ
Morn | Morning | *n.*	صَبَاحٌ . صُبْحٌ
Morose *a.*	عَبُوسٌ . نَكِدٌ
Moroseness *n.*	عُبُوسَةٌ . شَرَاسَةٌ
Morrow *n.*	غَدٌ . بُكْرَةُ
Morsel *n.*	لُقْمَةٌ . قِطْعَةٌ . صَغِيرَةٌ
Mortal *a.*	مَائِتٌ . فَانٍ . قَاتِلٌ
Mortals *n. pl.*	بَشَرٌ
Mortality *n.*	مَوْتٌ . هَلَاكٌ
Mortally *ad.*	لِلْمَوْتِ . مُمِيتًا
Mortar *n.*	طِينٌ . هَاوُنٌ . مِدْفَعٌ قَصِيرٌ
Mortgage *n.* or *v.t.*	رَهْنٌ . رَهَنَ ـ
Mortification *n.*	فَسَادٌ . قَهْرٌ . خَجَلٌ
Mortify *v. i.* or *t.*	فَسَدَ . أَذَلَّ . قَمَعَ ـ

Mosaic n. or a.	فُسَيْفِسَاءٌ . فُسَيْفِسِيٌّ
Moslem n.	مُسْلِمٌ
Mosque n.	جَامِعٌ . مَسْجِدٌ
Mosquito n.	نَامُوسَةٌ . بَعُوضَةٌ
Moss n.	طَحْلَبٌ . اشْنَةٌ
Most a.	أَكْثَرُ . الأَكْثَرُ
Mote n.	قَذًى . هَبْوَةٌ
Moth n.	فَرَاشَةٌ . عُثَّةٌ
Mother n.	أُمٌّ . وَالِدَةٌ
Mother-in-law n.	حَمَاةٌ
Motion n. or v. i.	حَرَكَةٌ . أَشَارَ إِلَى
Motive n.	بَاعِثٌ . دَاعٍ . مُوجِبٌ
Motley a.	مُلَوَّنٌ . مُتَنَوِّعٌ
Motor n.	مُحَرِّكٌ
Mottled a.	كَثِيرُ الْبُقَعِ الْمُلَوَّنَةِ
Motto n.	عِبَارَةٌ عُنْوَانِيَّةٌ . شِعَارٌ
Mould etc. see Mold etc.	
Mound n.	كُمَةٌ . تَلٌّ . مِتْرَاسٌ
Mount n. or v. t.	جَبَلٌ . صَعِدَ . رَكِبَ
Mountain n. or a.	جَبَلٌ . جَبَلِيٌّ
Mountaineer n.	سَاكِنُ الْجَبَلِ
Mountainous a.	كَثِيرُ الْجِبَالِ
Mountebank a.	مُشَعْبِذٌ . دَجَّالٌ
Mourn v. i. or t.	نَاحَ . حَزِنَ
Mourner n.	نَائِحٌ . نَادِبٌ . حَزِينٌ
Mournful a.	مَحْزُونٌ . مَكْرُوبٌ
Mourning n.	نَوْحٌ . حُزْنٌ . حِدَادٌ
Mouse n. (pl. Mice).	فَأْرَةٌ ج فِيرَانٌ
Moustache n.	شَارِبٌ ج شَوَارِبُ
Mouth n.	فَمٌ . فُوهٌ . مَدْخَلٌ
Mouthful n.	لُقْمَةٌ ج لُقَمٌ . اكْلَةٌ
Mouthpiece n.	فَمُ الْمِزْمَارِ وَمَا اشْبَهَ نَائِبٌ فِي الْكَلَامِ
Movable a.	مِمَّا يُحَرَّكُ او يُنْقَلُ
Movables n. pl.	بَضَائِعُ . اثَاثٌ
Move v. t. or i.	نَقَلَ . حَرَّكَ . تَحَرَّكَ
Movement n.	حَرَكَةٌ . تَحْرِيكٌ

Mow v. t. or n. حَشَّ ـِ . كَدَّسَ	Multiplicand n. أَلْمَضْرُوبُ (عَدَدٌ)
Much a. or ad. كَثِيرٌ . وَافِرٌ . كَثِيرًا	Multiplication n. أَلضَّرْبُ . تَكْثِيرٌ
Mucilage n. لُعَابٌ . صَمْغٌ ذَائِبٌ	Multiplicity n. تَضَاعُفٌ . تَعَدُّدٌ
Mucous a. مُخَاطِيٌّ	Multiplier n. أَلْمَضْرُوبُ فِيهِ
Mucus n. مُخَاطٌ	Multiply v. t. كَثَّرَ . ضَرب . إِزْدَادَ
Mud n. وَحْلٌ . طِينٌ . حَمْأَةٌ	Multitude n. جُمْهُورٌ . فَوْجٌ
Muddle v. t. عَكَّرَ . شَوَّشَ . إِرْتِبَاكٌ or n.	Mumble v. t. هَمَسَ ـِ . دَنْدَنَ
Muddy a. ذُو وَحَلٍ	Mummery n. سُخْرَةٌ . مُجُونٌ
Muff n. فَرْوَةٌ لِلْيَدَيْنِ	Mummy n. جُثَّةٌ مُحَنَّطَةٌ
Muffle v. t. سَتَرَ ـُ . أَنَّ ـُ . خَمَرَ	Mumps n. pl. إِلْتِهَابُ الْغُدَّةِ النَّكَفِيَّةِ
Mug n. كُوزٌ . قَدَحٌ . إِبْرِيقٌ	Munch v. t. or i. مَضَغَ ـَ . لَاكَ ـُ
Mulatto n. خِلَاسِيٌّ	Municipal a. بَلَدِي
Mulberry n. تُوتٌ . تُوتَةٌ	Municipality n. بَلَدِيَّةٌ . إِدَارَةُ مَدِينَةٍ
Mule n. بَغْلٌ ج بِغَالٌ	Mundane a. عَالَمِيٌّ . دُنْيَوِيٌّ
Muleteer n. بَغَّالٌ . مُكَارٍ	Munificence n. سَخَاءٌ . كَرَمٌ
Mulish a. عَنِيدٌ كَالْبَغْلِ	Munificent a. جَوَّادٌ . كَرِيمٌ جِدًّا
Multiform a. مُتَعَدِّدُ الْهَيْئَةِ	Munitions n. pl. ذَخَائِرُ حَرْبِيَّةٌ
Multiple n. عَدَدٌ يُقْسَمُ عَلَى غَيْرِهِ بِلَا بَاقٍ	Mural a. مُخَاطِيٌّ . سُورِيٌّ جِدَارِيٌّ

Murder *n.* or *v. t.*	قَتْلٌ . قَتَلَ ــَ
Murderer *n.*	قَاتِلٌ
Murderous *a.*	مُهْلِكٌ . قَاصِدُ ٱلْقَتْلِ
Murky *a.*	مُظْلِمٌ . كَدِرٌ (هَوَاءٌ)
Murmur *v. i.* or *n.*	تَذَمَّرَ . دَنْدَنَ
Murrain *n.*	وَبَا ٱلْمَوَاشِي
Muscle *n.*	عَضَلَةٌ . صَدَفٌ
Muscular *a.*	عَضَلِيٌّ
Muse *n.* or *v. t.*	إِلَاهَةُ ٱلشِّعْرِ . تَأَمَّلَ
Museum *n.*	مَعْرِضُ ٱلتُّحَفِ . مَتْحَفٌ
Mushroom *n.*	فُطْرٌ
Music *n.*	صِنَاعَةُ ٱلْأَلْحَانِ . مُوسِيقَى
Musical *a.*	مُوسِيقِيٌّ . مُطْرِبٌ
Musician *n.*	عَالِمٌ بِٱلْمُوسِيقَى
Musk *n.*	مِسْكٌ
Musket *n.*	بُنْدُقِيَّةٌ . بَارُودَةٌ
Muskmelon *n.*	شَمَّامٌ . بَطِّيخٌ أَصْفَرُ
Muslin *n.*	نَسِيجٌ رَقِيقٌ . شَاشٌ
Mussulman *n.*	مُسْلِمٌ
Must *v. i.* (*aux.*)	يَجِبُ . يَنْبَغِي
Mustard *n.*	خَرْدَلٌ
Muster *v. t.* or *i.*	حَشَدَ ــَ . جَمَعَ ــَ . إِجْتَمَعَ
Muster *n.*	حَشْدُ ٱلْعَسَاكِرِ . دَفْتَرُهُمْ
Musty *a.*	عَفِنٌ . فَاسِدٌ
Mutability *n.*	عَدَمُ ثَبَاتٍ أَوْ بَقَاءٍ
Mutable *a.*	مُتَغَيِّرٌ . مُتَقَلِّبٌ
Mute *a.* or *n.*	صَامِتٌ . أَخْرَسُ
Mutilate *v. t.*	جَدَعَ ــَ . جَذَمَ ــَ
Mutineer *n.* Mutinous *a.*	عَاصٍ . ثَائِرٌ . مُتَمَرِّدٌ
Mutiny *n.*	عِصْيَانٌ . ثَوْرَةٌ . فِتْنَةٌ
Mutter *v. t.*	هَمَسَ ــِ . دَمْدَمَ
Muttering *n.*	هَمْسٌ . دَمْدَمَةٌ
Mutton *n.*	لَحْمُ ضَأْنٍ
Mutual *a.*	مُشْتَرَكٌ . مُتَبَادِلٌ
Mutually *ad.*	إِشْتِرَاكًا . تَبَادُلًا
Muzzle *v. t.* or *n.*	كَمَّ ــُ . كِمَامٌ . فَمٌ

Myriad n.	رَبْوَةٌ . عَدَدٌ عَظِيمٌ	Mystery n.	سِرٌّ . لُغْزٌ
Myrrh n.	مُرٌّ	Mystic a. or n. Mystical a.	غَامِضٌ . خَفِيٌّ . صُوفِيٌّ
Myrtle n.	آسٌ	Mystify v. t.	حَيَّرَ وَخَاتَلَ
Myself pron.	نَفْسِي . ذَاتِي	Myth n.	خُرَافَةٌ . حِكَايَةٌ
Mysterious a.	غَرِيبٌ . سِرِّيٌّ	Mythology n.	عِلْمُ الخُرَافَاتِ . مَجْمُوعُهَا

N

Nag n. or v. t.	حِصَانٌ صَغِيرٌ . نَكَدَ	Nap n.	نَوْمَةٌ قَصِيرَةٌ . زَغَبَرٌ
Nail n. or v. t.	مِسْمَارٌ . ظُفْرٌ . سَمَّرَ	Nape n.	قَفَا العُنُقِ
Naive a.	مُخْلِصٌ . صَافِي القَلْبِ	Napkin n.	فُوطَةٌ . مِنْشَفَةٌ
Naked a.	عُرْيَانٌ . مَكْشُوفٌ	Narcotic a.	مُخَدِّرٌ . مُنَوِّمٌ
Nakedness n.	عُرْيٌ . عَوْرَةٌ	Narrate v. t.	حَدَّثَ . قَصَّ . رَوَى
Name n. or v. t.	إِسْمٌ . سَمَّى . ذَكَرَ	Narration Narrative n.	حَدِيثٌ . قِصَّةٌ . رِوَايَةٌ
Nameless a.	بِلَا اسْمٍ . مَجْهُولٌ	Narrator n.	مُحَدِّثٌ . رَاوٍ
Namely ad.	أَيْ . يَعْنِي	Narrow a.	ضَيِّقٌ . مَحْصُورٌ
Namesake n.	سَمِيٌّ	Narrow v. t. or i.	ضَيَّقَ . تَضَيَّقَ

Nasal a.	انْفِيٌّ . اغَنُّ	Nauseous a.	مُسَبِّبُ ٱلْغَثَيَانِ . كَرِيهَةٌ
Nasty a.	وَسِخٌ . قَذِرٌ . قَبِيحٌ	Nautical a.	مَنُوطٌ بِٱلسَّفَرِ بَحْرًا . نُوتِيٌّ
Natal a.	وَطَنِيٌّ . مَوْلِدِي	Naval a.	مَنُوطٌ بِالسُّفُنِ اوِ ٱلْبَوَارِجِ
Nation n.	أُمَّةٌ . شَعْبٌ	Nave n.	صَحْنُ ٱلْكَنِيسَةِ
National a.	أُمَمِيٌّ . وَطَنِيٌّ	Navel n.	سُرَّةٌ
Nationality n.	وَطَنِيَّةٌ . جِنْسِيَّةٌ	Navigable a.	صَالِحٌ لِسَيْرِ ٱلسُّفُنِ
Native a.	وَطَنِيٌّ . أَهْلِيٌّ	Navigate v. t.	مَأفِرٌ فِي سَفِينَةٍ . سَيَّرَهَا
Nativity a.	مَوْلِدٌ . وِلَادَةٌ	Navigation n.	ٱلسَّيْرُ فِي ٱلسُّفُنِ . عِلْمُهُ
Natural a.	طَبِيعِيٌّ . فِطْرِيٌّ . خَلْقِيٌّ	Navigator n.	قَائِدُ سَفِينَةٍ . مُدِيرُهَا
Naturalist n.	عَالِمٌ بِٱلطَّبِيعِيَّاتِ	Navy n.	أُسْطُولٌ . مَجْمُوعُ بَوَارِجٍ
Naturalize v. t.	ضَمَّ إِلَى تَبَعِيَّةِ دَوْلَةٍ	Nay ad.	لَا . كَلَّا
Naturalness n.	طَبِيعِيَّةٌ . عَدَمُ تَصَنُّعٍ	Nazarite n.	نَذِيرٌ
Nature n.	ٱلطَّبِيعَةُ . خِلْقَةٌ . مَاهِيَّةٌ	Near a. or v. t.	قَرِيبٌ . قَرُبَ . دَنَا
Naught n.	لَا شَيْءٌ . بَطَلَ . عَدَمٌ	Near Nearly } ad.	قَرِيبًا . تَقْرِيبًا
Naughtiness n.	تَمَرُّدٌ . رَدَاءَةٌ . شَرٌّ	Nearness n.	قُرْبٌ
Naughty a.	مُتَمَرِّدٌ . فَاسِدٌ . شِرِّيرٌ	Neat a.	نَظِيفٌ . مُرَتَّبٌ . بَقَرِيٌّ
Nausea n.	غَثَيَانٌ	Neatness n.	نَظَافَةٌ . إِتْقَانٌ
Nauseate v. t.	سَبَّبَ ٱلْغَثَيَانَ	Nebula n.	سَدِيمٌ

Nebular / Nebulous } a.	سَدِيمِيٌّ
Necessary a.	لَازِمٌ . ضَرُورِيٌّ . وَاجِبٌ
Necessitate v. t.	ألْزَمَ . احْوَجَ
Necessitous a.	مُحْتَاجٌ . مُفْتَقِرٌ
Necessity n.	حَاجَةٌ . عَوَزٌ . ضَرُورَةٌ
Neck n.	عُنُقٌ رَقَبَةٌ
Necklace n.	قِلَادَةٌ . عِقْدٌ
Necromancy n.	سِحْرٌ . خُرَافَةٌ
Necropolis n.	مَقْبَرَةٌ . مَدْفَنٌ
Nectar n.	شَرَابُ ٱلْآلِهَةِ . شَرَابٌ نَفِيسٌ
Need n. or v. t. or i.	حَاجَةٌ . فَاقَةٌ . إِحْتَاجَ
Needful a.	ضَرُورِيٌّ . لَازِمٌ
Needle n.	إِبْرَةٌ . مَسَلَّةٌ
Needless a.	لَا حَاجَةَ إِلَيْهِ
Needs ad.	لَا بُدَّ مِنْ
Needy a.	مُحْتَاجٌ . فَقِيرٌ
Nefarious a.	شَنِيعٌ . غَايَةٌ فِي ٱلشَّرِّ
Negation n.	نَفْيٌ . إِنْكَارٌ . سَلْبٌ

Negative a. or v. t.	نَافٍ . سَلْبِيٌّ . أَدْحَضَ . رَفَضَ
Neglect v. t. or n.	أهْمَلَ . تَغَافَلَ . إِهْمَالٌ
Neglectful / Negligent } a.	مُهْمِلٌ . مُتَغَافِلٌ
Negligence n.	إِهْمَالٌ . تَغَافُلٌ
Negotiate v. t.	تَاجَرَ . فَاوَضَ . قَاوَلَ
Negotiation n.	تَدْبِيرُ أمْرٍ . مُفَاوَضَةٌ
Negotiator n.	مُدَبِّرُ أمْرٍ أوْ مُعَاهَدَةٍ
Negro n.	زِنْجِيٌّ . عَبْدٌ . أسْوَدُ
Neigh v. t.	صَهَلَ . حَمْحَمَ
Neighbour n.	جَارٌ . قَرِيبٌ
Neighbouring a.	مُجَاوِرٌ
Neighbourhood n.	جِوَارٌ
Neither pro.	لَا . لَا أحَدَ (إِثْنَيْنِ)
Nephew n.	إِبْنُ أخٍ أوْ اخْتٍ
Nerve n. or v. t.	عَصَبٌ . قُوَّةٌ . قَوَّى
Nervous a.	عَصَبِيٌّ . سَرِيعُ ٱلتَّأَثُّرِ
Nest n.	عُشٌّ . وَكْرٌ
Nestle v. t.	اسْتَكَنَّ (فَرَّخَ) . آوَى

Net *n.* or *a.*	شَبَكَةٌ . شَرَكٌ . صَافٍ
Net *v. t.*	حَبَكَ ـُ . رِبحَ ـ رِبحاً خَالِصاً
Nether *a.*	أَسْفَلُ . جَحِيمِيّ
Netting *n.*	شَبَكَةٌ . شَبَكٌ
Nettle *n.* or *v. t.*	قُرَّاصٌ . قَرَصَ ـ . نَكَى
Neuralgia *n.*	وَجَعُ ٱلعَصَب
Neuter *n.*	لاَمُذَكَّرٌ ولاَمُؤَنَّثٌ . لاَزِمٌ
Neuter Neutral *a.* or *n.*	مُحَايِدٌ
Neutrality *n.*	حِيَادٌ . مُحَايَدَةٌ
Neutralize *v. t.*	أَبطَلَ فِعلَهُ
Never *ad.*	أَبَداً . قَطُّ (مَع نَفي)
Nevertheless *ad.*	مَعَ ذَلِكَ
New *a.*	جَدِيدٌ . حَدِيثٌ
Newness *n.*	جِدَّةٌ
News *n.*	أَخبَارٌ . حَوَادِثُ
Newspaper *n.*	جَرِيدَةٌ
Next *a.* or *ad.*	أَلتَّالِي . ٱلثَّانِي . قَادِمٌ . بَعدُ
Nib *n.*	رَأسٌ . طَرَفٌ
Nibble *v. t.*	قَرَضَ ـ . قَضِمَ ـ
Nice *a.*	لَذِيذٌ . حَسَنٌ . مُدَقَّقٌ
Nicety *a.*	دِقَّةٌ . رِقَّةٌ . تَأَنُّقٌ
Niche *n.*	مِشكَاةٌ
Nickel *n.*	مَعدِنٌ أَبيَض
Nickname *n.* or *v. t.*	مَقَبٌ . لَقَّب
Niece *n.*	بِنتُ أَخٍ أَو اختٍ
Niggard Niggardly *n.*	بَخِيلٌ . شَحِيحٌ
Nigh *a.* or *ad.*	قَرِيبٌ . قَرِيباً
Nighness *n.*	قُربٌ
Night *n.*	لَيلٌ ج لَيَال
Night-fall *n.*	عَشِيَّةٌ . غَسَقٌ
Nightingale *n.*	بُلبُل ج بَلاَبِل
Nightly *a.* or *ad.*	لَيلِيّ . كُلَّ لَيلَة
Nightmare *n.*	كَابُوسٌ . ضَاغُوطٌ
Nilometer *n.*	مِقيَاسٌ لِمَاءِ ٱلنِّيل
Nimble *a.*	خَفِيفٌ . حَرِكٌ . نَشِيطٌ
Nimbleness *n.*	خِفَّةٌ . نَشَاطٌ

17

Nine a.	تِسْعٌ . تِسْعَةٌ
Ninefold a.	تِسْعَةُ أَضْعَافٍ
Nineteen a.	تِسْعَةَ عَشَرَ . تِسْعُ عَشَرَةَ
Nineteenth a.	أَلتَّاسِعُ عَشَرَ
Ninetieth Ninety } a.	تِسْعُونَ
Ninth a.	أَلتَّاسِعُ . تِسْعٌ
Nip v. t. or n.	قَرَصَ ـُ قَرَسَ ـِ . قَرْص
Nippers n. pl.	مِلْقَطٌ صَغِيرٌ
Nipple n.	حَلَمَةٌ . بِزٌ
Nitre n.	مِلْحُ بَارُودٍ
No a. or ad.	لَا . لَيْسَ . كَلَّا
Nobility n.	شَرَفٌ . كَرَامَةٌ . الأَشْرَافُ
Noble a.	شَرِيفٌ . جَلِيلٌ . كَرِيمٌ
Nobleman n.	شَرِيفُ الأَصْلِ
Nobody n.	لَا أَحَدٌ . لَيْسَ أَحَدٌ
Nocturnal a.	لَيْلِيٌّ
Nod n. or v. t.	حَنِيَّةُ الرَّأْسِ . حَنَاهُ
Node n.	عُقْدَةٌ ج عُقَدٌ
Nodose Nodular } a.	ذُو عُقَدٍ
Noise n.	صَوْتٌ . ضَجَّةٌ . جَلَبَةٌ
Noiseless n.	بِلَا صَوْتٍ
Noisome a.	مُؤْذٍ . كَرِيهٌ . مُهْلِكٌ
Noisy a.	صَيَّاحٌ . صَوَّاتٌ
Nomad n. Nomadic a. }	بَدَوِيٌّ
Nomenclature n.	تَسْمِيَةٌ عِلْمِيَّةٌ
Nominal a.	إِسْمِيٌّ . بِالإِسْمِ فَقَطْ
Nominate v. t.	سَمَّى . عَيَّنَ
Nominative a.	فَاعِلٌ . مُبْتَدَا
Nominee n.	مُسَمًّى . مُعَيَّنٌ
Non-conductor n.	غَيْرُ مُوصِلٍ لِلْكَهْرَبَائِيَّةِ
None a.	لَا أَحَدٌ . لَيْسَ أَحَدٌ
Non-existence n.	عَدَمُ وُجُودٍ
Non-resident n.	غَيْرُ سَاكِنٍ مَحَلَّ مُعَيَّنٍ
Nonsense n.	هَذَيَانٌ . هَذْرٌ
Nonsensical a.	بِلَا مَعْنًى . هَذْرِيٌّ

Nook n.	زَاوِيَةٌ
Noon Noonday } n.	أَلظُّهْرُ . مُنْتَصَفُ ٱلنَّهَارِ
Noose n.	أُنْشُوطَةٌ . رِبْقَةٌ
Nor conj.	وَلاَ
Normal a.	قَانُونِيٌّ . طَبِيعِيٌّ
North n.	ٱلشِّمَالُ
North Northern } a.	شِمَالِيٌّ
Northward ad.	شِمَالاً
Nose n.	أَنْفٌ . مَنْخَرٌ
Nostril n.	مَنْخَرٌ
Not ad.	لاَ . مَا . لَيْسَ . لَمْ . لَنْ
Notable a.	شَهِيرٌ . وَجِيهَةٌ . عَجِيبٌ
Notary n.	مُسَجِّلُ ٱلصُّكُوكِ
Notation n.	تَرْتِيبُ ٱلأَرْقَامِ
Notch n. or v.t.	حَزَّةٌ . فَرْضٌ . فَرَّضَ
Note n. or v. t.	عَلاَمَةٌ . رُقْعَةٌ . كَتَبَ
Note-book n.	دَفْتَرُ تَذْكِرَةٍ
Noted a.	مُقَيَّدٌ . مَشْهُورٌ . شَائِعٌ
Noteworthy a.	مُسْتَحِقُّ ٱلذِّكْرِ
Nothing n.	لاَ شَيْءٌ
Nothingness n.	عَدَمٌ
Notice n.	إِعْلاَنٌ . إِلْتِفَاتٌ . تَنْبِيهٌ
Notice v. t.	لاَحَظَ . إِلْتَفَتَ إِلَى
Noticeable a.	مِمَّا يُلاَحَظُ . مِمَا يُذْكَرُ
Notification n.	تَنْبِيهٌ إِعْلاَنٌ إِخْطَارٌ
Notify v. t.	اخْبَرَ . أَعْلَنَ . أَعْلَمَ
Notion n.	فِكْرٌ . تَصَوُّرٌ . رَأْيٌ
Notional a.	وَهْمِيٌّ . خَيَالِيٌّ
Notoriety n.	شُهْرَةٌ . صِيتٌ رَدِيٌّ
Notorious a.	مَشْهُورٌ . سَيِّءُ ٱلصِّيتِ
Notwithstanding conj.	مَعْ أَنْ وَأَوْ
Nought n. see Naught.	
Noun n.	إِسْمٌ ج أَسْمَاءٌ
Nourish v. t.	قَاتَ ــُ . رَبَّى . غَذَى
Nourishment n.	قُوتٌ . غِذَاءٌ
Novel a. or n.	جَدِيدٌ . غَرِيبٌ . رِوَايَةٌ
Novelist n.	مُؤَلِّفُ ٱلرِّوَايَاتِ

Novelty n.	جِدَّةٌ . نَادِرَةٌ	Numb a. or v. t.	خَدَّرَ . خَدِرَ
November n.	تِشْرِينُ الثَّانِي (نُوفَمبِرْ)	Number n. or v. t.	عَدَدٌ . عِدَّةٌ . عَدَّ
Novice n.	مُبْتَدِئٌ . تِلْمِيذٌ جَدِيدٌ	Numberless a.	لَا يُعَدُّ أَوْ يُحْصَى
Novitiate n.	مُدَّةُ التَّلْمَذَةِ الإِبْتِدَائِيَّةِ	Numbers n.	سِفْرُ العَدَدِ (فِي التَّوْرَاةِ)
Now ad.	أَلآنَ . حَالاً	Numbness a.	خَدَرٌ
Nowadays ad.	فِي هَذِهِ الأَيَّامِ	Numeral n. or a.	عَدَدٌ . رَقْمٌ . عَدَدِيٌّ
Noway Nowise } n.	كَلاَّ . لاَ . أَلْبَتَّةَ	Numerate v. t.	عَدَّ . قَرَأَ الأَرْقَامَ
Nowhere ad.	غَيْرُ مَوْجُودٍ أَصْلاً	Numerator n.	صُورَةُ الكَسْرِ
Noxious a.	مُضِرٌّ . سَامٌّ . مُهْلِكٌ	Numeric Numerical } a.	عَدَدِيٌّ
Nozzle n.	أَنْفٌ . خُرْطُومٌ . طَرَفٌ	Numerous a.	كَثِيرٌ . عَدِيدٌ
Nucleus n.	(نَوَاةٌ) . مَرْكَزُ الجَوْهَرِ	Numismatics n.	عِلْمُ النُّقُودِ
Nudge v. t.	وَكَزَ بِالمَرْفِقِ	Numskull n.	بَلِيدٌ . أَبْلَهُ
Nudity n.	عَرَاءٌ . عُرْيٌ	Nun n.	رَاهِبَةٌ
Nugget n.	كُتْلَةٌ مِنْ تِبْرٍ . شَذْرَةٌ	Nuncio n.	قَاصِدُ البَابَا (نَائِبُهُ)
Nuisance n.	مَكْرَهَةٌ . مُكَدِّرٌ	Nunnery n.	دَيْرُ الرَّاهِبَاتِ
Null a.	بَاطِلٌ . سَاقِطٌ . غَيْرُ عَامِلٍ	Nuptial a.	زَوَاجِيٌّ . عُرْسِيٌّ
Nullify v. t.	أَبْطَلَ . أَلْغَى	Nuptials n.	عُرْسٌ
Nullity n.	بُطْلاَنٌ . سُقُوطٌ	Nurse n.	مُرْضِعٌ (ةٌ) مُمَرِّضَةٌ . مُرَبِّيَةٌ

Nurse *v. t.*	أَرْضَعَ . مَرَّضَ . رَبَّى
Nutmeg *n.*	جَوْزُ ٱلطِّيبِ،
Nursery *n.*	حُجْرَةُ ٱلْأَوْلَادِ.(مَشْتَلٌ)
Nutriment *n.*	غِذَآءٌ . قُوتٌ
Nursling *n.*	رَضِيعٌ
Nutrition *n.*	غِذَآءٌ . قُوتٌ . تَغْذِيَةٌ
Nurture *n.* or *v. t.*	تَرْبِيَةٌ . رَبَّى
Nutritious } *a.* Nutritive }	مُغَذٍّ
Nut *n.*	جَوْزَةٌ . بُنْدُقَةٌ
Nymph *n.*	إِلَاهَةُ ٱلْمَآءِ وَٱلْجِبَالِ

O

Oak *n.*	سِنْدِيَانٌ . بَلُّوطٌ
Obdurate *a.*	عَنِيدٌ. مُتَصَلِّبُ ٱلْقَلْبِ
Oaken *a.*	مِنْ سِنْدِيَانٍ
Obedience *n.*	طَاعَةٌ . إِذْعَانٌ
Oar *n.*	مِجْذَافٌ ج مَجَاذِيف
Obedient *a.*	مُطِيعٌ . خَاضِعٌ
Oarsman *n.*	جَذَّافٌ
Obeisance *n.*	سُجُودٌ . خُرُورٌ
Oasis *n.*	وَاحَةٌ ج وَاحَاتٌ
Obelisk *n.*	عَمُودٌ . مُرَبَّعٌ . مِسَلَّةٌ
Oats *n. pl.*	(شُوفَانٌ)
Obese *a.*	سَمِينٌ . شَحِيمٌ
Oath *n.*	قَسَمٌ . حَلَفٌ . يَمِينٌ
Obey *v. t.*	أَطَاعَ . خَضَعَ ـ لِ
Oatmeal *n.*	دَقِيقُ شُوفَانٍ
Obituary *n.*	تَرْجَمَةٌ مُخْتَصَرَةٌ لِمَيِّتٍ
Obduracy *n.*	عِنَادٌ . صَلَابَةُ ٱلْقَلْبِ

Object n.	شَيْءٌ . غَايَةٌ . مَرَامٌ . مَفْعُولٌ بِهِ
Object v. t.	إِعْتَرَضَ . قَاوَمَ
Objection n.	إِعْتِرَاضٌ . مَانِعٌ
Objectionable a.	غَيْرُ مَقْبُولٍ
Objective a.	خَارِجٌ عَنِ الْعَقْلِ
Objector n.	مُعْتَرِضٌ . مُقَاوِمٌ
Oblation n.	تَقْدِمَةٌ . قُرْبَانٌ
Obligation n.	فَرْضٌ . وُجُوبٌ . إِمْتِنَانٌ
Obligatory a.	مَفْرُوضٌ . وَاجِبٌ
Oblige v. t.	أَوْجَبَ . عَمِلَ مَعْرُوفًا
Obliged a.	مَمْنُونٌ . مُلْتَزِمٌ . شَاكِرٌ
Obliging a.	ذُو مَعْرُوفٍ . لَطِيفٌ
Oblique a.	مُنْحَرِفٌ . مَائِلٌ
Obliquity n.	إِنْحِرَافٌ . إِنْحِنَاءٌ
Obliterate v. t.	مَحَا . دَرَسَ بِـ
Oblivion n.	نِسْيَانٌ . عَفْوٌ
Oblivious a.	نَاسٍ . غَافِلٌ
Oblong a.	مُسْتَطِيلٌ

Obloquy n.	طَعْنٌ . لُؤْمٌ . ذَمٌّ
Obnoxious a.	مَكْرُوهٌ . مُعَرَّضٌ لِ
Obscene a.	قَبِيحٌ . فَاحِشٌ . مُفْسِدٌ
Obscenity n.	قَبَاحَةٌ . كَلَامٌ قَبِيحٌ
Obscure v. t. or a.	أَظْلَمَ . أَبْهَمَ . مُلْتَبِسٌ
Obscureness Obscurity } n.	ظُلْمَةٌ . غُمُوضٌ . إِلْتِبَاسٌ
Obsequies n. pl.	جِنَازَةٌ
Obsequious a.	خَاضِعٌ . ذَلِيلٌ
Observable a.	مِمَّا يُلَاحَظُ أَوْ يُرَاعَى
Observance n.	مُرَاعَاةٌ . حِفْظٌ . إِجْرَاءٌ
Observant a.	مُلَاحِظٌ . مُنْتَبِهٌ
Observation n.	مُلَاحَظَةٌ . مُرَاقَبَةٌ . رَصْدٌ
Observatory n.	مَرْصِدٌ فَلَكِيٌّ
Observe v. t.	لَاحَظَ . رَاعَى . رَصَدَ
Obsolete a.	غَيْرُ مُسْتَعْمَلٍ . مُهْمَلٌ
Obstacle n.	مَانِعٌ . عَائِقٌ
Obstetrics n.	عِلْمُ الْوِلَادَةِ وَالتَّوْلِيدِ

Obstinacy n. عِنَادٌ . إِصْرَارٌ . مُكَابَرَةٌ	Occupancy n. تَمَلُّكٌ . إِقَامَةٌ فِي
Obstinate a. عَنِيدٌ . مُصِرٌّ . مُكَابِرٌ	Occupant Occupier } n. سَاكِنٌ . مُتَمَتِّعٌ
Obstruct v. t. مَانَعَ . صَدَّ . عَاقَ	Occupation v. حِرْفَةٌ . إِحْتِلَالٌ . تَمَتُّعٌ
Obstruction n. مَانِعٌ . سَدٌّ . عَارِضٌ	Occupy v. t. حَلَّ فِي شَغَلَ . إِسْتَوْلَى
Obtain v. t. حَصَّلَ . نَالَ ـَ . أَدْرَكَ	Occur v. i. حَدَثَ . خَطَرَ بِالْبَالِ
Obtainable a. مُمْكِنٌ تَحْصِيلُهُ . يُنَالُ	Occurrence n. حَادِثَةٌ . حُدُوثٌ
Obtrude v. t. أَلَحَّ . تَدَاخَلَ . تَعَرَّضَ	Ocean n. الْبَحْرُ الْمُحِطُ . أُوقِيَانُوسٌ
Obtrusive a. فُضُولِيٌّ . مُتَدَاخِلٌ	Oceanic a. بَحْرِيٌّ
Obtuse a. كَلِيلٌ . بَلِيدٌ . مُنْفَرِجٌ	Oceanica n. جَزَائِرُ الْبَحْرِ الْمُحِيطِ
Obtuseness n. كَلٌّ . بَلَادَةٌ	Octagon n. شَكْلٌ مُثَمَّنٌ
Obverse n. وَجْهُ السِّكَّةِ أَوِ النُّقُودِ	Octagonal a. ذُو ثَمَانِي زَوَايَا
Obviate v. t. أَزَالَ . رَدَّ . نَجَّا مِنْ	Octangular a. مُثَمَّنُ الزَّوَايَا
Obvious a. ظَاهِرٌ . وَاضِحٌ	October n. تِشْرِينُ الأَوَّلُ (أُكْتُوبِر)
Occasion n. فُرْصَةٌ . سَبَبٌ . حَاجَةٌ . مَرَّةٌ	Octogenarian n. إِبْنُ ثَمَانِينَ سَنَةً
Occasional a. إِتِّفَاقِيٌّ . حَادِثٌ أَحْيَانًا	Ocular a. بَصَرِيٌّ . عَيَانِيٌّ
Occident n. الْغَرْبُ . الأَقْطَارُ الْغَرْبِيَّةُ	Oculist n. طَبِيبُ الْعُيُونِ
Occidental a. غَرْبِيٌّ . مَغْرِبِيٌّ	Odd a. فَرْدٌ . غَرِيبٌ . زَائِدٌ
Occult n. سِرِّيٌّ . مَكْتُومٌ	Oddity Oddness } n. غَرَابَةٌ . شُذُوذٌ

Ode n.	قَصِيدَةٌ . نَشِيدٌ
Odious a.	مَمْقُوتٌ . كَرِيهٌ . قَبِيحٌ
Odium n.	مَقْتٌ . كُرْهٌ . كَرَاهِيَةٌ
Odorous a.	ذَكِيُّ ٱلرَّائِحَةِ
Odour n.	رَائِحَةٌ
Of prep.	مِنْ . عَنْ . عَلَامَةُ ٱلْإِضَافَةِ
Off ad.	بَعِيدًا . عَلَى بُعْدٍ
Offal n.	سَقَطُ الذَّبِيحِ . زُبَالَةٌ
Offence / Offense } n.	إِغَاظَةٌ . غَيْظٌ . تَعَدٍّ
Offend v. t.	اغَاظَ . كَدَّرَ . اخْطَأَ
Offender n.	مُذْنِبٌ . مُكَدِّرٌ . خَاطِئٌ
Offensive a.	مُغِيظٌ . كَرِيهٌ . مُعْتَدٍ
Offer v. t. or i.	قَدَّمَ . أَهْدَى . عَرَضَ
Offer n.	إِهْدَاءٌ . عَرْضٌ . تَقْدِمَةٌ
Offering n.	ذَبِيحَةٌ . تَقْدِمَةٌ
Office n.	مَنْصِبٌ . خِدْمَةٌ . مَكْتَبٌ
Officer n.	مَأْمُورٌ . ضَابِطٌ
Official a. or n.	رَسْمِيٌّ . مَأْمُورٌ
Officiate v. i.	قَامَ بِخِدْمَةٍ أَوْ وَظِيفَةٍ
Officious a.	مُتَكَلِّفٌ . فُضُولِيٌّ
Officiousness n.	فُضُولٌ . تَعَرُّضٌ
Offscouring n.	سُقَاطَةٌ . نُفَايَةٌ . نَجَاسَةٌ
Offset v. t. or n.	وَازَنَ . بَادَلَ . بَدَلٌ
Offshoot n.	فَرْعٌ . عُسْلُجٌ
Offspring n.	ذُرِّيَّةٌ . نَسْلٌ
Oft / Often } ad.	كَثِيرًا مَا . مِرَارًا
Ogle v. t.	غَمَزَ ـِ عِشْقًا
Oh inter.	آهِ . اوَّاه
Oh that !	يَا لَيْتَ
Oil n. or v. t.	زَيْتٌ . دُهْنٌ . زَيَّتَ
Oil-cloth n.	مُشَمَّعٌ
Oily a.	دُهْنٌ . زَيْتِيٌّ
Ointment n.	دِهْنٌ . مَرْهَمٌ
Old a.	طَاعِنٌ فِي ٱلسِّنِّ . شَيْخٌ . عَتِيقٌ . قَدِيمٌ
Olden a.	قَدِيمٌ
Oleander n.	دَفْلَى . دِفْلٌ

Olive n.	زَيْتُونَةٌ	Oneness n.	وِحْدَانِيَّةٌ
Omelet n.	عِجَّةٌ	Onerous a.	ثَقِيلٌ . شَاقٌّ
Omen n.	فَأْلٌ . طِيَرَةٌ . عَلَامَةٌ	Onion n.	بَصَلَةٌ
Ominous a.	مُنْذِرٌ بِالسُّوءِ	Only a.	وَحِيدٌ . وَحْدَهُ . لَا غَيْرُ
Omission n.	إِهْمَالٌ . تَرْكٌ . إِسْقَاطٌ	Onset Onslaught } n.	هُجُومٌ . حَمْلَةٌ . بَطْشٌ
Omit v. t.	تَرَكَ ـُ . أَهْمَلَ . أَسْقَطَ	Onward Onwards } ad.	إِلَى قُدَّامٍ . تَقَدُّمًا
Omnibus n.	عَجَلَةٌ كَبِيرَةٌ	Onyx n.	جَزْعٌ (حَجَرٌ كَرِيمٌ)
Omnipotence n.	أَلْقُدْرَةُ عَلَى كُلِّ شَيْءٍ	Ooze v. i.	رَشَحَ ـَ . نَضَّ ـَ
Omnipotent a.	اَلْقَادِرُ عَلَى كُلِّ شَيْءٍ	Opaque a.	مُظْلِمٌ . غَيْرُ شَفَّافٍ
Omnipresence n.	أَلْحُضُورُ فِي كُلِّ مَكَانٍ	Open v. t. or i. or a.	فَتَحَ ـَ . إِنْفَتَحَ . مَفْتُوحٌ
Omnipresent a.	اَلْحَاضِرُ فِي كُلِّ مَكَانٍ	Opening n.	فَتْحَةٌ . شَقٌّ . بَابٌ
Omniscience n.	أَلْعِلْمُ بِكُلِّ شَيْءٍ	Openly ad.	عَلَانِيَةً . جِهَارًا
Omniscient a.	اَلْعَالِمُ بِكُلِّ شَيْءٍ	Openness n.	خُلُوصٌ . مُجَاهَرَةٌ
Omnivorous a.	آكِلٌ مِنْ كُلِّ شَيْءٍ	Opera n.	رِوَايَةٌ مُوسِيقِيَّةٌ
On pr. or ad.	عَلَى . عِنْدَ . إِلَى قُدَّامٍ	Operate v. i. or t.	جَرَى ـَ . أَثَّرَ . عَمِلَ ـَ
Once ad.	مَرَّةً . قَبْلاً . وَقْتًا مَّا	Operation n.	عَمَلٌ إِجْرَاءٌ . عَمَلِيَّةٌ
One a. or n.	وَاحِدَةٌ (ة) . أَحَدٌ . ذَاتٌ	Operative a.	عَامِلٌ . مُؤَثِّرٌ . عَمَلِيٌّ
One-eyed a.	أَعْوَرُ		

Operator n.	عَامِلٌ . جَرَّاحٌ
Ophthalmic a.	عَيْنِيٌّ
Ophthalmia n.	إِلْتِهَابُ ٱلْعَيْنِ . رَمَدٌ
Opiate n.	دَوَاءٌ أَفْيُونِيٌّ . مُنَوِّمٌ
Opinion n.	رَأْيٌ . ظَنٌّ . إِعْتِقَادٌ
Opinionated / Opinionative } a.	عَنِيدُ ٱلرَّأْي
Opium n.	أَفْيُونٌ
Opponent n.	خَصْمٌ . مُقَاوِمٌ
Opportune a.	فِي مَحَلِّهِ أَوْ حِينِهِ
Opportunity n.	فُرْصَةٌ
Oppose v. t.	ضَادَّ . عَارَضَ . مَانَعَ
Opposite a.	مُقَابِلٌ . حِذَاءَ . مُضَادٌّ
Opposition n.	مُضَادَّةٌ . مُعَارَضَةٌ
Oppress v. t.	ظَلَمَ ـ . بَغَى ـ . ضَايَقَ
Oppression n.	ظُلْمٌ . جَوْرٌ
Oppressive a. / Oppressor n. }	ظَالِمٌ . مُضَايِقٌ . بَاغٍ
Opprobrious a.	مَعِيبٌ . مُحَقِّرٌ . مُخْزٍ
Opprobrium n.	عَارٌ . عَيْبٌ . خِزْيٌ
Optic / Optical } a.	بَصَرِيٌّ . مُخْتَصٌّ بِعِلْمِ ٱلنُّور
Optician n.	صَانِعُ آلَاتٍ بَصَرِيَّةٍ
Optics n.	عِلْمُ ٱلنُّورِ وَٱلْبَصَر
Optimism n.	اَلتَّفَاؤُلُ بِٱلْخَيْرِ
Option n.	خِيَارٌ
Optional a.	إِخْتِبَارِيٌّ
Opulence n.	ثَرْوَةٌ . يَسَرٌ
Opulent a.	غَنِيٌّ . مُوسِرٌ
Or conj.	أَوْ . أَمْ
Oracle n.	وَحْيٌ . رَأْيٌ حَكِيمٌ
Oracular a.	مُتَكَلِّمٌ بِسُلْطَةٍ
Oral a.	شَفَاهِيٌّ . لَفْظِيٌّ
Orange n.	بُرْتُقَالٌ
Orang-outang n.	قِرْدٌ يُشْبِهُ ٱلْإِنْسَانَ
Oration n.	خُطْبَةٌ
Orator n.	خَطِيبٌ
Oratorical n.	خِطَابِيٌّ . بَلِيغٌ
Oratory n.	عِلْمُ ٱلْخِطَابَةِ . مُصَلًّى

Orb *n.*	كُرَةٌ
Orbit *n.*	مَدَارُ كَوْكَبٍ . تَجْوِيفُ الْعَيْنِ
Orchard *n.*	بُسْتَانٌ . حَدِيقَةٌ
Orchestra *n.*	جَمَاعَةُ عَازِفِينَ وَمَوْقِفُهُمْ
Ordain *v. t.*	أَقَامَ . أَمَرَ . رَسَمَ
Ordeal *n.*	إِمْتِحَانٌ شَدِيدٌ . مِحْنَةٌ
Order *v. t.*	أَمَرَ . رَتَّبَ . دَبَّرَ
Order *n.*	أَمْرٌ . تَرْتِيبٌ . رُتْبَةٌ
Orderly *a.* (مُرَاسَلَةٌ)	مُرَتَّبٌ . مُنْتَظِمٌ
Ordinance *n.*	سُنَّةٌ . فَرْضٌ . حُكْمٌ
Ordinarily *ad.*	إِعْتِيَادِيًّا . غَالِبًا
Ordinary *a.*	إِعْتِيَادِيٌّ . مَأْلُوفٌ
Ordination *n.*	إِقَامَةٌ . تَعْيِينٌ . رَسْمٌ
Ordnance *n.*	مَدَافِعُ وَمُتَعَلِّقَاتُهَا
Ore *n.*	خَلِيطٌ يُسْتَخْرَجُ ٱلْمَعْدِنُ مِنْهُ
Organ *n.* (أَرْغُنْ)	عُضْوٌ . وَاسِطَةٌ
Organic *a.*	عُضْوِيٌّ . آلِيٌّ . أَسَاسِيٌّ
Organism *n.*	بِنَاءٌ . آلِيٌّ
Organist *n.*	عَازِفٌ عَلَى ٱلْأَرْغُنِ
Organization *n.*	نِظَامٌ . تَرْتِيبٌ
Organize *v. t.*	نَظَّمَ . رَتَّبَ . جَهَّزَ
Orgies *n. pl.*	بَطَرٌ مُفْرِطٌ . سُكْرٌ
Orient *n.*	ٱلشَّرْقُ ٱلْأَقْطَارُ ٱلشَّرْقِيَّةُ
Oriental *a.* or *n.*	شَرْقِيٌّ . شَرْقِيُّ ٱلْأَوْطَانِ
Orientalism *n.*	إِصْطِلَاحٌ شَرْقِيٌّ
Orientalist *n.*	عَالِمٌ بِلُغَاتِ ٱلشَّرْقِ
Orifice *n.*	مَنْفَذٌ . فَتْحَةٌ
Origin *n.*	أَصْلٌ . مَبْدَأٌ . مَصْدَرٌ
Original *a.*	أَصْلِيٌّ . أَوَّلِيٌّ . غَرِيبٌ
Original *n.*	أَصْلٌ . صُورَةٌ أَصْلِيَّةٌ
Originality *n.*	أَصْلِيَّةٌ . إِبْدَاعٌ . ذَكَاءٌ
Originate *v. t.* or *i.*	أَبْدَعَ . أَوْجَدَ . نَشَأَ
Originator *n.*	مُبْدِعٌ . مُخْتَرِعٌ . مُبْتَكِرٌ
Orion *n.*	ٱلْجَبَّارُ . ٱلْجَوْزَاءُ
Ornament *n.*	زِينَةٌ . زَخْرَفَةٌ
Ornament *v. t.*	زَيَّنَ . زَخْرَفَ

Ornamental a.	زِينِيٌّ . مُزَيِّنٌ
Ornate a.	مُزَخْرَفٌ . مُزَوَّقٌ
Ornitho-logy n.	عِلْمٌ يُبْحَثُ فِيهِ عَنِ الطُّيُورِ
Orphan n.	يَتِيمٌ ج أَيْتَامٌ . يَتَامَى
Orphanage n.	دَارُ الْيَتَامَى
Orthodox a.	قَوِيمُ الْمَذْهَبِ (ارثوذكس)
Orthodoxy n.	صِحَّةُ الْمَذْهَبِ
Orthography n.	عِلْمُ التَّهْجِئَة
Oscillate v. i.	ذَبْذَبَ . إِرْتَجَحَ . خَطَرَ
Oscillation n.	ذَبْذَبَةٌ . إِرْتِجَاجٌ
Osseous a.	عَظْمِيٌّ
Ossify v. t. or i.	حَوَّلَهُ أَوْ تَحَوَّلَ عَظْمًا
Ostensible a.	ظَاهِرٌ . مُدَّعًى
Ostentation n.	تَفَاخُرٌ . مُبَاهَاةٌ
Ostentatious a.	مُتَفَاخِرٌ . مُتَبَاهٍ
Osteology n.	عِلْمُ الْعِظَامِ
Ostracise v. t.	نَفَى . طَارَدَ
Ostrich n.	نَعَامَةٌ

Other a.	آخَرُ . ذَاكَ
Otherwise ad.	وَإِلَّا . خِلَافًا لِذَلِكَ
Ottar n.	عِطْرٌ
Otter n.	كَلْبُ الْمَاءِ
Ottoman n.	عُثْمَانِيٌّ
Ought v. i.	وَجَبَ . لَزِمَ
Ounce n.	اوقِيَّةٌ انكليزيَّةٌ أَوْ طِبِّيَّةٌ
Our Ours } pro.	لَنَا . نَا
Ourselves pro. pl.	نَحْنُ . انْفُسُنَا
Oust v. t.	طَرَدَ . أَخْرَجَ
Out ad.	خَارِجًا
Outbid v. t.	زَايَدَ
Outbreak Outburst } n.	ثَوْرَةٌ . إِنْفِجَارٌ
Outcast n.	مَطْرُودٌ . مَنْفِيٌّ
Outcry n.	صِيَاحٌ . صُرَاخٌ
Outdo v. t.	فَاقَ . سَبَقَ
Outdoor a. Outdoors adv. }	خَارِجَ الْبَيْتِ
Outer a.	خَارِجِيٌّ

Outermost *a.*	ألأَبْعَدُ عَنِ ٱلمَرْكَزِ
Outfit *n.*	جَهَازٌ . لَوَازِمٌ
Outgrow *v. t.*	سَبَقَ نُمُوًّا . زَادَ عَلَى
Outhouse *n.*	بَيْتٌ خَارِجَ ٱلدَّارِ
Outlandish *a.*	غَرِيبٌ . بَرْبَرِيٌّ
Outlaw *n.*	فَاقِدُ ٱلحُقُوقِ ٱلشَّرْعِيَّةِ
Outlay *n.*	نَفَقَةٌ . مَصْرُوفٌ
Outlet *n.*	مَخْرَجٌ . مَنْفَذٌ . مَصَبٌّ
Outline *n.* or *v. t.*	رَسْمٌ مُخْتَصَرٌ . رَسَمَ —
Outlive *v. t.*	عَاشَ بَعْدَهُ
Outlook *n.*	مَنْظَرٌ . مُرَاقَبَةٌ
Outlying *a.*	بَعِيدٌ عَنِ ٱلمَرْكَزِ . خَارِجِيٌّ
Outmost *a.*	ألأَبْعَدُ عَنِ ٱلمَرْكَزِ
Outpost *n.*	مَرْكَزُ حَرَسٍ خَارِجِيٍّ
Outrage *v. t.*	فَضَحَ — . أَسَاءَ إِلَى
Outrage *n.*	فَظِيعَةٌ . إِهَانَةٌ . بَغْيٌ
Outrageous *a.*	فَظِيعٌ . مُفْرِطُ ٱلبَغْيِ
Outrider *n.*	فَارِسٌ . تَابِعٌ
Outright *ad.*	حَالاً . تَمَامًا
Outrun *v. t.*	سَبَقَ رَكْضًا
Outset *n.*	بَدَاءَةٌ . مَطْلَعٌ
Outside *n.*	أَلخَارِجُ ظَاهِرُهُ
Outskirt *n.*	ظَاهِرُ بَلَدٍ . ضَاحِيَةٌ
Outspread *v. t.*	بَسَطَ — . مَدَّ —
Outstanding *a.*	بَارِزٌ . غَيْرُ مَدْفُوعٍ
Outstrip *v. t.*	سَبَقَ —
Outward *a.* or *ad.*	خَارِجِيٌّ . ظَاهِرٌ . إِلَى خَارِجٍ
Outweigh *v. t.*	رَجَحَ — . زَادَ وَزْنًا .
Outwit *v. t.*	فَاقَ حِيلَةً
Outwork *n.*	اسْتِحْكَامٌ . خَارِجِيٌّ
Oval Ovate *a.*	بَيْضِيُّ ٱلأَشْكَالِ . اهَالَجِيٌّ
Ovary *n.*	مَبِيضٌ فِي ٱلنَّبَاتِ وَٱلحَيَوَانِ
Ovation *n.*	مَوْكِبٌ . إِكْرَامِيٌّ
Oven *n.*	فُرْنٌ . تَنُّورٌ
Over *pr.* or *ad.*	فَوْقُ . عَلَى . زِيَادَةً
Overbalance *v. t.*	رَجَحَ — . فَاقَ وَزْنًا

Overbearing a.	مُتَجَبِّرٌ . غَطَارِيسٌ
Overboard ad.	مِنَ السَّفِينَةِ . فِي الْبَحْرِ
Overcautious a.	زَائِدُ الْحَذَرِ
Overcharge v. t.	أَفْرَطَ فِي الثَّمَنِ أَوِ الْحِمْلِ
Overcoat n.	جُبَّةٌ فَوْقَانِيَّةٌ
Overcome v. t.	غَلَبَ ـِ . قَهَرَ ـَ
Overdo v. t.	أَفْرَطَ فِي الْعَمَلِ
Overdose n.	جُرْعَةٌ مُفْرِطَةٌ
Over-due a. (دين)	فَاتَتِ الِاسْتِحْقَاقِ
Overestimate v. t.	أَفْرَطَ فِي التَّقْدِيرِ
Overflow v.t. or n.	فَاضَ ـِ . فَيَضَانٌ
Over-grown a.	كَثِيرُ النَّبَاتِ . مُفْرِطُ النُّمُوِّ
Overhang v. t.	أَشْرَفَ عَلَى . بَرَزَ ـُ
Overhead ad.	فَوْقَ الرَّأْسِ
Overhear v. t.	سَمِعَ اتِّفَاقًا
Overland a.	بِالْبَرِّ (سَفَرٌ)
Overlay v. t.	غَشَّى ب
Overload v. t.	ثَقَّلَ الْحِمْلَ
Overlook v. t.	أَشْرَفَ عَلَى . أَهْمَلَ . عَفَا ـُ
Overmatch n.	أَقْدَرُ مِنْ
Overmuch a.	زَائِدٌ . مُفْرِطٌ
Overnight ad.	مُدَّةَ اللَّيْلِ الْمَاضِي
Overpay v. t.	أَوْفَى فَوْقَ الْحَقِّ
Overplus n.	فَضْلَةٌ . بَقِيَّةٌ . زِيَادَةٌ
Overpower v.t.	قَوِيَ عَلَى . قَهَرَ ـَ
Overrate v. t.	أَفْرَطَ فِي التَّثْمِينِ
Overreach v.t.	غَبَنَ ـِ جَاوَزَ
Overrule v. t.	أَبْطَلَ تَأْثِيرَهُ أَوْ حَوَّلَهُ
Overruling a.	مُتَسَلِّطٌ . ضَابِطٌ
Overrun v. t.	أَفْرَطَ . غَطَّى . غَزَا ـُ
Oversee v. t.	نَاظَرَ
Overseer n.	نَاظِرٌ . وَكِيلٌ
Overshoe n.	جُرْمُوقٌ (كَالُوش)
Oversight n.	إِهْمَالٌ . سَهْوٌ . مُنَاظَرَةٌ
Oversleep v. t.	تَأَخَّرَ فِي النَّوْمِ
Overspread v. t.	إِنْتَشَرَ عَلَى . غَطَّى

Overstep v. t.	جَاوَزَ . تَجَاوَزَ
Overt a.	ظَاهِرٌ . شَائِعٌ
Overtake v. t.	لَحِقَ ـَ . أَدْرَكَ . أَلَمَّ بِ
Overtask } Overtax } v. t.	كَلَّفَ فَوْقَ ٱلطَّاقَةِ
Overtax v. t.	أَفْرَطَ فِي ٱلضَّرِيبَةِ
Overthrow v. t.	قَلَبَ ـِ . هَزَمَ . هَدَمَ ـِ
Overtly ad.	ظَاهِرًا . جِهَارًا
Overtop v. t.	عَلَا ـُ . فَاقَ ـُ
Overture n.	عَرْضٌ . مُفَاوَضَةٌ . فَاتِحَةٌ
Overturn v. t.	قَلَبَ ـِ . نَكَّسَ
Overweening a.	مُعْجَبٌ بِنَفْسِهِ . مُزْهٍ
Overwhelm v. t.	غَمَرَ ـُ . قَهَرَ ـَ
Overwork v. t.	شَغَّلَ فَوْقَ ٱلطَّاقَةِ
Oviparous a.	بَائِضٌ . بَيُوضٌ
Ovum n.	بَيْضَةٌ . بِزْرَةٌ . جُرْثُومَةٌ
Owe v. t.	كَانَ مَدْيُونًا . عَلَيْهِ دَيْنٌ
Owing a.	مَدْيُونٌ . مَطْلُوبٌ . نَاشِئٌ عَنْ
Owl n.	بُومَةٌ ج بُومٌ
Own a. or v. t.	خَاصَّتُهُ . مَلَكَ ـِ . أَقَرَّ بِ
Owner n.	صَاحِبٌ . مَالِكٌ . رَبٌّ
Ownership n.	مِلْكٌ
Ox (pl. Oxen).	ثَوْرٌ
Oxalis n.	حُمَّاضٌ (نَبَاتٌ)
Oyster n.	نَوْعٌ مِنَ ٱلصَّدَفِ . مَحَارَةٌ

P

Pace n. or v. t.	خُطْوَةٌ . خَطَا . مَشَى ـِ
Pacer n.	رَهْوَانٌ (فَرَسٌ)
Pacific a. or n.	مُسَالِمٌ سِلْمِيٌّ . ٱلْبَحْرُ ٱلْمُحِيطُ
Pacify v. t.	سَالَمَ . هَدَّأَ

Pack v. t.	رَزَمَ ُ. حَزَمَ ُ. كَبَسَ ِ
Pack Package } n.	رِزمَةٌ . حُزمَةٌ . فَردَةٌ
Packet n.	حُزمَةٌ . سَفِينَةٌ سَرِيعَةٌ
Pack-horse n.	فَرَسٌ لِلحَملِ . كَدِيشٌ
Pack-saddle n.	جَلٌ (جَلَالٌ)
Pad n. or v. t.	وَسَادَةٌ . حَشَا . بَطَنَ
Paddle v. i. or n.	جَذَفَ . مِجذَافٌ
Padlock n.	قُفلٌ ج أَقفَالٌ
Pagan n.	وَثَنِيٌّ
Paganism n.	عِبَادَةُ الأَوثَانِ
Page n.	صَفحَةٌ . غُلَامٌ
Page v. t.	رَقَمَ الأَعدَادَ عَلَى الصَفحَاتِ
Pageant Pageantry } n.	مَوكِبٌ . إِحتِفَالٌ بِبَهَاءٍ
Pail n.	دَلوٌ . سَطلٌ
Pain n. or v. t.	وَجَعٌ . أَلَمٌ . أَوجَعَ
Painful a.	مُوجِعٌ . مُؤلِمٌ . مُكَدِّرٌ
Painless a.	بِلَا أَلَمٍ
Pains n.	إِعتِنَاءٌ . إِهتِمَامٌ . دِقَةٌ

Paint n. or v. t.	دِهَانٌ . دَهَنَ ُ . صَوَّرَ
Painter n.	دَهَّانٌ . مُصَوِّرٌ
Painting n.	دَهنٌ . تَصوِيرٌ . صُورَةٌ
Pair n. or v. t. or i.	زَوجٌ . زَاوَجَ . تَزَاوَجَ
Palace n.	قَصرٌ . بِلَاطُ المَلِكِ
Palanquin n.	تَختَرَوَانٌ
Palatable a.	مَقبُولٌ لِلذَّوقِ . لَذِيذٌ
Palate n.	حَنَكٌ . سَقفُ الحَلقِ
Palatial a.	جَلِيلٌ . عَظِيمٌ . قَصرِيٌّ
Pale a. or v. i.	مُصفَرٌّ . بَاهِتٌ . إِصفَرَّ
Paleness n.	إِصفِرَارٌ . بَهتُ اللَّونِ
Paleography n.	خَطُّ القُدَمَاءِ وَعِلمُهُ
Paleonto- logy n.	عِ مُ المُتَحَجِّرَاتِ الآلِيَّةِ
Palisade n.	سِيَاجٌ مِن أَوتَادٍ لِلدِّفَاعِ
Pall n.	غِطَاءُ النَّعشِ . رِدَاءٌ
Pallet n.	فِرَاشٌ حَقِيرٌ . لَوحُ مُصَوِّرٍ
Palliate v. t.	سَتَرَ أَو خَفَّفَ بِعُذرٍ
Palliative n.	مُسَكِّنُ وَجَعٍ

Pallid *a.*	مُصْفَرٌّ	Panel *n.*	لَوْحٌ . (حَشْوَة بَابٍ)
Palm *n.*	نَخْلٌ . رَاحَةُ ٱلْيَدِ	Pang *n.*	أَلَمٌ وَقْتِيٌّ شَدِيدٌ . مَخَاضٌ
Palm-Sunday *n.*	أَحَدُ ٱلشَّعَانِينِ	Panic *n.*	رَوْعٌ فَجَائِيٌّ بَاطِلٌ
Palpable *a.*	مَا يُلْمَسُ . وَاضِحٌ	Pannier *n.*	قُفَّةٌ . زِبِّيلٌ أَوْ زَنْبِيلٌ
Palpitate *v. i.*	خَفَقَ ُ	Panoply *n.*	دِرْعٌ كَامِلَةٌ
Palpitation *n.*	خَفَقَانٌ	Panorama *n.*	مَنْظَرٌ . شَامِلٌ
Palsied *a.*	مَفْلُوجٌ	Pant *v. i.*	نَهَجَ َ لَهِثَ َ
Palsy *n.*	فَالِجٌ	Pantalets Pantaloons *n.*	سَرَاوِيلُ سِرْوَالٌ
Paltry *n.*	حَقِيرٌ . خَسِيسٌ	Pantheism *n.*	مَذْهَبُ أُلُوهِيَّةِ ٱلْكَوْنِ
Pamper *v. t.*	أَشْبَعَ . فَتَقَ	Pantheist *n.*	مُعْتَقِدٌ بِأُلُوهِيَّةِ ٱلْكَوْنِ
Pamphlet *n.*	كُرَّاسَةٌ . رِسَالَةٌ	Panther *n.*	نَمِرٌ نَمِرٌ وَنَمُورَةٌ
Pan *n.*	طَاجَنٌ . لَكَنٌّ	Pantomime *n.*	تَشْخِيصٌ بِٱلْإِشَارَاتِ
Panacea *n.*	عِلَاجٌ لِكُلِّ دَاءٍ	Pantry *n.*	بَيْتُ ٱلْمُونَةِ
Pancreas *n.*	بَنْكَرْيَاسٌ	Papa *n.*	أَبٌّ . بَابَا
Pandemonium *n.*	مَجْمَعُ ٱلشَّيَاطِينِ	Papacy *n.*	ٱلْبَابَوِيَّةُ (مَذْهَبٌ)
Pander *v. i.*	صَدَمَ شَهَوَاتِ غَيْرِهِ	Papal *a.*	بَابَوِيٌّ
Pane *n.*	لَوْحٌ . زُجَاجٌ	Paper *n.* or *a.*	وَرَقٌ . جَرِيدَةٌ . مِنْ وَرَقٍ
Panegyric *n.*	مَدِيحٌ . تَبْجِيلٌ	Papist *n.*	بَابَوِيٌّ تَابِعُ ٱلْبَابَا

18

Papyrus *n.*	قَصَبٌ آ أَبَرْدِيّ . قِرْطَاسُهُ
Par *n.*	مُسَاوَاة . مُعَادَلَةُ آلقِيمَةِ
Parable *n.*	مَثَلٌ ج أَمْثَالٌ
Parabola *n.*	قَطْعٌ مَخْرُوطِيٌّ . شَلْجَمِيٌّ
Parade *n.* or *v. t.*	مَوْكِبٌ . إِحْتَفَلَ
Paradise *n.*	فِرْدَوْس . جَنَّة
Paradox *n.*	تَنَاقُضٌ بِٱلظَّاهِرِ فَقَطْ
Paragraph *n.*	فَقَرَة . فَصْلٌ . جُمْلَة
Parallel *n.* or *a.*	مُوَازَاة . مُشَابَهَة . مُوَازٍ
Parallelogram *n.*	مُرَبَّعٌ مُسْتَطِيلٌ
Paralysis *n.*	فَالِجٌ . شَلَل
Paralytic *a.*	مَفْلُوجٌ . أَشَلُّ
Paralyze *v. t.*	أَشَلَّ
Paramount *a.*	رَئِيسِيّ . ٱلأَعْظَمُ . فَائِقٌ
Paramour *n.*	عَاشِقٌ أَوْ عَاشِقَة
Parapet *n.*	مِتْرَاسٌ . سُورٌ
Paraphrase *n.* or *v.t.*	تَأْوِيل . فَسَّرَ
Parasite *n.*	نَبَات أَوْ حَيَوَان طُفَيْلِيٌّ

Parasol *n.*	شَمْسِيَّة صَغِيرَة
Parcel *n.* or *v. t.*	حُزْمَة . رَبْطَة . قِسْمٌ ــ قَسَّمَ
Parch *v. t.* or *i.*	جَفَّفَ . لَفَحَ ــ تَجَفَّفَ
Parchment *n.*	رِقٌّ مِنْ جِلْدٍ
Pardon *n.* or *v. t.*	عَفْوٌ . غُفْرَان . عَفَا ــ
Pardonable *n.*	مِمَّا يُغْفَرُ لَهُ . يُصْفَحُ عَنْهُ
Pare *v. t.*	قَشَّرَ ــ . جَلَفَ ــ . نَقَصَ
Parent *n.*	وَالِدٌ (ة) . مَنْشَأٌ
Parentage *n.*	أَصْلٌ . نَسَبٌ
Parental *a.*	وَالِدِيٌّ
Parenthesis *n.*	هِلَالَانِ وَجُمْلَة بَيْنَهُمَا
Parenthetical *a.*	مُعْتَرِضٌ
Paring *n.*	قِشْرَة . قُصَاصَة
Parish *n.*	أَبْرَشِيَّة
Parity *n.*	مُسَاوَاة . مُعَادَلَة . مُشَابَهَة
Park *n.*	مُنْتَزَه . غَابَة
Parley *n.* or *v. i.*	مُفَاوَضَة . إِئْتَمَرَ
Parliament *n.*	مَجْلِسُ آلنُوَّاب

Parliamentary a.	مَنُوطٌ بِالْبَارْلَمَنْتِ
Parlour n.	غُرْفَةُ الإِسْتِقْبَالِ
Parole n.	كَلَامُ شَرَفٍ . عَهْدٌ
Paroxysm n.	نَوْبَةُ مَرَضٍ . دَوْرٌ
Parricide n.	قَتْلُ آلِوَالِدَيْنِ أَوْقَاتِلُهُمَا
Parrot n.	بَبْغَاءُ
Parry v. t.	دَفَعَ ــ . جَانَبَ . إِجْتَنَبَ
Parse v. t.	أَعْرَبَ
Parsimonious n.	قَتُورٌ . شَحِيحٌ
Parsimony n.	قَتْرٌ . إِقْتِصَادٌ زَائِدٌ
Parsley n.	بَقْدُونِسٌ
Parsnip n.	جَزَرٌ أَبْيَضُ
Parson n.	قِسِّيسٌ . خُورِيٌّ
Parsonage n.	بَيْتُ القِسِّيسِ
Part n.	قِسْمٌ . حِصَّةٌ . جَانِبٌ
Part v. t. or i.	فَصَلَ ــِ . قَاسَمَ . إِفْتَرَقَ
Partake v. t.	إِشْتَرَكَ . تَنَاوَلَ
Partial a.	جِزْبِيٌّ . مُحَابٍ

Partially ad.	جُزْئِيًّا . بِمُحَابَاةٍ
Participant n.	مُشْتَرَكٌ . مُتَنَاوِلٌ
Participate v. t.	إِشْتَرَكَ . أَخَذَ حِصَّةً
Participation n.	إِشْتِرَاكٌ . إِتِّخَاذٌ
Participle n.	إِسْمُ فَاعِلٍ أَوْ مَفْعُولٍ
Particle n.	ذَرَّةٌ . دَقِيقَةٌ . حَرْفٌ
Particular a.	خَاصٌّ . مُدَقِّقٌ
Particular n.	مَادَّةٌ . خَاصَّةٌ . تَفَاصِيلُ
Particularity n.	خَاصِّيَّةٌ . دِقَّةٌ . تَفْصِيلٌ
Particularize v. t.	خَصَّصَ . فَصَّلَ . دَقَّقَ
Parting n.	إِفْتِرَاقٌ . وَدَاعٌ
Partisan n.	حَلِيفٌ . مُتَحَزِّبٌ
Partition n.	تَقْسِيمٌ . قِسْمَةٌ . حَاجِزٌ
Partly ad.	بَعْضًا . جُزْئِيًّا
Partner n.	شَرِيكٌ . رَفِيقٌ
Partnership n.	شِرْكَةٌ
Partridge n.	حَجَلٌ
Party n.	حِزْبٌ . جَمَاعَةٌ . فَرِيقٌ

Paschal *a.*	خاصٌّ بعيدِ ٱلْفِصْحِ
Pashalic *n.*	وِلَايَةُ بَاشا
Pass *n.*	مَمَرٌّ . تَذْكِرَةٌ . حَال
Pass *v. t.* or *i.*	إِجْتَازَ . عَبَرَ . عَبَّرَ . مَرَّ . مَرَّب
Passable *a.*	مِمَّا يُمَرُّ عَلَيْهِ . جَائِزٌ
Passage *n.*	مَمَرٌّ . مُرُورٌ . جُمْلَة
Passenger *n.*	مُسَافِرٌ . رَاكِبٌ
Passing *a.*	مَارٌّ . وَقْتِيٌّ . زَائِل
Passion *n.*	اِنْفِعَالٌ شَدِيدٌ . هَوًى
Passionate *a.*	سَرِيعُ ٱلْغَضَبِ . مُحْتَدٌّ
Passive *a.*	قَابِلِ تَأْثِيرٍ سَا . كِنْ . ٱلْمَجْهُول
Passover *n.*	عِيدُ ٱلْفِصْحِ
Passport *n.*	تَذْكِرَةُ ٱلْمُرُور
Past *pr.* or *a.* or *n.*	وَرَآءَ . عِبْرَ . مَاضٍ
Paste *n.* or *v. t.*	عَصِيدَةٌ . لَازِقَةٌ . أَلْزَقَ
Pasteboard *n.*	وَرَقٌ سَمِيكٌ . كَرْتُون
Pastime *n.*	لَعِبٌ . أَهْوٌ
Pastor *n.*	رَاعٍ . قِسِّيسٌ

Pastoral *a.*	رَعَوِيٌّ . قِسِّيسٌ
Pastry *n.*	كَعْكٌ . فَطَائِرُ
Pasturage Pasture } *n.*	مَرْعًى . مَرْتَع
Pat *v. t.* or *n.*	لَطَمَ خَفِيفًا وَلُطْفًا
Pat *a.*	فِي مَحَلِّه . غَايَةِ ٱلْمُوَافَقَة
Patch *n.* or *v. t.*	رُقْعَة . رَقَّعَ . رَفَأَ
Pate *n.*	رَأْس . هَامَة
Patent *n.* or *v. t.*	اِمْتِيَازٌ . أَعْطَى ٱمْتِيَازًا
Patent *a.*	وَاضِحٌ . جَلِيٌّ . جِهَارِيٌّ
Paternal *a.*	أَبَوِيٌّ . إِرْثِيٌّ
Paternity *n.*	أُبُوَّةٌ
Path *n.*	سَبِيل . صِرَاطٌ . سُلُوك
Pathetic *a.*	مُؤَثِّرٌ فِي ٱلْعَوَاطِف
Pathless *a.*	مَا لَا يُسْلَك . لَا طَرِيقَ فِيه
Pathology *n.*	عِلْمُ ٱلْأَمْرَاض
Pathos *n.*	مَا يُهَيِّجُ ٱلْعَوَاطِف
Pathway *n.*	مَسْلَك . طَرِيقٌ . مَمَرٌّ
Patience *n.*	صَبْرٌ . أَنَاة

Patient *a.* or *n.*	صَبُورٌ . مَرِيضٌ	Pause *n.* or *v.i.*	وَقَفَ . فَتْرَةٌ . وَقْفٌ
Patois *n.*	لَغْوٌ . لَهْجَةٌ غَيْرُ فَصِيحَةٍ	Pave *v. t.*	بَلَّطَ . رَصَفَ ـ . سَهَّلَ
Patriarch *n.*	رَئِيسُ ٱلآبَاءِ . بَطْرَكٌ	Pavement *n.*	بَلَاطٌ . رَصْفٌ . تَبْلِيطٌ
Patriarchate *a.*	بَطْرَكِيّةٌ	Pavillion *n.*	خَيْمَةٌ . مِظَلَّةٌ
Patrician *n.* or *a.*	نَجِيبٌ . شَرِيفٌ	Paw *n.* or *v. i.*	كَفُّ ٱلْحَيَوَانِ .بَحَثَ بِهِ
Patrimony *n.*	مِيرَاثٌ	Pawn *n.* or *v. t.*	رَهِينَةٌ . رَهَنَ ـ
Patriot *n.* Patriotic *a.*	مُحِبُّ ٱلْوَطَنِ	Pawnbroker *n.*	مُرْتَهِنٌ . مُسْتَرْهِنٌ
Patriotism *n.*	مَحَبَّةُ ٱلْوَطَنِ	Pay *n.* or *v. i.*	أُجْرَةٌ . أَوْفَى .ادَّى
Patrol *n.* or *v. i.*	عَسَسٌ . دَوْرِيَّةٌ . عَسَّ ـ	Payable *a.*	مُسْتَحِقٌّ . مَا يُوْفَى
Patron *n.*	وَلِيٌّ . مُحَامٍ . نَصِيرٌ	Paymaster *n.*	مُؤَدِّي ٱلاجْرَةِ
Patronage *n.*	مُوَالَاةٌ . مُحَامَاةٌ	Payment *n.*	إِيفَاءٌ . دَفْعٌ . قِسْطٌ
Patronize *v. t.*	وَالَى. عَضَّدَ ـ . أَيَّدَ	Pea *n.*	جُلُّبَانٌ . بَسَلَّةٌ
Pattern *n.* or *v. t.*	اَنْمُوذَجٌ. مِثَالٌ.تَمَثَّلَ	Peace *n.*	سَلَامٌ .صُلْحٌ . رَاحَةٌ
Paucity *n.*	قِلَّةٌ	Peaceable *a.*	مُسَالِمٌ . مُطْمَئِنٌّ
Paunch *n.*	بَطْنٌ . جَوْفٌ	Peaceful *a.*	سِلْمِيّ . سَاكِنٌ
Pauper *n.*	فَقِيرٌ. عَائِشٌ مِنْ صَدَقَاتٍ	Peacemaker *n.*	مُصَالِحٌ .صَانِعُ سَلَامٍ
Pauperism *n.*	فَقْرٌ . مَسْكَنَةٌ	Peach *n.*	دُرَاقِنٌ . (دُرَّاق . خَوْخ)
Pauperize *v. t.*	اَفْقَرَ	Peacock *n.*	طَاوُوسٌ ج طَوَاوِيسُ

Peak *n.*	قُمَّةٌ .رَأْسُ جَبَلٍ	Pedestrian *n.*	مَاشٍ
Peal *n.* or *v. i.*	صَوْت قَوِيٌّ. صَوَّتَ	Pedigree *n.*	نَسَبٌ
Pear *n.*	إِنْجَاصٌ. إِجَّاصٌ. كُمَّثْرَى	Peel *v. t.* or *n.*	قَشَرَ .جَرَّدَ. قِشْرَةٌ
Pearl *n.*	لُؤْلُؤَةٌ . دُرَّةٌ	Peep *v. i.* or *n.*	لَاصَ .سَارَقَ نَظَرَهُ .نَظْرَةٌ
Peasant *n.*	فَلاحٌ	Peer *n.*	نَظِيرٌ. شَرِيفٌ .قَرِينٌ
Peasantry *n.*	الْفَلَّاحُونَ	Peerage *n.*	رُتْبَةُ الشَّرَفَاءِ. جَمَاعَتُهُمْ
Pebble *n.*	حَصَاةٌ ج حَصَيَاتٌ وَحَصَى	Peerless *a.*	فَائِقٌ . لَا نَظِيرَ لَهُ
Peck *n.*	مِكْيَالٌ يَسَعُ نَحْوَ مُدٍّ	Peevish *a.*	نَكِدٌ
Pectoral *a.*	صَدْرِيٌّ	Peg *n.* or *v. t.*	وَتَدٌ .مِسْمَارٌ خَشَبِيٌّ. سَمَّرَهُ
Peculation *n.*	سَرْقَةٌ .إِخْتِلَاسٌ	Pelican *n.*	بَجَعٌ (طَائِرٌ)
Peculiar *a.*	خَاصٌّ . نَادِرٌ	Pelf *n.*	رِبْحٌ . مَالٌ. (خَاصَّةً) حَرَامٌ
Peculiarity *n.*	خَاصِّيَّةٌ .غَرَابَةٌ	Pellet *n.*	كُرَيَّةٌ .حَبَّةٌ
Pecuniary *a.*	مَالِيٌّ.مَنُوطٌ بِالدَّرَاهِمِ	Pell-mell *ad.*	شَذَرَ مَذَرَ
Pedagogue *n.*	مُعَلِّمُ أَوْلَادٍ	Pelt *v. t.*	رَمَى – .رَجَمَ –
Pedant *n.* Pedantic *a.*	مُتَظَاهِرٌ بِالْعِلْمِ	Peltry *n.*	جُنُودٌ
Peddle *v. t.*	دَارَ يَبِيعُ	Pen *n.* or *v. t.*	قَلَمٌ . زَرِيبَةٌ .كَتَبَ –
Peddler *n.*	عنقَاشٌ .بَيَّاعٌ	Penal *a.*	قِصَاصِيٌّ .جَزَائِيٌّ . عِقَابِيٌّ
Pedestal *n.*	قَاعِدَةُ عَمُودٍ	Penalty *n.*	قِصَاصٌ . عِقَابٌ

Penance *n.*	كَفَّارَة. عُقُوبَة. تَكْفِيرِيَّة
Pencil *n.* or *v. t.*	قَلَم . رَسَم بِهِ
Pendant *n.*	شَيْءٌ مُعَلَّقٌ . قُرْطٌ
Pendent *a.*	مُعَلَّقٌ . مُتَدَلٍّ
Pending *a.*	مُعَلَّقٌ . غَيْرُ مَقْضِيٍّ
Pendulum *n.*	رَقَّاصُ سَاعَةٍ
Penetrate *v. t.*	خَرَقَ ـِ . تَخَلَّلَ . أَدْرَكَ
Penetration *n.*	دُخُولٌ. فِطْنَةٌ. ذَكَاءٌ
Penetrating *a.*	نَافِذ. حَادٌّ . ذَكِيٌّ
Peninsula *n.*	شِبْهُ جَزِيرَةٍ
Peninsular *a.*	عَلَى صُورَةِ شِبْهُ جَزِيرَةٍ
Penitence *n.*	تَوْبَة. إِنْسِحَاقُ القَلْبِ
Penitent *a.*	تَائِبٌ. نَادِمٌ
Pentientiary *n.*	سِجْنٌ
Penknife *n.*	سِكِّينٌ صَغِيرٌ . (مَطْوًى)
Penman *n.*	عَالِمٌ بِالخَطِّ . كَاتِبٌ
Penmanship *n.*	صِنَاعَةُ الخَطِّ
Pennant / Pennon *n.*	رَايَةٌ . بَيْرَقٌ صَغِيرٌ
Penniless *a.*	فَقِيرٌ . مُفْلِسٌ
Penny *n.* (*pl.* pence)	نُقُودٌ أَنْكِلِيزِيَّةٌ =٢. بَارَةً
Pension *n.*	رَاتِبٌ . مَعَاشٌ تَقَاعُد
Pensioner *n.*	صَاحِبُ رَاتِبِ التَّقَاعُد
Pensive *n.*	مُتَفَكِّرٌ . مَشْغُولُ البَال
Pent-up *a.*	مَحْصُورٌ . مَحْجُوزٌ
Pentagon *n.* / Pentagonal *a.*	مُخَمَّسُ الزَّوَايَا
Pentateuch *n.*	اسْفَارُ مُوسَى الخَمْسَة
Pentecost *n.*	يَوْمُ الخَمْسِينَ. العَنْصَرَة
Penult *n.*	مَقْطَعُ الكَلِمَة قَبْلَ الاخِير
Penurious *n.*	بَخِيلٌ
Penury *a.*	فَقْرٌ . فَاقَة . عَوَزٌ
People *n.* or *v. t.*	شَعْبٌ. أَهْل. أَنَاس. عَمَّرَ
Pepper *n.* or *v. t.*	فُلْفُلٌ . فَلْفَلَ
Peppermint *n.*	ضَرْبٌ مِنَ النَّعْنَع
Peradventure *ad.*	لَعَلَّ . عَسَى
Perambulate *v. t.*	دَارَ ـ . طَافَ ـ
Perceivable *a.*	مَا يُرَى . مَا يُدْرَك

Perceive v. t. رَأَى ۔ شَعَرَ ۔ أَدْرَكَ	Perforate v. t. ثَقَبَ ۔ ۔ خَرَقَ ۔ ۔
Percent ad. بِالْمِئَة	Perforation n. ثَقْبٌ ۔ خَرْقٌ
Percentage n. نِسْبَةٌ فِي ٱلْمِئَة	Perforce ad. رَغْمًا ۔ جَبْرًا
Perceptible a. see Perceivable.	Perform v. t. عَمِلَ ۔ أَنْجَزَ ۔ أَجْرَى
Perception n. شُعُورٌ ۔ إِدْرَاكٌ	Performance n. عَمَلٌ ۔ إِنْجَازٌ
Perch v. t. جَثَمَ ۔	Performer n. عَامِلٌ ۔ مُشَخِّصٌ
Perchance ad. لَعَلَّ ۔ رُبَّمَا	Perfume n. or v. t. عَطَّرَ ۔ عَطَرَ
Percipient a. مُدْرِك ۔ شَاعِرٌ	Perfumery n. عِطْرٌ
Percolate v. i. or t. رَشَحَ ۔ ۔ صَفَّى	Perhaps ad. رُبَّمَا ۔ عَسَى ۔ لَعَلَّ
Percolation n. رَشْحٌ ۔ تَصْفِيَة	Pericardium n. شَغَافٌ ۔ غِلَافُ ٱلْقَلْبِ
Percussion n. طَرْقٌ ۔ صَدْمٌ ۔ قَرْعٌ	Peril n. or v. t. خَطَرٌ ۔ خَاطَرَ بِ
Perdition n. تَلَفٌ ۔ هَلَاكٌ	Perilous a. خَطِرٌ ۔ مُخْطِرٌ
Peremptory a. جَازِمٌ ۔ قَطْعِيٌّ	Period n. مُدَّة ۔ عَصْرٌ ۔ دَوْرٌ
Perennial a. مُسْتَمِرٌّ طُولَ ٱلسَّنَة	Periodic Periodical } a. دَوْرِيٌّ
Perfect a. تَامٌّ ۔ كَامِلٌ	Periodical n. نَشْرَة ۔ جَرِيدَة
Perfect v. t. كَمَّلَ ۔ أَنْجَزَ ۔ أَنْفَذَ	Periosteum n. سِمْحَاقٌ ۔ غِشَاءُ ٱلْعَظْمِ
Perfection n. كَمَالٌ ۔ سَلَامَة	Perish v. i. هَلَكَ ۔ ۔ بَادَ ۔ فَنِيَ ۔
Perfidious n. غَدَّارٌ ۔ خَوَّان	Perishable a. سَرِيعُ ٱلزَّوَالِ أَوِ ٱلْفَسَادِ
Perfidy n. غَدْرٌ ۔ خِيَانَة ۔ خِدَاعٌ	

Perjure v. t.	حَنَثَ ـ في . حَلَفَ ـ زُوراً
Perjury n.	حِنْثُ . يَمِينُ زُورٍ
Permanence ‹ n. Permanency	دَوَامٌ . بَقَاءٌ
Permanent a.	بَاقٍ . ثَابِتٌ . مُسْتَمِرٌّ
Permeable a.	مَا يَتَخَلَّلُ . مَا يَنْفُذُ فِيهِ
Permeate v. t.	تَخَلَّلَ . نَفَذَ ـ في
Permissible a.	مُبَاحٌ . جَائِزٌ
Permission n.	إِذْنٌ . رُخْصَةٌ
Permit v. t.	أَذِنَ ـ . سَمَحَ ـ
Pernicious a.	مُؤْذٍ . مُهْلِكٌ . مُفْسِدٌ
Perpendicular a.	عَمُودِيٌّ . قَائِمٌ
Perpetrate v. t.	فَعَلَ ـَ . ارْتَكَبَ
Perpetrator n.	فَاعِلٌ . مُرْتَكِبٌ
Perpetual a.	دَائِمٌ . مُسْتَمِرٌّ . مُؤَبَّدٌ
Perpetuate v. t.	أَدَامَ . خَلَّدَ
Perpetuity n.	دَوَامٌ . بَقَاءٌ
Perplex v. t.	بَهَتَ ـ . حَيَّرَ . شَوَّشَ
Perplexing a.	مُحَيِّرٌ . مُشَوِّشٌ . مُشْكِلٌ

Perplexity n.	حَيْرَةٌ . إِرْتِبَاكٌ
Perquisite n.	رَاتِبٌ إِضَافِيٌّ . عَرَضِيٌّ
Persecute v. t.	إِضْطَهَدَ . عَنَّتَ . ظَلَمَ ـِ
Persecution n.	إِضْطِهَادٌ . تَعَدٍّ
Persecutor n.	مُضْطَهِدٌ
Perseverance n.	مُوَاظَبَةٌ . مُدَاوَمَةٌ
Persevere v. t.	وَاظَبَ . دَاوَمَ . لَازَمَ
Persian a.	عَجَمِيٌّ . فَارِسِيٌّ
Persist v. i.	أَصَرَّ عَلَى . ثَابَرَ عَلَى
Persistence ‹ n. Persistency	إِصْرَارٌ . مُثَابَرَةٌ
Persistent ‹ a. Persisting	مُصِرٌّ . مُثَابِرٌ
Person n.	شَخْصٌ . أَلذَّاتُ . أُقْنُومٌ
Personal a.	شَخْصِيٌّ . ذَاتِيٌّ
Personate ‹ v. t. Personify	شَخَّصَ . مَثَّلَ
Personification n.	تَشْخِيصٌ
Perspicacity n.	ذَكَاءٌ . بَصِيرَةٌ
Perspicuous n.	جَلِيٌّ . وَاضِحٌ
Perspiration n.	عَرَقٌ . رَشِيحٌ

Perspire *v. i.*	عَرِقَ . رَشَحَ ـ
Persuade *v. t.*	أَقْنَعَ . حَمَلَ عَلَى
Persuasion *n.*	إِرْضَاءٌ . إِقْنَاعٌ . إِعْتِقَادٌ
Persuasive *a.*	مُقْنِضٌ . مُسْتَمِيلٌ
Pert *a.*	وَقِحٌ . سَلِيطٌ
Pertain *v. i.*	إِخْتَصَّ بِ
Pertinacious *a.*	مُصِرٌّ . عَنِيدٌ
Pertinacity *n.*	إِصْرَارٌ . عِنَادٌ
Pertinence Pertinency } *n.*	مُوَافَقَةٌ . مُلَاءَمَةٌ
Pertinent *a.*	سَدِيدٌ . مُنَاسِبٌ
Perturbation *n.*	قَلَقٌ . إِقْلَاقٌ
Perusal *n.*	قِرَاءَةٌ . مُطَالَعَةٌ
Peruse *v. t.*	قَرَأَ ـَ . طَالَعَ
Pervade *v. t.*	شَمِلَ ـُ . عَمَّ ـُ . تَخَلَّلَ
Pervasion *n.*	تَخَلُّلٌ . شُمُولٌ
Perverse *a.*	مُتَمَرِّدٌ . شَكِسٌ
Perversion *n.*	إِضْلَالٌ . إِفْسَادٌ . تَحْرِيفٌ
Perversity *n.*	عِنَادٌ . شَكَاسَةٌ

Pervert *v. t.*	أَضَلَّ . حَرَّفَ . أَفْسَدَ
Pest *a.*	وَبَآءٌ . ضَرَرٌ شَدِيدٌ
Pester *v. t.*	أَقْلَقَ . أَضْجَرَ . ازْعَجَ
Pest house *n.*	مُسْتَشْفًى لِأَمْرَاضٍ مُعْدِيَةٍ
Pestiferous Pestilential } *a.*	وَبَائِيٌّ مُضِرٌّ . مُفْسِدٌ
Pestilence *n.*	وَبَآءٌ
Pestilent *a.*	مُضِرٌّ . مُفْسِدٌ
Pestle *n.*	مِدَقَّةٌ . مِطْرَقَةٌ
Pet *n.* or *v. t.*	عَزِيزٌ . مُدَلَّلٌ . دَلَّلَ
Petal *n.*	وَرَقَةُ زَهْرَةٍ
Petiole *n.*	سَاقُ وَرَقَةٍ
Petition *n.*	طَلَبٌ . دُعَاءٌ . عَرِيضَةٌ
Petition *v. t.*	طَلَبَ ـُ . قَدَّمَ عَرِيضَةً
Petrifaction *n.*	تَحَجُّرٌ . مُحَجَّرَةٌ
Petrify *v. t.* or *i.*	حَجَّرَ . تَحَجَّرَ
Petroleum *n.*	زَيْتٌ مَعْدَنِيٌّ . بِتْرُولٌ
Petticoat *n.*	فُسْتَانٌ تَحْتِيٌّ . تَنُّورَةٌ
Pettish *a.*	نَكِدٌ . شَكِسٌ

Petty a.	صَغِيرٌ . طَفِيفٌ . دَنِيٌّ	Phenomenon n.	ظَاهِرَةٌ . حَادِثَةٌ
Petulance n.	نَكَدٌ . شَرَاسَةٌ	Phial n.	قَارُورَةٌ . (قِنِّينَةٌ)
Petulant a.	نَكِدٌ . شَرِسٌ . مُتَذَمِّرٌ	Philanthropist n.	مُحِبُّ ٱلْبَشَرِ
Pew n.	مَقْعَدٌ فِي كَنِيسَةٍ	Philanthropy n.	مَحَبَّةُ ٱلْبَشَرِ
Pewter n.	مُرَكَّبُ ٱلْقَصْدِيرِ وَٱلرَّصَاصِ	Philippic n.	خُطْبَةُ طَعْنٍ
Phalanx n.	كَتِيبَةٌ . كَثِيفَةٌ مُرَبَّعَةٌ	Philology n.	عِلْمُ ٱللُّغَةِ
Phantasm n.	تَصَوُّرٌ . خَيَالٌ	Philosopher n.	فَيْلَسُوفٌ
Phantom n.	طَيْفٌ . خَيَالٌ	Philosophic Philosophical } a.	فَلْسَفِيٌّ
Pharaoh n.	فِرْعَوْنٌ	Philsophy n.	فَلْسَفَةٌ
Pharissee n.	فَرِّيسِيٌّ	Phlegm n.	بَلْغَمٌ
Pharisaic a.	مِثْلُ ٱلْفَرِّيسِيِّ . مُرَاءٍ	Phlegmatic a.	بَلْغَمِيٌّ . بَارِدٌ
Pharisaism n.	رِيَاءٌ . مَذْهَبُ ٱلْفَرِّيسِيِّ	Phonetic a.	صَوْتِيٌّ
Pharmaceutic Pharmaceutical } a.	صَيْدَلِيٌّ أَجْزَائِيٌّ	Phosphorescent a.	مُضِيءٌ بِضَوْءٍ خَفِيفٍ
Pharmacist n.	صَيْدَلِيٌّ	Phosphorus n.	فَصْفُور
Pharmacopœia n.	ٱلْأَقْرَابَاذِين	Photograph n.	صُورَةٌ شَمْسِيَّةٌ
Pharmacy n.	أَجْزَائِيَّةٌ . صَيْدَلِيَّةٌ	Photography n.	ٱلتَّصْوِيرُ ٱلشَّمْسِيُّ
Pharos n.	مَنَارَةٌ	Phrase n.	عِبَارَةٌ . جُمْلَةٌ
Pharynx n.	بُلْعُومٌ	Phraseology n.	صُورَةُ ٱلْكَلَامِ
Phase n.	مَنْظَرٌ . صُورَةٌ . حَالٌ		

Phthisis *n.*	دَاءُ السَّلِّ	Piece *n.*	قِطْعَةٌ . جِزْءٌ
Physic *n.*	أَلطِّبُّ. دَوَاءٌ	Piecemeal *ad.*	قِطْعَةً فَقِطْعَةً
Physical *n.*	طَبِيعِيٌّ	Pier *n.*	دِعَامَةُ رَصِيفٍ مُمْتَدٌّ فِي ٱلْبَحْرِ
Physician *n.*	طَبِيبٌ	Pierce *v. t.*	خَرَقَ — . ثَقَبَ — . طَعَنَ
Physics *n.*	عِلْمُ ٱلطَّبِيعِيَّاتِ	Piercing *a.*	خَارِقٌ . حَادٌّ
Physiognomy *n.*	هَيْئَةُ ٱلْوَجْهِ	Piety *n.*	تَقْوَى . تَدَيُّنٌ
Physiology *n.*	عِلْمُ ٱلْفِسْيُولُوجِيَا	Pig *n.*	خِنَّوْصٌ. خِنْزِيرٌ صَغِيرٌ
Piazza *n.*	رُوَاقٌ . سَاحَةٌ	Pigeon *n.*	حَمَامَةٌ . يَمَامَةٌ
Pick *v. t.*	قَطَّ — . إِنْتَخَب	Pigmy *n.*	قَزَمُ ٱلْجِنْسِ
Pick Pick-axe } *n.*	مِعْوَل	Pike *n.*	رُمْحٌ . حَرْبَةٌ
Picket *n.*	وَتَدٌ . طَلِيعَةُ حَرَسٍ	Pile *n. or v. t.*	كُومَةٌ . وَتَدٌ. كَوَّمَ
Pickle *v. t.* or *n.*	كَبَسَ فِي خَلٍّ . كَبِيسٌ	Piles *n. pl.*	بَوَاسِيرُ
Picnic *n.*	تَنَزُّهٌ	Pilfer *v. t.*	سَرَقَ أَشْيَاءَ طَفِيفَةً
Pickpocket *n.*	لِصٌّ. نَشَّالٌ	Pilgrim *n.*	حَاجٌّ . زَائِرٌ
Pictorial *a.*	تَصَوُّرِيٌّ. صُورِيٌّ	Pilgrimage *n.*	حَجٌّ
Picture *n.*	صُورَةٌ	Pill *n.*	حَبَّةٌ (لِلْعِلَاجِ)
Picturesque *a.*	جَمِيلُ ٱلْمَنْظَرِ	Pillage *n. or v. t.*	نَهْبٌ سَلْبٌ نَهَبَ
Pie *n.*	نَوْعٌ مِنَ ٱلْحَلْوَى مَحْشُوٌّ	Pillar *n.*	عَمُودٌ. اسْطُوَانَةٌ

Pillow n.	مِخَدَّةٌ . وِسَادَةٌ	Pistil n.	مِدَقَّةُ ٱلزَّهْرِ
Pilot n. or v.t.	دَلِيلُ سَفِينَةٍ . هَدَى	Pistol n.	فَرْدٌ . طَبَنْجَة
Pimple n.	بَثْرَةٌ صَغِيرَةٌ	Pit n.	حُفْرَةٌ . هَاوِيَةٌ . نُقْرَةٌ
Pin n. or v. t.	دَبُّوسٌ . ضَبَطَ بِهِ	Pitch n.	قِيرٌ . دَرَجَةُ ٱلصَّوْتِ
Pinch v. t. or n.	قَبَضَ ــ قَرَصَ ــ ضَيَّقَ عَلَى	Pitch v. t.	طَلَى بِٱلْقِيرِ . رَمَى . وَقَّعَ
Pincers Pinchers n.	مَلْقَطٌ . كَمَّاشَةٌ	Pitch v. i. or t.	حَطَّ ــ نَزَلَ . ضَرَبَ
Pincushion n.	وِسَادَةٌ لِلدَّبَابِيسِ	Pitcher n.	إِبْرِيقٌ . كُوزٌ
Pine n. or v. t.	صَنَوْبَرٌ . نَحَلَ ــ . تَاقَ ــ	Pitfall n.	حُفْرَةُ صَيْدٍ . اغْوِيَّةٌ
Pink n. or a.	قَرَنْفُلٌ وَرْدِيُّ ٱللَّوْنِ	Pith n.	أُبٌّ . زُبْدَةٌ . خُلَاصَةٌ
Pinnacle n.	قِمَّةٌ . شُرْفَةٌ	Pithy a.	سَدِيدٌ
Pint n.	مِكْيَالٌ يَسَعُ نَحْوُ ٢٠٠ دِرْهَمٍ	Pitiable a.	مَا يُرْثَى لَهُ
Pioneer n.	مُمَهِّدُ ٱلطَّرِيقِ . مُتَقَدِّمٌ	Pitiful a.	شَفُوقٌ . زَهِيدٌ . حَقِيرٌ
Pious a.	تَقِيٌّ . مُتَدَيِّنٌ	Pitiless a.	بِلَا شَفَقَةٍ . صَارِمٌ
Pipe n.	قَسْطَلٌ . مِزْمَارٌ . قَصَبَةٌ	Pittance n.	مَبْلَغٌ زَهِيدٌ . صَدَقَةٌ زَهِيدَةٌ
Piper n.	زَمَّارٌ	Pity n. or v. t.	شَفَقَةٌ . أَشْفَقَ عَلَى
Pique n. or v.t.	غَيْظٌ . ضَجَرٌ . هَاجَ	Pivot n.	مِحْوَرٌ . مَدَارٌ
Pirates n.	لُصُوصُ ٱلْبَحْرِ . قُرْصَان	Placard n.	إِعْلَانٌ
Pistachio n.	فُسْتُقٌ	Placate v. t.	طَيَّبَ ٱلنَّفْسَ . سَكَّنَ غَيْظَهُ

Place n. or v. t.	مكَان . مَوْضِعٌ . وَضَعَ –
Placid a.	هَادِىءُ . سَاكِنٌ
Plagiarize v. i.	تَنَحَّلَ . إِنْتَحَلَ
Plague n.	طَاعونٌ . وَبَآءٌ . بَلِيَّة
Plague v. t.	أَزْعَجَ . عَنَى . كَدَّرَ
Plain n.	سَهْلٌ . مِهَادٌ
Plain a.	سَهْلٌ . وَاضِحٌ . بسيطٌ
Plainly ad.	جليا . بِإِخْلَاصٍ بِبَسَاطَةٍ
Plainness n.	وُضوحٌ . بَسَاطة . بَيَان
Plaint n.	شَكْوَى . حَنِينٌ
Plaintiff n.	مُدَّعٍ شَرْعِيٌّ
Plaintive a.	مُحْزِنٌ . حَزِينٌ
Plait v. t. or n.	ضَفَرَ – . ثَنَى – . ضَفِيرَة
Plan n.	تَدْبِيرٌ . قَصْدٌ . رَسْمٌ
Plan v. t.	دَبَّرَ . رَسَمَ — هَنَّا
Plane a. or n.	مُسَطَّحٌ . مِسْطَحٌ .(فَارَة) نَجَّارٍ
Planet n.	سَيَّارٌ (نَجْمَة)
Planetary a.	سَيَّارِيٌّ
Plank n.	لَوْحٌ سَمِيكٌ
Plant n. or v. t.	نَبْتٌ . غَرَسَ –
Plantation n.	مَنْبِت . مَزْرَعَة
Plaster n. or v. t.	طِينٌ . أَزْقَة . طَيَّنَ
Plastering n.	تَكْلِيسٌ . وَرَقَة
Plate n.	صَحْنٌ . آنِيَة فِضِّيَّة أَوْ ذَهَبِيَّة
Plate v. t.	قَلَّسَ بِمَعْدِنٍ
Plateau n.	سَهْل مُرْتَفَع . هَضَبَة
Platform n.	مِنْبَرٌ . سَطْحٌ مُرْتَفَع
Platter n.	قَصْعَة ج قِصَاعٌ
Plaudit n.	إِسْتِحْسَان . مَدْحٌ
Plausible a.	مُرْضٍ . مِمَّا يُصَدَّق
Play v. t.	لَعِبَ – . شَخَّصَ . عَزَفَ –
Play n.	لَعِبٌ . تَسْلِيَة
Playful a.	لَعُوبٌ . دَعِبٌ
Playfellow Playmate } n.	رَفِيقٌ فِي اللِّعْب
Plaything n.	لُعْبَة . العُوبة
Plea n.	حُجَّة . إِعْتِذَارٌ . دُعَاءٌ

Plead *v. i.*	إِحْتَجَّ . إِبْتَهَلَ . رَافَعَ
Pleasant Pleasing *a.*	سَارَّ . طَيِّبٌ . اَنِيسٌ
Pleasantry *n.*	مَزْحٌ . هَزْلٌ
Please *v. t.*	سَرَّ . أَرْضَى . أَعْجَبَ
Pleasure *n.*	سُرُورٌ . لَذَّةٌ . إِنْشِرَاحٌ
Plebeian *a.* or *n.*	عَامِّيٌّ . أَحَدُ الْعَوَامّ
Pledge *v. t.*	رَهَنَ . تَعَهَّدَ . عَرْبَنَ
Pledge *n.*	رَهْنٌ . عَهْدٌ . ضَمَانٌ
Plenary *a.*	تَامٌّ . كَامِلٌ . عَام
Plenipotentiary *n.*	سَفِيرٌ . مُطْلَقٌ
Plenteous Plentiful *a.*	وَافِرٌ . غَزِيرٌ . كَثِيرٌ
Plenty *n.*	وَفْرٌ . كَثْرَةٌ . غَزَارَةٌ
Pleurisy *n.*	دَاءُ ذَاتِ الْجَنْبِ
Pliable Pliant *a.*	لَيِّنٌ . مُدْعِنٌ
Plight *n.* or *v. t.*	عَهْدٌ . حَالٌ . عَهَدَ
Plod *v. t.*	سَعَى بِمَشَقَّةٍ . كَدَّ
Plot *n.*	مَكِيدَةٌ . مُؤَامَرَةٌ . بُقْعَة
Plot *v. t.* or *i.*	رَسَمَ . دَبَّرَ . إِحْتَالَ
Plow Plough *n.* or *v. t.*	مِحْرَاثٌ . حَرَثَ
Plowshare Ploughshare *n.*	سِكَّةُ مِحْرَاثٍ
Pluck *v. t.* or *n.*	قَلَعَ . قَطَفَ . شَجَاعَةٌ
Plug *n.* or *v. t.*	سِدَادٌ . سَدَّ
Plum *n.*	خَوْخٌ . خَوْخَةٌ (بَرْقُوق)
Plumage *n.*	رِيشٌ
Plume *n.*	رِيشَةٌ . وِسَامُ شَرَفٍ
Plummet *n.*	مِقْيَاسُ الْعُمْقِ . شَاقُولٌ
Plump *a.* or *ad.*	سَمِينٌ . مُشْحِمٌ . فَجْأَةٌ
Plunder *v. t.* or *n.*	نَهَبَ . سَلَبَ . غَنِيمَةٌ
Plunge *v. t.* or *i.*	غَمَسَ . غَطَسَ . خَاضَ
Plural *a.* or *n.*	أَكْثَرُ مِنْ وَاحِدٍ . الْجَمْع
Plurality *n.*	أَكْثَرِيَّةٌ . تَعَدُّدٌ
Plus *n.*	عَلَامَةُ الْجَمْعِ (+)
Ply *v. t.* or *n.*	أَلَحَّ . شَغَلَ . جَدَّ . ثَنْيَة
Pneumatics *n. sing.*	عِلْمُ الْهَوَاءِ
Pneumonia *n.*	دَاءُ ذَاتِ الرِّئَةِ
Poach *v. t.*	سَرَقَ صَيْدًا . نَهَبَ

Pocket n. or v. t.	جَيْبٌ . وَضَعَ فِيهِ
Pod n.	قَرْنَةُ نَبَاتٍ
Poem n.	قَصِيدَةٌ
Poesy n.	شِعْرٌ . عِلْمُ النَّظْمِ
Poet n.	شَاعِرٌ
Poetic } a. Poetical }	شِعْرِيٌّ . نَظْمِيٌّ
Poetry n.	شِعْرٌ . دِيوَانُ شِعْرٍ
Poignant a.	شَدِيدٌ . حَادٌّ . شَاقٌّ
Point n.	رَأْسٌ . نُقْطَةٌ . مُرَادٌ
Point v. t. or i.	أَشَارَ . سَنَّ . نَقَّطَ . وَجَّهَ
Pointer n.	دَلِيلٌ . كَلْبُ صَيْدٍ
Pointless n.	كَلِيلٌ . بِلَا مَعْنًى
Poise n.	ثِقْلٌ . مُوَازَنَةٌ
Poison n. or v. t.	سَمٌّ . سَمَّ
Poisonous a.	سَامٌّ
Poke n. or v. t.	دَفْعٌ . دَفَعَ . وَكَزَ
Poker n.	مِحْرَاكٌ
Polar n.	قُطْبِيٌّ
Polarity n.	الِإتِّجَاه نَحْوَ ٱلْقُطْب
Polarize v. t.	أَعْطَاهُ خَاصِّيَةَ ٱلِإتِّجَاه لِلْقُطْب
Pole n.	قُطْبٌ . قَضِيبٌ طَوِيل
Pole-star n.	نَجْمُ ٱلْقُطْب
Police n.	ضَابِطَة مَدِينَةٍ . بُولِيسٌ
Policy n.	سِيَاسَةٌ . تَدْبِيرٌ
Polish n. or v. t.	صَقْلٌ . صَقَلَ
Polite a.	أَدِيبٌ . أَنِيسٌ
Politeness n.	أَدَبٌ . أُنْسٌ
Politic a.	بَصِيرٌ . فَطِنٌ
Political a.	سِيَاسِيٌّ
Politics n. sing.	أُمُورُ ٱلسِّيَاسَة
Polity n.	نِظَامُ دَوْلَةٍ أَوْ سِيَاسَةٍ
Poll n. or v. t.	رَأْسٌ . إِنْتِخَابٌ . قَيَّدَ ٱلْأَسْمَاء
Pollen n.	هَبَاءُ أَسْدِيَة ٱلنَّبَات
Poll-tax n.	ضَرِيبَة عَلَى ٱلشَّخْص
Pollute v. t.	أَفْسَدَ . نَجَّسَ . وَسَّخَ
Pollution n.	نَجَاسَةٌ . رَجَاسَةٌ

Poltroon *n.*	جَبَانٌ . خَسِيسٌ
Polygamy *n.*	تَعَدُّدُ ٱلزَّوْجَاتِ . ضَرٌّ
Polygon *n.*	كَثِيرُ ٱلاضلَاعِ
Polysyllable *n.*	لَفْظَةٌ مُعَدَّدَةُ ٱلْمَقَاطِعِ
Polytheism *n.*	أَقْوَل بِكَثْرَةِ ٱلآلِهَةِ
Pomade *n.*	دِهَانُ ٱلشَّعْرِ
Pomegranate *n.*	رُمَّانَةٌ
Pommel *v. t.* or *n.*	ضَرَبَ — . قَرَبُوسٌ
Pomp *n.*	مُبَاهَاةٌ . مَوْكِبٌ
Pompous *a.*	مُبَاهٍ . فَخُورٌ . مُتَأَنِّهٌ
Pond *n.*	بِرْكَةٌ ج بِرَكٌ
Ponder *v. i.*	تَأَمَّلَ . تَفَكَّرَ
Ponderous *a.*	ثَقِيلٌ . مُهِمٌّ
Poniard *n.* or *v.t.*	خَنْجَرٌ . طَعَنَ بِهِ
Pontiff *n.*	حَبْرٌ . رَئِيسُ ٱلْكَهَنَةِ
Pontifical *a.*	حَبْرِيٌّ . بَابَوِيٌّ
Pony *n.*	فَرَسٌ صَغِيرٌ
Poodle *n.*	كَلْبٌ

Pool *n.*	بِرْكَةٌ . غَدِيرٌ
Poor *a.*	فَقِيرٌ . مِسْكِينٌ . حَقِيرٌ
Poorly *ad.*	بِحَالَةٍ سَيِّئَةٍ
Pop *n.* or *v.i.*	صَوْتُ ٱنْفِجَارٍ . إِنْفَجَرَ
Pope *n.*	بَابَا
Popery *n.*	مَذْهَبُ ٱلْبَابَا
Popish *a.*	بَابَوِيٌّ
Poplar *n.*	شَجَرُ ٱلْحَوْرِ
Poppy *n.*	خَشْخَاشٌ
Populace *n.*	ٱلْعَامَّةُ . رَعَاعُ ٱلنَّاسِ
Popular *a.*	مَقْبُولٌ عِنْدَ ٱلْجُمْهُورِ
Popularity *n.*	قَبُولٌ عِنْدَ ٱلنَّاسِ
Popularize *v. t.*	جَعَلَ مَقْبُولاً عِنْدَ ٱلنَّاسِ
Populate *v. t.*	أَعْمَرَ
Population *n.*	أَهْلٌ . سُكَّانٌ
Populous *a.*	كَثِيرُ ٱلسُّكَّانِ
Porcelain *n.*	خَزَفٌ صِينِيٌّ
Porch *n.*	رِوَاقٌ . إِيوَانٌ

Porcupine *n.*	قُنْفُذ ج قَنَافِذ	Portmanteau *n.*	صَنْدُوقُ سَفَرٍ صَغِيرٌ
Pore *n.*	مَسَمّ ج مَسَامّ	Portrait *n.*	صُورَة شَخْص
Pork *n.*	لَحْم خِنْزِير	Portray *v. t.*	صَوَّرَ . وَصَفَ —
Porous *a.*	ذو مَسَامّ	Position *n.*	مَقَام . مَرْكَز . حَال
Porridge *n.*	ثَرِيد. عَصِيدَة	Positive *a.*	أَكِيدٌ .مُتَيَقِّنٌ. جَازِم
Port *n.*	مِيمَاء. يَسَارُ سَفِينَةٍ. مُرْفَأ	Possess *v. t.*	مَلَكَ ـ حَازَ ـ. إِقْتَنَى
Portable *a.*	خَفِيف. يُمْكِنُ نَقْلُهُ	Possession *n.*	مُلْك. تَمَلُّك
Portage *n.*	نَقْل . اجْرَتُهُ	Possessive *a.*	مِلْكِيّ. أَلْمُضَافُ إِلَيْهِ
Portal *n.*	بَاب . مَدْخَل	Possessor *n.*	مَالِك. صَاحِب. رَبّ
Porte *n.*	البَابُ أَلْعَالِي	Possibility *n.*	إِمْكَان
Portend *v. t.*	دَلَّ عَلَى . أَنْبَأَ بِهِ	Possible *a.*	مُمْكِن . مُحْتَمَل
Portent *n.*	عَلَامَة سُوء . شُؤْم	Post *v. t.* (accounts)	شَطَّبَ حِسَابًا
Portentous *a.*	مُنْذِرٌ بِسُوء	Post *n.*	عُمُود . بَرِيد .مَنْصِب
Porter *n.*	حَمَّال. بَوَّاب(عَتَّال.شِيَّال)	Postage *n.*	اجْرَة الْبَرِيد
Port-hole *n.*	كُوَّة مِدْفَع فِي سَفِينَةٍ	Postal *a.*	مُخْتَصّ بِالبَرِيدِ
Portico *n.*	رُوَاق	Posterior *a.*	خَلْفِيّ . بَعْد .تَال
Portion *n. or v. t.*	جُزْء.حِصَّة.قَسَم	Posterity *n.*	ذُرِّيَّة. أَهْل الْمُسْتَقْبِل
Portly *a.*	جَسِيم.مَهِيب الْهَيْئَة	Post-haste *ad.*	بِغَايَةِ السُّرْعَةِ

Postman n.	ساعي ٱلْبَرِيدِ (بُوسْطَجِيٌّ)
Post-master n.	مُدِيرُ ٱلْبَرِيد
Post-office n.	مَرْكَزُ إِدَارَةِ ٱلْبَرِيد
Postpone v. t.	أَخَّرَ . أَجَّلَ
Postscript n.	ذَيْلٌ . مُلْحَق
Postulate n.	فَرْضٌ . قَضِيَّةٌ أَوَّلِيَّة
Posture n.	وَضْعٌ . هَيْئَة . حَالَة
Posy n.	زَهْرَة . بَاقَة
Pot n.	قِدْرٌ . مِرْجَلٌ
Potash n.	قِلْيٌ . قِلى
Potable a.	صَالِحٌ لِلشُّرْب
Potato n.	بَطَاطِسٌ
Potency n.	عِزَّة . قُوَّةٌ . صَوْلَة
Potent a.	قَوِيٌّ . مُقْتَدِرٌ . عَزِيز
Potentate n.	مُسَلَّط . مَلِك
Potential a.	مُمْكِنٌ وُجُوده
Potion n.	جُرْعَةٌ . شَرْبَة
Pottage n.	طَبِيخٌ مِنْ لَحْمٍ وخُضَرٍ

Potter n.	خَزَّافٌ . فَخَّارِيٌّ
Pottery n.	خَزَفٌ . فَخَّارٌ
Pouch n.	كِيسٌ . جِرَابٌ . حَوْصَلَة
Poultice n. or v. t.	لَزُوقٌ . عَالَجَ به
Poultry n.	دَجَاجٌ
Pounce v. i.	إِنْقَضَّ عَلَى
Pound n.	رِطْلٌ أَزْكَ يزِيُّ لِبِرَةً نكايِزِية
Pound v. t.	مَسْحُوقٌ — . دَقَّ
Pour v.t. or i.	صَبَّ . سَكَبَ . تَدَفَّقَ
Poverty n.	فَقْرٌ . فَاقَة
Powder n.	مَسْحُوقٌ . سَفُوفٌ . بَارُودٌ
Power n.	قُوَّة . قُدْرَة . سُلْطَان
Powerful a.	قَوِيٌّ . مُقْتَدِرٌ . قَدِيرٌ
Powerless a.	عَاجِز
Pox n.	أَلدَّاءُ ٱلزُّهْرِيُّ
Small-pox n.	أَلْجُدَرِيُّ
Practicability n.	إِمْكَانُ ٱلْعَمَل
Practicable a.	مُمْكِنٌ عَمَلُهُ

Practical a.	مُوافِقٌ لِلْحَالِ أَوِ الْمَعْمَل
Practice n. or v. t.	مُمَارَسَةٌ . عَادَة . مَارَس
Practitioner n.	طَبِيبٌ . عَامِل
Prairie n.	فَلَاةٌ ذَاتُ كَلَإٍ
Praise n. or v. t.	مَدْحٌ . حَمْد . مَدَح . سَبَّح
Praiseworthy a.	خَلِيقٌ بِالْمَدْح
Prance v. i.	شَبَّ ـُ (حِصَان)
Prate v. i.	هَذَرَ ـِ
Pratique n.	بَرَاءَةُ الصِّحَّةِ . بَرَاتِيكَه
Prattle n. or v. i.	ثَرْثَرَةُ الْوَلَدِ . ثَرْثَر
Pray v. t. or i.	تَوَسَّل . تَضَرَّع . صَلَّى
Prayer n.	تَوَسُّلٌ . طَلَبٌ . صَلَاة
Preach v. i. or t.	كَرَزَ ـِ . بَشَّرَ . وَعَظَ ـِ
Preacher n.	وَاعِظٌ . مُبَشِّر
Preamble n.	دِيبَاجَةٌ . مُقَدِّمَة
Precarious a.	غَيْرُ ثَابِتٍ أَوْ مَوْثُوقٍ بِهِ
Precaution n.	حَذَرٌ . إِحْتِيَاط
Precautional Precautionary a.	حَذَرِيٌّ إِحْتِيَاطِيّ

Precede v. t.	سَبَقَ ـُ . تَقَدَّم
Precedence Precedency n.	تَقَدُّمٌ . أَفْضَلِيَّة
Precedent a. or n.	مُقَدَّم . سَابِقَة
Precept n.	مَبْدَأ . سُنَّة . أَمْر
Preceptor n.	مُعَلِّم . مُهَذِّب
Precious a.	ثَمِين . عَزِيز . نَفِيس
Precipice n.	جُرْفٌ شَاهِق . وَهْدَة
Precipitance Precipitancy n.	عَجَلَة . تَهَوُّر
Precipitant a.	مُتَهَوِّر . عَجُول
Precipitate v. t.	رَسَّب . اعْجَل
Precipitate a. or n.	مُتَهَوِّر . رُسُوب
Precipitation n.	تَهَوُّر . تَرْسِيب
Precipitous a.	شَامِخ . عَجُول
Precise a.	مُدَقِّق . مَضْبُوط . مُتَأَنِّق
Preciseness Precision n.	ضَبْط . إِتْقَان
Preclude v. t.	مَنَع . أَغْلَق . سَدَّ عَلَى
Precocious a.	بَالِغٌ قَبْلَ أَوَانِه . مُبْتَسِر
Precociousness Precocity n.	بُلُوغٌ قَبْلَ الْوَقْت

Preconceive *v. t.*	سبق فتصوّر	Preemption *n.*	حقُّ اُلشُّفعة
Preconcerted *a.*	متفق عَليه سابقًا	Preengagement *n.*	تعهد . سا بق
Precursor *n.*	سابقٌ . علامةٌ . بشيرٌ	Preexistence *n.*	سبقُ اَلوُجودِ
Predaceous *a.*	عائشٌ باَ لصيدِ مفترس	Preexistent } Preexisting } *a.*	كَائنٌ سَابقًا
Predatory *n.*	ذَاهبٌ خَاطفٌ مفترسٌ	Preface *n.* or *v. t.*	مقدّمةٌ . صدّرَ . فتح
Predecessor *n.*	سابقٌ . سَالفٌ	Prefatory *a.*	إفتتَاحِيٌّ . ديبَاجِيٌّ
Predestinate } Predestine } *v. t.*	سبق فقضى قدّرَ	Prefer *v. t.*	آثرَ . فضّلَ . عرض —
Predetermine *v. t.*	سبق فحتّم	Preferable *a.*	أفضل . أوْلى
Predicament *n.*	حالٌ . ورْطةٌ	Preference *n.*	تفضيلٌ . إيثَارٌ
Predicate *n.*} or *v. t.*}	خبرٌ . مسنَد . اسنَد	Preferment *n.*	ترْقية . تقدُّم
Predict *v. t.*	أنبأ به	Prefigure *v. t.*	رمزَ إلى . سبق فمثّل
Prediction *n.*	نبوءةٌ . إنبَاءٌ	Prefix *v. t.*	صدّرَ . أدْخل علَى
Predispose *v. t.*	سبق فأمال أوْهيأ	Prefix *n.*	إضافةٌ إبتِدائِيَّةٌ
Predisposition *n.*	ميْل . سابق	Pregnancy *n.*	حبل . حمْل
Predominant *n.*	غالبٌ . مستعْل	Pregnant *a.*	حبْلى . متضمّن كثيرًا
Predominate *v. i.*	فاق . غلب ـ	Prejudge *v. t.*	حكم قبْل اَلفحص
Preeminence *n.*	أسْبقية	Prejudice *n.*	ميْل أوْحكم سَا بقٌ . ضرَرٌ
Preeminent *a.*	فائقٌ . سابقٌ	Prejudicial *a.*	مضرٌّ . موْذٍ

Prelate *n.*	أُسقُفٌ	Prepossessing *a.*	مُسْتَمِيل مُسْتَعْطِفٌ
Preliminary *a.*	إِفْتِتَاحِيٌّ	Prepossession *n.*	تَمَلُّكُ أَوْرَأيْ سَابِقٌ
Prelude *n.*	فَاتِحَة . مُقَدِّمَة	Preposterous *a.*	مُخَالِفُ ٱلْعَقْلِ . عَبَثٌ
Premature *a.*	قَبْلَ وَقْتِهِ . مُبْتَسَرٌ	Prerequisite *a.* or *n.*	لَازِمٌ . لُزُومٌ . سَابِقٌ
Premeditate *v. t.*	سَبَقَ فَتَأَمَّلَ	Prerogative *n.*	إِمْتِيَازٌ
Premeditated *a.*	عَمْدِيٌّ . مَقْصُودٌ	Presage *n.* or *v. t.*	إِنْذَارٌ . أَنْذَرَ
Premier *n.*	أَوَّلٌ . وَزِيرٌ أَوَّلٌ	Presbyter *n.*	قَسِيسٌ
Premise *v. t.* or *i.*	صَدَّرَ كَلَامَهُ بِ	Presbytery *n.*	مَشْيَخَةُ ٱلْكَنِيسَةِ
Premises *n. pl.*	مُقَدَّمَاتُ قِيَاسٍ	Prescribe *v. t.*	أَمَرَ . فَرَضَ . وَصَفَ
Premium *n.*	رِبًا . جَزَاءُ ٱلْإِكْرَامِيّ	Prescription *n.*	وَصْفَةُ عِلَاجٍ
Preoccupy *v. t.*	سَبَقَ فَمَلَكَ . شَغَلَ ٱلْبَالَ	Presence *n.*	حُضُورٌ . وُجُودٌ . حَضْرَةٌ
Preordain *v. t.*	سَبَقَ فَعَيَّنَ أَوْأَعَدَّ	Present *a.* or *n.*	حَاضِرٌ . ٱلْحَاضِرُ . هَدِيَّةٌ
Preparation *n.*	إِسْتِعْدَادٌ . تَهَيُّؤٌ	Present *v. t.*	أَهْدَى . أَظْهَرَ . قَدَّمَ
Preparative Preparatory *a.*	مُهَيِّئٌ . إِسْتِعْدَادِيٌّ	Presentation *n.*	إِهْدَاءٌ . تَقْدِيمٌ
Prepare *v. t.*	هَيَّأَ . أَعَدَّ	Presentiment *n.*	رَأْيٌ سَابِقٌ . هَاجِسٌ
Prepay *v. t.*	سَلَّفَ ٱلْأُجْرَةَ	Presently *ad.*	حَالًا . عَنْ قَرِيبٍ
Preponderate *v. i.*	رَجَحَ . زَادَ عَلَى	Preservation *n.*	حِفْظٌ . أَمْنٌ
Preposition *n.*	حَرْفُ جَرٍّ	Preserve *v. t.*	حَفِظَ . صَانَ

Preside *v. t.*	رَأَسَ . أَدَارَ
Presidency *n.*	رَآسَة
President *n.*	رَئِيسٌ
Press *v. t.*	ضَغَطَ ـَ كَبَسَ ـِ . حَثَّ ـُ
Press *n.*	مِكْبَسٌ . مَطْبَعَة
Pressing *a.*	مُهِمٌّ . ضَرُورِيٌّ
Pressure *n.*	ضَغْط . حَصْرٌ . إِلْحَاحٌ
Prestige *n.*	نُفُوذ . جَاه
Presumable *a.*	مُوَافِق اَلظَّنِّ . مُحْتَمَل
Presume *v. t.* or *i.*	ظَنَّ . خَمَّنَ . تَجَرَّأَ
Presumption *n.*	ظَنٌّ . تَجَبُّرٌ . تَرْجِيحٌ
Presumptive *a.*	مَظْنُونٌ . مُرَجَّحٌ
Presumptuous *a.*	مُتَجَبِّرٌ . مُعْجِبٌ
Presuppose *v.t.*	سَبَقَ فَظَنَّ أَوْ فَرَضَ
Pretend *v. t.*	إِدَّعَى . تَظَاهَرَ
Pretence Pretension } *n.*	إِدِّعَاءٌ . حُجَّة
Pretentious *a.*	مُبَالِغ فِي اَلاِدِّعَاء
Preternatural *a.*	فَوْق اَلطَّبِيعَة

Pretext *n.*	حُجَّة . إِدِّعَاءٌ . عُذْرٌ
Pretty *a.*	حَسَنٌ . جَمِيل . ظَرِيفٌ
Prevail *v. i.*	غَلَبَ . فَاقَ ـُ . عَمَّ ـُ
Prevalence *n.*	إِسْتِيلَاءٌ . إِنْتِشَارٌ
Prevalent Prevailing } *a.*	مُنْتَشِرٌ . مُشْتَلٌّ
Prevaricate *v. i.*	مَوَّهَ . وَارَبَ
Prevent *v. t.*	مَنَعَ ـَ . صَدَّ ـُ
Preventable *a.*	مِمَّا يُمْنَع
Preventative Preventive } *n. or a.*	مَانِع
Previous *a.*	سَابِق . سَالِف . مَاض
Prey *n.* or *v. t.*	فَرِيسَة . غَنِيمَة . إِفْتَرَسَ
Price *n.*	ثَمَن . سِعْر
Priceless *a.*	مَا لَا يُثَمَّنُ . فَوْق كُلّ ثَمَن
Prick *v. t.* or *n.*	نَخَسَ ـُ . نَخَرَ ـَ . نَخْسَة
Prickle *n.*	شُوَيْكَة
Prickly *a.*	كَثِيرُ الشَّوْك
Prickly-pear *n.*	صُبَّيْر (تِين بِشَوْكَه)
Pride *n.*	كِبْرِيَاءٌ . عِزَّةُ اَلنَّفْسِ

Priest *n.*	كَاهِنٌ . خُورِي	Prior *a.* or *n.*	سَابِقٌ . رَئِيسُ دَيْر
Priesthood *n.*	كَهَنُوتٌ	Prioress *n.*	رَئِيسَةُ دَيْر
Priestly *a.*	كَهْنُوتِيٌّ	Priority *n.*	أَسْبَقِيَّةٌ . تَقَدُّم
Prim *a.*	مُتَأَنِّق	Prism *n.*	مَوْشُورٌ . مَنْشُور
Primary *a.*	أَوَّلِيٌّ . أَصْلِيٌّ	Prismatic *n.*	مَوْشُورِي
Prime *a.* or *n.*	أَوَّلُ . الأَعْلَى دَرَجَةً	Prison *n.*	سِجْنٌ . حَبْس
Primer *n.*	كِتَابُ مَبَادِئَ	Prisoner *n.*	مَحْبُوسٌ . أَسِير
Primeval *a.*	مِنَ العُصُورِ الأُولَى	Privacy *a.*	إِنْفِرَادٌ . عُزْلَة . سِرٌّ
Primitive *a.*	إِبْتِدَائِيٌّ . أَصْلِيٌّ	Private *a.*	سِرِّيٌّ . مُنْفَرِدٌ . خَاصٌّ
Primness *n.*	تَأَنُّق	Privateer *n.*	سَفِينَةٌ حَرْبِيَّة خَاصَّة
Prince *n.*	أَمِيرٌ . إِبْنُ مَلِك	Privation *n.*	حِرْمَانٌ . عَوَزٌ . عَدَم
Princess *n.*	أَمِيرَة . إِبْنَةُ مَلِك	Privilege *n.*	إِمْتِيَازٌ . فَائِدَة . رُخْصَة
Principal *a.* or *n.*	أَعْظَمُ . أَوَّلُ . رَئِيس	Privily *ad.*	سِرًّا . خِفْيَة
Principality *n.*	سَلْطَنَة . إِمَارَة	Privy *a.* or *n.*	عَارِفٌ سِرًّا . خَاصٌّ . خَلَاء
Principle *n.*	مَبْدَأٌ . قَاعِدَة	Prize *n.* or *v. t.*	جَائِزَة . جِعَالَة . أَعَزَّ
Print *v. t.* or *n.*	طَبَعَ . وَسَمَ . أَثَر	Probability *n.*	تَرْجِيحٌ
Printer *n.*	طَبَّاعٌ . صَاحِبُ مَطْبَعَة	Probable *a.*	مُرَجَّحٌ
Printing *n.*	طَبْع	Probation *n.*	إِمْتِحَانٌ

Probe v. t. or n.	سَبَرَ ـِ . مِسبَارُ
Probity n.	إِستِقَامَة . أَمَانَة
Problem n.	مَسأَلَة . قَضِيَّة
Problematical a.	غَيرُ ظَاهِرٍ . مُبهَم
Proboscis n.	خُرطُوم
Proceed v. i.	تَقَدَّمَ . شَرَعَ فِي . صَدَرَ ـُ
Proceeding n.	عَمَل . تَصَرُّف
Proceeds n. pl.	حَاصِل . دَخل
Process n.	فِعل . كَيفِيَّة . طَرِيقَة
Procession n.	مَوكِب
Proclaim v. t.	نَادَى بِ . صَرَّحَ
Proclamation n.	مُنَادَاة . إِعلَان
Proclivity n.	مَيل . إِنعِطَاف
Procrastinate v. t. or i.	أَجَّلَ . تَأَخَّرَ
Procreate v. t.	وَلَدَ ـِ . أَنتَجَ
Procumbent a.	مُلقًى عَلَى وَجهِه
Procurable a.	مَا يُحَصَّل
Procure v. t.	حَصَّلَ . فَازَ بِ

Prodigal a.	مُسرِف . مُبَذِّر
Prodigality n.	تَبذِير . إِسرَاف
Prodigious a.	عَظِيم . عَجِيب
Prodigy a.	مُعجِزَة . آيَة
Produce v. t. or n.	أَنتَجَ . أَورَدَ . غَلَّة
Product n.	نَتِيجَة . حَاصِل
Productive a.	مُنتِج . مُثمِر . مُسَبِّب
Profanation n.	تَدنِيسُ مُقَدَّس
Profane a. or v. t.	دَنِس . دُنيَوِيّ . دَنَّسَ
Profaneness Profanity } n.	دَنَاسَة . تَجدِيف
Profess v. t.	أَقَرَّ . تَظَاهَرَ . قَالَ بِ
Profession n.	إِقرَار . عَقِيدَة . حِرفَة
Professor n.	مُقِرّ . أُستَاذ
Professorship n.	وَظِيفَة أُستَاذٍ
Proffer v. t. or n.	قَدَّمَ . أَدَّى . تَقدِيم
Proficiency n.	تَقَدُّم فِي العُلُوم
Proficient a.	مَاهِر . بَارِع
Profile n.	رَسم جَانِبِيّ لِلوَجهِ

Profit n. or v. i.	رِبْح . رَبِحَ ـَ
Profitable a.	مُكْسِب . مُفِيد
Profligacy n.	خَلاعَة . فُجُور
Profligate a.	خَلِيع . فَاجِر
Profound a.	عَمِيق . خَارِق . مُتَعَمِّق
Profuse a	وَافِر . مُفْرِط . فَيَّاض
Profusion n.	وَفْرَة . فَيْض . تَبْذِير
Progenitor n.	جَدّ . سَالَف
Progeny n.	ذُرِّيَّة . نَسْل
Prognosis n.	إِنْذَار بِنَتِيجَة مَرَض
Prognosticate v. t.	أَنْبَأَ أَوْ أَنْبَأَ بِهِ
Programme n.	لاَئِحَة . تَعْرِيف
Progress n.	تَقَدُّم . نَجَاح
Progress v. i.	تَقَدَّمَ . نَجَحَ ـَ
Progressive a.	مُتَقَدِّم . مُتَتَابِع
Prohibit v. t.	مَنَعَ ـَ . نَهَى ـَ . حَرَّمَ
Prohibition n.	نَهْي . مَقْع
Prohibitive } Prohibitory } a.	مَانِع . نَاهٍ

Project v. i. or t.	بَرَزَ ـُ . قَصَدَ ـِ . أَلْقَى
Project n.	قَصْد . تَدْبِير . مَشْرُوع
Projectile n.	مِرْمَاة . قِبْلَة
Prolific a.	مُثْمِر . مُنْتِج كَثِيراً
Prolix a.	مُسْهِب . مُمِلّ
Prolixity n.	إِسْهَاب . إِطْنَاب
Prolong v. t.	أَطَالَ . مَدَّ ـُ
Prolongation n.	إِطَالَة
Promenade n.	تَنَزُّه . مُنْتَزَه
Prominence } Prominency } n.	عُلُوّ . بُرُوز
Prominent a.	بَارِز . ظَاهِر . شَهِير
Promiscuous a.	مُخْتَلِط . غَيْر مُرَتَّب
Promise n. or v. t.	مَوْعِد . وَعْد . يَعِد
Promissory a.	وَعْدِيّ . تَعَهُّدِيّ
Promontory n.	رَأْس عَالٍ فِي ٱلْبَحْر
Promote v. t.	سَاعَدَ . نَجَّحَ . رَقَّى
Promotion n.	تَرْقِيَة . تَقْدِيم
Prompt a.	مُسْتَعِدّ . سَرِيع ٱلْفِعْل

Promptitude Promptness } n. إِسْتِعْدَاد. سُرْعَة	Prophet n. نَبِيّ ج أَنْبِيَاء
Promulgate v. t. نَشَرَ . أَذَاعَ	Prophetic Prophetical } a. نَبَوِيّ
Prone a. مُلْقًى عَلَى وَجْهِهِ . مَائِل. مُنْعَطِف	Propitiate v. t. إِسْتَعْطَفَ
Prong n. شُعْبَة	Propitiation n. إِسْتِعْطَاف. كَفَّارَة
Pronoun n. ضَمِير	Propitious a. مُنْعِم . مُوَافِق . مُفِيد
Pronounce v. t. لَفَظَ — . صَرَّحَ بِ	Proportion n. نِسْبَة. مُنَاسَبَة. حِصَّة
Pronunciation n. لَفْظ . نُطْق	Proportional Proportionate } a. نِسْبِيّ . مُتَنَاسِب
Proof n. بُرْهَان . بَيِّنَة . إِمْتِحَان	Proposal n. عَرْض. قَصْد . رَأْي
Proof a. مَا لاَ يُؤَثَّرُ فِيهِ	Propose v. t. عَرَضَ . قَدَّمَ
Proof-sheet n. مُسْوَدَّة	Proposition n. عَرْض. قَضِيَّة . مَطْلَب
Prop n. or v. t. دِعَامَة . سَنَد. دَعَمَ	Propound v. t. عَرَضَ — . طَرَحَ — . قَدَّمَ
Propagate v. t. وَلَدَ. نَشَرَ — اذَاعَ	Proprietor n. صَاحِب. رَبّ. مَالِك
Propel v. t. دَفَعَ — . سَاقَ —	Propriety n. لِيَاقَة . مُوَافَقَة
Propensity n. مَيْل. صَبْو . إِنْعِطَاف	Propulsion n. دَفْع . سَوْق
Proper a. لاَئِق . مُوَافِق. خَاصّ	Prorogue v. t. أَجَّلَ . أَخَّرَ
Property n. مِلْك . خَاصَّة . صِفَة	Prosaic Prosaical } a. نَثْرِيّ . مُمِلّ
Prophecy n. نُبُوَّة وَ نَبُوَّة	Proscribe v. t. حَرَّمَ . طَرَدَ —
Prophesy v. i. أَنْبَأَ . اخْبَرَ بالغَيْب	Prose n. نَثْر

Prosecute v. t.	تَتَبَّعَ . إِدَّعَى عَلَى
Prosecutor n.	مُدَّعٍ . مُوَاظِب
Proselyte n. or v. t.	دَخِيل . جَلَبَ إِلَى دِين
Prosody n.	عِلْمُ الْعَرُوضِ
Prospect n.	مَنْظَر . أَمَل . مُنْتَظَر
Prospective a.	مُسْتَقْبِل . مُنْتَظَر
Prosper v. i.	نَجَحَ — أَفْلَحَ
Prosperity n.	نَجَاح . فَلَاح
Prosperous a.	نَاجِح . مُفْلِح
Prostitute n.	عَاهِرَة . فَاجِرَة
Prostitute v. t.	إِسْتَعْمَلَ لِغَايَةٍ رَذِيلَةٍ
Prostrate a.	سَاجِد . مُتَمَدِّد
Prostrate v. t.	أَلْقَى . سَجَدَ — . خَوَّرَ
Prosy a.	مُمِلّ . مُضْجِر
Protect v. t.	حَمَى — . وَقَى — . صَانَ —
Protection n.	حِمَايَة . وِقَايَة
Protective a. Protector n.	حَامٍ . حَافِظ
Protectorate n.	حِمَايَة
Protegé n.	مَحْمِيّ . مَوْلِيّ
Protest v. i. or t.	أَكَّدَ . صَرَّحَ بِعَدَمِ قَبُول
Protestation n.	إِقَامَةُ الْحُجَّةِ تَأْكِيد
Protocol n.	لَائِحَة (بْرُوتُوكُول)
Protract v. t.	أَطَالَ . أَخَّرَ
Protrude v. t. or i.	أَخْرَجَ . بَرَزَ — . نَتَأَ —
Protuberance n.	نَوْء . بُرُوز
Proud a.	مُتَكَبِّر . مُشَامِخ . مُعْجِب
Prove v. t. or i.	بَرْهَنَ . جَرَّبَ . تَبَيَّنَ
Provender n.	عَلِيق . عَلَف
Proverb n.	مَثَل ج أَمْثَال
Proverbial a.	يُضْرَبُ بِهِ الْمَثَل
Provide v. t.	جَهَّزَ . قَدَّمَ . أَمَدَّ
Providence n.	عِنَايَة . تَدْبِير
Provident a.	ذُو عِنَايَةٍ . مُدَبِّر
Providential a.	مِنْ عِنَايَةِ اللّٰه
Province n.	إِقْلِيم . وِلَايَة
Provincial a.	إِقْلِيمِيّ . غَيْرُ مُهَذَّب

Provison n.	جِهَازٌ . مُؤْنَةٌ . شَرْطٌ
Provisional Provisionary } a.	وَفْقِيٌّ . شَرْطِيٌّ
Provocation n.	إِغَاظَةٌ . تَهْيِيجٌ
Provocative a.	مُهَيِّجٌ . مُحَرِّكٌ
Provoke v. t.	أَغَاظَ . هَيَّجَ . أَثَارَ
Prow n.	مُقَدَّمُ سَفِينَةٍ
Prowess n.	بَسَالَةٌ . شَجَاعَةٌ . سَطْوَةٌ
Prowl v. i.	جَالَ ـَ . جَالَ يَفْتَرِسُ
Proximate a.	أَلْأَقْرَبُ . سَابِقٌ أَوْ تَالٍ
Proximity n.	قُرْبٌ
Proxy n.	وَكِيلٌ . وَكَالَةٌ
Prudence n.	حَزْمٌ . بَصِيرَةٌ . إِحْتِيَاطٌ
Prudent a.	حَازِمٌ . فَطِنٌ . حَذِرٌ
Prudish a.	مُتَصَنِّعٌ بِالْحِشْمَةِ
Prune n. or v. t.	خَوْخَةٌ مُجَفَّفَةٌ . شَذَّبَ . قَضَّبَ
Pry v. i.	تَجَسَّسَ . رَفَعَ بِمِخْلٍ
Psalm n.	مَزْمُورٌ ج مَزَامِيرُ
Psalmist n.	مُؤَلِّفُ ٱلْمَزَامِيرِ . مُرَنِّمٌ
Psalter n.	كِتَابُ ٱلْمَزَامِيرِ
Psychic Psychical } a.	مَنُوطٌ بِالنَّفْسِ
Psychology n.	أَلْفَلْسَفَةُ ٱلْعَقْلِيَّةُ
Puberty n.	سِنُّ ٱلْبُلُوغِ
Public a. or n.	عُمُومِيٌّ . شَائِعٌ . ٱلْجُمْهُورُ
Publican n.	عَشَّارٌ . خَمَّارٌ
Publication n.	إِذَاعَةٌ . نَشْرٌ
Publicity n.	شُيُوعٌ . إِشْتِهَارٌ
Publish v. t.	نَشَرَ ـُ . أَشَاعَ
Pucker v.i. or n.	جَعَّدَ . جَعْدَةٌ . ثَنْيَةٌ
Puddle n.	مَنْقَعُ وَحَلٍ
Puerile a.	وَلَدِيٌّ . رَكِيكٌ . (صِبْيَانِيٌّ)
Puff n. or v. i.	نَفْخَةٌ . نَفَخَ ـَ
Pugilist n.	مُلَاكِمٌ
Pugnacious a.	خُصُومٌ . مُحِبُّ ٱلْمُنَازَعَةِ
Pull v. t.	شَدَّ ـُ . جَرَّ ـُ . قَلَعَ ـَ
Pulley n.	بَكَرَةٌ
Pulmonary Pulmonic } a.	رِئَوِيٌّ

Pulp n.	لُبٌّ . شَحْمٌ
Pulpit n.	مِنْبَرٌ
Pulsate v. i.	نَبَضَ
Pulsation n.	نَبْضَة . نَبْض
Pulse n.	أَلنَّبْضُ . أَلقْطَانِيُّ
Pulverize v. t.	سَحَقَ ـَ . دَقَّ ـُ
Pump n. or v.t.	طُلُمْبَةٌ . رَفَعَ مَاءً بِها
Pun n.	تَوْرِيَةٌ (فِي ٱلبيَان)
Punch v. t.	ثَقَبَ ـُ . دَفَعَ ـَ
Punch n.	نَوْعٌ مِنَ ٱلْمُسْكِرِ . مِثْقَب
Punctual a.	مُرَاعِي ٱلْوَقْت . مُدَقِّق
Punctuality n	أَلتَّدْقِيقُ فِي ٱلْمِيعَادِ
Punctuate v.t.	وَضَعَ عَلَامَاتِ ٱلْوَقْف
Puncture n. or v.t.	ثَقْبَة . ثَقَبَ ـُ
Pungent a.	حِرِّيفٌ . حَادٌّ
Punish v. t.	عَاقَبَ . قَاصَّ
Punishment n.	عِقَاب . قِصَاص
Punitive a.	عِقَابِيٌّ . قِصَاصِيٌّ
Punster n.	مَاهِرٌ بِٱلتَّوْرِيَةِ
Puny a.	هَزِيلٌ . ضَعِيف
Pup Puppy } n.	جَرْوُ كَلْبٍ
Pupil n.	تِلْمِيذٌ . بُؤْبُؤُ ٱلعَيْن
Puppet n.	أَلعُوبَةٌ
Pur or Purr v. i. or n.	خَرْخَرَةُ ٱلهِرِّ
Purchase v. t.	إِبْتَاعَ . إِشْتَرَى
Purchaser n.	مُشْتَرٍ
Pure a.	صَافٍ . طَاهِرٌ . صِرْفٌ
Purely ad.	فَقَطْ
Purgative a. or n.	مُطَهِّرٌ . مُسْهِل
Purgatory n.	ٱلمَطْهَرُ
Purge v. t.	طَهَّرَ . اسْهَل
Purification n.	تَطْهِير . غَسْل
Purify v. t.	طَهَّرَ . نَقَّى . مَحَّصَ
Purity n.	طَهَارَةٌ . نَقَاوَةٌ . عِفَّة
Purloin v. t.	إِخْتَلَسَ . سَرَقَ ـِ
Purple n. or a.	ارْجوَان . ارجوَانِيٌّ

Purport *n.* or *v. t.*	مَضْمُون . مَعْنًى . افَادَ
Purpose *n.* or *v. t.*	قَصْد . نِيَّة . قَصَدَ ـِ
Purposely *ad.*	عَمْدًا . قَصْدًا
Purse *n.*	كِيسُ دَرَاهِم
Pursue *v. t.*	تَبِع ـَ طَارَدَ . سَعَى فِي
Pursuit *n.*	مُطَارَدَة . إِتِّبَاع . حِرْفَة
Pursuance *n.*	إِتِّبَاع
Purvey *v. t.*	قَدَّمَ مُؤْنَةً . جَهَّز
Purveyor *n.*	مُجَهِّزُ آلْمُؤْنَة
Pus *n.*	صَدِيد . قَيْح . مِدَّة
Push *v. t.* or *n.*	دَفَعَ ـَ . حَرَّضَ . نَشَاط

Pusillanimity *n.*	جَبَانَة
Pusillanimous *a.*	جَبَانٌ صَغِيرُ آلنَّفْس
Puss Pussy *n.*	هِرٌّ . قِط
Pustule *n.*	بَثْرَة . دُمَّل
Put *v. t.*	وَضَعَ . جَعَلَ ـَ . حَرَّضَ
Putrefaction *n.*	فَسَاد . عُفُونَة
Putrefy *v. i.*	فَسَدَ ـُ عَفِنَ
Putrid *a.*	عَفِن . فَاسِد
Puzzle *n.* or *v. t.*	إِرْتِبَاك . حَيْرَة . حَيَّرَ
Pygmy *n.*	قَزَم جِنْسًا
Pyramid *n.*	هَرَم ج اهْرَام
Pyre *n.*	عُرْمَة وَقِيد

Q

Quack *v. i.* or *n.*	بَطْبَطَ . دَجَّال
Quackery *n.*	تَدْجِيل . مُخَاتَلَة
Quadrangle *n.*	مُرَبَّع . دَارٌ مُرَبَّعَة
Quadrant *n.*	رُبْعُ دَائِرَة
Quadratic *a.*	مُرَبَّعِيّ
Quadrilateral *a.*	ذُوأَرْبَعِ أَضْلَاعٍ
Quadroon *n.*	وَلَدُ أَبٍ ابْيَضَ وَأُمٍّ خَلَاسِيَة
Quadruped *n.*	ذُو أَرْبَعِ قَوَائِمَ
Quadruple *a.*	أَرْبَعَة أَضْعَافٍ
Quaff *v. t.*	شَرِبَ ـَ
Quagmire *n.*	نَقْع . حَمْأَة
Quail *n.* or *v. i.*	سَلْوَى (سِمَّان) . خَافَ
Quaint *a.*	غَرِيب . أَنِيق
Quake *v. i.*	إِرْتَعَدَ . رَعَشَ ـَ

Quakers *n. pl.*	طَائِفَة مِنَ الْمَسِيحِيِّينَ
Qualification *n.*	أَهْلِيَة . قَيْد
Qualify *v. t.*	أَهَّلَ . نَعَتَ ـَ . قَيَّدَ
Quality *n.*	صِفَة . خَصْلَة . نَبَالَة
Qualm *n.*	غَثَيَان . قَلَقُ الضَّمِيرِ
Quantity *n.*	مِقْدَار . كَمِّيَة
Quarantine *n.*	حَجْر صِحِّي
Quarrel *n.* or *v. i.*	خِصَام . خَاصَمَ
Quarrelsome *a.*	خَصُوم . مُحِكّ
Quarry *n.*	مَقْلَع . صَيْد
Quart *n.*	مِكْيَال وَهُوَ رُبْعُ جَالُونٍ
Quarter *n.*	رُبْع . جِهَة . مَحَلّ
Quarterly *a.* or *ad.*	كُلَّ ثَلَاثَةِ أَشْهُرٍ
Quartermaster *n.*	مَأْمُورُ الْمُونَة

Quartett } *n.* Quartet }	أَرْبَعَةٌ يُغَنُّونَ مَعًا
Quarto *n.*	كِتَابٌ مُرَبَّعُ ٱلشَّكْلِ
Quartz *n.*	ضَرْبٌ مِنَ ٱلْحَجَرِ ٱلصَّلْبِ
Quash *v. t.*	سَحَقَ ـ . أَبْطَلَ
Quaver *v. i.* or *n.*	رَجَّ (ٱلصَّوْتُ)
Quay *n.*	إِسْكَلَةٌ . بَنْط . رَصِيف
Queen *n.*	مَلِكَةٌ
Queer *a.*	غَيْرُ مَأْلُوفٍ . غَرِيبٌ
Queerness *n.*	غَرَابَةٌ
Quell *v. t.*	أَخْمَدَ . سَكَّنَ
Quench *v. t.*	أَطْفَأَ . أَرْوَى
Querulous *a.*	مُتَذَمِّرٌ . مُتَشَكٍّ
Query *n.* or *v. t.*	إِسْتِفْهَام سَأَلَ . شَكَّ
Quest *n.*	طَلَب . تَفْتِيش
Question *n.*	سُؤَالٌ . مَطْلَب . قَضِيَّةٌ
Question *v. t.*	سَأَلَ . إِرْتَابَ
Questionable *a.*	فِيهِ نَظَرٌ أَوْ رَيْبٌ
Quibble *n.* or *v. i.*	حِيلَةٌ . رَاوَغَ
Quibbler *n.*	مُرَاوِغٌ فِي ٱلْكَلَامِ
Quick *a.*	سَرِيعٌ . ذَكِيٌّ . حَيٌّ
Quicken *v. t.*	أَسْرَعَ . أَحْيَا . حَرَّكَ
Quicklime *n.*	كِلْسٌ غَيْرُ مَصْوَّلٍ
Quickness *n.*	سُرْعَة . عَجَلَة
Quicksand *n.*	رَمْلٌ يُغْرَقُ فِيهِ
Quicksilver *n.*	زِئْبَق
Quiescence *n.*	سُكُونٌ
Quiescent *a.*	سَاكِنٌ
Quiet *v. t.*	هَدَّأَ . سَكَّنَ . أَرَاحَ
Quiet *n.* or *a.*	سُكُون رَاحَة سَاكِنٌ
Quietness } *a.* Quietude }	هُدُوٌّ . سُكُونٌ
Quill *n.*	رِيشَةٌ . قَلَم رِيشَةٍ
Quilt *n.* or *v. t.*	لِحَاف . دِثَار . خَاطَ لِحَافًا
Quince *n.*	سَفَرْجَلَة ج سَفَارِج
Quinine *n.*	كِينَا
Quinsy *n.*	إِلْتِهَابُ ٱللَّوْزَتَيْنِ
Quintal *n.*	مِئَةُ لِيبْرَا

20

Quire n.	رِزْمَةُ وَرَق	Quondam a.	سَابِقٌ
Quit v. t.	تَرَكَ ـُ . قَضَى ٱلْوَاجِبَ	Quorum n.	عَدَدُ أَعْضَاءٍ كَافٍ لِلْأَشْغَالِ
Quit a.	مُحَرَّرٌ مِنْ . بَرِيءٌ مِنْ	Quota n.	حِصَّةٌ . نَصِيبٌ
Quite ad.	تَمَامًا بِالْكُلِّيَّةِ	Quotation n.	إِقْتِبَاسٌ
Quittance n.	تَبْرِئَةٌ مِنْ دَيْنٍ . وَصْلٌ	Quote v. t.	إِقْتَبَسَ. ذَكَرَ (سِعْرًا)
Quiver n. or v. i.	جَعْبَةٌ . إِهْتَزَّ. إِرْتَجَفَ	Quoth v. t.	قَالَ
Quiz v. t.	خَيَّرَ . سَخِرَ بِهِ	Quotient n.	خَارِجُ ٱلْقِسْمَةِ

R

Rabbi n.	مُعَلِّمٌ. حَاخَامٌ	Raceme n.	عُرْجُونٌ
Rabbinic Rabbinical a.	حَاخَامِي .تَلْمُودِي	Rack n.	آلَةُ تَعْذِيبٍ. عَذَابٌ .رَفٌّ
Rabbit n.	أَرْنَبٌ ج أَرَانِب	Racket n.	ضَجَّةٌ . جَلَبَةٌ
Rabble n.	رَعَاعٌ . أَوْبَاشٌ	Radiance n.	ضِيَاءٌ . بَهَاءٌ . لَمَعَانٌ
Rabid a.	هَائِجٌ . مَجْنُونٌ . كَلِبٌ	Radiant a.	لَامِعٌ . نَيِّرٌ
Race n.	سِبَاقٌ . جِنْسٌ . أَصْلٌ	Radiate v. i. or t.	شَعَّ . أَشَعَّ
Race v. i. or t.	سَابَقَ .جَعَلَ يُسَابِقُ	Radical a. or n.	أَصْلِيٌّ. جَوْهَرِي. أَصْل .جِذْر

Radicle *n.*	جُذَيْرٌ
Radish *n.*	فُجْلَةٌ
Radius *n.*	نِصفُ قُطْرٍ . كُعْبِرَةٌ
Raft *n.*	رَمَثٌ ج أَرْمَاثٌ
Rafter *n.*	رَافِدٌ ج رَوَافِد
Rag *n.*	خِرْقَةٌ . رِثَّةٌ
Rage *n.* or *v.i.*	غَيْظٌ . غَضَبٌ . إِغْتَاظَ
Ragged *a.*	رَثٌّ . بَالٍ
Raging *a.*	هَائِجٌ . ثَائِرٌ . حَنِقٌ
Raid *n.*	غَزْوَةٌ . غَارَةٌ
Rail *n.*	قَضِيبٌ حَدِيدٍ
Rail *v. t.* or *i.*	سَيَّجَ . عَيَّرَ . إِفْتَرَى
Railing *n.*	تَعْيِيرٌ . إِفْتِرَاءٌ . دَرَابْزُونٌ
Raillery *n.*	هَزْلٌ . مَزْحٌ . مُدَاعَبَةٌ
Railroad Railway } *n.*	سِكَّةٌ حَدِيدٍ
Raiment *n.*	لِبَاسٌ . كِسْوَةٌ
Rain *n.* or *v. i.*	مَطَرٌ . أَمْطَرَ
Rainbow *n.*	قَوْسُ قُزَحَ
Rainy *a.*	مُمْطِرٌ
Raise *v. t.*	رَفَعَ — . أَقَامَ . رَبَّى
Raisin *n.*	زَبِيبَةٌ ج زَبِيبٌ
Rake *n.*	خَلِيعٌ . مَجْرَفَةٌ كَالْمُشْطِ
Rally *v. t.*	ضَمَّ الشَّارِدِينَ . دَاعَبَ
Ram *n.*	كَبْشٌ . مِنْجَنِيقٌ . بُرْجُ الْحَمَلِ
Ramble *v. i.*	جَالَ . طَافَ —
Rambling *a.*	جَائِلٌ . غَيْرُ سَدِيدٍ
Ramify *v. t.* or *i.*	فَرَّعَ . تَفَرَّعَ . تَشَعَّبَ
Rampant *a.*	مُفْرِطٌ . غَيْرُ مَحْصُورٍ
Rampart *n.*	سُورٌ . مِتْرَاسٌ
Ramrod *n.*	مِدَكُّ البُنْدُقِيَّةِ
Rancid *a.*	زَنِخٌ
Rancour *n.*	حِقْدٌ . غِلٌّ . ضَغِينَةٌ
Rancorous *a.*	مُغِلٌّ . حَقُودٌ
Random *a.* or *n.*	عَاسِفٌ غَيْرُ تَعَمُّدٍ
Range *n.*	مَدًى . صَفٌّ
Range *v. t.* or *i.*	صَفَّ — جَالَ . طَافَ —

Rank a.	مُخْصِبْ . زِنْخْ . شَدِيدْ
Rank n. or v. i.	رُتْبَة . صَفْ . لَهْرَتبَة
Rankle v. i.	إِشْتَدَّ . إِحْتَدْ
Ransack v. t.	فَتَّشْ كَثِيراً . نَهَبَـ
Ransom n. or v. t.	فِدْيَة . إِفْتَدَى . فَكَّـ
Rant v. i.	أَفْرَطَ بالْكَلام
Rap n. or v. i.	لَكْمَة . ضَرَبَ . دَقَّـ
Rapacious a.	طَمَّاعْ . ضَارْ . سَالِبْ
Rapacity n.	طَمَعْ . إِخْتِطَافْ
Rape n.	إِغْتِصَابْ . فَضَحْ
Rapid a.	سَرِيعْ . مُسْرِعْ
Rapidity / Rapidness n.	سُرْعَة . عَجَلَة
Rapids n. pl.	سَيْلُ مَآءٍ سَرِيعْ
Rapier n.	سَيْفْ خَفِيفْ ضَيِّـقْ النَّصْلِ
Rapine n.	نَهْبْ . إِخْتِطَافْ
Rapture n.	سُرُورْ مُفْرِطْ
Rapturous a.	مُفْتَنْ . سَالِبُ الْعَقْل
Rare a.	نَادِر . نَفِيسْ . لَطِيفْ
Rarefy v. t. or i.	رَقَّقَ . لَطَّفْ
Rarely ad.	نَادِراً
Rareness / Rarity n.	قِلَّةُ الْوُجُودِ . نُدْرَة
Rascal n.	خَبِيثْ . مُحْتَالْ
Rascality n.	خُبْثْ . غَبِينَة
Rase v. t.	خَرَّبْ . هَدَّمْ . مَحَا ـ
Rash a.	هَيِّرْ . مِسْرَاعْ . عَجُولْ
Rashness n.	تَهَوُّرْ . عَدَمُ عِنَايَةٍ
Raspberry n.	ثَمَرُ الْعُلَّيْقِ
Rat n.	جُرَذ ج جُرْذَان
Ratan n.	خَيْزَرَانْ
Rate n.	سِعِر . كَمِّيَة . نِسْبَة
Rather ad.	بالْحَرِيِّ . أَكْثَر
Ratify v. t.	أَمْضَى . أَثْبَتَ . وَقَّعْ
Ratio n.	نِسْبَة . دَرَجَة
Ration n.	جِرَايَةُ الْجُنْدِي
Rational a.	نَاطِقْ . مُوَافِقْ للْعَقْل
Rationalist n.	قَائِلْ بِكَفَاءَةِ الْعَقْل دُونَ الْوَحْي

Ratsbane *n.*	سَمُّ ٱلْفَار
Rattle *v. i.* or *t.* or *n.*	صَلَّ ـِ . صَلِيلٌ
Ravage *v. t.*	نَهَبَ ـَ . خَرَّبَ
Rave *v. i.*	هَذَى ـِ . هَذَرَ ـِ
Ravel *v. t.* or *i.*	فَكَّكَ . حَلَّ ـُ . إِنْفَكَّ
Raven *n.*	غُرَابٌ ج غِرْبَانٌ
Ravenous *a.*	لَئِيمٌ . نَهِيمٌ . كَاسِرٌ
Ravine *n.*	وَادٍ عَمِيقٌ ضَيِّقٌ
Raving *a.*	هَاذٍ . هَائِجٌ
Ravish *v. t.*	خَطِفَ ـ إِغْتَصَبَ . أَفْتَنَ
Ravishment *n.*	إِغْتِصَابٌ . وَلَهٌ
Raw *a.*	نِيٌّ . غَيْرُ خَبِيرٍ . مَسْحُوجٌ
Rawhide *n.*	سَوْطٌ مِنْ جِلْدٍ غَيْرِ مَدْبُوغٍ
Ray *n.*	شُعَاعٌ . نَوْعٌ مِنَ ٱلسَّمَك
Raze *v. t.*	مَحَا ـ . هَدَّ تَمَامًا
Razor *n.*	مُوسَى ج مَوَاسٍ
Reach *v. t.* or *i.*	بَلَغَ ـُ . لَحِقَ . إِمْتَدَّ
React *v. t.* or *i.*	رَدَّ ٱلْفِعْل
Reaction *n.*	رَدُّ ٱلْفِعْل
Read *v. t.* or *i.*	قَرَأَ ـ . تَلَا ـُ
Readable *a.*	مُسْتَحِقٌّ ٱلْقِرَاءَةِ . يُقْرَأُ
Readily *ad.*	بِسُهُولَةٍ
Readiness *n.*	تَأَهُّبٌ . مُبَادَرَةٌ
Reading *n.*	قِرَاءَةٌ . مُطَالَعَةٌ
Readmit *v. t.*	عَادَ فَ دْخَلَ
Ready *a.*	مُسْتَعِدٌّ . حَاضِرٌ . مُهَيَّأٌ
Reaffirm *v. t.*	كَرَّرَ . عَادَ فَأَكَّدَ
Real *a.*	حَقِيقِيٌّ . فِعْلِيٌّ . صَحِيحٌ
Real-estate *n.*	ٱلْأَمْوَالُ غَيْرُ ٱلْمَنْقُولَةِ
Reality *n.*	حَقِيقَةٌ . وُجُودٌ
Realise *v. t.*	انْجَزَ . أَوْجَدَ . تَحَقَّقَ
Realm *n.*	مَمْلَكَةٌ
Ream *n.*	مَاعُونٌ (مِنَ ٱلْوَرَق)
Reanimate *v. t.*	أَحْيَا . أَنْعَشَ
Reap *v. t.* or *i.*	حَصَدَ ـ . حَصَّلَ . تَمَتَّعَ
Reaper *n.*	حَاصِدٌ . آلَةُ ٱلْحَصَادِ

Reappear v. i.	عَادَ فَظَهَرَ
Reappoint v. t.	عَيَّنَ ثَانِيَةً
Rear n. or a. or v. t.	مُؤَخَّرٌ . أَقَامَ . رَبَّى
Rear-guard n.	سَاقَةُ ٱلْجَيْشِ
Reason v. i. or t.	حَاجَّ . ٱسْتَدَلَّ . أَقْنَعَ
Reason n.	سَبَبٌ . بُرْهَانٌ . عَقْلٌ
Reasonable a.	مَعْقُولٌ . مُعْتَدِلٌ . عَاقِلٌ
Reasoning n.	مُحَاجَّةٌ . إِسْتِدْلَالٌ
Reassure v. t.	أَكَّدَ ثَانِيَةً . أَمَّنَ
Rebel n. or v. i.	خَائِنٌ . عَاصٍ عَطَى
Rebellion n.	عِصْيَانٌ
Rebellious a.	عَاصٍ
Rebound v. i. or n.	إِرْتَدَّ . إِرْتِدَادٌ
Rebuff n. or v. t.	رَدٌّ . رَفْضٌ . رَفَضَ
Rebuke v. t. or n.	وَبَّخَ . تَوْبِيخٌ زَجْرٌ
Rebut v. t.	رَدَّ دَلِيلاً . دَفَعَ
Recall v. t.	إِسْتَرْجَعَ . ذَكَّرَ . نَقَضَ
Recant v. t. or i.	إِرْتَدَّ عَنْ . أَنْكَرَ

Recapitulate v. t.	كَرَّرَ مُلَخِّصاً
Recede v. i.	رَجَعَ . تَقَهْقَرَ
Receipt n. or v. t.	وَصْلٌ . أَعْطَى وَصْلاً
Receive v. t.	قَبِلَ . قَبَضَ . نَالَ
Recent a.	حَدِيثٌ . جَدِيدٌ
Receptacle n.	وِعَاءٌ . غِلَافٌ
Reception n.	قَبُولٌ . إِسْتِقْبَالٌ . أَخْذٌ
Receptive a.	قَابِلٌ
Recess n.	إِعْتِزَالٌ . فَرَاغٌ . فَتْرَةٌ
Recipe n.	وَصْفَةُ دَوَاءٍ
Recipient n.	مُسْتَلِمٌ . قَابِلٌ . نَائِلٌ
Reciprocal a.	مُتَبَادِلٌ . مُعَاوِضٌ
Reciprocate v. t. or i.	عَاوَضَ . تَبَادَلَ
Reciprocity n.	تَبَادُلُ ٱلْفِعْلِ أَوِ ٱلْفَائِدَةِ
Recital n.	قِرَاءَةٌ . رِوَايَةٌ . قِصَّةٌ
Recitation n.	تِلَاوَةٌ عَنْ ظَهْرِ ٱلْقَلْبِ
Recite v. t.	قَرَأَ . تَلَا
Reckless a.	مُتَهَوِّرٌ . غَيْرُ مُبَالٍ

Reckon v. t.	حَسَبَ ـُ . أَحْصَى
Reckoning n.	حِساب . مُحاسَبَةٌ
Reclaim v. t.	إِسْتَرْجَعَ . أَصْلَحَ
Recline v. i.	إِتَّكَأَ . إِسْتَنَد
Recluse n. or a.	نَاسِكٌ . مُعْتَزِلٌ
Recognisable a.	مَا يُعرَفُ أَوْ يُمَيَّز
Recognise v. t.	عَرَفَ . قَبِلَ صَرِيحًا
Recoil v. i. or n.	إِرْتَدَّ . نَكَصَ ـُ
Recollect v. t.	ذَكَرَ ـُ . جَمَعَ ثَانِيَةً
Recollection n.	ذِكْر وَذِكْرَى
Recommence v. t.	بَدَأَ ثَانِيَةً
Recommend v. t.	وَصَّى بِهِ . مَدَحَ
Recompense v. t. or n.	جَازَى . مُجَازَاةٌ
Reconcile v. t.	صَالَحَ . وَفَّقَ بَيْنَ
Recondite a.	غَامِض . عَوِيص
Reconnaissance n.	إِسْتِطْلَاع
Reconnoiter v. t.	إِسْتَطْلَعَ . تَجَسَّسَ
Reconquer v. t.	فَتَحَ ـَ ثَانِيَةً

Reconsider v. t.	اعَادَ ٱلنَّظَرَ فِي
Reconsideration n.	مُرَاجَعَةٌ
Record v. t. or n.	كَتَبَ . دَوَّنَ . سِجِلّ
Recount v. t.	قَصَّ . رَوَى بِتَفْصِيل
Recourse n.	إِلْتِجَاءٌ . مَلْجَأٌ
Recover v. t. or i.	إِسْتَرَدَّ . تَعَافَى
Recoverable a.	قَابِلُ ٱلِاسْتِرْدَاد
Recovery n.	إِسْتِرْجَاعٌ . شِفَاءٌ
Recreant a. or n.	خَائِن . جَبَان . نَذْلٌ
Recreation n.	تَنَزُّه . تَسْلِيَة
Recriminate v. t. or i.	اتَّهَمَ . تَعَايِب
Recruit v. t. or i.	أَمَدَّ . جَدَّدَ . تَعَافَى
Recruit v. i. or n.	جَنَّدَ . عَسْكَرِي جَدِيد
Rectangle n.	مُرَبَّع مُسْتَطِيل قَائِمُ ٱلزَّوَايَا
Rectify v. t.	قَوَّمَ . أَصْلَحَ
Rectilinear a.	مُسْتَقِيمُ ٱلْخُطُوط
Rectitude n.	إِسْتِقَامَة
Rector n.	مُدِيرٌ . قِسِّيسُ أَبْرَشِيَّة

Rectory *n.*	كَنِيسَةُ أَبْرَشِيَّةٍ . بَيْتُ القِسِّيسِ
Rectum *n.*	المُسْتَقِيمُ (مِنَ الأَمْعَاءِ)
Recumbent *a.*	مُتَّكِئٌ
Recuperate *v. i.*	تَعَافَى
Recuperative *a.*	شَافٍ . مُعَافٍ
Recur *v. i.*	عَادَ . تَكَرَّرَ . إِلْتَجَأَ
Recurrence *n.*	عَوْدٌ . تَكْرَارٌ
Red *a.*	أَحْمَرُ
Redden *v. t. or i.*	حَمَّرَ . إِحْمَرَّ
Redeem *v. t.*	فَدَى . فَكَّ
Redeemer *n.*	فَادٍ . مُخَلِّصٌ
Redemption *n.*	فِدْيَةٌ . فِدَاءٌ
Redness *n.*	حُمْرَةٌ . إِحْمِرَارٌ
Redolent *a.*	فَائِحٌ . عَبِقٌ
Redouble *v. t.*	ضَاعَفَ . كَثَّرَ
Redoubt *n.*	مِتْرَاسٌ . حِصْنٌ
Redress *v. t.*	قَوَّمَ . عَدَلَ . أَنْصَفَ
Reduce *v. t*	قَبَّلَ . أَخْضَعَ . رَدَّ

Reduction *n.*	تَحْوِيلٌ (فِي الحِسَابِ) . رَدٌّ
Redundant *n.*	زَائِدٌ عَنِ اللُّزُومِ
Reduplicate *v. t.*	ضَاعَفَ
Re-echo *v. t. or i.*	رَدَّ الصَّدَى
Reed *n.*	قَصَبَةٌ . مِزْمَارٌ
Reef *n.*	سِلْسِلَةُ صُخُورٍ فِي المَاءِ
Reef *v. t.*	طَوَى ـ (القُلُوعَ)
Reek *v. i.*	فَاحَ بُخَارُهُ . بَخَرَ
Reel *n. or v. t. or i.*	مَكَبٌّ . كَبَّ . تَرَنَّحَ
Re-elect *v. t.*	إِنْتَخَبَ ثَانِيَةً
Re-embark *v. i. or t.*	نَزَلَ ثَانِيَةً فِي سَفِينَةٍ
Re-enforce *v. t.*	عَزَّزَ . أَمَدَّ
Re-engage *v. t.*	جَدَّدَ العَهْدَ أَوِ القِتَالَ
Re-enter *v. t.*	عَادَ فَدَخَلَ
Re-establish *v. t.*	عَادَ فَأَقَامَ أَوْ أَثْبَتَ
Re-examine *v. t.*	عَادَ فَفَحَصَ أَوِ امْتَحَنَ
Refectory *n.*	قَاعَةٌ لِلْأَكْلِ
Refer *v. t. or i.*	وَجَّهَ أَوْ أَشَارَ إِلَى

Referee *n.*	فَيْصَلٌ .حَكَمٌ	Refrangible *n.*	قَابِلُ ٱلْاِنْكِسَارِ
Reference *n.*	إِشَارَةٌ .شَاهِدٌ .عِلَاقَةٌ	Refresh *v. t.*	أَنْعَشَ .أَرَاحَ
Refine *v. t. or i.*	مَحَّصَ.هَذَّبَ .تَنَقَّى	Refreshment *n.*	إِنْعَاشٌ . طَعَامٌ
Refinement *n.*	أَدَبٌ . تَهْذِيبٌ	Refrigerator *n.* مُبَرِّدٌ	آلَةُ ٱلتَّبْرِيدِ .
Refinery *n.*	مَعْمَلُ ٱلتَّمْحِيصِ أَوِ ٱلتَّصْفِيَةِ	Refuge *n.*	مَلْجَأٌ . سَبِيلٌ لِلنَّجَاةِ
Refit *v. t.*	عَادَ فَجَهَّزَ . أَصْلَحَ	Refugee *n.*	مُلْتَجِئٌ .مُهَاجِرٌ .هَارِبٌ
Reflect *v. i. or t.*	تَأَمَّلَ . إِنْعَكَسَ	Refulgence } Refulgency }*n.*	لَمَعَانٌ . بَهَاءٌ
Reflective *a.*	مُتَأَمِّلٌ . عَاكِسٌ	Refulgent *a.*	بَهِيٌّ . نَيِّرٌ
Reflector *n.*	سَطْحٌ عَاكِسٌ . مِرْآةٌ	Refund *v. t.*	أَوْفَى . رَدَّ
Reflex *a.*	مَرْدُودٌ .مُنْعَكِسٌ	Refusal *n.*	رَفْضٌ .حَقُّ ٱلْأَخْذِ دُونَ غَيْرِهِ
Reflexive *a.*	مَائِلٌ إِلَى ٱلْوَرَاءِ أَوِ ٱلذَّاتِ	Refuse *n.*	سِقَاطَةٌ . نُفَايَةٌ
Reform *v. t.*	اَصْلَحَ .قَوَّمَ .جَدَّدَ	Refuse *v. t.*	أَبَى . رَفَضَ
Reform } Reformation }*n.*	إِصْلَاحٌ . تَجْدِيدٌ	Refute *v.t.*	أَدْحَضَ .نَقَضَ . رَدَّ
Reformatory *a. or n.*	مُصْلِحٌ (إِصْلَاحِيَّة)	Regain *v. t.*	إِسْتَرَدَّ . إِسْتَعَادَ
Reformer *n.*	مُصْلِحٌ	Regal *a.*	مَلَكِيٌّ
Refract *v. t.*	كَسَّرَ شُعَاعَ ٱلنُّورِ	Regale *v. t.*	أَوْلَمَ وَلِيمَةً فَاخِرَةً
Refraction *n.*	إِنْكِسَارُ ٱلنُّورِ	Regard *v. t.* or *n.*	لَاحَظَ . إِعْتَبَرَ . إِعْتِبَارٌ
Refractory *a.*	مُتَمَرِّدٌ . شَكِسٌ	Regardless *a.*	غَيْرُ مُكْتَرِثٍ . غَافِلٌ
Refrain *v. i.*	إِمْتَنَعَ . أَمْسَكَ عَنْ		

Regency *n.*	نِيَابَةُ مُلْكٍ
Regenerate *v. t.* or *a.*	جَدَّدَ مُتَجَدِّد
Regent *n.*	نَائِبُ ٱلْمَلِكِ
Regicide *n.*	قَاتِلُ مَلِكٍ . قَتَلَهُ
Regime *n.*	شَكْلُ حُكُومَةٍ
Regiment *n.*	كَتِيبَة . أَلَاي
Region *n.*	قُطْرٌ . جِهَةٌ
Register *n.* or *v. t.*	دَفْتَرٌ . سِجِلّ . سَجَّلَ
Regress Regression } *n.*	إِرْتِدَاد . تَقَهْقُر
Regret *n.* or *v. t.*	أَسِفَ تَأَسَّفَ عَلَى
Regular *a.*	قِيَاسِيٌّ عَلَى تَرْتِيب
Regularity *n.*	تَرْتِيبٌ . إِنْتِظَام
Regulate *v. t.*	رَتَّبَ . نَظَّمَ . دَبَّرَ
Regulation *n.*	قَانُون . نِظَام
Regulator *n.*	مُرَتِّب . آلَةُ ضَبْطٍ
Rehearse *v. t.*	قَصَّ . تَلَا مُرَاجَعَة
Reign *n.* or *v. i.*	مُلْك . مَلَكَ . إِسْتَوْلَى
Reimburse *v. t.*	أَوْفَى كَافَأَ
Rein *n.* or *v. t.*	عِنَان . عَنَّنَ . كَبَحَ
Reindeer *n.*	نَوْعٌ مِنَ ٱلْإِيِلِ
Reins *n. pl.*	كُلِّى
Reinstall Reinstate } *v. t.*	أَعَادَ إِلَى مَنْصِبِهِ
Reissue *v. t.* or *i.* or *n.*	عَادَ فَأَصْدَرَ
Reiterate *v. t.*	كَرَّرَ
Reject *v. t.*	نَبَذَ . رَفَضَ
Rejoice *v. i.* or *t.*	سُرَّ . فَرِحَ . فَرَّحَ
Rejoicing *n.*	فَرَح . سُرُور
Rejoin *v. t.* or *i.*	لَاقَى بَعْدَ فِرَاقٍ . أَجَابَ
Rejoinder *n.*	مُجَاوَبَة . جَوَاب
Rejuvenate *v. t.*	جَدَّدَ ٱلشَّبَابَ
Rekindle *v. t.*	أَشْعَلَ ثَانِيَةً
Relapse *v. i.* or *n.*	عَادَ إِلَى حَالَتِهِ . نُكِسَ نُكْس
Relate *v. t.* or *i.*	قَصَّ . حَدَّثَ . تَعَلَّقَ بِـ
Relation *n.*	نِسْبَة . رِوَايَة . نَسِيب
Relationship *n.*	قَرَابَة . نَسَب
Relative *n.* or *a.*	سَبِيب . مَوْصُول . نَسَبِي

Relax *v. t.* or *i.*	أَرْخَى. خَفَّفَ إِرْتَخَى
Relaxation *n.*	إِرْخَاءٌ إِرَاحَة فَرَحٌ
Relaxative Relaxing } *a.*	مُرْخٍ . مُلَيِّن
Relay *n.* or *v. t.*	بَدَلُ خَيْلٍ . عَادَ فَوَضَعَ
Release *v. t.* or *n.*	أَطْلَقَ . حَرَّرَ . إِطْلَاقٌ
Relent *v. i.*	رَقَّ لَهُ . سَامَحَ
Relentless *a.*	بِلَا رَحْمَةٍ أَوْ عَفْوٍ
Relevant *a.*	مُوَافِقٌ . فِي مَحَلِّهِ
Reliable *a.*	مَا يُمْكِنُ الرُّكُونُ إِلَيْهِ. مَوْثُوقٌ بِهِ
Reliance *n.*	ثِقَةٌ . إِعْتِمَادٌ . إِتِّكَالٌ
Relic *n.*	بَقِيَّةٌ . أَثَرٌ . ذَخِيرَة
Relief *n.*	إِسْعَافٌ , نَجْدَةٌ . إِرَاحَة
Relieve *v. t.*	أَرَاحَ . خَفَّفَ . أَمَدَّ
Religion *n.*	دِيَانَة . دِينٌ
Religious *a.*	دِينٌ . دِينِيٌّ
Relinquish *v. t.*	تَرَكَ . تَنَحَّى عَنْ
Relinquishment *n.*	تَرْكٌ
Relish *n.* or *v. t.*	لَذَّةُ طَعْمٍ . إِسْتَلَذَّ

Reluctance *n.*	نُفُورٌ . مُضَادَّة . كَرَاهَة
Reluctant *a.*	نَافِرٌ . غَيْرُ رَاضٍ
Rely *v. i.*	وَثِقَ بِ . إِتَّكَلَ عَلَى
Remain *v. i.*	بَقِيَ . دَامَ . مَكَثَ
Remainder *n.*	بَقِيَّة . فَضْلَة
Remains *n. pl.*	بَقَايَا . جِثَّة
Remand *v. t.*	أَعَادَ . رَدَّ
Remark *v. t.* or *n.*	لَاحَظَ. قَالَ . مُلَاحَظَة
Remarkable *a.*	مُسْتَحِقُّ النَّظَرِ كَمَشْهُور
Remediable *a.*	قَابِلُ الإِصْلَاحِ
Remedial *a.*	عِلَاجِيٌّ . مُصْلِحٌ
Remedy *n.* or *v. t.*	عِلَاجٌ . عَالَجَ
Remember *v. t.*	تَذَكَّرَ . ذَكَرَ
Remembrance *n.*	ذِكْرٌ . ذِكْرَى
Remind *v. t.*	ذَكَّرَ (فَكَّرَ)
Reminiscence *n.*	ذِكْرٌ . تَذْكَارٌ
Remiss *a.*	غَافِل . مُتَوَانٍ
Remission *n.*	غُفْرَانٌ . عَفْوٌ

Remit v. t.	رَدَّ . أَرْسَلَ . عَفَا _
Remittance n.	اِرْسالُ دَرَاهِم
Remittent a.	مُنْقَطِع . مُنَرَدِّدٌ
Remnant n.	فَضْلَة
Remonstrance n.	إِعْتِرَاضٌ
Remonstrate v. i.	إِعْتَرَضَ عَلَى . وَبَّخَ
Remorse n.	تَوْبِيخُ ٱلضَّمِيرِ
Remorseless a.	بِلا رَحْمَةٍ . قَاسٍ
Remote a.	بَعِيدٌ
Remoteness n.	بُعْدٌ
Remount v. t.	عَادَ فَصَعِدَ أَوْ رَكِبَ
Removal n.	نَقْلٌ . رَحِيلٌ . عَزْلٌ
Remove v. t. or i.	نَقَلَ . عَزَلَ . اِرْتَحَلَ
Remunerate v. t.	جَازَى . كَافَى
Remunerative a.	مُكَافٍ . مُرْبِحٌ
Renascence } Renaissance } n.	تَجْدِيدٌ . عَوْدَة
Rend v. t.	مَزَّقَ . شَقَّ _
Render v. t.	رَدَّ . أَعْطَى . صَبَرَ
Renegade n.	مُرْتَدٌّ . خَائِنٌ
Renew v. t.	جَدَّدَ
Renewable a.	قَابِلُ ٱلتَّجْدِيدِ
Renewal n.	تَجْدِيد
Renounce v. t.	رَفَضَ . نَبَذَ _
Renovate v. t.	جَدَّدَ
Renown n.	صِيتٌ شُهْرَةٌ ذِكْرٌ
Renowned a.	شَهِيرٌ
Rent v. t. or n.	آجَرَ . أُجْرَةٌ
Rent n. or a.	شَقٌّ . فَتْقٌ . مَشْقُوقٌ
Renunciation n.	رَفْضٌ . إِنْكَارٌ
Reorganize v. t.	رَتَّبَ أَوْ نَظَّمَ ثَانِيَةً
Repair v. t. or i.	أَصْلَحَ . رَمَّمَ . ذَهَبَ إِلَى
Reparation n.	تَصْلِيحٌ . تَعْوِيضٌ
Repass v. t. or i.	عَادَ فَاجْتَازَ أَوْ مَرَّ
Repast n.	أَكْلَةٌ . طَعَامٌ
Repay v. t.	وَفَى . يَفِي
Repel v. t. or i.	نَسَخَ — . أَلْغَى نَسْخَ

Repeat _v. t._	كَرَّرَ . ثَنَى
Repel _v. t._	دَفَعَ ــ . دَافَعَ
Repellent _a._	رَادَ . مُنفِّر
Repent _v. i._	تَابَ ــ . نَدِمَ ــ
Repentance _n._	تَوْبَة . نَدَامَة
Repentant _a._	تَائِبٌ . نَادِم
Repetition _n._	تَكْرَار
Repine _v. i._	تَشَكَّى . تَذَمَّرَ
Replace _v. t._	عَوَّضَ . اعادَ إِلَى مَكَانِه
Replenish _v. t._	مَلَأَ أَيضًا . سَدَّ ٱلعَوَز
Replete _a._	مَحْشُوٌّ . مُمْتَلئٌ . مُفعَم
Repletion _n._	مَفعُومة . إِمْتِلاءٌ
Reply _n._ or _v. t._	جَوَابٌ . جَاوَبَ . أَجَابَ
Report _v. t._	قَرَّرَ . أَخْبَرَ
Report _n._	تَقْرِير . خَبَر . صَوْت
Reporter _a._	مُقَرِّرٌ . مُخبِرٌ
Repose _v. i._ or _n._	إِسْتَرَاحَ . رَاحَة
Repository _n._	مَخْزَن . مُسْتَودَع
Repossess _v. t._	عَادَ فَمَلَك . إِسْتَرَدّ
Reprehend _v. t._	وَبَّخَ . لَامَ ــ
Reprehensible _a._	مُسْتَحِقُّ ٱللَّوْم
Represent _v. t._	مَثَّل . صَوَّرَ . نَابَ عَنْ
Representation _n._	صُورَة . نِيَابَة
Representative _n._ or _a._	نَائِبٌ . مُمَثِّل
Repress _v. t._	مَنَعَ ــ . قَهَرَ ــ . قَمَعَ ــ
Repressive _a._	قَاهِر . مَانِع
Reprieve _v. t._ or _n._	أَجَّلَ ٱلقِصَاصَ
Reprimand _v. t._ or _n._	وَبَّخَ . تَوْبِيخ
Reprint _v. t._ or _n._	طَبَعَ ثَانِيَةً
Reprisal _n._	أَخْذُ ٱلثَّأْر . إِنْتِقَام
Reproach _v. t._ or _n._	عَيَّرَ . عَار . تَعْيِير
Reprobate _n._	مَرْفُوضٌ . مَرْذُول
Reproduce _v. t._	جَدَّدَ . تَنَاسَل
Reproduction _n._	تَجْدِيدَ . تَنَاسُل
Reproductive _a._	مُجَدِّد . مُتَنَاسِل
Reproof _n._	تَوْبِيخ

Reprove v. t. وَبَّخَ . عَزَلَ ـِ . لَامَ ـَ	Requirement n. إِحْتِيَاجٌ . إِقْتِضَاءٌ . إِلزَامٌ
Reptile n. زَحَافَةٌ	Requisite a. مَطْلُوبٌ . لَازِمٌ
Republic n. جُمْهُورِيَّةٌ	Requisition n. إِقْتِضَاءٌ . إِلزَامٌ
Repulican a. جُمْهُورِي	Requital n. مُكَافَأَةٌ . جَزَآءٌ
Republicanism n. مَذْهَبُ ٱلْجُمْهُورِية	Requite v. t. كَافَأَ . جَازَى . عَوَّضَ
Republish v. t. أَصْدَرَ ثَانِيَةً	Rescind v. t. نَسَخَ ـَ . أَلْغَى
Repudiate v. t. رَفَضَ ـِ . أَنْكَرَ	Rescue v. t. or n. أَنْقَذَ . خَلَّصَ . نَجَّى
Repugnance) Repugnancy) n. كَرَاهَةٌ . نُفُورٌ	Research n. تَفْتِيشٌ . بَحْثٌ
Repugnant a. كَرِيهٌ . مُنَفِّرٌ	Resemblance n. مُشَابَهَةٌ
Repulse n. or v. t. رَدْعٌ . رَدَّ ـُ	Resemble v. t. شَابَهَ . مَاثَلَ . أَشْبَهَ
Repulsive a. رَادِعٌ . قَبِيحٌ . كَرِيهٌ	Resent v. t. إِسْتَاءَ . قَاوَمَ
Reputable a. حَسَنُ ٱلصِّيتِ . مُحْتَرَمٌ	Resentful a. مُغْتَاظٌ . حَقُودٌ
Reputation) Repute) n. صِيتٌ . ذِكْرٌ . شُهْرَةٌ	Reservation n. إِبْقَاءٌ . تَقْيِيدٌ
Reputed a. مَحْسُوبٌ . مَظْنُونٌ	Reserve v. t. حَفِظَ . اَبْقَى
Request n. or v. t. طَلَبٌ . طَلَبَ ـُ . إِلتَمَسَ	Reserved a. مَحْفُوظٌ . كَتُومٌ . مُتَحَفِّظٌ
Requiem n. تَرْزِمَةٌ اوْ قُدَّاسٌ لِأَجْلِ ٱلْمَوْتَى	Reservoir n. حَوْضٌ . صَهْرِيجٌ (خَزَان)
	Reset v. t. وَضَعَ ثَانِيَةً
Require v. t. إِحْتَاجَ . إِقْتَضَى . أَلْزَمَ	Reside v. i. سَكَنَ ـُ . اَقَامَ

Residence *n.*	إِقَامَةٌ . سُكْنَى	Resource *n.*	مَلْجَأٌ . وَسِيلَةٌ
Resident *a.*	سَاكِنٌ . مُتَوَطِّنٌ	Respect *v. t.* or *n.*	إِحْتَرَمَ . إِحْتِرَامٌ
Residual *a.*	بَاقٍ . فَاضِلٌ	Respectability *n.*	إِحْتِرَامٌ
Residue Residuum } *n.*	بَقِيَّةٌ . فَضْلَةٌ	Respecting *pr.*	بِخُصُوصِ . مِنْ جِهَةِ
Resign *v. t.*	تَخَلَّى عَنْ . سَلَّمَ	Respective *a.*	كُلٌّ عَلَى حِدَةٍ . نِسْبِيٌّ
Resignation *n.*	تَسْلِيمٌ	Respectable *a.*	مُحْتَرَمٌ . مُتَوَسِّطٌ
Resigned *a.*	صَبُورٌ	Respectful *a.*	مُحْتَرِمٌ . مُحْتَشِمٌ
Resin *n.*	رَاتِينَجٌ	Respiration *n.*	تَنَفُّسٌ . نَفَسٌ
Resist *v. t.*	قَاوَمَ . ضَادَّ . عَارَضَ	Respiratory *a.*	تَنَفُّسِيٌّ
Resistance *n.*	مُقَاوَمَةٌ	Respite *n.* or *v. t.*	فَتْرَةٌ . أَمْهَلَ
Resistless *a.*	مَا لَا يُقَاوَمُ	Resplendent *a.*	بَهِيٌّ . لَامِعٌ
Resolute *a.*	عَزُومٌ . ثَابِتُ الرَّأْي	Respond *v. i.*	أَجَابَ . وَافَقَ
Resolution *n.*	عَزْمٌ . تَقْرِيرٌ . حَلٌّ	Response *n.*	جَوَابٌ
Resolve *v. t.* or *n.*	عَزَمَ . حَلَّ . عَزْمٌ	Responsibility *n.*	مَسْؤُولِيَّةٌ
Resolvent *n.*	حَالٌّ . مُذِيبٌ	Responsible *a.*	مَسْؤُولٌ
Resonance *n.*	رَدُّ الصَّوْتِ . رَنِينٌ	Responsive *a.*	مُجِيبٌ . مُرِيدُ الْجَوَابِ
Resort *v. i.* or *n.*	إِلْتِجَأَ إِلَى . مُجْمَعٌ	Rest *v. t.* or *i.*	رَاحَ . إِسْتَرَاحَ
Resound *v. t.* or *i.*	أَذَاعَ الصِّيتَ . رَنَّ	Rest *n.*	سُكُونٌ . رَاحَةٌ . بَقِيَّةٌ

Restaurant n.	محلُّ طعَامٍ (مَطعَمٌ)
Restitution n.	رَدٌّ . تعوِيضٌ
Restive a.	قَلِقٌ . جَمُوحٌ
Restless a.	عديمُ ٱلرَّاحةِ . جَزِعٌ
Restoration n.	رَدٌّ . إِصْلاحٌ . شفاءٌ
Restorative a.	شافٍ . مقوٍّ
Restore v. t.	رَدَّ . جَدَّد
Restrain v. t.	منَعَ . حجَزَ
Restraint n.	حجْرٌ . مانِعٌ . ضبْطٌ
Restrict v. t.	حصَرَ . قصَرَ علَى
Restriction n.	حصْرٌ . قصْرٌ
Result v. i. or n.	نتَجَ مِنْ . نتيجةٌ
Resume v. t.	إِسْترَدَّ . عادَ إِلَى
Resumé n.	خُلاصةٌ . ملخَّصٌ
Resurrection n.	قيامةٌ . بعْثٌ
Resuscitate v. t.	أَحْيا . انعشَ
Retail v. t. or n.	باعَ بِٱلمُفرَّق
Retain v. t.	امسكَ . ضبطَ
Retainer n.	خادِمٌ . تابِعٌ
Retaliate v. i.	أَخذ ٱلثأْرَ . إِنْتقمَ
Retard v. t.	عاقَ . أَخَّر
Retention n.	إِمساكٌ . حجْزٌ
Retentive a.	حافِظٌ . ضابطٌ
Reticent a.	كَتُومٌ . كاظِمٌ
Retina n.	شبكيَّةُ ٱلعَيْنِ
Retinue n.	حشَمٌ . تبَعٌ
Retire v. i.	تقهقرَ . إِرْتدَ
Retirement n.	إِعْتِزَالٌ . تقاعُد
Retort v. t. or i.	رَدَّ بِٱلمِثلِ
Retort n.	رَدٌّ . إِنْبِيقٌ
Retrace v. t.	رَجَعَ علَى ٱلأَثرِ
Retract v. t.	إِسْترَدَّ قوْلاً
Retreat n. or v. i.	إِرْتِدادٌ . إِرْتدَ
Retrench v. t.	نقصَ . قلل ٱلمَصرُوف
Retribution n.	معاقبَةٌ . مُجَازَاة
Retributive / Retributory } a.	عقَابي

Retrieve v. t.	إِسْتَرَدَّ . أَصْلَحَ
Retroaction n.	رَدُّ ٱلْفِعْل
Retrograde a. or v. i.	مُرْتَدٌّ . تَقَهْقَرَ
Retrogression n.	إِرْتِدَادٌ . إِنْحِطَاطٌ
Retrospect Retrospection } n.	نَظَرٌ إِلَى ٱلْمَاضِي
Return v. t. or i.	رَجَّعَ . رَجَعَ
Return n.	رُجُوعٌ . تَعْوِيضٌ . رِبْحٌ
Reunion n.	إِجْتِمَاعٌ بَعْدَ فِرَاقٍ
Reunite v. t. or i.	ضَمَّ أَيْضاً . إِنْضَمَّ
Reveal v. t.	أَعْلَنَ . كَشَفَ . أَظْهَرَ
Revel n. or v. i.	بَطَرٌ . إِنْهَمَكَ بِاللَّذَّاتِ
Revelation n.	إِعْلَانٌ . وَحْيٌ . تَنْزِيلٌ
Revelry n.	بَطَرٌ . مَرَحٌ
Revenge n. or v. t.	إِنْتِقَامٌ . إِنْتَقَمَ
Revengeful v. i.	شَدِيدُ ٱلِانْتِقَامِ . ضَاغِنٌ
Revenue n.	دَخْلٌ
Reverberate v. i.	إِرْتَدَّ ٱلصَّوْتُ وَتَكَرَّرَ
Revere v. t.	إِحْتَرَمَ . وَقَّرَ
Reverence n.	إِحْتِرَامٌ
Reverend a.	مُوَقَّرٌ . مُحْتَرَمٌ
Reverent Reverential } a.	مُحْتَرِمٌ . إِحْتِرَامِيٌّ
Reverie Revery } n.	شُرُودُ ٱلْأَفْكَارِ . تَأَمُّلٌ
Reversal n.	قَلْبٌ . عَكْسٌ . نَقْضٌ
Reverse v. t.	قَلَبَ . عَكَسَ . أَبْطَلَ
Reverse n.	نَقِيضٌ . مُصِيبَةٌ . قَفاً
Revert v. i.	عَادَ . رَجَعَ
Review n. or v. t.	مُرَاجَعَةٌ . أَعَادَ ٱلنَّظَرَ
Revile v. t.	شَتَمَ . سَبَّ
Revisal Revision } n.	مُرَاجَعَةٌ . تَصْحِيحٌ
Revise v. t.	رَاجَعَ . نَقَّحَ . صَحَّحَ
Revisit v. t.	عَادَ فَزَارَ
Revival n.	إِنْتِعَاشٌ . تَجْدِيدٌ
Revive v. t. or i.	أَنْعَشَ . إِنْتَعَشَ
Revivify v. t.	أَحْيَا . جَعَلَهُ يَنْتَعِشُ
Revocation n.	فَسْخٌ . إِلْغَاءٌ
Revoke v. t.	نَقَضَ . أَلْغَى . فَسَخَ

Revolt v. i. or n.	عَصَى ـِ . عِصْيَانْ
Revolution n.	إِنْقِلَابْ . دَوَرَانْ
Revolutionary a.	آيِل لِلْفِتْنَةِ
Revolutionize v. t.	غَيَّرَ كُلِّيًا
Revolve v. t. or i.	ادَارَ . رَدَّدَ . دَارَ ـُ
Revulsion n.	رَدٌّ . نُفُورٌ شَدِيدٌ
Reward n. or v. t.	ثَوَابْ . جَازَى
Rewrite v. t.	عَادَ فَكَتَبَ
Rhetoric n.	عِلْمُ الْبَيَانِ
Rheumatism n.	دَآءُ الْمَفَاصِلِ
Rhinoceros n.	كَرْكَدَّنْ
Rhubarb n.	رَوَنْدْ او رُوَنْدْ
Rhyme n.	سَجْعْ . قَافِيَةْ
Rhythm n.	نَظْمُ الشِّعْرِ
Rib n.	ضِلْعْ ج ضُلُوعْ وا ضْلُعْ
Ribalbry n.	كَلَامْ رَذِيلْ أَو فَاحِشْ
Ribbed a.	مُضَلَّعْ . مُخَطَّطْ
Ribbon n.	شَرِيطْ ج شُرُطْ وشَرَائِط

Rice n.	ارُزّ . رُزّ
Rich a.	غَنِيّ . مُخْصِبْ . دَسِمْ
Riches n. pl.	غِنًى . ثَرْوَة . مَالْ
Richness n.	خَصْبْ . وُفُورْ . دَسَمْ
Rickets n. pl.	دَآءُ الْكُسَاحَةِ
Rickety a.	كَسِيحْ . رَكِيكْ
Rid v. t.	أَنْقَذَ . خَلَّصَ . نَجَّى
Riddle n.	لُغْزْ . أُحْجِيَّةْ
Ride v. t. or n.	رَكِبَ ـَ . رِكْبَةْ
Riding n.	رُكُوبْ
Ridge n.	ظَهْرْ . مُرْتَفِعْ
Ridicule n. or v. t.	هُزْءْ . سَخِرَ بِ
Ridiculous a.	مُضْحِكْ . سُخْرِيّ
Rifle n. or v. i.	بُنْدُقِيَّة مُضَلَّعَة . سَلَبَ ـ
Rift n. or v. t.	شَقّ . فُرْجَة . شَقَّ
Rig v. t.	جَهَّزَ السَّوَارِيَ . الْبَسَ
Rigging n.	جِهَازْ سَفِينَةْ
Right a. or n.	مُصِيبْ . مُسْتَقِيمْ . حَقّ . يَمِينْ

Right n.	صَوَابٌ. عَدْلٌ. إِمْتِيَازٌ	Rioter n. Riotous a.	مُشَاغِبٌ. خَلِيعٌ. بَطِرٌ
Righteous n.	بَارٌّ. تَقِيٌّ. صَالِحٌ	Rip v. t. or n.	فَتَقَ ـِ. مزق. فَتْقٌ
Righteousness n.	بِرٌّ	Ripe a.	نَاضِجٌ. مُسْتَوٍ. كَامِلٌ
Rightful a.	حَقٌّ. شَرْعِيٌّ. عَادِلٌ	Ripen v. t. or i.	أَنْضَجَ. نَضِجَ ـَ
Rigid a.	مُتَوَتِّرٌ. مُتَصَلِّبٌ	Ripeness n.	نَضْجٌ. كَمَالٌ. بُلُوغٌ
Rigidity Rigidness } n.	صَلَابَةٌ. عَدَمُ لُيُونَةٍ	Ripple n.	مَوْجَةٌ خَفِيفَةٌ
Rigour n.	عُنْفٌ. شدة. صَرَامَةٌ	Rise v. i.	إِرْتَفَعَ. قَامَ ـُ. أَشْرَقَ
Rigorous a.	شَدِيدٌ. عَنِيفٌ. صَارِمٌ	Rising n.	قِيَامٌ. طُلُوعٌ. إِرْتِفَاعٌ
Rill n.	سَاقِيَةٌ. جَدْوَلُ مَاءٍ	Risk n. or v. t.	خَطَرٌ. خَاطَرَ
Rim n.	حَافَةٌ	Rite n.	طَقْسٌ دِينِيٌّ. سُنَّةٌ
Rind n.	قِشْرٌ	Ritual a. or n.	طَقْسِيٌّ. كِتَابُ طُقُوسٍ
Ring n.	حَلْقَةٌ. خَاتَمٌ. رَنِينٌ	Rival n. or v. t.	مُنَاظِرٌ. سَابَقَ
Ring v. t. or i.	دَقَّ ـُ. رَنَّ ـِ. طَنَّ ـِ	Rivalry n.	مُسَابَقَةٌ. مُبَارَاةٌ
Ringleader n.	رَئِيسُ ثَوْرَةٍ	River n.	نَهْرٌ ج أَنْهُرٌ وَأَنْهَارٌ
Ringlet n.	جَعِيدَةُ شَعْرٍ	Rivet n. or v. t.	مِسْمَارُ مِبْجَنٍ. سَمَّرَ بِهِ
Ringworm n.	أَلْقُوبَاءُ	Rivulet n.	نُهَيْرٌ. سَاقِيَةٌ
Rinse v. t.	شَطَفَ ـِ. مَضْمَضَ	Road n.	طَرِيقٌ. سِكَّةٌ. دَرْبٌ
Riot n.	شَغْبٌ. فِتْنَةٌ. بَطَرٌ	Roadstead n.	مَرْسًى. مَرْفَأٌ

Roam v. i.	جَالَ ـُ . سَاحَ ـِ
Roan a. or n.	فَرَسٌ كُمَيْت مُبقَّع
Roar v. i. or n.	زَمْجَرَ . زَأَرَ ـَ . زَئِيرٌ
Roast v. t. or n.	شَوَى ـِ . مَشْوِي
Rob v. t.	سَلَبَ ـُ . نَهَبَ ـَ
Robber n.	لِصٌّ . سَرَّاق
Robbery n.	سَلْبٌ . سَرِقَة
Robe n. or v. t.	ثَوْبٌ . رِدَاءٌ . أَلْبَسَ
Robust a.	صَلِيعٌ . قَوِيُّ الجِسْم
Rock n. or v. t.	صَخْرَة . هَزَّ ـُ
Rocket n.	سَهْمٌ نَارِيٌّ
Rocky a.	صَخْرِيٌّ
Rod n.	عَصاً
Roe n.	اُنْثَى الأَيِّل
Rogue n.	مَكَّارٌ . غَدَّارٌ . خَبِيثٌ
Roguery n.	خُبْثٌ . مَكْرٌ . حِيَلٌ
Roil v. t.	عَكَّرَ . كَدَّرَ . هَيَّجَ
Roll v. t. or i.	دَحْرَجَ . تَدَحْرَجَ . طَوَى ـِ
Roll n.	دَرْجٌ . قَائِمَة . دَحْرَجَة
Roller n.	مِحْدَلَة
Romance n.	حِكَايَة . خُرَافَة
Romanism n.	عَقَائِد كَنِيسَة رُومِيَّة
Romp v. i. or n.	تَغَالَظَ في اللَّعِب . اِبْنَة سَلِيطَة
Roof n.	سَقْفٌ . سَطْحٌ
Room n.	مَكَانٌ . فَرَاغٌ . حُجْرَة
Roomy a.	فَسِيحٌ . رَحِيبٌ
Root n. or v. i.	جِذْرٌ . أَصْلٌ . تَأَصَّلَ
Root v. t.	نَبَشَ ـُ . إِسْتَأْصَلَ
Rope n.	حَبْلٌ . مَرَسٌ
Rose n.	وَرْدَة
Rosette n.	وَرْدَة مِنْ شَرِيطٍ
Rosin n.	رَاتِينَج
Rosy a.	وَرْدِيٌّ . مُحَمَّرٌ
Rot v. i. or t. or n.	فَسَدَ ـُ . تَعَفَّنَ
Rotary Rotatory a.	دَائِرٌ . دَوَّارٌ
Rotate v. i. or t.	دَارَ ـُ . أَدَارَ

Rotation *n.*	دَوَرَانٌ . تَنَاوُبٌ	Royalty *n.*	مَلَكِيَّة . مُلْك . ضَرِيبَة
Rotten *a.*	فَاسِدٌ . عَفِنٌ	Rub *v. t.*	فَرَكَ . مَسَحَ . إِحْتَكَّ
Rottenness *n.*	فَسَادٌ . عُفُونَةٌ	Rub *n.*	فَرْكٌ . حَكٌّ . صُعُوبَة
Rotund *a.*	كَرَوِيٌّ . مُسْتَدِيرٌ	Rubbish *n.*	رَدْمٌ . نُفَايَة . سَقَط
Rotundity *a.*	كَرَوِيَّة	Ruby *n.* or *a.*	يَاقُوتَة . يَاقُوتِيّ
Rough *a.*	خَشِنٌ . فَظٌّ . غَلِيظٌ	Rudder *n.*	دَفَّة السَّفِينَة
Roughness *n.*	حُشُونَة . غِلَاظَة	Ruddy *a.*	أَحْمَرُ . أَشْقَرُ
Round *a.* or *n.*	مُسْتَدِيرٌ . دَوْرٌ	Rude *a.*	فَظٌّ
Roundness *n.*	إِسْتِدَارَة . كَرَوِيَّة	Rudeness *n.*	غِلَاظَة . فَظَاظَة
Rouse *v. t.*	أَيْقَظَ . حَرَّكَ . حَرَّضَ	Rudiment *n.*	مَبْدَأ . اصْل
Rout *n.* or *v. t.*	هَزِيمَة . هَزَمَ	Rudimental Rudimentary } *a.*	إِبْتِدَائِي
Route *n.*	طَرِيق	Rue *v. t.*	أَسِفَ . نَدِمَ
Routine *n.*	أُسْلُوبٌ . عَادَة	Rue *n.* (plant)	سَذَابٌ
Rove *v. i.*	جَالَ . سَاحَ	Ruff *n.*	طَوْق ذُو كَشْكَشٍ
Row *n.*	صَفٌّ . شَغْبٌ . خِصَامٌ	Ruffian *n.*	خَبِيث . غَلِيظ . شَرِس
Row *v. t.*	جَذَفَ . قَذَفَ	Ruffle *v. t.*	تَنَفَّشَ . أَضْجَرَ
Royal *a.*	مَلَكِيٌّ . مُلُوكِيٌّ	Rug *n.*	سَجَّادَة . زُرْبِيَّة
Royalist *n.*	مَلَكِيُّ الحِزْب	Rugged *a.*	وَعْرٌ . خَشِن

Ruin v. t. or n.	خَرَبَ ـِ . خَرَابٌ
Ruinous a.	خَرَابِيٌّ
Rule n.	قَانُونٌ . قَاعِدَة . حُكْمٌ
Rule v. t.	حَكَمَ ـُ . سَطَرَ
Ruler n.	حَاكِمٌ . مُتَسَلِّطٌ . مِسْطَرَةٌ
Rumble v. i.	خَرَّ ـُ . قَرْقَرَ
Ruminant n.	حَيوانٌ مُجْتَرٌّ
Ruminate n. or v. i.	إِجْتَرَّ . تَأَمَّلَ
Rummage n. or v. t.	قَلَّبَ . فَتَّشَ
Rumour n.	إِشَاعَة . خَبَرٌ
Rump n.	عَجُزٌ . إِلْيَة
Rumple v. t.	جَعَّدَ . غَضَّنَ

Run v. i.	رَكَضَ ـُ . سَالَ ـِ . جَرَى ـِ
Runaway n.	هَارِبٌ . آبِقٌ . شَارِدٌ
Rupture n.	فَتْقٌ . شِقَاقٌ . إِنْفِجَارٌ
Rural a.	رِيفِيٌّ . غَيْرُ مَدَنِيٍّ
Ruse n.	حِيلَة
Rush n. or v. i.	إِقْتِحَامٌ . زَحْمَة . إِقْتَحَمَ
Rush n.	بَرْدِيٌّ (نَبَاتٌ)
Rust n. or v. i.	صَدَأٌ . صَدِئَ ـَ
Rustic a.	غَيْرُ مُهَذَّبٍ . خَشِنٌ
Rustle v. i.	جَرَّ ـُ . خَشْخَشَ
Rusty a.	صَدِئٌ
Ruthless a.	قَاسٍ . بِلَا رَأْفَةٍ

S

Sabbath n.	سَبْتٌ . يَوْمُ الْأَحَدِ
Sabre n.	سَيْفٌ ج سيوف

Sable n. or a.	سَمُّورٌ (طَائِرٌ) . أَسْوَدُ
Saccharine a.	سُكَّرِي

Sacerdotal *a.*	كَهَنُوتِيّ	Safety-valve *n.*	صِمَامُ آلَةٍ
Sack *n.* or *v. t.*	كِيسٌ . نَهَبَ ـُ	Saffron *n.*	زَعْفَرَان
Sackcloth Sacking } *n.*	خَيْشٌ . مِسْح	Sag *v. i.*	حَطَّ ـُ مِنْ ثِقَلٍ
Sacrament *n.*	سِرٌّ دِينِيّ	Sagacious *a.*	ذَكِيٌّ . فَطِنٌ
Sacred *a.*	مُقَدَّسٌ . دِينِيٌّ . مُحَرَّمٌ	Sagacity *n.*	ذَكَاءٌ . فِطْنَةٌ
Sacredness *n.*	قُدْسٌ . حُرْمِيَّةٌ	Sage *a.* or *n.*	حَكِيمٌ . فَطِينٌ . قَوِيْسَةٌ
Sacrifice *n.* or *v. t.*	ذَبِيحَةٌ . ذَبَحَ ـَ . ضَحَّى	Sail *n.* or *v. i.* or *t.*	قِلْعٌ . أَقْلَعَ . سَيَّرَ
Sacrificial *a.*	ذَبِيحِيّ . قُرْبَانِيّ	Sailor *n.*	نُوتِيّ . بَحْرِيّ . مَلَّاحٌ
Sacrilege *n.*	تَدْنِيسُ ٱلْمُقَدَّس	Saint *n.*	قَدِّيسٌ
Sad *a.*	حَزِينٌ . كَئِيبٌ . مَحْزُنٌ	Sake *n.*	قَصْدٌ . غَايَةٌ . شَأْنٌ
Sadden *v. t.*	أَحْزَنَ	Salad *n.*	سَلَطَةٌ
Saddle *n.*	سَرْجٌ . بَرْذَعَةٌ	Salary *n.*	رَاتِبٌ . مَعَاشٌ . مَاهِيَةٌ
Saddler *n.*	سَرَّاجٌ . (سَرُوجِي) بَرَاذِعِيّ	Sale *n.*	بَيْعٌ . رَوَاجٌ
Sadducee *n.*	صَدُّوقِيّ	Saleable *a.*	رَائِجٌ
Sadness *n.*	حُزْنٌ . كَآبَةٌ . غَمٌّ . لَهَفٌ	Salient *a.*	بَارِزٌ . ظَاهِرٌ
Safe *a.* or *n.*	سَالِمٌ . مَصُونٌ . آمِنٌ	Saline *a.*	مِلْحِيّ . مَالِحٌ
Safeguard *n.* or *v. t.*	حِمَايَةٌ . حَمَى ـِ	Saliva *n.*	لُعَابٌ . رِيقٌ
Safety *n.*	أَمْنٌ . سَلَامَةٌ . نَجَاةٌ	Sallow *a.*	مُصْفَرّ

Sallowness n.	إِصْفِرَارٌ . صُفْرَةٌ
Sally n. or v. i.	هُجُومٌ . هَجَمَ عَلَى
Saloon n.	غُرْفَةُ ٱسْتِقْبَالٍ
Salt n. or v. t.	مِلْحٌ . مَلَّحَ
Salt-cellar n.	مَمْلَحَةٌ
Saltness n.	مُلُوحَةٌ
Salt-petre n.	مِلْحُ البَارُودِ
Salubrious a.	نَافِعٌ لِلصِّحَةِ
Salubrity n.	مُلاَءَمَةٌ لِلصِّحَةِ
Salutary a.	مُفِيدٌ . نَافِعٌ
Salutation n.	تَحِيَّةٌ . سَلاَمٌ
Salute v. t. or n.	سَلَّمَ عَلَى . تَسْلِيمٌ
Salvation n.	خَلاَصٌ . نَجَاةٌ . إِنْقَاذٌ
Salve n.	مَرْهَمٌ . دُهْنٌ
Salver n.	طَبَقٌ ج أَطْبَاقٌ
Samaritan n.	سَامِرِيٌّ
Same n.	ذَات . نَفْسٌ . هُوَ هُوَ
Sameness n.	ذَاتِيَّةٌ . مُمَاثَلَةٌ

Sample n.	عَيِّنِيَّةٌ . (مَسْطَرَةٌ) . نَمُوذَجٌ
Sanative Sanatory } a.	شَافٍ . مُفِيدٌ لِلصِّحَةِ
Sanctification n.	تَقْدِيسٌ . تَطْهِيرٌ
Sanctify v. t.	قَدَّسَ . طَهَّرَ
Sanctimonious a.	مُتَظَاهِرٌ بِالتَّقْوَى
Sanction n. or v. t.	مُصَادَقَةٌ . أَثْبَتَ
Sanctity n.	قَدَاسَةٌ . قُدْسٌ
Sanctuary n.	مَقْدِسٌ . مَعْبَدٌ . مَلاَذٌ
Sand n.	رَمْلٌ ج رِمَالٌ
Sandal n.	حِذَاءٌ . نَعْلٌ
Sandal wood n.	صَنْدَلٌ
Sandal-fly n.	بَعُوضَةٌ (سُكَيْت)
Sandstone n.	حَجَرٌ رَمْلِيٌّ
Sandwich n.	لَحْمٌ بَيْنَ قِطْعَتَيْ خُبْزٍ
Sandy a.	رَمْلِيٌّ
Sane a.	سَلِيمُ ٱلْعَقْلِ
Sanguinary a.	دَمَوِيٌّ . سَفَّاكُ ٱلدَّمِ
Sanguine a.	وَاثِقٌ . كَثِيرُ ٱلرَّجَاءِ

Sanitary a.	صِحّيّ . مفيد لِلصِّحّة
Sanity n.	سلامةُ آلعَقل . صِحّتُه
Sap n. or v. t.	عصيرُ آلنّبَات . هَدَمَ آلاساس
Sapient a.	حكيمٌ . مُتَصَنِّعُ آلْحِكْمَة
Sapling n.	شجيرَة
Sapphire n.	ياقوتٌ ازرَقُ
Saracen n.	شَرقيٌّ . عَرَبيٌّ
Sarcasm n.	تَهكّمٌ . إِستِهزآءٌ
Sarcastic Sarcastical } a.	تَهكّمي
Sarcophagus n.	نَاوُوسٌ (تابوت قديم)
Sardonic a.	(ضَحكٌ) . تَهكّمي
Sash n.	زُنّارٌ . بَروَازِ نافِذَةٍ
Satan n.	إِبْليسُ . آلشَّيطَان
Satanic Satanical } a.	إِبْليسيٌّ . شَيطانيٌّ
Satchel n.	كيسٌ صغيرٌ
Satellite n.	تابعٌ . قَمَر
Sate Satiate } v. t.	شَبَّعَ . أَرضى . أَفعَم
Satiety n.	شَبَعٌ
Satin n.	أَطلَسُ حَرير
Satire n.	هِجَاءٌ
Satiric Satirical } a.	هِجَائيٌّ
Satirize v. t.	هجَا ـ
Satisfaction n.	رِضًى . إِرضَاءٌ
Satisfactory a.	مُرْضٍ . كَاف
Satisfy v. t.	أَرضى . أَقنعَ
Saturate v. t.	أَشرَبَ . أَشبَعَ
Saturday n.	يَومُ آلسَّبتِ
Saturn n.	زحَل
Sauce n.	مَرَقَة
Saucer n.	صَحنٌ صغيرٌ . سُكرُجَه
Saucy a.	وقحٌ . سليط
Saunter v. i.	مَشى مُتَكَاسِلا
Sausage n.	مَقَانِقُ . سجّقٌ
Savage n. or a.	هَمَجٌ . وَحشيٌّ . جاف
Savageness n.	تَوحُّشٌ . قَسَاوَة . هَمَجيه
Savant n.	علامَة

Save v.t. or pr.	خلّص . إِقْتَصَد . إِلا	Scaly a.	ذُو حَرَاشِفَ . حِرْ شَفِيٌّ
Saving a. or n.	مُقْتَصِد . إِقْتِصَادٌ . إِسْتِثْنَاءً	Scamp n.	خَبِيثٌ . شِرِّيرٌ
Saviour n.	مُخَلِّصٌ . فَادٍ	Scamper v. i.	رَكَضَ ـُ . فَرَّ
Savour n. or v. i.	طَعْمٌ . إِتَّصَفَ بِ	Scan v. t.	تَفَرَّسَ . وَزَنَ الشِّعْرَ
Savoury a.	لَذِيذٌ . طَيِّبٌ . زَكِيٌّ	Scandal n.	عَارٌ . إِفْتِرَاءً . فَضِيحَةٌ
Saw n. or v. t.	مِنْشَارٌ . نَشَرَ ـُ	Scandalize v. t.	فَضَحَ . إِفْتَرَى . اخْجَلَ
Sawyer n.	نَشَّارٌ	Scandalous a.	مَعِيبٌ . فَاضِحٌ . افْتِرَائِيٌّ
Say v. t.	قَالَ ـُ أَخْبَرَ	Scant {a. Scanty}	نَاقِصٌ . قَلِيلٌ
Saying n.	قَوْلٌ . مَثَلٌ	Scantiness {n. Scantness}	نَقْصٌ . قِلَّةٌ
Scab n.	جُلْبَةٌ	Scape-goat n.	حَامِلُ ذُنُوبِ غَيْرِه
Scabbard n.	غِمْدٌ . قِرَابٌ	Scar n.	نَدْبَةٌ . أَثَرُ جُرْحٍ
Scaffold n.	صِقَالَة	Scarce a.	نَادِرٌ . قَلِيلُ الْوُجُودِ
Scaffolding n.	صِقَالَاتٌ	Scarcely ad.	بِالجُهْدِ . نَادِراً
Scald v. t.	سَلَقَ ـُ . سَمَطَ ـِ	Scarcity n.	قِلَّةُ الْوُجُودِ . نُدْرَة
Scale n.	كِفَّةُ مِيزَانٍ . حَرْشَفٌ	Scare v. t.	خَوَّفَ . أَفْزَعَ . أَرْهَبَ
Scale v. t.	قَشَّرَ . تَسَوَّرَ . تَسَلَّقَ	Scarecrow n.	شَبَحٌ لِلتَّخْوِيفِ
Scalp n. or v. t.	فَرْوَةُ الرَّأْسِ . نَزَعَهَا	Scarf n.	وِشَاحٌ . حِمَالَة
Scalpel n.	مِشْرَطٌ ج مَشَارِطُ	Scarify v. t.	شَرَطَ ـِ . حَجَمَ ـُ

Scarlatina Scarlet-fever } n.	ٱلْحُمَّى ٱلْقِرْمِزِيَّة
Scarlet a. or n.	قِرْمِزِيٌّ . قِرْمِز
Scath Scathe } v. t.	آذَى . أَهْلَكَ
Scathless a.	غَيْرُ مُؤْذًى . سَالِم
Scatter v. t.	فَرَّقَ . بَدَّدَ
Scavenger n.	زَبَّال
Scene n.	مَنْظَر . فَصْل رِوَايَة
Scenery n.	مَنْظَر
Scent n. or v. t.	رَائِحَة . إِشْتَمَّ . عَطَّرَ
Sceptre n.	صَوْلَجَان . مُلْك
Sceptic n. Sceptical a. }	مُرْتَاب
Scepticism n.	إِرْتِيَاب . شَكّ
Schedule n.	قَائِمَة . جَدْوَل
Scheme n.	تَدْبِير . مَقْصَد . اسْلُوب
Scheme v. t.	دَبَّرَ . إِخْتَرَعَ . رَسَمَ
Schism n.	شِقَاق . إِخْتِلَاف
Schismatic n. or a.	رَافِضِيّ خَارِجِيّ
Scholar n.	تِلْمِيذ . طَالِب . عَالِم
Scholarly a.	عَالِم . عِلْمِيّ
Scholarship n.	عِلْم . مَال وَقْف لِلتِّلْمِيذِ
Scholastic a.	مَدْرَسِيّ
School n.	مَدْرَسَة . مَذْهَب
Schooling n.	تَدْرِيس . تَعْلِيم
School-master n.	مُعَلِّم مَدْرَسَة
Schooner n.	سَفِينَة ذَاتُ سَارِيَتَيْن
Science n.	عِلْم . فَنّ
Scientific Scientifical } a.	عِلْمِيّ
Scintillate v. i.	تَلَأْلَأَ . بَرَقَ ُ
Scissors n. pl.	مِقَصّ . مِقْرَاض
Scoff n. or v. i.	هُزْء . هَزَأَ ـَ
Scold v. t. or i.	وَبَّخَ . عَنَّف . زَجَرَ ـُ
Scolding n.	تَعْنِيف . زَجْر
Scoop n. or v. t.	مِغْرَفَة . غَرَف ِ . حَفَر ـُ
Scope n.	مَدًى . مَجَال . غَايَة
Scorch v. t.	حَرَقَ ِ . كَوَى . شَوَّطَ
Score n.	عِشْرُونَ . حِسَاب . شَأْن

Score *v. t.*	خَطَّطَ . قَيَّدَ فِي حِسَابٍ
Scorn *n.* or *v.t.*	إِحْتِقَارٌ . إِزْدَرَى بِ
Scorner Scornful	مُزْدَرٍ . مُحْتَقِرٌ
Scorpion *n.*	عَقْرَبٌ
Scoundrel *n.*	خَبِيثٌ . شِرِّيرٌ . قَبِيحٌ
Scour *v. t.*	جَلَى ـِ . طَافَ عَاجِلًا
Scourge *n.* or *v. t.*	سَوْطٌ . بَلِيَّةٌ . جَلَدَ ـِ
Scot-free *a.*	مُعْفًى مِنْ . سَالِمٌ
Scout *n.* or *v.t.*	جَاسُوسٌ . إِسْتَخَفَّ بِ
Scowl *n.* or *v. i.*	عُبُوسَةٌ . عَبَّسَ . كَلَحَ ـَ
Scragged Scraggy	خَشِنٌ . نَحِيفٌ
Scramble *n.* or *v. i.*	مُنَاوَشَةٌ . تَسَلُّقٌ
Scrap *n.*	قِطْعَةٌ صَغِيرَةٌ . حِتَّةٌ
Scrape *v. t.*	حَتَّ ـُ . كَشَطَ ـِ . حَكَّ ـُ
Scraper *n.*	مِكْشَطٌ . مِحَتٌّ
Scratch *v. t.* or *i.*	خَدَشَ ـِ . حَكَّ ـُ
Scratch *n.*	خَمْشٌ . خَدْشَةٌ
Scrawl *n.*	خَطٌّ رَدِيءٌ
Scream Screech	صَاحَ ـِ . صَيْحَةٌ
Screen *n.* or *v. t.*	سِتْرٌ . سَتَرَ ـِ
Screw *n.* or *v. t.*	(بُرْمَه) . شَدَّ بِهَا
Scribble *v.i.* or *t.*	أَسَاءَ خَطًّا وَمَعْنًى
Scribbler *n.*	مُؤَلِّفٌ رَكِيكٌ
Scribe *n.*	كَاتِبٌ
Scrimp *v. t.*	ضَيَّقَ . قَصَّرَ
Script *n.*	أَحْرُفُ طَبْعٍ شَبِيهَةٌ بِالْخَطِّ
Scriptural *a.*	مُطَابِقٌ لِلْكِتَابِ الْمُقَدَّسِ
Scripture *n.*	الْكِتَابُ الْمُقَدَّسُ
Scrofula *n.*	دَاءُ الْخَنَازِيرِ
Scrofulous *a.*	مُصَابٌ بِدَاءِ الْخَنَازِيرِ
Scroll *n.*	دَرْجٌ
Scrub *n.* or *v. t.*	خَسِيسٌ . جَلَى ـِ . مَسَحَ
Scruple *n.* or *v. i.*	شَكٌّ . إِرْتِيَابٌ . تَرَدَّدَ
Scrupulous *a.*	مُتَرَدِّدٌ . مُحْتَرِسٌ
Scrutinize *v. t.*	دَقَّقَ النَّظَرَ . تَفَحَّصَ
Scrutiny *n.*	فَحْصٌ مُدَقَّقٌ . إِنْعَامُ نَظَرٍ

Scuffle n. or v. t.	مُصَارَعَة . نَاوَشَ
Sculptor n.	نَحَّات . نَقَّاش
Sculpture n.	صِنَاعَةُ ٱلنحْتِ
Scum n. or v. t.	رَغْوَة . زَبَد . نَزَعَهَا
Scurf n.	هِبْرِيَة . قِشْرَةُ ٱلرَّأْسِ
Scurrilous a.	قَبِيحٌ . رَذِيلٌ . سَفِيهٌ
Scurvy n. or a.	دَاءُ ٱلْإِسْكَرْبُوطِ . خَسِيسٌ
Scuttle n. or v.t.	سَطْلُ فَحْمٍ . ثَقَبَ سَفِينَة لِتَغْرَقَ
Scythe n.	مِحْصَد . مِنْجَل
Sea a.	بَحْرٌ
Seaboard / Seacoast } n.	شَطُّ ٱلْبَحْرِ . رِيفٌ
Seafarer / Seafaring } n.	مَلَّاحٌ . بَحْرِيٌّ
Seal n. or v.	خَتْمٌ . خَاتَم خَتَمَ . عِجْلُ ٱلْبَحْرِ
Seam n.	دَرْزٌ . نَدْبَة . طَبَقَة
Seaman n.	بَحْرِيٌّ
Seamanship n.	مِلَاحَه
Seamstress a.	خَيَّاطَة
Seaport n.	مِينَاء . فُرْضَة
Sear v. t.	كَوَى ـ . جَفَّفَ . صَلَّبَ
Search v. t. or n.	فَتَّشَ . تَفَحَّصَ . تَفْتِيش
Searching a.	مُسْتَقْصٍ . مُدَقِّق . نَافِذ
Seasick a.	مُصَابٌ بِدُوَارِ ٱلْبَحْرِ
Seaside n.	سَاحِلُ ٱلْبَحْرِ . رِيفُهُ
Season n.	فَصْلٌ . وَقْتٌ . مُدَّة
Seasonable a.	فِي وَقْتِهِ . فِي مَحَلِّهِ
Seasoning n.	تَابَل . تَتْبِيل . تَجْفِيف
Seat n. or v. t.	مَقْعَد . مَجْلِس . أَجْلَسَ
Seaward ad.	إِلَى جِهَةِ ٱلْبَحْرِ
Secede v. i.	إِنْفَصَلَ . إِعْتَزَلَ . خَرَجَ ـ
Secession n.	إِنْفِصَال . خُرُوج
Seclude v. t.	حَجَبَ ـ . جَعَلَ بِعُزْلَةٍ
Seclusion n.	عُزْلَة . خُلُوّ
Second n.	ثَانِيَةٌ ج ثَوَانٍ
Second a. or n. or v. t.	الثَّانِي . أَيَّدَ
Secondary a.	ثَانَوِيٌّ . غَيْرُ مُهِمّ
Second-hand a.	مُسْتَعْمَل
Second-rate a.	مِنَ ٱلدَّرَجَةِ ٱلثَّانِيَة

Secrecy n.	سِرّ . كِتْمَان
Secret a. or n.	سِرِّيّ . مَكْتُومٌ . سِرٌّ
Secretary n.	كَاتِبٌ . نَاظِرُ دَائِرَةٍ
Secrete v. t.	اخْفَى . خَبَّأ . أَفْرَزَ
Secretion n.	إِخْفَاءٌ . إِفْرَازٌ
Sect n.	طَائِفَةٌ . شِيعَةٌ . مَذْهَبٌ
Sectarian a. / Sectary n.	طَائِفِيٌّ . تَحَزُّبِيٌّ
Section n.	قِطْعَةٌ . قِسْمٌ . فَصْلٌ
Secular a.	غَيْرُ دِينِيٍّ . عَالَمِيٌّ
Secularize v. t.	حَوَّلَ إِلَى غَايَةٍ عَالَمِيَّةٍ
Secure a. or v. t.	مُطْمَئِنٌّ . حَصَلَ . أَحْرَزَ
Security n.	أَمْنٌ طُمَأْنِينَةٌ . ضَمَانٌ
Sedate a.	رَزِينٌ . هَادِيٌّ
Sedative a. or n.	مُسَكِّنٌ
Sedentary a.	قَاعِدٌ . مُلَازِمُ الْجُلُوسِ
Sediment n.	رَاسِبٌ . ثُقْلٌ
Sedition n.	فِتْنَةٌ . ثَوْرَةٌ . شَغْبٌ
Seditious a.	مُشَاغِبٌ . مُهَيِّجٌ . مُثِيرٌ
Seduce v. t.	أَغْوَى . أَضَلَّ
Seductive a.	مُغْوٍ مُفْتِنٌ . مُضِلٌّ
Sedulous a.	كَدُودٌ . مُجْتَهِدٌ
See v. t. or n.	رَأَى ــ . نَظَرَ ــ . أَبْرَشِيَّةٌ
Seed n.	بِزْرٌ . زَرْعٌ . نَسْلٌ
Seedling n.	نَبَاتٌ مِنْ بِزْرَةٍ
Seed-time n.	أَبَانُ الزَّرْعِ
Seedy a.	كَثِيرُ الْبِزْرِ . بَالٍ
Seek v. t.	طَلَبَ ــ . فَتَّشَ . جَدَّ ــ
Seeing con.	بِمَا أَنْ
Seem v. i.	ظَهَرَ ــ . بَانَ ــ
Seemingly ad.	بِحَسَبِ الظَّاهِرِ
Seemly a.	لَائِقٌ . حَسَنٌ
Seer n.	رَائِي . نَبِيٌّ
Seethe v. t.	طَبَخَ ــ . غَلَى
Segment n.	قِطْعَةٌ
Segregate v. t.	فَصَلَ ــ . أَفْرَزَ
Seize v. t.	قَبَضَ ــ . خَطَفَ ــ . إِعْتَرَى

Seizure n.	قَبْضٌ . ضَبْطٌ	Seminary n.	مَدْرَسَةٌ
Seldom ad.	نَادِراً . قَلَمَا	Semitic a.	سَامِيٌّ
Select v. t. or a.	إِخْتَارَ . إِصْطَفَى . صَفِيٌّ	Senate n.	مَشْيَخَةٌ . مَجْلِسُ اعْيَان
Self n.	ذَاتٌ . نَفْسٌ	Senator n.	عُضْوُ مَجْلِسِ ٱلْأَعْيَان
Self-conceit n.	عُجْبٌ	Send v. t.	أَرْسَلَ . بَعَثَ ـَ
Self-denial n.	إِنْكَارُ ٱلذَّاتِ	Senility n.	شَيْخُوخَةٌ . كِبَرٌ
Self-evident a.	غَنِيٌّ عَنِ ٱلْبَيَانِ	Senior n. or a.	أَكْبَرُ عُمْراً . ٱلْمُتَقَدِّمُ
Selfish a.	مُحِبُّ ٱلذَّاتِ	Seniority n.	أَسْبَقِيَّةٌ سِنًّا أَوْ مَنْصِباً
Selfishness n.	مَحَبَّةُ ٱلذاتِ	Sensation n.	حِسٌّ . شُعُورٌ . تَأْثِيرٌ
Self-respect n.	إِحْتِرَامُ ٱلذاتِ	Sensational a.	مُهَيِّجُ ٱلْعَوَاطِفِ
Self-same a.	ذَاتٌ . بِعَيْنِهِ	Sense n.	حِسٌّ . حَاسَّةٌ . مَعْنًى
Self-will n.	عِنَادٌ	Senseless a.	بِلَاحِسٍّ أَوِمَعْنًى . مَغْشِيٌّ عَلَيْهِ
Sell v. t.	بَاعَ ـِ	Sensibility n.	حَاسِيَةٌ . رِقَّةُ ٱلنَّفْسِ
Semblance n.	شِبْهٌ . شَكْلٌ . صُورَةٌ	Sensible a.	حَسَّاسٌ . عَاقِلٌ . مَحْسُوسٌ
Semi n.	نِصْفٌ (فِي ٱلتَّرْكِيبِ)	Sensitive a.	دَقِيقُ ٱلْحِسِّ وَٱلٱنْفِعَالِ
Semi-annual a.	كُلَّ نِصْفِ سَنَةٍ	Sensual a. Sensualist n.	حَيَوَانِيٌّ . شَهَوَانِيٌّ
Semi-circle n.	نِصْفُ دَائِرَةٍ	Sensualism Sensuality } n.	شَهَوَانِيَّةٌ
Semicolon n.	عَلَامَةُ وَقْفٍ كَذَا (;)	Sentence n.	جُمْلَةٌ . قَضَاءٌ . حُكْمٌ

Sentient *n*.	حَسَّاسٌ. مُدْرِكٌ بِالْحَسِّ	Serenade *n.* or *v. t.*	عَزْفُ ٱلْمُوسِيقَى بِٱللَّيْلِ
Sentiment *n*.	حِسّ . عَاطِفَةٌ . مَعْنًى	Serene *a*.	هَادِئٌ . صَافٍ . رَصِينٌ
Sentinel⎫ Sentry⎬ *n*.	حَارِسٌ . خَفَرٌ	Serenity *n*.	صَفَآءٌ . هُدُوءٌ
Separable *a*.	قَابِلُ ٱلْفَصْلِ	Serf *n*.	عَبْدٌ
Separate *v. t.* or *a*.	فَصَلَ ـ مُنْفَصِلٌ	Sergeant *n*.	جَاوِيشٌ . شَاوِيشٌ
Separation *n*.	فَصْلٌ إِنْفِصَالٌ.مُفَارَقَةٌ	Serial *a.* or *n*.	مُتَتَابِعٌ.رِوَايَةٌ تُطْبَعُ أَجْزَاءً مُتَتَابِعَةً
Separatist *n*.	مُعْتَزِلٌ . مُنْشَقٌّ		
September *n*.	شَهْرُ أَيْلُولَ.(سبتمبر)	Series *n*.	نَسَقٌ. سِلْسِلَةٌ
Septennial *a*.	كُلَّ سَبْعِ سِنِينَ	Serious *a*.	رَزِينٌ.جَادٌّ . عَظِيمٌ
Septentrional *a*.	شِمَالِيٌّ	Sermon *n*.	مَوْعِظَةٌ
Septuagenarian *n*.	إِبْنُ ٧٠ سَنَةً	Serpent *n*.	حَيَّةٌ . ثُعْبَانٌ
Septuagint *n*.	أَلتَّرْجَمَةُ ٱلسَّبْعِينِيَّةُ	Serpentine *a*.	مُلْتَفٌّ كَٱلْحَيَّةِ
Sepulchre *n*.	قَبْرٌ. ضَرِيحٌ	Servant *n*.	خَادِمٌ . أَجِيرٌ
Sepulture *n*.	دَفْنٌ	Serve *v. t.*	خَدَمَ ـ.عَبَدَ.صَلَحَ لِ
Sequel *n*.	تَابِعٌ. تَالٍ . نَتِيجَةٌ	Service *n*.	خِدْمَةٌ. عِبَادَةٌ. مَعْرُوفٌ
Sequence *n*.	تَتَابُعٌ. تَالٍ	Serviceable *a*.	مُفِيدٌ. صَالِحٌ لِ
Sequester⎫ Sequestrate⎬ *v. t.*	ضَبَطَ ـُ. حَجَزَ ـُ	Servile *a*.	ذَلِيلٌ . خَاضِعٌ
Serdphic *a*.	مَلَائِكِيٌّ . بَهِيٌّ	Servility *n*.	تَذَلُّلٌ . عُبُودِيَّةٌ

Servitor n.	خَادِمٌ . تَابِعٌ
Servitude n.	عُبُودِيَّةٌ . رِقٌّ
Sesame n.	سِمْسِمٌ
Session n.	جَلْسَةٌ
Sesspool n.	بَالُوعَةٌ أَوْسَاخٍ
Set v.t. or i.	وَضَعَ ـِ . جَبَرَ ـُ . غَابَ ـِ
Set n.	طَقْمٌ . قَوْمٌ . حِزْبٌ
Settle v. i.	سَكَنَ ـُ . أَثْقَلَ . هَدَأَ
Settle v. t.	أَسْكَنَ . دَبَّرَ . أَنْجَزَ
Settlement n.	مَسْكَنٌ . تَسْوِيَةٌ
Settlings n. pl.	دُرْدِيٌّ . رُسُوبٌ
Seven a.	سَبْعٌ أَوْ سَبْعَـة
Seventh a.	سَابِعٌ
Seventeen a.	سَبْعَةَ عَشَرَ
Seventieth / Seventy } a.	سَبْعُونَ
Sever v. t.	فَصَلَ ـِ . قَطَعَ ـِ
Several a.	بَعْضٌ . بِضْعَةٌ . فَرْدٌ
Severally ad.	أَفْرَادًا . عَلَى حِدَةٍ

Severance n.	فَصْلٌ . قَطْعٌ
Severe a.	قَاسٍ . صَارِمٌ . شَدِيدٌ
Severity n.	صَرَامَةٌ . شِدَّةٌ . عُنْفٌ
Sew v. t.	خَاطَ ـِ . خَيَّطَ
Sewer n.	خَيَّاطٌ . بَالُوعَةٌ . سَرَبٌ
Sex n.	جِنْسٌ
Sextant n.	آلَةٌ لِقِيَاسِ الزَّوَايَا
Sexton n.	قَنْدَلَفْت . حَفَّارُ الْقُبُورِ
Sexual a.	جِنْسِيٌّ . مُمَيِّزُ الْجِنْسِ
Shabby a.	رَثِيثٌ . خَسِيسٌ
Shackle v. t.	قَيَّدَ . عَاقَ
Shackles n. pl.	قُيُودٌ . أَغْلَالٌ
Shade n. or v. t.	ظِلٌّ . خَيَالٌ . ظَلَّلَ
Shadow n.	ظِلٌّ . رَمْزٌ
Shadowy a.	مُظَلِّلٌ . وَهْمِيٌّ . مُبْهَمٌ
Shady a.	مُظَلِّلٌ . كَثِيرُ الظِّلِّ
Shaft n.	سَهْمٌ . بِئْرٌ . عَرِيشٌ
Shagged / Shaggy } a.	أَشْعَرُ . كَثٌّ

Shake *v. t.* or *i.* or *n.*	هزَّ ـِ. أَهْتَزَ. هزَّة
Shall *aux. v.*	فِعْلٌ إِضَافِيّ يَدُلُّ عَلَى ٱلِٱسْتِقْبَال
Shallow *a.*	قَلِيلُ ٱلْغَوْرِ . ضَعِيفٌ
Sham *n.* or *a.* or *v. i.*	تَصَنَّعَ . غِشٌّ
Shambles *n. pl.*	مَسْلَخٌ . مَجْزَرٌ
Shame *n.*	خِزْيٌ . عَارٌ . خَجَلٌ
Shamefaced *a.*	مُسْتَحٍ . خَجِل
Shameful *a.*	مُخْزٍ . مُعِيبٌ . قَبِيحٌ
Shameless *a.*	بِلَا حَيَاءٍ
Shank *n.*	سَاقٌ . يَدُ آلَةٍ
Shanty *n.*	كُوخٌ
Shape *v. t.* or *n.*	كَوَّنَ . صُورَة . هَيْئَة
Shapeless *a.*	بِلَا شَكْلٍ أَوْ تَرْتِيبٍ
Shapely *a.*	جَمِيلُ ٱلشَّكْلِ
Share *v. t.* or *i.*	قَاسَمَ . شَارَكَ
Share *n.*	حِصَّة . سَهْم . سِكَّة
Share-holder *n.*	صَاحِبُ سَهْمٍ

Shark *a.*	كَلْبُ ٱلْبَحْرِ
Sharp *a.*	حَادٌّ . حِرِّيفٌ . خَارِقٌ . ذَكِيّ
Sharpen *v. t.*	سَنَّ . أَنْهَضَ
Sharpness *n.*	حِدَّة . حِذْق . شِدَّة
Shatter *v. t.*	كَسَّرَ . قَصَفَ . أَبَادَ
Shave *v. t.*	حَلَقَ ـِ . غَبَنَ ـِ
Shaving *n.*	نِجَارَة . شَرِيحَة رَقِيقَة
Shawl *n.*	شَالٌ
She *pron.*	هِيَ
Sheaf *n.*	حُزْمَة قَمْحٍ
Shear *v. t.*	جَزَّ
Shears *n. pl.*	مِجَزّ . مِقَصّ
Sheath *n.*	غِلَافٌ . غِمْدٌ
Sheathe *v. t.*	غَلَفَ ـِ . غَمَدَ
Shed *v. t.*	سَفَكَ ـِ . ذَرَفَ ـِ . خَلَعَ ـِ
Sheep *n.*	غَنَم . ضَأْن . شَاة
Sheep-fold *n.*	حَظِيرَة . صِيرَة
Sheepish *a.*	مُسْتَحٍ . خَجِل

Sheer *a.*	مَحْضٌ . خَالِصٌ
Sheet *n.*	مُلَاءَةٌ . شَرْشَفٌ . طَلْحِيَّةٌ
Shelf *n.*	رَفٌّ ج رُفُوفٌ
Shell *n.*	قِشْرَةٌ . صَدَفَةٌ . قُنْبُلَةٌ
Shell *v. t.*	قَشَرَ ـُ . رَمَى بِٱلْقَنَابِلِ
Shell-fish *n.*	صَدَفٌ
Shelter *n.* or *v. t.*	مَأْوًى . آوَى . حَمَى ـِ
Shepherd *n.*	رَاعٍ ج رُعَاةٌ
Sherbet *n.*	شَرَابٌ
Sheriff *n.*	مَأْمُورٌ يُجْرِي ٱلْأَحْكَامَ
Shield *n.* or *v. t.*	تُرْسٌ . حَمَى ـِ . صَانَ
Shift *v. t.* or *n.*	نَقَلَ . غَيَّرَ . حِيلَةٌ
Shiftless *a.*	عَدِيمُ ٱلتَّدْبِيرِ . قَاصِرٌ
Shilling *n.*	بِـ ١‏٢ مِنَ ٱللِّيرَا ٱلْإِنْكِلِيزِيَّةِ
Shin *n.*	مُقَدَّمُ ٱلسَّاقِ
Shine *v. i.*	أَضَاءَ . أَشْرَقَ
Shingle *n.* or *v. t.*	لَوْحٌ رَقِيقٌ . غَطَّى بِهِ
Shining Shiny } *a.*	مُضِيٌّ لَامِعٌ
Ship *n.* or *v. t.*	سَفِينَةٌ . أَنْزَلَ فِيهَا
Shipment *n.*	إِرْسَالِيَّةٌ بِضَاعَةٍ
Shipping *n.*	مُجْتَمِعُ سُفُنٍ
Shipwreck *n.*	ٱنْكِسَارُ سَفِينَةٍ
Shire *n.*	مُقَاطَعَةٌ . لِوَاءٌ
Shirk *v. t.*	تَجَنَّبَ (ٱلْوَاجِبَ)
Shirt *n.* or *v. t.*	قَمِيصٌ ج قُمْصَانٌ . أَلْبَسَهُ
Shiver *v. i.* or *t.*	اِقْشَعَرَّ . حَطَمَ
Shoal *n.*	سِرْبٌ (سَمَكٍ) . ضَحْلٌ
Shock *n.* or *v. t.*	صَدْمَةٌ . رَجَّةٌ . ارْعَبَ
Shocking *a.*	هَائِلٌ . مُكَدِّرٌ
Shoe *n.* or *v. t.*	حِذَاءٌ . نَعْلٌ . نَعَلَ ـَ
Shoemaker *n.*	سَكَّافٌ . إِسْكَافٌ
Shoot *v. t.* or *i.*	أَطْلَقَ . رَمَى ـِ . فَرَّخَ
Shoot *n.*	فَرْخٌ . عُسْلُجٌ
Shop *n.*	دُكَّانٌ . حَانُوتٌ
Shop-keeper *n.*	صَاحِبُ دُكَّانٍ
Shopping *n.*	شِرَاءٌ . مِسْوَاقٌ

Shore n.	شَطّ . شَاطِئٌ	Shriek v. i. or n.	صَرَخَ ـُ . صُرَاخٌ
Short a.	قَصِيرٌ . نَاقِصٌ	Shrill a.	حَادُّ ٱلصَّوْتِ
Shorten v. t. or i.	قَصَّرَ . تَقَصَّرَ	Shrine n.	مَقَامٌ مُقَدَّسٌ . مَعْبَدٌ
Short-lived a.	قَصِيرُ ٱلْعُمْرِ	Shrink v. i.	تَقَلَّصَ . نَقَصَ . ٱشْمَأَزَّ
Shortness n.	قِصَرٌ . إِيجَازٌ	Shrivel v. t. or i.	غَضَّنَ . تَغَضَّنَ
Short-sighted a.	قَصِيرُ ٱلْبَصَرِ	Shroud n. or v.t.	كَفَنٌ . سَتَرَ . سَتَرَ
Shot n.	رَمِيَّةٌ . خُرْدُقٌ . رَامٍ	Shrub n.	نَجْمُ ٱلْأَشْجَارِ . شُجَيْرَةٌ
Should pret. of shall		Shrubbery n.	مُجْتَمَعُ أَنْجُمٍ
Shoulder n.	كَتِفٌ . مَنْكِبٌ	Shrubby a.	نَجْمِيٌّ . كَثِيرُ ٱلْأَنْجُمِ
Shout v. t. or n.	زَعَقَ ـَ . صَاحَ . هُتَافٌ	Shrug v. t. or n.	هَزَّ (ٱلْأَكْتَافَ)
Shove v. t. or n.	دَفَعَ ـ دَفْعَةٌ	Shudder n. or v. i.	ٱرْتِعَاشٌ . ٱرْتَجَفَ
Shovel n. or v. t.	مِجْرَفَةٌ . جَرَفَ ـُ	Shuffle v. t.	خَلَطَ . ٱحْتَالَ
Show v. t.	أَظْهَرَ . بَيَّنَ . هَدَى ـ	Shun v. t.	أَعْرَضَ عَن . ٱجْتَنَبَ
Show n.	مَعْرَضٌ . مَنْظَرٌ . تَظَاهُرٌ	Shut v. t. or i.	أَغْلَقَ . ٱنْغَلَقَ
Shower n.	مَطْرَةٌ	Shutter n.	دَرْفَةٌ
Showy a.	زَاهٍ . مُزَخْرَفٌ	Shuttle n.	مَكُوكٌ
Shred n. or v. t.	شِقَّةٌ . قِطْعَةٌ رَقِيقَةٌ . قَطَعَ	Shy a. or v.i.	مُسْتَحٍ . وَجِلٌ . أَجْفَلَ
Shrew n.	سَلِيطَةٌ . صَخَّابَةٌ	Shyness n.	حَيَاءٌ . وَجَلٌ
Shrewd a.	حَاذِقٌ . دَاهٍ		

Sibyl *n.* كَاهِنَةٌ . وَثَنِيَّةٌ . عَرَّافَةٌ	Sight *n.* نَظَرٌ . بَصَرٌ . مَنْظَرٌ
Sick *a.* مَرِيضٌ . عَلِيلٌ	Sightless *a.* أَعْمَى
Sicken *v. t. or i.* قَزَّزَ . مَرِضَ	Sightly *a.* ظَاهِرٌ . شَهِيٌّ لِلنَظَرِ
Sickish *a.* مُقَزِّزٌ	Sign *n.* عَلَامَةٌ . إِشَارَةٌ . آيَةٌ
Sickle *n.* مِنْجَلٌ	Sign *v. t. or i.* أَمْضَى . أَشَارَ إِلَى
Sickly *a.* وَخِيمٌ . سَقِيمٌ . ضَعِيفٌ	Signal *n. or a.* إِشَارَةٌ . مُمْتَازٌ
Sickness *n.* مَرَضٌ . عِلَّةٌ	Signalize *v. t.* مَيَّزَ . شَهَّرَ
Side *n.* جَانِبٌ . نَاحِيَةٌ . حِزْبٌ	Signature *n.* إِمْضَاءٌ
Sideboard *n.* خِزَانَةُ ٱلسُّفْرَةِ	Signet *n.* خَتْمٌ . خَاتِمٌ
Sidelong *a.* جَانِبِيٌّ . مُنْحَرِفٌ	Significance ⎱ *n.* مَعْنًى . اهَمِّيَّةٌ Significance ⎰
Sidereal *a.* كَوْكَبِيٌّ . نَجْمِيٌّ	Significant *a.* دَالٌّ . مُهِمٌّ
Side-saddle *n.* سَرْجٌ لِلنِّسَاءِ	Signification *n.* مَعْنًى . فَحْوَى
Sidewise *ad.* بِالْعَرْضِ . جَانِبًا	Signify *v. t.* أَفَادَ . عَنَى
Siege *n.* مُحَاصَرَةٌ . حِصَارٌ	Silence *n.* سُكُوتٌ . هُدُوٌّ . سُكُونٌ
Siesta *n.* قَيْلُولَةٌ	Silence *v. t.* أَسْكَتَ . أَفْحَمَ
Sieve *n.* مُنْخُلٌ . غِرْبَالٌ	Silent *a.* سَاكِتٌ . سَاكِنٌ
Sift *v. t.* غَرْبَلَ . تَفَحَّصَ	Silk *n.* حَرِيرٌ . سُنْدُسٌ
Sigh *v. i. or n.* تَنَهَّدَ . زَفَرَ . زَفِيرٌ	Silk ⎱ *a.* حَرِيرِيٌّ Silken ⎰

Silk-worm n.	دُودُ القَزّ	Simplify v. t.	جعله بسيطًا . سهَّل
Silky a.	ناعمٌ . أَملَسُ	Simply ad.	ببَساطَةٍ . فَقَطْ
Sill n.	اسكَفَّةٌ (اسفَلُ البَاب أَو الشُّبَاكِ)	Simulate v. t.	تَشبَّهَ . تَظاَهَرَ بِ
		Simultaneous a.	في وقتٍ واحِدٍ
Silliness n.	غَباوَةٌ . رُعُونَةٌ	Sin n. or v. i.	خطِيَّةٌ . أَخطَأَ
Silly a.	أَرعَنُ . غَبِي	Since ad. or pr. or con.	بعدَ . مُنذُ . لأَنَّ
Silver n. or a.	فضَّةٌ . فِضِّي	Sincere a.	مُخلِصٌ . نَصُوحٌ
Silversmith n.	صائِغٌ ج صَاغَةٌ	Sincerity n.	إِخلاصٌ . صفاَ النِّيَّةِ
Silvery a.	فِضِّيٌّ . كالفِضَّةِ	Sine n.	جيبٌ في (الهَندَسَةِ)
Similar a.	شَبِيهةٌ . مِثلٌ . مُشَاكِلٌ	Sinew n.	وَتَرٌ . أَصلُ قوَّةٍ
Similarity Similitude } n.	مُشَابَهَةٌ	Sinewy a.	قوِيٌّ . ضَلِيعٌ . عَضِلٌ
Simile n.	تَشبِيهٌ	Sinful a.	خاطِئٌ . أَثِيمٌ
Simmer v. t.	علَى ـ . بخِفَّةٍ	Sinfulness n.	خطِيَّةٌ . حَالَةُ الإِثمِ
Simony n.	شِراَءُ رُتَبِ الكَنِيسَةِ	Sing v. t.	رنَّمَ . غنَّى . رتَّلَ
Simoom n.	سَمُومٌ (ريحٌ)	Singe v. t.	مسَّتهُ النَّارُ قلِيلاً
Simper v. i.	تَبَسَّمَ كالأَبلَهِ	Singing n.	غِناَءٌ . تَرنِيمٌ
Simple a.	بَسِيطٌ . هيِّنٌ . واضِحٌ	Single a.	فردٌ . واحِدٌ . عازِبٌ
Simpleton n.	غَبِيٌّ . أَبلَهُ	Singleness n.	وَحدَةٌ . بَسَاطَةٌ
Simplicity n.	بَسَاطَةٌ . سَذَاجَةٌ		

Singular n.	مُفْرَدٌ . غَرِيبٌ . عَجِيبٌ	Sister-hood n.	جَمْعِيَّةُ نِسَاءٍ أَوْ رَاهِبَاتٍ
Singularity n.	وَحْدَةٌ . غَرَابَةٌ	Sit v. t.	جَلَسَ . آسْتَقَرَّ . حَضَنَ
Sinister a.	يَسَارٌ . مَشُومٌ	Site n.	مَوْقِعٌ . مَوْضِعٌ
Sink v. i. or t.	غَرِقَ . آنْحَطَّ . أَغْرَقَ	Sitting n.	جُلُوسٌ . جَلْسَةٌ
Sink n.	مَصَبٌّ . بَالُوعَةٌ	Situate Situated } a.	وَاقِعٌ
Sinking-fund n.	مَالٌ لِآسْتِهْلَاكِ دَيْنٍ	Situation n.	مَوْقِعٌ . مَنْصِبٌ . حَالٌ
Sinless a.	بِلَا خَطِيَّةٍ . بَارٌّ	Six a.	سِتَّةٌ أَوْ سِتٌّ
Sinner n.	خَاطِئٌ	Sixpence n.	نِصْفُ شِلِينٍ
Sinuosity n.	تَعَرُّجٌ	Sixteen a.	سِتَّةَ عَشَرَ
Sinuous a.	مُتَعَرِّجٌ	Sixteenth a.	اَلسَّادِسُ عَشَرَ
Sip n. or v. t.	مَصَّةٌ . تَمَصَّصَ	Sixth a.	سَادِسٌ
Sir n.	سَيِّدٌ	Sixty a.	سِتُّونَ
Sire n.	أَبٌ . مَوْلًى (لِلْمُلُوكِ)	Size n.	حَجْمٌ . قَدْرٌ . قَدٌّ
Siren n. or a.	جِنِّيَّةُ الْبَحْرِ . فَتَّانٌ	Skate n.	نَعْلٌ لِلسَّيْرِ عَلَى الْجَلِيدِ
Sirocco n.	رِيحٌ شَرْقِيَّةٌ . سَمُومٌ	Skein n.	شُلَّةُ خَيْطَانٍ . خُصْلَةٌ
Sirup n.	عَصِيرٌ مُحَلًّى . شَرَابٌ	Skeleton n.	هَيْكَلُ حَيَوَانٍ
Sister n.	أُخْتٌ . شَقِيقَةٌ	Skeptic etc. see Sceptic etc.	مُرْتَابٌ
Sister-in law n.	سِلْفَةٌ . أُخْتُ الزَّوْجِ أَوِ الزَّوْجَةِ	Sketch n. or v. t.	رَسْمٌ . رَسَمَ

Skiff n.	قَوَارِبُ . زَوْرَقٌ	Slack } v. t. Slacken } or i.	أَرْخَى . خَفَّ ـ
Skilfulness } Skill } n.	مَهَارَةٌ	Slackness n.	رَخَاءٌ . تَوَانٍ
Skilful } Skilled } a.	مَاهِرٌ . خَبِيرٌ	Slain pp. of slay	مَذْبُوحٌ
Skim v. t. or i.	نَزَعَ ـ الرَّغْوَةَ . سَفَّ ـ	Slake v. t.	رَوِيَ ـ . صَوَّلَ
Skin n. or v. t. ـ	جِلْدٌ . قِشْرٌ . سَلَخَ	Slam v. t.	أَغْلَقَ بِعُنْفٍ
Skinny a.	هَزِيلٌ . جِلْدِيٌّ	Slander v. t. or n.	نَمَّ ـ . نَمِيمَةٌ
Skip v. i. or t.	قَفَزَ ـ . فَاتَ . تَرَكَ	Slanderer n. } Slanderous a. }	نَمَّامٌ . مُفَتِرٌ
Skipper n.	رُبَّانُ سَفِينَةٍ صَغِيرَةٍ	Slang a.	كَلَامٌ عَامِّيٌّ
Skirmish n.	قِتَالٌ خَفِيفٌ	Slant v. i. or t.	مَالَ ـ . أَمَالَ
Skirt n.	هُدْبٌ . تُخْمٌ	Slanting a.	مَائِلٌ . غَيْرُ عَمُودِيٍّ
Skittish a.	جَفُولٌ	Slap v. t. or n.	لَطَمَ ـ . لَطْمَةٌ
Skulk v. i.	اِخْتَبَأَ دَهَاءً	Slash v. t. or n.	شَقَّ ـ . جَرَحَ ـ
Skull n.	جُمْجُمَةٌ	Slate n. or v. t.	لَوْحُ حَجَرٍ . غَطَّى بِهِ
Sky n.	جَوٌّ . جَلَدٌ . سَمَاءٌ	Slate-pencil n.	قَلَمُ حَجَرٍ
Sky-lark n.	قُنْبُرَةٌ ج قَنَابِرُ	Slaughter n. or v. t.	ذَبْحٌ . ذَبَحَ ـ
Sky-light n.	كُوَّةٌ فِي السَّقْفِ	Slave n.	عَبْدٌ . رَقِيقٌ . مَمْلُوكٌ
Slab n.	لَوْحُ حَجَرٍ أَوْ خَشَبٍ	Slaver n.	سَفِينَةٌ لِجَلْبِ الْعَبِيدِ
Slack a.	مُسْتَرْخٍ . مُتَغَافِلٌ	Slavery n.	عُبُودِيَّةٌ . رِقٌّ

Slavish a.	عَبْدِيٌّ . ذَلِيلٌ	Slight v. t.	أَهَانَ . آسْتَخَفَّ بِهِ
Slay v. t. (pp. Slain)	قَتَلَ ـ . ذَبَحَ	Slily ad.	بِحِيلَةٍ . إِخْتِلَاسًا . خَفِيَّةً
Sled Sledge } n.	مَرْكَبَةٌ لِلثَّلْجِ	Slim a.	رَقِيقٌ . أَهْيَفُ
Sledge n.	مِهَدَّةٌ	Slime n.	رَدْغَةٌ . وَحْلٌ خَفِيفٌ
Sleek a.	أَمْلَسُ . لَيِّنٌ	Sling n. or v. t. ـ	مِقْلَاعٌ . قَذَفَ بِهِ ـ
Sleep n. or v. i. ـ	نَوْمٌ . رُقَادٌ . نَامَ ـ	Slink v. i.	آنْسَلَّ
Sleepiness n.	نُعَاسٌ	Slip v. i. or n. ـ	زَلَقَ . زَلْقَةٌ ـ . زَلَّـةٌ
Sleepless a.	بِلَا نَوْمٍ	Slipper n.	أَشْيِنٌ . بَابُوجٌ
Sleepy a.	نَعْسَانُ	Slippery a.	زَلِقٌ . زَلْجٌ . مُتَقَلِّبٌ
Sleet n.	ثَلْجٌ وَمَطَرٌ مَعًا	Slit n. or v. t. ـ	شَرْمٌ . شَرَمَ ـ
Sleeve n.	كُمٌّ ج أَكْمَامٌ	Sliver n. or v. t. شَظِيًّا	شَظِيَّةٌ . شَقَّةٌ
Sleigh n.	مَرْكَبَةٌ لِلثَّلْجِ	Sloop n.	سَفِينَةٌ لَهَا سَارِيَةٌ وَاحِدَةٌ
Sleight n.	خِفَّةُ يَدٍ . حِيلَةٌ	Slope n.	احْدُورٌ . حَدُورٌ
Slender a.	أَهْيَفُ . دَقِيقٌ . ضَعِيفٌ	Sloppy a.	قَذِرٌ . وَحْلٌ
Slenderness n.	رِقَّةٌ . ضَعْفٌ	Sloth n. (حيوان)	كَسَلٌ . كَسْلَانُ
Slice n. or v. t.	شَرِيحَةُ لَحْمٍ . شَرَّحَ	Slothful a.	كَسْلَانُ . بَطِيءٌ
Slide v. i. or t.	زَلَجَ ـ زَلِقَ ـ أَزْلَقَ	Slough n.	مَحَلٌّ كَثِيرُ ٱلْوَحْلِ
Slight a. or n.	زَهِيدٌ . آسْتِخْفَافٌ	Sloven a.	غَيْرُ مُهَنْدَمٍ

Slovenly ad.	بِلاَ إِتْقَان
Slow a.	بَطِيٌّ
Slowness n.	بُطوٌ . تَأَخُّرٌ
Slug n.	كَسْلاَنٌ . بَزَّاقَة . عُرْيَانَة
Sluggard n. } Sluggish a. }	كَسْلاَنٌ . بَلِيدٌ
Sluice n.	مَنْفَذ ماءٍ في سَدٍّ
Slumber v. i. or n.	نَعَسَ ـَ . نام ـَ . نَوْمٌ
Slur v. t. or n.	اَسْتَخَفَّ . لَوَّثَ
Slut n.	بَذَّة
Sly a.	مُحْتَالٌ . إِدَاهٍ
Slyly ad.	حِيلَةً . خِفْيَةً
Slyness n.	دَهاءٌ . دَسٌّ . اَسْتِخْفاءٌ
Smack n.	سَفِينة صَغِيرة . قَبْلة قَوِيَّة
Small a.	صَغِيرٌ . دَقِيقٌ
Small-pox n.	جَدَرِيٌّ
Smart a.	نَشِيطٌ . نَبِيهٌ . حَاذِق
Smart v. i. or n.	تَأَلَّمَ شَدِيدًا . أَلَمٌ
Smartness n.	حَذَاقَة . حِدَّة

Smash v. t. or n.	كَسَّرَ . حَطَّمَ
Smattering n.	رُكَّكَة عِلْمٍ
Smear v. t.	لَطَخَ ـَ . وَسَّخَ
Smell n.	رَائِحَة . شَمٌّ . حاسّةُ
Smell v. t. or i.	شَمَّ ـُ . فَاحَ ـُ
Smelt v. t.	أَذَاب . أَمَاعَ
Smile v. i. or n.	تَبَسَّمَ . تَبَسُّمٌ
Smirch v. t.	وَسَّخَ . سَوَّدَ
Smite v. t.	ضَرَبَ ـُ . قَتَلَ ـِ . لَفَحَ ـَ
Smith n.	حَدَّادٌ . نَحَّاسٌ . صَائِغ
Smoke n. or v. t.	دُخَان . دَخَنَ
Smoker n.	شَارِبُ تُتُنٍ أَوْ دُخَانٍ
Smoky a.	مُدَخِّن . مُتَدَخِّن
Smooth a. or v. t.	مَلِسٌ . مُسْتَوٍ . مَلَّسَ
Smoothness n.	مَلاَسَة . اَسْتِواءٌ
Smother v. t.	خَنَقَ ـُ . أَطْفَأَ
Smoulder v. i.	اَحْتَرَقَ بِدُونِ لَهِيب
Smuggle v. t.	هَرَّبَ . اَدْخَلَ خُلْسَةً

Smutty *a.*	كَتِنٌ . وَسِخٌ
Snag *n.*	خَشَبَةٌ تصادِمُهَا سَفِينَةً . مَانِعٌ
Snail *n.*	بَزَّاقَةٌ . حَلَزُونَةٌ
Snake *n.*	حَيَّةٌ . أَفْعَى
Snap *v. t.* or *i.*	قَصَفَ ـِ . اِقْتَسَمَ بِصَوْتٍ
Snappish *a.*	نَكِدٌ . حَادُّ الْكَلَامِ
Snare *n.*	شَرَكٌ . مَكِيدَةٌ
Snarl *v. i.*	هَرَّ ـِ . هَمْهَمَ
Snatch *v. t.*	خَطِفَ ـَ
Sneak *v. i.*	اِنْسَلَّ . اِنْدَسَّ
Sneak *n.* Sneaking *n.*	ذَلِيلٌ . دَسِيسٌ
Sneer *v. i.* or *n.*	هَزَأَ . اِسْتَخَفَّ . هَزْءٌ
Sneeze *v. i.*	عَطَسَ ـِ
Sniff *v. t.*	اِشْتَمَّ . اِسْتَنْشَقَ
Snip *v. t.*	قَطَعَ ـَ . قَرَضَ ـِ
Snipe *n.*	نَوْعٌ مِنَ القَطَا
Snob *n.* Snobbish *a.*	مُتَظَارِفٌ . مُتَظَاهِرٌ بِالشَرَفِ
Snooze *v. i.*	نَامَ نَوْماً خَفِيفاً
Snore *v. i.*	شَخَرَ ـُ . خَرْخَرَ
Snort *v. i.*	نَخَرَ ـُ
Snout *n.*	خُرْطُومٌ . جِ خَرَاطِيمُ
Snow *n.* or *v. i.*	ثَلْجٌ . ثَلَجَ ـِ
Snow-drift *n.*	كُومَةُ ثَلْجٍ
Snowy *a.*	مُثْلِجٌ . أَبْيَضُ
Snub *v. t.*	عَامَلَ بِفَظَاظَةٍ . خَجَّلَ
Snuff *n.* or *v. t. i.*	سَعُوطٌ . نَزَعَ الذُبَالَةَ
Snuff-box *n.*	عِلْبَةُ السَّعُوطِ
Snuffers *n. pl.*	مِقْرَاضُ الفَتِيلَةِ
Snuffle *v. i.*	نَخَرَ ـِ
Snug *a.*	مُتَلَبِّدٌ . يُنَاسِبُ مَحَلُّهُ
Snuggle *v. i.*	اِسْتَكَنَّ
So *ad.*	كَذَا . هَكَذَا . كَذَلِكَ
Soak *v. t.* or *i.*	نَقَعَ ـَ . تَشَرَّبَ
Soap *n.* or *v. t.*	صَابُونٌ . عَامَلَ بِهِ
Soapsuds *n.*	رَغْوَةُ الصَابُونِ
Soar *v. i.*	اِسْتَعْلَى (طَيْرٌ)

Sob v. i. or n.	بَكَى مَعَ تَنَهُّدٍ
Sober Soberminded } a.	رَزِينٌ. صَاحٍ
Soberness Sobriety } n.	رَزَانَةٌ. تَعَفُّفٌ
Sociability n.	انْسٌ. عِشْرَةٌ
Sociable a.	انِيسٌ. أَلِيفٌ
Social a.	أَلِيفٌ. جَمْهُورِي
Socialism n.	مَذْهَبُ ٱلْإِشْتِرَاكِيِّينَ
Society n.	ٱلْهَيْئَةُ ٱلْإِجْتِمَاعِيَّةُ
Sock n.	جَوْرَبٌ
Socket n.	نُقْرَةٌ. تَجْوِيفٌ
Sod n.	مَدَرٌ فِيهِ جُذُورُ كَلَأٍ
Soda n.	ٱلْقِلَى. نَطْرُونٌ
Sodden a.	مَسْلُوقٌ. مَنْقُوعٌ
Sofa n.	مَقْعَدٌ. دِيوَانٌ
Soft a.	نَاعِمٌ. لَيِّنٌ. طِفْلٌ
Soften v. t. or i.	أَلَانَ. لَانَ
Softness n.	لِينٌ. نُعُومَةٌ
Soil v. t. or n.	لَطَّخَ ـ وَسَّخَ. تُرْبَةٌ
Sojourn v.i. or n.	تَغَرَّبَ. غُرْبَةٌ
Sojourner n.	مُتَغَرِّبٌ
Solace v. t. or n.	سَلَّى عَزَّى. سَلْوَى
Solar a.	شَمْسِيٌّ
Solder n. or v. t.	لِحَامٌ. لَحَمَ ـ
Soldier n.	عَسْكَرِيٌّ. جُنْدِيٌّ
Soldiery n.	عَسَاكِرُ
Sole n.	نَعْلٌ. أَسْفَلُ ٱلْقَدَمِ
Sole v. t. or a.	خَصَفَ ٱلنَّعْلَ. وَحِيدٌ
Solely ad.	فَقَطْ
Solemn n.	مُوَقَّرٌ. خَطِيرٌ
Solemnity n.	ٱحْتِفَالٌ. وَقَارٌ
Solemnize v. t.	ٱحْتَفَلَ. مَارَسَ سِرًّا
Solicit v. t.	تَوَسَّلَ. طَلَبَ ـ
Solicitation n.	تَوَسُّلٌ. ٱلْتِمَاسٌ
Solicitor n.	وَكِيلُ دَعَاوٍ
Solicitous a.	مُهْتَمٌّ. رَاغِبٌ فِي
Solicitude n.	هَمٌّ. رَغْبَةٌ

Solid a.	جَامِدٌ . مَتِينٌ . مُجَسَّمٌ	Some a.	بَعْضٌ
Solidify v. t. or i.	جَمَّدَ . تَجَمَّدَ	Somebody n.	وَاحِدٌ . أَحَدٌ مَّا
Solidity n.	جُمُودٌ . مَتَانَةٌ	Somehow ad.	كَيْفَمَا كَانَ
Soliloquize v. t.	كَلَّمَ نَفْسَهُ	Somersault } Somerest } n.	وَثْبَةُ ٱنْقِلَابٍ
Soliloquy n.	مُخَاطَبَةُ الذَّاتِ	Something n.	شَيْءٌ مَّا
Solitariness n.	تَوَحُّدٌ . ٱنْفِرَادٌ	Sometime ad.	وَقْتًا مَّا
Solitary a.	مُنْفَرِدٌ . مُعْتَزِلٌ	Sometimes ad.	أَحْيَانًا
Solitude n.	وَحْدَة . عُزْلَة	Somewhat ad. or n.	نَوْعًا . شَيْءٌ مَّا
Solo n.	غِنَاءُ شَخْصٍ وَحْدَهُ	Somewhere ad.	فِي مَكَانٍ مَّا
Solstice n.	نُقْطَةُ ٱنْقِلَابِ ٱلشَّمْسِ	Somnambulism n.	مَشْيٌ فِي ٱلنَّوْمِ
Soluble a.	قَابِلُ ٱلذَّوَبَانِ أَوِ ٱلْحَلِّ	Somnambulist n.	مَاشٍ فِي ٱلنَّوْمِ
Solution n.	حَلٌّ . مَحْلُولٌ	Somnolence n.	نُعَاسٌ
Solvable a.	قَابِلُ ٱلْحَلِّ أَوِ ٱلْوَفَاءِ	Son n.	ٱبْنٌ ج أَبْنَاءٌ وَبَنُونَ
Solve v. t.	حَلَّ أَوْ ضَحَ	Son-in-law n.	زَوْجُ ٱبْنَةٍ . صِهْرٌ
Solvency n.	قُدْرَةٌ عَلَى ٱلْوَفَاءِ	Song n.	أُغْنِيَّةٌ . نَشِيدٌ
Solvent a.	قَادِرٌ عَلَى ٱلْوَفَاءِ	Songster n.	مُغَنٍّ . مُغَرِّدٌ
Solvent n.	سَائِلٌ مُحَلِّلٌ أَوْ مُذَوِّبٌ	Sonnet n.	قَصِيدَةٌ قَصِيرَةٌ
Sombre a.	مُظْلِمٌ . مُغِمٌّ	Sonorous a.	صَائِتٌ . رَنَّانٌ

Sonship n.	بُنُوَّة	Sort n.	نَوْعٌ. صِنْفٌ. شَكْلٌ
Soon ad.	عَنْ قَرِيبٍ. سَرِيعًا	Sort v. t.	رَتَّبَ عَلَى اشْكَالِهِ
Soot n.	كَنْ. سُخَامٌ	Sot n. Sottish a. }	سِكِّيرٌ. أَبْلَهُ
Soothe v. t.	خَفَّفَ. لَاطَفَ. سَكَّنَ	Sought pp. (Seek)	مَطْلُوبٌ
Soothsayer n.	عَرَّافٌ. مُنَجِّمٌ	Soul n.	نَفْسٌ. رُوحٌ. حَيَاةٌ
Sooty a.	كَتِنِيٌّ. سُخَامِي	Soulless a.	بِلَا نَفْسٍ. خَسِيسٌ
Sophism Sophistry } n.	سَفْسَطَة	Sound a. or n.	صَحِيحٌ. صَوْتٌ. مَضِيقٌ
Sophist n. Sophistical a. }	سَفْسَطِيٌّ	Sound v. t. or i.	سَبَرَ. صَاتَ
Soporific n. or a.	مُنَوِّمٌ	Soundings n. pl.	قِيَاسُ عُمْقِ الْبَحْرِ
Sorcerer Sorceress } n.	سَاحِرٌ. سَاحِرَةٌ	Soundly ad.	جَيِّدًا بِصَوَابٍ
Sorcery n.	سِحْرٌ	Soundness n.	صِحَّةٌ. مَتَانَةٌ
Sordid a.	خَسِيسٌ. طَمَّاعٌ	Soup n.	شُوْرَبَةٌ
Sore a. or n.	مُؤْلِمٌ. شَدِيدٌ. قَرْحَةٌ	Sour a.	حَامِضٌ. شَكِسٌ
Sorely ad.	جِدًّا	Source n.	أَصْلٌ. مَصْدَرٌ. يَنْبُوعٌ
Sorrel a. or n.	أَشْقَرُ. حَمَّاضٌ	Sourness n.	حُمُوضَةٌ. شَكَاسَةٌ
Sorrow n. or v. i.	حُزْنٌ. حَزِنَ	Souse v. t.	غَطَّسَ. غَمَسَ
Sorrowful a.	حَزِينٌ. كَئِيبٌ	South n. or a.	جَنُوبٌ. جَنُوبِيٌّ
Sorry a.	مُكَدَّرٌ. آسِفٌ. مُتَحَسِّرٌ	South-east n.	الْجَنُوبُ الشَّرْقِيُّ

Southerly Southern } a.	جَنُوبِيٌّ	Sparkle v. i.	أَخْرَجَ شَرَراً . تَلَأْلَأَ
Southward ad.	جَنُوباً . إِلَى ٱلْجَنُوب	Sparrow n.	عُصْفُورٌ دُورِيٌّ
South-west n.	ٱلْجَنُوبُ ٱلْغَرْبِيُّ	Sparse a.	مَتَشَتِّتٌ مُتَفَرِّق
Souvenir n.	تَذْكَارٌ . تَذْكِرَةٌ	Spasm n.	تَشَنُّج
Souvereign n. or a.	مَلِكٌ . سُلْطَانِيٌّ	Spasmodic a.	تَشَنُّجِي . مُتَقَطِّعٌ
Souvereignty n.	مُلْكٌ . سَلْطَنَةٌ	Spatter v. t.	لَطَخَ ـَ
Sow n. or v. t.	خِنْزِيرَةٌ . زَرَعَ ـَ أَذَاعَ	Spawn n. or v. i.	بَيْضُ ٱلسَّمَكِ . بَاضَ ـِ
Space n.	خَلَاءٌ . مَسَافَةٌ . مُدَّةٌ	Speak v. i.	تَكَلَّمَ . نَطَقَ ـِ
Spacious a.	فَسِيحٌ . رَحِيبٌ	Speaker v.	مُتَكَلِّمٌ . رَئِيسُ مَجْلِسٍ
Spade n.	مِجْرَفَةٌ . مَرٌّ . لَوْحٌ	Spear n.	رُمْحٌ . حَرْبَةٌ
Span n. or v. t.	شِبْرٌ . قَاسَ بِهِ	Special v.	خَاصٌّ . خُصُوصِي
Spaniard n. Spanish a. }	إِسْبَنْيُولِيٌّ	Speciality n.	خُصُوصِيَّةٌ
Spaniel n.	نَوْعٌ مِنَ ٱلْكَلْب	Specie n.	نُقُودٌ . مَسْكُوكَات
Spank v. t.	لَطَمَ عَلَى ٱلْعَجِز	Species n.	نَوْعٌ ج أَنْوَاع
Spar n.	سَارِيَةٌ . حَجَرٌ مُتَبَلْوِرٌ	Specific a.	نَوْعِي . خُصُوصِيٌّ . جَازِمٌ
Spare a.	يَسِيرٌ . نَحِيفٌ . فَارِغ	Specification n.	تَخْصِيصٌ . تَعْرِيفٌ
Spare v. t.	عَفَّ عَنْ . ٱسْتَحْيَا . ٱقْتَصَدَ	Specify v. t.	خَصَّصَ . صَرَّحَ . عَرَّفَ
Spark n.	شَرَارَةٌ . جُزْءٌ يَسِيرٌ	Specimen n.	مِثَالٌ . مَسْطَرَةٌ . عَيِّنَةٌ

Specious a.	حَسَنٌ أَوْحَقٌّ بِالظَّاهِرِ
Speck n.	نُقْطَةٌ . لَطْخَةٌ
Speckled n.	مُنَقَّطٌ . أَرْقَطُ
Spectacle n.	مَنْظَرٌ . مَشْهَدٌ
Spectacles n. pl.	مِنْظَارٌ (عُوَيْنَاتٌ)
Spectator n.	شَاهِدٌ . مُتَفَرِّجٌ
Spectre n.	خَيَالٌ . طَيْفٌ
Speculate v. i.	تَأَمَّلَ . تَفَلْسَفَ
	اِبْتَاعَ بِانْتِظَارِ زِيَادَةِ الثَّمَنِ. ضَارَبَ
Speculative a.	نَظَرِيٌّ . فَلْسَفِيٌّ
Speculum n.	مِرْآةٌ . مِنْظَارٌ
Speech n.	كَلَامٌ . خِطَابٌ . لُغَةٌ
Speechless a.	صَامِتٌ . أَخْرَسُ
Speed n.	سُرْعَةٌ . فَلَاحٌ . تَوْفِيقٌ
Speedy a.	سَرِيعٌ
Spell n.	دَوْرٌ . بُرْهَةٌ
Spell v. t.	هَجَّى . تَهَجَّى
Speller n.	مُتَهَجٍّ . كِتَابٌ تَهْجِيَةٍ

Spend v. t.	صَرَفَ . أَنْفَقَ . أَفْرَغَ
Spendthrift n.	مُسْرِفٌ . مُبَذِّرٌ
Spew v. t. or i.	اِسْتَفْرَغَ . قَاءَ
Sphere n.	كُرَةٌ . دَائِرَةٌ . مَقَامٌ
Spheric }a. Spherical }	كَرَوِيٌّ
Spheroid n.	شِبْهُ كُرَةٍ
Sphinx n.	اِ بُو الْهَوْلِ
Spice n.	طِيبٌ تَابِلٌ
Spicy a.	تَابِلِيٌّ . حِرِّيفٌ . مُطَيَّبٌ
Spider n.	عَنْكَبُوتٌ . رُتَيْلَاءِ
Spike n. or v. t.	سُنْبُلَةٌ . مِسْمَارٌ كَبِيرٌ. سَمَّرَ بِهِ
Spikenard n.	نَارَدِينُ
Spill v. t. or i.	أَرَاقَ . كَبَّ ـُ . اِنْكَبَّ
Spin v. t. or i.	غَزَلَ ـِ . بَرَمَ ـُ
Spinach } n. Spinage }	إِسْبَانَخٌ
Spinal a.	فَقَرِيٌّ
Spindle n. or v. i.	مَغْزَلٌ . طَالَ . اِسْتَدَقَّ
Spine n.	الْعَمُودُ الْفَقَرِيُّ . شَوْكَةٌ

Spinster *n.*	اِمْرَأَةٌ . غَيْرُ مُتَزَوِّجَةٍ	Splice *v. t.* or *n.*	أَوْصَلَ الطَّرَفَيْنِ
Spiral *a.*	لَوْلَبِيٌّ	Splint Splinter } *n.*	شَظِيَّةٌ . جَبِيرَةٌ
Spire *n.*	بُرْجٌ بِهَيْئَةٍ مِسَلَّةٍ	Split *v. t.*	شَقَّ ـ . فَلَقَ ـ
Spirit *n.*	رُوحٌ . نَشَاطٌ . طَبْعٌ	Spoil *v. t.* or *i.*	نَهَبَ ـ أَفْسَدَ . فَسَدَ ـ
Spirited *a.*	نَشِيطٌ	Spoil *n.*	نَهْبٌ . غَنِيمَةٌ
Spiritless *a.*	خَائِرٌ . مُتَرَاخٍ	Spokesman *n.*	نَائِبٌ فِي التَّكَلُّمِ
Spiritual *a.*	رُوحِيٌّ . دِينِيٌّ	Spoliation *n.*	نَهْبٌ . تَسْلِيحٌ
Spirituality *a.*	رُوحَانِيَّةٌ	Sponge *n.* or *v. t.*	إِسْفَنْجَةٌ . سَفْنَجَ . مَسَحَ بِهَا
Spirituous *a.*	رُوحِيٌّ . مُسْكِرٌ		
Spit *n.* or *v. t.*	سَفُّودٌ . بُصَاقٌ بَصَقَ ـ	Spongy *a.*	إِسْفَنْجِيٌّ
Spite *n.* or *v. t.*	ضَغِينَةٌ . غِلٌّ . ضَغَنَ ـ حَقَدَ	Sponsor *n.*	كَفِيلٌ . إِشْبِينٌ
		Spontaniety *n.*	فِعْلٌ مِنْ تِلْقَاءِ النَّفْسِ
Spiteful *a.*	ضَغِنٌ . مُغِلٌّ . حَقُودٌ	Spontaneous *a.*	مِنَ النَّفْسِ رَأْسًا
Spittle *n.*	بُصَاقٌ . لُعَابٌ . تُفْلٌ	Spool *n.*	مِسْلَكَةٌ (بَكَرَةٌ)
Spittoon *n.*	مَبْصَقَةٌ	Spoon *n.*	مِلْعَقَةٌ ج مَلَاعِقُ
Splash *v. t.*	لَأَمَ السَّائِلَ فَرَشَّهُ	Spoonful *n.*	مِلْءُ مِلْعَقَةٍ
Spleen *n.*	طِحَالٌ . حِقْدٌ	Sporadic *a.*	مُتَوَحِّدٌ . مُتَفَرِّقٌ
Splendid *a.*	فَاخِرٌ . بَاهِرٌ . بَهِيٌّ	Spore *n.*	بِزْرَةٌ دَقِيقَةٌ جِدًّا
Splendour *n.*	بَهَاءٌ . رَوْنَقٌ . جَلَالٌ	Sport *n.*	لَعِبٌ . طَرَبٌ . صَيْدٌ

Sportsman n.	صَيَّادٌ
Spot n.	مَوْضِعٌ . بُقعَةٌ . لَطْخَةٌ
Spotless a.	طَاهِرٌ . بِلاعَيْب
Spotted a.	مُلطَّخٌ . أَرْقَطُ
Spouse n.	زَوْجٌ . زَوْجَةٌ
Spout n. or v. i.	صُنْبُورٌ . تَفْجَّرَ
Sprain n. or v. t.	وَثْيٌ . وَثَّى
Sprawl v. i.	اِسْتَلْقَى
Spray n.	رِشَاشُ الْمَاء
Spread v. t. or i.	نَشَرَ . اِنْتَشَرَ
Spree n.	سَكْرَةٌ
Sprig n.	شُعْبَةٌ . عُسْلُجٌ
Sprightful / Sprightly } a.	نَشِيطُ الْجَسَدِ والْعَقل
Spring v. i.	وَثَبَ . صَدَرَ . اِنْفَجَرَ
Spring n.	وَثْبَةٌ . نَبْعٌ . رَبِيعٌ . زُنْبُرُك
Sprinkle v. t. or i.	رَشَّ . نَضَحَ
Sprite n.	خَيَالٌ . طَيْفٌ
Sprout v. i. or n.	نَبَتَ . فَرَّخَ . فَرْخ
Spry a.	خَفِيفُ الْحَرَكَةِ . نَشِيطٌ
Spue v. i.	اِسْتَفْرَغَ . تَقَيَّأ
Spur n.	مِهْمَازٌ . ظَهْرٌ بَارِزٌ
Spur v. t.	حَثَّ . أَنْهَضَ . نَخَسَ
Spurious a.	كَاذِبٌ . مُزَوَّرٌ
Spurn v. t.	رَفَضَ . أَنِفَ مِنْ
Spurt v. t. or i.	فَجَّرَ . اِنْفَجَرَ
Spy n. or v. t.	جَاسُوسٌ . نَظَّرَ
Spyglass n.	نَظَّارَةٌ صَغِيرَةٌ
Squabble v. i.	شَاجَرَ . نَازَعَ
Squad n.	شِرْذِمَةٌ
Squadron n.	كُرْدُوسَةٌ . جَمَاعَةُ سُفُن
Squalid a.	قَذِرٌ . وَسِخٌ
Squall n. or v. t.	هَبَّةٌ قَوِيَّةٌ . صَرَخَ
Squalor n.	قَذَرٌ . وَسَخٌ
Squander v. t.	بَذَّرَ . أَسْرَفَ
Square a. or n.	مُرَبَّعٌ . عَادِلٌ . سَاحَةٌ
Square v. t.	رَبَّعَ . كَعَّبَ . سَدَّدَ

Squash *n.*	كُوسَى . لَقْطِين
Squat *v. t.*	قَعَدَ ٱلْقُرْفُصَى
Squeak *n.* or *v. i.*	صَرِيرٌ . صَرَّ ـ
Squeal *v. i.*	صَاحَ كَٱلْخِنْزِير
Squeeze *v. t.*	ضَغَطَ ـَ . عَصَرَ ـِ
Squint *v. i.* or *n.*	حَوِلَ ـَ . حَوَلٌ
Squint-eyed *a.*	أَحْوَلُ
Squirrel *n.*	سِنْجَابٌ
Stab *v. t.* or *n.*	طَعَنَ ـَ . طَعْنَةٌ
Stability *n.*	ثَبَاتٌ . رُسُوخٌ
Stable *n.* or *a.*	إِصْطَبْل . أَخُورٌ . ثَابِتٌ
Stack *n.* or *v. t.*	كُوْمَةٌ . كَوَّمَ
Staff *n.*	عُكَّازٌ . رُكْنٌ ج أَرْكَانٌ
Stag *n.*	ذَكَرُ ٱلْإِيَّل
Stage *n.*	دَكَّةٌ . دَرَجَةٌ . مَرْحَلَةٌ
Stagger *v. i.* or *t.*	تَرَنَّحَ . تَمَايَلَ . أَرَابَ
Stagnant *a.*	سَاكِنٌ . فَاسِدٌ . كَاسِدٌ
Stagnate *v.i.*	سَكَنَ ُ . فَسَدَ ُ . كَسَدَ
Staid *a.*	رَزِينٌ . رَصِينٌ
Stain *v. t.* or *n.*	صَبَغَ ـُ . لَطَخَ ـَ . لَطْخَةٌ
Stainless *a.*	بِلَا عَيْبٍ . نَقِيٌّ
Stairs Stair-case *n.*	مِعْرَجٌ . سُلَّمٌ
Stake *n.*	وَتَد . رَهْنٌ . إِسْتِشْهَادٌ
Stake *v. t.*	خَاطَرَ ـ . رَاهَنَ
Stale *a.*	تَافِهٌ . عَتِيقٌ
Stalk *n.*	سَاقُ نَبَاتٍ . رُجَيْلَةٍ
Stall *n.*	مَعْلَفٌ . دُكَّانٌ
Stallion *n.*	فَحْلٌ ج فُحُولٌ
Stalwart *a.*	قَوِيٌّ . شُجَاعٌ
Stamen *n.*	سَدَاةٌ ج أَسْدِيَةٌ
Stammer *v. i.*	تَمْتَمَ . لَجْلَجَ
Stamp *v. t.*	خَبَطَ ـ . طَبَعَ . رَسَمَ ـِ
Stamp *n.*	طَبْعٌ . رَسْمٌ . دَمْغَةٌ
Stampede *n.*	هَزِيمَةٌ
Stanch *a.* or *v. t.*	ثَابِتٌ . وَقَفَ نَزْفًا
Stand *v. i.*	وَقَفَ ـ . ثَبَتَ . بَقِيَ

Stand n.	مَوْقِفٌ. قَاعِدَةٌ. ثُبُوتٌ
Standard n.	عَلَمٌ. مِقْيَاسٌ. قَاعِدَةٌ
Standing a.	قَائِمٌ. ثَابِتٌ. دَائِمٌ
Stanza n.	دَوْرُ شِعْرٍ
Stable n. or a.	رَزَّةٌ. حَاصِلٌ. رَئِيسِيٌّ
Star n.	نَجْمَةٌ. كَوْكَبٌ
Starboard n.	عِين السَّفِينَةِ
Starch n. or v. t.	نَشَا. نَشَّى
Stare v. i.	تَفَرَّسَ. حَمْلَقَ
Stark a.	مَحْضٌ. كُلِّيٌّ. جَامِدٌ
Starlight n.	نُورُ النُّجُومِ
Starry a.	ذُو نُجُومٍ أَوْ كَثِيرِهَا
Start v. i. or t.	بَدَا. أَجْفَلَ. حَرَّكَ
Startle v. t.	جَفَلَ. أَرْعَشَ
Starvation n.	أَلْمَوْتُ جُوعاً
Starve v. i. or t.	مَاتَ أَوْ أَمَاتَ جُوعا
State n.	حَالٌ. وِلَايَةٌ. حُكُومَةٌ
State v. t.	قَالَ. قَصَّ. قَرَّرَ
Stateliness n.	أُبَّهَةٌ. جَلَالَةٌ
Stately a.	جَلِيلٌ. عَظِيمٌ. مُوَقَّرٌ
Statement n.	قَوْلٌ. تَقْرِيرٌ
Statesman n.	عَالِمٌ بِالسِّيَاسَةِ
Statesmanship n.	عِلْمُ السِّيَاسَةِ
Station n.	مَنْصِبٌ. رُتْبَةٌ. مَحَطَّةٌ
Station v. t.	وَضَعَ. نَصَبَ
Stationary a.	وَاقِفٌ. ثَابِتٌ
Stationery n.	أَدَوَاتُ الْكِتَابَةِ
Statistics n.	عِلْمُ الْإِحْصَاءِ أَوِ التَّعْدَادِ
Statuary n.	مُجْتَمَعُ تَمَاثِيلَ
Statue n.	تِمْثَالٌ
Stature n.	قَدٌّ. قَامَةٌ
Statute n.	سُنَّةٌ. نِظَامٌ
Stave v. t.	كَسَرَ. أَخَّرَ
Stave n.	لَوْحٌ. ضَيِّقٌ لِبَرْمِيلٍ
Stay v. i. or t.	اسْتَمَرَّ. وَقَفَ. دَعَمَ

Stead *n.*	عِوَضٌ . بَدَلٌ
Steadfast *a.*	ثَابِتٌ . رَاسِخٌ
Steadfastness Steadiness } *n.*	حَزْمٌ . ثَبَاتٌ
Steady *a.*	ثَابِتٌ . غَيْرُ مُتَقَلِّبٍ
Steak *n.*	شَرِيحَةُ لَحْمٍ
Steel *v. t.* or *i.*	سَرَقَ . اِنْسَلَّ
Stealth *n.*	اِنْسِلَالٌ . اِخْتِلَاسٌ
Stealthy *a.*	مُنْسَلٌّ . مُخْتَلِسٌ
Steam *n.* or *v. i.*	بُخَارٌ . بَخَّرَ
Steam-boat Steamer } *n.*	بَاخِرَةٌ . وَابُورٌ
Steam-engine *n.*	آلَةٌ بُخَارِيَّةٌ
Steed *n.*	جَوَادٌ ج جِيَادٌ
Steel *n.* or *v. t.*	فُولَاذٌ . قَسَّى
Steelyard *n.*	قَبَّانٌ
Steep *a.* or *v. t*	مُنْحَدِرٌ جِدًّا . نَقَعَ
Steeple *n.*	مَنَارَةُ كَنِيسَةٍ
Steepness *n.*	شِدَّةُ انْحِدَارٍ
Steer *v. t.*	أَدَارَ سَفِينَةً
Stellar *a.*	نَجْمِيّ
Stem *v. t.*	وَقَفَ . دَفَعَ
Stem *n.*	سَاقٌ . مُقَدَّمُ سَفِينَةٍ
Stench *n.*	رَائِحَةٌ قَبِيحَةٌ
Step *n.* or *v. i.*	خُطْوَةٌ . خَطَا
Step-child *n.*	وَلَدُ الزَّوْجِ أَوِ الزَّوْجَةِ
Step-father *n.*	زَوْجُ الأُمِّ . رَابٌّ
Step-mother *n.*	زَوْجَةُ الأَبِ . رَابَّةٌ
Stepping-stone *n.*	وَسِيلَةٌ . مِرْقَاةٌ
Sterile *a.*	عَقِيمٌ . أَجْدَبُ
Sterility *n.*	جَدْبٌ . عُقْمٌ
Sterling *n.* or *a.*	دَرَاهِمُ إِنْكِلِيزِيَّةٌ . حَقِيقِيّ
Stern *n.* or *a.*	مُؤَخَّرٌ . عَبُوسٌ
Sternness *n.*	عُبُوسٌ
Stethoscope *a.*	مُسْتَقْصِيَةٌ . صَدْرِيَّةٌ
Stew *v. t.* or *n.*	سَلَقَ . رُوَيْدًا . يُخْنَةٌ
Steward *n.*	وَكِيلٌ . قَهْرَمَانٌ
Stewardship *n.*	وَكَالَةٌ . قَهْرَمَةٌ

Stick n. or v.t.	قَضِيبٌ. الزَق. طَعَن
Stickiness n.	لُزوجَة
Stickle v. i.	نَازَعَ مُكابَرةً
Sticky a.	لَزِجٌ. دَبِقٌ
Stiff a.	جَامِدٌ. صُلْبٌ. مُتَيَبِّسٌ
Stiffen v. t. or i.	جَمَّدَ. جَمَدَ
Stiffness n.	جُمودٌ. اِشْتِدادٌ. صَلاَبَةٌ
Stiff-necked a.	صُلْبُ الرَّقَبَةِ
Stifle v.	أَطْفَأَ. سَكَّنَ. خَنَقَ
Stigma n.	عَيْبٌ. سِمَةٌ
Stigmatize v.	عَيَّبَ. وَسَمَ
Still v. t. or a.	سَكَّنَ. سَاكِنٌ. سَاكِتٌ
Still ad.	إِلَى الآنَ. مَعَ ذَلِكَ
Still-born a.	(وَلَدٌ) سِقْطٌ
Stillness n.	سُكونٌ. هُدوٌّ
Stimulant a. or n. Stimulative a.	مُنبِّهٌ. مُنَشِّطٌ
Stimulate v. t.	نَبَّهَ. حَرَّضَ
Stimulation n.	تَحْرِيضٌ. تَهْيِيجٌ
Stimulus n.	مُنبِّهٌ. مُحَرِّكٌ
Sting n. or v. t.	لَسْعَةٌ. لَسَعَ
Stinginess n.	بُخْلٌ. شُحٌّ
Stingy a.	بَخِيلٌ. شَحِيحٌ
Stink n. or v. i.	نَتَانَةٌ. نَتَنَ
Stint v. t. or a.	حَدَّدَ. حَدَّ. عَمَل مَحْدُودٌ
Stipend v.	رَاتِبٌ. مَعَاشٌ
Stipulate v. i.	اِشْتَرَطَ
Stipulation n.	شَرْطٌ. إِتِّفاقٌ
Stir v. i. or t.	تَحَرَّكَ. حَرَّكَ. هَزَّ
Stirrup n.	رِكَابٌ ج رُكُبٌ
Stitch v. t.	خَاطَ. دَرَزَ
Stock n.	أَصْلٌ. مَالٌ. سِلْعَةٌ
Stock v. t.	جَهَّزَ. ذَخَرَ
Stockade n.	سِيَاجٌ لِلتَّحْصِينِ
Stock-holder n.	صَاحِبُ أَسْهُمٍ
Stocking n.	جَوْرَبٌ
Stocks n. pl.	أَسْهُمٌ مَالِيَّةٌ. مِقْطَرَةٌ

Stocky a.	ضَخْمٌ . قَوِيُّ ٱلْجِسْمِ
Stoic a. or n.	غَيْرُ مُبَالٍ بِمَا يَحْدُثُ
Stoicism n.	مَذْهَبُ غَيْرِ ٱلْمُكْتَرِثِينَ بِٱلدَّهْرِ
Stole, Stolen, *see* Steal.	
Stolid a.	بَلِيدٌ . أَبْلَهُ
Stolidity n.	بَلَادَةٌ . بَلَاهَةٌ
Stomach n. or v. t.	مَعِدَةٌ . ٱحْتَمَلَ
Stone n. or v. t.	حَجَرٌ . نَوَاةٌ . رَجَمَ . أَخْرَجَ ٱلْبِزْرَةَ أَوِ ٱلنَّوَاةَ
Stone-cutter n.	نَحَّاتٌ
Stone-ware n.	آنِيَةٌ حَجَرِيَّة
Stony a.	مُحْجِرٌ
Stool n.	كُرْسِيٌّ لِلرِّجْلَيْنِ . إِسْكَمْلَةٌ
Stoop v. i.	ٱنْحَنَى . خَضَعَ –
Stop v. t. or i.	وَقَفَ . وَقَّفَ –
Stop n.	وَقْفٌ . وُقُوفٌ . سَدٌّ
Stoppage n.	وَقْفٌ . تَوْقِيفٌ
Stopper / Stopple } n.	سِدَادٌ . صِمَامٌ

Storage n.	خَزْنٌ . ٱدِّخَارٌ
Store n. or v. t.	كَمِّيَّةٌ . مُؤْنَةٌ . ذَخَرَ . مَخْزَنٌ
Storied a.	مَقُولٌ فِي رِوَايَةٍ . ذُو طَبَقَاتٍ
Stork n.	بَجَعٌ
Storm n.	نَوْءٌ . عَاصِفٌ . هُجُومٌ
Storm v. t. or i.	هَجَمَ عَلَى . عَصَفَ
Stormy a.	عَاصِفٌ . كَثِيرُ ٱلْأَنْوَاءِ
Story n.	قِصَّةٌ . طَبَقَةُ بَيْتٍ
Stout a.	قَوِيٌّ . جَسُورٌ . سَمِينٌ
Stoutness n.	قُوَّةٌ . شِدَّةٌ . سِمَنٌ
Stove n.	وِجَاقٌ . مَوْقِدٌ
Stow v. t.	خَزَنَ – . عَبَّى
Straddle v. i. or t.	فَجَّ – . رَكِبَ –
Straggle v. i.	شَرَدَ – . عَنْ . هَامَ –
Straggler n.	شَارِدٌ
Straight a. or ad.	مُسْتَقِيمٌ . رَأْسًا
Straighten v. t.	قَوَّمَ . سَوَّى
Straightforwad a.	مُسْتَقِيمٌ . عَادِلٌ

Straightway ad.	حَالاً . عَلَى الْفَوْرِ	Stratum n.	طَبَقَةٌ
Strain v. t.	شَدَّ ـُ . وَنَّى ـِ . صَفَّى	Straw n.	قَشٌّ . تِبْن
Strain n.	جَهْدٌ . اسْلُوبٌ	Strawberry n.	ثَمَرُ كَالتُّوتِ. فَرَاوْلاً
Strainer n.	مِصْفَاةٌ	Stray v. i.	ضَلَّ ـِ . شَرَدَ ـُ تَاهَ ـِ
Strait a. or n.	ضَيِّقٌ. ضَيْقَةٌ. مَضِيقٌ	Streak n.	خَطٌّ
Straiten v. t.	ضَيَّقَ . شَدَّ	Streaked / Streaky } a.	مُخَطَّطٌ
Strand n.	شَطٌّ . طَاقُ حَبْلٍ	Stream n. or v. i.	مَجْرًى . نَهْرٌ. سَالَ ـِ
Strange a.	غَرِيبٌ. عَجِيبٌ	Streamlet n.	نُهَيْرٌ. سَاقِيَةٌ
Strangeness n.	غَرَابَةٌ	Street n.	طَرِيقٌ . زُقَاقٌ. شَارِعٌ
Stranger n.	غَرِيبٌ. أَجْنَبِيٌّ	Strength n.	قُوَّة . مَتَانَةٌ
Strangle v. t.	خَنَقَ ـُ	Strengthen v. t.	قَوَّى . شَدَّدَ
Strangulation n.	خَنَقٌ . اِخْتِنَاقٌ	Strenuous a.	عَزُومٌ. مُجِدٌّ
Strap n. or v. t.	سَيْرٌ. شَدَّ بِهِ	Stress n.	ضَغْطٌ . شِدَّةٌ
Strapping a.	طَوِيلٌ . خَلِيعٌ	Stretch v. t. or i.	مَدَّ ـُ . وَسَّعَ . إِمْتَدَّ
Strata n. pl.	طَبَقَاتٌ . صُفُوفٌ	Stretch n.	اِمْتِدَادٌ . اِتِّسَاعٌ
Stratagem n.	حِيلَةٌ . مَكِيدَةٌ	Strew v. t.	بَذَرَ . فَرَّقَ . نَشَرَ
Strategy n.	عِلْمُ إِدَارَةِ الْحَرْبِ	Stricken a.	مُصَابٌ. مُتَضَايِقٌ
Stratification n.	نَضْدُ الطَّبَقَاتِ	Strict a.	مُدَقِّقٌ. مُشَدِّدٌ .صَارِمٌ

Strictly *ad.*	بضَبْطٍ بطَريقَةٍ اِمَةٍ بِالتَمَامِ	Stroke *v. t.*	دَاكَ ـُ . لَاطَفَ
Strictness *n.*	تَدْقيقٌ . تَشْديدٌ	Stroll *v. i.*	جَالَ ـُ . عَارَ ـِ
Stricture *n.*	تَنْكيتٌ . تَضْييقٌ	Strong *a.*	قَوِيٌّ . مَتينٌ . شَديدٌ
Stride *n.* or *v. i.*	خُطْوَةٌ طَويلَةٌ	Stronghold *n.*	حِصْنٌ . مَعْقِلٌ
Strife *n.*	نِزَاعٌ . مُنَاظَرَةٌ	Structure *n.*	هَيْئَةٌ . بِنْيَةٌ . بِنَاءٌ
Strike *v. t.*	ضَرَبَ ـِ . أَثَّرَ . اصَابَ	Struggle *v. i.*	جَدَّ . عَارَكَ
Striking *a.*	مُؤَثِّرٌ . غَريبٌ	Struggle *n.*	عِرَاكٌ
String *n.*	خَيْطٌ . وَتَرٌ . سِلْسِلَةٌ	Strumpet *n.*	عَاهِرَةٌ . فَاجِرَةٌ
String *v. t.*	جَهَّزَ بِوَتَرٍ . صَفَّ	Strut *v. i.*	تَبَخْتَرَ . تَخَطَّرَ
Stringent *a.*	مُشَدَّدٌ . خَطيرٌ . مُهِمٌّ	Stubble *n.*	هَشيمٌ
Stringy *a.*	ليفِيٌّ . خَيْطِيٌّ	Stubborn *a.*	عَنيدٌ . مَاردٌ
Strip *v. t.*	عَرَّى . قَشَرَ . نَزَعَ ـِ	Stucco *n.* or *v. i.*	جَصٌّ . طَلَى بِهِ
Strip *n.*	قِطْعَةٌ ضَيِّقَةٌ . سَيْرٌ	Stud *n.*	طَوَالَةُ خَيْلٍ . زِرٌّ
Stripe *n.*	قَلَمٌ . خَطٌّ . ضَرْبَةُ سَوْطٍ	Studded *a.*	مُرَصَّعٌ
Striped *a.*	مُخَطَّطٌ	Student *n.*	تِلْميذٌ . طَالِبُ عِلْمٍ
Stripling *n.*	وَلَدٌ . غُلَامٌ	Studied *a.*	مَدْرُوسٌ . مُهَيَّأً . مُدَبَّرٌ
Strive *v. i.*	جَدَّ . كَدَّ . اِجْتَهَدَ	Studious *a.*	مُجِدٌّ فِي الدَّرْسِ
Stroke *n.*	ضَرْبَةٌ . مُصِيبَةٌ . إِصَابَةٌ	Study *n.* or *v. t.*	دَرْسٌ . دَرَسَ ـُ

Stuff n.	مادةٌ. مَتَاعٌ. قُمَاشٌ	Stylish a.	بِحَسبِ الزِّيِّ. انيقٌ
Stuff v. t.	حَشَا. أَفْعَمَ	Suasive a.	مقْنعٌ
Stuffing n.	حَشْوٌ	Suavity n.	لَطَافَة. أَدَبٌ. عُذوبةٌ
Stultify v. t.	جهَّلَ. حَمَّقَ	Subdivide v. t.	جزَّأَ ايضًا
Stumble v. i.	عَثَرَ. زَلَّ. كَبَا	Subdivision n.	تَجْزِئَةُ الْمُجزإِ
Stumbling-block n.	حَجَرُ عَثْرَةٍ	Subdue v. t.	أَخْضَعَ. غَلَبَ
Stump n.	قَرْمِيَّةٌ ج قَرَامِيُّ	Subject n.	تابِعٌ. مَوضوعٌ. فَاعِلٌ
Stun v. t.	دَوَّخَ. حَيَّرَ. بَهَّتَ	Subject v. t. or a.	خضَعَ. خَاضِعٌ. تحت
Stunt v. t.	وَقَّفَ عَنِ النموّ	Subjection n.	إِخْضَاعٌ. خُضوعٌ
Stupefy v. t.	أَدْخَلَ. بَهَّتَ. خدر	Subjective a.	باطِنيٌّ. ذِهْنِيّ
Stupendous a.	عظِيمٌ جدًّا. عَجِيبٌ	Subjoin v. t.	لْحَقَ بِهِ. ذَيَّلَ
Stupid a.	بَلِيدٌ. أَبْلَهُ. أَخْرَقُ	Subjugate v. t.	أَخْضَعَ. قَهَرَ
Stupidity n.	خُرْقٌ. بَلاهَةٌ	Subjunctive a.	مُلْحقٌ. مَوْصُولٌ بِهِ
Stupor n.	سُبَاتٌ. خَدَرٌ	Sublime a.	سَامٍ. جَلِيلٌ. رَفِيعٌ
Sturdy a.	قَوِيٌّ. عَزومٌ	Sublimity n.	سُمُوٌّ. جَلالَةٌ. رِفْعَةٌ
Stutter v. i.	تمَتَمَ. لَجْلَجَ	Submerge v. t.	أَغْرَقَ. غطَّسَ
Sty n.	زَرِيبَةُ الْخَنَازِير. شحَّاذُ الْعَيْن	Submersion n.	تَغْطِيسٌ
Style n.	اسْلُوبٌ. عِبَارَةٌ. زَيٌّ	Submission n.	خُضوعٌ. تسْلِيمٌ

Submissive *a*.	خَاضِعٌ. طَائِعٌ
Submit *v. i. or t.*	خَضَعَ ــَ. سَلَّمَ
Subordinate *a*.	تَابِعٌ. دُونٌ. ثَانَوِي
Subordination *n*.	خُضُوعٌ. تَبَعِيَّةٌ
Suborn *v. t.*	حَمَلَ عَلَى حَلْفِ زُورٍ
Subscribe *v.t. or i.*	أَمْضَى. رَضِيَ بِهِ. اِشْتَرَكَ فِي
Subscriber *n*.	مُشْتَرِكٌ
Subscription *n*.	قِيمَةُ اِشْتِرَاكٍ
Subsequent *a*.	تَالٍ. تَابِعٌ
Subsequently *ad*.	بَعْدُ. مِنْ بَعْدُ
Subserve *v. t.*	خَدَمَ ــِ. أَفَادَ
Subservient *a*.	مُفِيدٌ لَهُ. خَاضِعٌ
Subside *v. i.*	خَمَدَ ــُ. سَكَنَ ــُ
Subsidence *n*.	سُكُونٌ. هُبُوطٌ
Subsidiary *a*.	مُعَاوِنٌ. إِضَافِيٌّ
Subsidize *v.t.*	أَعَانَ بِدَرَاهِمَ لِخِدْمَةٍ
Subsidy *n*.	إِعَانَةٌ مَالِيَّةٌ
Subsist *v. i.*	اِقْتَاتَ. بَقِيَ ــَ. وُجِدَ

Subsistence *n*.	مَعِيشَةٌ. وُجُودٌ
Substance *n*.	مَادَّةٌ. جَوْهَرٌ. خُلَاصَةٌ
Substantial *a*.	حَقِيقِيٌّ. جَوْهَرِيٌّ
Substantiate *v. t.*	أَثْبَتَ. حَقَّقَ
Substantive *n. or a*.	اِسْمٌ. حَقِيقِيٌّ
Substitute *n. or v. t.*	عِوَضٌ. أَبْدَلَ
Substitution *n*.	إِبْدَالٌ
Substruction Substructure } *n*.	بِنَاءٌ تَحْتِي. أَسَاسٌ
Subtend *v. t.*	قَاطَعَ مِنْ أَسْفَلَ أَوْ مُقَابِلًا
Subterfuge *n*.	مُوَارَبَةٌ. حِيلَةٌ
Subterranean Subterraneous } *a*.	تَحْتَ الْأَرْضِ
Subtle *a*.	دَاهٍ. مُحْتَالٌ. مَكَّارٌ
Subtilty Subtlety } *n*.	حِيلَةٌ. دَهَاءٌ
Subtract *v. t.*	طَرَحَ ــَ. أَسْقَطَ مِنْ
Subtraction *n*.	طَرْحٌ
Subtrahend *n*.	اَلْمَطْرُوحُ
Suburban *a*.	مِنْ سَوَادِ مَدِينَةٍ
Suburbs *n. pl.*	سَوَادُ مَدِينَةٍ

Subversion n.	قَلْبٌ . هَدْمٌ . تَحْرِيفٌ
Subversive a.	مُخَرِّبٌ . مُحَرِّفٌ
Subvert v. t.	قَلَبَ ـ . خَرَّبَ . حَرَّفَ
Succeed v. t. or i.	تَبِعَ ـ حَلَّ مَحَلَّهُ . نَجَحَ
Success n.	نَجَاحٌ . فَوْزٌ
Successful a.	نَاجِحٌ . ظَافِرٌ
Succession n.	تَتَابُعٌ . خِلَافَةٌ
Successive a.	مُتَتَابِعٌ . مُتَعَاقِبٌ
Successor n.	تَابِعٌ . خَلَفٌ . خَلِيفَةٌ
Succinct a.	مُوجَزٌ . مُلَخَّصٌ
Succour n. or v. t.	إِغَاثَةٌ . أَغَاثَ . أَعَانَ
Succulent a.	غَضٌّ
Succumb v. i.	خَضَعَ . مَاتَ
Such a.	كَذَا . كَهَذَا . مِثْلُ هَذَا
Suck v. t.	رَضَعَ ـ اِمْتَصَّ
Sucker n.	فَرْخٌ . عُسْلُجٌ . نَوْعٌ مِنَ السَّمَكِ
Suckle v. t.	أَرْضَعَ

Suckling n.	رَضِيعٌ ج رُضَّعٌ
Suction n.	مَصٌّ
Sudden a.	فُجَائِيٌّ . بَاغِتٌ
Suddenly ad.	بَغْتَةً
Sue v. t.	اِدَّعَى عَلَيْهِ . حَاكَمَ . طَلَبَ
Suet n.	شَحْمٌ
Suffer v. t. or i.	اِحْتَمَلَ . قَسِيَ . رَخَّصَ
Sufferable a.	مَا يُحْتَمَل
Sufferance n.	رُخْصَة . اِحْتِمَالٌ
Sufferer n.	مُصَابٌ . مُكَابِدٌ . مُتَأَلِّمٌ
Suffering n.	أَلَمٌ . ضِيقٌ . عَذَابٌ
Suffice v. i. or t.	كَفَى ـ . أَغْنَى
Sufficiency n.	كِفَايَةٌ . مُكْنَةٌ
Sufficient a.	كَافٍ . مُغْنٍ
Suffix n.	مُضَافٌ إِلَى آخِرِهِ
Suffocate v. t.	خَنَقَ . فَطَّسَ
Suffocation n.	خَنْقٌ . اِخْتِنَاق
Suffrage n.	حَقُّ صَوْتِ الاِنْتِخَابِ

Suffuse v. t.	نْشَرَ ـُ . أَفْشَى
Sugar n.	سُكَّرٌ
Sugar-basin} n. Sugar bowl}	سُكَّرِيَّةٌ
Sugar-cane n.	قَصَبُ السُّكَّرِ
Sugar-loaf n.	رَأْسُ سُكَّرٍ
Sugar-plum n.	مُلَبَّسٌ
Suggest v. t	أَوْعَزَ . قَدَّمَ رَأْيًا
Suggestion n.	تَقْدِيمُ رَأْيٍ . تَلْمِيحٌ
Suggestive a.	مُلَمِّحٌ . مُشِيرٌ إِلَى
Suicidal n.	آئِلٌ لِقَتْلِ النَّفْسِ
Suicide n	قَتْلُ النَّفْسِ . اِنْتِحَارٌ
Suit n. or v. t.	حُلَّةُ ثِيَابٍ . دَعْوَى . نَاسَبَ
Suitable a.	مُوَافِقٌ . مُنَاسِبٌ
Suitableness n.	مُنَاسَبَةٌ
Suite n.	حَشَمٌ . طَقْمٌ
Suitor n.	طَالِبٌ . مُحِبٌّ . صَاحِبُ دَعْوَى
Sulky } Sullen } a.	عَبُوسٌ . حَرِيدٌ
Sully v. t.	لَطَخَ . ثَلَمَ الصِّيتَ

Sulphur n.	كِبْرِيتٌ
Sulphureous } Sulphurous } a.	كِبْرِيتِيٌّ
Sultriness n. } Sultry a. }	عَكٌّ
Sum n.	مَجْمُوعٌ . حَاصِلٌ
Sumach n.	سُمَّاقٌ (شَجَرَةٌ)
Summarily ad.	مُلَخَّصًا . حَالًا
Summary n. or a.	مُلَخَّصٌ
Summer n.	صَيْفٌ . قَيْظٌ
Summit n.	قِمَّةٌ . رَأْسٌ
Summon v. t.	اِسْتَدْعَى . اِسْتَحْضَرَ
Summons n. sing.	اِسْتِحْضَارٌ
Sumptuous a.	فَاخِرٌ . بَهِيٌّ . ثَمِينٌ
Sun n. or v. t.	شَمْسٌ . شَمَّسَ
Sun-beam n.	شُعَاعُ الشَّمْسِ
Sunday n.	يَوْمُ الأَحَدِ
Sunder v. t.	فَصَلَ ـِ
Sun-dial n.	سَاعَةٌ شَمْسِيَّةٌ
Sundries n. pl.	أَشْيَاءٌ شَتَّى

Sundry a.	شَتَّى
Sunken a.	غارِقٌ . تَحْتَ اَلْمَاءِ
Sunlight n.	نُورُ اَلشَّمْسِ
Sunlit a.	مُنَوَّرٌ مِنَ اَلشَّمْسِ
Sunny a.	شَمْسٌ . مُعَرَّضٌ لِلشَّمْسِ
Sunrise n.	شُرُوقُ اَلشَّمْسِ
Sunset n.	غُرُوبُ اَلشَّمْسِ
Sunshine n.	ضَوْءُ اَلشَّمْسِ
Sun-stroke n.	رُعْنٌ
Sup v. i.	تَعَشَّى
Superabundance n.	وَفْرَةٌ . فَرْطٌ
Superabundant a.	مُفْرِطٌ . وَافِرٌ
Superannuated a.	عاجِزٌ مِنَ اَلْكِبَرِ
Superb a.	فاخِرٌ . نَفِيسٌ . بَهِيٌّ
Supercilious a.	مُتَغَطْرِسٌ . مُتَجَبِّرٌ
Supereminent a.	فائِقٌ جِدًّا
Supererogatory a.	نافِلِيٌّ
Superficial a.	سَطْحِيٌّ . ظاهِرِيٌّ
Superfine a.	نَفِيسٌ جِدًّا . سامٍ
Superfluity n.	زِيادَةٌ . فَضْلٌ
Superfluous a.	زائِدٌ . فَوْقَ اَللاَزِمِ
Superintend v. t.	ناظَرَ . تَوَكَّلَ عَلَى
Superintendence n.	مُناظَرَةٌ
Superintendent n.	ناظِرٌ . وَكِيلٌ
Superior a. or n.	فائِقٌ . أَعْظَمُ . رَئِيسٌ
Superiority n.	سَبْقٌ . أَفْضَلِيَّةٌ
Superla- tive a.	اَلْأَفْضَلُ . أَفْعَلُ اَلتَّفْضِيلِ
Supernatural a.	فَوْقَ اَلطَّبِيعَةِ
Superscribe v. t.	عَنْوَنَ
Superscription n.	عُنْوانٌ
Supersede v. t.	عَزَّلَ – . أَلْغَى
Supernal n.	عَلْوِيٌّ . سَماوِيٌّ
Superstition n.	وَهْمٌ . خُرَافَةٌ
Superstitious n.	مُتَوَهِّمٌ . خُرَافِيٌّ
Superstructure n.	بِناءٌ فَوْقَ غَيْرِهِ
Supervene v. i.	حَدَثَ عَرَضًا

Supervise v. t.	ناظَرَ . رَاقَبَ
Supervisor n.	نَاظِرٌ . مُنَاظِرٌ
Supine a.	مُتَكَاسِلٌ . غَيْرُ مُكْتَرِثٍ
Supineness n.	تَوَانٍ . تَهَامُلٌ
Supper n.	عَشَاءٌ
Supplant v. t.	اَسْتَبْدَلَ حِيلَةً
Supple a.	مَرِنٌ . لَيِّنٌ . مُنْقَادٌ
Supplement n.	مُلْحَقٌ . إِضَافَةٌ
Supplemental Supplementary } a.	إِضَافِيٌّ
Suppleness n.	مُرُونَةٌ . لِيُونَةٌ
Suppliant Supplicant } a.	مُتَوَسِّلٌ . مُتَضَرِّعٌ
Supplicate v. t.	تَوَسَّلَ . تَضَرَّعَ إِلَى
Supplication n.	تَوَسُّلٌ . اِلْتِمَاسٌ
Supplies n. pl. Supply n. }	مُونَةٌ . ذَخِيرَةٌ . كَفَاءَةٌ
Supply v. t.	جَهَّزَ . قَدَّمَ . أَوْرَدَ
Support v. t.	عَضَدَ . عَالَ . أَمَدَّ
Support n.	سَنَدٌ . عَوْلٌ . عَضُدٌ
Supportable a.	يُحْتَمَلُ . يُطَاقُ

Supposable a.	مَظْنُونٌ . مُحْتَمَلٌ
Suppose v. t.	ظَنَّ _ فَرَضَ _
Supposition n.	ظَنٌّ . فَرْضٌ
Suppositious a.	غَيْرُ حَقِيقِيٍّ . مَظْنُونٌ
Suppress v. t.	أَخْمَدَ . أَبْطَلَ . مَنَعَ _
Suppression n.	اِبْطَالٌ . إِخْمَادٌ
Suppurate v. i.	قَاحَ _ تَقَيَّحَ
Supremacy n.	سُلْطَة . رِيَاسَةٌ تَفَوُّقٌ
Supreme a.	الأَعْظَمُ . مُطْلَقُ التَّسَلُّطِ
Sure a.	اكِيدٌ . يَقِينٌ . مُحَقَّقٌ
Surety n.	أَمْنٌ . كَفَالَةٌ . يَقِينٌ
Surf n.	أَمْوَاجٌ عَلَى الشَّطِّ
Surface n.	سَطْحٌ . وَجْهٌ
Surfeit n. or v. t.	كِظَّةٌ . كَظَّ _
Surge n. or v. i.	مَوْجٌ عَظِيمٌ . تَمَوَّجَ
Surgeon n.	جَرَّاحٌ
Surgery n.	عِلْمُ الجِرَاحَةِ
Surgical a.	جِرَاحِيٌّ

Surly *a.*	شَكِسٌ . فَظٌّ	Suspect *v. t.*	اتَّهَمَ . اشْتَبَهَ
Surmise *n.* or *v. t.*	حَدَسٌ . خَمَّنَ	Suspend *v. t.*	وَقَفَ . أَجَّلَ . عَلَّق
Surmount *v. t.*	عَلَا يَدَاُو . غَلَبَ ــِ	Suspense *n.*	تَرَدُّدٌ . حِيْرَةٌ
Surname *n.*	اسْمُ الْعَائِلَةِ . لَقَبٌ	Suspension *n.*	تَوْقِيفٌ . تَعْطِيل
Surpass *v. t.*	سَبَقَ ــُ . فَاقَ ــَ	Suspension *n.*	تُهْمَةٌ . شُبْهَةٌ
Surpassing *a.*	فَائِقٌ . جَيِّدٌ جِدًّا	Suspicious *a.*	ظَنَّانُ . مُشْتَبَهٌ
Surplus *n.*	فَضْلَةٌ . بَقِيَّةٌ	Sustain *v. t.*	احْتَمَلَ . سَنَدَ ــُ . عَضَدَ ــُ
Surprise *n.* or *v. t.*	تَعَجُّبٌ . جَا . ادْهَشَ	Sustenance *n.*	قُوتٌ . عَضِد
Surrender *v. t.* or *n.*	سَلَّمَ . تَسْلِيم	Suture *n.*	دَرْز
Surreptitious *a.*	مَا يُفْعَلُ خُلْسَةً أَوْ غَدْرًا	Suzerain *n.*	دَوْلَى
Surround *v. t.*	احَاطَ بِهِ . احْدَق	Swab *n.* or *v. t.*	مِمْسَحَةٌ . مَسَحَ بِهَا
Survey *v. t.*	عَايَنَ . فَحَصَ ــَ . مَسَحَ ــَ	Swaddle *v. t.* or *n.*	قَمَطَ . قِمَاط
Survey Surveying *n.*	مَسْحٌ . مِسَاحَةٌ	Swagger *v. i.* or *n.*	تَغَطْرَسَ . غَطْرَسَةٌ
Surveyor *n.*	مَسَّاحٌ	Swain *n.*	فَلاحٌ . فَلاحٌ عَاشِقٌ
Survival *n.*	بَقَاءٌ بَعْدَ آخَرَ	Swallow *v. t.* or *n.*	ازْدَرَدَ . سُنُونُو
Survive *v. t.*	عَاشَ بَعْدَهُ	Swamp *n.*	مُسْتَنْقَعٌ . سَبَخَةٌ . غَمْقَةٌ
Susceptibility *n.*	حِسٌّ . تَأَثُّرٌ	Swan *n.*	نَوْعٌ مِنَ الاوَزِّ
Susceptible *a.*	مُحِسٌّ . مُتَأَثِّرٌ . قَابِلٌ	Sward *n.*	جَزْمَةٌ . ارْضٌ كَثِيرَةُ الْكَلَإِ

Swarm n. or v. i.	ثَوَّلَ . اِزْدَحَمَ
Swarthy a.	أَسْمَرُ
Sway v. t. or i.	مَلَكَ . أَمَالَ . تَمَايَلَ
Swear v. i.	حَلَفَ . أَقْسَمَ . شَتَمَ
Swearing n.	حَلْف . تَحْذِيف
Sweat n. or v. i.	عَرَقٌ . عَرِقَ
Sweep v. t.	كَنَسَ . جَرَفَ
Sweepings n. pl.	كُنَاسَةٌ . زُبَالَةٌ
Sweet a. or n.	حُلْوٌ . عَذْبٌ . حَلْوَى
Sweeten v.t. or i.	حَلَّى . حَلَا
Sweetheart n.	عَاشِقٌ (ة) مَعْشُوق (ة)
Sweetmeat n.	حَلْوَى ج حَلَاوَى
Sweetness n.	حَلَاوَةٌ . عُذُوبَة
Swell v. i. or n.	اِنْتَفَخَ . وَرِمَ . عُبَابٌ
Swelling n.	وَرَمٌ
Swelter v. i.	تَضَايَقَ مِنَ الْحَرِّ
Swerve v.	مَالَ . اِنْحَرَفَ
Swift a.	سَرِيعٌ
Swiftness n.	سُرْعَةٌ
Swim v. i.	سَبَحَ
Swimming n.	سِبَاحَةٌ
Swimmingly ad.	جَيِّدًا . بِتَوْفِيقٍ
Swindle v. t. or n.	غَبَنَ . غَدَرَ
Swine n.	خِنْزِيرٌ ج خَنَازِيرُ
Swing v. t. or i.	اِرْجَحَ . اِرْتَجَحَ . تَمَايَلَ
Swing n.	أُرْجُوحَةٌ . مَرْجُوحَةٌ
Switch n.	قَضِيبٌ لَيِّنٌ
Swoon v. i. or n.	غُشِيَ عَلَيْهِ . غَشْيَةٌ
Swoop v. i.	اِنْقَضَّ عَلَى
Sword n.	سَيْفٌ . ج سُيُوفٌ . حُسَامٌ
Sycamore n.	جُمَّيْزٌ . جُمَّيْزَةٌ
Sycophant n.	مُدَاهِنٌ
Syllable n.	مَقْطَعُ كَلِمَةٍ
Syllabus n.	خُلَاصَةٌ . مُخْتَصَرٌ
Syllogism n.	قِيَاسٌ مَنْطِقِى
Sylvant a.	غَابِيٌّ

Symbol *n.*	رَمْزٌ . مِثَالٌ . عَلَامَةٌ
Symbolic Symbolical } *a.*	رَمْزِيٌّ . اِسْتِعَارِيٌّ
Symmetrical *a.*	مُتَنَاسِبُ الْأَجْزَاءِ
Symmetry *n.*	تَنَاسُبُ الْأَجْزَاءِ
Sympathetic	مُشْتَرِكٌ فِي شُعُورِ غَيْرِهِ
Sympathize *v. i.*	اِشْتَرَكَ فِي شُعُورِهِ
Sympathy *n.*	إِشْتِرَاكٌ فِي شُعُورِهِ
Symptom *n.*	عَلَامَةٌ . عَرَضُ مَرَضٍ
Synagogue *n.*	مَجْمَعُ الْيَهُودِ
Synchronism *n.*	اِتِّفَاقٌ فِي الْوَقْتِ
Syndicate *n.*	وَكَالَةٌ أَوْ شِرْكَةٌ لِإِجْرَاءِ أَشْغَالٍ

Synonym Synonyme } *a.*	كَلِمَةٌ مُتَرَادِفَةٌ
Synonymous *a.*	مُتَرَادِفٌ
Synopsis *n.*	مُلَخَّصٌ . خُلَاصَةٌ
Synoptic Synoptical } *a.*	مُلَخِّصِيٌّ . شَامِلٌ
Syntax *n.*	عِلْمُ النَّحْوِ
Synthesis *n.*	تَرْكِيبٌ . تَأْلِيفُ الْأَفْكَارِ
Syriac *a.*	سِرْيَانِيٌّ
Syringe *n.* or *v. i.*	مِحْقَنَةٌ . عَالَجَ بِهَا
Syrup *n.*	عَصِيرٌ . مُحَلًّى . شَرَابٌ
System *n.*	تَرْتِيبٌ . نِظَامٌ . مَذْهَبٌ
Systematic Systematical } *a.*	نِظَامِيٌّ . تَرْتِيبِيٌّ
Systematize *v. t.*	نَظَّمَ . رَتَّبَ

T

Tabernacle *n.*	خَيْمَةٌ . مَظَلَّا
Table *n.*	مَائِدَةٌ . سُفْرَةٌ . جَدْوَلٌ
Tableau *n.*	صُورَةٌ . تَشْخِيصٌ

Table-land *n.*	نَجْدٌ . هَضْبَةٌ . صَعِيدٌ
Tablet *n.*	لَوْحٌ لِلْكِتَابَةِ
Tabular *a.*	مُسَطَّحٌ . جَدْوَلِيٌّ

Tacit a.	سَاكِتٌ . مُضَمَّنٌ . مَفْهُومٌ
Taciturn a.	سَكُوتٌ . كَتُومٌ
Taciturnity n.	سُكُوت
Tack n.	مِسْمَارٌ صَغِيرٌ. مَجْرَى السَّفِينَة
Tack v. t.	سَمَّرَ خَفِيفًا. غَيَّرَ مَجْرَى السَّفِينَة
Tackle n. or v. t.	جَهَازٌ. آلَاتٌ. قَبَضَ . شَدَّ
Tackling n.	جِهَازُ السَّوَارِي وَالْقُلُوع
Tact n.	مَهَارَةٌ . لَبَاقَةٌ . فِرَاسَةٌ
Tactical a.	مُخْتَصٌّ بِتَنْظِيمِ الْجُيُوشِ
Tactics n. sing.	عِلْمُ تَنْظِيمِ الْجُيُوشِ
Tadpole n.	وَلَدُ الضِّفْدَع
Tail n.	ذَنَبٌ . ذَيْلٌ . مُؤَخَّر
Tailor n.	خَيَّاط
Taint v. t. or n.	شَابَ ـُ لَطْخَة
Take v. t.	أَخَذَ ـُ تَنَاوَلَ
Taking a. or n.	جَاذِبٌ . أَخْذٌ
Tale n.	قِصَّةٌ . حِكَايَةٌ . رِوَايَةٌ
Tale-bearer n.	نَمَّامٌ . وَاشٍ

Talent n.	وَزْنَةٌ . مَوْهَبَةٌ
Talented a.	ذَكِيٌّ . لَوْذَعِيٌّ
Talisman n.	طَلْسَمٌ ج طَلَاسِيم
Talk n. or v. i.	كَلَامٌ . تَكَلَّمَ
Talkative a.	كَثِيرُ الْكَلَام
Tall a.	طَوِيلُ الْقَامَةِ . عَالٍ
Talness n.	طُولٌ . عُلُوٌّ
Tallow n.	شَحْمٌ
Tally v. i.	طَابَقَ . اتَّفَقَ
Tallon n.	مِخْلَبٌ . ظُفْرٌ
Tamable a.	مَا يُؤْنَسُ . يُطَبَّعُ . يُذَلَّلُ
Tame a. or v. t.	دَاجِنٌ . ذَلُولٌ. ذَلَّلَ
Tamely ad.	تَذَلُّلًا
Tamper v. i.	تَدَاخَلَ فِي . لَعِبَ فِي
Tan n. or v. t.	دِبْغَةٌ . دَبَغَ ـُ
Tangent n.	خَطٌّ مُمَاسٌّ لِقَوْس
Tangible a.	مَا يُمَسُّ أَوْ يُلْمَسُ. مَحْسُوس
Tangle v. t. or n.	شَبَّكَ . عُقْدَة

Tank *n.*	حَوْضٌ . بِرْكَةٌ
Tanner *n.*	دَبَّاغٌ
Tannery *n.*	مَدْبَغَةٌ . دِبَاغَةٌ
Tantalize *v. t.*	عَذَّبَ بِرَجَاءِ ٱلْمُسْتَحِيلِ
Tantamount *a.*	مُسَاوٍ
Tap *n.*	دَقَّ ُ خَفِيفاً . بَزَلَ ُ
Tape *n.*	شَرِيطٌ
Taper *n. or v. i.*	شَمْعَةٌ . ٱسْتَدَقَّ
Tap-root *n.*	ٱلْجِذْرُ ٱلْأَصْلِيُّ ٱلْمُسْتَقِيمُ
Tapestry *n.*	أَنْسِجَةٌ مُوَشَّاةٌ لِلتَّعْلِيقِ
Tapeworm *n.*	الدُّودَةُ ٱلْعَرِيضَةُ
Tar *n. or v. t.*	قَطْرَانٌ طَلَى بِهِ . نُورِي
Tardiness *n.*	تَأَخُّرٌ . بُطُوءٌ
Tardy *a.*	مُتَأَخِّرٌ . بَطِيءٌ
Tare *n.*	زُوَانٌ
Target *n.*	هَدَفٌ . تُرْسٌ صَغِيرٌ
Tariff *n.*	تَعْرِيفٌ . جَدْوَلُ جَمَارِكَ
Tarnish *v. t.*	كَدَّرَ ٱللَّوْنَ . لَطَّخَ
Tarry *v. i.*	مَكَثَ ُ . أَبْطَأَ
Tart *a. or n.*	حَامِضٌ . حَادٌّ . فَطِيرَةٌ
Tartar *n.*	طَارْطِيرٌ . تَتَرِي
Tartness *n.*	حُمُوضَةٌ . حِدَّةٌ
Task *n.*	شُغْلٌ مَفْرُوضٌ . عَمَلٌ شَاقٌّ
Tassel *n.*	شَرَّابَةٌ . زُرٌّ
Taste *v. t. or n.*	ذَاقَ ُ . ذَوْقٌ . مَشْرَبٌ
Tasteful *a.* Tasty	بِحَسَبِ ٱلذَّوْقِ . أَنِيقٌ
Tasteless *a.*	بِلَا طَعْمٍ . تَافِهٌ
Tatter *v. t. or n.*	مَزَّقَ . خِرْقَةٌ . رِثَّةٌ
Tattle *v. i.*	هَذَرَ . فَضَحَ ٱلسِّرَّ
Taunt *v. t.*	عَيَّرَ عَنَّفَ
Tavern *n.*	فُنْدُقٌ . حَانَةٌ
Tawdry *a.*	مُتَظَرِّفٌ بِلَا ذَوْقٍ
Tawny *a.*	أَسْمَرُ
Tax *n.*	ضَرِيبَةٌ . رَسْمٌ
Taxable *a.*	تَحْتَ ضَرِيبَةٍ أَوْ رَسْمٍ
Taxation *n.*	ٱلضَّرَائِبُ بِجُمْلَتِهَا

Tea n.	شَايٌ	Teeth n. pl. of Tooth	أَسْنَانٌ
Teach v. t.	عَلَّمَ . دَرَّسَ	Teetotal- ism n.	اَلْاِمْتِنَاعُ عَنِ ٱلْمُسْكِرَاتِ
Teachable a.	قَابِلُ ٱلتَّعْلِيمِ . طَوْعٌ	Telegram n.	رِسَالَةٌ بَرْقِيَّةٌ
Teacher n.	مُعَلِّمٌ . مُدَرِّسٌ	Telegraph n.	سِلْكٌ بَرْقِيٌّ
Team n.	ثَوْرُ ٱلْحِرَاثَةِ . قِطَارُ دَوَابَّ	Telephone n.	آلَةٌ لِلتَّكَلُّمِ عَلَى بُعْدٍ
Tea-pot n.	إِبْرِيقُ شَايٍ	Telescope n.	نَظَّارَةٌ . مِنْظَرٌ
Tear n.	دَمْعَةٌ . شَرْمٌ . مَزْقَةٌ	Tell v. t. or i.	خَبَّرَ . حَدَّثَ . قَالَ
Tear v. t.	مَزَّقَ . شَقَّ ـُ	Tell-tale n.	وَاشٍ
Tearful a.	دَمِيعٌ	Temerity n.	تَهَوُّرٌ . اِعْتِسَافٌ
Tease v. t.	نَكَّدَ . أَضْجَرَ	Temper n.	طَبْعٌ . خُلُقٌ
Teat n.	حَلَمَةُ حَيَوَانٍ . بِزٌّ	Temper v. t.	مَزَجَ ـُ لَطَّفَ . عَدَّلَ
Technical a.	صِنَاعِيٌّ . اِصْطِلَاحِيٌّ	Temperament n.	مِزَاجٌ
Technology n.	اَلْبَحْثُ عَنِ ٱلصِّنَاعَاتِ وَحُدُودِهَا	Temperance n.	اِعْتِدَالٌ . عِفَّةٌ
Tedious a.	مُتْعِبٌ . مُمِلٌّ . مُطَوَّلٌ	Temperate a.	مُعْتَدِلٌ . عَفِيفٌ
Tediousness Tedium } n.	مَلَلٌ . ضَجَرٌ	Temperature n.	دَرَجَةُ ٱلْحَرَارَةِ
Teem v. i.	غَصَّ ـُ . أَنْتَجَ كَثِيرًا	Tempest n.	عَاصِفَةٌ . نَوْءٌ
		Tempestuous a.	عَاصِفٌ . زَوْبَعِيٌّ
Teens n. pl.	اَلْعُمْرُ بَيْنَ ١٣ و ١٩ سَنَةً	Temple n.	هَيْكَلٌ . صُدْغٌ

Temporal a.	زَمَنِيٌّ . صُدْغِيٌّ
Temporarily ad.	وَقْتِيًا
Temporary a.	وَقْتِيٌّ . إِلَى حِينٍ
Temporise v. i.	دَارَ مَعَ الْأَحْوَالِ
Tempt v. t.	جَرَّبَ . أَغْوَى
Temptation n.	تَجْرِبَة
Tempter n.	مُجَرِّبٌ
Ten a.	عَشَرَة . عَشْر
Tenable a.	قَابِلُ التَّمَسُّكِ بِهِ أَوِ الْإِثْبَاتِ
Tenacity n.	تَمَسُّكٌ . تَشَبُّث
Tenant n.	مُسْتَأْجِرٌ
Tenantry n.	مُسْتَأْجِرُو املَاك
Tend v. t. or i.	آلَ . مَالَ إِلَى . إِعْتَنَى بِ
Tendency n.	مَيْلٌ . انْعِطَافٌ
Tender a.	غَضٌّ . طَرِيٌّ . حَنُونٌ
Tender n. or v. t.	عَرْضُ سِعْرٍ . عَرَضَ
Tenderness n.	حَنُوٌّ . رِقَّة
Tendon n.	وَتَرٌ
Tendril n.	عَسْلُج لَوْلَبِيٌّ لِلتَّعَايِيق
Tenement n.	مَسْكِنٌ مُسْتَأْجَرٌ
Tenet n.	عَقِيدَة . مَذْهَبٌ
Tenfold n.	عَشَرَةُ أَضْعَافٍ
Tennis n.	نَوْعٌ مِنْ لِعْبِ الْكُرَة
Tenor n.	فَحْوَى . سِيَاق
Tense a. or n.	مَشْدُودٌ . زَمَانُ الْفِعْلِ
Tension n.	شَدٌّ . اشْتِدَادٌ
Tent n.	خَيْمَة . صِيوَانٌ . فُسْطَاطٌ
Tentacle n.	قَرْنُ الْحَشَرَتِ
Tentative a.	تَجْرِيبِي
Tenth a.	عَاشِرٌ
Tenuity n.	رِقَّة . لَطَافَة
Tenure n.	اسْتِئْجَارُ
Tepid a.	فَاتِرٌ
Terebinth n.	شَجَرُ الْبُطْمِ
Term n.	عِبَارَة . مُدة . شَرْط . حَدٌّ
Term v. t.	سَمَّى . دَعَا

Terminal a.	في ٱلطَّرَفِ . آخِرُ	Testator n.	مُوصٍ
Terminate v. t.	أَنهَى . إِنتَهَى	Testicle n.	خِصيَة ج خُصى
Termination n.	إِنهآءٌ . نِهايَةٌ	Testify v. t.	شَهِدَ ـ
Terminus n.	تَخم . طَرَفٌ . حَدٌّ	Testimonial a. } Testimony n. }	شَهَادَةٌ
Terrace n.	سَطحُ بَيتٍ . دَكَّةٌ	Testiness n.	حِدَّةٌ . شَكاسَةٌ
Terra-Cotta n.	فَخَّارٌ	Tetanus n.	دَآءُ ٱلكُزاز
Terrestrial a.	أَرضِيٌّ	Tether v. t.	شَكَلَ ـ . شَكَلَ
Terrible a.	مُخِيفٌ . هَائِلٌ	Teutonic a.	جَرمَانِيٌّ
Terrier n.	ضَربٌ مِنْ كِلابِ ٱلصَّيدِ	Text n.	مَتن . مَوضُوعٌ
Terrific a.	مُسَبِّبُ خَوفٍ شَدِيدٍ	Text-book n.	كِتَابُ دَرسٍ
Terrify v. t.	خَوَّفَ . فَزَّعَ	Textile a.	مَنسُوجٌ . نَسِيجِيٌّ
Territory n.	إِقلِيمٌ . أَرضُ مَملَكَةٍ	Texture n.	نَسِيجٌ
Terror n.	هَولٌ . فَزَعٌ	Than conj.	مِنْ (بَعدَ أَفعَلِ ٱلتَّفضِيلِ)
Terse a.	أَنيقُ ٱلعِبَارَةِ . مُوجَزُهَا	Thank v. t.	شَكَرَ ـ . أَثنَى عَلَى
Terseness n.	إِيجَازٌ	Thankful a.	شَاكِرٌ . شَكُورٌ
Test n. or v. t.	امتِحَانٌ . جَرَّبَ	Thankfulness n.	شُكرَانٌ . شُكرٌ
Testament n.	عَهدٌ . وَصِيَّةٌ	Thankless a.	عَدِيمُ ٱلشُّكرِ
Testamentary a.	مَنُوطٌ بِوَصِيَّةٍ	Thanks n.	

Thanksgiving *n.*   شُكْرٌ . حَمْدٌ

That *pron.* or *conj.*   ذَلِكَ . أَنْ

Thatch *n.* or *v. t.*   غِمَآءٌ . غَمَى ـُ

Thaw *v. i.* or *t.*   ذَابَ ـُ . أَذَابَ

The *def. article.*   أَلْ التَّعْرِيف

Theatre *n.*   مَسْرَحٌ . مَلْعَبٌ

Theatric   } *a.*
Theatrical   مَسْرَحِيّ

Thee *p. pron.*   كَ (ضَمِيرُ ٱلْمُخَاطَب)

Theft *n.*   سَرِقَة

Theirs *a. pron.*   الذِي لَهُمْ

Theism *n.*   ٱلْإِعْتِقَادُ بِوُجُود اللّٰه

Theist *n.*   مُعْتَقِدٌ بِاللّٰه

Them *p. pron.*   هُمْ . هُنَّ (مَنْصُوبٌ اومَجْرُور)

Theme *n.*   مَوْضُوع . جُمْلَة . مَقَالَة

Themselves *pron. pl.*   هُمْ أَنْفُسُهُمْ

Then *ad.*   عِنْدَ ذَلِكَ . حِينَئِذٍ . إِذًا

Thence *ad.*   مِنْ هُنَاكَ

Thenceforth   } *ad.*
Thenceforward   مِنْ ذَلِكَ ٱلْوَقْتِ

Theodolite *n.*   آلَةٌ لِلْمِسَّاحَة

Theologian *n.*   عَالِمٌ بِاللّٰاهُوتِ

Theologic   } *a.*
Theological   لَاهُوتِيّ

Theology *n.*   عِلْمُ ٱللّٰاهُوت

Theorem *n.*   قَضِيَّة هَنْدَسِيَّة

Theoretic   } *a.*
Theorotical   نَظَرِي . تَصَوُّرِي

Theorise *v. i.*   نَظَر فِي . إِرْتَأَى

Theory *n.*   نَظَرِيَّة . رَأْيٌ

Therapeutic *a.*   عِلَاجِيّ . شِفَائِيّ

There *ad.*   هُنَاكَ . حَرْفُ ٱلْإِبْتِدَآء

Thereabout *ad.*   تَقْرِيبًا

Thereafter *ad.*   بَعْدَ ذَلِكَ . ثُمَّ

Thereby *ad.*   بِذَلِكَ . لِذَلِكَ

Therefore *ad.*   لِذَلِكَ . لِأَجْلِ ذَلِك

Therein *ad.*   فِي ذَلِكَ . هُنَاكَ

Thereof *ad.*   مِنْ ذَلِكَ . مِنْهُ

Thereupon *ad.*   حِينَئِذٍ . عِنْدَ ذَلِكَ

Therewith *ad.*   لِذَلِكَ . بِه

Thermal a.	مَنُوطٌ بِالْحَرِّ	Thing n.	شَيْءٌ . أَمْرٌ
Thermometer n.	مِيزَانُ الْحَرَارَةِ	Think v. i. or t.	أَفْتَكَرَ . ظَنَّ
Thesaurus n.	خِزَانَةٌ . قَامُوسٌ جَامِعٌ	Third a. or n.	ثَالِثٌ . ثَالِثٌ
These pron. pl. of this	هٰؤُلَاءِ	Thirst n. or v. i.	عَطِشَ عَطَشٌ ـَ
Thesis n.	مَوْضُوعٌ . مَبْحَثٌ . مَقَالَةٌ	Thirsty a.	عَطْشَانُ م عَطْشَى
They pl. pron.	هُمْ هُنَّ (مَرْفُوعٌ)	Thirteen a.	ثَلٰثَةَ عَشَرَ
Thick a.	سَمِيكٌ . كَثِيفٌ . ثَخِينٌ	Thirteenth a.	الثَّالِثُ عَشَرَ
Thicken v. t. or i.	سَمَّكَ . كَثَّفَ	Thirtieth a.	الثَّلَاثُونَ
Thicket n.	أَجَمَةٌ . دَغَل	Thirty a.	ثَلَاثُونَ
Thickness n.	سَمْكٌ . كَثَافَةٌ	This pron.	هٰذَا . هٰذِهِ
Thick-set a.	ضَخْمٌ	Thistle n.	شَوْكٌ . حَسَكٌ
Thief n.	سَارِقٌ . لِصٌّ	Thither ad.	إِلَى هُنَاكَ
Thieve v. i.	لَصَّ ـَ	Thong n.	سَيْرٌ . شِرَاكٌ
Thievish a.	مُتَلَصِّصٌ	Thorax n.	الصَّدْرُ
Thigh n.	فَخْذٌ ج أَفْخَاذٌ	Thorn n.	شَوْكٌ . اشِرَاكٌ
Thimble n.	قِمْعٌ . كِشْتِبَانٌ	Thorny a.	كَثِيرُ الشَّوْكِ . عَسِرٌ
Thin a.	رَقِيقٌ . نَحِيفٌ .	Thorough a.	كَامِلٌ . شَامِلٌ
Thine a. pron.	لَكَ . الَّذِي لَكَ	Thoroughfare n.	سِكَّةٌ . شَارِعٌ

Those pl. of that	اوائِكَ
Thou pron.	أَنت
Though conj.	مَعْ ان . وَلَوْ . وَان
Thought n.	فِكْرٌ . رَأْيٌ
Thoughtful a.	مُتَفَكِّرٌ . رَزِينٌ . مُهْتَمٌ
Thoughtless a.	طائِشٌ . غَافِلٌ
Thousand a. or n.	أَلْفٌ
Thousandth n.	الأَلْفُ
Thraldom) Thralldom) n.	عُبُودِيَّةٌ . رِقٌّ
Thrash v. t.	دَرَسَ الحُبُوبَ . ضَرَبَ
Thread n. or v. t.	خَيْطٌ . أَدْخَلَهُ فِي إِبْرَةٍ
Threadbare a.	بَالٍ
Threat n.	تَهْدِيدٌ . وَعِيد
Threaten v. t. or i.	هَدَّدَ . أَوْعَدَ . هَمَّ بِ
Threatening a.	مُهَدِّدٌ . مُوشِكٌ
Three a.	ثَلاثَةٌ . ثَلاثَةٌ . ثَلاثٌ
Threefold a.	ثَلاثَةَ أَضْعَافٍ
Threescore a.	سِتُّونَ
Thresh v. t.	دَرَسَ الحُبُوبَ
Threshold n.	أُسْكُفَّةٌ . مَدْخَلٌ
Thrice ad.	ثَلاثَ مَرَّاتٍ
Thrift n.	نَجَاحٌ . اقْتِصَادٌ
Thriftless a.	عَدِيمُ التَّدْبِيرِ وَالنَّجَاحِ
Thrifty a.	نَاجِحٌ . مُقْتَصِدٌ
Thrill v. t. or n.	حَرَّكَ . هَاجَ . اهْتِزَازٌ
Thrilling a.	مُهِيِّجٌ . مُؤَثِّرٌ جِدًّا
Thrive v. i.	نَجَحَ . أَفْلَحَ
Throat n.	حُلْقُومٌ . بُلْعُومٌ . حَلْقٌ
Throb v. i.	خَفَقَ . اخْتَلَجَ
Throe n.	أَلَمٌ شَدِيدٌ . مَخَاضٌ
Throne n.	عَرْشٌ
Throng n. or v. t. or i.	زَحْمَةٌ . تَقَاطَرَ
Throttle v. t.	خَنَقَ
Through pr.	مِنَ الأَوَّلِ إِلَى الآخِرِ . بِوَاسِطَةٍ
Throughout pr. or ad.	فِي كُلِّهِ
Throw v. t. or n.	رَمَى . رَمْيَةٌ

Thrust v. t. or n.	دَفَعَ. طَعَنَ ـُ دَفْعَةٌ
Thumb n. or v. t.	إِبْهَامٌ ج أَبَاهِيم . وَسَّخَ بِهَا
Thump n. or v. t.	ضَرَبَ . وَكَزَ . ضَرْبَةٌ
Thunder n. or v. i.	رَعْدٌ . رَعَدَ ـَ
Thunder-bolt n.	صَاعِقَةٌ
Thunder-struck a.	صَعِقَ . مَدْهُوشٌ
Thursday n.	يَوْمُ الخَمِيسِ
Thus ad.	هٰكَذَا . كَذَا
Thwart v. t.	عَارَضَ . عَطَّلَ
Thy poss. pron.	لَكَ
Thyme n.	سَعْتَر
Thyself pron.	أَنْتَ نَفْسُكَ
Tick n. or v. i.	قُرَّادَةٌ . تَكْتَكَ
Ticket n.	تَذْكِرَةُ إِجَازَةٍ
Tickle v. t.	دَغْدَغَ
Tide n.	مَدُّ البَحْرِ وَجَزْرُهُ
Tidings n. pl.	أَخْبَارٌ
Tidy a.	نَظِيفٌ . مُرَتَّبٌ
Tie v. t.	رَبَطَ ـِ . عَقَدَ ـِ . قَيَّدَ
Tier n.	طَبَقَةٌ . صَفٌّ
Tiger mas. Tigress fem. } n.	نَمِرٌ . نِمْرَةٌ ج نُمُورٌ
Tight a.	شَدِيدٌ . مَشْدُودٌ
Tighten v. t.	شَدَّ ـُ أَحْكَمَ . مَكَّنَ
Tile n. or v. t.	قِرْمِيدَةٌ . غَطَّى بِهَا
Till ad. or n.	حَتَّى . إِلَى . صُنْدُوق دَرَاهِم
Till v. t.	حَرَثَ ـُ . فَلَحَ ـَ
Tillage n.	حِرَاثَةٌ . وَفِلَاحَةٌ
Tilt v. t.	أَمَالَ . طَأْطَأَ ـَ
Timber n.	خَشَبٌ
Time n.	زَمَانٌ . وَقْتٌ مَرَّة
Timely ad.	فِي وَقْتِهِ . فِي مَحَلِّهِ
Time-piece n.	سَاعَةٌ
Timid Timorous } a.	خَائِفٌ . جَبَانٌ
Timidity n.	جَبَانَةٌ . حَيَاءٌ
Tin n.	قَصْدِيرٌ . تَنَكٌ . صَفِيحٌ
Tincture n.	صِبْغَةٌ . أَوُن

Tinder n.	صُوفَانٌ
Tinge v. t.	لَوَّنَ خَفِيفاً
Tingle v. i.	تَأَلَّمَ شَدِيداً
Tinker n. or v. t.	سِنْكَرِيٌّ . اصْلَحَ أَوْعِيَة
Tinkle v. i.	طَنَّ ـ
Tinkling n.	طَنِينٌ
Tinman } Tinner } n.	تِنْكَارِيٌّ
Tinsel n. or a.	بَهْرَجٌ . لَامِعٌ
Tint n.	لَوْنٌ خَفِيفٌ
Tiny a.	صَغِيرٌ جِدّاً . زَهِيدٌ
Tip n. or v. t.	طَرَفٌ . رَأْسٌ . أَمَالَ
Tippler n.	سِكِّيرٌ
Tipsy a.	سَكْرَانُ
Tiptoe n.	أَطْرَافُ أَصَابِعِ الْقَدَمِ
Tiptop n.	اعْلَاهُ . سَامٍ غَايَةً في الْجُودَةِ
Tirade n.	شَتْمٌ
Tire v. t. or n.	اتْعَبَ . طَبَانٌ
Tired a.	مُتْعَبٌ
Tiresome a.	مُتْعِبٌ . مُمِلٌّ
Tissue n.	نَسِيجٌ
Tithe v. t. or n.	عَشَّرَ . عُشْرٌ
Title n.	لَقَبٌ . عِنْوَانٌ . حَقٌّ
Titular a.	بِالْإِسْمِ فَقَطْ . اسْمِيٌّ
To pr.	إِلَى . نَحْوَ . لِ
Toad n.	نَوْعٌ مِنَ الضِّفْدَعِ
Toadstool n.	فِطْرٌ
Toast v. t. or n.	حَمَّصَ . خُبْزٌ مُحَمَّصٌ
Tobacco n.	تَبْغٌ . تُتُنٌ . دُخَانٌ
To-day n.	الْيَوْمُ
Toddle v. i.	دَبَّ ـ
Toddy n.	شَرَابٌ مُسْكِرٌ
Toe n.	اصْبُعُ الْقَدَمِ
Together ad.	مَعًا
Toil v. i. or n.	تَعِبَ ـ تَعَبٌ . كَدٌّ
Toilet n.	زِينَةُ لِبَاسٍ . مَائِدَةٌ لِلْبْسِ
Toilsome a.	مُتْعِبٌ . شَاقٌّ

Token n.	تَذْكِرَةٌ . عَلَامَةٌ	Tonnage n.	وَزْنُمَا تَسَعُهُ سَفِينَةٌ
Tolerable a.	مُحْتَمَلٌ . مُعْتَدِلٌ	Tonsil n.	لَوْزَةُ الْحَلْقِ
Tolerance } n. Toleration }	اِحْتِمَالٌ . تَسَامُحٌ	Tonsure n.	حَلْقُ قِمَّةِ الرَّأْسِ
Tolerate v. t.	أَبَاحَ . اِحْتَمَلَ	Too ad.	بِزِيَادَةٍ . أَيْضًا
Toll n. or v. t.	رَسْمٌ . دَقَّ	Tool n.	آلَةٌ . أَدَاةٌ
Tomahawk n.	فَأْسٌ حَرْبِيَّةٌ لِلْهُنُودِ	Tooth n.	سِنٌّ . نَابٌ . ضِرْسٌ
Tomato n.	(بَنْدُورَةٌ . طَمَاطِمُ)	Toothache n.	وَجَعُ الْأَسْنَانِ
Tomb n.	قَبْرٌ . ضَرِيحٌ	Toothless a.	بِلَا أَسْنَانٍ
Tombstone n.	حَجَرُ قَبْرٍ	Tooth-pick n.	سِوَاكٌ
Tome n.	كِتَابٌ . مُجَلَّدٌ	Toothsome a.	اللَّذِيذُ
To-morrow n.	اَلْغَدُ	Top n.	قِمَّةٌ . سَطْحٌ . دُوَّامَةٌ . (نَخْلَةٌ)
Ton n.	وَزْنٌ = ٢٠٠٠ لِيبْرًا	Toper n.	سِكِّيرٌ
Tone n.	صَوْتٌ . نَغْمَةٌ	Tophet n.	اَلْجَحِيمُ
Tongs n. pl.	مِلْقَطٌ	Topic n.	مَوْضُوعٌ . مَبْحَثٌ
Tongue n.	لِسَانٌ . لُغَةٌ	Topical a.	مَحَلِّيٌّ . مَوْضُوعِيٌّ
Tongue-tied a.	مَعْقُودُ اللِّسَانِ	Topmost a.	اَلْأَعْلَى
Tonic a. or n.	مُقَوٍّ	Topography n.	تَخْطِيطٌ . وَصْفٌ
To-night n.	هَذِهِ اللَّيْلَةَ	Topple v. i.	اِهْتَزَّ . اِنْقَلَبَ

Torch n.	مِشْعَلٌ	Touching a.	لامِسٌ . مُؤَثِّرٌ
Torment n. or v. t.	عَذابٌ . عَذَّبَ	Touchy a.	سَرِيعُ الْغَيْظِ
Tormenter | Tormentor \} n.	مُعَذِّبٌ	Tough a.	صَابٌ . قَاسٍ
Tornado n.	زَوْبَعَةٌ	Toughen v. t.	صَابَ . قَسَّى
Torpedo n.	لَغْمٌ بَحْرِيٌّ. فَنَرَةٌ (سَمَكَةٌ)	Tour n.	سِياحَةٌ . سَفْرَةٌ
Torpid a.	ثَقِيلُ الْحَرَكَةِ	Tourist n.	سائِحٌ . مُسافِرٌ
Torpidity | Torpor \} n.	سُباتٌ . ثِقَلٌ	Tournament n.	تَطَاعُنٌ لَعِبِيٌّ
Torrent n.	سَيْلٌ	Tow n. or v. t.	مُشاقَةُ الْكَتَّانِ . جَرَّ
Torrid a.	حَارٌّ جِدًّا	Toward | Towards \} prep.	إِلَى . نَحْوَ
Tortoise n.	سُلَحْفاةٌ ـ سَلاحِفُ	Towel n.	مِنْشَفَةٌ
Tortuous a.	مُعَوَّجٌ	Tower n. or v. t.	بُرْجٌ . ارْتَفَعَ
Torture n.	عَذابٌ . تَعْذِيبٌ	Towering a.	عالٍ . مُرْتَفِعٌ
Toss v. t. or i.	طَرَحَ ـ . انْقَلَبَ	Tow-line n.	حَبْلُ الْجَرِّ (لِسَفِينَةٍ)
Total a. or n.	كُلِّيٌّ . جُمْلَةٌ . مَجْمُوعٌ	Town n.	بَلْدَةٌ . مَدِينَةٌ
Totality n.	كُلِّيَّةٌ . جُمْلَةٌ	Township n.	بَلْدَةٌ مَعَ ضَواحِيها
Totally ad.	بِأَسْرِهِ . جُمْلَةً	Toxicology n.	عِلْمُ السُّمُومِ
Totter v. i.	اهْتَزَّ . هَمَّ بِالسُّقُوطِ	Toy n. or v. t.	لُعْبَةٌ . لاعَبَ . عَبِثَ
Touch v. i.	مَسَّ ـ . لَمَسَ ـ	Trace v. t.	رَسَمَ ـ . اسْتَقْصَى

Trace n.	أَثَرٌ . عَلَامَةٌ . رَسْمٌ	Tragic { Tragical } a.	هَائِلٌ . فَظِيعٌ
Traces n. pl.	سُيُورُ الخَيْلِ	Trail v. t. or i.	جَرَّ . اِنْسَحَبَ
Traceable a.	مَا يُسْتَدَلُّ عَلَيْهِ	Train v. t.	هَذَّبَ . أَدَّبَ
Track v. t.	تَأَثَّرَ . اِقْتَفَى	Trait n.	صِفَةٌ . عَلَامَةُ خُلُقٍ
Track n.	مَسْلَكٌ . أَثَرٌ . أَثَرُ قَدَمٍ	Traitor n. { Traitorous a. }	خَائِنٌ
Trackless a.	لَا مَسْلَكَ فِيهِ وَلَا أَثَرَ	Trammel v. t. or n.	عَاقَ . أَوْثَقَ . عَائِقٌ
Tract n.	إِقْلِيمٌ . مَقَالَةٌ	Trample v. t.	دَاسَ . اِزْدَرَى بِ
Tractable a.	طَوْعٌ . طَائِعٌ	Trance n.	غَيْبَةٌ
Tractability n.	طَوْعِيَّةٌ . اِنْقِيَادٌ	Tranquil a.	هَادِئٌ مُسْتَرِيحٌ
Traction n.	جَذْبٌ . مَدٌّ . جَرٌّ	Tranquilize { Tranquillize } v. t.	هَدَّأَ . أَمَّنَ
Trade n. or v. i.	تِجَارَةٌ . حِرْفَةٌ تَاجَرَ	Tranquillity n.	هُدُوءٌ
Trade-mark n.	عَلَامَةُ بَضَائِعَ	Transact v. t.	قَضَى بِ . أَجْرَى
Trader { Tradesman } n.	تَاجِرٌ رِجْلُ تِجَارٍ	Transaction n.	عَمَلٌ . أَمْرٌ
Tradition n.	تَقْلِيدٌ . حَدِيثٌ	Transcend v. t.	فَاقَ . جَاوَزَ
Traditional { Traditionary } n.	تَقْلِيدِيٌّ	Transcendent a.	فَائِقٌ
Traduce v. t.	نَمَّ بِ . عَابَ بِ	Transcribe v. t.	نَسَخَ . نَقَلَ
Traffic n.	تِجَارَةٌ . مُعَامَلَةٌ	Transcript n.	نُسْخَةٌ
Tragedy n.	رِوَايَةٌ أَوْ حَادِثَةٌ هَائِلَةٌ	Transcription n.	نَسْخٌ

Transfer *v. t.* or *n.*	نَقَلَ ـُ . نَقْل
Transferable *a.*	قَابِلُ ٱلنقْلِ أَوِ ٱلتحْوِيلِ
Transference *n.*	نقْل . تَحْوِيل
Transfigure *v. t.*	جَلَّى . غَيَّرَ ٱلشَّكْلَ
Transfix *v. t.*	خَرَقَ ـِ . اَنْفَذَ فِي
Transform *v. t.*	غَيَّرَ . حَوَّلَ
Transformation *n.*	تَغْيِير
Transgress *v. t.*	خَالَفَ . تَعَدَّى
Transgression *n.*	تَعَدٍّ . خَطِيَّة
Transgressor *n.*	خَاطِئٌ . مُخَالِفٌ
Tranship *v. t.*	نَقَلَ مِنْ سَفِينَةٍ إِلَى اخْرَى
Transient *a.*	وَقْتِيّ . زَائِل
Transit *n.*	عُبُور . اِجْتِيَاز
Transition *n.*	عُبُور . اَنْتِقَال
Transitive *a.*	مُتَعَدٍّ (فعل)
Transitory *a.*	وَقْتِي . زَائِل
Translatable *a.*	قَابِلُ ٱلتَّرْجَمَة
Translate *v.*	تَرْجَمَ . نَقَلَ ـ
Translation *n.*	تَرْجَمَة . نَقْل
Translator *n.*	مُتَرْجِم
Translucent *a.*	شَفَّافُ بَعْضِ ٱلشُّفُوفِ
Transmarine *a.*	مَا وَرَاءَ ٱلْبَحْرِ
Transmigrate *v. t.*	هَاجَرَ . اَنْتَقَلَ
Transmigration *n.*	مُهَاجَرَة . تَنَاسُخ
Transmission *n.*	إِرْسَال . اِنْفَاذ
Transmit *v. t.*	أَرْسَلَ . أَنْفَذَ إِلَى
Transmutation *n.*	تَحْوِيل . تَحَوُّل
Transparency *n.*	شُفُوف
Transparent *a.*	شَفَّاف . وَاضِح
Transpire *v. i.*	حَدَثَ ـُ . ذَاعَ ـِ
Transplant *v. t.*	نَقَلَ ـُ غَرْسًا
Transport *n.*	نَقْل . سَفِينَةُ نَقْلٍ . طَرَب
Transport *v. t.*	نَقَلَ ـُ . أَبْهَجَ
Transportation *n.*	نَقْل . نَفْي
Transpose *v. t.*	بَدَّلَ . عَكَسَ ـِ
Transposition *n.*	تَبْدِيلُ ٱلْمَكَانِ

Transverse *a.*	مُعَارِضٌ
Trap *n.* or *v. t.*	مَصِيدَةٌ . صَادَ بِهَا
Trapdoor *n.*	بَابٌ مَخْفِيٌّ
Trapezium *n.*	مُرَبَّعٌ مُنْحَرِفٌ
Trappings *n. pl.*	عُدَّةُ زِينَةٍ لِلْخَيْلِ خَاصَّةً
Trash *n.*	نُفَايَةٌ . سَقَطٌ
Trashy *a.*	بَاطِلٌ . خَسِيسٌ
Travail *v.i.* or *n.*	تَعِبَ ــ . تَمَخَّضَ مَخَاضٌ
Travel *v. i.*	سَافَرَ ــ . سَاحَ ــ
Traveller *n.*	مُسَافِرٌ . سَائِحٌ
Traverse *v. t.*	قَطَعَ ــ . عَارَضَ
Tray *n.*	طَبَقٌ . صِينِيَّةٌ
Treacherous *a.*	خَائِنٌ . غَادِرٌ
Treachery *n.*	خِيَانَةٌ ، غَدْرٌ
Treacle *n.*	دُبْسٌ
Tread *v. i.* (trod)	دَاسَ ــ
Treason *n.*	خِيَانَةٌ
Treasonable *a.*	ذُو خِيَانَةٍ
Treasure *n.* or *v. t.*	كَنْزٌ . ذَخَرَ ــ
Treasurer *n.*	أَمِينُ الصَّنْدُوقِ . خَازِنٌ
Treasury *n.*	خِزْنَةٌ . بَيْتُ الْمَالِ
Treat *v. t.* or *i.*	عَامَلَ . بَحَثَ ــ . عَالَجَ
Treatise *n.*	مَقَالَةٌ . رِسَالَةٌ
Treatment *n.*	مُعَامَلَةٌ . مُعَالَجَةٌ
Treaty *n.*	مُعَاهَدَةٌ
Treble *a.* or *v. t.* or *i.*	مُثَلَّثٌ . ثَلَّثَ . تَثَلَّثَ
Tree *n.*	شَجَرَةٌ
Trellis *n.*	عَرِيشٌ . شُبَّاكٌ
Tremble *v. i.*	إِرْتَجَفَ . إِرْتَعَدَ
Tremendous *a.*	عَظِيمٌ . هَائِلٌ
Tremor *n.*	قُشَعْرِيرَةٌ . رَجْفَةٌ
Tremulous *a.*	مُرْتَجِفٌ . مُرْتَعِشٌ
Trench *n.*	خَنْدَقٌ ج خَنَادِقُ
Trepidation *n.*	إِرْتِجَافٌ . فَزَعٌ
Trespass *v. i.* or *n.*	تَعَدَّى . أَخْطَأَ . تَعَدٍّ
Tress *n.*	خُصْلَةٌ . ضَفِيرَةٌ

Triad n.	إِتِّحَادُ ثَلْثَةٍ فِي وَاحِدٍ
Trial n.	تَجْرِبَةٌ . مُحَاكَمَةٌ . بَلِيَّةٌ
Triangle n.	مُثَلَّثٌ
Triangular a.	مُثَلَّثُ ٱلشَّكْلِ
Tribe n.	قَبِيلَةٌ . سِبْطٌ . جِنْسٌ
Tribulation n.	ضِيقٌ . شِدَّةٌ
Tribunal n.	مَحْكَمَةٌ . مَجْلِسٌ . دِيوَانٌ
Tribune n.	حَاكِمٌ . رُومَانِيٌّ . مِنْبَرٌ
Tributary a.	تَحْتَ ٱلْجِزْيَةِ . فَرْعُ نَهْرٍ
Tribute n.	جِزْيَةٌ . خَرَاجٌ
Trice n.	لَحْظَةٌ . لَمْحَةٌ
Trick n.	حِيلَةٌ . مَكِيدَةٌ
Trickery n.	إِحْتِيَالٌ . خِدَاعٌ
Trickish a.	مُحْتَالٌ . غَشَّاشٌ
Trickle v. i.	نَضَّ . نَزَّ
Tri-coloured a.	ذُو ثَلَاثَةِ أَلْوَانٍ
Trident n.	صَوْلَجَانٌ ذُو ثَلَثِ شَوَكَاتٍ
Triennial a.	كُلَّ ثَلَاثِ سِنِينٍ

Trifle n. or v. t.	شَيْءٌ زَهِيدٌ . عَبَثَ
Trifling n.	زَهِيدٌ مَالَا يُعْتَبَرُ . عَبَثٌ
Triform a.	مُثَلَّثُ ٱلشَّكْلِ
Trigger n.	زِنَادُ ٱلْبُنْدُقِيَّةِ
Trigonometry n.	عِلْمُ ٱلْمُثَلَّثَاتِ
Trilateral a.	ذُو ثَلَاثَةِ جَوَانِبَ
Triliteral a.	ذُو ثَلَاثَةِ أَحْرُفٍ
Trill n. or v. t.	تَطْرِيبٌ . طَرَّبَ
Trim a. or v. t.	أَنِيقٌ . قَصَّ . زَيَّنَ
Trimming n.	زِينَةٌ (خَرْجٌ)
Trinity n.	ثَالُوثٌ
Trinket n.	حِلْيَةٌ . شَيْءٌ زَهِيدٌ
Trio n.	ثَلَثَةٌ مُتَّحِدُونَ
Trip v. i.	مَشَى بِخِفَّةٍ . عَثَرَ . كَبَا
Trip n.	عَثْرَةٌ . سَفْرَةٌ
Triple a.	مُثَلَّثٌ . ثُلَاثِيٌّ
Triplet n.	ثَلَثَةُ أَبْيَاتِ شِعْرٍ عَلَى قَافِيَةٍ وَاحِدَةٍ
Tripod n.	ذُو ثَلَاثِ قَوَائِمَ

Trisyllabic a. } Trisyllable n. }	ذات ثُلُثَةِ مَقَاطِع
Trite a.	كَثِيرُ الِاسْتِعْمَالِ. مُبْتَذَلٌ
Triumph n. or v. i.	نَصْرَة. إِنْتَصَرَ
Triumphal } Triumphant } a.	مَنْصُورٌ. نَصْرِيٌّ
Triumvirate n.	حُكْمُ ثَلُثَةٍ
Triune n.	مُثَلَّثُ الأَقَانِيمِ. ثَالُوثِيٌّ
Trivial a.	زَهِيدٌ. حَقِيرٌ
Trodden pp. of tread.	مَدُوسٌ
Troop n.	جَمَاعَة. كَتِيبَةٌ
Trooper n.	جُنْدِيٌّ. فَارِسٌ
Trophy n.	عَلَامَةُ نُصْرَةٍ
Tropic n.	مِنْطَقَةٌ حَارَّةٌ
Tropical a.	مُخْتَصٌّ بِالْمِنْطَقَةِ الْحَارَّةِ
Trot v. i. or n.	خَبَّ. خَبَبٌ
Trouble v. t. or n.	كَدَّرَ. أَزْعَجَ. ضِيقٌ
Troublesome a.	مُكَدِّرٌ. شَاقٌّ
Troublous a.	مُضْطَرِبٌ. شَاقٌّ
Trough n.	حَوْضٌ

Trousers } Trowsers } n.	سَرَاوِيلُ
Trousseau n.	جَهَازُ عَرُوسٍ
Trowel n.	مِلْعَقَةُ الْبَنَّاءِ
Truant a. or n.	كَسْلَانٌ يُهْمِلُ الْوَاجِبَاتِ
Truce n.	هُدْنَة
Trudge v. i.	مَشَى. تَعِبَ فِي الْمَشْيِ
True a.	حَقِيقِيٌّ. أَكِيدٌ. أَمِينٌ. صَحِيحٌ
Truly ad.	حَقًّا
Trump } Trumpet } n.	بُوقٌ
Trumpery n.	خِدَاعٌ. عَبَثٌ
Trumpeter n.	بَوَّاقٌ
Truncate } Truncated } a.	أَقْطَعُ مَجْزُومٌ
Trunk n.	صَنْدُوقٌ. سَاقٌ. خُرْطُومٌ
Trust n.	ثِقَةٌ وَدِيعَة. إِئْتِمَانٌ
Trust v. i. or t.	وَثِقَ. صَدَّقَ
Trustee n.	وَكِيلٌ. أَمِينٌ
Trustful a.	وَاثِقٌ
Trustiness n.	أَمَانَة

Trusty Trustworthy } a.	أَمِينٌ . مَوْثُوقٌ بِهِ
Truth n.	حَقٌّ . صِدْقٌ . صَوَابٌ
Truthful a.	صَادِقٌ
Try v. t. or i.	جَرَّبَ . حَاوَلَ
Trying a.	مُجَرِّبٌ . شَاقٌّ . مُكَدِّر
Tub n.	مِرْجَل
Tube n.	انْبُوبَة
Tubercle n.	عُجْرَة . دَرَنَة
Tubercular Tuberculous } a.	دَرَنِي
Tuck n. or v. t.	ثِنْيَة . طَيَّة . طَوَى ــ
Tuesday n.	يَوْمُ الثَّلَاثَاء
Tuft n.	خُصْلَة . قُنْبَرَة
Tug v. t. or i.	شَدَّ ــ . جَذَبَ ــ
Tug-boat n.	وَابُورٌ جَرَّارٌ
Tuition n.	اجْرَةُ تَعْلِيم
Tulip n.	ضَرْبٌ مِنَ الزَّنْبَق
Tumble v. i.	سَقَطَ ــ هَبَطَ ــ تَقَلَّبَ
Tumbler n.	قَدَحٌ ج اقْدَاح

Tumid a.	مُنْتَفِخٌ . وَارِمٌ
Tumour n.	وَرَمٌ . خُرَاجٌ
Tumult n.	شَغَبٌ . ضَجَّة . جَلَبَة
Tumultuary Tumultuous } a.	شَاغِبٌ
Tune n. or v. t.	نَغْمَة . لَحْنٌ . أَوْقَعَ
Tunnel n. or v. t.	سِرْدَابٌ . سَرَبٌ حَفَرَهُ
Turban n.	عِمَامَة . لَفَّة
Turbid a.	عَكِرٌ . كَدِرٌ
Turbulence Turbulency } n.	تَشْوِيشٌ . شَغَبٌ
Turbulent a.	مُشَاغِبٌ . مُهَيِّجٌ
Turf n.	ارْضٌ كَثِيرَةُ الْكَلَإِ
Turgid a.	وَارِمٌ . مُنْتَفِخٌ
Turkey n.	تُرْكِيَّا . دِيكٌ رُومِيٌّ
Turquoise n.	فَيْرُوزٌ
Turmoil n.	إِضْطِرَابٌ . شَغَبٌ
Turn v. t. or i.	خَرَطَ ــ . أَدَارَ . دَارَ ــ
Turn n.	دَوْرَة . بَرْمَة
Turner n.	خَرَّاطٌ

Turnip *n.*	لِفْت
Turnkey *n.*	بَوَّابُ سِجْن
Turpentine *n.*	رَاتِينِجُ الصَّنَوْبَر
Turpitude *n.*	قَبَاحَة
Turret *n.*	بُرْج
Turreted *a.*	ذو أَبْرَاج
Turtle *n.*	سُلَحْفَاة
Turtledove *n.*	حَمَامَة . يَمَامَة
Tusk *n.*	نَابٌ ج أَنْيَابٌ
Tussle *n.*	مُصَارَعَة
Tutelage *n.*	حِمَايَة . وَكَالَة
Tutelar Tutelary } *a.*	حَافِظ . مُحَامٍ
Tutor *n.*	مُعَلِّم . مُهَذِّب
Twain *n.*	إِثْنَان م إِثْنَتَان
Twang *v. i. or n.*	رَنَّ ـِ . رَنِين
Tweezers *n. pl.*	مِلْقَطٌ صَغِير
Twelfth *a.*	أَلثَّانِي عَشَر
Twelve *a.*	إِثْنَا عَشَرَ وَاثْنَتَاعَشَرَة
Twentieth *a.*	أَلْعِشْرُونَ
Twenty *a.*	عِشْرُون
Twice *ad.*	مَرَّتَيْن
Twig *n.*	عُسْلُوج ج عَسَالِيجُ
Twilight *n.*	شَفَق
Twin *n.*	تَوْأَم
Twine *n.* or *v. t.*	خَيْط دَوْبَارَة . قَتَلَ ـِ
Twinge *v. i. or n.*	تَأَلَّمَ . أَلَم
Twinkle *v. i.*	تَلَأْلَأَ . لَمَعَ ـَ
Twinkle Twinkling } *n.*	لَأْلَأَة . لَمَعَان
Twirl *v. t. or i.*	بَرَمَ ـِ دَوَّرَ . دَارَ
Twist *v. t.*	فَتَلَ ـِ . جَدَلَ ـِ . حَرَّفَ ـِ
Twitch *v. t. or n.*	شَدَّ بِهِ بَغْتَةً
Twitter *v. i.*	غَرَّدَ
Two *a.*	إِثْنَان م إِثْنَتَان
Two-edged *a.*	ذو حَدَّيْن
Twofold *a.*	مُثَنًّى . مُضَاعَف
Tympanum *n.*	طَبْلَةُ الآذُن

Type *n.*	رَمْزٌ . صُورَةٌ . حَرْفُ طَبْعٍ
Typhoid *a.* or *n.*	الْحُمَّى التِّيفُودِيَّةُ
Typhus *a.* or *n.*	الْحُمَّى التِّيفُوسِيَّةُ
Typical *a.*	رَمْزِيٌّ . مِثَالِيٌّ
Typify *v. t.*	رَمَزَ . اشَارَ إِلَى
Typographical *a.*	مَنُوطٌ بِالطَّبْعِ

Typography *n.*	صِنَاعَةُ الطَّبْعِ
Tyrannical } *a.* Tyrannic	ظَالِمٌ . طَاغٍ
Tyrannize *v. t.*	ظَلَمَ ـ
Tyranny *n.*	ظُلْمٌ . بَغْيٌ
Tyrant *n.*	ظَالِمٌ . طَاغٍ . بَاغٍ

U

Ubiquity *n.*	حُضُورٌ فِي كُلِّ مَكَانٍ
Udder *n.*	ضَرْعٌ ج ضُرُوعٌ
Ugliness *n.*	بَشَاعَةٌ . قَبَاحَةُ الْمَنْظَرِ
Ugly *a.*	قَبِيحُ الْمَنْظَرِ
Ulcer *n.*	قُرْحَةٌ
Ulcerate *v. i.*	تَقَرَّحَ
Ulceration *n.*	تَقَرُّحٌ
Ulna *n.*	زَنْدٌ
Ulterior *a.*	أَبْعَدُ . وَرَاءَهُ

Ultimate *a.*	الْأَبْعَدُ . نِهَائِيٌّ
Ultimatum *n.*	قَرَارٌ نِهَائِيٌّ
Ultra *a.*	مُفْرِطٌ . مُتَجَاوِزٌ الْحَدِّ
Umbel *n.*	صِيوَانُ أَزْهَارٍ
Umbelliferous *a.*	صِيوَانِيٌّ
Umbrage *n.*	غَيْظٌ . حِقْدٌ
Umbrageous *a.*	ظَلِيلٌ
Umbrella *n.*	شَمْسِيَّةٌ
Umpire *n.*	فَيْصَلٌ . حَكَمٌ

Un	حَرْفُ نَفْيٍ فِي اَلتَّرْكِيبِ
Unable *a.*	غَيْرُ قَادِرٍ
Unabridged *a.*	غَيْرُ مُخْتَصَرٍ . مُطَوَّلٌ
Unacceptable *a.*	غَيْرُ مَقْبُولٍ
Unaccommodating *a.*	غَيْرُ مُسَاهِلٍ
Unaccompanied *a.*	غَيْرُ مُرَافِقٍ
Unaccountable *a.*	غَيْرُ مَسْؤُولٍ . غَيْرُ مَفْهُومٍ
Unaccustomed *a.*	غَيْرُ مُعْتَادٍ
Unacknowledged *a.*	غَيْرُ مُسَلَّمٍ بِهِ
Unacquainted *a.*	غَيْرُ عَارِفٍ بِهِ
Unadvisable *a.*	غَيْرُ مُوَافِقٍ
Unaffected *a.*	غَيْرُ مُؤَثِّرٍ
Unaided *a.*	غَيْرُ مُسَاعَدٍ . وَحْدَهُ
Unalterable *a.*	مَالَا يَتَغَيَّرُ . ثَابِتٌ
Unamiable *a.*	غَيْرُ لَطِيفٍ . شَرِسٌ
Unanimity *n.*	إِجْمَاعُ الرَّأْيِ
Unanimous *a.*	مُجْمِعُ الرَّأْيِ
Unanswerable *a.*	مَالَا يُرَدُّ عَلَيْهِ
Unappreciated *a.*	غَيْرُ مُعْتَبَرٍ
Unapproachable *a.*	مَالَا يُدْنَى مِنْهُ
Unappropriated *a.*	غَيْرُ مُخَصَّصٍ
Unarmed *a.*	غَيْرُ مُتَسَلِّحٍ
Unasked *a.*	غَيْرُ مَطْلُوبٍ
Unaspiring *a.*	غَيْرُ طَالِبِ الرِّفْعَةِ
Unassailable *a.*	لَا يُهَاجَمُ . مَنِيعٌ
Unassisted *a.*	غَيْرُ مُسَاعَدٍ . وَحْدَهُ
Unassuming *a.*	غَيْرُ مُعْجِبٍ . مُتَوَاضِعٌ
Unattainable *a.*	لَا يُحَصَّلُ
Unattended *a.*	غَيْرُ مُرَافَقٍ . وَحْدَهُ
Unauthorised *a.*	غَيْرُ مُبَاحٍ
Unavailing *a.*	غَيْرُ مُفِيدٍ . عَبَثٌ
Unavoidable *a.*	مَالَا بُدَّ مِنْهُ
Unaware *a.*	غَيْرُ عَارِفٍ
Unawares *ad.*	عَلَى غَفْلَةٍ
Unbar *v. t.*	رَفَعَ المِغْلَاقَ . فَتَحَ

Unbecoming *a.*	غَيْرُ لَائِقٍ
Unbelief *n.*	عَدَمُ إِيمَانٍ أَوْ تَصْدِيقٍ
Unbeliever *n.* Unbelieving *a.*	غَيْرُ مُؤْمِنٍ
Unbending *a.*	مُتَصَلِّبٌ
Unbiassed *a.*	غَيْرُ مُتَحَامِلٍ أَوْ مُتَحَزِّبٍ
Unbind *a.*	حَلَّ . فَكَّ
Unblemished *a.*	بِلَا عَيْبٍ
Unblushing *a.*	بِلَا حَيَاءٍ . وَقِحٌ
Unbolt *v. t.*	فَتَحَ الْمِغْلَاقَ
Unborn *a.*	غَيْرُ مَوْلُودٍ
Unbosom *v. t.*	صَرَّحَ بِهِ . أَقَرَّ
Unbounded *a.*	غَيْرُ مَحْدُودٍ
Unbridle *v. i.*	فَكَّ اللِّجَامَ . أَطْلَقَ
Unbroken *a.*	غَيْرُ مُنْقَطِعٍ
Unbuckle *v. t.*	فَكَّ الْإِبْزِيمَ
Unburden *v. t.*	نَزَعَ حِمْلًا . أَرَاحَ
Unburied *a.*	غَيْرُ مَدْفُونٍ
Unbutton *v. t.*	فَكَّ الْأَزْرَارَ

Uncanonical *a.*	غَيْرُ قَانُونِيٍّ
Unceasing *a.*	غَيْرُ مُنْقَطِعٍ . دَائِمٌ
Unceremonious *a.*	عَدِيمُ التَّكْلِيفِ
Uncertain *a.*	غَيْرُ مُؤَكِّدٍ . مَشْكُوكٌ فِيهِ
Uncertainty *n.*	عَدَمُ يَقِينٍ . شَكٌّ
Unchain *v. t.*	فَكَّ الْقَيْدَ أَوِ الزِّنْجِيرَ
Unchangeable Unchanging } *a.*	غَيْرُ مُتَغَيِّرٍ
Uncharitable *a.*	عَدِيمُ الْمَحَبَّةِ
Unchaste *a.*	غَيْرُ عَفِيفٍ . نَجِسٌ
Unchristian *a.*	مُخَالِفُ الْمَسِيحِيَّةِ
Uncivil *a.*	غَيْرُ أَنِيسٍ . فَظٌّ
Uncivilized *a.*	غَيْرُ مُتَمَدِّنٍ
Uncle *n.*	عَمٌّ . خَالٌ
Unclean *a.*	غَيْرُ طَاهِرٍ . نَجِسٌ
Uncleanness *n.*	نَجَاسَةٌ
Unclose *v. t.*	فَتَحَ . كَشَفَ
Uncoil *v. t.*	فَكَّ الْمُلْتَفَّ . أَرْخَى
Uncomely *a.*	غَيْرُ كَيِّسٍ أَوْ ظَرِيفٍ

Uncomfortable a.	غَيْرُ مُسْتَرِيحٍ شَاقٌّ
Uncommon a.	غَيْرُ مَعْهُودٍ . نَادِرٌ
Uncomplaining a.	غَيْرُ شَاكٍ
Uncompromising a.	غَيْرُ مُتَرَاضٍ . عَنِيدٌ
Unconcern n.	عَدَمُ ٱكْتِرَاثٍ
Unconditional a.	بِلاَ شَرْطٍ . مُطْلَقٌ
Uncongenial a.	غَيْرُ مُؤَانِسٍ
Unconqurable a.	لاَ يُغْلَبُ
Unconscious a.	غَيْرُ شَاعِرٍ او عَالِمٍ
Unconsciousness n.	غَيْبَةٌ
Unconstitutional a.	مُخَالِفُ ٱلنِّظَامِ
Uncontrolkble / Uncontrolled } a.	لاَ يُضْبَطُ
Unconverted a.	غَيْرُ تَائِبٍ أَوْ مُتَغَيِّرٍ
Uncork v. t.	أَخْرَجَ ٱلسِّدَادَ
Uncorrupt / Uncorrupted } a.	غَيْرُ فَاسِدٍ / غَيْرُ مَرْضٍ
Uncounted a.	غَيْرُ مَعْدُودٍ
Uncourteous a.	عَدِيمُ ٱلأُنْسِ . فَظٌّ
Uncouth a.	غَيْرُ مَأْلُوفٍ . أَخْرَقُ
Uncover v. t.	كَشَفَ ـ . فَتَحَ ـَ
Unction n.	مَسْحَةٌ
Unctuous a.	دِهْنٌ . ذُو زَيْتٍ
Uncultivated a.	غَيْرُ مَحْرُوثٍ . غَيْرُ مُهَذَّبٍ
Uncut a.	غَيْرُ مَقْصُوصٍ أَوْ مَقْطُوعٍ
Undaunted a.	جَسُورٌ . غَيْرُ خَائِفٍ
Undeceive v. t.	أَزَالَ ٱلْغُرُورَ وَٱلْغَلَطَ
Undecided a.	مُتَرَدِّدٌ
Undefiled a.	غَيْرُ مُدَنَّسٍ . طَاهِرٌ
Undefined a.	غَيْرُ مَحْدُودٍ
Undeniable a.	لاَ يُنْكَرُ
Under prep.	تَحْتَ
Underbid v. i.	عَرَضَ أَقَلَّ
Underbrush n.	أَنْجُمُ تَحْتَ شَجَرٍ
Undercurrent n.	مَجْرًى تَحْتَ ٱلْمَاءِ
Undergo v. i.	إِحْتَمَلَ . قَاسَى
Undergraduate n.	تِلْمِيذُ مَدْرَسَةٍ
Underground v.	تَحْتَ ٱلأَرْضِ

Undergrowth n.	شُجَيْرَات تَحْتَ شَجَرٍ
Underhand a. Underhanded	مَسْتُورٌ . غَادِرٌ
Underlie v. t.	وُجِدَ تَحْتَ
Underline v. t.	خَطَّ تَحْتَ ٱلسَّطْرِ
Underling n.	شَخْصٌ دُونٌ . أَجِيرٌ
Undermine v. t.	حَفَرَ تَحْتَ . نَقَضَ ـُ
Underneath ad.	تَحْتَ
Underpinning n.	حِجَارَةُ ٱلْأَسَاسِ
Underrate v. t.	إِسْتَصْغَرَ . إِسْتَخَفَّ
Underscore v. t.	رَسَمَ تَحْتَهُ خَطًّا
Undersell v. t.	بَاعَ بِأَقَلِّ ثَمَنٍ
Understand v. t.	فَهِمَ ـَ . أَدْرَكَ
Understanding n.	ذِهْنٌ . إِدْرَاكٌ
Undertake v. t.	تَعَاطَى إِلْتَزَمَ
Undertaker n.	مُدَبِّرُ ٱلدَّفْنِ
Undertaking n.	مَسْعًى . مَشْرُوعٌ
Undertone n.	صَوْتٌ مُنْخَفِضٌ
Undervalue v. t.	بَخَسَ ـَ إِسْتَخَفَّ بِهِ

Undeserved a.	غَيْرُ مُسْتَحَقٍّ
Undeserving a.	غَيْرُ مُسْتَحِقٍّ
Undesigned a.	غَيْرُ مَقْصُودٍ . إِتِّفَاقِيٌّ
Undesirable a.	غَيْرُ شَهِيٍّ أَوْ مَرْغُوبٍ فِيهِ
Undeviating a.	غَيْرُ مُنْحَرِفٍ . مُسْتَقِيمٌ
Undignified a.	غَيْرُ لَائِقٍ ٱلشَّأْنِ
Undisguisied a.	غَيْرُ مُسْتَتِرٍ . ظَاهِرٌ
Undismayed a.	غَيْرُ خَائِفٍ
Undivided a.	غَيْرُ مُنْقَسِمٍ . مُتَّحِدٌ
Undo v. t.	حَلَّ ـُ . أَبْطَلَ . عَكَسَ ـِ
Undone a.	مُعَطَّلٌ . هَالِكٌ
Undoubted a.	لَا رَيْبَ فِيهِ . مُقَرَّرٌ
Undress v. t.	نَزَعَ ٱلثِّيَابَ . خَلَعَ ـَ
Undue a.	مُفْرِطٌ . زَائِدٌ
Undulated a.	مُتَمَوِّجٌ غَيْرُ مُسْتَوٍ
Undulation n.	تَمَوُّجٌ
Unduly ad.	بِزِيَادَةٍ . فِي غَيْرِ مَحَلِّهِ
Undutiful a.	غَيْرُ مُطِيعٍ

Undying a.	غَيْرُ مَائِتٍ . خَالِدٌ
Unearth v. t.	نَبَشَ ـُ . كَشَفَ ـِ
Unearthly n.	غَيْرُ طَبِيعِيّ
Uneasiness n.	إِضْطِرَابٌ . هَمٌّ . قَلَقٌ
Uneasy a.	غَيْرُ مُسْتَرِيحٍ . مُهْتَمٌّ
Uneducated a.	غَيْرُ مُهَذَّبٍ . أُمِّيّ
Unembarrassed a.	غَيْرُ مُرْتَبِكٍ
Unending a.	غَيْرُ مُتَنَاهٍ
Unengaged a.	غَيْرُ مَرْبُوطٍ . مُتَفَرِّغٌ
Unenlightened a.	جَاهِلٌ
Unenviable a.	غَيْرُ شَهِيّ . مَكْرُوهٌ
Unequal a.	غَيْرُ مُتَسَاوٍ . عَاجِزٌ
Unequalled a.	فَرِيدٌ . فَائِقٌ
Unequivocal a.	غَيْرُ مُبْهَمٍ . صَرِيحٌ
Unerring a.	غَيْرُ مُخْطِئٍ . مُصِيبٌ
Uneven a.	غَيْرُ مُسْتَوٍ
Unevenness n.	عَدَمُ آسْتِوَاءٍ
Unexpected a.	غَيْرُ مُنْتَظَرٍ
Unexpressed a.	غَيْرُ مَنْطُوقٍ بِهِ
Unfaded / Unfading a.	غَيْرُ ذَابِلٍ
Unfailing a.	غَيْرُ مُنْقَضٍ . بَاقٍ
Unfair a.	غَيْرُ عَادِلٍ
Unfairness n.	عَدَمُ إِنْصَافٍ
Unfaithful n.	غَيْرُ أَمِينٍ
Unfaithfulness n.	عَدَمُ امَانَةٍ
Unfashionable a.	خِلَافُ الزِّيّ
Unfasten v. t.	فَكَّ ـُ . حَلَّ ـُ
Unfathomable a.	مَا لَا يُسْبَرُ
Unfavourable a.	مُخَالِفُ الْمَطْلُوبِ
Unfeeling a.	غَيْرُ مُتَأَثِّرٍ . بِلَا رَحْمَةٍ
Unfeigned a.	بِلَا رِيَاءٍ . مُخْلِصٌ
Unfelt a.	غَيْرُ مَشْعُورٍ بِهِ
Unfilial a.	غَيْرُ لَائِقٍ بِالْبَنِينَ
Unfinished a.	غَيْرُ مُتَمَّمٍ أَوْ مُنْجَزٍ
Unfit a.	غَيْرُ لَائِقٍ . غَيْرُ أَهْلٍ
Unfold v. t.	نَشَرَ ـُ كَشَفَ ـِ فَسَّرَ

Unforeseen a.	غَيْرُ مُنْتَظَرٍ
Unforetold a.	غَيْرُ مُخْبَرٍ بِهِ
Unforgiven a.	غَيْرُ مَغْفُورٍ
Unfortunate a.	نَحِسٌ . مَنْكُودُ ٱلْحَظِّ
Unfounded a.	بِلَا أَسَاسٍ
Unfrequent a.	نَادِرٌ
Unfrequented a.	غَيْرُ مُتَرَدَّدٍ إِلَيْهِ
Unfriendly a.	غَيْرُ وَدُودٍ . خَصِيمٌ
Unfruitful a.	غَيْرُ مُثْمِرٍ
Unfurl v. t.	نَشَرَ
Ungainly a.	أَخْرَقُ
Ungenerous a.	غَيْرُ كَرِيمٍ . شَحِيحٌ
Ungentlemanly a.	غَيْرُ أَدِيبٍ
Ungodlin ess n.	عَدَمُ تَقْوًى . شَرٌّ
Ungodly a.	عَدِيمُ ٱلتَّقْوَى . شِرِّيرٌ
Ungovernable a.	مَا لَا يُضْبَطُ
Ungraceful a.	غَيْرُ ظَرِيفٍ . أَخْرَقُ
Ungracious a.	غَيْرُ لَطِيفٍ . سَيِّئٌ
Ungrammatical a.	مُخَالِفٌ لِعِلْمِ ٱلنَّحْوِ
Ungrateful a.	غَيْرُ شَكُورٍ . كَنُودٌ
Ungratefulness n.	عَدَمُ ٱلشُّكْرِ
Ungrounded a.	مَا لَا أَصْلَ لَهُ
Unguarded a.	غَيْرُ مَصُونٍ مُتَغَافِلٍ
Unguent n.	دُهْنٌ . مَرْهَمٌ
Unhallowed a.	غَيْرُ مُقَدَّسٍ . مُحَرَّمٌ
Unhappiness n.	غَمٌّ . كَدَرٌ
Unhappy a.	مَغْمُومٌ . تَعِيسٌ
Unharness v. i.	نَزَعَ عُدَّةَ ٱلْخَيْلِ
Unhealthful } a. Unhealthy }	غَيْرُ مُوَافِقٍ ٱلصِّحَّةِ وَخِيمٌ
Unheard a.	غَيْرُ مَسْمُوعٍ
Unheeded a.	غَيْرُ مُكْتَرَثٍ لَهُ
Unhesitating a.	غَيْرُ مُتَرَدِّدٍ
Unhinge v. t.	خَلَعَ
Unhitch v. t.	فَكَّ . حَلَّ
Unholy a.	غَيْرُ مُقَدَّسٍ . دَنِسٌ

Unhonoured a.	غَيْرُ مُكَرَّم
Unhook v. t.	فَكَّ ـُ
Unhorse v. t.	رَمَى عَنِ ٱلْفَرَس
Unhurt a.	غَيْرُ مُؤْذًى. سَلِيمٌ
Unicorn n.	وَحِيدُ ٱلْقَرْن
Uniform a.,	عَلَى نَسَقٍ وَاحِدٍ
Uniform n.	بِذْلَةٌ رَسْمِيَّة
Uniformity n.	وَحْدَةُ ٱلشَّكْلِ أَوِ ٱلنِّظَام
Unimpeachable a.	مَا لَا يُعَاب
Unimportant a.	غَيْرُ مُهِمٍّ
Unimproving a.	غَيْرُ مُتَقَدِّم
Uninhabitable a.	مَا لَا يُسْكَنُ
Unintelligible a.	مَا لَا يُفْهَم
Unintended } a. Unintentional }	غَيْرُ مَقْصُودٍ
Uninteresting a.	غَيْرُ ٱللَّذِيذِ. مُمِلٌّ
Uninterrupted a.	غَيْرُ مُنْقَطِعٍ
Uninvited a.	غَيْرُ مَدْعُوٍّ. طُفَيْلِي
Union n.	إِتِّحَادٌ. ضَمُّ صِلَة

Unionist n.	مُرِيدُ ٱلِٱتِّحَادِ
Unique a.	فَرِيدٌ. وَحِيدٌ
Unison n.	إِتِّفَاقُ ٱلْأَصْوَات
Unit n.	فَرْدٌ. وَاحِدٌ
Unitarian n.	مُوَحِّدٌ. مُنْكِرُ ٱلثَّالُوث
Unite v.t. or i.	ضَمَّ ـُ. وَصَلَ. إِتَّحَدَ
United a.	مُتَّحِدٌ. مُتَّصِلٌ
Unity n.	وَحْدَانِية. وَحْدَة
Univalve n. Univalvular a. }	ذُو مِصْرَاعٍ وَاحِدٍ
Universal a.	عَامٌّ. شَامِلٌ
Universalist n.	ٱلْقَائِلُ بِخَلَاصِ ٱلْجَمِيع
Universality n.	عُمُومِيَّة. كُلِّيَّة
Universe n.	ٱلْكَوَنُ
University n.	مَدْرَسَةٌ جَامِعَة
Unjust a.	غَيْرُ عَادِلٍ. ظَالِمٌ
Unjustifiable a.	مَا لَا يُبَرَّرُ أَوْ يُعْذَر
Unkind a.	عَدِيمُ ٱلْمَعْرُوفِ. مُسِيء
Unkindness n.	إِسَاءَة

Unknowingly ad.	سَهْواً . غَفْلَةً	Unlucky a.	خَسِ . مَشْؤُومٌ
Unknown a.	غَيْرُ مَعْرُوفٍ . مَجْهُولٌ	Unman v. t.	اوهَنَ . خَوَّفَ
Unlace v. t.	حَلَّ الشَّرِيطَ	Unmanageable a.	مَالاَ يُضْبَطُ
Unlade v. i.	فَرَّغَ مَرْكَبًا	Unmanly a.	قَلِيلُ الْمُرُوَّةِ . خَنِثٌ
Unlawful a.	غَيْرُ شَرْعِيٍّ أَوْ جَائِزٍ	Unmannered ⎱ a. Unmannerly ⎰	قَلِيلُ الأَدَبِ
Unlearn v. t.	تَعَلَّمَ خِلاَفَةٌ . نَسِيَ	Unmarried a.	عَازِبٌ
Unlearned a.	أُمِّيٌّ . مَدْنِسِيٌّ	Unmask v. t.	كَشَفَ السِّتَارَ
Unleavened a.	غَيْرُ مُخْتَمِرٍ . فَطِيرٌ	Unmeaning a.	بِلا مَعْنًى
Unless cong.	مَالَمْ لَوْ لَمْ . إِنْ لَمْ	Unmerciful a.	بِلا شَفَقَةٍ
Unlettered a.	أُمِّيٌّ	Unmerited a.	غَيْرُ مُسْتَوْجِبٍ
Unlike a.	غَيْرُ مُشَابِهٍ . مُخَالِفٌ	Unmindful a.	مُتَغَافِلٌ
Unlikely ad.	بَعِيدُ الْوُقُوعِ	Unmingled a.	غَيْرُ مَمْزُوجٍ . صِرْفٌ
Unlikeness n.	عَدَمُ مُشَابَهَةٍ	Unmitigated a.	غَيْرُ مُلَطَّفٍ . مَحْضٌ
Unlimited a.	غَيْرُ مَحْدُودٍ	Unmotherly a.	مُخَالِفٌ لِصِفَةِ الأُمِّ
Unload v. t.	حَطَّ الْحِمْلَ . فَرَّغَهُ	Unmurmuring a.	غَيْرُ مُتَذَمِّرٍ
Unlock v. t.	فَتَحَ قُفْلاً	Unmusical a.	غَيْرُ مُطْرِبٍ
Unloveliness n.	عَدَمُ جَمَالٍ أَوْ لُطْفٍ	Unnatural a.	غَيْرُ طَبِيعِيٍّ
Unlovely a.	غَيْرُ جَمِيلٍ . غَيْرُ مَحْبُوبٍ	Unnecessary a.	غَيْرُ لازِمٍ

Unneighbourly a.	مُخَالِفُ حَقِّ القَرِيبِ
Unnerve v. t.	أَوْهَنَ
Unnumbered a.	غَيْرُ مَعْدُودٍ
Unobjectionable a.	مَا لَا يُعْتَرَضُ عَلَيْهِ
Unobservable a.	مَا لَا يُلَاحَظُ
Unobserving a.	غَيْرُ مُلَاحِظٍ أَوْ مُنْتَبِهٍ
Unobtrusive a.	غَيْرُ فَضُولِيٍّ
Unoccupied a.	غَيْرُ مَشْغُولٍ . فَارِغٌ
Unoffending a.	غَيْرُ مُكَدِّرٍ
Unofficial a.	غَيْرُ رَسْمِيٍّ
Unostentatious a.	غَيْرُ مُتَفَاخِرٍ
Unpack v. i.	فَكَّ المَحْزُومَ أَوِ المُعَبَّى
Unpaid a.	غَيْرُ مَدْفُوعٍ
Unpalatable a.	غَيْرُ لَذِيذٍ
Unparalleled a.	لَا مَثِيلَ لَهُ
Unpardonable a.	لَا يُغْفَرُ
Unparliamentary a.	مُخَالِفُ قَانُونِ مَجْلِسٍ
Unphilosophical a.	مُخَالِفُ الفَلْسَفَةِ
Unpitied a.	غَيْرُ مَشْفُوقٍ عَلَيْهِ
Unpitying a.	غَيْرُ شَفُوقٍ
Unpleasant a.	غَيْرُ مُرْضٍ كَرِيهٌ
Unpleasantness a.	كَدَرٌ
Unpoetical a.	عَدِيمُ رُوحِ الشِّعْرِ
Unpolished a.	غَيْرُ مَصْقُولٍ أَوْ مُهَذَّبٍ
Unpolite a.	غَيْرُ أَدِيبٍ
Unpolluted a.	غَيْرُ مُفْسَدٍ . طَاهِرٌ
Unpopular a.	غَيْرُ مَقْبُولٍ عِنْدَ النَّاسِ
Unprecedented a.	لَا سَابِقَ لَهُ
Unprejudiced a.	خَالٍ مِنَ الغَرَضِ
Unpremeditated a.	غَيْرُ مَقْصُودٍ
Unprepared a.	غَيْرُ مُسْتَعِدٍّ
Unpretending a.	مُتَوَاضِعٌ . بَسِيطٌ
Unprincipled a.	غَيْرُ مُرَاعِي الحَقِّ
Unprinted a.	غَيْرُ مَطْبُوعٍ
Unproductive a.	غَيْرُ مُثْمِرٍ . عَقِيمٌ
Unprofitable a.	غَيْرُ مُرَبِّحٍ أَوْ مُفِيدٍ

Unpromising a.	مَا لَا أَمَلَ فِيهِ
Unpropitious a.	غَيْرُ مُوَافِقٍ
Unprotected a.	غَيْرُ مَصُونٍ
Unpublished a.	غَيْرُ مَنْشُورٍ أَوْ مُذَاعٍ
Unqualified a.	غَيْرُ أَهْلٍ لَه
Unquenchable a.	مَا لَا يُطْفَأ
Unquestionable a.	مَا لَا رَيْبَ فِيهِ
Unravel v. t.	حَلَّ ـُ . فَكَّ ـُ
Unreal a.	غَيْرُ حَقِيقِيٍّ . وَهْمِيٌّ
Unreasonable a.	لَا يُوَافِقُ الْعَقْلَ . غَيْرُ عَادِلٍ
Unredemeed a.	غَيْرُ مَفْدِيٍّ أَوْ مُوفَى
Unregenerate a.	غَيْرُ مُتَجَدِّدِ الْقَلْبِ
Unregistered a.	غَيْرُ مُسَجَّلٍ
Unrelenting a.	غَيْرُ مُسَامِحٍ . مُصِرٌّ
Unremitting a.	مُسْتَمِرٌّ
Unrepenting a.	غَيْرُ تَائِبٍ
Unrequited a.	غَيْرُ مُكَافَأٍ
Unreserved a.	غَيْرُ كَتُومٍ . مُخْلِصٌ
Unresisting a.	غَيْرُ مُقَاوِمٍ
Unrestrained a.	غَيْرُ مَحْصُورٍ
Unrewarded a.	غَيْرُ مُجَازَى
Unrighteous a.	غَيْرُ بَارٍّ . أَثِيمٌ
Unrighteousness n.	إِثْمٌ
Unripe a.	غَيْرُ نَاضِجٍ . فِجٌّ
Unrivalled a.	لَا مَثِيلَ لَهُ
Unrobe v. t.	خَلَعَ الثِّيَابَ
Unroll v. t.	فَتَحَ دَرْجًا . نَشَرَهُ
Unroof v. t.	رَفَعَ السَّطْحَ عن
Unruffled a.	غَيْرُ مُهَيَّجٍ . هَادِئٌ
Unruly a.	مَا لَا يُضْبَطُ . عَنِيد
Unsaddle v. t.	رَفَعَ السَّرْجَ عَنْهُ
Unsafe a.	غَيْرُ أَمِينٍ . مُخْطِرٌ
Unsaid a.	غَيْرُ مَقُولٍ
Unsaleable a.	مَا لَا يُبَاعُ . كَاسِدٌ
Unsanctified a.	غَيْرُ مُقَدَّسٍ أَوْ مُطَهَّرٍ
Unsatisfactory a. Unsatisfying	غَيْرُ مُرْضٍ

Unsavoury a.	غَيْرُ مَقْبُول لِلذَّوْقِ
Unsay v. t.	أَبْطَلَ ٱلْقَوْلَ
Unscrew v. t.	فَكَّ ٱللَّوْلَبَ
Unscriptural a.	ضِدُّ ٱلْكِتَابِ ٱلْمُقَدَّسِ
Unseal v. t.	فَكَّ ٱلْخَتْمَ
Unsearchable a.	مَا لاَ يُفْحَصُ اوْ يُسْتَقْصَى
Unseasonable a.	فِي غَيْرِ آنِهِ
Unseemly a.	غَيْرُ لاَئِقٍ
Unseen a.	غَيْرُ مَنْظُورٍ
Unselfish a.	غَيْرُ مُحِبِّ ٱلذَّاتِ
Unserviceable a.	غَيْرُ نَافِعٍ
Unsettle v. t.	أَزْعَجَ . شَوَّشَ
Unshaken a.	غَيْرُ مُزَعْزَعٍ
Unsheathe v. t.	إِسْتَلَّ مِنْ غِمْدِهِ
Unshod a.	حَافٍ
Unshrinking a.	غَيْرُ مُرْتَدٍّ . جَسُورٌ
Unsightliness n.	قَبَاحَةُ ٱلْمَنْظَرِ . بَشَاعَةٌ
Unsightly a.	قَبِيحُ ٱلْمَنْظَرِ . بَشِعٌ

Unskillfull } n. Unskilful }	غَيْرُ مَاهِرٍ
Unsociable a.	غَيْرُ أَلِيفٍ
Unsocial a.	غَيْرُ أَلِيفٍ . آبِد
Unsold a.	مَا لَمْ يُبَعْ
Unsolicited a.	غَيْرُ مَطْلُوبٍ
Unsophisticated a.	بَسِيطٌ . سَاذِجٌ
Unsought a.	غَيْرُ مَطْلُوبٍ
Unsound a.	غَيْرُ صَحِيحٍ أَوْ سَالِمٍ
Unsoundness n.	إِخْتِلاَلٌ . إِعْتِلاَلٌ
Unsparing a.	غَيْرُ مُقْتَصِدٍ . قَاسٍ
Unspeakable a.	مَا لاَ يُنْطَقُ بِهِ
Unspent a.	غَيْرُ مَصْرُوفٍ . بَاقٍ
Unspotted a.	غَيْرُ مُلَطَّخٍ . طَاهِرٌ
Unstable a.	غَيْرُ ثَابِتٍ . مُتَرَدِّدٌ
Unstained a.	غَيْرُ مُلَوَّثٍ . بِلاَ عَيْبٍ
Unsteady a.	غَيْرُ ثَابِتٍ . مُتَقَلِّبٌ
Unstinted a.	غَيْرُ مَحْدُودٍ
Unstrung a.	مَحْلُولٌ : مُرْخِيٌّ

26

Unsubstantial a.	غَيْرُ حَقِيقيٍّ أَوْ مَتِين
Unsuccessful a.	غَيْرُ نَاجِح
Unsuitable ⎫ a. Unsuited ⎬	غَيْرُ مُلائِم
Unsullied a.	غَيْرُ مَعِيب
Unsupported a.	غَيْرُ مُسْنَد
Unsurpassed a.	مَالَمْ يَفُقْهُ شَيْ
Unsusceptible a.	غَيْرُ حَاسّ
Unsuspicious a.	غَيْرُ ظَنَّان . وَاثِق
Unsystematic a.	غَيْرُ مُنْتَظِم
Unstained a	غَيْرُ فَاسِد
Untasted a.	غَيْرُ مَذُوق
Untaught a.	غَيْرُ مُعَلَّم . أُمِّيّ
Untenable a.	مَالاَ يُؤَيَّد . بَاطِل
Unthankful a.	غَيْرُ شَكُور
Unthankfulness a.	عَدَمُ شُكْر
Unthinking ⎫ a. Unthoughtful ⎬	غَيْرُ مُنْتَبِه . غَافِل
Unthrifty a.	غَيْرُ مُقْتَصِد
Untidy a.	غَيْرُ نَظِيف او مُرَتَّب

Untie v. t.	حَلَّ عَقْدَة
Until prep.	حَتَّى . إِلَى . أَنْ . إِلَى
Untimely a.	فِي غَيْرِ وَقْتِهِ
Untiring a.	مَالاَ يَتْعَبُ أَوْ يَكِلُّ
Unto prep.	حَتَّى . إِلَى
Untold a.	غَيْرُ مَذْكُور . غَيْرُ مُحْصَى
Untoward a.	مَشْؤُوم . شَاقّ
Untractable a.	مَالاَ يَضْبَط . عَنِيد
Untried a.	غَيْرُ مُخْتَبَر
Untrodden a.	غَيْرُ مَسْلُوك
Untrue a.	كَاذِبٌ غَيْرُ امِين
Untruth n.	كِذْبٌ
Untruthful a.	كَاذِبٌ
Untwist v. t.	حَلَّ المَفْتُول
Unused a.	غَيْرُ مُسْتَعْمَل
Unusual a.	نَادِرٌ . شَاذ
Unutterable a.	مَالاَ يُنْطَق بِهِ
Unveil v. t.	كَشَفَ البُرْقَعَ . بَيَّنَ

Unvarnished a.	غَيْرُ مَدْهُونٍ . بَسِيطٌ
Unvaried } a. Unvarying }	غَيْرُ مُتَغَيِّرٍ
Unwarlike a.	غَيْرُ جَدِيرٍ بِالْحَرْبِ
Unwarrantable } a. Unwarranted }	غَيْرُ جَائِزٍ
Unwary a.	غَيْرُ مُتَحَذِّرٍ . عَاقِلٌ
Unwearied a.	غَيْرُ مُتْعَبٍ
Unwelcome a.	غَيْرُ مُرَحَّبٍ بِهِ
Unwell a.	مَرِيضٌ
Unwept a.	غَيْرُ مَأْسُوفٍ عَلَيْهِ
Unwholesome a.	ضَارٌّ بِالصِّحَّةِ
Unwieldy a.	ضَخْمٌ . ثَقِيلٌ
Unwilling a.	غَيْرُ رَاضٍ
Unwind v. t.	حَلَّ الْمَلْفُوفَ
Unwise a.	غَيْرُ حَكِيمٍ
Unwittingly ad.	بِلَا مَعْرِفَةٍ أَوْ قَصْدٍ
Unwomanly a.	غَيْرُ لَائِقٍ بِالْمَرْأَةِ
Unwonted a.	غَيْرُ مُعْتَادٍ . نَادِرٌ
Unworn a.	غَيْرُ مَلْبُوسٍ
Unworthily ad.	بِلَا اسْتِحْقَاقٍ
Unworthiness n.	عَدَمُ اسْتِحْقَاقٍ
Unworthy a.	غَيْرُ لَائِقٍ أَوْ مُسْتَحِقٍّ
Unwritten a.	غَيْرُ مَكْتُوبٍ . شَفَهِيٌّ
Unyielding a.	غَيْرُ مُذْعِنٍ . ثَابِتٌ
Unyoke v. t.	رَفَعَ النِّيرَ
Up ad.	إِلَى فَوْقٍ . فَوْقُ
Upbraid v. t.	وَبَّخَ . لَامَ ـُ
Upheaval n.	إِرْتِفَاعٌ . إِنْدِفَاعٌ
Upheave v. t.	رَفَعَ ـ
Uphill a.	عَسِيرٌ . شَاقٌّ
Uphold v. t.	سَنَدَ . أَيَّدَ . عَضَدَ ـُ
Upholder n.	مُؤَيِّدٌ . عَاضِدٌ . ظَهِيرٌ
Upholsterer n.	مُنَجِّدٌ
Upholstery n.	مَفْرُوشَاتٌ
Upland n.	نَجْدٌ . صَعِيدٌ
Uplift v. t.	رَفَعَ . رَقَّى
Upon prep.	عَلَى . عِنْدَ . حِينَ

Upper a.	أَعْلَى . عَلَوِيٌّ . فَوْقَانِيٌّ	Urgent a.	مُلِحّ . ضَرُورِيٌّ
Upperhand n.	أَسْبَقِيَّة . غَلَبَة	Urinary a.	بَوْلِيٌّ
Uppermost a.	الْأَعْلَى	Urine n.	بَوْل
Upright a.	مُسْتَقِيم . قَائِم	Urn n.	جَرَّة . قَارُورَة
Uprightness n.	إِسْتِقَامَة	Us pron.	ضَمِيرٌ مُتَّصِل (نَا)
Uproar n.	شَغَب . ضَجَّة . ضَوْضَاء	Usage n.	اِسْتِعْمَال . عَادَة
Uproot v. t.	قَلَعَ . إِسْتَأْصَلَ	Use n. or v. t.	إِسْتِعْمَال . إِسْتَعْمَلَ
Upset v. t.	قَلَبَ . نَكَسَ	Useful a.	مُفِيد . نَافِع
Upshot n.	نَتِيجَة . عَاقِبَة	Usefulness n.	مَنْفَعَة . فَائِدَة
Upside-down a.	مَقْلُوب	Useless a.	بِلَا فَائِدَة
Upstart n. or a.	حَدِيثُ النِّعْمَة	Usher n. or v. t.	عَرِيف . أَدْخَلَ
Upward } Upwards } ad.	إِلَى فَوْق	Usual a.	إِعْتِيَادِيّ . دَارِج . جَارٍ
Urban a.	مَدَنِيّ	Usurer n.	مُرَاب
Urbane a.	مُهَذَّب . لَطِيف . أَنِيس	Usurp v. t.	إِغْتَصَبَ
Urbanity n.	أَدَب . أُنْس	Usurpation n.	إِغْتِصَاب
Urchin n.	وَلَد خَبِيث . قُنْفُذ	Usurper n.	مُغْتَصِب
Urge v. t.	حَرَّضَ . حَثَّ	Usury n.	رِبًا
Urgency n.	لَجَاجَة . ضَرُورَة	Utensil n.	آلَة . وِعَاء

Utility n.	فَائِدَة . نَفْعٌ	Utterly ad.	تَمَامًا بِالْكُلِّيَّةِ
Utmost a.	الأَقْصَى	Uttermost a.	الأَقْصَى . الأَبْعَدُ
Utter v. t.	نَطَقَ ـِ . فَاهَ ـَ بِهِ	Uxorious a.	مُفْرِطُ الْحُبِّ لِزَوْجَتِهِ
Utterance n.	نُطْقٌ		

V

Vacancy n.	فَرَاغ . مَنْصِبٌ خَالٍ	Vagabondage n.	بَطَالَة
Vacant a.	فَارِغ . خَالٍ	Vagary n.	تَصَوُّرٌ بَاطِلٌ . وَهْمٌ
Vacate a.	اخْلَى . تَرَكَ ـُ	Vagrancy n.	جَوَلَانُ الْمُتَسَوِّل
Vacation n.	فَرَاغ . بَطَالَة . فُرْصَة	Vagrant n.	تَائِهٌ . بَطَّالٌ . (مُعْتَرٌّ)
Vaccinate v. t.	طَعَّمَ	Vague a.	مُبْهَمٌ . غَيْرُ وَاضِح
Vaccination n.	تَطْعِيم	Vail n.	بُرْقُعٌ . قِنَاعٌ
Vaccine n.	مَادَّة لِلتَّطْعِيم	Vain a.	بَاطِل . مُعْجَبٌ
Vacillate v. i.	تَرَدَّدَ	Vainglorious a.	مُتَصَلِّفٌ
Vacillation n.	تَرَدُّدٌ	Vale n.	وَادٍ . وَهْدٌ
Vacuity Vacuum } n.	فَرَاغ . خَلَاءٌ	Valedictory n.	خِطَابٌ وِدَاعِيٌّ
Vagabond n.	طَوَّاف . بَطَّالٌ . (مُتَشَرِّدٌ)	Valet n.	خَادِمٌ شَخْصِيٌّ

Valiant *a.*	بَاسِل . شُجَاعٌ	Vanish *v. i.*	إِخْتَفَى . زَالَ ـ
Valid *a.*	ثَابِت . شَرْعِيٌّ . حَقِيقِيٌّ	Vanity *n.*	عُجْبٌ . تَكَبُّرٌ بُطْلٌ
Validity *n.*	ثُبُوتٌ . شَرْعِيَّة	Vanquish *v. t.*	قَهَرَ ـ غَلَبَ ـ
Valise *n.*	صُنْدُوقُ سَفَرٍ صَغِيرٌ	Vantage-ground *n.*	مَقَامٌ أَفْضَلُ
Valley *n.*	وَادٍ ج أَوْدِية	Vapid *a.*	تَافِهٌ نَاشِفٌ بِلَاطَعْمٍ
Valorous *a.*	بَاسِل . شُجَاعٌ	Vapour *n.*	بُخَارٌ
Valour *n.*	شَجَاعَة . بَسَالَة إِقْدَامٌ	Vapour-bath *n.*	حَمَّامٌ بُخَارِي
Valuable *a.*	ثَمِين	Vaporize *v. t.*	حَوَّلَ إِلَى بُخَارٍ
Valuation *n.*	تَثْمِين . تَقْدِيرٌ	Variable *a.*	مُتَغَيِّرٌ . مُتَقَلِّبٌ
Value *n.*	ثَمَن . قِيمَة أَهَمِّيَّة	Variableness *n.*	تَغَيُّرٌ . تَقَلُّبٌ
Value *v. t.*	ثَمَّنَ . إِعْتَبَرَ	Variance *n.*	إِخْتِلَافٌ . خِلَافٌ
Valve *n.*	صِمَامٌ	Variation *n.*	تَغَيُّرٌ . إِخْتِلَافٌ . فَرْقٌ
Vampire *n.*	وَطْوَاطٌ كَبِيرٌ	Variegate *v. t.*	لَوَّنَ . رَقَّشَ ـ
Van *n.*	طَلِيعَةُ الْجَيْشِ . عَرَبَة	Variety *n.*	نَوْعٌ . شَكْلٌ . تَنَوُّعٌ
Vandal *n.*	بَرْبَرِيٌّ مُخَرِّبٌ	Varioloid *n.*	جَدَرِي خَفِيفٌ
Vandalism *n.*	تَخْرِيبٌ بَرْبَرِيٌّ	Various *n.*	مُتَنَوِّعٌ . شَتَّى .
Vane *n.*	دَوَّارَةٌ تَدُلُّ عَلَى جِهَةِ الرِّيحِ	Varlet *a.*	دَنِيٌّ . خَبِيثٌ
Vanguard *n.*	طَلِيعَةُ جَيْش	Varnish *n.*	نَوْعٌ مِنَ الصَّبْغِ (فَرْنِيش)

Vary v. t. or i.	غَيَّرَ . نَوَّعَ . تَغَيَّرَ
Vase n.	إِنَاءٌ . ظَرْفٌ
Vassal n.	تَابِعٌ . مُزَارِعٌ تَابِعٌ
Vassalage n.	خُضُوعٌ . عُبُودِيَّةٌ
Vast a.	عَظِيمٌ . فَسِيحٌ . عَدِيدٌ
Vastness n.	عَظَمَةٌ . اِتِّسَاعٌ
Vat n.	حَوْضٌ ج أَحْوَاضٌ
Vault n.	قَبْوٌ . قُبَّةٌ . خَشْخَاشَةٌ
Vault v. t. or i.	عَقْدَ . قَفَزَ
Vaulted n.	مُقَبَّبٌ . مَقْبُوٌّ
Vaunt v. i.	اِفْتَخَرَ . تَصَلَّبَ
Veal n.	لَحْمُ عِجْلٍ
Veer v. t. or i.	أَدَارَ . دَارَ
Vegetable n.	نَبَاتٌ . خُضْرَةٌ . بَقْلٌ
Vegetate v. t.	نَبَتَ . نَمَا كَالْبُقُولِ
Vegetation n.	عُشْبٌ . نَبَاتٌ
Vehemence n.	شِدَّةٌ . عُنْفٌ
Vehement a.	عَنِيفٌ . مُشَدِّدٌ
Vehicle n.	مَرْكَبَةٌ . عَرَبَةٌ
Veil n.	بُرْقُعٌ . نِقَابٌ . قِنَاعٌ
Veil v. t.	تَنَقَّبَتْ . حَجَبَ
Vein n.	عِرْقٌ . وَرِيدٌ
Veined / Veiny a.	ذُو عُرُوقٍ أَوْ أَوْرِدَةٍ
Vellum n.	رَقٌّ لِلْكِتَابَةِ
Velocity n.	سُرْعَةُ السَّيْرِ
Velvet n.	مُخْمَلٌ . قَطِيفَةٌ
Velvety a.	مُخْمَلِيٌّ . أَمْلَسُ
Venality n.	اِرْتِشَاءٌ . اَلْمَيْلُ إِلَيْهِ
Vend v. t.	بَاعَ
Vender / Vendor n.	بَائِعٌ
Veneer v. t.	لَبَّسَ . غَشَّى
Venerable a.	مُحْتَرَمٌ . وَقُورٌ
Venerate v. t.	اِحْتَرَمَ . وَقَّرَ
Veneration n.	اِحْتِرَامٌ . تَوْقِيرٌ
Venereal a.	زُهْرِيٌّ
Vengeance n.	نِقْمَةٌ . ثَأْرٌ

Vengeful n.	مُنْتَقِمٌ . حَقُودٌ
Venial n.	مِمَّا يُغْفَرُ أو يُعْذَرُ . زَهِيدٌ
Venison n.	لَحْمُ الصَّيْدِ
Venom n.	سُمٌّ . حِقْدٌ
Venomous a.	سَامٌّ . حَقُودٌ
Venous a.	وَرِيدِيٌّ (لِلدَّمِ)
Vent n.	مَنْفَذٌ . إِظْهَارٌ . نُطْقٌ
Vent v. t.	نَفَثَ ــُ . أَظْهَرَ (حِقْدًا)
Ventilate v. t.	هَوَّى عَرَضَ لِلْهَوَاءِ
Ventilation n.	تَهْوِيَةٌ
Ventilator n.	مَنْفَذٌ لِلْهَوَاءِ
Ventriloquism n.	اَلتَّكَلُّمُ مِنَ الْجَوْفِ
Ventriloquist n.	مُتَكَلِّمٌ مِنَ الْجَوْفِ
Venture n. or v. t.	مُخَاطَرَةٌ تَجَرَّأَ
Venturesome Venturous a.	مُخَاطِرٌ . جَسُورٌ
Venus a.	اَلزَّهْرَةُ . الإِلَهَةُ الْعِشْقِ
Veracious a.	صَادِقٌ
Veracity n.	صِدْقٌ

Veranda n.	رِوَاقٌ ج أُرْوِقَةٌ
Verb n.	فِعْلٌ ج أَفْعَالٌ
Verbal a.	فِعْلِيٌّ . لَفْظِيٌّ
Verbally ad.	شِفَاهًا . لَفْظًا
Verbatim ad.	حَرْفِيًّا
Verbosity n.	كَثْرَةُ الْكَلَامِ
Verdant a.	أَخْضَرُ . غَبِيٌّ . نَضِرٌ
Verdict n.	حُكْمٌ . قَضَاءٌ . فَتْوَى
Verdigris n.	زِنْجَارٌ
Verdure n.	خُضْرَةٌ
Verge n.	حَافَةٌ . حَرْفٌ . حَدٌّ
Verge v. i.	إِقْتَرَبَ . مَالَ ــِ
Verification n.	تَحْقِيقٌ . إِثْبَاتٌ
Verify v. t.	حَقَّقَ
Verily ad.	حَقًّا
Verisimilitude n.	مُشَابَهَةٌ إِمْكَانِيَّةٌ
Veritable a.	حَقِيقِيٌّ . وَاقِعٌ
Verity n.	حَقٌّ . حَقِيقَةٌ . صِدْقٌ

Vermillion *n.*	زِنْجَفْرٌ. حُمْرَةٌ	Vespers *n. pl.*	صَلَاةُ الْمَسَاءِ
Vermin *n.*	حَشَرَاتٌ خَبِيثَةٌ	Vessel *n.*	مَرْكَبٌ. سَفِينَةٌ. وِعَاءٌ
Vernacular *a.*	وَطَنِيّ (لُغَةٌ)	Vest *n.*	صَدْرِيَّةٌ. صَدْرَةٌ
Vernal *a.*	رَبِيعِيّ	Vestal *a.* or *n.*	عَفِيفٌ. عَذْرَاءُ
Versatile *a.*	مُتَقَلِّبٌ. مَاهِرٌ	Vested *a.*	ثَابِتٌ. مُعَيَّنٌ. مُقَلَّدٌ
Versatility *n.*	مَهَارَةٌ	Vestibule *n.*	دِهْلِيزٌ
Verse *n.*	بَيْتُ شِعْرٍ. دَوْرٌ	Vestige *n.*	أَثَرٌ. رَسْمٌ
Versed *a.*	حَاذِقٌ. خَبِيرٌ. عَالِمٌ	Vestment *n.*	لِبَاسٌ. حُلَّةٌ
Versification *n.*	نَظْمٌ	Vesture *n.*	ثَوْبٌ. لِبَاسٌ
Versify *v. i.* or *t.*	نَظَمَ ـِ. شَعَّرَ ـُ	Veteran *a.*	مُجَرَّبٌ. مُتَمَرِّنٌ
Version *n.*	تَرْجَمَةٌ	Veterinary *a.*	مَنُوطٌ بِطِبِّ الْحَيَوَانَاتِ
Vertebra *n.*	فِقْرَةٌ ج فِقَارٌ	Veto *n.* or *v. t.*	نَهْيٌ. مَنْعٌ. رَفْضٌ. رَفَضَ
Vertebral *a.*	فِقْرِيّ	Vex *v. t.*	أَضْجَرَ. كَدَّرَ. أَغَاظَ
Vertebrate *a.*	ذُو فِقْرَاتٍ أَوْ فِقَارٍ	Vexation *n.*	كَدَرٌ. مُضَايَقَةٌ
Vertex *n.*	قِمَّةٌ. رَأْسٌ	Vexatious *n.*	مُضَايِقٌ. مُكَدِّرٌ
Vertical *a.*	عَمُودِيّ	Viaduct *n.*	سِكَّةٌ مُرْتَفِعَةٌ. جِسْرٌ
Vertigo *n.*	دُوَارٌ	Vial *n.*	قَارُورَةٌ. جَامٌ
Very *a.* or *ad.*	حَقِيقِيّ. ذَاتٌ. جِدًّا	Viands *n. pl.*	أَطْعِمَةٌ

Vibrate v. t. or i.	رَجَّ ـ . إِرْتَجَ . إِهْتَزَّ
Vibration n.	إِهْتِزَازٌ
Vicar n.	نَائِبٌ . خُورِيٌّ . قِسِّيسٌ
Vicarious n.	نَائِبٌ . مُوَكَّلٌ
Vice n.	رَذِيلَةٌ . شَرٌّ . مِلْزَمَةٌ . عِوَضٌ
Vice-admiral n.	نَائِبٌ . رَئِيسُ أُسْطُولٍ
Vicegerent n.	نَائِبٌ
Viceroy n.	نَائِبُ مَلِكٍ
Vicinage ⎱ n. Vicinity ⎰	جُوَارٌ
Vicious a.	فَاسِدٌ . شِرِّيرٌ . خَلِيعٌ
Vicissitude n.	تَقَلُّبٌ
Victim n.	قَتِيلٌ . ذَبِيحٌ
Victor n. Victorious a. ⎰	قَاهِرٌ . غَالِبٌ . مَنْصُورٌ
Victory n.	نَصْرٌ . غَلَبَةٌ . فَوْزٌ
Victual v. t.	زَوَّدَ . مَوَّنَ
Victuals n. pl.	طَعَامٌ . مَأْكُولَاتٌ
Vie v. i.	بَارَى . سَابَقَ . نَافَسَ
View v. t.	نَظَرَ ـ . رَأَى ـ . تَطَلَّعَ

View n.	مَنْظَرٌ . رَأْيٌ
Vigil n.	سَهَرٌ . صَلَاةٌ سَهَرِيَّةٌ
Vigilance n.	مُرَاقَبَةٌ . سَهَرٌ
Vigilant a.	سَاهِرٌ . حَذِرٌ . مُنْتَبِهٌ
Vigorous a.	قَوِيٌّ . نَشِيطٌ . شَدِيدٌ
Vigour n.	شِدَّةٌ . قُوَّةٌ . نَشَاطٌ
Vile a.	رَذِيلٌ . نَجِسٌ . قَبِيحٌ
Vileness n.	قَبَاحَةٌ . خَسَاسَةٌ
Vilify v. t.	عَابَ ـ . شَتَمَ ـ
Villa n.	دَارُ سَكَنٍ خَارِجَ ٱلْمَدِينَةِ
Village n.	قَرْيَةٌ . ضَيْعَةٌ
Villager n.	قَرَوِيٌّ
Villain n. Villainous a. ⎰	خَبِيثٌ . شِرِّيرٌ
Villainy ⎱ n. Villany ⎰	خُبْثٌ . شَرٌّ
Vindicate v. t.	بَرَّأَ . بَرَّرَ . ثَبَّتَ
Vindication n.	تَبْرِئَةٌ . إِثْبَاتٌ
Vindictive a.	ضَغِنٌ . طَالِبُ ٱلْاِنْتِقَامِ
Vine n.	كَرْمَةٌ . زَرَجُونٌ . دَالِيَةٌ

Vinegar n.	خَلّ
Vineyard n.	كَرْم
Vintage n.	قِطَاف. حَاصِلُ ٱلْكَرْمِ
Viol Viola } n.	كَمَنْجَةٌ كَبِيرَةٌ
Violate v. i.	خَالَفَ. نَكَثَ ـ اغْتَصَبَ
Violation n.	مُخَالَفَة. نَكْثٌ
Violence n.	عُنْفٌ. قُوَّةٌ. غَصْبٌ
Violent a.	عَنِيفٌ. شَدِيدٌ. ظَلُومٌ
Violet n. or a.	بَنَفْسَجَة. بَنَفْسَجِيّ
Violin n.	كَمَنْجَة
Viper n.	أَفْعَى. صِلّ
Virago n.	سَلِيطَة
Virgin n.	عَذْرَاء
Virginity n.	عُذْرَة
Virile a.	رَجُلِيّ. مَرْئِيّ
Virility n.	رُجُولِيَّة
Virtual a.	حَقِيقِيّ. بِٱلْحَقِيقَة
Virtue n.	فَضِيلَة. جُودَة. قُوَّة
Virtuous a.	عَفِيفٌ. نَقِيّ. صَالِحٌ
Virulence n.	شِدَّة. عُنْف. سَلَاقَة
Virulent a.	شَدِيدٌ. عَنِيفٌ. سَامّ
Virus n.	سَمّ. صَدِيدٌ
Visage n.	مُحَيّا. وَجْه. طَلْعَة
Viscera n. pl.	أَحْشَاء
Viscid Viscous } a.	لَزِج. دِبِق
Viscount n.	أَمِير. رُتْبَة أَمِيرِيَّة
Visibility n.	إِمْكَانِيَّة نَظَرِهِ. ظُهُور
Visible v. t.	مَا يُنْظَرُ. ظَاهِرٌ
Vision n.	نَظَر. رُؤْيَة. رُؤْيَا
Visionary a.	خَيَالِيّ. وَهْمِيّ
Visit n. or v. t.	زِيَارَة. زَارَ ـ. اِفْتَقَدَ
Visitation n.	اِفْتِقَاد. مُصِيبَة
Visitor n.	زَائِر. ضَيْف. مُفَتِّش
Vista n.	مَنْظَر (إِلَى بَعِيدٍ)
Visual a.	مَرْئِيّ. نَظَرِيّ. بَصَرِيّ
Vital a.	حَيَوِيّ. ضَرُورِيّ

Vitality n.	حَيَوِيَّةٌ رُوحُ ٱلْحَيَاةِ
Vitals n. pl.	اَلْأَحْشَاءُ ٱلرَّئِيسِيَّة
Vitiate v. t.	أَفْسَدَ . أَبْطَلَ
Vitreous a.	زُجَاجِيٌّ
Vitriol n.	زَاجٌ . شَبٌّ
Vituperate v, t.	شَتَمَ ـُ . طَعَنَ ـَ
Vivacious a.	خَفِيفٌ . مَرِحٌ . ذَكِيٌّ
Vivacity n.	خِفَّةٌ . مَرَحٌ . نَشَاطٌ
Vivid a.	بَرَّاقٌ . مُؤَثِّرٌ
Vividness n.	وُضُوحٌ . لَمَعَانٌ
Vivify v. t.	أَحْيَا . أَنْعَشَ
Vivisection n.	تَشْرِيحُ ٱلْجِسْمِ ٱلْحَيِّ
Vixen n.	سَلِيطَةٌ . وَقِحَةٌ
Viz ad.	أَيْ . يَعْنِي
Vizier n.	وَزِيرٌ
Vocabulary n.	قَامُوسٌ مُوجَزٌ
Vocal a.	صَوْتِيٌّ . مَلْفُوظٌ
Vocalize v. t.	لَفَظَ ـِ . حَرَّكَ (الحروف)
Vocation n.	حِرْفَةٌ . وَظِيفَةٌ . دَعْوَةٌ
Vociferate v. t.	صَاحَ ـِ . صَرَخَ ـُ
Vociferous a.	صَائِحٌ . هَاتِفٌ
Voice n.	صَوْتٌ . صِيغَةُ ٱلْمَعْلُومِ أَوِ ٱلْمَجْهُولِ
Void a. or n.	فَارِغٌ . خَالٍ . بَاطِلٌ . خَلَاءٌ
Volatile a.	طَيَّارٌ . مُتَقَلِّبٌ
Volcanic a.	بُرْكَانِيٌّ
Volcano a.	بُرْكَانٌ . جَبَلُ نَارٍ
Volition n.	إِرَادَةٌ . إِخْتِيَارٌ
Volley n.	إِطْلَاقُ أَسْلِحَةٍ كَثِيرَةٍ مَعًا
Volublity n.	كَثْرَةُ ٱلْكَلَامِ
Voluble a.	كَثِيرُ ٱلْكَلَامِ
Volume n.	مُجَلَّدٌ . جِرْمٌ . سِعَةٌ
Voluminous a.	كَثِيرٌ . مُطَوَّلٌ
Voluntary a.	إِخْتِيَارِيٌّ . طَوْعِيٌّ
Volunteer n.	مُتَطَوِّعٌ . مُتَبَرِّعٌ
Voluptuary n. } Voluptuous a. }	شَهْوَانِيٌّ . مُتَنَعِّمٌ
Vomit v. t. or n.	إِسْتَفْرَغَ . قَيْءٌ

Voracious *a.*	نَهِمٌ . أَهْيَمُ . شَرِهٌ
Voracity *n.*	نَهْمَةٌ . شَرَهٌ
Vortex *n.*	دُرْدُورٌ
Votary *n.*	مُتَعَبِّدٌ . نَذِيرٌ
Vote *n.* or *v. i.*	صَوْتٌ فِي ٱلْاِنْتِخَابِ
Voter *n.*	مَنْ لَهُ حَقٌّ فِي ٱلْاِنْتِخَابِ
Votive *a.*	نَذْرِيٌّ
Vouch *v. t.* or *i.*	أَثْبَتَ . شَهِدَ
Voucher *n.*	شَاهِدٌ . بَيِّنَةٌ
Vouchsafe *v. t.*	مَنَحَ . أَنْعَمَ عَلَى . وَهَبَ
Vow *n.* or *v. t.*	نَذْرٌ . نَذَرَ
Vowel *n.*	حَرْفُ عِلَّةٍ
Voyage *n.* or *v. i.*	سَفَرٌ . سَافَرَ
Voyager *n.*	مُسَافِرٌ
Vulgar *a.*	دَارِجٌ . دَنِيٌّ . خَسِيسٌ
Vulgarism *n.*	إِصْطِلَاحٌ دَارِجٌ
Vulgarity *n.*	دَنَاءَةٌ . قِلَّةُ أَدَبٍ
Vulnerable *a.*	قَابِلُ ٱلْجَرْحِ وَٱلطَّعْنِ
Vulture *n.*	نَسْرٌ . شُوحَةٌ
Vying *See* Vie	مُنَافِسٌ
Vulgate *n.*	تَرْجَمَةُ ٱلْكِتَابِ ٱلْمُقَدَّسِ ٱللَّاتِينِيَّةُ

W

Wabble *v. i.*	تَرَنَّحَ . تَمَايَلَ
Wad *n.* or *v. t.*	حَشْوَةٌ . حَشَاكَا
Wadded *a.*	مَحْشُوٌّ
Waddle *v. i.*	تَمَايَلَ فِي ٱلْمَشْيِ
Wade *v. i.*	خَاضَ
Wafer *n.*	بُرْشَانَةٌ

Waft v. t.	حَمَلَ ـِ (اَلرِّيحُ)
Wage n. or v. t.	مَازِحٌ . هَزَّ ـُ . بَصْبَصَ
Wage v. t.	رَاهَنَ . إِسْتَأْجَرَ . حَارَبَ
Wager n. or v. t.	رَهْنٌ . رَاهَنَ
Wages n. pl.	أَجْرٌ . كِرَاءٌ
Waggish a.	مَازِحٌ . مَاجِنٌ
Waggon n.	مَرْكَبَةٌ . عَرَبَةٌ
Waif n.	لَقِيطٌ
Wail v. i. or n.	وَلْوَلَ . عَوَّلَ . عَوِيلٌ
Waist n.	خَصْرٌ . حَقْوٌ
Waistcoat n.	صُدْرَةٌ . صَدْرِيَّةٌ
Wait v. i.	إِنْتَظَرَ . إِسْتَأْنَى . تَرَبَّصَ
Waiter n.	خَادِمٌ . طَبَقٌ
Waiting-maid n.	خَادِمَةٌ . جَارِيَةٌ
Waive v. t.	تَرَكَ ـُ . خَلَّى . تَنَحَّى عَنْ
Wake v. i.	إِسْتَيْقَظَ . إِنْتَبَهَ
Wake n.	حِرَاسَةُ مَيِّتٍ . أَثَرُ سَفِينَةٍ
Wakeful a.	يَقِظٌ . سَاهِرٌ
Waken v. i. or t.	تَيَقَّظَ . أَيْقَظَ . نَبَّهَ
Walk v. t. or n.	مَشَى ـِ . مَشْيٌ . مَمْشًى
Wall n. or v. t.	حَائِطٌ . سُورٌ . حَوَّطَ
Wallet n.	جِرَابٌ . كِيسٌ . قَلْعٌ
Wallow v. i.	تَمَرَّغَ
Walnut n.	جَوْزَةٌ . شَجَرُ الْجَوْزِ
Waltz n.	نَوْعٌ مِنَ الرَّقْصِ
Wan n.	أَصْفَرُ مُصْفَرٌّ
Wand n.	قَضِيبٌ صَوْلَجَانٌ
Wander v. i.	تَاهَ ـِ . ضَلَّ ـِ . حَادَ ـِ
Wanderer n.	تَائِهٌ . ضَالٌّ . جَائِلٌ
Wane v. i.	تَنَاقَصَ . إِنْحَطَّ
Want v. t. or i.	إِحْتَاجَ . اِرَادَ نَقَصَ ـُ
Want n.	حَاجَةٌ . فَاقَةٌ . نَقْصٌ
Wanting a.	نَاقِصٌ مَفْقُودٌ
Wanton a.	فَاجِرٌ . بَطِرٌ . لَاهٍ
War n. or v. i.	حَرْبٌ . حَارَبَ
Warble v. i.	غَرَّدَ

Warbler Warbling } n.	مُغَرِّدٌ
Ward n.	حِرَاسَةٌ . قَاصِرٌ لَهُ وَصِيٌّ
Warden n.	حَافِظٌ . وَكِيلٌ
Wardrobe n.	خِزَانَةُ ثِيَابٍ . لِبَاسٌ
Wares n. pl.	سِلَعٌ . بَضَائِعُ
Warehouse n.	مَخْزَنٌ
Warfare n.	مُحَارَبَةٌ . مُجَاهَدَةٌ
Warily ad.	بِحَذَرٍ . مُتَحَذِّراً
Wariness n.	حَذَرٌ . إِحْتِيَاطٌ
Warlike a.	حَرْبِيٌّ . مُحِبُّ ٱلْحَرْبِ
Warm a. or v.t.	دَافِئٌ . حَارٌّ . سَخَّنَ
Warmly ad.	بِحَمَاسَةٍ . بِغَيْرَةٍ
Warmth n.	دِفْءٌ . حَرَارَةٌ
Warn v.t.	حَذَّرَ . أَنْذَرَ
Warning n.	إِنْذَارٌ . إِخْطَارٌ
Warp n. or v. t.	سَدَاةٌ . حَرَّفَ
Warrant n.	تَفْوِيضٌ . إِجَازَةٌ . أَمْرٌ
Warrant v. t.	كَفَلَ . ضَمِنَ . بَرَّرَ
Warrantable a.	جَائِزٌ
Warrior n.	مُحَارِبٌ . جُنْدِيٌّ
Wart n.	ثُؤْلُولٌ ج ثَآلِيل
Wary a.	مُتَحَذِّرٌ . مُحْتَرِسٌ . بَصِيرٌ
Was see Be.	كَانَ يَكُونُ
Wash v. t. or i.	غَسَلَ . إِغْتَسَلَ
Wash n.	غَسْلٌ . غَسْلَةٌ
Washer-woman n.	غَسَّالَةٌ
Washing n.	غَسْلٌ . غَسَالَةٌ . غَسِيلٌ
Wasp n.	زُنْبُورٌ ج زَنَابِيرُ
Waspish a.	نَكِدٌ . سَرِيعُ ٱلْغَيْظِ
Waste v. t. or i.	أَسْرَفَ . بَذَّرَ . ضَنِيَ
Waste n.	إِسْرَافٌ . خَرَابٌ . صَحْرَاءُ
Wasteful a.	مُسْرِفٌ . مُبَذِّرٌ
Watch n.	خَفِيرٌ . هَزِيعٌ . سَاعَةٌ
Watch v. t. or i.	حَرَسَ . رَاقَبَ . سَهِرَ
Watchful v.	مُرَاقِبٌ . حَذِرٌ . مُنْتَبِهٌ
Watch-maker n.	سَاعَاتِيٌّ

Watchman n.	حَارِسٌ . رَقِيبٌ
Watch-tower n.	بُرْجُ الرَّقِيبِ
Watchword n.	شِعَارٌ
Water n. or v. i.	مَآءٌ . سَقَى ـ
Water-course n.	مَجْرَى مَآءٍ
Water-cress n.	قُرَّةُ الْعَيْنِ (نبات)
Waterfall n.	شَلَّالٌ
Water-melon n.	بِطِّيخٌ أَحْمَرُ
Waterproof n.	مُشَمَّعٌ
Water-spout n.	عَمُودُ مَاءٍ
Watery a.	مَائِيٌّ . خَفِيفٌ . تَافِهٌ
Wave n. or v.t. or i.	مَوْجٌ . هَزَّ . هَاجَ ـ
Waver v. i.	تَرَدَّدَ . إِرْتَابَ . تَمَايَلَ
Wavy a.	مُتَمَوِّجٌ
Wax n. or v.t. or i.	شَمْعٌ . أَشْمَعَ . زَادَ ـ
Waxen a.	شَمْعِيٌّ
Waxwork n.	صُوَرٌ أَوْ شُخُوصٌ شَمْعِيَّةٌ
Way n.	طَرِيقٌ . مِنْوَالٌ . وَسِيلَةٌ

Wayfarer Wayfaring } n.	مُسَافِرٌ . إِبْنُ السَّبِيلِ
Waylay v. t.	اكْمَنَ لَهُ
Wayward a.	جَامِحٌ غَيْرُ مُطِيعٍ
We pron. pl.	نَحْنُ
Weak a.	ضَعِيفٌ . وَاهِنٌ . وَمُرْتَخٍ
Weaken v. t.	أَضْعَفَ . أَوْهَنَ
Weakness n.	ضَعْفٌ . وَهْنٌ . سَقَمٌ
Weal n.	خَيْرٌ . سَعَادَةٌ
Wealth n.	ثَرْوَةٌ . غِنًى . وَفْرَةٌ
Wealthy a.	غَنِيٌّ . ذُو ثَرْوَةٍ
Wean v. t.	فَطَمَ ـ
Weapon n.	سِلَاحٌ
Wear v. t.	لَبِسَ ـ . أَبْلَى
Weariness n.	تَعَبٌ . ضَنْكٌ . إِعْيَاءٌ
Wearisome a.	مُتْعِبٌ . مُمِلٌّ
Weary a. or v. t.	تَعِبٌ . أَتْعَبَ . ازْعج
Weasel n.	إِبْنُ عِرْسٍ . نِمْسٌ
Weather n.	حَالَةُ الْجَوِّ . طَقْسٌ

Weather-cock n.	دَوَّارَةُ الرِّيحِ
Weave v. t.	حَاكَ . نَسَجَ ـِ
Weaver n.	حَائِكٌ . نَسَّاجٌ
Web n.	نَسِيجٌ
Wed v. t. or i.	تَزَوَّجَ
Wedding n.	عُرْسٌ
Wedge n.	سَفَنٌ
Wedlock n.	زِيجَةٌ . زَوَاجٌ
Wednesday n.	يَوْمُ الأَرْبِعَاءِ
Weld n. or v. t.	عُشْبٌ بَرِّي . قَلَعَ
Week n.	أُسْبُوعٌ
Weekday a.	غَيْرُ يَوْمِ الأَحَدِ
Weekly a. or ad.	اسْبُوعِيٌّ . أُسْبُوعِيًّا
Weep v. i.	بَكَى
Weevil n.	سُوسٌ
Weigh v. t.	وَزَنَ ـِ . تَأَمَّلَ . ثَقُلَ ـَ
Weight n.	وَزْنٌ . ثِقْلٌ . أَهَمِّيَّةٌ
Weighty a.	ثَقِيلٌ . مُهِمٌّ

Weir n.	سَدُّ نَهْرٍ
Weird a.	غَيْرُ طَبِيعِيٍّ . غَرِيبٌ
Welcome n. or a.	تَأْهِيلٌ . مُتَرَحَّبٌ بِهِ
Weld v. t.	لَحَمَ ـَ
Welfare n. Well-being	خَيْرٌ . حَظٌّ . سَلَامَةٌ
Well a. or ad.	مُعَافَى . جَيِّدٌ . حَسَنًا
Well n. or v. i.	بِئْرٌ . نَبَعَ ـَ
Well-bred a.	مُهَذَّبٌ . حَسَنُ التَّرْبِيَةِ
Well-nigh ad.	تَقْرِيبًا
Well-spring n.	نَبْعٌ
Welter v. i.	تَمَرَّغَ . تَقَلَّبَ
Wen n.	سِلْعَةٌ . غُدَّةٌ
Wench n.	جَارِيَةٌ
Went See Go.	ذَهَبَ ـَ
Were See Be.	كَانُوا
West n.	مَغْرِبٌ . غَرْبٌ
Western a.	غَرْبِيٌّ
Westward ad.	غَرْبًا . نَحْوُ الغَرْبِ

Wet *a.*	مَبْلُول . رَطْبٌ . مَاطِرٌ	Whereby *ad.*	أَلَّذِي بِهِ . مِنْ حَيْثُ
Wether *n.*	كَبْشٌ خَصِيٌّ	Wherefore *ad.*	لِذَلِكَ . مِنْ ثَمَّ . لِمَاذَا
Whale *n.*	حُوتٌ	Wherein *ad.*	حَيْثُ أَيْنَ
Wharf *n.*	إِسْكِلَة . (رَصِيفٌ)	Whereof *ad.*	أَلَّذِي مِنْهُ
What *pron.*	مَا . مَاذَا	Whereon Whereupon } *ad.*	إِذْ ذَاكَ . عِنْدَ ذَاكَ
Whatever Whatsoever } *pron.*	مَهْمَا . كُلَّمَا	Wheresoever Wherever } *ad.*	حَيْثُمَا . أَيْنَمَا
Wheat *n.*	قَمْحٌ . بُرٌّ . حِنْطَةٌ	Whereto Whereunto } *ad.*	إِلَى حَيْثُ
Wheedle *v. t.*	دَاهَنَ . دَارَى . تَمَلَّقَ	Wherewith Wherewithal } *ad.*	مَا بِهِ . بِمَا
Wheel *n.*	دُولَابٌ (عَجَلَةٌ)	Whet *v. t.*	سَنَّ . هَيَّجَ . شَوَّقَ
Wheel-barrow *n.*	عَجَلَةُ الْيَدِ	Whether *pron.* or *conj.*	أَيُّهُمَا . إِنْ كَانَ
Whelp *n.*	شِبْلٌ . جَرْوٌ	Whetstone *n.*	مِسَنٌّ . مِشْحَذٌ . صَلْبٌ
When *ad.*	مَتَى . لَمَّا . عِنْدَمَا	Whey *n.*	مَصْلٌ
Whence *ad.*	مِنْ أَيْنَ . مِنْ حَيْثُ	Which *pron.*	مَا . مَنْ . أَلَّذِي
Whenever Whensoever } *ad.*	كُلَّمَا . مَتَى مَا	Which-ever Which-so-ever } *pron.*	أَيُّمَا . هَذَا أَوْ ذَاكَ
Where *ad.*	أَيْنَ . إِلَى أَيْنَ . حَيْثُ	Whiff *n.*	نَفْحَةٌ . نَفْسٌ
Whereabouts *ad.* or *n.*	أَيْنَ . مَكَانٌ	Whig *n.*	مِنْ حِزْبِ الْأَحْرَارِ الْإِنْكِلِيزِ
Whereas *conj.*	بِمَا أَنْ . عَلَى أَنَّ	While *n.*	مُدَّةٌ . وَقْتٌ . حِينٌ
Whereat *ad.*	عِنْدَ ذَلِكَ		

While Whilst } *ad.*	بَيْنَمَا . حِينَمَا . لَمَّا . إِذْ
Whim *n.*	وَهْمٌ . تَصَوُّرٌ بَاطِلٌ
Whimper *v. i.*	بَكَى خَفِيفًا كَالْوَلَدِ
Whimsical *a.*	وَهْمِيٌّ . غَرِيبٌ
Whine *v. i.* or *n.*	هَرَّ ـِ . هَرِيرٌ
Whip *n.* or *v. t.*	سَوْطٌ . سَاطَ ـُ
Whir *v. i.*	دَارَ بِصَوْتٍ . خَرَّ
Whirl *v. t.* or *i.*	دَوَّرَ ـُ دَارَ
Whirlpool *n.*	دَرْدُورٌ
Whirlwind *n.*	زَوْبَعَةٌ
Whisker *n.*	لِحْيَةُ الْعَارِضِ
Whisk *v. t.*	حَرَّكَ . جَرَفَ بِسُرْعَةٍ
Whisky *n.*	نَوْعٌ مِنَ الْعَرَقِ . وِسْكِي
Whisper *n.* or *v. i.*	وَسْوَسَةٌ . سَارَّ
Whistle *v. i.* or *n.*	صَفَرَ ـِ . صَافُورَةٌ
Whit *n.*	قُطْمَةٌ . ذَرَّةٌ . بَتَّةً
White *a.* or *n.*	أَبْيَضُ . بَيَاضٌ
Whiten *v. t.* or *i.*	بَيَّضَ . إِبْيَضَّ
Whiteness *n.*	بَيَاضٌ
Whitewash *n.*	بَيَاضُ الْجِيرِ
Whither *ad.*	إِلَى أَيْنَ
Whithersoever *ad.*	أَيْنَمَا . حَيْثُمَا
Whitish *a.*	ضَارِبٌ إِلَى الْبَيَاضِ
Whittle *v. t.*	قَشَرَ بِسِكِّينٍ . بَرَى ـِ
Whiz *n.* or *v. i.*	صَفِيرُ السَّهْمِ . صَفَرَ ـِ
Who *rel.* or *int.* pron.	الَّذِي . أَلَّتِي . مَنْ
Whoever *rel. pron.*	مَنْ . كُلُّ مَنْ
Whole *a.*	كُلٌّ . صَحِيحٌ . كَامِلٌ
Wholesale *n.* or *a.*	بَيْعٌ بِالْجُمْلَةِ
Wholesome *a.*	سَلِيمٌ . مُوَافِقُ الصِّحَّةِ
Wholly *ad.*	جُمْلَةً . كَافَّةً . تَمَامًا
Whom *pron. See* Who.	أَلَّذِي
Whoop *n.* or *v. i.*	صِيَاحٌ . صَاحَ ـِ . زَعَقَ
Whooping-cough *n.*	دَاءُ الشَّهْقَةِ
Whore *n.*	زَانِيَةٌ . عَاهِرَةٌ . فَاجِرَةٌ
Whoredom *n.*	عَهْرٌ . فُجُورٌ

Whose *poss. pron.* See Who [er.	Wilderness *n.* بَرِّيَّة . بَادِيَة
Whosoever *rel. pron.* See Whoev-	
Why *ad.* لِمَ . لِمَاذَا	Wildly *ad.* بِجُنُون . طَيْشًا
Wick *n.* فَتِيلَة . شَعِيلَة	Wile *n.* حِيلَة .. مَكِيدَة . خُدْعَة
Wicked *a.* شِرِّيرٌ . أَثِيمٌ . طَالِحٌ	Wilful *a.* عَنِيدٌ
Wickedness *n.* شَرٌّ . إِثْمٌ	Wilfulness *n.* عِنَادٌ
Wicket *n.* بَابٌ صَغِيرٌ	Will *v. i.* سَوْفَ
Wide *a.* وَاسِعٌ . فَسِيحٌ . عَرِيضٌ	Will *v. t.* أَرَادَ . أَوْصَى . إِرَادَة . وَصِيَّة or *n.*
Widely *ad.* جِدًّا . شَائِعًا . اِتِّسَاعًا	Willing *a.* رَاضٍ . مُرِيدٌ
Widen *v. t. or i.* وَسَّعَ . اِتَّسَعَ	Willingness *n.* رِضًى . قَبُول
Widow *n.* أَرْمَلَة ج أَرَامِلُ	Willow *n.* صَفْصَاف
Widower *n.* اِرْمَل	Wilt *v. i.* ذَمَلَ -
Widowhood *n.* تَرَمُّل	Wily *a.* بَكَّارٌ . مُخْتَالٌ . خَدَّاعٌ
Width *n.* عَرْضٌ . اِتِّسَاعٌ	Win *v. t.* رَبِحَ - . فَازَ بِـ . أَرْضَى
Wield *v. t.* اِسْتَعْمَلَ . أَدَارَ . دَبَّرَ	Wince *v. i.* جَفَلَ عَنْ
Wife *n.* زَوْجَة . قَرِينَة . إِمْرَأَة	Wind *n.* رِيحٌ
Wig *n.* شَعْرٌ مُسْتَعَارٌ	Wind *v. t. or i.* فَتَلَ ِ . دَارَ -
Wigwam *n.* كُوخُ الْهُنُودِ	Winding-sheet *n.* كَفَنٌ ج اكْفَان
Wild *a.* بَرِّيٌّ . وَحْشِيٌّ . فَالِت	Windlass *n.* آلَةٌ لِرَفْعِ الْأَثْقَالِ

Windmill n.	طَاحُونْ تُدِيرُهُ ٱلرِّيحُ
Window n.	طَاقَةٌ . كَوَّةٌ . شُبَّاكٌ
Windpipe n.	قَصَبَةُ ٱلرِّئَةِ
Windward ad.	إِلَى جِهَةِ ٱلرِّيحِ
Windy a.	كَثِيرُ ٱلرِّيحِ . بَاطِلٌ
Wine n.	خَمْرٌ . نَبِيذٌ
Wine-bibber n.	شِرِّيبُ خَمْرٍ
Wine-glass n.	قَدَحٌ . كَأْسٌ
Wing n.	جَنَاحٌ . كَنَفٌ
Wink v. i.	طَرَفَ ـِ . تَغَاضَى عَنْ
Winner n.	فَائِزٌ . غَالِبٌ
Winning a.	مُرْضٍ . مُسْتَمِيلُ ٱلْقَلْبِ
Winnow v. t.	ذَرَّى
Winter n.	فَصْلُ ٱلشِّتَاءِ
Wintery } Wintry } a.	شَتْوِيٌّ . شَاتٍ . بَارِدٌ
Wipe v. t.	مَسَحَ ـَ نَظَّفَ . مَحَا ـ
Wire n. or v. t.	شَرِيطٌ . سِلْكٌ . رَاسَلَ بِهِ
Wiry a.	شَرِيطِيٌّ . ضَلِيعٌ . قَوِيٌّ

Wisdom n.	حِكْمَةٌ . فِطْنَةٌ
Wise a.	حَكِيمٌ . عَاقِلٌ
Wish v. t. or n.	اِرَادَ تَمَنَّى . إِرَادَةٌ . بُغْيَةٌ
Wistful a.	تَائِقٌ . رَاغِبٌ
Wit n.	ذَكَاءٌ . حِذْقٌ . بَصِيرَةٌ
Witch n.	سَاحِرَةٌ
Witchcraft n.	سِحْرٌ . كِهَانَةٌ
Wichery n.	سِحْرٌ . فُتُونٌ
With prep.	مَعَ . بِ . عِنْدَ . مِنْ
Withal ad.	أَيْضًا . مَعَ كُلِّهِ
Withdraw v. t. or i.	اِسْتَرَدَّ . اِرْتَدَّ
Withdrawal n.	اِسْتِرْجَاعٌ . اِرْتِدَادٌ
Wither v. t. or i.	أَذْبَلَ . ذَبَلَ ـُ
Withers n. pl.	حَارِكٌ (عَظْمٌ بِأَعْلَى ٱلظَّهْرِ)
Withhold v. t.	أَمْسَكَ عَنْ
Within prep.	دَاخِل . فِي . ضِمْنَ
Without prep.	خَارِجٌ . بِدُونِ . مَالَمْ
Withstand v. t.	قَاوَمَ . ثَبَتَ ضِدَّ

Witless *a.*	غَبِيّ . أَخْرَقُ
Witness *n.* or *v. i.*	شَاهِدٌ . شَهَادَةٌ . شَاهَدَ
Witticism *n.*	مُلْحَةٌ
Wittingly *ad.*	قَصْداً . بِعِلْمٍ
Witty *a.*	ذَكِيٌّ . ظَرِيفٌ
Wives *n. pl. See* Wife	زَوْجَاتٌ
Wizard *n.*	سَاحِرٌ
Woe *n.*	وَيْلٌ . بَلِيَّةٌ . حُزْنٌ
Woe-begone *a.*	حَزِينٌ . مَغْمُومٌ
Woeful ⎫ Woful ⎭ *a.*	حَزِينٌ . مُحْزِن
Wolf *n.*	ذِئْبٌ ج ذِئَابٌ
Woman *n.* (*pl.* Women).	مَرْأَةٌ . إِمْرَأَةٌ
Womanhood *n.*	حَالَةُ ٱلْمَرْأَةِ . ٱلنِّسَاءُ
Woman-kind *n.*	جِنْسُ ٱلنِّسَاءِ
Womb *n.*	رَحِمٌ ج أَرْحَامٌ
Wonder *n.*	تَعَجُّبٌ . غَرِيبَةٌ . مُعْجِزَةٌ
Wonderful ⎫ Wondrous ⎭ *a.*	عَجِيبٌ . مُدْهِشٌ
Wont *a.* or *n.*	مُعْتَادٌ . عَادَةٌ
Wonted *a.*	مُعْتَادٌ
Woo *v. t.*	تَوَدَّدَ إِلَى . إِسْتَعْطَفَ
Wood *n.*	خَشَبٌ . خَطَبٌ . غَابَةٌ
Woodcock *n.*	دُجَاجُ ٱلْأَرْضِ
Woodcut *n.*	نَقْشٌ عَلَى خَشَبٍ
Wooded *a.*	ذُو أَشْجَارٍ
Wooden *a.*	خَشَبِيٌّ . مِنْ خَشَبٍ
Woodman *n.*	حَطَّابٌ
Woody *a.*	خَشَبِيٌّ . كَثِيرُ ٱلْأَشْجَارِ
Woof *n.*	لُحْمَةٌ
Wool *n.*	صُوفٌ
Woollen *a.*	صُوفِيٌّ . مِنْ صُوفٍ
Woolly *a.*	صُوفِيٌّ . ذُو صُوفٍ
Word *n.*	كَلِمَةٌ . وَعْدٌ . أَمْرٌ
Wording *n.*	عِبَارَةٌ . تَرْكِيبُ عِبَارَةٍ
Wordy *a.*	كَثِيرُ ٱلْكَلَامِ
Work *n.* or *v. i.*	شُغْلٌ . عَمَلٌ . إِشْتَغَلَ
Worker ⎫ Workman ⎭ *a.*	صَانِعٌ . فَاعِلٌ

Workmanship n.	صَنْعَةٌ . عَمَلٌ
Workshop n.	مَعْمَلٌ . دُكَّانُ شُغْلٍ
World n.	عَالَمٌ . دُنْيَا
Worldliness n.	مَحَبَّةُ الدُّنْيَا
Worldly n.	مُحِبُّ الدُّنْيَا . دُنْيَوِيٌّ
Worm n.	دُودَةٌ ج دُودٌ . دِيدَانٌ
Worm-eaten a.	مُسَوَّسٌ
Wormy a.	مُدَوَّدٌ . كَثِيرُ الدُّودِ
Worn pp.	مَلْبُوسٌ . تَعِبٌ . مَنْهُوكٌ
Worry v. t. or i.	كَدَّرَ . أَهَمَّ . إِهْتَمَّ
Worse a. or ad.	أَرْدَأُ . شَرٌّ
Worship n. or v. t.	عِبَادَةٌ . عَبَدَ
Worshipper n.	عَابِدٌ . سَاجِدٌ
Worst a. or v. t.	الأَرْدَأُ . غَلَبَ
Worsted n. or a.	غَزْلٌ صُوفِيٌّ
Worth n. or a.	قِيمَةٌ . مُعَادِلٌ . مُسْتَحِقٌّ
Worthily ad.	بِاسْتِحْقَاقٍ . بِلِيَاقَةٍ
Worthless a.	بِلَا قِيمَةٍ . غَيْرُ نَافِعٍ

Worthy a.	مُسْتَحِقٌّ . أَهْلٌ . فَاضِلٌ
Would (See Will.)	سَوْفَ . يَالَيْتَ
Wound n. or v. t.	جُرْحٌ . جَرَحَ
Wound pp. of Wind.	مَفْتُولٌ . مَلْفُوفٌ
Wove } Woven } See Weave.	مَنْسُوجٌ
Wrangle v. i.	نَازَعَ . شَاجَرَ
Wrap v. t.	لَفَّ
Wrapper } Wrapping } n.	لِفَافَةٌ . غِلَافٌ
Wrath n.	غَيْظٌ . سُخْطٌ . غَضَبٌ
Wrathful a.	غَضُوبٌ . سَاخِطٌ . مُغْتَاظٌ
Wreak v.	أَنْزَلَ عَلَى . أَحَلَّ بِهِ
Wreathe n.	اكْلِيلُ أَزْهَارٍ . ضَفِيرَةٌ
Wreathe v. t.	ضَفَرَ . لَفَّ
Wreck v. t. or n.	كَسَّرَ . خَرَّبَ . كَسْرٌ
Wren n.	ضَرْبٌ مِنَ العَصَافِيرِ
Wrench v. t.	لَوَّى . إِغْتَصَبَ
Wrest v. t.	إِغْتَصَبَ . خَطَفَ . حَرَّفَ
Wrestle v. i.	صَارَعَ

Wrestling n.	مُصَارَعَةٌ	Writing n.	كِتَابٌ . كِتَابَةٌ
Wretch n.	شَقِيٌّ . خَبِيثٌ . حَقِيرٌ	Written a.	مَكْتُوبٌ . خَطِّيٌّ
Wretched a.	شَقِيٌّ . تَعِسٌ . بَائِسٌ	Wrong n.	ظُلْمٌ . ضَرَرٌ . خَطَأٌ
Wriggle v. i.	تَلَوَّى	Wrong n.	غَيْرُ صَحِيحٍ . مُخْطِئٌ
Wright n.	صَانِعٌ	Wrong v. t.	ظَلَمَ . أَضَرَّ . أَسَاءَ إِلَى
Wring v. t.	عَصَرَ . إِغْتَصَبَ	Wrongful a.	مُضِرٌّ . ظَالِمٌ . غَيْرُ عَادِلٍ
Wrinkle n. or v. t.	جَعْدَةٌ . تَجَعَّدَ	Wroth a.	مُغْتَاظٌ . غَضْبَانُ
Wrist n.	مِعْصَمٌ . رُسْغٌ	Wrought a.	مَصْنُوعٌ
Write n.	كَتَبَ . حَرَّرَ . أَلَّفَ	Wrung See Wring.	مَعْصُورٌ
Writer n.	كَاتِبٌ . مُؤَلِّفٌ	Wry a.	أَزْوَرُ . مُعَوَّجٌ
Writhe v. t.	تَلَوَّى		

Y

Yacht n.	سَفِينَةٌ صَغِيرَةٌ لِلتَّنَزُّهِ . يَخْتٌ	Yawn v. i. or n.	تَثَاءَبَ . تَثَاؤُبٌ
Yard n.	ذِرَاعٌ إِنْكِلِيزِيٌّ	Ye p. pron.	أَنْتُمْ . أَنْتُنَّ
Yarn n.	غَزْلٌ . قِصَّةٌ . أَوِيلَةٌ	Yea ad.	نَعَمْ
Yawl n.	زَوْرَقٌ	Year n.	سَنَةٌ . عَامٌ

Yearling *n.*	حَوْليٌّ . إِبْنُ سَنَةٍ
Yearly *a.*	سَنَوِيٌّ
Yearn *v. i.*	إِشْتَاقَ إِلَى . حَنَّ ـِ
Yearning *n.*	حَنِينٌ . شَوْقٌ
Yeast *n.*	خَمِيرٌ
Yell *v. i.* or *n.*	صَاحَ ـِ . صَيْحَةٌ
Yellow *a.*	أَصْفَرُ
Yellowish *a.*	ضَارِبٌ إِلَى الصُّفْرَةِ
Yelp *v. i.*	هَرَّ ـِ . نَبَحَ ـَ
Yeoman *n.*	فَلَّاحٌ . صَاحِبُ مُلْكٍ
Yes *ad.*	نَعَمْ . بَلَى
Yesterday *ad.*	الْبَارِحَةَ . أَمْسِ
Yet *conj.*	مَعَ ذَلِكَ . بَعْدُ
Yield *v. t.* or *i.*	أَنْتَجَ . سَلَّمَ . أَذْعَنَ
Yielding *a.* or *p. pr.*	مُذْعِنٌ . لَيِّنٌ . مُنْتِجٌ
Yoke *n.* or *v. t.*	نِيرٌ . وَضَعَ النِّيرَ
Yoke-fellow *n.*	أَلِيفٌ . شَرِيكٌ
Yolk } *n.* Yelk }	مُحُّ الْبَيْضِ (الصُّفَار)
Yon *a.* Yonder *ad.* }	هُنَاكَ . ذَلِكَ
Yore *ad.*	قَدِيمًا
You *p. pron.*	أَنْتُمْ . أَنْتُنَّ
Young *a.* or *n.*	صَغِيرُ الْعُمْرِ . دِفْلٌ
Younger *a.*	أَصْغَرُ عُمْرًا
Youngest *n.*	الْأَصْغَرُ عُمْرًا
Youngster *n.*	صَبِيٌّ . فَتًى
Your *poss. pron.*	كَ . كُمْ . كُنَّ . كُمَا
Yours *pross. pron.*	لَكَ . لَكُمْ . لَكُنَّ
Yourself *p. pron.*	أَنْتَ نَفْسُكَ
Youth *n.*	حَدَاثَةٌ صَبْوَةٌ
Youthful *a.*	حَدِيثُ السِّنِّ . شَابٌّ

Z

Zeal *n.*	غَيرة . مُرُوَّة . إقْدَام
Zealot *n.*) Zealous *a.* (	غَيُور
Zebra *n.*	فَرَس وَحشِيّ مُخَطَّط
Zenith *n.*	سَمتُ الرَّأسِ
Zephyr *n.*	نَسِيم
Zero *n.*	صِفر
Zest *n.*	شَهِيَّة . لَذَّة
Zigzag *a.* or *n.*	مُتَعَرِّج . تَعَرِيج
Zinc *n.*	تُوتِيَا
Zion *n.*	صِهيَوْن
Zodiac *n.*	مِنطَقَة البُرُوج
Zone *n.*	مِنطَقَة
Zoological *a.*	مَنُوط بِعِلمِ الحَيَوَان
Zoologist *n.*	عَالِم بِالحَيَوَان
Zoology *n.*	عِلمُ الحَيَوَان

SUPPLEMENT

ENGLISH-ARABIC

advertisement n.	إِعْلَانٌ
advertising agency n.	وَكَالَةُ الْإِشْهَارِ
aerial n.	هَوَائِيّ
aeronautics n.	طَيَرَانٌ
aggression n.	إِعْتِدَاءٌ
aggressor n.	مُعْتَدٍ
airbase n.	قَائِدَةٌ جَوِّيَّةٌ
air conditioner n.	بَرَّادَةٌ
air-conditioning n.	تَكْيِيفُ الْهَوَاءِ
aircraft n.	طَائِرَةٌ
,, carrier n.	حَامِلَةُ الطَّائِرَاتِ
airfield n.	مَطَارٌ
air mail n.	الْبَرِيدُ الْجَوِّيُّ
airplane n.	طَائِرَةٌ
airport n.	مِينَا جَوِّيَّةٌ

air raid n.	غَارَةٌ جَوِّيَّةٌ
airtight a.	حَاجِبُ الْهَوَاءِ
air warden n.	حَارِسُ الْمُقَاوَمَةِ الْجَوِّيَّةِ
alert n.	إِشَارَةُ الْخَطَرِ
alternate current n.	تَيَّارٌ مُتَبَادَلٌ
ameliorate v.	أَصْلَحَ
amortization n.	إِسْتِهْلَاكٌ
amortize v.	إِسْتَهْلَكَ
amplifier n.	مُكَبِّرٌ
analogy n.	مُمَاثَلَةٌ
analysis n.	تَحْلِيلٌ
anesthesia n.	تَخْدِيرٌ
anesthesize v.	خَدَّرَ
anesthetic n.	مُخَدِّرٌ
annex v.	أَلْحَقَ

annexation *n.*	إِلْحَاق	arthritis *n.*	إِلْتِهَابُ الْمَفَاصِلِ
anonymous *a.*	بِدُونَ اسْم	aseptic *a.*	مُعَقَّم
antagonism *n.*	مُقَاوَمَةٌ	aspirin *n.*	أَسْبِيرِين
antisemite *n.*, anti- semitic *a.*	ذُو اللَّاسَامِيَّة	assimilate *v.*	مَثَّل
		assimilation *n.*	تَمَثُّل
antisemitism *n.*	لَاسَامِيَّةٌ	atheism *n.*	كُفْرَان
apartment house *n.*	مَنْزِلٌ	atheist *n.*	كَافِرٌ
appendectomy *n.*	جَذْمُ الزَّائِدَة الدُّودِيَّة	atmospheric *a.*	جَوِّيٌّ
		atom bomb *n.*	قُنْبُلَةٌ ذَرِّيَّةٌ
appendix *n.*	زَائِدَةٌ دُودِيَّةٌ	atomic *a.*	ذَرِّيٌّ
appetizer *n.*	مُشَهٍّ	atomic fission *n.*	شَقُّ الذَّرَّةِ
arbitration *n.*	تَحْكِيم	atomic warfare *n.*	مُحَارَبَةٌ ذَرِّيَّة
arbitration board *n.*	لَجْنَةٌ تَحْكِيمِيَّةٌ	atomizer *n.*	عَقَّارَةٌ
		audition *n.*	سَمَاع
arbitrator *n.*	مُحَكِّم	aureomycin *n.*	أُورِيُومِيسِين
armored car *n.*	سَيَّارَةٌ مُصَفَّحَةٌ	author *n.*	مُؤَلِّف

authorization n.	إِجَازَةٌ	bank rate n.	سِعْرُ الْفَائِدَة
authorize v.	أَجَازَ	barbed wire n.	سِلْكٌ شَائِكٌ
automatic a.	مُتَحَرِّكٌ بِذَاتِه	battle fatigue n.	ضَنَى الْحَرْب
automobile n.	سَيَّارَةٌ	beachhead n.	قَائِدَةٌ حَرْبِيَّةٌ
autonomous a.	مُسْتَقِلٌّ	bearish a.	نُزُولِيٌّ
autonomy n.	إِسْتِقْلَالٌ	beautician n.	صَاحِبُ دَارِ الزِّينَة
autopsy n.	تَشْرِيحٌ	bicycle n.	دَرَّاجَةٌ
aviator n.	طَيَّارٌ	bifocals n. pl.	نَظَّارَاتٌ ذَوَاتُ نُقْطَتَى اجْتِمَاعِ النُّور
bacillus n.	جُرْثُومَةٌ		
backlog n.	بَقَايَا عَمَل	big shot n.	رَجُلٌ مُهِمٌّ
bacteriology n.	عِلْمُ الْجَرَاثِيم	billion n.	أَلْفُ مِلْيُون
ball bearing n.	لُقْمَةٌ ذَاتُ كُرًى	bimonthly a.	مَا يَظْهَرُ كُلَّ شَهْرَيْن
balloon n.	مِنْطَادٌ	biochemical a.	مُخْتَصٌّ بِالْكِيمِيَاء الْاحيائية
ball point pen n.	قَلَمُ الْحِبْرِ الْجَافّ		
band leader n.	مُدِيرُ الْجَوْق		
bank account n.	حِسَابٌ	biochemistry n.	كِيمِيَاءٌ أَحْيَائِيَّةٌ

biology *n.*	عِلْمُ الْاَحْياءِ
bipartisan *a.*	لِكِلَي الْحِزْبَيْنِ
bisexual *a.*	لِكِلَي الْجِنْسَيْنِ
blackboard *n.*	سَبُّورَةٌ
black list *n.*	قائِمَةٌ سَوْدَاءُ
blacklist *v.*	قاطَعَ
blockade *n.*	مُحاصَرَةٌ
blood bank *n.*	مَخْزَنُ الدَّمِ
blood group *n.*	صَفُّ الدَّمِ
blood test *n.*	فَحْصُ الدَّمِ
blood transfusion *n.*	نَقْلُ الدَّمِ
blueprint *n.*	رَسْمٌ هَنْدَسِيٌّ
board of education *n.*	مَصْلَحَةُ التَّرْبِيَةِ
board of health *n.*	مَصْلَحَةُ الصِّحَّةِ
bomber *n.*	مَقْنَبِلَةٌ
bomb sight *n.*	آلَةٌ تَصْوِيبِيَّةٌ لِلْقَذْفِ بِالْقَنابِلِ
boner *n.*	غَلْظَةٌ كَبِيرَةٌ
book jacket *n.*	لَفافَةُ الْكِتابِ
book review *n.*	اِنْتِقادٌ
boost *n.*	اِكْثارٌ
boric acid *n.*	حامِضٌ بُورِقِيٌّ
box office *n.*	صُنْدُوقُ سِينَماءَ أَوْ مَرْسَحٍ
boycott *v.*	قاطَعَ
boyscout *n.*	كَشْفِيٌّ
brass hat *n.*	ضابِطٌ عالٍ
bra(ssiere) *n.*	عَنْتَرَى
bridgehead *n.*	رَأْسُ الْجِسْرِ
broadcast *n.*	اِذاعَةٌ
broadcast *v.*	أَذاعَ
broker *n.*	سِمْسارٌ

brokerage n.	سَمْسَرَةٌ	camouflage v.	أَخْفَى
bronchitis n.	نَزْلَةٌ صَدْرِيَّةٌ	can opener n.	فَتَّاحَةٌ
budget n. (pol.)	مُقَرَّرُ الْمِيزَانِيَّة	canopy n.	مِظَلَّةٌ
		capitalism n.	رَأْسَمَالِيَّةٌ
buffer state n.	دَوْلَةٌ مُتَوَسِّطَةٌ وَمُتَحَايِدَةٌ	capitalist n.	رَأْسَمَالِيٌّ
bulldozer n.	آلَةٌ لِبِنَاءِ الطُّرُق	cardiac a.	قَلْبِيٌّ
bungalow n.	دَارٌ خَارِجَ الْمَدِينَة	cardiogram n.	رَسْمٌ قَلْبِيٌّ
bunker n.	مَلْجَأٌ عَسْكَرِيٌّ	carfare n.	ثَمَنُ التَّذْكِرَة
bureaucracy n.	نَسَقٌ مُوَظَّفِيٌّ	cartoon n.	صُورَةٌ هَزْلِيَّةٌ
bus n.	حَافِلَةٌ	cash register n.	صُنْدُوقٌ مُسَجِّلٌ
cablegram n.	بَرْقِيَّةٌ	catalogue n.	قَائِمَةٌ
caesarian section n.	عَمَلِيَّةٌ قَيْصَرِيَّةٌ	ceiling price n.	مُعْظَمُ الثَّمَن
calculating machine n.	آلَةٌ حَاسِبَةٌ	certificate of origin n.	تَذْكِرَةُ الْأَصْل
calorie n.	حَرَارِيَّةٌ	chain reaction n.	رَدُّ الْفِعْل الْمُسَلْسَل
camera n.	آلَةُ التَّصْوِير		

chauffeur *n.*	سَائِقٌ
checkroom *n.*	غُرْفَةٌ لِحِفْظِ الثِّيَابِ
checkup *n.* (med.)	فَحْصٌ
chiropodist *n.*	إِخْتِصَاصِيٌّ لِمُعَالَجَةِ الأَقْدَامِ
class-conscious *a.*	مُدْرِكٌ طَبَقَتَهُ
classified ad *n.*	إِعْلَانٌ مُبَوَّبٌ
class struggle *n.*	حَرْبُ الطَّبَقَاتِ
coalition *n.*	تَحَالُفٌ
codefendant *n.*	شَرِيكُ الْمُدَّعَى عَلَيْهِ
coed *n.*	تِلْمِيذَةٌ
coefficient *n.*	مُعَدَّلٌ
cold war *n.*	اَلْحَرْبُ الْبَرِيدَةُ
cold wave *n.*	دَوْرَةُ الْبَرْدِ
collateral *n.*	جَانِبِيٌّ

collective agreement *n.*	مُعَاهَدَةٌ جَمَاعِيَّةٌ
collective security *n.*	الأَمْنُ الْمُشْتَرَكُ
commander-in-chief *n.*	قَائِدٌ عَامٌ
commentator *n.*	مُفَسِّرُ الأَخْبَارِ
commercial college *n.*	مَدْرَسَةٌ تِجَارِيَّةٌ
commissar *n.*	مُعْتَمَدٌ شِيُوعِيٌّ
communism *n.*	شِيُوعِيَّةٌ
communist *n.*	شِيُوعِيٌّ
compartment *n.*	شُقَّةٌ
concentration camp *n.*	مُعَسْكَرُ الْاِعْتِقَالِ,
contraceptive *n.*	مُضَادَّاتٌ لِلْحَبَلِ

co-operative n.	جَمعِيَّةٌ تَعَاونِيَّةٌ	dehydrated a.	مُجَرَّدٌ عَن المَاء
correligionist n.	شَرِيكُ الدِّين	demobilization n.	حَلُّ الجَيْشِن .
coughdrop n.	بَستِيلِيَّةٌ لِلسُّعلَة	demobilize v.	حَلُّ الجَيْش
crematory n.	مَحَلُّ إِحرَاقِ الجُثَث	democracy n.	دِيموقْرَاطِيَّةٌ
current n.	تَيَّارٌ	democrat n.	دِيموقْرَاطِى
cutthroat n.	سَفَّاح	democratic a.	دِيموقْرَاطِيٌّ
cyclotron n.	سِيكلو تُرُون	depth charge n.	قَنْبَلَةٌ مُضَادَّةٌ لِلغَوَّاصَات
darkroom n.	حُجرَةٌ مُظلِمَةٌ لَتوضِيح تَصَاوِير	derrick n.	مِرْفَعَةٌ
deadline n.	مِيعَادٌ آخِرٌ	detective story n.	رِوَايَةٌ بُولِيسِيَّةٌ
death rate n.	نِسبَةُ المَوت	detergent n.	مُطَهِّرٌ
decode v.	قَرَأَ مَكتُوباً شِفرِيّاً	devaluation n.	تَنزِيلٌ نَقدِيٌّ
deep freeze n.	بَرَّادَةٌ شَدِيدَةٌ	develop v.	تَطَوَّرَ
defrost v.	أَذَابَ الجَلِيدَ فِى خِزَانَة الثَّلج	diabetes n.	مَرَضُ البَول السُّكَّرِيّ
		diagnose v.	شَخَّصَ مَرَضاً
		diagnosis n.	تَشخِيصُ مَرَض

diagnostician *n*.	طَبِيب تَشْخِيصِيّ
dialectic *a*.	مَنْطِقِيّ
diathermy *n*.	عِلَاج كَهْرَبَائِيّ
dictaphone *n*.	آلَة اسْتِكْتَابِيَّة
dictatorship *n*.	اِسْتِبْدَاد
differential calculus *n*.	حِسَاب التَّفَاضُل
dining car *n*.	عَرَبَة الْأَكْل
directory *n*.	دَلِيل.
disarmament *n*.	نَزْع السِّلَاح
disinfectant *n*.	مُعَقِّم
dive bomber *n*.	طَائِرَة الِانْقِضَاض
dividend *n*. (profit share)	حِصَّة فِي الرِّبْح
doublecross *v*.	خَانَ
double talk *n*.	كَلَام ذِى لِسَانَيْن
doughboy *n*.	عَسْكَرِيّ أَمِيرِكِيّ
driveway *n*.	مَدْخَل لِلسَّيَّارَات
druggist *n*.	عَطَّار
drugstore *n*.	دُكَّان الْعَطَّارَة
duty-free *a*.	خَالِص مِنَ الْكُمْرُوك
earmark *v*.	خَصَّصَ
earphone *n*.	سَمَّاعَة
editor *n*.	مُحَرِّر
editorial *n*.	اِفْتِتَاحِيَّة
efficiency *n*.	اِقْتِدَار
electrician *n*.	كَهْرَبَائِيّ
electrification *n*.	كَهْرَبَة
electrocute *v*.	قَتَلَ بِالْكَهْرَبَاء
electrocution *n*.	قَتْل بِالْكَهْرَبَاء
electrode *n*.	عَمُود كَهْرَبَائِيّ

electromagnet *n.* مِغْنَطِيسٌ كَهْرَبَائِيُّ	eraser *n.* مِمْحَاةٌ
electron *n.* كَهْرَبٌ	escalator *n.* سُلَّمٌ مُتَحَرِّكٌ
electronic *a.* كَهَارِبِيٌّ	executive *n.* مُنَفِّذٌ
electronics *n.* عِلْمُ الْكَهَارِبِ	extremist *n.* مُتَطَرِّفٌ
	fascism *n.* فَاشِيَّةٌ
elementary school *n.* مَدْرَسَةٌ أَوَّلِيَّةٌ	fascist *n.* فَاشِيٌّ
elevated railway *n.* سِكَّةُ الْحَدِيدِ الْمُرْتَفِعَةُ	fertilizer *n.* سَمَادٌ
	feudalism *n.* إِقْطَاعِيَّةٌ
elevator *n.* مِصْعَدَةٌ	fighter bomber *n.* طَائِرَةُ الْقِتَالِ الْقَذَّافَةُ
emergency exit *n.* مَخْرَجٌ عِنْدَ الضَّرُورَةِ	figurehead *n.* رَئِيسٌ بِالإِسْمِ
emotions *n.* حِسِّيَاتٌ	filing cabinet *n.* خِزَانَةُ الْمِلَفَّاتِ
employment agency *n.* مَكْتَبُ التَّخْدِيمِ	fingerprint *n.* طَابِعُ الأَصَابِعِ
	fingerprint *v.* أَخَذَ طَابِعَ الأَصَابِعِ
encyclopedia *n.* دَائِرَةُ الْمَعَارِفِ	fire department *n.* إِطْفَائِيَّةٌ
endocrine gland *n.* غُدَّةٌ صَمَّاءُ	fire escape *n.* سُلَّمُ النَّجَاةِ
enemy alien *n.* أَجْنَبِيٌّ عُدَائِيٌّ	

fire extinguisher n.	مِطْفَأَة	garbage can n.	صُنْدُوقُ الْقُمَامَة
fire power n.	قُوَّةُ النَّار	gas attack n.	هُجُومٌ بِالْغَاز
firing squad n.	فِرْقَةُ الْإِعْدَام	gasoline n.	بِنْزِين
first aid n.	إِسْعَاف	gas station n.	مَحَلُّ الْبِنْزِين
fission n.	شَقّ	general delivery n.	يَطْلُبُ مِنَ الْبُوسْطَة
fissionable a.	مَا يَقْدِرْ أَنْ يَشَقَّ		
flame thrower n.	رَامِى اللَّهِيب	general staff n.	هَيْئَةُ أَرْكَانِ الْحَرْب
		generator n.	مُوَلِّد
flirt n.	مُغَازَلَة	gentile n.	غَيْرُ الْيَهُودِيّ
flirt v.	غَازَل		
floodlight n.	نُورٌ كَشَّاف	glamour girl n.	جَارِيَةٌ جَاذِبَةٌ
fluorescent a.	فُلُورِى	glider n.	طَائِرَةٌ شِرَاعِيَّةٌ
forced landing n.	نُزُولٌ مَجْبُور	golf n.	كُلَف
fountain pen n.	قَلَمُ الْحِبْر	grippe n.	نَزْلَةٌ وَافِدَةٌ
frankfurter n.	مَقَانِقُ صَغِيرٌ	ground floor n.	الطَّبَقَةُ السُّفْلَى
		hack a.	رَثّ
freshman n.	طَالِبُ السَّنَةِ الْأُولَى	handout n.	هَدِيَّةٌ

hangar *n*.	وَكْرٌ	high frequency *n*.	تَوَاتُرٌ عَالٍ
hanger *n*.	عَلَّاقٌ	highlight *n*.	اَلتَّقَطَةُ الْهُمَى
hangover *n*.	غَشَيَانٌ بَعْدَ الشُّرْبِ	high pressure *n*. high tension *n*.	ضَغْطٌ عَالٍ
hay fever *n*.	نَزْلَةٌ يُسَبِّبُهَا نَوْعُ عُشْبٍ	highway *n*.	طَرِيقٌ عَامٌّ
headline *n*.	تَرْوِيسَةٌ	hike *n*.	جَوْلَةٌ
health insurance *n*.	تَأْمِينٌ ضِدَّ الْأَمْرَاضِ	holding company *n*.	شِرْكَةُ الشِّرْكَاتِ
heater *n*.	آلَةُ التَّسْخِينِ	holdup *n*.	نَهْبٌ
heating *n*.	تَسْخِينٌ	honeydew melon *n*.	بَطِّيخٌ أَصْفَرُ
heatwave *n*.	دَوْرَةُ الْحَرَارَةِ	hoodlum *n*.	وَغْدٌ
heavyweight *n*.	وَزْنٌ ثَقِيلٌ	hookup *n*.	تَوْصِيلٌ مُتَكَاثِرٌ
heckler *n*.	مُقَاطِعُ الْكَلَامِ	hormone *n*.	هُورْمُونٌ
helicopter *n*.	طَائِرَةٌ عَمُودِيَّةٌ	horoscope *n*.	طَالِعٌ فِي التَّنْجِيمِ
hemorrhage *n*.	نَزِيفٌ	horsepower *n*.	قُوَّةُ حِصَانٍ
highball *n*.	وِيسْكِى	hot dog *n*.	مَقَانِقُ مَقْلِيٌّ

housewarming *n.*	عيدُ ٱلْإِنْتقال إلى بَيْت جَديد
hush money *n.*	رِشْوَةٌ
hydrant *n.*	حنفيّةٌ فى شارعٍ للإطفائيّة
hydraulic *a.*	مائىّ
hydroelectric *a.*	عن ٱلْكَهْرَباءِ ٱلْمَائيّة
hydrogen *n.*	هيدرُوجين
hydroplane *n.*	طائرةٌ بحريّةٌ
hygiene *n.*	علْم الصّحّة
hypertrophy *n.*	زيادَةٌ مفْرطَةٌ
hypnosis *n.*	تنْويم
hypodermic *a.*	تحْت ٱلْأَديم

hysteria *n.*	هسْتيريا
icebox *n.*	خزانةُ ٱلثَّلج
ice breaker *n.*	حاطمةُ ٱلجَليد
identification *n.*	تذْكرةُ إنْبَات ٱلشّخْصيّة
ideology *n.*	نسَقُ ٱلْأَفْكار
ignition *n.*	إلْهابُ
incinerator *n.*	آلةٌ لحَرْق ٱلفَضَلات
Inc. *a.*	شركةٌ مسَجّلةٌ
incubator *n.*	آلةُ ٱلتّفْريخ
industrial *a.*	صناعى
industrialize *v.*	جهّز بصنائغ
infantile paralysis *n.*	ٱلشَّلَل ٱلطّفْلىّ

إِحْسَاس		interior decorator n.	مُزَخْرِف
inferiority complex n.		internee n.	أَسِير
اَلْإِنْحِطَاط		iodine n.	يُود
infiltrate v.	إِسْتَرَقَ إِلَى	IOU n.	سَنَد
inflation n.	تَضَخُّم نَقْدِيّ	I.Q. n.	دَرَجَةُ الْعَقْل
infrared a.	دُونَ الْأَحْمَر	iron curtain n.	اَلسِّتَارُ الْحَدِيدِيّ
initiative n.	حَافِز	isolationism n.	عُزْلَة سِيَاسِيَّة
injection n.	حُقْنَة	isolationist n.	تَابِع الْعُزْلَة السِّيَاسِيَّة
in-laws n.	أَلْحَمَوَان	jackpot n.	اَلْفَوْزُ الْأَكْبَرُ فِى الْمُقَامَرَة
insecticide n.	مُضَادَّات حَشَرِيَّة	jalopy n.	سَيَّارَة رَثَّة
installment plan n.	تَدْبِير نَجْمِى	jaywalk v.	مَشَى عَلَى غَفْلَة
insulator n.	عَازِل	jazz n.	جَزّ
insulin n.	إِبْنْسُولِين	jeep n.	سَيَّارَة «جِيب»
شُرْكَة		jet plane n.	طَائِرَة نَفَّاثَة
insurance company n.		jet propulsion n.	اَلتَّسْيِيرُ النَّفَّاثِى
اَلتَّأْمِين			
intake n.	مَدْخَل		

jig saw puzzle n.	لُغْزُ قُطَعٍ كَثِيرَةٍ
jurisdiction n.	إِخْتِصَاصٌ
juror n.	مُحَلَّفٌ
juvenile a.	صِبْيَانِيٌّ
kerosene n.	نَفْطٌ
kindergarten n.	رَوْضَةُ الْأَطْفَالِ
know-how n.	مَعْرِفَةٌ وَاخْتِبَارٌ
labor market n.	سُوقُ الْعَمَلِ
landslide n.	إِنْهِيَالُ الْأَرْضِ
layer cake n.	نَوْعُ كَعْكٍ
layette n.	ثِيَابٌ لِطِفْلٍ وَلِيدٍ
lay-off n.	رَفْتٌ
layout n.	تَرْتِيبٌ
League of Nations n.	عُصْبَةُ الْأُمَمِ
leftover n.	بَقَايَا

lending library n.	مَكْتَبَةٌ إِعَارِيَّةٌ
lens n.	عَدَسَةٌ
liability insurence n.	تَأْمِينٌ عَلَى الْمَسُوولِيَّةِ
life expectancy n.	إِنْتِظَارُ الْحَيَاةِ
life insurance n.	تَأْمِينٌ عَلَى الْحَيَاةِ
lighter n.	قَدَّاحٌ
lipstick n.	مَرُودٌ
living wage n.	أَجْرُ كَافٍ
loudspeaker n.	حَاكٍ
lubricating oil n.	زَيْتُ تَشْحِيمٍ
mailbox n.	صُنْدُوقٌ لِلْمَكَاتِيبِ
make-up n.	زِينَةُ الْوَجْهِ
maneuver n.	مُنَاوَرَةٌ
manicure n.	تَنْظِيفُ الْأَظْفَارِ

markdown n.	تَنْزِيلُ الثَّمَنِ	moderator n.	مُرَتَّب
mechanized n.	مِيكَانِى	motion picture n.	صُورَةٌ مُتَحَرِّكَةٌ
meningitis n.	أَلْإِلْتِهَابُ السَّحَائِى	motorbike n.	عَجَلَةٌ نَارِيَّةٌ
menu n.	قَائِمَةُ الطَّعَامِ	motorboat n.	قَارِبٌ نَارِى
	أَلْبَحْرِيَّةُ	motorcade n.	مَوْكِبُ سَيَّارَاتٍ
merchant marine n.	التِّجَارِيَّةُ	motorist n.	سَائِقُ سَيَّارَةٍ
	إِبْدَالُ الْمَوَادِّ فِى	motor plough n.	مِحْرَاثٌ آلِى
metabolism n.	الْجِسْمِ	motor truck n.	سَيَّارَةُ النَّقْلِ
microfilm n.	مِيكْرُوفِلْم	museum n.	مُتْحَف
microphone n.	مِصْوَات	narcosis n.	تَنْوِيم
microscope n.	مِجْهَر	Nazi n.	نَازِى
military police n.	أَلشُّرْطَةُ الْعَسْكَرِيَّةُ	neon light n.	ضَوْءٌ نِيُونِى
		network n.	شَبَكَةٌ
mine sweeper n.	لَاقِطَةُ الْأَلْغَام	neuralgia n.	نِيُورَالْجِيَّةٌ
minimum wage n.	أَلْأَجْرُ الْأَصْغَرُ	newscast n.	إِذَاعَةُ الْأَخْبَارِ
mixup n.	إِرْتِبَاك	newsreel n.	جَرِيدَةٌ نَاطِقَةٌ

newsstand *n.*	دُكّانُ جَرَائِدَ	parachute *n.*	مِظَلَّةٌ وَاقِيَةٌ
nonaggression pact *n.*	مُعَاهَدَةُ عَدَمِ الِإعْتِدَاء	parachutist *n.*	جُنْدِيُّ الْمِظَلَّةِ
		paralysis *n.*	فَالِجٌ
notarize *v.*	شَهِدَ قَانُونِيًّا	paranoia *n.*	جُنُونٌ
nuclear physics *n.*	عِلْمُ الذَّرَّاتِ	paratrooper *n.*	جُنْدِيُّ الْمِظَلَّةِ
nudism *n.*	عُرْيَانِيَّةٌ	parking lot *n.*	مَوْقِفٌ
nursery school *n.*	رَوْضَةُ الْأَطْفَالِ	patent *n.*	إِجَازَةُ الْحَصْرِ
nutritionist *n.*	إِخْتِصَاصِيٌّ بِالْغِذَاء	patrolman *n.*	شُرْطِيٌّ
nylon *n.*	نَيْلُونٌ	pediatrician *n.*	طَبِيبُ أَمْرَاضِ الْأَطْفَالِ
obstetrician *n.*	طَبِيبٌ مُوَلِّدٌ		
off limits *n.*	مُحَرَّمٌ عَلَى الْعَسَاكِرِ	pediatrics *n.*	أَلطِّبُّ الطِّفْلِيُّ
overpass *n.*	مَعْبَرٌ	pedicure *n.*	تَنْظِيفُ أَظْفَارِ الْأَرْجُلِ
pajamas *n. pl.*	بِيجَامَا	penicillin *n.*	بِنِيسِلِّين
pancake *n.*	كَعْكَةُ طَاجِنٍ	percolator *n.*	مِصْفَاةُ الْقَهْوَةِ
panel discussion *n.*	مُبَاحَثَةٌ عُمُومِيَّةٌ	periscope *n.*	مِنْظَرُ الْغَوَّاصَةِ

permanent wave n.	تَمْوِيجٌ	pinup (girl) n.	تَصْوِيرَةٌ جَارِيَةٍ الْمُعَلَّقَةُ بِالْجِدَارِ
petty officer n.	ضَابِطُ الصَّفِّ		
phone n.	تِلِيفُونٌ	plainclothes man n.	مُخْبِرٌ شُرْطِيٌّ
phonograph n.	حَاكٍ	plebiscite n.	إِسْتِفْتَاءُ الشَّعْبِ
phony a., n.	كَاذِبٌ	plutonium n.	بلُوتُونِيُومٌ
photostat n.	نُسْخَةٌ فُوتُوغْرَافِيَّةٌ	pneumatic a.	هَوَائِيٌّ
physics n.	عِلْمُ الطَّبِيعَةِ	poison ivy n.	السُّمَّاقُ السَّامُّ
physiognomy n.	سَحْنَةٌ	polio(myelitis) n.	الشَّلَلُ الطِّفْلِيُّ
physiology n.	عِلْمُ وَظَائِفِ الْأَعْضَاءِ	pornography n.	تَأْلِيفٌ فَحَّاشٌ
picket n.	صَفُّ مُضْرِبِينَ	potential a.	مُمْكِنٌ
picnic n.	أَكْلٌ فِي الْعَرَاءِ	potential n.	إِمْكَانِيَّةٌ
piecework n.	الْعَمَلُ بِالْقِطَعِ	pressure cooker n.	طَنْجَرَةٌ ذَاتُ بُخَارٍ مَضْغُوطٍ
pigment n.	صِبَاغٌ	price-cutting n.	تَنْزِيلُ الْأَثْمَانِ بِالتَّزَاحُمِ
pinch-hit n.	بَدَلٌ		

professional a.	مُحْتَرِف	quinine n.	كِينَا
profiteer n.	رَابِح	racket n.	شَرِكَةُ مُذْنِبِين
propaganda n.	دَعَاوَة	racketeer n.	جَانٍ
propeller n.	مِرْوَحَة	radar n.	رَادَار
protein n.	بْرُوتِئِين	radiator n.	آلَةٌ مُسَخِّنَة
pseudonym n.	إِسْم مُسْتَعَار	radio n.	لَاسِلْكِيّ
psychiatry n.	أَلطِّبُّ النَّفْسَانِي	turn on the radio	فَتَحَ
psychoanalysis n.	تَحْلِيل نَفْسِي	turn off the radio	قَطَعَ
psychopath n.	مَرِيض نَفْسِي	radio v.	أَذَاعَ
public prosecutor n.	نَائِب عَام	radioactive a.	ذُو رَادِيُوم فَاعِل
pullover n.	سُتْرَةٌ صُوفِيَّة	radio broadcast n.	إِذَاعَة لَاسِلْكِيَّة
pulp magazine n.	مَجَلَّة رَائِجَة	radio frequency n.	تَوَاتُر لَاسِلْكِي
pursuit plane n.	طَائِرَةُ الْمُطَارَدَة	radiogram n.	رِسَالَة لَاسِلْكِيَّة
quantum theory n.	نَظَرِيَّةُ الْكَمّ	radio network n.	شَبَكَة لَاسِلْكِيَّة
questionnaire n.	وَرَقَةُ سُؤَالَات	radio station n.	مَحَطَّة لَاسِلْكِيَّة
		radio transmitter n.	مُرْسِلَة

radium *n.*	رَادِيُومٌ
rate of exchange *n.*	سِعْرُ الصَّرْفِ
rationalize *v.*	وَجَدَ سَبَبًا فِى الذِّهْنِ
rationing *n.*	حَصْرُ التَّمْوِينِ
rear light *n.*	ضَوْءٌ خَلْفِىٌّ
rebroadcast *n.*	إِعَادَةُ إِذَاعَةٍ
receiver *n.*	قَابِلٌ
(in bankruptcy)	مُسْتَقْبِلُ أَمْوَالِ الْإِفْلَاسِ؛
(tel.)	سَمَّاعَةٌ؛
(radio)	مُسْتَقْبِلٌ
receptionist *n.*	مُسْتَخْدِمَةُ الْإِسْتِقْبَالِ
reconnaissance *n.* (mil.)	إِسْتِكْشَافٌ
record *n.* (phonograph)	أُسْطُوَانَةٌ
record changer *n.*	مُبْدِلُ الْاِسْطُوَانَاتِ

red tape *n.*	إِجْرَاءَاتٌ عَقِيمَةٌ
reference book *n.*	كِتَابُ الْمَرْجِعِ
refrigerator *n.*	خِزَانَةُ الثَّلْجِ
refugee *n.*	مُلْتَجِئٌ
refund *n.*	رَدُّ النُّقُودِ
refund *v.*	رَدَّ
registration *n.*	تَسْجِيلٌ
relativity *n.*	نِسْبِيَّةٌ
rental library *n.*	مَكْتَبَةٌ إِعَارِيَّةٌ
reorganization *n.*	إِعَادَةُ التَّنْظِيمِ
reporter *n.*	مُخْبِرُ جَرِيدَةٍ
rest room *n.*	مُسْتَرَاحٌ
retroactive *a.*	فَاعِلٌ إِلَى الْمَاضِى
reviewer *n.*	نَقَّادٌ
revolutionize *v.*	قَلَّبَ

revolver *n.*	مُسَدَّس
revue *n.*	إِسْتِعْرَاض
rheumatism *n.*	رَثْيَة
ringleader *n.*	زَعِيم
rocket *n.*	صَارُوخ
roller skate *n.*	مَزْلَقَان ذَوَا عَجَلَاتٍ
rolling mill *n.*	آلَةُ التَّصْفِيح
roundtrip *n.*	جَوْلَةٌ وَعَوْدَة
saccharine *n.*	سَكَّارِين
safety belt *n.*	حِزَامُ الْأَمْن
safety pin *n.*	دَبُّوس إِنْكِلِيزِي
sanitarium *n.*	مَصَحّ
satellite country *n.*	بِلَادٌ مُتَوَقِّفَة
saxophone *n.*	سَكْسُوفْرن
scholarship *n.* (grant)	مَنْحُ نَفَقَةٍ لِتِلْمِيذ

Scotch tape *n.*	شَرِيطٌ غِرَائِي
scrapbook *n.*	كَشْكُول
screen actor *n.*	مُمَثِّل سِينِمَائِي
searchlight *n.*	نُورٌ كَاشِف
secret service *n.*	الْخِدْمَةُ السِّرِّيَّة
semifinal *n.*	مُبَارَاةُ نِصْف نِهَائِي
semimonthly *a.*	نِصْف شَهْرِي
semimonthly *n.*	مَجَلَّةُ نِصْف شَهْرِيَّة
serialization *n.*	نَشْرٌ بِتَسَلْسُل
serialize *v.*	نَشَرَ بِتَسَلْسُل
serviceman *n.*	عَسْكَرِي
sewing machine *n.*	آلَةُ الْخِيَاطَة
sex appeal *n.*	جَذْبٌ جِنْسِي
shack *n.*	كُوخ
shipping room *n.*	غُرْفَةُ الشَّحْن

shock troops *n. pl.*	عَسَاكِرُ الْهِجُوم
short-change *v.* (cheat)	غَبَنَ
short circuit *n.*	دَائِرَة قَصِيرَة
shorthand *n.*	تَدْمِيج
short wave *n.*	مَوْج قَصِير
shower bath *n.*	مِنْضَح
sibling *n.*	طِفْل
side dish *n.*	طَعَام جَانِبِى
side line *n.*	شُغْل جَانِبِى
sightseeing *n.*	تَفَرُّج
signatory powers *n. pl.*	الدُّوَل الْمُوَقِّعَة
signpost *n.*	نَصَبَة
silkscreen *n.*	حِجَاب حَرِيرِى
skyscraper *n.*	نَاطِحَةُ السَّحَاب

skywriting *n.*	كِتَابَة عَلَى السَّمَاء
slacks *n. pl.*	جِنْس بِنْطَلُون
slick magazine *n.*	مَجَلَّة ظَرِيفَة
slot machine *n.*	آلَةُ لَعِبِ الْقِمَار
small change *n.*	فُرَاطَة
snapshot *n.*	صُورَة حَالِيَّة
soccer *n.*	لَعِبُ كُرَةِ الْقَدَم
socialism *n.*	إِشْتِرَاكِيَّة
socialist *n*, socialist(ic) *a.*	إِشْتِرَاكِى
socialized medicine *n.*	الطِّبّ الْمُشْتَرَك
sociology *n.*	عِلْم الْإِجْتِمَاع
social security *n.*	تَأْمِين اجْتِمَاعِى
social service *n.*, social work *n.*	خِدْمَة اجْتِمَاعِيَّة
soda fountain (counter) *n.*	مَائِدَةُ الْأَشْرِبَة

sophisticated a.	أَدِيبٌ	sport n.	رِيَاضَةٌ
soundtrack n.	شَرِيطٌ نَاطِقٌ	spotter n.	مُرَاقِبٌ
Soviet Union n.	إِتِّحَادُ السُّوفْيِت	spring n. (techn.)	لَوْلَبٌ
space ship n.	سَفِينَةٌ فَضَائِيَّةٌ	standardization n.	تَسْوِيَةٌ بِمِقْيَاسٍ أَحَدٍ
space travel n.	سَفَرٌ فِي الفَضَاءِ		
spank v.	ضَرَبَ طِفْلًا	standardize v.	سَوَّى بِمِقْيَاسٍ أَحَدٍ
spark plug n.	شَمْعَةُ الشَّرَارَةِ	standard of living n.	مُسْتَوَى الحَيَاةِ
spastic a.	تَشَنُّجِيٌّ	standing room n.	فُسْحَةُ الوَاقِفِينَ
special delivery n.	تَوْزِيعٌ مُسْتَعْجِلٌ	stateroom n.	قَمَرَةُ الدَّرَجَةِ الأُولَى
specialist n.	إِخْتِصَاصِيٌّ	statistician n.	إِحْصَائِيٌّ
spectroscope n.	مِطْيَافٌ	statistics n.	إِحْصَائِيَّةٌ
sponsor n.	كَفِيلٌ	steam shovel n.	مِجْرَافٌ بُخَارِيٌّ
sponsor v.	كَفَلَ	stenographer n.	مُدَمِّجٌ
spool n.	مِكَبٌّ	stenography n.	تَدْمِيجٌ
sporadic a.	مُتَفَرِّقٌ	sterilization n.	تَعْقِيمٌ

stickup n.	لُصوصيّة
stockbroker n.	سِمسارُ الأسهُم
stock market n.	سوقُ الأسهُم
storage n.	تخزين
streetwalker n.	عاهِرة
stretcher n.	مِحفَّة
strikebreaker n.	كاسِرُ الإضْراب
studio n.	مُحتَرَف
stuffed shirt n. (fig.)	رَجُل مُتكبِّر
subconscions n.	ألعقل الباطِن
subcontract n.	عَقد فَرعي
subcontractor n.	مُقاوِل فَرعي
submarine n.	غَوّاصة
subsidiary n. (fin.)	شرِكة مُساعِدة
subsidize v.	قدَّم إعانةً

subsidy n.	إعانة
substandard a.	تحت المِقياس
subtenant n.	مُكتَرٍ ثانٍ
subversive a.	ثوروي
subway n.	سِكّة تحت الأرض
suitcase n.	حقيبة
sunlamp n.	مِصباح ضَوءٍ فَوقَ البنفسجي
supreme commander n.	ألقائدُ العامُّ
suspender n.	رِبطة السّاق
suspension bridge n.	جِسر مُعلَّق
switchboard n.	مَركَز التّليفون
swivel chair n.	كُرسي دائر
syndicate n.	نَقابة

synopsis *n.*	تَلْخِيص
tabloid *n.*	جَرِيدَة صَغِيرَة الْحَجْم
tail spin *n.*	شَقْلَبَة طَائِرَة
tail wind *n.*	رِيح وَرَائِيَّة
take-off *n.* (av.)	صُعُود
take off *v.* (av.)	صَعِدَ
talcum powder *n.*	ذَرِيرَة طَلْقِيَّة
tank *n.* (mil.)	دَبَّابَة
tank destroyer *n.*	مِدْفَع مُضَادّ لِلدَّبَّابَات
task force *n.*	قُوَّة عِرَاك
tax-exempt *a.*	مُعَافًى مِنَ الْمُكُوس
taxicab *n.*	سَيَّارَة الْأُجْرَة
taxpayer *n.*	دَافِع الضَّرَائِب
tear bomb *n.*	قُنْبُلَة دَمْعِيَّة

technology *n.*	هَنْدَسَة
telecast *n.*	إِذَاعَة تَلْفَزِيَّة
telecast *v.*	أَذَاعَ بِالتَّلْفَزَة
telepathy *n.*	تَبَادُل الْخَوَاطِر
telephone receiver *n.*	سَمَّاعَة
televise *v.*	تَلْفَزَ
television *n.*	تَلْفَرَة
tenement house *n.*	مَنْزِل
terrorism *n.*	إِرْهَاب
terrorist *n.*	إِرْهَابِي
terrorize *v.*	أَرْهَبَ
therapy *n.*	طَرِيقَة الشِّفَاء
thyroid gland *n.*	غُدَّة دَرَقِيَّة
tideland *n.*	الْبَرّ الَّذِي يَغْطُوه مَدّ الْبَحْر
time exposure *n.*	تَصْوِير وَقْتِي

time table n.	مَوَاقِيتُ	trade mark n.	عَلَامَةٌ تِجَارِيَّةٌ
tip-off n.	إِشَارَةٌ	trade union n.	نِقَابَةُ الْعُمَّالِ
toaster n.	مُقَمِّرٌ كَهْرَبَائِيٌّ	traffic jam n.	إِرْتِبَاكُ الْحَرَكَةِ
tonsilectomy n.	جَذْمُ اللَّوْزَتَيْنِ	traffic light n.	سِرَاجُ الْحَرَكَةِ
toothpaste n.	مَعْجُونُ الْأَسْنَانِ	trainee n.	مُدَرَّبٌ
topnotch a.	فَائِقٌ	travelers' check n.	حَوَالَةٌ سَفَرِيَّةٌ
top-secret a.	سِرِّيٌّ جِدًّا	trial balloon n.	تَجْرِيبٌ
		trolley car n.	تَرَامٌ
topsoil n.	طَبَقَةُ التُّرْبَةِ الْفَوْقَانِيَّةُ	trouble-shooter n.	مُسَهِّلُ الْمَصَاعِبِ
torpedo n.	حَرَّاقَةٌ	trustee n.	أَمِينٌ
torpedoboat n.	نَسَّافَةٌ	tuberculosis n.	تَدَرُّنٌ
totalitarianism n.	اَلْحُكْمُ الْمُطْلَقُ	tugboat n.	رَقَّاسٌ
touch-and-go a. [risky]	خَطِرٌ	turnstile n.	بَابٌ دَوَّارٌ
tourist class n.	اَلدَّرَجَةُ الثَّالِثَةُ فِي سَفِينَةٍ	tycoon n.	ذُو نُفُوذٍ كَثِيرٍ
		typescript n.	مَكْتُوبٌ بِآلَةِ الْكِتَابَةِ
track meet n.	سِبَاقٌ	typesetting n.	اَلْحُرُوفُ الْمَجْمُوعَةُ

typewriter *n.*	آلَةُ الكِتَابَةِ	vacuum cleaner *n.*	مِنْفَضَةٌ
typewriting *n.*	كِتَابَةٌ بِالآلَةِ	vegetarian *n.*	نَبَاتِى
underdeveloped *a.*	بِدُونَ تَطَوُّرٍ كَافٍ	vending machine *n.*	آلَةُ البَيعِ
underdog *n.*	مُضْطَرٌ	venereal disease *n.*	مَرَضٌ سِرِّى
underground *n.* (polit.)	حَرَكَةٌ سِيَاسِيَّةٌ	ventilator *n.*	مِهْوَاةٌ
	سِرِّيَّةٌ	visual aid *n.*	مِعْوَانٌ نَظَرِى
underprivileged *a.*	مِسْكِين	visualize *v.*	تَصَوَّرَ
unemployment *n.*	تَعَطُّل	vocational school *n.*	مَدْرَسَةُ الصَّنَائِعِ
union *n.* (labor)	نِقَابَة		
unionize *v.*	نَظَّمَ نِقَابَةً	wage earner *n.*	كَاسِبٌ
upkeep *n.*	حِفْظ	waiting room *n.*	غُرْفَةُ الإنْتِظَارِ
utopian *a.*	خِيَالِى	walkout *n.*	إِضْرَابٌ
vacationist *n.*	مُفْرِص	walkover *n.*	نَصْرٌ سَهْلٌ
vaccinate *v.*	لَقَّحَ	want ad *n.*	إِعْلاَنُ الطَّلَبِ
vaccination *n.*	تَلْقِيح	warmonger *n.*	مُحَرِّضٌ لِلْحَرْبِ

washed-up a.	مُضْنًى	wisecrack n.	نُكْتَة
washing machine n.	آلَةُ الْغَسْل	wisecrack v.	نَكَّتَ
washout n. (sl.) [failure]	فَشَل	wristwatch n.	سَاعَةُ يَدٍ
water closet n.	مِرْحَاض	xenophobia n.	كَرَاهَةُ الْأَجَانِب
white-collar worker n.	عَامِلٌ بِعَقْلِه	x-ray n.	أَشِعَّةُ رِنْتِجِن أَوْ إِكْس
wholesaler n.	تَاجِرُ الْجُمْلَة	xylophone n.	آلَةٌ مُوسِيقِيَّة
wireless a.	لَاسِلْكِيٌّ	Yugoslavia n.	يُوكُوسْلَافِيَا

ARABIC–ENGLISH
AND
ENGLISH–ARABIC
DICTIONARY

JOHN WORTABET, M. D.
AND
HARVEY PORTER, Ph.D.

*With a Supplement of Modern Words
and New Meanings by*

JOHN L. MISH, Ph.D.
Chief, Oriental Division, New York Public Library

FREDERICK UNGAR PUBLISHING CO.
NEW YORK

ARABIC-ENGLISH DICTIONARY.

ا

As a numerical sign = 1.	أ
Particle of interrogation.	أ
Father.	أَبٌ مث أَبَوَانِ ج آبَاءُ
Month of August.	آبٌ
Fatherly, paternal.	أَبَوِيٌّ
Fatherhood.	أُبُوَّة
Time, eternity (future).	أَبَدُ
For ever.	أَبَدَ الآبِدِينَ
Ever; always.	أَبَدًا
Eternal.	أَبَدِيٌّ وَمُؤَبَّدٌ
Eternity, perpetuity.	أَبَدِيَّة
Needle.	إِبْرَةٌ ج إِبَرُ
Needle-case.	مِئْبَرٌ ج مَآبِرُ
Pure gold.	إِبْرِيزٌ
Diocese.	أَبْرَشِيَّة

Water-jug.	إِبْرِيقٌ ج أَبَارِيقُ
Buckle, clasp.	إِبْزِيمٌ ج أَبَازِيمُ
Arm-pit.	إِبْطٌ ج آبَاطُ
To run away.	اَبَقَ يَابِقُ
Runaway (slave).	آبِقٌ
Camels (coll noun).	إِبْلٌ
Satan.	إِبْلِيسُ ج أَبَالِسَةُ
To praise the dead.	أَبَّنَ
Time or season of a thing.	إِبَانَ
Son.	إِبْنٌ ج أَبْنَاءُ وَبَنُونَ
Daughter.	إِبْنَةٌ أَوْ بِنْتٌ ج بَنَاتُ
Ebony.	أَبَنُوسٌ
Beauty. Greatness.	أُبَّهَة
To refuse, refrain.	أَبَى يَأْبَى
Refusing, disdaining.	أَبِيٌّ

A kind of tamarisk.	أُثْلٌ
To sin.	اَثِمَ يَاثَمُ
To accuse of sin.	أَثَّمَ
Sin, crime.	إِثْمٌ ج آثَامٌ
Guilty.	أَثِيمٌ ج أَثَمَاءُ
Sin, crime.	مَأْثَمَةٌ ومَأْثَمٌ ج مَآثِمُ
To burn, blaze.	أَجَّ يَؤُجُّ أَجِيجاً
To pay; let on hire.	أَجَرَ يَأْجُرُ
To pay, let for money.	آجَرَ
To hire, take on hire.	إِسْتَأْجَرَ
Recompense.	أَجْرٌ ج اجورٌ
Wages, salary.	أُجْرَةٌ وَأَجْرَةٌ
Baked bricks.	آجُرٌّ
Lease, hire, rent.	إِيجَارٌ
Hired labourer.	أَجِيرٌ ج أُجَرَاءُ
Landlord.	مُوجِرٌ وَمُؤَاجِرٌ
Tenant.	مُسْتَأْجِرٌ
Pear (fruit).	إِجَّاصٌ وَإِنْجَاصٌ
To delay, tarry.	أَجِلَ يَأْجَلُ

Refusal, rejection.	إِبَاءٌ
She-ass.	أَتَانٌ ج أُتُنٌ وَأُتْنٌ
Oven, furnace.	أَتُونٌ ج اتُنٌ
To come, arrive.	أَتَى يَأْتِي
To give; requite.	آتَى إِيتَاءً
To happen.	تَأَتَّى
Arrival, coming.	إِتْيَانٌ
Comer, one who arrives.	آتٍ
The future; coming next.	الآتِي
To abound.	أَثَّ يَئِثُّ
Household furniture.	أَثَاثٌ
To choose.	أَثَرَ يَأْثُرُ
To impress.	أَثَّرَ فِي
To choose, prefer.	آثَرَ
To follow one's tracks	تَأَثَّرَ
Trace, impression.	أَثَرٌ ج آثَارٌ
Influence; impression.	تَأْثِيرٌ
Memorable deed.	مَأْثَرَةٌ ج مَآثِرُ
Impressive.	مُؤَثِّرٌ

To tarry, delay.	تَأَخَّرَ	To grant a delay.	أَجَّلَ
Other, another.	آخَرُ م اخْرَى	Appointed time.	الأَجَلَ
End, last.	آخِرٌ ج أَوَاخِرُ	Cause, reason, sake.	أَجْلٌ
The future life.	الآخِرَة	Postponed, future.	آجِلٌ
Last, extreme.	أَخِيرٌ ج أَخِيرُون	Thicket, jungle.	أَجَمٌ ج آجَامٌ
At the end, finally, lastly.	أَخِيرًا	To unify.	أَحَّدَ وَوَحَّدَ
Posterior part.	مُؤَخَّرٌ	To unite with ; join.	إِتَّحَدَ بِ
Brotherhood.	إِخَاءٌ وَأُخُوَّة	One.	أَحَدٌ م إِحْدَى ج آحَادٌ
Brother.	أَخٌ ج إِخْوَةٌ وَإِخْوَانٌ	Sunday.	الأَحَدُ
Sister.	أُخْتٌ ج أَخَوَاتٌ	Units.	آحَادٌ
Fraternal, brotherly.	أَخَوِيٌّ	Union ; agreement.	إِتِّحَادٌ
Stable.	أَخُورٌ	To take.	أَخَذَ يَأْخُذُ
To be educated.	أَدُبَ يَأْدُبُ	To begin, to say.	أَخَذَ يَقُولُ
To invite to a meal.	أَدَبَ يَأْدِبُ	To seize, take hold of.	أَخَذَ بِ
To discipline, chastise.	أَدَّبَ	To aid, assist.	أَخَذَ بِيَدِهِ
Become well-educated.	تَأَدَّبَ	To blame.	آخَذَ مُؤَاخَذَةً بِ أَوْ عَلَى
Liberal education.	أَدَبٌ ج آدَابٌ	To take to himself.	إِتَّخَذَ
Polite literature.	عِلْمُ الأَدَبِ	Source. Way.	مَأْخَذٌ ج مَآخِذُ
Chastisement.	تَأْدِيبٌ	To postpone.	أَخَّرَ تَأْخِيرًا

Moral. Polite.	أَدَبِيّ
Literary, learned.	أَدِيبٌ ج أُدَبَاءُ
Condiment, seasoning.	إِدَامٌ
Human skin.	أَدَمَةٌ
Dark or tawny colour.	أُدْمَةٌ
Human being.	آدَمِيّ
To give up, deliver.	أَدَّى
To bring to	أَدَّى إِلَى
Payment, discharge.	أَدَاءُ
Tool, utensil.	أَدَاةٌ ج أَدَوَاتٌ
When. Lo.	إِذْ
Behold! When.	إِذَا
Therefore.	إِذًا وَإِذَنْ
March (month).	آذَارُ
To give leave to.	أَذِنَ لِ يَأْذَنُ
To call to prayer.	أَذَّنَ
To ask permission.	إِسْتَأْذَنَ
Permission, leave.	اِذْنٌ
Ear. Handle.	اِذْنٌ وَأُذُنٌ ج آذَانٌ

The Moslem call to prayer.	أَذَانٌ
Minaret.	مِئْذَنَةٌ وَمَأْذَنَةٌ ج مَآذِنُ
One who calls to prayer.	مُؤَذِّنٌ
To injure, annoy.	آذَى إِيذَاءً
Injury, damage.	أَذًى وَأَذِيَّةٌ
Hurtful, harmful.	مُؤْذٍ
Need, want.	أَرَبٌ ج آرَابٌ
In pieces, limb by limb.	إِرْبًا إِرْبًا
Groin.	أُرْبِيَّةٌ
Purpose.	مَأْرَبَةٌ وَمَأْرَبٌ ج مَآرِبُ
Europe.	اورُبَّا
European.	أُورُبِّيّ
Inheritance. (See وَرِثَ)	إِرْثٌ
Purple (n).	أُرْجُوَانٌ
Purple (adj).	اِرْجُوَانِيّ
To date; write a history.	أَرَّخَ
Epoch, history.	تَأْرِيخٌ ج تَوَارِيخُ
Historian.	مُؤَرِّخٌ
Dated	مُؤَرَّخٌ

To be founded, built.	تَأَسَّسَ	Ardeb, (corn measure).	إِرْدَبٌّ
Foundation.	اسَاسٌ ج أُسُسٌ	Cedar or pine (tree).	أُزْزٌ
Fundamental.	اسَاسِيٌّ	Rice.	أُزٌّ وَأُرُزٌّ ورُزٌ
Founder.	مُؤَسِّسٌ	Earth, soil, land.	أَرْضٌ
Founded, established.	مُؤَسَّسٌ	Terrestrial.	أَرْضِيٌّ
Spinach, spinage.	أُسْبَانَخٌ	To be sleepless.	أَرِقَ يَأْرَقُ
Master, professor.	استَاذٌ ج أَسَاتِذَةٌ وَأَسَاتِيذُ	Wakefulness; insomnia.	أَرَقٌ
Lion.	اَسَدٌ ج اسُودٌ	Hare, rabbit	ارنبٌ ج أَرَانِبُ
To take captive.	اسَرَ يَأْسِرُ	To flow.	ازَب يَازِب ازْبًا
To submit as a captive.	إِسْتَأْسَرَ	Drain.	مِيزَابٌ ج مَيَازِيبُ
All, the whole of.	بِأَسْرِهِ	To assist, strengthen.	ازَرَ
Captivity, retention.	أَسْرٌ	A long wrapper, veil.	إِزَارٌ
Near relations.	اسرَةٌ	Succour, assistance.	مُؤَازَرَةٌ
Captive.	أَسِيرٌ ج اسَرَاءُ وَأَسْرَى	An apron.	مِئْزَرٌ ج مَآزِرُ
Stable.	إِسْطَبلٌ ج إِسْطَبلَاتٌ	Eternity.	أَزَلٌ وَأَزَلِيَّةٌ
Fleet.	أُسْطُولٌ ج اساطِيلُ	Eternal (of past time).	ازَلِيٌّ
To regret.	أَسِفَ وَتَأَسَّفَ	Distress ; draught.	أَزْمَةٌ
Sorrow, grief, regret.	أَسَفٌ	In front, opposite to.	إِزَاءَ
Oh ! Alas !	اسَفِيْ وَيَا أَسَفَا	To found.	أَسَّسَ

Sponge.	إِسْفِنْج
Harbour.	إِسْكِلَة ج أَسَاكِلُ
Name ; noun.	إِسْم ج أَسْمَاء
To be grieved.	أَسِيَ يَأْسَى
Grief, sorrow.	اسًى وَأَسَاً
To be firmly rooted.	أَصَلَ يَأْصُلُ
To be firmly rooted.	تَأَصَّلَ
To extirpate.	إِسْتَأْصَلَ
Root ; principle.	أَصْلٌ ج أُصُولٌ
Radical, original.	أَصْلِيّ
Noble ; judicious.	أَصِيلٌ
Evening.	الْأَصِيل
Franks.	إِفْرَنْج وَإِفْرَنْجَة
A European.	إِفْرَنْجِيّ
Horizon ; region.	أُفُقٌ ج آفَاقٌ
To tell a lie.	أَفَكَ يَأْفِكُ
A lie.	إِفْكٌ وَإِفْكَة
To disappear, set.	أَفَلَ يَأْفُلُ
Opium.	أَفْيُونٌ

Camomile.	أَقْحُوَانٌ
Oke.	اقة ج اقَقُ وَاقَاتٌ
To assure.	أَكَّدَ
To be assured.	تَأَكَّدَ
Firm ; certain.	أَكِيدٌ
Assurance, certitude,	تَأْكِيدٌ
To eat.	أَكَلَ يَأْكُلُ
A morsel, mouthful.	ا كْلَة
Corroding ulcer.	آ كِلَةٌ وَأَ كَلَة
Glutton.	أَكِيلٌ وَأَ كُولٌ
Food.	مَأْكَلٌ ج مَآكِل
Hill. Mound.	أَ كَمَةٌ ج آ كَامٌ
The (definite article).	أَلْ
Is it not so ? Surely.	اَلَا
That-not.	أَلَّا أَنْ لا
Unless, except.	إِلَّا
Who, which (Masc).	الَّذِي مث اللذَان ج الَّذِينَ
Who, Which (Fem).	التِي ج اللَّوَاتِي

A god, divinity.	إِلهٌ ج آلِهَةٌ	To be accustomed	أَلِفَ يَأْلَفُ
God ; the One True God.	اللهُ	To be friendly.	آلَفَ
To deify.	أَلَهَ	To compile a book.	أَلَّفَ
O God !	اللهُمَّ	To be united.	تَأَلَّفَ
Divinity.	أُلوهةٌ وَالوهية	Friend, companion.	إِلْفٌ وَأَلِيفٌ
Rump.	أَلْيَةٌ ج الاَيَا وَأَلْيَاتٌ	Thousand.	أَلْفٌ ج اُلوفٌ وآلَافٌ
Regiment.	الأَيْ ج اَلآيَاتٌ	Friendship, alliance.	اُلْفَةٌ
To, unto, until.	إِلَى	Accord, harmony.	إِئْتِلافٌ
Until, till.	إِلَى أَنْ	Compilation.	تَأْلِيفٌ ج تَآلِيفُ
Until when ? How long ?	إِلَى مَتَى	Customary, usual.	مَأْلوفٌ
To seek ; lead.	أَمَّ يَؤُمُّ	Friendship, familiarity.	مُوَالَفَةٌ
Mother.	اُمٌّ ج امَاتٌ وَامَّهَاتٌ	Author (of a book).	مُوَلِّفٌ
Before, in-front.	أَمَامَ	Book. Composed.	مُوَلَّفٌ
Imam, leader.	إِمَامٌ ج أَئِمَّة	To suffer, feel pain.	أَلِمَ يَأْلَمُ
Nation, people.	اُمَّةٌ ج اُمَمٌ	To pain, cause pain.	أَلَمَ وَآلَمَ
Maternal, Illiterate.	اُمِّيٌّ	To feel pain, ache.	تَأَلَّمَ
But, but as to.	أَمَّا	Pain, grief, ache.	أَلَمٌ ج آلَامٌ
Either, or.	إِمَّا ـ وَإِمَّا	Painful.	أَلِيمٌ وَمُؤْلِمٌ
Limit, end, term	أَمَدٌ ج آمَادٌ	Diamond.	اَلمَاسٌ

To entrust.	أَمَّنَ وَآمَنَهُ عَلَى	To order, command.	أَمَرَ يَأْمُرُ
To believe in.	آمَنَ إِيمَانًا بِ	To consult.	آمَرَ مُؤَامَرَةً في
To protect	امَنَهُ	Command, order.	أَمْرٌ ج أَوَامِرُ
To trust, rely upon.	إِئْتَمَنَ	Matter, affair.	أَمْرٌ ج اُمُورٌ
Safety, protection.	أَمْنٌ وَأَمَانٌ	Prefecture, power.	إِمَارَةٌ
Safe, secure.	آمِنٌ	Chief, prince.	أَمِيرٌ ج أُمَرَاءُ
Faithfulness, fidelity.	أَمَانَةٌ	Colonel.	أَمِيرُ الأَيِ
Faithful.	أَمِينٌ ج اُمَنَاءُ	Admiral.	أَمِيرُ البَحْرِ
Treasurer.	أَمِينُ الصَّنْدُوق	Caliph.	أَمِيرُ المُؤْمِنِينَ
Amen; so be it.	آمِينَ وأَمِينَ	Princely.	أَمِيرِيٌّ
Creed, belief.	إِيمَانٌ	Taxes.	المَالُ الأَمِيرِيُّ
Trustworthy.	مَأْمُونٌ	Sub-governor.	مَأْمُورٌ
Believer, faithful.	مُؤْمِنٌ	Yesterday.	أَمْسِ
Female slave.	أَمَةٌ ج إِمَاءٌ	To hope, hope for.	أَمَلَ يَأْمُلُ
That (particle).	أَنْ وَأَنَّ	To meditate, reflect upon.	تَأَمَّلَ
If. Not.	إِنْ	Hope, desire.	أَمَلٌ ج آمَالٌ
Certainly, truly.	أَنَّ وَإِنَّ	Hoped, expected.	مَأْمُولٌ
Only, but. Verily.	إِنَّمَا	To be faithful.	أَمِنَ يَأْمَنُ
To groan; moan.	أَنَّ يَئِنُّ أَنِينًا	To be or feel safe.	أَمِنَ يَأْمَنُ

Dislike. Scorn.	أَنَفَةٌ	I, we.	أَنَا ج نَحْنُ
Disdainful.	أَنُوفٌ	Thou.	أَنْتَ ج أَنْتُمْ م أَنْتِ ج أَنْتُنَّ
Court of appeal.	مَجْلِسُ ٱلِٱسْتِئْنَافِ	You two, both of you.	أَنْتُمَا
To be pleased.	أَنِقَ بِ يَأْنَقُ	Female.	أُنْثَى ج إِنَاثٌ وَأَنَاثَى
To be dainty.	تَأَنَّقَ	Feminine, effeminate.	مُؤَنَّثٌ
Men, mankind.	أَنَامٌ وَآنَامٌ	The Gospel.	أَلْإِنْجِيلُ
To act deliberately.	تَأَنَّى	To be polite, affable.	أَنِسَ يَأْنَسُ
Patience, deliberateness.	أَنَاةٌ	To be sociable.	آنَسَ مُؤَانَسَةً
Vessel.	إِنَاءٌ ج آنِيَةٌ وَأَوَانٍ	To cheer.	آنَسَ إِينَاسًا
Deliberateness.	تَأَنٍّ	Social life. Cheerfulness.	أُنْسٌ
Deliberate, careful.	مُتَأَنٍّ	Mankind.	إِنْسٌ
Anise.	أَنِيسُونٌ	Man.	إِنْسَانٌ ج أُنَاسٌ
Whence ?	أَنَّى = مِنْ أَيْنَ	Human ; polite.	إِنْسَانِيٌّ
Ah ! Alas !	آهِ وَآهَا	Humanity ; politeness.	إِنْسَانِيَّةٌ
To equip, get one ready.	أَهَبَ	Friendly, gentle.	أَنِيسٌ وَمُؤَانِسٌ
To get ready.	تَأَهَّبَ لِ	To hate, disdain.	أَنِفَ يَأْنَفُ
Apparatus, tools.	أُهْبَةٌ ج اهَبٌ	To recommence; appeal.	إِسْتَأْنَفَ
To render fit for.	اهَّلَ لِ	Nose.	أَنْفٌ ج أُنَافٌ وَآنُوفٌ
To bid welcome.	أَهَّلَ بِهِ	Little while age.	آنِفًا

To marry.	تَأَهَّلَ
To deserve, merit.	إِسْتَأَهَلَ
Welcome !	أَهْلاً وَسَهْلاً
Family ; relations.	أَهْلٌ ج أَهَالٍ
Worthy of, fit for.	أَهْلٌ لِ
Domestic.	أَهْلِيٌّ
Aptitude, fitness.	اهْلِيَّة
Deserving, meriting.	مُسْتَأْهِلٌ
Or, unless.	أَوْ
To return.	آبَ يَؤُوبُ إِيَاباً
Geese.	إِوَز
Myrtle.	آسٌ
Injury, damage.	آفَةٌ ج آفَاتٌ
To result in.	آلَ يَؤُولُ
To explain, make clear.	أَوَّلَ
Family ; kinsfolk.	آلٌ
Instrument.	آلَةٌ ج آلَاتٌ
Organic.	آلِيٌّ
First, beginning.	أَوَّلُ ج أَوَائِل

Firstly, in the first place.	أَوَّلاً
Successively.	أَوَّلاً فَأَوَّلاً
Those, these.	اوْلَئِكَ
Province.	إِيَالَة ج إِيَالَاتٌ
Interpretation.	تَأْوِيلٌ
End, result, issue.	مَآلٌ
Time.	آنٌ وَاوَانٌ
Now at present.	أَلآنَ
Porch, hall.	إِيوَانٌ إِيوَانَاتٌ
To resort for shelter.	أَوَى يَأْوِي
Abode shelter.	مَأْوًى ج مَآوٍ
Jackal.	إِبْنُ آوَى
That is to say; namely.	أَيْ
Whoever, whichever.	أَيُّ
Sign ; miracle.	آيَةٌ ج آيَاتٌ
Him.	إِيَّاهُ
Me.	إِيَّايَ
To strengthen, aid.	أَيَّدَ
May (month).	أَيَّار

Its time comes.	آنَ يَئِينُ	To despair.	ايَسَ يَأْيِسُ
Where ? whither ?	أَيْنَ	Despair.	إِيَاسٌ
Whither ; everywhere.	أَيْنَمَا	Despairing.	أَيِسٌ وَآيِسٌ
Whither ? where ?	إِلَى أَيْنَ	Deer, stag.	ايَّلٌ وَإِيَّلٌ
From whence ?	مِنْ أَيْنَ	September.	أَيْلُولُ

ب

Well, cistern.	بِئْرٌ ج آبَارٌ	As a numerical sign 2.	ب
Para (coin).	بَارَةٌ ج بَارَاتٌ	With, during, by, at, in.	ب
Gunpowder.	بَارُودٌ	By God !	بِٱللهِ
Gun.	بَارُودَةٌ ج بَوَارِيد	By reason of, inasmuch.	بِمَا أَنْ
Falcon, hawk.	بَازٌ	Pope ; father.	بَابَا ج بَابَاوَات
Market.	بَازَارٌ	Papal.	بَابَوِيٌّ وَبَابَاوِيٌّ
Cloth-merchant.	بَازِرْگَانٌ	Pupil of the eye.	بُؤْبُؤُ ٱلْعَيْنِ
Evil ! Bad, very bad. !	بِئْسَ	Slipper.	بَابُوجٌ ج بَوَابِيج
Courage , boldness.	بَأْسٌ	Camomile.	بَابُونَجٌ
Misfortune.	بَأْسٌ وَبُؤْسٌ	Egg-plant.	بَاذِنْجَانٌ

Stork.	بَجَعٌ
To be great.	بَجُلَ يَبْجُلُ بَجَالَةً
To honour, praise.	بَجَّلَ
To be hoarse.	بَحَّ يَبَحُّ بَحًّا
Hoarseness ; rough voice.	بُحَّة
Hoarse.	أَبَحُّ وَمَبْحُوحٌ
To investigate.	بَحَثَ عَنْ
To discuss.	بَاحَثَ وَتَبَاحَثَ
Examination, enquiry.	بَحْثٌ
Research.	مَبْحَثٌ ج مَبَاحِثُ
Discussion, controversy.	مُبَاحَثَة
To scatter.	بَحْثَرَ
Sea.	بَحْرٌ ج أَبْحُرٌ وَبُحُورٌ
The Atlantic Ocean.	بَحْرُ الظُّلُمَاتِ
The Red Sea.	اَلْبَحْرُ الأَحْمَرُ
The Black Sea.	اَلْبَحْرُ الأَسْوَدُ
The Caspian Sea.	بَحْرُ الْخَزَرِ
The Pacific Ocean.	اَلْبَحْرُ الْمُحِيط
The Mediterranean.	اَلْبَحْرُ الْمُتَوَسِّطُ اوْ بَحْرُ الرُّومِ

Misfortune, distress.	اَلْبَأْسَاء
Unfortunate, poor.	بَائِسٌ
Pasha.	بَاشَا ج بَاشَاوَاتٌ
Sparrow-hawk.	بَاشَقٌ ج بَوَاشِقُ
Bunch of flowers, bouquet.	بَاقَةٌ
Bale (of merchandise).	بَالَةٌ
Okra.	بَامِيا وَبَامِيَةٌ
Parrot.	بَبْغَاءٌ ج بَبْغَاوَاتٌ
To cut off ; decide.	بَتَّ يَبُتُّ
Irrevocably; not at all.	اَلْبَتَّةَ وَبَتَّةً
To cut off; amputate.	بَتَرَ يَبْتِرُ
Virgin.	بَتُولٌ
Virginity.	بُتُولِيَّة
To disperse, publish.	بَثَّ يَبُثُّ
To be divulged, spread.	إِنْبَثَّ
Pustule.	بَثْرٌ ج بُثُورٌ
To break out.	بَثَقَ يَبْثِقُ
To proceed from.	إِنْبَثَقَ مِنْ
To dawn.	إِنْبَثَقَ الْفَجْرُ

To disperse ; squander.	بدّد
To be dispersed.	تَبَدَّد
To be arbitrary.	إسْتَبَدَّ
By all means, necessarily.	لَابُدَّ
To begin ; create.	بَدَأَ يَبْدَأُ
To give precedence.	بَدَا
To create ; produce.	أَبْدَأَ
To begin, commence.	إِبْتَدَأَ بِ
Beginning.	بَدْء وَبَدَاءَة
Initial, primary.	إِبْتِدَائِيّ
Principle.	مَبْدَأ ج مَبَادِي
Dissipation ; pride.	بَدَخ
To hasten towards.	بَدَرَ إلى
To hasten.	بَادَرَ وَآبْتَدَرَ
Full moon.	بَدْر ج بُدُور
Thrashing-floor.	بَيْدَر ج بَيَادِر
To originate.	بَدَعَ يَبْدَعُ
To originate.	أَبْدَعَ وَآبْتَدَعَ
Innovation.	بِدْعَة ج بِدَع

Basin, pool.	بَحْرَة ج بِحَار
Lake.	بَحَيْرَة ج بُحَيْرَات
Nautical.	بَحْرِيّ
Sailor.	بَحْرِيّ ج بَحْرِيَّة
Fortune, good luck.	بَخْت
To swagger.	بَخْتَرَ وَتَبَخْتَرَ
To steam.	بَخَرَ يَبْخَرُ بَخْرًا
To fumigate, steam.	بَخَّرَ
Steamship.	بَاخِرَة ج بَوَاخِر
Vapour steam.	بُخَار ج أَبْخِرَة
Incense.	بَخُور
Cyclamen (plant).	بَخُور مَرْيَم
Having a foul breath.	أَبْخَر
Censer.	مِبْخَرَة ج مَبَاخِر
To diminish.	بَخَسَ يَبْخَسُ
Defective, low price.	بَخْس
To be miserly.	بَخِلَ يَبْخَلُ
Avarice, stinginess.	بُخْل
Miser ; miserly.	بَخِيل ج بُخَلَاء

Nomads, bedouins.	اَلْبَدْو	Astonishing.	بَدِيعٌ
Desert.	بَادِيَةٌ ج بَوَاد	Rhetoric.	عِلْمُ الْبَدِيعِ
Desert life ; desert.	بَدَاوَةٌ	Invention.	إِبْدَاعٌ وَابْتِدَاعٌ
Beduin ; nomad.	بَدَوِيٌّ	Inventor. Creator.	مُبْدِعٌ
To be proud.	بَذَخ يَبْذَخ	To change, exchange.	بَدَّلَ يَبْدُلُ
Pride, haughtiness.	بَذَخ	To be changed or altered.	تَبَدَّلَ
To sow ; disperse.	بَذَرَ يَبْذُر	To take in exchange.	إِسْتَبْدَلَ
Seed, grain.	بَذْرٌ ج بِذَارٌ	Substitute.	بَدَلٌ وَبَدِيلٌ
Dissipation, prodigality.	تَبْذِيرٌ	Instead of.	بَدَلَ أَنْ
Prodigal.	مُبَذِّرٌ	In exchange for.	بَدَلًا مِنْ
To give.	بَذَلَ يَبْذُلُ	Reciprocity.	تَبَادُلٌ
Generous gift, present.	بَذْلٌ	Reciprocal	مُتَبَادَلٌ
To justify.	بَرَّرَ	Body, trunk.	بَدَنٌ ج اَبْدَانٌ
To be justified.	تَبَرَّرَ	To come suddenly.	بَدَهَ ج يَبْدَهُ
Goodness, piety.	بِرٌّ	Intuitive knowledge.	بَدَاهَةٌ
Wheat.	بُرٌّ	Intuitively.	بَدِيهَا. عَلَى الْبَدِيهَةِ
Land as opposed to sea.	بَرٌّ	Axiom.	بَدِيهِيَّةٌ
By land and by sea.	بَرًّا وَبَحْرًا	To appear.	بَدَا يَبْدُو
Just, pious.	بَارٌّ ج أَبْرَارٌ	To make plain, reveal.	أَبْدَى

To continue, persevere.	ما بَرِح	External.	بَرَّانِيّ ج بَرَّانِيُّون
To cause pain.	بَرَّحَ	Wild (tree or animal).	بَرِّيّ
Yesterday.	الْبَارِحُ وَالْبَارِحَةُ	Desert, waste.	بَرِّيَّة ج بَرَارِيّ
Day before yes- terday.	الْبَارِحَة ٱلأولى ⟩ اوَّل ٱلْبَارِحَةِ ⟨	Justification.	تَبْرِيرٌ
To become cold.	بَرَدَ يَبْرُدُ	To create.	بَرَأَ يَبْرا
To file (iron).	بَرَدَ	To be innocent of. Recover from an illness.	بَرَأَ وَبَرِئَ يَبْرا
To make cool or cold.	بَرَّدَ	To acquit.	بَرَّأَ مِن
Cold.	بَرْدٌ	Recovery, cure.	بُرْءٌ وبُرْءٌ
Hail ; hail stones.	بَرَدٌ	Innocent.	بَرِيءٌ ج أبرِياء
Fever and ague.	بُرَداء وبردِيَّة	Immunity. Document.	بَراءَة
Reed, papyrus reed.	بَرْدِيّ	Creator (God).	ٱلْبَارِى
Cold.	بَارِدٌ	Creature, creation.	بَرِيَّة ج بَرَايَا
Freshness, coolness.	بُرودَة	Native of Barbary.	بَرْبَرِيّ
Courier, post.	بَرِيدٌ ج بُرُد	Oranges.	بُرْقَانٌ وبُردقَانٌ
File.	مِبْرَدٌ ج مَبَارِدُ	Tower, castle.	بُرْجٌ ج بُروجٌ
Donkey-saddle.	بُرْدعَة	Signs of zodiac.	بُروجُ ٱلأَفْلاكِ
To appear, issue.	بَرَزَ يَبْرِز	Man-of-war.	بارِجَة ج بوارِج
To go to battle.	بارَزَ	To part from.	بَرِح يَبْرَح

To publish, bring out.	أَبْرَزَ	Flea.	بُرْغُوثٌ ج بَرَاغِيثُ
Combat, duel.	بِرَازٌ وَمُبَارَزَةٌ	Small flies ; gnats.	بَرْغَشٌ
Appearance.	بُرُوزٌ	A small fly ; gnat.	بَرْغَشَةٌ
Champion ; fighter.	مُبَارِزٌ	Wheat coarsely ground.	بُرْغُلٌ
Isthmus.	بَرْزَخٌ ج بَرَازِخُ	Screw.	بُرْغِيٌّ ج بَرَاغِيُّ
Alexandrian clover.	بِرْسِيمٌ	To flash, lighten.	بَرَقَ يَبْرُقُ
Stramonium.	بَرْشٌ	To flash, gleam.	أَبْرَقَ
Piebald, spotted.	أَبْرَشُ م بَرْشَاءُ	Lightning.	بَرْقٌ ج بُرُوقٌ
Soft-boiled egg.	بِرِشْتٌ	Borax.	بُورَقٌ
Wafer.	بُرْشَانٌ	To veil the face.	بَرْقَعَ
Leprosy.	بَرَصٌ	A lady's veil.	بُرْقُعٌ ج بَرَاقِعُ
Leper.	أَبْرَصُ م بَرْصَاءُ ج بُرْصٌ	Yellow plum ; apricot.	بَرْقُوقٌ
To bribe.	بَرْطَلَ بِرْطَلَةٌ	Ewer.	إِبْرِيقٌ ج أَبَارِيق
Bribe.	بِرْطِيلٌ ج بَرَاطِيل	To kneel.	بَرَكَ يَبْرُكُ
To excel.	بَرَعَ يَبْرَعُ	To bless.	بَارَكَ فِي أَوْ عَلَى
To bestow of free will.	تَبَرَّعَ بِ	To seek blessing.	تَبَرَّكَ بِ
Distinguished ; perfect.	بَارِعٌ	To be blessed.	تَبَارَكَ
Distinction ; elegance.	بَرَاعَةٌ	Blessing.	بَرَكَةٌ ج بَرَكَاتٌ
Bud.	بُرْعُمٌ ج بَرَاعِم	Pool, pond ; tank.	بِرْكَةٌ ج بِرَكٌ

Creation, universe. بَرِيَّةٌ ج بَرَايَا	Blessed. مُبَارَكٌ
Mended or cut (pen). مَبْرِيٌّ	Compasses. بِرْكَارٌ وَبِيكَارٌ
Linen or cotton clothes. بَزٌّ	Volcano. بُرْكَانٌ ج برَاكِينَ
Udder, nipple. بِزٌّ ج أَبْزَازٌ	To twist. بَرَمَ يَبْرُمُ
Seed, grain. بِزْرٌ ج بُزُورٌ	To make firm. أَبْرَمَ
A grain or seed. بِزْرَةٌ	Gimlet; augur. بِبْرَمٌ وَبَرِّيمَةٌ
To peep forth (sun). بَزَغَ يَبْزَغُ	Affirmed, assured. مُبْرَمٌ
Rising of sun or moon. بُزُوغٌ	Twisted cord. مَبْرُومٌ
To spit. بَزَقَ يَبْزُقُ بَزْقًا	Barrel ; cask. بِرْمِيلٌ ج بَرَامِيلُ
Spittle, saliva. بُزَاقٌ	A kind of cloak. بُرْنُسٌ
Snail. (coll. بَزَّاقٌ) بَزَّاقَةٌ	Hat. بُرْنَيْطَةٌ
Spittoon. مَبْزَقَةٌ	Space of time. بُرْهَةٌ
To split. Tap a cask. بَزَلَ يَبْزُلُ	To prove بَرْهَنَ عَلَى أَوْ عَنْ
Perforator. بِزَالٌ وَمَبْزَلٌ	To be demonstrated. تَبَرْهَنَ
Buckle. إِبْزِيمٌ	Proof, evidence. بُرْهَانٌ ج بَرَاهِينُ
Bath-tub. الإِبْزَنُ ج أَبَازِنُ	Demonstrated, proved. مُبَرْهَنٌ
Cat. بَسٌّ بَسَّةٌ (بَسِينٌ بَسِينَةٌ)	Frame. بِرْوَازٌ ج بَرَاوِيزُ
Garden ; orchard. بُسْتَانٌ ج بَسَاتِينَ	To pare ; emaciate. بَرَى يَبْرِي
Gardener. بُسْتَانِيّ	To vie with. بَارَى وَانْبَرَى

Epidermis ; cuticle.	بَشَرَةٌ	Piles.	بَاسُورٌ
Man ; mankind ; humanity.	بَشَرٌ	To spread out ; cheer.	بَسَطَ يَبْسُطُ
Mankind, men.	الْبَشَرُ	To be cheerful, merry.	إِنْبَسَطَ
Good news.	بُشْرَى	Carpet.	بِسَاطٌ ج بُسُطٌ
Human.	بَشَرِيٌّ	Simple.	بَسِيطٌ ج بُسَطَاءُ
Good news ; gospel.	بِشَارَةٌ ج بَشَائِرُ	The Earth.	الْبَسِيطَةُ
Bearer of good news.	بَشِيرٌ	Cheerfulness.	إِنْبِسَاطٌ وبَسْطٌ
Announcer of news ; preacher.	مُبَشِّرٌ	Extended ; happy.	مَبْسُوطٌ
To be ugly, deformed.	بَشِعَ يَبْشَعُ	To spit.	بَسَقَ يَبْسُقُ بَسْقاً
Bad taste (food); ugliness.	بَشَاعَةٌ	To be brave.	بَسُلَ يَبْسُلُ
Ugly ; repulsive.	بَشِعٌ وبَشِيعٌ	Bold, brave.	بَاسِلٌ ج بُسَلَاءُ
Indigestion.	بَشَمٌ	Bravery ; heroism.	بَسَالَةٌ
Lotus (plant).	بَشْنِينٌ	To smile.	بَسَمَ يَبْسِمُ وتَبَسَّمَ وابْتَسَمَ
To shine, glitter.	بَصَّ يَبِصُّ	Smile.	تَبَسُّمٌ وابْتِسَامٌ
A live coal.	بَصَّةٌ	To be cheerful.	بَشَّ
Spy.	بَصَّاصٌ ج بَصَّاصُونَ	Cheerfulness of face, gentleness.	بَشَاشَةٌ
To see.	بَصَرَ يَبْصُرُ بَصِرَ يَبْصَرُ	To rejoice at.	بَشِرَ يَبْشَرُ
To consider, observe.	تَبَصَّرَ	To announce good news.	بَشَّرَ
Sight.	بَصَرٌ ج أَبْصَارٌ	To manage an affair.	بَاشَرَ

Musk-melon.	بِطِّيخٌ أَصْفَر	Intelligent.	بَصِيرٌ ج بُصَراءُ
To exult.	بَطِرَ يَبْطَرُ بَطَراً	Consideration ; reflection.	تَبَصُّرٌ
Exultation. Wantonness.	بَطَرٌ	To spit.	بَصَقَ يَبْصُقُ بَصْقاً
Toshoe animals	بَيْطَرَ	Spittle, saliva.	بُصَاقٌ
Farrier.	بَيْطارٌ ج بَياطِرة	Onion ; bulb.	بَصَلٌ
Veterinary art .	بَيْطَرَةٌ	To cut, incise.	بَضَعَ يَبْضَعُ
Battery (of cannons).	بَطّاريّةٌ	A small number.	بِضْعٌ وبِضْعَةٌ
Patriarch.	بَطْرَكٌ ج بَطارِكَةٌ	A few days.	بِضْعَةُ أَيّامٍ
Patriarchate.	بَطْرَكِيَّةٌ وبَطْرَكِيَّةٌ	Merchandise.	بِضَاعَةٌ ج بَضائِعُ
To assault.	بَطَشَ يَبْطِشُ بِ	Knife ; lancet.	مِبْضَعٌ ج مَباضِعُ
Power ; violence.	بَطْشٌ	To lance a tumour.	بَطَّ يَبُطُّ
A marked ticket.	بِطَاقَةٌ	Duck.	بَطَّةٌ ج بَطٌّ
To cease.	بَطَلَ يَبْطُلُ	Bottle.	بَطَّةٌ ج بَطَطٌ
To repeal, abolish.	بَطَلَ وأَبْطَلَ	To linger.	بَطُؤَ يَبْطُؤُ
Vanity ; lie.	بُطْلٌ وبُطْلانٌ	To be slow, dally.	تَباطَأَ في
Hero.	بَطَلٌ ج أَبْطَالٌ	Slowness.	بَطَاءٌ وبُطْءٌ وبُطُوءٌ
False, vain, useless.	بَاطِلٌ	Slow, tardy, dilatory.	بَطِيءٌ
Lazy, idle ; useless.	بَطّالٌ	Water-course.	بَطْحَاءُ وبَطِيحَةٌ
Idleness ; holidays.	بِطَالَةٌ	Water-melon.	بِطِّيخٌ أَحْمَر

Then ; afterwards ; after.	بَعْدُ	Abolition, repeal.	إِبْطَالٌ
Distant ; far.	بَعِيدٌ	Marine muscle.	بَطْلَيْنُوسٌ
Camel.	بَعِيرٌ ج بُعْوانٌ	Terebinth.	بُطْمٌ
To scatter, dissipate.	بَعْزَقَ	To line (clothes).	بَطَنَ وأَبْطَنَ
Portion, part ; some.	بَعْضٌ	Belly, abdomen.	بَطْنٌ ج بُطُونٌ
Gnats, mosquitoes.	بَعُوضٌ	Inner lining.	بِطَانَةٌ
A gnat or mosquito.	بَعُوضَةٌ	Inner, hidden.	باطِنٌ ج بَواطِنُ
Husband, wife.	بَعْلٌ ج بُعُولٌ	Internally, secretly.	باطِنًا
Unwatered land.	بَعْلٌ	To send.	بَعَثَ يَبْعَثُ إلى
To take by surprise.	بَغَتَ يَبْغَتُ وباغَتَ	To raise the dead.	بَعَثَ
Surprise.	بَغْتَةٌ ج بَغَتَاتٌ	Cause, motive.	باعِثٌ
Suddenly, unexpectedly.	بَغْتَةً	Sent. Envoy.	مَبْعُوثٌ
Strait.	بوغازٌ ج بَوَاغِيزُ	To scatter, uncover.	بَعْثَرَ
To hate, detest.	أَبْغَضَ	To be far distant.	بَعُدَ يَبْعُدُ
Hatred ; enmity.	بُغْضٌ	To make distant.	بَعَّدُوا أَبْعَدَ
Violent hatred.	بِغْضَةٌ وبَغْضَاءُ	To be far from.	تَبَاعَدَ عَن
One who hates.	مُبْغِضٌ	To go far from.	إبْتَعَدَ عَن
Mule.	بَغْلٌ ج بِغالٌ وأَبْغالٌ	To regard improbable.	إسْتَبْعَدَ
Muleteer.	بَغَّالٌ	Distance ; interval.	بُعْدٌ

To remain ; continue.	بَقِيَ يَبْقَى	Necklace.	بَغْمَة
To preserve.	أَبْقَى وَاَسْتَبْقَى	To seek ; desire.	بَغَى يَبْغِي
To be left.	تَبَقَّى	To be unjust ; oppress.	بَغَى عَلَى
Continuance, uration.	بَقَاء	It is desirable.	يَنْبَغِي أَنْ
Remainder.	بَقِيَّة ج بَقَايَا	Injustice ; aggression.	بَغْي
Remaining.	باقٍ ج بَاقُونَ	Wish, desire.	بُغَاء وَابْتِغَاء
The Everlasting (God).	الْبَاقِي	Anything wished for or sought.	بُغْيَة وَبِغْيَة
Vetch.	بَاقِيَة	Unjust aggressor.	بَاغٍ ج بُغَاة
More enduring.	أَبْقَى	Bundle of clothes.	بُقْجَة ج بُقَجٌ
To reprove, scold.	بَكَّتَ	Parsley.	بَقْدُونَسٌ
To come early.	بَكَّرَ وَبَا كَرَ	Oxen.	بَقَرٌ ج أَبْقَارٌ
First-born ; virgin.	بِكْرٌ ج أَبْكَارٌ	Cow.	بَقَرَة ج بَقَرَاتٌ
Dawn ; to-morrow.	بُكْرَة	Box-tree.	بَقْسٌ
Pulley.	بَكَرَة ج بَكَرٌ	To be spotted.	بَقِعَ يَبْقَعُ بَقَعًا
Virginity.	بَكَارَة	Spots, stains.	بُقَعٌ
Early.	بَاكِرًا	Piece of land.	بُقْعَة ج بُقَعٌ وَبِقَاعٌ
First fruits.	بَاكُورَة	Vegetables, herbs.	بَقْلٌ ج بُقُولٌ
To be dumb.	بَكِمَ يَبْكَمُ	Green-grocer.	بَقَّالٌ
To cause to be silent.	أَبْكَمَ	Logwood.	بَقَّمٌ

Devil, Satan.	اِبْلِيسٌ ج أَبَالِسَة	Dumbness.	بَكَم
Balsam, balm.	بَلْسَم	Dumb ; mute.	أَبْكَم ج بُكْم
Elder-tree.	بَلَسَان	To weep.	بَكَى يَبْكِي
To tax illegally.	بَلَص يَبْلُص	To cause to weep.	بَكَّى وأَبْكَى
Oppressive taxation.	بَلْص	Weeping.	بُكَاءٌ وبُكًى
To pave with flage-stones.	بَلَّط	But ; nay but.	بَلْ
Axe, battle-axe.	بَلْطَة	To wet, moisten.	بَلَّ يَبُلُّ
Flag-stones ; pavement.	بَلَاط	To become wet	تَبَلَّل وابْتَلَّ
Oak-tree, acron.	بَلُّوط	Wet, moistened.	مَبْلُولٌ ومَبَلَّل
Sapper, executioner.	بَلْطَجِيّ	To mix, confound.	بَلْبَل
Act of paving.	تَبْلِيط	Nightingale.	بُلْبُل ج بَلَابِل
Paver.	مُبَلِّط	Intense anxiety.	بَلْبَال
Paved.	مُبَلَّط	Dates (Coll.)	بَلَح
To swallow.	بَلَع يَبْلَع	To be stupid.	بَلُد يَبْلُد
Swallowing.	بَلْعٌ وابْتِلَاع	Town ; land.	بَلَدٌ ج بِلَادٌ وبُلْدَان
Sink, sewer, gutter.	بَالُوعَة	Native ; urban.	بَلَدِيّ
Gullet.	بُلْعُوم	Stupidity ; dullness.	بَلَادَة
To reach, attain.	بَلَغ يَبْلُغ بُلُوغًا	Imbecile, stupid.	بَلِيدٌ وأَبْلَد
To inform.	بَلَّغ	Crystal.	بِلُّورٌ وبَلُّورٌ

Yes, certainly.	بَكَى	To exaggerate.	بَالَغَ فِي
Trial. Grief ; calamity.	بَلَاءِ	Mature ; of full age.	بَالِغ
Affliction.	بَلْوَى ج بَلَايَا	Message.	بَلَاغ
Used up ; rotten.	بَال	Elegance of style.	بَلَاغَة
Wherewith ?	بِمَ	Rhetoric.	عِلْم آلبَلَاغَةِ
Because, inasmuch as	بِمَا ان	Arrival, maturity.	بُلُوغ
Coffee-berries ; coffee.	بُنّ	Eloquent efficacious.	بَلِيغ
Fingers.	بَنَان	Sum, amount.	مَبْلَغ ج مَبَالِغ
To drug, stupefy.	بَنَّج	Exaggeration.	مُبَالَغَة
Henbane, Hyoscyamus.	بَنْج	Phlegm.	بَلْغَم ج بَلَاغِم
Section. Banner.	بَنْد ج بُنُود	Phlegmatic.	بَلْغَمِي
Tomatoes.	بَنْدُورَة	Spotted.	أَبْلَق م بَلْقَاء ج بُلْق
Flag, banner.	بَنْدِيرَة	A thorny plant.	بَلَّان
Hazel-nut.	بُنْدُقَة و بُنْدُق	Stupidity, idiocy.	بَلَه وبَلَاهَة
Musket, gun.	بُنْدُقِيَة	Stupid ; simple-ton, idiot.	أَبْلَه م بَلْهَاء ج بُلْه
Bastard.	بُنْدُوق ج بَنَادِيق	To test, try ; afflict.	بَلَا يَبْلُو
Violet (plant).	بَنَفْسَج	To decay.	بَلِي يَبْلَى
Violet (colour).	بَنَفْسَجِي	To be attentive to.	بَالَى بِ
Ring-finger.	بَنْصِر ج بَنَاصِر	Decay ; rottenness.	بِلَى

To be dazzled.	بَهَرَ	Seat. Bank.	بنك ج بُنُوكة
Beautiful, admirable.	باهرٌ	To construct, build.	بني يَبني
Heavy, distressing.	باهظٌ	To adopt a son.	تبنَّى
To supplicate.	اِبْتَهَلَ إلى	Building, edifice.	بناءٌ وبِنايةٌ
Supplication.	اِبْتِهالٌ	In consequence of.	بناءً على
Rope-dancer.	بهلوانٌ	Mason.	بنَّاءٌ ج بنَّاؤُونَ
To be doubtful.	أَبهمَ واسْتَبهَم	Form ; constitution.	بِنية
Brute, beast.	بهيمةٌ ج بهائم	Son, boy.	إبنٌ ج بنونَ وأَبناءٌ
Doubt ; ambiguity.	إبهامٌ	Daughter.	إبنةٌ وبِنتٌ ج بنَاتٌ
Thumb.	إبهامٌ ج أَباهم	Traveller, wayfarer.	إبنُ السَّبيل
Ambiguous ; doubtful.	مُبهَم	Built. Indeclinable.	مَبني
To be beautiful.	بهَا يَبهُو	To be astonished ; faded.	بَهِتَ يَبهَت
To rival in beauty.	باهَى	To astonish, perplex.	بهَت يَبهَت
Beauty, brilliancy.	بهاءٌ	Lie ; slander.	بُهتان
Beautiful splendid.	بهيٌّ	To rejoice, cheer.	بهَج وأَبهَج
Door. Chapter.	بابٌ ج أَبوابٌ	To rejoice at.	بهَج وأَبتَهَج
The Sublime Porte.	البابُ العَالي	Joy, gladness ; beauty	بهجة
Door-keeper.	بوَّابٌ	Cheering ; causing joy.	مُبهِج
Large door, gate.	بوَّابة	To shine.	بهَر يَبهَر

Storehouse.	بائِكَة ج بَوَائِك	To be known.	باحَ يَبُوح
To micturate. Melt ; flow.	بالَ يَبُول	To divulge.	باحَ ب
Condition ; mind ; thought.	بالٌ	To allow.	أَباحَ
To occur to mind	خَطَر بِبَال	To consider lawful.	إِسْتِبَاح
Bale.	بالَة	Revealing, licence.	إِباحَة
Urine.	بَوْل	Permissable ; lawful.	مُباح
Steel.	بُولَاذ (فُولَاذ)	To abate ; fade.	باخَ يَبُوخ
An owl.	بُومَة	To perish.	بارَ يَبُور
Bill ; order ; receipt.	بُولِيصَة ج بَوَالِص	Uncultivated land.	بُور
The Egyptian willow.	بانٌ	Destruction, ruin.	بَوَار
Distance ; difference.	بَوْن	Borax ; natron.	بُورَق
To pass the night.	باتَ يَبِيت	Falcon, hawk.	بازِ ج بِيزَان
House, room. Verse of poetry.	بَيْت ج بِيُوت وأَ بْيَات	To kiss.	باسَ يَبُوس بَوْساً
Water-closet ; latrine ; privy.	بَيْت الْمَاء بَيْت الْخَلَاء بَيْت الْفَضَاء	Post ; mail.	بُوسْطَة
		Postman.	بُوسْطَجِي
		A fathom.	باع ج ا بْوَاع
Public treasury.	بَيْت الْمَال	Generous. Able.	طَوِيل الْبَاع
Cobweb.	بَيْت الْعَنْكَبُوت	To blow a trumpet.	بَوَّق
Jerusalem.	بيْت الْمَقدِس	Trumpet ; shell.	بُوق ج ا بْوَاق

To shoe a horse.	بيطر	The Kaaba in Mecca.	أَلبَيْت اَلحَرام
To sell.	باع يبيع	House, night's lodging.	مَبِيت
To swear fealty.	بايع مبايعة	To perish, vanish.	بَاد يبِيد
To buy from.	إبتاع مِن	To destroy, annihilate.	أبَاد
Selling, sale.	بيع	Desert.	بيداء جبيد
Church, synagogue.	بِيعة ج بِيع	Foot-soldier.	بَيَّادي بَيَّادة
Seller.	بائِع ج باعة	But, although.	بَيدأَن
Seller.	بَيَّاع	Thrashing-floor.	بَيدَر
Sale ; place of sale.	مَبِيع	Well of water.	بِير
Bey.	بَيك وبَك	Banner.	بَيرق بَيارق
Pair of compasses.	بِيكار	To lay eggs.	بَاض يَبِيض
Elder (tree).	بَيسان	To whiten, bleach.	بَيَّض
Hospital.	بيمارستان	To become white.	إبيَضّ
To be distinct, separate.	بان يَبِين	Eggs.	بَيض ج بيوض
To render clear ; explain.	بَيَّن	An egg. Testicle.	بَيضة
To quit, abandon.	بايَن	Oval, ovate ; elliptical.	بَيضي
To be clear, lucid.	تبَيَّن	Whiteness.	بَياض
Between, among.	بَينَ	White.	أبَيض م بيضاء ج بيض
Middling.	بين بَين	Tinner; white-washer.	مبَيِّض

Evidence.	بَيِّنَةٌ ج بَيِّنَاتٌ	Whilst, while.	بَيْنَا وَبَيْنَمَا
Difference ; contrast.	تَبَايُن	Explanation.	بَيَان
Clear, evident.	مُبِيْنٌ وبَيّن	A branch of Rhetoric.	عِلْم ٱلْبَيَان
		Distinct, evident.	بَائِنٌ وبَيّنٌ

ت (T)

Native gold.	تِبْر	As a numeral sign=400	ت
To follow.	تَبِـعَ يَتْبَعُ وٱتَّبَعَ	I swear by God.	تَٱللّٰه
To cause to follow.	أَتْبَعَ	Chest. Coffin.	تَابُوت ج تَوَابِيت
To follow.	تَابَعَ مُتَابَعَةً عَلَى	Once ; sometimes.	تَارَة
To follow up.	تَتَبَّع	Twin.	تَوْأَمَةٌ ج تَوَائِمُ
To follow consecutively.	تَتَابَع	Twins ; double.	تَوْأَم
Follower.	تَبَعٌ ج اتْبَاعٌ	The sign of Gemini.	ٱلتَّوْأَمَان
Successive.	مُتَتَابِـعٌ	To suffer loss.	تَبَّ يَتِبُّ
Tobacco.	تَبْغ	To be established.	إِسْتَتَبَّ
To season (a dish).	تَبَّل وتَابَلَ	Evil be to him !	تَبًّا لَهُ

To confine, limit.	تَخَم يَتْخِم تَخْمًا
Adjoin, border upon.	تاخَم
To cause indigestion.	أَتْخَم
Boundary.	تَخْم ج تُخوم
Adjoining.	مُتاخِم
Indigestion.	تَخْمة
To cover with earth.	تَرَّب
Earth, dust.	تُراب ج أَتْرِبة
Cemetery. Soil.	تُرْبة ج تُرَب
Citron.	اتْرُجّ واتْرُنْج
To translate.	تَرْجَم
Translation.	تَرْجَمة
Dragoman, interpreter.	تُرْجُمان
Translator, interpreter.	مُتَرْجِم
Translated, interpreted.	مُتَرْجَم
Sorrow, grief.	تَرَح ج أَتْراح
Shield.	تُرْس ج أَتْراس
Bulwark.	مِتْراس ج مَتاريس
Arsenal.	تَرْسانة وتَرْسِخانة

Condiments.	تَوَابِل
Seasoned (dish.)	مُتَبَّل
Straw.	تِبْن
Tartars (coll.)	تَتَر
A Tartar.	تَتَرِيّ
One after another.	تَتْرى
Tobacco	تُتُن
To trade.	تَجَر يَتْجِر وتاجَر
Commerce, trade.	تِجارة
Merchant.	تاجِر ج تُجّار
Commerce.	مَتْجَر ج مَتاجِر
In front of, opposite to.	تُجاه
Under, below, beneath.	تَحْت
Inferior, placed below.	تَحْتانِيّ
To present with.	أَتْحَف ب
Precious object, gift.	تُحْفة
Bench ; bedstead.	تَخْت ج تُخوت
Palanquin.	تَخْتَرَوان
Capital of a kingdom.	تَخْت المُلْك

To become tired.	آمب يَتْعَبُ	Channel, canal.	تَرْعَةٌ ج تُرَع
To give trouble ; tire.	أَتْعَبَ	Luxury ; ease.	تَرَفٌ وتُرْفَةٌ
Fatigue, toil.	تَعَبٌ ج أَتْعَابٌ	Collar-bone, clavicle.	تَرْقُوَةٌ
Tired, fatigued.	تَعِبٌ	To abandon, allow.	تَرَكَ يَتْرُكُ
Toilsome, fatiguing.	مُتْعِبٌ	To leave to, bequeath.	تَرَكَ لِ
Fatigued.	مُتْعَبٌ	Abandoning leaving.	تَرْكٌ
To stumble	تَعِسَ يَتْعَسُ	Turk.	تُرْكٌ ج أَتْرَاكٌ
Misfortune.	تَعْسٌ وَتَعَاسَةٌ	A turk ; Turkish.	تُرْكِيٌّ
Unhappy, unlucky.	تَعِسٌ	Estate of one dead.	تَرِكَةٌ وتَرْكَةٌ
Apple.	تُفَّاحٌ	Abandoned, omitted.	مَتْرُوكٌ
An apple, apple-tree.	تُفَّاحَةٌ	Lupine.	تُرْمُسٌ
To spit.	تَفَلَ يَتْفِلُ	Theriac ; antidote.	تِرْيَاقٌ
Spittle, saliva.	تُفْلٌ	Nine.	تِسْعَةٌ م تِسْعٌ
Spittoon.	مَتْفَلَةٌ	A ninth (part).	تُسْعٌ
To be mean, foolish.	تَفِهَ يَتْفَهُ	Ninth (ord. num.)	تَاسِعٌ
Insipidity.	تَفَاهَةٌ	Ninety, ninetieth.	تِسْعُونَ
To arrange skilfully.	أَتْقَنَ	October.	تِشْرِينُ الأَوَّلُ
Perfection (of a work).	تَقَانَةٌ	November.	تِشْرِينُ الثَّانِي
Skilful elaboration.	إِتْقَانٌ	Come !	تَعَالَ

Completion, end.	تَمَامٌ	Skilfully made.	متقن
Completely.	تَمَامًا وبِالتَّمَام	Pious.	تَقِيّ
Talisman, amulet	تَمِيمَةٌ ج تَمَائِم	Piety.	تقوى
Perfect, complete.	تَامٌّ م تَامَّةٌ	Small hill.	تَلٌّ ج تِلَالٌ
Complement.	تَتِمَّةٌ	To perish.	تَلِفَ يَتْلَفُ تَلَفًا
Stammerer.	تَمْتَامٌ	To ruin.	أَتْلَفَ
Ripe dates.	تَمْرٌ ج تُمُورٌ	Destruction.	تَلَفٌ
Tamarind (fruit).	تَمْرٌ هِنْدِيّ	Destroyer, waster.	مُتْلِفٌ
July.	تَمُوز وتَمُّوز	Squanderer.	مِتْلَافٌ
Crocodile.	تِمْسَاحٌ ج تَمَاسِيحُ	That (fem.)	تِلْك
Dragon.	تِنِّينٌ ج تَنَانِين	Furrow, rut.	تَلَمٌ ج اتْلَامٌ
Persian tobacco.	تَنْبَكُ	To be a pupil.	تَلْمَذَ
Idler, lazy.	تَنْبَلٌ ج تَنَابِلُ	Disciple, pupil.	تِلْمِيذٌ ج تَلَامِيذ
Oven-pit.	تَنُّورٌ ج تَنَانِيرُ	To follow ; succeed.	تَلَا يَتْلُو تُلُوًّا
Tin.	تَنَكُ	To read ; recite.	تَلَا يَتْلُو تِلَاوَةً
To suspect, accuse.	أَتْهَم وآتَّهَم	Reading, recitation.	تِلَاوَةٌ
Suspicion. Accusation.	تُهْمَةٌ	Following, next.	تَالٍ
To repent.	تَابَ يَتُوب	To be complete.	تَمَّ يَتِمُّ
Repentence ; penitence.	تَوْبَةٌ	To complete, finish.	تَمَّمَ وأَتَمَّ

Passion, desire.	تَوْقٌ وَتَوَقَانٌ	Repentant, penitent.	تَائِبٌ
Yearning, desiring.	تَائِقٌ	White mulberry.	تُوتٌ
To lose one's way.	تَاهَ يَتُوهُ	Black mulberry.	تُوتٌ شَامِيٌّ
A strong, deep current.	تَيَّارٌ	Blackberry.	تُوتُ الْعُلَّيْقِ
To be appointed, decreed to.	تَاحَ وَأَتَاحَ ل	Zinc.	تُوتِيَاءُ
He-goat.	تَيْسٌ ج تُيُوسٌ	To crown.	تَوَّجَ
Figs ; fig-trees.	تِينٌ	To be crowned.	تَتَوَّجَ
A fig, a fig tree.	تِينَةٌ	Crown, diadem.	تَاجٌ ج تِيجَانٌ
To be proud. Wander.	تَاهَ يَتِيهُ	Pentateuch. Bible.	تَوْرَاةٌ
Desert. Pride.	تِيهٌ	One time.	تَارَةً
Lost, wandering. Proud.	تَائِهٌ	To long for, desire.	تَاقَ يَتُوقُ إِلَى

ث

Wart.	ثُؤْلُولٌ ج ثَآلِيلُ	As a numeral sign = 500	ث
To stand firm.	ثَبَتَ يَثْبُتُ	To yawn.	تَثَاءَبَ تَثَاؤُبًا
To be certain, assured.	ثَبَتَ عِنْدَ	Revenge.	ثَأْرٌ ثَارَ ج اثَارٌ

To prove.	ثَبَّتَ وَأَثْبَتَ	Fox.	ثَعْلَبٌ ج ثَعَالِبُ
Firmness. Reality.	ثَبَاتٌ وَثُبُوتٌ	Alopecia, falling of hair.	دَاءُ الثَّعْلَبِ
Firm ; certain sure.	ثَابِتٌ	To make a breach.	ثَغَرَ يَثْغَرُ
Fixed star.	ثَابِتَةٌ ج ثَوَابِتُ	Frontier. Mouth.	ثَغْرٌ ج ثُغُورٌ
Firm ; proved.	مُثْبَتٌ وَثَابِتٌ	Opening ; breach.	ثُغْرَةٌ ج ثُغُورٌ
To persevere in.	ثَابَرَ عَلَى مُثَابَرَةٍ	Sediment, dregs.	ثُقْلٌ
Assiduous, persevering.	مُثَابِرٌ	To pierce.	ثَقَبَ يَثْقُبُ ثَقْبًا
To be thick.	ثَخُنَ يَثْخُنُ	To be pierced.	تَثَقَّبَ وَانْثَقَبَ
To make slaughter.	أَثْخَنَ	Hole.	ثَقْبٌ ج ثُقُوبٌ
Thickness; hardness.	ثُخْنٌ وَثُخُونَةٌ	Penetrating.	ثَاقِبٌ
Thick, firm.	ثَخِينٌ ج ثِخَانٌ	Gimlet, drill.	مِثْقَبٌ ج مَقَابِبُ
Breast (mamma).	ثَدْيٌ ج ثُدِيٌّ	Pierced, perforated.	مَثْقُوبٌ
Omentum, caul.	ثَرْبٌ ج ثُرُوبٌ	To be skilful.	ثَقِفَ يَثْقَفُ
Bread with broth.	ثَرِيدٌ	Sagacity, intelligence.	ثَقَافَةٌ
To abound in wealth.	ثَرِيَ وَأَثْرَى	Well-made; educated.	مُثَقَّفٌ
Wealth, riches.	ثَرَاءٌ وَثَرْوَةٌ	To be heavy.	ثَقُلَ يَثْقُلُ
The Pleiades.	ثُرَيَّا	To make heavy.	ثَقَّلَ
Moisture ; earth.	ثَرًى ج أَثْرَاءٌ	To burden, annoy.	ثَقَلَ عَلَى
Large serpent.	ثُعْبَانٌ ج ثَعَابِينُ	To deem heavy	إِسْتَثْقَلَ

Triangular ; triangle.	مُثَلَّثٌ	Weight, burden.	ثِقْلٌ ج أَثْقَالٌ
Trinity.	ثَالُوثٌ	Mankind and geni.	اَلثَّقَلَانِ
Trigonometry.	عِلْمُ الْمُثَلَّثَاتِ	Heavy.	ثَقِيلٌ ج ثُقَلَاءُ وَثِقَالٌ
To snow.	ثَلَجَ يَثْلِجُ وَاَثْلَجَ	Overburdened.	مُثْقَلٌ
Snow.	ثَلْجٌ ج ثُلُوجٌ	1⅖ dirhems.	مِثْقَالٌ ج مَثَاقِيلُ
Icy cold.	ثَلِجٌ	Mother bereft of children.	ثَاكِلٌ وَثَكْلَى
To blunt.	ثَلَمَ يَثْلِمُ ثَلْمًا وَثَلَّمَ	To blame, censure.	ثَلَبَ يَثْلِبُ
To be blunted.	ثَلِمَ وَتَثَلَّمَ وَاَثْلَمَ	Censure, reproach.	ثَلْبٌ
Furrow ; breach.	ثُلْمٌ	Fault, vice.	مَثْلَبَةٌ ج مَثَالِبُ
Yonder ; there.	ثَمَّ	To make three.	ثَلَّثَ
Then ; moreover.	ثُمَّ وَثُمَّتْ	To become three.	أَثْلَثَ
Antimony.	إِثْمِدٌ	Third part, third.	ثُلْثٌ وَثُلُثٌ
To bear fruit.	ثَمَرَ يَثْمُرُ وَأَثْمَرَ	Third.	ثَالِثٌ
Fruit.	ثَمَرٌ ج أَثْمَارٌ وَثِمَارٌ	Thirdly.	ثَالِثًا
A fruit.	ثَمَرَةٌ ج ثَمَرٌ وَثَمَرَاتٌ	Thrice, three times.	ثَلَاثًا
Productive, fruitful.	مُثْمِرٌ	Tuesday.	اَلثُّلَاثَاءُ وَالثُّلَثَاءُ
Intoxication.	ثَمَلٌ	Three.	ثَلَاثَةٌ أَوْ ثَلْثَةٌ م ثَلَاثٌ
To value, estimate.	ثَمَّنَ	Triliteral.	ثُلَاثِيٌّ
Price, value.	ثَمَنٌ ج أَثْمَانٌ	Thirty.	ثَلَاثُونَ وَثَلَثُونَ

Two.	إِثْنَان م ثِنْتَان وَآثْنَتَان
Monday.	يَوْمُ الإِثْنَيْنِ
Exception, exclusion.	إِسْتِثْنَاء
Exceptional.	إِسْتِثْنَائِيّ
Put in the dual, (noun).	مُثَنّى
The dual.	اَلْمُثْنّى
Excpeted, excluded.	مُسْتَثْنّى
To reward, recompense.	ثَوَّبَ
To reward.	أَثَابَ إِثَابَة
Garment.	ثَوْبٌ ج ثِيَابٌ وَاثْوَابٌ
Reward, recompense.	ثَوَابٌ
To rise up ; break out.	ثَارَ يَثُور
To stir up ; rouse.	ثَوَّرَ وَأَثَار
Bull, ox.	ثَوْرٌ ج أَثْوَارٌ وَثِيرَان
Excitement. Mutiny.	ثَوْرَة
Garlic.	ثُومٌ
To abide. To die.	ثَوَى يَثْوِي
Abode.	مَثْوًى ج مَثَاوٍ
Woman freed from her husband	ثَيِّبٌ ج ثَيِّبَات

Eighth part.	ثُمْنٌ ج أَثْمَان
Eighth.	ثَامِن
Eight.	ثَمَانِيَة م ثَمَانٍ
Eighty.	ثَمَانُون
Costly, precious.	ثَمِينٌ وَمُثْمِنٌ
Valuation, estimation.	تَثْمِين
Estimator appraiser.	وَمُثَمِّن
Octagon. Estimated.	مُثَمَّن
To fold, double.	ثَنَى يَثْنِي ثَنْياً
To dissuade.	ثَنَى عَنْ
To make two.	ثَنَّى
To praise a person.	أَثْنَى عَلَى
To be bent, folded.	إِنْثَنَى
To desist from.	إِنْثَنَى عَنْ
To exclude.	إِسْتَثْنَى مِنْ
Praise, eulogy.	ثَنَاءٌ ج أَثْنِيَة
Second.	ثَانٍ م ثَانِيَة
Secondly.	ثَانِياً وَثَانِيَةً
Second, (time).	فِي إِثْنَاءِ ج ثَوَانٍ
Meanwhile.	ثَانِبَة ذَلِكَ

ج

The Angel Gabriel.	جِبْرِيلُ
Gypsum.	جِبْسٌ
To form, knead.	جَبَلَ يَجْبِلُ
Mountain.	جَبَلٌ ج أَجْبَالٌ وَجِبَالٌ
Natural temper.	جِبْلَةٌ وَجَبْلَةٌ
Mountainous.	جَبَلِيٌّ
Natural, inborn.	جِبِلِّيٌّ
Kneaded ; formed.	مَجْبُولٌ
To be timid, cowardly.	جَبُنَ يَجْبُنُ
To become curdled.	تَجَبَّنَ
Cowardice.	جُبْنٌ وَجَبَانَةٌ
Cheese.	جُبْنٌ وَجِبْنٌ
Brow forehead.	جَبِينٌ
Coward.	جَبَانٌ ج جُبَنَاءُ
Burying-ground.	جَبَّانَةٌ
Brow, forehead.	جَبْهَةٌ
To gather taxes.	جَبَا يَجْبُو وَيَجْبِي
To choose.	إِجْتَبَى

As a numeral sign = 3.	ج
Primate of Christians.	جَاثَلِيقٌ
Agitation, commotion.	جَاشٌ
To lop ; cut off.	جَبَّ يَجُبُّ
A deep well.	جُبٌّ ج أَجْبَابٌ
A long coat.	جُبَّةٌ ج جِبَبٌ
To set a broken bone. To repair.	جَبَرَ يَجْبِرُ
To force, compel.	جَبَرَ عَلَى
To set a broken bone.	جَبَّرَ
To constrain, force.	أَجْبَرَ عَلَى
To be haughty.	تَجَبَّرَ عَلَى
Compulsion.	جَبْرٌ
Algebra.	أَلْجَبْرُ
Bandage ; splint.	جَبِيرَةٌ ج جَبَائِرُ
Strong, Proud.	جَبَّارٌ ج جَبَابِرَةٌ
God. Orion.	أَلْجَبَّارُ
Bone-setter.	مُجَبِّرٌ
Set (bone) ; constrained.	مَجْبُورٌ

Fortune, success.	جَدّ	Tribute, tax.	جِبَايَة ج جِبَايَات
Exertion, seriousness.	جِدّ	Tax-gatherer.	جَابٍ
Much ; very ; seriously.	جِدًّا	Corpse ; body.	جُثّة ج جُثَث
Grandfather.	جَدّ ج جُدُود	To kneel.	جَثَا يَجْثُو جُثُوًّا
Grandmother.	جَدّة ج جَدّات	To deny ; disbelieve.	جَحَدَ يَجْحَد
New, recent.	جَدِيد ج جُدُد	Denying. An apostate.	جَاحِد
Drought ; dearth.	جَدْب	Unbelief ; denial.	جُحُود
Sterile, bare.	أَجْدَب م جَدْبَاء	Den, hole.	جُحْر ج أَجْحَار وَأَجْحِرَة
Imbecile, idiot.	مَجْدُوب	Foal of an ass.	جَحْش ج جِحَاش
Grave.	جَدَث ج أَجْدَاث	To protrude (eye).	جَحَظَ ـَ جُحُوظًا
Wall, enclosure.	جِدَار ج جُدُر	To look sharply at.	جَحَظَ إِلَى
Small-box.	جَدَرِيّ	To injure ; oppress.	أَجْحَفَ بِ
Fit, worthy of.	جَدِير بِ	Damage ; injury.	إِجْحَاف
More worthy, fitted.	أَجْدَر	Large fire ; hell.	جَحِيم
To cut off, main.	جَدَعَ يَجْدَع	To exert oneself.	جَدَّ يَجِدّ
Mutilation.	جَدْع	To be new.	جَدَّ جِدَّة
Maimed, mutilated.	أَجْدَع	To renew ; restore.	جَدَّدَ
To row.	جَدَفَ	To be renewed, restored.	تَجَدَّد
To blaspheme.	جَدَفَ عَلَى	To become new.	إِسْتَجَدَّ

Oar.	مِجْذَافٌ مَجَاذِيفُ	Blasphemy.	تَجْدِيفٌ ج تَجَادِيفُ
To cut off.	جَذَمَ يَجْذِم وَجَذَمَ	Oar, paddle.	مِجْذَافٌ ج مَجَاذِيفُ
Leprosy.	جُذَامٌ	To twist.	جَدَلَ يَجْدُلُ جَدْلاً
Leper.	أَجْذَمُ ج جُذْمَى	To braid the hair.	جَدَّلَ
To draw, drag.	جَرَّ يَجُرُّ جَرًّا	To contend, dispute.	جَادَلَ
To be pulled, drawn.	إِنْجَرَّ	Contention, dispute.	جِدَالٌ وَمُجَادَاةٌ
To chew the cud.	إِجْتَرَّ	Brook. List.	جَدْوَلٌ ج جَدَاوِلُ
And so on, et cetera.	هَلُمَّ جَرًّا	Plaited, twisted.	مَجْدُولٌ
Prepositions.	حُرُوفُ ٱلْجَرِّ	To be useful, profitable.	اجْدَى
Mechanics.	جَرُّ ٱلْأَثْقَالِ	Gift. Benefit.	جَدْوَى
Earthen jar.	جَرَّةٌ ج جِرَارٌ	Kid. Capricorn.	جَدْيٌ ج جِدَاءٌ
Preposition and case governed by it.	جَارٌّ وَمَجْرُورٌ	To draw ; attract.	جَذَبَ يَجْذِبُ
Large army.	جَيْشٌ جَرَّارٌ	To be drawn, attracted.	إِنْجَذَبَ
Sin, crime.	جَرِيرَةٌ ج جَرَائِرُ	Power of attraction.	قُوَّةٌ جَاذِبَةٌ
Milky-way.	ٱلْمَجَرَّةُ	To lop, cut off.	جَذَرَ يَجْذِر
To be bold.	جَرُؤَ يَجْرُؤُ جَرَاءَةً	Root, origin. Root of number.	جَذْرٌ ج جُذُورٌ
To embolden, encourage.	جَرَّأَ	Lad, youth.	جَذَعٌ وَجِذْعَانٌ
To bare, venture.	إِجْتَرَأَ	Trunk of tree.	جِذْعٌ
Boldness, courage.	جُرْأَةٌ وَجَرَاءَةٌ	To row (a boat).	جَذَفَ يَجْذِفُ

To strip, abstract.	جَرَّدَ	To have the itch.	جَرِبَ يَجْرَبُ
To be stripped, bared.	تَجَرَّدَ	To put to the test, try.	جَرَّبَ
Locusts.	جَرَادٌ	Itch, scabies.	جَرَبٌ
Branch of palm-tree.	جَرِيدٌ	Leathern sack.	جِرَابٌ ج أَجْرِبَةٌ
Naked, hairless.	اجْرَدُ م جَرْدَاءُ	Suffering from itch.	أَجْرَبُ
Separated ; bare, naked.	مُجَرَّدٌ	A corn-measure.	جَرِيبٌ ج أَجْرِبَةٌ
Solely for.	مُجَرَّدًا لِ	Trial, experiment; temptation.	تَجْرِبَةٌ ج تَجَارِبُ
Abstractions.	مُجَرَّدَاتٌ	Tried, tested.	مُجَرَّبٌ
Field-rat.	جُرَذٌ ج جِرْذَانٌ	Root ; germ.	جُرْثُومَةٌ ج جَرَاثِيمُ
Bundle of sticks.	جُرْزَةٌ	Cress, water-cress.	جِرْجِيرٌ
Bell.	جَرَسٌ ج أَجْرَاسٌ	To wound, hurt.	جَرَحَ يَجْرَحُ
To bruise ; bray.	جَرَشَ يَجْرُشُ	Wound, cut.	جُرْحٌ ج جُرُوحٌ
Hand-mill.	جَارُوشٌ ج جَوَارِيشُ	Wound.	جِرَاحَةٌ ج جِرَاحٌ
To swallow.	جَرَعَ يَجْرَعُ وَاجْتَرَعَ	Surgery.	عِلْمُ الْجِرَاحَةِ
Draught of water.	جُرْعَةٌ	Surgeon.	جَرَّاحٌ وَجِرَاحِيٌّ
To sweep away.	جَرَفَ يَجْرُفُ	Wounded.	جَرِيحٌ ج جَرْحَى
Shovel ; hoe.	مِجْرَفَةٌ	Beast of prey.	جَارِحَةٌ ج جَوَارِحُ
To commit a crime.	جَرَمَ وَأَجْرَمَ	Wounded.	مَجْرُوحٌ ج مَجَارِيحُ
To impute a crime falsely.	تَجَرَّمَ	Covered with wounds.	مُجَرَّحٌ

Fleece, shorn wool.	جَزَّة
Shearer.	جَزَّاز
Shears, scissors.	مَجَزّ
Shorn, cut.	مَجْزُوز
To divide into portions.	جَزّا
To be divided into parts.	تَجَزّا
Part, portion.	جُزْء ج أَجْزَاء
Partial, particular.	جُزْئِي
Particular proposition.	جُزْئِيّة
Details, parts ; trifles.	جُزْئِيَّات
Apothecary, druggist.	أَجْزَائِي
Pharmacy.	أَجْزَائِيّة
Divided into parts.	مُتَجَزِّى
To slaughter, kill.	جَزَرَ يَجْزُر
To ebb (sea).	جَزَرَ يَجْزُر جَزْراً
Slaughter. Ebb.	جَزْر
Carrots.	جَزَر
Butcher ; slaughterer.	جَزَّار
Island.	جَزِيرة ج جَزَائِر وَجُزُر

Sin, crime.	جُرْم ج جُرُوم وَأَجْرَام
Body, bulk.	جُرْم ج أَجْرَام
The celestial bodies.	الأَجْرَام الفَلَكِيّة
Boat, lighter.	جُرْم ج جُرُوم
Verily, truly.	لَا جَرَم
Sin, guilt, crime.	جَرِيمة ج جَرَائِم
Criminal, guilty.	مُجْرِم
Mortar, basin.	جُرْن ج أَجْرَان
Cub, whelp.	جَرْو ج أَجْرِية
To flow.	جَرَى يَجْرِي جَرْياً وَجَرَيَاناً
To cause to flow.	جَرَّى وَأَجْرَى
To carry out, execute.	أَجْرَى
To agree with.	جَارَى في
Rations of a soldier.	جِرَاية
Running ; current.	جَارٍ
Slave-girl, girl.	جَارِية
Execution of an order.	إِجْرَاء
Course ; duct.	مَجْرَى ج مَجَارٍ
To shear, cut, mow.	جَزَّ يَجُزّ

Peninsula.	شبْهُ جَزِيرَةٍ	Tax on a tributary ; land tax.	جِزْيَةٌ
Algiers.	اَلْجَزَائِر	To touch.	جَسَّ يَجِسُّ وَآجْتَسَّ
Slaughter-house.	مَجْزَرٌ ج مَجَازِر	To spy out.	جَسَّ وَتَجَسَّسَ
To grow impatient.	جَزِعَ يَجْزَعُ	Spy.	جَاسُوسٌ ج جَوَاسِيسُ
Impatience, grief.	جَزَعٌ وَجُزُوعٌ	To assume a body.	تَجَسَّدَ
Impatient.	جَزِعٌ وَجَزُوعٌ	Body, flesh.	جَسَدٌ ج أَجْسَادٌ
At random, by conjecture.	جَزْفٌ وَمُجَازَفَةً وَجِزَافًا	Corporeal.	جَسَدِيٌّ وَجُسْدَانِيٌّ
		Incarnation.	تَجَسُّدٌ
To abound.	جَزُلَ يَجْزُلُ جَزَالَةً	To dare venture.	جَسَرَ يَجْسُرُ
To give largely.	أَجْزَلَ	To venture boldly.	تَجَاسَرَ
Abundant ; much.	جَزِيل	Bridge. Dike.	جِسْرٌ ج أَجْسُرٌ
Very venerable.	جَزِيلُ الْاَحْتِرَام	Courage, audacity.	جَسَارَةٌ
To decide ; make binding.	جَزَمَ يَجْزِمُ جَزْمًا	Bold, courageous.	جَسُورٌ
Boot.	جَزْمَةٌ ج جَزْمَات	Courage, audacity.	تَجَاسُرٌ
Decisive.	جَازِمٌ ج جَوَازِمُ	To be large.	جَسُمَ جَسَامَةً
To recompense.	جَزَى يَجْزِي	To assume a form.	تَجَسَّمَ
To reward.	جَازَى	Body.	جِسْمٌ ج أَجْسَامٌ
To be rewarded or punished.	تَجَازَى	Bodily ; material.	جُسْمَانِي
Requital, reward.	جَزَاءٌ وَمُجَازَاةٌ	Importance.	جَسَامَةٌ

Eyelid. جَفْنٌ ج جُفُونٌ وَأَجْفَانٌ	Large. Important. جَسِيمٌ
To treat rudely. جَفَا يَجْفُو جَفَاءً	Solid, corporeal, bulky. مُجَسَّمٌ
To shun, turn away from. جَافَى	To belch, eruct. جَشَأَ وَتَجَشَّأَ
Harshness. جَفْوَةٌ وجَفَاءٌ	Eructation. جُشَاءٌ
Thick, coarse, rude. جَافٍ	To undertake a difficult task. جَشِمَ وتَجَشَّمَ
To be great. جَلَّ يَجِلُّ جَلَالًا	Gypsum ; mortar. جَصٌّ
To disdain. جَلَّ وَتَجَالَّ عَنْ	Quiver. جَعْبَةٌ ج جِعَابٌ
To honour, magnify. اجَلَّ	To be curly (hair). جَعُدَ يَجْعُدُ
Pack-saddle. جَلٌّ ج أَجْلَالٌ	To be curly, wrinkled. تَجَعَّدَ
The gist of a matter. جَلُّ الْأَمْرِ	Buffoon ; low fellow. جُعَيْدِيٌّ
Splendour, majesty. جَلَالٌ	To put, place, make. جَعَلَ يَجْعَلُ
Maker of pack-saddles. جَلَالَاتِيٌّ	He began to weep. جَعَلَ يَبْكِي
Human greatness ; majesty. جَلَالَةٌ	Pay, wages; bribe. جَعَالَةٌ وَجُعْلٌ
Great. جَلِيلٌ ج أَجِلَّاءُ	To become dry. جَفَّ يَجِفُّ جَفَافًا
Book ; review. مَجَلَّةٌ	To dry cause to dry. جَفَّفَ
To gather ; bring. جَلَبَ يَجْلُبُ	To become dry. تَجَفَّفَ
To be led, imported. إِنْجَلَبَ	Dry, withered, جَافٌّ وَجَفِيفٌ
Importation, import. جَلْبٌ	To be frightened, shy. جَفَلَ وَأَجْفَلَ
Camlour, noise, tumult. جَلَبٌ	To put to flight ; frighten. جَفَّلَ

Hoar-frost, ice.	جَلِيدٌ	Imported slaves, cattle.	جَلَبٌ
Book-binder.	مُجَلِّدٌ	Scab. Hunger, distress.	جُلْبَةٌ
Bound in leather, book.	مُجَلَّدٌ	Clamour, tumult.	جَلَبَةٌ
To sit, sit up.	جَلَسَ يَجْلِسُ	Cattle or slave-dealer.	جَلَّابٌ
To sit in company with.	جَالَسَ	Julep, raisin-water.	جُلَّابٌ
To cause to sit.	أَجْلَسَ	Drawn ; imported.	مَجْلُوبٌ
A single sitting ; session.	جَلْسَةٌ	Little bell.	جُلْجُلٌ ج جَلَاجِلُ
Sitting. Straight.	جَالِسٌ	Baldness on the temples.	جَلَحَةٌ
Act of sitting.	جُلُوسٌ	Bald on the temples.	أَجْلَحُ
Companion.	جَلِيسٌ ج جُلَسَاءُ	To whet (a razor).	جَلَخَ وَجَلَّخَ
Council.	مَجْلِسٌ ج مَجَالِسُ	Grindstone.	جَلْخٌ
Council of ministers.	مَجْلِسُ ٱلْوُزَرَاءِ	To scourge.	جَلَدَ يَجْلِدُ جَلْداً
Court of the First Instance.	ٱلْمَجْلِسُ ٱلْاِبْتِدَائِيُّ	To be frozen.	جَلَدَ يَجْلُدُ جَلْداً
Court of Appeal.	مَجْلِسُ ٱلْاِسْتِئْنَافِ	To bind a book.	جَلَّدَ
Mixed Tribunal.	ٱلْمَجْلِسُ ٱلْمُخْتَلَطُ	To bear patiently.	تَجَلَّدَ
Council of war.	مَجْلِسٌ حَرْبِيٌّ	Endurance. Firmament.	جَلَدٌ
To tear, scrape.	جَلَفَ يَجْلِفُ جَلْفاً	Skin, hide, leather.	جِلْدٌ ج جُلُودٌ
Large sack.	جُوَالِقٌ ج جَوَالِيقُ	Endurance.	جَلَادَةٌ وَجُلُودَةٌ
Catapult.	مِنْجَلِيقٌ وَمِنْجَنِيقٌ	Executioner.	جَلَّادٌ

Mineral, solid.	جَمَادٌ
The fifth and sixth months of the Mohammedan year.	جُمَادَى ٱلاوَّلِ ، ٱلآخِرَة
Live coal. Tribe.	جَمْرَةٌ ج جَمْرٌ
Carbuncle (disease).	جَمْرَةٌ
Censer ; fire-pan.	مِجْمَرَةٌ ج مَجَامِرُ
Sycamore.	جَمَّيْزٌ وجُمَّيْزَى
Buffalo.	جَامُوسٌ ج جَوَامِيسُ
To gather, add.	جَمَعَ يَجْمَعُ
To bring together.	جَمَعَ بَيْنَ
To agree upon.	أَجْمَعُوا عَلَى
To assemble, be gathered.	تَجَمَّعَ وٱجْتَمَعَ
Assembly ; plural.	جَمْعٌ ج جُمُوعٌ
Whole plural.	ٱلْجَمْعُ ٱلسَّالِمُ
Broken plural.	جَمْعُ ٱلتَّكْسِيرِ
Week.	جُمْعَةٌ ج جُمَعٌ
Friday.	ٱلْجُمْعَةُ
Party ; community.	جَمَاعَةٌ
Collector ; comprehensive.	جَامِعٌ

To polish ; remove.	جَلَا يَجْلُو
To become evident.	جَلَا لِ
To depart.	جَلَا عَنْ
To emigrate.	أَجْلَى
To appear.	تَجَلَّى لِ
To be disclosed.	إِنْجَلَى
Clearness. Emigration.	جَلَاءٌ
Clear, evident, manifest.	جَلِيٌّ
Clearly, evidently.	جَلِيًّا
Transfiguration.	ٱلتَّجَلِّي (عِيدُ)
Polished, planed.	مَجْلُوٌّ و مَجْلِيٌّ
To polish.	جَلَى يَجْلِي جَلْيًا
Great number, crowd.	جَمٌّ غَفِيرٌ
Skull.	جُمْجُمَةٌ ج جَمَاجِمُ
To be restive, runaway (horse).	جَمَحَ يَجْمَحُ
Refractory.	جَامِحٌ و جَمُوحٌ
To congeal, harden.	جَمَدَ يَجْمُدُ
Underived word.	جَامِدٌ ج جَوَامِدُ
The mineral kingdom	ٱلْجَوَامِدُ

Sum, total; summary.	مُجْمَل
Multitude.	جُمْهُور ج جَمَاهِير
Republican.	جُمْهُورِي
Republic.	جُمْهُورِيَّة
To be dark (night).	جَنَّ يَجِنُّ
To become mad.	جَنَّ
To madden.	جَنَّ وَأَجَنَّ
Demons, genii.	جِنّ وَجَان وَجِنَّة
Garden, paradise.	جَنَّة ج جَنَّات
Heart, mind.	جَنَان ج أَجْنَان
Madness, insanity.	جُنُون
Embryo, fœtus.	جَنِين ج أَجِنَّة
Small garden.	جُنَيْنَة
Shield.	مِجَنّ ج مَجَانّ
Mad, insane.	مَجْنُون ج مَجَانِين
To shun, avoid.	تَجَنَّبَ وَاجْتَنَبَ
Side, flank.	جَنْب ج جُنُوب
Pleurisy.	ذَاتُ الجَنْبِ
Flank, part.	جَانِب ج جَوَانِب

Mosque.	جَامِع ج جَوَامِع
All, the whole of.	جَمِيع
All; altogether.	جَمِيعًا
Company; committee.	جَمْعِيَّة
All, whole.	أَجْمَع ج أَجْمَعُون
Unanimity.	إِجْمَاع
Assembly, gathering.	إِجْتِمَاع
Confluence. Society of learned men.	مَجْمَع ج مَجَامِع
United, total.	مَجْمُوع ج مَجَامِيع
Pay, salary.	جَامِكِيَّة
To embellish, adorn.	جَمَّلَ
To treat with affability.	جَامَلَ
Camel.	جَمَل ج جِمَال
Sum, total. Sentence, phrase, paragraph.	جُمْلَة ج جُمَل
In the aggregate.	بِالجُمْلَة
Beauty, grace.	جَمَال
Camel-driver.	جَمَّال
Handsome, good deed.	جَمِيل
Generally speaking.	بِالإِجْمَال

To make similar.	جَنَّسَ	Mild, gentle.	لَيْنُ الْجَانِبِ
To appear similar.	جَانَسَ	Title of respect.	جَنَابٌ
Genus, kind, race, sex ; nationality.	جِنْسٌ ج أَجْنَاسٌ	South ; south wind.	جَنُوبٌ
Generic noun.	إِسْمٌ جِنْسِيٌّ	Southern.	جَنُوبِيٌّ
Nationality.	جِنْسِيَّة	Foreign.	أَجْنَبِيٌّ ج أَجَانِبُ
Of the same kind.	مُجَانِس	Act of avoiding.	إِجْتِنَابٌ وَتَجَنُّبٌ
To act unjustly.	جَنِفَ وَأَجْنَفَ	To incline towards.	جَنَحَ يَجْنَحُ
Wrong, injustice.	جَنَفٌ	Wing.	جَنَاحٌ ج أَجْنِحَة
Coarse linen.	جِنْفَاصٌ وَجَنْفِيصٌ	Sin, crime, guilt.	جُنَاحٌ
Catapult.	مَنْجَنِيقٌ ج مَجَانِقُ وَمَجَانِيقُ	To levy troops.	جَنَّدَ
To gather (fruit).	جَنَى ـ وَأَجْتَنَى	To be enlisted, enrolled.	تَجَنَّدَ
To commit a crime.	جَنَى جِنَايَةً	Army.	جُنْدٌ ج جُنُودٌ
To accuse falsely.	تَجَنَّى عَلَى	A soldier.	جُنْدِيٌّ
A gatherer. Criminal.	جَانٍ	Grasshopper.	جُنْدُبٌ ج جَنَادِبُ
Crime ; sin.	جِنَايَةٌ	To throw a man down.	جَنْدَلَ
To toil.	جَهَدَ	A kind of plum.	جَنَرِيك
To weary, fatigue.	جَهَّدَ	Funeral, corps.	جَنَازَةٌ ج جَنَائِزُ
To struggle.	جَاهَدَ مُجَاهَدَةً وَجِهَادًا	Funeral rites.	جِنَازٌ ج جَنَانِيزُ
To strive after.	إِجْتَهَدَ فِي	Verdigris.	جُنْزَارٌ

To affect ignorance.	تَجَاهَل	Exertion, effort.	جهْدٌ
To deem one ignorant.	إِسْتَجْهَلَ	He did his best.	أَفْرَغَ جَهْدَهُ
Ignorance. Folly.	جَهْلٌ وَجَهَالَةٌ	Combat, struggle.	جِهَادٌ
Ignorant, fool.	جَاهِلٌ	Military.	جِهَادِيٌّ
Pre-islamic age.	أَلْجَاهِلِيَّة	Diligence, effort.	إِجْتِهَادٌ
Unknown. Passive verb.	مَجْهُولٌ	Champion.	مجَاهِدٌ
Hell.	جهَنم	To publish.	جهَرَ بِ
Hellish, infernal.	جهَنِّيٌّ	To be dazzled.	جهِرَ يَجْهَر
Sky, atmosphere.	جوٌّ	To declare publicly.	جَاهَرَ بِ
To travel.	جَابَ يَجُوب	To appear in public.	تَجَاهَرَ
To answer, reply.	جَاوَب	Publicly, openly.	جهْرًا وَجِهَارًا
To answer, respond.	أَجَابَ	Day-blind.	اجْهَرُ م جَهْرَاء
To answer ; listen to.	إِسْتَجَابَ	Microscope.	مجْهَرٌ
Answer reply.	جَوَابٌ ج أَجْوِبَة	To equip, fit out.	جهَّزَ
Compliance.	إِجَابَةٌ وَاسْتِجَابَةٌ	To get ready.	تجهَّزَ
Answerer.	مجِيبٌ وَمسْتَجِيبٌ	Trousseau. Requi- sites, apparatus.	جهَازٌ ج أَجْهِزَة
Answered (prayer).	مسْتَجَابٌ	Equipment, expedition.	تجْهِيزٌ
Broadcloth.	جُوخٌ ج أَجْوَاخٌ	To be ignorant.	جهِلَ يَجْهَل
Cloth-maker or dealer.	جوَّاخٌ	To impute ignorance.	جهَّلَ

Stocking.	جَوْرَبٌ ج جَوَارِبَ	To excel.	جَادَ يَجُودُ جُوْدَةً
To pass, travel.	جَازَ يَجُوزُ	To give abundantly.	جَادَ جُوداً
To be allowable.	جَازَ جَوَازاً	To make good.	جَوَّدَ
To allow ; permit.	جَوَّزَ	Liberality, generosity.	جُودٌ
To exceed.	جَاوَزَ مُجَاوَزَةً	Goodness, excellence.	جُوْدَةٌ
To allow ; permit.	أَجَازَ إِجَازَةً	Generous.	جَوَادٌ ج أَجْوَادٌ
To exceed the bounds.	تَجَاوَزَ	Fleet (horse).	جَوَادٌ ج جِيَادٌ
To overlook.	تَجَاوَزَ عَنْ	Good, excellent.	جَيِّدٌ ج جِيَادٌ
To pass by.	إِجْتَازَ بِ	Very well.	جَيِّداً
Nut, nut-tree. Walnut.	جَوْزٌ	To oppress.	جَارَ يَجُورُ عَلَى
Cocoa-nut.	جَوْزٌ هِنْدِيٌّ	To be contiguous.	جَاوَرَ
Nutmeg.	جَوْزُ الطِّيبِ	To save ; protect.	أَجَارَ إِجَارَةً
Twins. Orion.	الجَوْزَاءُ	To be neighbours.	تَجَاوَرَ
Passing ; lawful.	جَائِزٌ	To seek protection.	إِسْتَجَارَ
Lawfulness ; passage.	جَوَازٌ	Neighbour.	جَارٌ ج جِيرَانٌ
Present, prize.	جَائِزَةٌ ج جَوَائِزُ	Oppression, tyranny.	جَوْرٌ
Permission ; licence.	إِجَازَةٌ	Neighbourhood, vicinity.	جِوَارٌ
Passage. Figurative.	مَجَازٌ	Neighbour ; contiguous.	مُجَاوِرٌ
Metaphoric.	مَجَازِيّ	Protector, defender.	مُجِيرٌ

Honour, rank, dignity	جَاهٌ	Coat of mail.	جَوْشَنٌ ج جَوَاشِنُ
Jewels, pearls. Essence, nature element.	جَوْهَرٌ ج جَوَاهِر	To be hungry.	جَاعَ يَجُوعُ
Atom ; monad.	اَلْجَوْهَر ٱلْفَرْدُ	To starve.	جَوَّعَ وَأَجَاعَ
		Hunger.	جُوعٌ
A jewel, pearl.	جَوْهَرَةٌ	Hungry.	جَائِعٌ ج جِيَاعٌ
Jeweller. Essential.	جَوْهَرِيٌّ	Famine ; hunger.	مَجَاعَةٌ
Interior, inward.	جَوَّانِيٌّ	To hollow.	جَوَّفَ
To come, arrive.	جَاءَ يَجِيءُ	Cavity. Belly.	جَوْفٌ ج أَجْوَافٌ
To bring.	جَاءَ بِ	Empty, hollow.	اجْوَف
Act of coming, arrival.	مَجِيءٌ	Cavity.	تَجْوِيفٌ ج تَجَاوِيفُ
Pocket, Sinus.	جَيْبٌ ج جِيُوبٌ		
Neck.	جِيدٌ ج أَجْيَادٌ وَجِيودٌ	Hollow, empty.	مَجَوَّفٌ
Gypsum ; quicklime.	جِيرٌ	Crowd.	جَوْقَةٌ ج جَوْقَاتٌ
To collect an army.	جَيَّشَ	To travel.	جَالَ يَجُولُ
The soul.	جَأْشٌ وجَاشٌ	Travelling roaming.	جَائِلٌ
Army.	جَيْشٌ ج جِيُوشٌ	Act of travelling about.	جَوَلَانٌ
Corpse, carcass.	جِيفَةٌ ج جِيَفٌ	Range ; sphere of action.	مَجَالٌ
Race ; generation.	جِيلٌ ج أَجْيَالٌ	Vessel, tray.	جَامٌ ج جَامَاتٌ

ح

High priest, the Pope.	الْحَبْرُ الْأَعْظَمُ
Ink.	حِبْرٌ
Joy, gladness, happiness.	حُبُورٌ
Inkstand.	مَحْبَرَةٌ ج مَحَابِرُ
To imprison.	حَبَسَ يَحْبِسُ
To restrain.	حَبَسَ عَنْ
Prison.	حَبْسٌ ج حُبُوسٌ
Imprisonment.	حَبْسٌ وَآحْتِبَاسٌ
Retention.	إِحْتِبَاسٌ
Imprisoned ; arrested.	مَحْبُوسٌ
The Abyssinians.	حَبَشٌ وَحَبَشَةٌ
An Abyssinian.	حَبَشِيٌّ
Abyssinia.	بِلَادُ الْحَبَشِ وَالْحَبَشَةُ
To fail ; perish.	حَبَطَ يَحْبَطُ
Failure.	حُبُوطٌ
Basil, penny-royal.	حَبَقٌ
To weave ; unite.	حَبَكَ يَحْبُكُ

As a numeral sign = 8.	ح
To love.	حَبَّ يَحِبُّ حِبًّا وَحُبًّا
To make lovable.	حَبَّبَ إِلَى
To love ; like.	أَحَبَّ
To show love.	تَحَبَّبَ
To prefer.	إِسْتَحَبَّ عَلَى
Grain ; seed ; berry; pill ; pustule.	حَبٌّ ج حُبُوبٌ
Love, friendship.	حُبٌّ وَمَحَبَّةٌ
A grain.	حَبَّةٌ ج حَبَّاتٌ
Lover ; beloved.	حَبِيبٌ ج احِبَّاءُ
With all my heart.	حُبًّا وَكَرَامَةً
Dearer ; preferable.	أَحَبُّ
Lover ; friend.	مُحِبٌّ
Beloved ; liked.	مَحْبُوبٌ
Well done.	حَبَّذَا . يَاحَبَّذَا
To be glad.	حَبِرَ يَحْبَرُ حُبُورًا
Learned, good man.	حَبْرٌ ج أَحْبَارٌ

To decide, decree.	حَتَمَ يَحْتِمُ
To decide ; order.	حَتَمَ بِ
To compel.	حَتَمَ عَلَى
Final decision.	حَتْمٌ ج حُتُومٌ
Decided, fixed.	مَحْتُومٌ
To exhort, instigate.	حَثَّ يَحُثُّ
Instigation.	حَثٌّ وَإِحْثَاثٌ
To go as a pilgrim to Mecca.	حَجَّ يَحِجُّ
To overcome in argument.	حَجَّهُ
To dispute, contend with.	حَاجَّ
To offer as a proof.	إِحْتَجَّ بِ
To argue against.	إِحْتَجَّ عَلَى
Pilgrimage to Mecca.	حَجٌّ وَحِجَّةٌ
Proof ; title, deed. Pretext, excuse.	حُجَّةٌ ج حُجَجٌ
The last month of the Mohammedan year.	ذُو الحِجَّةِ
Pilgrim to Mecca.	حَاجٌّ ج حُجَّاجٌ
To hide, cover.	حَجَبَ يَحْجُبُ
To prevent.	حَجَبَ عَنْ
To conceal one's self.	إِحْتَجَبَ

Well woven ; strong.	مَحْبُوكٌ
To conceive (woman).	حَبِلَتْ تَحْبَلُ
To be entangled.	تَحَبَّلَ
Rope, cable.	حَبْلٌ ج حِبَالٌ
Jugular vein.	حَبْلُ الوَرِيدِ
Pregnancy, conception.	حَبَلٌ
Net, snare.	أُحْبُولَةٌ ج حَبَائِلُ
Pregnant (woman).	حُبْلَى ج حَبَالَى
Rope-maker.	حَبَّالٌ
To creep, crawl.	حَبَا يَحْبُو
To bepartial to.	حَابَى
Partiality, favour.	مُحَابَاةٌ
Partial.	مُحَابٍ
To rub off.	حَتَّ يَحُتُّ حَتًّا
Bit of anything.	حَتَّةٌ ج حَتَتٌ
Until, to, as far as, even.	حَتَّى
So that.	حَتَّى أَنْ
Death.	حَتْفٌ ج حُتُوفٌ
Natural death.	حَتْفَ أَنْفِهِ

To hop, leap.	حَجَلَ يَحْجِل
Partridge.	حَجَلّ ج حِجْلَانّ
Having white foot, or feet, (horse).	مُحَجَّلّ
To cup, scarify.	حَجَمَ يَحْجِم
To be cupped.	إِحْتَجَمَ
Bulk ; size.	حَجْمّ ج حُجُومّ
Art of cupping, cupping.	حِجَامَة
Cupper.	حَجَّامّ
Cupping instrument.	مِحْجَمّ
To propose riddles.	تَحَاجَى
Intelligence.	حِجًى ج أَحْجَاءّ
Enigma ; riddle.	أُحْجِيَّة ج أَحَاجِيّ
To confine, define.	حَدَّ يَحُدّ
To go into mourning.	حَدَّ حِدَادًا
To confine ; define ; sharpen.	حَدَّدَ
To look sharply.	أَحَدَّ ٱلنَّظَرَ
To be limited ; defined.	تَحَدَّدَ
To be excited.	إِحْتَدَّ
Limit, boundary.	حَدّ ج حُدُودّ

Partition; veil.	حِجَابّ ج حُجُبّ
Diaphragm.	ٱلْحِجَابُ ٱلْحَاجِزّ
Chamberlain. Door-keeper.	حَاجِبّ ج حُجَّابّ
Eye-brow.	حَاجِبّ ج حَوَاجِب
To prevent, restrain.	حَجَرَ يَحْجِر
To be turned into stone.	تَحَجَّرَ
Prevention, prohibition.	حَجْرّ
Stone.	حَجَرّ ج أَحْجَارّ وَحِجَارَة
Nitrate of silver.	حَجَر جَهَنَّم
Chamber ; sepulchre.	حُجْرَة
Stone-cutter.	حَجَّارّ ج حَجَّارُون
Larynx.	حَنْجَرَة ج حَنَاجِر
To prevent, hinder.	حَجَزَ يَحْجِز
To separate.	حَجَزَ بَيْن
To sequester goods.	حَجَزَ عَلَى
Prevention, restraint.	حَجْزّ
Arabia Petroea, Hijas.	ٱلْحِجَاز
A barrier.	حَاجِزّ ج حَوَاجِزّ
Hindered, prevented.	مَحْجُوز

Event.	حَادِثَةٌ ج حَوَادِثُ
Newness, youth.	حَدَاثَةٌ
New, recent.	حَدِيثٌ
Story, tale. Mohammedan tradition.	حَدِيثٌ ج أَحَادِيثُ
Tale.	احْدُوثَةٌ ج أَحَادِيثُ
Conversation.	مُحَادَثَةٌ
To descend.	إنْحَدَرَ
Descent.	حُدُورٌ وَآنْحِدَارٌ
To surmise.	حَدَسَ يَحْدِسُ فِي
Conjecture; guess.	حَدْسٌ
Hypotheses.	حَدَسِيَّاتٌ
To surround, enclose.	أَحْدَقَ بِ
To look sharply at.	حَدَّقَ إِلَى
The pupil of the eye.	حَدَقَةٌ
Garden.	حَدِيقَةٌ ج حَدَائِقُ
Glow (of a fire).	حَدَمٌ وَحَدَمٌ
Growing with heat.	مُحْتَدِمٌ
Camel-driver.	حَادٍ ج حُدَاةٌ

Impetuosity ; acerbity.	حِدَّةٌ
Sharp, pointed ; pungent.	حَادٌّ
Acute angle.	زَاوِيَةٌ حَادَّةٌ
Mourning.	حِدَادٌ
Blacksmith.	حَدَّادٌ
Iron.	حَدِيدٌ
A piece of iron.	حَدِيدَةٌ
Demarcation.	تَحْدِيدٌ
Limited ; bounded.	مَحْدُودٌ
Kite (hawk).	حِدَأَةٌ ج حِدَاءٌ
To become convex.	تَحَدَّبَ
To be hump-backed.	إحْدَوْدَبَ
Hump-backed.	أَحْدَبُ م حَدْبَاءُ
Convex ; bulging.	مُحَدَّبٌ
To happen, occur.	حَدَثَ يَحْدُثُ
To tell ; relate.	حَدَّثَ
To converse.	حَادَثَ مُحَادَثَةً
To cause to exist.	أَحْدَثَ
To converse together.	تَحَادَثَ

Placed opposite ; vis-a-vis.	مُحَاذ
To be hot.	حَرَّ يَحِرُّ
To set free, free (a slave).	حَرَّرَ
To be set free, freed.	تَحَرَّرَ
Heat.	حَرّ
Freeman ; noble.	حُرّ ج أَحْرَارٌ
Heat warmth.	حَرَارَة
Liberty, freedom.	حُرِّيَّة
Silk ; silk-stuff.	حَرِير
Letter, note.	تَحْرِير ج تَحَارِير
Hot, burning ; fervent.	حَارّ
Liberated ; set free.	مُحَرَّر
Heated (with anger, etc.)	مَحْرُور
To fight.	حَارَبَ مُحَارَبَة
To fight one another.	تَحَارَب
War, battle.	حَرْب ج حُرُوب
Enemy's territory.	دَارُ الحَرْب
Chameleon.	حِرْبَاء ج حَرَابِيّ
Lance ; bayonet.	حَرْبَة ج حِرَاب

The eleventh.	حَادِي عَشَر
To be cautious.	حَذِرَ يَحْذَر
To warn.	حَذَّر
To be cautious.	تَحَذَّرَ وَاحْتَذَرَ
Caution ; distrust.	حَذَرٌ وَحَذَرٌ
Cautious.	حَذِر ج حَذِرون
Take care !	حَذَار
A thing to be avoided.	مَحْذُور
To cut off ; drop.	حَذَفَ يَحْذِف
To throw at.	حَذَفَ ب
Elision ; suppression.	حَذْف
Cut off ; suppressed.	مَحْذُوف
To be skilful.	حَذَقَ يَحْذِق
Sharpness, skill.	حِذْق
Sharp ; clever.	حَاذِق ج حُذَّاق
To imitate, emulate.	حَذَا يَحْذُو حَذْواً
To be opposite to.	حَاذَى
Opposite to ; vis-à-vis.	حِذَاء
Shoe, sandal.	حِذَاء ج أَحْذِيَة

To be cautioned.	تَحَرَّسَ وَاَحْتَرَسَ	Place of prayer.	مِحْرَابٌ
Watch, guard.	حَرَاسَةٌ	To till.	حَرَثَ يَحْرُثُ حَرْثًا
Watchman, guard.	حَارِسٌ ج حُرَّاسٌ	Agriculture.	حِرَاثَةٌ
To excite discord.	حَرَّشَ بَيْنَ	Ploughman.	حَارِثٌ وَحَرَّاثٌ
To meddle with.	تَحَرَّشَ بِ	A plough.	مِحْرَثٌ وَمِحْرَاثٌ
Wood, thicket.	حُرْشٌ ج أَحْرَاشٌ	To be in difficulty.	حَرِجَ يَحْرَجُ
To covet eagerly.	حَرَصَ يَحْرِصُ	To be forbidden.	حَرِجَ عَلَى
Greed, cupidity.	حِرْصٌ	Narrow. Forbidden.	حَرِجٌ
Covetous.	حَرِيصٌ ج حُرَصَاءُ	No blame or sin.	لَا حَرَجَ
To incite, instigate.	حَرَّضَ عَلَى	Auction.	حَرَاجٌ
To turn from.	حَرَفَ يَحْرِفُ عَنْ	To be angry.	حَرَدَ يَحْرَدُ
To falsify, garble.	حَرَّفَ	Anger, grudge, hatred.	حَرَدٌ
To deviate from.	إِنْحَرَفَ عَنْ	Lizard.	حِرْذَوْنٌ ج حَرَاذِينَ
To earn sustenance.	إِحْتَرَفَ	To guard carefully.	حَرَزَ يَحْرِزُ
Edge, border.	حَرْفٌ ج حِرَفٌ	To guard. Obtain.	أَحْرَزَ
Letter, particle (in grammer).		To guard against.	تَحَرَّزَ وَاَحْتَرَزَ
	حَرْفٌ ج حُرُوفٌ وَأَحْرُفٌ	Caution ; amulet.	حِرْزٌ
Literal.	حَرْفِيٌّ	Fortified ; valued.	حَرِيز
Trade, craft.	حِرْفَةٌ ج حِرَفٌ	To guard, watch.	حَرَسَ يَحْرُسُ

To refuse, forbid.	حَرَمَ يَحْرُمُ	Pungency.	عَرَافَة
To be unlawful.	حَرَمَ يَحْرُمُ	Sharp, pungent.	حِرِّيفُ
To forbid.	حَرَّمَ	Falsified.	مُحَرَّفٌ
To be forbidden.	تَحَرَّمَ	Oblique ; trapezium	مُنْحَرِفٌ
To honour, venerate.	إِحْتَرَمَ	To burn.	حَرِقَ يَحْرَقُ وَاحْرَقَ
To hold as unlawful.	إِسْتَحْرَمَ	To be burned.	احْتَرَقَ وَتَحَرَّقَ
Excommunication.	حِرْمٌ	Heat, burning pain.	حُرْقَةٌ
Sacred (territory).	حَرَمٌ	Heat, conflagration.	حَرِيقٌ
Sacred territory at Mecca.	الحَرَمُ	Blister ; tinder	حَرَّاقَةٌ ج حَرَّاقَاتٌ
Mecca and Medina.	الحَرَمَانِ	Hip-bone.	حَرْقَفَةٌ ج حَرَاقِفُ
Sacredness. Wife.	حُرْمَةٌ ج حُرَمٌ	To be in motion.	حَرَكَ يَحْرُكُ
Unlawful, sacred.	حَرَامٌ	To move a thing	حَرَّكَ
El Kaaba.	ألمَسْجِدُ الحَرَامُ	To be moved.	تَحَرَّكَ
The month.	الشَّهْرُ الحَرَامُ . مُحَرَّمٌ	Brisk, nimble.	حَرِكٌ
Robber, thief.	حَرَامِيٌّ ج حَرَامِيَّةٌ	Motion ; gesture.	حَرَكَةٌ ج حَرَكَاتٌ
Women of a household.	حَرِيمٌ	Vowel-point.	(ٌ)
Unlawful ; first month of the Moslem year.	مُحَرَّمٌ	Motion.	حِرَاكٌ
Denied, refused. Excommunicated.	مَحْرُومٌ	Withers of a horse.	حَارِكٌ
Venerable, respected.	مُحْتَرَمٌ	Act of moving.	تَحْرِيكٌ

To rear and kick.	حَرَنَ يَحْرُنُ	Belt, girth.	حِزَامٌ ج أَحْزِمَةٌ
Restive, refractory.	حَرُونٌ	Prudent, resolute.	حَازِمٌ
To be adapted to.	حَرِيَ بِ	Belt, girth.	مِحْزَمٌ ج مَحَازِم
To seek, aim at.	تَحَرَّى	To grieve.	حَزَنَ يَحْزِنُ
Suitable, proper for.	حَرِيٌّ بِ	To be grieved.	حَزِنَ يَحْزَنُ
More suited, better.	أَحْرَى	To grieve another.	أَحْزَنَ
How much more.	كَمْ بِالْحَرِيِّ	Sadness.	حُزْنٌ ج أَحْزَانٌ
Rather.	بِالأَحْرَى	Sad, sorrowful.	حَزِينٌ
To cut, incise, notch.	حَزَّ يَحُزّ	Sad thing, sorrowful.	مُحْزِنٌ
Dandruff, scurff.	حَزَازٌ وَحَزَازَةٌ	Saddened, grieved.	مَحْزُونٌ
To collect parties.	حَزَّبَ	To feel ; perceive.	حَسَّ يَحِسُّ
Troop ; party.	حِزْبٌ ج أَحْزَابٌ	To feel ; perceive.	أَحَسَّ بِ
Leagued ; partisan.	مُتَحَزِّبٌ	Perception, sense.	حِسٌّ
To guess, compute.	حَزَرَ يَحْزِر	Perceptible.	حِسِّيٌّ وَمَحْسُوسٌ
June (month).	حَزِيرَانُ	Faculty of each of the five senses ; feeling.	حَاسَّةٌ ج حَوَاسٌّ
To tie together.	حَزَمَ يَحْزِم	The five senses.	الْحَوَاسُّ الْخَمْسُ
To be firm, prudent.	حَزُمَ يَحْزُم	Curry-comb.	مِحَسَّةٌ
Bundle, parcel.	حُزْمَةٌ ج حُزَمٌ	To count.	حَسَبَ يَحْسُبُ
Firmness, resolution, discretion.	حَزْمٌ		

To cut off ; stop.	حَسَمَ يَحْسِم	To suppose, consider.	حَسِبَ يَحْسِب
Sharp sword.	حُسَامٌ	To account with.	حَاسَبَ
To be handsome.	حَسُنَ يَحْسُن	To settle an account.	تَحَاسَبَ
To embellish, adorn.	حَسَّنَ	Sufficient ; sufficiency.	حَسْب
To treat well.	حَاسَنَ	According to.	بِحَسَب
To do a thing well.	أَحْسَنَ	Honour ; pedigree.	حَسَب
To confer a benefit.	أَحْسَنَ إِلَى	Account, calculation.	حِسَابٌ
To approve.	إِسْتَحْسَنَ	Arithmetic.	عِلْمُ الْحِسَابِ
Beauty ; good.	حُسْنٌ ج مَحَاسِن	Noble	حَسِيبٌ ج حُسَبَاء
Beautiful ; good.	حَسَنٌ ج حِسَان	Counted, calculated.	مَحْسُوبٌ
Good deed.	حَسَنَةٌ ج حَسَنَاتٌ	To envy.	حَسَدَ يَحْسُد
Goldfinch.	حَسُّونٌ	Envy, grudge.	حَسَد
More beautiful, better.	أَحْسَنَ	Envious.	حَاسِد وَحَسُود ج حُسَّادٌ
How beautiful.	مَا أَحْسَنَ	Envied ; object of envy.	مَحْسُود
Benefit, beneficence.	إِحْسَانٌ	To grieve for.	حَسَرَ يَحْسُر عَلَى
Good deeds or qualities.	مَحَاسِن	To feel regret.	تَحَسَّرَ عَلَى
To cut hay.	حَشَّ يَحُشُّ حَشًّا	Grief.	حَسْرَةٌ ج حَسَرَاتٌ
Smoker of hashish.	حَشَّاشٌ	Alas !	يَا حَسْرَتِي . وَاحَسْرَتَاه
Grass; hay. Hashish.	حَشِيشٌ	Hatred. Thistle.	حَسَكٌ

Part, share.	حِصّةٌ ج حِصَصٌ	To assemble, v. t.	حَشَدَ يَحْشُدُ
Stones, firewood.	حَصَبٌ	To be assembled.	إِحْتَشَدَ
Measles.	حَصْبَةٌ	Troop, assembly.	حَشْدٌ
To mow, reap.	حَصَدَ يَحْصُدُ	Places of assembling.	مَحَاشِدُ
Mower, reaper.	حَاصِدٌ وَحَصّادٌ	To assemble.	حَشَرَ يَحْشُرُ حَشْرًا
Harvest, harvest-time.	حَصَادٌ	Day of Judgment.	يَوْمُ الْحَشْرِ
Mown, reaped.	حَصِيدٌ وَمَحْصُودٌ	Place of gathering.	مَحْشَرٌ ج مَحَاشِرُ
To confine, restrict.	حَصَرَ يَحْصُرُ	Insect.	حَشَرَةٌ ج حَشَرَاتٌ
To besiege.	حَاصَرَ مُحَاصَرَةً	To stand in awe. or shame.	إِحْتَشَمَ
Restriction ; confinement.	حَصْرٌ	Attendants, retinue.	حَشَمٌ
Strictly speaking.	بِالْحَصْرِ	Reverence ; modesty.	حِشْمَةٌ
Siege, blockade.	حِصَارٌ وَمُحَاصَرَةٌ	Reverence ; modesty.	إِحْتِشَامٌ
Maker or seller of mats.	حَصَرِيٌّ	To stuff, cram.	حَشَا يَحْشُو
Mat.	حَصِيرٌ وَحَصِيرَةٌ ج حَصَائِرُ	To be filled.	إِحْتَشَى وَانْحَشَى
Besieger ; blockader.	مُحَاصِرٌ	Viscera, bowels.	حَشًا ج أَحْشَاءٌ
Besieged ; restricted.	مَحْصُورٌ	Stuffing, wadding.	حَشْوٌ
Green grapes.	حِصْرِمٌ	To abstain, disdain.	تَحَاشَى عَنْ
Sound judgment.	حَصَافَةٌ	Except. God forbid!	حَاشَا
To happen to one.	حَصَلَ ـ لُ	Annotation. Followers.	حَاشِيَةٌ ج حَوَاشٍ

To be present.	حَضَرَ يَحْضُرُ	To obtain, acquire.	حَصَلَ عَلَى
To come.	حَضَرَ إِلَى	To be obtained.	تَحَصَّلَ
To bring.	حَضَّرَ وَأَحْضَرَ	Result.	حَاصِلٌ ج حَوَاصِلُ
To be ready.	تَحَضَّرَ	The result ; in short.	الْحَاصِلُ
To cause to come.	إِسْتَحْضَرَ	Acquisition.	تَحْصِيلٌ
Towns, cultivated land.	حَضَرٌ	Result, produce.	مَحْصُولٌ ج مَحَاصِيلُ
Presence. Highness.	حَضْرَةٌ	To be fortified.	حَصُنَ يَحْصُنُ
Present, ready.	حَاضِرٌ	To fortify.	حَصَّنَ
Present tense.	الْحَاضِرُ	To be entrenched.	تَحَصَّنَ
Approach of death.	مُحْتَضَرٌ	Fortress.	حِصْنٌ ج حُصُونٌ
To embrace.	حَضَنَ يَحْضُنُ	Horse.	حِصَانٌ ج حُصُنٌ وَأَحْصِنَةٌ
Bosom.	حِضْنٌ ج حُضُونٌ	Strongly fortified.	حَصِينٌ
Nursing ; incubation.	حِضَانَةٌ	Fox.	أَبُو الْحُصَيْنِ
To fall, go down.	حَطَّ يَحُطُّ	To count, number.	أَحْصَى
To put down.	حَطَّ	Small pebbles.	حَصًى
To descend, fall.	إِنْحَطَّ	Small pebble.	حَصَاةٌ
Falling.	إِنْحِطَاطٌ	Innumerable.	غَيْرُ مُحْصًى
Railway station.	مَحَطٌّ وَمَحَطَّةٌ	To instigate, incite.	حَضَّ يَحُضُّ
Fallen, depressed.	مُنْحَطٌّ	Foot of a mountain.	حَضِيضٌ

Surrounded.	مَحْفُوفٌ	Placed, laid, deposited.	مَحْطُوطٌ
Grandson.	حَفِيدٌ ج حَفَدَةٌ	To collect fire-wood.	إِحْتَطَبَ
To dig.	حَفَرَ يَحْفِرُ وَآحْتَفَرَ	Fuel, wood.	حَطَبٌ
Ditch, pit.	حُفْرَةٌ ج حُفَرٌ	Wood-cutter.	حَطَّابٌ
Hoof.	حَافِرٌ ج حَوَافِرُ	To break.	حَطَمَ يَحْطِمُ وَحَطَّمَ
Grave-digger.	حَفَّارٌ	To crumble.	تَحَطَّمَ وَآنْحَطَمَ
Dug, dug out.	مَحْفُورٌ	Piece, fragment.	حِطْمَةٌ وَحُطَامٌ
To guard, keep.	حَفِظَ يَحْفَظُ	Goods or vanities of this world.	حُطَامُ آلدُّنْيَا
To be careful of.	حَافَظَ عَلَى	To be fortunate.	حَظَّ يَحَظُّ
To be watchful.	تَحَفَّظَ	Happiness.	حَظٌّ ج حُظُوظٌ
Guard; careful watch.	حِفْظٌ	Happy.	مَحْظُوظٌ
Truss.	حِفَاظٌ	To forbid.	حَظَرَ يَحْظُرُ عَلَى
Memory.	(أَلْقُوَّةُ) آلْحَافِظَةُ	Enclosure.	حَظِيرَةٌ ج حَظَائِرُ
Guardian, keeper.	مُحَافِظٌ	Prohibited things.	مَحْظُورَاتٌ
Guardianship.	مُحَافَظَةٌ	To obtain.	حَظِيَ يَحْظَى ب
Guarded, preserved.	مَحْفُوظٌ	To encompass.	حَفَّ ب
To gather, assemble.	حَفَلَ يَحْفِلُ	Dry bread.	خُبْزٌ حَافٌّ
To receive with honour.	إِحْتَفَلَ لَهُ	Edge, rim, border.	حَافَّةٌ
To give attention to.	إِحْتَفَلَ ب	Kind of litter.	مَحَفَّةٌ

Socket.	حَقٌّ ج حِقَاقٌ	Large assembly ; care.	حَفْلٌ
Case, casket.	حُقَّةٌ ج حُقَقٌ	Entirely full (hall &c.)	حَافِلٌ
Reality, truth. ssence.	حَقِيقَةٌ ج حَقَائِقُ	Celebration ; pomp.	إِحْتِفَالٌ
Truly.	حَقِيقَةً وَفِي الْحَقِيقَةِ	Assembly.	مَحْفِلٌ ج مَحَافِلُ
Real ; proper (sense).	حَقِيقِيٌّ	Place of assembly.	مُحْتَفَلٌ
More worthy of.	اَحَقُّ ب	Handful.	حَفْنَةٌ ج حَفَنَاتٌ
Merit.	إِسْتِحْقَاقٌ ج إِسْتِحْقَاقَاتٌ	To go bare-foot.	حَفِيَ يَحْفَى
Verification.	تَحْقِيقٌ	To show joy and honour.	حَفِيَ وَاحْتَفَى ب
Verified, confirmed.	مُحَقَّقٌ	Bare-footedness.	حَفَاءٌ وَحُفْوَةٌ
Worthy of, deserving.	مُسْتَحِقٌّ	Bare-foot ; unshod.	حَافٍ
A long time.	حُقْبٌ ج أَحْقَابٌ	To be true, right.	حَقَّ يَحِقُّ
Saddle-bag.	حَقِيبَةٌ	To verify, confirm.	حَقَّقَ
To bear spite.	حَقَدَ يَحْقِدُ	To assure one's self.	تَحَقَّقَ
Hatred, grudge, spite.	حِقْدٌ	To deserve ; fall due.	إِسْتَحَقَّ
Spiteful.	حَاقِدٌ وَحَقُودٌ	Right ; truth ; obligation, worth ; true ; truthful.	حَقٌّ ج حُقُوقٌ
To despise.	حَقَرَ يَحْقِرُ وَاحْتَقَرَ	Duty.	حَقٌّ عَلَى
To be contemptible.	حَقُرَ يَحْقُرُ	Worthy of.	حَقٌّ ب
Contempt ; vileness.	حَقَارَةٌ	Truly, indeed.	حَقًّا وَبِالْحَقِّ
Despised ; mean ; paltry.	حَقِيرٌ		

To do a thing well.	أَحْكَمَ	Field.	حَقْلٌ ج حُقُولٌ
To go together to law.	تَحَاكَمَ	To retain. Inject.	حَقَنَ يَحْقِن
Judgment ;	حُكْمٌ ج أَحْكَامٌ	To be congested.	إِحْتَقَنَ
government ; authority, rule.		Clyster ; syringe.	حُقْنَةٌ ج حُقَنٌ
Wisdom.	حِكْمَةٌ ج حِكَمٌ		
Judge ; governor.	حَاكِمٌ	Waist ; loins.	حَقْوٌ ج حِقَاءٌ
Judgment ; govern-	حُكُومَةٌ	To rub, scrape.	حَكَّ يَحُكُّ
ment.		To rub against.	إِحْتَكَّ بِ
Wise.	حَكِيمٌ ج حُكَمَاءُ	Rubbing ; scratching.	حَكٌّ
Well made.	مُحْكَمٌ	Magnetic compass.	حَكٌّ
Tribunal.	مَحْكَمَةٌ ج مَحَاكِمُ	An itching.	حِكَّةٌ وَحُكَاكٌ
To tell, relate.	حَكَى يَحْكِي	Touchstone.	مِحَكٌّ
To resemble.	حَاكَى وَحَاكَى	To withhold	تَحَكَّرَ وَاحْتَكَرَ
Story, tale, narrative.	حِكَايَةٌ	grain for sale at high prices.	
To alight, abide.	حَلَّ يَحُلُّ	Usurious grain-trade.	حُكْرَةٌ
To solve (a problem)	حَلَّ يَحُلُّ حَلًّا	To give judgment.	حَكَمَ يَحْكُم
dissolve (a solid) ; loosen.		To judge in favour of.	حَكَمَ لِ
To come upon one.	حَلَّ عَلَى	To judge against.	حَكَمَ عَلَى
To be lawful.	حَلَّ يَحِلُّ	To appoint one to judge.	حَكَّمَ
To permit. Analyze.	حَلَّلَ	To contest in law.	حَاكَمَ
To allow, permit.	أَحَلَّ		

To card cotton.	حَلَجَ يَحْلِج	To deem lawful.	إِسْتَحَلّ
Carding of cotton.	حِلَاجَة	A solving, dissolving.	حَلّ
Cotton-carder.	حَلَّاج	Lawful.	حِلّ
Instrument for carding.	مِحْلَج	Garment.	حُلَّة ج حُلَل
Snail.	حَلَزُون	Lawful ; right.	حَلَال
Spiral.	حَلَزُونِيّ	An alighting, abiding.	حُلُول
To swear.	حَلَفَ يَحْلِف	Husband ; wife.	حَلِيل م حَلِيلَة
To make swear.	حَلَّف وَآسْتَحْلَف	Deeming lawful.	إِسْتِحْلَال
To be in league with.	حَالَف	Dissolving ; analysis.	تَحْلِيل
To confederate.	تَحَالَف	Place ; quarter.	مَحَلّ ج مَحَال
Oath ; league.	حِلْف	Inn ; stopping-place.	مَحَلَّة
Confederate.	حَلِيف ج حُلَفَاء	To milk.	حَلَبَ يَحْلُب
Alliance.	تَحَالُف وَمُحَالَفَة	To flow ; exude.	تَحَلَّب وَآنْحَلَب
To shave.	حَلَقَ يَحْلِق	Aleppo.	حَلَب
Throat, palate.	حَلْق ج حُلُوق	Fenugreek.	حُلْبَة
Guttural letters.	حُرُوف ٱلْحَلْق	Milkman.	حَالِب وَحَلَّاب
Circle ; link, ear-ring.	حَلْقَة	Fresh milk.	حَلِيب
Barber.	حَلَّاق	Emulsion.	مُسْتَحْلَب
Barber's trade.	حِلَاقَة	Assafoetida.	حِلْتِيت

— ٥ —

Sweetened, sugared.	مُحَلَّى	Shaved, shorn.	حَليق ج خلْقَى
To be adorned.	حَلِيَ يَحْلَى	Shaved.	مَحْلوقٌ
To adorn (with jewels).	حَلَّى	Throat.	حُلْقُومٌ ج حَلَاقيم
To gild.	حَلَّى بِذَهَب	Intense blackness.	حَلَكٌ
To be adorned.	تَحَلَّى	Very black.	حَالِكٌ
Jewels ; ornaments.	حَلْيٌ ج حُلِيّ	To dream.	حَلَمَ يَحْلُمُ
Adornment.	حِلْيَةٌ ج حِلًى	To be gentle, mild.	حَلُمَ يَحْلُمُ
To have fever.	حُمَّ	Gentleness, clemency.	حِلْمٌ
To take a bath.	إِسْتَحَمَّ	Dream, vision.	حُلْمٌ ج أَحْلَامٌ
Fever.	حُمَّى ج حُمَّيَات	Teat, nipple.	حَلَمَةٌ
Thermal spring.	حَمَّة	Gentle, mild.	حَليمٌ ج حُلَمَاء
Fate ; death.	حِمَامٌ	To be sweet.	حَلَا يَحْلُو
Dove ; pigeon.	حَمَامَةٌ ج حَمَامٌ	To sweeten.	حَلَّى تَحْلِيَةً
Bath.	حَمَّامٌ ج حَمَّامَاتٌ	To find sweet.	إِسْتَحْلَى
Suffering from fever.	مَحْمومٌ	Sweet, agreable.	حُلْوٌ
To praise ; thank.	حَمَدَ يَحْمَدُ	Present ; gratuity.	حُلْوَانٌ
Praise ; thanks.	حَمْدٌ	Confectioner.	حَلْوَانِيٌّ
Praise be to God.	أَلْحَمْدُ لله	Sweetmeats.	حَلْوَى
Praised.	حَميدٌ	Sweetness.	حَلَاوَةٌ

Acidity ; sourness.	حُموضَةٌ	Praised, praiseworthy.	مَحْمُودٌ
Sorrel (plant).	حُماضٌ وَخُمَّيْضٌ	To dye red ; redden.	حَمَّرَ
Acidulated, acid, sour.	مُحَمَّضٌ	To become red; blush.	إِحْمَرَّ
To be foolish.	حَمَقَ يَحْمَقُ	Bitumen.	حُمَّرٌ
Stupidity, folly.	حُمْقٌ وَحَماقَةٌ	Redness. Erysipelas.	حُمْرَةٌ
Chicken-pox.	حماقٌ	Ass, donkey.	حِمارٌ ج حَميرٌ
Stupid, foolish.	اَحْمَقُ	Wild ass.	حِمارُ الْوَحْشِ
To carry, lift.	حَمَلَ يَحْمِلُ	Ass-driver.	حَمّارٌ ج حَمارَةٌ
To conceive (woman).	حَمَلَتْ	Red.	اَحْمَرُ م حَمْراءُ ج حُمْرٌ
To attack, charge.	حَمَلَ على	Rubefacient.	مُحَمِّرٌ
To bear fruit.	حَمَلَ يَحْمِلُ	To be hard in religion, etc.	حَمَسَ يَحْمَسُ
To overflow (river).	حَمَلَ النَّهْرُ	To irritate.	حَمَسَ وَأَحْمَسَ
To burden, load.	حَمَّلَ	Bravery energy.	حَماسَةٌ
To suffer patiently.	تَحَمَّلَ	To roast, toast.	حَمَّصَ
To bear, suffer.	إِحْتَمَلَ	To be roasted.	تَحَمَّصَ
To be possible.	إِحْتَمَلَ أَنْ	Hems (city).	حِمْصُ
Carrying. Pregnancy.	حَمْلٌ	Chick-peas.	حِمَّصٌ
Burden, load.	حِمْلٌ ج أَحْمالٌ	To be sour, acid.	حَمَضَ يَحْمَضُ
Lamb.	حَمَلٌ ج حُمْلانٌ	Acid ; sour.	حامِضٌ

Guard, garrison.	حَامِيَةٌ
Protection. Protégé,	حَمَايَة
Heated.	مُحْمًى
Protector ; advocate.	مُحَامٍ
To yearn.	حَنَّ يَحِنُّ إِلَى
To have compassion.	تَحَنَّنَ عَلَى
Compassionate, tender.	حَنَّانٌ وَحَنُونٌ
To dye with *Henna*.	حَنَّأَ
The plant *henna*.	حِنَّاءُ
Shop.	حَانُوتٌ ج حَوَانِيتُ
To break an oath.	حَنِثَ يَحْنَثُ
Perjury. Sin, crime.	حِنْثٌ
A perjurer.	حَانِثٌ
Snake.	حَنَشٌ ج أَحْنَاشٌ
To embalm.	حَنَّطَ وَأَحْنَطَ
Wheat.	حِنْطَةٌ
Colocynth.	حَنْظَلٌ
Tap.	حَنَفِيَّةٌ
To be enraged.	حَنِقَ يَحْنَقُ

Sign of the Ram (Aries).	أَلحَمَلُ
Attack ; charge in battle.	حَمْلَةٌ
Porter.	حَمَّالٌ
Patience ; endurance.	إِحْتِمَالٌ
Litter.	مَحْمِلٌ ج مَحَامِلُ
Borne ; suffered.	مَحْمُولٌ
Bearable. Possible.	مُحْتَمَلٌ
Father-in-law.	حَمٌو ج أَحْمَاءُ
Mother-in-law.	حَمَاةٌ ج حَمَوَاتٌ
To protect, defend.	حَمَى يَحْمِي
To be very hot.	حَمِيَ يَحْمَى
To make hot.	أَحْمَى إِحْمَاءً
To defend.	حَامَى عَنْ
To protect one's self.	إِحْتَمَى
Interdicted place.	حِمًى ج أَحْمَاءُ
Care of diet.	حِمْيَةٌ
Anger, rage. Disdain.	حَمِيَّةٌ
Venom, sting.	حُمَةٌ
Protector. Hot.	حَامٍ

Leather. Poplar tree.	حَوْرٌ	Violent anger ; spite.	حَنَقٌ
Disciple of a prophet.	حَوَارِيٌّ	To make wise.	حَنَكَ وَأَحْنَكَ
A quarter of a town.	حَارَةٌ	Palate.	حَنَكٌ ج احْنَاكٌ
Panier. Oyster.	مَحَارَةٌ	Experienced.	مُحَنَّكٌ
Pivot.	مِحْوَرٌ ج مَحَاوِر	To bend, incline.	حَنَى يَحْنِي
Conversation ; debate.	مُحَاوَرَةٌ	To be bent.	تَحَنَّى وَانْحَنَى
To get ; possess.	حَازَ يَحُوزُ	Tenderness, compassion.	حَنُوٌّ
To drow aside from.	إِنْحَازَ عَنْ	Wine-house, tavern.	حَانِيَةٌ
To turn to and join.	إِنْحَازَ إِلَى	Bent, crooked ; inclined.	مُنْحَنٍ
Space occupied by a body	حَيِّزٌ	Large fish. Whale.	حُوتٌ ج حِيتَانٌ
To gather, collect.	حَوَّشَ	To compel.	أَحْوَجَ
To be taken in.	إِنْحَاشَ	To want, need, require.	إِحْتَاجَ
Fold ; court.	حَوْشٌ ج احْوَاشٌ	Want ;	حَاجَةٌ ج حَاجَات وَحَوَائِج
Mixed people ; rabble.	حَوْشٌ	need ; necessity ; object ; desire.	
Saddle-girth, girdle.	حِيَاصَةٌ	Want ; having need.	إِحْتِيَاجٌ
Stomach of a bird.	حَوْصَلَةٌ	In want or need of.	مُحْتَاجٌ إِلَى
Reservoir, tank.	حَوْضٌ ج أَحْوَاضٌ	To overcome.	اسْتَحْوَذَ عَلَى
To surround ; enclose.	حَوَّطَ	Coachman, cabman.	حُوذِيٌّ
To invest, surround.	احَاطَ ب	To be bewildered.	حَارَ يَحَارُ
		To converse, debate.	حَاوَرَ

State, condition. حَالَةٌ ج حَالَاتٌ	Wall. حَائِطٌ ج حِيطَانٌ
Power. Year. حَوْلٌ ج أَحْوَالٌ	Investment. Caution. إِحْتِيَاطٌ
All around, around. حَوْلَ	Circumference. مُحِيطٌ
Squint. حَوَلٌ	The ocean. اَلْبَحْرُ اَلْمُحِيطُ
Transfer of a debt. حَوَالَةٌ	Edge, border. حَافَةٌ ج حَافَاتٌ
Stratagem ; means. حِيلَةٌ ج حِيَلٌ	To surround. حَاقَ يَحُوقُ بِ
Mechanics. عِلْمُ اَلْحِيَلِ	To strike out, erase. حَوَّقَ
In front of, opposite to. حِيَالَ	To weave. حَاكَ يَحُوكُ
Squint-eyed. أَحْوَلُ م حَوْلَاءُ	Weaver. حَائِكٌ ج حَاكَةٌ
More cunning, crafty. أَحْيَلُ	The art of weaving. حِيَاكَةٌ
Transferring. تَحْوِيلٌ	To be changed. حَالَ وَتَحَوَّلَ
Absurd, unreasonable. مُحَالٌ	To come between. حَالَ بَيْنَ
Undoubtedly. لَا مَحَالَةَ	To change, alter. حَوَّلَ إِلَى
Cunning, sly, wily. مُحْتَالٌ	To attempt. حَاوَلَ
Impossible ; absurd. مُسْتَحِيلٌ	To use stratagem. اِحْتَالَ
To run around ; hover. حَامَ يَحُومُ	To be changed. Absurd. اِسْتَحَالَ
Wine-shop. حَانَةٌ وَحَانُوتٌ	State, condition. حَالٌ ج أَحْوَالٌ
Eve (mother of mankind). حَوَّاءُ	Immediately. حَالًا وَفِي اَلْحَالِ
To possess ; contain. حَوَى يَحْوِي	As soon as. حَالَمَا

Injustice, oppression. حَيْفٌ	To comprise. إِحْتَوَى عَلَى
To surround, befall. حَاقَ يَحِيقُ بِ	Snake-charmer. Containing. حَاوٍ.
Strength, power, might. حَيْلٌ	Where, where there. حَيْثُ
To draw near (time). حَانَ يَحِينُ	Wherever. حَيْثُمَا
Wine-house, tavern. حَانٌ وَحَانَةٌ	In respect of, since. مِنْ حَيْثُ
Time, season. حِينٌ ج أَحْيَانٌ	So that. بِحَيْثُ انْ
Instantaneously ; at once. لِلْحِينِ	To deviate ; turn aside. حَادَ يَحِيدُ
From time to time. أَحْيَانًا	To avoid, shun. حَايَدَ مُحَايَدَةً
Then ; at that time. حِينَئِذٍ	To be bewildered. حَارَ يَحَارُ
To live. حَيِيَ يَحْيَا حَيَاةً	To bewilder, perplex. حَيَّرَ
To be ashamed of. حَيِيَ حَيَاءً مِنْ	To be perplexed. تَحَيَّرَ فِي
To salute, greet. حَيَّا تَحِيَّةً	Perplexity. حِيرَةٌ وَتَحَيُّرٌ
To bring to life. أَحْيَا	Street ; quarter. حَارَةٌ ج حَارَاتٌ
To spare one's life. إِسْتَحْيَا	Confused, perplexed. حَائِرٌ
To be ashamed. إِسْتَحْيَا وَٱسْتَحَى	Planet. مُتَحَيِّرَةٌ ج مُتَحَيِّرَاتٌ
Come ! come quickly ! حَيَّ	Space occupied by a body. حَيِّزٌ
Shame ; modesty. حَيَاءٌ	To menstruate. حَاضَتْ تَحِيضُ
Life ; life-time. حَيَاةٌ أَوْ حَيَوَةٌ	Menstruation ; menses. حَيْضٌ
Alive. Tribe.	To be unjust. حَافَ يَحِيفُ
Quarter of a town. حَيٌّ ج أَحْيَاءٌ	

Vital.	حَيَوِيّ	Snake.	حَيَّةٌ ج حَيَاتٌ
Greeting.	تَحِيَّةٌ ج تَحِيَّاتٌ	Animal.	حَيَوَانٌ ج حَيَوَانَاتٌ
Face.	مُحَيَّا	Zoology.	عِلْمُ الْحَيَوَانِ
Vivifying, giving life.	مُحْيٍ	Animal (*Adj.*)	حَيَوَانِيّ

خ

To test, try, prove.	خَبَرَ يَخْبُرُ	As a numeral sign = 600.	خ
To negotiate.	خَابَرَ	To trot, amble.	خَبَّ يَخُبُّ
To inform.	خَبَّرَ وَأَخْبَرَ بِ	Ambling pace, trot.	خَبَبٌ
To learn by experience.	إِخْتَبَرَ	To conceal, hide.	خَبَا يَخْبَأُ وَخَمَّأً
To ask for information	إِسْتَخْبَرَ	To be concealed.	إِخْتَبَأَ وَتَخَبَّأَ
New report.	خَبَرٌ ج اخْبَارٌ	Small tent.	خِبَاءٌ ج أَخْبِئَةٌ
Knowledge ; experience.	خِبْرَةٌ	Large jug.	خَابِيَةٌ ج خَوَابٍ
Report ; story.	خَبَرِيَّةٌ	A hiding place.	مَخْبَأٌ ج مَخَابِئُ
Well informed.	خَبِيرٌ ج خُبَرَاءُ	To be corrupt.	خَبُثَ يَخْبُثُ
Better informed.	أَخْبَرُ	Wickedness.	خُبْثٌ وَخَبَاثَةٌ
To bake bread.	خَبَزَ يَخْبِزُ	Vile, malicious.	خَبِيثٌ ج خُبَثَاءُ
Bread.	خُبْزٌ	Infamous actions.	خَبَائِثُ
Loaf of bread.	خُبْزَةٌ	A cause of evil.	مَخْبَثَةٌ

End, conclusion.	خِتَامٌ ج خُتُمٌ	Baker's trade.	خِبازَةٌ
Sealed ; closed.	مَخْتومٌ	Baker.	خَبّازٌ م خَبّازَةٌ
To circumcise.	خَتَنَ يَخْتِنُ	Mallow (plant).	خُبّازَى وَخُبَّيْزَةٌ
To be circumcised.	إِخْتَتَنَ	Any thing baked.	مَخْبوزٌ وَخَبيزٌ
Any relation on side of wife.	خَتَنٌ	To mix ; bungle.	خَبَصَ يَخْبِصُ
Noble lady.	خَاتونٌ ج خَوَاتينُ	Rash bungler.	خَبّاصٌ
Circumcision.	خِتَانٌ وَخِتَانَةٌ	To strike.	خَبَطَ يَخْبِطُ
To coagulate.	خَثَرَ يَخْثُرُ وَتَخَثَّرَ	At random.	خَبْطَ عَشْوَاءَ
To thicken.	خَثَّرَ وَاخْثَرَ	To be or make insane.	خَبِلَ يَخْبَلُ
Sediment, dregs.	خُثَارَةٌ	Mad, insane.	خَبِلٌ وَأَخْبَلُ وَمُخَبَّلٌ
Coagulated ; thickened.	خَاثِرٌ	Fatigued ; weakened.	مَخْبولٌ
To be ashamed, blush.	خَجِلَ يَخْجَلُ	Tent of wool.	خِبَاءٌ ج أَخْبِيَةٌ
To put to shame.	خَجَّلَ وَأَخْجَلَ	Large jug, jar.	خَابِيَةٌ ج خَوَابٍ
Shame, confusion.	خَجَلٌ	To cheat.	خَتَلَ يَخْتِلُ وَخَاتَلَ
Modest, bashful.	خَجْلَانٌ وَمَخْجولٌ	Fraud, deceit.	مُخَاتَلَةٌ
Cheek.	خَدٌّ ج خُدودٌ	To seal, stamp.	خَتَمَ يَخْتِمُ
Furrow, pit.	خَدٌّ وَاخْدودٌ	To conclude, terminate.	خَتَمَ
Furrow, track.	خُدَّةٌ ج خُدَدٌ	Seal-ring, signet.	خَاتِمٌ ج خَوَاتِمُ
Small cushion.	خُدَيْدِيَةٌ	End, conclusion.	خَاتِمَةٌ

Servant.	خَادِمْ ج خَدَمْ وَخَدَّامْ	Cushion, pillow.	مِخَدَّةْ
Friend.	خِدْنْ ج أَخْدَانْ	To be benumbed.	خَدِرَ يَخْدَرُ
Prince, viceroy.	خَدِيْوِي	To benumb.	خَدَّرَ
To forsake.	خَذَلَ يَخْذُلُ خَذْلاً	Curtain, veil.	خِدْرْ ج خُدُورْ
To be forsaken.	إِنْخَذَلَ	Numbness ; stupefaction.	تَخْدَرْ
Forsaken, unaided.	مَخْذُولْ	Sedative, anæsthetic.	مُخَدِّرْ
To gurgle, rumble.	خَرَّ يَخِرُّ	Girl kept in seclusion.	مُخَدَّرَةْ
To prostrate one's self.	خَرَّ لِ	To scratch.	خَدَشَ يَخْدِشُ خَدْشاً
Gurgling, murmur.	خَرِيرْ	To deceive.	خَدَعَ يَخْدَعُ وَخَادَعَ
To ease the bowels.	خَرِئَ يَخْرَا	Deceit, guile.	خَدْعَةْ
Excrement.	خُرْءْ وَخِرَاءْ	To be deceived.	إِنْخَدَعَ
To be ruined.	خَرِبَ يَخْرَبُ	Deceit.	خَدِيعَةْ ج خَدَائِع
To demolish, ruin.	خَرَّبَ يُخَرِّب	Impostor ; deceitful.	خَادِعْ
To be destroyed.	تَخَرَّبَ	Impostor, great cheat.	خَدَّاعْ
A ruin, waste.	خِرْبَةْ ج خِرَبْ	Chamber.	مُخْدَعْ ج مُخَادِع
Devastation ; ruin.	خَرَابْ	Deceived, deluded.	مَخْدُوعْ
Carob-tree.	خَرُّوبْ وَخُرْنُوبْ	To serve.	خَدَمَ يَخْدُم خِدْمَةً
Devastation, destruction.	تَخْرِيبْ	To employ.	إِسْتَخْدَمَ
To scratch a writing.	خَرْبَشَ	Service ; official duty.	خِدْمَةْ

Awl.	مُخْرَزٌ ج مَخَارِزُ	Hellebore.	خَرْبَقٌ
To be dumb.	خَرِسَ يَخْرَسُ	To get out ; emerge.	خَرَجَ يَخْرُجُ
Dumbness.	خَرَسٌ	To take out ; expel.	أَخْرَجَ
Dumb.	أَخْرَسُ	To be well trained.	تَخَرَّجَ
Ear-ring.	خُرْصٌ ج خِرْصَان	To draw out, extract.	إِسْتَخْرَجَ
To turn on a lathe.	خَرَطَ يَخْرُطُ	Expenditure.	خَرْجٌ
To unsheathe a sword.	إِخْتَرَطَ	Saddle-bags.	خُرْجٌ ج أَخْرَاجٌ
Trade of a turner.	خِرَاطَةٌ	Exterior, quotient.	خَارِجٌ
Shavings of a lathe.	خُرَاطَةٌ	Foreign affairs.	الأُمُورُ الْخَارِجِيَّةُ
Turner. Liar.	خَرَّاطٌ	Land-tax ; tribute, tax.	خَرَاجٌ
Lathe.	مَخْرَطَةٌ ج مَخَارِطُ	Abscess.	خُرَاجٌ ج خُرَاجَاتٌ
Cone.	مَخْرُوطٌ	Outlet ; issue.	مَخْرَجٌ
Conical.	مَخْرُوطِيٌّ	Skilful, well-trained.	مُخَرَّجٌ
Snout.	خُرْطُومٌ ج خَرَاطِيمُ	To rattle, snore.	خَرْخَرَ
To invent, devise.	إِخْتَرَعَ	Small shot.	خُرْدُقٌ
Castor-oil-plant.	خِرْوَعٌ	Mustard.	خَرْدَلٌ
Invention.	إِخْتِرَاعٌ ج إِخْتِرَاعَاتٌ	To pierce ; bore.	خَرَزَ يَخْرُزُ
To dote from old age.	خَرِفَ يَخْرَفُ	Small shells, beads.	خَرَزٌ
Dotage.	خَرَفٌ وَخَرَافَةٌ	Vertebræ of the back.	خَرَزَاتُ الظَّهْرِ

See. خَرُّوبٌ	خَرْنُوبٌ	Doting, idiotic.	خَرِفٌ وَخَرْفَانُ
Silk-stuff.	خَزٌّ ج خُزُوزٌ	Fictitious tale, fable.	خَرَافَةٌ
Caspian Sea.	بَحْرُ الْخَزَرِ	Lamb, sheep.	خَرُوفٌ ج خِرَافٌ
Ratan, Bamboo.	خَيْزُرَانٌ	Autumn.	خَرِيفٌ
A fable. خَزَعْبَلَةٌ ج خَزَعْبَلَاتٌ		To pierce.	خَرَقَ يَخْرُقُ خَرْقًا
Earthenware, pottery.	خَزَفٌ	To be pierced.	إِنْخَرَقَ
Potter.	خَزَفِيٌّ وَخَزَّافٌ	To traverse.	إِخْتَرَقَ
To penetrate ; tear.	خَزَقَ يَخْزِقُ	Rent, hole.	خَرْقٌ ج خُرُوقٌ
To impale.	خَوْزَقَ	Stupid, awkward.	خَرِقٌ وَأَخْرَقُ
To cut off.	خَزَلَ يَخْزِلُ خَزْلًا	Rag, tatter.	خِرْقَةٌ ج خِرَقٌ
To pierce the nose.	خَزَمَ يَخْزِمُ	Unusual.	خَارِقٌ ج خَوَارِقُ
Nose-ring.	خِزَامٌ	To slit. Fail.	خَرَمَ يَخْرِمُ
Lavender. Hyacinth.	خُزَامَى	To embroider.	خَرَّمَ
To store, hoard.	خَزَنَ يَخْزِنُ	To be torn, slit, pierced.	إِنْخَرَمَ
Treasury.	خِزْنَةٌ وَخِزَانَةٌ	Bore.	خُرْمٌ ج خُرُومٌ
Treasure. خِزْنَةٌ وَخَزِينَةٌ ج خَزَائِنُ		Acromion (anatomy).	الأَخْرَمُ
Library.	خِزَانَةُ الْكُتُبِ	Embroidery.	تَخْرِيمٌ
Armoury.	خِزَانَةُ السِّلَاحِ	Embroidered, chased.	مُخَرَّمٌ
Treasurer.	خَازِنٌ ج خَزَنَةٌ	To scratch.	خَرْمَشَ

Timber-wood.	خَشَبٌ	Magazine.	مَخْزَنٌ ج مَخَازِنُ
A piece of wood.	خَشَبَةٌ	To subdue.	خَزَا يَخْزُو وخَزْواً
Coarse ; hard.	خَشَبٌ	To be despised.	خَزِيَ يَخْزَى
Wood-seller.	خَشَّابٌ	To be ashamed of.	خَزِيَ مِنْ
To rustle ; clink.	خَشْخَشَ	Shame, disgrace.	خِزْيٌ
Poppy.	خَشْخَاشٌ	Shameful thing.	خِزْيَةٌ
Charnel-house.	خَشْخَاشَةٌ	To be mean.	خَسَّ يَخِسُّ خَسَاسَةً
Refuse.	خُشَارٌ وخُشَارَةٌ	Lettuce.	خَسٌّ
Te be submissive.	خَشَعَ يَخْشَعُ	Vile, mean (miserly).	خَسِيسٌ
To humble one's self.	تَخَشَّعَ	To lose.	خَسِرَ يَخْسَرُ
Lowliness ; humility.	خُشُوعٌ	To cause loss, damage.	خَسَّرَ
Humble.	خَاشِعٌ ج خَاشِعُونَ	Loss.	خُسْرٌ وخَسَارَةٌ وخُسْرَانٌ
Young gazelle.	خِشْفٌ وخَشْفَةٌ	Losing, loser.	خَاسِرٌ
Bat (animal).	خُشَّافٌ	To sink into the earth and vanish. Be eclipsed.	خَسَفَ يَخْسِفُ
Nose.	خَشْمٌ . خَيْشُومٌ ج خَيَاشِيمُ	To be eclipsed.	إِنْخَسَفَ
To be rough.	خَشُنَ يَخْشُنُ	Eclipse.	خُسُوفٌ
To treat one harshly.	خَاشَنَ	Eclipsed.	مَخْسُوفٌ
Roughness.	خُشْنَةٌ وخُشُونَةٌ	To enter, penetrate.	خَشَّ يَخُشُّ
Rough.	خَشِنٌ ج خِشَانٌ		

To abridge	إختصَرَ	To fear, dread.	خَشِيَ يَخْشَى
Waist.	خَصْرٌ ج خُصُورٌ	Fear.	خَشْيَةٌ وَخِشْيَانٌ
Side ; flank.	خَاصِرَةٌ ج خَوَاصِرُ	For fear that.	خَشْيَةَ أَنْ
Abridgment.	إختِصَارٌ	Fearful.	خَاشٍ وَخَشْيَانٌ
In short ; briefly.	بِالإختِصَارِ	To distinguish by ب	خَصَّ يَخُصُّ
Whip, staff.	مِخْصَرَةٌ ج مَخَاصِرُ	To be special to.	خَصَّ خُصُوصاً
Abridged ; compend.	مُختَصَرٌ	To assign.	خَصَّصَ ب
Habit, quality.	خَصْلَةٌ ج خِصَالٌ	To be one's property.	إختَصَّ ب
Lock of hair. Bunch.	خُصْلَةٌ ج خُصَلٌ	Hut, booth.	خُصٌّ ج خِصَاصٌ
To dispute, contend with.	خَاصَمَ	Special to.	خَاصٌّ لِ وب
Adversary.	خَصْمٌ ج خُصُومٌ	Quality, property.	خَاصَّةٌ ج خَوَاصُّ
Adversary.	خَصِيمٌ ج خُصَمَاءُ	Particularly.	خَاصَّةً
Dispute, quarrel.	خِصَامٌ	The notables.	الخَاصَّةُ والخَوَاصُّ
To geld, castrate.	خَصَى يَخْصِي	Particular property.	خَاصِّيَّةٌ
Eunuch.	خَصِيٌّ ج خِصْيَانٌ	Especially.	عَلَى الخُصُوصِ وَخُصُوصاً
Testicle.	خُصْيَةٌ ج خُصَى	Special, particular.	خُصُوصِيٌّ
To stir (water).	خَضَّ وَخَضْخَضَ	To be fertile.	خَصَبَ يَخْصَبُ
To dye.	خَضَبَ يَخْضِبُ	Fertility.	خِصْبٌ
To be dyed.	تَخَضَّبَ وَاختَضَبَ	Fertile.	خَصِبٌ وَمُخْصِبٌ

To err, sin.	خَطِئَ يَخْطَأُ	Dye, colour.	خِضَابٌ
To charge with mistake.	خَطَّأَ	To be green.	خَضِرَ يَخْضَرُ
To err, transgress ; miss one's aim.	أَخْطَأَ	To become green.	خَضَّرَ
Error ; sin, mistake.	خَطَأٌ وَخَطَاءٌ	Greenness. Vegetables.	خُضْرَةٌ ج خُضَرٌ
Sin.	خَطِيئَةٌ ج خَطَايَا	Green.	أَخْضَرُ م خَضْرَاءُ ج خُضْرٌ
Sinner.	خَاطِئٌ ج خَطَّاةٌ وَخُطَاةٌ	Fruits ; herbs.	خُضْرَاوَاتٌ
Erring, missing.	مُخْطِئٌ	To submit ; obey.	خَضَعَ يَخْضَعُ
To make a speech.	خَطَبَ يَخْطُبُ	To subdue.	خَضَّعَ وَأَخْضَعَ
To betroth, ask in marrigae.	خَطَبَ يَخْطُبُ	To humble one's self.	تَخَضَّعَ
To talk or converse with.	خَاطَبَ	Submissive.	خَاضِعٌ وَخَضُوعٌ
Calamity.	خَطْبٌ ج خُطُوبٌ	Submission.	خُضُوعٌ
Address, speech.	خُطْبَةٌ وَخِطَابٌ	To trace ; write.	خَطَّ يَخُطُّ
Betrothal.	خِطْبَةٌ	To mark with lines.	خَطَّطَ
Preacher.	خَطِيبٌ ج خُطَبَاءُ	Line, streak.	خَطٌّ ج خُطُوطٌ
Second person, (Gram.)	مُخَاطَبٌ	Equator.	خَطُّ ٱلِٱسْتِوَاءِ
To occur to his mind.	خَطَرَ لَهُ	Equinoctial line.	خَطُّ ٱلِٱعْتِدَالِ
To expose to danger.	خَاطَرَ ب	Meridian.	خَطُّ نِصْفِ ٱلنَّهَارِ
Danger, risk.	خَطَرٌ ج أَخْطَارٌ	Imperial edict.	خَطٌّ شَرِيفٌ
Thought, idea.	خَاطِرٌ ج خَوَاطِرُ	Affair. Line of action.	خُطَّةٌ

Lightness ; agility.	خِفَّةٌ	Admonition, warning.	إِخْطَارٌ
Light (in weight) ; quick.	خَفِيفٌ	Great ; important.	خَطِيرٌ
Slighting, despising.	إِسْتِخْفَافٌ	Dangerous.	مُخْطِرٌ وَخَطِرٌ
Alleviating, lightening.	تَخْفِيفٌ	Risks, dangers, perils.	مَخَاطِرُ
To protect, guard.	خَفَرَ يَخْفُرُ	To seize, abduct.	خَطَفَ يَخْطَفُ
Sentry, guard.	خَفَرٌ	To snatch away, rob.	إِخْتَطَفَ
Sentry, escort.	خَفِيرٌ ج خُفَرَاءُ	Robbery ; abduction.	خَطْفٌ
Bat (animal).	خُفَّاشٌ ج خَفَافِيشُ	Seizing with violence.	خَاطِفٌ
To depress, lower.	خَفَضَ يَخْفِضُ	Swallow (bird).	خُطَّافٌ ج خَطَاطِيفُ
To let down, lower.	خَفَّضَ	To muzzle.	خَطَمَ يَخْطِمُ
To become low.	إِنْخَفَضَ	Marsh-mallow.	خَطْمِيٌّ
Abasement.	خَفْضٌ	To step, walk.	خَطَا يَخْطُو
To beat. Flutter.	خَفَقَ يَخْفِقُ	To pass beyond.	تَخَطَّى
To fail, miss.	أَخْفَقَ	Step, pace.	خُطْوَةٌ ج خُطْوَاتٌ
Palpitation.	خَفَقَانٌ	Sin, transgression.	خَطِيَّةٌ
To be hidden.	خَفِيَ يَخْفَى خَفَاءً	To be light (in weight).	خَفَّ يَخِفُّ
To go out of sight.	خَفِيَ خَفْيَةً	To make light, ease.	خَفَّفَ
To conceal.	أَخْفَى إِخْفَاءً	To make light of.	إِسْتَخَفَّ
To be concealed.	تَخَفَّى	Boot, shoe.	خُفٌّ ج اخْفَافٌ

To tremble, quiver.	إِخْتَلَجَ	To disappear.	إِخْتَفَى مِنْ
Bay, gulf; canal.	خَلِيجٌ ج خُلْجَانٌ	Secret; unperceived.	خَفًّا وَخَفَاءٌ
To be displaced.	تَخَلْخَلَ	Concealed, secret.	خَفًّا ج خَفَايَا
Ankle-ring.	خَلْخَالٌ ج جلاخيل	Secretly; in secret.	خُفْيَةٌ
To be eternal.	خَلَدَ يَخْلُدُ	King.	خَاقَانُ ج خَوَاقِينُ
Eternity; immortality.	خُلُودٌ	To become vinegar.	خَلَّ
Mole (animal).	خُلْدٌ ج مَنَاجِذ	To be remiss in, neglect.	اخَلَّ بِـ
Everlasting.	خَالِدٌ وَمُخَلَّدٌ	To penetrate, enter.	تَخَلَّلَ فِي
To steal.	خَلَسَ يَخْلُسُ وَآخْتَلَسَ	To be shaky, faulty.	اخْتَلَّ
Theft, robbery.	إِخْتِلَاسٌ	Vinegar. Slit, rent.	خَلٌّ
Thief, robber.	مُخْتَلِسٌ وخَالِسٌ	Intimate friend.	خِلٌّ ج أَخْلَالٌ
To be pure. Escape.	خَلَصَ يَخْلُصُ	Defect; injury.	خَلَلٌ
To deliver, rescue, save.	خَلَّصَ	Quality, habit.	خَلَّةٌ ج خِلَالٌ
To be sincere.	أَخْلَصَ	Friend.	خَلِيلٌ ج أَخِلَّاءٌ وَخِلَّانٌ
To be saved; escape.	تَخَلَّصَ	Mental disorder; fault.	إِخْتِلَالٌ
Rescue; salvation.	خَلَاصٌ	Leading to disorder.	مُخِلٌّ
Essence; extract.	خُلَاصَةٌ	Claw, talon.	مِخْلَبٌ ج مَخَالِبُ
Pure, unmixed; free.	خَالِصٌ	To quiver.	خَلَجَ يَخْلُجُ خَلْجًا
Sincerity.	إِخْلَاصٌ وَخُلُوصٌ	To contend with.	خَالَجَ

To remain behind.	تَخَلَّفَ عَنْ
To disagree.	تَخَالَفَ وَآخْتَلَفَ
Behind, after.	خَلْفَ
Successor, descendant.	خَلَفٌ
Difference.	خِلْفَةٌ وَاخْتِلافٌ
Disagreement.	خِلافٌ
Contrary to that.	خِلافًا لِذلِكَ
Caliphate. Succession.	خِلافَةٌ
Successor. Caliph.	خَلِيفَةٌ ج خُلَفَاءُ
Opposition.	مُخَالَفَةٌ
Varied, different.	مُخْتَلِفٌ
To create.	خَلَقَ يَخْلُقُ خَلْقًا
To be worn out.	خَلَقَ يَخْلُقُ
To be adapted to.	خَلُقَ بِ وَلِ
To invent, forge lies.	إِخْتَلَقَ
To affect, feign.	تَخَلَّقَ بِ
Creation ; creatures. Mankind.	خَلْقٌ
Natural shape.	خِلْقَةٌ ج خِلَقٌ
Inbron quality.	خُلُقٌ ج أَخْلاقٌ

Sincere.	مُخْلِصٌ
The Saviour.	الْمُخَلِّصُ
To mix, mingle.	خَلَطَ يَخْلِطُ
To confuse, disorder.	خَلَّطَ
To associate with.	خَالَطَ وَتَخَالَطَ
To be mixed, mingled.	إِخْتَلَطَ
Mixture.	خَلْطٌ ج أَخْلاطٌ
Social intercourse.	خُلْطَةٌ
To cast off, strip. Depose ; unhinge ; dislocate.	خَلَعَ يَخْلَعُ
To disjoint, pull to pieces.	خَلَّعَ
To be removed ; dislocated.	إِنْخَلَعَ
Dislocation. Deposition.	خَلْعٌ
Robe of honour.	خِلْعَةٌ ج خِلَعٌ
Disorderly life. Vice.	خَلاعَةٌ
Unhinged ; feeble, weak.	مُخَلَّعٌ
To succeed ; replace.	خَلَفَ يَخْلُفُ
To leave behind.	خَلَّفَ
To oppose.	خَالَفَ مُخَالَفَةً وَخِلافًا
To break one's promise.	أَخْلَفَ الْوَعْدَ

Empty, vacant. Free.	خَال	Congenital.	خِلقِيّ
Past ages.	اَلقُرُون اَلخَالِيَة	Creator (God).	خَالِق وَخَلَاق
Feed-bag (for animals).	مِخلَاة	Fit, suitable.	خَلِيق ج خُلَقَاء ب
To be putrid.	خَمَّ يَخِمّ	Creature.	خَلِيقَة ج خَلَائِق
To examine a country.	خَمَّ يَخُمّ خَمًّا	Created things.	أَلمَخلُوقَات
Hen-coop.	خُمّ	To be vacant ; alone.	خَلَا يَخلُو
To subside ; abate.	خَمَدَ يَخمَدَ	To be free from.	خَلَا مِن وَعَن
Silent ; dead.	خَامِد	To meet privately.	خَلَاب
Abatement, subsidence.	خُمُود	To leave, let alone.	خَلَّى
To veil, conceal.	خَمَرَ يَخمُر	To vacate a place.	اِخلَاه
To conceal. Leaven.	خَمَّر	To withdraw from.	تَخَلَّى عَن
To be mixed with.	خَامَر	To confine himself to.	تَخَلَّى لِ
To veil the head, face.	تَخَمَّر	Empty space ; solitude.	خَلَاء
To ferment ; rise (dough).	اِختَمَر	Water-closet.	بَيت اَلخَلَاء
Wine.	خَمر وَخَمرَة	Except.	خَلَا وَمَا خَلَا
Covering ; veil.	خِمَار ج خُمُر	Emptiness.	خُلُوّ
Leaven.	خَمِير وَخَمِيرَة	Privacy, solitude.	خَلوَة
Wine-merchant.	خَمَّار	Aside, apart.	عَلَى خَلوَةٍ
Wine-shop.	خَمَّارَة	Bee-hive ; cell.	خَلِيَّة ج خَلَايَا

Nasal twang.	خُنَّة	Fermented.	مُخَمَّر
Sunffles (disease).	خُنَان	To be the fifth.	خَمَس يَخْمُس
To be effeminate.	خَنِثَ يَخْنَث	To make pentagonal.	خَمَّسَ
Hermaphrodite.	خُنْثَى	The fifth part.	خُمْس ج أَخْمَاس
Poniard.	خَنْجَر ج خَنَاجِر	Five.	خَمْسَة م خَمْس
Trench, moat.	خَنْدَق ج خَنَادِق	Fifth.	خَامِس
Canals of the Nile.	خَنَادِل	Fifty, fiftieth.	خَمْسُونَ
Hog, pig.	خِنْزِير ج خَنَازِير	Thursday.	يَوْمُ الْخَمِيس
Wild boar.	خِنْزِير بَرِّيّ	Pentagon. Pentagonal.	مُخَمَّس
Scrofula.	دَاءُ الْخَنَازِير	To scratch.	خَمَش يَخْمِش
The stars.	أَلْخُنَّس	Hollow of the foot.	أَلْأَخْمَص
Satan.	أَلْخَنَّاس	To limp.	خَمَع يَخْمَع
Fern (plant).	خُنْشَار	Nap of cloth.	خَمْل
Sucking, pig.	خِنَّوْص ج خَنَانِيص	To be obscure (man).	خَمَل يَخْمُل
The little finger.	خِنْصِر ج خَنَاصِر	Villi of stomach.	خَمْل الْمِعْدَة
Black beetle	خُنْفَسَاء ج خَنَافِس	Velvet.	مُخْمَل
To strangle.	خَنَق يَخْنُق	To surmise.	خَمَنَ يَخْمُنُ وخَمَّنَ
To be strangled.	إِخْتَنَق وَانْخَنَق	By supposition.	عَلَى التَّخْمِين
Quinsy (disease).	خُنَاق	To snuffle.	خَنَّ يَخِنُّ خَنِينًا

Timid, fearing.	خَائِفٌ
Intimidation.	تَخْوِيفٌ
Fearful, perilous.	مُخَوَّفٌ
Terrible, inspiring fear.	مُخِيفٌ
Cause of fear.	مَخَافَةٌ ج مَخَاوِفُ
To bestow upon.	خَوَّلَ
Maternal uncle.	خَالٌ ج أَخْوَالٌ
Mole on the face.	خَالٌ ج خِيلَانٌ
Maternal aunt.	خَالَةٌ ج خَالَاتٌ
Steward.	خَوْلِيٌّ ج خَوَلٌ
Calico.	خَامٌ
To be unfaithful.	خَانَ يَخُونُ
To accuse of treachery.	خَوَّنَ
Inn (Prince).	خَانٌ ج خَانَاتٌ
Deceit, treachery.	خَوْنٌ وَخِيَانَةٌ
Table for food.	خِوَانٌ ج أَخْوِنَةٌ
Unfaithful, traitor.	خَائِنٌ
Treacherous.	خَؤُونٌ وَخَوَّانٌ
To be waste, empty.	خَوَى يَخْوِي

Strangled.	خَنِقٌ وَمَخْنُوقٌ
Foul words.	الْمُخْنَى
Suffocation ; asphyxia.	إِخْتِنَاقٌ
(Mister, Mr.	خَوَاجَه خَوَاجَاتٌ)
(Teacher.	خوجَه ج خوجَاتٌ)
Plum ; peach.	خَوْخٌ
Helmet.	خُوذَةٌ ج خُوَذٌ
To bellow.	خَارَ يَخُورُ
To fail (strength).	خَارَ خَوُّورًا
Bellowing of cattle.	خُوَارٌ
Curate, person.	خُورِيٌّ ج خَوَارِنَةٌ
To be unsaleable.	خَاسَ يَخُوسُ
Leaves of the plam-tree.	خُوصٌ
Having a deformed eye.	أَخْوَصُ
To wade ; ford.	خَاضَ يَخُوضُ
Ford.	مَخَاضَةٌ ج مَخَاوِضُ
To fear, be afraid of.	خَافَ يَخَافُ
To frighten.	خَوَّفَ وَأَخَافَ
Fear, fright.	خَوْفٌ وَمَخَافَةٌ وَخِيفَةٌ

Zinc.	خَارِصِينِي	Empty, hollow ; void.	خَاوٍ
Coarse canvas.	خَيْشٌ	To be disappointed.	خَابَ يَخِيب
Large sack.	خَيْشَةٌ ج خَيْشَاتٌ	To disappoint.	خَيَّبَ وَاخَاب
To sew.	خَاطَ يَخِيط وَخَيَّطَ	Failure, disappointment.	خَيْبَة
Thread.	خَيْطٌ ج خُيُوطٌ وَخِيطَانٌ	Frustrated.	خَائِبٌ
Needle-work, sewing.	خِيَاطَة	To deem better ; prefer.	خَيَّرَ عَلَى
Tailor.	خَيَّاط	To give one a choice.	خَيَّرَ
Sewn, stitched.	مَخِيطٌ وَمَخْيُوطٌ	To choose, select, prefer.	إِخْتَار
To conceive; imagine.	خَالَ يَخَال	A good thing.	خَيْرٌ ج خِيَارٌ
To seem to.	خُيِّلَ ل وَإِلَى	Better than.	خَيْرٌ مِنْ
To imagine, fancy.	تَخَيَّلَ	The best of men.	خَيْرُ النَّاس
Horse ; cavalry.	خَيْلٌ ج خُيُول	Good, benevolent.	خَيْرِيٌّ
Spectre, phantom.	خَيَالٌ ج اخْيِلَة	Choice. Cucumber.	خِيَارٌ
Imaginary ideal.	خَيَالِيٌّ	Good, liberal.	خَيْرٌ
Faculty of imagination.	الأُمْخَيِّلَة	Better ; preferable.	خَيْرٌ (الاخيَرُ)
Horseman.	خَيَّالٌ ج خَيَّالَة	Choice, election.	اِخْتِيَارٌ
To pitch a tent ; abide.	خَيَّمَ	Voluntary.	اِخْتِيَارِيٌّ
Unbleached cloth.	خَامٌ	Free to choose.	مُخَيَّرٌ
Tent ; booth.	خَيْمَةٌ ج خِيَامٌ	Preferred.	مُخْتَارٌ

د

Thick juice of grapes.	دِبْسٌ
Mace. Pin.	دَبُّوسٌ ج دَبَابِيس
To tan (leather).	دَبَغَ يَدْبَغ
Trade of a tanner.	دِبَاغَة
Tanner.	دَبَّاغ
Tannery.	مَدْبَغَة ج مَدَابِغ
Tanned.	مَدْبُوغ
To adhere to.	دَبِقَ يَدْبَقُ ب
Glue, bird-lime.	دِبْقٌ
To be effaced.	دَثَرَ يَدْثُرُ
To cover with a blanket.	دَثَّرَ
To be destroyed.	إِنْدَثَرَ
That which perishes.	دَاثِرٌ
Poultry.	دُجَاجٌ
A hen.	دُجَاجَةٌ
Turkey.	دُجَاجُ الْهِنْدِ

As a numerical sign=4.	د
State, condition ; habit.	دَابٌ
To crawl, creep.	دَبَّ يَدِبُّ
Bear (animal).	دُبٌّ ج أَدْبَابٌ
Animal ; beast.	دَابَّةٌ ج دَوَابٌّ
Little animal ; reptile.	دُوَيْبَّة
Silk brocade.	دِيبَاجٌ
Introduction, preface.	دِيبَاجَةٌ
To tread, crawl.	دَبْدَبَ
To plan ; manage well.	دَبَّرَ
To go back, retreat.	أَدْبَرَ
To regard attentively.	تَدَبَّرَ
Back, hind part.	دُبْرٌ ج أَدْبَارٌ
Management.	تَدْبِيرٌ ج تَدَابِيرُ
One who turns back.	مُدْبِرٌ
Administrator ; director.	مُدَبِّرٌ

To enter.	دَخَلَ يَدْخُل	Woodcock.	دُجَاجُ آلأَرْضِ
To be included.	دخل تحت وَفِي	Partridge.	دُجَاجُ آلبَرِّ
To cause to enter.	أَدْخَلَ	Completely armed.	مُدَجَّجٌ
To intermeddle.	تَدَاخَلَ فِي	To lie ; cheat.	دجَلَ يَدْجُل
Income, revenue.	دَخْلٌ	Liar ; imposter ; quack.	دَجَّالٌ
I beseech you.	دَخْلَكَ وَدَخِيلَكَ	Tigris (river).	دِجْلة
Interior, inside.	دَاخِلٌ	To be cloudy, dark. To become tame.	دَجَنَ يَدْجُن
Home Secretary.	وَزِيرُ آلدَّاخِلِيَّةِ	To abide.	دَجَنَ دُجُونًاب
Stranger. Guest.	دَخِيلٌ ج دُخَلَاءُ	Darkness.	دُجْنَةٌ ج دُجَنٌ
Door ; access.	مَدْخَلٌ ج مَدَاخِلُ	Tame animal.	دَاجِنٌ ج دَوَاجِنُ
Revenue.	مَدْخُولٌ ج مَدَاخِيل	Darkness.	دُجًى
To smoke.	دَخَنَ وَدَخَّنَ وَأَدْخَنَ	To drive away.	دَحَرَ يَدْحَر
Millet.	دُخْنٌ	To roll down (tran).	دَحْرَجَ
Smoke. Tobacco.	دُخَانٌ	To be rolled.	تَدَحْرَجَ
Chimney.	مَدْخَنَةٌ ج مَدَاخِنُ	Lucern.	دُحَيْرِجَة
To flow copiously.	دَرَّ يَدِرُّ	Whitlow.	دَاحِسٌ
Copious flow of milk.	دَرٌّ	To force into.	دَحَشَ يَدْحَش
How exquisite !	لله دَرُّهُ	To rebut, refute.	أَدْحَضَ
Pearl. Parrot.	دُرَّةٌ ج دُرَّاتٌ	To be refuted, rebutted.	إِنْدَحَضَ

To sew, stitch.	دَرَزَ يَدْرُزُ	Copious flow.	مِدْرَارٌ
Seam.	دَرْزٌ ج دُرُوزٌ	To guide, direct.	دَرَّبَ
Druze.	دُرْزِيٌّ ج دُرُوزٌ	To be practised in.	تَدَرَّبَ
To efface.	دَرَسَ يَدْرُسُ	Path ; way.	دَرْبٌ ج دُرُوبٌ
To read, study.	دَرَسَ يَدْرُسُ	Training ; drill.	تَدْرِيبٌ
To tread out corn, thresh.	دَرَسَ	Trained ; excercised.	مُدَرَّبٌ
To study or read under a teacher.	دَرَسَ عَلَى	Balustrade.	دَرَبْزِينٌ وَدَرَابِزُون
To teach, lecture.	دَرَّسَ	To proceed gradually.	درج يَدْرُجُ
To be effaced.	إِنْدَرَسَ	To introduce.	أَدْرَجَ وَدَرَّجَ في
Lesson. study.	دَرْسٌ ج دُرُوسٌ	To proceed by degrees.	تَدَرَّجَ
Threshing.	دِرَاسٌ وَدِرَاسَةٌ	Roll of Paper.	دَرْجٌ ج أَدْرَاجٌ
School.	مَدْرَسَةٌ ج مَدَارِسُ	Box, case.	دُرْجٌ ج أَدْرَاجٌ
Teacher, professor.	مُدَرِّسٌ	Road, path.	دَرْجٌ ج ادرَاجٌ وَدِرَاجٌ
To put on a coat of mail.	إِدَّرَعَ وَتَدَرَّعَ	Step; degree.	دَرَجَةٌ ج دَرَجَاتٌ
Coat of mail.	دِرْعٌ ج دُرُوعٌ	Gradually.	تَدْرِيجاً وَبِالتَّدْرِيجِ
Armoured.	مُدَرَّعٌ	Common, current.	دَارِجٌ
Water jug.	دَوْرَقٌ ج دَوَارِقُ	Francolin.	دُرَّاجٌ
Peach.	دُرَاقِنٌ وَدُرَّاقٌ	To lie unconscious.	انْدَرَجَ
To make responsible for.	دَرَّكَ	Elm.	دَرْدَارٌ

To overtake. دَارَكَ	A game. Copper دَسْتٌ ج دُسُوتٌ pot,
To reach ; comprehend. أَدْرَكَ	Rule, regulation. دُستورٌ
To overtake ; rectify. تَدَارَكَ	Town, دَسْكَرَةٌ ج دَسَاكِرُ village.
To seek to obviate. إِسْتَدْرَكَ	To be fatty. دَسِمَ يَدْسَمُ
Comprehension. إِدْرَاكٌ	Fat, grease. دَسَمٌ ودُسُومَةٌ
To be filthy. دَرِنَ يَدْرَنُ	To dismiss ; leave. دَشَرَ
Dirt. Tubercle. دَرَنٌ ج أَدْرَانٌ	Let ! (imp. from. وَدَعَ) دَعْ
Polluted, dirty, دَرِنٌ	To sport, jest with. دَعَبَ وَدَاعَبَ
Drachm ; money. دِرْهَمٌ ج دَرَاهِم	Wickedness. دَعَرٌ ودِعَارَةٌ
Dervish. دَرْوِيشٌ ج دَرَاوِيشُ	To tread under foot. دَعَسَ يَدْعَسُ
To know. دَرَى يَدْرِي	A track, foot-print. دَعْسَةٌ
To treat kindly, cajole. دَارَى	To rup. دَعَكَ يَدْعَكُ
To acquaint, inform. أدرى بِ	To contend with. دَاعَكَ مُدَاعَكَةً
Knowledge. دِرَايَةٌ	To prop. دَعَمَ يَدْعَمُ دَعْمًا
To hide, insert. دَسَّ يَدُسُّ	Support, prop. دِعَامَةٌ ج دَعَائِم
To plot against. دَسَّ عَلَى	To call ; pray, دَعَا يَدْعُو
To be hidden, concealed. إِنْدَسَّ	To invite. دَعَا دَعْوَةً
Spy. دَاسُوسٌ ج دَوَاسِيسُ	To pray for. دَعَا لِ
Intrigue. دَسِيسَةٌ ج دَسَائِسُ	To invoke a curse upon. دَعَا عَلَى

Heat, warmth.	دِفْءٌ	To claim ; pretend.	إِدَّعَى بِ
Register. Account-book.	دَفْتَرٌ ج دَفَاتِرُ	To claim against.	إِدَّعَى عَلى
Minister of Finances.	دَفْتَرْدَارٌ	To call, invite.	إِسْتَدْعَى
To push back.	دَفَرَ يَدْفِرُ	Call ; prayer.	دُعَاءٌ ج أَدْعِيَة
Juniper tree.	دِفْرَان	Invocation ; invitation. Imprecation.	دَعْوَةٌ
To push.	دَفَشَ يَدْفِش	Claim ; law-suit.	دَعْوَى ج دَعَاوٍ
To push back, repel.	دَفَعَ يَدْفَعُ	Calling. Preacher.	دَاعٍ ج دُعَاة
To hand over to.	دَفَعَ إِلَى وَكَل	Cause ; motive.	دَاعِيَةٌ ج دَوَاعٍ
To contend with. Defer.	دَافَعَ	Claim, pretention.	إِدِّعَاءٌ
To protect, defend.	دَافَعَ عَنْ	Pretender ; plaintiff.	مُدَّعٍ
To be thrust back.	إِنْدَفَعَ	Defendant.	مُدَّعًى عَلَيْهِ
Pushing back. Payment.	دَفْعٌ	*To tickle.	دَغْدَغَ دَغْدَغَةً
Expulsive force.	قُوَّةٌ دَافِعَةٌ	Darkness ; nightfall.	دَغَشٌ
Cannon.	مِدْفَعٌ ج مَدَافِع	Corruption. Thicket.	دَغَلٌ ج أَدْغَالٌ
To pour forth (water).	دَفَقَ يَدْفُقُ	Tambourine.	دَفٌّ ج دُفُوفٌ
To be poured out.	تَدَفَّقَ وَٱنْدَفَقَ	Side. Rudder.	دَفَّةٌ
Overflowing.	مُتَدَفِّقٌ	To be warm.	دَفِئَ يَدْفَأُ
Oleander.	دِفْلٌ وَدِفْلى	To warm.	دَفَّأَ وَأَدْفَأَ
To bury ; conceal.	دَفَنَ يَدْفِنُ	To warm one's self.	تَدَفَّأَ

To be blackish.	دَكَنَ يَدْكَنُ	To be buried.	إِندَفَنَ
Blackish colour.	دُكْنَةٌ	Burying, burial.	دَفْنٌ
Shop.	دُكَّانٌ ج دَكَاكِينُ	Buried treasure.	دَفِينَةٌ ج دَفَائِنُ
Shop-keeper.	دُكَّنْجِيٌّ	Tomb.	مَدْفَنٌ ج مَدَافِنُ
Blackish.	أَدْكَنُ م دَكْنَاءُ	To be fine, thin.	دَقَّ يَدِقُّ
To point out, show.	دَلَّ يَدُلُّ عَلى	To crush ; knock.	دَقَّ يَدُقُّ
To spoil (a child).	دَلَّلَ	To ring the bell.	دَقَّ الجَرَس
To sell at auction.	دَلَّلَ عَلى	To be precise.	دَقَقَ
To be coquettish.	تَدَلَّلَ	To examine minutely.	دَقَّقَ النَّظَرَ
To seek, or to find a proof.	إِستَدَلَّ عَلى	Exactness, accuracy.	دِقَّةٌ
Coquetry.	دَلالٌ	Pestle.	مَدَقٌّ ومِدَقَّةٌ
Broker, auctioneer.	دَلّالٌ	Fine : thin. Fine flour.	دَقِيقٌ ج أَدِقَّةٌ ودِقَاقٌ
Sign, proof.	دَلِيلٌ ج أَدِلَّةٌ	Minute (time).	دَقِيقَةٌ د قَائِقُ
Guide.	دَلِيلٌ ج أَدِلاءُ	Exactness, precision.	تَدْقِيقٌ
Plane-tree.	دُلْبٌ	Exact, precise.	مُدَقِّقٌ
Water-wheel.	دُولابٌ ج دَوَالِيبُ	To demolish. To charge a gun.	دَكَّ يَدُكُّ
Deceit.	دَلَسٌ ودُلْسَةٌ	Wide bench, seat.	دَكَّةٌ
To loll the tongue.	دَلَعَ لِسَانَهُ	Ramrod.	مِدَكٌّ
To leak.	دَلَفَ يَدْلِفُ دَلْفًا	Loaded (gun).	مَدْكُوكٌ

To murmur against.	دَمْدَمَ عَلَى	Dolphin.	دُلْفِينٌ ج دَلَافِينُ
To perish utterly.	دَمَرَ يَدْمُرُ	To pour out (a liquid).	دَلَقَ يَدْلُقُ
To annihilate, destroy.	دَمَرَ وَدَمَّرَ	To rub.	دَلَكَ يَدْلُكُ دَلْكًا ب
Destruction, annihilation.	دَمَارٌ	Rubbing stone.	مَدْلَكٌ وَمَدْلَكَةٌ
Palmyra.	تَدْمُرُ	To be very dark.	أَدْلَهَمَّ
To be dense, (darkness).	دَمَسَ يَدْمُسُ	Very black.	مُدْلَهِمٌّ
To conceal, bury.	دَمَسَ يَدْمُسُ	To draw a bucket.	دَلَا يَدْلُو
Dark, (night).	دَامِسٌ	To let down.	دَلَّى وَأَدْلَى
Damascus.	دِمَشْقُ	To be let down.	تَدَلَّى
To shed tears, (eyes).	دَمَعَ يَدْمَعُ	Bucket.	دَلْوٌ ج دِلَاءٌ
Tears.	دَمْعٌ ج دُمُوعٌ وَأَدْمُعٌ	Aquarius.	الدَّلْوُ
A tear, a drop.	دَمْعَةٌ	Grape-vine.	دَالِيَةٌ ج دَوَالٍ
To mark by branding.	دَمَغَ يَدْمَغُ	Blood.	دَمٌ
Mark, brand.	دِمْغَةٌ	Bloody.	دَمَوِيٌّ
Brain.	دِمَاغٌ ج أَدْمِغَةٌ	To be gentle.	دَمُثَ يَدْمُثُ
To manure land.	دَمَلَ يَدْمُلُ	Mild, soft.	دَمْثٌ وَدَمِيثٌ
To be healed.	دَمَلَ يَدْمُلُ وَانْدَمَلَ	Gentleness, delicacy.	دَمَاثَةٌ
Pustule, boil.	دُمَّلٌ ج دَمَامِلُ	To be joined.	دَمَجَ يَدْمُجُ وَانْدَمَجَ
Manure.	دَمَالٌ	Compact.	مُدْمَجٌ وَمُنْدَمِجٌ

Soiled, foul.	دَنِسٌ ج ادْنَاسٌ	Bracelet.	دمْلجٌ ج دَمَالجُ
To be near death.	أَدْنَفَ	To manure land.	دمَّنَ وَدَمَّنَ
To perish with cold.	دَنِقَ يَدْنَقُ	To be permanent.	دمِنَ يَدْمَنُ
Small coin.	دانقٌ ج دَوانقُ	To persevere in, cleave to.	ادَّمَنَ
To approach.	دَنا يَدْنو	Constant practice.	إدْمَانٌ
Nearness ; proximity.	دَناوَةٌ	Addicted to.	مُدْمِنٌ
Meanness, baseness.	دَنَايَةٌ	To bleed, flow (blood).	دَمِيَ يَدْمِي
Vile. Near.	دَنِيٌ ج أَدْنِيَاهُ	To cause to bleed.	دَمَّى وَادْمَى
Anything base.	دَنِيَّةٌ ج دَنَايَا	Blood.	دَمٌ ج دِمَاهُ
The (present) world.	دنيَا	Bloody.	دَمِيٌ وَدَمَوِيٌ
Worldly.	دُنْيَوِيٌّ	Large wine-jar.	دَنٌّ ج دنَانٌ
Nearer. Viler, worse.	ادْنى	To be low, vile.	دَنا يَدْنُا
Time ; age.	دَهْرٌ ج دهُورٌ	Meanness ; weakness.	دَنَاءَةٌ
For ever and ever.	دَهْرُ الدَّاهِرِينَ	Low ; worthless.	دَنِيٌ ج أَدْنِيَاهُ
To be bewildered.	دَهِشَ يَدْهَشُ	A gold coin.	دِينَارٌ ج دَنَانِيرُ
To perplex.	دُهِّشَ وَأَدْهَشَ	To be defiled.	دَنِسَ يَدْنَسُ
Astounded.	دَهِشٌ وَمَدهُوشٌ	To stain, pollute.	دَنَّسَ
Confusion ; perplexity.	دَهْشَةٌ	To be defiled.	تَدَنَّسَ
Vestibule.	دهليزٌ ج دهاليزُ	Filth, pollution.	دَنَسٌ ج أَدْنَاسٌ

Gout.	دَاءُ ٱلْمُلُوكِ
Hydrophobia.	دَاءُ ٱلْكَلَبِ
Elephantiasis.	دَاءُ ٱلْفِيل
To be giddy, sea sick.	دَاخَ يَدُوخُ
To subdue, conquer.	دَوَّخَ
Giddiness.	دَوْخَة
A worm.	دُودَة ج دِيدَانٌ وَدُودٌ
Silk-worm.	دُودَةُ ٱلْقَزِّ
David.	دَاوُدُ
To revolve, circulate.	دَارَ يَدُورُ
To set going; administer.	اَدَارَ
To be round.	تَدَوَّرَ وَٱسْتَدَارَ
House.	دَارٌ ج دُورٌ وَدِيَارٌ
The world to come.	دَارُ ٱلْبَقَاء
The world that is.	دَارُ ٱلْفَنَاء
The two worlds (of time and eternity).	ٱلدَّارَانِ
Turn; age, period.	دَوْرٌ ج اَدْوَارٌ
Rotation, circulation.	دَوَرَانٌ
Sparrow.	دُورِيٌّ

To scatter.	دَهَكَ يَدْهَكُ دَهْكًا
To come unexpectedly.	دَهَمَ يَدْهَمُ
Blackness.	دُهْمَة
Black (horse).	أَدْهَمُ
To anoint, paint.	دَهَنَ يَدْهُن
To beguile; coax.	دَاهَنَ
To be anointed.	تَدَهَّنَ
Oil, grease.	دُهْنٌ ج أَدْهَانٌ
Paint. Ointment.	دِهَانٌ وَدَهُونٌ
Painter.	دَهَّانٌ
Dissimulation; flattery.	مُدَاهَنَة
Painted.	مُدَهَّنٌ وَمَدْهُونٌ
To be sly, subtle.	دَهِيَ يَدْهَى
Cunning, craft.	دَهَاء
Calamity.	دَاهِيَةٌ ج دَوَاهٍ
Sagacious, cunning.	دَاهٍ وَدَاهِيَةٌ
To throw down.	دَهْوَرَ
To tumble down.	تَدَهْوَرَ
Illness, disease.	دَاء ج أَدْوَاء

By turns, alternately.	مُدَاوَلَةٌ
Used, employed commonly.	مُتَدَاوَلٌ
To continue ; endure.	دَامَ يَدُومُ
As long as it stands.	مَادَامَ قَائِمًا
To persist in.	دَاوَمَ عَلَى
To prolong.	أَدَامَ
To continue.	إِسْتَدَامَ
Continuance.	دَوَامٌ وَدَيْمُومَةٌ
The ban palm.	دَوْمٌ
Continually ; for ever.	عَلَى ٱلدَّوَام
Spinning-top.	دُوَّامَةٌ
Continuing, lasting.	دَائِمٌ
Always.	دَائِمًا
Wine.	مُدَامٌ وَمُدَامَةٌ
Perseverance.	مُدَاوَمَةٌ
To write out.	دَوَّن
Beneath. Before, behind.	دُونَ
Except.	دُونَ أَنْ

Revolving ; roaming.	دَائِرٌ
Circle; or bit of a planet. Calamity. Department.	دَائِرَةٌ ج دَوَائِرُ
Encyclopedia.	دَائِرَةُ ٱلْعُلُومِ
Giddiness.	دُوَارٌ
Convent.	دَيْرٌ ج أَدْيِرَةٌ
Administration.	إِدَارَةٌ
Circular form.	إِسْتِدَارَةٌ
Pivot, axis.	مَدَارٌ
Round, circular.	مُدَوَّرٌ وَمُسْتَدِيرٌ
Inspector ; director.	مُدِيرٌ
Territory of a Mudir.	مُدِيرِيَّةٌ
To tread, trample.	دَاسَ يَدُوسُ
To be trodden upon.	إِنْدَاسَ
Shoe, sandal.	مَدَاسٌ
To alternate.	دَاوَلَ مُدَاوَلَةً
To do by turns.	تَدَاوَلَ
Dynasty ; empire.	دَوْلَةٌ ج دُوَلٌ
Vine, grapes.	دَوَالِيٌّ

To judge, requite. Follow a religion.	دَانَ دِينًا	Without.	بِدُونٍ وَمِنْ دُونِ
To submit, yield to.	دانَ لِ	Low, mean, vile, bad.	دُونٌ
To lend money.	دَيَّنَ وَأَدَانَ	Take it !	دُونَكَ
To borrow.	تَدَيَّنَ وَاسْتَدَانَ مِنْ	Court of justice ; tribunal Poems.	دِيوَانٌ ج دَوَاوِينُ
To follow a religion.	تَدَيَّنَ بِ	Inserted, registered.	مُدَوَّنٌ
Debt, loan.	دَيْنٌ ج دُيُونٌ	To treat medically.	دَاوَى
Religion ; belief.	دَيْنٌ ج ادْيَانٌ . دِيَانَةٌ ج دِيَانَاتٌ	Medicine, remedy.	دَوَاءٌ ج أَدْوِيَةٌ
The Judgment Day.	يَوْمُ الدِّينِ	Inkstand.	دَوَاةٌ وَدَوَايَةٌ
Judgment.	دَيْنُونَةٌ	Hum, buzz; rustling.	دَوِيٌّ
Debtor ; creditor.	دَائِنٌ	Treatment, cure.	مُدَاوَةٌ
Judge.	دَيَّانٌ	Physician.	مُدَاوٍ
City. (see مدن)	مَدِينَةٌ	Cock.	دِيكٌ ج دُيُوكٌ
Debtor.	مَدْيُونٌ ج مَدْيُونُون	To borrow ; lend.	دَانَ يَدِينُ

ذ

Slaughtered.	ذَبِيحٌ
Sacrifice.	ذَبِيحَةٌ ج ذَبَائِحُ
Alter.	مَذْبَحٌ ج مَذَابِحُ
Slaughtered, immolated.	مَذْبُوحٌ
To swing to and fro.	ذَبْذَبَ
Wavering.	مُذَبْذِبٌ وَمُتَذَبْذِبٌ
To wither.	ذَبَلَ يَذْبُلُ ذُبُولاً
To cause to wither, dry up.	أَذْبَلَ
Withered, withering.	ذَابِلٌ
To treasure up.	ذَخَرَ يَذْخَرُ وَآذَخَرَ
Treasure ; stores.	ذُخْرٌ ج أَذْخَارٌ وَذَخِيرَةٌ ج ذَخَائِرُ
To scatter, sprinkle.	ذَرَّ يَذُرُّ ذَرًّا
Young or small ants.	ذَرٌّ
An atom.	ذَرَّةٌ
Descendants.	ذُرِّيَةٌ ج ذَرَارِيُّ

As a numeral sign=700.	ذ
This, this one.	ذَا ج اولاَءِ
That, that one.	ذَاكَ ج اولئِكَ
That, that one.	ذلِكَ ج اوْلاَئِكَ
What ? Why ?	لِمَاذَا مَاذَا
Thus, like this.	كَذَا
This.	هذَا مث هذَانِ ج هَوْلاَءِ
Thus, like this.	هكَذَا
Wolf.	ذِئْبٌ ج ذِ ئَابٌ
To repel ; defend.	ذَبَّ يَذُبُّ عَنْ
Fly.	ذُبَابٌ ج ذِبَّانٌ
A fly.	ذُبَابَةٌ
To slaughter, slay.	ذَبَحَ يَذْبَحُ
To kill one another.	تَذَابَحَ
Act of slaughtering.	ذَبْحٌ
Angina, croup.	ذِبْحَةٌ

Bewildered ; frightened. مَذْعُورٌ	Spanish fly. ذِرَّاحٌ ج ذَرَارِيح
To obey. ذَعِنَ يَذْعَنُ وَأَذْعَنَ لِ	To scatter, strew. ذَرْذَرَ
To confess, submit. اذْعَنَ بِ	Power, capacity. ذَرْعٌ
Submission. إِذْعَانٌ	To be unable. ضَاقَ ذَرْعًا
Obedient, submissive. مُذْعِنٌ	Arm ; cubit. ذِرَاعٌ ج أَذْرُعٌ
Strong odour. ذَفَرٌ	Sudden, rapid. ذَرِيعٌ
Chin ; beard. ذَقْنٌ ج ذُقُونٌ	To flow; shed (tears). ذَرَفَ يَذْرِفُ
To remember. ذَكَرَ يَذْكُرُ	To winnow ; scatter. ذَرَى يَذْرِي
To mention, relate. ذَكَرَ	To winnow. ذَرَّى وَأَذْرَى
To remind of. ذَكَّرَ وَأَذْكَرَ	To seek shelter. ذَرَّى وَاسْتَذْرَى
To confer with. ذَاكَرَ فِي	A kind of millet. ذُرَةٌ
To remember, think of. تَذَكَّرَ	Maize. ذُرَةٌ صَفْرَاءُ
To confer together. تَذَاكَرَ فِي	Dispersed dust. Shelter. ذَرًى
Memory ; praise. Mention. ذِكْرٌ	Summit. ذَرْوَةٌ ج ذُرًى
Male. Male organ. ذَكَرٌ ج ذُكُورٌ	Winnowing fork. مِذْرًى
Remembrance. ذِكْرَى	To frighten. ذَعَرَ يَذْعَرُ وَأَذْعَرَ
Faculty of memory. ذَاكِرَةٌ	To be terrified. ذَعِرَ وَانْذَعَرَ
Permit, passport. تَذْكِرَةٌ ج تَذَاكِرُ	Fright, terror. ذُعْرٌ
Remembrance. تَذْكَارٌ	Bewilderment. ذَعَرٌ

Protected tributaries. أَهْلُ ٱلذِّمةِ	Frequent remembrance. تذَكُّر
Conscience ; moral sense. ذِمةٌ	Conference. مُذاكرةٌ
Blamed ; censured. ذَميمٌ	Masculine, (word). مُذَكَّرٌ
Blameworthy action. مَذَمةٌ	Mentioned. Praised. مذْكورٌ
Blamed ; censured. مذمومٌ	To be quick, (in intellect). ذَكِيَ يَذكى
To murmur against. تذَمَّرَ عَلى	Quick understanding. ذَكاءٌ
To be guilty. أَذْنَبَ	Intelligent. ذَكيٌّ ج أَذكِياءٌ
Crime guilt. ذَنبٌ ج ذُنوبٌ	Quicker in perception. أَذكى
Tail, extremity. ذَنبٌ ج أَذْنابٌ	To be low ; submissive. ذَلَّ يَذِلُّ
Comet. نَجمٌ ذو ذَنَب	To humble, humiliate. ذَلَّ وَأَذَلَّ
Guilty ; criminal. مُذْنِبٌ	To render tractable. ذَلَّلَ
To go, depart. ذَهَبَ يَذهَب	To humble one's self. تذَلَّلَ
To think, believe. ذَهَبَ إِلى	Submissiveness. ذُلٌّ
To gild. ذَهَّبَ وَأَذْهَبَ	Humiliation. ذُلٌّ وَمَذَلَّةٌ
To cause to disappear. أَذْهَبَ	Low, abject. ذَليلٌ ج أَذلاءٌ
Gold. ذَهَبٌ	This ; that. (see ذا) ذَلِكَ
Golden, of gold. ذَهَبيٌّ	To blame, censure. ذَمَّ يَذُمُّ
Nile-boat. ذَهَبيةٌ	Blame, rebuke. ذَمٌّ وَمَذَمةٌ
Going ; passing. ذاهِبٌ	Covenant ; security. ذِمةٌ ج ذِمَمٌ

Selfishness.	مَحَبّة ٱلذات	Departure.	ذَهَابٌ
To dissolve, melt.	ذَابَ يَذُوبُ	Gilt.	مذهَّبٌ
To cause to melt.	ذَوَّبَ وَاذابَ	Way. Creed.	مَذهبٌ ج مَذَاهبُ
Melting, in a fluid state.	ذَائِبٌ	To embrace a creed.	تَمَذهَبَ
Manager.	مِذوَدٌ ج مَذَاوِد	Gold powder.	ماء ٱلذهَب
To taste; try.	ذَاقَ يَذُوقُ	To forget, neglect.	ذَهَلَ يَذهَلُ عَنْ
To give to taste.	أَذاقَ	To be astonished.	ذَهَلَ وَٱنذَهَلَ
Taste, sense of taste.	ذَوقٌ	To cause to forget.	أَذهلَ عَنْ
Sound taste.	ذَوقٌ سَلِيمٌ	Astonishment.	إنذهَالٌ
Flavour.	مَذَاقٌ	Astonished, bewildered.	منذَهِلٌ
That, yonder. (See اذا)	ذَاكَ	Mind, intellect.	ذِهنٌ ج أَذهَانٌ
To wither, (plant).	ذَوَى يَذوِي	Intellectual, subjective.	ذِهنِيّ
This, (fem. of كَا)	ذِي وَهذِي	Master, possessor.	ذُو ج ذَوُو
To be public, (news).	ذَاعَ يَذِيعُ	Essence; person, self.	ذَاتٌ
To make public.	اذَاع وَب	To the right.	ذَاتَ ٱليمِين
Publication.	إذَاعَة	On a certain day.	ذَاتَ يَومٍ
To add an appendix.	ذَيَّلَ	In person.	بذَاتِه
Tail, skirt. Fringes. Appendix.	ذَيلٌ ج ذُيُولٌ	In itself.	فِي ذَاتِه
Appendix, supplement.	تَذيِيل	Essential, personal.	ذَاتِيّ

ر

Compassionate.	رَؤُوفٌ وَرَئِفٌ
White antelope.	رِئْمٌ ج آرَامٌ
To see, perceive ; judge.	رَأَى يَرَى
To have a vision.	رَأَى رُؤْيَا
To dissemble.	رَاءَى مُرَاءَاةً
Do you suppose ?	يَا تَرَى
To show.	أَرَى إِرَاءَةً
To appear to.	تَرَأَّى وَتَرَاءَى لِ
To consider.	إِرْتَأَى
Opinion ; view.	رَأْيٌ ج آرَاءٌ
Military banner.	رَايَةٌ
Hypocrisy.	رِيَاءٌ
Lung.	رِئَةٌ ج رِئَاتٌ
Inflammation of lung.	ذَاتُ الرِّئَةِ
Dream, vision.	رُؤْيَا ج رُؤًى
Act of seeing.	رُؤْيَةٌ ج رُؤًى

As a numeral sign=200.	ر
Resin.	رَاتِينَجٌ
To be a chief.	رَأَسَ يَرْأَسُ
To make one a leader.	رَأَّسَ
To become a chief.	تَرَأَّسَ
Head ; peak ; cape ;	رَأْسٌ ج رُؤُوسٌ
chief, leader ; principal part.	
Directly ; completely.	رَأْسًا
Most willingly.	عَلَى الرَّأْسِ وَالْعَيْنِ
Capital ; stock.	رَأْسُ الْمَالِ
Headship, authority.	رَآسَةٌ وَرِيَاسَةٌ
President, chief.	رَئِيسٌ ج رُؤَسَاءُ
The vital organs.	الْأَعْضَاءُ الرَّئِيسَةُ
Under authority.	مَرْؤُوسٌ
To show pity.	رَأَفَ يَرْأَفُ
Compassion, pity, mercy.	رَأْفَةٌ

To tie, bind, fasten.	رَبَطَ يَرْبِطُ	Mirror.	مِرْآةٌ ج مَرَايَا
To agree upon.	تَرَابَطَ	Hypocrite.	مُرَاءٍ
To be tied.	إِرْتَبَطَ	Hypocrisy.	مُرَاءَاةٌ
Bundle, parcel.	رَبْطَةٌ ج رَبَطَاتٌ	Lord, master.	رَبٌّ ج أَرْبَابٌ
Highway-robber.	رَابِطُ ٱلدَّرْب	The Lord.	أَلرَّبُّ
Bond, rope.	رِبَاطٌ ج رُبُطٌ	Syrup.	رُبٌّ ج رِبَابٌ
Connective, copula.	رَابِطَةٌ	Often. Seldom.	رُبَّ وَرُبَّمَا
Stable.	مِرْبَطٌ ج مَرَابِطُ	Divine. Rabbi.	رَبَّانِيٌّ
Cord, rope; halter.	مِرْبَطٌ	A kind of violoncello.	رَبَابٌ
Pasture freely in.	رَبَعَ بِ	Captain of ship; chief.	رُبَّانٌ
To square.	رَبَّعَ	To gain.	رَبِحَ يَرْبَحُ رِبْحًا
To sit cross-legged.	تَرَبَّعَ	To cause one to gain.	رَبَّحَ
Fourth part.	رُبْعٌ ج ارْبَاعٌ	Profit, gain.	رِبْحٌ ج أَرْبَاحٌ
Medium in stature.	رَبْعَةٌ	A kind of sorrel (plant).	رِيَاسٌ
Fourth.	رَابِعٌ رَابِعَةٌ	To wait, expect.	تَرَبَّصَ
Quadrilateral.	رُبَاعِيٌّ	Pure, refined, (silver).	رُوبَاصٌ
Spring-time.	رَبِيعٌ	To lie in wait.	رَبَضَ يَرْبِضُ
The third month	رَبِيعُ ٱلأَوَّلُ	Suburb.	رَبَضٌ ج أَرْبَاضٌ
of the Mohammedan year.		Enclosure.	مَرْبِضٌ ج مَرَابِضُ

Usury, interest.	رِبَا وَرِبَاءُ	The fourth month.	رَبِيعُ ٱلْآخِرُ
Asthma, panting.	رَبْوٌ	Four.	أَرْبَعَةٌ م أَرْبَعٌ
Hill, height.	رَبْوَةٌ ج رُبًى	Quadrupeds.	ذَوَاتُ ٱلْأَرْبَعِ
Ten thousand.	رَبْوَةٌ ج رَبَوَاتٌ	Wednesday.	ٱلْأَرْبَعَاءُ
Hill, height.	رَابِيَةٌ ج رَوَابٍ	Forty.	أَرْبَعُونَ
Education, training.	تَرْبِيَةٌ	Square form or number.	مُرَبَّعٌ
Groin.	ارْبِيَةٌ	Of medium stature.	مَرْبُوعٌ
Usurer.	مُرَابٍ	Jerboa.	يَرْبُوعٌ ج يَرَابِيعُ
Educator, trainer.	مُرَبٍّ	To entangle, bind.	رَبَقَ يَرْبُقُ رَبْقًا
Educated, trained up.	مُرَبًّى	Loop, noose.	رِبْقٌ وَرِبْقَةٌ
To set in order.	رَتَّبَ	To mix, confuse.	رَبَكَ يَرْبُكُ
To be arranged.	تَرَتَّبَ	To be entangled.	رَبِكَ وَٱرْتَبَكَ
To result from.	تَرَتَّبَ عَلَى	Confused, entangled.	مُرْتَبِكٌ
Rank, position.	رُتْبَةٌ ج رُتَبٌ	Captain of a ship.	رُبَّانٌ
Salary, pension.	رَاتِبٌ	To increase ; grow.	رَبَا يَرْبُو
Arrangement, order.	تَرْتِيبٌ	To nourish ; train up.	رَبَّى
Grade, rank.	مَرْتَبَةٌ ج مَرَاتِبُ	To take usury.	رَابَى مُرَابَاةً
To live in abundance.	رَتِعَ يَرْتَعُ	To increase v. t.	أَرْبَى
To repair.	رَتَقَ يَرْتُقُ رَتْقًا	To be brought up.	تَرَبَّى

Swing.	أُرْجُوحَةٌ	To sing.	رَتَّلَ
Preference, probability.	تَرْجِيحٌ	Large spider.	رُتَيْلَاءُ ج رُتَيْلَاوَاتٌ
A poetical metre.	رَجَزٌ	Singing, chanting.	تَرْتِيلٌ ج تَرَاتِيلُ
Poem of رَجَزٌ metre.	أُرْجُوزَةٌ	To be ragged.	رَثَّ يَرِثُّ
To defile one's self.	رَجَسَ يَرْجَسُ	Worn out. Rags.	رَثٌّ
Pollution.	رِجْسٌ وَرَجَسٌ وَرَجَاسَةٌ	Squalor, raggedness.	رَثَاثَةٌ
Dirty, foul.	رَجِسٌ	To bewail (the dead).	رَثَى يَرْثِي
To return.	رَجَعَ يَرْجِعُ	To sympathize with, pity.	رَثَى لِ
To have recourse to.	رَجَعَ إِلَى	Elegy.	رِثَاءٌ
To renounce.	رَجَعَ عَنْ	Elegy.	مَرْثِيَةٌ وَمَرْثَاةٌ ج مَرَاثٍ
To restore.	رَجَّعَ	To move, shake.	رَجَّ يَرُجُّ
To review.	رَاجَعَ	Agitation, trembling.	إِرْتِجَاجٌ
To restore.	أَرْجَعَ	To put off, defer.	أَرْجَأَ
To reclaim.	إِسْتَرْجَعَ	The seventh month of the Moslem year.	رَجَبٌ
Return.	رُجُوعٌ	To over-weigh.	رَجَحَ يَرْجَحُ
Review, repetition.	مُرَاجَعَةٌ	To prefer.	رَجَّحَ عَلَى
To quake, tremble.	رَجَفَ يَرْجُفُ	To be more probable.	تَرَجَّحَ
To shake, agitate.	أَرْجَفَ	Outweighing, preferable.	رَاجِحٌ
To tremble.	إِرْتَجَفَ	Preferable, more probable.	أَرْجَحُ

To hope, expect.	رَجَا يَرْجُو
To hope for.	تَرَجَّى وَآرْتَجَى
To beg, entreat.	تَرَجَّى
To put off, defer.	أَرْجَى
Hope.	رَجَاءٌ
To be spacious (place).	رَحِبَ يَرْحَبُ
To make wide.	رَحَّبَ وَأَرْحَبَ
To welcome.	رَحَّبَ وَتَرَحَّبَ ب
Ample, spacious.	رَحْبٌ وَرَحِيبٌ
Welcome.	تَرْحَابٌ
Welcome !	مَرْحَبًا بِكَ
wash.	رَحَضَ يَرْحَضُ
Wash-tub, water, closet.	مِرْحَاضٌ ج مَرَاحِيضُ
Choice wine.	رُحَاقٌ ورَحِيقٌ
To depart, migrate.	رَحَلَ يَرْحَلُ وَآرْتَحَلَ
Pack-saddle.	رَحْلٌ ج رِحَالٌ
Journey.	رِحْلَةٌ وَآرْتِحَالٌ
Migration.	رَحِيلٌ وَآرْتِحَالٌ
Traveller.	رَاحِلٌ ج رُحَّلٌ

Trembling, shaking.	رَجْفَةٌ
Seditious rumours.	أَرَاجِيفُ
To go on foot.	رَجَل يَرْجَلُ
To dismount.	تَرَجَّلَ
To speak extempore.	إِرْتَجَلَ
Foot, leg.	رِجْلٌ ج أَرْجُلٌ
A man.	رَجُلٌ ج رِجَالٌ
Pedestrain.	رَجِلٌ وَرَاجِلٌ
Manliness ; virility.	رُجُولِيَّةٌ
Extemporizing.	إِرْتِجَالٌ
Caldron.	مَرْجَلٌ ج مَرَاجِلُ
Improvised (speech).	مُرْتَجَلٌ
To stone ; kill.	رَجَمَ يَرْجُمُ
To guess.	رَجَمَ بِالْغَيْبِ
To be heaped up.	إِرْتَجَمَ
Heap of stones.	رَجَمٌ ج رِجَامٌ
Tomb-stone.	رُجْمَةٌ ج رُجَمٌ
Stoned, killed. Cursed.	رَجِيمٌ
Coral.	مَرْجَانٌ

Soft, tender. رَخْصٌ م رَخْصَةٌ	Great traveller. رَحَّالٌ وَرَحَّالَةٌ
Cheapness of price. رُخْصٌ	Day's journey. مَرْحَلَةٌ ج مَرَاحِلُ
Cheap. Soft, tender. رَخِيصٌ	To pity, to be merciful. رَحِمَ يَرْحَمُ
To be soft (voice). رَخُمَ يَرْخُمُ	To have, or pray for, pity for one. تَرَحَّمَ عَلَى
Marble. رُخَامٌ	To implore pity. إِسْتَرْحَمَ
Soft (voice). رَخِيمٌ وَرَخُمٌ	Uterus, womb. رَحِمٌ ج أَرْحَامٌ
Elision of last letter of a word. تَرْخِيمٌ	Pity, compassion. رَحْمَةٌ
To be soft, flaccid. رَخِيَ يَرْخَى	Compassion. رَحِيمٌ ج رُحَمَاءُ
To loosen, let down. أَرْخَى	The Merciful. الرَّحْمَانُ الرَّحِيمُ
To flag, be slow. تَرَاخَى	Act of mercy. مَرْحَمَةٌ ج مَرَاحِمُ
To become lax. إِرْتَخَى وَاسْتَرْخَى	Deceased (person). مَرْحُومٌ
Relaxation ; abundance. رَخَاءٌ	Mill-stone. رَحًى ج أَرْحَاءٌ
Lax, soft, loose. رَخْوٌ	A fabulons bird. رُخ
Softness, slackness. رَخَاوَةٌ	Saddle. رَخْتٌ ج رُخُوتٌ
Free from care. رَخِيُّ البَالِ	To be cheap. رَخُصَ يَرْخُصُ
Relaxation. إِرْتِخَاءٌ وَاسْتِرْخَاءٌ	To be soft, supple. رَخُصَ رَخَاصَةً
To return, send back, turn away. Refer. رَدَّ يَرُدُّ	To lower the price. رَخَّصَ
To ponder ; repeat. رَدَّدَ	To allow, permit. رَخَّصَ لِ
To frequent (a place). تَرَدَّدَ إِلَى	To consider a thing cheap. To ask leave. إِسْتَرْخَصَ

Restrain, prevent.	رَدَعَ يَرْدَعُ عَنْ	To waver ; hesitate.	تَرَدَّدَ فِي
To be restrained.	إِرْتَدَعَ عَنْ	To go back, retreat, revert.	إِرْتَدَّ
To follow.	رَدَفَ يَرْدُفُ	To be converted to.	إِرْتَدَّ إِلَى
To be synonymous, (words).	تَرَادَفَ	To depart from.	إِرْتَدَّ عَنْ
The reserves, (soldiers).	رَدِيفٌ	To reclaim ; revoke.	اِسْتَرَدَّ
Synonymous (words).	مُتَرَادِفٌ	Repulse. Return. Reply.	رَدٌّ
To stop, fill up.	رَدَمَ يَرْدِمُ	Conversion to.	إِرْتِدَادٌ إِلَى
To be stopped up.	إِرْتَدَمَ	Apostasy.	إِرْتِدَادٌ عَنْ
Ruins of a wall, debris.	رَدْمٌ	Reclamation, recovery.	اِسْتِرْدَادٌ
To spin. Purr (cat).	رَدَنَ يَرْدُنُ	Frequenting. Wavering.	تَرَدُّدٌ
Sleeve.	رُدْنٌ ج أَرْدَانٌ	Setting aside, repelling.	مَرَدٌّ
The Jordan.	الأُرْدُنُّ	Convert ; apostate.	مُرْتَدٌّ
Spindle.	مِرْدَنٌ ج مَرَادِنُ	Vacillating, hesitating.	مُتَرَدِّدٌ
A large hall.	رَدْهَةٌ ج رِدَاهٌ	Rejected ; refuted.	مَرْدُودٌ
To perish.	رَدِيَ يَرْدَى رَدًى	Divorced woman.	مَرْدُودَةٌ
To put on a mantle.	تَرَدَّى	Evil, malice.	رَدَاءَةٌ وَرَدَاوَةٌ
Mantle, cloak.	رِدَاءٌ ج أَرْدِيَةٌ	Bad, wicked.	رَدِيءٌ ج أَرْدِيَاءُ
Enveloped in a mantle.	مُتَرَدٍّ	Worse, more wicked.	أَرْدَأُ
To be mean, base.	رَذَلَ يَرْذُلُ	Corn measure.	أُرْدَبٌّ

Blessed with worldly goods.	مَرْزُوقٌ	To reject.	رَذَلَ يَرْذُلُ رَذْلاً
To wrap up a package.	رَزَمَ يَرْزِمُ	Ignoble, base.	رَذِيلٌ ج رُذَلاَءُ
Package, bale.	رِزْمَةٌ ج رِزَمٌ	Vileness.	رَذَالَةٌ ج رَزَالاَتٌ
To be grave, dignified.	رَزُنَ يَرْزُنُ	Vice.	رَذِيلَةٌ ج رذَائِلُ
Gravity, dignity.	رَزَانَةٌ	Rice.	رُزٌّ (أَرُزٌّ *for*)
Weighty, grave, calm.	رَزِينٌ	Iron peg.	رَزَّةٌ ج رَزَّاتٌ
Almanac.	رُزْنَامَةٌ	To diminish. Afflict.	رَزَأَ يَرْزَأُ
To settle down. (liquid).	رَسَبَ يَرْسُبُ	Misfortune.	رَزِيئَةٌ ج رَزَايَا
Sediment.	رُسُوبٌ وَرُسَابَةٌ	Iron rod.	إِرْزَبَّةٌ وَمِرْزَبَةٌ
Theatre.	مَرْسَحٌ ج مَرَاسِحُ	Satrap.	مَرْزُبَانٌ ج مَرَازِبَةٌ
To be firm, stable.	رَسَخَ يَرْسَخُ	To fall from fatigue.	رَزَحَ يَرْزَحُ
Firm, stable.	رَاسِخٌ ج رَاسِخُونَ	Extreme fatigue.	رُزُوحٌ
Well instructed.	رَاسِخٌ فِي ٱلْعِلْمِ	Fatigued, exhausted.	رَازِحٌ
The ankle, wrist.	رُسْغٌ ج أَرْسَاغٌ	District.	رُزْدَاقٌ ج رُزْدَاقَاتٌ
To correspond about.	رَاسَلَ	To grant, bestow.	رَزَقَ يَرْزُقُ
To dismiss, send.	أَرْسَلَ	To receive means of life.	إِرْتَزَقَ
To hang loose, (hair).	إِسْتَرْسَلَ	To seek means of life.	إِسْتَرْزَقَ
Message, letter, epistle. Mission.	رِسَالَةٌ ج رَسَائِلُ	Means of living.	رِزْقٌ ج أَرْزَاقٌ
Messenger, apostle.	رَسُولٌ ج رُسُلٌ	God.	ٱلرَّازِقُ وَٱلرَّزَّاقُ

To be trained for.	تَرَاشَحَ لِ	One sent, missionary.	مُرْسَلٌ
Cold in the heat.	رَشْحٌ	Correspondent.	مُرَاسِلٌ
Trained. Candidate.	مُرَشَّحٌ	Correspondence.	مُرَاسَلَةٌ
To direct, guide.	أَرْشَدَ	To trace ; design.	رَسَمَ يَرْسِمُ عَلَى
To ask for guidance.	إِسْتَرْشَدَ	To prescribe, enjoin.	رَسَمَ لِ
Rectitude. Maturity.	رُشْد	To ordain to a sacred office.	رَسَمَ رِسَامَةً
Cress, pepperwort.	رَشَادٌ	Trace ; sign. Tax.	رَسْمٌ ج رُسُومٌ
Follower of right way.	رَاشِدٌ وَرَشِيدٌ	Official, authoritative.	رَسْمِيٌّ
To sip. suck.	رَشَفَ يَرْشُفُ	Marked. Ordained.	مَرْسُومٌ
To hurl (a weapon).	رَشَقَ يَرْشُقُ	Halter.	رَسَنٌ ج أَرْسُنٌ وَأَرْسَانٌ
Fine, elegant form.	رَشِيقٌ	To be firm.	رَسَا يَرْسُو
Elegance of from.	رَشَاقَةٌ	To cast anchor.	أَرْسَى إِرْسَاءً
Window.	رَوْشَنٌ ج رَوَاشِنُ	At anchor, (ship).	رَاسٍ
To bribe.	رَشَا يَرْشُو رَشْوًا	Port. Anchorage.	مَرْسًى ج مَرَاسٍ
To receive a bribe.	إِرْتَشَى	Anchor.	مِرْسَاةٌ ج مَرَاسٍ
To ask for a bribe.	إِسْتَرْشَى	To sprinkle.	رَشَّ يَرُشُّ
Bribe.	رَشْوَةٌ ج رُشًى	Watering-pot.	مِرَشَّةٌ ج مِرَشَّاتٌ
To press, squeeze.	رَصَّ يَرُصُّ	To exude, ooze.	رَشَحَ يَرْشَحُ رَشْحًا
To overlay with lead.	رَصَّصَ	To train, bring up.	رَشَّحَ لِ

To pound, bruise.	رَضَّ يَرُضُّ	Lead.	رَصَاصٌ
To be bruised.	تَرَضَّضَ وَارْتَضَّ	Piece of lead ; bullet.	رَصَاصَةٌ
Bruise, contusion.	رَضٌّ وَرَضَّةٌ	Lead-colour.	رَصَاصِيٌّ
Saliva.	رُضَابٌ	Firm, compact.	مَرْصُوصٌ
To submit.	رَضَخَ يَرْضَخُ رَضْخًا خَالِ	To watch for.	رَصَدَ يَرْصُدُ
To nurse (infant).	رَضِعَ يَرْضَعُ	To lie in wait for.	رَصَدَ لِ
To nurse, (mother).	أَرْضَعَ	To observe, watch.	تَرَصَّدَ
Infant at the breast.	رَضِيعٌ	Watching, observation.	رَصْدٌ
Act of nursing a child.	إِرْضَاعٌ	Balance of account.	رَصِيدٌ
Wet-nurse.	مُرْضِعَةٌ ج مُرْضِعَاتٌ	Observatory.	مَرْصَدٌ ج مَرَاصِدُ
To be pleased.	رَضِيَ يَرْضَى	Highway, lurking-place.	مِرْصَادٌ
To consent to.	رَضِيَ بِ	To set with jewels	رَصَّعَ
To satisfy, conciliate.	رَاضَى	Inlaid with gold-work.	مُرَصَّعٌ
To satisfy, please.	أَرْضَى إِرْضَاءً	To pave.	رَصَفَ يَرْصُفُ رَصْفًا
To be content with.	إِرْتَضَى	Firmness, solidity.	رَصَافَةٌ
Satisfaction.	رِضًى وَرِضْوَانٌ	Firm. Paved road.	رَصِيفٌ
Satisfied, content.	رَاضٍ ج رَاضُونَ	To be solid, grave.	رَصُنَ يَرْصُنُ
Comfortable life.	عِيشَةٌ رَاضِيَةٌ	Gravity, sedateness.	رَصَانَةٌ
Mutual agreement.	تَرَاضٍ	Firm, dignified, grave.	رَصِينٌ

A trembling, shaking.	رَعْشٌ	Satisfying, pleasing.	مُرْض
To bleed, (nose).	رَعِفَ يَرْعَفُ	To be moist, damp.	رَطُبَ يَرْطُبُ
Bleeding from the nose.	رُعَافٌ	To moisten; cool.	رَطَّبَ
Sun-stroke.	رَعْنٌ	To be moistened.	تَرَطَّبَ
Stupidity	رَعَنٌ وَرُعُونَةٌ	Fresh, ripe dates.	رُطَبٌ
To graze; tend (cattle).	رَعَى يَرْعَى	Moisture; humidity.	رُطُوبَةٌ
Rule (subjects). Have regard to.		449.28 grammes.	رَطْلٌ ج أَرْطَالٌ
To have regard for.	رَاعَى	To stick in mire.	إِرْتَطَمَ
To pasture, graze.	إِرْتَعَى وَتَرَعَّى	The rabble, dregs of men.	رَعَاعٌ
Guarding; pasturing.	رِعَايَةٌ	To frighten.	رَعَبَ يَرْعَبُ
Subjects (of a ruler).	رَعِيَّةٌ ج رَعَايَا	To terrify.	رَعَبَ وَأَرْعَبَ
Shepherd. Pastor.	رَاعٍ ج رُعَاةٌ	To be frightened.	إِرْتَعَبَ
Pasturage, pasture.	مَرْعًى ج مَرَاعٍ	Fright, fear.	رُعْبٌ وَرُعُبٌ
Observed, regarded.	مَرْعِيٌّ	Causing fear.	رَاعِبٌ وَمُرْعِبٌ
Out of regard for.	مُرَاعَاةً ل	To thunder.	رَعَدَ يَرْعُدُ
To desire, long for.	رَغِبَ يَرْغَبُ فِي	To tremble, be afraid.	إِرْتَعَدَ
To have no desire for, refrain from.	رَغِبَ عَنْ	Thunder.	رَعْدٌ ج رُعُودٌ
To implore, entreat.	رَغِبَ إِلَى	To tremble.	رَعَشَ يَرْعَشُ وَارْتَعَشَ
To inspire with desire.	رَغَّبَ	To cause to tremble.	أَرْعَشَ

Assistance.	رِفْدٌ ج أَرْفَادٌ
Cushion ; bandage.	رِفَادَةٌ
To flap the wings.	رَفْرَفَ
To kick.	رَفَسَ يَرْفِسُ
A kick.	رَفْسَةٌ
To shovel.	رَفَشَ يَرْفُشُ رَفْشاً
Winnowing-shovel.	رَفْشٌ
To leave, reject	رَفَضَ يَرْفُضُ
To be separated, disperse.	إِرْفَضَّ
One who rejects.	رَافِضٌ ج رَفَضَةٌ
A fanatic.	مُتَرَفِّضٌ
Rejected.	مَرْفُوضٌ
To raise ; take away.	رَفَعَ يَرْفَعُ
To be exalted.	رَفُعَ يَرْفُعُ
To present to ; inform.	رَفَعَ إِلَى
To cite before a judge.	رَافَعَ إِلَى
To bring a cause together before a judge.	تَرَافَعَ
To rise high ; carried off.	إِرْتَفَعَ
Act of raising, elevating.	رَفْعٌ

Strong desire, eagerness.	رَغْبَةٌ
A desired object.	رَغِيبَةٌ ج رَغَائِبُ
Comfortable, easy.	رَغْدٌ وَرَغِيدٌ
Loaf (of bread).	رَغِيفٌ ج أَرْغِفَةٌ
To humiliate, vex ; force.	أَرْغَمَ
In spite of him.	رَغْماً عَنْهُ
To effervesce, froth.	رَغَا يَرْغُو
Foam, froth, cream.	رَغْوَةٌ
To shine ; flutter.	رَفَّ يَرِفُّ
Flock. Shelf.	رَفٌّ ج رُفُوفٌ
To mend (a garment).	رَفَأَ يَرْفَأُ
To make peace between.	رَفَأَ بَيْنَ
Peace, concord, accord.	رِفَاءٌ
Harbour for ships.	مَرْفَأٌ
To refuse, reject.	رَفَتَ يَرْفُتُ
Permit (for goods).	رَفْتِيَّةٌ
To rise, swell (dough).	رَفَخَ
To aid. Dress (a wound).	رَفَدَ يَرْفِدُ
To ask help.	إِسْتَرْفَدَ

— ٨ —

To become a slave.	رقَّ رقًّا	High rank, dignity.	رِفْعَة
To make thin, fine.	رقق وارَقّ	High, elevated.	رَفِيع
To enslave.	إِسْتَرَقّ	Elevation, height.	إِرْتِفَاع
Slavery.	رِقّ	Carnival.	مَرْفَع ج مَرَافِع
Parchment ; paper.	رِقّ ج رُقُوق	Raised up. Carried off.	مَرْفُوع
Fineness. Compassion.	رِقّة	To be gentle towards.	رَفِقَ يَرْفَقُ ب
Tender-heartedness.	رِقّة ٱلْقَلْب	To accompany one.	رَافَقَ
Thin bread.	رُقَاق ج رِقَاق	To treat with kindness.	تَرَفَّقَ ب
Thin. Slave.	رَقِيق ج رِقَاق	To be companions.	تَرَافَقَ
Not rich.	رَقِيقُ ٱلْحَال	Kindness, compassion.	رِفْق
To watch, observe.	رَقَبَ يَرْقُبُ	Company.	رِفْقَة ج رِفَق
To guard, keep. Observe.	رَاقَبَ	Companion.	رَفِيق ج رُفَقَاء
To expect, look for.	تَرَقَّبَ	Elbow.	مِرْفَق ومَرْفِق ج مَرَافِق
Neck. Slave.	رَقَبَة ج رِقَاب	Water-closet	مُرْتَفَق
Guardian.	رَقِيب ج رُقَبَاء	To live in luxury.	رَفَهَ يَرْفَهُ
Watch-tower.	مَرْقَب ج مَرَاقِب	To be comfortable, (life).	رَفُهَ يَرْفُهُ
Telescope.	مِرْقَب	Good living.	رَفَاهَة ورَفَاهِية
To sleep.	رَقَدَ يَرْقُدُ	To be thin, fine.	دَقَّ يَرِقُّ
To put to sleep.	أَرْقَدَ	To pity one.	رَقَّ لَهُ

Numerical sign.	رَقَمٌ ج ارْقَامٌ	Sleep.	رُقَادْ
Indian numerals.	الرّقمُ آلهِنْديُّ	Bed ; dormitory.	مَرْقَدٌ ج مَرَاقَدُ
Written. Embroidered.	مَرْقُومٌ	To variegate.	رَقَشَ يَرْقُشُ وَرَقَشَ
Clavicle. collar-bone.	تَرْقُوَةٌ	To be embellished.	تَرْقَشَ
To ascend, rise.	رَقِيَ يَرْقَى	Variegated.	ارْقَشُ رَقْشَاءُ ج رُقْشٌ
To use magic.	رَقَى يَرْقِي رُقْيَةً	To dance.	رَقَصَ يَرْقُصُ رَقْصاً
To raise high, elevate.	رَقَّى	To cause to dance.	رَقَّصَ وَأَرْقَصَ
To rise high.	تَرَقَّى وَآرْتَقَى فِي وَإِلَى	Dancing, leaping.	رَقْصٌ
Magic, incantation.	رُقْيَةٌ	Dancer. Pendulum.	رَقَّاصٌ
Charmer, magician.	رَاقٍ ج رُقَاةٌ	To be spotted.	تَرَقَّطَ
Rising, progress.	تَرَقٍّ وَآرْتِقَاءٌ	Spotted.	ارْقَطُ م رقْطَاءُ ج رُقْطٌ
Ladder, stairs.	مَرْقًى وَدِرْقَاةٌ ج مَرَاقٍ	To patch.	رَقَعَ يَرْقَعُ وَرَقَّعَ
To be weak.	رَكَّ يَرُكُّ رَكَاكَةً	To be foolish.	رَقُعَ يَرْقُعُ رَقَاعَةً
To make a foundation.	رَكَّ يَرُكُّ	Patch scrap.	رُقْعَةٌ ج رِقَاعٌ
Rubble used in masonry.	رَكَّةٌ	Folly, stupidity.	رَقَاعَةٌ
Weak.	رَكِيكٌ ج رُكَاكٌ	Firmament.	رَقِيعٌ
Pressed.	مَرْكُوكٌ	Patched, mended.	مُرَقَّعٌ
To ride ; embark.	رَكِبَ يَرْكَبُ	To write.	رَقَمَ يَرْقُمُ رَقْماً
To follow one's fancy.	رَكِبَ هَوَاهُ	To mark with stripes.	رَقَمَ وَرَقَّمَ

To vie with in running.	رَاكَضَ
Good runner.	رَكوضٌ
To bow (in prayer) ; kneel.	رَكَعَ يَرْكَعُ
To cause one to bow.	رَكَّعَ وَأَرْكَعَ
Bowing in (prayer).	رَكْعَةٌ ج رَكَعَاتٌ
To heap up.	رَكَمَ يَرْكُمُ رَكْمًا
To be heaped up.	تَرَاكَمَ وَارْتَكَمَ
Heap, pile.	رَكْمٌ وَرُكَامٌ
To rely upon.	رَكَنَ يَرْكُنُ إِلَى
To trust in.	أَرْكَنَ إِلَى
To take to fight.	أَرْكَنَ إِلَى الفِرَارِ
Support, prop.	رُكْنٌ ج أَرْكَانٌ
The elements (of things).	الأركَانُ
Firmness ; gravity.	رُكُونَةٌ وَرَكَانَةٌ
To rely upon.	تَرَكَّى وَارْتَكَى عَلَى
Small vessel.	رَكْوَةٌ ج رَكْوَةٌ
Well.	رَكِيَّةٌ ج رَكَايَا
To mend, restore.	رَمَّ يَرُمُّ وَرَمَّمَ
To become decayed.	رَمَّ وَأَرَمَّ

To brave danger.	رَكِبَ اللَّيلَ
To compose, mix.	رَكَّبَ
To be constructed, mixed.	تَرَكَّبَ
To commit a crime.	إِرْتَكَبَ
Band of horsemen.	رَكْبٌ
Knee.	رُكْبَةٌ ج رُكَبٌ
Stirrup.	رِكَابٌ ج رُكُبٌ
Rider. Passenger.	رَاكِبٌ ج رُكَّابٌ
Composition, structure.	تَرْكِيبٌ
Ship, vessel.	مَرْكَبٌ ج مَرَاكِبُ
Carriage.	مَرْكَبَةٌ
Shoes.	مَرْكُوبٌ ج مَرَاكِيبُ
Compound. Joined.	مُرَكَّبٌ
To be still, motionless.	رَكَدَ يَرْكُدُ
Still, stagnant.	رَاكِدٌ
To fix in (the ground).	رَكَزَ يَرْكُزُ
Prop, buttress.	رَكِيزَةٌ ج رَكَائِزُ
Centre.	مَرْكَزٌ ج مَرَاكِزُ
To run.	رَكَضَ يَرْكُضُ رَكْضًا

To be very hot.	رَمَضَ يَرْمَض	To be repaired by degrees.	تَرَمَّم
Intense heat.	رَمْضَاء	Altogether.	بِرُمَّتِه
The ninth month of the Moslem year.	رَمَضَان	Decayed bones.	رُمَّة ج رِمَم
To glance furtively.	رَمَقَ يَرْمُقُ	Decayed (bone).	رَمِيم
The last breath of life.	رَمَق	Lance, spear.	رُمْح ج رِمَاح
To put sand into.	رَمَلَ	Lancer, spearman.	رَامِح
To become sandy.	أَرْمَلَ	To have sore eyes.	رَمِدَ يَرْمَدُ
To become a widow or widower.	أَرْمَلَ وَتَرَمَّلَ	Ophthalmia.	رَمَد
Sand.	رَمْل ج رِمَال وَارْمَال	Ashes.	رَمَاد
Hour-glass.	سَاعَة رَمَايَة	Having ophthalmia.	رَمْدَان
Widower; widow.	أَرْمَل ج أَرْمَلَة	Grey, ash-coloured.	رَمَادِيّ
Pomegranate.	رُمَّان	To indicate by a sign.	رَمَزَ يَرْمُز
The Armenians.	ألأَرْمَن	To be intelligent.	رَمَزَ يَرْمُز رَمَازَة
Armenian.	ارْمَنِيّ	Sign. Allegory.	رَمْز ج رُمُوز
To throw; hit; accuse.	رَمَى يَرْمِي	Model, specimen.	رَامُوز ج رَوَامِيز
To be thrown.	إِرْتَمَى أَرْتِمَاء	Alluded to.	مَرْمُوز إِلَيْه
Throw, hit.	رَمْيَة ج رَمِيَات	To conceal; bury.	رَمَسَ يَرْمُس
Archer, slinger.	رَامٍ ج رُمَاة	Tomb, grave.	رَمْس ج رُمُوس
Sagittarius (of the Zodiac).	الرَّامِي	Lupine (herb).	تُرْمُس

Fearful, awful.	رَهِيبٌ
Dust. Excitement.	رَهَجٌ
To assemble, congregate.	إِرْتَهَطَ
Company of men.	رَهْطٌ ج أَرْهُطٌ
To be thin, sharp.	رَهُفَ يَرْهُفُ
Thin, slender.	رَهِيفٌ ومُرْهَفٌ
To approach puberty.	رَاهَقَ
Boy at puberty.	مُرَاهِقٌ
Ointment.	مَرْهَمٌ ج مَرَاهِمُ
To be firm.	رَهَنَ يَرْهُنُ رَهْنًا
To pledge with.	رَهَنَ عِنْدَ
To bet, lay a wager.	رَاهَنَ
To bet together.	تَرَاهَنَ
To receive a pledge.	إِرْتَهَنَ
To require a pledge.	إِسْتَرْهَنَ
Pledge, mortgage.	رَهْنٌ ج رِهَانٌ
Fixed, stable, durable.	رَاهِنٌ
Pledged.	رَهِينٌ ومُرْتَهَنٌ ومَرْهُونٌ
Pledge, security.	رَهِينةٌ ج رَهَائِن

Instrument for throwing (projectile, arrow).	مِرْمًى ج مَرَامٍ
Arrow, missile.	مِرْمَاةٌ ج مَرَامٍ
To twang, ring.	رَنَّ يَرِنُّ رَنِينًا
Sound, tone, echo.	رَنِينٌ ورَنَّةٌ
Hare.	أَرْنَبٌ ج أَرَانِبُ
To make giddy, (wine).	رَنَّحَ
To stagger.	تَرَنَّحَ
Lustre, brilliancy.	رَوْنَقٌ
To sing.	رَنَّمَ يُرَنِّمُ ورَمَّ وتَرَنَّمَ
Poem. Hymn.	تَرْنِيمةٌ
Singing, psalmody.	تَرْنِيمٌ
To fear, dread.	رَهَبَ يَرْهَبُ رَهْبَةً
To frighten.	رَهَّبَ وأَرْهَبَ
To become a monk.	تَرَهَّبَ
Fear.	رَهْبةٌ
Monachism.	رَهْبَنةٌ ورَهْبَانِيةٌ
Monk.	رَاهِبٌ ج رُهْبَانٌ
Nun.	رَاهِبةٌ ج رَاهِبَاتٌ

Long-suffering.	طَوِيلُ الرُّوحِ	Ambling-horse.	رَهْوَانٌ
Spiritual, incorporeal.	رُوحَانِيٌّ	To curdle, (milk.)	رَابَ يَرُوبُ
Wind. Odour.	رِيحٌ ج رِيَاحٌ	Curdled ; churned.	رَائِبٌ وَمُرَوَّبٌ
Whitlow.	رِيحُ الشَّوْكَةِ	Ferment of; milk.	رَوْبَةٌ
Odour. Puff of wind.	رِيحَةٌ	To void excre- ment, (horse).	رَاثَ يَرُوثُ رَوْثًا
Myrtle.	رَيْحَانٌ ج رَيَاحِينُ	To be current.	رَاجَ يَرُوجُ
Odour.	رَائِحَةٌ ج رَوَائِحُ	To put in circulation·	رَوَّجَ
Generous, liberal.	أَرِيحِيّ	Currency. Good market.	رَوَاجٌ
Cattle-fold.	مُرَاحٌ	Selling well. Current.	رَائِجٌ
Fan.	مِرْوَحٌ وَمِرْوَحَةٌ ج مَرَاوِحُ	To go, depart.	رَاحَ يَرُوحُ
Water-closet.	مُسْتَرَاحٌ	To give rest.	أَرَاحَ إِرَاحَةً
To ask for. Seek (food).	رَادَ يَرُودُ	To be pleased.	إِرْتَاحَ
To beguile, seduce ; entice.	رَاوَدَ	To rest.	إِسْتَرَاحَ
To wish, desire.	أَرَادَ	Wine. Mirth.	رَاحٌ
To mean, intend.	أَرَادَ بِ	Rest ease, quietude.	رَاحَةٌ
Slowly, gently.	رُوَيْدًا	Palm of the hand.	رَاحَةٌ رَاحَاتٌ
Will ; volition.	إِرَادَةٌ	Water-closet.	بَيْتُ الرَّاحَةِ
Voluntary.	إِرَادِي	Breath, spirit.	رُوحٌ ج أَرْوَاحٌ
Desired. Purpose · meaning.	مُرَادٌ	The Holy Spirit.	رُوحُ الْقُدُسِ

Mediterranean Sea.	بَحْرُ آلرُّومِ	To train, discipline.	رَوَّضَ
Rafter.	رُومِيَّةٌ جَ رَوَامِيُّ	Garden, flower-bed.	رَوْضٌ
Desire, purpose.	مَرَامٌ	Meadow.	رَوْضَةٌ جَ رِيَاضٌ
Rhubarb.	رَوَنْدٌ وَرَاوَنْدٌ	Exercise, training.	رِيَاضَةٌ
To report, quote.	رَوَى يَرْوِي رِوَايَةً	Mathematics.	عِلْمُ آلرِّيَاضَاتِ
To quench one's thirst.	رَوِيَ يَرْوَى	To fear.	رَاعَ يَرُوعُ وَآرْتَاعَ
To consider attentively.	تَرَوَّى	To frighten.	رَاعَ وَرَوَّعَ وَارَاعَ
To quench thirst.	أَرْوَى إِرْوَاءً	Fear, fright.	رَوْعٌ وَرَوْعَةٌ
Narration, tale.	رِوَايَةٌ	To act slyly.	رَاغَ يَرُوغُ رَوْغًا
Narrator.	رَاوٍ جَ رُوَاةٌ وَرَاوُونَ	To employ a ruse.	رَاوَغَ
Rain ; irrigation.	رِيٌّ	Ruse, trick.	مُرَاوَغَةٌ
Well watered.	رَيَّانُ	To be clear, limpid.	رَاقَ يَرُوقُ
Well watered. Cited.	مَرْوِيٌّ	To render clear, clarify.	رَوَّقَ
To make doubtful.	رَابَ يَرِيبُ	To pour out or forth.	أَرَاقَ
To trouble, disquiet.	أَرَابَ	To breakfast.	اتَرَوَّقَ
To have doubts.	إِرْتَابَ	Tent, portico.	رِوَاقٌ جَ أُرْوِقَةٌ
Doubt.	رَيْبٌ وَرَيْبَةٌ جَ رِيَبٌ	Clear, limpid, pure.	رَائِقٌ
Doubt, hesitation.	اِرْتِيَابٌ	To desire strongly.	رَامَ يَرُومُ
Causing, doubt.	مُرِيبٌ	Roman. Greek.	رُومٌ جَ ارْوَامٌ

To pour out.	رَاقَ يَرِيقُ	As long as ; while.	رَيْثَمَا
To pour out a liquid.	أَرَاقَ	Feathers.	رِيشْ ج رِيَاش
Saliva.	رِيقٌ	A feather.	رِيشَةٌ
Before breakfast.	عَلَى الرِّيق	Furniture, goods.	رِيَاشٌ
To droll (child).	رَالَ يَرِيلُ رَيلاً	The best part.	رَيْعَانٌ
Saliva. Dollar.	رِيَالٌ	A fertile land	رِيفٌ ج أَرْيَافٌ
White gazelle or antelope.	رِيمٌ	along the banks of a river.	
Flag ; standard.	رَايَةٌ ج رَايَاتٌ	Sea-coast.	رِيفُ الْبَحرِ

ز

Raisins, dried figs.	زَبِيبٌ	As a numeral sign=7.	ز
Hairy.	أَزَبُّ م زَبَاءِ	Nap of cloth.	زُوبرٌ وَزُوبَرٌ
Fertile year.	عَامٌ أَزَبُّ	Mercury, quicksilver.	زِئْبَقٌ
To churn (butter).	زَبَدَ يَزْبُدُ	To roar (lion).	زَارَ يَزْأَرُ وَزَئَرَ
To foam, froth.	زَبَدَ وَازْبَدَ	Roaring ; angry ; enemy.	زَائِرٌ
Foam, froth.	زَبَدٌ	Tares, (seed and plant).	زَوَانٌ
Butter.	زُبْدٌ وَزُبْدَةٌ	**Hairiness, Down.**	زَبَبٌ

Glass-merchant.	زِجَاجِيٌّ	Cream.	زُبْدَة
Having long eyebrows.	أَزَجُّ م زَجَّاء	A kind of perfume ; civet.	زَبَادٌ
To forbid. Rebuke.	زَجَرَ يَزْجُرُ	Foaming. Enraged.	مُزْبِدٌ
To be forbidden.	إِنْزَجَرَ	Psalms of David.	زَبُورٌ ج زُبُرٌ
Play. Uproar.	زَجَلٌ	Powerful man.	زِيرٌ
Carrier-pigeons.	حَمَامُ الزَّاجِلِ	Chrysolite.	زَبَرْجَدٌ
To remove a thing.	زَحَّ يَزُحُّ	A whirlwind.	زَوْبَعَة ج زَوَابِعُ
To strain in breathing.	زَحَرَ يَزْحَرُ	To manure.	زَبَلَ يَزْبِلُ وَزَبَّلَ
Straining. Dysentery.	زَحِيرٌ	Manure.	زِبْلٌ وَزِبْلَة
To remove a thing.	زَحْزَحَ عَنْ	Dirt ; sweepings.	زُبَالَة
To march. Creep.	زَحَفَ يَزْحَفُ	Manure-gatherer.	زَبَّالٌ
Marching. An army.	زَحْفٌ	Basket, pannier.	زِنْبِيلٌ ج زَنَابِيل
Reptiles.	الزَّحَّافَةُ وَالزَّحَّافَاتُ	Dung-hill.	مَزْبَلَة ج مَزَابِلُ
To depart ; retire.	زَحَلَ يَزْحَلُ عَنْ	Customer.	زَبُونٌ ج زَبَائِنُ
To move a thing.	زَحَّلَ وَازْحَلَ	To thrust with a lance.	زَجَّ يَزُجُّ زَجًّا
The planet Saturn.	زُحَلُ	Point of a spear.	زُجٌّ ج زِجَاجٌ
To crowd ; press.	زَحَمَ يَزْحَمُ وَزَاحَمَ	Glass ; glass vessels.	زُجَاجٌ
To be crowded.	تَزَاحَمَ وَازْدَحَمَ	Piece, or cup, of glass.	زُجَاجَة
Pressure ; throng.	زَحْمَة وَزِحَامٌ	Glass-manufacturer.	زُجَّاجٌ

To sow ; plant.	زَرَعَ يَزْرَعُ	Full ; copious.	زَاخِرٌ
To sow in shares.	زَارَعَ مُزَارَعَة	Munitions of war.	زَخِيرَةٌ ج زَخَائِرُ
Seed. Off-spring.	زَرْعٌ ج زُرُوعٌ	To adorn.	زَخْرَفَ زَخْرَفَةً
Husbandman.	زَارِعٌ ج زُرَّاعٌ	Vain show.	زُخْرُفٌ ج زَخَارِفُ
Seed. Agriculture.	زِرَاعَةٌ	Adorned with tinsel.	مُزَخْرَفٌ
Plantation.	مَزْرَعَةٌ ج مَزَارِعُ	Whip of thong. Strap.	زَخْمَةٌ
Giraffe.	زَرَافَةٌ ج زُرَافَى	To button.	زَرَّ يَزُرُّ زَرًّا وَزَرَّرَ
To thrust ; dung, (bird).	زَرَقَ يَزْرُقُ	Button. Knob.	زِرٌّ ج أَزْرَارٌ
To become blue.	إِزْرَقَّ آزْرِقَاقًا	To make a sheep-fold.	زَرَبَ يَزْرُبُ
Blue (colour).	زُرْقَةٌ	To flow ; leak.	زَرِبَ يَزْرَبُ زَرْبًا
Sky ; heavens.	أَلزَّرْقَاءُ	Payment for stabling.	زَرَابَةٌ
A black singing bird.	زُرَيْقٌ	Flod for cattle ; lurking place.	زَرِيبَةٌ ج زَرَائِبُ
A kind of bread-salad.	زُرَيْقَاءُ	Narrow street.	زَارُوبٌ ج زَوَارِيبُ
Blue.	أَزْرَقُم زَرْقَاءُ ج زُرْق	Water-course.	مِزْرَابٌ ج مَزَارِيبُ
Bitter enemy.	عَدُوٌّ ازْرَقُ	To swallow.	زَرِدَ يَزْرَدُ وَازْدَرَدَ
Short spear.	مِزْرَاقٌ ج مَزَارِيقُ	Coat of mail.	زَرَدٌ ج زُرُودٌ
To press, vex.	زَرَكَ يَزْرُكُ	Ring, or link of a chain.	زَرَدَةٌ
Crowd, throng.	زَرْكَةٌ	A kind of pudding.	زُرْدَى
To embroider.	زَرْكَشَ	Starling.	زُرْزُورٌ ج زَرَازِيرُ

Saffron.	زَعْفَرَانٌ	Brocade of silk.	زَرْكَشٌ
To cry out, shout.	زَعَقَ يَزْعَقُ	Arsenic.	زِرْنِيخٌ
To frighten.	زَعَقَ بِ وَأَزْعَقَ	To reproach.	زَرَى يَزْرِي عَلَى
Thunderbolt. (see صَاعِقَةٌ)	زَاعِقَةٌ	To despise.	اِزْدَرَى اِزْدِرَاءً بِ
To be angry ; bored.	زَعِلَ يَزْعَلُ	Contemptible.	زَرِيٌّ
Angry, bored.	زَعْلَانُ	Despiser.	مُزْدَرٍ
To assert.	زَعَمَ يَزْعَمُ زَعْمًا	To cheat by tricks.	زَعْبَرَ زَعْبَرَةً
Assertion.	زَعْمٌ وَزُعْمَةٌ	Juggler.	مُزَعْبِرٌ
Honour. Authority.	زَعَامَةٌ	Thyme. (see صَعْتَر)	زَعْتَرٌ
Chief. Spokesman.	زَعِيمٌ	To disturb.	زَعَجَ يَزْعَجُ وَأَزْعَجَ
Fin.	زَعْنِفَةٌ ج زَعَانِفُ	To be troubled.	اِنْزَعَجَ
Down ; fine hair, feathers.	زَغَبٌ	Agitation ; trouble.	زَعَجٌ وَانْزِعَاجٌ
Nap of cloth.	زِغْبَرٌ وَزَغْبَرٌ	Medlar (tree and fruit).	زُعْرُورٌ
To adulterate.	زَغَلَ يَزْغَلُ زَغْلًا	Thin haired. Thief.	أَزْعَرُ ج زُعْرَانٌ
Young pigeon.	زُغْلُولٌ ج زَغَالِيلُ	To shake ; move.	زَعْزَعَ
To lead a bride home.	زَفَّ يَزِفُّ	To be shaken ; moved.	تَزَعْزَعَ
Procession of joy.	زِفَّةٌ	Violent wind.	زَعْزَعٌ ج زَعَازِعُ
To cover with pitch.	زَفَتَ	Inconstant ; unstable.	مُتَزَعْزِعٌ
Pitch.	زِفْتٌ	Quick in killing.	زُعَافٌ

A slip ; fault.	زَلَلٌ
A fault, fall.	زَلَّةٌ ج زَلَات
Clear, pure, cool (water). (White of an egg).	زُلَالٌ
Tortoise.	(زُلَحِفَةٌ زَلاحِفُ)
To shake.	زَلْزَلَ زِلْزَالًا وَزَلْزَالًا
Earth-quake.	زَلْزَلَةٌ ج زلازِلُ
To strip one's self.	(تَزَلَّطَ)
Throat.	زُلْعُومٌ ج زَلاعِيمُ
To exaggerate.	زَلَّفَ
To bring near.	أَزْلَفَ
Nearness.	زُلْفَةٌ وَزُلْفَى
To slip, glide.	زَلَقَ يَزْلِقُ زَلقًا
Slippery (place).	زَلِقٌ ومَزْلَقَةٌ
Diarrhœa.	زَلَقُ آلامِعَاءِ
A kind of fish.	زَلِيقٌ
Arrow for devining.	زَلَمٌ ج أَزْلَامٌ
Man. Footman.	(زَلَمَةٌ ج زِلْمٌ)
To tighten. Strap.	زَمَّ يَزُمُّ زمًا
Halter. Shoe-strap.	زِمَامٌ ج ازمَّة

Covered with pitch.	مُزَفَّتٌ
To expire breath.	زَفَرَ يَزْفِرُ
Deep sigh.	زَفْرَةٌ ج زَفَرَاتٌ
Expiration. Deep sigh.	زَفِيرٌ
Oleaster.	زَيْزَفُونٌ
Water-skin.	زِقٌّ ج زِقَاقٌ
Street, lane.	زُقَاقٌ ج ازِقَّة
A sack made of hair.	زكِيبَةٌ
A wine-skin.	زُكْرَةٌ ج زُكُرٌ
To tickle.	زَكْزَكَ
To have a cold in the head.	زُكِمَ
A cold in the head ; catarrh.	زُكَامٌ وَزُكْمَةٌ
To consider.	زَكَنَ يَزْكُنُ
To be pure.	زَكَا يَزْكُو
To give alms. Justify.	زَكَّى
To be justified.	تَزَكَّى
Alms.	زَكْوَةٌ (زَكَاةٌ) ج زُكًا
Pure ; just.	زَكِيٌّ ج أَزْكِيَاء
To stumble ; slip.	زَلَّ يَزِلُّ زَلًّا

Intense cold.	زَمْهَرِيرٌ
To scorn ; frown.	تَزَنْبَرَ عَلَى
Wasp ; hornet.	زُنْبُورٌ ج زَنَابِيرُ
Spring of a watch.	زُنْبُرُكٌ
Lily. Iris, (flower and plant).	زَنْبَقٌ
The black races.	زِنْجٌ ج زُنُوجٌ
A black ; negro.	زِنْجِيٌّ
Ginger.	زَنْجَبِيلٌ
To bind with a chain.	زَنْجَرَ
Verdigris.	زِنْجَارٌ
Chain.	زِنْجِيرٌ (جِنْزِيرٌ) ج زَنَاجِيرُ
Book-keeping.	حِسَابُ ٱلزِّنْجِيرِ
Cinnabar.	زُنْجُفْرٌ و زِنْجَفْرٌ
To become rancid.	زَنِخَ يَزْنَخُ
Ulna (bone).	زَنْدٌ ج زَنَادٌ
Steel for atriking fire.	زَنَادٌ
To disbelive religion.	تَزَنْدَقَ
Unbeliever.	زِنْدِيقٌ ج زَنَادِقَة
To gird one's self.	تَزَنَّرَ

To shout ; roar.	زَمْجَرَ زَمْجَرَةً
To play on a reed.	زَمَّرَ يُزَمِّرُ
Musical reed.	زَمْرٌ ج زُمُورٌ
Group ; party.	زُمْرَةٌ ج زُمَرٌ
A piper.	زَمَّارٌ
A pipe.	زَمَّارَةٌ و مِزْمَارٌ ج مَزَامِيرُ
Epiglottis.	لِسَانُ ٱلْمِزْمَارِ
Psalm.	مَزْمُورٌ ج مَزَامِيرُ
Emerald.	زُمُرُّدٌ
To be about to happen.	أَزْمَعَ
About to happen.	مُزْمِعٌ
Beast of burden.	زَامِلَةٌ ج زَوَامِلُ
Comrade ; companion.	زَمِيلٌ ج زُمَلَاءُ
Chisel.	إِزْمِيلٌ ج أَزَامِيلُ
To continue a long time.	أَزْمَنَ
Time.	زَمَنٌ و زَمَانٌ ج أَزْمِنَةٌ
Temporal ; transient.	زَمَنِيٌّ
Chronic disease.	مُزْمِنٌ (مَرَضٌ)
To be inflamed.	زَمْهَرَ وَٱزْمَهَرَّ

Lute. Timbrel.	مِزْهَرٌ ج مَزَاهِرُ
To vanish.	زَهَقَ يَزْهَقُ زُهُوقاً
To blossom.	زَهَا يَزْهُو زَهْواً وازْهَى
Pomp of this world.	زَهَا الدُّنْيَا
Quantity ; number.	زُهَاءُ
About a hundred.	زُهَاءُ مِئَةٍ
Beautiful ; bright.	زَاهٍ
To give in marriage.	زَوَّجَ
To marry a woman.	تَزَوَّجَ
Copperas ; vitriol.	زَاجٌ
Husband. Pair.	زَوْجٌ ج أَزْوَاجٌ
Pair, couple.	زَوْجَانِ
Wife.	زَوْجَةٌ ج زَوْجَاتٌ
Marriage.	زَوَاجٌ وزِيجَةٌ
Married.	مُزَوَّجٌ ومُتَزَوِّجٌ
Double ; doubled.	مُزْدَوِجٌ
To leave its place.	زَاحَ يَزُوحُ
To move from its place.	أَزَاحَ
To provide food for journey.	زَوَّدَ

Girdle.	زِنَارٌ ج زَنَانِيرُ
Melia (tree).	زَنْزَلَخْتُ (أَزْدَرَخْتُ)
Necklace. Shackle.	زِنَاقٌ
To commit adultery.	زَنَى يَزْنِي
Adulterer.	زَانٍ ج زُنَاةٌ
Munition.	(زَهْبٌ وزُهْبَةٌ)
To renounce.	زَهَدَ يَزْهَدُ (فِي وعَنْ)
To become an ascetic.	تَزَهَّدَ
Indifference.	زُهْدٌ
Ascetic ; indifferent.	زَاهِدٌ ج زُهَّادٌ
Little. Insignificant.	زَهِيدٌ
To shine.	زَهَرَ يَزْهَرُ زُهُوراً
To blossom ; flourish.	أَزْهَرَ
Flower.	زَهْرَةٌ ج أَزْهَارٌ
Dice.	زَهْرُ التَّرْدِ
The planet Venus.	الزُّهْرَةُ
A Mosque in Cairo.	الْجَامِعُ الأَزْهَرُ
A graduate of الأَزْهَرِ	أَزْهَرِيٌّ
In blossom ; flourishing.	مُزْهِرٌ

Embellished, decorated.	مُزَوَّق	To take provisions.	تَزَوَّد
To pass away ; cease.	زَالَ يَزُولُ	Food for the journey.	زَاد
To continue.	مَا زَالَ وَلَا يَزَالُ	Sack for food.	مِزْوَد ج مَزَاوِد
To remove.	زَوَّلَ وَأَزَالَ	Water-skin.	مَزَاد ج مَزَاوِد
To strive, prevail.	زَاوَلَ مُزَاوَلَة	To visit.	زَارَ يَزُورُ زِيَارَةً وَمَزَاراً
Disappearance. Cessation.	زَوَالٌ	To falsify ; forge.	زَوَّرَ
Vanishing ; transient.	زَائِلٌ	Falsehood.	زُورٌ
Juice.	زُومٌ	Visitor. Pilgrim.	زَائِرٌ ج زُوَّارٌ
To be apart ; removed.	إِنْزَوَى	Baghdad.	الزَّوْرَاءُ
Tares.	زُوَانٌ	Visit. Pilgrimage.	زِيَارَة
Angle, corner.	زَاوِيَة ج زَوَايَا	Crooked.	ازْوَرَّ
Acute angle.	زَاوِيَة حَادَّة	Falsification ; forgery.	تَزْوِير
Obtuse angle.	زَاوِيَة مُنْفَرِجَة	Shrine.	مَزَار ج مَزَارَات
Right anlge.	زَاوِيَة قَائِمَة	Falsifier ; counterfeiter.	مُزَوِّر
Quicksilver.	زِيبَق وَزِئْبَق	Falsified ; conterfeited.	مُزَوَّر
To oil.	زَيَّتَ	Small boat.	زَوْرَق ج زَوَارِق
Oil.	زَيْت ج زُيُوت	To deviate.	زَاغَ يَزُوغُ زَوْغاً
Olive (tree and fruit).	زَيْتُون	Hyssop (plant).	زُوفَا وَزُوفِي
Olive-coloured.	زَيْتُونِيّ	To embellish.	زَوَّقَ تَزْوِيقاً

Large water-jar.	زِيرٌ ج أَزْيَارٌ
A kind of cricket.	زِير
To deviate.	زَاغَ يَزِيغُ زَيغَانًا وزِيغًا
To cause to deviate.	أَزَاغَ
A kind of crow.	زَاغٌ ج زِيغَانٌ
To be counterfeit.	زَافَ يَزِيفُ
To counterfeit money.	زَيَّفَ
Counterfeit.	زَائِفٌ ج زِيُوفٌ
To adorn.	زَانَ يَزِينُ وَزَيَّنَ
To be adorned.	تَزَيَّنَ تَزَيَّنَا وَازْدَانَ
Ornament ; finery.	زِينَةٌ ج زِيَنٌ
Barber ; hair-dresser.	مُزَيِّنٌ
To assume the costume, or habits of others.	تَزَيَّا بِ
Form. Costume.	زِيٌّ ج أَزْيَاء

Astronomical tables. Plumb-line.	زِيج
To depart ; deviate.	زَاحَ يَزِيحُ
To move away ; remove.	أَزَاحَ
Line.	زِيحٌ ج أَزْيَاحٌ
To increase, (v. t. & i.)	زَادَ يَزِيد
To exceed.	زَادَ عَنْ وعَلَى
To bid higher.	زَايَدَ
To increase gradually.	تَزَايَدَ
To be increased.	إِزْدَادَ
An increase.	زِيَادَةٌ ج زِيَادَاتٌ
In excess ; superfluous.	زَائِدٌ
More ; more abundant.	أَزْيَدُ
Auction.	مَزَادٌ ج مَزَادَاتٌ
Increased.	مَزِيدٌ ج مَزِيدَاتٌ

س

Cause, reason ; سَبَبٌ ج أَسْبَابٌ	As a numeral sign = 60. س
means ; means of living.	Remaining ; the rest ; all. سَائِرٌ
Causality. سَبَبِيَّة	To ask ; request. سَأَلَ يَسْأَلُ
Forefinger, index. سَبَّابَةٌ	To beg (alms). تَسَأَلَ وَتَسَوَّلَ
Caused. مُسَبَّبٌ وَمُتَسَبَّبٌ عَنْ	Question, request. سُؤَالٌ
Trader. مُتَسَبَّبٌ	Questioner. Beggar. سَائِلٌ
Sabbath. Saturday. سَبْتٌ ج سُبُوتٌ	Question ; request. مَسْأَلَةٌ ج مَسَائِلُ
Heavy sleep, lethargy. سُبَاتٌ	Questioned. Responsible. مَسْؤُولٌ
To swim, float. سَبَحَ يَسْبَحُ سِبَاحَةً	Responsibility. مَسْؤُولِيَّةٌ
To praise, magnify God. سَبَّحَ	To loathe. سَئِمَ يَسْأَمُ مِنْ
Praise be to God ! سُبْحَانَ ٱللّٰه	To revile, defame. سَبَّ يَسُبُّ
Rosary. سُبْحَةٌ ج سُبَحٌ وَسُبْحَاتٌ	To cause, occasion. سَبَّبَ
Swimming floating. سِبَاحَةٌ	To be caused. تَسَبَّبَ
Ships. Stars. سَابِحَاتٌ	To live by. تَسَبَّبَ بِ
Fleet horses سَوَابِحُ	Abuse, invective. سَبٌّ

Heptagon.	مُسَبَّع	Hymn.	تَسْبِحَة ج تَسابِيح
To give abundantly.	أَسْبَغَ على	Act of praising God.	تَسْبِيح
To go before, precede.	سَبَق يَسْبِق	Rosary.	مَسْبَحَة ج مَسابِح
To go hastily to one.	سَبَق إلى	Salty, marshy (sod).	سَبِخ
To try to precede.	سابَق سِباقاً	Salty, marsh.	سَبْخة ج سِباخ
To contend for precedence.	تَسابَق	To probe. Try, test.	سَبَر يَسْبُر
Previous, former.	سابِق	Probing, sounding.	سَبْر
Formerly, before, of old.	سابِقاً	Surgeon's probe.	مِسْبَر ج مَسابِر
Antecedent.	سابِقة ج سَوابِق	Tribe Jewish).	سِبْط ج أَسْباط
Racing ; a race.	سِباق ومُسابَقة	February (month).	شُباط
To melt metals; cast into a mould.	سَبَك يَسْبِك سَبْكاً	To make (in) seven.	سَبَّع
Melted; moulded.	سَبِيك ومَسْبُوك	To become seven.	أَسْبَع
Ingot.	سَبِيكة ج سَبائِك	Seven.	سَبْعة م سَبْع
Foundery.	مَسْبَك ج مَسابِك	Seventh part.	سُبْع ج أَسْباع
To lower the veil ; let fall.	أَسْبَلَ	Beast of prey.	سَبُع ج سِباع
To put forth ears, (grains).	أَسْبَلَ الزَّرْع	Seventh.	سابِع
Ears of grain.	سَبَل	Composed of seven.	سُباعي
Road, way ; manner; means. Public fountain.	سَبِيل ج سُبُل	Seventy ; seventieth.	سَبْعُون
		Week.	أُسْبُوع ج أَسابِيع

Mosque.	مَسْجِدٌ ج مَسَاجِدُ	Traveller, wayfarer.	إِبْنُ السَّبِيلِ
Turbidness ; agitation.	سَجَسٌ	Spinage.	سَبَانِخٌ وَاسْبَاناخٌ
To coo ; rhyme.	سَجَعَ يَسْجَعُ	To take prisoner, captivate.	سَبِي يَسْبِي
Rhymed prose.	سَجْعٌ وَتَسْجِيعٌ	Captives. Booty.	سَبْيٌ وَسَبِيٌّ ج سَبَايَا
Rhymed (prose).	مُسَجَّعٌ وَمَسْجُوعٌ	Six.	سِتَّةٌ م سِتٌّ
Curtain, veil.	سَجْفٌ ج سُجُوفٌ	Lady.	(سِتٌّ ج سِتَّاتٌ)
To register, record.	سَجَّلَ	Sixty ; sixtieth.	سِتُّونَ
Record ; scroll.	سِجِلٌّ ج سِجِلَّاتٌ	To cover, veil.	سَتَرَ يَسْتُرُ
To flow, stream.	سَجَمَ يَسْجُمُ وَاْنَسَجَمَ	To be covered.	تَسَتَّرَ وَاسْتَتَرَ
To shed.	سَجَمَ يَسْجُمُ وَأَسْجَمَ	Veil, curtain, cover.	سِتْرٌ ج سُتُورٌ
Flowing effusion.	إِنْسِجَامٌ	Veil, cover.	سِتَارٌ ج سُتُرٌ
To imprison.	سَجَنَ يَسْجُنُ سَجْنًا	God who covers sins.	السَّتَّارُ
Prison.	سِجْنٌ ج سُجُونٌ	Concealed. Understood, (pronoun).	مُسْتَتِرٌ
Jailor.	سَجَّانٌ	Constantinople.	الأَِسْتَانَةُ
Imprisoned.	سَجِينٌ ج سُجَنَاءُ	Anus, podex.	إِسْتٌ ج أَسْتَاهٌ
Natural disposition.	سَجِيَّةٌ ج سَجَايَا	To worship, adore.	سَجَدَ يَسْجُدُ
To flow.	سَحَّ يَسُحُّ سَحًّا	Worshipper.	سَاجِدٌ ج سُجَّدٌ
To drag, trail.	سَحَبَ يَسْحَبُ سَحْبًا	Prayer-carpet.	سَجَّادَةٌ
To be dragged, drawn.	إِنْسَحَبَ	Prostration, adoration.	سُجُودٌ

To compel to labour without wages.	سَخَّرَ يَسْخَرُ وَسَخَّرَ
To laugh at, mock.	سَخِرَ يَسْخَرُ مِنْ
Compulsory labour.	سُخْرَةٌ
To be angry.	سَخِطَ يَسْخَطُ وَتَسَخَّطَ
To provoke to anger.	اَسْخَطَ
Anger, displeasure.	سَخْطٌ وَسَخَطٌ
To be weak.	سَخُفَ يَسْخُفُ سَخَافَةً
Shallowness, weakness.	سَخَافَةٌ
To blacken with soot.	سَخَّمَ
Soot, crock.	سُخَامٌ
To be hot ; have. fever.	سَخُنَ يَسْخُنُ
To warm, heat.	سَخَّنَ وَأَسْخَنَ
Heat. Fever ; illness.	سُخُونَةٌ
Warm, hot.	سُخْنٌ
Hot ; sick, ill.	سَاخِنٌ ج سُخَانٌ
So be liberal.	سَخَا يَسْخُو وَسَخِيَ يَسْخَى
Generosity.	سَخَاءٌ وَسَخَاوَةٌ
Generous, liberal.	سَخِيٌّ ج اسْخِيَاءُ

Cloud.	سَحَابٌ وَسَحَابَةٌ ج سُحُبٌ
To scratch, rub off.	سَحَجَ يَسْحَجُ
To be rubbed off.	تَسَحَّجَ وَأَنْسَحَجَ
Dysentery.	سَحْجٌ
To bewitch, fascinate.	سَحَرَ يَسْحَرُ
To take a morning meal.	تَسَحَّرَ
Magic, enchantment.	سِحْرٌ
Early daybreak.	سَحَرٌ ج أَسْحَارٌ
Sorcerer, magician.	سَاحِرٌ ج سَحَرَةٌ
Wooden box.	سَحَّارَةٌ
Meal before daybreak.	سُحُورٌ
To pound, crush.	سَحَقَ يَسْحَقُ
To be crushed.	تَسَحَّقَ وَأَنْسَحَقَ
Bruised, powdered.	مَسْحُوقٌ
Contrition.	إِنْسِحَاقُ ٱلْقَلْبِ
Shore ; coast.	سَاحِلٌ ج سَوَاحِلُ
To break, crush.	سَحَنَ يَسْحَنُ
Aspect ; complexion.	سَحْنَةٌ
Tanned leather.	سِخْتِيَانٌ

To close, stop up.	سَدَّ يَسُدُّ سَدًّا
To take the place of.	سَدَّ مَسَدًّا
Balance, pay an account.	سَدَّدَ
To be stopped.	إِنْسَدَّ وَآسْتَدَّ
To collect a debt.	إِسْتَدَّ
Barrier ; dam.	سد ج اسْدَادٌ
Vestibule, porch.	سُدّة
A stopper, a cork.	سِدَادَةٌ
Right, true.	سد وسَدِيدٌ
Stopped, corked.	مَسْدُودٌ
Simplicity of mind.	سَدَاجَة
A species of lotus.	سِدْرٌ ج سُدُورٌ
To be the sixth.	سدَس يَسْدِسُ
To make six.	سَدَّسَ
Sixth part.	سُدُسٌ ج اسْدَاسٌ
Sixth.	سادِسٌ
Consisting of six.	سُدَاسِيٌّ
Hexagon.	مُسَدَّسٌ
To let down.	سدل يَسْدُلُ واسْدَلَ

To be let down.	تَسَدَّلَ واَنْسَدَلَ
Mist. Nebula.	سَدِيمٌ
In vain, to no purpose.	سُدًى
Warp (of cloth).	سُدَاةٌ ج أَسْدِيَةٌ
Rue-plant.	سَذَابٌ
To gladden, cheer.	سَرَّ يَسُرُّ
To rejoice at.	سُرَّ سُرُورًا ب
To cheer, gladden.	اسرّ
To impart a secret.	سَارَّ مُسَارَّةً
To keep secret, conceal.	أَسَرَّ
To confide a secret to.	اسرّ إلى
Secret, mystery.	سِرٌّ ج أَسْرَارٌ
Secretary.	كَاتِمُ الأَسْرَار
Navel.	سُرَّةٌ ج سُرَّاتٌ وسُرُورٌ
Happy state of life.	سَرَّاءُ
Mysterious, secret.	سِرِّيٌّ
Joy, pleasure.	سُرُورٌ ومَسَرَّةٌ
Bed, cradle ; throne.	سَرِيرٌ ج اسِرَّةٌ
Hidden thought.	سَرِيرَةٌ ج سَرَائِرُ

Pasture.	مَسْرَح ج مَسَارِح	Concubine.	سَرِّيَّة ج سَرَارِيُّ
Comb.	مِسْرَح ج مَسَارِح	Joy, pleasure.	مَسَرَّة ج مَسَرَّات
Cellar, vault.	سِرْدَابٌ ج سَرَادِيبُ	Happy, pleased.	مَسْرُورٌ
Strip of leather.	سَرِيدَة ج سَرَائِدُ	To drive to pasture.	سَرَّبَ
Awning.	سُرَادِق ج سُرَادِقَات	Troop, flock.	سِرْبٌ ج أَسْرَابٌ
Sticking-paste. (for	سِرَاسٌ (شِرَاس	Aqueduct, canal.	سَرَبٌ ج اَسْرَابٌ
Way, street, road.	سِرَاطٌ وَصِرَاطٌ	Mirage.	سَرَابٌ
Crab. Cancer.	سَرَطَان	Shirt; dress.	سِرْبَالٌ ج سَرَابِيلُ
Cancer (of the Zodiac).	اَلسَّرَطَان	To saddle (a horse).	سَرَجَ يَسْرُجُ
To hasten, hurry.	سَرُعَ يَسْرُعُ	Saddle.	سَرْجٌ ج سُرُوجٌ
To hasten to do.	اِسْرَعَ فِي	Dung, manure.	سِرْجِين
Quickness, haste, speed.	سُرْعَة	Lamp, torch.	سِرَاجٌ ج سُرُجٌ
Quick, rapid, swift.	سَرِيع	Glow-worm.	سِرَاجُ اللَّيْلِ
To be extravagant, act immoderately.	أَسْرَفَ	Glanders. Saddlery.	سِرَاجَة
Extravagance.	سَرَفٌ وَإِسْرَافٌ	Saddler.	سَرَّاجٌ وَسُرُوجِي
A spendthrift.	مُسْرِف	Sesame oil.	سِيرَج وَشِيرَج
To steal, rob.	سَرَقَ يَسْرِقُ	Lamp-stand.	مِسْرَجَة ج مَسَارِج
To steal away.	إِنْسَرَقَ	To pasture at will.	سَرَحَ يَسْرَحُ
Theft, robbery.	سِرْقَة وَسَرِقَة	To send away; set free.	سَرَّحَ

Flat, plane, even.	مُسَطَّحٌ
To write.	سَطَرَ يَسْطُرُ
Line ; row.	سَطْرٌ ج اسْطُرٌ وسُطُورٌ
Large knife.	سَاطُورٌ ج سَوَاطِيرُ
Fable, legend.	اسْطُورَةٌ ج أَسَاطِيرُ
Ruler (for lines). Sample.	مِسْطَرَةٌ
New wine.	مُسْطَارٌ
Authority, guardianship.	سَيْطَرَةٌ
To rise ; gleam.	سَطَعَ يَسْطَعُ
Pail, bucket.	سَطْلٌ
Ship of war. Fleet.	اسْطُولٌ
To stop up, bar.	سَطَمَ يَسْطِمُ
Cork, stopper ; bolt.	سِطَامٌ
Cylinder.	اسْطُوَانَةٌ ج اسَاطِينُ
Cylindrical.	اسْطُوَانِيٌّ
To attack ; assail.	سَطَا يَسْطُو عَلَى
Attack ; power.	سَطْوَةٌ ج سَطَوَاتٌ
Thyme (plant).	سَعْتَرٌ (أَوْ صَعْتَرٌ)
To be fortunate.	سَعَدَ يَسْعَدُ

Thing stolen.	سَرِقَةٌ وسُرَاقَةٌ
Thief.	سَارِقٌ ج سُرَّاقٌ وسَرَقَةٌ
Great thief.	سَرَّاقٌ
Dung.	سِرْقِينٌ
Continuing endlessly.	سَرْمَدٌ
Eternal.	سَرْمَدِيٌّ
Cypress (tree).	سَرْوٌ
Liberal, noble.	سَرِيٌّ ج سَرَاةٌ
Trowsers.	سِرْوَالٌ ج سَرَاوِيلُ
To travel.	سَرَى يَسْرِي
To cause to travel.	أَسْرَى بِ
Night-journey.	سُرَى
Night-traveller.	سَارٍ ج سُرَاةٌ
Column ; mast.	سَارِيَةٌ ج سَوَارٍ
Palace.	سَرَايَا ج سَرَايَاتٌ
The Syriac language.	السُّرْيَانِيَّةُ
To spread out.	سَطَحَ يَسْطَحُ وسَطَّحَ
To be spread out.	تَسَطَّحَ
Surface ; terrace.	سَطْحٌ ج سُطُوحٌ

To help, assist.	سَاعَدَ
To make happy.	أَسْعَدَ
Luck, success.	سَعْدٌ ج سُعُودٌ
Monkey.	سَعْدَانٌ ج سَعَادِينُ
Fore-arm.	سَاعِدٌ ج سَوَاعِد
Happiness, felicity.	سَعَادَةٌ
Your Excellency.	سَعَادَتُكَ
Fortunate.	سَعِيدٌ ج سُعَدَاءُ
To light a fire.	سَعَرَ يَسْعَرُ
To fix, estimate a price.	سَعَّرَ
To be fixed, (price).	تَسَعَّرَ
To blaze, spread.	إِسْتَعَرَ
Price.	سِعْرٌ ج أَسْعَارٌ
Flame, blaze. Fire.	سَعِيرٌ
Snuff.	سَعُوطٌ
To assist.	سَعَفَ يَسْعَفُ وَأَسْعَفَ بِ
To assist, help.	سَاعَفَ
Branches of palm-tree.	سَعَفٌ
To cough.	سَعَلَ يَسْعُلُ سُعَالاً

Cough.	سُعَالٌ
To run. Seek.	سَعَى يَسْعَى سَعْيًا
To calumniate.	سَعَى بِ
Effort, exertion.	سَعْيٌ
Messenger.	سَاعٍ ج سُعَاةٌ
Effort ; enterprise.	مَسْعًى ج مَسَاعٍ
Medicine (in powder).	سَفُوفٌ
Bill of exchange.	سَفْتَجَةٌ ج سَفَاتِجُ
To shed.	سَفَحَ يَسْفَحُ سُفُوحًا وَسَفْحًا
To fornicate.	سَافَحَ
Foot of a mountain.	سَفْحٌ
Fornication.	سِفَاحٌ
Roasting-fork.	سَفُّودٌ ج سَفَافِيدُ
To travel.	سَفَرَ يَسْفُرُ سَفْرًا
To send on a journey.	سَفَّرَ
To depart, travel.	سَافَرَ
To shine, (dawn).	أَسْفَرَ
Written book.	سِفْرٌ ج أَسْفَارٌ
Journey.	سَفَرٌ ج أَسْفَارٌ

Baseness, vileness.	سَفَالَة
Low, vile.	سَافِلٌ ج سَفَلَة
The lowest part.	اسفَلُ
Wedge.	سَفِينٌ وَإِسْفِينٌ
Ship, boat.	سَفِينَة ج سُفُن
Sponge.	سَفَنْج وَسِفَنْج
To be foolish.	سَفَه يَسْفَه سَفْهًا
To revile.	تَسَفَّه عَلَى
Stupidity.	سَفَه وَسَفَاهَة
Stupid, foolish.	سَفِيه ج سُفَهَاء
To fall, fall down.	سَقَط يَسْقُط
To cause to fall, let fall. Discount. Subtract.	أَسْقَطَ
To fall by degrees.	تَسَاقَطَ
Refuse. Defect.	سَقَط ج أَسْقَاط
Fall, slip, fault, error.	سَقْطَة
Low, worthless.	سَاقِط ج سُقَّاط
Refuse, what is rejected.	سُقَاطَة
Door-latch.	سَقَّاطَة
Falling, downfall.	سُقُوط

A journey.	سَفْرَة ج سَفَرَات
Table-cloth; table.	سُفْرَة
Traveller.	مُسَافِر
Embassy.	سَفَارَة
Ambassador.	سَفِير ج سُفَرَاء
Quince.	سَفَرْجَل ج سَفَارِج
Sophism.	سَفْسَطَة وَسِفْسَطَة
Sophistical ; sophist.	سَفْسَطِيّ
To shut, slap.	سَفَق يَسْفِق
Thick, compact.	سَفِيق
Impudent, insolent.	سَفِيق الوَجْهِ
To shed.	سَفَك يَسْفِك سَفْكًا
To be shed.	إِنْسَفَك
Blood-shedder.	سَفَّاك لِلدِّمَاء
Shed, (blood, &c.)	مَسْفُوك
To be low, sink.	سَفُل يَسْفُل
To be mean.	سَفُل سَفَالَة
The lowest part, bottom.	سِفْل
The lower part.	سُفْلِيّ

Cup-bearer.	سَاق	Discount. Subtraction.	إسْقَاطٌ
Water-wheel. Irrigation-canal.	سَاقِيَةٌ ج سَوَاقٍ	Native place.	مَسْقَطُ الرَّأْسِ
Dropsy.	إسْتِسْقَاءٌ	To roof.	سَقَفَ يَسْقُفُ سَقْفًا وَسَقَّفَ
Dropsical.	مُسْتَسْقٍ	Roof ; ceiling.	سَقْفٌ ج سقوفٌ
To coin money.	سَكَّ ٱلنُّقُودَ	Porch, roof.	سَقِيفَةٌ ج سَقَائِفُ
Ploughshare. Road, high road. Coined money.	سِكَّةٌ ج سِكَكٌ	Bishop.	أُسْقُفٌ ج أَسَاقِفَةٌ
Railway.	سِكَّةُ حَدِيدٍ	Bishopric.	اسْقُفِيَّةٌ
To pour out ; melt.	سَكَبَ يَسْكُبُ	A Slavonian.	سِقْلَبِيٌّ ج سَقَالِبَةٌ
To flow.	سَكَبَ سُكُوبًا وَانْسَكَبَ	To be weak, diseased.	سَقِمَ يَسْقَمُ
Melting, flowing.	سَكْبٌ	To make ill.	أَسْقَمَ
To be silent, still.	سَكَتَ يَسْكُتُ	Disease, illness.	سُقْمٌ ج اسْقَامٌ
To silence, still.	سَكَتَ وَأَسْكَتَ	Diseased, weak.	سَقِيمٌ ج سُقَمَاءُ
Silence ; pause.	سَكْتٌ وَسُكُوتٌ	Scammony, (plant).	سَقَمُونِيا
Apoplexy. A pause.	سَكْتَةٌ	To give to drink, irrigate.	سَقَى يَسْقِي
Silent, reserved.	سَكُوتٌ	To draw water ; ask for water.	إسْتَقَى
To become intoxicated.	سَكِرَ يَسْكَرُ	To be dropsical.	إسْتَسْقَى
To intoxicate.	سَكَرَ وَأَسْكَرَ	Giving to drink, watering.	سَقْيٌ
Drunkenness.	سُكْرٌ	Water-skin.	سِقَاءٌ ج أَسْقِيَةٌ
		Water-carrier.	سَقَّاءٌ ج سَقَّاؤُونَ

Poverty ; lowliness.	مِسْكَنَة	Agony of death.	سَكْرَةُ آلْمَوْتِ
Inhabited; possessed.	مَسْكُون	Wooden lock to a door.	سَكْرَة
The world.	أَلْمَسْكُونَة	Sugar.	سُكَّر
Poor ; lowly.	مِسْكِين ج مَسَاكِين	Intoxicated.	سَكْرَان ج سُكَارَى
To draw a sword.	سَلَّ يَسُلُّ وَآسْتَلَّ	Habitual drunkard.	سِكِّير
To slip away.	تَسَلَّلَ وَآنْسَلَّ	Trade of a shoemaker.	سِكَافَة
Basket.	سَلٌّ وَسَلَّة ج سِلَال	Shoemaker.	إِسْكَاف ج أَسَاكِفَة
Consumption, (disease).	دَاءُ آلسَّلِّ	Threshold.	أُسْكُفَّة
Offspring, progeny.	سُلَالَة	To subside.	سَكَنَ يَسْكُنُ سُكُونًا
Child ; male offspring.	سَلِيل	To dwell in.	سَكَنَ سَكَنًا وفِي
Large needle. Obelisk.	مِسَلَّة	To rely upon, trust in.	سَكَنَ إِلَى
Unsheathed. Phthisical.	مَسْلُول	To calm, pacify, quiet.	سَكَنَ
To melt, clarify (butter).	سَلَأَ يَسْلَا	To make to dwell.	أَسْكَنَ
To rob. Seize.	سَلَبَ يَسْلُبُ وَآسْتَلَبَ	Habitation.	سَكَن
Robbery. Negation.	سَلْب	An inhabitant.	سَاكِن ج سُكَّان
Robbed, plundered.	مَسْلُوب	Rest, quiescence.	سُكُون
Method, way.	أُسْلُوب ج أَسَالِيب	Knife.	سِكِّين ج سَكَاكِين
To arm equip.	سَلَّح ب	Quiet.	سَكِينَة
To arm one's self.	تَسَلَّح	House. abode.	مَسْكَن ج مَسَاكِن

Sultan. سُلْطَانُ ج سَلَاطِينُ	Arms, weapons. سِلَاحُ ج أَسْلِحَةُ
Imperial. سُلْطَانِيٌّ	Tortoise. سِلَحْفَاةُ ج سَلَاحِفُ
High road. طَرِيقٌ سُلْطَانِيٌّ	To skin, flay. سَلَخَ يَسْلُخُ سَلْخًا
Article for sale. سِلْعَةُ ج سِلَعُ	To be stripped off. اِنْسَلَخَ
To pass away ; precede. سَلَفَ يَسْلُفُ	End of (the month). سَلْخٌ وَمَنْسَلَخٌ
To give in advance. سَلَفَ وَأَسْلَفَ	Slaughter-house. مَسْلَخٌ مَسَالِخُ
To borrow ; تَسَلَّفَ وَاسْتَلَفَ	To be loose, docile. سَاسَ يَسْلَسُ
receive payment in advance.	Docility. سَلَسٌ وَسَلَاسَةٌ
Payment in advance. سَلَفٌ	Docile ; compliant. سَلِسٌ
Predecessor. سَلَفٌ ج أَسْلَافٌ	To chain. سَلْسَلَ ب
Vanguard of army. سُلَافُ الْعَسْكَرِ	To trace a pedigree. سَلْسَلَ إِلَى
Preceding ; former. سَالِفٌ	Chain. سِلْسِلَةُ ج سَلَاسِلُ
To boil. سَلَقَ يَسْلُقُ سَلْقًا	Artificial fountain. سَلْسَبِيلٌ
To scale or climb a wall. تَسَلَّقَ	A continued series. تَسَلْسُلٌ
Ulceration of eye-lids. سُلَاقٌ	To make one a ruler. سَلَّطَهُ
Greyhound. سَلُوقِيٌّ	To overcome ; rule. تَسَلَّطَ عَلَى
Natural trait. سَلِيقَةُ ج سَلَائِقُ	Rule, dominion. سَلْطَةٌ وَتَسَلُّطٌ
Naturally, instinctively. بِالسَّلِيقَةِ	Power, dominion. سَلْطَنَةٌ
Boiled. مَسْلُوقٌ	Absolute power. سُلْطَانٌ

To travel, enter. Behave.	سَلَكَ يَسْلُك
To make to enter.	أَسْلَكَ
String ; wire.	سِلْكٌ ج أَسْلَاكٌ
Conduct, behaviour.	سُلُوكٌ
Good manners.	عِلْمُ السُّلُوك
Ordinary, usual, current.	سَالِكٌ
Path road.	مَسْلَكٌ ج مَسَالِكُ
To be sound, safe.	سَلِمَ يَسْلَمُ
To be free from.	سَلِمَ مِنْ
Tsave ; preser ove.	سَلِمَ مِنْ
To admit.	سَلِمَ بِ
To surrender, yield.	سَلِمَ لِ
To give over, hand to.	سَلَّمَ إِلَى
To salute, greet.	سَلَّمَ عَلَى
To keep peace with.	سَالَمَ
To deliver up.	أَسْلَمَ
To profess Islâm.	أَسْلَمَ
To take possession of.	تَسَلَّمَ
To yield, surrender.	إِسْتَسْلَمَ

Peace, reconciliation.	سِلْمٌ
Ladder, stairs.	سُلَّمٌ ج سَلَالِمُ
Peace, well-being.	سَلَامٌ وَسَلَامَةٌ
Greeting ; salutation.	سَلَامٌ
Sound and safe.	سَالِمٌ
Sound plural.	أَلْجَمْعُ السَّالِمُ
Sound, safe.	سَلِيمٌ ج سُلَمَاءُ
Corrosive sublimate.	سُلَيْمَانِيّ
More secure, safer.	أَسْلَمُ
Religion of Islâm.	الإِسْلَامُ
Delivery ; surrender.	تَسْلِيمٌ
Moslem.	مُسْلِمٌ ج مُسْلِمُونَ
Delivered ; conceded.	مُسَلَّمٌ
To forget.	سَلَا يَسْلُو
To divert, cheer, amuse.	سَلَّى
To be diverted.	تَسَلَّى
Diversion.	سَلْوَةٌ وَتَسْلِيَةٌ وَتَسَلٍّ
Quail. Consolation.	سَلْوَى
Consolation.	سُلْوَانٌ

Semolino.	سَمِيذٌ وسَمِيد
To be brownish.	سَمِرَ يَسْمَرُ واسْمَرَّ
To nail.	سَمَرَ وَسَمَّرَ
To converse with.	سَامَرَ وتَسَامَرَ
Brownish colour.	سُمْرَةٌ
Samaria (in Palestine).	أَلسَّامِرَةُ
Samaritan.	سَامِرِيٌّ
Sable (animal).	سَمُّورٌ
Brownish.	أَسْمَرُ م سَمْرَاءُ ج سُمْرٌ
Nail. Foot-corn.	مِسْمَارٌ ج مَسَامِيرُ
To act as a broker.	سَمْسَرَ
Brokerage ; fee of a broker.	سَمْسَرَةٌ
Broker.	سِمْسَارٌ ج سَمَاسِرَةٌ
Sesame.	سِمْسِمٌ
Sesamoid bone.	سِمْسِمَانِيٌّ
To strap with thongs.	سَمَطَ
Thong.	سِمْطٌ ج سُمُوطٌ
Table-cloth.	سِمَاطٌ ج أَسْمِطَةٌ
To hear, listen.	سَمِعَ يَسْمَعُ واسْتَمَعَ

To poison.	سَمَّ يَسُمُّ سَمًّا
Hole. Poison.	سَمٌّ ج سُمُومٌ
Arsenic ; ratsbane.	سَمُّ الفَارِ
Poisonous.	سَامٌّ
Hot wind.	سَمُومٌ
Holes ; pores.	مَسَامٌّ
Poisoned.	مَسْمُومٌ
Way ; manner.	سَمْتٌ
Azimuth.	أَلسَّمْتُ ج سُمُوتٌ
Zenith.	سَمْتُ الرَّأْسِ
To be ugly.	سَمُجَ يَسْمُجُ سَمَاجَةً
Ugly, horrid ; foul.	سَمْجٌ وسَمِيجٌ
To grant, permit ; pardon.	سَمَحَ يَسْمَحُ
To pardon, excuse.	سَامَحَ
Kindness ; grace.	سَمَاحٌ وسَمَاحَةٌ
Allowed ; permitted.	مَسْمُوحٌ بِهِ
Periosteum.	سِمْحَاقٌ
To manure the soil.	سَمَّدَ
Manure.	سَمَادٌ

Fat, corpulent. سَمِينٌ ج سِمَانٌ	To hear of. سِمِعَ ب
To be high ; rise high. سَمَا يَسْمُو	To accept, obey. سَمِعَ لِ و من
Give a name ; name. سَمَّى	Sense of hearing. سَمْعٌ
To be named ; mentioned. تَسَمَّى	You shall be obeyed. سَمْعًا وَطَاعَةً
Name ; noun. إِسْمٌ ج أَسْمَاءٌ	Report, fame. سُمْعَةٌ
The name of God. إِسْمُ الْجَلَالَةِ	Irregular, traditional. سَمَاعِيٌّ
Height ; greatness. سُمُوٌّ	The hearer of all (God). السَّمِيعُ
Heaven. سَمَاءٌ ج سَمَوَاتٌ	Sumach, (tree and fruit). سُمَّاقٌ
Heavenly. سَمَاوِيٌّ وَسَمَائِيٌّ	To become thick. سَمُكَ سَمَاكَةً
High ; sublime. سَامٍ ج سُمَاةٌ	To thicken, make thick. سَمَّكَ
Grand vizierial order. أَمْرٌ سَامٍ	Depth, thickness. سُمْكٌ وسَمَاكَةٌ
Named, determined. مُسَمَّى	Fish. سَمَكٌ ج اسْمَاكٌ
To sharpen, whet. سَنَّ يَسُنُّ	A fish. سَمَكَةٌ
To introduce a law. سَنَّ سُنَّةً	Deep, thick. سَمِيكٌ
To become aged. اسَنَّ	To grow fat. سَمِنَ يَسْمَنُ سِمَنًا
Tooth. Age in life. سِنٌّ ج اسْنَانٌ	To butter; fatten. سَمَّنَ
To become old. طَعَنَ فِي السِّنِّ	Clarified butter. سَمْنٌ
Law ; usage. سُنَّةٌ ج سُنَنٌ	Seller of butter. Grocer. سَمَّانٌ
Head of a spear. سِنَانٌ ج أَسِنَّةٌ	Quail. (سُمَنَةٌ ج سُمَنٌ وَسَمَامِنُ)

Predicate.	المُسْنَد	A Sunnite.	سُنّيٌّ ج سُنّية
Subject.	ٱلْمُسْنَدُ إِلَيْهِ	Whet-stone.	مِسَنّ
Sandarach.	سِنْدَرُوسٌ	Advanced in age.	مُسِنّ
Silk brocade ; fine silk.	سُنْدُسٌ	Skiff, small boat.	سُنْبُوقٌ
Cat.	سِنَّوْرٌ ج سَنَانِيرُ	An ear of corn.	سُنْبُلَة ج سنابل
Acacia (Nilotica).	سَنْط	Virgo (of the Zodiac).	السُّنْبُلَة
A kind of harp.	سِنْطِيرٌ وَسَنْطُورٌ	Squirrel.	سِنْجَابٌ
Tinker.	سَنْكَرِيٌّ ج سَنَاكِرَة	Standard, flag.	سِنْجَقٌ ج سَنَاجِقُ
Hump of camel.	سَنَامٌ ج أَسْنِمَة	To occur to the mind.	سَنَحَ يَسْنَحُ
Raised ; convex.	مُسَنَّم	To dissuade.	سَنَحَ عَن
To ascend. Be easy.	تَسَنَّى	Socket of a tooth.	سِنْخٌ ج اسْنَاخٌ
Brightness, gleaming.	سَنًى	To lean upon.	سَنَدَ يَسْنُدُ وَ ٱسْتَنَدَ إِلَى
Sublimity ; high rank.	سَنَاءٌ	To support firmly.	سَنَّدَ
Senna, (plant).	سَنَا مَكَّة	To ascribe, trace up.	أَسْنَدَ إِلَى
Year.	سَنَة سِنُونَ وَسَنَوَاتٌ	Support ; refuge.	سَنَدٌ ج أَسْنَادٌ
High, sublime, noble.	سَنِيٌّ	Anvil.	سِنْدَانٌ ج سَنَادِينُ
Annual, yearly.	سَنَوِيٌّ	Evergreen oak ; ilex.	سِنْدِيَانٌ
Swallow.	سُنُونُو	Cushion, pillow.	مِسْنَدٌ ج مَسَانِدُ
To be lengthy, prolix.	أَسْهَبَ	Supported, propped.	مُسْنَدٌ

Purgative, laxative.	مُسْهِل	To give largely.	اسْهَبَ فِي الْعَطَاء
Arrow.	سَهْم ج سِهَام	Prolixity; amplification.	اِسْهَاب
Lot, share.	سَهْم ج اسْهُم	Loquacious; diffuse.	مُسْهِب
Sagittarius.	سَهْم الرَّامِي	To be sleepless.	سَهِدَ يَسْهَد
To overlook, neglect.	سَهَا يَسْهُو عَنْ	To deprive of sleep.	سَهَّدَا
Oversight, forgetfulness.	سَهْو	Sleeplessness.	سَهْد وَسُهَاد
Thoughtlessly.	سَهْوًا	To keep awake.	سَهِر يَسْهَر
Forgetful, negligent.	سَاهٍ	Awake.	سَاهِر وَسَهْرَان
To be evil, bad.	سَاءَ يَسُوء	To be level; easy.	سَهُلَ يَسْهُل
To treat badly; offend.	سَاءَ سُوءًا	To smooth; facilitate.	سَهَّلَ
To be evil to; offend.	أَسَاءَ إِلَى	To be level; become easy.	تَسَهَّلَ
To suspect evil.	أَسَاءَ الظَّنَّ	To be accommodating.	تَسَاهَلَ
Evil.	سُوء ج أَسْوَاء وَمَسَاوِئ	To regard as easy.	اِسْتَسْهَلَ
Evil, bad.	سَيِّئ م سَيِّئَة	Plain; level.	سَهْل ج سُهُول
Sin; calamity.	سَيِّئَة ج سَيِّئَات	Gentle.	سَهْل الْخُلُق
Teak-tree.	سَاج	Easy; smooth, soft.	سَهْل
See under. سيح	سَاحَ يَسُوح	Ease, facility. Evenness.	سُهُولَة
Court; yard.	سَاحَة ج سَاحَات	Canopus, (star).	سُهَيْل
Traveller.	سَائِح ج سَيَّاح	Diarrhœa.	إِسْهَال

To rule a people. To groom a horse.	سَاسَ يَسُوسُ
To be moth-eaten.	سَوَّسَ
Moth, worm. Liquorice.	سُوسٌ
Political administration.	سِيَاسَةٌ
Groom.	سَائِسٌ ج سَاسَةٌ وَسُوَّاسٌ
Lily.	سُوسَنٌ وَسُوسَانٌ
To whip.	سَاطَ يَسُوطُ سَوْطًا
Whip, lash.	سَوْطٌ ج سِيَاطٌ
Hour. Watch.	سَاعَةٌ ج سَاعَاتٌ
Sun-dial.	سَاعَةٌ شَمْسِيَّةٌ
Hour-glass.	سَاعَةٌ رَمْلِيَّةٌ
Watch-maker.	سَاعَاتِيٌّ
To be permitted, lawful.	سَاغَ لَ
To allow, permit.	سَوَّغَ لَ
Lawful, allowable.	سَائِغٌ
To put off, defer.	سَوَّفَ
Row, course.	سَافٌ ج سَافَاتٌ
A particle which changes the *present* tense into a future; *e.g.* Thou shalt see.	سَوْفَ ترَى

To rule.	سَادَ يَسُودُ سِيَادَةً
To become black.	إِسْوَدَّ
To blacken; write a rough draft.	سَوَّدَ
To be blackened.	تَسَوَّدَ
Dominion; honour.	سُؤْدَدٌ وَسِيَادَةٌ
Black bile. Melancholy.	سَوْدَاءُ
Sudan (country).	بِلَادُ السُّودَانِ
Blackness. Large number.	سَوَادٌ
Power, authority.	سِيَادَةٌ
Master, lord.	سَيِّدٌ ج سَادَةٌ
Black.	أَسْوَدُ م سَوْدَاءُ ج سُودٌ
First copy, rough draft.	مُسْوَدَّةٌ
Glass bottle.	مُسَوَّدَةٌ ج مُسَوَّدَاتٌ
To wall in a town.	سَوَّرَ
Wall, ramparts.	سُورٌ ج أَسْوَارٌ
Chapter of Koran.	سُورَةٌ ج سُوَرٌ
Syria.	سُورِيَّةٌ
Bracelet.	سِوَارٌ وَأُسْوَارٌ ج أَسْوِرَةٌ
Surrounded with walls.	مُسَوَّرٌ

To be ripe, well cooked.	إِسْتَوَى	Distance.	مَسَافَةٌ
To sit upon.	إِسْتَوَى عَلَى	To drive, urge on.	سَاقَ يَسُوقُ
Just, right. Same, alike.	سَوَاءٌ	To lead to.	سَاقَ إِلَى
Alike, equally.	عَلَى حَدٍّ سَوَاءٍ	To be driven, urged on.	إِنْسَاقَ
Equally ; together.	سَوِيَّةً وَسَوَاءٌ	Leg. Stem سُوقٌ وَسِيقَانٌ ج سَاقٌ
Chiefly, principally.	لَا سِيَّمَا	(of a plant). Side of a triangle.
Equally, alike, (both).	هُمَا سِيَّانِ	Market.	سُوقٌ ج أَسْوَاق
Equator.	خَطُّ الْإِسْتِوَاءِ	Fine flour.	سُوَيْق
Equaliy. Moderation.	مُسَاوَاةٌ	Logical connection.	سِيَاقٌ
Equal.	مُسَاوٍ وَمُتَسَاوٍ	Driver, driving.	سَائِقٌ
Common gender.	مُسْتَوٍ	To clean one's teeth.	تَسَوَّكَ
To set free.	سَيَّبَ	Toothpick.	سِوَاكٌ وَمِسْوَاكٌ
Left free, at liberty.	سَائِبٌ	To deceive, incite to evil.	سَوَّلَ لِ
Unguarded ; free.	مُسَيَّبٌ	To compel.	سَامَ يَسُومُ
To hedge in, enclose.	سَيَّجَ	To bargain.	سَاوَمَ مُسَاوَمَةً
Hedge.	سِيَاجٌ ج سِيَاجَاتٌ	Sign, mark.	سِيمَةٌ وَسِيمَاءُ
Surrounded by a hedge.	مُسَيَّجٌ	To be worth.	سَوِيَ يَسْوَى وَسَاوَى
To travel. Flow.	سَاحَ يَسِيحُ	To adjust, rectify.	سَوَّى تَسْوِيَةً
Long journery.	سِيَاحَة	To be equal.	سَاوَى وَآسْتَوَى

Journey, road.	مَسِيرٌ	Traveller.	سَائِحٌ ج سِيَّاحٌ
Sword.	سَيْفٌ ج سُيُوفٌ	Great traveller.	سِيَّاحٌ
To flow ; become liquid.	سَالَ يَسِيلُ	Area.	مَسَاحَةٌ
To liquify.	سَيَّلَ وَأَسَالَ	Land surveying.	عِلْمُ ٱلْمَسَاحَة
Stream ; torrent.	سَيْلٌ ج سُيُولٌ	Large knife.	سِيخٌ ج أَسْيَاخٌ
Flow ; flux.	سَيَلَانٌ	To go ; travel.	سَارَ يَسِير
Ceylon.	سَيْلَانٌ	To carry away.	سَارَ ب
Ruby ; carbuncle.	سِيلَانٌ	Journey. Thong.	سَيْرٌ ج سِيُورٌ
		Conduct. Biography.	سِيرَةٌ ج سِيَرٌ
Liquid, fluid.	سَائِلٌ ج سَوَائِلُ	Current, customary.	سَائِرٌ
Water-course.	مَسِيلٌ	Planet.	سَيَّارَةٌ ج سَيَّارَاتٌ

ش

Young woman.	شَابَّة ج شَابَّات	As a numeral sign=300.	ش
Youth.	شَبَابٌ وَشَبِيبَةٌ	To be inauspicious.	شَوُمَ وَشُئِمَ
A reed or musical pipe.	شَبَّابَة	To take as a bad omen.	تَشَاءَمَ
To take firm hold.	تَشَبَّثَ ب	Evil omen, ill luck.	شُؤْمٌ
Dill (plant).	شِبِثٌّ	Syria. Damascus.	الشَّامُ
Object of vision.	شَبَحٌ ج أَشْبَاحٌ	Syrian. Damascene.	شَامِيٌّ
A horse's shackle.	شِبْحَةٌ	Nature, disposition.	شِئْمَةٌ
Span.	شِبْرٌ ج أَشْبَارٌ	Inauspicious, unlucky.	مَشْوُمٌ
To scarify.	شَبَّطَ	Thing ; state ; honour.	شَأْنٌ
February.	شُبَاطُ وَسُبَاطُ	Of great importance.	عَظِيمُ الشَّأْنِ
To be satiated.	شَبِعَ يَشْبَعُ	White falcon.	شَاهِينٌ ج شَوَاهِينُ
To satiate, satisfy.	أَشْبَعَ	To grow up, (youth).	شَبَّ يَشِبُّ
Satiety, satiation.	شِبَعٌ	To blaze (fire, war).	شَبَّ يَشُبُّ
Satiated, satisfied.	شَبْعَان	Vitriol. Alum.	شَبٌّ
To entwine, entangle.	شَبَكَ يَشْبِكُ	Young man.	شَابٌّ ج شُبَّانٌ

Resemblance.	مُشَابَهَة	To be entangled.	تَشَبَّكَ وَٱشْتَبَكَ
To be scattered.	شَتَّ يَشِتُّ	Fishing-net.	شَبَكَة ج شَبَك
To scatter.	شَتَّ وَشَتَّتَ وَأَشَتَّ	Window.	شُبَّاك ج شَبَابِيك
To be dispersed.	تَشَتَّتَ	Cub of a lion.	شِبْل ج أَشْبَال
Disunion.	شَتٌّ وَشَتَات	Groomsman.	شَبِين م شَبِينَة
Great is the difference !	شَتَّان	To liken, compare.	شَبَّهَ ب
Various things.	أَشْيَاء شَتَّى	To resemble.	شَابَهَ وَأَشْبَهَ
Nursery-plant.	شَتْلَة	To imitate.	تَشَبَّهَ ب
Plant-nursery.	مَشْتَل	To resemble one another.	تَشَابَهَ
To revile.	شَتَمَ يَشْتِمُ شَتْمًا	To be obscure.	إِشْتَبَهَ
Defamation.	شَتِيمَة ج شَتَائِم	To be in doubt.	إِشْتَبَهَ فِي
Reviled.	شَتِيم وَمَشْتُوم	A similar person or thing.	شِبْه
To pass the winter.	شَتَا يَشْتُو وَشَتِّي	Similarity ; likeness.	شَبَه
Winter ; rain.	شِتَاء	Point of resemblance.	وَجْهُ ٱلشَّبَه
Pertaining to winter.	شَتَوِيّ	Doubt, suspicion.	شُبْهَة ج شُبُهَات
Wintry ; rainy.	شَاتٍ	Resembling, like.	شَبِيه
Winter abode.	مَشْتًى	Ambiguity ; doubt.	اِشْتِبَاه
To wound the head.	شَجَّ يَشُجُّ	Comparison ; metaphor.	تَشْبِيه
Wound in the head.	شَجَّة	Doubtful, obscure.	مُشْتَبَه

To be niggardly.	شَحَّ يَشِحُّ شَحًّا
To contend together.	تَشَاحَّ
Avarice, covetousness.	شُحٌّ
Avaricious.	شَحِيحٌ ج شِحَاحٌ
Incontestable.	لَا مُشَاحَّةَ فِي
To ask for alms, beg.	شَحَدَ يَشْحَدُ
Mendicity.	شِحَاذَةٌ
Importunate beggar.	شَحَّاذٌ
Stye on the eyelid.	شَحَّاذُ الْعَيْنِ
To drag along.	شَحَطَ يَشْحَطُ
Grease, lard, fat.	شَحْمٌ ج شُحُومٌ
Lobe of the ear.	شَحْمَةُ الْأُذُنِ
To fill, load.	شَحَنَ يَشْحَنُ وأَشْحَنَ بِ
To treat with enmity.	شَاحَنَ
Freight, cargo.	شَحْنٌ وَشَحْنَةٌ
Hatred, enmity.	شَحْنَاءُ وَشِحْنَةٌ
Garrison.	شِحْنَةٌ
Hatred, enmity.	مُشَاحَنَةٌ
To micturate.	شَخَّ يَشُخُّ شَخًّا

To become woody.	شَجَّرَ
To quarrel with.	شَاجَرَ مُشَاجَرَةً
To abound in trees.	شَجِرَ
To dispute, quarrel.	تَشَاجَرَ
Tree; shrub, bush.	شَجَرٌ ج أَشْجَارٌ
A tree.	شَجَرَةٌ
Abounding in trees.	شَجِرٌ وَمُشْجِرٌ
Dispute, contest.	مُشَاجَرَةٌ
To be brave.	شَجُعَ يَشْجُعُ شَجَاعَةً
To encourage, embolden.	شَجَّعَ
To take courage.	تَشَجَّعَ
Courage, bravery.	شَجَاعَةٌ
Brave, bold.	شُجَاعٌ ج شُجْعَانٌ
To grieve. Coo.	شَجَنَ يَشْجُنُ شَجْنًا
Grief.	شَجَنٌ ج شُجُونٌ
To cause anguish.	شَجَا يَشْجُو
To be grieved.	شَجِيَ يَشْجَى شَجًا
Anxiety, grief.	شَجًا وَشَجْوٌ
Grieved, anxious, sad.	شَجٍ وَشَجِيٌّ

Blacker.	أَشَدُّ سَوَاداً
More or most angry.	أَشَدُّ غَضَباً
Violence. Strength.	إِشْتِدَادٌ
Cheek.	شِدْقٌ
Deacon	شِدْيَاقٌ ج شَدَايِقَة
Diffuse in speech.	مُتَشَدِّقٌ
A young gazelle.	شَادِنٌ
To sing.	شَدَا يَشْدُو وَأَشْدَى
To be exceptional.	شَذَّ يَشُذُّ
Irregular, rare.	شَاذٌّ ج شَوَاذ
Irregularity ; rarity.	شُذُوذٌ
Anything bad, evil.	شَرٌّ ج شُرُورٌ
Wicked. Worse.'	شَرٌّ ج أَشْرَارٌ
A spark.	شَرَارَةٌ
Bad, wicked.	شَرِيرٌ ج أَشْرَارٌ
Very wicked.	شِرِّيرٌ ج شِرِّيرُونَ
The Evil One, Satan.	الشِّرِّيرُ
To drink, swallow.	شَرِبَ يَشْرَبُ
To smoke tobacco.	شَرِبَ الدُّخَّانَ

Urine.	شِخَاخٌ
To snore ; snort.	شَخَرَ يَشْخِرُ شَخِيراً
To gaze at.	شَخَصَ بِبَصَرِهِ إِلَى
To go from .. to ..	شَخَصَ مِنْ وَإِلَى
To distinguish.	شَخَّصَ
To be distinct.	تَشَخَّصَ
Person, individual.	شَخْصٌ ج أَشْخَاصٌ
Diagnosis of (disease).	تَشْخِيصٌ
To strap, bind.	شَدَّ يَشُدُّ شَدًّا
To bind fast, strengthen.	شَدَّدَ
To treat with severity.	شَدَّدَ عَلَى
To be strengthened.	تَشَدَّدَ وَاشْتَدَّ
To be strong, intense.	إِشْتَدَّ
Violence, intensity.	شِدَّةٌ
Hardship, distress.	شِدَّةٌ ج شَدَائِدُ
Name of the sign (ّ).	شَدَّةٌ
Violent, strong.	شَدِيدٌ ج اشِدَّاء
Courageous, brave.	شَدِيدُ الْبَأْسِ
More intense, stronger.	أَشَدُّ

Long slice of meat.	شَرِيحٌ وَشَرِيحَةٌ	To saturate.	شَرَّبَ
Dissection.	تَشْرِيح	To absorb, imbibe.	تَشَرَّبَ
Anatomy.	عِلْمُ التَّشْرِيح	Act of drinking.	شِرْبٌ
Anatomist.	مُشَرِّحٌ ج مُشَرِّحُونَ	Draught. Water-jug.	شَرْبَةٌ
Prime of youth.	شَرْخ	Drink, beverage.	شَرَابٌ ج أَشْرِبَةٌ
To flee, take fright.	شَرَدَ يَشْرُدُ	Syrup.	شَرَابٌ
To depart from.	شَرَدَ عَنْ	Tassel.	شَرَّابَةٌ ج شَرَارِيب
Roaming, fugitive.	شَارِدٌ	Moustache.	شَارِبٌ ج شَوَارِبُ
Strange, unusual.	شَوَارِدُ	Addicted to drink.	شِرِّيبٌ
Small number of men.	شِرْذِمَةٌ	Inclination.	مَشْرَبٌ ج مَشَارِبُ
To be ill-natured.	شَرِسَ يَشْرَسُ	To entangle, confuse.	شَرْبَكَ
Ill-natured.	شَرِسٌ	A species of fir.	شَرْبِين
Sticking-paste.	شِرَاسٌ وَسِرَاسٌ	To baste.	شَرَّجَ
Extremity of a rib.	شُرْسُوف	Sesame-oil.	شِيرَجٌ وَسِيرَجٌ
Epigastric region.	أَلْقِسْمُ الشَّرَاسِيفِيُّ	To explain.	شَرَحَ يَشْرَحُ
Root.	شِرْسٌ ج شُرُوس	To dissect.	شَرَّحَ
A fringe.	شَرْشَرَةٌ ج شَرَاشِرُ	To be enlarged. Happy.	إِنْشَرَحَ
Bed-sheet.	شَرْشَفٌ ج شَرَاشِفُ	Commentary.	شَرْحٌ ج شُرُوحٌ
To stipulate.	شَرَطَ يَشْرُطُوَاشْتَرَطَ	Commentator.	شَارِحٌ ج شُرَّاحٌ

To be noble.	شَرُفَ يَشْرُف	To make incisions.	شَرَطَ وَشَرَّطَ
To be high.	شَرَفَ يَشْرُفُ شَرَفاً	To stipulate with.	شَارَطَ وَتَشَارَطَ
To exalt, honour.	شَرَّفَ	Condition, stipula- tion, contract.	شَرْطُ ج شُرُوطُ
To be near to ; overtop.	أَشْرَفَ عَلَى	Guard's-man.	شُرْطِيّ ج شُرْطَة
To be honoured.	تَشَرَّفَ	Wire ; tape.	شَرِيطَ ج شُرُط
Elevated place. Eminence.	شَرَفٌ ج أَشْرَافٌ	Bistoury.	مِشْرَط ج مَشَارِط
Honour, nobility ; height.	شَرَفٌ	Stipulation. Betting.	مُشَارَطَة
Battlement.	شُرْفَة ج شُرُفَات	To make a law.	شَرَعَ يَشْرَعُ وَاشْتَرَعَ
Noble.	شَرِيفٌ ج أَشْرَافٌ	To begin.	شَرَعَ شُرُوعاً
An edict by the Sultan's own hand.	أَلْخَطُّ الشَّرِيف	He began to say.	شَرَعَ يَقُول
Projecting, overlooking.	مُشْرِفٌ	To engage in an affair.	شَرَعَ في
To rise (sun).	شَرَقَ يَشْرُقُ	Divine or religious law.	شَرْعٌ
To go eastward.	شَرَّقَ	Legitimate, legal.	شَرْعِيّ
To rise, shine, beam.	أَشْرَقَ	Main street. Legislator.	شَارِعٌ ج شَوَارِع
East ; Orient.	شَرْق	A sail.	شِرَاعٌ ج أَشْرِعَة
Eastern ; Oriental.	شَرْقِيّ	Law, statute.	شَرِيعَة ج شَرَائِع
East ; Orient. Levant.	مَشْرِقٌ ج مَشَارِق	Jordan (river).	أَلشَّرِيعَة
To share with.	شَارَكَ مُشَارَكَةً	Deuteronomy.	تَثْنِيَة الاشْتِرَاع
To take a partner.	أَشْرَكَ في	Legislator.	مُشْتَرِع

To buy.	إِشْتَرَى
Purchase.	شِرَاءٌ وَشِرًى
Nettle-rash ; urticaria.	شَرَى
Artery.	شَرْيَانٌ ج شَرَايِين
Buyer.	شَارٍ وَمُشْتَرٍ ج شُرَاةٌ
Jupiter (planet).	اَلْمُشْتَرِي
To look askance at.	شَزَرَ يَشْزُرُ إِلَى
To be distant.	شَسَعَ يَشْسَعُ شُسُوعاً
Very remote, distant.	شَاسِعٌ
Water-closet.	(شُشْمَةٌ)
Sample.	(شُشْنَةٌ)
Fish-hook.	شِصٌّ ج شُصُوصٌ
To go beyond bounds.	شَطَّ فِي
Shore, bank.	شَطٌّ ج شُطُوطٌ
Excess. Injustice.	شَطَطٌ
Shore. Coast.	شَاطِئٌ ج شَوَاطِئ
To cut into strips. Deviate.	شَطَبَ يَشْطُبُ
To divide, halve.	شَطَرَ يَشْطُرُ
To balve with another.	شَاطَرَ

To be a polytheist.	أَشْرَكَ بِاللهِ
To share.	اِشَارَكَ وَاَشْتَرَكَ
Polytheism.	تَشْرِكٌ
Snare.	شِرَكٌ ج أَشْرَاك
Company ; partnership.	شُرْكَةٌ
Shoe-string.	شِرَاكٌ ج شُرُكٌ
Partner.	شَرِيك ج شُرَكَاء
Polytheist, idolater.	مُشْرِك
Associate. Subscriber.	مُشْتَرَك
Common to several.	مُشْتَرَك
To split, slit.	شَرَمَ يَشْرِمُ شَرْماً
To be split.	شُرِمَ وَتَشَرَّمَ وَاْنْشَرَمَ
Split, rent.	شَرْمٌ ج شُرُومٌ
Cocoon.	شَرْنَقَةٌ ج شَرَانِق
To be greedy for.	شَرِهَ يَشْرَهُ إِلَى
Inordinate desire.	شَرَهٌ وَشَرَاهَة
Greedy. Glutton.	شَرِهٌ وَشَرْهَانُ
Trowsers.	شِرْوَالٌ وَسِرْوَالٌ
To buy.	شَرَى يَشْرِي شِرَاءً وَشِرًى

Ramified. مُشَعَّبٌ	Half ; part. شَطْرٌ ج شُطُورٌ
To juggle. شَعْبَذَ	Wicked ; sharper. شَاطِرٌ ج شُطَّارٌ
Juggler. مُشَعْبِذٌ	Divided into halves. مَشْطُورٌ
To be dishevelled. شَعِثَ وَتَشَعَّثَ	Adjacent, neighbouring. مُشَاطِرٌ
To know ; feel. شَعَرَ يَشْعُرُ بِ	Chess. شَطْرَنْجٌ
To inform. أَشْعَرَهُ ب	To wash ; rinse. شَطَفَ يَشْطُفُ شَطْفًا
Poetry, verse. شِعْرٌ ج أَشْعَارٌ	To be rebellious. شَيْطَنَ وَتَشَيْطَنَ
Hair. شَعْرٌ ج شُعُورٌ	Devilishness. شَيْطَنَةٌ
A hair. شَعْرَةٌ ج شَعَرَاتٌ	Satan, devil. شَيْطَانٌ ج شَيَاطِين
Poetical. شِعْرِيٌّ	Splinter. Fibula. شَظِيَّةٌ ج شَظَايَا
Sirius, Dog-Star. أَلشِّعْرَى	To disperse. شَعَّ يَشِعُّ شُعَاعًا
Would that I knew ! لَيْتَ شِعْرِي	To be dispersed. شَعَّ يَشِعُّ
Hairy, shaggy. أَشْعَرُ ج شُعْرٌ	To emit rays. أَشَعَّ
Rites. شِعَارٌ وَشَعَائِرُ	Sun-beam. شُعَاعٌ ج أَشِعَّةٌ وَشُعَاعٌ
Trellis-work. شَعْرِيَّةٌ ج شَعْرِيَّاتٌ	To ramify. تَشَعَّبَ وَاْنْشَعَبَ
Poet. شَاعِرٌ ج شُعَرَاءُ	Mountain-pass. شِعْبٌ ج شِعَابٌ
Knowing, perceiving. شَعُورٌ	People, nation. شَعْبٌ ج شُعُوبٌ
Barley. شَعِيرٌ	Branch. Portion. شُعْبَةٌ ج شُعَبٌ
Sense (sight, &c.) مَشْعَرٌ ج مَشَاعِرُ	The eighth lunar month. شَعْبَانُ

To busy, occupy much. شَغَّلَ	To kindle. شَعَلَ يَشْعَلُ وَشَعَّلَ وَاشْعَلَ
To be occupied. To act. إِشْتَغَلَ	To be kindled. شَعَلَ وَاشْتَعَلَ
Occupation, work. شُغْلٌ ج أَشْغَالٌ	To be enraged. إِشْتَعَلَ غَضَبًا
Busying affair. شَاغِلٌ ج شَوَاغِلُ	Firebrand, flame. شُعْلَةٌ ج شُعَلٌ
Occupation. إِشْتِغَالٌ	Burning wick. شُعَيْلَةٌ ج شُعَلٌ
Occupied ; busy. مَشْغُولٌ	Conflagration. إِشْتِعَالٌ
To be very fine, transparent. شَفَّ يَشِفُّ	Lamp ; torch. مِشْعَلٌ ج مَشَاعِلُ
Thin, fine dress. شَفٌّ ج شُفُوفٌ	Palm-Sunday. عِيدُ الشَّعَانِين
Transparent. شَفَّافٌ	To juggle. شَعْوَذَ
Transparency. شُفُوفٌ	Jugglery. شَعْوَذَة
Edge, border. شَفْرٌ ج أَشْفَارٌ	Juggler. مُشَعْوِذٌ
Blade. شَفْرَةٌ ج شِفَارٌ	To stir up discord, evil. شَغَبَ يَشْغَبُ
Border of a valley. شَفِيرُ الْوَادِي	Discord, tumult ; revolt. شَغْبٌ
To plead, intercede. Couple, double. شَفَعَ يَشْفَعُ	To inflame with love. شَغَفَ حُبًّا
To make double. شَفَّعَ	To be smitten. شَغِفَ بِ
Right of pre-emption. شُفْعَةٌ	Passionate love. شَغَفٌ
Intercession, mediation. شَفَاعَةٌ	Passionately taken up. مَشْغُوفٌ
Intercessor. شَافِعٌ وَشَفِيعٌ ج شُفَعَاءُ	To occupy. شَغَلَ يَشْغَلُ
To pity. شَفِقَ يَشْفَقُ وَأَشْفَقَ عَلَى	To divert from. شَغَلَ عَنْ

To split into pieces	شَقَقَ	Evening twilight.	شَفَقٌ
To be split or separated.	إِنْشَقَّ	Compassion ; tenderness.	شَفَقَة
Split, rent ; crack.	شَقٌّ ج شُقُوقٌ	Compasionate.	شَفُوقٌ وَشَفِيقٌ
Great hardship.	شَقٌّ وَمَشَقَّة	To speak mouth to mouth.	شَافَهَ
Half, one side of a thing.	شِقٌّ	Lip. شَفَةٌ ج شِفَاةٌ وَشَفِهَاتٌ وَشَفَوَاتٌ	
Piece of cloth.	شُقَّةٌ ج شِقَقٌ	Labiat.	شَفَهِيٌّ وَشَفَوِيٌّ
Troublesome, hard.	شَاقٌّ	By word of mouth. مُشَافَهَةً وَشِفَاهاً	
Separation, discord.	شِقَاق	To cure, heal. شَفَى يَشْفِي شِفَاءً مِنْ	
Full brother.	شَقِيقٌ ج أَشِقَّاء	To be very near.	أَشْفَى عَلَى
Red anemone.	شَقَائِقُ النُّعْمَان	To recover (one's health).	إِشْتَفَى
Derivation of a word.	إِشْتِقَاقٌ	To seek a cure.	إِسْتَشْفَى
Separation, division.	إِنْشِقَاقٌ	Cure, recovery.	شِفَاءٌ
Great hardship.	مَشَقَّةٌ ج مَشَاقٌّ	Brink, edge, extremity.	شَفاً
Derived (word).	مُشْتَقٌّ	Curing, healing.	شَافٍ
Light red, sorrel colour.	شُقْرَةٌ	A clear answer.	جَوَابٌ شَافٍ
Of fair complexion, sorrel.	أَشْقَرُ	Hospital. مُسْتَشْفًى وَدَارُ الشِّفَاء	
The green wood pecker.	شَقَرَّاقٌ	To split, cleave.	شَقَّ يَشُقُّ شَقّاً
Verbosity.	شَقْشَقَةُ اللِّسَان	To trouble, distress. شَقَّ مَشَقَّةً عَلَى	
		To rebel.	شَقَّ العَصَا

Thankful.	شَاكِرٌ وَشَكُورٌ	To pile up.	شَقَعَ يَشْقَعُ شَقْعًا
Hemlock.	شَوْكَرَانٌ وَشَيْكَرَانٌ	To split, cut into pieces.	شَقَفَ
To be stubborn.	شَكِسَ يَشْكَسُ	Earthen pot ; piece.	شَقْفَةٌ ج شَقَفٌ
Refractory.	شَكِسٌ وَشَكْسٌ	To lift up.	شَقَلَ يَشْقِلُ شَقْلًا
To be obscure.	شَكَلَ يَشْكُلُ وَاشْكَلَ عَلَى	To be miserable.	شَقِيَ يَشْقَى
To tether, tie up.	شَكَلَ وَشَكَّلَ	To labour, toil.	شَقِيَ فِي
To resemble.	شَاكَلَ	To struggle with.	شَاقَى
To be fashioned, shaped.	تَشَكَّلَ	To make miserable.	أَشْقَى
To resemble one another.	تَشَاكَلَ	Misery.	شَقًا وَشَقَاءٌ وَشَقَاوَةٌ
To be ambiguous.	إِشْتَكَلَ	Miserable.	شَقِيٌّ ج أَشْقِيَاءُ
To deem dubious.	إِسْتَشْكَلَ	To doubt.	شَكَّ يَشُكُّ وَتَشَكَّكَ فِي
Likeness ; form.	شَكْلٌ ج أَشْكَالٌ	To pierce through.	شَكَّ
Fashion. Kind, sort. Vowel point.		To throw into doubt.	شَكَّكَ فِي
Tether.	شِكَالٌ ج شُكُلٌ	Uncertainty, doubt.	شَكٌّ ج شُكُوكٌ
Side. Way.	شَاكِلَةٌ ج شَوَاكِلُ	Thrust (of a lance, &c.)	شَكَّةٌ
Resemblance.	مُشَاكَلَةٌ وَتَشَاكُلٌ	Armed.	شَاكُّ السِّلَاحِ
Difficulty.	مُشْكِلٌ ج مَشَاكِلُ	Doubtful, uncertain.	مَشْكُوكٌ فِيهِ
Mouth-bit.	شَكِيمَةٌ	To thank.	شَكَرَ يَشْكُرُ وَتَشَكَّرَ لِ
To complain to.	شَكَا يَشْكُو إِلَى	Thanks.	شُكْرٌ وَشُكْرَانٌ ج شُكُورٌ

To disappoint. شَمَّتَ	To complain of pain. شكا أَلَمًا
To be high, lofty. شَمَخَ يَشْمَخُ	To complain. تشكّى وَٱشْتكىإِلَى
To be high; be proud. تَشامَخَ	Complaint; accusation. شكاية
High; proud. شامِخ ج شُمَّخ	Plaintiff. شاكٍ ومُشْتَكٍ
Pride, haughtiness. تَشامُخ	Accused. مشْكُوٌّ ومُشْتَكى عَليْهِ
Proud, haughty. مُتشامِخ	To be paralyzed. شلَّ يَشلُّ وَشلَّ
To tuck up a garment. شَمَّرَ يشَمِّر	To paralyze, disable. أَشلَّ
To be ready for. تَشمَّرَ وَٱنْشَمَرَل	Paralysis. شلَل
Fennel. شمْرَة وَشمَار	Cataract. شلّال ج شلالات
To abhor. شمِزَ يَشْمِزُ مِنْ	To strip, undress. شلَحَ يَشْلَحُ
To shrink from. اشْمأَزَّ ٱشْمِئْزَازًا	To strip, plunder. شلَّح
To be sunny. شَمِسَ يَشْمُسُ وَأَشْمَسَ	Mantle. مشْلَح
To be restive. شمَسَ يَشْمُسُ	Body after decay. شِلْوٌ ج أَشْلاءٌ
To expose in the sun. شمَّسَ	Darnel-grass. شيْلَم
Sun. شمْس ج شُموس	To smell. شمَّ يَشُمُّ شمًّا
Solar. شمْسي	To make one smell. شمَّمَ وَأَشمَّ
Umbrella; sun-shade. شمْسية	Sense of smell. شمّ
Deacon. شمَّاس ج شمَامسة	A fragrant, striped melon. شمَّام
Restive, refractory. شموس	To rejoice شمِتَ يشْمَتُ شمَاتَةَ ب
	at the affliction of an enemy.

To hate, detest. شَنَأَ وَشَنِئَ يَشْنَا	Exposed to the sun. مُشَمَّسٌ
Hatred, detestation. شَنْءٌ	Whiteness, hoariness. شَمَطٌ
Hater, enemy. شَانِئٌ ج شُنَّاءُ	Gray-haired, graizzled. أَشْمَطُ
Hated ; hateful. مَشْنُوءٌ	To wax ; cover with wax. شَمَّعَ
Moustache. شَنَبٌ ج اشْنَابٌ	Wax. شَمْعٌ ج شُمُوعٌ
A grain-measure. شُنْبُلٌ ج شَنَابِلُ	Wax-candle. شَمْعَةٌ ج شَمَعَاتٌ
Spasmodic contraction. تَشَنُّجٌ	Waxed. Oil-cloth. مُشَمَّعٌ
Nature, disposition. شِنْشِنَةٌ ج شَنَاشِنُ	Candlestick. شَمْعَدَانٌ
To be bad. شَنُعَ يَشْنُعُ شَنَاعَةً	To shift to north. شَمَلَ يَشْمُلُ
To disgrace, revile. شَنَّعَ شَنَّعًا	To take the left side. شَمَلَ يَشْمُلُ
To accuse him of evil. شَنَّعَ عَلَيْهِ	To include, contain. شَمَلَ يَشْمُلُ
To regard as foul. إِسْتَشْنَعَ	To comprise, contain. إِشْتَمَلَ عَلَى
Infamy, ugliness. شُنْعَةٌ وَشَنَاعَةٌ	Union. شَمْلٌ
Foul, ugly. شَنِعٌ شَنِيعٌ وَأَشْنَعُ	Comprehensive ; general. شَامِلٌ
To embellish. شَنَّفَ	Left side ; north. شِمَالٌ
Ear-ring. شَنْفٌ ج شُنُوفٌ	Northern, northerly. شِمَالِيٌّ
To hang. شَنَقَ يَشْنِقُ شَنْقًا	Endowed. Included. مَشْمُولٌ
Hanging. شَنَقٌ	Beet (root). شَمَنْدَرٌ وَشْمَنْدَرٌ
Longing, yearning. شَنِقٌ وَشَانِقٌ	To attack. شَنَّ وَأَشَنَّ الغَارَةَ عَلَى

Vision, sight, scene.	مُشَاهَدَة	Cord, rope.	شِنَاقٌ ج أَشْنِقَة
To make public.	شَهَرَ يَشْهُرُ	Gibbet, gallows.	مِشْنَقَة ج مَشَانِقُ
To make known, publish.	أَشْهَرَ	Hanged.	مَشْنُوقٌ
To become known ; be celebrated ; notorius.	إِشْتَهَرَ	Gray colour.	شُهْبَة وَشَهَبٌ
Month.	شَهْرٌ ج شُهُورٌ وَأَشْهُرٌ	Meteor.	شِهَابٌ ج شُهُبٌ
Celebrity, fame, repute.	شُهْرَة	Gray.	أَشْهَبُ م شَهْبَاءُ ج شُهْبٌ
Celebrated, notorious.	شَهِيرٌ	Aleppo.	أَلشَّهْبَاءُ
Well-known.	مَشْهُورٌ ج مَشَاهِيرُ	To witness, be present.	شَهِدَ يَشْهَدُ
According to usage.	عَلَى الْمَشْهُورِ	To witness against.	شَهِدَ يَشْهَدُ عَلَى
To draw the breath.	شَهَقَ يَشْهَقُ	To bear witness to.	شَهِدَ بِ
A single cry.	شَهْقَة	To be an eye-witness ; see.	شَاهَدَ
High, lofty.	شَاهِقٌ ج شَوَاهِقُ	Call to witness.	أَشْهَدَ وَٱسْتَشْهَدَ
Inspiration and expiration in breathing.	أَلشَّهِيقُ وَٱلزَّفِيرُ	To die as a martyr.	أُسْتُشْهِدَ
A mixture of two colours.	شُهْلٌ	Honeycomb.	شُهْدٌ ج شِهَادٌ
To be sagacious.	شَهُمَ يَشْهُمُ	Eye-witness.	شَاهِدٌ ج شُهُودٌ
Honourable.	شَهْمٌ ج شِهَامٌ	Testimony. Diploma.	شَهَادَة
Sagacity. Honour.	شَهَامَة	Martyrdom.	شَهَادَة وَٱسْتِشْهَادٌ
Falcon.	شَاهِينٌ ج شَوَاهِينُ	Witness. Martyr.	شَهِيدٌ ج شُهَدَاءُ
		Assembly. Aspect.	مَشْهَدٌ

To crave for.	شَهَا يَشْهُو
To excite a desire.	شَهَّى
To desire eagerly.	إِشْتَهَى
Strong desire, appetite, passion, lust.	شَهْوَةٌ ج شَهَوَاتٌ
Desired, pleasant.	شَهِيٌّ وَمُشْتَهَى
Sensual.	شَهْوَانِيٌّ
More desirable, delicious.	أَشْهَى
Desire, craving.	إِشْتِهَاءٌ
Craved.	مُشْتَهًى ج مُشْتَهِيَات
To mix.	شَابَ يَشُوبُ شَوْبًا
Blemish.	شَائِبَةٌ ج شَوَائِب
A species of kite.	شُوحَةٌ
To point out or at.	أَشَارَ إِلَى
To counsel, advise.	أَشَارَ عَلَى بِ
To consult.	شَاوَرَ وَاسْتَشَارَ
To consult together.	تَشَاوَر عَلَى
Consultation.	مَشُورَةٌ وَمَشْوَرَةٌ
Councillors.	أَهْلُ الشُّورَى

Council.	مَجْلِسُ الشُّورَى
Sign; signal; allusion.	إِشَارَةٌ
Demonstrative pronoun.	إِسْمُ الإِشَارَةِ
Indicated, referred to.	مُشَارٌ إِلَيْهِ
Councillor; minister.	مُشِيرٌ
Councillor.	مُسْتَشَارٌ
Soup.	شُورَبَةٌ
To trouble, confuse.	شَوَّشَ
To be confused; sick.	تَشَوَّشَ
Thin muslin.	شَاشٌ
Sergeant.	شَاوِيشٌ (جَاوِيشٌ)
Hair of head.	شُوشَةٌ
Confusion. Sickness.	تَشْوِيشٌ
Confused. Ill.	مُشَوَّشٌ
Squint-eyed.	أَشْوَصُ م شَوْصَاء
To see.	شَافَ يَشُوفُ شَوْفًا
To show.	شَوَّفَ
To fill with longing.	شَاقَ وَشَوَّقَ إِلَى
To long for.	تَشَوَّقَ وَاشْتَاقَ إِلَى

To roast, broil (meat). شَوَى يَشْوِي	Strong desire. شَوْقٌ ج أَشْوَاقْ
To be roasted, grilled. إِنْشَوَى	Desirable, charming. شَائِقْ
Roasted, grilled. شَوِي وَمَشْوِيّ	Ardently longing. مُشْتَاقْ
Gridiron. مِشْوًى ومِشْوَاةْ	To pierce with a thorn. شَاكَ وَشَوَّكَ
To will, wish, desire. شَاءَ يَشَاء	Thorns, prickles. شَوْكْ ج أَشْوَاكْ
Thing, something. شِيءْ ج أَشْيَاء	A thorn, sting. شَوْكَة
Gradually. شَيْئًا فَشَيْئًا	Shawl. شَالْ ج شَالَاتْ
A small thing ; a little. (شَوَيَّة)	Desert. شَوْلْ ج أَشْوَالْ
Will, wish, desire. مَشِيئَة	Large sack. شُوَالْ ج شُوَالَاتْ
To become gray. شَابَ يَشِيبْ	The tenth lunar month. شَوَّالْ
To make gray. أَشَابَ وَشَيَّبَ	Watch-tower. Barn. شُونَة ج شُوَنْ
Old age. شَيْبْ وَمَشِيبْ	To disfigure. شَوَّهَ
White or hoary beard. شَيْبَة	To be ugly, disfigured. تَشَوَّهَ
Hoary ; old. شَائِبْ وَأَشْيَبْ	Deformity, ugliness. شَوَهْ
Cotton-prints. شِيتْ	Deformed ugly. أَشْوَهُ م شَوْهَاء
Artemesia ; wormwood. شِيحْ	King ; Shah, (Persian). شَاهْ
To grow old. شَاخَ يَشِيخْ وَشَيَّخَ	Royal, imperial. شَاهَانِيّ
Old man, Sheikh. شِيخْ ج شُيُوخْ	Sheep, lamb. شَاةْ ج شَاه وشِيَاهْ
Religious Chief of the Moslems. شِيخْ آلإِسْلَامْ	Ugly, deformed. Stupid. شَوَّ

A Shite.	شِيعِيّ	Old age.	شِيخُوخَةٌ
Public ; common.	شَائِعٌ وَمُشَاعٌ	Republic. Senate.	مَشِيخَةٌ
Partisan of.	مُشَايِعُ لِ	To build up.	شَادَ يَشِيدُ وَشِيَّدَ
To lift up, carry.	شَالَ يَشِيلُ شَيْلًا	High, elevated.	مَشِيدٌ وَمُشَيَّدٌ
To trade of a porter.	شِيَالَةٌ	To be slightly burnt.	شَاطَ يَشِيطُ
A porter.	شَيَّالٌ	To get angry.	إِسْتَشَاطَ عَلَى
Black spot ; mole.	شَامَةٌ ج شَامَاتٌ	Satan, devil.	شَيْطَانٌ
Syria.	أَلشَّامُ	Inflamed by anger.	مُسْتَشِيطٌ
Character, nature.	شِيمَةٌ ج شِيَمٌ	To be spread abroad.	شَاعَ يَشِيعُ
Of noble qualities.	كَرِيمُ ٱلشِّيَمِ	To publish.	شَاعَ بِ وَأَشَاعَ
To disgrace.	شَانَ يَشِينُ شَيْنًا	To see a guest off.	شَيَّعَ
A disgraceful thing.	شَيْنٌ	To escort, follow.	شَايَعَ
Tea.	شَايٌ	To publish the news.	أَشَاعَ ٱلْخَبَرَ
		Party, sect ; the Shites.	شِيعَةٌ

ص

He became learned.	أَصْبَحَ عَالِمًا
To take to doing.	أَصْبَحَ يَفْعَل
Dawn. Morning.	صُبْحٌ ج أَصْبَاحٌ
Early part of forenoon.	صُبْحَة
Morning.	صَبَاحٌ
Beauty, comeliness.	صَبَاحَة
Morning.	صَبِيحَة
Lamp.	مِصْبَاحٌ ج مَصَابِيحُ
To be patient. Confine.	صَبَرَ يَصْبِرُ
To ask one to be patient. Embalm Ballast.	صَبَّرَ
To be patient.	تَصَبَّرَ وَاصْطَبَرَ
Patience, endurance.	صَبْرٌ
Aloe. Aloe-plant.	صَبْرٌ وَصَبِرٌ
Patient.	صَابِرٌ ج صَابِرُونَ
Very patient.	صَبَّارٌ وَصَبُورٌ

As a numeral sign=90.	ص
To pour out.	صَبَّ يَصُبُّ صَبًّا
To dart or rush upon.	صَبَّ عَلَى
To be in love.	صَبَّ يَصَبُّ صَبَابَةً
To descend.	أَصَبَّ
To be poured out. Incline.	اِنْصَبَّ
Longing lover.	صَبٌّ
Catarrh of the nose.	صُبَّة
Excessive love or desire.	صَبَابَة
Poured forth.	صَبِيبٌ
Mouth of a river.	مَصَبٌّ
Sabian.	صَابِئٌ ج صَابِئُونَ
To be handsome.	صَبُحَ يَصْبُحُ
To bid good morning.	صَبَّحَ
To rise in the morning.	أَصْبَحَ

Youth.	صَبْوَةٌ	Cactus.	صَبَّيْرٌ
Boy, youth.	صَبِيٌّ ج صُبْيَانٌ	Ballast (of a ship).	صَابُورَةٌ
Young woman.	صَبِيَّةٌ ج صَبَايَا	A kind of basket.	صَابُورِيَّةٌ
To recover from disease. To be sound ; true.	صَحَّ يَصِحُّ	Finger, toe.	أُصْبُعٌ ج أَصَابِعُ
		Gridiron.	مِصْبَعٌ
To cure a sick person. Correct; render sound.	صَحَّحَ تَصْحِيحًا	To dye, colour.	صَبَغَ يَصْبُغُ
Health. Soundness. Truth.	صِحَّةٌ	To be baptized ; dyed.	إِصْطَبَغَ
Healthy, sound. True.	صَحِيحٌ ج أَصِحَّاءُ	Dye ; paint.	صِبْغٌ وَصِبَاغٌ
Chapter.	إِصْحَاحٌ ج إِصْحَاحَاتٌ	Dye. Religion. Baptism.	صِبْغَةٌ
Correction.	تَصْحِيحٌ	Dyer.	صَبَّاغٌ
To accompany.	صَحِبَ يَصْحَبُ وَصَاحَبَ	Art of dyeing.	صِبَاغَةٌ
To take the part of.	تَصَحَّبَ لِ	A dye-house.	مَصْبَغَةٌ
To associate with.	تَصَاحَبَ مَعَ	To wash with soap.	صَبَّنَ وَصَوْبَنَ
To associate together.	إِصْطَحَبَ	Soap-maker.	صَبَّانٌ
Companionship.	صُحْبَةٌ	Soap.	صَابُونٌ
Friend. Owner.	صَاحِبٌ ج أَصْحَابٌ	Soap factory.	مَصْبَنَةٌ
Wealthy.	صَاحِبُ مَالٍ	To incline to, long for.	صَبَا ﺑـ إِلَى
Accompanied.	مَصْحُوبٌ	Light east-wind.	الصَّبَا
Desert.	صَحْرَاءُ ج صَحْرَاوَاتٌ	Youth, boyhood. Love.	الصِّبَا

Subject in hand.	صَدَدٌ
Pus ; matter.	صَدِيدٌ
To become rusty.	صَدِئَ يَصْدَأُ
To confront ; face.	تَصَدَّى لِ
Rust.	صَدَأٌ
To sing.	صَدَحَ يَصْدَحُ
Singer.	صَادِحٌ
To take place ; occur.	صَدَرَ ُ
To proceed from.	صَدَرَ مِنْ
To arise, result from.	صَدَرَ عَنْ
To go to.	صَدَرَ إِلَى
To begin (a book) with.	صَدَّرَ بِ
To show forth ; issue.	أَصْدَرَ
Chest ; bosom.	صَدْرٌ ج صُدُورٌ
The first part. Chief.	
Prime Minister.	اَلصَّدْرُ الأَعْظَمُ
Vest.	صَدْرِيَّةٌ صَدَارَةٌ
The office of Prime Minister.	صَدَارَةٌ
Going out.	صَادِرٌ
(opp. to وارد coming in).	

To alter a word.	صحَّفَ تَصْحِيفًا
Large plate.	صَحْفَةٌ ج صِحَافٌ
A written page.	صَحِيفَةٌ ج صَحَائِفُ
The Koran.	مُصْحَفٌ ج مَصَاحِفُ
Plate (for food).	صَحْنٌ ج صُحُونٌ
Court (of a house).	صَحْنُ الدَّارِ
To become clear (sky)	صَحَا يَصْحُو وصَحِيَ يَصْحَى
To recover consciousness after intoxication or sleep.	
To rouse.	أَصْحَى
Fair weather ; clear sky.	صَحْوٌ
Mental clearness.	صَحْوَةٌ
Clear (sky) ; conscious.	صَاحٍ
To shout, clamour.	صَخِبَ
Clamourous.	صَخِبٌ وصَخُوبٌ
Rock.	صَخْرٌ وصَخْرَةٌ ج صُخُورٌ
Rocky ; stony.	صَخِرٌ ومُصْخِرٌ
To turn away from.	صَدَّ يَصُدُّ عَنْ
To oppose ; prevent.	صَدَّ صَدًّا
Aversion ; opposition	صَدٌّ

To ratify, confirm.	صَادَقَ عَلَى	Origin; source. Noun of action.	مَصْدَر ج مَصَادِر
To give alms, charity.	تَصَدَّقَ	To have a sprain.	صُدِعَ وَصُدِّعَ
Truth; veracity; sincerity.	صِدْق	To trouble; annoy.	صَدَّعَ
Alms; charity.	صَدَقَة ج صَدَقَات	To be sprained.	اِنْصَدَعَ
Dower given to a wife.	صَدَاق	Fissure. Sprain.	صَدْع ج صُدُوع
True friendship.	صَدَاقَة	Headache.	صُدَاع
True, sincere.	صَادِق	To incline to.	صَدَغَ يَصْدَغُ إِلَى
True friend.	صَدِيق ج أَصْدِقَاء	Temple; temporal region.	صُدْغ ج أَصْدَاغ
Righteous.	صِدِّيق ج صِدِّيقُون	To meet by chance.	صَدَفَ يَصْدِفُ
More, most, true.	أَصْدَق	To encounter.	صَادَفَ مُصَادَفَة
Belief; faith. Verification.	تَصْدِيق	To happen by chance.	تَصَدَّفَ
Believer. Verifying. Confirming.	مُصَدِّق	To meet together.	تَصَادَفَ
One who gives alms.	مُتَصَدِّق	Sea-shells.	صَدَف
An apothecary's trade.	صَيْدَلَة	A see-shell.	صَدَفَة ج صَدَفَات
Druggist.	صَيْدَلَانِيّ ج صَيَادِلَة	Chance.	صِدْفَة ج صِدَف
A pharmacy.	صَيْدَلِيَّة	To say the truth.	صَدَقَ يَصْدُقُ
To strike; repel.	صَدَمَ يَصْدِمُ	It applies correctly to.	يَصْدُقُ عَلَى
To dash against; thrust.	صَادَمَ	To believe. Verify.	صَدَّقَ
		To treat as a friend.	صَادَقَ

Intense cold.	صَرْصَر	To collide.	تَصَادَم وَاصْطَدَم
A cockroach.	صُرْصُر وصُرْصُور	Shock, collision.	صَدْمَة
Violent, cold wind.	رِيحٌ صَرْصَر	To return an echo.	أَصْدَى إِصْدَاء
Way; path.	صِرَاط	Echo; sound.	صَدًى ج أَصْدَاء
To strike down.	صَرَع يَصْرَع	To tie up.	صَرَّ يَصُرُّ صَرًّا
To have a fit.	صُرِع	Creak; chirp; tingle.	صَرَّ يَصِرُّ
To wrestle.	صَارَع وَتَصَارَع	To persist in.	أَصَرَّ عَلَى
To be thrown down.	إِنْصَرَع	Parcel; packet.	صُرَّة ج صُرَر
Epilepsy.	صَرْع	Persistence.	إِصْرَار
Epileptic.	صَرِيع وَمَصْرُوع	Grating noise.	صَرِير
Hemistich.	مِصْرَاع ج مَصَارِيع	To be pure, clear.	صَرُخ يَصْرُخ
Half of a folding door.		To make clear proclaim.	صَرَّح
Wrestler, combatant.	مُصَارِع	Pure, clear. Explicit.	صَرِيح
To send away;	صَرَف يَصْرِف	Clearness. Purity.	صَرَاحَة
change or spend (money).		Clear expression.	تَصْرِيح
To avert from.	صَرَف عَن	To cry out.	صَرَخ يَصْرُخ
To turn him to.	صَرَفَهُ إِلَى	A loud cry.	صَرْخَة
To conjugate, decline.	صَرَّف	Cries, screams.	صُرَاخ وَصَرِيخ
To commit to.	صَرَّف فِي	Crying out.	صَارِخ
To be inflected.	تَصَرَّف		

To carry out.	تَصَرَّفَ فِي	Severity.	صَرَامَةٌ
To depart; be inflected.	إِنْصَرَفَ	Shoe.	(صِرْمَايَةٌ ج صَرَامِيٌّ)
Etymology.	صَرْفٌ	The past year.	اَلْعَامُ ٱلْمُنْصَرِمُ
Pure, unmixed.	صِرْفٌ	Mast.	صَارٍ وَصَارِيَةٌ ج صَوَارٍ
Evils of fortune.	صُرُوفُ ٱلدَّهْرِ	Platform.	مِصْطَبَّةٌ ج مَصَاطِبُ
Broker's trade ; brokerage.	صَرَافَةٌ	To be difficult.	صَعُبَ يَصْعُبُ
Money-changer.	صَرَّافٌ ج صَيَارِفَةٌ	To make difficult.	صَعَّبَ وَتَصَعَّبَ
Departing, going off.	إِنْصِرَافٌ	To find difficult.	إِسْتَصْعَبَ
Freedom of action.	تَصَرُّفٌ	To be difficult.	تَصَعَّبَ وَاسْتَصْعَبَ
Inflection of words.	تَصْرِيفٌ	Difficult, hard.	صَعْبٌ ج صِعَابٌ
Vicissitudes of time.	تَصَارِيفُ ٱلدَّهْرِ	Difficulty.	صُعُوبَةٌ
Expense.	مَصْرُوفٌ مَصَارِيفُ	Difficulties, troubles.	مَصَاعِبُ
Having free action.	مُتَصَرِّفٌ	Thyme.	صَعْتَرٌ (أَوْ سَعْتَرٌ)
Inflected word. Governor.		To ascend.	صَعِدَ يَصْعَدُ صُعُوداً
A governor's district.	مُتَصَرِّفِيَّةٌ	To take or carry up.	صَعِدَ بِ
A word capable of inflection.	مُتَصَرِّفٌ	To cause to ascend.	أَصْعَدَ
To cut off, sever.	صَرَمَ يَصْرِمُ	Distress, calamity.	صَعْدَاءُ
To cease.	تَصَرَّمَ وَٱنْصَرَمَ	Sighing, deep sigh.	صُعَدَاءُ
Sharp severe.	صَارِمٌ ج صَوَارِمُ	Henceforth.	مِنَ ٱلْآنَ فَصَاعِداً

Noun in the diminutive form. مُصَغَّرٌ	Earth. Elevated land. صَعِيدٌ
To incline to. صَغَا يَصْغُو إِلَى	Upper Egypt. صَعِيدُ مِصْرَ
To listen to. صَغَا وَأَصْغَى إِلَى	Place of ascent. مَصْعَدٌ ج مَصَاعِدُ
Attention, listening. إِصْغَاءٌ	Vehement sound, cry. صَعْقٌ
To set in a line. صَفَّ يَصُفُّ	Thunderbolt. صَاعِقَةٌ ج صَوَاعِقُ
To take position in line. إِصْطَفَّ	Poor, pauper. صُعْلُوكٌ أج صَعَالِيكُ
Row, line, class. صَفٌّ ج صُفُوفٌ	To be small. صَغُرَ يَصْغُرُ
Line of battle. مَصَفٌّ ج مَصَافٌّ	To be base. صَغَرَ يَصْغُرُ
To consider, examine. صَفَحَ ــ	To make small. صَغَّرَ وَأَصْغَرَ
To turn away from, leave. Pardon, forgive. صَفَحَ ــ عَنْ	To change a noun into the diminutive form. صَغَّرَ الإِسْمَ
To cover with plates (metal). صَفَّحَ	To become small, or base. تَصَاغَرَ
To clap the hands. صَفَّحَ بِالْيَدِ	To esteem as little. إِسْتَصْغَرَ
To take by the hands (in saluting). صَافَحَ مُصَافَحَةً وَصِفَاحًا	Smallness. صِغَرٌ وصَغَارَةٌ
To examine attentively. تَصَفَّحَ	Adject. صَاغِرٌ ج صَاغِرُونَ
Forgiveness. صَفْحٌ	Little, small. صَغِيرٌ ج صِغَارٌ
To disregard. ضَرَبَ عَنْهُ صَفْحًا	A small sin. صَغِيرَةٌ ج صَغَائِرُ
Page of a book. صَفْحَةٌ ج صَفَحَاتٌ	Smaller, younger; least. أَصْغَرُ
Generous, forgiving. صَفُوحٌ	The minor proposition of a syllogism. الصُّغْرَى
	Act of diminishing. تَصْغِيرٌ

Yellow.	أَصْفَرُ م صَفْرَاءُ ج صُفْرٌ
(Yellow) bile.	صَفْرَاءُ
A poor man, destitute.	مُصْفِرٌ
Desert, plain.	صَفْصَفٌ
Willow, osier.	صَفْصَافٌ
To slap.	صَفَعَ يَصْفَعُ صَفْعاً
A slap.	صَفْعَةٌ
To strike ; flap.	صَفَقَ يَصْفِقُ صَفْقاً
To be strong.	صَفُقَ يَصْفُقُ صَفَاقَةً
To clap the hands.	صَفَّقَ
To agree upon.	اصْفَقَ عَلَى
They ratified a compact.	تَصَافَقُوا
Side, flank, face.	صَفْقٌ ج صُفُوقٌ
Contract, bargain.	صَفْقَةٌ
Fascia ; aponeurosis.	صِفَاقٌ
Thick, firm (texture).	صَفِيقٌ
Scrotum.	صَفَنٌ ج أَصْفَانٌ
Saphena vein.	صَافِنٌ ج صَوَافِنُ
To be clear.	صَفَا يَصْفُو

Plate of metal.	صَفِيحَةٌ ج صَفَائِحُ
Grasp of the hand.	مُصَافَحَةٌ
Broad, flat. Plated.	مُصَفَّحٌ
To shackle, fetter.	صَفَدَ يَصْفِدُ
Bond, fetter.	صَفْدٌ ج أَصْفَادٌ
To whistle.	صَفَرَ يَصْفِرُ صَفِيراً
To be empty.	صَفِرَ يَصْفَرُ صَفَراً
To make, or dye, yellow.	صَفَّرَ
To make vacant.	صَفَّرَ وَأَصْفَرَ
To become poor.	أَصْفَرَ
To become yellow, pale.	إِصْفَرَّ
Empty.	صُفْرٌ ج أَصْفَارٌ
Having nothing.	صِفْرُ الْيَدَيْنِ
Zero.	صِفْرٌ وَسِفْرٌ ج أَصْفَارٌ
Second month of lunar year.	صَفَرٌ
Yellowness, paleness.	صُفْرَةٌ
Whistle.	صَافُورَةٌ وَصُفَّيْرَةٌ
Yolk of an egg.	صَفَارُ الْبَيْضِ
Golden oriole.	صُفَارِيَّةٌ

Hoar-frost.	صَقِيع	To purify, filter.	صَفَّى وَأَصْفَى
To polish, give lustre.	صَقَلَ يَصْقُلُ	To be sincere.	صَافَى وَأَصْفَى آلوُدَّ
Staging.	صَقَالَة ج صَقَائِل	To choose, select.	إِصْطَفَى
Polisher.	صَقَّال ج صَيَاقِلَة	Smooth stone.	صَفَا ج أَصْفَاء
Polished. Sword.	صَقِيل	Serenity of life, pleasure.	صَفَاء
Sclav.	صَقْلِيّ ج صَقَالِبَة	Clearness.	صَفْوُ وَصَفَاء وَصَفْوَة
To strike coin (money).	صَكَّ يَصُكُّ	Pure ; chosen.	صَفِيّ ج أَصْفِيَاء
To trip, stumble.	صَكَّ يَصُكُّ	Pure, lear, climpid.	صَافٍ
To strike each other.	إِصْطَكَّ	Strainer.	مِصْفَاة ج مَصَافٍ
A legal deed.	صَكّ ج صُكُوك	Purified, filtered.	مُصَفَّى
Deadly serpent.	صِلّ ج أَصْلَال	Chosen.	مُصْطَفَى
To crucify.	صَلَبَ يَصْلُبُ صَلْبًا	To strike.	صَقَرَ يَصْقُرُ
To become hard, tough.	صَلَبَ يَصْلُبُ	Hawk.	صَقْر ج أَصْقُر
To render hard. To make the sign of the cross.	صَلَّبَ	Hell.	صَقَر
To become hard, firm.	تَصَلَّبَ	A pickaxe.	صَاقُور
Crucifixion.	صَلْب وَتَصْلِيب	To be covered with frost.	صُقِعَ
The loins.	صُلْب ج أَصْلَاب	To be cold, icy.	صَقِعَ
Hardness, firmness.	صَلَابَة	Region, district.	صُقْع ج اصْقَاع
Cross.	صَلِيب ج صُلْبَان	Intenseness of cold.	صَقْعَة

Crusader.	صَلِيبِيٌّ ج صَلِيبِيَّة
Crosswise.	مُصَالَبَةٌ
Crossing at right angles.	مُصَلَّبٌ
Crucified.	مَصْلُوبٌ ج مَصَالِيبُ
Fair ; wide.	صَلْت
Sceptre.	صَوْلَجَانٌ وَصَوْلَجَانَة
To be good, right.	صَلَحَ يَصْلَحُ
To be suitable, good for.	صَلَحَ لِ
To make peace.	صَالَحَ مُصَالَحَةً
To agree upon.	صَالَحَ عَلَى
To repair, improve.	أَصْلَحَ
To make peace between (two parties).	أَصْلَحَ بَيْنَ
To be reconciled.	تَصَالَحَ وَاصْطَلَحَ
To become better.	اِصْطَلَحَ
To agree upon. ...	اِصْطَلَحَ عَلى
Peace, reconciliation.	صُلْح
Good ; fit ; just. (one's good, self-interest).	صَالِح
A good deed.	صَالِحَةٌ ج صَالِحَات
Goodness, virtue.	صَلَاح

Reformation ; improvement.	إِصْلَاح
Technical use.	اِصْطِلَاح
Conventional.	اِصْطِلَاحِيٌّ
Peacemaker, reformer.	مُصْلِح
Advantage. Department.	مَصْلَحَةٌ ج مَصَالِح
Reconciliation.	مُصَالَحَة
To be hard.	صَلَدَ يَصْلِدُ صَلَداً
To sound.	صَلْصَلَ وَتَصَلْصَلَ
Clay.	صِلْصَال
Baldness of the head.	صَلَح
Bald spot.	صَلْعَةٌ وَصُلْعَة
Bald.	أَصْلَعُ م صَلْعَاءُ ج صُلْع
Abbreviation of the formula:	صَلْعَم
	صَلَّى اللّٰهُ عَلَيْهِ وَسَلَّم
To boast.	صَلَفَ يَصْلَفُ وَتَصَلَّفَ
Boasting.	صَلَف
To pray.	صَلَّى صَلَاةً أَوْ صَلَوةً
To pray for ; bless.	صَلَّى عَلَى
Prayer. Mercy.	صَلَاةٌ ج صَلَوَاتٌ

Place of prayer.	مُصَلًّى
One who prays.	مُصَلٍّ
To roast, broil.	صَلَى يَصْلِي
To put into the fire.	أَصْلَى
To warm one's self by the fire.	تَصَلَّى وَاصْطَلَى بِالنَّارِ
Fuel ; fire.	صِلَاءٌ
To stop (a flask).	صَمَّ يَصُمُّ صَمًّا
To become deaf.	صَمَّ وَأَصَمَّ
To determine upon.	صَمَّمَ عَلَى
Deafness.	صَمَمٌ
Stopper, cork. Valve.	صِمَامٌ
Most sincerely.	مِنْ صَمِيمِ القَلْبِ
Deaf.	أَصَمُّ م صَمَّاءُ ج صُمٌّ
Hard stone.	حَجَرٌ أَصَمُّ
A surd root.	جَذْرٌ أَصَمُّ
To be silent.	صَمَتَ يَصْمُتُ صَمْتًا
To silence.	صَمَّتَ وَأَصْمَتَ
Silence.	صَمْتٌ وَصُمَاتٌ وَصُمُوتٌ
Solid (not hollow).	مُصْمَتٌ

Canal of the ear.	صِمَاخٌ ج أَصْمِخَةٌ
To arrange ; adorn.	صَمَدَ يَصْمُدُ صَمْدًا
To lay up, save.	صَمَّدَ
Solid ; not hollow.	صَمَدٌ
The Eternal (God).	الصَّمَدُ
Cell of a recluse.	صَوْمَعَةٌ ج صَوَامِعُ
To gum, put gum into.	صَمَّغَ
Gum.	صَمْغٌ ج صُمُوغٌ
Gum Arabic.	الصَّمْغُ العَرَبِيُّ
To have a fetid odour.	أَصَنَّ
Stench.	صِنَّةٌ وَصِنَانٌ
Tube, pipe.	صُنْبُورٌ
Pine tree.	صَنَوْبَرٌ
Cone-shaped.	صَنَوْبَرِيٌّ
Cymbal.	صَنْجٌ ج صُنُوجٌ
Valiant.	صِنْدِيدٌ ج صَنَادِيدُ
Chest, trunk.	صُنْدُوقٌ ج صَنَادِيقُ
Sandal-wood.	صَنْدَلٌ
Fish-hook.	صِنَّارَةٌ ج صَنَانِيرُ

Sort, kind.	صِنْفٌ ج صُنُوفٌ	To make; construct.	صَنَعَ يَصْنَعُ
Literary work.	مُصَنَّفٌ ج مُصَنَّفَاتٌ	To arrange skilfully.	صَنَّعَ
Author.	مُصَنِّفٌ	To coax, flatter.	صَانَعَ مُصَانَعَةً
Idol. Camel's hump.	صَنَمٌ ج أَصْنَامٌ	To effect good manners.	تَصَنَّعَ
Hush ! Be silent !	صَهْ	To make ; have made.	إِصْطَنَعَ
A reddish colour.	صُهْبٌ وَصُهْبَةٌ	Act of making ; deed.	صُنْعٌ
Reddish.	أَصْهَبُ م صَهْبَاءُ ج صُهْبٌ	Good deed ; benefit.	صُنْعٌ
A very cold day.	يَوْمٌ أَصْهَبُ	Work. Carft, trade.	صَنْعَةٌ
(Red) wine.	ٱلصَّهْبَاءُ	Craft,	صِنَاعَةٌ ج صِنَاعَاتٌ
To melt. Smite.	صَهَرَ يَصْهَرُ	trade, industry. Art.	
To become related. to by marriage.	صَاهَرَ	Artisans.	أَصْحَابُ ٱلْحِرَفَ
Son-in-law, brother-in-law.	صِهْرٌ ج أَصْهَارٌ	Maker, artisan.	صَانِعٌ ج صُنَّاعٌ
Water-tank.	صِهْرِيجٌ ج صَهَارِيجُ	Artificial.	صِنَاعِيٌّ
To neigh (horse).	صَهَلَ يَصْهِلُ	Deed. Good deed.	صَنِيعَةٌ ج صَنَائِعُ
Neighing.	صَهِيلٌ وَصُهَالٌ	Affectation.	تَصَنُّعٌ
To hit the mark.	صَابَ ـُ وَأَصَابَ	Factory.	مَصْنَعٌ وَمَصْنَعَةٌ ج مَصَانِعُ
To approve. Point, aim.	صَوَّبَ	Affected ; artificial.	مُصَنَّعٌ
To attain one's purpose.	أَصَابَ	Made. Fabricated.	مَصْنُوعٌ
		To assort ; compose.	صَنَّفَ

Sculptor. Painter.	مُصَوِّرٌ	To be right.	أَصَابَ فِي قَوْلِهِ
Young chick.	صُوصٌ ج صِيصَانٌ	To do right.	أَصَابَ فِي عَمَلِهِ
To measure grain.	صَاعَ يَصُوعُ	To assail, smite.	أَضَابَ
A measure for grain.	صَاعٌ	To descend, (rain).	أَنْصَابَ
To form, fashion.	صَاغَ يَصُوغُ صَوْغًا	To hold to be right.	إِسْتَصْوَبَ
Pure, unmixed.	صَاغٍ	Side, course, direction.	صَوْبٌ
Money at its legal value.	صَاغٌ	Right, correct.	صَائِبٌ وَمُصِيبٌ
Grammatical form.	صِيغَةٌ ج صِيغٌ	What is right, correct.	صَوَابٌ
Goldsmith.	صَائِغٌ ج صَاغَةٌ وَصِيَّاغٌ	Struck, stricken.	مُصَابٌ
Goldsmith's art.	صِيَاغَةٌ	Affliction.	مُصِيبَةٌ ج مَصَائِبُ
Jewelry.	مَصَاغٌ	To make a noise.	صَاتَ يَصُوتُ وَصَوَّتَ
To become a Sûfi.	تَصَوَّفَ	Sound, voice.	صَوْتٌ ج أَصْوَاتٌ
Wool.	صُوفٌ ج أَصْوَافٌ	Reputation, fame.	صِيتٌ
A tuft of wool.	صُوفَةٌ	To fashion, shape, picture.	صَوَّرَ
Tinder, agaric.	صُوفَانٌ	To imagine.	صَوَّرَ لَهُ
Religious mystic ; Sûfi.	صُوفِيٌّ	To be formed. To imagine.	تَصَوَّرَ
To overpower, subdue.	صَالَ يَصُولُ عَلَى	Tyre (city). Horn, trumpet.	صُورٌ
To clean wheat.	صَوَّلَ ٱلْحِنْطَةَ	Picture, form.	صُورَةٌ ج صُوَرٌ
To soak, slake.	صَوَّلَ	Imagination, idea.	تَصَوُّرٌ

Cry ; crowing of a cock.	صِيَاحٌ	Power ; rule ; force.	صَوْلَةٌ
Cry, shout.	صَيْحَةٌ	Rubbish, refuse matter.	صَوَالَةٌ
Clamorous (man).	صَيَّاحٌ	Implement for	مِصْوَلٌ ج مَصَاوِلُ
To hunt; صَادَ يَصِيدُ وَتَصَيَّدَ وَٱصْطَادَ		cleaning wheat ; trough.	
trap, snare ; catch fish		Sceptre.	صَوْلَجَانٌ
Hunting, fishing ; game.	صَيْدٌ	To fast.	صَامَ يَصُومُ صَوْمًا وَصِيَامًا
Hunter, fisherman.	صَيَّادٌ	To abstain from.	صَامَ عَنْ
Sidon (city).	صَيْدَاء	To cause to fast.	صَوَّمَ
Trap, snare.	مِصْيَدَةٌ ج مَصَايِدُ	Fast ; abstinence.	صَوْمٌ وَصِيَامٌ
Prey taken in hunting.	مَصِيدٌ	Fasting.	صَائِمٌ ج صُوَّامٌ وَصِيَّمٌ
Pharmacy.	صَيْدَلَةٌ	Hermit's cell.	صَوْمَعَةٌ ج صَوَامِعُ
Druggist.	صَيْدَلَانِيٌّ	To keep, preserve, guard.	صَانَ يَصُونُ
To become ; change into.	صَارَ يَصِيرُ	To enclose with a wall.	صَوَّنَ
To happen to, befall.	صَارَ لَهُ	Act of preserving.	صَوْنٌ وَصِيَانَةٌ
To begin to do.	صَارَ يَفْعَلُ	Flint, flint-stone.	صَوَّانَةٌ ج صَوَّانٌ
To arrive at.	صَارَ مَصِيرًا إِلَى	Guarded, preserved.	مَصُونٌ
To cause to become.	صَيَّرَ	To cry out ; crow, (cock).	صَاحَ يَصِيحُ
Fold (for sheep).	صِيرَةٌ ج صِيَرٌ	To call out to.	صَاحَ بِ
Act of becoming.	صَيْرُورَةٌ	To cry out against.	صَاحَ عَلَى

China.	أَلصِّين	Destination, end, result.	مَصِيرْ
Chinese, Chinese porcelain.	صِينِيّ	To pass the summer.	صَافَ يَصِيفُ
Tray.	صِينِيَّة	Summer.	صَيْفْ
Large tent. Pavilion.	صِيوَانْ	Belonging to summer.	صَيْفِيّ
External ear.	صِيوَانُ ٱلأُذُن	A hot day.	يَوْمٌ صَائِفْ
		Summer residence.	مَصِيفْ

ض

To guard. Do a thing well ; perfect.	ضَبَطَ يَضْبِطُ ضَبْطاً	As a numeral sign=800.	ض
To withhold, restrain.	ضَبَطَ عَلَى	To shout in battle.	ضَاضاً
Exactness, correctness.	ضَبْطْ	Shouts of war.	ضَوْضَى وَضَوْضَاء
Rule ; canon.	ضَابِطْ ج ضَوَابِطُ	Thin ; small.	ضَئِيلْ ج ضُؤَلَاء
Military officer.	ضَابِطْ ج ضُبَّاط	Sheep, (coll noun).	ضَأْن
Almighty (God).	ضَابِطُ ٱلْكُلِّ	To grasp, keep.	ضَبَّ وَاضَبَّ عَلَى
Policeman.	ضَابِطِيّ ج ضَابِطِيَّة	Lizard.	ضَبّ ج ضِبَابْ
		Mist ; thin cloud.	ضَبَابَة ج ضَبَابْ

To make one laugh. أَضْحَكَ	Written sentence, مضبطة ج مضَابِط decision. (law).
Pleasantry. ضُحْكَة وَاضْحُوكَة	Well-regulated ; exact. مَضْبُوط
Comic, causing laughter. مُضْحِك	Hyena. ضَبْع وَضَبُع ج ضِبَاع
To appear. ضَحا يَضْحُو ضَحْواً	To cry, shout. ضَجَّ يَضِجّ وَأَضَجَّ
To come in the morning. ضَحَّى	To contend with. ضَاجَّ
To sacrifice an animal. ضَحَّى ب	Tumult, cry. ضَجَّة وَضَجِيج
To show, reveal. أَضْحى وَضَحَّى عَنْ	To be irri- ضَجِرَ يَضْجَرُ وَتَضَجَّرَ مِنْ
He took to laughing. أَضْحَى يَضْحَك	tated, impatient, bored.
ضَحَاء وَضَحْوَة وَضَحِى وَضَحِيَّة	To bore, vex, distress. أَضْجَرَ
Early morning after sunrise.	Uneasiness. ضَجَر وَضَجْرَة
Sacrifice. ضَحِيَّة ج ضَحَايا	Uneasy ; irritable. ضَجِر وَمُتَضَجِّر
Suburb, region. ضَاحِيَة ج ضَوَاحِ	Vexing, distressing. مُضْجِر
Bright ; cloudless. أَضْحَى م ضَحْياء	To lie down. ضَجَعَ يَضْجَعُ وَأَضْجَعَ
Day of sacrifice. يَوْمُ الأَضْحَى	To lie with (a woman). ضَاجَعَ
(tenth of the month. (ذُو الْحِجَّة	To make one to lie down. أَضْجَعَ
To be large. ضَخُمَ يَضْخُمُ	Bed-fellow. ضَجِيع
Large bulk ; corpulence. ضَخَامَة	Bed, bed- مَضْجَع ج مَضَاجِع chamber.
Large ; heavy. ضَخْم ج ضِخَام	To laugh. ضَحِك يَضْحَك ضَحِكاً
To overcome. ضَدَّ يَضُدّ	To laugh at. ضَحِك مِنْ وَعَلَى

Injurious, harmful.	مُضِرٌّ	To oppose.	ضَادَّ مُضَادَّةً
Injury ; means of harm.	مَضَرَّةٌ	To disagree.	تَضَادَّ تَضَادًّا
To strike.	ضَرَبَ يَضْرِبُ ضَرْبًا	Contrary ; enemy.	ضِدٌّ ج أَضْدَادٌ
Multiply, (*Arith*). Pitch (tent). Strike (money).		Two opposites.	ضِدَّانِ
To impose a tax.	ضَرَبَ عَلَى	Contrast ; opposition.	تَضَادٌّ
To overlook.	ضَرَبَ عَنْهُ صَفْحًا	To injure.	ضَرَّ يَضُرُّ وَأَضَرَّ بِ
To incline to blackness.	ضَرَبَ إِلَى ٱلسَّوَادِ	To receive an injury.	تَضَرَّرَ
To blow a trumpet.	ضَرَبَ فِي ٱلْبُوقِ	To force, compel.	اِضْطَرَّ إِلَى
To travel.	ضَرَبَ فِي ٱلْأَرْضِ	To be forced.	اضْطُرَّ إِلَى
To give a parable.	ضَرَبَ مَثَلًا	Harm ; evil.	ضُرٌّ وَضَرَرٌ
To be silent.	أَضْرَبَ	Adversity.	ضَرَّاءُ
To quit, cease.	أَضْرَبَ عَنْ	A fellow-wife to a woman's husband.	ضَرَّةُ ٱلْمَرْأَةِ ج ضَرَائِرُ
To speculate.	ضَارَبَ مُضَارَبَةً	Necessity.	ضَرُورَةٌ ج ضَرُورَاتٌ
To fight together.	تَضَارَبَ	Necessarily.	بِالضَّرُورَةِ وَضَرُورَةً
To be agitated.	اِضْطَرَبَ	Indispensable.	ضَرُورِيٌّ
To be confused.	اِضْطَرَبَ ٱلأمْرُ	Necessary things.	ضَرُورِيَّاتٌ
Multiplication. (*Arith*).	ضَرْبٌ	Blind.	ضَرِيرٌ ج أَضِرَّاءُ
Kind, form.	ضَرْبٌ ج ضُرُوبٌ	Necessity.	اِضْطِرَارٌ

Udder.	ضَرْعٌ ج ضُرُوعٌ	A blow, stroke.	ضَرْبَةٌ ج ضَرَبَاتٌ
Prayer with humility.	تَضَرُّعٌ	Striking. Multiplier.	ضَارِبٌ
Present-future tense.	مُضَارِعٌ	Impost, tax.	ضَرِيبَةٌ ج ضَرَائِبُ
of verbs; (e.g.	(يَضْرِبُ)	Agitation.	إِضْطِرَابٌ
Lion. Brave man.	ضِرْغَامٌ	Large tent.	مَضْرَبٌ ج مَضَارِبُ
To burn, blaze.	ضَرِمَ يَضْرَمُ وَأَضْطَرَمَ	Struck. Multiplicand.	مَضْرُوبٌ
To kindle a fire.	أَضْرَمَ	Sharer in traffic.	مُضَارِبٌ
To be kindled.	إِضْطَرَمَ	Agitated, confused.	مُضْطَرِبٌ
Firewood. Blazing.	ضِرَامٌ	To smear.	ضَرَجَ يَضْرُجُ ضَرْجًا
Blazing.	مُضْطَرِمٌ	To dye red. Adorn.	ضَرَّجَ
Rapacious animal.	ضَارٍ ج ضَوَارٍ	Grave.	ضَرِيحٌ ج ضَرَائِحُ
Humiliation, (from	ضَعَةٌ (وَضَعَ).	To be set on edge (teeth).	ضَرِسَ يَضْرَسُ
To pull down, rase.	ضَعْضَعَ ضَعْضَعَةٌ	To contend with.	ضَارَسَ
To be weak, feeble.	ضَعُفَ يَضْعُفُ	Molar tooth.	ضِرْسٌ ج أَضْرَاسٌ
Te double.	ضَعَّفَ يُضَعِّفُ وَضَاعَفَ	Wisdom teeth.	أَضْرَاسُ الْعَقْلِ
To weaken, enfeeble.	أَضْعَفَ	Experienced man.	مُضَرَّسٌ
To be doubled.	تَضَاعَفَ	To beseech.	ضَرَعَ يَضْرَعُ إِلَى
Weakness, feebleness.	ضُعْفٌ	To resemble.	ضَارَعَ مُضَارَعَةً
Double.	ضِعْفٌ ج أَضْعَافٌ	To beseech.	تَضَرَّعَ إِلَى

Error.	ضَلٌّ وَضَلَالٌ وَضَلَالَة
Strayed; erring.	ضَالٌّ ج ضَالُّونَ
A stray animal.	ضَالَّة
Error.	اضْلُولَة ج اضَالِيل
Leading astray.	مُضِلٌّ
Cause of error.	مَضَلَّة
To be strong.	ضَلُعَ يَضْلُعُ ضَلَاعَة
To be full, strong.	تَضَلَّعَ
Rib. Side of a triangle, &c.	ضِلْع ج ضُلُوع وَأَضْلَاع وَأَضْلُع (م)
Strong, powerful; large.	ضَلِيع
Ribbed; striped.	مُضَلَّع
To join, add. To vocalize a letter with. ( ) .	ضَمَّ يَضُمُّ ضَمًّا
To grasp, seize.	ضَمَّ عَلَى
To be joined, annexed.	إِنْضَمَّ
The vowel-point. ( ).	ضَمّ وَضَمَّة
Collected, joined. Having the vowel-point.	مَضْمُوم
To vanish.	إِضْمَحَلَّ

Weak, feeble.	ضَعِيف ج ضُعَفَاء
To mix, confuse.	ضَغَثَ يَضْغَثُ
To press, squeeze.	ضَغَطَ يَضْغَطُ ضَغْطًا
To be pressed.	أِنْضَغَطَ
Pressure. Compulsion.	ضَغْطَة
Night-mare.	ضَاغُوط
To bear malice.	ضَغِنَ يَضْغَنُ عَلَى
To bear malice or hatred against each other.	تَضَاغَنَ
Spiteful, malevolent.	ضَغِن
Hatred, malice.	ضِغْن ج أَضْغَان
Malice, spite.	ضَغِينَة ج ضَغَائِن
Side of a river.	ضِفَّة
Frog.	ضِفْدَع ج ضَفَادِع
To braid, plait.	ضَفَرَ يَضْفِرُ وَضَفَرَ
To be braided, twisted.	إِنْضَفَرَ
Braid; tress.	ضَفِيرَة ج ضَفَائِر
To be ample.	ضَفَا يَضْفُو
To err; wander from.	ضَلَّ يَضِلُّ
To lead into error.	ضَلَّ إِضْلَالًا

To be avaricious.	ضَنَّ يَضَنُّ ضَنَّا
A prized thing.	ضَنٌّ ج ضَنَائِن
Avaricious, stingy.	ضَنِين
To be larrow; feebne.	ضَنُكَ يَضْنُكُ
Distress. Narrowness.	ضَنْكٌ
To be sickly.	ضَنِيَ يَضْنَى ضَنًى
To suffer, endure.	ضَاَنَى مُضَانَاةً
To consume (disease).	أَضْنَى
To be consumed slowly.	إِنْضَنَى
Disease ; weakness.	ضَنًى
Sickly, emaciated.	مُضْنًى
To overcome.	ضَهَدَ يَضْهَدُ
To maltreat ; persecute	إِضْطَهَدَ
Presecution.	إِضْطِهَاد
Persecutor.	مُضْطَهِد
To resemble.	ضَاهَى مُضَاهَاةً
To shine ; glitter.	ضَاءَ يَضُوءُ
To illuminate.	ضَوَّأَ تَضْوِئَة
To shine.	أَضَاءَ إِضَاءَة

To dress a wound.	ضَمَدَ يَضْمِدُ وَضَمَّدَ
Dressing for a wound.	ضِمَاد
Bandage.	ضِمَادَة
To be thin, emaciated.	ضَمُرَ يَضْمُرُ
To conceal, hide.	أَضْمَرَ
To resolve.	أَضْمَرَ فِي نَفْسِهِ
To be shrivelled.	تَضَمَّرَ وَٱنْضَمَرَ
Emaciation, atrophy.	ضُمُور
Secret thought.	ضَمِير ج ضَمَائِر
Heart, Conscience. Pronoun.	
Secret; understood. (Gram).	مُضْمَر
To stand surety. To farm or rent.	ضَمِنَ يَضْمَنُ
To make one responsible for. To put in; inclose.	ضَمَّنَ
To include, comprise.	تَضَمَّنَ
Within. Inclosed.	ضِمْن
Suretyship. Responsibility.	ضَمَان
Responsible for.	ضَامِن وَضَمِين
Sense ; meaning.	مَضْمُون ج مَضَامِين
Ensured ; assured.	

Annexation.	إِضَافَةٌ	To seek light.	إِسْتَضَاءَ
Two nouns اَلْمُضَافُ وَالْمُضَافُ إِلَيْهِ		Light.	ضِيَاءٌ وَضَوْءٌ ج أَضْوَاءٌ
in the construct state (e.g.		Light-giving ; brilliant.	مُضِيءٌ
(كِتَابُ زَيْدٍ		Tumult of war.	ضَوْضَى وَضَوْضَاءُ
Host.	مُضِيفٌ	To injure.	ضَارَ يَضِيرُ ضَيْرًا
Hospitable.	مِضْيَافٌ	To suffer pain.	تَضَوَّرَ
To be narrow.	ضَاقَ يَضِيقُ ضِيقًا	To be lost ; perish.	ضَاعَ يَضِيعُ
To be inabequate.	ضَاقَ عَنْ	To lose. Destroy.	ضَيَّعَ وَأَضَاعَ
To make narrow.	ضَيَّقَ	Lost. Neglected.	ضَائِعٌ
To annoy ; oppress.	ضَايَقَ	Unmissed.	ضِيَاعًا
To feel oppressed.	تَضَايَقَ	Village.	ضَيْعَةٌ ج ضِيَعٌ وَضِيَاعٌ
Narrowness. Distress.	ضِيقٌ	To be a guest.	ضَافَ يَضِيفُ
Poverty. Misery.	ضِيقَةٌ	To treat with hospitality.	أَضَافَ
Narrow ; contracted.	ضَيِّقٌ	To join, add. To put a noun in the construct state.	أَضَافَ إِلَى
Narrower.	أَضْيَقُ	To be joined.	إِنْضَافَ إِلَى
Narrowplace.	مَضِيقٌ ج مَضَايِقُ	To seek hospitality.	إِسْتَضَافَ
To oppress.	ضَامَ يَضِيمُ ضَيْمًا	Guest.	ضَيْفٌ ج أَضْيَافٌ وَضُيُوفٌ
Wrong ; injury.	ضَيْمٌ	Entertainment.	ضِيَافَةٌ

ط

Cooked.	مَطْبُوخٌ
Tiberias.	طَبَرِيَّة
Battalion.	طَابُورٌ
Chalk.	طَبَاشِيرُ
To stamp. Print.	طَبَعَ يَطْبَعُ
To break in (a horse).	طَبَّعَ
To assume a character.	تَطَبَّعَ
To be imprinted.	إِنْطَبَعَ
Natural disposition.	طَبْعٌ ج طِبَاعٌ
Art of printing.	طِبَاعَةٌ
Nature.	طَبِيعَةٌ ج طَبَائِعُ
Natural. Naturalist.	طَبِيعِيٌّ
Physics.	عِلْمُ الطَّبِيعِيَّات
Printing-press.	مَطْبَعَةٌ ج مَطَابِعُ
Impressed, printed.	مَطْبُوعٌ

As a numeral sign = 9.	ط
To bend down.	طَاطَا
To be depressed, abased.	تَطَاطَأ
To treat the sich.	طَبَّ تَطْبِيبًا
Medical treatment.	طِبٌّ
The science of medicine.	عِلْمُ الطِّبِّ
Medical.	طِبِّيٌّ
Physician.	طَبِيبٌ ج أَطِبَّاءُ
To cook.	طَبَخَ يَطْبُخُ طَبْخًا
To be cooked.	اِنْطَبَخَ
Cooking. Food cooked.	طَبْخٌ
Cook.	طَبَّاخٌ
Art of cookery.	طَبَاخَةٌ
Cooked food.	طَبِيخٌ
Kitchen.	مَطْبَخٌ ج مَطَابِخُ

Straining.	طَحَارٌ وَطَحِيرٌ	To fit, suit.	طَابَقَ مُطَابَقَةً
Spleen.	طِحَالٌ ج طُحُلٌ	To make to agree.	طَبَّقَ وَطَابَقَ بَيْنَ
Water-moss.	طُحْلُبٌ وَطِحْلِبٌ	To cover, close, shut.	أَطْبَقَ
To rush upon.	طَحَمَ يَطْحَمُ عَلَى	To agree upon.	أَطْبَقَ عَلَى
Impetuous ; violent.	طَحُومٌ	To agree.	تَطَابَقَ
To grind (flour).	طَحَنَ يَطْحَنُ طَحْنًا	To apply to something.	إِنْطَبَقَ عَلَى
Miller.	طَحَّانٌ	Suitable, conformable to.	طِبْقٌ
Mill.	طَاحُونٌ وَطَاحُونَةٌ ج طَوَاحِينُ	Cover. Tray.	طَبَقٌ ج أَطْبَاقٌ
Grinders, (teeth).	طَوَاحِنُ	Layer ; stratum.	طَبَقَةٌ ج طَبَقَاتٌ
Flour.	طَحِينٌ	Class ; Grade. Stage.	
Dregs of sesame-oil.	طَحِينَةٌ	A hard year	سَنَةٌ مُطَبِّقَةٌ
Mill-machine.	مِطْحَنَةٌ	Conformable to.	مُطَابِقٌ
Mill.	مِطْحَنَةٌ ج مَطَاحِنُ	Agreement, accord.	مُطَابَقَةٌ
All ; every one.	طُرًّا	To beat the drum.	طَبَّلَ
To happen to.	طَرَأَ يَطْرَأُ عَلَى	Drum.	طَبْلٌ ج طُبُولٌ
To overwhelm with praise.	أَطْرَأَ	Drummer.	طَبَّالٌ
Fresh, juicy, moist.	طَرِيءٌ	Pistol.	طَبَنْجَةٌ ج طَبَنْجَاتٌ
Unexpected calamity.	طَارِئَةٌ	To fry.	طَجَنَ يَطْجُنُ طَجْنًا
Exaggerated praise.	إِطْرَاءٌ	Frying-pan.	طَاجِنٌ ج طَوَاجِنُ
		To strain in breathing.	طَحَرَ يَطْحُرُ

To follow regularly.	إِطَّرَدَ
To digress.	إِسْتَطْرَدَ آسْتِطْرَاداً
Bale of goods.	طَرْدٌ ج طُرُودٌ
Attack ; charge ; pursuit.	طِرَادٌ
Expelled, outcast.	طَرِيدٌ
Chased game.	طَرِيدَةٌ ج طَرَائِدُ
Having no exception.	مُطَّرِدٌ
To embroider.	طَرَّزَ
Form, shape, manner.	طَرْزٌ
Mode, manner.	طِرَازٌ
Embroiderer.	طَرَّازٌ ومُطَرِّزٌ
Embroidered.	مُطَرَّزٌ
To be deaf.	طَرِشَ يَطْرَشُ
To whitewash.	(طَرَشَ يَطْرُشُ)
Deafness.	طَرَشٌ
Lime for whitewashing.	(طَرْشٌ)
Whitewasher.	(طَرَّاشٌ)
Deaf.	أَطْرَشُ م طَرْشَاء ج طُرْشٌ
A high pointed cap.	طَرْطُورٌ

To be joyful.	طَرِبَ يَطْرَبُ طَرَباً
To sing, chant, trill.	طَرَّبَ
To gladden.	طَرَّبَ وأَطْرَبَ
Mirth, glee.	طَرَبٌ
One who feels merry.	طَرِبٌ
Exciting mirth or delight.	مُطْرِبٌ
Red cap, fez.	طَرْبُوشٌ ج طَرَابِيشُ
To throw. Subtract.	طَرَحَ يَطْرَحُ
Casting. Subtraction.	طَرْحٌ
Abortion, miscarriage.	طِرْحٌ
Veil worn by a female.	طَرْحَةٌ
Sheet of paper.	طَرْحِيَّةُ وَرَقٍ
Cushion to sit on.	طَرَّاحَةٌ
Cast down.	طَرِيحَةٌ ج طَرْحَى
Place.	مَطْرَحٌ ج مَطَارِحُ
Tarragon.	طَرْخُونٌ (نَبَاتٌ)
To drive awry ; chase.	طَرَدَ يَطْرُدُ
To attack, charge, assault.	طَارَدَ
To be sent away.	اِنْطَرَدَ

Cabin of a ship.	طَارِمَةٌ	To hurt the eye.	طَرَفَ يَطْرِفُ
To soften, moisten.	طَرَّى	To go to an extreme.	تَطَرَّفَ
To praise highly.	أَطْرَى إِطْرَاءً	The eye.	طَرْفٌ
Tender; fresh; juicy.	طَرِي	The eyelid.	طَرْفُ الْعَيْنِ
طَسْتٌ وَطَشْتٌ ج طُسُوتٌ وَطُشُوتٌ		Side. End part.	طَرَفٌ ج اطْرَافٌ
Basin for washing.		Limbs, extremities.	الاطْرَافُ
To graft. Vaccinate.	طَعَّمَ	Choice subjects of conversation.	أَطْرَافُ الْحَدِيثِ
To give food.	أَطْعَمَ	The lower classes.	أَطْرَافُ النَّاسِ
To be grafted, inoculated.	تَطَعَّمَ	Twinkling of an eye.	طَرْفَةٌ
To taste.	إِسْتَطْعَمَ	Tamarisk (tree).	طَرْفَاءُ
Taste; flavour.	طَعْمٌ ج طُعُومٌ	To strike, knock.	طَرَقَ يَطْرُقُ طَرْقًا
Bait thrown to fish.	طُعْمٌ	To be silent.	أَطْرَقَ
Food.	طَعَامٌ ج أَطْعِمَةٌ	To find or seek a way.	تَطَرَّقَ إِلَى
Food. Place of food.	مَطْعَمٌ ج مَطَاعِمُ	To take a way.	إِسْتَطْرَقَ
Thrust, pierce.	طَعَنَ يَطْعَنُ بِ	Calamity; evil.	طَارِقَةٌ ج طَوَارِقُ
To defame.	طَعَنَ فِي وَعَلَى	Way; road, path.	طَرِيقٌ ج طُرُقٌ
To become old.	طَعَنَ فِي السِّنِّ	Way; manner.	طَرِيقَةٌ ج طَرَائِقُ
A thrust.	طَعْنَةٌ	Hammer.	مِطْرَقَةٌ ج مَطَارِقُ
Plague.	طَاعُونٌ ج طَوَاعِينُ	Beaten (road).	مَطْرُوقٌ وَ مُسْتَطْرَقٌ

Time before sunset.	طَفَلٌ
Infant.	طِفْلٌ ج اَطْفَالٌ
Infancy. Childhood.	طُفُولِيَّةٌ
Intruder.	طُفَيْلِيٌّ
To rise high, (water).	طَفَا يَطْفُو
To float.	طَفَا فَوْقَ الْمَاءِ
Scum.	طُفَاوَةٌ
To make a sound.	طَقَّ يَطُقُّ
Weather. Religious rite.	طَقْسٌ ج طُقُوسٌ
To make a noise.	طَقْطَقَ طَقْطَقَةٌ
Suit of clothes. Set.	طَقْمٌ ج طُقُومَةٌ
To look down upon.	أَطَلَّ عَلَى
Finest rain ; dew.	طَلٌّ
Overlooking place.	مَطَلٌّ
To seek ; ask ; desire.	طَلَبَ يَطْلُبُ
To beseech ; pray.	طَلَبَ إِلَى
To demand ; claim.	طَالَبَ
To demand repeatedly.	تَطَلَّبَ
Desire. Request.	طَلَبٌ وَطِلْبَةٌ

The Turkish Imperial cypher.	طُغْرَاءٌ ج طُغْرَاءَاتٌ
A company ; order.	طُغْمَةٌ
To overflow.	طَغَا يَطْغُو
Highly wicked.	طَاغٍ ج طُغَاةٌ
Idol. Tempter.	الطَّاغُوتُ
To look down upon.	أَطَفَّ عَلَى
Small quantity.	طَفِيفٌ
To put out (fire) ; allay.	أَطْفَأَ
To be extinguished.	اِنْطَفَأَ اَنْطَفَأَ
To be full ; overflow.	طَفَحَ يَطْفَحُ
To fill to overflowing.	طَفَّحَ واَطْفَحَ
Ove flowing.	طَفْحَانُ وَطَافِحٌ
To jump, leap.	طَفَرَ يَطْفِرُ طَفْراً
A leap. Eruption.	طَفْرَةٌ
To commence to do.	طَفِقَ يَفْعَلُ
To have a child, (woman).	أَطْفَلَ
To approach setting.	أَطْفَلَتِ الشَّمْسُ
To intrude.	تَطَفَّلَ

To inform.	أَطْلَعَ عَلَى	Seeker.	طَالِبٌ ج طُلَّابٌ وَطَلَبَةٌ
To look at, or for.	تَطَلَّعَ إِلَى	A student.	طَالِبُ عِلْمٍ
To know, see.	إِطَّلَعَ عَلَى	Demand ; desire.	مَطْلَبٌ ج مَطَالِبُ
To examine.	إِسْتَطْلَعَ	Claim. Object	مَطْلُوبٌ ج مَطَالِيبُ
Spadix, spathe.	طَلْعٌ	sought or desired.	
Face. Aspect.	طَلْعَةٌ	To be wicked.	طَلَحَ يَطْلَحُ طَلَاحًا
Star (of fortune).	طَالِعٌ ج طَوَالِعُ	A kind of thorny acacia.	طَلْحٌ
Rising ; appearance.	طُلُوعٌ	Wicked.	طَالِحٌ ج طُلَّحٌ وَطَالِحُونَ
Vanguard.	طَلِيعَةٌ ج طَلَائِعُ	Wickedness.	طَلَاحٌ
First line of a poem.	مَطْلَعٌ	Sheet of paper.	طَلْحِيَةٌ ج طَلَاحِيٌّ
To be freed.	طَلَقَ يَطْلُقُ	To blot. Obliterate.	طَلَسَ يَطْلِسُ
To have a cheerful face.	طَلُقَ يَطْلُقُ	Satin. Atlas.	أَطْلَسُ
To divorce (his wife).	طَلَّقَ	A particular	طَيْلَسَانٌ ج طَيَالِسَةٌ
To free, liberate.	أَطْلَقَ	robe worn by learned men.	
To generalize.	أَطْلَقَ ٱلْقَوْلَ	To write a talisman.	طَلْسَمَ
To permit him.	أَطْلَقَ لَهُ	Talisman.	طَلْسَمٌ ج طَلَاسِيمُ
To be applied ; apply.	أُطْلِقَ	To rise, (sun). Sprout.	طَلَعَ يَطْلُعُ
To go, depart.	إِنْطَلَقَ	To ascend.	طَلَعَ وَطَلِعَ يَطْلَعُ
Pains of childbirth.	طَلْقٌ	To study ; read.	طَالَعَ مُطَالَعَةً
		To appear. Sprout.	أَطْلَعَ

Accumulated.	مُطَهَّرٌ	Liberal.	طَلْقُ ٱلْيَدَيْنِ
To efface.	طَمَسَ يَطْمُسُ وَطَمَّسَ	Cheerful.	طَلْقُ ٱلْوَجْهِ
To be effaced.	تَطَمَّسَ وَٱنْطَمَسَ	Eloquent.	طَلْقُ ٱللِّسَانِ
Obliterated.	طَمِيسٌ وَمَطْمُوسٌ	Divorce.	طَلَاقٌ
To covet, hope.	طَمِعَ يَطْمَعُ فِي وَب	Divorced (woman).	طَالِقٌ وَطَالِقَةٌ
Covetousness ; avidity.	طَمَعٌ	Absolutely.	عَلَى ٱلْإِطْلَافِ وَمُطْلَقًا
A coveted object.	طَمَعٌ ج أَطْمَاعٌ	Free. Absolute.	مُطْلَقٌ
Covetous.	طَامِعٌ وَطَمِعٌ وَطَمَّاعٌ	Loaf of bread.	طُلْمَةٌ ج طُلَمٌ
Thing coveted.	مَطْمَعٌ ج مَطَامِعُ	Beauty ; grace.	طَلَاوَةٌ
To tranquillize ; reassure.	طَمَّنَ	To anoint ; cover with.	طَلَى يَطْلِي
To be low, (land). To be free from disquietude.	إِطْمَأَنَّ	Ointment ; tar ; plaster.	طِلَاءٌ
To abide, dwell.	إِطْمَأَنَّ بِٱلْمَوْضِعِ	Smeared, covered.	مَطْلِيٌّ
To trust implicitly.	إِطْمَأَنَّ إِلَى	Calamity.	طَامَّةٌ
Tranquility.	طُمَأْنِينَةٌ وَٱطْمِئْنَانٌ	To cover up.	طَمَّ يَطُمُّ طَمًّا
Tranquil ; composed.	مُطْمَئِنٌّ	To be filled, covered up.	إِنْطَمَّ
To rise high, (water).	طَمَا يَطْمُو	Menstruation ; menses.	طَمْثٌ
High (water, sea).	طَامٍ	To gaze at.	طَمَحَ يَطْمَحُ إِلَى
To buzz ; ring.	طَنَّ يَطِنُّ طَنِينًا	Aspring. Proud.	طَامِحٌ وَطَمُوحٌ
Humming ; ringing.	طَنِينٌ	To bury, conceal.	طَمَرَ يَطْمُرُ

Brick, canon.	طوبٌ	Sonorous. Wide-spread.	طَنَّانٌ
Gunner ; artillery-man.	طُوبْجِيٌّ	To be eloquent ; exert one's self in.	أَطْنَبَ في
Blessedness.	طُوبَى	Tent-rope.	طُنُبٌ ج أَطْنَابٌ
To perish.	طَاحَ يَطُوحُ	Superfluity, prolixity.	إِطْنَابٌ
To mislead.	طَوَّحَ وَأَطَاحَ	An immoderate praiser.	مُطْنِبٌ
To wander ; perish.	تَطَوَّحَ	Made fast with ropes.	مُطَنَّبٌ
Adversities.	طَوَائِحُ وَمَطَاوِحُ	Tambour.	طُنْبُورٌ ج طَنَابِيرُ
High mountain.	طَوْدٌ ج أَطْوَادٌ	A cooking pan.	طَنْجَرَةٌ ج طَنَاجِرُ
Lofty ; rising high.	مُنْطَادٌ	To hum, ring.	طَنَّنَ طَنْطَنَةً
Time after time.	طَوْراً بَعْدَ طَوْرٍ	Peak.	طَنَفٌ ج أَطْنَافٌ
State, manner.	طَوْرٌ ج أَطْوَارٌ	A carpet.	طِنْفِسَةٌ ج طَنَافِسُ
Mountain.	طَوْرٌ	To be clean, pure.	طَهَرَ يَطْهُرُ
Mount Sinai.	ٱلطُّورُ	To cleanse. Circumcise.	طَهَّرَ
Drinking-cup.	طَاسٌ ج طَاسَاتٌ	To be cleansed, purified.	تَطَهَّرَ
Peacock.	طَاوُوسٌ ج طَوَاوِيسُ	Purity. Holiness.	طَهَارَةٌ
Frivolity.	طَوْشٌ	Pure. Holy.	طَاهِرٌ ج أَطْهَارٌ
Eunuch; gelding.	طَوَاشٍ ج طَوَاشِيَةٌ	Purgatory.	مُطَهَّرٌ
To obey.	طَاعَ يَطُوعُ وَأَطَاعَ	Purified.	مُطَهَّرٌ
To consent; follow.	طَاوَعَ مُطَاوَعَةً	A cook.	طَاهٍ ج طُهَاةٌ

To put a collar on.	طَوَّقَ	To volunteer.	تَطَوَّعَ
Window.	طَاقٌ ج طَاقَاتٌ	To be able.	إِسْتَطَاعَ
Collar.	طَوْقٌ ج أَطْوَاقٌ	Obedient.	طَوْعٌ وَطَائِعٌ
Ability. Window.	طَاقَةٌ	Voluntarily ; willingly.	طَوْعاً
Ability ; power.	إِطَاقَةٌ	Obedience ; submission.	طَاعَةٌ
To be long.	طَالَ يَطُولُ طُولاً	More submissive.	طَوْعٌ
To lengthen.	طَوَّلَ وَأَطَالَ	Ability ; power.	إِسْتَطَاعَةٌ
Defer, put off.	طَاوَلَ فِي	Voluntary action.	تَطَوُّعٌ
To wrong.	تَطَاوَل عَلَى	Obeyed. Accepted.	مُطَاعٌ
To be long, extend.	إِسْتَطَالَ	To go around. طَافَ يَطُوفُ حَوْلَ وَفِي
During a long time.	طَالَمَا	To travel. Circumambulate.
Length. Duration.	طُولٌ	To lead around.	طَوَّفَ
Longitude.	خُطُوطُ ٱلطُّولِ	To surround.	أَطَافَ بِ
Advantage ; benefit.	طَائِلٌ	Night-police. Raft.	طَوْفٌ
Table.	طَاوِلَةٌ	Flood ; deluge.	طُوفَانٌ
Long. Tall.	طَوِيلٌ ج طِوَالٌ	Party, sect.	طَائِفَةٌ ج طَوَائِفُ
Competent.	طَوِيلُ ٱلْبَاعِ	Circumambulation.	طَوَافٌ
Longer.	أَطْوَلُ	A Mecca guide.	مُطَوِّفٌ
Lengthening.	تَطْوِيلٌ	To be able.	حَقَّ يَطُوقُ وَمَا أَطَاقَ

Blessedness.	طُوبَى	Parallelogram.	مُسْتَطِيلٌ
To fly, (bird).	طَارَ يَطِيرُ طَيَرَاناً	To fold, fold up.	طَوَى يَطْوِي طَيًّا
To hasten to...	طَارَ الَى	To suffer hunger.	طَوِيَ يَطْوَى
To make to fly.	طَيَّرَ أَوْ أَطَارَ	To be folded up.	إِنْطَوَى
To draw a bad omen.	تَطَيَّرَ	Folding. Traversing.	طَيٌّ
To be dispersed.	تَطَايَرَ تَطَايُراً	Within it.	فِي طَيِّهِ
Evil augury or omen.	طَيَّرَ	Hunger.	طَوًى
Flight (of birds, &c.)	طَيَرَانٌ	Folded up.	مَطْوِيٌّ
Bird.	طَائِرٌ ج طَيْرٌ وَطُيُورٌ	To be good.	طَابَ يَطِيبُ طِيبًا
Paper-kite.	طَيَّارَاتٌ	To be cheerful.	طَابَتْ نَفْسُهُ
Spreading.	مُسْتَطِيرٌ	To perfume.	طَيَّبَ
To be light-headed.	طَاشَ يَطِيشُ	To be perfumed.	تَطَيَّبَ
To miss, (an arrow).	طَاشَ عَنْ	To find good.	إِسْتَطَابَ وَ اسْتَطْيَبَ
Frivolity.	طَيْشٌ وَطَيَشَانٌ	Perfume.	طِيبٌ ج أَطْيَابٌ
Light, fickle, frivolous.	طَائِشٌ	Ball used in play.	(طَابَةٌ)
Apparition ; spectre.	طَيْفٌ	Good. In good health	طَيِّبٌ
To plaster with clay.	طَيَّنَ	Cheerful, happy.	طَيِّبُ النَّفْسِ
Clay ; mortar.	طِينٌ ج أَطْيَانٌ	A good thing.	طَيِّبَةٌ ج طَيِّبَاتٌ
A lump of clay.	طِينَةٌ	A tax on houses, &c.	(طَابُو)
Plasterer.	طَيَّانٌ	How good it is !	مَا أَطْيَبَهُ

ظ

Success ; victory.	ظَفَرٌ
Victorious ; conqueror.	مُظَفَّرٌ
To continue.	ظَلَّ يَظِلُ
To continue to act.	ظَلَّ يَفْعَلُ
To cover ; shade.	ظَلَّلَ وَأَظَلَّ
To be in the shade of.	تَظَلَّلَ بِ
To seek the shade.	إِسْتَظَلَّ بِ
Shade ; protection.	ظِلٌّ ج أَظْلَالٌ
Cover. Cloud.	ظُلَّةٌ ج ظِلَالٌ
Cloud.	ظَلَالٌ وَظِلَالٌ وظِلَالَةٌ .
Giving shade,	ظَلِيلٌ وَمُظِلٌّ
Shady. Cloudy.	مُظِلٌّ وَمُظَلَّلٌ
Tent. Umbrella.	مَظَلَّةٌ ج مَظَالُّ
Hoof.	ظِلْفٌ ج ظُلُوفٌ وأَظْلَافٌ
To wrong ; oppress.	ظَلَمَ يَظْلِمُ

As a numeral sign=900.	ط
Gazelle.	ظَبْيٌ م ظَبْيَةٌ ج ظِبَاءٌ
To adorn, embellish.	ظَرَّفَ
To deem beautiful.	إِسْتَظْرَفَ
Vessel, receptacle.	ظَرْفٌ ج ظُرُوفٌ
Adverbial noun of time or place.	
Beautiful. Witty.	ظَرِيفٌ ج ظُرَفَاءُ
To travel.	ظَعَنَ يَظْعَنُ ظَعْنًا
Camel.	ظَعُونٌ ج ظُعْنٌ
Litter for woman.	ظَعِينَةٌ ج أَظْعَانٌ
To scratch with the nail.	ظَفَرَ يَظْفِرُ
To obtain. Overcome.	ظَفِرَ بِ وَعَلَى
To give victory.	ظَفَّرَ وَأَظْفَرَ
Nail ; claw ; hoof.	ظُفْرٌ ج أَظْفَارٌ
Pterygium.	ظَفَرٌ وَظَفَرَةٌ

Suspicion.	ظَنَّةٌ ج ظِنَنٌ	To be dark.	ظَلِمَ يَظْلَمُ وَأَظْلَمَ
Presumption.	مَظِنَّةٌ	To accuse of injustice.	ظَلَّمَ
Supposed.	مَظْنُونٌ	To accuse of injustice.	تَظَلَّمَ مِنْ
Probable propositions.	مَظْنُونَاتٌ	To suffer injustice.	انْظَلَمَ
To appear.	ظَهَرَ يَظْهَرُ ظُهُورًا	Injustice ; oppression.	ظُلْمٌ
To overcome, subdue.	ظَهَرَ عَلَى	Darkness.	ظُلْمَةٌ ج ظُلُمَاتٌ
To aid, assist.	ظَاهَرَ مُظَاهَرَةً	Atlantic Ocean.	بَحْرُ الظُّلُمَاتِ
To show, manifest.	أَظْهَرَ	Tyrant.	ظَالِمٌ ج ظَالِمُونَ وَظَلَمَةٌ
To show forth.	تَظَاهَرَ بِ	Darkness.	ظَلَامٌ وَظَلْمَاءُ
To seek help or aid.	إِسْتَظْهَرَ بِ	Great tyrant.	ظَلَّامٌ وَظَلُومٌ
To overcome.	إِسْتَظْهَرَ عَلَى	Wrong ; injustice.	مَظْلَمَةٌ ج مَظَالِمُ
Back.	ظَهْرٌ ج ظُهُورٌ	Wronged.	مَظْلُومٌ وَظَلِيمٌ
From memory.	عَنْ ظَهْرِ الْقَلْبِ	Dark ; obscure.	ظَالِمٌ
Mid-day ; noon.	ظُهْرٌ ج أَظْهَارٌ	To be thirsty.	ظَمِئَ يَظْمَأُ
Clear ; evident. External.	ظَاهِرٌ	Thirst. Longing.	ظَمَأٌ ج أَظْمَاءٌ
Apparently.	فِي الظَّاهِرِ	Thirsty ; desirous.	ظَمِئٌ وَظَمْآنُ
Phenomenon.	ظَاهِرَةٌ ج ظَوَاهِرُ	To suppose.	ظَنَّ يَظُنُّ ظَنًّا
Appearance.	ظُهُورٌ	To suspect.	ظَنَّ وَاظَّنَّ وَأَظَنَّ بِ
Mid-day ; hour of noon.	ظَهِيرَةٌ	Supposition	ظَنٌّ ج ظُنُونٌ
Disclosure, manifestation.	إِظْهَارٌ		

ع

Religious worship.	عِبَادَة
Slavery, servitude.	عُبُودِيَّة
Self-consecration to God.	تَعَبُّد
Place of worship.	مَعْبَد ج مَعَابِد
Object of worship.	مَعْبُود
To pass; pass away.	عَبَرَ يَعْبُر
To cause to pass over.	عَبَّرَ
To explain.	عَبَّرَ عَنْ
To consider.	إِعْتَبَرَ
To take warning from.	اِعْتَبَرَ بِ
On the other side.	عَبْرَ
Tear; sobbing.	عَبْرَة ج عَبَرَات
Admonition.	عِبْرَة ج عِبَر
Hebrew.	عِبْرِيّ وَعِبْرَانِيّ
A wayfarer.	عَابِر سَبِيل

As a numeral sign = 70.	ع
Covering of bosom.	عُبّ ج عِبَاب
Torrent, billows.	عُبَاب
To care for.	عَبَأَ يَعْبَا عَبْأ
Woollen cloak.	عَبَاء وَعَبَاءَة ج أَعْبِئَة
To play.	عَبِثَ يَعْبَث عَبَثًا
Play, sport. Useless.	عَبَث
To no purpose, in vain.	عَبَثًا
To worship, adore.	عَبَدَ يَعْبُد
To take one as a slave.	تَعَبَّد
To devote one's self to ...	تَعَبَّد لِ
To enslave.	إِسْتَعْبَد
Servant, slave.	عَبْد ج عَبِيد
Mankind.	أَلْعِبَاد
Worshipper.	عَابِد ج عَبَدَة وَعُبَّاد

Fine, excellent.	عَبْقَرِيٌّ
To pack (goods).	عِبَأَ يَعْبُوْ وَعَبَّى
To be filled ; arranged.	تَعَبَّى
To importune ; rebuke.	عَتَّ يَعُتُّ
To blame, censure.	عَتَبَ يَعْتِبُ عَلَى
To blame, censure.	عَاتَبَ مُعَاتَبَةً
Threshold.	عَتَبَةٌ ج عَتَبَاتٌ
Blame.	عِتَابٌ وَمَعْتَبَةٌ ج مَعَاتِبُ
To be ready.	عَتَدَ يَعْتِدُ عَتَادًا
About to happen ; ready.	عَتِيدٌ
To become old.	عَتِقَ يَعْتِقُ عَتْقًا
To set free.	عَتَقَ يَعْتِقُ
To make old, let grow old.	عَتَّقَ
To set free, emancipate.	أَعْتَقَ
Antiquity, oldness.	عِتْقٌ
Emancipation.	عَتْقٌ وَعَتَاقٌ
Shoulder.	عَاتِقٌ ج عَوَاتِقٌ
Old. Emancipated.	عَتِيقٌ ج عِتَاقٌ
Kept long, made old.	مُعَتَّقٌ

Expression. Style, diction.	عِبَارَةٌ
This means.	هٰذَا عِبَارَةٌ عَنْ
Act of passing over.	عُبُورٌ
Perfume.	عَبِيرٌ
Consideration, regard.	إِعْتِبَارٌ
Explanation.	تَعْبِيرٌ
Ferry, passage.	مَعْبَرٌ ج مَعَابِرُ
Esteemed ; important.	مُعْتَبَرٌ
To frown.	عَبَسَ يَعْبِسُ
Austere, stern.	عَابِسٌ وَعَبُوسٌ
Very stern. Lion.	عَبَّاسٌ
Frowning, sternness.	عُبُوسٌ
To injure.	عَبَطَ يَعْبِطُ عَبْطًا
To carry off in the flower of one's age, (death).	أَعْبَطَ وَأَعْتَبَطَ
A pure lie.	عَبْطٌ
An act without reason.	إِعْتِبَاطٌ
To be diffused, (perfume).	عَبِقَ –
Sense of suffocation.	عَبْقَةٌ

Acting corruptly. عاثٍ ج عثاةٌ	Freed, emancipated. مَعْتُوقْ
To cry out. عَجَّ يَعِجُّ عَجًّا وَعَجِيجًا	Shoulder-pole. عَتَلَةْ
To raise the dust, (wind). عَجَّ	Porter. عَتَّالْ ج عَتَّالَةْ
Outcry, clamour. عَجَّ وَعَجِيجْ	Porterage. عِتَالَةْ
Omelet. (عِجَّةْ)	To become dark. عَتِم يَعْتِم وَعَتِم
Dust, smoke. عَجَاجْ وَعَجَاجَةْ	Darkness of night. عَتِم وَعَتَمَةْ
عَجِبَ يَعْجَب عَجَبًا مِنْ وَل وَتَعَجَّبْ	Obscure, dark. مُعْتِم وَمُعْتِم
To wonder at. وَٱسْتَعْجَب مِنْ	To be idiotic. عَتَهَ عَتَاهَة
To cause to wonder. عَجَّبْ وَأَعْجَبْ	Idiocy, stupidity. أَعْتَهْ وَعَتَاهَة
To please. أَعْجَب	Idiot ; mad. مَعْتُوهْ
To be vain, conceited. اعْجَب بِنَفْسِهِ	To be proud, rebel. عَتَا يَعْتُو عُتُوًّا
Pride, vanity, self-conceit. عُجْب	Proud rebellious. عَاتٍ ج عُتَاةْ
Astonishment. عَجَب	Moth-worm. عَتَّةْ ج عَتّ
Very wonderful. عَجَب وَعُجَاب	To stumble, trip. عَثَر يَعْثُر عَثْرًا
O wonderful يَا لِلْعَجَب	To stumble upon. عَثَر يَعْثُر عَلَى
Wonderful, extraordinary. عَجِيب	To cause to stumble. عَثَّر وَأَعْثَر
عَجِيبَة ج عَجَائِب وَأَعْجُوبَة ج أَعَاجِيب	A false step. عَثْرَة ج عَثَرَاتْ
Wonderful thing, marvel.	Young bastard. Serpent. عُثْمَان
More wonderful. أَعْجَب	To do evil, mischief. عَثَا يَعْثُو عُثُوًّا

Cart ; wheel.	عجلة ج عجل
Hasty, quick.	عجول
More hasty, expeditious.	أعجل
Hastened, accelerated.	معجّل
Foreigners. *sp.* Persians.	عجم
Persia.	أعجم وبلاد العجم
Foreign origin of a word.	عجمة
Foreigner.	أعجميّ ج أعجام
Marked with vowel-points (letters). Obscure.	معجم
To knead (dough).	عجن يعجن عجنا
The perinæum.	عجان
Kneaded ; dough.	عجين
Kneading-trough.	معجن ج معاجن
Pastry.	معجّنات
Electuary.	معجون ج معاجن
Pressed dates.	عجوة
To number ; regard.	عدّ يعدّ
To prepare, make ready.	أعدّ
To be multiplied.	تعدّد

Wonder, astonishment.	تعجّب
Vain, self-conceited.	معجب بنفسه
Knot, knob.	عجرة ج عجر
A kind of melon.	عجور
To act haughtily.	تعجرف على
Coarseness, rudeness.	عجرفة
To lack strength.	عجز يعجز عجزا
To render unable.	عجّز واعجز
Weakness, impotence. Second hemistich of a verse.	عجز
The posterior part.	عجز ج أعجاز
Feeble.	عاجز ج عواجز
Old woman.	عجوز ج عجائز
Miracle.	معجزة ج معجزات
To be lean.	عجف يعجف عجفا
Very lean.	عجف م عجفاء ج عجاف
To hasten.	عجل يعجل واستعجل
To press one on.	عجّل واستعجل
Haste.	عجل وعجلة واستعجال
Calf.	عجل ج عجول

To be valued at.	تَعَدَّل	Of no account.	لا يُعتَدُّ بهِ
To be equal, (two things).	تَعَادَل	To be ready, prepare.	اِسْتَعَدَّ
To turn aside from.	إِنْعَدَل عَن	Number.	عَدَدٌ ج أَعْدَادٌ
To become right.	إِعْتَدَل	Implements.	عُدَّةٌ ج عُدَدٌ
Equity, justice.	عَدْلٌ	Numerous.	عَدِيدٌ
Just, equable.	عَادِلٌ ج عُدُولٌ	Preparation.	إِسْتِعْدَادٌ
Justice, equity.	عَدَالَةٌ	Enumeration.	تَعَدَادٌ
Like, equal.	عَدِيلٌ وَعِدْلٌ	Reday, prepared.	مَعَدٌّ
Bag, sack.	عَدِيلَةٌ	Important.	مُعْتَدٌّ به
Equality, equity. Moderation. Equinox.	إِعْتِدَالٌ	Numbered, counted.	مَعْدُودٌ
Equinoctial.	إِعْتِدَالِيٌّ	Reday, prepared.	مُسْتَعِدٌّ
Equal, like.	مُعَادِل	Lentils.	عَدَسٌ
Equation. Equilibrium.	مُعَادَلَةٌ	Lens. A small pustule.	عَدَسَةٌ
Average.	مُعَدَّلٌ	Lenticular.	عَدَسِيٌّ
Temperate, moderate.	مُعْتَدِلٌ	To act justly.	عَدَلَ يَعْدِلُ عَدْلاً
To lack, want.	عَدِمَ يَعْدَمُ عَدَمًا	To deviate.	عَدَلَ عُدُولاً عَن
To deprive of ; annihilate.	أَعْدَمَ	To act with equity.	عَدَلَ بَيْن
To cease to exist.	إِنْعَدَم	To make just, equal.	عَدَّلَ
Non-existence.	عَدَمٌ	To be equal to.	عَادَلَ مُعَادَلَة

Hostility, enmity.	عَدَاوَةٌ
Enemy.	عَدُوٌّ ج أَعْدَاءٌ وأَعَادٍ وعُدىً
Injustice.	إِعْتِدَاءٌ وَتَعَدٍّ
Infectious, contagious.	مُعْدٍ
Unjust.	مُتَعَدٍّ ومُعْتَدٍ عَلَى
Transitive (verb).	مُتَعَدٍّ
To be sweet.	عَذُبَ يَعْذُبُ عُذُوبَةً
To punish, torment.	عَذَّبَ
To be punished ; suffer.	تَعَذَّبَ
Sweet, (water).	عَذْبٌ
Punishment ; torment.	عَذَابٌ
Sweetness, agreableness.	عُذُوبَةٌ
To excuse.	عَذَرَ يَعْذِرُ
To apologize.	تَعَذَّرَ وَأْعْتَذَرَ
To be impossible.	تَعَذَّرَ عَلَى
To ask to be excused.	إِسْتَعْذَرَ
Excuse, apology.	عُذْرٌ ج أَعْذَارٌ
Virgin.	عَذْرَاءُ ج عَذَارَى
The sign Virgo.	العَذْرَاءُ

Lacking.	عَدِيمٌ ج عُدَمَاءُ
Non-existent.	مَعْدُومٌ
To manure land.	عَدَنَ وَعَدَّنَ
Eden. Abode.	عَدْنٌ
Paradise.	جَنَّاتُ عَدْنٍ
Mine. Metal, mineral. Origin, source.	مَعْدِنٌ ج مَعَادِنُ
Mineral, metallic.	مَعْدِنِيٌّ
To run.	عَدَا يَعْدُو عَدْواً
To pass beyond it.	عَدَاهُ
To cause to go beyond.	عَدَّى
To treat with enmity.	عَادَى
To infect (disease).	أَعْدَى
To pass the limit ; transgress. Be transitive (verb).	تَعَدَّى
To be hostile toward.	إِعْتَدَى عَلَى
Except.	عَدَا وَمَا عَدَا
Hostile party.	عُدًى (قَوْمٌ)
Infection or contagion.	عَدْوَى
Gross injustice.	عُدْوَانٌ

Coachman.	عَرَبَجِيٌّ
Syntax ; parsing.	إِعْرَابٌ
Bedouin.	أَعْرَابِيٌّ ج أَعْرَابٌ
Declinable, capable of receiving all the vowel-points.	مُعْرَبٌ
Arabicized.	مُعَرَّبٌ
To embroil, trouble.	عَرْبَسَ
To give a pledge.	عَرْبَنَ
Pledge.	عُرْبُونٌ ج عَرَابِينُ
To ascend, mount.	عَرَجَ يَعْرُجُ فِي
To be taken up.	عُرِجَ بِهِ
To limp, be lame.	عَرِجَ عَرَجًا
To halt, stop at.	عَرَّجَ وَتَعَرَّجَ عَلَى
To incline, decline.	إِنْعَرَجَ
Lameness.	عَرَجٌ وَعَرَجَانٌ
Lame.	أَعْرَجُ م عَرْجَاءُ ج عُرْجٌ
Sloping, Bend.	مُنْعَرَجٌ
Booth.	عِرْزَالٌ ج عَرَازِيلُ
Husband, wife.	عِرْسٌ ج أَعْرَاسٌ

Halter. Cheek.	عِذَارٌ ج عُذُرٌ
To throw off restraint.	خَلَعَ الْعِذَارَ
Excuse pretext.	إِعْتِذَارٌ
Difficulty, impossibility.	تَعَذُّرٌ
Excuse.	مَعْذِرَةٌ ج مَعَاذِرُ
Excused, excuseable.	مَعْذُورٌ
To blame.	عَذَلَ يَعْذُلُ عَذْلاً
To blame one's self.	إِعْتَذَلَ وَتَعَذَّلَ
Censure, blame.	عَذْلٌ وَعَذَلٌ
One who blames.	عَاذِلٌ ج عُذَّالٌ
Salubrious, (land).	عَذِيَةٌ (أَرْضٌ)
To arabicize a foreign word.	عَرَّبَ
To speak clearly.	أَعْرَبَ
To become an Arab.	تَعَرَّبَ وَاسْتَعْرَبَ
The Arabs.	أَلْعَرَبُ وَعِرْبَانٌ
The pure Arabs.	أَلْعَرَبُ الْعَرْبَاءُ
Carriage, coach.	عَرَبَةٌ وَعَرَبَانَةٌ
Arabic ; An Arabian.	عَرَبِيٌّ
The Arabic language.	أَلْعَرَبِيَّةُ

Breadth, width.	عَرْضٌ ج عُرُوضٌ	Wedding.	عِرْسٌ ج أَعْرَاسٌ
Latitude.	خُطُوطُ الْعَرْضِ	Weasel.	إِبْنُ عِرْسٍ
Day of Judgment.	يَوْمُ الْعَرْضِ	Bridegroom.	عَرِيسٌ ج عُرْسٌ
Petition.	عَرْضُحَالٍ ج عَرْضُحَالَاتٍ	Bride.	عَرُوسٌ ج عَرَائِسُ
Honour.	عِرْضٌ ج أَعْرَاضٌ	Throne. Booth.	عَرْشٌ ج عُرُوشٌ
Accident.	عَرَضٌ ج اعْرَاضٌ	Grape-vine.	عَرِيشٌ ج عَرَائِشُ
By chance, accidentally.	عَرَضًا	Court of a house.	عَرْصَةٌ ج أَعْرَاصٌ
Accidental.	عَرْضِيٌّ	To happen.	عَرَضَ يَعْرِضُ
Cross-beam.	عَارِضَةٌ ج عَوَارِضُ	To offer.	عَرَضَ عَلَى
Science of prosody.	عِلْمُ الْعَرُوضِ	To be wide, broad.	عَرُضَ يَعْرُضُ
Broad.	عَرِيضٌ ج عِرَاضٌ	To make broad.	عَرَّضَ
Opposition, objection.	إِعْتِرَاضٌ	To expose to.	عَرَّضَ لِ
Exposition.	مَعْرِضٌ	To oppose ; contradict.	عَارَضَ
Opposition, contradiction.	مُعَارَضَةٌ	To turn away from.	أَعْرَضَ عَنْ
Offered, presented.	مَعْرُوضٌ	To be exposed.	تَعَرَّضَ وَآعْتَرَضَ
Transverse; obstructing.	مُعْتَرِضٌ	To interfere in.	تَعَرَّضَ لِ
Parenthetic clause.	جُمْلَةٌ مُعْتَرِضَةٌ	To review an army.	إِعْتَرَضَ الْجُنْدَ
Juniper-tree.	عَرْعَرٌ	To be in the way of.	إِعْتَرَضَ دُونَ
To know.	عَرَفَ يَعْرِفُ	To oppose, object to.	اعْتَرَضَ عَلَى

To make known. Define.	عَرَّفَ	To sweat.	عَرِقَ يَعْرَقٍ عَرَقًا
To be known.	تَعَرَّفَ	To cause to sweat.	عَرَّقَ
To acknowledge.	إِعْتَرَفَ ب	Extend its roots, (tree).	أَعْرَقَ
Odour, (sp. fragrant).	عَرْفٌ	Sweat. Distilled spirits.	عَرَقٌ
Comb of a cock.	عرفٌ	Root. Vein.	عِرْقٌ ج عُرُوقٌ
Cock's-comb, (plant).	عرفُ الدّيكِ	Sweating, perspiring.	عَرْقَانُ
Common usage.	عُرْفِيٌّ	Irak.	بِلادُ الْعِرَاقِ
Mount Arafât.	عَرَفَاتٌ	Rooted. Noble.	عَرِيقٌ
Knowing. Skilled.	عَارِفٌ	Diaphoretic.	مُعَرِّقٌ
The diviner's art.	عِرَافَةٌ	To hamstring (a beast).	عَرْقَبَ
Diviner, astrologer.	عَرَّافٌ	Hamstring.	عُرْقُوبٌ ج عَرَاقِيبُ
Overseer.	عَرِيفٌ ج عُرَفَاءُ	To confuse, complicate.	عَرْقَلَ
Confession.	إِعْتِرَافٌ	To be dangled, confused.	تَعَرْقَلَ
Tariff. Defining.	تَعْرِيفٌ ج تَعْرِيفَاتٌ	Difficulties.	عَرَاقِيل
The definite article.	حرفُ التّعْرِيفِ	To rub.	عَرَكَ يَعْرُكُ عَرْكًا
Knowledge.	مَعْرِفَةٌ ج مَعَارِفُ	To fight.	عَارَكَ مُعَارَكَةً وَعِرَاكًا
Determinate, noun.		Nature.	عَرِيكَةٌ ج عَرَائِكُ
Determinate, definite.	مُعَرَّفٌ	Gentle, tractable.	لَيّنُ الْعَرِيكَةِ
Known. Kindness.	مَعْرُوفٌ	Battle.	مَعْرَكَةٌ ج مَعَارِكُ

To become powerful. تَعَزَّزَ	A heap. عُرْمَةٌ ج عُرَمٌ
To overcome. إِعْتَزَّ وَٱسْتَعَزَّ عَلَى	Numerous, (army). عَرَمْرَمٌ
Might. Honour. عِزٌّ وَعِزَّةٌ	Covert, lair. عَرِين وَعَرِينةٌ
Self-respect. عِزَّةُ النَّفْسِ	To be fall. عَرَا ــ وَٱعْتَرَى
Mighty ; noble ; dear. عَزِيزٌ ج أَعِزَّاءُ	Loop, button-loop. عُرْوَةٌ ج عُرًى
The mighty God. أَلْعَزِيزُ	The firmest support. العُرْوَةُ الوُثْقَى
Governor of Egypt. عَزِيزُ مِصْرَ	Overtaken (by). مُعْتَرًى
Dear, or dearer. أَعَزُّ	To be naked ; free from. عَرِي يَعْرَى
Celibacy. عُزْبَةٌ وَعُزُوبَةٌ	To strip, denude. عَرَّى وَأَعْرَى
To be celibate. عَزَبَ يَعْزُب	To be stripped. تَعَرَّى
Unmarried. أَعْزَب وَمَعْزَبَاءُ ج عُزْب	Nakedness. عُرْيٌ وَعُرْيَةٌ
To punish ; reprove. عَزَّرَ	Naked ; free from. عَارٍ ج عُرَاة
Punishment. تَعْزِيرٌ	Naked. عُرْيَانٌ ج عُرْيَانُونَ
The angel of death. عِزْرَائِيل	Naked, denuded. مُعَرًّى
To play upon عَزَفَ يَعْزِف	To be mighty, noble. عَزَّ يَعِزُّ
a musical instrument.	To be distressing to. عَزَّ عَلَيْهِ
To furrow (the عَزَقَ يَعْزِق عَزْقًا	God, exalted and أَللهُ عَزَّ وَجَلَّ
earth).	magnified (be His name!).
A hoe. مِعْزَقٌ وَمِعْزَقَةٌ ج مَعَازِقُ	To render powerful. عَزَّزَ
To set aside ; depose. عَزَلَ يَعْزِل	To love. أَعَزَّ

Consoled, comforted.	مُعَزًّى	To clean out.	عَزَّلَ
To ascribe, attribute.	عَزَى يَعْزُو	To separate one's self.	إِعْتَزَلَ
To patrol.	عَسَّ يَعُسُّ وَآعْتَسَّ	Removal (of an officer).	عَزْلٌ
Night-patrol.	عَسٌّ وَعَسَسٌ	Retirement. seclusion.	عُزْلَةٌ
Male-bee. Chief.	يَعْسُوبٌ	Retirement.	إِعْتِزَالٌ وَآنْعِزَالٌ
Bax-thorn.	عَوْسَجٌ	Place of seclusion.	مَعْزِلٌ
Gold. Gem.	عَسْجَدٌ	Away, aloof from.	بِمَعْزِلٍ عَنْ
To be difficult for.	عَسُرَ يَعْسُرُ عُسْرًا عَلَى	Seceder.	مُعْتَزِلٌ
To make difficult.	عَسَّرَ	Removed, separated.	مَعْزُولٌ
To treat harshly.	عَاسَرَ	To resolve to do.	عَزَمَ يَعْزِمُ عَلَى
To become poor.	أَعْسَرَ	To invite. Recite charms.	عَزَّمَ
To become difficult.	تَعَسَّرَ	Resolution, firm purpose.	عَزْمٌ
To find difficult.	إِسْتَعْسَرَ	Firm, resolute.	عَازِمٌ ج عَزَمَةٌ
Difficulty.	عُسْرٌ وَعُسْرَى وَمَعْسُرَةٌ	Magician, charmer.	عَزَّامٌ وَمُعَزِّمٌ
Difficult, hard.	عَسِرٌ وَعَسِيرٌ	Determined, resolute.	عَزُومٌ
Left-handed.	أَعْسَرُ مِعْسَرَاءُ	To comfort.	عَزَّى تَعْزِيَةً
Poor, indigent.	مُعْسِرٌ	To be comforted.	تَعَزَّى
To treat unjustly.	عَسَفَ يَعْسِفُ	Patience. Mourning.	عَزَاءٌ
Injustice, oppression.	عَسْفٌ	Comforter, consoler.	مُعَزٍّ

Tithe ; a tenth. عُشْر ج أَعْشَار	To form a camp. عَسْكَر
Social intercourse. عِشْرَة ومُعَاشَرَة	Army, troops. عَسْكَر ج عَسَاكِر
Ten. عَشَرَة م عَشْر ج عَشَرَات	Soldier. عَسْكَرِيّ ج عَسَاكِر
Twenty. عِشْرُونَ	Military service. عَسْكَرِيَّة
Tenth. عَاشِر	Military camp. مُعَسْكَر
Tithe-gatherer. عَشَّار ج عَشَّارُونَ	Honey. عَسَل
Associate, friend. عَشِير ج عُشَرَاء	To make honey, (bees). عَسَّل
Kinsfolk. عَشِيرَة ج عَشَائِر	Tender shoot. عُسْلُج ج عَسَالِج
Decimal. (arith.) أَعْشَارِيّ	Stiffness of the wrist. عَسَم
Community. مَعْشَر ج مَعَاشِر	Having stiff wrist or ankle. أَعْسَم
Familiar friend. مُعَاشِر	To become hard. عَسَا يَعْسُو
Companionship. مُعَاشَرَة	Thick, coarse, rough. عَاسٍ
To love passionately. عَشِق يَعْشَق	It may be that, perhaps. عَسَى أَنْ
Passionate love. عِشْق ومَعْشَق	To make a nest. عَشَّ وأَعَشَّ
Beloved one. عَشِيق ومَعْشُوق	Bird's nest. عُشّ ج أَعْشَاش
Passionate lover. عَاشِق ج عُشَّاق	To produce herbage. أَعْشَب
To sup. عَشَا يَعْشُو وتَعَشَّى	Green herb. عُشْب ج اعشاب
Weakness of sight. عَشًا وعَشَاوَة	To take tithes. عَشَر وعَشَّر
Supper. عَشَاء	To consort with. عَاشَر
	To associate together. تَعَاشَر

The Eucharist.	اَلْعَشَاء اَلسِّرِّيُّ	Bound, tied.	مَعْصُوبٌ
Evening.	عَشِيَّةٌ ج عَشَايَا	To press, squeeze.	عَصَرَ يَعْصِرُ
Yesterday evening.	عَشِيَّةُ أَمْسِ	To be contemporary with.	عَاصَرَ
Darkness of night.	عَشْوَةٌ وَعَشْوَاءُ	To be pressed.	تَعَصَّرَ وَاَنْعَصَرَ
Cook.	عَشِّي	A time, period.	عَصْرٌ ج أَعْصُرٌ
To bind up.	عَصَبَ وَعَصَّبَ	Latter part of the day.	عَصْرٌ
To defend a cause.	تَعَصَّبَ فِي	The afternoon prayer.	صَلَاةُ الْعَصْرِ
To take the part of.	تَعَصَّبَ لِ	Juice, extract.	عَصِيرٌ وَعُصَارَةٌ
To league against.	تَعَصَّبَ عَلَى	A press.	مَعْصَرَةٌ ج مَعَاصِرُ
To be leagued.	إِعْتَصَبَ	Contemporary.	مُعَاصِرٌ
Sinew. Nerve.	عَصَبٌ ج أَعْصَابٌ	Tail-bone.	عُصْعُصٌ ج عَصَاعِصُ
Male relations.	عَصَبَةٌ ج عَصَبَاتٌ	To blow violently.	عَصَفَ يَعْصِفُ
Troop, band.	عِصَبَةٌ ج عِصَبٌ	Hurricane.	عَاصِفَةٌ ج عَوَاصِفُ
Nervous.	عَصَبِي	Chaff, straw.	عُصَافَةٌ
Partisanship. Male relations.	عَصَبِيَّةٌ	Safflower.	عُصْفُرٌ
Bandage. Troop.	عِصَابَةٌ ج عَصَائِبُ	Small bird.	عُصْفُورٌ ج عَصَافِيرُ
Obstinacy, fanaticism.	تَعَصُّبٌ	To prevent ; defend.	عَصَمَ يَعْصِمُ
A zealous partisan.	مُتَعَصِّبٌ	To take refuge.	اعْتَصَمَ وَاسْتَعْصَمَ
		Prevention, defence.	عِصْمَةٌ

Muscle.	عَضَلَة ج عَضَل وَعَضَلَات	Capital of a country.	عَاصِمَة
Severe; difficult.	عُضَال وَمُعْضِل	Wrist.	مِعْصَم ج مَعَاصِم
Difficult case.	مُعْضِلَة ج مُعْضِلَات	Preserved, protected.	مَعْصُوم
Member, limb.	عِضْو ج أَعْضَاء	Staff, rod, cane.	عَصَا ج عِصِيّ
To perish.	عَطِبَ يَعْطَبُ عَطَبًا	Knot-grass.	عَصَا الرَّاعِي
To destroy. Damage.	أَعْطَب	To disobey, rebel.	عَصَى يَعْصِي
To perfume.	عَطَّرَ	Rebellious.	عَاصٍ ج عُصَاة
To perfume one's self.	تَعَطَّرَ	The river Orontes.	نَهْر العَاصِي
Perfume.	عِطْر ج أَعْطَار	Disobedience.	عِصْيَان وَمَعْصِيَة
Ottar of roses.	عِطْر الوَرْدِ	To bite.	عَضَّ يَعَضُّ عَضًّا
Aromatic.	عَطِر م عَطِرَة	To defame.	عَضَّ بِلِسَانِه
Grocer.	عَطَّار ج عَطَّارُون	To aid, assist.	عَضَدَ يَعْضُدُ وَعَاضَدَ
Grocery.	عَطَارَة	To aid one another.	تَعَاضَدَ
The planet Mercury,	عُطَارِدُ	To seek assistance of.	إِعْتَضَدَ بِ
To sneeze.	عَطَسَ يَعْطِسُ	Aid Assistance.	عَضْد ج أَعْضَاد
To make one sneeze.	عَطَّسَ	The upper arm.	عِضْد ج أَعْضَاد
A sneezing.	عَطْسَة وَعُطَاس	Side, side-post.	عِضَادَة
Snaff.	عَطُوس	To be difficult.	عَضَلَ وَأَعْضَلَ
To thirst.	عَطِشَ يَعْطَشُ عَطَشًا	Muscular.	عَضِل

Damage and loss.	عُطْلٌ وَضَرَرٌ	To cause to thirst.	عَطْشَ وَأَ عْطَشَ
Interest on money.	عُطْلُ آلْمَال	Thirst.	عَطْشٌ
Vacant time.	مُعْطَلَةٌ وَعَطَالَةٌ	Thirsty.	عَطْشَانُ ج عَطَاشَى
Spoiled, useless.	عَاطِلٌ	To incline towards.	عَطَفَ يَعْطِفُ إِلَى
Without work ; useless.	مُعَطَّلٌ	To be kind to.	عَطَفَ وَتَعَطَّفَ عَلَى
Mouldiness.	عَطَنٌ وَعَطْنَةٌ	To join one word to	عَطَفَ كَلِمَةً
Mouldy.	عَطِنٌ وَمَدْطَنٌ	another by a conjunction.	
To give present, offer.	أَعْطَى	To turn away from.	عَطَفَ عَنْ
To beg.	تِعَطَّى وَآسْتَعْطَى	To be bent, inclined.	إِنْعَطَفَ
To engage in.	تَعَاطَى	To seek favour.	إِسْتَعْطَفَ
Gift.	عَطًا وَعَطَاءٌ وَعَطِيَّةٌ	A conjunction.	حَرْفُ عَطْفٍ
Giver.	مُعْطٍ	Side, flank.	عَطْفٌ ج أَعْطَافٌ
To be great, large.	عَظُمَ يَعْظُمُ	Conjunctive particle.	عَاطِفٌ
To be hard upon.	عَظُمَ عَلَى	Kindness, pity.	عَاطِفَةٌ ج عَوَاطِفُ
To make large ; magnify.	عَظَّمَ	Joined ; inclined.	مَعْطُوفٌ
To be great ; proud.	تَعَظَّمَ	A word to which an-	مَعْطُوفٌ عَلَيْهِ
To magnify one's self.	تَعَاظَمَ	other is joined by a conjunction.	
To regard as great.	إِسْتَعْظَمَ	A bend.	مُنْعَطَفٌ
		To be without work. Be spoiled.	عَطَلَ وَتَعَطَّلَ
Bone.	عَظْمٌ ج عِظَامٌ	To leave unemployed. Ruin.	عَطَّلَ

Decayed.	عَفِنٌ وَمَعْفُونٌ وَمُعَفَّنٌ	Pride ; majesty.	عِظَمٌ وَعَظَمَةٌ
Putrid, mouldy.	مُتَعَفِّنٌ	Great.	عَظِيمٌ ج عُظَمَاءُ وَعِظَامٌ
To pardon, forgive.	عَفَا يَعْفُو عَنْ	The Great (God).	الْعَظِيمُ
To restore to health.	عَافَى	A great thing.	عَظِيمَةٌ ج عَظَائِمُ
Bravo ! Well done.	عَافَاكَ	Greater.	أَعْظَمُ م عُظْمَى
To exempt, excuse.	أَعْفَى مِنْ	Greater, or chief part.	مُعْظَمٌ
To be restored to health.	تَعَافَى	Exalted, made great.	مُعَظَّمٌ
To ask to be released.	إِسْتَعْفَى	To abstain from wrong.	عَفَّ يَعِفُّ عَنْ
Pardon, amnesty. Young ass.	عَفْوٌ	Virtuous.	عَفِيفٌ ج أَعِفَّاءُ
Spontaneously ; easily.	عَفْوًا	Continence, chastity.	عِفَّةٌ
Health.	عَافِيَةٌ ج عَوَافٍ وَعَافِيَاتٌ	To cover with dust.	عَفَرَ يَعْفِرُ
Resignation.	إِسْتِعْفَاءٌ	Dust.	عَفَرٌ وَعَفْرٌ
Restoration to health.	مُعَافَاةٌ	Demon.	عِفْرِيتٌ ج عَفَارِيتٌ
Convalescent.	مُتَعَافٍ	To heap up.	عَفَشَ يَعْفِشُ
Cornelian.	عَقِيقٌ	Trash. Baggage.	عَفْشٌ
To succeed.	عَقَبَ ـُ عَقْبًا	Galls.	عَفْصٌ
To follow.	عَقَّبَ وَأَعْقَبَ وَاعْتَقَبَ	To become decayed, rotten, mouldy.	عَفِنَ يَعْفَنُ وَعَفُنَ وَتَعَفَّنَ
To punish.	عَاقَبَ		
To follow out.	تَعَقَّبَ	Mildew.	وَعَفُونَةٌ

Article of faith.	عَقِيدَةٌ ج عَقَائِدُ
Belief, creed.	إِعْتِقَادٌ
Bond, contract, union.	إِنْعِقَادٌ
Obscurity, complexity.	تَعْقِيدٌ
Very knotty ; tangled.	مُعَقَّدٌ
Doctrine, belief.	مُعْتَقَدٌ
To cut, wound.	عَقَرَ يَعْقِرُ عَقْرًا
To persevere in.	عَاقَرَ
To be wounded.	إِنْعَقَرَ
Wounding, wound.	عَقْرٌ
Barrenness.	عُقْرٌ وعِقْرَةٌ وَعَقَارَةٌ
Barren.	عَاقِرٌ ج عَوَاقِرُ
Real estate.	عَقَارٌ ج عَقَارَاتٌ
A drug.	عَقَّارٌ ج عَقَاقِيرُ
Scorpion.	عَقْرَبٌ ج عَقَارِبُ
Scorpion (of the zodiac).	اَلْعَقْرَبُ
To plait (the hair).	عَقَصَ يَعْقِصُ
To sting.	(عَقَصَ يَعْقِصُ وَعَقَّصَ)
Plait (of hair).	عَقِيصَةٌ ج عَقَائِصُ

To follow (one another).	تَعَاقَبَ
Heel of foot.	عَقِبٌ ج أَعْقَابٌ
Mountain road.	عَقَبَةٌ ج عِقَابٌ
End, issue.	عُقْبَى
End, result.	عَاقِبَةٌ ج عَوَاقِبُ
Punishment.	عِقَابٌ وَمُعَاقَبَةٌ
Eagle.	عُقَابٌ ج أَعْقُبٌ وَعِقْبَانٌ
That which follows.	عَقِيبٌ
To tie, knot. Conclude. Ratify.	عَقَدَ يَعْقِدُ
To determine upon.	عَقَدَ عَلَى
To make a contract with.	عَاقَدَ
To be complicated.	تَعَقَّدَ
To unite in a contract.	تَعَاقَدَ
To believe firmly.	إِعْتَقَدَ
Contract. Vault.	عَقْدٌ ج عُقُودٌ
Necklace.	عِقْدٌ ج عُقُودٌ
Knot. Joint.	عُقْدَةٌ ج عُقَدٌ
Maker of silk-cord.	عَقَّادٌ
Ally, confederate.	عَقِيدَةٌ

Barren, sterile.	عَقِيمٌ ج عُقُمٌ	Hair-filet.	عِقَاصٌ
Acre, (town).	عَكَّةُ وَعَكَّاءُ	To crook, bend.	عَقَفَ يَقِفُ
To become turbid.	عَكِرَ يَعْكُرُ وَتَعَكَّرَ	To become bent.	تَعَقَّفَ وَآنْعَقَفَ
To render turbid.	عَكَّرَ وَأَعْكَرَ	Bent, hooked.	أَعْقَفُ وَمَعْقُوفٌ
Dregs, lees, sediment.	عَكَرٌ	To bind.	عَقَلَ يَعْقِلُ وَآعْتَقَلَ
Troubled, turbid.	عَكِرٌ وَمُعَكَّرٌ	To understand.	عَقَلَ مَعْقُولاً
To lean upon (a staff.)	عَكَزَ وَتَعَكَّزَ عَلَى	To conceive, know.	تَعَقَّلَ
Staff ; crosier.	عُكَازٌ ج عَكَاكِيزُ	To withhold, restrain.	إِعْتَقَلَ
To reverse, invert.	عَكَسَ يَعْكِسُ	Mind, intellect.	عَقْلٌ ج عُقُولٌ
To invert, oppose.	عَاكَسَ	Rational ; mental.	عَقْلِيٌّ
To be inverted, reflected.	إِنْعَكَسَ	Intelligent.	عَاقِلٌ ج عُقَّالٌ وَعُقَلَاءُ
Inversion, reflection.	إِنْعِكَاسٌ	Rope cord.	عِقَالٌ ج عُقُلٌ
On the contrary.	بِالْعَكْسِ	A noble woman.	عَقِيلَةٌ ج عَقَائِلُ
Thick, dense.	عَكِشٌ	Fortress, refuge.	مَعْقِلٌ ج مَعَاقِلُ
To detain.	عَكَفَ يَعْكُفُ عَكْفًا	Intelligible, reasonable.	مَعْقُولٌ
To persevere in.	عَكَفَ عَلَى	Mental science.	عِلْمُ الْمَعْقُولَاتِ
To abide in.	عَكَفَ وَآعْتَكَفَ فِي	To be barren.	عَقُمَ يَعْقُمُ
Keeping to.	عَاكِفٌ	To render barren.	عَقَّمَ وَأَعْقَمَ
Religious seclusion.	إِعْتِكَافٌ	Barrenness.	عُقْمٌ

Dispute, contention.	مُعَالَجَةُ	To tie up. Muzzle.	عَكَمَ يَعْكِمُ
To feed (a beast).	عَلَفَ يَعْلِفُ	To become ill.	عَلَّ عِلَّة
Fodder (for beasts).	عَلَفٌ	To Divert. Account for.	عَلَّلَ بِ
Seller of provender.	عَلَّافٌ	To offer excuses.	تَعَلَّلَ
Manger.	مَعْلَفٌ ج مَعَالِفُ	To divert one's self.	تَعَلَّلَ بِ
Fattened (animal),	مُعَلَّفٌ	To become diseased, sick.	إِعْتَلَّ
To hang to.	عَلِقَ يَعْلَقُ وَاْعتَلَقَ بِ	May-be, perhaps.	عَلَّ وَلَعَلَّ
To conceive, (woman).	عَلِقَ عُلُوقًا	Cause. Malady.	عِلَّةٌ ج عِلَلٌ
To love.	عَلِقَ عُلُوقًا بِه	The weak letters.	حُرُوفُ العِلَّة
To begin to do.	عَلِقَ يَعْلَقُ	Upper chamber.	عِلِّيَّةٌ ج عَلَالِيُّ
To attach.	عَلَّقَ	Sick, diseased.	عَلِيلٌ وَمَعْلُولٌ
To note down.	عَلَّقَ فِي	Assignment of a cause.	تَعْلِيلٌ
To be attached to.	تَعَلَّقَ بِ	Ill, diseased. Containing one of the weak letters.	مُعْتَلٌّ
Leech.	عَلَقَةٌ ج عَلَقَاتٌ وَعَلَقٌ		
Connection.	عَلَاقَةٌ ج عَلَائِقُ	Small box.	عُلْبَةٌ ج عُلَبٌ
Forage, for animals.	عَلِيقٌ	To work at. Treat (a disease).	عَالَجَ
Climbing plant ; brier.	عُلَّيْقٌ	To take medical treatment.	تَعَالَجَ
Connection.	تَعَلُّقٌ	To strive with one another.	تَعَالَجَ
Attached, suspended.	مُعَلَّقٌ	Treatment of disease. Remedy, cure,	عِلَاجٌ وَمُعَالَجَةٌ

Learned, savant.	عَلِيمٌ ج عُلَمَاء	Attached to.	مُتَعَلِّقٌ بِـ
Announcement, notice.	إِعْلَامٌ	Very bitter plant.	عَلْقَمٌ
Instruction. Doctrine.	تَعْلِيمٌ	To chew.	عَلَكَ يَعْلُكُ عَلْكًا
Instructions; orders.	تَعْلِيمَاتٌ	To know, perceive.	عَلِمَ يَعْلَمُ
Taught. Marked.	مُعَلَّمٌ	To teach. To mark.	عَلَّمَ
Teacher, master.	مُعَلِّمٌ	To inform.	أَعْلَمَ
Known. Active voice,	مَعْلُومٌ	To learn.	تَعَلَّمَ
(verb). Certainly, of course.		To desire to know; ask.	إِسْتَعْلَمَ
To be open, manifest.	عَلَنَ يَعْلُنُ	Sign. Banner.	عَلَمٌ ج أَعْلَامٌ
To publish, reveal.	أَعْلَنَ	Proper name.	إِسْمُ عَلَمٍ
To be manifest.	إِعْتَانَ وَاسْتَعْلَنَ	Science, knowledge.	عِلْمٌ ج عُلُومٌ
Manifest, open.	عَلِنٌ وَعَالِنٌ	Scientific.	عِلْمِي
Openly, publicly.	عَلَانِيَةٌ	Knowing; learned.	عَالِمٌ ج عُلَمَاء
Manifestation, announce-ment. Advertisement.	إِعْلَانٌ	World.	عَالَمٌ ج عَوَالِمُ وَعَالَمُونَ
To be high; ascend.	عَلَا يَعْلُو	The animal kingdom.	عَالَمُ الْحَيَوَانِ
To overcome.	عَلَا عَلَى	The vegetable kingdom.	عَالَمُ النَّبَاتِ
To elevate.	عَلَّى وَأَعْلَى	The mineral kingdom.	عَالَمُ الْمَعَادِنِ
To be elevated.	تَعَلَّى وَتَعَالَى	Very learned.	عَلَّامٌ وَعَلَّامَةٌ
God, the exalted one.	اللهُ تَعَالَى	Sign, mark.	عَلَامَةٌ

In his time.	عَلَى عَهْدِهِ	Come ! come here !	تَعَالَ
By means of.	عَلَى يَدِ فُلَانٍ	To rise high.	اِعْتَلَى وَآسْتَعْلَى
To be general ; include.	عَمَّ يَعُمُّ	Nobility ; eminence.	عَلَاءٌ وَعُلى
To generalize.	عَمَّمَ	Height. Grandeur.	عُلُوٌّ
Paternal uncle.	عَمٌّ ج أَعْمَامٌ	In addition to.	عَلَاوَةٌ
Paternal aunt.	عَمَّةٌ ج عَمَّاتٌ	High ; elevated ; noble.	عَلِيٌّ ج عَلِيُّونَ
Cousin on the father's side. Husband.	إِبْنُ ٱلْعَمِّ	God, the most High.	ٱلْعَلِيُّ
Cousin on the father's side. Wife.	بِنْتُ ٱلْعَمِّ	Upper chamber.	عِلِّيَّةٌ ج عَلَالِيُّ
For what ?	عَمَّ (عَنْ ما)	High, sublime.	عَالٍ
For whom ?	عَمَّنْ (عَنْ مَنْ)	The Sublime Porte.	اَلْبَابُ ٱلْعَالِي
General, universal.	عَامٌّ	Higher, nobler.	أَعْلَى ج أَعَالٍ
The common people.	اَلْعَامَّةُ	The exalted, (God).	ٱلْمُتَعَالِي
They all came.	جَاءَ ٱلْقَوْمُ عَامَّةً	To address a letter.	عَلْوَنَ
To common people.	اَلْعَوَامُّ	Address ; title.	عُلْوَانٌ
Vulgar, common.	عَامِّيٌّ	To ascend.	عَلَا يَعْلِي عَلْيًا وَعُلِيًّا
Turban.	عِمَامَةٌ ج عَمَائِمُ	Upon, with, for, at.	عَلَى
Universality, totality.	عُمُومٌ	You ought to do ...	عَلَيْكَ أَنْ تَفْعَلَ
In general, universally.	عُمُومًا	He is in debt.	عَلَيْهِ دَيْنٌ

To make inhabited.	أَعْمَرَ	General, universal.	عُمُومِيّ
To be flourishing.	عَمَرَ يَعْمُرُ	More common or general.	أَعَمّ
To build, construct.	عَمَّرَ	Turbaned.	مُعَمَّم وَمُتَعَمِّم
To colonize.	أَعْمَرَ وَٱسْتَعْمَرَ	To prop up, support.	عَمَدَ يَعْمُدُ
Life-time ; age.	عُمْر ج أَعْمَار	To intend, purpose.	عَمَدَ وَتَعَمَّدَ
By my life !	لَعَمْرِي	To aim at, seek, repair to.	عَمَدَ إِلَى
Prosperity of a land. Civilization.	عُمْرَان	To baptize.	عَمَدَ وَعَمَّدَ
Edifice. Cultivation.	عِمَارَة ج عَمَائِر	To be baptized.	تَعَمَّدَ وَٱعْتَمَدَ
Inhabited.	عَامِر وَعَمِير وَمَعْمُور	To depend upon.	ٱعْتَمَدَ عَلَى
Mason.	مِعْمَار وَمِعْمَارِيّ ج مِعْمَارِيَّة	Intentionally.	عَمْدًا وَتَعَمُّدًا
Colony.	مُسْتَعْمَرَة	Prop. Committee.	عُمْدَة
Weakness of sight.	عَمَش	Column, pillar.	عَمُود ج أَعْمِدَة
Weak in sight.	أَعْمَش	Perpendicular line.	خَطّ عَمُودِيّ
To be deep.	عَمُقَ يَعْمُقُ	Representative.	مُعْتَمَد
To make deep.	عَمَّقَ وَأَعْمَقَ	Baptism.	مَعْمُودِيَّة
To go deeply into.	تَعَمَّقَ فِي	To live a long time.	عَمَرَ يَعْمُرُ
Depth.	عُمْق وَعَمْق ج أَعْمَاق	To be inhabited.	عَمَرَ يَعْمُرُ
Deep, profound.	عَمِيق	To inhabit.	عَمَرَ عِمَارَة
To work, do, make.	عَمِلَ يَعْمَل	To build.	عَمَرَ عِمَارَة

Made. Governed (word). مَعْمُول	To act upon. عَمِلَ في
To become blind. عَمِيَ يَعْمَى	To deal with. Treat. عَامَلَ
To be blind to. عَمِيَ عَنْ	To employ, use, exert. اعْمَلَ
To be obscure to. عَمِيَ الأُمْرُ عَلَى	To deal with one another. تَعَامَلَ
To render blind. اعْمَى	To labour, work. إعْتَمَلَ
To feign blindness. تَعَامَى	To use ; employ. إسْتَعْمَلَ
Blindness. عَمَى	Work, service, عَمَلٌ ج اعْمَال
Blind. أعْمَى م عَمْيَاء ج عُمْي	deed, action ; occupation.
For, from, at. عَنْ	An evil deed. عَمْلَة
He left us. ذَهَب عَنَّا	Money. عُمْلَة
After a little while. عَنْ قَلِيلِ	Practical. Artificial. عَمَلِي
To the last man. عَنْ آخِرِهِمْ	Operation. عَمَلِيَّة
At his right hand. عَنْ يَمِينِه	Workman, doer. عَامِلٌ ج عُمَّال
Life for life. نَفْسٌ عَنْ نَفْسٍ	A word that. عَامِلٌ ج عَوَامِلُ
Because of a promise. عَنْ وَعْدٍ	governs another (in gram.)
To appear. عَنَّ يَعِنَّ عَنَّا	Commercial agent. عَمِيلٌ
Clouds. عَنَانٌ	Use, employment. إسْتِعْمَالٌ
Reins. عِنَانٌ ج اعِنة	Mill, factory. مَعْمَلٌ ج مَعَامِلُ
Grapes. عِنَبٌ	Transaction. مُعَامَلَةٌ ج مُعَامَلَاتٌ
	Manner of treatment.

Simple, elemental.	عُنْصُرِيٌّ	Jujube tree and fruit.	عَتَابٌ
Wild onion ; squill.	عُنْصُل	Ambergris. Ship-hold. A kind of Mimosa.	عَنْبَر
To be harsh ; rude.	عَنُفَ يَعْنُفُ	To treat with rigour.	عَنَّتَ
To upbraid.	عَنَّفَ وَأَعْنَفَ	At, near, with, on.	عِنْدَ
Roughness, harshness.	عُنْفَ	I came from him.	جِئْتُ مِنْ عِنْدِهِ
Violently.	عَنْفًا	At sunrise.	عِنْدَ طُلُوعِ الشَّمْسِ
The first of a thing.	عُنْفُوَانٌ	He sat with him.	جَلَسَ عِنْدَهُ
Prime of youth.	عُنْفُوَانُ الشَّبَابِ	I have property.	عِنْدِي مَالٌ
Harsh, violent.	عَنِيفٌ	Such is my opinion.	عِنْدِي كَذَا
To embrace.	عَانَقَ وَاعْتَنَقَ	When it happened.	عِنْدَ مَا صَارَ
Neck.	عُنُقٌ ج اعْنَاقٌ	Then ; thereupon.	عِنْدَ ذَلِكَ
Embrace.	عِنَاقٌ وَمُعَانَقَةٌ	To be obstinate.	عَنَدَ يَعْنُدُ
Fabulous bird ; griffin.	الْعَنْقَاءُ	To resist.	عَانَدَ عِنَادًا وَمُعَانَدَةً
Bunch.	عُنْقُودٌ ج عَنَاقِيدُ	To oppose one another.	تَعَانَدَ
Spider.	عَنْكَبُوتٌ ج عَنَاكِبُ	Obstinate.	عَنِيدٌ ج عُنُدٌ وَمُعَانِدٌ
To trouble, distress.	عَنَا يَعْنُو	She-goat.	عَنْزٌ ج عُنُوزٌ وَعِنَازٌ
To submit to.	عَنَا (ل)	Element. Origin.	عُنْصُرٌ ج عَنَاصِرُ
To subdue.	عَنَّى وَاعْنَى	Feast of Pentecost.	الْعَنْصَرَةُ
Force, violence.	عَنْوَةٌ		

To make an engagement.	تَعَاهَدَ
Covenant, agreement. Time, epoch.	عَهْدٌ ج عُهُودٌ
The Old Testament.	اَلْعَهْدُ الْقَدِيمُ
The New Testament.	اَلْعَهْدُ الْجَدِيدُ
Presumptive heir.	وَلِيُّ الْعَهْدِ
Compact. Responsibility.	عُهْدَةٌ
Treaty, alliance.	مُعَاهَدَةٌ
Stipulated. Known.	مَعْهُودٌ
Debauchery.	عَهْرٌ وَعَهَارَةٌ
To stop ; pass by.	عَاجَ يَعُوجُ
To crook, bend, contort.	عَوَّجَ
To become bent.	تَعَوَّجَ وَاعْوَجَّ
Ivory.	عَاجٌ
Crookedness.	عِوَجٌ وَاعْوِجَاجٌ
Crooked.	أَعْوَجُ م عَوْجَاءُ ج عُوجٌ
Crooked, tortuous.	مُعَوَّجٌ
To return to.	عَادَ يَعُودُ إِلَى
To repeat.	عَادَ وَأَعَادَ
To visit (the sick).	عَادَ عِيَادَةً

Captive ; submissive.	عَانٍ ج عُنَاةٌ
To address a letter.	عَنْوَنَ
Title ; address.	عُنْوَانٌ
To mean, intend.	عَنَى يَعْنِي
To concern.	عُنِيَ عِنَايَةً
To distress, afflict.	عَنَّى وَأَعْنَى
To suffer, endure.	عَانَى
To care for, manage.	اِعْتَنَى بِ
Difficulty, trouble.	عَنَاءٌ
Care, solicitude.	عِنَايَةٌ وَاعْتِنَاءٌ
Divine Providence.	اَلْعِنَايَةُ الْإِلَهِيَّةُ
Meaning, sense.	مَعْنًى ج مَعَانٍ
Rhetoric.	عِلْمُ الْمَعَانِي
Ideal, mental.	مَعْنَوِيٌّ
To know.	عَهِدَ يَعْهَدُ عَهْدًا
To enjoin, charge.	عَهِدَ إِلَى
To make an agreement.	عَاهَدَ
To swear to one.	عَاهَدَهُ
To be careful of.	تَعَهَّدَ وَتَعَاهَدَ

Refuge, asylum.	مَعَاذٌ وَمَعَاذَةٌ	To accustom.	عَوَّدَ
God forbid !	مَعَاذَ اللّٰه	To restore.	أَعَادَ إِلَى
To lose one eye.	عَوِرَ وَٱعْوَرَّ	To be accustomed.	تَعَوَّدَ وَٱعْتَادَ
To lend.	أَعَارَ	Custom.	عَادَةٌ ج عَادَاتٌ
To borrow.	إِسْتَعَارَ	Old. Customary.	عَادِيٌّ
Private parts.	عَوْرَةٌ ج عَوْرَاتٌ	Ancient monuments.	أَلْعَادِيَّاتُ
Loan ; act of lending.	إِعَارَةٌ	Return ; repetition.	عَوْدٌ
Borrowing. Metaphor.	إِسْتِعَارَةٌ	Stick. Lute.	عُودٌ ج عِيدَانٌ
Metaphorical.	إِسْتِعَارِيٌّ	Aloes-wood.	أَلْعُودُ
One-eyed.	أَعْوَرُ م عَوْرَاءُ ج عُورٌ	Festival, feast-day.	عِيدٌ ج أَعْيَادٌ
Borrowed. Metaphorical.	مُسْتَعَارٌ	A visitor, (sp. of the sick).	عَائِدٌ
To want, lack.	عَازَ يَعُوزُ وَأَعْوَزَ	Benefit ; utility.	عَائِدَةٌ ج عَوَائِدُ
He needed it.	أَعْوَزَهُ ٱلشَّيْءُ	Repetition.	إِعَادَةٌ
Fortune has reduced him to poverty.	أَعْوَزَهُ ٱلدَّهْرُ	Habitual, customary.	إِعْتِيَادِيٌّ
Poverty, need.	عَوَزٌ	The future life.	أَلْمَعَادُ
Needy.	عَوِزٌ وَعَائِزٌ وَأَعْوَزُ وَمُعْوِزٌ	Habituated.	مُعَوَّدٌ وَمُعْتَادٌ
Wants.	مَعَاوِزُ	To seek protection.	عَاذَ يَعُوذُ بِ
To be difficult.	عَوِصَ يَعْوَصُ	Taking refuge.	عَوْذٌ وَعِيَاذٌ

To rely upon.	عَوَّلَ عَلَى وَبِ
To sustain a family.	أَعَالَ
Wailing.	عَوْلٌ وَعَوْلَةٌ وَعَوِيلٌ
Family.	عَائِلَةٌ ج عَائِلَاتٌ
A family, household.	عِيَالٌ
Pickaxe.	مِعْوَلٌ ج مَعَاوِلُ
To swim, float.	عَامَ يَعُومُ عَوْمًا
A year.	عَامٌ ج أَعْوَامٌ
Swimming.	عَائِمٌ
To aid, assist.	عَاوَنَ وَأَعَانَ عَلَى
To give mutual aid.	تَعَاوَنَ
To seek the aid of.	إِسْتَعَانَ بِ
Aid, assistance.	عَوْنٌ وَمَعُونَةٌ
Aider, assistant.	عَوْنٌ ج أَعْوَانٌ
Aid, assistance.	إِعَانَةٌ وَمُعَاوَنَةٌ
Assistant, coadjutor.	مُعَاوِنٌ
Bane, pest, blight.	عَاهَةٌ
To howl, bark.	عَوَى يَعْوِي عُوَاءً

Difficulty, obscurity.	عَوَصٌ
Difficult.	عَوِيصٌ م عَوْصَاءُ
To give something in exchange.	عَاضَ يَعُوضُ وَعَوَّضَ
To receive in compensation for.	تَعَوَّضَ وَاعْتَاضَ عَنْ أَوْ مِنْ
Thing in exchange.	عِوَضٌ
Compensation.	عِوَضٌ وَتَعْوِيضٌ
Instead of.	عِوَضًا عَنْ أَوْ مِنْ
To hinder.	عَاقَ يَعُوقُ وَعَوَّقَ وَأَعَاقَ
To be hindered.	تَعَوَّقَ
Delay.	عَاقَةٌ
Obstacle.	عَائِقٌ وَعَائِقَةٌ ج عَوَائِقُ
Capella (star).	أَلْعَيُّوقُ
Act of retarding.	إِعَاقَةٌ وَتَعْوِيقٌ
To support ; nourish.	عَالَ يَعُولُ
To be unfaithful in.	عَالَ فِي
His patience was exhausted.	عَالَ وَعِيلَ صَبْرُهُ
To wail.	عَوَّلَ وَأَعْوَلَ وَاعْتَوَلَ

To seek means of living.	تَعَيَّشَ	Howling, crying, barking.	عُوَاء
Life.	عَيْشٌ وَعِيشَةٌ	To be faulty.	عَابَ يَعِيبُ
Wheat, bread, food.	عَيْشٌ	To find fault with.	عَابَ وَعَيَّبَ
Living, living well.	عَائِشٌ	Blemish; shame.	عَيْبٌ ج عُيُوبٌ
Means of living.	مَعَاشٌ وَمَعِيشَةٌ	Defective, faulty.	عَائِبٌ
To cry out, shout.	عَيَّطَ	Shameful.	مَعِيبٌ وَمَعِيوبٌ
Shouting.	عِيَاطٌ	To act corruptly.	عَاثَ يَعِيثُ
To dislike.	عَافَ يَعَافُ وَيَعِيفُ	To celebrate a feast.	عَيَّدَ
To become poor.	عَالَ يَعِيلُ	Feast, festival.	عِيدٌ ج أَعْيَادٌ
To have a large family.	أَعْيَلَ	Christmas.	عِيدُ الْمِيلَادِ
Family.	عَائِلَةٌ ج عِيَالٌ	To go about; journey.	عَارَ يَعِيرُ
Having a large family.	مُعْيِلٌ	To upbraid, reproach. To verify by weighing.	عَيَّرَ
To appoint; specify.	عَيَّنَ	Disgrace, shame.	عَارٌ
To see.	عَايَنَ مُعَايَنَةً وَعِيَانًا	Standard of weight.	عِيَارٌ
To be specified; appointed.	تَعَيَّنَ	Jesus (Christ).	عِيسَى
Eye. Self.	عَيْنٌ ج أَعْيُنٌ وَعُيُونٌ	Christian.	عِيسَوِيٌّ
The chief men, notables.	الْأَعْيَانُ	To live.	عَاشَ يَعِيشُ عَيْشًا
Fountain.	عَيْنٌ ج عُيُونٌ	To nourish.	عَيَّشَ وَأَعَاشَ

A rhomboid.	الشَّبِيهُ بِالْمُعَيَّن	It is he himself.	هُوَ هُوَ عَيْنُهُ
Designated, appointed.	مُتَعَيِّن	Certain knowledge.	عَيْنُ الْيَقِين
Bane, scourge, blight.	عَاهَة	Act of seeing.	عِيَانٌ ومُعَايَنَة
To be unable.	عَيِيَ يَعْيَى عَيًّا	Clearly, evidently.	عِيَانًا
To be disabled ; disable.	أَعْيَا	Occular (witness).	عِيَانِيّ
Weakness, disease.	عَيَاء	Spectacles, eye-glasses.	عُوَيْنَات
Weak.	عَيٌّ ج أَعْيَاء	Specification, designation.	تَعْيِين
Weak, incapable, sick.	عَيَّانٌ	Designated, appointed.	مُعَيَّن
		A rhombus, (geom.).	مُعَيَّن

غ

To become dust-coloured.	إِغْبَرَّ	As a numeral sign=1000.	غ
Dust.	غَبْرَة وغِبْرَة وغَبَار	To visit at intervals.	غَبَّ ُ
Remaining. Passing away.	غَابِر	At intervals.	غِبًّا
Dust-coloured.	أَغْبَرُ م غَبْرَاء ج غُبْر	After.	غِبَّ
Duskiness.	غَبَس وغُبْسَة	To raise the dust.	غَبَّرَ وأَغْبَرَ
Ash-coloured.	أَغْبَسُ م غَبْسَاء	To become dusty.	تَغَبَّرَ

Small pistol.	غَدَّارَةٌ ج غَدَّارَاتٌ	To be in a happy state.	إِغْتَبَطَ
Pool of water.	غَدِيرٌ ج غُدْرَانٌ	Happy state.	غِبْطٌ وَغِبْطَةٌ
To go forth early.	غَدَا يَغْدُو	Channel of water.	غَبِيطٌ ج غُبُطٌ
To breakfast.	تَغَدَّى	Fortunate ; blessed.	مَغْبُوطٌ
To give breakfast.	غَدَّى	To cheat.	غَبَنَ يَغْبِنُ غَبْنًا
To-morrow.	غَدًا وَفِي الْغَدِ	To conceal.	غَبَنَ وَاغْتَبَنَ
Day after to-morrow.	بَعْدَ الْغَدِ	To be deceived, or cheated.	إِنْغَبَنَ
Morning meal ; lunch.	غَدَاءٌ	Fraud, deceit.	غَبْنٌ وَغَبِينَةٌ
Early morning.	غُدْوٌ وَغَدَاةٌ	To be hidden from.	غَبِيَ عَلَى
To nourish (food).	غَذَا ـ وَغَذَّى	Ignorance, heedlessness.	غَبَاوَةٌ
To be fed.	تَغَذَّى وَاغْتَذَى	Ignorant, stupid.	غَبِيٌّ ج أَغْبِيَاءٌ
Food nutriment.	غِذَاءٌ ج أَغْذِيَةٌ	Lean, meagre.	غَثٌّ وَغَثِيثٌ
Nourishing (food).	مُغِذٍّ	Ash-colour.	غُثْمَةٌ
To beguile.	غَرَّ يَغُرُّ غُرُورًا	To be nauseated.	غَثَا يَغْثِي غَثَيَانًا
To be deceived.	إِغْتَرَّ	Wen ; gland.	غُدَّةٌ ج غُدَدٌ
White mark on the forehead of a horse. The new moon. The best of anything.	غُرَّةٌ ج غُرَرٌ	To deceive.	غَدَرَ يَغْدِرُ غَدْرًا بِ
Very deceitful.	غَرَّارٌ وَغَرُورٌ	To leave, abandon.	غَادَرَ
Unexperienced, ignorant.	غِرٌّ ج أَغْرَارٌ	Perfidy, treachery.	غَدْرٌ
		Treacherous.	غَادِرٌ وَغَدَّارٌ

Sieve.	غِرْبَالٌ ج غَرَابِيلُ	False things, vanities.	غُرُورٌ
To warble.	غَرِدَ يَغْرُدُ وَغَرَّدَ	Beautiful. Noble.	أَغَرُّ م غَرَّاءُ
To prick.	غَرَزَ يَغْرِزُ غَرْزاً ب	Deceived, deluded.	مَغْرُورٌ
To insert.	غَرَزَ وَغَرَّزَ وَأَغْرَزَ	To depart ; set (sun).	غَرَبَ يَغْرُبُ
Nature ; natural, innate quality.	غَرِيزَةٌ ج غَرَائِزُ	To go west.	غَرَّبَ وَأَغْرَبَ
Natural, innate.	غَرِيزِيٌّ	To go to a strange land.	تَغَرَّبَ
To plant.	غَرَسَ يَغْرِسُ غَرْساً	To regard as strange.	إِسْتَغْرَبَ
To be planted.	إِنْغَرَسَ	The west.	غَرْبٌ
Planted tree.	غَرْسٌ ج أَغْرَاسٌ	Travelling in a foreign land.	غُرْبَةٌ وتَغَرُّبٌ وَاغْتِرَابٌ
Plantation.	مَغْرِسٌ ج مَغَارِسُ		
Planted (tree).	مَغْرُوسٌ	A crow.	غُرَابٌ ج غِرْبَانٌ
Piastre.	غِرْشٌ ج غُرُوشٌ	Strangeness, obscurity.	غَرَابَةٌ
Aim, object.	غَرَضٌ ج أَغْرَاضٌ	Setting, sun-set.	غُرُوبٌ
To gargle.	غَرْغَرَ	A stranger.	غَرِيبٌ ج غُرَبَاءُ
A gargle.	غَرْغَرَةٌ	Strange event.	غَرِيبَةٌ ج غَرَائِب
To dip out with a ladle.	غَرَفَ يَغْرُفُ وَاغْتَرَفَ	The west.	مَغْرِبٌ ج مَغَارِبُ
		Hour of sun-set.	مَغْرِبُ الشَّمْسِ
Upper chamber.	غُرْفَةٌ ج غُرَفٌ	Moor, Arab of N. W. Africa.	مَغْرِبِيٌّ ج مَغَارِبَةٌ
Handful.	غُرْفَةٌ ج غِرَافٌ	To sift ; disperse.	غَرْبَلَ

No wonder !	لاَ غَرْوَ	Ladle.	مِغْرَفَةٌ ج مَغَارِفُ
Incitement, instigation.	إِغْرَاءٌ	To sink, be drowned.	غَرِقَ يَغْرَقُ
Glue pot.	مِغْرَاةٌ	To drown.	غَرَّقَ وَأَغْرَقَ
To prick.	غَزَّ يَغُزُّ ب	To take in, comprise.	إِسْتَغْرَقَ
Gaza, (town).	غَزَّةُ	Drowning, sinking.	غَرَقٌ
To be copious.	غَزُرَ يَغْزُرُ	Drowned.	غَرِيقٌ ج غَرْقَى
Abundance.	غَزَارَةٌ	To pay a tax, fine.	غَرِمَ يَغْرَمُ
Abundant.	غَزِيرٌ ج غِزَارٌ	To impose a fine.	غَرَّمَ وَأَغْرَمَ
To spin.	غَزَلَ يَغْزِلُ غَزْلاً	To be very fond of.	اغْرِمَ ب
To say amatory words.	تَغَزَّلَ	To pay a tax ; fine.	تَغَرَّمَ
Spun thread or yarn.	غَزْلٌ	Fine, tax ; loss.	غَرَامَةٌ
Amatory words.	غَزَلٌ وَتَغَزُّلٌ	Fond attachment.	غَرَامٌ
Gazelle.	غَزَالٌ ج غِزْلاَنٌ	Debtor ; litigant.	غَرِيمٌ ج غُرَمَاءُ
Female gazelle. The sun.	غَزَالَةٌ	Eagerly desirous.	مُغْرَمٌ
Spindle.	مِغْزَلٌ ج مَغَازِلُ	Crane ; stork.	غُرْنُوقٌ ج غَرَانِقُ
Spun.	مَغْزُولٌ	To glue.	غَرَا يَغْرُو وَغَرَّى
To wage war, invade the enemy's country.	غَزَا يَغْزُو	To incite, urge.	أَغْرَى
		To be glued.	تَغَرَّى
Military expedition.	غَزْوٌ	Glue.	غِرَاءٌ

An incursion. غَزْوَةٌ ج غَزَوَاتٌ	To cover, conceal. غَشِيَ يَغْشَى
Warrior ; invader. غَازٍ ج غُزَاةٌ	To be dark, (night). غَشِيَ وَأَغْشَى
Sense, meaning. مَغْزَى الْكَلَامِ	He swooned. غُشِيَ عَلَيْهِ غَشَيَانًا
To become very dark. غَسَقَ يَغْسِقُ	To put a covering upon. غَشَّى
Early darkness of night. غَسَقٌ	Cover ; membrane. غِشَاءٌ ج أَغْشِيَةٌ
To wash. غَسَلَ يَغْسِلُ وَغَسَّلَ	Swoon. غَشْيَةٌ وَغَشَيَانٌ
To be washed. إِنْغَسَلَ	Covered, enveloped. مَغْشِيٌّ وَمُغَشًّى
To wash one's self. إِغْتَسَلَ	Swooning, senseless. مَغْشِيٌّ عَلَيْهِ
Washing, ablution. غُسْلٌ	To be choked. غَصَّ يَغَصُّ
Washerwoman. غَسَّالَةٌ	To choke. Grieve. أَغَصَّ
Clothes that are washed. غَسِيلٌ	Choking. Grief. غُصَّةٌ ج غُصَصٌ
To deceive, falsify. غَشَّ يَغُشُّ	To force. غَصَبَ يَغْصِبُ غَصْبًا عَلَى
To be deceived. إِنْغَشَّ	To take by violence.
Deceit, dishonesty, fraud. غِشٌّ	To violate. غَصَبَ وَٱغْتَصَبَ مِنْ
Deceitful. غَاشٌّ وَغَشَّاشٌ	Violence. غَصْبٌ
Deceived ; falsified. مَغْشُوشٌ	In spite of him. غَصْبًا عَنْهُ
Inexperience. غَشَمٌ	Oppressor. غَاصِبٌ وَمُغْتَصِبٌ
Inexperienced. غَشِيمٌ ج غُشَمَاءُ	Violence, tyranny. إِغْتِصَابٌ
Film (on the eyes) غِشَاوَةٌ	Forced. مَغْصُوبٌ وَمُغْتَصَبٌ

To snore.	غَطَّ يَغِطّ غَطِيطًا
To be plunged, immersed.	إِنْغَطَّ
To be proud.	غَطْرَسَ غَطْرَسَةً
To immerse. To plunge.	غَطَسَ يَغْطِسُ غَطْسًا في
To immerse.	غَطَّسَ
Feast of Epiphany.	عِيدُ الغِطَاسِ
Diver.	غَطَّاسٌ
Bath-tub.	مِغْطَسٌ ج مَغَاطِسُ
Magnet.	مِغْنَطِيسٌ وَمَغْنَاطِيسٌ
To cover up, conceal.	غَطَّى
To be covered, concealed.	تَغَطَّى
Cover, covering.	غِطَاءٌ ج أَغْطِيَةٌ
To cover, veil.	غَفَرَ ـ وَغَفَّرَ
To forgive, pardon.	غَفَرَ ـ لِ
To ask for pardon.	إِسْتَغْفَرَ
Guard, escort.	غَفَرٌ
Pardon, forgiveness.	غُفْرَانٌ
Forgiving, (God).	غَفَّارٌ وَغَفُورٌ

Branch, twig.	غُصْنٌ ج أَغْصَانٌ
To be fresh (plant).	غَضَّ يَغِضُّ
To take no notice.	غَضَّ الطَّرْفَ
Fresh, juicy, luxuriant.	غَضٌّ
To be angry.	غَضِبَ يَغْضَبُ
To make angry.	غَاضَبَ وَأَغْضَبَ
To be angry.	تَغَضَّبَ
Anger, rage, passion.	غَضَبٌ
Angry, enraged.	غَضْبَانُ ج غَضْبَى
Stern, austere, angry.	غَضُوبٌ
Object of anger.	مَغْضُوبٌ عَلَيْهِ
Ease of life, affluence.	غَضَارَةٌ
Cartilage.	غُضْرُوفٌ ج غَضَارِيفُ
Wrinkle, fold.	غَضْنٌ
During.	فِي غُضُونِ كَذَا
To become dark.	غَضَا يَغْضُو
To close the eyes to.	أَغْضَى عَنْهُ
To neglect, disregard.	تَغَاضَى عَنْ
To immerse, dip.	غَطَّ يَغِطّ غَطًّا

Burning of love &c.	غَلِيلٌ	Guard, sentinel.	غَفِيرٌ وَخَفِيرٌ
Proceeds, غَلَّةٌ ج غَلَّاتٌ وَغِلَالٌ		Pardon, forgiveness.	مَغْفِرَةٌ
revenue from land, crops.		To be heedless of.	غَفَلَ يَغْفُلُ عَنْ
Burning of love or grief.	غَلِيلٌ	To make one unmindful.	أَغْفَلَ
Fruitful, productive.	مُغِلٌّ	Forget, disregard.	أَغْفَلَ
Manacled, shackled.	مَغْلُولٌ	To be unmindful of.	تَغَافَلَ عَنْ
To conquer, subdue.	غَلَبَ يَغْلِبُ	To watch for one's	إِسْتَغْفَلَ
To contend for victory.	غَالَبَ	unmindfulness.	
To prevail, overcome.	تَغَلَّبَ عَلَى	Heedlessness. غَفْلٌ وَغَفْلَةٌ وَغُفُولٌ	
To be overcome, defeated.	إِنْغَلَبَ	Unawares. غَفْلَةً وَعَلَى غَفْلَةٍ	
Victory, conquest.	غَلَبَةٌ	Unmindful, heedless.	غَافِلٌ
Victor, conqueror. غَالِبٌ ج غَلَبَةٌ		Simpleton.	مُغَفَّلٌ
Usually. غَالِبًا وَفِي الْغَالِبِ		To sleep. غَفَا يَغْفُو وَعَفِيَ يَغْفَى	
Conquered, overcome.	مَغْلُوبٌ	Sleepy ; sleeping.	غَافٍ
The last darkness of night.	غَلَسٌ	To fetter, shackle.	غَلَّ يَغُلُّ
At early dawn.	غَلَسًا	To yield income.	أَغَلَّ وَغَلَّ
To make a mistake.	غَلِطَ يَغْلَطُ	To take the proceeds.	إِسْتَغَلَّ
To accuse one of mistake.	غَلَّطَ	Rancour, malice.	غِلٌّ وَغَلِيلٌ
Mistake, error. غَلَطٌ ج أَغْلَاطٌ		Manacle, shackle. غُلٌّ ج أَغْلَالٌ	

Boy, youth.	غُلَامٌ ج غِلْمَانٌ
Tortoise.	غَيْلَمٌ
To become calm, (sea).	غَلَنَ
Quiet, calmness of the sea.	(غَلِينَة)
To be excessive.	غَلَا يَغْلُو غُلُوًّا
To be high in price.	غَلَا غَلَاءً
To make the price high.	غَلَّى
To go too far.	غَالَى مُغَالَاةً فِي
To find it high-priced.	إِسْتَغْلَى
High price ; dearness.	غَلَاءٌ
Excess, exaggeration.	غُلُوٌّ
Furlong.	غَلْوَةٌ ج غَلَوَاتٌ
High-priced, dear.	غَالٍ
Of higher price, dearer.	أَغْلَى
To boil (pot).	غَلَى يَغْلِي
To cause to boil.	غَلَّى وَأَغْلَى
Boiling, ebullition.	غَلْيٌ وَغَلَيَانٌ
Tobacco-pipe.	غَلْيُونٌ ج غَلَايِينُ
Vessel for heating water.	غَلَّايَة

Single mistake, fault.	غَلْطَة
Erroneous.	مُغَلِّط وَمَغْلُوط
Sophism.	مُغَالَطَة
To be thick, bulky.	غَلُظَ يَغْلُظ
To be hard, severe.	غَلُظَ عَلَى
To be rough, uncivil.	أَغْلَظَ لَهُ
Thickness, incivility.	غِلَاظَة
Thick ; rough.	غَلِيظٌ ج غِلَاظٌ
To put into an envelope.	غَلَّفَ
To have a cover.	تَغَلَّفَ وَاغْتَلَفَ
Covering, sheath.	غِلَافٌ ج غُلُفٌ
Envelope.	(مُغَلَّفٌ ج مُغَلَّفَاتٌ
Uncircumcised.	أَغْلَفُ ج غُلْفٌ
To close, shut.	أَغْلَقَ
To be closed, shut.	إِنْغَلَقَ
Lock.	غَلْقٌ ج أَغْلَاقٌ
Closed, locked.	مُغْلَقٌ
Balance of account.	غِلَاقَة حِسَاب

To immerse, dip. غَمَسَ يَغْمِسُ	To cover, to grieve. غَمَّ يَغُمُّ
To be plunged. إِنْغَمَسَ وَاغْتَمَسَ	To be grieved. إِنْغَمَّ وَاغْتَمَّ
To be obscure. غَمُضَ يَغْمُضُ	Grief, sorrow. غَمٌّ ج غُمُومٌ
To shut (the eyes). غَمَّضَ وَاغْمَضَ	Clouds, (coll). غَمَامٌ ج غَمَائِمُ
To be closed, (eye). إِنْغَمَضَ	A cloud. غَمَامَةٌ
Obscure. غَامِضٌ ج غَوَامِضُ	Sorrowful, mournful. مُغِمٌّ
Closed (eye). Obscure. مُغَمَّضٌ	Afflicted, grieved. مَغْمُومٌ
Depth. (غُمْقٌ)	To sheathe; cover. غَمَدَ يَغْمِدُ وَأَغْمَدَ
Deep. (غَمِيقٌ)	To cover, veil. غَمَّدَ وَتَغَمَّدَ
To swoon. غُمِيَ عَلَيْهِ وَاغْمِيَ عَلَيْهِ	Scabbard, sheath. غِمْدٌ ج أَغْمَادٌ
Swooning, swoon. غَمْيٌ وَإِغْمَاءٌ	To submerge (water). غَمَرَ يَغْمُرُ
In a swoon. مُغْمًى عَلَيْهِ	To be abundant. غَمَرَ يَغْمُرُ
To be coquettish. غَنِجَ –	To be submerged. إِنْغَمَرَ وَاغْتَمَرَ
Coquetry. غَنْجٌ وَغِنَاجٌ	Abundant (water). غَمْرٌ
Coquette. غَنِجَةٌ وَغَنُوجَةٌ	Deep water. Difficulty. غَمْرَةٌ
To plunder ; obtain. غَنِمَ يَغْنَمُ	Pangs of death. غَمَرَاتُ ٱلْمَوْتِ
To give a free gift. غَنَّمَ	To wink. Press. غَمَزَ يَغْمِزُ غَمْزًا
To seize as spoil. إِغْتَنَمَ	Sign made with the eye. غَمْزٌ

To seize the opportunity.	إِغْتَنَمَ وَاسْتَغْنَمَ الفُرْصَةَ	Very dark, black.	غَيْهَبٌ ج غَيَاهِبُ
Booty.	غُنْمٌ وَغَنِيمَةٌ ج غَنَائِمُ	To aid, succour.	غَاثَ يَغُوثُ وَأَغَاثَ
Sheep (coll.).	غَنَمٌ ج أَغْنَامٌ	To seek aid.	إِسْتَغَاثَ وَب
Shepherd.	غَنَّامٌ	Aid, succour.	غَوْثٌ وَإِغَاثَةٌ
Spoiler ; successful.	غَانِمٌ	Request of aid.	إِسْتِغَاثَةٌ
To be rich.	غَنِيَ يَغْنَى	To sink deep.	غَارَ يَغُورُ
To be content with.	غَنِيَ بِ	To attack, invade.	أَغَارَ عَلَى
To be in no need of.	غَنِيَ عَنْ	Laurel (plant).	غَارٌ
To sing, chant.	غَنَّى	Raid, incursion.	غَارَةٌ ج غَارَاتٌ
To free from want.	أَغْنَى	He made a raid.	شَنَّ الغَارَةَ
To become rich.	إِغْتَنَى وَاسْتَغْنَى	Bottom, depth. Low land.	غَوْرٌ
To be in no need of.	إِسْتَغْنَى عَنْ	Cave, cavern.	مَغَارَةٌ ج مَغَائِرُ
Wealth, opulence.	غِنًى وَغَنَاءٌ	To plunge into.	غَاصَ يَغُوصُ فِي
He cannot do without it.	مَا لَهُ عَنْهُ غِنًى	To plunge dip (v.t.).	غَوَّصَ
Song.	غِنَاءٌ وَأُغْنِيَّةٌ ج أَغَانٍ وَأَغَانِيُّ	One who plunges.	غَائِصٌ
Rich, opulent.	غَنِيٌّ ج أَغْنِيَاءُ	Diver, (sp. pearl-fisher).	غَوَّاصٌ
Beautiful woman.	غَانِيَةٌ ج غَوَانٍ	Deep.	(غَوِيصٌ)
Singer.	مُغَنٍّ ج مُغَنِّيَة	To dig, excavate. Sink.	غَاطَ يَغُوطُ

To void excrement.	تَغَوَّطَ	To conceal from.	غَيَّبَ عَنْ
Low ground.	غَوْطٌ وَغَوْطَةٌ	Absence.	غَيْبٌ وَغَيْبَةٌ وَغِيَابٌ
Excrement, fæces.	غَائِطٌ	Hidden thing.	غَيْبٌ ج غُيُوبٌ
To destroy.	غَالَ يَغُولُ وَاَغْتَالَ	From memory.	غَيْبًا وَعَلَى ٱلْغَائِبِ
To slay covertly.	إِغْتَالَ	The unseen world.	عَالَمُ ٱلْغَيْبِ
Goblin, demon.	غُولٌ ج غِيلَانٌ	Forest.	غَابَةٌ ج غَابَاتٌ
Evil, mischief.	غَائِلَةٌ ج غَوَائِلُ	Calumny, backbiting.	غِيبَةٌ
To err.	غَوِيَ يَغْوَى غَوًى	Absent, hidden.	غَائِبٌ
To seduce.	غَوَى وَأَغْوَى	Time or place of the setting of the sun.	مَغِيبُ ٱلشَّمْسِ
To be led into error.	إِنْغَوَى	To water with rain.	غَاثَ يَغِيثُ
Error, leading astray.	غَيٌّ وَغَوَايَةٌ	Rain.	غَيْثٌ ج غُيُوثٌ
Error.	غِيَّةٌ ج غِيَّاتٌ	Fresh, tender (woman)	غَادَةٌ
Erring ; deceiver.	غَاوٍ ج غُوَاةٌ	Tender.	أَغْيَدُ م غَيْدَاءُ ج غِيدٌ
To be absent, distant.	غَابَ يَغِيبُ	To be jealous.	غَارَ يَغَارُ
To set ; disappear.	غَابَ غِيَابًا	To alter, change.	غَيَّرَ
To lose one's reason.	غَابَ عَنِ ٱلصَّوَابِ	To make jealous.	أَغَارَ
To slander.	غَابَ وَٱغْتَابَ	To be changed.	تَغَيَّرَ
To go away, travel.	غَابَ وَتَغَسَّ	To differ.	غَايَرَ وَتَغَايَرَ

Anger, rage, wrath.	غَيْظُ	Other ; another. Except.	غَيْرُ
Angry, enraged.	مُغْتَاظٌ	Et cætera.	وَغَيْرُ ذٰلِكَ
Crow, raven.	غَاقٌ	Not pure, impure.	غَيْرُ خَالِصٍ
Lock.	(غَالٌ ج غَالَاتٌ)	Without that.	مِنْ غَيْرِ ذٰلِكَ
Thicket, jungle.	غِيلٌ ج أَغْيَالٌ	Although.	غَيْرَ أَنْ
Subterfuge, deception.	غِيلَةٌ	Nothing else.	لَا غَيْرُ
Rancour, malice ; evil.	غَائِلَةٌ	Jealously ; zeal.	غَيْرَةٌ
To be cloudy.	غَامَ وَأَغْيَمَ وَتَغَيَّمَ	Very jealous.	غَيُورٌ
Clouds (*coll.*)	غَيْمٌ ج غُيُومٌ	Unhealthy (climate).	(مِغْيَارٌ)
Extremity, term. Ultimate object.	غَايَةٌ ج غَايَاتٌ	Thicket, wood.	غَيْضَةٌ ج غِيَاضٌ
Extremely.	إِلَى ٱلْغَايَةِ	To anger, enrage.	غَاظَ يَغِيظُ وَأَغَاظَ
		To become angry.	إِغْتَاظَ وَتَغَيَّظَ

ف

And ; then. As a numeral sign=80.	ف
Heart ; soul ; mind.	فُوَاُدٌ ج أَفْئِدَة
Rat ; mouse.	فَأْرٌ ج فِئْرَان
A mouse.	فَأْرَةٌ ج فَأْرَات
Axe ; hatchet.	فَأْسٌ ج فُؤُوس
To draw a favourable augury.	تَفَأَّلَ وَتَفَاءَلَ ب
Good or evil omen.	فَأْلٌ وَتَفَاؤُل
Company, band.	فِئَةٌ ج فِئَات
To break in pieces.	فَتَّ يَفُتُّ
To be crumbled.	تَفَتَّتَ وَاَنْفَتَّ
Small pieces ; crumbs.	فُتَاتٌ
Crumbled.	فَتِيتٌ وَمَفْتُوت
To cease from.	فَتِئَ يَفْتَأُ عَنْ
He continued to do.	مَا فَتِئَ يَفْعَل

To open. Conquer (a country).	فَتَحَ يَفْتَح
To succour. Reveal.	فَتَحَ عَلَى
To address one first.	فَاتَحَ
To be opened.	تَفَتَّحَ وَاَنْفَتَحَ
To open, commence. Attack and conquer (a land).	إِفْتَتَحَ
To begin. Seek succour.	إِسْتَفْتَحَ
Victory, conquest.	فَتْحٌ ج فُتُوح
Conquered countries.	فُتُوحَات
The short vowel fatha.( )	فَتْحَة
An opening.	فَتْحَة
Conqueror. Light-coloured.	فَاتِح
Introduction, preface.	فَاتِحَة
First chapter of the Koran.	أَلْفَاتِحَة
He who opens, conquers.	فَتَّاح

Rupture, hernia. Rent. فَتْقٌ وَفِتاقٌ	Introduction. Conquest. افتِتاحٌ
Ruptured, ripped. مَفْتُوقٌ	Introductory. افْتِتاحِيٌّ
To assault ; kill. فَتَكَ ب	Key. مِفْتاحٌ ج مَفاتِيحُ
Bold, daring. فاتِكٌ ج فُتّاكٌ	Opened. Vocalized by مَفْتُوحٌ
To twist. فَتَلَ يَفْتِلُ فَتْلاً وَفَتَّلَ	the vowel *fatha*.
To be twisted. تَفَتَّلَ وَاَنْفَتَلَ	To subside ; be tepid. فَتَرَ يَفْتُر
Twister (of rope, &c.) فَتّالٌ	To desist ; abate. فَتَرَ عَنْ
Twisted (rope, &c.) فَتِيلٌ وَمَفْتُولٌ	To allay. Make tepid. فَتَّرَ
Wick of a lamp. فَتِيلةٌ ج فَتائِلُ	Measure between extended فِتْرٌ
To please ; infatuate. فَتَنَ يَفْتِنُ	thumb and index finger.
To please ; seduce. أَفْتَنَ	Intermission. فَتْرَةٌ ج فَتَرات
To lead, or to be led, افْتَتَنَ	Languid ; lukewarm. فاتِرٌ
into error.	Lukewarmness, languor. فُتُورٌ
Seduction. Trial, affliction. فِتْنةٌ	To examine, investigate. فَتَّشَ
Sedition.	Examination, inquest. تَفْتِيشٌ
Seducer ; charmer. فاتِنٌ ج فُتّانٌ	Examiner, inspector. مُفَتِّشٌ
Infatuated ; seduced. مَفْتُونٌ	To crumble (*v.t.*). (فَتَّتَ)
To be young. فَتِيَ يَفْتَى فَتًى وَفَتاءً	To cleave, slit, rip. فَتَقَ يَفْتُقُ وفَتَّقَ
To answer أَفْتَى (العالِمُ) في مَسْأَلةٍ	To be split ; ripped. تَفَتَّقَ وَاَنْفَتَقَ
a learned question.	

To suffer pain from loss. فَجِعَ	To affect youth. تَفْتَى
To grieve, complain. تَفَجَّعَ	To ask the solution of a إِسْتَفْتَى
Calamitous. فَاجِعٌ وَفَجُوعٌ	learned question, sp. judicial.
Great calamity. فَاجِعَةٌ ج فَوَاجِعُ	A young man. فَتًى ج فِتْيَانٌ
Radish (plant). فِجْلٌ	A young woman. فَتَاةٌ ج فَتَيَاتٌ
To notch, blunt. فَجَمَ يَفْجِمُ فَجْمًا	Manliness, generosity. فُتُوَّةٌ
To be excessive ; foul. فَحُشَ يَفْحُشُ	Judicial sentence. فَتْوَى ج فَتَاوٍ
To use foul words. فَحُشَ وَأَفْحَشَ	A lawyer. Mufti. مُفْتٍ (ٱلْمُفْتِي)
Shameless evil. Excess. فُحْشٌ	Way, path. فَجٌّ ج فِجَاجٌ
Evil. Excessive. فَاحِشٌ	Unripe (fruit). فِجٌّ وَفِيجٌ
Atrocious sin. فَاحِشَةٌ ج فَوَاحِشُ	To attack or فَجَأَ يَفْجَأُ وَفَاجَأَ befall suddenly.
To examine. فَحَصَ - وَتَفَحَّصَ	Suddenly ; unawares. فُجَاءَةٌ
Examination. (فَحْصٌ ج فُحُوصٌ)	To give exit to water. فَجَرَ يَفْجُرُ
To become formidable. اِسْتَفْحَلَ	To live in open sin. فَجَرَ يَفْجُرُ
Male. Strong man. فَحْلٌ ج فُحُولٌ	To flaw. Dawn. تَفَجَّرَ وَٱنْفَجَرَ
Elites in science. فُحُولُ ٱلْعُلَمَاءِ	Dawn, day-break. فَجْرٌ
To be silence. فَحَمَ يَفْحَمُ	Wicked (man). فَاجِرٌ ج فُجَّارٌ
To blacken. فَحَّمَ	Great wickedness. فُجُورٌ
	To give pain. فَجَعَ يَفْجَعُ فَجْمًا

Glorious trait.	مَفْخَرَةٌ ج مَفَاخِرُ	To silence by argument.	أَفْحَمَ
To be great.	فَخُمَ يَفْخُمُ فَخَامَةٌ	Charcoal.	فَحْمٌ
To show great honour.	فَخَّمَ	Coal.	فَحْمُ الْحَجَرِ أَوْ فَحْمٌ حَجَرِيٌّ
Highly honoured.	مُفَخَّمٌ	Seller of charcoal.	فَحَّامٌ ج فَحَّامَةٌ
Club-footed.	أَفْدَعُ ج فُدْعٌ	Blackness ; darkness.	فَحْمَةٌ
To wound the head.	فَدَغَ يَفْدَغُ	(Answer) that silences.	مُفْحِمٌ
Yoke of	فَدَّانٌ وفِدَّانٌ ج فَدَادِينُ	Meaning ; sense.	فَحْوَى وَفَحْوَاءُ
oxen. Field-measure, acre.		Trap, snare.	فَخٌّ ج فِخَاخٌ وفُخُوخٌ
Plum-line.	فَادِنٌ ج فَوَادِنُ	To break through.	فَخَتَ يَفْخَتُ
To redeem, ransom.	فَدَى يَفْدِي	To be perforated.	إِنْفَخَتَ
To ransom.	إِفْتَدَى	Hole, break, perforation.	فَخْتٌ
Ransom. Redemption.	فِدَاءٌ	Thigh. Sub-tribe.	فَخْذٌ ج أَفْخَاذٌ
May it be a ransom to you !	فِدَاكَ	To glory, boast.	فَخِرَ يَفْخَرُ وَافْتَخَرَ
The Redeemer.	الْفَادِي	To prefer.	فَخَرَ وفَخَّرَ وأَفْخَرَ عَلَى
To become apart.	فَذَّ يَفِذُّ	To compete or vie with.	فَاخَرَ
One alone, single.	فَذٌّ	Glory, excellence.	فَخْرٌ
One by one.	فَذَاذَى وَفُذَاذاً	Glorious ; excellent.	فَاخِرٌ
Resumé, gist.	فَذْلَكَةٌ	Pottery ; earthen-ware.	فَخَّارٌ
To flee ; escape.	فَرَّ يَفِرُّ فَرًّا	Potter.	فَخَّارِيٌّ وفَاخُورِيٌّ

Over-garment.	فُرْجِيَّة	Fleeing, fugitive.	فَارّ وَفَرَّارّ
Chicken.	فَرُّوجّ ج فَرَارِيجُ	Snipe, quail.	فُرِّيّ
Open. Relieved.	مَفْرُوجّ	Flight ; escape.	فِرَارّ
Diverging.	مُنْفَرِجّ	Escape. Place of escape.	مَفَرّ
Obtuse angle.	اَلزَّاوِيَةُ الْمُنْفَرِجَةُ	Wildass ; onager.	فَرَأْ وَفَرَاءّ
To rejoice.	فَرِحَ يَفْرَحُ فَرَحًا بِ	The Euphrates (river).	اَلْفُرَاتِ
To make glad.	فَرَّحَ وَأَفْرَحَ	Fork.	(فُرْتَيْكَةّ)
Joy, gladness, happiness.	فَرَحّ	Storm at sea.	(فُرْتُونَةّ)
Happy, glad.	فَرِحّ ج فَرِحُونَ	Excrement, fæces.	فَرْثّ
Glad, rejoicing.	فَرْحَانُّ م فَرْحَانَةّ	To relieve.	فَرَجَ يَفْرِجُ فَرْجًا
To sprout ; hatch.	فَرَّخَ وَأَفْرَخَ	To separate.	أَفْرَجَ بَيْنَ
Sprout. Chick	فَرْخّ ج فُرُوخّ	To make place for.	فَرَجَ لِ
Chicken.	فَرْخَةّ	To open ; widen. Relieve.	فَرَّجَ
To separate one's self.	فَرَدَ عَنْ	To show,	فَرَّجَ عَلَى
To make single ; set apart.	أَفْرَدَ	To see a new thing.	تَفَرَّجَ
To be alone.	تَفَرَّدَ وَانْفَرَدَ	To be opened, separate ; to diverge. Be relieved.	انْفَرَجَ
To seek privacy.	إِسْتَفْرَدَ	Relief.	فَرَجّ
One ; one of a pair. Individual.	فَرْدّ ج أَفْرَادّ	Opening Show.	فُرْجَةّ ج فُرَجّ

Atom ; monad.	اَلْجَوْهَرُ ٱلْفَرْد
Pistol.	فَرْدٌ ج فُرُودَة
Bale of goods.	فَرْدَة
One by one.	فُرَاداً وَفُرَادَى
Unique, matchless.	فَرِيدٌ
Precious gem.	فَرِيدَةٌ ج فَرَائِدُ
Singular number (gram.).	مُفْرَدٌ
Alone; insolated.	مُنْفَرِدٌ
Paradise.	فِرْدَوْسٌ ج فَرَادِيس
To set aside.	فَرَزَ يَفْرِزُ وَأَفْرَزَ
To go aside, or away.	إِنْفَرَزَ
Cornice, frieze.	إِفْرِيزٌ ج أَفَارِيز
To perceive ; gaze	تَفَرَّس
To capture (prey).	اِفْتَرَس
Horse.	فَرَسٌ ج أَفْرَاسٌ
Hippopotamus.	فَرَسُ ٱلْبَحْر
Horseman.	فَارِسٌ ج فُرْسَان
Persia.	بِلَادُ فَارِسَ وبِلَادُ ٱلْفُرْسِ
Persian.	فَارِسِيٌّ وَفُرْسِيٌّ ج فُرْسٌ

The Persian language.	اَلْفَارِسِيَّة
Horsemanship.	فَرَاسَة وفُرُوسَة
Skilful discernment.	فِرَاسَة
Physiognomy.	عِلْمُ ٱلْفِرَاسَةِ
Prey (of a lion).	فَرِيسَة
Pharisee.	فَرِّيسِيٌّ ج فَرِّيسِيُّونَ
Parasang; league.	فَرْسَخ ج فَرَاسِيخ
To spread out.	فَرَشَ يَفْرِش
To be spread out.	إِفْتَرَشَ وَٱنْفَرَشَ
House-furniture.	فَرْشٌ وَمَفْرُوشٌ
Brush.	فُرْشَة
Bed.	فِرَاشٌ وفَرْشَةٌ ج فُرُشٌ
Moth ; butterfly.	فَرَاشَة ج فَرَاشٌ
Furnished (house).	مَفْرُوشٌ
To separate the feet.	فَرْشَخَ
Occasion; chance.	فُرْصَة ج فُرَصٌ
To avail one's self of an opportunity.	إِنْتَهَزَ ٱلْفُرْصَة
To appoint ; ordain.	فَرَضَ يَفْرِض
Estimate ; suppose. Allot.	

To flatten ; make broad.	فَرْطَحَ	To notch, cut.	فَرَضَ وفَرَّضَ
Broad ; flattened.	مُفَرْطَحُ	To impose.	فَرَضَ وآفْتَرَضَ عَلَى
To derive, deduce.	فَرَّعَ مِنْ	To enact (a law).	إِفْتَرَضَ
To ramify ; branch forth.	تَفَرَّعَ	Decree. Supposition.	فَرْضُ ج فُرُوضُ
Branch. Derivative.	فَرْعُ ج فُرُوعُ	On the supposition.	عَلَى فَرَضٍ
Hatchet.	فَرَّاعَةُ	Harbour.	فُرْضَةُ ج فُرَضُ
To be very proud.	تَفَرْعَنَ	Ordinance; duty. Alloted portion.	فَرِيضَةُ ج فَرَائِضُ
Pharaoh.	فِرْعَوْنُ ج فَرَاعِنَةُ	The science of the laws of inheritance.	عِلْمُ الفَرَائِضِ
To be empty, vacant.	فَرَغَ يَفْرُغَ	Enactment. Supposition.	إِفْتِرَاضُ
To finish a thing.	فَرَغَ مِنْ	Supposed. Enacted.	مَفْرُوضُ
To pour out. Empty.	فَرَّغَ وأَفْرَغَ	To lose an opportunity.	فَرَطَ يَفْرُطُ
To be free from, be at leisure.	تَفَرَّغَ مِنْ	To do a thing hastily.	فَرَطَ مِنْ
To devote one's self to.	تَفَرَّغَ لِ	To miss ; neglect.	فَرَّطَ (في)
To exhaust ; vomit.	إِسْتَفْرَغَ	To go to excess.	أَفْرَطَ افْرَاطًا
Empty, vacant.	فِرِغُ وفَارِغُ	Excess.	فَرْطُ ج أَفْرَاطُ
Emptiness ; cessation.	فَرَاغُ	Cheap.	فَرْطُ
To flap the wings.	فَرْفَرَ فَرْفَرَةُ	Excessive, immoderate.	مُفْرِطُ
Light-headed, noisy.	فَرْفَارُ		

To rub.	فَرَكَ يَفْرُكُ فَرْكًا	To divide. Distinguish.	فَرَقَ يَفْرُق بَيْنَ
To be mature, (grain).	أَفْرَكَ	To scatter ; disperse.	فَرَّقَ
To be rubbed and pressed.	إِنْفَرَكَ	To distribute among.	فَرَّقَ عَلَى
To become full (grain).	إِسْتَفْرَكَ	To stir up dissension.	فَرَّقَ بَيْنَ
Act of rubbing ; friction.	فَرْك	To abandon. Die.	فَارَقَ
Rubbed soft grain.	فَرِيكُ	To be separated.	تَفَرَّقَ وَآفْتَرَقَ
To mince.	فَرَمَ يَفْرِم فَرْمًا	To leave one another.	تَفَارَقَ
To change the teeth, (child).	فَرَّمَ	To be separated from.	إِنْفَرَقَ عَنْ
A small piece.	(فَرْمَةٌ)	Difference, distinction.	فَرْقٌ
Firman.	فَرَمَانُ	The Koran.	الْفُرْقَانُ
Oven.	فُرْنٌ ج أَفْرَانُ	Party of men.	فِرْقَةٌ ج فِرَقٌ
Baker.	فَرَّانٌ	Separation.	فُرْقَةٌ وَآفْتِرَاقٌ
Europeans. Franks.	إِفْرَنْجٌ وَفِرِنْجٌ	Separation. Death.	فِرَاقٌ
France.	فَرَنْسَا	General of a division.	فَرِيقٌ
French.	فَرَنْسِيٌّ فَرَنْسَاوِيٌّ	Africa.	أَفْرِيقِيَّةُ
To line with fur.	فَرَّى تَفْرِيَة	Separation, dispersion.	تَفْرِيقٌ
Garment of fur.	فَرْوٌ ج فِرَاءُ	In parts, in detail.	بِالتَّفْرِيق
Scalp. Fur-cloak.	فَرْوَةٌ	A point from	مَفْرِقٌ ج مَفَارِقُ
Furrier.	فَرَّاءُ	which a road branches.	

To make roomy, wide.	فَسَّحَ	To fabricate a lie.	إِفْتَرَى الْكَذِب
His bosom was dilated (with joy).	إِنْفَسَحَ صَدْرُه	Wilful lie.	فِرْيَةٌ ج فِرًى
Space; court-yard.	فُسْحَةٌ ج فُسَح	Unusual thing.	فَرِيٌّ
Spaciousness, width.	فَسَاحَة	To be excited.	فَزَّ
Spacious, roomy, ample.	فَسِيحٌ	To frighten, disturb.	فَزَّ وَأَفَزَّ
To annul, abrogate.	فَسَخَ يَفْسَخ	To excite, incite.	إِسْتَفَزَّ
To split.	فَسَّخَ	To cut; break.	فَزَرَ يَفْزِرُ فَزْرًا
To be annulled, split.	إِنْفَسَخ	To be afraid.	فَزِعَ يَفْزَع فَزَعًا
Abrogation. Separation.	فَسْخٌ	To flee for help to.	فَزِعَ الى
A part, a piece.	فَسْخَةٌ	To frighten.	فَزَّعَ وَأَفْزَع
Salted fish.	فَسِيخٌ	Fear; fright.	فَزَعٌ
To become corrupt.	فَسَدَ يَفْسُد	Frightened, afraid.	فَزِعٌ
To corrupt.	فَسَّدَ وَأَفْسَد	Refuge. Succour.	مَفْزَعٌ
To stir up strife.	أَفْسَدَ بَيْن	Pistachio (tree and fruit).	فُسْتُقٌ
To be corrupted, bad.	إِنْفَسَد	Basin; reservoir.	فُسْتُقِيَّة
Corruption, mischief.	فَسَادٌ	Female gown.	فُسْتَانٌ ج فَسَاتِين
Invalidity. Decomposition.		To make place for; permit.	فَسَحَ يَفْسَح وَأَفْسَحَ لَهُ فِي
Bad. Invalid. Spoilt.	فَاسِدٌ	To be spacious, (place).	فَسُحَ يَفْسُح
Causing mischief or strife.	مُفْسِدٌ		

To be faint-hearted.	فَشِلَ يَفْشَلُ	Cause of evil.	مَفْسَدة ج مَفَاسِد
To fail, be disappointed.	تَفَشَّلَ	To make plain ; explain.	فَسَّرَ
Disappointment.	فَشَلٌ	To seek an explanation.	إِسْتَفْسَرَ
To be spread.	فَشَا يَفْشُو فُشُوًّا	Explanation.	تَفْسِيرٌ ج تَفَاسِير
To spread. Divulge.	أَفْشَى	Pavilion ; tent.	فُسْطَاط
To become wide ; extend.	تَفَشَّى	Phosphorus.	فُسْفُور وفُصْفُور
Stone or gem of a signet-ring. Lobe.	فَصّ ج فُصُوص	Bugs ; bed-bugs.	فَسَافِس
A species of clover.	فِصَّة	Mosaic-pavement.	فُسَيْفِسَاء
To break forth, (light).	فَصَحَ يَفْصَحُ	To be impious.	فَسَقَ يَفْسُقُ
To appear clearly.	أَفْصَحَ	Impiety.	فِسْقٌ وفُسُوقٌ
To affect eloquence.	تَفَاصَحَ	Impious, dissolute.	فَاسِقٌ
Passover ; Easter.	فِصْحٌ	Adulteress.	فَاسِقة
Lucidity ; eloquence.	فَصَاحة	To pick a lock.	فَشَّ يَفُشُّ فَشًّا
Elegant speaker.	فَصِيحٌ ج فُصَحَاء	To vent one's anger.	فَشَّ خُلْهُ
To open a vein.	فَصَدَ يَفْصِدُ فَصْدًا	Do take a wide step.	فَشَخَ يَفْشَخُ
To be bled.	إِنْفَصَدَ	A step.	فَشْخة
Bleeder, phlebotomist.	فَصَّاد	To talk incoherently.	فَشَرَ وفَشَّرَ
		Incoherent talk ; babbling.	فَشَّارٌ
		Cartridge.	فَشَكَة ج فَشَك)

Cut out. Detailed.	مُفَصَّلٌ	A person who is bled.	مَفْصُودٌ
In detail.	مُفَصَّلًا	Lancet.	مَفْصَدٌ
Hinge.	مَفْصَلَةٌ ج مَصَلَّاتٌ	To cut off ; separate.	فَصَلَ يَفْصِلُ
Detached.	مَفْصُولٌ وَمُنْفَصِلٌ	Decide a disputed point.	
		To divide into parts.	فَصَّلَ
To break, crack.	فَصَمَ يَفْصِمُ	To bargain for a price.	فَاصَلَ
To be broken, cracked.	إِنْفَصَمَ	To expire ; die.	أَفْصَلَ
To break open.	فَضَّ يَفُضُّ فَضًّا	To be separated ; detatched.	إِنْفَصَلَ
To cover with silver.	فَضَّض	To go away from.	إِنْفَصَلَ عَنْ
To be dispersed.	إِنْفَضَّ	Separation. Chapter.	فَصْلٌ ج فُصُولٌ
Silver. Para.	فِضَّةٌ	A season of the year.	
To divulge, disgrace.	فَضَحَ يَفْضَحُ	That which separates.	فَاصِلٌ
Disgrace.	فَضِيحَةٌ ج فَضَائِحُ	Decisive judgment.	حُكْمٌ فَاصِلٌ
To remain over.	فَضَلَ يَفْضُلُ	Family ; species.	فَصِيلَةٌ ج فَصَائِلُ
To excel, surpass.	فَضَلَ وَعَلَى	Judge, arbiter.	فَيْصَلٌ ج فَيَاصِلُ
To prefer.	فَضَّلَ عَلَى	Detailed statement.	تَفْصِيلٌ ج تَفَاصِيلُ
To show favour.	أَفْضَلَ وَتَفَضَّلَ	In detail.	بِالتَّفْصِيلِ
Do me the favour.	تَفَضَّلْ	Joint.	مَفْصِلٌ ج مَفَاصِلُ
To leave a part.	إِسْتَفْضَلَ مِنْ	Rheumatism.	دَاءُ المَفَاصِلِ

To reach, Lead to.	أدْضَى إلى	Excess Favour.	فَضْلٌ ج فُضُولٌ
To have leisure for.	تَفَضَّى لِ	Superiority, excellence.	
Open space.	فَضَاءٌ	Besides.	فَضْلاً عَن
Empty; unoccupied.	فاض	Portion remaining.	فَضْلَةٌ
To create, (God).	فَطَرَ	Superior; excellent.	فَاضِلٌ وَفَضِيلٌ
To break one's fast.	فَطَرَ وأفْطَرَ	Officiousness.	فُضُولٌ
To be broken.	تَفَطَّرَ وَانْفَطَرَ	Meddlesome.	فُضُولِيٌّ
Fungus.	فِطْرٌ	Virtue. Excellence.	فَضِيلَةٌ ج فَضَائِل
Feast of Ramadan.	عيد الفِطْر	Better.	أفْضَلُ ج أفاضِل
Innate quality.	فِطْرَةٌ ج فِطَرٌ	The best.	الأفْضَلُ
Creator.	فَاطِرٌ	Calculus	حِسَابُ التَّمَامِ وَالتَّفَاضُلِ
Midday, meal.	فُطُورٌ	(integral and differential).	
Unleavened.	فَطِيرٌ	Preference.	تَفْضِيلٌ
Jewish feast of un-leavened bread.	عيدُ الفِطْر	Adjective in the	إسْمُ التَّفْضِيلِ
Pastry-cake.	فَطِيرَةٌ ج فَطَائِرُ	comparative degree, as :	أكْبَرُ
To die.	فَطَسَ يَفْطِسُ فُطوساً	Preferable.	مُفَضَّلٌ
To be suffocated.	فَطَسَ يَفْطَسُ	Distinguished for excellence.	مِفْضَالٌ
To kill. Suffocate.	فَطَّسَ	To be empty.	فَضَا يَفْضُو فَضَاءً
Flat-nosed.	أفْطَسُ م فَطْسَاءُ ج فُطْسٌ	To empty, turn out.	فَضَّى

Doer. Agent or subject of the verb. فَاعِلْ ج فَعَلَةْ	To wean (an infant). فَطَمَ يَفْطِمِ
Noun of agent. إِسْمُ ٱلْفَاعِلِ	To be weaned. إِنْفَطَمَ
Agent or subject of the passive verb. نَائِبُ ٱلْفَاعِلِ	To cease from. إِنْفَطَمَ عَنْ
Effective, efficient. فَعَّالْ	Weaning. فِطَامْ
Influence, impression. إِنْفِعَالْ ج إِنْفِعَالَاتْ	Weaned (child). فَطِيمْ وَمَفْطُومْ
Emotion. إِنْفِعَالْ نَفْسَانِيّ	To remember; consider. Understand. فَطَنَ يَفْطِنُ بِ
Foot (in prosody). تَفْعِيلْ ج تَفَاعِيل	To remind. فَطَّنَ بِ
Something done. مَفْعُولْ ج مَفَاعِيل	To understand. Remember. تَفَطَّنَ ل
Impression; influence.	Understanding; sagacity. فِطْنَةْ
Object of transitive verb. مَفْعُولْ بِه	Intelligent. فَطِنْ وَفَطِينْ
Noun of patient. إِسْمُ ٱلْمَفْعُولِ	To be rough, rude. فَظَّ يَفَظُّ فَظَاظَةْ
Invented. Done purposely. مُفْتَعَلْ	Rough, rude. فَظّ ج فِظَاظ
To fill (a vessel). فَعَمَ يَفْعَمِ	To be horrid. فَظُعَ يَفْظُعُ فَظَاعَةْ
To be full. فَعِمَ يَفْعَمِ فَعُومَة	Atrocious; horrid. فَظِعْ وَفَظِيعْ
Filled, full. مُفْعَمْ	To do; perform; act. فَعَلَ يَفْعَل
Viper. أَفْعَى وَأَفْعُوانْ ج أَفَاعٍ	To be affected. Be done. إِنْفَعَلَ
To open (the mouth). فَغَرَ يَفْغَرُ	To forge; invent. اِفْتَعَلَ
To open. فَغَرَ وَأَفْغَرَ	Act, deed. Verb. فِعْلْ ج أَفْعَالْ
To open (an abscess). Put out an eye. فَقَأَ يَفْقَأ	

Only.	فَقَطْ	To burst; break.	تَفَقَّأَ وَآنْفَقَأَ
To die from heat or grief.	فَقَعَ	To lose.	فَقَدَ يَفْقِدُ فَقْدًا وَفُقْدَانًا
To be cleft or rent.	إِنْفَقَعَ	To deprive of, cause to lose.	أَفْقَدَ
Very bright-coloured.	فَاقِعٌ	To seek a lost object.	تَفَقَّدَ
Bubble of air.	فُقَّاعَةٌ ج فَقَاقِيع	To miss, fail to find. Visit a sick person.	إِفْتَقَدَ
Unripe figs.	(فَقِيع)	Lost object. Dead.	فَقِيدٌ وَمَفْقُودٌ
Excessive poverty.	فَقْرٌ مُفْقِعٌ	To slit, perforate.	فَقَرَ يَفْقِرُ
To be full, (vessel).	فَقِمَ يَفْقَمُ	To impoverish.	أَفْقَرَ
To become very serious.	تَفَاقَمَ	To become poor.	إِفْتَقَرَ
Seal. (sea-animal).	فُقْمَةٌ وَفِقْمَةٌ	To need.	إِفْتَقَرَ إِلَى
To understand.	فَقِهَ يَفْقَهُ فِقْهًا	Poverty; need.	فَقْرٌ
To be skilled in the Law.	فَقُهَ يَفْقُهُ	Vertebra.	فَقْرَةٌ ج فِقَرٌ
To teach.	فَقَّهَ وَأَفْقَهَ	Poor; needy.	فَقِيرٌ ج فُقَرَاء
To understand; learn.	تَفَقَّهَ	To hatch eggs (bird).	فَقَسَ يَفْقِسُ فَقْسًا
Knowledge; intelligence.	فِقْهٌ	To be hatched.	تَفَقَّسَ وَآنْفَقَسَ
Science of Law.	عِلْمُ الْفِقْه	Small melon.	فُقُّوسٌ
Understanding; learning.	فَقَاهَةٌ	To break open.	فَقَشَ يَفْقِشُ فَقْشًا
Skilled in Law.	فَقِيهٌ ج فُقَهَاء		

To blunt or notch. فَلَّ يَفِلُّ فَلاً	To separate; untie. فَكَّ يَفُكُّ فَكًّا
Arabian Jasmine. فُلٌّ	To separate ; disentangle. فَكَّكَ
To free, liberate. فَلَتَ يَفْلِتُ	To be separated ; untied. إِنْفَكَّ
To escape أَفْلَتَ وتَفَلَّتَ وٱنْفَلَتَ	Not to cease. مَا ٱنْفَكَّ
To spring on. تَفَلَّتَ عَلَى	To seek redemption. إِسْتَفَكَّ
Escape. فَلَتٌ	Jaw-bone. فَكٌّ ج فُكُوكٌ
Sudden event. فَلْتَةٌ	To think فَكَّرَ يُفَكِّرُ وفَكَّرَ
Suddenly. Undesignedly. فَلْتَةً	of ; consider. وتَفَكَّرَ وٱفْتَكَرَ فِي
Vagabond. (فَلْتِيٌّ)	To remind. (فَكَّرَ)
Loose, free. فَالَتٌ	Thought ; reflection. فِكْرٌ ج أَفْكَارٌ
Improper language. (كَلَامٌ فَالَتٌ)	Very thoughtful. فِكِّيرٌ
To be paralyzed. فُلِجَ وٱنْفَلَجَ	Latch. (فَاكُورَةٌ ج فَوَاكِيرُ)
To shine, (day break). اِنْفَلَجَ	To be gay. فَكِهَ يَفْكَهُ فَكَاهَةً
Paralysis ; palsy. فَالِجٌ	To cheer by wit. فَكَّهَ
Paralysed ; paralytic. مَفْلُوجٌ	To enjoy. تَفَكَّهَ بِ
To plough ; till. فَلَحَ يَفْلَحُ	To jest with another. تَنَاكَهَ
To prosper; be successful. أَفْلَحَ	Merry ; cheerful. فَكِهٌ ج فَكِهُونَ
Furrow. فَلْحٌ ج فُلُوحٌ	Fruit. فَاكِهَةٌ ج فَوَاكِهُ
Prosperity ; success. فَلَاحٌ	Jesting ; merriment. فَكَاهَةٌ

To spread out.	(فَلَشَ)	Agriculture.	فِلَاحَة
To be spread out.	(إِنفَلَشَ)	Farmer, peasant.	فَلَّاحٌ ج فَلَّاحُونَ
To escape from.	(فَلَصَ يَفْلَصُ مِنْ)	A piece.	فِلذة ج أَفْلَاذ
To escape.	افْلَص وتَفَلَّص وآنْفَلَص	A sweet pastry.	فَالُوذ وَفَالُوذَج
To flatten, make broad.	فَلطَح	Steel.	فُولَاذٌ (بُولَادٌ)
Flattened ; broad.	مفَلطَح	Bronze. Metal.	فِلِزّ
To pepper.	فَلفَل	To proclaim bankrupt.	فَلَّسَ
Pepper (tree or fruit).	فُلفُل وَفِلفِل	To become bankrupt.	أَفْلَسَ
Pepper plant.	فَلِيفِلَة	A small coin.	فَلَسٌ ج فُلُوس
Peppered.	مفَلفَل	Pl. scales of fish. Money.	
To cleave ; split.	فَلَق يَفْلِق	Insolvency, bankruptcy.	إِفْلَاسٌ
To be skilled in.	أَفْلَق وَآفتَلَق	Bankrupt ; penniless.	مُفْلِس
To be split, cleft.	تَفَلَّق وَآنفَلَق	Palestine.	فِلِسطِين
The dawn broke.	انفَلَق الصّبْح	To philosophize.	تَفَلسَف
Dawn. Stocks.	فَلَق ج أَفلَاق	Philosophy.	فَلسَفَة
Lobe. Cotyledon.	فِلَة ج فِلَق	Physics.	الفَلسَفَة الطَّبِيعِيَّة
Distinguished (poet).	مفلِق	Psychology.	الفَلَة العَقلِيَّة
To augur or predict.	فَلَّكَ وتَفَلَّكَ	Philosophical.	فَلسَفِيّ
Ship. Noah's ark.	فُلكٌ	Philosopher.	فَيلَسُوف ج فَلَاسِفة

Inn ; hotel.	فُنْدُقْ ج فَنَادِقْ	Celestial sphere.	فَلَكْ ج أَفْلَاكْ
Lantern. Light-house.	فَنَارْ ج فَنَارَاتْ	Astronomy.	عِلْمُ الفَلَكْ
Lantern. Lamp.	فَانُوسْ ج فوانيسُ	Astronomer.	فَلَكِيّ
To perish.	أَفْنِي يَفْنَى	Small ship ; boat.	(فَلُوكَةْ)
To annihilate ; destroy.	أَفْنَى	A certain person.	فُلَانْ
Destruction. Vanishing.	فَنَاءْ	Such and such.	فُلَانِيّ
Transient ; perishing.	فَانْ	Open space ; the open air.	(فَلَا)
Panther ; lynx.	فَهْدْ ج فُهُودْ	Foal.	فِلْوْ ج فَلَاوَى وأَفْلَاءْ
To make index.	فَهْرَس	Open country.	فَلَاةْ ج فَلَوَاتْ
Cata-	فِهْرِس وَفِهْرِسْتْ ج فَهَارِس	To clean from lice.	فَلَّى
logue. Index, table of contents.		Cork. Bottle-cork.	فِلِّينْ
To understand.	فَهِمَ يَفْهَمْ	God-son.	فَلْيُونْ
To make understand.	فَهَّم وأَفْهَم	Mouth. (see فوه)	فَمْ وَفُمْ
To be understood.	إِنْفَهَم	Form ; kind. Art.	فَنّ ج فُنُونْ
To seek to know.	إِسْتَفْهَم	To be accomplished.	تَفَنَّن
Understanding.	فَهْم	Accomplished ; skilful.	مُتَفَنِّن
Very intelligent.	فَهِيم وَفَهَّامة	Small cup.	فِنْجَانْ ج فَنَاجِين
Interrogation.	إِسْتِفْهَامْ	To state in detail. Accuse of untruth or error.	فَنَّد
Interrogative pronoun.	إِسْمُ اسْتِفْهَامْ	Branch. Taper.	فَنَدْ فُنُودْ

To float.	(فاش يَفُوش فَوْشًا)	Understood. Meaning.	مَفْهُومٌ
To commit to.	فَوَّضَ إلى	To pass. Miss.	فَاتَ يَفُوتُ
To converse with.	فاوض	To make pass ; omit.	فَوَّتَ
To converse together.	تَفَاوَض	To differ ; be dissimilar.	تَفَاوَتَ
Anarchy.	فَوْضَى	Passing ; missing.	فَوْتٌ وفَوَاتٌ
Conversation.	مُفَاوَضَةٌ	Dissimilarity ; difference.	تَفَاوُتٌ
Napkin ; towel.	فُوطَةٌ ج فُوَطٌ	Troop ; company.	فَوْجٌ ج أَفْوَاجٌ
To surpass; excel.	فاقَ يَفُوقُ	In troops, crowds.	أَفْوَاجًا أَفْوَاجًا
To hiccough.	فَاقَ فَوَاقًا	To be diffused, (odour).	فاحَ يَفُوحُ
To awake.	أَفاقَ واسْتفاقَ مِن	To boil.	فارَ يَفُورُ فَوْرًا وفُورَانًا
Above ; upon ; beyond.	فَوْقُ	To make boil.	أَفَارَ وفَوَّرَ
Upwards.	إلى فَوْقُ	Mice.	فَارٌ ج فِيرَانٌ
And upwards.	فَما فَوْقُ	Mouse. Carpenter's plane.	فَارَةٌ
Poverty ; want ; need.	فَاقَةٌ	Immediately ; at once.	عَلَى الْفَوْر
What is above.	فَوْقَانِيٌّ	Jet d'eau ; fountain.	فَوَّارَةٌ
Hiccough.	فُوَاقٌ	To win, succeed.	فازَ يَفُوزُ
Surpassing, excelling.	فَائِقٌ	To obtain ; attain.	فازَ بِ
Beyond description.	فَائِقُ الْوَصْف	Success. Escape.	فَوْزٌ
Horse-beans. (sing.	فُولٌ (فُولَةٌ	Desert.	مَفَازَةٌ ج مَفَازَاتٌ ومَفَاوِزُ

— ١٧ —

Cook or seller of beans.	فَوَّالٌ
Garlic.	فُومٌ
To speak ; utter.	فَاهَ يَفُوهُ وتَفَوَّهَ
Mouth.	فُوهٌ وفَمٌ ج أَفْواهٌ وأَفْمامٌ
Madder-root.	فُوَّةٌ وفُوَّةٌ
Opening.	فُوَّهَةٌ ج فُوَّهاتٌ وأَفْواهٌ
In, among, with, at.	فِي
To shade.	فَاءَ وفَيَّأَ
To shade one's self.	تَفَيَّأَ
Shadow.	فَيْءٌ ج أَفْياءٌ
Party ; company.	فِئَةٌ ج فِئَاتٌ
To flow.	فَاحَ يَفِيحُ فَيْحًا وفِيحَانًا
To spill, shed.	أَفَاحَ
Wide ; extensive.	أَفْيَحُ م فَيْحاءُ
To benefit ; serve ; mean.	أَفَادَ
To be benefited ; acquire.	إِسْتَفَادَ

Benefit ; use ; profit. Interest (on money).	فَائِدَةٌ ج فَوائِدُ
Bestowal of benefit.	إِفَادَةٌ
Beneficial ; useful.	مُفِيدٌ
Turquoise (stone).	فَيْرُوزٌ
See under فَصْل.	فَيْصَلٌ
To abound ; overflow, (river.) Be full, (vessel).	فَاضَ يَفِيضُ فَيْضًا
To pour (water) ; fill.	أَفَاضَ
Abundance.	فَيْضٌ ج فُيوضٌ
Periodic overflow or inundation of the Nile.	فَيَضَانُ النِّيل
Waterless desert.	فَيْفَاءُ ج فَيَافٍ
Elephant.	فِيلٌ ج أَفْيالٌ وفِيَلَةٌ
An army-corps.	فَيْلَقٌ ج فَيَالِقُ
Why? Wherefore?	فِيمَ (فِي ما)
To be niggardly.	فَانَ يَفِينُ فَيْنًا

ق

To bury, inter.	قَبَرَ يَقْبِرُ قَبْرًا
Grave, sepulchre.	قَبْرٌ ج قُبُورٌ
Sky-lark, lark.	قُنْبُرَةٌ ج قَنَابِر
Capers.	قَبَّرٌ
Cemetery.	مَقْبَرَةٌ ج مَقَابِر
Interred, buried.	مَقْبُورٌ
Cyprus (island).	قُبْرُس
Of Cyprus ; Cypriote.	قُبْرُسِيٌّ
To seek fire, or knowledge, from.	قَبَسَ يَقْبِسُ واقْتَبَسَ من
To quote an author.	إِقْتَبَسَ من
A coal, a fire-brand.	قَبْسَةٌ
To seize, grasp ; arrest. To contract.	قَبَضَ يَقْبِضُ
To receive (money).	قَبَضَ

As a numeral sign=100.	ق
To make convex.	قَبَّبَ
Collar (to a shirt, &c.).	(قَبَّةٌ)
Cupola, dome.	قُبَّةٌ ج قِبَبٌ
Large steelyard.	قَبَّانٌ ج قَبَابِين
Surmounted with a dome.	مُقَبَّبٌ
To be ugly, vile.	قَبُحَ يَقْبُحُ
To render, or deem ugly.	قَبَّحَ
To revile, insult.	قَابَحَ
To act meanly, shamefully.	أَقْبَحَ
To detest, abhor.	إِسْتَقْبَحَ
Ugliness, foulness.	قُبْحٌ وقَبَاحَةٌ
Fie on him !	قُبْحًا لهُ
Ugly, infamous.	قَبِيحٌ ج قِبَاحٌ
Vile action.	قَبِيحَةٌ ج قَبَائِح

To kiss.	قَبَّلَ	God caused him to die.	قَبَضَهُ
To correspond to ; meet.	قَابَلَ	To die.	قُبِضَ
To compare, collate.	قَابَلَ بِ	To make a payment to.	قَبَّضَ
To receive, accept.	تَقَبَّلَ	To shrink.	تَقَبَّضَ واَنقَبَضَ
To meet ; be compared.	تَقَابَلَ	Grasping, taking posses-	قَبْضٌ
To go to meet, receive.	إِستَقبَلَ	sion. Constipation.	
Previously.	قبلُ وَقَبْلاً ومِن قَبْلُ	A grasp ; handful.	قَبْضَةٌ
Side, direction.	قِبَلٌ	Handle, haft, hilt.	قَبْضَةٌ
With respect to ; from.	مِن قِبَلهِ	Astringent.	قَابِضٌ
Direction of Mecca. South.	قِبلَةٌ	Contraction, constipation.	إِنقِبَاضٌ
Kiss.	قُبلَةٌ ج قُبَلٌ . وتَقبِيلٌ	Handle, hilt.	مَقبِضٌ ج مَقَابِض
Southern.	قِبلِيٌّ	Seized ; received. Dead.	مَقبُوضٌ
Capable of, subject to.	قَابِلٌ لِ	Copts.	قِبطٌ واَقبَاط
Midwife. Receiver.	قَابِلةٌ ج قَوابِلُ	A Copt ; Coptic.	قِبطِيٌّ
Capacity ; appetite.	قَابِليَّةٌ	Hood, cowl.	قِبعٌ وقُبَّعةٌ
Over against.	قُبَالةٌ	Clogs.	قَبقَابٌ ج قَبَاقِيب
Midwifery.	قِبَالة	To receive, accept,	قَبِلَ يَقبَلُ قَبُولاً
Consent ; reception.	قَبُولٌ	admit ; consent, agree to.	
As regards this.	مِن هذا اَلقَبيلِ	To take up.	أَقبَلَ عَلى
		To approach, be near.	أَقبَلَ

Avarice, economy.	قِبْر وَتَقْتِير
Parsimonious, economical.	قَاتِر وَمقْتِر
To kill, murder.	قَتَل يَقْتُل
To fight against.	قَاتَل مَقَاتَلَة
To combat with one another, fight.	تَقَاتَل وَاقْتَتَل
To seek death, stake one's life.	إسْتَقْتَل
Murder ; execution.	قَتْل
Murderer, assassin.	قَاتِل ج قَتَلَة
Battle, combat.	قِتَال وَمقَاتَلَة
Deadly, causing death.	قَتَّال
Killed.	قَتِيل ج قَتْلَى . وَمقْتُول
Vital part (of the body).	مَقْتَل
Warrior, combatant.	مقَاتِل
Darkness.	قَتَام
Dark-coloured.	قَاتِم وَأقْتَم
Cucumber.	قِثَّاء
Elaterium.	قِثَّاء الحِمَار
To cough.	(قَحَّ يَقِحّ)
Pure, unmixed.	قُحّ ج اقْحَاح

Tribe.	قَبِيلَة ج قَبَائِل
Approach. Prosperity.	إقْبَال
The future. Reception.	إسْتِقْبَال
Meeting. Collation (of two texts). Antithesis.	مقَابَلَة
Coming, approaching.	مقْبِل
Opposite to, in front of.	مقَابِل
Accepted ; received.	مقْبُول
The future ; Facing.	مستَقْبَل
To weigh with steelyard.	قَبَن
Steelyard.	قَبَّان
Trade of a weigher.	قَبَانَة
One who weighs.	قَبَّانِيّ
Weighing.	قَبُونَة
To bend, curve.	قَبَا يَقْبُو قَبْواً
Outer garment.	قَبَاء ج أقْبِيَة
Vault.	قَبْو ج أقْبِيَة
Small pack-saddle.	قَتَب ج أقْتَاب
To be niggardly.	قَتَر وَأقْتَر عَلَى

Verily he prospers.	قَدْ أَفْلَحَ
To cut, cleave.	قَدَّ يَقُدُّ قَدًّا
To cut and dry (meat).	قَدَّد
To be cut and dried.	تَقَدَّد
To be cut, slit, divided.	إِنْقَدَّ
Stature, size.	قَدٌّ ج قُدُودٌ
Equal to in measure.	عَلَى قَدِّه
Goodly in form.	حَسَنُ ٱلْقَدِّ
Cured meat.	قَدِيدٌ ومُقَدَّدٌ
To bore, pierce.	قَدَحَ يَقْدَحُ
To strike fire.	قَدَحَ وَٱقْتَدَحَ
To revile, censure.	قَدَحَ فِي
Drinking-cup.	قَدَحٌ ج أَقْدَاحٌ
Slanderer, calumniator.	قَادِحٌ
Gimlet.	مِقْدَحٌ ومِقْدَاحٌ
To be able.	قَدَرَ يَقْدِرُ عَلَى
To measure; compute.	قَدَرَ وقَدَّر
To decree for.	قَدَرَ وقَدَّرَ عَلَى
To prepare, assign.	قَدَرَ لِ

A cough.	(قَحَّة)
Cough. Prostitute.	قَحْبَةٌ ج قِحَابٌ
To be rainless.	قَحِطَ يَقْحَطُ وأَقْحَطَ
Drought, famine.	قَحْطٌ
Year of drought.	عَامٌ مُقْحِطٌ
To sweep away.	قَحَفَ يَقْحَفُ
Skull.	قِحْفٌ ج أَقْحَافٌ
What is swept away.	قُحَافَةٌ
Winnowing-fan; dust-pan.	مِقْحَفَةٌ
To dry up, wither.	قَحِلَ يَقْحَلُ قَحْلاً
To dry, cause to wither.	أَقْحَلَ
Dryness, aridity.	قُحُولَةٌ
To rush.	قَحَمَ يَقْحَمُ قُحُومًا فِي
To draw near to.	قَحَمَ إِلَى
To rush upon.	إِقْتَحَمَ
Anthemis, camomile.	أُقْحُوَان
Particle, e. g. Zeid has just risen.	قَدْ. قَدْ قَامَ زَيْدٌ
The liar sometimes peaks the truth.	قَدْ يَصْدُقُ الْكَذُوب

To hallow ; sanctify.	قَدَّس
To be purified, sanctified.	تَقَدَّس
Holiness.	قُدْسٌ وقداسةٌ
Jerusalem.	القُدْس
The Holy Ghost.	(أَلروحُ القُدس)
Mass, liturgy.	قداسٌ ج قداديس
The All-Holy (God).	القدوس
Saint.	قدّيسٌ ج قدّيسونَ
Sanctification.	تقديسٌ
Jerusalem.	بيت المَقدس
Sanctified.	مقدسٌ ومتقدّسٌ
The Holy Bible.	أَلكتابُ المقدَّس
To arrive from.	قدِم يقدم من
To be old.	قدم يقدم . وتقادم
To prefer (a thing).	قدَّمهُ عَلَى
To present, offer to.	قدم ل
To undertake boldly.	أقدم على
To advance, lead.	تقدَّم
To advance towards.	تقدَّم إلى

To put a value upon.	قدَّر
To enable.	قدر على
To be preordained.	تقدَّر
To be powerful, or rich.	اقتَدر
Quantity, measure.	قَدْر
Fate ; divine decree. Powder, position.	قدْرٌ ج أَقْدار
Cooking-pot.	قدْرٌ ج قُدور
Might, power, authority.	قدرةٌ
Powerful ; able.	قَادرٌ وقديرٌ
The Omnipotent.	أَلقدير
Predestination.	تقديرٌ ج تقادير
Suppositon. Implied meaning. Evaluation.	
Hypothetically.	تقديراً
Quantity, fixed measure.	مقدارٌ
As much as.	بِمقدارِ ما
Power, ability.	مقدرةٌ
Valuer, estimator.	مقدّرٌ
Predestinated.	مقدَّرٌ ومقدورٌ

Antiquity, oldness, &c. تَقَادُمٌ	To surpass. تَقَدَّمَ عَلَى
Front part, fore part. مُقَدَّمٌ	Antiquity. قِدْمٌ وَقِدْمَةٌ
Advance guard of مُقَدَّمَةٌ	Precedence. قِدَمٌ
(an army). Preface ; premise.	Foot. قَدَمٌ ج أَقْدَامٌ
One who is in advance. مُتَقَدِّمٌ	Priority, precedence. قُدْمَةٌ
Afore-mentioned. مُتَقَدِّمٌ ذِكْرُهُ	Comer ; coming. قَادِمٌ
Courageous, energetic. مِقْدَامٌ	In front of, before. قُدَّامٌ
To imitate, emulate. اِقْتَدَى بِ	Courageous, bold. قَدُومٌ ج قُدُمٌ
Model for imitation. قُدْوَةٌ	Hatchet, adze. قَدُومٌ وَقَدُّومٌ
Way, manner. قِدْيَةٌ	Ancient, old. قَدِيمٌ ج قُدَمَاءُ
Imitation. اِقْتِدَاءٌ	The Eternal (God). الْقَدِيمُ
To be unclean. قَذِرَ يَقْذَرُ وَقَذُرَ يَقْذُرُ	Formerly. قَدِيمًا وَفِي الْقَدِيمِ
To foul, render unclean. قَذَّرَ	In olden times. مِنَ الْقَدِيمِ
Filth. قَذَرٌ ج أَقْذَارٌ وَقَاذُورَةٌ	More ancient. أَقْدَمُ ج أَقْدَمُونَ
Dirty, filthy ; unclean. قَذِرٌ	The ancients. الْأَقْدَمُونَ
To throw. Row. قَذَفَ يَقْذِفُ	Boldness ; diligence. إِقْدَامٌ
To accuse of. قَذَفَ بِ	Present ; offering. تَقْدِمَةٌ ج تَقَادِمُ
Throwing ; abusing. قَذْفٌ	Presenting, offering. تَقْدِيمٌ
Rower. قَذَّافٌ	Pre-eminence ; progress. تَقَدُّمٌ

Affirmation ; confession.	إِقْرَار	Oar.	مِقْذَاف ومِقْذَف ج مَقَاذِيف
Report.	تَقْرِير	Mote, or small particle.	قَذَى
Residence.	مَقَرّ ومُسْتَقَرّ	To stay, dwell.	قَرَّ يَقِرّ
To read.	قَرَأَ يَقْرَأُ قِرَاءَة	To persist, persevere in.	قَرَّ عَلَى
To study with (a teacher).	قَرَأَ عَلَى	He was content.	قَرَّ عَيْنًا
To send, or deliver, a greeting.	أَقْرَأَهُ السَّلَام	To settle, fix, establish.	قَرَّر
		To cause one to stay.	قَرَّر وأَقَرَّ
To investigate.	إِسْتَقْرَأَ	To cause one to confess. To settle, fix.	قَرَّر
Act of reading.	قِرَاءَة ج قِرَاءَات	To decide upon.	قَرَّر في نَفْسِهِ أَنْ
The Coran.	الْقُرْآن	To confess, avow.	أَقَرَّ ب
Reader, reciter.	قَارِئ ج قُرَّاء	To refresh, console.	أَقَرَّ عَيْنَهِ
Read, recited.	مَقْرُوء ومِقْرَيّ ومَقْرُوّ	To be stated, determined.	تَقَرَّر
To approach.	قَرُب يَقْرُب الى ومِنْ	To dwell, inhabit.	إِسْتَقَرَّ في
To bring near ; offer.	قَرَّب	Water-cress. Darling.	قُرَّة الْعَيْن
To be near to.	قَارَبَ	Dwelling ; stability.	قَرَار
To be on the point of.	قَارَب أَنْ	Refrain, (music).	قَرَار
To approach.	تَقَرَّب تَقَرُّبًا إِلَى	Continent, firm-land.	قَارَّة
To be near one another.	تَقَارَب	Glass bottle.	قَارُورَة ج قَوَارِير
To approach.	إِقْتَرَب	Consoled, content.	قَرِير الْعَيْن

Pure (water).	قَرَاحٌ	Nearness.	قُرْبٌ
Talent, genius.	قَرِيحَةٌ ج قَرَائِح	Near ; soon.	عَن قُرْب
Ape, monkey.	قِرْدٌ ج قُرُودٌ	In the vicinity of.	بِالْقُرْبِ مِن
Tick, (insect).	قُرَادٌ ج أَقْرِدَةٌ	Skin-bag.	قِرْبَةٌ ج قِرَبَاتٌ وَقِرَبٌ
To burn, blaze (coal).	قَرِدَح	Offering to God.	قُرْبَانٌ ج قَرَابِين
Armourer.	قَرْدَاحِيٌّ وَقَرْدَحْجِيٌّ	Sheath, scabbard.	قِرَابٌ ج اقْرِبَةٌ
To freeze.	قَرِسَ يَقْرَسُ قَرْسًا	Kinship ; relations.	قَرَابَةٌ وَقُرْبَى
Intense cold.	قَارِسٌ وَقَرِيسٌ	Boat, skiff.	قَارِبٌ ج قَوَارِب
A kind of plum.	(قَرَاسِيَا)	Near ; related ;	قَرِيبٌ ج أَقْرِبَاءُ
To curdle (milk).	قَرَشَ الْحَلِيبَ	neighbour, followman ; relation.	
Piastre.	قِرْشٌ ج قُرُوشٌ	Shortly, soon.	عَن قَرِيب
Tribe of Koreish.	قُرَيْشٌ	Nearer ; more probable.	أَقْرَبُ
Sweet curd.	قُرَيْشَةٌ	Approximation.	تَقْرِيبٌ
Rich.	(مُقْرِشٌ)	Approximately.	تَقْرِيبًا وَبِالتَّقْرِيب
To pinch.	قَرَصَ يَقْرُصُ قَرْصًا	Pommel.	قَرْبُوسٌ ج قَرَابِيس
To cut out (dough).	قَرَّصَ	To wound.	قَرَحَ يَقْرَحُ قَرْحًا
Disc ; cake.	قُرْصٌ ج أَقْرَاصٌ	To finish teething (horse).	قَرِحَ يَقْرَحُ
Nettle (plant).	قُرَّاصٌ وَ(قُرَّيْصٌ)	To invent ; improvise. Demand.	إِقْتَرَحَ
Corsairs, pirates.	قُرْصَانٌ	A wound ; an ulcer.	قَرْحَةٌ

To fight.	قَارَعَ مقارعةً وقِرَاعاً	To cut ; nibble.	قَرَضَ يَقْرِض
To cast lots, or play dice.	تَقَارَع	To lend one money.	أَقْرَض
To cast lots for.	إِقْتَرَع فِي وعَلَى	To die out, perish.	إِنْقَرَض
Knocking. Gourd.	قَرْع	To borrow.	إِقْتَرَض وآسْتَقْرَض
Baldness ; scald-head.	قَرْعَة	Loan, debt.	قَرْض ج قُروض
A gourd, Chemical retort.	قُرْعَة	Cuttings, clippings.	قُرَاصَة
Lot. Ballot.	قُرْعة ج قُرَع	Poetry.	قَرِيض
He wins.	أَلْقُرعةُ لَه	Scissors.	مِقْراض ج مَقَاريض
He loses.	الْقُرعةُ عَلَيه	To cut.	قَرَط يَقْرِط
Middle part of the way.	قَارِعَة	To give little to.	قَرَّطَ عَلَى
Day of judgement.	القَارِعَة	Ear-ring. Cluster.	قُرْط ج أَقْراط
Bald, scald-headed. Bare.	أَقْرَع	Carat, inch.	قِيراط ج قَراريط
Whip, knocker.	مِقْرَعة ج مَقَارع	Cordova (in Spain).	قُرْطُبة
To suspect, blame.	قِرَف وقَرَّف ب	Paper.	قُرْطَاس ج قراطيس
To loathe.	قَرِف يَقْرَف قَرَفاً	Reed-basket.	قُرْطَلّ ج قراطل
To cause disgust.	أَقْرَف	To laud, eulogize.	قَرَّظَ
To commit (a crime).	إِقْتَرَف	Eulogy. Panegyric.	تَقْريظ
Disgust, loathing.	قَرَف	To knock, rap.	قَرَعَ يَقْرَع قَرْعاً
Suspicion. Cinnamon.	قِرْفة	To scold, rebuke.	قَرَّعَ

Of a crimson colour.	قِرْمِزِيٌّ	Disgusting.	مُقْرِفٌ
A Karmathian.	قِرْمِطِيٌّ	To cluck, (hen).	قَرَقَ يَقْرِق قَرْقاً
Sect of Karmathians.	قَرَامِطَةٌ	Hernia in the scrotum.	(قَرْقٌ)
To join.	قَرَنَ يَقْرِن قِرْناً بِ	Sitting-hen.	(قُرْقَةٌ)
To join together.	أَقْوَنَ	To dry, become hard.	(قَرْقَدَ)
To be joined ; married.	إِقْتَرَنَ بِ	Squirrel.	قَرْقَذانٌ وقَرْقَدونٌ
Horn. Century, age.	قَرْنٌ ج قُرونٌ	To rumble, (stomach).	قَرْقَرَ
Alexander the Great.	ذو القَرْنَينِ	Rumbling.	قَرْقَرَةٌ ج قَرَاقِرُ
Rhinoceros.	وحيد القَرَن	Lamb.	(قَرْقورٌ)
One's equal.	قِرْنٌ ج أَقْرانٌ	To gnaw at.	(قَرْقَش)
Projecting angle or corner.	قُرْنَةٌ	To cut into small pieces.	(قَرْقَطَ)
Close union.	قِرانٌ ومُقَارَنَةٌ	To rumble, clatter.	(قَرْقَع)
Comrade ; husband.	قَرينٌ ج قُرَناءُ	A rattling, rumbling.	(قَرْقَعَةٌ)
Wife. Context.	قَرينَةٌ ج قَرائِنُ	To gnaw off.	قَرِمَ يَقْرُم قَرْماً
Horned ; angled.	مُقَرَّنٌ	The Crimea.	القِرْم
Joined, yoked.	مَقْرونٌ ومُقْتَرِنٌ	Stump of a tree.	قِرْمَةٌ ج قِرْمٌ
Cauliflower.	قَرْنَبيطٌ (قَنْبيطٌ)	Tile, brick.	قِرْميدٌ
Cloves. Carnation (plant).	قَرَنْفُلٌ	Cochineal ; crimson.	قِرْمِزٌ
Cloves.	كَبْشُ القَرَنْفل		

قَسٌّ ج قُسوسٌ. وقسِّيسٌ ج قسِّيسونَ
Clergyman, minister.

Sebesten plum. مِقْساسٌ
Cordia Myxa L.

To force, compel. قَسَرَ يَقْسِر

Violence, compulsion. قَسْرٌ

By force. قَسْرًا

To act قَسَطَ يَقْسِط قَسْطًا وقُسوطًا
unjustly, swerve from what is
right, to separate, distribute.

To do justice. قَسَطَ يَقْسِط وأَقْسَطَ

To pay by instalments. قَسَّطَ

To divide equally. تَقَسَّطَ بَيْنَ

Justice ; just, equitable. قِسْطٌ

Part, portion. قِسْطٌ ج أَقْساطٌ

Pipe, conduit. قَسْطَلٌ ج قَساطِل

To divide. قَسَمَ يَقْسِم قَسْمًا وقَسَّمَ

To share mutually. قاسَمَ

To swear by God. أَقْسَمَ باللّٰه

To be divided, separated. تَقَسَّمَ

To share. تَقاسَمَ وَانْقَسَمَ

A pink, carnation. قَرَنْفُلَة

To follow out. قَرَا ـُ. وَاسْتَقْرَى

Analogy. (See اِسْتَقْرَأَ) اِسْتِقْراءٌ

To receive hospitably. قَرَا يَقْري

Entertainment ; feasting. قِرًى

Village. قَرْيَةٌ ج قُرًى

To feel aversion to. قَزَّ يَقَزّ عَنْ

Raw-silk, floss silk. قَزٌّ

Silk-worm. دودُ القَزّ

Glass, glass-ware. قَزازٌ (زُجاجٌ)

Silk, or glass merchant. قَزّازٌ

Iris (of the eye). قَزَحِيَّةٌ

Tin. قَزْديرٌ (عوض : قَصْديرٌ)

To limp. قَزَلَ يَقْزِل قَزْلًا

Limping. قَزَلٌ

Lame. أَقْزَلُ قَزْلاءُ ج قُزْلٌ

To be small, mean. قَزُمَ يَقْزُم

Mean, dwarfish. قَزْمٌ وقُزْمٌ

Cleaner (sweeper).	قَشَّاشٌ	To take mutual oaths.	تَقَاسَم
Broom.	مِقَشَّةٌ	To be divided.	إِنْقَسَم
Demijohn.	مِقَشِّشَةٌ	Oath.	قَسَمٌ ج أَقْسَامٌ
Chapped skin.	قَشَبٌ	Part; share.	قِسْمٌ ج أَقْسَامٌ
Cream.	قِشْدَةٌ	Division, share, lot.	قِسْمَةٌ ج قِسَمٌ
To peel, skin.	قَشَرَ يَقْشِرُ قَشْرًا	Quotient, (arith.).	خَارِجُ الْقِسْمَةِ
To be peeled.	تَقَشَّر وَاقْشَرَّ	Sharer ; lot.	قَسِيمٌ ج أَقْسِمَاءُ
Rind, bark, shell.	قِشْرٌ ج قُشُورٌ	Divided, distributed.	مُقَسَّمٌ
A rind, bark, shell.	قِشْرَةٌ وقِشَارَةٌ	Dividend (arith.).	مَقْسُومٌ
Peeled.	مُقَشَّرٌ	Divisor, (arith.).	مَقْسُومٌ عَلَيْهِ
To strip off.	قَشَطَ يَقْشِطُ قَشْطًا عَن	To be hard, unyielding.	قَسَا يَقْسُو
To strip; rob.	قَشَّطَ	To harden.	قَسَّى وأَقْسَى
To be stripped.	تَقَشَّطَ وَانْقَشَطَ	To endure, suffer.	قَاسَى
Sugar-candy. Cream.	(قِشْطَةٌ)	Hard-heartedness.	قَسَاوَةٌ
Leather strap.	(قِشَاطٌ)	Hard, severe.	قَاسٍ ج قُسَاةٌ
To see.	(قَشِعَ يَقْشَعُ)	To gather, collect. Sweep. Skim.	قَشَّ يَقُشُّ
To be dispersed, (clouds).	أَقْشَع	Straw.	قَشٌّ
To be dispelled.	أَقْشَعَ عَن	A single straw.	قَشَّة

Sugar-cane.	قَصَب السُّكَّر
A reed or cane. City ; capital.	قَصَبَة ج قَصَب
Œsophagus.	قَصَبَة المَرِيء
Windpipe.	قَصَبَة الرِّئَة
Bone of the nose.	قَصَبَة الأَنف
Butcher's trade.	قِصَابَة
Butcher.	قَصَّاب
Slaughter-house.	مَقْصَبَة
To purpose; repair to.	قَصَد يَقْصِد
To economise.	قَصَد وَاقْتَصَد فِي
Intention, purpose, aim.	قَصْد
Visitor. Legate.	قَاصِد ج قُصَّاد
Intended, desired.	مَقْصُود
A poem.	قَصِيدَة ج قَصَائِد
Moderation ; economy.	اِقْتِصَاد
Intention, aim.	مَقْصِد ج مَقَاصِد
Tin.	قَصْدِير
To be short.	قَصُر يَقْصُر
To lack power.	قَصَر أَو قَصَر عَن

To be seen. Dispelled.	اِنْقَشَع
To shudder, shiver.	اِقْشَعَرَّ
Shudder ; shivering.	قُشَعْرِيرَة
To be wretched.	قَشَف يَقْشَف قَشَافَة
To lead an ascetic life.	تَقَشَّف
Life in misery.	قَشَف
Ascetic.	مُتَقَشِّف
Barrack.	(قِشْلَة)
To cut off, clip.	قَصَّ يَقُصُّ قَصًّا
To tell ; narrate.	قَصَّ يَقُصُّ عَلَى
To punish.	قَاصَّ مُقَاصَّة وَقِصَاصًا
To be clipped, cut off.	اِنْقَصَّ
To take vengeance. Tell.	اِقْتَصَّ
Sternum.	قَصّ
Tale, story.	قِصَّة ج قِصَص
Punishment.	قِصَاص
Cuttings ; parings.	قُصَاصَة
Scissors.	مِقَصّ ج مَقَاصّ
Reeds. Thread of gold.	قَصَب

Abbreviation ; neglect.	تَقصِيرٌ	To shorten.	قَصَّرَ وَأَقصَرَ
Limited. Bleached.	مَقصُورٌ	To bleach.	قَصَرَ قَصراً وَقِصارةً
A large room.	مَقصُورةٌ ج مَقاصِير	To shut up, confine.	قَصَرهُ في
Large dish.	قَصعةٌ ج قَصعَاتٌ	To limit, restrict.	قَصَرَ على
To break.	قَصَفَ يَقصِفُ قَصفاً	To lag, fall short of.	قَصَّرَ في
To roar, (thunder).	قَصَفَ يَقصِفُ	To desist from.	أَقصَرَ عن
To be broken.	تَقصَّفَ وَانقَصَفَ	To shrink, contract.	تَقَصَّرَ
Brittle, easily broken.	قَصِفٌ	To limit one's self to.	إِقتَصَرَ عَلَى
Breaking, roaring.	قَاصِفٌ	Shortness.	قَصرٌ وَقِصَرٌ
Pleasure-house.	مَقصَفٌ	Remissness.	قُصُورٌ
To cut off, mow.	قَصَلَ يَقصِلُ قَصلاً	End (of an affair).	قُصَارى
Stubble, chaff.	قَصَلٌ وَقِصَالةٌ	Castle, palace.	قَصرٌ ج قُصُورٌ
Green food for animals.	قَصِيلٌ	Minor, under age.	قَاصِرٌ
To break in pieces.	قَصَمَ يَقصِمُ قَصماً	Powerless.	قَاصِرُ اليَد
To be broken.	تَقَصَّمَ وَانقَصَمَ	Fuller, bleecher.	قَصَّارٌ
Brittle, fragile.	قَصِيمٌ	Art of bleaching.	قِصَارةٌ
Broken shattered.	قَصِيمٌ وَمَقصُومٌ	Cæsar, emperor.	قَيصَرٌ ج قَيَاصِرةٌ
To be very distant.	قَصَا يَقصُو	Short; small.	قَصِيرٌ ج قِصَارٌ
To penetrate deeply ; follow out to the end.	تَقَصَّى وَاستَقصى في	Shorter.	أَقصَرُ م قُصرى ج أَقَاصِرُ

To require.	قَضَى عَلَى	Distance.	قَصًا وقَصَاء
To die.	قَضَى أَوْ قَضَى أَجَلهُ أَوْ نَحْبَهُ	Very distant.	قَاصٍ ج أَقْصَاء
To spend the time.	قَضَى الزَّمَانَ	Investigation.	إِسْتِقْصَاء
To pay a debt.	قَضَى الدَّيْنَ	More distant.	أَقْصَى مقصُوى ج أَقَاصٍ
To judge in favour of.	قَضَى لِ	The extreme end ; highest purpose.	الغَايَةُ القُصْوَى
To fulfil a purpose.	قَضَى الوَطَر	The uttermost parts of the earth.	أَقَاصِي الأَرْضِ
To execute, carry out.	قَضَى	To break, crush.	قَضَّ يَقُضُّ قَضًّا
To summon before a judge.	قَاضَى	To swoop down (bird). To fall.	إِنْقَضَّ
To be carried out ; cease.	إِنْقَضَى	To cut off, prune.	قَضَبَ وَاقْتَضَبَ
They had a law-suit.	تَقَاضَيَا	To be pruned.	تَقَضَّبَ وَانْقَضَبَ
To be required ; necessary.	إِقْتَضَى	Prunings.	قُضَابَة
Judgment.	قَضًى وقَضَاء ج أَقْضِيَة	Rod, stick.	قَضِيب ج قُضْبَان
Event ; fact, matter ; question, proposition.	قَضِيَّة ج قَضَايَا	Improvised (speech).	مُقْتَضَب
A judge.	قَاضٍ ج قُضَاة	To nibble at, gnaw.	قَضِمَ يَقْضَم
Supreme Judge.	قَاضِي القُضَاةِ	Roasted peas.	(قَضَامَةً أَوْ قَضَامِيّ)
Death.	القَاضِيَة	To decide, fulfil (a duty) ; satisfy (a want) ; execute (an order).	قَضَى يَقْضِي
End ; completion.	إِنْقِضَاء		
Exigency ; requisite.	إِقْتِضَاء	To judge.	قَضَى بَيْنَ يَقْضِي

To come from all sides.	تَقَاطَرَ
To distil.	إِسْتَقْطَرَ
Dropping.	قَطْرٌ وَقَطَرَانٌ
Rain ; drops.	قَطْرٌ
Side, region. Diameter.	قُطْرٌ ج أَقْطَارٌ
Diameter of a circle.	قُطْرُ الدَّائِرَةِ
Diagonal of a square or parallelogram.	قُطْرُ الْمُرَبَّعِ اوْ الْمُسْتَطِيلِ
A drop. Collyrium.	قَطْرَةٌ
Liquid pitch ; tar.	قَطْرَانٌ
File or string ; train.	قِطَارٌ
Distillation.	تَقْطِيرٌ
Hand-cuffs ; stocks.	مِقْطَرَةٌ
To cut off, cross.	قَطَعَ يَقْطَعُ قَطْعًا
To carry on highway robbery.	قَطَعَ الطَّرِيقَ
To sever ; prevent.	قَطَعَ عَنْ
To assign a portion.	قَطَعَ لَهُ
To speak decisively.	قَطَعَ فِي الْقَوْلِ
To cut off entirely.	قَطَّعَ

Accomplished.	مَقْضِيّ
Required, necessary.	مُقْتَضَى
In conformity with.	بِمُقْتَضَى
To cut (a reed-pen).	قَطَّ يَقُطُّ
Never, not at all.	قَطُّ وَقَطْ
I never saw him.	مَا رَأَيْتُهُ قَطُّ
Tom-cat, cat.	قِطٌّ ج قِطَاطٌ
Female cat.	قِطَّةٌ
To frown.	قَطَبَ يَقْطِبُ قَطْبًا. وَقَطَّبَ
Axis, pivot.	قُطْبٌ ج قُطُوبٌ
Pole, pole-star. Leader.	قُطْبٌ
Pole-star.	نَجْمَةُ الْقُطْبِ
One of the earth's poles.	قُطْبَةٌ
Polar.	قُطْبِيّ
One who frowns.	قَاطِبٌ وَقَطُوبٌ
All together.	قَاطِبَةً
To trickle.	قَطَرَ يَقْطُرُ قَطْرًا
To place in line or file.	قَطَرَ يَقْطُرُ
To fall in drops.	تَقَطَّرَ

Lent.	قَطَاعَةٌ ج قَطَائِعُ	To scan poetry.	قَطَّعَ ٱلشِّعْرَ
Herd, flock.	قَطِيعٌ ج قُطْعَانٌ	To while away time.	قَطَّعَ ٱلزَّمَانَ
Fief-land. Tax.	قَطِيعَةٌ ج قَطَائِعُ	To separate from.	قَاطَعَ
Separation ; interruption.	إِنْقِطَاعٌ	To take across (a river). Give land as a fief.	أَقْطَعَ
Scanning.	تَقْطِيعٌ تَقَاطِيعُ	To be cut off.	تَقَطَّعَ وَٱنْقَطَعَ
Syllable.	مَقْطَعٌ ج مَقَاطِعُ	To be interrupted ; cease.	إِنْقَطَعَ
Ford of a river.	مَقْطَعُ ٱلنَّهْرِ	To be devoted to.	إِنْقَطَعَ إِلَى
Province.	مُقَاطَعَةٌ ج مُقَاطَعَاتٌ	To cut off a part.	إِقْتَطَعَ مِنْ
Work by the job.	(بِٱلْمُقَاطَعَةِ)	Amputation. Section. Size.	قَطْعٌ
Cut into pieces.	مُقَطَّعٌ	Hyperbola.	قَطْعٌ زَائِدٌ
Separated, detached.	مُنْقَطِعٌ	Ellipse.	قَطْعٌ نَاقِصٌ
Cut off ; amputated.	مَقْطُوعٌ	Parabola.	قَطْعٌ مُكَافٍ
To cull, pluck, gather.	قَطَفَ يَقْطِفُ وَٱقْتَطَفَ	Conic section.	قَطْعُ ٱلْمَخْرُوطِ
Act of gathering fruit.	قَطْفٌ	Certainly ; not at all.	قَطْعًا
Time of gathering.	قِطَافٌ	A part, piece.	قِطْعَةٌ ج قِطَعٌ
A kind of sweet cake	قَطَائِفُ	Sharp ; decisive.	قَاطِعٌ
Basket, panier.	مِقْطَفٌ	Opposite side of a river.	(قَاطِعُ ٱلنَّهْرِ)
To cut off.	قَطَمَ يَقْطِمُ قَطْمًا	Highway-man.	قَاطِعُ ٱلطَّرِيقِ

Infirm ; cripple. مُقْعَد	Piece, fragment. قُطَيْمَة
Pensioner. Neglectful. مُتَقَاعِد	To inhabit (a place). قَطَنَ يَقْطُنُ فِي
To be deep. قَعُرَ يَقْعُرُ قَعَارَةً	Loins ; lumbar region. قَطَن
To make concave. قَعَّرَ	Cotton. قُطْن ج أَقْطَان
To dig deep. قَعَّرَ وَأَقْعَرَ	Settled inhabitant. قَاطِن ج قُطَّان
Bottom ; depth. قَعْر ج قُعُور	Pumpkin, squash. يَقْطِين
Dug ; hollow ; concave. مُقَعَّر	A kind of snipe. قَطَاة ج قَطًا
To clatter, rattle. قَعْقَعَ ج قَعْقَعَة	To sit down ; dwell. قَعَدَ يَقْعُد
Magpie. قَعْقَع وَقُعْقُع ج قَعَاقِعَان	To lie in wait for. قَعَدَ لِ
Large basket, panier. قُفَّة ج قِفَف	To desist from. قَعَدَ عَن
To track. قَفَرَ يَقْفُرُ قَفْراً وَتَقَفَّرَ وَاقْتَفَرَ	To cause to sit, seat. اَقْعَدَ
To be waste, deserted. اَقْفَرَ	To be unable to walk. اَقْعَدَ
Desert, waste (land). قَفْر ج قِفَار	To neglect. تَقَعَّدَ وَتَقَاعَدَ عَن
Bee-hive ; basket. قَفِير ج قُفْرَان	Eleventh month of the Arabian year. ذُو القَعْدَة
To jump, leap. قَفَزَ يَقْفِزُ قَفْزاً	Foundation, base; rule, canon ; model. قَاعِدَة ج قَوَاعِد
Jump, leap. قَفْزَة ج قَفَزَات	Capital of a country. قَاعِدَة البِلَاد
A certain measure. قَفِيز ج أَقْفِزَة	Sitting ; inactivity. قُعُود
Bird-cage ; coop. قَفَص ج أَقْفَاص	A place of sitting. مَقْعَد ج مَقَاعِد

To be little in quantity,	قَلَّ يَقِلُّ	To shiver from cold.	قَهْقَفَ
be scarce, happen rarely.		To return.	قَفَلَ يَقْفِلُ قُفُولاً
Rarely,	قَلَّمَا (قَلَّ مَا)	To guard, lock up.	قَفَّلَ يُقَفِّلُ تَقْفِلاً
To bear, carry.	قَلَّ قَلاًّ وَأَقَلَّ	To lock, shut.	قَفَلَ وَأَقْفَلَ
To diminish, lessen.	قَلَّلَ وَأَقَلَّ	To cause to return.	أَقْفَلَ عَنْ
To have little property.	أَقَلَّ	To be locked, bolted.	إِنْقَفَلَ
To find small, paltry.	إِسْتَقَلَّ	Lock, bolt. Caravan.	قُفْلٌ ج أَقْفَالٌ
To be independent.	إِسْتَقَلَّ بِ	Caravan.	قَافِلَةٌ ج قَوَافِلُ
Earthen water-jug.	قُلَّةٌ ج قُلَلٌ	Vein in the arm.	قَيْفَالٌ
Littleness, small quantity.	قِلَّةٌ	To walk behind, follow.	قَفَا يَقْفُو
Plural which signifies	جَمْعُ الْقِلَّةِ	To send after.	قَفَّى بِ
from 3 to 10 objects.		To follow, imitate.	تَقَفَّى وَاقْتَفَى
A (monk's) cell.	قِلِّيَّةٌ وَقِلاَّيَةٌ	To prefer, select, chose.	اقْتَفَى
Few, little, scarce.	قَلِيلٌ ج قَلِيلُونَ	Back side, reverse.	قَفاً وَقَفَاءٌ
Rarely, seldom, slightly.	قَلِيلاً	Rhyme, (final word).	قَافِيَةٌ ج قَوَافٍ
Less, rarer.	أَقَلُّ	Imitation ; preference.	إِفْتَفَاءٌ
Least, rarest.	الْأَقَلُّ	Rhymed prose.	أَلْكَلاَمُ الْمُقَفَّى
Poor, having but little.	أَقَلُّ وَمُقِلٌّ	Rhymed prose.	
Diminishing, lessening.	تَقْلِيلٌ	Cardamon.	قَاقُلَّة
Independence.	إِسْتِقْلاَلٌ		

To wind round ; adorn. قَلَّدَ	Independent. مُسْتَقِلٌّ
Imitate.	To change, alter. To قَلَبَ يَقْلِبُ
To undertake an affair. تَقَلَّدَ الأَمْرَ	overturn ; overthrow.
To put on the sword. تَقَلَّدَ السَّيْفَ	To manipulate ; prove. قَلَّبَ
Necklace ; collar. قِلَادَةٌ ج قَلَائِدُ	To be turned ; be fickle. تَقَلَّبَ
Imitation. Church تَقْلِيدٌ ج تَقَالِيد	To be turned upside down. اِنْقَلَبَ
tradition.	To return to. إِنْقَلَبَ إِلَى
Imitator, counterfeiter. مُقَلِّدٌ	Change of letters (in gram). قَلْبٌ
Imitated, counterfeited. مُقَلَّدٌ	Heart, mind, قَلْبٌ ج قُلُوبٌ
Management of مَقَالِيدُ الأُمُورِ	thought ; centre, core.
affairs.	Sincere, earnest, hearty. قَلْبِيٌّ
Red Sea. بَحْرُ القُلْزُمِ	Mould, cast, last. قَالَبٌ ج قَوَالِبُ
Hood, cap. قَلَنْسُوَةٌ	Loaf of sugar. قَالَبُ سُكَّرٍ
Eel. أَنْقَلِيسُ وَإِنْقِلِيسُ	Revolution ; overthrow. إِنْقِلَابٌ
To contract, shrink. قَلَصَ يَقْلِصُ	Solstice. إِنْقِلَابُ الشَّمْسِ
To be wrinkled, shrunk. تَقَلَّصَ	Change ; inconstancy. تَقَلُّبٌ
To tear from its place, قَلَعَ يَقْلَعُ	Vicissitudes. تَقَلُّبَاتٌ
pull out, uproot.	Turned, turned over. مَقْلُوبٌ
To set sail. أَقْلَعَ	
To withdraw from. أَقْلَعَ عَنْ	
To be taken away. إِنْقَلَعَ	Final resting place. مُنْقَلَبٌ
To pull out, uproot. إِقْتَلَعَ	

To pare (the nails).	قَلَمَ ـ وَقَلَّمَ	Sail.	قِلْعٌ ج قُلُوعٌ
Pen; handwriting. Style.	قَلَمٌ ج أَقْلَامٌ	Castle, fortress.	قَلْعَةٌ ج قِلَاعٌ
Pencil.	قَلَمُ رُصَاصٍ	Sores in the mouth, (aphthæ)·	قُلَاعٌ
Slate-pencil.	قَلَمُ حَجَرٍ	Stone-quarry.	مَقْلَعٌ ج مَقَالِعُ
Parings (of nails &c.).	قُلَامَةٌ	Sling.	مِقْلَاعٌ ج مَقَالِيعُ
Region, tract, province; climate.	إِقْلِيمٌ ج أَقَالِيمُ	Uprooted, pulled out.	مَقْلُوعٌ
Cut, pared.	مُقَلَّمٌ	To circumcise.	قَلَفَ يَقْلِفُ
Pen-case.	مِقْلَمَةٌ	To calk a ship.	قَلَفَ وَقَلَّفَ
Cowl, cap.	قَلَنْسُوَةٌ ج قَلَانِسُ	Prepuce.	قَلَفَةٌ وَقُلْفَةٌ ج قُلَفٌ
To fry.	قَلَا يَقْلُو وقَلَوْا وَقَلَى يَقْلِي قَلْيًا	Trade of calking ships.	قِلَافَةٌ
Ash of alkaline plants.	قِلًى وَقِلْي	Uncircumcised.	أَقْلَفُ
Cell of a monk.	قَلَّايَةٌ	To be agitated.	قَلِقَ يَقْلَقُ قَلَقًا
Fried food.	قَلِيَّةٌ	To agitate, disturb.	أَقْلَقَ
A frying-pan.	مِقْلًى وَمِقْلَاةٌ	Disquietude, trouble.	قَلَقٌ
Fried, roasted.	مَقْلِيٌّ وَمُقْلًى	Disturbed; restless.	قَلِقٌ
Summit, top.	قِمَّةٌ ج قِمَمٌ	Colocassia (plant).	قُلْقَاسٌ
Wheat.	قَمْحٌ	To move, shake.	قَلْقَلَ قَلْقَالًا
Grain of wheat; grain (weight).	قَمْحَةٌ	To be moved, shaken.	تَقَلْقَلَ
		Agitation.	قَلْقَلَةٌ

Shirt.	قَمِيصٌ ج أَقْمِصَةٌ وَقُمْصَانٌ
Transmigration (soul).	تَقَمُّصٌ
To bind ; swaddle.	قَمَطَ وَقَمَّطَ
Swaddling-cloth.	قِمَاطٌ ج قُمُطٌ
Bound up, swaddled.	مُقَمَّطٌ
To tame, subdue.	قَمَعَ يَقْمَعُ وَأَقْمَعَ
To prevent.	قَمَعَ وَأَقْمَعَ عَنْ
To be subdued, tamed.	إِنْقَمَعَ
Subjugating.	قَمْعٌ وَإِقْمَاعٌ
Funnel.	قِمْعٌ ج أَقْمَاعٌ
To murmur, find fault.	تَقَمْقَمَ
Jar, cup; flask.	قُمْقُمٌ ج قَمَاقِمُ
Lice, vermin.	قَمْلٌ
Infested with lice.	قَمِلٌ وُمَقْمَلٌ
A louse.	قَمْلَةٌ
Very small insects.	قُمَّلٌ
Oven to heat baths.	قَمِينٌ
Poultry-house, hen-coop.	قُنٌّ

To play a game of chance.	قَمَرَ يَقْمُرُ
To gamble.	قَامَرَ مُقَامَرَةً وَقِمَاراً
To be moonlight.	أَقْمَرَ
To play at dice.	تَقَامَرَ
Moon.	قَمَرٌ ج أَقْمَارٌ
Moonlit (night).	قَمْرَةٌ
Lunar ; moonlike.	قَمَرِيٌّ
Small window.	قَمَرِيَّةٌ
Gambling.	قِمَارٌ
Moonlit (night).	مُقْمِرَةٌ
Gambler.	مُقَامِرٌ
To jump.	قَمَزَ يَقْمُزُ قَمْزاً
To dive.	قَمَسَ يَقْمُسُ قَمْساً
Dictionary.	قَامُوسٌ ج قَوَامِيسُ
Whip.	قَمْشَةٌ
Woven stuff.	قُمَاشٌ ج أَقْمِشَةٌ
Household things.	قُمَاشُ البَيْتِ
To jump, leap.	قَمَصَ يَقْمِصُ
To transmigrate (soul).	تَقَمَّصَ

Hunter. قَانِصٌ وَقَنَّاصٌ	Small mountain. Peak. قُنَّةٌ ج قُنَنٌ
Crop, gizzard. قَانِصَةٌ ج قَوَانِصُ	Rule, canon, law. تَقَانُونٌ ج قَوَانِينُ
	Kind of harp.
Consul. قُنْصُلٌ ج قَنَاصِلُ	Canonical, legal. قَانُونِيٌّ
Consulate. قُنْصُلِيَّةٌ وَقُنْصُلاَتُو	Glass bottle, phial. قِنِّينَةٌ ج قَنَانِيٌّ
To despair. قَنَطَ يَقْنِطُ وَقَنَطَ يَقْنَطُ	To be very red. قَنَأَ يَقْنَأُ قُنُوءٌ
To throw into despair. قَنَّطَ	Very dark red. أَحْمَرُ قَانِئٌ
Despair. قَنَطٌ وَقُنُوطٌ	Hemp ; coarse rope. قِنَّبٌ
Discouraged ; despairing. قَنِطٌ	Lark. قُنْبَرَاءُ وَقُنْبَرَةٌ ج قَنَابِرُ
To fall from a horse. قَنْطَرَ وَتَقَنْطَرَ	Crest of a cock. قُنْبُرَةٌ ج قَنَابِرُ
Arch. قَنْطَرَةٌ ج قَنَاطِرُ	Cauliflower. قُنَّبِيطٌ وَقَرْنَبِيطٌ
100 rottles. قِنْطَارٌ ج قَنَاطِيرُ	Bomb-shell. قُنْبُلَةٌ ج قَنَابِلُ
Centaury. قِنْطَارِيُونٌ	To obey God. قَنَتَ يَقْنُتُ وَأَقْنَتَ
Collected together. مُقَنْطَرٌ	To eat sparingly. قَنَتَ يَقْنِتُ قَنَاتَةً
To be contented. قَنِعَ يَقْنَعُ	Pious. قَانِتٌ م قَانِتَةٌ
To convince, persuade. قَنَّعَ وَأَقْنَعَ	Piety, submission to God. قُنُوتٌ
To veil one's self. تَقَنَّعَ	Lamp. قِنْدِيلٌ ج قَنَادِيلُ
To be content. To be persuaded, convinced. إِقْتَنَعَ ب	To hunt. قَنَصَ يَقْنِصُ وَأَقْتَنَصَ
	Hunting. قَنْصٌ وَأَقْتِنَاصٌ
Content, temperate. قَنِعٌ وَقَنُوعٌ	Prey ; game. قَنَصٌ وَقَنِيصٌ

Cairo, *i.e. Victirx.*	أَلْقَاهِرَةُ	Contented.	قَانِعٌ
God, the Almighty.	أَلْقَهَّارُ	Veil for the head.	قِنَاعٌ ج قُنُعٌ
Forced, conquered.	مَقْهُورٌ	Contentedness.	قَنَاعَةٌ وَقُنُوعٌ
Steward.	قَهْرَمَانٌ ج قَهَارِمَةٌ	Wearing an iron helmet.	مِقْنَعٌ
To go backwards.	قَهْقَرَ وَتَقَهْقَرَ	Porcupine.	قِنْفَذٌ ج قَنَافِذُ
Retrograde movement.	قَهْقَرَى	To acquire.	قَنَا يَقْنُو وَٱقْتَنَى
Pile of stones.	قُهْقُورٌ (وَقَعْقُورٌ)	To dig a canal.	قَنَّى
To laugh immoderately.	قَهْقَهَ	To give one possession.	أَقْنَى
Immoderate laughter.	قَهْقَهَة	Acquisition ; possession.	قُنْوَةٌ
Coffee. Wine.	قَهْوَةٌ	Canal. Lance.	قَنَاةٌ ج قَنَوَاتٌ
Coffee-house ; café.	قَهْوَةٌ ج قَهَوَاتٌ	That which is acquired.	قِنْيَةٌ ج رِقْنِى
Coffee-house keeper.	(قَهْوَجِيٌّ)	Possessor, proprietor, owner.	قَانٍ
A bow's length.	قَابُ قَوْسٍ	Having an aquiline nose.	أَقْنَى
Ring-worm, tetter.	قُوبَاءُ	To subdue, oppress.	قَهَرَ يَقْهَرُ
To nourish, feed.	قَاتَ يَقُوتُ	To treat with violence.	قَاهَرَ
To be nourished.	تَقَوَّتَ وَٱقْتَاتَ	Violence ; oppression.	قَهْرٌ
Food, victuals.	قُوتٌ ج أَقْوَاتٌ	By force, inspite of.	قَهْرًا
Sustainer, guardian.	مُقِيتٌ	Victor, conqueror.	قَاهِرٌ

To lead, guide.	قَادَ يَقُودُ وَآقْتَادَ
To be guided, led.	إِنْقَادَ وَآقْتَادَ
To obey.	إِنْقَادَ لِ
Leading, guiding.	قَوْدٌ وَقِيَادَةٌ
Guide ; leader.	قَائِدٌ ج قُوَّادٌ
Halter.	مِقْوَدٌ ج مَقَاوِدُ
Led, guided.	مَقُودٌ وَمَقْوُودٌ
Small, isolated mountain.	قَارَةٌ ج قَارَاتٌ
A thing with a hole in its middle.	مُقَوَّرٌ
To measure.	قَاسَ يَقُوسُ وَآقْتَاسَ
To be bent.	قَوِسَ يَقْوَسُ وَتَقَوَّسَ
To shoot with a gun.	(قَوَّسَ)
To be shot, fired.	(تَقَوَّسَ)
Bow, arc.	قَوْسٌ ج قِسِيٌّ وَأَقْوَاسٌ
Rainbow.	قَوْسُ قُزَحَ
Cavass ; archer.	قَوَّاسٌ ج قَوَّاسَةٌ
Sage (plant).	قَوَيْسَةٌ
Crupper.	(قُوشٌ ج أَقْوَاشٌ)

To demolish.	قَاضَ وَقَوَّضَ
Exchange.	قَوْضٌ
Plain ; bottom-land.	قَاعٌ ج قِيعَ
Courtyard. Hall.	قَاعَةٌ ج قَاعَاتٌ
To cackle (hen).	قَاقَ يَقُوقُ قَوْقًا
Cylindrical hat.	قَاوُوقٌ ج قَوَاوِيقُ
To speak, say, propose.	قَالَ يَقُولُ
To give as an opinion.	قَالَ بِ
To speak against.	قَالَ عَلَى
It is said, has been said.	قِيلَ
To argue, bargain with.	قَاوَلَ
To make a false report.	تَقَوَّلَ
To converse together.	تَقَاوَلَ
Talk.	قَالٌ وَقِيلٌ
Saying, word, speech ; promise.	قَوْلٌ ج أَقْوَالٌ وَأَقَاوِيلُ
Author of a saying.	قَائِلٌ
Treatise ; chapter ; article.	مَقَالَةٌ
Said ; word, sentence.	مَقُولٌ

To be upright, straight. اِسْتَقَامَ	Conference. Contract. مُقَاوَلَةٌ
People ; company. قَوْمٌ ج أَقْوَامٌ	Colic. قُولَنْجٌ
The enemy. أَلْقَوْمُ	Colon (intestine). أَلْقُولُونُ
Consistence. قَوَامٌ	To rise ; stand. قَامَ يَقُومُ
Support ; sustenance. قِوَامٌ	To rise against, revolt. قَامَ عَلَى
Stature ; fathom. قَامَةٌ ج قَامَاتٌ	To rise to honour one. قَامَ لِ
Price, value, worth. قِيمَةٌ ج قِيَمٌ	To take one's place. قَامَ مَقَامَهُ
Upright, vertical ; firm. قَائِمٌ	To carry on (a matter). قَامَ بِ
Governor. Lt.-Colonel. قَائِمَقَام	To keep a promise. قَامَ بِوَعْدِهِ
Right-angled. قَائِمُ الزَّاوِيَةِ	She began to cry. قَامَتْ نَنُوحُ
Right angle. زَاوِيَةٌ قَائِمَةٌ	To erect ; straighten. قَوَّمَ
Foot of a quadruped. قَائِمَةٌ ج قَوَائِمُ	To oppose, dispute with. قَاوَمَ
List, catalogue. قَائِمَةٌ ج قَوَائِمُ	To set up ; establish. أَقَامَ
Resurrection. قِيَامَةٌ	To stay (in a place). أَقَامَ بِ
Manager ; agent. قَيِّمٌ	To persevere in. اقَامَ عَلَى
Straight ; true. قَوِيمٌ ج قِيَامٌ	To appoint to. أَقَامَهُ عَلَى
The Self-Existent (God) أَلْقَيُّومُ	He brought a أَقَامَ عَلَيْهِ الدَّعْوَى charge against him.
Abiding ; preforming. إِقَامَةٌ	To be straightened. تَقَوَّمَ

Act of strengthening.	تَقْوِيَة
Strengthening, fortifying.	مُقَوّ
To vomit.	قَاءَ يَقِيءُ قَيْئًا
To make vomit.	قَيَّأَ تَقْيِئَة وَأَقَاءَ
Act of vomiting.	قَيْء
Emetic.	مُقَيِّء
Guitar.	قِيثَار ج قَيَاثِير
To suppurate.	قَاحَ يَقِيحُ وَقَيَّحَ وَتَقَيَّحَ
Pus, suppuration.	قَيْح
To bind. Register. To restrict. (the sense of a word).	قَيَّدَ
To be bound, registered.	تَقَيَّدَ
To be bound to.	تَقَيَّدَ ب
Fetter, chain, limit.	قَيْد ج قُيُود
Limitation, restriction. Registration.	تَقْيِيد
Bound ; Registered.	مُقَيَّد
Pitch, tar.	قِير وَقَار
Cyrene.	أَلْقَيْرَوَان
To measure, compare.	قَاسَ يَقِيسُ

Uprightness ; rectitude.	إِسْتِقَامَة
Calendar.	تَقْوِيمُ ٱلسَّنَة
Valuation of a country for purposes of taxation.	تَقْوِيمُ ٱلْبِلَادِ
Place, rank, office.	مُقَام
Resisting ; adversary.	مُقَاوِم
Resistance, opposition.	مُقَاوَمَة
Straight. Upright.	مُسْتَقِيم
To be, or grow, strong.	قَوِيَ يَقْوَى
To be able to do it.	قَوِيَ عَلَى ٱلْأَمْرِ
To strengthen.	قَوَّى
To grow strong.	تَقَوَّى وَٱسْتَقْوَى
Strength, faculty, ability ; potentiality.	قُوَّة ج قُوَّات وَقُوًى
The mental faculties.	أَلْقُوَى ٱلْعَقْلِيَّة
Perception.	أَلْقُوَّةُ ٱلنَّظَرِيَّة
Reasoning.	أَلْقُوَّةُ ٱلْعَمَلِيَّة
Memory.	أَلْقُوَّةُ ٱلْحَافِظَة
Strong, powerful.	قَوِيّ ج أَقْوِيَاء

Silk-cord.	(قيطانٌ)
To be very hot.	قاظَ يَقيظُ قَيظاً
Heat of summer. Drought.	قَيظٌ
Maple (tree).	قَيقَبٌ
To take a siesta.	قالَ يَقيلُ
To abrogate a sale.	أَقالَ
To seek abrogation.	إِسْتَقالَ
Hydrocele.	قِيلةٌ
Mid-day nap, siesta.	قَيْلولَةٌ
Annulment of a bargain.	إِقالَةٌ
Place of a mid-day nap.	مَقيلٌ
Maid-servant. Female singer.	قَيْنَةٌ

To measure.	قايَسَ مُقايَسةً
To compare a thing with another.	قايَسَ بَيْنَ
To be measured.	إِنْقاسَ
Measure ; rule, analogy. Syllogism.	قِياسٌ ج أَقْيِسةٌ
According to rule.	قِياسِيٌّ
Estimate by analogy.	مُقايَسةٌ
A measure.	مِقْياسٌ ج مَقاييسُ
Nilometer.	مِقْياسُ النِّيلِ
To exchange for.	قاضَ ـِ مِنْ
To exchange with.	قايَضَ مُقايَضةً
To be broken down.	تَقَيَّضَ
Exchange.	قِياضٌ ومَقايَضةٌ

ك

To invert ; overthrow.	كَبَّ يَكُبُّ كَبَّا
To be intent upon.	أَكَبَّ عَلَى
To fall prostrate.	إِنْكَبَّ
Ball of thread.	كُبَّةٌ ج كُبَبٌ
Broiled bits of meat.	كَبَابٌ
Cubeb.	كَبَابَةٌ (نبات)
Hedge-hog.	كَبَابَةُ الشَّوْكِ
Thread-reel.	مِكَبٌّ ج مِكَبَّاتٌ
Over-coat.	كَبُّوتٌ ج كَبَابِيتُ
To pull in a horse.	كَبَحَ يَكْبَحُ
To restrain, prevent.	كَبَحَ عَنْ
To be in the zenith.	كَبَّدَ وَتَكَبَّدَ
To suffer, endure.	كَابَدَ

As a numeral sign=20.	ك
Pronominal suffix.	كَ وَكِ
He struck thee.	ضَرَبَكَ
Thy book.	كِتَابُكِ
As, like.	كَ
Like a lion.	كَالأَسَدِ
To be sad.	كَئِبَ يَكْأَبُ وَاكْتَأَبَ
Grief, sorrow.	كَأْبٌ وَكَآبَةٌ
Grieved.	كَئِبٌ وَكَئِيبٌ وَمُكْتَئِبٌ
Cup.	كَأْسٌ ج كَاسَاتٌ وَكُؤُوسٌ
Death.	كَأْسُ المَنِيَّةِ
As if, as though.	كَأَنَّ وَكَأَنْ
As if Zeid were a lion.	كَأَنَّ زَيْدًا أَسَدٌ

God is great !	اللهُ أَكْبَرُ
The grandees.	الأَكَابِرُ
Pride, haughtiness.	تَكَبُّرُ
Magnifying God.	تَكْبِيرُ
Proud, haughty.	مُتَكَبِّرُ
Sulphur ; matches.	كِبْرِيت
Sulphuretted.	مُكَبْرَتُ
To press. Surprise.	كَبَسَ يَكْبِسُ
To train an animal.	كَبَّسَ
To be pressed, squeezed.	تَكَبَّسَ
Assault. Pressure.	كَبْسُ
A sudden attack.	كَبْسَةُ
Nightmare.	كَابُوسُ ج كَوَابِيسُ
Pickles.	كَبِيس
Leap year.	سَنَةٌ كَبِيسَةٌ
Hand-press.	مِكْبَسٌ ج مَكَابِسُ
Assailed, pressed. Pickled.	مَكْبُوسُ
To grasp.	كَبَشَ يَكْبِشُ كَبْشًا

The middle of the sky.	كَبِدُ
Liver.	كَبِدُ وَكَبْدٌ ج أَكْبَادُ وَكُبُودُ
Interior ; middle.	كَبِدُ
Citron.	كَبَّادُ
To be advanced in age.	كَبِرَ يَكْبَرُ
To be large ; grow.	كَبُرَ يَكْبُرُ
It became formid-able to him.	كَبُرَ عَلَيْهِ الأَمْرُ
To enlarge ; magnify.	كَبَّرَ
To grow proud.	تَكَبَّرَ وَاسْتَكْبَرَ
To deem great.	إِسْتَكْبَرَ
Greatness, glory, pride.	كُبْرُ
Greatness, advanced age.	كِبَرُ
Caper-bush.	كَبَرُ وَ(كَبَّارُ وَقَبَّارُ)
Major proposition, (logic).	كُبْرَى
Greatness ; pride.	كِبْرِيَاءُ
Great, large.	كَبِيرُ ج كِبَارُ وَكُبَرَاءُ
Great crime.	كَبِيرَةُ ج كَبَائِرُ
Greater ; older.	أَكْبَرُ

To enrol one's self.	اِكْتَتَبَ	Ram, male sheep.	كَبْشٌ ج كِبَاشٌ
To ask to write.	اِسْتَكْتَبَ	Mulberry-fruit.	كَبْشُ ٱلتُّوتِ
Book-seller.	كُتُبِيّ	Cloves.	كَبْشُ ٱلقَرُنْفُلِ
Writer, clerk.	كَاتِبٌ ج كُتَّابٌ	A handful.	(كَبْشَةٌ)
Writing, book.	كِتَابٌ ج كُتُبٌ	To bind, fetter.	كَبَّلَ يَكْبِلُ وَ كَبَّلَ
Christians. Jews.	أَهْلُ ٱلْكِتَابِ	To be fettered.	تَكَبَّلَ
School.	كُتَّابٌ ج كَتَاتِيبُ	Heavy fetter.	كَبْلٌ ج كُبُولٌ
Writing ; calligraphy.	كِتَابَةٌ	Fettered.	مُكَبَّلٌ وَ مَكْبُولٌ
Squadron.	كَتِيبَةٌ ج كَتَائِبُ	Horse-blanket.	(كُوبَانٌ)
School. Office.	مَكْتَبٌ ج مَكَاتِبُ	To fall , trip.	كَبَا يَكْبُو كَبْوًا
Library ; study.	مَكْتَبَةٌ ج مَكَاتِبُ	Trip, stumble.	كَبْوَةٌ
Correspondent.	مُكَاتِبٌ	Charpie, lint.	كَتِيتٌ
Correspondence by letter.	مُكَاتَبَةٌ	To write.	كَتَبَ يَكْتُبُ كِتَابَةً
Inscribed, registered.	مُكْتَتِبٌ	To prescribe, appoint.	كَتَبَ عَلَى
Written ; letter.	مَكْتُوبٌ ج مَكَاتِيبُ	To arrange troops in order.	كَتَّبَ
Crippled. Whole.	أَكْتَعُ م كَتْعَاءُ ج كُتْعٌ	To correspond with.	كَاتَبَ
To tie the hands back.	كَتَّفَ	To assemble in squadrons.	تَكَتَّبَ
To cross the arms.	تَكَنَّفَ	To write to one another.	تَكَاتَبَ

To regard as much. إِسْتَكْثَرَ	Shoulder. كَتِفْ ج أَكْتَافْ
To thank. إِسْتَكْثَرَ بِخَيْرِه	Heap, lump. كُتْلَةْ ج كُتَلْ
Great number, plenty, abundance كُثْرْ وَكَثْرَةْ	Catholic. كَاثُولِيكِيّْ ج كَاثُولِيكْ
Much, many ; abundant. كَثِيرْ	To conceal, hide. كَتَمَ يَكْتُمْ
Abundantly, often, very. كَثِيرًا	To be concealed, hidden. إِنْكَتَمَ
Tragacanth, goat's thorn. كَثِيرَاء	To confide a secret. إِسْتَكْتَمَ
More, more frequent. أَكْثَرْ	Concealing. كَتْمْ وَكِتْمَانْ
Most people. أَكْثَرُ ٱلنَّاسِ	Private secretary. كَاتِمُ ٱلْأَسْرَارِ
Growth, increase. تَكَاثُرْ	Constipation, costiveness. كَتَامْ
Rich. مُكْثِرْ	Kept secret. مَكْتُومْ وَمُكْتَتَمْ
To be thick, dense. كَثُفَ يَكْثُفْ	Flax, linen. كَتَّانْ
Thickness, denseness. كَثَافَةْ	Linseed. بِزْرُ كَتَّانْ
Thick, dense, compact. كَثِيفْ	Thick, dense. كَثْ وَكَثِيثْ
To apply colly- rium, or paint, to one's eyes. تَكَحَّلَ وَٱكْتَحَلَ	To be much, many ; increase, multiply. كَثُرَ يَكْثُرْ
An eye-salve or paint. كُحْلْ	To increase ; do too much. كَثَّرَ
Black antimony-powder. كَحَالْ	To be rich ; increase, grow. أَكْثَرَ
Horse of best breed. كَحِيلْ ج كَحَائِلْ	To speak much. أَكْثَرَ فِي ٱلْكَلَامِ
	To increase multiply. تَكَاثَرَ

Scar.	كَدْمٌ ج كُدُومٌ
To yoke oxen.	كَدَنَ يَكْدُنُ
Thus, like this.	كَذَا وَكَذَلِكَ
So and so.	كَذَا أَوْكَذَا
To lie, speak falsely.	كَذَبَ يَكْذِبُ
To accuse of lying.	كَذَّبَ
To discredit a thing.	كَذَّبَ
To contra-dict	كَذَّبَ وَأَكْذَبَ نَفْسَهُ
one's self ; belie one's self.	
Lie, fraud.	كِذبُواْ كْذوو بَةٌ ج أَكَاذِيبُ
Liar.	كَذُوبٌ وَكَاذِبٌ وَ كَذَّابٌ
More false.	أَكْذَبُ
Falsely accused.	مَكْذُوبٌ عَلَيْهِ
Falsehood.	مَكْذَبَةٌ ج مَكَاذِيبُ
To return.	كَرَّ يَكُرُّ كُرُوراً
To return against.	كَرَّ كَرًّا
To repeat. Purify, refine.	كَرَّرَ
To be repeated.	تَكَرَّرَ

Having.	أَكْحَلُ م كَحْلَاءُ ج كُحْلُ
the eye-lashes black.	
Pencil with	مَكْحَلٌ ومِكْحَالٌ
which the kohl is applied.	
Vessel contain-ing the kohl.	مَكْحَلَةٌ ج مَكَاحِلُ
Secretary.	كَاخِيَةٌ ج كَوَاخٍ
To toil hard. To weary.	كَدَّ يَكُدُّ
Toil ; effort, exertion.	كَدُّ
Laborious.	كَدُودٌ
To be muddy, turbid.	كَدِرَ يَكْدَرُ
To trouble ; make turbid.	كَدَّرَ
To be troubled ; muddy.	تَكَدَّرَ
Turbidness ; vexation.	كَدَرٌ
Troubled ; turbid.	كَدِرٌ وَمُكَدَّرٌ
To heap reaped grain.	كَدَسَ يَكْدِسُ
Heap of grain.	كُدْسٌ ج أَكْدَاسٌ
To bite (horse).	كَدَشَ يَكْدِشُ
Pack-horse.	كَدِيشٌ ج كُدْشٌ
To bite.	كَدَمَ يَكْدُمُ كَدْماً

To look after.	اِكْتَرَثَ لِ وَب	Return, return to attack.	كَرَّ
Leek.	كُرَّاثٌ	Turn, time.	كَرَّةٌ ج كَرَّاتٌ
Georgia.	بِلَادُ اَلْكُرْج	Globe, ball.	كُرَةٌ ج كُرَاتٌ
Georgian.	كُرْجِيٌّ	Succession of ages.	كُرُورُ اَلدُّهُورِ
Kurd.	كُرْدٌ وَأَكْرَادٌ	Repetition.	تِكْرَارٌ وَتَكْرِيرٌ
A Kurd.	كُرْدِيٌّ	Repeatedly.	تَكْرَاراً
Neck chain.	(كُرْدَانٌ)	Repeated. Refined.	مُكَرَّر
To divide into squadrons.	كَرْدَسَ	To grieve.	كَرَبَ يَكْرُبُ كَرْباً
The Kurds country.	كُرْدِسْتَانُ	To offect with sorrow.	أَكْرَبَ
Squardon.	كُرْدُوسَةٌ ج كَرَادِيسُ	To be in distress, grief.	اِكْتَرَبَ
To preach.	كَرَزَ يَكْرِزُ كَرْزاً	Grief, sorrow.	كَرْبٌ ج كُرُوبٌ
Preaching.	كَرْزٌ وَكِرَازَةٌ	Cherub.	كَرُوبٌ
Cherry, cherry tree.	كَرَزٌ	Grieved.	كَرِيبٌ وَمَكْرُوبٌ
The leading ram.	كَرَّازٌ	Horse-whip.	كُرْبَاجٌ ج كَرَابِيجُ
Earthen flask.	كَرَّازٌ وَكَرَّارٌ	To impose a quarantine.	كَرْتَنَ
To consecrate.	(كَرَّسَ)	To be kept in quarantine.	تَكَرْتَنَ
To be devoted to God.	تَكَرَّسَ	Quarantine.	كَرَنْتِينَةٌ
Pamphlet.	كُرَّاسَةٌ ج كَرَارِيسُ	Paste-board.	كَرْتُونٌ

Grace, liberality.	كَرَمٌ	Chair.	كُرْسِيٌّ ج كَرَاسِيٌّ وَكَرَاسٍ
Vine (grape).	كَرْمٌ ج كُرُومٌ	Carriage.	(كَرُّوسَةٌ ج كَرُّوسَاتٌ)
A vine-tree.	كَرْمَةٌ	Consecration, dedication.	(تَكْرِيسٌ)
Vine-dresser.	كَرَّامٌ	Vetch.	كِرْسِنَّةٌ
Generosity ; honour.	كَرَامَةٌ	To be wrinkled.	كَرِشَ يَكْرَشُ وَتَكَرَّشَ
Most gladly !	حَبًّا وَكَرَامَةً	Stomach.	كِرْشٌ ج كُرُوشٌ
Noble, liberal.	كَرِيمٌ ج كِرَامٌ	To sip water.	كَرَعَ يَكْرَعُ
Precious object.	كَرِيمَةٌ	Celery.	كَرَفْسٌ
More noble, or generous.	اكْرَمُ	Distilling-retort.	كَرَكَةٌ
Respect, reverence.	إِكْرَامٌ	Crane (bird).	كُرْكِيٌّ ج كَرَاكِيٌّ
For the sake of.	إِكْرَامًا لِ	To disarrange, confuse.	كَرْكَبَ
Honouring, honour.	تَكْرِيمٌ	Rhinoceros.	كَرْكَدَّنٌ
Honoured.	مَكْرُمٌ وَمُكَرَّمٌ	To laugh loud.	كَرْكَرَ
Noble action.	مَكْرُمَةٌ ج مَكَارِمُ	Saffron.	كُرْكُمٌ
Cabbage.	كُرُنْبٌ وَكَرَنْبٌ	To be generous, noble.	كَرُمَ يَكْرُمُ
To loathe, abhor.	كَرِهَ يَكْرَهُ	To exalt, honour.	كَرَّمَ وَأَكْرَمَ
To be loathsome.	كَرُهَ يَكْرُهُ	How generous he is !	مَا أَكْرَمَهُ
To render hateful.	كَرَّهَ	To act generously.	تَكَرَّمَ

Muleteer.	مُكَارٍ ج مُكَارُون	To force one to ..	أَكْرَه عَلَى
Hirer out, letter.	مُكْرٍ	To loathe.	تَكَرَّه وَتَكَارَه
Hired, rented, let.	مُكْرًى	To find loathsome.	إِسْتَكْرَه
To dry up; become rigid.	كَزَّ يَكُزُّ	Aversion, disgust.	كُرْه وَكَرَاهَة
Tetanus.	كُزَاز وَكُزَّاز	Detestable.	كَرِه وَكَرِيه
Coriander.	كُزْبُرة وَكُزْبَرة	Adversity.	كَرِيهَة ج كَرَائِه
To earn ; acquire.	كَسَب يَكْسِب	Compulsion.	إِكْرَاه
To bestow; give.	كَسَب وَأَكْسَب	Abhorred, detested.	مَكْرُوه
To seek gain ; acquire.	إِكْتَسَب	Caraway.	كَرْوِيَا وَكَرَاوِيَا
Earnings, gain.	كَسْب	To slumber.	كَرِي يَكْرَى كَرًى
Acquiring, earning.	إِكْتِسَاب	To let, rent.	كَارَى وَأَكْرَى
Acquired.	إِكْتِسَابِي	To hire, rent.	إِكْتَرَى وَإَسْتَكْرَى
Gain, profit.	مَكْسَب ج مَكَاسِب	Hire, wages ; rent.	كِرَاء وَكَرْوَة
Acquired.	مَكْسُوب وَمُكْتَسَب	Globe, ball.	كُرَة ج كُرَات وَكُرًى
Chestnut.	(كَسْتَنَا)	Terrestrial globe.	كُرَة الأَرْض
To cut off.	كَسَح يَكْسَح كَسْحًا	Globular, spherical.	كُرَوِيّ
To be crippled.	كَسِح يَكْسَح كَسَحًا	Act of renting, letting.	إِكْرَاء
Rickets. Sweepings.	كُسَاحَة	Act of hiring.	إِكْتِرَاء

Broken plural.	جَمْعُ التَّكْسِير	Lame, crippled.	كَسِيح ج كُسْحَان
Broken into pieces.	مُكَسَّر	A cripple.	أُكْسَح م كَسْحاء ج كُسْح
Routed ; bankrupt.	مَكْسُور	To sell badly.	كَسَدَ يَكْسُدُ
To be eclipsed.	كَسَفَ وَٱنْكَسَفَ	Worthless ; selling badly.	كَاسِد
Eclipse.	كَسُوف وَٱنْكِسَاف	To break ; rout, defeat.	كَسَرَ يَكْسِرُ
Heavy-hearted.	كَاسِفُ ٱلْبَال	To break into pieces.	كَسَّرَ
Eclipsed.	مَكْسُوف وَمُنْكَسِف	To seek an abatement.	كَاسَرَ
To be lazy.	كَسِلَ يَكْسَلُ وَ تَكَاسَلَ	To be broken into pieces.	تَكَسَّرَ
Laziness, idleness.	كَسَل وَ تَكَاسُل	To be broken ; routed ; become a bankrupt, fail.	إِنْكَسَرَ
Lazy, idle.	كَسْلَان ج كَسَالَى	Breach, fracture.	كَسْر
Mode, fashion.	كِسْم	Fraction (arith).	كَسْر ج كُسُور
To clothe.	كَسَا يَكْسُو وَأَكْسَى	Fragment.	كِسْرَة ج كِسَر
To be dressed, clothed.	إِكْتَسَى	The vowel. (ِ)	كَسْرَة ج كَسَرَات
Garment, dress.	كِسَاء ج أَكْسِية	A fracture ; defeat.	
Clothing, dress.	كُسْوَة ج كُسَى	Chosroes.	كِسْرَى ج أَكَاسِرَة
To frown. Chase away.	(كَشَّ)	Bird of prey.	كَاسِرَة ج كَوَاسِر
Lock of hair.	كَشَّة	A fragment.	كُسَارَة
A thimble.	(كِشْتِبَان)	Elixir.	إِكْسِير
		Defeat ; bankruptcy.	إِنْكِسَار

A beggar's bag.	كَشْكُولُ	To disperse.	كَشَحَ ـِ
Currants.	كِشْمِشُ	To retire from.	إِنْكَشَحَ عَنْ
To surfeit (food).	كَظَّ يَكُظُّ	Flank ; waist.	كَشْحُ ج كُشُوحُ
Indigestion ; surfeit.	كَظَّةُ	To snarl (beast).	كَشَرَ عَنْ نَابِهِ
To shut ; restrain.	كَظَمَ يَكْظِمُ	To strip ; scrape.	كَشَطَ يَكْشِطُ
Silent, speechless.	كَاظِمُ	To be dispersed (clouds).	تَكَشَّطَ
Suppressing anger.	كَظِيمُ	To be taken off.	إِنْكَشَطَ
To cube (a number).	كَعَّبَ	To uncover.	كَشَفَ يَكْشِفُ وَكَشَّفَ
Ankle. Cube, (arith).	كَعْبُ	To reveal, disclose.	كَاشَفَ بِ
The kaba in Mecca.	أَلْكَعْبَةُ	To be uncovered.	إِنْكَشَفَ
Cubic ; cube.	مُكَعَّبُ	To discover ; find out.	إِكْتَشَفَ
The radius (bone).	كُعْبُرَةُ	To try to discover.	إِسْتَكْشَفَ
Biscuit, cake, bun.	كَعْكُ	Unveiling, revealing.	كَشْفُ
To muzzle.	كَعَمَ يَكْعِمُ	Overseer. Test.	(كَاشِفُ ج كَشَفَةُ)
Muzzle of the camel.	كِعَامُ	Uncovered, disclosed.	مَكْشُوفُ
Muzzled.	كَعِيمُ وَمَكْعُومُ	Discovery.	إِكْتِشَافُ ج إِكْتِشَافَاتُ
To be timid.	كَعَا يَكْعُو	Discoverer.	مُكْتَشِفُ
To defy.	(كَعَى)	Ruffle of a garment.	كَشْكَشُ

Paper.	كَاغِدٌ
To hem, seam.	كَفَّ يَكُفُّ كَفًّا
To prevent. To cease.	كَفَّ عَنْ
To become blind.	كُفَّ بَصَرُهُ
To abstain from.	إِنْكَفَّ عَنْ
Palm of hand.	كَفٌّ ج كُفُوفٌ
Scale (of a balance).	كَفَّةٌ
Silk handkerchief.	كَفِيَّةٌ
All.	كَاَفَّةً
Equal ; daily bread.	كَفَافٌ
Blind.	كَفِيفٌ وَمَكْفُوفٌ ج مَكَافِيفُ
To reward.	كَافَأَ مُكَافَأَةً وَكِفَاءً
To retreat ; turn back.	إِنْكَفَأَ
Equality, likeness.	كَفْأً وَكَفَاءَةٌ
Equal, like.	كَفْءٌ وَكُفْوٌ
To face.	كَفَحَ يَكْفَحُ وَكَافَحَ
To fight for, defend.	كَافَحَ عَنْ
To drive back.	أَكْفَحَ عَنْ

To encounter one another.	تَكَافَحَ
Battle, combat.	كِفَاحٌ وَمُكَافَحَةٌ
To cover.	كَفَرَ يَكْفِرُ وَكَفَّرَ
To be an infidel.	كَفَرَ يَكْفُرُ
To renounce, deny.	كَفَرَ بِ
To expiate.	كَفَّرَ
Village, hamlet.	كَفْرٌ ج كُفُورٌ
Unbelief ; infidelity.	كُفْرٌ
Infidel.	كَافِرٌ ج كُفَّارٌ وَكَفَرَةٌ
Camphor.	كَافُورٌ
Atonement ; expiation.	كَفَّارَةٌ
Atonement ; expiation.	تَكْفِيرٌ
To take charge of.	كَفَلَ يَكْفُلُ
To stand security.	كَفَلَ يَكْفِلُ
To make one give bail.	كَفَّلَ
To guarantee.	تَكَفَّلَ لَهُ بِ
Buttocks.	كَفَلٌ ج أَكْفَالٌ
One who stands bail.	كَافِلٌ

To be crowned.	تَكَلَّلَ
Weariness ; dulness.	كَلٌّ وَكَلَالٌ
Blunt ; dim.	كَلٌّ وَكَلِيلٌ
All ; each, every.	كُلٌّ
Both of. (كِلْتَا) dual fem	كِلَا
No ! by no means.	كَلَّا
Cannon ball.	كُلَّة ج كُلَلٌ
As often as, whenever.	كُلَّمَا
Universal, general.	كُلِّيٌّ م كُلِّيَّة
General term, (logic).	اَلْكُلِّيَّة
Altogether, entirely.	بِالْكُلِّيَّة
Fatigued ; dim ; blunt.	كَالٌّ
Crown ; umbel.	إِكْلِيل ج أَكَالِيل
Crowned.	مُكَلَّل
Forage ; herbage.	كَلَأ
To have hydrophobia.	كَلِبَ
Dog.	كَلْب ج كِلَاب
Shark.	كَلْبُ الْبَحْر

God.	اَلْكَافِل
Bail, security, pledge.	كَفَالَة
A surety.	كَفِيل كُفَلَاء
Guaranteed.	مَكْفُول
To be very dark (night).	إِكْفَهَرَّ
To shroud the dead.	كَفَن
Shroud.	كَفَن ج أَكْفَان
To suffice ; satisfy.	كَفَى يَكْفِي
To prevent evil.	كَفَاهُ الشَّرَّ
To recompense.	كَافَى بِ
To be contented.	إِكْتَفَى
Sufficient.	كَفِيٌّ وَكَافٍ
Sufficient quantity.	كِفَايَة
Recompense, requital.	مُكَافَأَة
To be tired, weary.	كَلَّ يَكِلُّ
To be dim, dull.	كَلَّ وَكَلَّلَ
To crown. To join in wedlock, marry.	كَلَّلَ
To fatigue ; to dim.	أَكَلَّ

To be freckled. كَلِفَ يَكْلَفُ كَلَفَأ	Beaver. كَلْبُ ٱلْمَاءِ
To be devoted to. كَلِفَ ب	Canis major. أَلْكَلْبُ ٱلْأَكْبَرُ
To impose a difficult matter upon one. كَلَّفَ وَإِلَى	Canis minor. أَلْكَلْبُ ٱلْأَصْغَرُ
To cost. كَلَّفَ	Hydrophobia. كَلْبٌ
To take the trouble (to do anything). كَلَّفَ خَاطِرَهُ	Seized with hydrophobia. كَلِبٌ
Please do this ! كَلِّفْ خَاطِرَكَ	Female dog, bitch. كَلْبَةٌ
To take pains. تَكَلَّفَ	Tongs, forceps. كَلْبَتَانِ
Ardent love. Freckles. كَلَفٌ	Hook ; grapnel. كُلَّابٌ جْ كَلَالِيبُ
Trouble, labour, كُلْفَةٌ جْ كُلَفٌ	See : كِلَا Both, (fem). كِلْتَا
hardship. Cost, expense.	To frown. كَلَحَ يَكْلَحُ وَأَكْلَحَ وَتَكَلَّحَ
Freckled ; maculated. أَكْلَفُ	
Trouble. تَكْلِيفٌ جْ تَكَالِيفُ	Austere, severe. كَالِحٌ
Without ceremony. بِلَا تَكْلِيفٍ	To plaster with lime. كَلَّسَ
Expensive. مُكْلِفٌ وَمُكَلِّفٌ	Lime mortar. كِلْسٌ
Responsible agent. مُكَلَّفٌ	Sock, stocking. (كَلْسَةٌ)
Intruder. مُتَكَلِّفٌ	Lime-kiln. كَلَّاسَةٌ
Raft. كَلَكٌ	Lime-burner; plasterer. مُكَلِّسٌ
To wound. كَلَمَ يَكْلُمُ وَكَلَّمَ	Plastered with lime. مُكَلَّسٌ
	Eel. أَنْكَلِيسٌ

To muzzle (an animal).	كَمَّ	To speak ; speak to.	كَلَّمَ
Quantity.	كَمٌّ وَكَمِيَّةٌ ج كَمِيَّاتٌ	To converse with.	كَالَمَ
Calyx, spathe.	كِمٌّ ج أَكْمَامٌ	To talk, converse.	تَكَلَّمَ
Sleeve.	كُمٌّ ج أَكْمَامٌ	Wound.	كَلْمٌ ج كُلُومٌ وَكِلَامٌ
Muzzle.	كِمَامَةٌ وَكِمَامٌ	Incomplete sentence.	كَلِمٌ
Muzzled.	مَكْمُومٌ	Word, sentence.	كَلِمَةٌ ج كَلِمَاتٌ
Truffle.	كَمْءٌ وَكَمْأَةٌ	Speech, saying.	كَلَامٌ
Bill ; cheque.	كَمْبِيَالَةٌ	Talking, speech.	تَكَلُّمٌ
Rate, or bill of exchange.	كَمْبِيُو	Speaker, 1st person, (gram).	مُتَكَلِّمٌ
Dark brown, bay.	كُمَيْتٌ	Wounded.	مَكْلُومٌ وَكَلِيمٌ
Pear.	كُمِّثْرَى	Both. (dual).	كِلَامٌ كِلَا
A pear.	كُمَّثْرَاةٌ ج كُمَّثْرِيَّاتٌ	Kidney.	كُلْيَةٌ ج كُلًى
Scum ; film.	كِمْحَةٌ	How much ? How many ?	كَمْ
To be sad.	كَمِدَ يَكْمَدُ كَمَدًا	How many men ?	كَمْ رَجُلًا
To make sad.	أَكْمَدَ	Pronominal suffix.	كُمْ
Change of colour.	كَمَدٌ وَكُمْدَةٌ	Your book (pl. m.).	كِتَابُكُمْ
Concealed grief.		Your book (dual).	كِتَابُكُمَا
A kind of belt.	كَمَرٌ ج أَكْمَارٌ	As, even as, just as.	كَمَا
Duty ; custom-house.	كُمْرُكْ		

Place of ambush.	مَكْمَنْ ج مَكَامِنْ	Receiver of customs.	كَمَرُ كَجِيّ
Hidden, concealed.	مُكْتَمِنْ	Chyme.	كَيْمُوسْ
Violin.	كَمَنْجَـة	To grasp.	(كَشَ)
Blindness.	كَمَهْ	To be wrinkled.	إِنْكَمَشْ وَتَكَمَّشْ
Blind.	أَكْمَهُ م كَمْهَاء ج كَمَهْ	A handful.	(كَمْشَةْ)
Pronominal suffix.	كُنّ	Carpenter's pincers.	(كَمَّاشَةْ)
Your book, (fem).	كِتَابُـكُنّ	كَمَلَ يَكْمُلُ وَتَكَمَّلَ وَتَكَامَلَ وَاكْتَمَلَ	
To conceal, secrete.	كَنَّ يَكُنّ	To be complete, finished.	
To be concealed.	إِكْتَنَّ	To finish, complete.	كَمَّلَ وَأَكْمَلَ
To retire ; be quiet.	إِسْتَكَنَّ	Entire, complete.	كَامِلْ
Cover, shelter.	كِنّ ج أَكْنَانْ	Perfection.	كَمَالْ
Son's wife.	كَنَّةْ ج كَنَائِنْ	Finishing ; perfecting.	تَكْمِيلْ
Roof for shelter.	كَنَّةْ ج كِنَانْ	Completed, finished.	مُكَمَّلْ
Hearth, stove.	كَانُونْ ج كَوَانِينْ	To hide ; hide one's self.	كَمَنَ ـُ وَاكْتَمَنَ
December.	كَانُونُ الأَوَّلْ	To lie in ambush.	اكْمَنَ ل
January.	كَانُونُ الثَّانِي	Ambush.	كَمْنَةْ ج كِمَانْ
Concealed.	كَنِينْ وَمَكْنُونْ	State of being hidden.	كُمُونْ
Callousness (of hand).	كَنَبْ	Cumin.	كَمُّونْ
		Hidden ; ambush.	كَمِينْ ج كُمَنَاء

Canaan.	كَنْعَانٌ	Ingratitude.	كَنُودٌ
The Canaanites.	ٱلْكَنْعَانِيُّونَ	Frankincense.	كُنْدُرٌ
To shelter.	كَنَفَ يَكْنُفُ كَنْفًا	Shoe.	(كُنْدُرَةٌ ج كَنَادِرُ)
To surround.	تَكَنَّفَ وَٱكْتَنَفَ	Hem, border.	كِنَارٌ
Refuge.	كَنَفٌ جأ كْنَافٌ	Canary bird.	كَنَارِيٌّ
A kind of sweet pastry.	كَنَافَةٌ	Lute, harp.	كَنَّارَةٌ ج كَنَّارَاتٌ
Privy, sewer.	كَنِيفٌ ج كُنُفٌ	To treasure, store.	كَنَزَ يَكْنِزُ
Substance, essence.	كُنْهٌ	To be firm, hard.	ٱكْتَنَزَ
To hint at.	كَنَى يَكْنِي كِنَايَةً عَنْ	Treasure.	كَنْزٌ ج كُنُوزٌ
To give a surname.	كَنَّى بِ	Firm and compact.	مُكْتَنِزٌ
To take a surname.	تَكَنَّى بِ	Hidden, buried (treasure).	مَكْنُوزٌ
Surname. Epithet.	كُنْيَةٌ	To sweep.	كَنَسَ يَكْنِسُ كَنْسًا وَكَنَّسَ
Metaphor, metonomy.	كِنَايَةٌ	Sweeper.	كَنَّاسٌ
Instead or in place of.	كِنَايَةً عَنْ	Sweepings.	كُنَاسَةٌ
To electrify.	كَهْرَبَ	Synagogue.	كَنِيسٌ
Yellow amber.	كَهْرَبَاءُ	Church.	كَنِيسَةٌ ج كَنَائِسُ
Electric.	كَهْرَبَائِيٌّ	Ecclesiastical.	كَنَائِسِيٌّ وَكَنَسِيٌّ
Electricity.	كَهْرَبَائِيَّةٌ	Broom.	مِكْنَسَةٌ ج مَكَانِسُ

Small district.	كُورَة ج كُور
Bee-hive	كُوَارَة نَحْلٍ
Quarantine.	كُورَنْتِينَا
Petroleum. Gas.	كَازٌ
Drinking-mug.	كُوزٌ ج أَكْوَازٌ
Drinking-cup.	كَاسٌ ج كُوسٌ
Vegetable marrow.	كُوسَا
Elbow.	كُوعٌ ج أَكْوَاعٌ
Kufa (city).	ٱلْكُوفَةُ
Kufic (writing) ; of Kufa.	كُوفِيٌّ
Head-wrapper.	كُوفِيَّة
Planet, star.	كَوْكَبٌ ج كَوَاكِبُ
A party ; assembly.	كَوْكَبَة
To make a heap.	كَوَّمَ
A heap.	كُومَة ج كُوَمٌ وأَكْوَام
To be, exist.	كَانَ يَكُونُ
He had wealth.	كَانَ لَهُ مَالٌ
He was standing.	كَانَ قَائِمًا

Electrified.	مُكَهْرَب
Cavern, cave.	كَهْف ج كُهُوف
To be middle-aged.	كَهَلَ يَكْهَلُ
Middle-aged.	كَهْل ج كُهُول
Mature age.	كُهُولَة وَكُهُولِيَّة
To divine, foretell.	كَهَنَ يَكْهُنُ
Soothsayer ; priest.	كَاهِن ج كَهَنَة
Soothsaying ; divination.	كَهَانَة
Priesthood.	كَهَنُوت
A large cup.	كُوبٌ ج أَكْوَابٌ
A horse cloth.	(كُوبَانٌ)
Stern of ship ; helm.	كَوْثَل
Hut.	كُوخٌ ج أَكْوَاخٌ
To restrain, hinder.	كَادَ يَكُودُ كَوْدًا
He almost did.	كَادَ يَفْعَلُ
He hardly did.	مَا كَادَ يَفْعَلُ
Art, profession.	كَارٌ ج كَارَاتٌ
Furnace, forge.	كُورٌ ج أَكْوَارٌ

He was doing.	كَانَ يَفْعَلُ	To be cauterised.	إِكْتَوَى
He had said.	كَانَ قَدْ قَالَ	Cauterisation, ironing.	كَيّ
To create, form.	كَوَّنَ	Smoothing-iron.	مِكْوَاةٌ ج مَكَاوٍ
To be created, formed.	تَكَوَّنَ	Cauterised ; ironed.	مَكْوِيٌّ
Existence, nature.	كِيَانٌ	In order that.	كَيْ وَلِكَيْ
Nature ; universe.	كَوْنٌ جأ كْوَان	In order not...	كَيْ لَا وَلِكَيْ لَا
Being ; creature.	كَائِنٌ	So and so.	كَيْتَ وَكَيْتَ
Incident, event.	كَائِنَةٌ ج كَائِنَاتٌ	To deceive...	كَادَ يَكِيدُ كَيْدًا وَكَايَدَ
All created things.	أَلْكَائِنَاتُ	Stratagem, guile.	كَيْدٌ
Formation, creation.	تَكْوِينٌ	Same as. كَيْدٌ	مَكِيدَةٌ ج مَكَائِدُ
Book of Genesis.	سِفْرُ التَّكْوِينِ	To be shrewd.	كَاسَ يَكِيسُ
Place.	مَكَانٌ ج أَمْكِنَةٌ وَأَمَاكِنُ	To put into a bag.	كَيَّسَ
Adverb of place.	ظَرْفُ الْمَكَانِ	Intelligence.	كَيْسٌ وَكِيَاسَةٌ
Place ; rank.	مَكَانَةٌ ج مَكَانَاتٌ	Bag, purse.	كِيسٌ ج أَكْيَاسٌ
Creator.	مُكَوِّنٌ	Clever ; handsome.	كَيِّسٌ
Window.	كُوَّةٌ ج كُوَّاتٌ وَكُوًى	Handsome, pretty.	(كُوَيِّسٌ)
To burn, cauterise.	كَوَى يَكْوِي	More handsome.	اكْوَسُ
(To iron clothes).	كَوَى	To take a special form.	تَكَيَّفَ

One who measures.	كَيَّالٌ	How; in what way?	كَيْفَ
Measure of capacity.	مَكْيَلٌ	Enjoyment. Quality.	(كَيْف)
Measured.	مَكِيلٌ وَمَكْيُولٌ	Howsoever.	كَيْفَمَا كَانَ
Chyle.	كَيْلُوسٌ	Quality; form.	كَيْفِيَّةٌ ج كَيْفِيَّاتٌ
In order that.	كَيْمَا (كَيْ مَا)	To measure.	كَالَ يَكِيلُ وَكَيَّلَ
Chemistry.	كِيمِيَا وَكِيمِيَاء	To measure out.	إِكْتَالَ
Chemist; chemical.	كِيمِيّ	Measure of grains = 6 mudds.	كَيْلٌ ج أَكْيَال (٦ أَمْدَادٍ)
Quinine.	كِينَا	A small measure.	كَيْلَة ج كَيْلَاتٌ
Cinchona bark.	خَشَبُ ٱلْكِينَا	Measuring, weighing.	كِيَالَة

ل

By thy life!	لَعَمْرُكَ	As a numeral sign = 30.	ل
No; not.	لَا	To, for.	لِ
Neither, nor.	لَا وَلَا	Let him write.	لِيَكْتُبْ

Assembled, gathered.	مُلْتَثِمٌ	No, there is not or no...	لَاتَ
To stay in.	أَلَبَّ بِ	An Arabian godess.	أَللَّاتَ
Marrow, pith.	لُبٌّ ج لُبُوبٌ	Lapis lazuli.	لَازَوَرْدٌ
Heart ; mind.	لُبٌّ ج أَلْبَابٌ	Azure-blue.	لَازَوَرْدِيٌّ
Intelligent.	لَبِيبٌ ج أَلِبَّاءُ	Angel.	مَلَأْكٌ وَمَلَكٌ ج مَلَائِكَةٌ
First milk.	لِبَاءٌ	To shine, glitter.	لَأْلَأَ وَتَلَأْلَأَ
Lioness.	لَبُؤَةٌ ج لَبُؤَاتٌ	Pearls.	لُؤْلُؤٌ
To tarry, abide in.	لَبَثَ يَلْبَثُ بِ	A pearl.	لُؤْلُؤَةٌ ج لَآلِئُ
He did not delay to do.	مَالَبِثَ أَنْ فَعَلَ	Pearl-coloured.	لُؤْلُؤِيٌّ
A tarrying.	لَبْثٌ وَلُبْثٌ وَلَبَاثٌ	To bind up a wound.	لَأَمَ يَلَأِمُ
A short stay, delay.	لُبْثَةٌ	To be of a low character.	لَؤُمَ
To beat. To abuse.	لَبَخَ يَلْبَخُ	To agree with.	لَاءَمَ
Persea (tree).	لَبَخَ (وَلَبَخٌ)	To reconcile.	لَاءَمَ بَيْنَ
Poultice, cataplasm.	أَبْخَةٌ ج لَبَخَاتٌ	To assemble. Unite. v. i.	إِلْتَأَمَ
To abide, dwell in.	لَبَدَ وَأَلْبَدَ بِ	Avarice, meanness.	لُؤْمٌ
To cram, compress.	لَبَّدَ	Base, sordid.	لَئِيمٌ ج لِئَامٌ
To be compact together.	تَلَبَّدَ	Convenient ; suitable.	مُلَائِمٌ
To stick to, cleave to.	تَلَبَّدَ بِ	Suitableness.	مُلَاءَمَة

A kick.	لَبْطَةٌ
To fit, become one.	لَبَقَ بِ
Wit and cleverness.	لَقٌ وَلَبَاقَةٌ
Skilful, clever.	ابِقٌ وَلَبيقٌ
To mix; confuse.	لَبَكَ يَلْبُكُ وَلَبَّكَ
To be confused, embarrassed.	تَلَبَّكَ وَٱلْتَبَكَ
Confused affair.	ابَكٌ وَلبْكَةٌ
Embarrassed.	مُلتَبِكٌ وَمَلْبُوكٌ
Egyptian bean.	لَبْلاَبٌ
Milk; sour milk. Sap.	لَبَنٌ ج أَلْبَانٌ
Brick, tile.	إِنٌ وَلِبْنٌ
A brick.	لَبَنَةٌ
Mount Lebanon.	لَبْنَان
Of Mount Lebanon.	لَبْنَانِيٌّ
Frankincence. Pine.	لُبَانٌ
Brick-maker. Milk-man.	لَبَّانٌ
Lioness.	لَبْوَةٌ ج لَبَوَاتٌ
To obey, respond.	لَبَّى

To be pressed closely.	إِلتَبَدَ
Cap of cloth or felt.	لَبَّادَةٌ
To make obscure.	لَبَسَ يَلْبِسُ عَلَى
To put on a dress.	لَبِسَ يَلْبَسُ
To render obscure. To clothe.	لَبَّسَ
To cover, clothe.	أَلْبَسَ
To be dark, obscure.	إِلتَبَسَ
To be confused with.	إِلتَبَسَ بِ
Ambiguity.	لَبْسٌ وَٱلتِبَاسٌ
Clothing, dress.	لُبْسٌ ج لُبُوسٌ
Garment.	لِبَاسٌ ج أَلْبِسَةٌ
Clothing.	مَلْبَسٌ ج مَلاَبِسٌ
Obscure ; doubtful.	مُلتَبِسٌ
Sugar-plums.	(مَلَبَّسٌ)
Garment.	مَلْبُوسٌ ج مَلاَبِيسُ
To collect pell-mell.	(لَبَّشَ)
Baggage, chattels.	لَبَشٌ
To kick.	لَطَأَ يَلْطَأُ لَطْأً

Here I am!	لَبَّيْكَ
To speak nonsense.	لَتَّ يَلُتُّ لَتًّا
Two idols.	أَللَّاتُ وَالْعُزَّى
Who, which (fem).	اَلَّتِي مث اَللَّتَانِ
	ج اَللَّوَاتِي
To stammer, lisp.	لَثِغَ يَلْثَغُ
Stammering, lisping.	لَثَغٌ وَلُثْغَةٌ
Lisper.	اَلْثَغُ م لَثْغَاءُ ج لُثْغٌ
To kiss.	لَثَمَ يَلْثِمُ وَلَثِمَ يَلْثَمُ لَثْمًا
To muffle the mouth.	لَثَمَ وَلَثَّمَ
A kiss.	لُثْمَةٌ
Veil.	لِثَامٌ
Gums (of the teeth).	لِثَةٌ ج لِثَاتٌ
To persist, persevere.	لَجَّ يَلِجُّ
To importune.	لَجَّ عَلَى
To wrangle with.	لَاجَّ
High sea; the deep.	لُجَّةٌ ج لُجَجٌ
Pertinacious.	لَاجٌّ وَلَجُوجٌ
Pertinacity.	لَجَاجٌ وَلَجَاجَةٌ

To take refuge in, repair to.	لَجَأَ يَلْجَأُ وَلَجِئَ
	يَلْجَأُ وَالْتَجَأَ إِلَى
To force, compel.	لَجَّأَ وَأَلْجَأَ إِلَى
To defend, protect.	أَلْجَأَ
Refuge.	لَجَأٌ وَمَلْجَأٌ ج مَلَاجِئُ
Seeking shelter.	لَاجِئٌ وَمُلْتَجِئٌ
To stammer.	لَجْلَجَ وَتَلَجْلَجَ
One who stutters.	لَجْلَاجٌ
To bridle (a horse).	لَجَمَ وَأَلْجَمَ
To be bridled.	اِلْتَجَمَ
Bridle, curb.	لِجَامٌ ج أَلْجِمَةٌ وَلُجُمٌ
Bridled.	مُلْجَمٌ
Committee.	لَجْنَةٌ
To be close, near.	لَحَّ يَلِحُّ لَحًّا
To persist in one's demands.	أَلَحَّ فِي اَلسُّؤَالِ
To importune, press.	أَلَحَّ عَلَيْهِ
Importunity; persistence.	إِلْحَاحٌ
One who insists.	مُلِحٌّ وَمِلْحَاحٌ

To pursue, follow.	لَاحَقَ	To bury.	لَحَدَ يَلْحَدُ لَحْدًا وَأَلْحَدَ
To annex, join to.	أَلْحَقَ ب	To swerve from.	أَلْحَدَ عَنْ
To reach ; be annexed.	إِلْتَحَقَ ب	To apostatize.	أَلْحَدَ وَالْتَحَدَ
Overtaking, reaching.	لَاحِقٌ	A grave.	لَحْدٌ ج أَلْحَادٌ وَلُحُودٌ
Adding ; annexing.	الْحَاقٌ	Apostasy ; heresy.	إِلْحَادٌ
Appendix ; supplement.	مُلْحَقٌ	An apostate.	مُلْحِدٌ ج مُلْحِدُونَ
To be fleshy.	لَحِمَ يَلْحَمُ لَحْمًا	To lick.	لَحَسَ ـَ لَحْسًا
To be killed, massacred.	لَحِمَ لَحْمًا	To regard, observe.	لَحَظَ يَلْحَظُ لَحْظًا
To solder.	لَحَمَ يَلْحُمُ لَحْمًا	To look at attentively.	لَاحَظَ
To join, unite.	لَاحَمَ وَأَلْحَمَ ب	Glance, moment.	لَحْظَةٌ
To kill one another.	تَلَاحَمَ	Observation.	مُلَاحَظَةٌ
To be soldered, united.	إِلْتَحَمَ	Regarded.	مَلْحُوظٌ ج مَلْحُوظَاتٌ
To grow bloody, (combat).	الْتَحَمَ	To wrap up	لَحَفَ يَلْحَفُ
Flesh, meat.	لَحْمٌ ج لُحُومٌ	To wrap one's self up.	إِلْتَحَفَ
Woof (of a stuff).	لُحْمَةٌ ج لَحَمٌ	Foot of a mountain.	لَحْفٌ
Solder.	لَحَامٌ	Cover, blanket.	لِحَافٌ ج لُحُفٌ
Butcher ; flesh-monger.	لَحَّامٌ	An outer dress.	مِلْحَفَةٌ ج مَلَاحِفُ
Union ; alliance.	إِلْتِحَامٌ	To reach, overtake.	لَحِقَ يَلْحَقُ

Sting, poisonous bite.	لَدْغَة	Combat, battle. مَلْحَمَة ج مَلَاحِم
To be pliable, flexible. لَدُنَ يَلْدُنُ		To make grammatical لَحَنَ يَلْحَنُ mistakes in speaking.
Soft ; supple. أَدْنٌ ج لِدْنٌ		To chant. لَحَّنَ فِي ٱلْقِرَاءَةِ
At, by, to, with, near to. لَدُنْ		Tone ; chant, air. لَحْنٌ ج أَلْحَان
Softness, flexibility. لَدَانَةٌ وَلُدُونَةٌ		Error of pronunciation.
At, by, to, with. لَدَى		Musical art. صِنَاعَةُ ٱلْأَلْحَان
Near or by thee ; to thee. لَدَيْكَ		Chanting. تَلْحِينٌ
To be sweet, agreeable. لَذَّ يَلَذُّ		To let one's beard grow. إِلْتَحَى
To enjoy. لَذَّ وَٱلْتَذَّ وَاسْتَلَذَّ بِ		Jaw-bone. لَحْيٌ مُثـ لَحْيَان ج لُحِيٌّ
To delight. تَلَذَّذَ		Bark, (sp. inner bark). لِحَاءٌ
Pleasure, delight. لَذَّةٌ ج لَذَّاتُ		Beard. لِحْيَةٌ ج لِحَى
Sweet, pleasant. لَذِيذٌ		Wild salsify. لِحْيَةُ ٱلتَّيْسِ
Delight, pleasure. مَلَذَّةٌ ج مَلَاذُّ		Obscurity in speech. لُخَّةٌ
To burn, brand. لَذَعَ يَلْذَعُ لَذْعًا		To extract ; sum up. لَخَّصَ
To feel a burning pain. إِلْتَذَعَ		Abstract. Explanation. تَلْخِيصٌ
A burn. لَذْعَةٌ		Summary, abstract مُلَخَّصٌ
Stinging pungent. لَذَّاعٌ		To quarrel ; oppose. لَدَّ يَلَدُّ لَدًّا
Ingenious ; witty. لُوْذَعٌ وَلُوْذَعِي		Violent in opposition. أَلَدُّ
		To sting, bite. لَدَغَ يَلْدَغُ لَدْغًا

Necessary, unavoidable.	لَا زِم	Latakia (*city*).	اَللَّاذِقِيَّةُ
Intransitive verb (*Gram.*).		Who, which.	اَلَّذِي مث اَللَّذَانِ ج اَلَّذِينَ
Necessity.	لُزُومٌ		
Compulsion.	اِلْزَامٌ	To press.	لَزَّ يَلُزُّ لَزًّا
Necessity;	اِلْتِزَامٌ ج اِلْتِزَامَاتٌ	To adhere to it.	اِلْتَزَّ بِهِ
obligation. Renting; farming		Necessary; constant.	لَازِبٌ
Hand-vice; (مِلْزَمَةٌ ج. مَلَازِمُ)		To stick, adhere.	لَزَجَ يَلْزَجُ
press.			
Lieutenant (*mil.*).	مُلَازِم	Viscid, sticky, cohesive.	لَزِجٌ
Assiduity, application.	مُلَازَمَةٌ	Viscidity, stickiness.	لُزُوجَةٌ
Obliged, compelled.	مَلْزُومٌ	To stick to.	لَزِقَ يَلْزَقُ وَ اِلْتَزَقَ بِ
Farmer of revenues.	مُلْتَزِمٌ	To adhere to another.	لَازَقَ
To sting.	لَسَعَ يَلْسَعُ لَسْعًا	To glue together.	أَلْزَقَ وَ لَزَّقَ
To be eloquent.	لَسِنَ يَلْسَنُ لَسَنًا	That which adjoins.	لَزِيقٌ
Eloquent.	لَسِنٌ ج لُسْنٌ	Poultice, plaster.	لَزْقَةٌ وَ اَزْرُوقٌ
Tongue; language.	لِسَانٌ ج أَلْسُنٌ	To adhere to; persist	لَزِمَ يَلْزَمُ
Cape of land.		in; be necessary, follow of	
Epiglottis.	لِسَانُ اَلْمِزْمَارِ	necessity.	
Speaking for itself.	لِسَانُ اَلْحَالِ	To cling to, persevere in.	لَازَمَ
By word of mouth.	لِسَانًا	To impose as a duty,	أَلْزَمَ إِلْزَامًا
Double dealer, false.	ذُو لِسَانَيْنِ	compel.	
Lingual.	لِسَانِيّ	To be responsible; be	اِلْتَزَمَ
		forced. To farm taxes.	
		To find necessary.	اِسْتَلْزَمَ

To find pretty or nice.	إِسْتَلْطَفَ
Friendliness. Favour.	لُطْفٌ
Light illness.	حَرَكَةٌ لُطْفٍ
Delicacy. Tenuity.	لَطَافَةٌ
Graceful ; kind. Rare (not dense).	لَطِيفٌ ج لُطَفَاء
God.	أَللَّطِيفُ
Witty saying.	لَطِيفَةٌ ج لَطَائِفُ
Friendliness ; courtesy.	تَلَطُّفٌ
Friendly treatment.	مُلَاطَفَةٌ
To slap.	لَطَمَ يَلْطُمُ لَطْمًا
To clash, collide.	تَلَاطَمَ وَٱلْتَطَمَ
Slap on the face.	لَطْمَةٌ ج لَطَمَاتٌ
To take shelter.	لَطَا يَلْطُو
To cleave to.	لَظَّ يَلُظ
To blaze (fire).	لَظِيَ يَلْظَى لَظًى
To be enflamed.	تَلَظَّى وَٱلْتَظَى
Fire ; flame	لَظًى
To play, sport, jest.	لَعِبَ ـَ لَعِبًا

To destroy, annihilate.	لَاشَى
To vanish, perish.	تَلَاشَى
Annihilation.	مُلَاشَاةٌ وَتَلَاشٍ
Thief, robber.	لِصٌّ ج أُصُوصٌ
Robbery, thieving.	أُصُوصِيَّةٌ
To stick to.	لَصِقَ يَلْصَقُ وَٱلْتَصَقَ بِ
To cling to, be devoted to	لَاصَقَ
To fasten, join.	أَلْصَقَ بِ
A dressing (for wounds).	أُصُوقٌ
Contiguous.	مُلَاصِقٌ
Contiguity, adherence.	مُلَاصَقَةٌ
To soil with.	لَطَخَ يَلْطَخُ وَلَطَّخَ بِ
To be soiled with.	تَلَطَّخَ بِ
A soil, stain.	لَطْخَةٌ
To be kind.	لَطَفَ يَلْطُفُ بِ
To soften, mitigate.	أَطَفَ
To treat with kindness.	لَاطَفَ
To be polite, courteous to.	تَلَطَّفَ لِ

It may be that Zeid is standing.	اَعَلَّ زَيْداً قَائِمٌ	To play, sport with.	لَاعَبَ
To shine, gleam.	اَعْلَمَ وَتَلَعْلَمَ	Play, sport.	لَعِبٌ وَلَاعِبٌ
To curse.	لَعَنَ يَلْعَنُ لَعْنَا	Gambling.	لَعِبُ الْقِمَار
To curse one another.	تَلَاعَنَ	A game, sport.	لُعْبَةٌ ج لُعَبٌ
Imprecation.	لَعْنٌ وَلَعْنَةٌ ج لَعَنَاتٌ	Saliva, spittle. Mucilage.	لُعَابٌ
Satan.	اَللَّعِينُ	Mucilaginous, slimy.	لُعَابِيٌّ
Cursed.	مَلْعُونٌ ج مَلَاعِينُ	Professional player.	لَعَّابٌ وَلَعِيبٌ
To be very tired.	لَغِبَ ـ	Play, pleasantry.	اُلْعُوبَةٌ
To chase long.	تَلَغَّبَ	Sporting, jesting.	تَلَاعُبٌ
Riddle; enigma.	لُغْزٌ ج اَلْغَازٌ	Place to play in.	مَلْعَبٌ ج مَلَاعِبٌ
Enigmatic, ambiguous.	مُلْغَزٌ	Toy, plaything.	مِلْعَبَةٌ
To speak indistinctly.	لَغَطَ يَلْغَطُ	A trick in play.	(مَلْعُوبٌ ج مَلَاعِيبُ)
Noise; sound.	لَغَطٌ ج اَلْغَاطٌ	To pain, burn.	لَعَجَ يَلْعَجُ لَعْجًا
Mine, blast.	لُغْمٌ ج لُغُومٌ	Burning pain.	لَاعِجٌ ج لَوَاعِجُ
Miner; blaster.	لُغْمَجِيٌّ	To lick.	لَعِقَ يَلْعَقُ لَعْقًا
To speak.	لَغَا يَلْغُو	Electuary.	لَعُوقٌ
To exclude, abolish.	اَلْغَى	Spoon.	مِلْعَقَةٌ ج مَلَاعِقُ
Language, dialect; idiom, expression.	لُغَةٌ ج لُغَاتٌ	Perhaps, may be.	لَعَلَّ وَعَلَّ

اقَبْ

٣١٤

علْمُ اللُّغَة

To burn, scorch. لَفَحَ يَلْفَحُ لَفْحًا	Lexicography. علْمُ اللُّغَة
Scorching. لَفُوحٌ وَلاَ فِحْ ج أَوَافِحُ	Lexicographers. أَهْلُ اللُّغَة
Mandrake (plant). لَفَّاحٌ	Faulty language, nonsense. لَغْوٌ
To pronounce. Dei. لَفَظَ يَلْفَظُ	Etymological ; linguistic. لُغَوِي
To utter. لَفَظَ وَتَلَفَّظَ ب	Abolishing, annulling. إِلْغَاء
Utterance ; word. لَفْظٌ ج أَلْفَاظٌ	Suppressed, abolished. مُلْغَى
As regards the لَفْظًا وَمَعْنًى	To wrap up, roll. لَفَّ يَلُفُّ لَفًّا
wording and the meaning.	
A word ; an لَفْظَةٌ ج لَفَظَاتٌ	To wrap one's self up. اِلْتَفَّ
utterance.	
Verbal. لَفْظِيٌّ	To be entwined. اِلْتَفَّ
To seam. لَفَقَ يَلْفُقُ لَفْقًا	A turban. (لَفَّةٌ ج لَفَّاتٌ)
To interpolate, falsify, lie. لَفَّقَ	Bandage. لِفَافَةٌ ج لَفَائِف
Embellished by falsehood. مُلَفَّقٌ	Mixed crowd. لَفِيفٌ
To wrap up, envelop. لَفْلَفَ	Wrapped up. Cabbage. مَلْفُوفٌ
Convolutions of تَلَافِيفُ الدِّمَاغِ the brain.	To twist, turn. لَفَتَ يَلْفِتُ لَفْتًا
To find. أَلْفَى إِلْفَاء	To consider, regard. اِلْتَفَتَ إِلَى
To mend ; take up. تَلَا فَى	Turnip, rape. لِفْتٌ
To give a title لَقَّبَ ب	Side-glance. لَفْتَةٌ ج لَفَتَات
Surname ; title. لَقَبٌ ج أَلْقَابٌ	Attention ; favour. اِلْتِفَاتٌ

To swallow.	تَلَقَّمَ وَٱلْتَقَمَ
Morsel, mouthful.	لُقْمَة ج لُقَم
To understand readily.	لَقِنَ يَلْقَنُ
To instruct, teach.	لَقَّنَ
To learn.	تَلَقَّنَ
Of quick understanding.	لَقِنٌ
Facial paralysis.	لَقْوَة
To meet ; see, find.	لَقِيَ يَلْقَى
To go to meet, meet.	لَاقَى لِقَاءً
To throw away, fling.	ٱلْقَى بِ
To cast away from.	أَلْقَى عَنْ
To propound, propose.	أَلْقَى عَلَى
To receive. To encounter.	تَلَقَّى
To meet one another.	تَلَاقَى وَٱلْتَقَى
To lie on one's back.	إِسْتَلْقَى عَلَى
Towards.	تِلْقَاء
Spontaneously.	مِنْ تِلْقَاءِ نَفْسِهِ
Mutual encounter.	تَلَاقٍ

Surnamed ; having a title.	مُلَقَّبٌ
To fecundate.	لَقَحَ يَلْقَحُ لَقْحاً
To be fecundated.	لَقِحَ يَلْقَحُ لَقْحاً
To fecundate.	لَقَّحَ وَأَلْقَحَ
Fecundation.	لَقْحٌ
Pollen.	لَقَاحٌ
To delay, be late.	(تَلَقَّسَ)
To pick up ; glean.	لَقَطَ يَلْقُطُ
To glean. Catch.	تَلَقَّطَ وَٱلْتَقَطَ
Freed slave.	لَاقِطٌ م لَاقِطَة
Picking up ; gleaning.	لِقَاطٌ
What is picked up.	لُقَاطَة
Foundling.	لَقِيطٌ ج لُقَطَاء
Pincers ; tongs.	مِلْقَطٌ ج مَلَاقِط
To snatch away.	ٱقَفَ وَٱلْتَقَفَ
Stork.	لَقْلَقٌ وَلَقْلَاقٌ ج لَقَالِقُ
To swallow.	لَقِمَ يَلْقَمُ لَقْماً
To feed.	لَقَّمَ وَالْقَمَ

Was it not?	أَلَمْ وَأَفَلَمْ وَأَوَلَمْ
To gather, amass.	لَمَّ يَلُمُّ لَمًّا
To come upon, befall.	أَلَمَّ بِ
When. Not yet.	لَمَّا
Inasmuch as...	لَمَّا كَانَ
Why?	لِمَاذَا (لِمَا ـ ذَا)
Calamity; misfortune.	لَمَّةٌ
Lock of hair.	لِمَّةٌ ج لِمَمٌ وَلِمَامٌ
Slight madness.	لَمَمٌ
Knowledge, experience.	إِلْمَامٌ
Calamity; chance.	مُلِمَّةٌ ج مُلِمَّاتٌ
Collected. Slightly mad.	مَلْمُومٌ
Light meal before lunch.	لُمْحَةٌ
To glance at.	لَمَحَ يَلْمَحُ إِلَى
To direct the sight.	لَمَحَ بِالْبَصَرِ
To shine, gleam.	لَمَحَ يَلْمَحُ
To hint at, suggest.	لَمَّحَ إِلَى
A glance resemblance.	لَمْحَةٌ

The day of resur-rection.	يَوْمُ التَّلَاقِي
Leaning or resting upon.	مُلْقًى عَلَى
Meeting-place.	مُلْقًى وَمُلْتَقًى
Meeting.	مُلَاقَاةٌ
Lac (resin); sealing wax.	لَكٌّ
Ten millions. Lac.	الْمَكُّ ج أَلْكَاكٌ
To push, thrust.	لَكَزَ يَلْكُزُ لَكْزًا
To be vile.	لَكِعَ يَلْكَعُ لَكْعًا وَلَكَاعَةً
Dirty, vile, abject.	لَكِعٌ م لَكَاءِ
To strike with the fist.	لَكَمَ يَلْكُمُ لَكْمًا
Boxing, fighting.	مُلَاكَمَةٌ
But, yet, however.	لَكِنْ وَلَكِنَّ
Large copper basin.	(لَكَنٌ ج أَلْكَانٌ)
Stam-merer.	أَلْكَنُ م لَكْنَاءُ ج لُكْنٌ
In order that.	لِكَيْ وَلِكَيْمَا
Not, not yet.	لَمْ
He has not eaten.	لَمْ يَأْكُلْ
Why? (*for* لِمَا)	لِمْ

To be gathered. تَلَمْلَمَ	Gleaming, shining. لَامِحٌ ولُمُوحٌ
A numerous army. لمْلَمٌ	Allusion, hint. تَلْمِيحٌ
Not. By no means. لَنْ	Points of resemblance. مَلَامِحُ
To flame, blaze(fire). لَهِبَ يَلْهَبُ	To touch. لَمَسَ يَلْمِسُ لَمْسًا ولَا مَسَ
To make to blaze. لَهَّبَ وَأَلْهَبَ	To seek for repeatedly. تَلَمَّسَ
To flame, blaze. تَلَهَّبَ وَالْتَهَبَ	To entreat, ask for. إِلْتَمَسَ مِنْ
Flame. لَهَبٌ ولَهِيبٌ	Touch, feeling. لَمْسٌ ومَلْمَسٌ
Inflammation. إِلْتِهَابٌ ج إِلْتِهَابَاتُ	Entreaty supplication. إِلْتِمَاسٌ
The divine nature. أَللّاهُوتُ	Touched. مَلْمُوسٌ
Theology. عِلْمُ اللّاهُوت	To shine, flash. لَمَعَ يَلْمَعُ وَالْتَمَعَ
Theologian. لَاهُوتِيٌّ	To beckon with. أَلْمَعَ بِ
To pant. Thirst. لَهَثَ يَلْهَثُ	Flash, brightness. لَمْعٌ ولَمَعَانٌ
Thirsty ; out of breath. لَهْثَانُ	A small quantity. لَمْعَةٌ ج لُمَعٌ
To be addicted to. لَهِجَ يَلْهَجُ بِ	That which shines. لَامِعٌ ج لُمَّعٌ
To be taken up with. لَهِجَ بِ	Having a sharp genius. أَلْمَعِيٌّ
Voice, tone. لَهْجَةٌ	Genius, wit. أَلْمَعِيَّةٌ
To regret. لَهِفَ يَلْهَفُ وتَلَهَّفَ عَلَى	Mottled, spotted. مُلَمَّعٌ
Regret, grief, sadness. لَهْفٌ	To gather, get together. لَمْلَمَ

Unless ; if not.	لَوْ لَمْ	Oh ! Alas !	يا لَهْفَاهَ وَيَالَهْفِي عَلَى
Were it not for...	لَوْلاَ وَلَوْ ما	Grieved.	لَهْفانُ م لَهْفَى
To thirst. Be restless.	لاَبَ يَلُوبُ	To swallow at one gulp.	لَهِمَ يَلْهَمُ وَٱلْتَهَم
Beans.	لُوبَاءُ وَلُوبِيَا	To inspire.	اَلْهَمَ
Pl. of. اَللَّتِي	أَللَّوَاتِي	Greedy, voracious.	لَهِمٌ
To stain ; soil. Mix.	لَوَّثَ	Divine guidance.	إِلْهامُ ج إِلْهَامَات
To be soiled.	تَلَوَّثَ تَلَوُّثَا	To play.	لَهَا يَلْهُو لَهْواً
To glimmer ; appear.	لاَحَ يَلُوحُ	To be infatuated with.	لَهِبَ
Plate ; tablet. Shoulder-blade.	لَوْحٌ ج أَلْوَاحٌ	To forget ; neglect.	(لَهَا عَنْ)
Schedule.	لاَئِحَةٌ ج لَوَائِح	To preoccupy.	لَهَّى وَأَلْهَى (عَنْ)
Appearances.	أَوَائِحُ	To be diverted.	تَلاهَى وَٱلْتَهَى
To take refuge in (ب)	لاَذَ يَلُوذُ	Amusement ; diversion.	لَهْوٌ
Refuge ; fortress.	مَلاَذٌ	Soft palate.	لَهَاةٌ ج لَهَوَات
Almond (tree and fruit).	لَوْزٌ	Palatial.	لَهَوِيٌّ
The tonsils.	(أَللَّوْزَتَان)	Diverted, thoughtless.	لاَهٍ
To taste.	لاَسَ يَلُوسُ لَوْساً	Amusement.	مَلْهًى ج مَلاهٍ
To be impatient.	لاَعَ يَلُوعُ	If. O that.	لَوْ
To torture.	لَوَّعَ تَلْوِيعًا	Although, though.	وَلَوْ

Changeful.	مُتَلَوِّنٌ	Pain ; anguish ; torture.	اوْعَةٌ
Lavander.	(لَوَنْدَا)	A plant, the Arum.	لُوفٌ
To twist.	لَوَى يَلْوِي لَيًّا	To masticate.	لَاكَ يَلُوكُ اوْكًا
To bend.	لَوَّى وَأَلْوَى	Hotel (Ital).	(لُوكَنْدَةٌ)
To be bent, deflected.	إِلْتَوَى	Were it not for....	لَوْلَا
Flag, standard. District.	لِوَاءٌ ج أَلْوِيَةٌ	Screw.	لَوْلَبٌ ج لَوَالِبُ
A general of the army.	أَمِيرُ اللِّوَاءِ	Spiral.	لَوْلَبِيٌّ
Curvature.	إِلْتِوَاءٌ	To blame censure.	لَامَ يَلُومُ لَوْمًا
O that ! Would that !	لَيْتَ	To blame ; one another.	تَلَاوَمَ
Would that Zeid were going !	لَيْتَ زَيْدٌ ذَاهِبٌ	Blame ; censure.	لَوْمٌ
Would that I had done it !	لَيْتَنِي فَعَلْتُهُ	Blamer ; censurer.	لَائِمٌ
Lion.	لَيْثٌ ج لُيُوثٌ	Blame ; censure.	مَلَامٌ وَمَلَامَةٌ
Not.	لَيْسَ	Blamable ; reprehensible.	مَلُومٌ
God is not unjust.	لَيْسَ اللّٰهُ بِظَالِمٍ	Hyoid bone.	الْعَظْمُ اللَّامِيُّ
Fiber of palm, &c.	لِيفٌ	State-prison.	(أُومَانٌ)
To be fit, suitable.	لَاقَ يَلِيقُ	To colour.	لَوَّنَ تَلْوِينًا
Suitable, proper.	لَائِقٌ	To be coloured.	تَلَوَّنَ
Night.	لَيْلٌ ج لَيَالٍ . وَلَيْلَةٌ ج لَيْلَاتٌ	Colour. Kind.	لَوْنٌ ج أَلْوَانٌ

To coax, conciliate.	تَلَيَّنَ لَهُ	Lest. (*From* لَا)	لِثَلَّا (لِأَنْ ـ لَا)
Tender, flexible.	لِيَنُّ ج لَيِّنُونُ	Lest he should say.	لِثَلَّا يَقُولُ
Softness. Diarrhœa.	لِيَنُّ	Lemon.	ايمُونُ
Softness, pliability.	لِيَنُونَةُ	To be soft, tender.	لَانَ يَلِينُ
Laxative, aperient.	مُلَيِّنُ	To soften.	لَيَّنَ تَلْيِينًا وَأَلَانَ إِلَاةَ
Portico.	(لِيوَانُ) إِيوَانُ	To conciliate.	لَايَنَ مُلَايَنَةً
		To become soft, tender.	تَلَيَّنَ

م

How beautiful!	مَا أَجْمَلَهُ	As a numeral sign = 40.	م
I do not know.	مَا أَدْرِي	What?	مَا
What?	مَاذَا	What has he done?	مَا فَعَلَ
What art thou doing?	مَاذَا تَفْعَلُ	What he has done.	مَا صَنَعَ
Why hast thou come?	لِمَاذَا جِئْتَ	A certain affair.	أَمْرُ مَا
Nature, essence.	مَاهِيَّةٌ	As long as I live.	مَا دُمْتُ حَيًّا

When, at the time when. مَتَى مَا	Wages, pay. مَاهِيَّةٌ ج مَاهِيَات
To resemble. مَثَلَ يَمْثُلُ وَمَاثَل	Water (see موه) مَاءٌ ج مِيَاه
To compare to. مَثَلَ وَمَاثَلَ بِ	Inner angle of the eye. مُوقٌ
To stand before. مَثَلَ يَمْثُلُ بَيْنَ يَدَيْهِ someone.	To provide. مَأَنَ يَمْأَنُ مَأْنًا
He imagined (a thing). تَمَثَّلَ لَهُ	Provisions. مَؤُونَةٌ وَمُؤْنَةٌ ج مُؤَن
To imitate. تَمَثَّلَ بِ	One hundred. مِئَةٌ وَمَائَةٌ ج مِئَات
To resemble each other. تَمَاثَل	Centenary. مِئَوِيٌّ
To be nearly convalescent. تَمَاثَلَ مِنْ عِلَّتِهِ	Metre (measure). مِتْرٌ ج اَمْتَار
To obey order. إِمْتَثَلَ ٱلْأَمْرَ	To grant. مَتَّعَ وَأَمْتَعَ بِ
Similar, like. مِثْلٌ ج أَمْثَال	To enjoy. تَمَتَّعَ بِ وَمِنْ
As well as. مِثْلَمَا	Enjoyment, privilege. مُتْعَةٌ ج مُتَع
Proverb; a saying. مَثَلٌ ج أَمْثَال	Furniture, effects. مَتَاعٌ ج اَمْتِعَة
To give an example. ضَرَبَ مَثَلًا	Enjoyment, privilege. تَمَتُّع وَٱسْتِمْتَاع
Model. Example. مِثَالٌ ج اَمْثِلَة	To be firm. مَتَنَ يَمْتُنُ مَتَانَة
Lesson. (مَثَالَة ج مَثَالَات وَمَثَائِل)	Text of a book. مَتْنٌ
Resembling. مَثِيلٌ ج مُثَل	Solidity, firmness. مَتَانَة
The best. أَمْثَلُ م مُثْلَى ج اَمَاثِل	Strong, solid, robust. مَتِين
Example. Lesson. أُمْثُولَة	When? When. مَتَى

Buffoon, jester.	مُجَّان	Image, figure.	تِمْثال ج تَماثِيل
Gratuitously ; freely.	مُجَّاناً	Assimilation. Analogy.	تَمْثِيل
Yolk of an egg.	مُحّ	Bladder.	مَثانة ج مَثانَات
Litter, panier.	مُحّارة	To spit ; reject.	مَجّ يَمُجّ مَجًّا
To purify.	مَحَص يَمْحَص مَحْصاً ب	To be great, glorious.	مَجَد يَمْجُد
To purify.To try, prove.	مَحَّص	To glorify ; exalt, honour.	مَجَّد
To be sincere.	مَحَض يَمْحَض مَحْضاً لهُ	To be glorified, praised.	تَمَجَّد
Pure, unmixed.	مَحْض	Glory, praise.	مَجْد ج أَمْجاد
To blot out, efface.	مَحَق يَمْحَق مَحْقاً	Glorification, praising.	تَمْجِيد
To be effaced.	إِمَّحَق واَّمَّحَق	Noble, glorious.	مَجِيد وماجِد
Perdition, annihilation.	مَحْق	The Glorious (God).	أَلمَجِيد
Waning of the moon.	مُحاق	More glorious.	أَمْجَد ج أَماجِد
To brawl, dispute.	مَحَك يَمْحَك مَحْكاً	Hungarian.	مَجَر
To quarrel with one.	ماحَكهُ	Hungary.	بِلادُ ٱلمَجَر
A quarrel, brawl.	مُماحَكة	Magians.	مَجُوس
Quarrelsome.	مَحِك وماحِك	Creed of the Magians.	أَلمَجُوسِيَّة
To be sterile.	مَحَل يَمْحَل وأَمْحَل	Code, book, (see جِلّ)	مَجَلَّة
Sterility, barrenness.	مَحْل	To jest.	مَجَن يَمْجُن مُجُوناً

Butter-milk.	مخيض
A churning-vessel.	ممخض
To blow the nose.	مخط يمخط
Mucus.	مخاط
Gossamer.	مخاط الشيطان أو الشمس
Mucous.	مخاطي
Lever.	مخل ج أمخال ومخول
To rinse the mouth.	(مخمض فاه وتمخمض)
To spread, extend.	مد يمد مدا
To dip the pen in ink.	مد القلم
To help, aid, assist.	مد وأمد
To reach ; extend to.	إمتد إلى
To be extended, lie down.	تمدد
To seek help.	إستمد
Tide ; flux.	مد ج مدود
The sign. (آ)	مد ومدة
A dry measure.	مد ج أمداد
Period ; while.	مدة ج مدد

Cunning, deceitful.	محال
Barren, unfruitful.	ماحل وممحل
To try, test.	محن يمحن محنا
To try, examine.	إمتحن
Trial, affliction.	محنة ج محن
Experience ; examination.	إمتحان
To efface, blot out.	محا يمحو محوا
To be blotted out.	امحى (إنمحى)
Effected ; blotted out.	ممحو
A wiper.	ممحاة
Marrow ; brain.	مخ ج مخاخ
To plough the water.	مخر يمخر
A ship.	ماخرة ج مواخر
Wine shop. House of ill-fame.	ماخور
To churn.	مخض يمخض مخضا
To suffer the pains of childbirth.	مخضت تمخض وتمخضت
To be churned.	تمخض وامتخض
Labour of childbirth.	مخاض

Medina (in Arabia).	اَلْمَدِينَةُ	Assistance.	مَدَدٌ وَإِمْدَادٌ
Bagdad.	مَدِينَةُ ٱلسَّلَام	Ink. Oil (f a lamp).	مِدَادٌ
Citizen, townsman.	مَدَنِيّ	Matter.	مَادَّةٌ ج مَوَادُّ
To grant one a delay.	مَادَى	Material.	مَادِّيّ
To take a long time.	تَمَادَى	Long.	مَدِيدٌ
Distance, extent ; end.	مَدَى	Extensin ; dilatatin.	تَمَدُّدٌ
Large knife.	مُدْيَةٌ ج مُدًى	Prolonged ; extended.	مُمْتَدّ
Since.	مُذْ	A letter with. (ٓ) مَدَّة	مَمْدُودٌ
To become rotten.	مَذِرَ يَمْذَرُ	To braise, extol.	مَدَحَ يَمْدَحُ
To disperse, scatter.	مَذَّرَ	To praise, Be extended.	إِمْتَدَحَ
Hither and thither.	شَذَرَ مَذَرَ	Eulogy.	مَدْحٌ .وَمَدِيحٌ ج مَدَائِحُ
Spoilt, rotten (egg) ; foul.	مَذِرٌ	Panegyrist.	مَادِحٌ وَمَدَّاحٌ
Insincere, dissembler.	مُمَاذِق	Village, town, city.	مَدَرٌ
To pass, pass by.	مَرَّ يَمُرُّ	Inhabitants of towns.	أَهْلُ ٱلْمَدَرِ
To embitter, make bitter.	مَرَّرَ	To build cities ; civilize.	مَدَّنَ
He caused him to pass.	أَمَرَّهُ	To become civilized.	تَمَدَّنَ
To continue ; last.	إِسْتَمَرَّ	Refinement, civilizatin.	تَمَدُّنٌ
Course, succession.	مَرٌّ وَمُرُورٌ	City, town.	مَدِينَةٌ ج مُدُنٌ وَمَدَائِنُ

To be very gay.	تَمِرحَ يَمرَحُ
Very gay.	مَرِحَ ج مَرْحى وَمَرَاحى
(See رحب)	مَرحَباً
To anoint.	مَرِخَ يَمرَخُ مَرخاً
Liniment.	مَرُوخ
Mars (planet).	اَلْمِرّيخُ
To rebel, revolt.	مَرَدَ يَمرُدُ وَتَمَرَّدَ
To be proud, insolent.	تَمَرَّدَ عَلى
Rebellious.	مارِدٌ ج مَرَدَة
Beardless (youth).	أَمرَدُ ج مُرْدٌ
Marjoram.	مَردَقُوشٌ ومَرْزَنْجُوشٌ
To steep, soak.	مَرَسَ يَمرُسُ
To exercise, practice.	مارَسَ
Rope, cord.	مَرَسَةٌ ج مَرَسٌ وأَمراسٌ
Exercise, practice.	مُمارَسةٌ
Myrtle-tree.	مَرْسِين
Hospital.	مارِستانٌ
To fall ill, be sick.	مَرِضَ يَمرَضُ

Bitter. Myrrh (plant).	مُرّ
Once.	مَرّةٌ ج مِرارٌ وَمَرّاتٌ
Several times, often.	مِرارا
Gall; bile.	مِرّةٌ ج مِرَرٌ
Aforesaid.	اَلْمارُّ ذِكرُه
Bitterness. Gall-bladder.	مَرارةٌ
More bitter.	أَمرُّ
Passage; pathway.	مَمَرّ
Continued, continual.	مُستَمِرّ
To be healthy (food).	مَرِئَ يَمرَأُ
Man.	مَرءٌ وأَمرُؤٌ
Woman.	مَرأَةٌ واَمرَأَة
Courage, bravery.	مُروءَةٌ ومُرُوّةٌ
Gullet, œsophagus.	مَرِيّ
To moisten, soak.	مَرَثَ يَمرُثُ
Meadow, pasture.	مَرْجٌ ج مُرُوجٌ
Confusion, disorder.	هَرجٌ وَمَرجٌ
Coral.	مَرْجانٌ

Elastic, flexible.	مِرِنٌ	To nurse the sick.	مَرَّضَ
Elasticity, flexibility.	مُرُونَةٌ	To make ill, or sick.	أَمْرَضَ
Maronite.	مَارُونِيٌّ ج مَوَارِنَةٌ	To feign illness.	تَمَارَضَ
Practice; exercise.	تَمْرِينٌ وتَمِرَنٌ	Disease, illness.	مَرَضٌ ج امْرَاضٌ
Trained; inured.	مُمَرَّنٌ	Sick, ill.	مَرِيضٌ ج مَرْضَى
Ointment.	مَرْهَمٌ ج مَرَاهِمُ	To pull out (hair).	مَرَطَ يَمْرُطُ مَرْطًا
Saint (Syriac).	مَار ومَارِي	Scanty-haired.	أَمْرَطُ م مَرْطَاءُ
Dispute, quarrel.	مِرْيَةٌ	To graze (cattle).	مَرَغَ يَمْرَغُ مَرْغًا
To suck.	مَزَّ يَمُزُّ مَزًّا	To roll one in the dust.	مَرَّغَ
Sourish. Insipid.	مَزٌّ ومَزَّةٌ	To roll in the dust.	تَمَرَّغَ
To mix.	مَزَجَ يَمْزُجُ مَزْجًا	To penetrate, pass.	مَرَقَ يَمْرُقُ مِنْ
To associate with.	مَازَجَ	Broth; gravy, sauce.	مَرَقٌ ومَرَقَةٌ
To get mixed with...	إِمْتَزَجَ بِ	A heretic.	مَارِقٌ
Mixture, amalgamation.	إِمْتِزَاجٌ	Marble.	مَرْمَرٌ
Mixture, alloy.	مَزِيجٌ	To become elastic.	مَرَنَ يَمْرُنُ
Temperament.	مِزَاجٌ ج امْزِجَةٌ	To be accustomed to.	مَرَنَ عَلَى
To joke, jest.	مَزَحَ يَمْزَحُ مَزْحًا	To train, habituate.	مَرَّنَ عَلَى
To jest together.	تَمَازَحَ	To be habituated to.	تَمَرَّنَ عَلَى

Jesting, bantering.	مِزَاحٌ
A kind of beer.	مِزْرٌ
To tear to pieces.	مَزَّقَ يُمَزِّقُ وَمَزَّقَ
To disperse (a crowd).	مَزَّقَ
To be torn into pieces.	تَمَزَّقَ
Merit; trait.	مَزِيَّةٌ ج مَزَايَا
To touch.	مَسَّ يَمَسُّ مَسًّا
To touch one another.	تَمَاسَّ
Touch; contact. Insanity.	مَسٌّ
Urgent business.	حَاجَةٌ مَاسَّةٌ
Tangent (geom.).	مُمَاسٌّ
Touched. Insane.	مَمْسُوسٌ
A kind of shoe.	مِسْتٌ ج مُسُوتٌ
To wipe; anoint.	مَسَحَ يَمْسَحُ مَسْحًا
To measure land.	مَسَحَ الأَرْضَ
Wiping. Anointing.	مَسْحٌ
Sack-cloth.	مِسْحٌ ج مُسُوحٌ
Land-survey.	مِسَاحَةٌ

Mensuration.	عِلْمُ الْمِسَاحَةِ
Anointed.	مَسِيحٌ ج مُسَحَاءُ وَمَسْحَى
Christ, the Messiah.	الْمَسِيحُ
Antichrist.	الْمَسِيحُ الدَّجَّالُ
Christian.	مَسِيحِيٌّ ج مَسِيحِيُّونَ
Christianity.	الْمَسِيحِيَّةُ
Land-surveyor.	مَسَّاحٌ ج مَسَّاحُونَ
Flat barren land.	مَسْحَاءُ
Crocodile.	تِمْسَاحٌ ج تَمَاسِيحُ
To change; distort.	مَسَخَ يَمْسَخُ مَسْخًا
Distorted, corrupted.	مَسْخٌ
To plait or twist.	مَسَدَ يَمْسُدُ
To rub with the hand.	(مَسَّدَ)
Cord of fibres.	مَسَدٌ ج مِسَادٌ
Massage.	(تَمْسِيد)
To hold, seize.	مَسَكَ يَمْسُكُ وَأَمْسَكَ
To retain, hold back.	أَمْسَكَ
To refrain from.	أَمْسَكَ عَن

To walk with one.	ماشى	Musk.	مِسْك
Walking, marching.	مَشْيٌ	Avarice. Abstinence.	إِمْسَاكٌ
Walker on foot; foot-soldier.	مَاشٍ ج مُشَاةٌ	Scented with musk.	مُمَسَّكٌ
Flocks, cattle.	ماشيةٌ ج مَواشٍ	To wish one good evening.	مَسَّى
Corridor.	مَمْشًى ج مَمَاشٍ	To enter into the evening.	أَمْسَى
To suck; sip.	مَصَّ يَمُصُّ وَآمْتَصَّ	Eve, evening.	مَسَاءٌ
To absorb.	إِمْتَصَّ	Good evening.	مَساءَ ٱلْـخَيْر
What is sucked.	مُصَّةٌ ومُصَاصٌ	To comb (the hair).	مَشَطَ يَمْشُطُ وَمَشَّطَ
Sugar-cane.	(قَصَبُ ٱلْمَصِّ)	Comb; rake.	مِشْطٌ ج أَمْشَاطٌ
Twine, pack-thread.	خَيْط مِصِيصٍ	Instep of the foot.	مُشْط ٱلرِّجْلِ
Siphon; sucking tube.	مِمَصٌّ	Hair-dresser.	مَاشِطٌ م مَاشِطَةٌ
Absorption.	إِمْتِصَاصٌ	Slenderness.	مَشَقٌ
To build cities.	مَصَّرَ	The refuse of silk.	مُشَاقَةٌ
Egypt. Cairo.	مِصْرٌ	Slim, Slender.	مَمْشُوقٌ
Great city. Limits.	مِصْرٌ ج أَمْصَارٌ	Apricots.	مِشْمِشٌ
Egyptian.	مِصْرِيٌّ ج مِصْرِيُّونَ	An apricot.	مِشْمِشَةٌ
Intestines.	مُصْرَانٌ ج مَصَارِينُ	To walk; go.	مَشَى يَمْشِي و تَمَشَّى
Mastic (kind of gum).	مُصْطَكَى	To cause to walk.	مَشَّى وأَمْشَى

To drop, trickle.	مَصَل يَمْصُل
Whey. Serum.	مَصْلٌ
To cause pain.	مَضَّ يَمَضُّ وَأَمَضَّ
Pain, grief.	مَضٌّ وَمَضَّةٌ وَمَضَض
To masticate, chew.	مَضَغَ يَمْضَغ
Mastication, chewing.	مَضْغ
Morsel.	مَضْغَةٌ ج مُضَغ
To rinse, wash.	مَضْمَضَ
To pass; go, depart.	مَضَى يَمْضِي
To sign (a letter).	مَضَى على
To take, carry off.	مَضَى بِ
To execute, accomplish.	أَمْضَى
To pass off, carried cut.	عَضَّى
Execution, Signature.	إِمْضَاءُ
The past; past tense.	الْمَاضِي
Signer; subscriber.	مُمْضٍ
To draw; stretch.	مَطَّ يَمُطّ
To rain.	مَطَر يَمْطُر وَامْطَر

To pray for rain.	إِسْتَمْطَر
Rain; heavy rain.	مَطَرٌ ج امْطَار
Rainy (weather).	مَاطِرٌ وَمُمْطِرٌ
A water-skin.	مَطْرَةٌ
Bishop.	مُطْرَانٌ ج مَطَارِنَة
To defer, put off.	مَطَلَ وَمَاطَل
Delay, putting off.	مَطْلٌ وَمُمَاطَلَة
One who puts off.	مُمَاطِلٌ
Deferred.	مَمْطُولٌ
To mount, ride.	أَمْطَى وَامْتَطَى
Beast of burden.	مَطِيَّةٌ ج مَطَايَا
With, together with.	مَعَ وَمَعْ
Nevertheless, yet.	مع ذَلِك
Although.	مع أَنْ
Together, simultaneously.	مَعًا
Company, attendance.	مَعِيَّة
Stomach.	مَعِدَةٌ وَمِعْدَةٌ ج مِعَد
Goats (coll noun).	مَعْزٌ وَمَعْزَى

To draw (a sword).	إِمْتَطَ
To speak indistinctly.	مَغْمَغَ ٱلْكَلَامَ
To magnetize.	(مَغْطَسَ)
The magnet.	مَغْنَطِيسٌ
To hate, detest.	مَقَتَ يَمْقُتُ مَقْتًا
Hatred; aversion.	مَقْتٌ
Hated, detested.	مَقِيتٌ وَمَمْقُوتٌ
Sebesten (*Cordia myxa*).	مُقَّاسٌ
To look at.	مَقَلَ يَمْقُلُ مَقْلًا
The eye; eye-ball.	مُقْلَةٌ ج مُقَلٌ
Mecca (city in Arabia).	مَكَّةُ
Meccan.	مَكِّيٌّ وَمَكَّاوِيٌّ
Weaving-shuttle.	مَكُّوكٌ
To abide, dwell.	مَكَثَ يَمْكُثُ
Sojourn, stay.	مَكْثٌ
To deceive.	مَكَرَ يَمْكُرُ وَمَاكَرَ
Trick, deceit, fraud.	مَكْرٌ
Cunning, deceitful.	مَاكِرٌ ج مَكَرَةٌ

A goat.	مَاعِزٌ ج مَوَاعِزُ
Goat-herd.	مَعَّازٌ
To crush.	(مَعَسَ يَمْعَسُ مَعْسًا)
To pull out (hair).	مَعَطَ يَمْعَطُ
Hairless.	أَمْعَطُ م مَعْطَاءُ ج مُعْطٌ
To rub.	مَعَكَ يَمْعَكُ مَعْكًا
To delay paying.	مَاعَكَ بِدَيْنِهِ
Tumult of battle.	مَعْمَعَةٌ ج مَعَامِعُ
To consider.	أَمْعَنَ ٱلنَّظَرَ. وَ تَمَعَّنَ
Consideration.	إِمْعَانٌ وَتَمَعُّنٌ
Utensil; boat.	مَاعُونٌ ج مَوَاعِينُ
Running water.	مَعِينٌ ج مُعُنٌ
Intestine.	مَعِيٌّ وَمِعًى ج أَمْعَاءُ
Red earth for dyeing.	مَغْرَةٌ
To suffer from colic.	مُغِصَ
Colic gripes.	مَغْصٌ
To stretch.	مَغَطَ يَمْغَطُ. وَمَغَّطَ
To be stretched.	تَمَغَّطَ وَٱمْتَغَطَ

To tire of.	مَلَّ يَمَلُّ مِنْ	Deceiver ; trickster.	مَكَّارُ
To cause weariness.	أَمَلَّ	To collect taxes.	مَكَسَ وَمَكَّسَ
To be restless, tired.	تَمَلَّلَ	Custom duties.	مَكْسٌ ج مُكُوسٌ
A religion, creed.	مِلَّةٌ ج مِلَلٌ	Tax-gatherer.	مَاكِسٌ وَمَكَّاسٌ
Weariness.	مَلَلٌ ومَلالٌ ومَلالَةٌ	To be strong.	مَكُنَ يَمْكُنُ
Mollah, a Turkish judge.	مُلَّا	To strengthen.	مَكَّنَ
Acorn-tree ; kind of oak.	مَلُّولٌ	To enable.	مَكَّنَ وَامْكَنَ مِنْ
To fill up.	مَلَأَ يَمْلَأُ مَلَأً	To be possible for (him).	أَمْكَنَهُ
To be filled.	مَلِئَ يَمْلَأُ وَامْتَلَأ مِنْ	It is possible that...	يُمْكِنُ أَنْ
To fill, fill up.	مَلَّأَ تَمْلِئَةً	To be stable, firm, solid.	تَمَكَّنَ
Quantity which fills up.	مِلْءٌ	To be able, overcome.	تَمَكَّنَ مِنْ
An assembly.	مَلأٌ ج أَمْلاءٌ	Possibility. Power.	مَكِنَةٌ
A kind of garment.	مُلاءَةٌ وَمِلايَةٌ	Place ; station.	مَكانٌ ج أَمَاكِنُ
Full.	مَلآنُ م مَلأَى وَمَلآنَةٌ	Influence ; power.	مَكانَةٌ
Fullness Plethora.	إِمْتِلاءٌ	Possibility ; power.	إِمْكانٌ
Full.	مَمْلُوءٌ وَمَمْلُوٌّ وَمُمْتَلِئٌ	Possible.	مُمْكِنٌ
To salt (food.)	مَلَحَ يَمْلَحُ ومَلَّحَ	Declinable noun.	مُتَمَكِّنٌ
To be salty. Be beautiful.	مَلُحَ يَمْلُحُ مُلُوحَةً	To tack, baste.	مَلَّ يَمُلُّ مَلاًّ

To plaster.	مَلَطَ يَمْلُط وَمَلَّطَ	How handsome he is !	ما أَمْلَحَهُ
Plaster.	مِلاطٌ	Salt.	مِلْحٌ ج أَمْلاحٌ
Malta (Island).	مالِطَةُ	Pleasant anecdote.	مُلْحَةٌ ج مُلَحٌ
Maltese.	مالِطِيٌّ	Beauty, goodliness.	مَلاحَةٌ
Scanty-haired.	أَمْلَطُ م مَلْطاءُ	The art of navigation.	مِلاحَةٌ
To flatter.	مَلَقَ يَمْلُقُ . ومااَقَ	Sailor. Salt merchant.	مَلّاحٌ
To flatter, cajole.	تَمَلَّقَ تَمَلُّقاً	Salt-works, salt mine.	مَلّاحَةٌ
Flattery.	مَلَقٌ وتَمْلِيقٌ وتَمَلُّقٌ	Saltness.	مُلوحَةٌ
Adulator, flatterer.	مَلِقٌ ومَلّاقٌ	Goodly, pretty.	مَلِيحٌ ج مِلاحٌ
To possess.	مَلَكَ يَمْلِكُ وتَمَلَّكَ	Salted.	مُمَلَّحٌ
To reign or rule over.	مَلَكَ على	Salt-cellar.	مَمْلَحَةٌ ج مَمالِحُ
To give in possession.	مَلَّكَ	Jew's mallow.	مَلوخِيَّةٌ ومُلوخِيا
To rule, possess.	تَمَلَّكَ	To be smooth.	مَلُسَ يَمْلُسُ
To abstain from.	تَمالَكَ عَنْ	To make smooth.	مَلَّسَ
Property ; goods.	مِلْكٌ ج أَمْلاكٌ	Twilight, dawn.	مَلَسُ الظَّلام
Power, authority, reign.	مُلْكٌ	Smoothness.	مَلاسَةٌ
Angle.	مَلَكٌ ومَلاكٌ ج مَلائِكَةٌ	Smooth.	أَمْلَسُ م مَلْساءُ ج مُلْسٌ
King.	مَلِكٌ ج مُلوكٌ	To escape.	مَلَصَ وتَمَلَّصَ مِنْ

Some *of* them say. مِنْهُمْ مَنْ يَقُول	Queen. ملِكة
He drew nigh *to* him. قَرُبَ مِنهُ	Custom, habit. ملَكة ج مَلَكات
Better *than.* أَفْضَلُ مِنْ	Royalty. Kingdom. ملكُوتُ
He came at once. جاءَ مِنْ ساعَتِه	Royal, Kingly. ملكِيُّ وَمُلُوكِيُّ
To be gracious. مَنَّ يَمُنُّ وَاَمْتَنَّ	Possessor, proprietor. مالِكُّ
To reproach for benefits. مَنَّ وَمَنَّنَ	Heron (bird). مالِكُ الْحَزين
Gift, benefit. Manna. مَنُّ	Possessor. King. مليكٌ ج ملكاء
By the grace of God. بِمَنِّه تَعالى	Kingdom. مملَكة ج ممالِكُ
Grace, bounty. منةٌ ج مِنن	Mamluk. مملُوكٌ ج مَمَاليكُ
Generous. منّانُ	To be restless. تملمَلَ
God, the Giver of good. اَلْمَنّانُ	Melancholy ; black bile. ملنخوليا
Death. Ill-fortune. اَلْمَنُونُ	To dictate a writing. أَملى عَلى
Reproach for benefit. إِمتِنانُ	A long time. مليًّا مِن الدهر
Under obligation. (مَمنُونُ)	Dictation. إِملاءٌ ج اَمال
Obligation. (مَمنُونية)	Million. مليونُ ج مَلايين
Battering-ram. مَنجنيقٌ وَمَنجليقُ	For what ? From what ? ممَّا (مِنْ ما)
To give, grant. مَنَح يَمنَح مَنحًا	Who ? Whoever. مَنْ
Gift, favour. منحةٌ ج مِنَح	From ; of ; for ; than. مِنْ

Wish, vain wish.	اِمْنِيَّةٌ ج أَمَانِيُّ	Since.	مُنْذُ وَمُذْ
Soul, life.	مُهْجَةٌ ج مُهَجٌ	To refuse; prohibit.	مَنَعَ يَمْنَعُ عَنْ وَمِنْ
To level; prepare.	مَهَّدَ يَمْهَدُ وَمَهَّدَ	To be inaccessible.	مَنُعَ يَمْنُعُ
To be made easy.	تَمَهَّدَ	To refuse; oppose.	مَانَعَ
Bed; child's cradle.	مَهْدٌ ج مُهُودٌ	To abstain from.	تَمَنَّعَ عَنْ
To be skilful.	مَهَرَ يَمْهَرُ	To intrench one's self.	تَمَنَّعَ بِ
To become skilful.	تَمَهَّرَ	To be impossible.	اِمْتَنَعَ
Dowry.	مَهْرٌ ج مُهُورٌ	To refrain from.	اِمْتَنَعَ وَتَمَنَّعَ
Foal. Signet.	مُهْرٌ ج مِهَارٌ	Prevention.	مَنْعٌ
Seal-bearer, secretary.	مُهْرُدَارٌ	Impregnable, inaccessible.	مَنِيعٌ
Filly.	مُهْرَةٌ ج مُهُرَاتٌ	Something which prevents.	مَانِعٌ
Skilfulness, dexterity.	مَهَارَةٌ	Impossible.	مُمْتَنِعٌ
Skilful.	مَاهِرٌ ج مَهَرَةٌ	Interdicted, prohibited.	مَمْنُوعٌ
To act slowly.	مَهَلَ يَمْهَلُ . وَتَمَهَّلَ	To grant one's desire.	مَنَّى تَمْنِيَةً
To grant a delay.	مَهَّلَ وَأَمْهَلَ	To wish, desire.	تَمَنَّى
To ask for a delay.	اِسْتَمْهَلَ	A measure.	مِنْجَاجٌ أَمْنَاهٌ
Deliberate action.	مَهْلٌ	Death. Destiny.	مَنِيَّةٌ ج مَنَايَا
Go slowly; softly!	مَهْلًا	Wish, desire.	مُنْيَةٌ ج مُنًى

Bold, desperate.	مُسْتَمِيتٌ	Concession of a delay.	إِمْهَالٌ
To be agitated.	ماجَ يَمُوجُ وتَمَوَّجَ	Slowness, delay.	تَمَهُّلٌ
Wave, billow.	مَوْجٌ ج أَمْوَاجٌ	Whatever.	مَهْمَا
Commotion ; fluctuation.	تَمَوُّجٌ	To serve. Overwork.	مَهَنَ يَمْهَنُ
A hospital; asylum.	مَارِسْتَانٌ	To employ. Despise.	اِمْتَهَنَ
Banana (tree or fruit).	مَوْزٌ	Art, trade.	مِهْنَةٌ ج مِهَنٌ
Diamond.	ماسٌ	Antelope.	مَهَاةٌ ج مَهَا
A razor.	مُوسَى أَوْ مُوسًى	To die, expire.	مَاتَ يَمُوتُ مَوْتًا
	و (مُوسٌ) ج مَوَاسٍ	To kill.	مَوَّتَ وَأَماتَ
Moses.	مُوسَى	To feign death.	تَمَاوَتَ
Music.	مُوسِيقَى	To act desperately.	اِسْتَمَاتَ
Musician. Musical.	مُوسِيقِي	Death, decease.	مَوْتٌ ومَوْتَةٌ
Indian peas.	مَاشٌ	Cattle-plague.	مَوْتَانٌ ومُوتَانٌ
Inner angle of the eye.	مُوقٌ	Dying.	مَائِتٌ ج مَائِتُونَ
To be wealthy, rich.	مَالَ يَمُولُ	Dead.	مَيْتٌ ومَيِّتٌ ج أَمْوَاتٌ
To become rich.	تَمَوَّلَ	Kind of death.	مِيتَةٌ
Goods, riches.	مَالٌ ج أَمْوَالٌ	Death, decease.	مَمَاتٌ
Public Treasury.	بَيْتُ ٱلْمَالِ	Deadly, mortal, fatal.	مُمِيتٌ

To seek a gift.	اِسْتَماح
A table.	مائِدَة ج مَائِدَات وموائِد
Race-field; arena.	مِيدَان ج مَيَادِين
Taxes.	مِيرِيّ أَوْ مِيرَة (أَمِيرِيّ)
To detect, distinguish.	مَيَّز
To be distinguished.	تَمَيَّز واِمْتَاز
Separation ; distinction.	تَمْيِيز
The age of reason.	سِنّ التَّمْيِيز
Distinction; privilege ; preference.	اِمْتِياز
Distinguishing.	مُتَمَيِّز
Distinguished.	مُتَمَيِّز ومُمْتَاز
Hackberry tree.	مَيْس
To flow (liquid).	مَاعَ يَمِيع
Incense, perfume. Balm.	مِيعَة
Fluid, liquid.	مَائِع
To be inclined to.	مَال يَمِيل إلى
To deviate from.	مَال عَنْ
To be adverse to...	مَال عَلى

Financial ; pecuniary.	مالِيّ
Finance; ministry of...	الْمَالِيَة
Minister of Finance.	وَزِير الْمَالِيَة
A wealthy man.	مُتَمَوِّل
A kind of bitumen.	مُومِيا
Mummy.	مُومِيَة ج مُومِيَات
To furnish.	مَان يَمُون . ومَوَّن
To lay in a store.	تَمَوَّن
Provisions.	مُونَة (مُؤْنَة)
Store-room.	بَيْت الْمُونَة
To gild, or silver.	مَوَّه
To falsify (news).	مَوَّه
Water.	مَاء ج امْوَاه ومِيَاه
Watery; fluid. Aquatic.	مَائِيّ
Nature, essence. Salary.	مَاهِيَة
Falsified (narrative).	مُمَوَّه
Equivocation.	تَمْوِيَة
To give a gift.	مَاح يَمِيح

Bent, inclined.	مَائِلٌ	To decline, (sun).	مَالَ يَمِيلُ
Very much inclined.	مَيَّالٌ	To reel in walking.	تَمَايَلَ
To lie, tell a falsehood.	مَانَ يَمِين	To conciliate.	إِسْتَمَالَ
A lie, falsehood.	مَيْن ج مُيُونٌ	To incline, bend.	مَيَّلَ وَأَمَالَ
A harbour, port. Enamel.	مِينَا	Inclination.	مَيْلٌ ج مُيُولٌ
		A probe. A mile.	مِيلٌ ج أَمْيَالٌ

ن

To lead to.	نَبَأ ب	As a numeral sign=50.	ن
To announce, inform.	نَبَأَ وَأَنْبَأَ	Cocoa-nut.	نَأَرَجِيلٌ وَنَارِجِيلٌ
To prophesy; foretell.	تَنَبَّأَ	To be far from.	نَأَى يَنْأَى عَن
To seek information.	إِسْتَنْبَأَ	To go far from.	اِنْتَأَى عَن
News; information.	نَبَأ ج أَنْبَاء	One who is far away, remote.	نَاءٍ
A prophecy.	نُبُوَّةٌ وَنَبْوَةٌ	A tube, pipe.	أُنْبُوبٌ ج أَنَابِيب
Prophetic.	نَبَوِيٌّ	To assault.	نَبَا عَلَى

A store; granary.	نِبْرٌ ج أَنَابِر	A prophet. نَبِيٌّ ج أَنْبِيَاه وَنَبِيُّونَ
Emphasis (in speaking).	نَبْرَةٌ	To sprout (plant). نَبَتَ يَنْبُتُ
Stage, pulpit.	مِنْبَرٌ ج مَنَابِرُ	To cause to sprout. أَنْبَتَ
A lamp.	نِبْرَاسٌ ج نَبَارِيس	A plant; herb; sprout. نَبْتٌ
To unearth, dig up.	نَبَشَ يَنْبُشُ	Plant, vegetation. نَبَاتٌ ج نَبَاتَاتُ
Earth or pit dug out.	نَبِيشَةٌ	Botany. عِلْمُ النَبَاتِ
A digger.	نَبَّاشٌ	The vegetable world. عَالَمُ النَّبَاتِ
To pulsate, throb.	نَبَضَ يَنْبِضُ	Botanist. Vegetable. نَبَاتِيٌّ
Pulsation; pulse.	نَبْضٌ	Sprouting, germinating. نَابِتٌ
A throb, pulsation.	نَبْضَةٌ	A club. نَبُّوتٌ ج نَبَابِيتُ
To invent (something).	إِسْتَنْبَطَ	Herbarium. Origin. مَنْبِتٌ ج مَنَابِتُ
The Nabathæns.	نَبَطٌ ج أَنْبَاط	To bark (dog). نَبَحَ يَنْبِحُ نَبْحًا
A vulgar word.	كَلِمَةٌ نَبَطِيَّةٌ	Barking. نِبَاحٌ
Discovery, invention.	إِسْتِنْبَاطُ	To throw; give up. نَبَذَ يَنْبِذُ
To spring, gush (water).	نَبَعَ يَنْبِعُ	The rabble, mob. أَنْبَاذُ النَّاسِ
Spring of water.	نَبْعٌ	Section, article. نُبْذَةٌ ج نُبَذٌ
Source, origin.	مَنْبَعٌ ج مَنَابِعُ	Wine. نَبِيذٌ ج أَنْبِذَة
A fountain.	يَنْبُوعٌ ج يَنَابِيع	To speak loud. نَبَرَ يَنْبِرُ نَبْرًا

Attention; wakefulness.	إِنْتِبَاهٌ	To arise ; appear.	نَبَغَ يَنْبَغُ
Warning. Notice.	تَنْبِيهٌ	Distinguished.	نَابِغَةٌ ج نَوَابِغُ
Awake, Attentive.	مُتَنَبِّهٌ وَمُنْتَبِهٌ	Chemical retrot.	اِنْبِيقٌ ج أَنَابِيقُ
To project.	نَتَأَ يَنْتَأُ نُتُوءًا	To shoot arrows.	نَبَلَ يَنْبُلُ نَبْلًا
Projecting; jutting out.	نَاتِئٌ	To have genius, skill.	نَبُلَ يَنْبُلُ
To bring forth.	نَتَجَ يَنْتِجُ	To become skilful.	تَنَبَّلَ
To arise, result from...	نَتَجَ عَنْ	Arrows, darts.	نَبْلٌ ج نِبَالٌ
To deduce, infer.	إِسْتَنْتَجَ	Highly intelligent.	نَبِيلٌ ج نِبَالٌ
Conclusion. Result; consequence.	نَتِيجَةٌ ج نَتَائِجُ	An arrow, dart.	نَبْلَةٌ
To pull, snatch.	نَتَرَ يَنْتُرُ	Ability; ; superiority.	نَبَالَةٌ
To snatch, pluck.	نَتَشَ يَنْتِشُ نَتْشًا	To perceive.	نَبِهَ يَنْبَهُ نَبْهًا لِ
To pluck, pull out.	نَتَفَ يَنْتِفُ	To awake.	نَبَهَ نَبْهًا مِنَ النَّوْمِ
To be plucked off.	تَنَتَّفَ	To wake ; one up.	نَبَّهَ مِنَ النَّوْمِ
A small quantity.	نُتْفَةٌ ج نُتَفٌ	To warn inform.	نَبَّهَ عَلَى أَوْ إِلَى
To stink.	نَتَنَ يَنْتُنُ نَتْنًا وَأَنْتَنَ	To awake.	تَنَبَّهَ وَانْتَبَهَ
Stench.	نَتَنٌ وَنَتَانَةٌ	To be awake to.	تَنَبَّهَ لِ
Stinking, putrid.	نَتِنٌ وَمُنْتِنٌ	To perceive.	إِنْتَبَهَ لِ
Tuberosity.	نُتُوءٌ ج نُتُوءَاتٌ	Celebrity. Intelligence.	نَبَاهَةٌ

High land.	نَجْد ج أَنْجُد	Swollen. Projecting.	نَاتِ
Help, succour.	نَجْدَة ج نَجَدَات	To disperse, scatter.	نَثَرَ يَنْثُر
An upholsterer.	نَجَّاد و مِنْجَد	To be scattered.	تَنَاثَرَ وَ ٱنْتَثَرَ
To plane (wood).	نَجَرَ يَنْجُر	Prose, (opp. to نَظْم).	نَثْر
Carpentry.	نِجَارَة	Gilly-flower.	مَنْثُور
Shavings chips of wood.	نُجَارَة	To be noble.	نَجُبَ يَنْجُب
Carpenter.	نَجَّار ج نَجَّارُون	To choose, select.	إِنْتَجَب
To finish a thing.	نَجَزَ يَنْجُز وَنَجَّزَ	Nobility.	نَجَابَة
To come to an end.	نَجِزَ يَنْجَز	Noble.	نَجِيب ج نُجَبَاه
To achieve; accomplish.	أَنْجَزَ	The choicest parts.	نَجَائِب
Achievement.	نَجْز ونِجَاز	To succeed, prosper.	نَجَحَ يَنْجَح
Ready, present.	نَاجِز وَنَجِيز	To give success.	نَجَّح وَأَنْجَح
To be impure.	نَجِس يَنْجَس نَجَساً	Success, prosperity.	نُجْح وَنَجَاح
To defile, pollute.	نَجَّس وَأَنْجَس	Successful, thriving.	نَاجِح
To become polluted.	تَنَجَّس	To help, aid.	نَجَد يَنْجُد. وَأَنْجَد
Filth. Legal impurity.	نَجَاسَة	To upholster.	نَجَّد
Impure, filthy.	نَجِس ج أَنْجَاس	To bring help to.	نَاجَد مُنَاجَدَة
Title of the Abyssinian kings.	النَّجَاشِيّ	To invoke assistance.	إِسْتَنْجَد

An asylum.	مَنْجَى ج مَناجٍ	To benefit, profit.	نَجَعَ يَنْجَعُ
Secret communication.	مُناجاة	Profitable, useful. Dark red blood.	نَجِيع
To weep, cry, wail.	نَحَبَ يَنْحَبُ	Child, son.	نَجْل ج أَنْجال
Bitter weeping. Death.	نَحْب	Gospel.	إِنْجِيل ج أَناجِيل
To die.	قَضَى نَحْبَهُ	Evangelical ; evangelist.	إِنْجِيلِيّ
Wailing. Lamenation.	نَحِيب	A sickle.	مِنْجَل ج مَناجِل
To cut, hew, carve.	نَحَتَ يَنْحَتُ	To appear.	نَجَمَ يَنْجُمُ وأَنْجَمَ
Fragments, chips.	نُحاتَة	To arise, or result from.	نَجَمَ عَنْ
Stone-cutter. Sculptor.	نَحَّات	A star. Shrub.	نَجْم ج أَنْجُم ونُجُوم
Cut, hewed.	نَحِيت ومَنْحُوت	Astronomy.	عِلْمُ النُّجُوم
Sculptor's chisel.	مِنْحَت ج مَناحِت	Astrology.	عِلْمُ التَّنْجِيم
To kill (an animal).	نَحَرَ يَنْحَرُ	Astronomer. Astrologer.	مُنَجِّم
To contend together.	تَناحَرَ	Mine. Source.	مَنْجَم ج مَناجِم
To commit suicide.	إِنْتَحَرَ	To escape.	نَجا يَنْجُو نَجاة
Skilled.	نِحْرِير ج نَحارِير	To confide a secret to.	ناجَى
Lower part of neck.	نَحْر ج نُحُور	To save deliver.	نَجَّى وأَنْجَى مِن
Throat.	مَنْحَر	To commune secretly.	تَناجَى
To cover with copper.	نَحَسَ	Deliverance.	نَجاة ونَجاه

Thin, emaciated.	نَحِيلٌ	Ill-luck.	نَحْسٌ ج نُحُوسٌ
We.	نَحْنُ	Unlucky.	نَحْسٌ وَمَنْحُوسٌ
To move towards.	نَحَا يَنْحُو	Brass.	نُحَاسٌ
To send away.	نَحَى عَنْ	Copper.	نُحَاسٌ أَحْمَرُ
To go aside.	تَنَحَّى عَنْ	A piece of copper.	نُحَاسَةٌ
Towards. Nearly, about. For example.	نَحْوَ	A copper merchant.	نُحَّاسٌ
Region. Method.	نَحْوٌ ج أَنْحَاءُ	To be slim.	نَحِفَ يَنْحَفُ نَحَافَةً
Grammar, *sp.* syntax.	عِلْمُ النَّحْوِ	To make thin.	أَنْحَفَ
Grammarian.	نَاحٍ ج نُحَاةٌ	Leanness ; slenderness.	نَحَافَةٌ
Grammatical.	نَحْوِيٌّ	Thin, meagre.	نَحِيفٌ ج نِحَافٌ
Side, direction.	نَاحِيَةٌ ج نَوَاحٍ	To become thin.	نَحَلَ يَنْحَلُ
To select.	نَخَبَ يَنْخُبُ وَانْتَخَبَ	To make thin.	أَنْحَلَ
Choice, election.	نُخَبٌ وَانْتِخَابٌ	To plagiarize.	تَنَحَّلَ وَانْتَحَلَ
Chosen. Choice.	نُخْبَةٌ ج نُخَبٌ	To embrace a religion.	انْتَحَلَ
Elector.	مُنْتَخِبٌ	Bees.	نَحْلٌ
Chosen ; elected.	مُنْتَخَبٌ	A bee.	نَحْلَةٌ
To snore ; snort.	نَخَرَ يَنْخِرُ	A religious sect.	نِحْلَةٌ ج نِحَلٌ
To be rotten.	نَخِرَ يَنْخَرُ نَخَرًا	Thinness, leanness.	نُحُولٌ

Pride. Sense of honour.	نَخْوَةٌ	Rotten, decayed.	نَخِرٌ وَ نَاخِرٌ
To expose one's faults.	نَدَّدَ بِ	Nostril ; nose.	مِنْخَرٌ ج مَنَاخِيرُ
A kind of perfume.	نِدٌّ	To prick with.	نَخَرَ يَنْخَرُ بِ
Similar to, an equal.	نِدٌّ ج أَنْدَادٌ	To prick.	نَخَسَ يَنْخَسُ نَخْسًا
To weep, lament.	نَدَبَ يَندِبُ	Cattle-trade ; slave-trade.	نَخَاسَةٌ
To call, appoint.	نَدَبَ وَاَنْتَدَبَ	Cattle, or slave trader.	نَخَّاسٌ
To be cicatrized.	نَدِبَ يَنْدَبُ	A goad, spur.	مَنْخَسٌ ج مَنَاخِسُ
To respond to a call.	إِنْتَدَبَ لِ	To hawk, clear the throat.	تَنَخَّعَ
Scar.	نَدْبَةٌ ج نُدُوبٌ وَأَنْدَابٌ	Marrow. Brain.	نُخَاعٌ ج نُخُعٌ
An elegy, a lamentation.	نَدَبَةٌ	Phlegm, mucus.	نُخَاعَةٌ
A weeper, lamenter.	نَادِبٌ	To sift, bolt flour.	نَخَلَ يَنْخُلُ
Mourned. Commissioner.	مَنْدُوبٌ	The palm-tree.	نَخْلٌ وَنَخِيلٌ
Liberty of action.	مَنْدُوحَةٌ	A palm-tree.	نَخْلَةٌ
To be rare.	نَدَرَ يَنْدُرُ	Bran.	نُخَالَةٌ
Rarity ; infrequency.	نُدْرَةٌ	A sieve.	مُنْخُلٌ ج مَنَاخِلُ
A rare thing.	نَادِرٌ ج نَوَادِرُ	To blow the nose.	تَنَخَّمَ
Rarely, seldom.	نَادِرًا وَفِي النَّادِرِ	Mucus ; phlegm.	نُخَامَةٌ
To card (cotton).	نَدَفَ يَندِفُ	To incite, instigate.	نَخَى وَأَنْخَى

Moisture. Dew.	نَدًى ج أَنْدَاء	Trade of carding.	نِدَافَةٌ
Call. Proclamation.	نِدَاء	Wool or cotton carder.	نَدَّافٌ
Vocative particle.	حَرْفُ ٱلنِّدَاءِ	Carded.	مَنْدُوفٌ
An assembly, a meeting.	نَدْوَةٌ	A towel. Veil.	مَنْدِيلٌ ج مَنَادِيلُ
Place of assembly.	نَادٍ ج أَنْدِيَةٌ	Andalusia. Spain.	ٱلأَنْدَلُسُ
A public crier.	مُنَادٍ	Andalusian.	اندلُسِيٌّ
Assembly-hall.	مُنْتَدًى	To regret.	نَدِمَ يَنْدَمُ وَتَنَدَّمَ عَلى
To make a vow; dedicate.	نَذَرَ	To associate with.	نَادَمَ مُنَادَمَةً
To warn.	أَنْذَرَ إِنْذَاراً ب	Regret, repentance.	نَدَمٌ وَنَدَامَةٌ
A vow.	نَذْرٌ ج نُذُورٌ	Repentant contrite.	نَادِمٌ
A warning. Prognosis.	إِنْذَارٌ	Associate, friend.	نَدِيمٌ ج نُدَمَاء
Vowed. Preacher.	نَذِيرٌ ج نُذُرٌ	To be wet.	نَدِيَ يَنْدَى
Vowed, consecrated.	مَنْذُورٌ	To dampen, wet.	نَدَّى تَنْدِيَةً
To be abject.	نَذُلَ يَنْذُلُ نَذَالَةً	To call.	نَادَى مُنَادَاةً وَنِدَاءً
Vile, mean.	نَذْلٌ ج أَنْذَالٌ	To proclaim ; publish.	نَادَى ب
Narcissus (plant).	نَرْجِسٌ	To be liberal.	أَنْدَى إِنْدَاءً
Cocoa-nut.	نَارِجِيلٌ وَنَأْرَجِيلٌ	Ta become wet.	تَنَدَّى
Nargileh.	نَارَجِيلَةٌ	To assemble v.i	اِنْتَدَى

Backgammon.	نَرْدٌ
Spikenard.	نَارَدِين" وَنَرْدِين"
Orange.	نَارَنْجٌ
Thrashing-harrow.	نَوْرَجٌ
To exude.	نَزَّ يَنِزُّ نَزًّا
Leakage.	نَزٌّ ج نُزُوزٌ
To exhaust a well.	نَزَحَ يَنْزَحُ
To emigrate.	نَزَحَ بِهِ وَانْتَزَحَ
Distant, Emigrant.	نَازِحٌ وَنَزِيحٌ
Little ; mean.	نَزْرٌ
To remove.	نَزَعَ يَنْزَعُ وَآنْتَزَعَ
To fight, dispute with.	نَازَعَ
To contend among themselves.	تَنَازَعَ
To be taken away.	إنْتَزَعَ
Agony of death.	نَزْعٌ وَنِزَاعٌ
Contention.	نِزَاعٌ وَمُنَازَعَةٌ
Taken away, removed.	مَنْزُوعٌ
To be exhausted (well).	نَزَفَ ــ

To have a flow of blood.	نَزَفَ
Hemorrhage	نَزْفُ الدَّمِ
Quick, hot-tempered.	نَزِقٌ
A falling star.	نَيْزَكُ ج نَيَازِكُ
To descend.	نَزَلَ يَنْزِلُ نُزُولاً
To stop at a place.	نَزَلَ فِي وَعَلَى
To bring down.	نَزَّلَ وَأَنْزَلَ
To reveal.	نَزَّلَ وَأَنْزَلَ عَلَى
To fight with.	نَازَلَ
To renounce.	تَنَزَّلَ عَنْ
To condescend.	تَنَازَلَ
To seek or offer hospitaliy.	اسْتَنْزَلَ
Place where men gather.	نَزْلٌ
Guests.	نُزُولٌ ج أَنْزَالٌ
A cold in the head.	نَزْلَةٌ
Calamity.	نَازِلَةٌ ج نَوَازِلُ
A guest.	نَزِيلٌ ج نُزَلَاءُ
A revelation.	إنْزَالٌ وَتَنْزِيلٌ

Relation, affinity. نِسْبَةٌ ج نِسَبٌ	Condescension, affability. تَنَازُلٌ
Kinsman. نَسِيبٌ ج أَنْسِبَاء	Hostlery ; house. مَنْزِلٌ ج مَنَازِلُ
Proportion. مُنَاسَبَةٌ وَتَنَاسُبٌ	Domestic economy. تَدْبِيرُ ٱلْمَنْزِلِ
Suited to, convenient. مُنَاسِبٌ	Degree, rank. مَنْزِلَةٌ
Proportioned. مُتَنَاسِبٌ	To abstain from evil. نَزَهَ يَنْزَهُ
Ascribed, imputed. مَنْسُوبٌ إِلَى	To walk, divert one's self. تَنَزَّهَ
Human nature. نَاسُوتٌ	To be free from. تَنَزَّهَ عَنْ
To weave. نَسَجَ يَنْسِجُ نَسْجًا	Purity of the soul. نُزْهٌ وَنَزَاهَةٌ
To be woven. إِنْتَسَجَ	Pure, upright. نَزِيهٌ ج نُزَهَاء
The art of weaving. نِسَاجَةٌ	Amusement. نُزْهَةٌ ج نُزَهٌ
Weaver. نَسَّاجٌ	Place of recreation. مُنْتَزَهٌ
Woven tissue. نَسِيجٌ ج نُسُجٌ	To attribute, ascribe. نَسَبَ إِلَى
Loom. مِنْسَجٌ	To resemble. Be suitable. نَاسَبَ
Woven ; tissue. مَنْسُوجٌ	To correspond with. تَنَاسَبَ
To abrogate. نَسَخَ يَنْسَخُ نَسْخًا abolish To copy, transcribe.	To trace one's genealogy. إِنْتَسَبَ
To follow successively. تَنَاسَخَ	To approve. إِسْتَنْسَبَ
To copy a (book). إِنْتَسَخَ وَٱسْتَنْسَخَ	Lineage. نَسَبٌ ج أَنْسَابٌ
To annul, abrogate. إِنْتَسَخَ	Arithmetical proportion. نُسْبَةٌ

Abrogation. Transcribing. نَسْخٌ	A hermit's life. نُسْكٌ وَنَسْكٌ
Copy ; manuscript, نُسْخَةٌ ج نُسَخٌ	A hermit. نَاسِكٌ ج نُسَّاكٌ
Transmigration of souls. تَنَاسُخٌ	To beget. نَسَلَ يَنْسُلُ نَسْلاً
Abolished. Copied. مَنْسُوخٌ	To multiply (men). تَنَاسَلَ
An eagle ; vulture. نَسْرٌ ج نُسُورٌ	Posterity, progeny. نَسْلٌ
A fistula, sinus. نَاسُورٌ ج نَوَاسِيرُ	Descent by generation. تَنَاسُلٌ
Beak of a bird. مِنْسَرٌ ج مَنَاسِيرُ	To blow gently. نَسَمَ يَنْسِمُ
A scented white rose. نِسْرِينٌ	To breathe. تَنَسَّمَ
Nestorian. نُسْطُورِيٌّ ج نَسَاطِرَةٌ	Breath of life. Man. نَسَمَةٌ ج نَسَمَاتٌ
To demolish winnow. نَسَفَ يَنْسِفُ	A soft breeze. نَسِيمٌ
Chaff. Froth. نُسَافَةٌ	An ape. نِسْنَاسٌ
Winnowing-fan. مِنْسَفٌ ج مَنَاسِفُ	Women. نُسْوَةٌ وَنِسَاءٌ وَنِسْوَانٌ
A razing machine. مِنْسَفَةٌ	Sciatica. عِرْقُ النَّسَا
To compose. نَسَقَ يَنْسُقُ نَسْقًا	To forget. نَسِيَ يَنْسَى نَسْيًا وَنِسْيَانًا
To place in order; arrange. نَسَّقَ	To cause to forget. نَسَّى وَأَنْسَى
To be arranged. تَنَسَّقَ وَتَنَاسَقَ	To feign forgetfulness. نَاسَى
Order ; system, method. نَسَقٌ	Forgetfulness. نَسْوَةٌ وَنِسْيَانٌ
To lead an ascetic's life. نَسَكَ وَتَنَسَّكَ	Forgotten. مَنْسِيٌّ

Chanting. Song.	نَشِيد	To dry up ; ooze.	نَشَّ يَنِشُّ
The Song of Songs.	نَشِيدُ ٱلْأَنْشَادِ	Blotting-paper.	وَرَق نَشَّاش
A poem. Song.	نَشِيدَة ج نَشَائِد	To grow up.	نَشَأَ يَنْشَأُ وَنَشُوَ يَنْشُو
Ammonia.	نِشَادِر وَنُوشَادِر	(child). To live, orginate. Rise.	
		To follow, proceed from.	نَشَأَ مِن
To spread out. To saw.	نَشَرَ يَنْشُر	To create ; originate.	أَنْشَأَ
To publish.	نَشَر يَنْشُر	Train up.	
To resuscitate,	نَشَرَ يَنْشُر	He began to say.	أَنْشَأَ يَقُول
raise to life.		Growing, developing.	نُشُوّ
To be extended.	تَنَشَّرَ وَٱنْتَشَر	Growing. Resulting.	نَاشِئ
To be published.	إِنْتَشَرَ	Composition ; style.	إِنْشَاء
Resurrection. Publication.	نَشْر	Origination.	
		Native country. Source.	مَنْشَأ
Day of Resurrection.	يَوْمُ ٱلنُّشُور	A creator. Author.	مُنْشِئ
A written open paper.	نَشْرَة	To break out (war).	نَشِبَ ـ بَيْن
Shavings, saw-dust.	نِشَارَة	An arrow (of wood).	نَشَّاب
Art of sawing.	نِشَارَة	An archer.	نَشَّاب
Dissemination.	إِنْتِشَار	To seek a lost object.	نَشَدَ يَنْشُد
Dispersed.	مَنْشُور وَمُنْتَشِر	To abjure by God.	نَشَدَهُ ٱللّٰه
A saw.	مِنْشَار ج مَنَاشِير	To cause to swear.	نَاشَدَ
Prism. Circular.	مَنْشُور	To recite (verses).	أَنْشَدَ

To be drunk. نَشِيَ ــ نَشْوًا وَنَشْوَةً	Prismatic form. مِنْشُورِيّ
To smell. Be drunk. نَشِيَ وَاسْتَنْشَى	To be active. نَشِطَ يَنْشَطُ. وَتَنَشَّطَ
To starch (linen). نَشَّى	To knot (a cord). نَشَطَ يَنْشِطُ
Starch. نَشَا وَنَشَاء	To encourage in. نَشَّطَ إِلَى وَفِي
Odour. Exhiliration of wine. نَشْوَةٌ	Ardour, energy. نَشَاطٌ
Drunk. نَشْوَان م نَشْوَى ج نَشَاوَى	Active, energetic. نَشِيطٌ ج نِشَاطٌ
To dictate a writing نَصَّ ــ ُ ل	A knot, noose. أُنْشُوطَةٌ ج أَنَاشِيط
Text (of a book). نَصّ ج نُصُوص	To become dry. نَشَفَ يَنْشَفُ
Clearly stated. مَنْصُوص عَلَيْه	To dry, wipe (the body). تَنَشَّفَ
To fix, plant ; raise. نَصَبَ يَنْصِبُ	Dry. نَاشِفٌ
To strive, toil. نَصِبَ ــ نَصَبًا	Wiping, drying up. تَنْشِيفٌ
To appoint to an office. نَصَّبَ	A towel. مِنْشَفَةٌ ج مَنَاشِفُ
To resist, oppose. نَاصَبَ	To inhale. نَشِقَ يَنْشَقُ. وَاسْتَنْشَقَ
To rise ; stand erect. إِنْتَصَبَ	To cause one to inhale. أَنْشَقَ
Idol, statue. نَصَبٌ ج أَنْصَابٌ	Snuff. نَشُوقٌ
Before my eye. نَصْبَ عَيْنِي	To snatch ; steal. نَشَلَ يَنْشُلُ وَانْتَشَلَ
Origin Handle. نِصَابٌ ج نُصُب	A pickpocket. نَشَّالٌ
Swindler. نَصَّابٌ	A ladle. مِنْشَلٌ وَمِنْشَالٌ ج مَنَاشِلُ

To seek aid from.	إِسْتَنْصَرَ بِ	Portion ; lot.	نَصِيبٌ ج أَنْصِبَةٌ
Help. Victory.	نَصْرٌ وَنُصْرَةٌ	Fatiguing, toilsome.	نَاصِبٌ
A Christian.	نَصْرَانِيٌّ ج نَصَارَى	Rank ; place.	مَنْصِبٌ ج مَنَاصِبُ
Christianity.	أَلنَّصْرَانِيَّةُ	Elevated, erected.	مَنْصُوبٌ
Victory, triumph.	إِنْتِصَارٌ	To listen to.	نَصَتَ يَنْصِتُ وَأَنْصَتَ ل
Helper.	نَاصِرٌ ج نَصَّارٌ وَأَنْصَارٌ	To silence.	أَنْصَتَ
Helper.	نَصِيرٌ ج نُصَرَاءُ	To listen.	نَصَّتَ
Victorious, conquering.	مُنْتَصِرٌ	To advise, counsel.	نَصَحَ يَنْصَحُ
Aided Conqueror.	مَنْصُورٌ	To act sincerely.	نَصَحَ نَصْحًا
To be pure, unmixed.	نَصَعَ يَنْصَعُ	To receive advice.	إِنْتَصَحَ
Pure, unmixed (color)	نَاصِعٌ	A sincere adviser.	نَاصِحٌ
To divide into two halves.	نَصَّفَ	Sincere.	نَصُوحٌ وَنَصِيحٌ
To be just, equitable.	أَنْصَفَ	Advice, counsel.	نَصِيحَةٌ ج نَصَائِحُ
To get one's due.	إِنْتَصَفَ	To assist aid.	نَصَرَ يَنْصُرُ
To be mid-day.	إِنْتَصَفَ ٱلنَّهَارُ	To become a Christian.	تَنَصَّرَ
Half, Middle.	نِصْفٌ ج أَنْصَافٌ	To strive to assist.	تَنَصَّرَ ل
Justice, equity.	إِنْصَافٌ	To help one another.	تَنَاصَرَ
Middle (of anything).	مُنْتَصَفٌ	To conquer, vanquish.	اِنْتَصَرَ عَلَى

To jump, skip.	(نَطَّ يَنِطّ نَطًّا)	To come out.	(نَصَلَ يَنْصُلُ نُصُولاً)
To butt.	نَطَحَ يَنْطَحُ نَطْحًا	Blade ; arrow-head.	نَصْلٌ ج نِصَالٌ
To butt one another.	تَنَاطَحَ	Forelock.	نَاصِيَةٌ ج نَوَاصٍ
Butted ; gored.	نَطِيحٌ وَمَنْطُوحٌ	To ooze, flow out.	نَضَّ يَنِضّ نَضًّا
To guard. To wait.	نَطَرَ يَنْطُرُ	Remainder, rest.	نُضَاضَةٌ
Keeper (of gardens).	نَاطُورٌ ج نَوَاطِيرُ	To be well cooked ; ripe.	نَضِجَ يَنْضَجُ
A watch-tower.	مَنْطَرَةٌ ج مَنَاطِرُ	Cooked well, ripe.	نَاضِجٌ
Very learned.	نِطِسٌ وَنِطَاسِيّ	Of mature judgment.	نَضِيجُ الرَّأْيِ
To speak utter.	نَطَقَ يَنْطِقُ	To ooze ; exude.	نَضَحَ يَنْضَحُ نَضْحًا
To gird.	نَطَّقَ	To sprinkle with.	نَضَحَ ب
To gird one's self.	تَنَطَّقَ وَٱنْتَطَقَ	To pile up.	نَضَدَ يَنْضِدُ . وَنَضَّدَ
To question, examine.	إِسْتَنْطَقَ	Laid in layers.	نَضِيدٌ وَمَنْضُودٌ
Speech ; articulation.	نُطْقٌ	To be soft. Blooming.	نَضَرَ يَنْضُرُ
Belt, girdle.	نِطَاقٌ ج نُطُقٌ	Bloom, freshness.	نَضْرَةٌ وَنَضَارَةٌ
Endowed with speech.	نَاطِقٌ	Blooming, verdant.	نَضِرٌ وَنَضِيرٌ
The human soul.	أَلنَّفْسُ النَّاطِقَةُ	To defend.	نَاضَلَ عَنْ
Speech, language. Logic.	مَنْطِقٌ	Combat.	نِضَالٌ وَمُنَاضَلَةٌ
Logical. Logician.	مَنْطِقِيّ	A horse-shoe.	نَضِيرَةٌ

Minister of Works. نَاظِرُ الاشْغَال	A girdle, belt. مِنْطَقَة ج مَنَاطِق
Minister of نَاظِرُ المَعَارِفِ العُمُومِية Public Instruction.	The Zodiac. مِنْطَقَة البُرُوج
Minister of Finance. نَاظِرُ المَالِية	Proper signification. مَنْطُوق
Minister of Foreign نَاظِرُ الخَارِجِية Affairs.	Examiner (law). مُسْتَنْطِق
Minister of the نَاظِرُ الدَّاخِلِية Interior.	To foment. نَطَلَ يَنْطُلُ · وَنَطَّلَ
Minister of War. نَاظِرُ الحَرْبِية	A fomentation. نَطُول ج نُطُولَات
Minister of Justice. نَاظِرُ الحَقَّانِية	To see, look at. نَظَرَ يَنْظُرُ وَإِلَى
Administration. Ministry. نَظَارَة	To consider. نَظَرَ يَنْظُرُ فِي
A telescope. نَظَّارَة وَنَاظُور	To resemble ; rival. نَاظَرَ
Spectacles. نَظَّارَات	Debate. Superintend, inspect.
Similar, equal to. نَظِير ج نُظَرَاء	To debate with one تَنَاظَرَ another.
Expectation. إِنْتِظَار وَاسْتِنْظَار	To expect. إِنْتَظَرَ وَاسْتَنْظَرَ
View. Aspect. مَنْظَر ج مَنَاظِر	Vision. Favour. نَظَر ج أَنْظَار
Speculum. مِنْظَار	As regards. نَظَرًا وَبِالنَّظَرِ إِلَى
Similar to. Inspector. مُنَاظِر	A look, a glance. نَظْرَة
Rivalry, Inspection. مُنَاظَرَة	Theoretical. Subjective. نَظَرِيّ
To be clean ; comely. نَظُفَ يَنْظُفُ	A problem. نَظَرِية ج نَظَرِيَات
To cleanse, purify. نَظَّفَ	Inspector, Director. نَاظِر ج نُظَّار
	Prime Minister. نَاظِرُ النُّظَّار

To make sleepy. أَنْعَسَ	To become clean. تَنَظَّفَ
To feign sleep. تَنَاعَسَ	Cleanliness. Beauty. نَظَافَةٌ
Sleepiness; drowsiness نُعَاسٌ	Clean; comely. نَظِيفٌ ج نُظَفَاءُ
Sleepy. نَاعِسٌ وَنَعْسَانُ ج نُعَّسٌ	To arrange ; compose (verses). نَظَمَ ـ
To cheer, refresh. نَعَشَ يَنْعَشُ . وَأَنْعَشَ	To be arranged. تَنَظَّمَ وَاْنَتَظَمَ
To be revived, animated. اِنْتَعَشَ	Arrangement. Poetry. نَظْمٌ
Bier. نَعْشٌ	System , method. نِظَامٌ ج أَنْظِمَـةٌ
Ursa Major. بَنَات نَعْشٍ الـكُبْرَى	Well-arranged. مُنَظَّمٌ
To croak, (crow). نَعَقَ يَنْعَقُ	Arranged, composed. مَنْظُومٌ
To shoe (an animal). نَعَلَ يَنْعَلُ نَعْلًا	To describe. نَعَتَ يَنْعَتُ نَعْتًا
Shoe. Horse-shoe. نَعْلٌ ج نِعَالٌ	Qualification; attribute. نَعْتٌ
To live in ease. نَعِمَ يَنْعَمُ	Adjective. نَعْتٌ ج نُعُوتٌ
To be soft to the touch. نَعُمَ يَنْعُمُ	A qualified noun. مَنْعُوتٌ
Excellent man ! نِعْمَ الرَّجُلُ	A sheep, an ewe. نَعْجَـةٌ ج نِعَاجٌ
Excellent! Good ! نِعِمَّا	A kind of finch (bird). نُعَّارٌ
To make one easy in life. نَعَّمَ	Earthen cooler. (نَعَارَةٌ ج نَعَائِرُ)
To bestow, confer on. أَنْعَمَ عَلَيْهِ	Irrigating wheel. نَاعُورَةٌ ج نَوَاعِير
To enjoy life ; enjoy. تَنَعَّمَ	To grow sleepy. نَعَسَ يَنْعَسُ

To be annoyed (in life).	تَنَغَّص	Yes, certainly, assuredly.	نَعَم
To be inflamed, (wound).	نَغِل يَنْغَل	Cattle, camles.	نَعَم ج أَنْعام
Bastard. Hinny.	نَغْل	Blessing, favour.	نِعْمَة ج نِعَم
To sing softly.	نَغَم يَنْغَم . وَنَغَّم	Opulent, rich.	وَاسِعُ النِّعْمَة
Melody, tune.	نَغْمَة ج نَغَمات	An ostrich.	نَعامَة ج نَعائِم ونَعامات
To spit out.	نَفَث يَنْفُث	Softness, smoothness.	نُعُومة
Expectoration. Puff.	نَفْث	Anemone.	شَقائِقُ النُّعْمان
To blow (wind).	نَفَح يَنْفَح نَفْحًا	Soft, tender.	ناعِم م ناعِمَة
A breath. A gift.	نَفْحَة ج نَفَحات	Contented, tranquil.	نَعِيمُ البال
To blow with the mouth.	نَفَخ يَنْفُخ	Goodness, favour.	إنْعام ج إنْعامات
To be puffed up proud.	إنْتَفَخ	Luxury; enjoyment.	تَنَعُّم
Breath, puff; blowing.	نَفْخ	Benefactor ; beneficent.	مُنْعِم
A water-bubble. Vesicle.	نَفّاخة	Mint (plant).	نَعْنَع ونَعْناع
Bellows.	مِنْفاخ ومِنْفَخ ج مَنافِخ	To announce death.	نَعى يَنْعى
Inflated, swollen,	مَنْفوخ	News of death.	نَعِيَة
To be spent, consumed.	نَفِد يَنْفَد	Announcer of death.	ناعٍ ج نُعاة
To consume.	أَنْفَد وآسْتَنْفَد	To be troubled.	نَغِص يَنْغَص نَغْصًا
To pierce through.	نَفَذ يَنْفُذ مِن	To trouble, vex.	نَغَّص وأَنْغَص عَلى

Soul, self. نَفْسٌ ج نُفُوسٌ وَأَنْفُسٌ	To be executed (an order). نَفَذَ
He himself came. جَاءَ نَفْسُهُ	To reach, arrive at. نَفَذَ إِلَى
A woman at child-birth. نُفَسَاءُ	To send, execute. نَفَّذَ وَأَنْفَذَ
The thing itself. نَفْسُ ٱلشَّيِّ	Execution; efficiency. نَفَاذٌ وَنُفُوذٌ
Breath. Style. نَفَسٌ ج أَنْفَاسٌ	Efficacious, effective. نَافِذٌ
Confinement, child-birth. نِفَاسٌ	Window. نَافِذَةٌ ج نَوَافِذُ
Respiration, breathing. تَنَفُّسٌ	Outlet, passage. مَنْفَذٌ ج مَنَافِذُ
A valuable thing. نَفِيسٌ ج نَفَائِسُ	To turn away from. نَفَرَ يَنْفِرُ مِنْ
More precious. أَنْفَسُ	To cause aversion. نَفَّرَ
To teaze (cotton). نَفَشَ ـ وَنَفَّشَ	To have mutual aversion. تَنَافَرَ
To bristle (hair), ruffle (feathers). تَنَفَّشَ	A number of men. نَفَرٌ ج أَنْفَارٌ
To shake, shake off. نَفَضَ ـ وَنَفَّضَ	Contest, repulsion. تَنَافُرٌ
A plate for ashes. مِنْفَضَةٌ ج مَنَافِضُ	A trumpet, bugle. نَفِيرٌ
Matches. نَفْطٌ	To be precious. نَفُسَ يَنْفُسُ
Naptha, bitumen. نِفْطٌ	To give birth. نَفِسَتْ تَنْفَسُ
Pustule, vesicle. نَفْطَةٌ	To breathe. تَنَفَّسَ
A vesicating medicine. مُنَفِّطٌ	To sigh deeply. تَنَفَّسَ ٱلصُّعَدَاء
To be useful. نَفَعَ يَنْفَعُ نَفْعًا	To contend together. تَنَافَسَ

To be excluded, rejected. إِنْتَفَى	To profit by. إِنْتَفَعَ بِ وَمِنْ
Banishment. Negation. نَفْيٌ	To seek benefit. إِسْتَنْفَعَ
Particle of negation. حَرْفُ ٱلنَّفْيِ	Advantage, benefit. نَفْعٌ وَمَنْفَعَةٌ
Rejected as useless. نُفَاوَةٌ وَنُفَايَة	Useful, profitable. نَافِعٌ
Excluded. Exiled. مَنْفِيٌّ	To have a brisk sale نَفَقَ يَنْفُقُ نَفَاقًا. To be exhausted.
Incompatibility. تَنَاف ومنافَاةٌ	To sell well. نَفَّقَ وَأَنْفَقَ
Exile. مَنْفِيٌّ ج مُنَاف	To be hypocritical. نَافَقَ
To dig through. نَقَبَ يَنْقُبُ نَقْبًا	To exhaust one's means. انفَقَ
To travel over. نَقَبَ في	Cost, expenses. نَفَقَةٌ ج نَفَقَاتٌ
To examine. نَقَبَ عَن	Selling briskly. نَافِقٌ
To put on a veil. تَنَقَّبَ وَانْتَقَبَ	Hypocrisy. نِفَاقٌ وَمُنَافَقَةٌ
A hole in a wall. نَقْبٌ ج انْقَابُ	A hypocrite ; deceiver. مُنَافِقٌ
Veil of a woman. نِقَاب ج نُقُبٌ	A supererogatory deed. نَفْلٌ
Chief. Magistrate. نَقِيب ج نُقَبَاهٴ	Booty. Present. نَفْلٌ ج أَنْفَالٌ
Worthy deed. مَنْقَبَةٌ ج مَنَاقِبُ	Clover. نَفْلَةٌ
To revise, correct. نَقَّحَ وَأَنْقَحَ	To expel ; deny, exclude. نَفَى يَنْفِي
Revision, correction. تَنْقِيحٌ	To banish, exile. نَفَى مِنْ
To peck (bird). نَقَدَ يَنْقُدُ نَقْدًا	To oppose, be incompatible. نَافَى

Gout.	نِقرسُ	To pay in cash.	نَقد لِ
To skip.	نَقزَ يَنقِزُ	To sort, pick out.	نَقَدَ وَتَنَقَّدَ
A church-bell.	ناقوسُ ج نوَاقيسُ	Ready money, cash.	نَقدُ
To paint; sculpture.	نَقشَ يَنقُشُ	Money, cash.	نُقُودُ وَنَقدِيَّةُ
To reckon with.	ناقَشَ مُناقشَةً	Testing ; criticism.	إِنتِقادُ
Painting. Tracing.	نَقشُ ج نُقوشُ	Beak (of a bird).	منقادُ ج مَناقيدُ
Painting. Sculpture.	نِقاشَةُ	To deliver, save.	نَقَذَ يَنقِذُ وأَنقَذَ
Painter. Engraver.	نَقّاشُ	Rescue, deliverance.	نَقَذُ
Brush. Chisel.	منقَشُ وَمِنقاشُ	Deliverer.	مُنقِذُ
To reduce, decrease.	نَقَصَ يَنقُصُ	To cut into (stone, wood) ; peck (bird).	نَقَرَ يَنقُرُ
To decrease gradually.	تَناقَصَ	To examine.	نَقَرَ وَنَقَّرَ عَن
To defame.	إِنتَقَصَ	To dispute with.	ناقَرَ مُناقَرَةً
Diminution ; loss.	نَقصُ وَنُقصانُ	Cavity. Carving.	نَقرُ
Diminished, defective.	ناقِصُ	Hollow, cavity.	نَقرَةُ ج نَقرُ
Fault ; vice.	نَقيصَةُ ج نَقائِصُ	Sculptor, carver.	نَقّارُ
To demolish; annul.	نَقَضَ يَنقُضُ	A small tambourine.	(نَقّارَةُ وَنُقَيرَةُ)
To contradict.	ناقَضَ	Hunting-horn.	ناقورُ ج نوَاقيرُ
To be annulled.	إِنتَقَضَ	Beak of a bird.	منقارُ ج مَناقيرُ

To die.	إِنْتَقَلَ إِلَى رَحْمَةِ اللهِ	Destruction, dissolution.	نَقْضٌ
Transpsrt. Quotation.	نَقْلٌ	Beam, joist.	نَقْضَةٌ
Narrator. Bearer. Copyist.	نَاقِلٌ	The contrary, opposite.	نَقِيضٌ
Movable (estate).	مُنْتَقِلٌ	Contrariety.	تَنَاقُضٌ وَمُنَاقَضَةٌ
Transferred ; quoted.	مَنْقُولٌ	To mark with dots.	نَقَطَ يَنْقُطُ وَنَقَّطَ
To punish, chastise.	إِنْتَقَلَ مِنْ	Dot of a letter.	نُقْطَةٌ ج نُقَطٌ
Vengeance.	نَقِمَةٌ وَانْتِقَامٌ	Geometrical point. A drop.	
An avenger.	نَاقِمٌ وَمُنْتَقِمٌ	Centre of a circle.	نُقْطَةُ الدَّائِرَةِ
To recover (from illness).	نَقِهَ يَنْقَهُ نَقَهًا	Epilepsy.	دَاءُ النُّقْطَةِ
Convalescent.	نَاقِهٌ وَنَقِهٌ ج نَقَّهٌ	To soak, macerate.	نَقَعَ يَنْقَعُ
To be pure.	نَقِيَ يَنْقَى	To become stagnant.	إِسْتَنْقَعَ
To clean, purify.	نَقَّى وَأَنْقَى	Penetrating, pervading.	نَاقِعٌ
To choose, select.	تَنَقَّى وَانْتَقَى	Infusion.	نَقِيعٌ وَمَنْقُوعٌ
To cleanse one's body.	إِسْتَنْقَى	Dried apricots.	(نَقُوعٌ)
Purity. Innocence.	نَقَاءٌ وَنَقَاوَةٌ	A marsh, swamp.	مُسْتَنْقَعٌ وَنَقْعٌ
Pure. clean. Innocent.	نَقِيٌّ	To take out.	إِنْتَقَفَ
Purer, cleaner.	أَنْقَى	To remove, transport.	نَقَلَ يَنْقُلُ
To afflict.	نَكَبَ يَنْكُبُ نَكْبًا	To copy from ; quote.	نَقَلَ عَنْ
		To emigrate.	انْتَقَلَ مِنْ إِلَى

Unfortunate.	مَنْكُودُ آلْحَظِّ	To swerve from.	نَكَبَ عَنْ
To be ignorant of.	نَكِرَ يَنْكَرُ	Adversity.	نَكْبَةٌ ج نَكَبَاتٌ
To deny.	أَنْكَرَ	Shoulder; side.	مَنْكِبٌ ج مَنَاكِبُ
To disapprove of.	أَنْكَرَ عَلَى	Afflicted, smitten.	مَنْكُوبٌ
To be disguised.	تَنَكَّرَ	To find fault with.	نَكَّتَ عَلَى
To deny. To censure.	إِسْتَنْكَرَ	Speck. Witty saying.	نُكْتَةٌ ج نُكَتٌ
Cunning.	نُكْرٌ وَنَكَارَةٌ	Criticism.	تَنْكِيتٌ
Indefinite noun.	نَكِرَةٌ ج نَكِرَاتٌ	To break a compact.	نَكَثَ يَنْكِثُ
Denial. Repudiation.	إِنْكَارٌ	To be broken (promise).	إِنْتَكَثَ
Disguise.	تَنَكُّرٌ	Broken, violated.	مَنْكُوثٌ
Illicit deed.	مُنْكَرٌ ج مُنْكَرَاتٌ	To marry.	نَكَحَ يَنْكَحُ نِكَاحاً
Indeterminate noun.	مُنَكَّرٌ	To give in marriage.	أَنْكَحَ
To push; prick.	نَكَزَ يَنْكُزُ نَكَزَاً	Marriage contract.	نِكَاحٌ
To upset.	نَكَسَ يَنْكُسُ وَنَكَّسَ	To be hard.	نَكِدَ ـَ نَكَداً
To be upset, inverted.	تَنَكَّسَ	To molest, annoy.	نَكَّدَ وَنَاكَدَ
To have a relapse.	نُكِسَ وَآنْتَكَسَ	To molest each other.	تَنَاكَدَ
A relapse.	نُكْسٌ وَآنْتِكَاسٌ	Irritable, peevish.	نَكِدٌ م نَكْدَاءُ
Reversed.	مَنْكُوسٌ وَمُنْتَكِسٌ	Annoyance, molestation.	تَنْكِيدٌ

Ichneumon; weasel.	نِمْس ج نُمُوس	To exhaust, To dig.	نَكَشَ يَنْكُشُ
Law. Mosquito.	نَامُوس ج نَوَامِيسُ	Pickaxe.	مِنْكَاش ج مَنَاكِيشُ
Mosquito-net.	نَامُوسِيَّة	To withdraw from.	نَكَصَ يَنْكُصُ عَنْ
Freckles.	نَمَش	To turn back.	نَكَصَ عَلَى عَقِبَيْهِ
A straight sword.	أَنْمِشَة	To abstain from, reject.	نَكَفَ يَنْكُفُ عَنْ
Freckled.	نَمِش م نَمْشَاء ج نُمْش	To discuss, contend.	تَنَاكَفَ
Cropped grass.	نَمِيص	To disdain, scorn.	إِسْتَنْكَفَ
Manner; fashion.	نَمَط ج نِمَاط	To punish severely.	نَكَّلَ وَنَكَّلَ بِ
To write well, embellish.	نَمَّقَ	A strong fetter.	نِكْل ج أَنْكَال
To be numb.	نَمِلَ ـ نَمَلًا	Chastisement; warning.	نَكَال
An ant. A pustule.	نَمْلَة ج نَمْل	Smell of breath.	نَكْهَة
Tip of the finger.	أَنْمُلَة ج أَنَامِل	To overcome; vex.	نَكَى يَنْكِي نِكَايَةً
To embellish, adorn.	نَمْنَمَ	To make mischief.	نَمَّ ـ بَيْنَ
To grow, develop.	نَمَا يَنْمُو	A calumniator.	نَمَّام وَنَمُوم
To attribute, ascribe, to.	نَمَا إِلَى	Calumny, slander.	نَمِيمَة ج نَمَائِم
Growth, increase.	نُمُوّ	To mark with numbers.	(نَمَّرَ)
Example.	نَمُوذَج ج نَمُوذَجَات	Leopard; panther. Tiger.	نِمْر ج نُمُورَة
To grow, increase.	نَمَى يَنْمِي	Number (For).	(نِمْرَة ج نِمَر)

Day.	نَهَارٌ ج نُهُرٌ	To ascribe to one.	نَمَى إلى
To be near.	نَهَزَ يَنْهَزُ نَهْزاً	To cause to grow.	أَنْمَى
To approach, be close to.	نَاهَزَ	To trace one's origin to.	إِنْتَمَى إلى
To seize an opportunity.	إِنْتَهَزَ	Growing, increasing.	نَامٍ
Opportunity.	نُهْزَةٌ ج نُهَزٌ	To plunder.	نَهَبَ يَنْهَبُ وَاَنْتَهَبَ
To bite.	نَهَشَ يَنْهَشُ نَهْشاً	Pillage, rapine.	نَهْبٌ
To rise, get up.	نَهَضَ يَنْهَضُ. عَنْ	Booty, plunder, spoil.	نَهْبَةٌ
To revolt, rise against.	نَهَضَ عَلَى	Pillager, depredator,	نَهَّابٌ
To rush towards.	نَهَضَ إلى	Pillaged, plundered.	مَنْهُوبٌ
To urge ; cause to rise,	أَنْهَضَ	To follow (the way).	نَهَجَ يَنْهَجُ
To rise up.	إِنْتَهَضَ	To be out of breath:	نَهِجَ يَنْهَجُ
To urge, incite.	إِسْتَنْهَضَ لِ	Rapid breathing, panting.	نَهَجٌ
Lifting ; rising.	نُهُوضٌ	A plain road. Way.	مِنْهَجٌ ومِنْهَاجٌ ج مَنَاهِجُ
To bray.	نَهَقَ يَنْهَقُ نُهَاقاً وَنَهِيقاً	To contend with in battle.	نَاهَدَ
To overcome, wear out.	نَهَكَ يَنْهَكُ	To sigh, groan.	تَنَهَّدَ
To defame.	نَهَكَ عِرْضَهُ وَاَنْتَهَكَ	To flow.	نَهَرَ يَنْهَرُ نَهْراً
To weaken.	نَهَكَ وَاَنْتَهَكَ	To chide, check.	نَهَرَ وَاَنْتَهَرَ
Enfeebled, weakened.	مَنْهُوكٌ	River.	نَهْرٌ ج أَنْهُرٌ وَأَنْهَارٌ

To drink.	نَهِلَ يَنْهَلُ نَهَلاً
A watering place.	مَنْهَلُ ج مَنَاهِلُ
To be ravenous.	نَهِمَ يَنْهَمُ
An insatiable avidity.	نَهْمٌ
Greedy ; glutton.	نَهِمٌ وَنَهِيمٌ
To prohibit.	نَهَى يَنْهَى عَنْ
To accomplish, achieve.	أَنْهَى
To inform.	أَنْهَى إِلَى
To lead to.	إِنْتَهَى إِلَى
To be completed.	تَنَاهَى وَاْنْتَهَى
To abstain from.	تَنَاهَى وَاْنْتَهَى عَنْ
Prohibition, interdiction.	نَهْيٌ
Intelligence.	نُهَى
End, utmost.	نِهَايَةٌ ج نِهَايَاتٌ
One who forbids.	نَاهٍ
What a man !	نَاهِيكَ مِنْ رَجُلٍ
End, termination ; limit.	إِنْتِهَاءٌ
Prohibited.	مَنْهِيٌّ عَنْهُ

Prohibited things.	أَلْمَنَاهِي
Infinite ; endless.	غَيْرُ مُتَنَاهٍ
End, extremity ; limit.	مُنْتَهَى
The final plural.	مُنْتَهَى ٱلْجُمُوعِ
Storm ; tempest.	نَوْءٌ ج أَنْوَاءٌ
To take one's place.	نَابَ يَنُوبُ عَنْ
To repent.	نَابَ وَأَنَابَ إِلَى ٱلله
To overtake, befall.	نَابَ وَاْنْتَابَ
To appoint a substitute.	أَنَابَ
To do a thing in turn.	تَنَاوَبَ عَلَى
The Nubians.	نُوبٌ وَنُوبَةٌ
A Nubian.	نُوبِيٌّ
A turn ; time.	نَوْبَةٌ ج نُوَبٌ
Musical concert.	نَوْبَةٌ ج نَوْبَاتٌ
Lieutenancy, vicarship.	نِيَابَةٌ
In place of, instead of.	نِيَابَةً عَنْ
Substitute, deputy.	نَائِبٌ ج نُوَّابٌ
The subject of a passive verb.	نَائِبُ ٱلْفَاعِلِ

Light.	نُورٌ ج أَنْوَارٌ	Parliament.	مجلسُ ٱلنوَّاب
Gipsy.	نُورِيٌّ ج نَورٌ	Misfortune.	نائبةٌ ج نَوائبُ
Illumination.	إِنَارَةٌ وَتَنْوِيرٌ	Mariner, sailor.	نُوتِيٌّ ج نُوتِيَّةٌ
Shining, bright.	نَيِّرٌ م نَيِّرَةٌ	To wail ; coo (pigeon).	نَاحَ يَنُوحُ
Giving light ; shining.	مُنِيرٌ	To bewail the dead.	نَاحَ عَلَى
A light-house. Minaret.	مَنَارَةٌ	Lamentation.	نَوْحٌ وَنُوَاحٌ وَنِياحٌ
A threshing-harrow.	نَوْرَج	A mourner, weeper.	نَائِحٌ
Men; people. (for اَنَاسٌ)	نَاسٌ	Wailing women.	نَائِحَةٌ ج نَوائِحُ وَنَائِحاتٌ
Sarcophagus.	نَاوُوسٌ ج نَوَاوِيسُ	To cause a camel to kneel.	أَنَاخَ
To engage in a combat.	نَاوَشَ	To abide in a place.	أَنَاخَ بِالمَكانِ
To attack one another.	تَنَاوَشَ	Climate.	مَناخٌ ج مَناخَاتٌ
To take out.	إِنتاشَ	To shine, sparkle.	نَارَ يَنُورُ وَأَنَارَ
To flee away.	نَاصَ يَنُوصُ عَنْ	To flower, blossom (plant).	نَوَّرَ وَأَنَارَ
A refuge, an asylum.	مَناصٌ	To light up.	نَوَّرَ وَأَنَارَ
To suspend to.	نَاطَ يَنُوطُ وَأَنَاطَ	To be enlightened by.	إِسْتَنَارَ بِ
Dependent on.	مَنُوطٌ بِ	Fire.	نَارٌ ج نِيرانٌ
To divide, classify, specify.	نَوَّعَ	A volcano.	جَبَلُ ٱلنَّار
To be of different kinds.	تَنَوَّع	A steam-ship.	مَرْكَبُ أَلنَّار

Sleep, slumber.	نَوْمٌ	Kind, sort species.	نَوْعٌ ج أَنْوَاعٌ
Sleeping ; sleeper.	نَائِمٌ ج نِيَام	Diversified ; diverse,	مُتَنَوِّعٌ
Sleep. A dream.	مَنَامٌ	To overlook, surmount.	نَافَ ــ عَلَى
A dormitory.	مَنَامٌ وَمَنَامَةٌ	More, upwards of.	نَيّفٌ وَنَيّفٌ
Hypnotic, soporific.	مُنَوّمٌ	Upwards of ten.	عَشَرَةٌ وَنَيّفٌ
To mark with the.	نَوَّنَ تَنْوِينًا	Water-lily.	نَوْفَرٌ
double vowels (ٌ) (ٍ) و (ً).		Jet d'eau.	نَوْفَرَةٌ
A dimple on chin.	نُونَةٌ	She-camel.	نَاقَةٌ ج نُوقٌ وَنِيَاقٌ
To purpose, resolve.	نَوَى يَنْوِي	Dainty, fastidious.	نَيِّقٌ
Distance, absence.	نَوًى	To give to, hand over.	نَاوَلَ
A fruit stone. Nucleus.	نَوَاةٌ ج نَوًى	To procure for one.	أَنَالَ
Intention.	نِيَّةٌ ج نِيَّاتٌ	To obtain, receive.	تَنَاوَلَ
Intended, purposed.	مَنْوِيٌّ	A loom.	نَوْلٌ ج أَنْوَال
Raw, underdone.	نِيءٌ وَنِيٌّ	Freight money.	نَاوُلُونُ
Canine tooth ; tusk.	نَابٌ ج أَنْيَابٌ	Mode, manner, fashion.	مِنْوَالٌ
To give rest.	(نَيَّحَ)	To sleep.	نَامَ يَنَامُ نَوْمًا وَنِيَامًا
To die.	تَنَيَّحَ	To put to sleep.	نَوَّمَ وَأَنَامَ
Yoke.	نِيرٌ ج أَنْيَارٌ وَنِيرَانٌ	To feign sleep	تَنَاوَمَ

To obtain, acquire. نَالَ يَنالُ	Woof. نَيرُ ج أَنيارُ
To cause to obtain. نَالَ وَأَنَالَ	Tooth-gum. نَيرة
Indigo-plant ; indigo. نيلُ	April. نيسانُ
The Nile. أَلنّيلُ	A decoration. نَيشانُ ج نَياشينُ
Nenuphar, lotus. نيلُوفَر وَزِينوفَر	To surpass, exceed. نَافَ يَنيفُ عَلَى
Nineveh. نينَوَى	Eminence, (title of honour). نيافة
A kind of flute. نَايُ ج نَايَاتُ	See under نَيّفُ وَنيفُ . نُوف

٨

Suppose I said. هَبني قلت	As a numeral sign = 5. ﻫ
To blow (wind). هَبَّ يَهَبُّ	His, him, it. ﻩ
To shake (a sword). هَبَّ وَأَهَبَّ	Her, it. هَا
To begin to do. هَبَّ يَفْعَلُ	Lo ! Behold ! هَا
To awake from sleep. هَبَّ مِنَ النَّوْم	Take thou ! Here you are ! هَاكَ
Fine dust in the air. هَبَابُ	Grant ! (Imp. of هَبْ . وَهَبَ

To defame, disgrace.	هَتَكَ سِتَرَه
To be disclosed, divulged.	تَهتَّكَ
Solution of continuity.	هَتْكُ
Disgrace, dishonour.	(هَتيكةٌ)
Rapid, quick (march).	هَجّاجٌ
To subside.	هَجَأ يَهجَا هَجأً
To spell (a ward).	تَهجَّأ
To forsake, renounce.	هَجَر يَهجُر
To emigrate.	هاجَر مِن
Forsaking.	هَجرٌ وهِجرانٌ
Separation; flight.	هِجرةٌ
The Hegira, Moslem Era.	ألهِجرةُ
Hot mid-day.	هاجِرةٌ وهَجيرةٌ
Emigrant.	مُهاجِرٌ
Emigration.	مُهاجَرةٌ
Deserted, forsaken.	مَهجورٌ
To occur to the mind.	هَجَس يَهجِس
A troubled thought.	هاجِسٌ

Blowing (of wind).	هُبوبٌ
Place of blowing of wind.	مَهَبٌّ
Flesh, a piece of meat.	هَبْرٌ
A wind raising dust.	ريحٌ هُبارِيّةٌ
Flakes. Scurf.	هِبرِيّةٌ
To descend ; fall.	هَبَط يَهبِط
To cause to come down.	أهبَطَ
Fall ; abatement.	هَبْطٌ وهُبوطٌ
A fall; a descent.	هَبْطةٌ
To take a vapour bath.	(تَهبَّل)
Vapour; steam.	(هَبْلةٌ)
Fumigation.	(تَهبيلٌ)
Dust flying in the air.	هَباءٌ
To defame.	هَتَر يَهتِر هَترأً
To be reckless; neglect.	إستَهتَر
To call, shout.	هَتَف يَهتِف هُتافاً
Call, cry, shauting.	هُتافٌ
To tear off ; divulge.	هَتَك يَهتِك

To be pulled down.	اِنْهَدَّ إِ	To sleep; subside.	هَجَعَ يَهْجَعُ هُجُوعًا
Destruction, demolition.	هَدٌّ	Part of the night.	هَجِيعٌ مِنَ اللَّيْلِ
Threatening.	تَهْدِيدٌ وتَهَدُّدٌ	To assail, surprise.	هَجَمَ يَهْجِمُ عَلَى
Sledge-hammer.	مِهَدَّةٌ	To attack suddenly.	هَاجَمَ
To subside, calm down.	هَدَأَ يَهْدَأ	A surprise, sudden attack.	هَجْمَةٌ
To calm, appease.	هَدَّأَ تَهْدِئَةً	Sudden attack or surprise.	هُجُومٌ
Rest, tranquillity, quiet.	هُدُوءٌ	To be low, vile.	هَجُنَ يَهْجُنُ هُجْنَةً
Eye-lashes; fringe.	هُدْبٌ ج أَهْدَاب	To consider mean.	اِسْتَهْجَنَ
To be spent uselessly. Squander.	هَدَرَ يَهْدِرُ	Fault, meanness.	هُجْنَةٌ
Roaring (of waves, &c.)	هَدِيرٌ	Fast dromedary.	هِجِّينٌ
To approach.	هَدَفَ يَهْدِفُ إِلَى	To mock, ridicule.	هَجَا يَهْجُو هَجْوًا
Target, aim.	هَدَفٌ ج أَهْدَاف	To spell.	هَجَا وهَجَّى وتَهَجَّى
To let down.	هَدَلَ ـ هَدْلًا	A satire, lampoon.	هِجَاءٌ
To hang down.	هَدِلَ وتَهَدَّلَ	Spelling.	هِجَاءٌ وتَهْجِيَةٌ وتَهَجٍّ
A bovine epidemic. Rinderpest.	أَبُو هَدْلَانَ	The alphabet.	حُرُوفُ الهِجَاءِ
To pull down.	هَدَمَ يَهْدِمُ هَدْمًا	Satire.	هَجْوَةٌ واهْجِيَّةٌ ج أَهَاجِي
To be destroyed.	تَهَدَّمَ وانْهَدَمَ	To pull down, demolish.	أَهَدَّ يَهُدُّ
Destruction, demolition.	هَدْمٌ	To threaten, menace.	هَدَّدَ وتَهَدَّدَ

هذان Dual of هذا	(هدوم) Clothes, garments.
هذَّب To trim; improve.	هادِمُ ٱللَّذاتِ Death.
تَهذَّب To be educated; improved.	مهدوم Destroyed, demolished.
تهذيب Education. Correction.	هادَنَ To come to an agreement.
مهذَّب ومتهذب Refined. polished.	تهادَنَ To make a truce.
هذَرَ يهذرُ هذْرًا To babble,	هدْنَة ومُهادَنَة Armistice, truce.
هذه Fem of هذا	هدْهُد ج هَداهِد Hoopoo (bird).
هذَى يهذي To talk irrationally.	هدى يهدي To lead aright, guide.
هذاءُ وَهذيان Delirium.	أهدى To give a present.
هرَّ ج هررة A cat.	تهادى To make mutual presents.
هرَّة ج هرر A she-cat.	اهتدى To be rightly guided.
هَرير Whining, yelping.	إستهدى To ask for guidance.
هرىءَ يَهرا To become tattered,	هداية وهُدًى The right path.
هرب يهربُ To run away, flee.	هدِيَّة ج هدايا A present, gift.
هرَّب To put to flight; smuggle.	هادٍ ج هُداة Guide, leader,
هرب Escape, flight.	مهديّ Rightly guided, offered.
هارب A fugitive.	هذَّ ـ هذيذًا في To ponder over.
مهرب ج مهارب Place of refuge.	هذا م هذه وَهذي This.

To walk fast.	هَرْوَلَ	To joke, jest.	هَرَّجَ
A cudgel.	هِرَاوَةٌ ج هَرَاوَى	Agitation, tumult.	هَرْجٌ
To wear out.	(هَرَى يَهْرِي هَرْيًا)	Jester ; buffoon.	هَارِجٌ وَمُهَرِّجٌ
To get worn out.	(إِهْتَرَى)	To pound, crush.	هَرَسَ يَهْرُسُ
Granary.	هُرْيٌ ج أَهْرَاءُ	To excite discord.	هَرَّشَ بَيْنَ
To shake, brandish.	هَزَّ يَهُزُّ هَزًّا	To sport.	تَهَارَشَ وَاهْتَرَشَ
Ta be shaken.	إِهْتَزَّ وَاُهْتُزَّ	Tumult, row.	هِرَاشٌ
Earthquake.	هَزَّةٌ	Heretic.	هِرْطُوقِيٌّ ج هَرَاطِقَةٌ
Sound. Rustling.	هَزِيزٌ	To walk fast.	هَرَعَ يَهْرَعُ هَرَعًا
To mock at.	هَزَأَ وَهَزِئَ يَهْزَأُ بِ	To pour out.	هَرَقَ يَهْرِقُ ٠ وَهَرَّقَ
To ridicule.	تَهَزَّأَ وَاسْتَهْزَأَ بِ	Effusion, shedding.	إِهْرَاقٌ
Mockery.	هُزْءٌ وَهُزُوءٌ وَاسْتِهْزَاءٌ	Heraclius (Emperor).	هِرَقْلُ
Part of the night.	هَزِيجٌ مِنَ اللَّيْلِ	To be decrepit.	هَرِمَ يَهْرَمُ
A song.	اهْزُوجَةٌ ج أَهَازِيجُ	To cut, hash.	هَرَمَ يَهْرِمُ ٠ وَهَرَّمَ
Part of the night.	هَزِيعٌ مِنَ اللَّيْلِ	To render one old.	هَرَّمَ وَأَهْرَمَ
Fear. Tumult.	هَيْزَعَةٌ	Decrepitude.	هَرَمٌ
To joke, jest.	هَزَلَ يَهْزِلُ هَزْلاً	A pyramid.	هَرَمٌ ج أَهْرَامٌ
To emaciate.	هَزَلَ هُزْلاً ٠ وَهَزَّلَ	Very old.	هَرِمٌ ج هَرِمُونَ

To oppress. هَضَمَ وتَهَضَّمَ وآهْتَضَمَ	To be emaciated. هزَلَ يَهزُلُ
To wrong. هَضَمَ حقَّهُ	Sport, jest, joke. هزْلٌ وهزَالَةٌ
To be digested (food). إنْهَضَمَ	Thinness, emaciation. هزَالٌ
Digestion. هَضْمٌ وآنْهِضَام	Thin, meagre. هزِيل و مَهزُول
Indigestion. سُوءُ ٱلهَضْمِ	To put to flight. هزَمَ يَهزِم
Injury, wrong. هَضِيمَةٌ ج هَضَائِم	To be put to flight. إنْهزَام
To rain. هَطَلَ يَهطِلُ هَطلًا	Rout, defeat. هزْمٌ وهزِيمة
Fine but continuous rain. هَطْلٌ	Thunder. Rain. هزِيم
To rustle; walk quickly. هَفَّ يَهِفُّ	To shake, agitate. هزْهَزَ
To long for. هَفَّ إلى	To be cheerful. هشَّ يَهِشُّ
To fly up and down. هَفَّت يَهِفِت	Joyous cheerful. هشّ
To rush to, or into. تَهافَت عَلى	Tender, soft. هشّ وهَشَاشٌ
A slip, fault. هَفوةٌ ج هَفَوَات	To roam about. (هشَلَ يَهشِل هَشْلًا)
Famished. هَاف	To drive away, expel. (هَشَلَ)
Thus, so. هكَذَا	To crush, break. هشَمَ يَهشِمُ وهشَّمَ
To mock at, deride. تَهكَّمَ عَلى	To be crushed. تَهشَّم وانْهشَمَ
Mockery. Irony. Sarcasm. تَهكُّمٌ	A hill. هَضْبةٌ ج هِضَابٌ
Particle of Interrogation. هلْ	To break. To digest. هَضَمَ يَهضِمُ

Dangerous place.	مَهْلَكَة	Did you write ?	هَلْ كَتَبْتَ
Here ! Come here !	هَلُمَّ	Is not ? Why not ?	هَلَّا
And so on, *et cœtera*.	هَلُمَّ جَرًّا	Come! Hasten!	حَيَّ هَلْ
Jelly.	هُلَام	To appear, (new moon).	هَلَّ يَهُلُّ
Jelly-like, gelatinous.	هُلَامِيّ	To praise God.	هَلَّلَ
They ; their ; them.	هُمْ	To exult, be joyous.	تَهَلَّلَ
Their book.	كِتَابُهُمْ	To pour down (rain).	إِنْهَلَّ
He struck them.	ضَرَبَهُمْ	The new moon.	هِلٌّ وَهَلَّة
To cause anxiety.	هَمَّ يَهُمُّ . وَأَهَمَّ	New moon. Crescent.	هِلَال
To desire, seek.	هَمَّ يَهُمُّ هَمَّاب	Semi-lunar, crescentic.	هِلَالِيّ
To be grieved.	إِهْتَمَّ	Act of parising God.	تَهْلِيل
To take pains in...	إِهْتَمَّ بِ	Elliptical. Oval.	أَهْلِيلَجِيّ
To be solicitous about	إِهْتَمَّ لِ	To perish, die.	هَلَكَ يَهْلَكُ
Care, anxiety.	هَمٌّ ج هُمُوم	To ruin. destroy.	هَلَكَ وَأَهْلَكَ
Concern ; energy.	هِمَّة ج هِمَم	To squander, exhaust.	إِسْتَهْلَكَ
Reptile, insect.	هَامَّة ج هَوَامُّ	Ruin, loss. Death.	هَلَاك
Energetic.	هُمَام	Perishing, lost, dead.	هَالِك
More important.	أَهَمُّ	Perdition, ruin.	تَهْلُكَة

To rain quietly.	هَمَلَ يَهْمُلُ	Care, effort.	إهْتِمامٌ
To neglect, forget.	أهْمَلَ	Important matter.	مُهِمٌّ ج مَهامٌّ
To be negligent.	(تَهامَلَ في)	Provisions, necessaries.	مُهِمّاتٌ
Negligence, carelessness.	(تَهامُلٌ)	Preoccupied, anxious.	مَهْمُومٌ
Unused, obsolete (word).	مُهْمَلٌ	Stupid, savage people.	هَمَجٌ
Neglected.	مُهْمَلٌ	To subside.	هَمَدَ يَهْمُدُ هُمُوداً
To mumble, mutter.	هَمْهَمَ	To extinguish ; clam.	هَمَّدَ وأهْمَدَ
To fall, flow, run.	هَمَا يَهْمُو	To pour out.	هَمَرَ يَهْمُرُ
Belt.	هِمْيانٌ ج هَمايِينُ	To be poured out, flow.	إنْهَمَرَ
Royal.	هَمايُونٌ وهَمايُونِيٌّ	To beat ; push.	هَمَزَ يَهْمِزُ هَمْزاً
They ; their · them, fem.	هُنَّ	A hemza = (ء)	هَمْزَةٌ ج هَمَزاتٌ
To congratulate.	هَنَّا بِ	A spur, goad.	مِهْمازٌ ج مَهامِيزُ
To enjoy, relish.	هَنِئَ يَهْنَأ بِ	Marked with a hemza.	مَهْمُوزٌ
To enjoy, relish.	تَهَنَّأ تَهَنُّؤاً بِ	To mumble.	هَمَسَ يَهْمِسُ هَمْساً
Wholesome. Pleasant.	هَنِيءٌ	Margin of a book.	هامِشٌ
Congratulation.	تَهْنِئَةٌ	To shed tears.	هَمَعَ يَهْمَعُ
India, the Indies.	ألْهِنْدُ	To press, urge.	هَمَكَ يَهْمُكُ
Cocoa-nut.	جَوْزُ الْهِنْد	To be engrossed in.	إنْهَمَكَ في

Camel-litter.	هَوْدَج ج هوادِج	An Indian.	هِنديّ ج هنُود
Lo ! Behold !	هُوَذَا	Endive, wild chicory.	هِنْدباءٌ
To roll down, fall down.	تَهوَّرَ	To make a plan.	هَنْدَسَ
To rush imprudently.	تَهوَّرَ	Engineering. Architecture.	هَنْدَسَةٌ
Rashness. Collapse.	تَهوُّر	Geometry.	عِلمُ آلهندَسةِ
Folly. Passionate desire.	هَوَسٌ	Geometrical.	هَنْدسيٌّ
Scorched green wheat. (هَوِيسٌ)		Geometrician, Architect. Engineer.	مُهَنْدِسٌ
To be agitated ; (bark).	هَاشَ يَهوشُ	To arrange, adorn.	هَنْدَمَ
Tumult.	هَوْشَةٌ ج هَوْشاتٌ	Here (adv).	هُنا وَهَهُنا
To vomit.	هَاعَ يَهَاعُ و يَهوعُ هوْعاً	There, yonder.	هُنا وَهُنالِكَ
To frighten.	هَالَ يَهُولُ	A little while, trifle.	هُنيةٌ وَهُنَيْهةٌ
To threaten with.	هوَّلَ عَليهِ بِ	He, it.	هُوَ
To be terrified.	إهْتَالَ	An abyss.	هُوَّةٌ ج هوَتٌ
Terror, fright.	هَوْلٌ ج أهْوالٌ	To become a Jew.	هَادَ وَتَهوَّدَ
The sphinx.	أبوُ آلهوْلِ	To abate price.	هَاوَدَ
Frightful, terrible.	هَائِلٌ وَمَهوُلٌ	Jews.	يهوُد
Halo (of moon).	هَالَةٌ ج هَالاتٌ	Jew.	يَهوُديٌّ
Head. Chief.	هَامَةٌ ج هَامَاتٌ	Jewess. Judea.	يَهوديّةٌ

Ringing in the ears.	هَوِيٌّ	To be easy.	هَانَ يَهُونُ هَوْناً عَلى
Air, atmosphere.	هَوَاءٌ ج أَهْوِيَةٌ	To be despised.	هَانَ يَهُونُ هُوناً
Atmospherical.	هَوَائِيٌّ	To facilitate.	هَوَّنَ على
The lower world ; hades.	الأَهَاوِيَةُ	To despise.	أَهَانَ
She, it ; they.	هِيَ ج هُنَّ	To neglect.	تَهَاوَنَ بِ
To prepare.	هَيَّا تَهِيئَةً	Contemptibleness.	هَوَانٌ
To be prepared for.	تَهَيَّأَ لِ	Disdain ; insult.	إِهَانَةٌ ج إِهَانَاتٌ
Form, aspect.	هَيْئَةٌ ج هَيْئَاتٌ	Negligence ; idleness.	تَهَاوُنٌ
Astronomy.	عِلْمُ الهَيْئَةِ	Mortar (for pounding).	هَاوُنٌ
To fear ; revere.	هَابَ يَهَابُ وآهْتَابَ	Light, easy to do.	هَيِّنٌ وهَيْنٌ
Imp. of هَابَ and وَهَبَ	هَبْ	Lighter, easier.	أَهْوَنُ
Respect, awe, veneration.	هَيْبَةٌ	Disdained ; injured.	مُهَانٌ
More respected.	أَهْيَبُ	Contempt, shame.	مَهَانَةٌ
Venerable ; respected.	مَهِيبٌ	To fall.	هَوَى يَهْوِي هَوِيّاً
Fear ; veneration, respect.	مَهَابَةٌ	To love ; desire.	هَوِيَ يَهْوَى
Give !	هَاتِ ج هَاتُوا	To ventilate.	هَوَّى تَهْوِيَةً
To be agitated, excited.	هَلِجَ يَهْلِجُ	To fall down ; descend.	أَهْوَى
To excite, agitate.	هَاجَ وهَيَّجَ	Passionate desire.	هَوًى ج أَهْوَاءٌ

To be agitated. تَهيَّجِ وَ آهْتَاجَ	To love passionately. هَام يَهيم
Agitation, excitement. هَيجَانُ	Passionate love. هيام
Battle, combat ; strife. هَيجَاء	Love stricken. هَائِم ج هيّم و هيَام
Agitated, excited. هَائِج	Starless night. لَيلُ أَهْيَم
Diarrhœa. هيضَة	Heart lost in love. قلبٌ مُستهَام
Slim. أَهْيَفُ م هَيفَاء ج هيف	God (the Protector). ألمُهَيْمِن
Temple ; alter. هيكل ج هيَاكل	Easy. هَيّن و هَيّن
The skeleton. الهَيكلُ العظمِيُّ	Far ! Far away ! هَيهَاتَ
Matter. هيُولى	Come ! Quick ! هيّا وَهيّ
Material (adj). هيُولِيّ وَهيُولانِيّ	

و

As a numeral sign = 6. و	Shame. Dishonour. إِبَة
And. و	Pestilence. وَبَاء وَوَبَاء ج أُوبِئَة وَأَوْبَاء
By God ! وَٱللّٰه	Epidemic ; pestiiential. وَبَائِيّ
Oh ! Ah ! Alas ! وا	Pestilential. وَبِيء وَمَوْبُوء

Cord of a circle. وَتَر وَوتَر	To rebuke, reprimand. وبّخ
String of a bow, or وَتَر ج أَوْتَار	Scolding, rebuking. تَوْبِيخ
musical instrument. Tendon	Cony. وبْر ج وبُور وَوبَار
Succession. تَوَاتُر	Soft hair (of animals). وبْر
Repeated at intervals. مُتَوَاتِر	Nomad people. أَهْلُ الوبَر
Often, repeatedly. مُتَوَاتِراً	Low people. وبْش ج أَوْبَاش
A bruise or wound. وَثْء وَوَثَاءَة	To rain. وبَل يَبِل وَبْلاً
To leap. وثَب يَثِب وَثْباً وَوُثُوباً	To be unhealthy, وبَل يَوْبَل
A leap, jump. An assault. وَثْبَة	(land).
To rely upon. وثِق يَثِق بِ	A heavy shower. وَبْل وَوَابِل
To be firm. وثُق يَوْثُق وَثَاقَة	Unhealthiness. Hardship. وبَال
To make firm. وثَّق	Unhealthy. Hard. وَبِيل
To make a covenant with. وَاثَقَ	To make firm. وتَد يَتِد وَوَتَّد
To fetter, tie fast. أَوْثَق بِالوِثَاقِ	Wooden peg. A kind وتَد ج أَوْتَاد
To trust, rely upon. إِسْتَوْثَق مِنْ	of foot (Prosody).
Confidence. ثِقَة	Mountains. أَوْتَادُ الأَرْضِ
A tie, fetter, rope, strap. وِثَاق	To string a bow. وتَر وَوَتَّر وَأَوْتَر
Firm or solid. Reliable. وَثِيق	To be strained hard. تَوَتَّر
Compact, alliance وَثِيقَة ج وَثَائِق	To follow one another. تَوَاتَر
	Single ; odd number. وَتَر

To be ; to exist.	وجد	Firmer, firmest.	أوثقم وُثْقَى
To create, produce.	أوْجَد إِيجاداً	The strongest hold.	أَلْعُرْوَةُ الوُثقى
To be grieved for.	توجَّد لِ	Covenant.	ميثاقٌ ج مَواثيقُ
Wealth, competence.	جدَّةٌ	An idol.	وثنٌ ج أوْثانٌ
Love ; joy ; grief.	وجد	Idolater ; heathen.	وثنيٌّ ج وَثَنيُّونَ
Inner consciousness.	وُجدانٌ	A sprain.	وثي
Existence.	وجود	To be necessary, due.	وجَب يجب
Found ; existing.	مَوْجودٌ	To make binding.	أوْجَبَ
Existing things.	ألموْجُوداتُ	To be worthy of.	إِستوْجَبَ
Grotto, cave.	وجرٌ ج أوْجَارٌ	A set of the same kind.	وَجْبَةٌ
Den, lair.	وِجَارٌ ج أوْجِرة	Necessity, duty.	وجوب
To be brief in speech.	وجَز يجز	Affirmation.	إِيجابٌ
To abbreviate, abridge.	أوْجَزَ	Affirmative, positive.	إِيجابيٌّ
Abridged, concise.	وجيزٌ ومو جز	Necessary, obligatory.	وجبٌ
Conciseness, brevity.	إِيجَازٌ	Duty.	وَاجبٌ ج وَاجباتٌ
To feel pain.	وجَع يوجَع ويِيجع	Cause, motive, reason.	موجبٌ
To cause or inflict pain.	أوْجَعَ	According to.	بموجبِ
		To find.	وجدَ يجد

Face. Chief. وجه ج أوْجه وَوجوه	To feel pain. توجَّع
Manner. Aim. Surface.	
To do for God. عمله لوجهِ الله	To feel pain for. توجَّع لـ
In some manner. بوجهٍ	Beer, ale. جعة
Side. Dimension. جهة ج جهات (Geom).	Pain. Disease. وجع ج أوْجاع
Concerning. من جهتهِ	Painful ; sore. وجيع ومموْجع
Consideration, position. وَجاهة	Fire-place, hearth. وجاق وأوْجاق
Opposite to, in front of. تجاه	To fear. وجل يوْجَل
Chief, prince. وَجيه ج وجهاء	Fear, terror. وجل ج أوْجال
Going, turning to. متوجّه	Timorous. وجل ج وجلون
To be alone. وَحد يَحد	Cheek (face). وجنة ج وَجنات
To reduce to one ; unify. وَحَّد	Mallet. ميجنة ج مَواجن
To be one, single, alone. توحَّد	To be respected. وجه يوْجه
To be united. إتَّحد	To turn a thing towards. وَجَّه
Separately. على حِدَةٍ	To send. وَجَّه
Alone. وَحْدَه	To meet one. واجه مواجهة
Unity, being unique. وَحْدانية	To repair to. توجَّه نحو وَإلى
Solitude, isolation. وَحْدة	To have an interview. (تَواجَة)
	To turn towards.

Savage, brute-like. مُتَوَحِّش	One; single; unique. وَاحِد
Thin mud, mire. وَحْل ج وُحُول	The only one. الوَاحِد
Muddy, miry. وَحِل	One. أَحَد م إِحْدَى ج آحَاد
To be spiteful. وَحِنَ يَحِن	Sunday. الأَحَد
To inspire. Send. أَوْحَى إِلَى	Unique. وَحِيد م وَحِيدَة
Divine inspiration. وَحْي	Union ; harmony ; accord. إِتِّحَاد
Haste, hurry. وَحَى	Unification. Belief in the unity of God. تَوْحِيد
To find fault with. وَاخَذ مُوَاخَذَةً	Isolation, solitude. تَوَحُّد
Excuse me. (لَا تُوَاخِذْنِي)	A unitarian. تَوَحَّد
To prick. وَخَزَ يَخِز وَخْزًا	Isolated, alone. One. مُتَوَحِّد
To be grizzled. وَخَطَهُ الشَّيْب	To be unpeopled. وَحَشَ وَتَوَحَّش
To be unhealthy. وَخَمَ يَوْخَم	To grow savage. تَوَحَّش
To surfeit (food). أَتْخَم	To feel lonely. إِسْتَوْحَش
To be ill (from food). إِتَّخَم	Wild beast. وَحْش ج وُحُوش
Dirty unclean. وَخِيم وَوَخِم	Onager, wild ass. حِمَار وَحْش
Indigestion. تُخَمَة	Grief ; solitude. وَحْشَة
To seek diligently. وَخَّى وَتَوَخَّى	Wild, ferocious cruel. وَحْشِيّ
To fraternize with. (وَاخَى مُوَاخَاةً)	Savage state. Barbarity. تَوَحُّش

Mildness, gentleness.	وَدَاعَة	To love ; wish for.	وَدَّ يَوَدُّ
Rest, quiet ; gentleness.	دَعَة	To show love to.	تَوَدَّدَ إِلَى
Quiet, gentle	وَدِيع ج وُدَعَاء	To have mutual love.	تَوَادَّ تَوَادًّا
Deposit ; trust, charge.	وَدِيعَة	Love ; friendship.	وُدٌّ وَوِدَادٌ
Depositor.	مُسْتَوْدِع	It is my wish.	بِوُدِّي (بِدِّي)
Depository.	مُسْتَوْدَع	Lover, affectionate.	وُدٌّ وَوَدُودٌ
Race-field.	مَيْدَان ج مَيَادِين	Affection, friendship.	مَوَدَّة
To send.	وَدَّى	Mutual, love.	مُوَادَّة وَتَوَادٌّ
To perish.	أَوْدَى إِيدَاءً	Jugular vein.	وَدَاج مث وَدَاجَان
Blood-money.	دِيَة ج دِيَاتٌ	To forsake, leave.	وَدَعَ يَدَعُ
Valley.	وَادٍ ج أَوْدِيَة	Let me, allow me !	دَعْنِي
Let him alone,	وَذَرَ — ذَرْهُ	To take leave of.	وَدَّعَ يُودِّع
Behind. Beyond.	وَرَاءَ	To conciliate.	وَدَّعَ وِدَاعًا
To equivocate.	وَارَبَ مُوَارَبَة	To deposit with.	أَوْدَعَ عِنْدَ
Obliquity. Diagonal.	(وَرْبٌ)	To bid farewell. Deposit.	إِسْتَوْدَعَ
To inherit.	وَرِثَ يَرِثُ إِرْثًا وَوِرَاثَةً	White shell.	وَدَعَة ج وَدَعَاتٌ
To bequeath.	وَرَّثَ وَأَوْرَثَ	Bidding adieu, farewell.	وَدَاعٌ
To bring on (an evil).	أَوْرَثَ		

To throw into difficulty.	وَرَّطَ	To inherit.	تَوَارَثَ
To fall into difficulty.	تَوَرَّطَ	Inheritance.	إِرْثٌ وَوِرَاثَةٌ
Difficulty.	وَرْطَةٌ ج وَرَطَاتٌ	Heir.	وَارِثٌ ج وَرَثَةٌ وَوُرَّاثٌ
To be pious.	وَرِعَ يَرِعُ	Inherited ; hereditary.	مَوْرُوثٌ
Fear of God. Piety.	وَرَعٌ	Inheritance.	مِيرَاثٌ ج مَوَارِيثُ
A pious man.	وَرِعٌ ج أَوْرَاعٌ	To come, arrive.	وَرَدَ يَرِدُ وُرُودًا
Foliage, paper.	وَرَقٌ ج أَوْرَاقٌ	Flower. Rose.	وَرْدٌ ج وُرُودٌ
To put forth leaves.	أَوْرَقَ	A rose.	وَرْدَةٌ
A leaf (of a tree) ; a piece of paper ; ticket.	وَرَقَةٌ	Cockroach.	بِنْتُ وَرْدَانَ
Stationer. Plasterer.	مُوَرِّقٌ	Red, rose-coloured.	وَرْدِيٌّ
Hip bone ; hip.	وَرِكٌ وَوِرْكٌ	Coming, arriving.	وَارِدٌ
A large lizard.	وَرَلٌ ج وِرْلَانٌ	Revenue.	إِيرَادَاتٌ
To swell.	وَرِمَ يَرِمُ وَرَمًا . وَتَوَرَّمَ	Vein.	وَرِيدٌ ج اوْرِدَةٌ
To cause to swell.	وَرَّمَ	Jugular vein.	حَبْلُ الوَرِيدِ
Swelling. Tumour.	وَرَمٌ ج أَوْرَامٌ	Access, entrance.	مَوْرِدٌ ج مَوَارِدُ
Bee-eater (bird).	وَرْوَارٌ ج وَرَاوِيرُ	Of a rose colour, rosy.	مُوَرَّدٌ
To conceal.	وَرَّى وَوَارَى	Brick, restless.	وَرْشٌ
To hide one's self.	تَوَارَى عَن	Work-shop.	(وَرْشَةٌ)

To be divided, distributed.	تَوَزَّع	Creatures ; mankind.	وَرَى
Scotch broom.	(وَزَّال)	Behind,	وَرَاء
To weigh.	وَزَنَ يَزِنُ وَزْنًا وَزِنَةً	The Pentateuch. Bible.	تَوْرَاةُ
To compose (a verse) according to measure scan.	وَزَنَ الشِّعْرَ	Using a word in a double sense.	تَوْرِيَةُ
To be heavy.	وَزُنَ يَوْزُنُ وَزَانَةً	Geese.	وَزّ (اوز)
To be equal in weight.	وَازَنَ	A goose,	وَزَّة
To compare.	وَازَنَ بَيْن	To flow.	وَزَبَ يَزِبُ وُزُوبًا
To be equal in weight.	تَوَازَنَ	Water-drain.	مِيزَابٌ ج مَيَازِيبُ
Weighing ; weigh.	وَزْن وَزْنَة	To commit a sin,	وَزَرَ يَزِرُ
Weight; measure; metre of a verse.	وَزْن ج أَوْزَانُ	To aid, help.	وَازَرَ عَلَى
A weight. Talent.	وَزْنَة ج وَزَنَات	To become a vizier.	تَوَزَّرَ
A weigher. Of full weight,	وَازِن	To put on a وِزْرة .	إِتَّزَرَ
Prudent, reflecting.	وَزِينُ الرَّأْي	Burden. Crime.	وِزْر ج أَوْزَار
Equal, equivalent to,	مُوَازِن	Loin-cloth.	وِزْرَة ج وِزْرَات
Equilibrium.	مُوَازَنَة	Office of a vizier.	وِزَارَة
Weighed ; measured.	مَوْزُون	Vizier.	وَزِير ج وَزَرَاء
Scales, balance. Standard. Measure.	مِيزَان ج مَوَازِين	Assistant.	مُوَازِر
Libra (zodiac).	أَلمِيزَان	To distribute.	وَزَّعَ وَأَوْزَعَ بَيْن

Mediator. وَسِيط ج وُسَطَاء	To correspond to, be parallel with. وَازَى
The middle finger. الْوُسْطَى	To correspond to, تَوَازَى
Intermediate. Mediator. مُتَوَسِّط	Correspondence. مُوَازَاة
Mediterranean. الْبَحْرُ الْمُتَوَسِّط	Parallel (line). مُتَوَازٍ
To be spacious, wide. وَسِعَ يَوْسَع	To be foul, soiled, وَسِخَ يَوْسَخ
To contain, hold. وَسِعَ يَسَع سَعَةً	To soil, وَسَّخَ وَأَوْسَخ
Thou canst not. لَا يَسَعُكَ اَنْ	Dirt, uncleanness. وَسَخ ج أَوْسَاخ
To widen, enlarge. وَسَّع وَأَوْسَع	Dirty, unclean, soiled. وَسِخ
To enrich (God). وَسَّعَ وَأَوْسَع عَلَى	To prop with a pillow. وَسَد
To be at ease. تَوَسَّعَ فِي	A pillow, cushion. وِسَادٌ ج وُسُد
To be enlarged. إِتَّسَع وَاسْتَوْسَع	A pillow. وِسَادَة ج وَسَادَات
Power, ability. وُسْعٌ وَسِعَةٌ	To put in the middle. وَسَّط
Width ; capacity. سَعَة وَاتِّسَاع	To take a middle position. تَوَسَّط
Extent, dilatation. إِتِّسَاع	To mediate between. تَوَسَّطَ بَيْن
Spacious. وَاسِع وَوَسِيع وَمُتَّسِع	Middle, centre. وَسْطٌ وَوَسَط
Wider, more vast. اوْسَع	Means. وَاسِطَة ج وَسَائِط
Rich, wealthy, opulent. مُوسِع	By means of, through. بِوَاسِطَة
To load; to freight. وَسَقَ يَسِقُ وَسْقًا	Intermediation. وَسَاطَة وَتَوَسُّط

To adorn.	وَشَّحَ
To put on.	تَوَشَّحَ وَاتَّشَحَ
A sash set with jewels.	وُشَاحٌ
Double-rhymed poetry.	مُوَشَّحَةٌ
To saw (wood).	وَشَرَ يَشِرُ
A prism.	مَوْشُورٌ ج مَوَاشِيرُ
A saw.	مِيشَارٌ
To be quick.	وَشُكَ يَوْشُكُ وَشْكًا
To be on the point of.	أَوْشَكَ أَنْ
Celerity ; haste, hurry.	وَشْكٌ
Swift ; on the point of.	وَشِيكٌ
To tattoo.	وَشَمَ يَشِمُ وَشْمًا وَوَشَّمَ
To whisper.	وَشْوَشَ وَتَوَشْوَشَ
To embellish.	وَشَى يَشِى . وَوَشَّى
To slander.	وَشَى بِفُلانٍ إِلَى
Slanderer.	وَاشٍ ج وُشَاةٌ وَوَاشُونَ
Coloured ; embroiderd.	مُوَشَّى
Illnes, pain.	وَصَبٌ ج أَوْصَابٌ

A load ; cargo.	وَسْقٌ ج أَوْسَاقٌ
Freighted, loaded.	مَوْسُوقٌ
To implore, seek.	تَوَسَّلَ إِلَى
Means.	وَسِيلَةٌ ج وَسَائِلُ
Supplication.	تَوَسُّلٌ
To brand.	وَسَمَ يَسِمُ وَسْمًا وَسِمَةً
Sign, mark.	وَسْمٌ ج وُسُومٌ . سِمَةٌ ج سِمَاتٌ
Badge of honour.	وِسَامٌ
Season.	مَوْسِمٌ ج مَوَاسِمُ
Marked. Branded.	مَوْسُومٌ
To slumber.	وَسِنَ يَوْسَنُ
Slumber; unconsciousness.	سِنَةٌ
To suggest wicked things.	وَسْوَسَ
Hallucination.	وَسْوَاسٌ ج وَسَاوِسُ
Satan.	إِلْوَسْوَاسُ
A razor.	مُوسَى وَ (مُوس)
Moses.	مُوسَى
Mosaic; a Jew.	مُوسَوِيٌّ

To be continuous.	إِتَّصَلَ	To shut, close (a door).	أُوْصَدَ
To arrive at, reach.	إِتَّصَلَ إِلَى	Shut, closed.	مُوصَدٌ
To be united to.	إِتَّصَلَ بِ	To describe, qualify.	وَصَفَ يَصِفُ
Connection, Receipt.	وَصلٌ	To prescribe medicine	وَصَفَ لِ
Junction, union.	وُصلَةٌ وَاَتِّصَالٌ	to a sick person, (physician).	
Union of the friends.	وِصَالٌ	To be qualified.	إِتَّصَفَ
Union. Gift.	صِلَةٌ ج صِلَاتٌ	Description.	وَصْفٌ ج أَوْصَافٌ
Arrival. Receipt.	وُصُولٌ ج وُصُولَاتٌ	Prescription of physician.	وَصْفَةٌ
Continuity ; connexion.	إِتِّصَالٌ	Descriptive.	وَصْفِيٌّ
Continuity. Union.	مُوَاصَلَةٌ	Quality ; adjective.	صِفَةٌ ج صِفَاتٌ
Connective.	مُوصِلٌ	Young servant.	وَصِيفٌ ج وُصَفَاء
Joined. Continual.	مُتَّصِلٌ	Qualified noun.	مَوْصُوفٌ
Suffixed pronoun.	الضَّمِيرُ الْمُتَّصِلُ	To unite, join.	وَصَلَ يَصِلُ بِ
United, joined.	مَوْصُولٌ	To reach, arrive at.	وَصَلَ إِلَى
Relative Pronoun.	أَلِاسْمُ الْمَوْصُولُ	To give, bestow.	وَصَلَ
Fault ; shame.	وَصْمٌ وَوَصْمَةٌ	To bring to.	وَصَلَ وَأَوْصَلَ إِلَى
To peep through a hole.	وَصْوَصَ	To persevere in.	وَاصَلَ
To bequeath.	وَصَّى وَأَوْصَى	To arrive at.	تَوَصَّلَ إِلَى
		To be joined.	تَوَاصَلَ

Clear exposition. إيضاحٌ وتوضيحٌ	To recommend. وصّى إلى بِ
Evident, manifest, clear. مُتَّضِحٌ	To charge, commend. وصَّى وأَوْصَى
To lay put down. وضَعَ يَضَعُ	A testator, وصِيٌّ ج أَوْصِياء
To give birth. وضَعَتْ تَضَعُ	Executor of a will. Guardian.
To humiliate, abase. وضَعَ فُلانًا	An order, charge. وَصِيَّةٌ ج وَصَايا
	Will, testament.
To be humble. تواضَعَ وٱتَّضَعَ	Testator. مُوصٍ
To be humbled. ٱتَّضَعَ	What is bequeathed. مُوصًى بِهِ
Position, site. وضْعٌ ج أَوْضاعٌ	A legatee, legatory. مُوصًى لَهُ
Humiliation. ضَعَةٌ	To be clean. وَضُؤَ يَوْضُؤُ وُضُوءًا
Laying down. Founder. واضِعٌ	To perform ablutions. تَوَضَّأَ
Humble, low. وَضِيعٌ ج وُضَعاء	Water for ablutions. وَضُوءٌ
Humility. تواضُعٌ وٱتِّضاعٌ	Cleanliness ; beauty. وَضاءَةٌ
Place, site, spot. مَوْضِعٌ ج مَواضِعُ	Ablutions before prayers. تَوَضُّؤٌ
	To be clear, evident. وضَحَ يَضِحُ
Humble, meek. مُتَّضِعٌ ومُتَواضِعٌ	To explain clearly. وضَّحَ وأَوْضَحَ
Object; subject. مَوْضُوعٌ ج مَواضيعُ	To become clear. تَوَضَّحَ وٱتَّضَحَ
To tread upon. وطِئَ يَطَأُ	To ask for explanation. ٱسْتَوْضَحَ
To mount. وطِئَ (الفَرَس)	Distinctness. وُضوحٌ وٱتِّضاحٌ
To prepare, render easy. وطَّأَ	Clear, manifest, evident. واضِحٌ

Perseverance, assiduity. مُواظَبَةٌ	To agree upon. وَاطَأَ وَتَوَاطَأَ عَلَى
To give an office to one. وَظَّفَ	Low ground. وَطَاءٌ وَوَطْءٌ
To be employed. تَوَظَّفَ	Pressure, violence. وَطْأَةٌ
Pay, Office, func- وَظِيفَةٌ جوَظَائِفُ tion, employment.	Low. وَاطِىءٌ
Physiology. عِلمُ وَظَائِفِ ٱلأَعْضَاءِ	Foot-stool. مَوْطِىءٌ ج مَوَاطِىءُ
Functionary ; official. مُتَوَظِّفٌ	To fix, make firm. وَطَدَ يَطِدُ وَوَطَّدَ
To take up wholly. وَعَبَ يَعِبُ	To be made firm, fixed. تَوَطَّدَ
To fill up; complete. أَوْعَبَ إِيعَابًا	Mountains. أَوْطَادٌ
To contain, hold. إِسْتَوْعَبَ	Firm, solid, immovable. وَطِيدٌ
To promise. وَعَدَ يَعِدُ	Object purpose. وَطَرٌ ج أَوْطَارٌ
To make an appointment. وَاعَدَ	To reside in. وَطَنَ يَطِنُ وَأَوْطَنَ بِ
To threaten· تَوَعَّدَ	To inhabit. وَطَّنَ وَٱسْتَوْطَنَ
To promise one another. تَوَاعَدَ	To resolve. وَطَّنَ نفسهُ
A promise. عِدَةٌ وَوَعْدٌ جوُعُودٌ	Native place. وَطَنٌ ج أَوْطَانٌ
Menaces, threats. وَعِيدٌ	Abode, home. مَوْطِنٌ ج مَوَاطِنُ
Appointed time مَوْعِدٌ ج مَوَاعِدُ	A bat. وَطْوَاطٌ ج وَطَاوِيطُ
Appointed time or place. مِيعَادٌ	To lower, let down. وَطَّى
Rugged place. وَعْرٌ ج وُعُورٌ	وَظَبَ يَظِبُ وظوبًا وَوَاظَبَ عَلَى
	To persevere in.

Rugged, difficult.	وعر
To intimate.	وَعَزَ- وَأوْعَزَ إِليه في
To exhort, warn.	وَعَظَ يَعِظ
To listen to warning.	إِتَّعَظَ
Sermon; exhortation.	وعظٌ وَعِظَةٌ وَمَوعِظَةٌ
A preacher.	واعِظٌ ج وعَّاظ
To be ill, indisposed.	تَوَعَّك
An illness.	وَعْكَةٌ
Antelope.	وعلٌ ج أوْعَال
Good morning.	وَعِمَ — عِمْ صَباحاً
To gather; contain.	وَعَى يَعِي
To put into a vessel.	أوْعَى إِيعاءً
To be careful.	تَوَقَّى وَآسْتَوْعَى
Attention, care.	وَعْيٌ
Vessel, receptacle.	وِعَاءٌ ج أوْعِية
Remembering. Cautious.	وَاعٍ
To be very hot.	وغِرَ يَغِرُ وَغَراً
Intense heat. Anger.	وغْرٌ
Tumult; battle.	وَغَى وَوَغْي
To come, arrive.	وَفَدَ يَفِدُ عَلى
To send (an envoy).	وَفَدَ وأوْفَدَ
A deputation.	وفدٌ ج وُفُود
Epidemic.	وَافِدٌ ج وُفُود
To increase, multiply.	وَفَرَ يَفِرُ
To economise; save.	وَفَّر
Wealth, affluence.	وَفْرٌ ج وُفُور
Economy; saving.	وَفْرٌ وَتَوْفِيرٌ
Abundant, plentiful.	وَافِرٌ
More abundant.	أوْفَرُ
To make fit. To assist.	وَفَّقَ
To reconcile.	وَفَّقَ وَوَافَقَ بَيْن
To agree or accord with.	وَافَقَ
To succeed.	تَوَفَّقَ
To agree together.	تَوَافَقَ في
To agree upon.	إِتَّفَقَ عَلى أوْ في
To happen, occur.	إِتَّفَقَ لِ

Accord, agreement.	وِفْقٌ وَوِفَاقٌ
In accordance with.	وِفْقًا لـ
Agreement, fitness.	مُوَافَقَةٌ
Coincidence. Accord.	إِتِّفَاقٌ
Accidental, by chance.	اِتِّفَاقِي
Success. Prosperity.	تَوْفِيقٌ
Convenient, suitable.	مُوَافِقٌ
Prosperous, successful.	مُتَوَفِّقٌ
To keep one's promise. To pay a debt.	وَفَى يَفِي وَأَوْفَى
To be perfect, complete.	وَفَى وَفِيًّا
To come to, meet.	وَافَى
To pay the whole.	وَفَّى حَقَّهُ
To die.	تُوُفِّيَ وَتَوَفَّاهُ اللهُ
Payment of a dept.	وَفَاءٌ وَإِيفَاءٌ
Death, decease.	وَفَاةٌ ج وَفَيَاتٌ
Complete.	وَافٍ
Cavity, hole.	وَقْبٌ ج أَوْقَابٌ
To appoint a time.	وَقْتٌ وَوَقَّتَ

Time, season.	وَقْتٌ ج أَوْقَاتٌ
Then, at that time.	وَقْتَئِذٍ
Immediately.	لِلْوَقْتِ وَلِوَقْتِهِ
Temporal, provisional.	وَقْتِيٌّ
To be impudent.	وَقَحَ يَقِحُ وَتَوَقَّحَ
Impudent, brazen-faced.	وَقِحٌ
Impudence.	وَقَاحَةٌ وَقِحَةٌ
To burn, blaze (a fire).	وَقَدَ يَقِدُ. وَتَوَقَّدَ وَاتَّقَدَ
To kindle (a fire) ; light.	أَوْقَدَ
Fuel.	وَقُودٌ وَوَقِيدٌ
Fire-grate.	مَوْقِدٌ وَمَوْقِدَةٌ
Lit, kindled.	مَوْقُودٌ وَمُتَّقِدٌ
To honour, respect.	وَقَّرَ
To load (an animal).	أَوْقَرَ إِيقَارًا
Load, burden.	وِقْرٌ ج أَوْقَارٌ
Dignified bearing.	وَقَارٌ
Venerable.	وَقُورٌ
To fall, fall down.	وَقَعَ يَقَعُ

To endow.	وَقَفَ لَ وَعلى
To inform. Know.	وَقَفَ وُقُوفاً على
To seize. To arrest.	وَقَّفَ وَأَوْقف
To contend with.	وَاقَفَ في
To hesitate.	تَوَقَّفَ في
To abstain from·	تَوَقَّفَ عَنْ
To depend on.	تَوَقَّفَ عَلى
Endowment.	وَقفٌ ج أَوْقافٌ
Standing. Pause.	وَاقِفٌ ج وُقُوفٌ
Standing ; stopping.	وقُوفُ
Hesitation ; arrest.	تَوَقُّف
Suspension ; arrest.	تَوْقيف
A stand, station.	مَوْقِفٌ ج مَوَاقِفُ
Dependent on, stopped. Endowed.	مَوْقُوفُ
To guard, protect.	وقى يَقي
To be on one's guard.	تَوَقَّى وَاتَّقى
To fear God.	إتَّقى يَتَّقي
Protection.	وقايَةُ وَوقاءُ

To happen, occur to one.	وقعَ لِ
To slander, insult one.	وقعَ في
To attack, assail.	وقعَ وَأَوْقعَ بِ
To let fall. Seal, sign.	وقَّعَ
To charge, rush upon.	واقعَ
To tune, put in tune.	أَوْقعَ
To expect.	تَوقَّعَ وَاسنوْقَعَ
To fight together.	تَواقعَ
To beseech humbly.	تَواقعَ عَلى
Event. Battle.	وَقعة ج وَقَماتٌ
Imploring help.	وقيعُ
Actually, in fact.	في الْوَاقع
Event, catastrophe.	وَاقعةٌ
Harmony of sounds.	إيقاع
Expectation ; hope.	تَوقع
Signature.	توقيعٌ ج تَوَاقيع
Place.	مَوقعٌ ج مواقع
To stop ; stand.	وَقفَ يَقِفُ

Fear of God, piety.	تقًى وتقْوى	To sell at a loss.	بَاعَ بالوَكس
Pious, God-fearing.	تقيّ ج أتقياء	To drop, trickle.	وَكَف يَكِف
Sixty drams. A pharmaceutical ounce.	اوْقية ج أواقٍ	Trickling, leaking.	وَكْفٌ
A man who fears God.	متّقٍ	To confide to.	وكل يَكِلُ إلى
To lean upon.	توَكّأ واتّكأ عَلى	To appoint as an agent.	وَكّلَ
To sit leaning on the side.	اتّكأ	To trust in.	توَكّلَ واتّكلَ على
A staff ; a couch.	متّكأ ج متّكآت	Agency.	وكالة ج وكالات
To advance slowly.	وكب يَكِب	Substitute, agent.	وَكيل ج وكلاء
A procession.	موكب ج مَواكب	Trust, confidence.	إتّكال
To affirm, confirm.	وكّد وأكّد	Committed to.	موْكُول إلى
To be confirmed.	توَكّد وتأكّد	To enter.	ولَج يَلِج ولُوجا وَفي
Certain, affirmed.	أكيد ومؤكّد	To commit to.	ولّج وإلى
Affirmation, confirmation. Emphasis.	توْكيد وتأكيد	To beget bring, forth.	ولد يَلِد
Certatinly.	بالتّأكيد	To act as a midwife.	ولّد
Nest of a bird.	وكر ج أوْكار	To originate from.	توَلّد مِن
To push, thrust.	وكز ــ	Child, son.	وَلد ج أوْلاد
To be defective.	وكس ــ	Birth, parturition.	ولادة
Diminution of value ; loss.	وكْس	Midwifery.	عِلمُ الوِلادَةِ

Grief, passion, love. وَلَهٌ	Father ; sire. وَالِدٌ ج وَالِدُونَ
Overcome with grief. وَلْهَانُم وَلَهَى	Mother ; dam. وَالِدَةٌ ج وَالِدَاتٌ
To wail, lament. وَلْوَلَ وَلْوَلَةً	Father and mother. ٱلْوَالِدَانِ
To follow. وَلِيَ وَوَلِيَ يَلِي	Generation. مَوْلِدٌ ج مَوَالِدُ
To rule. وَلِيَ وِلَايَةً وَعَلَى	Birthday. مِيلَادٌ ج مَوَالِيدُ
To make one a ruler. وَلَّى	Christmas. عِيدُ ٱلْمِيلَادِ
To turn away from. وَلَّى عَن	Unclassical (word) مُوَلَّدَةٌ
He turned and fled. وَلَّى هَارِبًا	Midwife. مُوَلِّدَةٌ
He turned his face. وَلَّى وَجْهَهُ	Born. Child. مَوْلُودٌ ج مَوَالِيدُ
To help, protect. وَالَى مُوَالَاةً	To be attached to. وَلِعَ يَوْلَعُ بِ
To do a good deed. أَوْلَى مَعْرُوفًا	To light or kindle. وَلَّعَ
To take charge of. تَوَلَّى	Material for lighting with. (وَلْعَةٌ)
To follow one another. تَوَالَى	Violent love, passion. وَلَعٌ
To take possession. إِسْتَوْلَى	Passionately addicted. مُولَعٌ بِ
Master, lord. وَلِيٌّ ج أَوْلِيَاءُ	To associate with. وَالَفَ مُوَالَفَةً
Friend of God. وَلِيُّ ٱللهِ	To entertain. أَوْلَمَ
Province. Rule. وِلَايَةٌ ج وِلَايَاتٌ	Entertainment. وَلِيمَةٌ ج وَلَائِمُ
Heir apparent. وَلِيُّ ٱلْعَهْدِ	To grieve much. وَلِهَ يَلَهُ

Lazy, languid ; slow.	مُتَوَان	Benefactor.	وَلِيُّ ٱلنِعَمِ
Enamel.	مينا	Ruler, governor.	وَال ج وُلاةٌ
Port, harbour.	مينا وَميناء ج مَوَان	More deserving, fit.	أَوْلَى بِ
To grant, give.	وَهب يَهَب	Master, lord.	مَوْلَى ج مَوَال
Grant ! (Imp. of وَهَبُ)	هَبْ	Invested with power.	مُتَوَلٍّ
To ask for a present.	إِستَوْهَب	Successive.	مُتَوَال
Gift, present.	هِبةٌ ج هِباتُ	A Sheïte.	مُتَوَال ج مُتاوِلةٌ
Donation, gift.	مَوْهِبةٌ ج مَواهِبُ	To beckon to.	وَمَأَ يَمَأُ . وَأَوْمَأَ إِلَى
Mohammedan Wahhabite.	وهَّابِيٌّ	Indication by sign.	وَمَأُ وَإِيمَاء
To blaze, burn.	وَهَج يَهِج	Indicated.	ألمُومَا إِلَيْهِ
To kindle (a fire).	أَوْهَج إِيهاجًا	A prostitute.	مُومِسةٌ ومُومِسُ
To glow burn.	تَوَهَّج	To flash.	وَمَض يَمِض . وَأَوْمَض
Glow, heat (of fire, sun).	وَهَجُ	Lightning; flash; gleam.	وَميضُ
Intensely glowing.	وهَّاج	To reprove, reprimand.	وَنَب
Deep pit ; abyss.	وهدة ج وَهَدُ	To be faint, weak.	وَنَى يَنِي.وَوَنِي
To lead into evil.	وهَّط وأَوْهَط	To relax one's efforts.	تَوَانَى فِي
To rush rashly into.	تَوَهَّط فِي	Fatigue, faintness.	وَنًى وَوَناء
Precipice, abyss.	وهْطةٌ ج وهْطُ	Slowness, slackness.	تَوَانٍ

Terror, fear, fright.	وَهَلٌ وَوَهلَةٌ
At first sight.	أوَّل وهلةٍ
To imagine, fancy.	أوهم يَهم
To lead into error.	وهَّم وأوهم
To suspect, accuse.	إتَّهم بِ
To suppose, imagine.	توهَّم
To be suspected.	إتُّهم ب
Opinion, idea.	وَهمٌ ج أوهام
The imagination.	القُوَّة الوَهمية
Imaginary, hypothetical.	وَهمي
Ambiguity. Misleading.	إيهامٌ
Suspicion, charge.	تُهمة ج تُهم
Suspected person.	متَّهم
Fanciful imagination.	توهُّم

To be weak.	وَهَن يَهن . وَوهَن ــ
To weaken.	وهَّن وأوهن
Weak, frail.	واهنُ ج وهنُ
To be weak.	وَهى ووَهي يَهي
To weaken, break.	أوهى
Feeble, frail.	واهٍ مواهيه ُج واهون
Wonderful! Alas!	واها لِ
Woe to you!	ويكَ
Oasis.	واحةٌ ج واحات
Woe to!	ويحٌ ويلُ
Disaster, calamity.	وَيلٌ
Woe to me!	وَيلي
Disgrace.	ويلةٌ ج ويلات

ي

As a numeral sign = 10.	ي
My, me, *e. g.*	ي
My book.	كِتَابِي
With me.	مَعِي
He struck me.	ضَرَبَنِي
A particle of relation, e.g.	يّ
Egyptian.	مِصْرِيّ
Interjection, O *e.g.*	يا
O Zeid !	يا زَيْدُ
To despair of.	يَئِس يَيْأَس وَيَيْئِس مِنْ
Despair, loss of hope.	يَأْسٌ
Despairing.	يَؤُوس وَيَؤُوس
To dry up, wither.	يَبِس يَيْبَس
To cause to dry.	يَبَّس وَأَيْبَس

To dry land.	أَيْبَس وَآلْيَابِسة
Dry.	يَابِس
Dryness.	يُبُوسة
To make one an orphan.	يَتَّم
To become an orphan.	تَيَّتَم
State of orphanage.	يُتْم
Orphan.	يَتِيم ج يَتَامَى وَأَيْتَام
A rare pearl.	دُرَّة يَتِيمة
A kind of stew.	(يَخْنَة)
Hand; arm. Power. Handle.	يَد ج أَيْدٍ وَأَيَاد
By force.	عَنْ يَد
In his presence.	بَيْن يَدَيْه
He is well versed.	لَهُ يَد بَيْضَاء
Power, influence.	أَلْيَد الطُّولَى

Arrest, interdicted.	(يَسَقْ)
A cavass (*Turk*).	(يسقجيّ)
Jasmine (jessamine).	يا سَمِين
Male bee. Chief.	يَعسوب
Fontanelle.	يَافوخ
A young man. Lad.	يافِع ج يَفَعَة
Ruby.	ياقوت
To be awake.	يقظَ يِيقظَ
To awaken.	يَقَّظ وأيقظَ
To wake up.	تيقَّظ واسْتيقظَ
Wakefulness. Attention.	يَقظَة
Awake, watchful.	يَقظ ويَقظان
To be certain, sure.	يَقن يِيقَن
To believe firmly.	أيقن واسْتيقَن
To know, be sure of.	تيقَّن
Certain belief, conviction.	يَقين
He is sure of it.	هو على يقينٍ منهُ
Certainly, undoubtedly.	يَقينًا
Certain knowledge.	علمُ اليقين

Manual.	يَدِيٌّ ويَدوِيٌّ
Scattered.	ايدِي سَبا
Jerboa (animal).	يَربوع
Glow-worm. Reed-pen.	يرّاع
Jaundice. Blight.	يرقان
To he easy.	يسر يِيسر يُسْرًا
To facilitate, make easy.	يَسَّر
To become easy.	تيَسَّر واسْتيْسر
To be feasible to one.	تيَسَّر لَهُ
Facility, ease; affluence.	يُسْر
Left. side. Ease.	يسار ج يُسْر
Easy. Small quantity.	يسير
More easy.	أيسر
The left side.	الأيسر واليُسرى
Rich, affluent.	موسر ج مياسير
Gambling.	مَيْسِر
Ease, affluence, wealth.	مَيْسرة
Left side.	مَيْسرة ج مياسر
Feasible, easy	مَيْسور ج مياسير

Fountain.	يَنْبُوعٌ	Indubitable truth.	حَقُّ اَلْيَقِين
Anise.	يَانَسُونٌ (أَنِيسُونٌ)	Certain truths ; axioms.	يَقِينِيَّاتٌ
To ripen (fruit).	يَنِعَ يَيْنَعُ . وَأَيْنَعَ	Confident, sure.	مُوقِنٌ
Ripe (fruit).	يَانِعٌ وَيَنِيعٌ ج يُنَّعٌ	Sea, ocean.	يَمٌّ ج يُمُومٌ
Jew (See هُودٌ)	يَهُودِيٌّ ج يَهُودٌ .	Wood-pigeon.	يَمَامٌ وَيَمَامَةٌ
Day. Time ; season	يَوْمٌ ج أَيَّامٌ	To go to the right.	يَمَّنَ وَيَامَنَ
Day by day.	يَوْمًا فَيَوْمًا	To seek a blessing.	تَيَمَّنَ ب
The same day.	مِنْ يَوْمِهِ	To exact an oath.	إِسْتَيْمَنَ
Once, some day.	يَوْمًا مَا	Blessing, success, luck.	يُمْنٌ
On a certain day, once.	ذَاتَ يَوْم	Right side or hand.	يَمْنَةٌ
To-day.	أَلْيَوْمُ	Yemen (Arabia Felix).	اَلْيَمَنُ
Daily.	يَوْمِيٌّ	Right hand.	يُمْنَى ج يُمْنِيَاتٌ
Day by day, daily.	يَوْمِيًّا	Right side, right hand.	يَمِينٌ
On that day.	يَوْمَئِذٍ	Oath.	يَمِينٌ ج أَيْمُنٌ وَأَيْمَانٌ
Jonah.	يُونُس (يُونَانٌ)	By God.	أَيْمُ وَأَيْمُ اَللّٰه
The Greek nation.	أَلْيُونَانُ	The South.	اَلتَّيْمَنُ
Greece.	بِلَادُ اَلْيُونَان	Right Side. Right wing of an army.	مَيْمَنَةٌ ج مَيَامِنُ
Greek. Grecian	يُونَانِيٌّ ج يُونَانِيُّونَ	Fortunate.	مَيْمُونٌ ج مَيَامِينُ
The Greek language.	أَلْيُونَانِيَّةُ	Auspicious.	مَيْمُونُ اَلطَّائِرِ

SUPPLEMENT

ARABIC-ENGLISH

It was impossible, for technical reasons, to follow the conventional arrangement according to roots in this Arabic-English supplement. The words are, therefore, arranged strictly alphabetically.

nutritionist n.	إِخْتِصَاصِيّ بِالْغِذَاءِ	metabolism n.	إِبْدَالُ الْمَوَادِّ فِي الْجِسْمِ
chiropodist n.	إِخْتِصَاصِيّ لِمُعَالَجَةِ الْأَقْدَامِ	Soviet Union n.	إِتِّحَادُ السُّوفِيتِ
		authorize v.	أَجَازَ
fingerprint v.	أَخَذَ طَابِعَ الْأَصَابِعِ	authorization n.	إِجَازَةٌ
camouflage v.	أَخْفَى	patent n.	إِجَازَةُ الْحَصْرِ
defrost v.	أَذَابَ الْجَلِيدَ فِي خِزَانَةِ الثَّلْجِ	living wage n.	أَجْرُ كَافٍ
broadcast v.	أَذَاعَ	minimum wage n.	الْأَجْرُ الْأَصْغَرُ
telecast v.	أَذَاعَ بِالتِّلْفَزَةِ	red tape n.	إِجْرَاءَاتٌ عَقِيمَةٌ
broadcast n.	إِذَاعَةٌ	enemy alien n.	أَجْنَبِيّ عَدَائِيّ
newscast n.	إِذَاعَةُ الْأَخْبَارِ		إِحْسَاسٌ
telecast n.	إِذَاعَةٌ تِلْفَزِيَّةٌ	inferiority complex n.	
radio broadcast n.	إِذَاعَةٌ لَاسِلْكِيَّةٌ		الْإِنْحِطَاط
mixup n.	إِرْتِبَاكٌ	statistician n.	إِحْصَائِيّ
traffic jam n.	إِرْتِبَاكُ الْحَرَكَةِ	statistics n.	إِحْصَائِيَّةٌ
terrorism n.	إِرْهَابٌ	jurisdiction n.	إِخْتِصَاص
terrorist n.	إِرْهَابِيّ	specialist n.	إِخْتِصَاصِيّ

alert *n.*	إِشَارَةُ الْخَطَرِ	terrorize *v.*	أَرْهَبَ
socialist *n,* socialist(ic) *a.*	إِشْتِرَاكِيٌّ	aspirin *n.*	أَسْبِيرِين
socialism *n.*	إِشْتِرَاكِيَّة	dictatorship *n.*	إِسْتِبْدَادٌ
x-ray *n.*	أَشِعَّة رِنْتِجِن أَوْ إِكْس	infiltrate *v.*	إِسْتَرَقَ إِلَى
ameliorate *v.*	أَصْلَحَ	revue *n.*	إِسْتِعْرَاض
walkout *n.*	إِضْرَابٌ	plebiscite *n.*	إِسْتِفْتَاءُ الشَّعْبِ
fire department *n.*	إِطْفَائِيَّة	autonomy *n.*	إِسْتِقْلَالٌ
rebroadcast *n.*	إِعَادَةُ إِذَاعَةٍ	reconnaissance *n.* (mil.)	إِسْتِكْشَافٌ
reorganization *n.*	إِعَادَةُ التَّنْظِيمِ	amortization *n.*	إِسْتِهْلَاك
subsidy *n.*	إِعَانَة	amortize *v.*	إِسْتَهْلَكَ
aggression *n.*	إِعْتِدَاءٌ	record *n.* (phonograph)	أُسْطُوَانَة
advertisement *n.*	إِعْلَانٌ	first aid *n.*	إِسْعَافٌ
want ad *n.*	إِعْلَانُ الطَّلَبِ	pseudonym *n.*	إِسْم مُسْتَعَار
classified ad *n.*	إِعْلَانٌ مُبَوَّب	internee *n.*	أَسِير
editorial *n.*	إِفْتِتَاحِيَّة	tip-off *n.*	إِشَارَة

incinerator n.	آلَةٌ لِحَرْقِ الْفَضَلَاتِ	efficiency n.	إِقْتِدَارٌ
sewing machine n.	آلَةُ الْخِيَاطَةِ	feudalism n.	إِقْطَاعِيَّةٌ
washing machine n.	آلَةُ الْغَسْلِ	boost n.	إِكْثَارٌ
typewriter n.	آلَةُ الْكِتَابَةِ	arthritis n.	إِلْتِهَابُ الْمَفَاصِلِ
slot machine n.	آلَةُ لَعِبِ الْقِمَارِ	meningitis n.	أَلْاِلْتِهَابُ السِّحَائِيُّ
radiator n.	آلَةٌ مُسَخِّنَةٌ	annexation n.	إِلْحَاقٌ
ignition n.	إِلْهَابٌ	annex v.	أَلْحَقَ
potential n.	إِمْكَانِيَّةٌ	billion n.	أَلْفُ مَلْيُونٍ
collective security n.	الْأَمْنُ الْمُشْتَرَكُ	dictaphone n.	آلَةٌ اسْتِكْتَابِيَّةٌ
		vending machine n.	آلَةُ الْبَيْعِ
trustee n.	أَمِينٌ	heater n.	آلَةُ التَّسْخِينِ
life expectancy n.	إِنْتِظَارُ الْحَيَاةِ	rolling mill n.	آلَةُ التَّصْفِيحِ
book review n.	إِنْتِقَادٌ	camera n.	آلَةُ التَّصْوِيرِ
landslide n.	إِنْهِيَالُ الْأَرْضِ	incubator n.	آلَةُ التَّفْرِيخِ
aureomycin n.	أُورِيُومِيسِين	calculating machine n.	آلَةٌ حَاسِبَةٌ
insulin n.	إِنْسُولِين		

gasoline *n.*	بَنْزِين	turnstile *n.*	بَاب دَوَّار
penicillin *n.*	بِنِيسِلِّين		أَلْبَحْرِيَّة
pajamas *n. pl.*	بِيجاما	merchant marine *n.*	التِّجارِيَّة
wholesaler *n.*	تاجِرُ الْجُمْلَة	pinch-hit *n.*	بَدَل
pornography *n.*	تَأْلِيف فَحَّاش	anonymous *a.*	بِدُونَ اسْم
social security *n.*	تَأْمِين اجْتِماعِى	underdeveloped *a.*	بِدُونَ تَطَوُّر كَافٍ
	تَأْمِين ضِدَّ	air conditioner *n.*	بَرَّادَة
health insurance *n.*	الأَمْراض	cablegram *n.*	بَرْقِيَّة
life insurance *n.*	تَأْمِين عَلَى الْحَياة	air mail *n.*	أَلْبَرِيد الْجَوِّىّ
	تَأْمِين عَلَى	protein *n.*	بُروتِين
liability insurence *n.*	المَسْؤُولِيَّة	coughdrop *n.*	بَسْتِيلِيَّة لِلسُّعْلَة
telepathy *n.*	تَبادُل الْخَواطِر	honeydew melon *n.*	بِطِّيخ أَصْفَر
trial balloon *n.*	تَجْرِيب	leftover *n.*	بَقايا
		backlog *n.*	بَقايا عَمَل .
coalition *n.*	تَحالُف	satellite country *n.*	بِلاد مُتَوَقِّفَة
substandard *a.*	تَحْتَ الْمِقْيَاس	plutonium *n.*	بُلُوتُونِيُوم

heating *n.*	تَسْخِين	arbitration *n.*	تَحْكِيم
jet propulsion *n.*	اَلتَّسْيِيرُ النَّفَّاثِي	analysis *n.*	تَحْلِيل
standardization *n.*	تَسْوِيَةٌ بِمِقْيَاسٍ أَحَد	psychoanalysis *n.*	تَحْلِيل نَفْسِي
		anesthesia *n.*	تَخْدِير
diagnosis *n.*	تَشْخِيص مَرَضٍ	storage *n.*	تَخْزِين
autopsy *n.*	تَشْرِيح	installment plan *n.*	تَدْبِير نَجْمِي
spastic *a.*	تَشَنُّجِي	tuberculosis *n.*	تَدَرُّن
visualize *v.*	تَصَوَّر	shorthand *n.*	تَدْمِيج
time exposure *n.*	تَصْوِير وَقْتِي	certificate of origin *n.*	تَذْكِرَةُ الْأَصْل
inflation *n.*	تَضَخُّم نَقْدِي		
develop *v.*	تَطَوَّر	identification *n.*	تَذْكِرَةُ إِثْبَات الشَّخْصِيَّة
unemployment *n.*	تَعَطُّل	trolley car *n.*	تْرَام
sterilization *n.*	تَعْقِيم	layout *n.*	تَرْتِيب
sightseeing *n.*	تَفَرُّج	headline *n.*	تَرْوِيسَة
air-conditioning *n.*	تَكْيِيفُ الْهَوَاء	registration *n.*	تَسْجِيل

high frequency *n.*	تَواتُرٌ عالٍ	synopsis *n.*	تَلْخيصٌ
radio frequency *n.*	تَواتُرٌ لاسِلْكيٌّ	televise *v.*	تَلْفَزَ
special delivery *n.*	تَوْزيعٌ مُسْتَعْجِلٌ	television *n.*	تَلْفَزَةٌ
hookup *n.*	تَوْصيلٌ مُتَكاثِرٌ	vaccination *n.*	تَلْقيحٌ
current *n.*	تيّارٌ	coed *n.*	تِلْميذَةٌ
alternate current *n.*	تيّارٌ مُتَبادِلٌ	phone *n.*	تِليفونٌ
carfare *n.*	ثَمَنُ التَّذْكِرَة	permanent wave *n.*	تَمْويجٌ
subversive *a.*	ثَوْرَوِيٌّ	price-cutting *n.*	تَنْزيلُ الأَثْمانِ بِالتَّزاحُمِ
layette *n.*	ثيابٌ لِطِفْلٍ وَليدٍ	markdown *n.*	تَنْزيلُ الثَّمَنِ
collateral *n.*	جانِبيٌّ	devaluation *n.*	تَنْزيلٌ نَقْدِيٌّ
sex appeal *n.*	جَذْبٌ جِنْسِيٌّ	manicure *n.*	تَنْظيفُ الأَظْفارِ
appendectomy *n.*	جَذْمُ الزَّائِدَة الدُوديّة	pedicure *n.*	تَنْظيفُ أَظْفارِ الأَرْجُلِ
tonsilectomy *n.*	جَذْمُ اللَّوْزَتَيْنِ	hypnosis *n.*	تَنْويمٌ
bacillus *n.*	جُرْثومَةٌ	narcosis *n.*	تَنْويمٌ

boric acid n.	حَامِضٌ بُورْقِيٌّ	newsreel n.	جَرِيدَةٌ نَاطِقَةٌ
aircraft carrier n.	حَامِلَةُ الطَّائِرَات	suspension bridge n.	جِسْرٌ مُعَلَّقٌ
silkscreen n.	حِجَابٌ حَرِيرِىٌّ	co-operative n.	جَمْعِيَّةٌ تَعَاوُنِيَّةٌ
darkroom n.	حُجْرَةٌ مُظْلِمَةٌ لَتِوْضِيحِ تَصَاوِير	parachutist n.	جُنْدِى المَظَلَّة
		industrialize v.	جَهَّزَ بِصَنَائِعَ
calorie n.	حَرَارِيَّةٌ	hike n.	جَوْلَةٌ
torpedo n.	حَرَّاقَةٌ	roundtrip n.	جَوْلَةٌ وَعَوْدَةٌ
cold war n.	الحَرْبُ البَرِيدَةُ	atmospheric a.	جَوِّىٌّ
class struggle n.	حَرْبُ الطَّبَقَات	airtight a.	حَاجِبُ الهَوَاءِ
underground n. (polit.)	حَرَكَةٌ سِيَاسِيَّةٌ سِرِّيَّةٌ .	air warden n.	حَارِسُ المُقَاوَمَة الجَوِّيَة
typesetting n.	الحُرُوفُ المَجْمُوعَةُ	ice breaker n.	حَاطِمَةُ الجَلِيد
safety belt n.	حِزَامُ الأَمْنِ	initiative n.	حَافِزٌ
bank account n.	حِسَابٌ	bus n.	حَافِلَةٌ
differential calculus n.	حِسَابُ التَّفَاصُل	phonograph n.	حَاكٍ
		loudspeaker n.	حَاكٍ

secret service n.	أَلْخِدْمَةُ السِّرِّيَّةُ	emotions n.	حِسِّيَات
icebox n.	خِزَانَةُ الثَّلْجِ	rationing n.	حَصْرُ التَّمْوِين
refrigerator n.	خِزَانَةُ الثَّلْجِ	dividend n. (profit share)	حِصّة فِى الرِّبْح
filing cabinet n.	خِزَانَةُ الْمِلَفَّات	upkeep n.	حِفْظ
earmark v.	خَصَّص	injection n.	حُقْنَة
touch-and-go a. [risky]	خَطِر	suitcase n.	حَقِيبَة
utopian a.	خَيَالِىّ	totalitarianism n.	أَلْحُكْمُ الْمُطْلَق
taxpayer n.	دَافِعُ الضَّرَائِب	demobilization n.	حَلُّ الْجَيْشِن
short circuit n.	دَائِرَة قَصِيرَة	demobilize v.	حَلَّ الْجَيْش
encyclopedia n.	دَائِرَةُ الْمَعَارِف	in-laws n.	أَلْحَمَوَان
tank n. (mil.)	دَبَّابَة	travelers' check n.	حَوَالَة سَفَرِيَّة
safety pin n.	دَبُّوس إِنْكِلِيزِىّ	duty-free a.	خَالِصٌ مِنَ الْكُمْرُوك
bicycle n.	دَرَّاجَة	doublecross v.	خَانَ
tourist class n.	أَلدَّرَجَةُ الثَّالِثَةُ فِى سَفِينة	anesthesize v.	خَدَّر
I.Q. n.	دَرَجَةُ الْعَقْل	social service n., social work n.	خِدْمَةٌ اجْتِمَاعِيَّة

profiteer *n.*	رَابِح	propaganda *n.*	دَعَاوَة
bridgehead *n.*	رَأْسُ الجِسْرِ	newsstand *n.*	دُكَّانُ جَرَائِدَ
capitalist *n.*	رَأْسْمَالِيٌّ	drugstore *n.*	دُكَّانُ العِطَارَة
capitalism *n.*	رَأْسْمَالِيَّة	directory *n.*	دَلِيل
flame thrower *n.*	رَامِى اللَّهِيبِ	cold wave *n.*	دَوْرَةُ البَرْدِ
figurehead *n.*	رَئِيس بِالإِسْمِ	heatwave *n.*	دَوْرَةُ الحَرَارَة
suspender *n.*	رِبْطَةُ السَّاقِ	signatory powers *n. pl.*	أَلدُّوَل المُوَقِّعَة
hack *a.*	رَث	buffer state *n.*	دَوْلَةٌ مُتَوَسِّطَة وَمُتَحَايِدَة
rheumatism *n.*	رَنِيَة	infrared *a.*	دُونَ الأَحْمَرِ
refund *v.*	رَدَّ	atomic *a.*	ذَرِّى
chain reaction *n.*	رَدُّالفِعْلِ المُسَلْسَل	talcum powder *n.*	ذَرِيرَة طَلْقِيَّة
refund *n.*	رَدُّ النُّقُودِ	radioactive *a.*	ذُو رَادِيُوم فَاعِل
radiogram *n.*	رِسَالة لاسِلْكِيَّة	antisemite *n.*, anti-semitic *a.*	ذُو اللَّاسَامِيَّة
cardiogram *n.*	رَسْم قَلْبِيٌّ		

chauffeur *n.*	سَائِقٌ	blueprint *n.*	رَسْم هَنْدَسِيّ
motorist *n.*	سَائِقُ سَيَّارَةٍ	hush money *n.*	رِشْوَةٌ
track meet *n.*	سِبَاقٌ	tugboat *n.*	رَقَّاسٌ
blackboard *n.*	سَبُّورَةٌ	lay-off *n.*	رَفْتٌ
iron curtain *n.*	أَلسِّتَارُ ٱلْحَدِيدِيّ	detective story *n.*	رِوَايَةٌ بُولِيسِيَّةٌ
pullover *n.*	سَتْرَةٌ صُوفِيَّةٌ	kindergarten *n.*	رَوْضَةُ ٱلْأَطْفَال
physiognomy *n.*	سَحْنَةٌ	nursery school *n.*	رَوْضَةُ ٱلْأَطْفَال
traffic light *n.*	سِرَاجُ ٱلْحَرَكَةِ	sport *n.*	رِيَاضَةٌ
top-secret *a.*	سِرِّيّ جِدًّا	tail wind *n.*	رِيح وَرَائِيَّةٌ
rate of exchange *n.*	سِعْرُ ٱلصَّرْف	appendix *n.*	زَائِدَةٌ دُودِيَّةٌ
bank rate *n.*	سِعْرُ ٱلْفَائِدَةِ	ringleader *n.*	زَعِيمٌ
cutthroat *n.*	سَفَّاحٌ	hypertrophy *n.*	زِيَادَةٌ مُفْرِطَةٌ
space travel *n.*	سَفَرٌ فِى ٱلْفَضَاءِ	lubricating oil *n.*	زَيْت تَشْحِيمٍ
space ship *n.*	سَفِينَةٌ فَضَائِيَّةٌ	make-up *n.*	زِينَةُ ٱلْوَجْهِ
saccharine *n.*	سَكَادِين	wristwatch *n.*	سَاعَةُ يَدٍ

standardize v.	سَوَّى بِمِقْيَاسٍ أَحَدٍ	subway n.	سِكَّةٌ تَحْتَ ٱلْأَرْضِ
automobile n.	سَيَّارَةٌ	elevated railway n.	سِكَّةُ ٱلْحَدِيدِ
taxicab n.	سَيَّارَةُ ٱلْأُجْرَةِ		ٱلْمُرْتَفِعَةُ
armored car n.	سَيَّارَةٌ مُصَفَّحَةٌ	barbed wire n.	سِلْكٌ شَائِكٌ
motor truck n.	سَيَّارَةُ ٱلنَّقْلِ	escalator n.	سُلَّمٌ مُتَحَرِّكٌ
network n.	شَبَكَةٌ	fire escape n.	سُلَّمُ ٱلنَّجَاةِ
radio network n.	شَبَكَةٌ لَاسِلْكِيَّةٌ	fertilizer n.	سَمَادٌ
diagnose v.	شَخَّصَ مَرَضًا	audition n.	سَمَاعٌ
military police n.	ٱلشُّرْطَةُ ٱلْعَسْكَرِيَّةُ	telephone receiver n.	سَمَّاعَةٌ
patrolman n.	شُرْطِيٌّ	poison ivy n.	ٱلسُّمَّاقُ ٱلسَّامُّ
insurance company n.	شَرِكَةُ ٱلتَّأْمِينِ	broker n.	سِمْسَارٌ
		stockbroker n.	سِمْسَارُ ٱلْأَسْهُمِ
holding company n.	شَرِكَةُ ٱلشَّرِكَاتِ	brokerage n.	سِمْسَرَةٌ
		IOU n.	سَنَدٌ
subsidiary n. (fin.)	شَرِكَةٌ مُسَاعِدَةٌ	stock market n.	سُوقُ ٱلْأَسْهُمِ
Inc. a.	شَرِكَةٌ مُسَجَّلَةٌ	labor market n.	سُوقُ ٱلْعَمَلِ

pigment *n*.	صِبَاغٌ	Scotch tape *n*.	شَرِيطٌ غِرَائِيٌّ
juvenile *a*.	صِبْيَانِيٌّ	soundtrack *n*.	شَرِيطٌ نَاطِقٌ
take off *v*. (av.)	صَعِدَ	correligionist *n*.	شَرِيكُ الدِّينِ
take-off *n*. (av.)	صُعُودٌ	codefendant *n*.	شَرِيكُ الْمُدَّعَى عَلَيْهِ
blood group *n*.	صَفُّ الدَّمِ	side line *n*.	شُغْلٌ جَانِبِيٌّ
industrial *a*.	صِنَاعِيٌّ	fission *n*.	شَقٌّ
box office *n*.	صُنْدُوقُ سِينَمَاءَ أَوْ مَرْسَحٍ	atomic fission *n*.	شَقُّ الذَّرَّةِ
garbage can *n*.	صُنْدُوقُ الْقُمَامَةِ	compartment *n*.	شُقَّةٌ
cash register *n*.	صُنْدُوقٌ مُسَجِّلٌ	tail spin *n*.	شَقْلَبَةُ طَائِرَةٍ
mailbox *n*.	صُنْدُوقٌ لِلْمَكَاتِيبِ	polio(myelitis) *n*. infantile paralysis *n*.	أَلشَّلَلُ الطِّفْلِيُّ
snapshot *n*.	صُورَةٌ حَالِيَّةٌ	spark plug *n*.	شَمْعَةُ الشَّرَارَةِ
motion picture *n*.	صُورَةٌ مُتَحَرِّكَةٌ	notarize *v*.	شَهِدَ قَانُونِيًّا
cartoon *n*.	صُورَةٌ هَزْلِيَّةٌ	communist *n*.	شِيُوعِيٌّ
petty officer *n*.	ضَابِطُ الصَّفِّ	communism *n*.	شِيُوعِيَّةٌ
spank *v*.	ضَرَبَ طِفْلًا	beautician *n*.	صَاحِبُ دَارِ الزِّينَةِ
high pressure *n*. high tension *n*.	ضَغْطٌ عَالٍ	rocket *n*.	صَارُوخٌ

أَلطِّبُّ	socialized medicine n.	ضَنَى ٱلْحَرْب	battle fatigue n.
ٱلْمُشْتَرَكُ		ضَوْءٌ خَلْفِيٌّ	rear light n.
أَلطِّبُّ ٱلنَّفْسَانِيُّ	psychiatry n.	ضَوْءٌ نيونِيٌّ	neon light n.
طَبَقَةُ ٱلتُّرْبَةِ ٱلْفَوْقَانِيَّةُ	topsoil n.	طَابِعُ ٱلْأَصَابِعِ	fingerprint n.
ٱلطَّبَقَةُ ٱلسُّفْلَى	ground floor n.	طَالِبُ ٱلسَّنَةِ ٱلْأُولَى	freshman n.
طَبِيبُ أَمْرَاضِ		طَالِعٌ فِي ٱلتَّنْجِيمِ	horoscope n.
ٱلْأَطْفَالِ	pediatrician n.	طَائِرَةٌ	airplane n. aircraft n.
طَبِيبٌ تَشْخِيصِيٌّ	diagnostician n.	طَائِرَةُ ٱلْإِنْقِضَاضِ	dive bomber n.
طَبِيبٌ مُوَلِّدٌ	obstetrician n.	طَائِرَةٌ بَحْرِيَّةٌ	hydroplane n.
طَرِيقٌ عَامٌّ	highway n.	طَائِرَةٌ شِرَاعِيَّةٌ	glider n.
طَرِيقَةُ ٱلشِّفَاءِ	therapy n.	طَائِرَةٌ عَمُودِيَّةٌ	helicopter n.
طَعَامٌ جَانِبِيٌّ	side dish n.	طَائِرَةُ ٱلْقِتَالِ	fighter bomber n.
طِفْلٌ	sibling n.	ٱلْقَذَّافَةُ	
طَيَّارٌ	aviator n.	طَائِرَةُ ٱلْمُطَارَدَةِ	pursuit plane n.
طَيَرَانٌ	aeronautics n.	طَائِرَةٌ نَفَّاثَةٌ	jet plane n.
عَازِلٌ	insulator n.	أَلطِّبُّ ٱلطَّفَلِيُّ	pediatrics n.

biology *n.*	عِلْمُ الْأَحْيَاءِ	streetwalker *n.*	عَاهِرَةٌ
bacteriology *n.*	عِلْمُ الْجَرَانِيم	motorbike *n.*	عَجَلَةٌ نَارِيَّةٌ
nuclear physics *n.*	عِلْمُ الذَّرَّات	lens *n.*	عَدَسَةٌ
hygiene *n.*	عِلْمُ الصَّحَّة	dining car *n.*	عَرَبَةُ الْأَكْلِ
physics *n.*	عِلْمُ الطَّبِيعَة	nudism *n.*	عُرْيَانِيَّةٌ
electronics *n.*	عِلْمُ الْكَهَارِب	isolationism *n.*	عُزْلَةٌ سِيَاسِيَّةٌ
physiology *n.*	عِلْمُ وَظَائِفِ الْأَعْضَاءِ	shock troops *n. pl.*	عَسَاكِرُ الْهُجُوم
piecework *n.*	اَلْعَمَلُ بِالْقِطَع	League of Nations *n.*	عُصْبَةُ الْأُمَم
caesarian section *n.*	عَمَلِيَّةٌ قَيْصَرِيَّةٌ	druggist *n.*	عَطَّارٌ
electrode *n.*	عَمُودٌ كَهْرُبَائِيٌّ	atomizer *n.*	عَفَّارَةٌ
bra(ssiere) *n.*	عَنْتَرَى	subcontract *n.*	عَقْدٌ فَرْعِيٌّ
air raid *n.*	غَارَةٌ جَوِّيَّةٌ	subconscions *n.*	اَلْعَقْلُ الْبَاطِن
flirt *v.*	غَازَلَ	diathermy *n.*	عِلَاجٌ كَهْرُبَائِيٌّ
thyroid gland *n.*	غُدَّةٌ دَرَقِيَّةٌ	hanger *n.*	عَلَّاقٌ
endocrine gland *n.*	غُدَّةٌ صَمَّاءُ	trade mark *n.*	عَلَامَةٌ تِجَارِيَّةٌ
waiting room *n.*	غُرْفَةُ الْإِنْتِظَار	sociology *n.*	عِلْمُ الْإِجْتِمَاع

standing room n.	فُسْحَةُ الْوَاقِفِينَ	shipping room n.	غُرْفَةُ الشَّحْنِ	
washout n. (sl.) [failure]	فَشَلٌ	checkroom n.	غُرْفَةٌ لِحِفْظِ الثِّيَابِ	
fluorescent a.	فْلُورِىٌّ	hangover n.	غَشَيَانٌ بَعْدَ الشُّرْبِ	
jackpot n.	أَلْفَوْزُ الْأَكْبَرُ فِى الْمُقَامَرَةِ	boner n.	غَلْطَةٌ كَبِيرَةٌ	
receiver n.	قَابِلٌ	submarine n.	غَوَّاصَةٌ	
motorboat n.	قَارِبٌ نَارِىٌّ	fascist n.	فَاشِىٌّ	
		fascism n.	فَاشِيَّةٌ	
boycott v.	قَاطَعَ	retroactive a.	فَاعِلٌ إِلَى الْمَاضِى	
supreme commander n.	أَلْقَائِدُ الْعَامُّ	paralysis n.	فَالِجٌ	
airbase n.	قَائِدَةٌ جَوِّيَّةٌ	topnotch a.	فَائِقٌ	
		can opener n.	فَتَّاحَةٌ	
catalogue n.	قَائِمَةٌ	turn on the radio	فَتَحَ	
black list n.	قَائِمَةٌ سَوْدَاءُ	checkup n. (med.)	فَحَصَ	
menu n.	قَائِمَةُ الطَّعَامِ	blood test n.	فَحْصُ الدَّمِ	
electrocute v.	قَتَلَ بِالْكَهْرَبَاءِ	small change n.	فُرَاطَةٌ	
electrocution n.	قَتْلٌ بِالْكَهْرَبَاءِ	firing squad n.	فِرْقَةُ الْإِعْدَامِ	

phony *a.*, *n.*	كَاذِبٌ	lighter *n.*	قَدَّاحٌ
wage earner *n.*	كَاسِبٌ	subsidize *v.*	قَدَّمَ إِعَانَةً
strikebreaker *n.*	كَاسِرُ الْإِضْرَابِ	decode *v.*	قَرَأَ مَكْتُوبًا شِفْرِيًّا
atheist *n.*	كَافِرٌ	turn off the radio	قَطَعَ
reference book *n.*	كِتَابُ الْمَرْجِعِ	revolutionize *v.*	قَلَّبَ
typewriting *n.*	كِتَابَةٌ بِالْآلَةِ	cardiac *a.*	قَلْبِيٌّ
skywriting *n.*	كِتَابَةٌ عَلَى السَّمَاءِ	fountain pen *n.*	قَلَمُ الْحِبْرِ
xenophobia *n.*	كَرَاهَةُ الْأَجَانِبِ	ball point pen *n.*	قَلَمُ الْحِبْرِ الْجَافّ
swivel chair *n.*	كُرْسِيٌّ دَائِرٌ	stateroom *n.*	قَمَرَةُ الدَّرَجَةِ الْأُولَى
boyscout *n.*	كَشْفِيٌّ	tear bomb *n.*	قُنْبُلَةٌ دَمْعِيَّةٌ
		atom bomb *n.*	قُنْبُلَةٌ ذَرِّيَّةٌ
scrapbook *n.*	كَشْكُولٌ	depth charge *n.*	قُنْبُلَةٌ مُضَادَّةٌ
pancake *n.*	كَعْكَةُ طَاجِنٍ		لِلْغَوَّاصَاتِ
atheism *n.*	كُفْرَانٌ	horsepower *n.*	قُوَّةُ حِصَانٍ
sponsor *v.*	كَفَلَ	task force *n.*	قُوَّةُ عِرَاكٍ
sponsor *n.*	كَفِيلٌ	fire power *n.*	قُوَّةُ النَّارِ

vaccinate v.	لَقَّحَ	double talk n.	كَلَامٌ ذِى لِسَانَيْنِ
ball bearing n.	لُقْمَةٌ ذَاتَ كُرًى	electron n.	كَهْرَب
spring n. (techn.)	لَوْلَب	electrician n.	كَهْرَبَائِى
hydraulic a.	مَائِى	electrification n.	كَهْرَبَة
semifinal n.	مُبَارَاةُ نِصْفِ نِهَائِيٍّ	electronic a.	كَهَارِبِى
record changer n.	مُبَدِّلُ الْأَسْطُوَانَات	shack n.	كُوخٌ
museum n.	مُتْحَف	biochemistry n.	كِيمِيَاءُ أَحْيَائِيَّةٌ
automatic a.	مُتَحَرِّكٌ بِذَاتِه	quinine n.	كِينَا
extremist n.	مُتَطَرِّفٌ	antisemitism n.	لَاسَامِيَّةٌ
sporadic a.	مُتَفَرِّق	radio n., wireless a.	لَاسِلْكِىٌّ
assimilate v.	مَثَّل	mine sweeper n.	لَاقِطَةُ الْأَلْغَام
steam shovel n.	مِجْرَافٌ بُخَارِى	arbitration board n.	لَجْنَةٌ تَحْكِيمِيَّةٌ
dehydrated a.	مُجَرَّدٌ عَنِ الْمَاءِ	stickup n.	لُصُوصِيَّةٌ
semimonthly n.	مَجَلَّةُ نِصْفِ شَهْرِيَّةٍ	soccer n.	لَعِبُ كُرَةِ الْقَدَم
microscope n.	مِجْهَر	book jacket n.	لِفَافَةُ الْكِتَاب
atomic warfare n.	مُحَارَبَةٌ ذَرِّيَّةٌ	jig saw puzzle n.	لُغْزُ قُطَعٍ كَثِيرَة

anesthetic *n.*	مُخَدِّر	blockade *n.*	مُحَاصَرَة
emergency exit *n.*	مَخْرَج عِنْدَ الضَّرُورَة	professional *a.*	مُحْتَرِف
blood bank *n.*	مَخْزَنُ الدَّم	studio *n.*	مُحْتَرَف
intake *n.*	مَدْخَل	motor plough *n.*	مِحْرَاث آلِيّ
driveway *n.*	مَدْخَل لِلسَّيَّارَات	editor *n.*	مُحَرِّر
trainee *n.*	مُدَرَّب	warmonger *n.*	مُحَرِّض لِلْحَرْب
elementary school *n.*	مَدْرَسَة أَوَّلِيَّة	off limits *n.*	مُحَرَّم عَلَى الْعَسَاكِر
commercial college *n.*	مَدْرَسَة تِجَارِيَّة	radio station *n.*	مَحَطَّة لَاسِلْكِيَّة
vocational school *n.*	مَدْرَسَة الصَّنَائِع	stretcher *n.*	مِحَفَّة
		arbitrator *n.*	مُحَكِّم
class-conscious *a.*	مُدْرِك طَبَقَتَه	crematory *n.*	مَحَلّ إِحْرَاق الْجُثَث
tank destroyer *n.*	مِدْفَع مُضَادّ لِلدَّبَّابَات	gas station *n.*	مَحَلّ الْبَنْزِين
stenographer *n.*	مُدَمِّج	juror *n.*	مُحَلَّف
		reporter *n.*	مُخْبِر جَرِيدَة
band leader *n.*	مُدِيرُ الْجَوْق	plainclothes man *n.*	مُخْبِر شُرْطِيّ

receiver n. (radio)	مُسْتَقْبِل	spotter n.	مُرَاقِب
	مُسْتَقْبِل أَمْوَال	moderator n.	مُرَتِّب
(in bankruptcy)	;الإِفْلَاس	water closet n.	مِرْحَاض
autonomous a.	مُسْتَقِلّ	radio transmitter n.	مُرْسِلَة
standard of living n.	مُسْتَوَى الْحَيَاة	diabetes n.	مَرَض الْبَوْل السُّكَّرِيّ
revolver n.	مُسَدِّس	venereal disease n.	مَرَض سِرِّيّ
appetizer n.	مُشَهٍّ	derrick n.	مِرْفَعَة
jaywalk v.	مَشَى عَلَى غَفْلَة	switchboard n.	مَرْكَز التِّلِيفُون
	مِصْبَاح ضَوْء فَوْق	propeller n.	مِرْوَحَة
sunlamp n.	الْبَنَفْسَجِي	lipstick n.	مَرُود
sanitarium n.	مَصَحّ	psychopath n.	مَرِيض نَفْسِي
elevator n.	مِصْعَدَة	interior decorator n.	مُزَخْرِف
percolator n.	مِصْفَاة الْقَهْوَة	roller skate n.	مَزْلَقَان ذَوَا عَجَلَات
board of education n.	مَصْلَحَة	receptionist n.	مُسْتَخْدِمَة الإِسْتِقْبَال
	التَّرْبِيَة	rest room n.	مُسْتَرَاح

commissar n.	مُعْتَمَدٌ شُيُوعِىٌّ		board of health n.	مَصْلَحَةُ الصِّحَّةِ
toothpaste n.	مَعْجُونُ الأَسْنَانِ		microphone n.	مِصْوَاتٌ
coefficient n.	مُعَدَّلٌ		contraceptive n.	مُضَادَّاتٌ لِلْحَبَلِ
concentration camp n.	مُعَسْكَرُ الاِعْتِقَالِ،		insecticide n.	مُضَادَّاتٌ حَشَرِيَّةٌ
			airfield n.	مَطَارٌ
ceiling price n.	مُعْظَمُ الثَّمَنِ		fire extinguisher n.	مِطْفَأَةٌ
disinfectant n.	مُعَقِّمٌ		detergent n.	مُطَهِّرٌ
aseptic a.	مُعَقَّمٌ		spectroscope n.	مِطْيَافٌ
visual aid n.	مِعْوَانٌ نَظَرِى		parachute n.	مِظَلَّةٌ وَاقِيَةٌ
flirt n.	مُغَازَلَةٌ		tax-exempt a.	مُعَافًى مِنَ الْمُكُوسِ
electromagnet n.	مِغْنَطِيسٌ كَهْرُبَائِى		collective agreement n.	مُعَاهَدَةٌ جَمَاعِيَّةٌ
vacationist n.	مُفَرِّصٌ		nonaggression pact n.	مُعَاهَدَةٌ عَدَمِ الاِعْتِدَاءِ
commentator n.	مُفَسِّرُ الأَخْبَارِ		overpass n.	مَعْبَرٌ
heckler n.	مُقَاطِعُ الْكَلَامِ		aggressor n.	مُعْتَدٍ
subcontractor n.	مُقَاوِلٌ فَرْعِى			

potential a.	مُمْكِنٌ	antagonism n.	مُقَاوَمَةٌ
maneuver n.	مُنَاوَرَةٌ	budget n. (pol.)	مُقَرَّرُ الْمِيزَانِيَّةِ
scholarship n. (grant)	مِنْحُ نَفَقَةٍ لِتِلْمِيذٍ	toaster n.	مُقَمِّرٌ كَهْرَبَائِيٌّ
		bomber n.	مُقْنِبلَةٌ
apartment house n. tenement house n.	مَنْزِلٌ	spool n.	مِكَبٌّ
shower bath n.	مِنْضَحٌ	amplifier n.	مُكَبِّرٌ
balloon n.	مِنْطَادٌ	employment agency n.	مَكْتَبُ التَّخْدِيمِ
dialectic a.	مِنْطِقِيٌّ	lending library n.	
periscope n.	مِنْظَرُ الْغَوَّاصَةِ	rental library n.	مَكْتَبَةٌ إِعَارِيَّةٌ
executive n.	مُنَفِّذٌ	subtenant n.	مُكْتَرٍ ثَانٍ
vacuum cleaner n.	مِنْفَضَةٌ	typescript n.	مَكْتُوبٌ بِآلَةِ الْكِتَابَةِ
ventilator n.	مِهْوَاةٌ	refugee n.	مُلْتَجِئٌ
time table n.	مَوَاقِيتُ	bunker n.	مَلْجَأٌ عَسْكَرِيٌّ
short wave n.	مَوْجٌ قَصِيرٌ	analogy n.	مُمَاثَلَةٌ
parking lot n.	مَوْقِفٌ	screen actor n.	مُمَثِّلٌ سِينَمَائِيٌّ
motorcade n.	مَوْكِبُ سَيَّارَاتٍ	eraser n.	مِمْحَاةٌ

relativity n.	نِسْبِيَّةٌ	generator n.	مُوَلِّدٌ
photostat n.	نُسْخَةٌ فُوتوغْرَافِيَّةٌ	author n.	مُؤَلِّفٌ
ideology n.	نَسَقُ الأَفْكَارِ	deadline n.	مِيعَادٌ آخِرٌ
bureaucracy n.	نَسَقُ مُوَظَّفِيٍّ	mechanized a.	مِيكَانِيٌّ
serialization n.	نَشْرٌ بِتَسَلْسُلٍ	airport n.	مِينَا جَوِّيَّةٌ
serialize v.	نَشْرٌ بِتَسَلْسُلٍ	skyscraper n.	نَاطِحَةُ السَّحَابِ
signpost n.	نَصْبَةٌ	public prosecutor n.	نَائِبٌ عَامٌّ
semimonthly a.	نِصْفُ شَهْرِيٍّ	vegetarian n.	نَبَاتِيٌّ
quantum theory n.	نَظَرِيَّةُ الكَمِّ	disarmament n.	نَزْعُ السِّلَاحِ
kerosene n.	نِفْطٌ	bronchitis n.	نَزْلَةٌ صَدْرِيَّةٌ
syndicate n.	نِقَابَةٌ	grippe n.	نَزْلَةٌ وَافِدَةٌ
union n. (labor)	نِقَابَةٌ	forced landing n.	نُزُولٌ مَجْبُورٌ
trade union n.	نِقَابَةُ العُمَّالِ	bearish a.	نُزُولِيٌّ
reviewer n.	نَقَّادٌ	hemorrhage n.	نَزِيفٌ
blood transfusion n.	نَقْلُ الدَّمِ	torpedoboat n.	نَسَّافَةٌ
		death rate n.	نِسْبَةُ المَوْتِ

hydrogen *n*.	هيدَرُوجِين	wisecrack *v*.	نَكَّت
general staff *n*.	هَيئَةُ أَرْكَانِ الْحَرْبِ	wisecrack *n*.	نَكْتَة
questionnaire *n*.	وَرَقَةُ سُؤَالاتٍ	holdup *n*.	نَهب
heavyweight *n*.	وَزْنٌ ثقِيل	searchlight *n*.	نُورٌ كَاشِفٌ
hoodlum *n*.	وَغْدٌ	floodlight *n*.	نُورٌ كَشَّافٌ
hangar *n*.	وَكْرٌ	gas attack *n*.	هجُومٌ بِالغَازِ
advertising agency *n*.	وَكَالَةُ الإِشْهَارِ	technology *n*.	هَنْدَسَة
		pneumatic *a*.	هَوَائِي
iodine *n*.	يُود	aerial *n*.	هَوَائِيّ
		hormone *n*.	هُورْمُون